REVIEWS

You have done a magnificent job of research. The book rings with authority and integrity. It is the most definitive account of the first four months of the Korean War that I have seen, towering over the U.S. Army's official combat history of that time period. Congratulations.
    – Clay Blair,
    author, *The Forgotten War*

I read every page and found it fascinating, with compelling accounts of action and heroism, many of which had never before been told. You are to be congratulated, not only for a tremendous piece of historical research but also for the manner in which you combined and sorted, deciding "what happened when" and "what goes where."
    – COL Harry J. Maihafer, USA, Ret.,
    author, *From the Hudson to the Yalu*

Fighting on the Brink is a worthy addition to the history of the Korean War. It is the most detailed account of the first four months of the Korean War available.
    – LTC Arthur W. Connor, Jr.,
    Army Advisory Group
    Maxwell AFB, AL

Fighting on the Brink stands alone in its importance to the military history of the Korean War, and places Uzal Ent in the front rank of military historians.
    – COL Robert W. Hill, USA, Ret.
    Tropic Lightning Flashes,
    25th Infantry Division publication review

Fighting on the Brink provides very useful information about the first four months of the Korean War. The level of detail you furnished on both individual soldiers and events is extremely valuable to the International Commemorations Committee, especially as we plan events honoring those who served in defense of the Pusan Perimeter.
    – LTG Claude M. Kicklighter, USA, Ret.
    Deputy Under Secretary of the Army
    (International Affairs)

FIGHTING ON THE BRINK: DEFENSE OF THE PUSAN PERIMETER

by Brig. Gen. Uzal W. Ent (Ret.)

TURNER PUBLISHING COMPANY

Turner Publishing Company
412 Broadway
P.O. Box 3101
Paducah, KY 42002-3101
(502) 443-0121

Copyright © 1996 by Uzal W. Ent
All rights reserved.
Publishing Rights: Turner Publishing
Company

Turner Publishing Company Staff:
Coordinator: Julie Agnew Thomas
Designer: Lora Ann Lauder

Library of Congress
Catalog Card Number: 95-60552

ISBN: 978-1-68162-089-3

Additional copies may be purchased directly
from Turner Publishing Company.

This publication was compiled using available
information. The publisher regrets it cannot assume liability for errors or omissions.

Table of Contents

Dedication

Brig. Gen. Uzal W. Ent
Penna National Guard (Ret.)

This book is humbly dedicated to the men who served and fought in defense of the Pusan Perimeter (and the battles leading to its formation) during the Korean War.

I have eaten your bread and salt,
I have drunk your water and wine,
The deaths ye died I have watched beside,
And the lives that ye led were mine.

I served in a rifle platoon in the Pusan Perimeter. This excerpt of a poem by Rudyard Kipling aptly expresses my relationship to the other soldiers and Marines who were there.

Uzal W. Ent
January 1994

Introduction

For more than 20 years I have been a student of the Korean War. I realized that, except for the official Army and Marine histories, little which is definitive had been written about one of the *most critical campaigns* of the entire war — the defense of the Pusan Perimeter. In the 40-odd years since it was fought, only one book has been written about that bloody, epic struggle, Edwin P. Hoyt's *The Pusan Perimeter*. This was a "popular" history, taken from books in print at the time.

A number of books and studies have been published on other aspects of the Korean War, but this campaign, which was vital to the U.S./U.N. success in the war, almost has been overlooked. Had we failed in this campaign, there would have been no Inchon landing... there would have been nothing more. The war would have been lost at the outset!

I have set out to correct that omission. My research has included all the standard books, many newspaper and magazine articles of the time, official records, plus special reports and studies. But of more importance are the recollections and experiences of the men who fought those early battles. This book includes hundreds of these.

This book will include:

- What occupation duty in Korea, Japan and Okinawa was really like.
- The development of the North and South Korean armed forces.
- The Republic of Korea Army's (ROKA) delaying actions in the first few weeks of the war.
- American battles leading to the formation of the Perimeter.
- The defense of the Pusan Perimeter, including GEN Walton H. Walker's plan for the defense and why it couldn't be implemented.
- The breakout from the Perimeter.

Within this narrative are woven the experiences and recollections of hundreds of U.S. soldiers and Marines who fought the battles. I hope I have brought the human element into what otherwise would be a dry recounting of historical facts and figures. What will make this book "live" are the accounts of those men who took part in the life-and-death struggles of that long-ago war.

In short, this book examines aspects of the early Korean War battles and the Perimeter defense and breakout, neither of which have never before been adequately explored or explained. Hopefully, this examination will put a different perspective on the first three months of the Korean War.

PART ONE

BEFORE THE EVENT

To make an army victorious in battle it is necessary to inspire them with confidence, so as to make them believe the victory will be theirs under any circumstances. But to give such an army confidence they must be well-armed and disciplined, and the men must know each other.

Niccolo Machiavelli, *"The Discourses"*

The Occupation of Japan

COL Charles Tench, of General of the Army Douglas MacArthur's staff, with a contingent of 30 officers and 120 enlisted men landed on the battle-scarred runway at Atasugi, Japan on Aug. 28, 1945, beginning the U.S. occupation of Japan. When Tench and his party arrived, the Japanese Armed Forces numbered over 6.9 million men. Of this number, 3.5 million were located in the home islands. They were supported by hundreds of ships and over 6,000 combat aircraft. It would seem apparent that an armed invasion of Japan before the war's end would have led to great slaughter on both sides.

Japan consists of four large islands: Hokkaido in the north; the main island of Honshu in the center; Kyushu and Shikoku in the south. There are over 3,000 smaller islands. Nearly three-quarters of the total area of 142,771 square miles is covered by extremely rugged hills and mountains. Over 250 peaks rise above 6,500 feet; with the highest, Mount Fuji, at 12,385 feet.

The Americans discovered that Japanese leadership almost had been destroyed. Further, heavy U.S. bombing had killed hundreds of thousands of civilians and injured even more. Firebombing had leveled vast areas of Tokyo, killing more people as each of the atomic bombs did at Hiroshima and Nagasaki. There was no organized medical care, food distribution or emergency aid for the sick, injured and homeless. Factories and rail systems were in shambles. The economy was crippled. Japan and the Japanese were in horrendous condition, and in no position to help themselves.

Richard G. Jones (HHC, 25th Div.) arrived in Japan shortly after the occupation began. He recalled that it took three days to go by train from Yokohama to Osaka, because of the damaged rail system. Once the lines were repaired, a trip could normally be made in less than a day.

The Japanese were very wary of the Americans, expecting them to loot, steal, rape their women and kill all the men. They were unprepared for the generosity and friendliness of American soldiers, who helped distribute food, blankets, medical supplies and other goods to the civilian population. GIs handed out chocolate bars, chewing gum and other "goodies" to Japanese children. There were other humane acts. In one case, three U.S. soldiers gave first-aid to a girl who had been badly injured by a Japanese street car and were said to have taken her to a hospital. These kinds of actions won over the Japanese and went far to ensure a peaceful, happy relationship with the Americans.

Donald L. Massey enlisted in the Army in 1946 at the age of 17. He had just four weeks of basic training before being sent to Japan and Battery C, 64th Field Artillery Battalion (FAB) at Nara, in south central Honshu. Massey remembered the first haircut he and his buddies got by a Japanese barber: "The straight razor seemed to be as big as a sword and we were concerned he might decide to take one of us out for his Emperor."

When a fire broke out in an old Japanese barracks used by the 64th FAB, the local Japanese fire department attempted to respond. The engine, propelled by steam, could not negotiate the slight hill leading to the burning barracks. The firemen tried, without success, to push the engine up the hill. The old barracks burned to the ground.

Once, Massey's unit was called out for a reported riot. They arrived in full combat gear only to hear that the "riot" was only a pushing match between two political opponents. The U.S., under the leadership of GEN Douglas MacArthur and his Occupation Military Government staff provided governmental, economic, public health, welfare, security and scientific direction to and for the Japanese from the outset of the occupation.

GEN MacArthur is often characterized as an aloof, proud, vain man, but with great imagination, initiative (sometimes to a fault) and great ambition, who was convinced that he was always right. His service to the U.S. and its Army is difficult to assess. Most people remember him for his "I shall return" speech to the Filipinos during World War II. Others recall his island-hopping counter-offensive against the Japanese later in the war. There are those who praise the Inchon landing, or curse his division of forces in Korea between the U.S. Eighth Army and the U.S. X Corps at a critical time in the Korean War.

Perhaps MacArthur's greatest achievement was his conduct of the occupation of Japan. He combined his innate aloofness, absolutely correct demeanor and behavior with an uncanny sense of what would work and would not work in Japan, a proud warrior-nation which had been crushed in a horrible, bloody war. He skillfully promulgated common-sense rules and regulations for the conduct of his troops, and created a strict, yet kind, humane and orderly life for the people of Japan. He demonstrated a vision, combined with the will and means, to set Japan on a new course, ultimately bringing it into a position of world commercial and industrial leadership. It is often said that both the U. S. and Japan were exceptionally fortunate that a man of MacArthur's vision, courage and drive was there to lead the occupation.

One of the first tasks for Occupation authorities was the location and rehabilitation of Allied prisoners of war (POW). By the end of September 1945, 32,624 POWs had been freed in Japan.

Occupation authorities oversaw the demobilization of Japan's armed forces. By July 31, l948, they had returned almost 6.4 million Japanese servicemen to civilian life, including those who had been in Korea, Manchuria, China and the various islands of the Pacific.

These authorities also oversaw the collection and disposal of Japanese war materiel. M o s t aircraft, tanks, mortars, artillery pieces, ships and other weapons were destroyed. Some small arms, binoculars, sabers and bayonets were retained for issue as souvenirs to U.S. soldiers of the occupation.

Since the Japanese were impoverished, all Japanese stores of food, extensive stocks of uniforms, rubber boots, garrison coats, medicines, blankets and other items were returned to the Japanese government. (This included 21 million pairs of socks, 7 million woolen blankets and more than 5 million pairs of leather shoes.)

Coincident with the repatriation of Allied POWs, demobilization and disarmament of the Japanese armed forces and the destruction of their war materiel, Occupation authorities also oversaw the repatriation of Japanese civilians from Korea and other areas of the world, as well as the return of Korean civilians from Japan.

In September 1945 there were approximately 1,356,400 Koreans in Japan. By May 1947, 935,370 had been returned to Korea. Between Oct. 1, 1945, and Dec. 31, 1946, 5,103,300 Japanese were repatriated. Occupation authorities supervised their return, and made arrangements to assimilate them into the population with a minimum of confusion and loss of time.

A small number of American officers and enlisted men, plus some civil service personnel, were assigned to military government duties. This Military Government organization, known later as Civil Affairs, was designed to first fill the Japanese civil government void, then to assist Japanese civil authorities as the latter took over more and more authority and responsibility. U.S. military occupation troops were deeply involved in supporting and assisting civil affairs officials.

Emerging from their fear of U.S. soldiers, the Japanese planned restaurants, theaters, dance halls, recreation centers and other entertainment facilities for American soldiers. Occupation authorities, in cooperation with the American Red Cross and Army Special Services, set up clubs, snack bars, took over hotels, theaters, golf clubs, parks and other facilities to provide a variety of supervised recreational outlets for occupation personnel.

Many historians and others, writing about the early days of the Korean War, maligned and slandered the soldiers of the U.S. Eighth Army in Japan as soft and ill-trained, or dismissed them all as beer-guzzling skirt-chasers.

Perhaps there were too many means of recreation and diversion available to the young occupation soldier. But, whatever they were in 1949 and 1950, these soldiers were the product of their leadership and training. This is particularly true of the leadership which set the policy and missions of the Army in Japan. Soldiers are not responsible for their state of training; that is the duty of their leaders, starting at the policy/mission level. The American soldiers in Japan were no better or worse than other young U.S. servicemen all over the world. But their state of individual and unit training was not at a satisfactory level for combat.

The mission of both the U.S. Sixth and Eighth Armies in Japan was occupation duty, to support military government and its policies and procedures. As the number of troops was reduced in Japan, the Sixth Army was deactivated. All combat troops there were placed under the command of Eighth Army. Prior to 1949 more than 90 percent of the average soldier's duty time was

9

devoted to fulfilling the occupation mission. Only some range firing and other low-level training, such as military courtesy and discipline, were conducted through these years, sandwiched between occupation responsibilities. Many units attempted to go beyond these basic military subjects, but they were often frustrated by factors over which they had no control.

Records provide some insight into the variety of tasks the men were called upon to perform – all of which served to degrade their combat effectiveness. The experiences of the 7th Cavalry Regiment, 1st Cavalry Division, are fairly typical:

The 7th Cavalry's first mission in Tokyo in 1945 was to take control of central city then locate, investigate and report "all Japanese installations that had contributed to the nation's war effort," including all arsenals, factories, barracks and storage areas. In addition, the Division was helping to demobilize the Japanese armed forces and inventorying all lumber mills in its zone to determine production capacity and lumber stocks on hand.

The location and destruction of weapons, aircraft, ammunition and other war supplies and equipment was continued into 1946. The 7th Cavalry also manned guard posts at the Imperial Palace grounds. The strength of the regiment continued to decline. Many of the few replacements received had not undergone a complete basic training course, but were integrated into the regiment's training program. Meantime, the Cavalry Division's area of control in central Honshu was expanded from four to eleven prefectures when the 97th Infantry Division was inactivated. Occupation continued to be the primary mission in 1947.

By the beginning of 1948, records show, organizational strength of commands in Japan fell dangerously low, hampering them in carrying out occupational patrols and sentry duties. The Cavalry performed occupation tasks as diverse as seizing and transporting under guard over 1,000 carats of diamonds, and the surveillance of Japanese labor demonstrations. Training was squeezed between non-military occupation duties again this year.

In February 1948, 1st Cavalry Division sent a recruiting team back to the U.S. Between March 15 and May 7, 1948, the team enlisted 3,384 men specifically for the 1st Cavalry Division.

The experience of 1st Cavalry Division in loss of personnel was not unique. Two factors seriously hampered both occupation and training efforts throughout Japan, Korea and Okinawa:

1. Far East strength was allowed to fall. Starting in 1945 with some 400,000 men, by June 1950, it stood at 108,500 men. The four combat divisions remaining in Eighth Army at that time numbered a mere 47,050 men. Those divisions were short 28,150 men of full strength, less than 2/3 the strength they should have to go to war.

2. The annual personnel turnover rate between 1945 and 1949 was 43 percent. In 1950, prior to the Korean War, the Far east Command continued to experience the same turnover rate!

The experience of Richard G. Jones points up the results of this rapid turnover of personnel and decline in strength. When he arrived in Ja-

pan in 1946, he was assigned as Chief Clerk in the G1 Section (Personnel and Administration) of the 25th Infantry Division in Osaka. "I was just 19 years old," he wrote, "and had only a few months in the Army and took over the job from a Technical Sergeant who was going home." He was given the job because he had worked after school for three months in a bank and, therefore, was considered to have some office experience. "Several other raw recruits, just out of basic training, were assigned to me at the same time," he said.

Finally in 1949, GEN MacArthur recognized that the Japanese were now able to assume more and more of the civilian administration of their country, and that he needn't rely so heavily on combat units to support occupation tasks. In April he changed the troop mission from that of sternly rigid occupation to one of "friendly protective guidance." The Eighth Army's combat divisions were progressively relieved of occupation duties and directed to undergo training which would lead to an effective, integrated air-ground-sea fighting team.

The date of July 31, 1950 was set for Army divisions in his command to complete Regimental Combat Team (RCT) field exercises and develop effective air-ground combat procedures. A battalion of each division was to complete amphibious landing exercises by Oct. 31.

These proficiency levels were to be attained:
1. Dec. 15, 1949 — Company (battery) level.
2. May 15, 1950 — Battalion (squadron) level.
3. July 31, 1950 — Regimental level.
4. Dec. 31, 1950 — Division level.
5. Combined and joint operations training (including amphibious exercises) were to take place concurrent with RCT and division level training.

This was an excellent program of progressive training, allowing plenty of time to attain each phase — on paper. But too many factors continued to severely hamper the realistic attainment of the projected levels of training:

1. Personnel turnover remained too high.
2. All commands were considerably understrength.
3. Many officers and enlisted men were absent on special duty (SD), detached service (DS) or temporary duty (TDY). Many occupation duties remained, requiring personnel from line units be detailed to these tasks. Also, each division ran special schools and refresh-courses for their officers and enlisted men, requiring men from line units to run these schools. Then there were unit athletes, who often were excused from military training.
4. Divisions and subordinate commands did not have all their units authorized under tables of organization and equipment. (Eleven of the 12 infantry regiments in Eighth Army had only two of their three battalions. None of the regiments had its tank company. Division tank battalions had only one of three authorized tank companies. These tank companies were equipped with light tanks, not the authorized heavy M-26 type. These light tanks were no match for the Russian T-34s they soon would face in Korea. Artillery battalions had only two of three authorized firing batteries. In short, each division could deploy only two-thirds of its wartime infantry

and artillery firepower and only 14 percent of its tank firepower.

5. There were severe shortages of certain crew-served weapons and equipment. For example, Eighth Army had only 21 of its authorized 226 recoilless rifles. Radios, mortars and spare machinegun barrels all were in short supply.

6. Troops in training had a great amount of unserviceable weapons and equipment: 10,000 of 18,000 jeeps were unserviceable. Only 4,441 of the 13,780 two and one-half ton trucks on hand could run. Ninety percent of weapons and 75 percent of automotive equipment in the four divisions had been rebuilt from WWII Pacific battle leftovers, and too much of it was still unserviceable. Further, according to BG Eugene M. Lynch, USA, Ret., who served in Japan before the war, priority of rebuilt equipment at that time went to the Chinese Nationalists on Taiwan and the French in Indochina (Vietnam). Lynch became GEN Walton Walker's pilot during the Korean War.

7. Many of the training areas were too small for proper training. Most could accommodate platoon and company operations, a few up to battalion-size. No areas existed for organizational training above the regimental level.

On Aug. 8, 1949 a training area was acquired on the slopes of Mt. Fuji. This could barely accommodate regimental-sized exercises, but with no live firing. The relatively small number of training areas required some units to undergo some training out of sequence. For example, the 7th Cavalry Regiment had to complete battalion tests before completing individual basic training, in order to use the division's only large-enough training area at Mt. Fuji.

Because of constraints on the Army's training program at the time, soldiers often arrived at their assigned unit without completing basic training. As a result, unit officers and NCOs had to devote time and attention to teaching these young soldiers the skills which they already should have learned.

Another problem was with the intelligence and character ratings of many replacements arriving in the Far East Command in 1949. In April 1949, 43 percent of the enlisted personnel in that command were rated in Class IV and V on the Army Classification Test, the lowest levels of aptitude. Commands in Japan often had to resort to evaluating and discharging men as unfit, necessitating the appointment of so-called "368 Boards" to evaluate individuals for dismissal from the Army for "undesirable traits of character." This produced a further drain on the time of officers who should have been with their units in training. One two-battalion regiment was discharging two to three men per week via these boards.

Most enlisted men were several years younger than their WWII counterparts. It came as no surprise to discover that a young man had enlisted at the age of 17, or even as young as 15. This could have been a factor contributing to their getting into trouble and ending with a Bad Conduct Discharge for "undesirable traits of character."

A third was the Army's Career Guidance Program for officers and non-commissioned officers. Many officers who possessed the leadership and training abilities necessary for the proper development of combat units had been given directed military occupation specialties (MOS) that prohibited them from commanding troops where they were needed. Likewise, experienced enlisted men could not be reassigned from one career field to another. In spite of this, most units had good, experienced leaders. Many commands lost these leaders in their first or second battles in Korea, then suffered terrible casualties when inexperienced men tried to fill in.

A fourth was the mandatory requirement for "Troop Information and Education." These sessions, usually conducted by a platoon leader or NCO, lasted about an hour, but required prior preparation by the session leader. The sessions dealt with current events or some other topic deemed of importance or interest by higher authorities, but often did little except infringe on already limited training time.

The divisions of Eighth Army were deployed in regimental- or battalion-sized garrisons throughout the country, generally near metropolitan areas. With the Japanese economy in shambles, and the 1950 exchange rate of 360 Japanese Yen to one U.S. dollar, even a private's pay of $50 a month was princely.

Recreational activities, some of which could be classified as vices, occupied the soldiers' during off duty time. These included cabarets, sight-seeing, movies on base, USO Clubs, sports, "shacking up," bar-hopping, or just getting together with comrades. Many temptations faced the young occupation soldier. Prostitution was then legal in Japan. Every city had a number of cabarets catering to the men with many prostitutes frequented these establishments. A few men worked the black market by selling their cigarettes to the Japanese. Some men became involved with drugs.

Some commands sometimes made an effort to provide the men with supervised recreation in the form of platoon parties. For example, a platoon party in the 27th Infantry, Camp Sakai, worked like this:

The platoon would request the platoon leader to sponsor a party, to be held in one of the cabarets in Osaka from 9 p.m. to midnight, usually on a Friday or Saturday. These parties rarely occurred more than two or three times a year in any one platoon. The platoon leader was required to write a letter to the Division Provost Marshal (PM) in Osaka, identifying the platoon, the officer sponsoring the party and where and when the event would take place. The PM is the equivalent of a community chief of police. The letter had to be approved at the company, battalion and regimental levels, but the PM could disapprove the request if the platoon had been unruly or had any incidents during its last party. If approval was granted, the platoon leader donated $10 and each of the 36 men or so $5 to buy snacks and soft drinks from the PX and rent the cabaret. This rental granted exclusive use of the dance hall by the platoon, a band and beer in liter bottles; whiskey was prohibited. About half the men had their own girlfriends, so typically, a 36-man platoon needed to hire only about 18 girls as dance partners. The total cost for these additional girls was only a few dollars.

The company First Sergeant was always invited to these affairs, with the platoon leader,

platoon sergeant and other senior NCOs acting as chaperones. The men and girls had to stay in the dance hall or adjoining restrooms. No "hanky-panky" was permitted.

The platoon was transported to and from the party in 2 1/2-ton trucks. The girls dressed up in gowns and had a great time. Most of them did not drink beer; that's why soft drinks were brought along.

In spite of the distractions, often unserviceable or improper weapons and equipment, inadequate training areas, personnel shortages and turnover, the men took tactical training very seriously and tried to do the job right. Because most of them never took part in live-firing unit exercises, they never experienced the sounds of battles. The training was unrealistic.

The recollections and experiences of some of the officers and enlisted men who were members of the Eighth Army in Japan before the Korean War will give some idea of what duty there was really like.

In Dec. 1949, CPT Logan Weston was assigned to Co. D, 17th Infantry Regiment in Sendai, part of the 7th Infantry Division, garrisoning the island of Hokkaido.

Weston had just 63 men in the unit. Full TO&E called for 160. Co. D was the battalion's heavy weapons company and included a machine gun platoon with both heavy and light .30-cal machine guns, a 75mm recoilless rifle platoon and an 81mm mortar platoon.

"From December 1949 to June 1950, I was never able to muster more than 48 men," he wrote. "We had to juggle men from machineguns to recoilless rifles to mortars for our annual tests. Needless to say, we did poorly. The balance of my assigned strength was away on (other) duty type activities. They were on detached service, by orders of higher authority, performing duties which had nothing to do with the weapons company. This was typical in 1948 through 1950. The practice was crippling to unit integrity, cohesion and training."

CPT Joseph W. "Bill" Terman arrived in Japan in early July 1949. Like Weston, who was a member of Merrill's Marauders in WW II, Terman was also a combat veteran, having served in the 150th FAB, 38th Infantry Division in the Pacific. Although a Reserve officer, not Regular Army, Terman was a professional and had high standards.

He was assigned to the 31st FAB, 7th Division, which was at Chitose, Hokkaido. The division's heavy tank battalion, the 77th, equipped with light tanks, was also at Chitose. In a few months he was given command of Battery B.

In a letter to his parents, he once wrote: "We have a very real problem in welding together a good, efficient military team over here. It certainly is a sharp contrast to the problem we had in 1941 and '42 and with more difficulties.... The quality of the men we have, with some outstanding exceptions, is so terribly inferior to the men we had then, the procuring of supplies and equipment erratic and inadequate, and, perhaps most discouraging, the virus of insidious bureaucracy permeating the voluminous paper administration is time-consuming in the extreme...."

CPT Terman is not making a personal attack on his men, but he knew that most of the men in

his battery had not completed grade school and only seven had completed high school. He believed that was the most in any battery of the battalion.

Shortly after she arrived in Japan to join her husband, Terman's wife, Leota, began teaching remedial reading and arithmetic to uneducated soldiers on the post. In a letter home, she wrote, "The grade level ranges from one to fourth grade. We are attempting to get all men to fifth grade level."

As with all other commands in Japan at the time, there was a large turnover of officers at Chitose. In mid-May 1950, there were only four officers at the post who had been there longer than Terman, who had been there nine months. This rapid and frequent turnover of leadership undermined the pursuit of effective training programs throughout the commands of Eighth Army.

The experience of LT Posey L. Starkey is remarkably similar to that of CPT Terman. Starkey was assigned to Co. D, 27th Infantry Regiment at Camp Sakai, Honshu, in July 1949. The 27th was part of the 25th Infantry Division. His platoon was composed of mostly 18- to 20-year-olds. "I recall there were several who were not literate," he wrote, "and their squad leaders would read and write their mail for them."

Starkey: "Our training at Sakai seemed to be largely garrison drills in subjects that were little advanced from advanced individual training.... We spent countless hours in gun drill... and similar elementary subjects. It was not until we went to the Fuji training area that I recall much tactical training. We did some firing but it seemed to be mostly 1,000-inch range work along with individual weapon qualification.

"We had our first real tactical training and field firing at Fuji.... We didn't talk about 'grazing fire,' we actually did it. We walked final protective lines and drew range based on real terrain. And we were away from the distractions of Sakai and garrison life."

1SG George S. Hearn was also a combat veteran of WWII, having served in China. He was assigned to the 27th at different times between 1947 and 1950.

In February 1947, he was transferred from Beijing to Co. B, 27th Infantry. Most of the members of the company were 18-month enlisted men. There were only two senior sergeants in the company and some platoons were led by privates first class (PFCs). "Early in 1948," he recalled, "the regiment was down in strength and Service Company and Regimental Headquarters were the only active companies.... The 1st Battalion was inactive with [a] lieutenant, a supply sergeant and [Hearn] as 1st Sergeant."

Hearn came to the U.S. in mid-July 1948, but returned to Japan in December. He was assigned as 1st Sergeant of Company B. He discovered that the 1st and 2d Battalions had "filled with new re-enlistees and... NCOs.... Most of our training was parade-ground type," with "maybe two weeks field training" during the summer," he said.

Harold E. Dill entered the Army in the Spring of 1945. On Jan. 25, 1949, he won a direct commission and an opportunity to become a Regular Army officer. In early Summer 1949, he was assigned to Co. B, 21st Infantry, Camp Wood,

Entrance to Camp Sakai, Japan. Home of the 27th Infantry Regt. (Courtesy of Richard S. Majcher, C/27 Infantry)

A view looking northeast from a hill near Camp Gifu, Honshu, Japan, 1948. (Courtesy of William Gott, former CPT 24th Infantry)

Pup tents at Camp McNair, 1949. (Source: Skirmish, Red, White and Blue, Ed Daily, Turner, 1992)

Wakiyama Rifle Range, June 1950. L-R: PVT Hulbert (blown up in Korea by a direct hit by an artillery round); PVT Tolbert; PFC Bell; Daniel Cooper. Cooper had just tied a 2/27th Inf record with the rifle. (Courtesy of Daniel Cooper, G/27 Infantry)

Guard Mount Inspection Co. A, 29th Infantry Regiment, Camp Napunja, Okinawa, 1949. (Courtesy of Jesus Rodriguez, A/29 Infantry)

Mt. Fuji Training Area near Gotemba, for elements of the 25th Infantry Division, 1949. (Courtesy of Harold Lederer (Deceased), A and C/27 Infantry)

13

Men of Btry B, 31st FAB, 7th Division prepare for inspection, Spring, 1950. (Photo by CPT Joseph W. Terman [KIA aug. 22, 1950]) (Courtesy of Dr. james W. Terman, M.D., son of CPT Joseph W. Terman)

Japanese K.P.s, Camp Sakai, May 1950. (Courtesy of Daniel Cooper, G/27 Infantry)

Osaka PX building about 1948, during the time the 25th Division Headquarters was in Osaka. (Courtesy of Milton Melhourn, Jr., 28 MP Co.)

Bolo Point, Okinawa, 1949. Left to Right: Man on left unidentified; Jesus Rodriguez; Alfredo [no last name given]; Manuel Gonzolas [KIA, Korea]. All were members of Co. A, 29th Infantry Regt. (Courtesy of Jesus Rodriguez, A/29 Infantry) near Kumamoto, Kyushu, part of the 24th Infantry Division, garrisoning Kyushu. His battalion training included air transportability and passing its field test.

James W. Dodgen, who enlisted in 1948 at the age of 16, was a member of Co. B, 7th Cavalry Regiment, part of the 1st Cavalry Division in northern Honshu. His battalion also underwent air transportability training, plus some amphibious warfare training just before the outbreak of the Korean War.

Company cooks usually worked one or two days, then were off one or two days. But these work days were very long — 12 hours or more. Gerald Gingery was the honor graduate of his cooks' and bakers' class at Ft. Knox, KY, in 1949. Sent to Japan in June, he became a cook in Co. H, 5th Cavalry Regiment, Camp McGill, Takayama, Honshu, part of the 1st Cavalry Division. As a cook, he recalled, he had considerable free time. At first, he said he was "apprehensive about the Japanese people," but soon befriended a number of them. Gerald spent much of his free time visiting shrines, temples and other sights. "All in all," he considered that "this was probably the very best of times in my Army life."

Twice between June 1949 and June 1950, his outfit went on "maneuvers" at Camp McNair, the 1st Cavalry's training area at Mt. Fuji.

About the only positive factor in getting the men out for training was that all Army garrisons in Japan employed Japanese nationals. Barbers, tailors, carpenters, kitchen police (KP) in unit mess halls, etc., were all handled by Japanese civilians. The men of each unit contributed money to pay KPs. In Gingery's unit, it was $10 per month per man. Without these paid KPs, four to six soldiers would have to be detailed daily to this task from every company or battery.

This, then, is a "snapshot" of occupation duty in Japan. Hampered in proper training by a multitude of factors, over which regimental, battalion and unit officers and NCOs had no control, most of them tried to do the best job possible.

The Occupation of Okinawa

The island of Okinawa is the largest island of Japan's Ryukyu Island chain, which extends from Japan to Taiwan. Okinawa is 67 miles long and ranges from 2 to 16 miles wide.

At the outbreak of the Korean War, the U.S. Army garrison included one combat organization, the three-battalion 29th Infantry Regiment. Like all Far East commands, the 29th was under-strength.

Regimental HQ, 1st and 3d Battalions was located at Camp Napunja, near Ishikawa, in the narrow 2-mile wide part of the island. The 2d Battalion was stationed at Awashi, a town some 8 or 10 miles south of Ishikawa. The men lived in quonset huts, constructed of curved sheets of corrugated metal, forming a building which resembled a half-circle when viewed from the ends. Each end of the building was pierced by doors and windows, and some huts also had a few windows along the curved walls.

Parts of Okinawa had been destroyed in the heavy fighting for the island in 1945. The people of the island were in about the same state as those in Japan. By 1949, however, they, too, had partially recovered.

The 29th, by this time, was dividing its time between low-level training and occupation duties. Okinawa was considered a hardship tour, somewhat over a year, but with no dependents. The same problems as in Japan inhibited the accomplishment of both training and occupation missions.

Frank F. Byrne (MSG, USA, Ret.), assigned to Co. K, had only five men in a squad that should have numbered nine. Three of the five were "jocks" — athletes. As a result, he wrote, "when we mustered for the day's training, I had two riflemen." He "found out later the rest of the command [regiment] was the same as my squad — under-manned, under-trained, under-equipped."

Harold Gamble, a Navy corpsman (medic) with the Marines in WWII during the invasion of Okinawa, was assigned to the 29th Regiment's Medical Company in April 1950. "Little had changed," he recalled, "Some rebuilding; the people were quite poor. The cities of Naha [capital of the island] and Shuri [a nearby town] were rebuilding.... Okinawa was a hardship tour...."

Dennis R. Nicewanger arrived on Okinawa as a new 2LT in January 1950. Duty was boring to him. Leisure consisted of swimming or touring the island in a jeep, visiting WWII battle grounds. "The daily routine... rotated around two events... either on guard duty... or conducting individual and small unit training," he declared. The 29th was the only Infantry command on the island, and was therefore called upon for security missions — to the detriment of training. "[We] found ourselves walking and conducting guard duty[at ammo dumps, supply depots, vehicle parks and other logistical centers] about every four or five days," he continued. "Each battalion was required to provide a company sized unit, 150 or so men, for guard duty, about every 4 or 5 days."

Training consisted of individual, squad and section exercises, and the preparation of bunkers and foxholes. Nicewanger's unit was able to conduct just one exercise between January and July 1950 in which they fired their weapons.

The experiences of these men show there was little difference between duty in Japan and duty in Okinawa; in both, training did not achieve the top priority that it should have had.

The Occupation of Korea

Korea is a mountainous peninsula of some 85,000 square miles, which juts from the Asiatic land mass like an ill-shapen thumb. It is

15

KOREA

Scale 1: 4,000,000 or
63.13 Miles to the Inch

STATUTE MILES

bounded on the north by the Yalu and Tum-en Rivers, on the east by the Sea of Japan, the Korea Strait in the south and by the Yellow Sea on the west. Some 500 miles of China and 11 miles of Russia border Korea in the north, along the rivers.

Korea is about the size of Utah but is shaped somewhat like Florida. The east coast is characterized by high mountains, which end abruptly in deep water. There are few harbors and little tide. On the west coast, however, the irregular shore line provides many harbors, and a tide of some 32 feet at Inchon.

The high Taebaek Range runs down the east coast like a massive spine. The range gradually falls in elevation as it trends southward. Almost all of Korea south of the narrow waist from Pyongyang to Wonsan slopes westward from Taebaek. As a result, the drainage and direction of flow of all sizable rivers is generally southwest.

At the time of the U.S. occupation and the Korean War, every mountain valley, no matter how small, was terraced, irrigated and cultivated. Even so, only 20 percent of Korea was arable land, mostly in the south and west. Rice, barley and soybeans, in that order, were the principal crops. Most rice was grown in the south, where the climate permitted two crops annually.

The country's population in 1950 was about 30 million. Of these, 21 million lived south of the 38th parallel and 9 million resided north of it. North Korea comprised 58 percent of the land area in 1950.

Summers in Korea are hot and humid, with a monsoon season generally from June to September. Winters are very cold, due to the winds coming from the interior of northern Asia. At the Chosin Reservoir in North Korea in December 1950, the Marines and soldiers experienced -40 degree temperatures.

Korea, also known as the "Hermit Kingdom," or Chosen, "The Land of the Morning Calm," had been successively ruled by China and Japan. From 1904 until 1945, Japan occupied Korea in a ruthless stranglehold, annexing the country as a colony in 1910. Only Japanese was taught in schools, although only 20 percent of the Korean people at the time could read or write. Japanese colonization of Korea was encouraged. They exploited the people and the land, and integrated Korea's industry with that of Japan.

The Japanese did attempt to modernize Korea, building roads, bridges, railroads, dams and factories. In spite of their efforts, most roads were dirt. A one-and-a-half-lane dirt road was considered a highway. The 750,000 Japanese residing in Korea were complete masters of the country, its people, its economy and its government. Koreans were dominated and exploited in their own country by the hated Japanese.

Most South Koreans at the time were farmers. Everyone in the family who could, worked in the paddies or fields. Rice was planted by hand, one plant at a time, pushed into the mud at the bottom of the paddy. It also was harvested by hand with a small sickle.

In rural areas people often relieved themselves by the side of the road, or in the fields where they worked. "Waste boxes" were provided in the cities of both Japan and Korea. These were public toilets consisting of an open ditch

about 18 inches wide and 3 to 4 feet long. When the ditch got full, a "honey dipper" would empty the accumulated material into a bucket. These buckets were picked up by wagons resembling a huge barrel on four wheels, called "honey carts" or "honey wagons." They carried their cargo to the country to be used as fertilizer in the paddies and fields. Farmers stored this product in shallow "honey wells" for future use. The smell of human feces was pervasive in the summer throughout much of Japan and Korea.

Farm houses and village dwellings were one story buildings constructed of mud and small sticks. Wooden rafters supported thatched roofs. Usually, the kitchen was at one end of the house and a few feet lower than the other one or two rooms. The kitchen fire kept the remainder of the house warm in winter (and summer) because the "chimney" ran under the floor of the room(s), then up the outside wall at the opposite end of the house. Some houses had an overhang to form a porch. A low wall often connected the house to outbuildings for oxen and the family toilet. There was no running water or electricity. One or two oil lamps, which gave off ribbons of black smoke, usually provided what light was necessary.

Most of this agrarian population had never been more than a few miles from their ancestral home areas. As a result, they had absolutely no concept of anything beyond their narrow, parochial lives. Forty years of repression and cruelty by the Japanese had further sapped any glimmer of independence or initiative from most Koreans.

As a result, the arrival of the Americans, with their fast-paced ways, vast wealth, food, jeeps, tanks and other trappings was overwhelming to the Koreans. On the other hand, the primitive and backward condition of the country, coupled with alien religions, philosophies and language was somewhat of a shock to the Americans. Further, the country smelled bad!

While the Soviet Union considered Korea to be of strategic value after WWII, the U.S. did not. The country had a relatively small population and no important industries or natural resources. Russia sought to control all of Korea and opposed the influence of any other country in that nation. The Soviets entered the war against Japan on Aug. 9, 1945, defeating Japanese troops in Manchuria. The proximity of Russian troops to Korea there and in Siberia forced U.S. planners to hastily accept the surrender of Japanese troops in Korea.

The U.S. State-War-Navy Coordinating Committee (SWNCC) met in Washington, D.C. on Aug. 10, 1945, in order to issue appropriate orders to GEN MacArthur. Finally, the Chief of the War Department's Operations Division Policy Section, COL Charles H. Bonesteel, was given 30 minutes to make a recommendation on how this could be done. Looking at a map, he noted that the 38th parallel cut Korea approximately in half, so he, therefore, proposed that the U.S. accept surrender of Japanese forces south of that line and the Soviets handle surrenders north of it. His recommendation was adopted and carried out. No one at the time envisioned that the 38th parallel would serve any other purpose — least of all to delineate the border between two nations — North Korea and

South Korea. But that is exactly what it did. Families were split and provinces divided arbitrarily by this line. No thought was given, nor expected to be given, to defensible terrain on either side of this line. The 38th parallel, like other longitudinal and latitudinal lines, exists on maps solely for geographic and navigational purposes.

When GEN MacArthur, commanding all U.S. forces in the Far East, received this order, he designated LTG John R. Hodge's XXIV Corps (6th, 7th and 40th Infantry Divisions) to occupy the area of Korea south of the 38th and accept the surrender of all Japanese troops in that area. Subsequently, the Corps became a military occupation force in South Korea. The force, under LTG Hodge, was designated U.S. Army Forces in Korea (USAFIK). A small Corps advance party landed at Kimpo Airfield near Seoul at about noon on Sept. 4, 1945. Most of the Corps landed at Inchon four days later.

The 40th Division was deactivated in early 1946, leaving the 6th and 7th to carry on. Duties of these two divisions included handling the military government of South Korea, the establishment of a civil government composed of Koreans, the establishment and training of a civilian police force (constabulary), as well as a national defense organization. In addition, the two divisions were tasked with security along the border with North Korea and the internal security of the South. Training to maintain and sharpen military skills was subordinated to these occupation missions.

Both the 6th and 7th Divisions were deployed over wide areas of South Korea. The 7th Division's 32d Infantry Regiment was sent to guard the 38th parallel. At first, the relationship with Soviet troops across the border was very cordial, but soon the border became an "iron curtain," manned on both sides by armed troops.

The 38th parallel was outposted by a series of reinforced rifle squads of about 14 men each. The men lived in quonset huts. Gasoline-driven pumps provided running water, and stand-up generators were ready to provide electricity when power from the North was shut off. Rations, mail, PX and other supplies were delivered periodically by truck. Each of these tiny units manned outposts, listening posts and patrolled a segment of the border. Patrols also came from the parent company. Many of these companies were located by themselves, isolated in tiny unit enclaves. They guarded against wholesale movement of goods to the North, provided guides for escapees from there and detected Northern guerrillas and raiders. Outpost duty was rotated frequently among commands of the occupying force. The men on outpost duty had to be alert and soldier. Theirs was a very important mission. Behind them were companies, battalions and regiments, ready to reinforce, when necessary.

U.S. authorities did what they could to bring a little stateside atmosphere to the men. A number of service clubs, operated by the Red Cross and Army Special Services, helped somewhat. Seoul boasted the "Hourglass Club," "Marble Hall," "Lanyard Lodge," "Quadrangle Club" and "Leisure Lodge." Camp Uijongbu, north of Seoul, had "Hillside Hut" and Munsan "Club Munsan." Further south at Taejon were the "Chunchon Club" and "Club Attu."

With the establishment of a South Korean Constabulary came missions for the 6th and 7th Divisions to organize, and staff training schools for Constabulary recruits. By 1948, for example, the 6th ran a weapons school at Taegu and a cannon school at Chinhae. The 7th had another cannon school for the Constabulary at Seoul.

Coincident with these activities by the occupying force, the U.S. was establishing what became known as the Korean Military Advisory Group (KMAG — pronounced Kay-mag). Initially, these men served as advisers to the Constabulary, and later, the South Korean Army. By the time of the Korean War, KMAG was authorized 181 officers, seven warrant officers, a nurse and 283 enlisted men.

The experiences and recollections of some former members of the Korean occupation forces provide some concept of what duty there entailed in 1948 and 1949.

Richard H. Stinson served in the Korean occupation in 1948 and 1949 as a member of Battery C, 48th FAB. The government of South Korea, under President Syngman Rhee, was just forming. Pro-Communist elements in the country were attacking military installations and trains carrying supplies, so Americans had to provide armed guards on these supply trains.

The guard details were composed of men from the 31st Infantry, 48th and 57th FAB and the 13th Combat Engineer Battalion. Usually, a detail of about five men was sent from each organization to the Seoul railyards. Each man was armed with an M2 automatic carbine for artillerymen and engineers or an M1 rifle for infantrymen, and carried a full field pack. The combined force was divided and placed on boxcars. Each car-group was given C-rations a 5-gallon can of water — and ample ammunition.

The train traveled by way of Suwon, south through Osan to Taejon, then southeast to Taegu and south from there to Pusan. The route was reversed on the way back to Seoul. The round trip took from 10 to 14 days.

The Army guards stayed in their assigned cars during the trip. If a train was attacked, as they often were, the defenders attempted to get the attackers in a cross-fire — which they often did. On one trip Stinson was stabbed in the back. He was treated at the Wonju hospital and put back on the train. Although he went back to Korea in 1950 as a member of the 555th FAB and again in 1951 with the 196th FAB, this is the only wound Stinson suffered.

On another trip, Korean bandits (or guerrillas) hit the train at a curve near a mountain. They "came down from the mountain, shooting and carrying torches," Stinson wrote. "But like rehearsal, we caught them in a crossfire and shot the _____ out of them. Word got out that we meant business...."

Occupation forces also set up unannounced roadblocks along the main roads, with the objective of retrieving stolen U.S. property and equipment.

In the 48th FAB, a gun crew, without its howitzer, and an auto mechanic usually were employed on a roadblock. When a Korean vehicle was pulled to the side of the road and inspected, every piece of U.S. or GI equipment found on the vehicle was removed on the spot. "They had everything," Stinson recalled, "from tires, radia-

tors, generators, starters, batteries, [engine] blocks, transmissions, etc."

Occasionally, an entire 2 1/2-ton truck or jeep (1/4-ton) was stopped and taken from the Korean driver. On one occasion, an electric generator large enough "to supply a house with lights" was retrieved. When a truck was seized or a vehicle made inoperable because of the removal of American parts, the occupants had no recourse but to continue their journey on foot. If a Korean employee of an American installation was found to have stolen goods, his identification card was taken and he was fired on the spot, and his card was sent to where he had worked. When South Korean security forces were trained, they took over road-block and train-guard duty.

In 1948, occupation duty in Korea was a nononsense job, even on a pass into town. In the 48th Field, the orders were to go in numbers of 5 or more. The shuttle bus to town had an armed guard riding shotgun.

Robert B. Hardin enlisted in the Army in February 1948 and arrived in Korea in May. He was assigned to the U.N. unit which guarded the Duk Soo Palace in Seoul, the home of Korea's ancient rulers. Later, he was assigned to Company I, 32d Infantry Regiment. Duties included "guard duty all over Seoul," he observed, mixed with some training.

Gene McClure also arrived in Korea in May 1948. He had enlisted in the Army on Dec. 18, 1947, when only 15 years old. Between May 1948 and May 1949, he served successively in the 506th Post Engineers (6th Division) in Taegu, the 31st Infantry (7th Division) at Seoul, the 7th Division stockade at Seoul (as a guard) and when it was activated, the 5th Regimental Combat Team (RCT). McClure subsequently served in Korea with Co. H, 5th RCT.

The pro-Communist movement's agents in South Korea often attempted to foment disorder. On one occasion in 1948, they incited a mutiny in a South Korean Constabulary unit. The mutineers attacked McClure's camp. One U.S. soldier was killed, but the firing alerted the garrison, and infantrymen manned the camp's perimeter until South Korean police arrived and quelled the mutiny.

Another time, McClure and a buddy were walking back to camp from town. As they approached the camp, a soldier ran from a side street, followed by a large crowd of angry Koreans and a Korean policeman with a carbine. The policeman called to the fleeing soldier, but he kept running and tried to climb over the camp fence. The policeman fired one shot, hitting the soldier in the head, killing him instantly. McClure and his friend jumped into a drainage ditch along the road as the policeman stood waving his carbine about and pointing it in their general direction. He soon left.

An American Army sergeant, who had been posting guards at the camp's front gate ran up. When told what happened, he followed the Korean into the police station and seized him. The sergeant then marched him into the Army camp at gunpoint. Investigation revealed that the dead soldier had been accused of cheating a Korean merchant out of some money and was running away.

Seventeen-year-old Sal Napolitano arrived in Korea in January 1948 and was assigned to the 31st FAB, which was performing military po-

lice duty. He recalled that the most serious problems for the occupation authorities were prostitution, theft, the black market and civilian riots.

As 1948 turned into 1949, the troops in Korea spent more time in training than heretofore. In the 48th Field this included what artillerymen call the "Cannoneer's Hop." In this exercise, members of an artillery gun crew rotated jobs on command. In this way, the crew cross-trained in the different tasks of each member. There were also classes in forward observation and the operation of a Fire Direction Center (FDC).

South Korea held a general election on May 10, 1948, forming a 200-representative National Assembly. During its first meeting on May 31, the Assembly elected Syngman Rhee chairman. On July 12, they adopted the Constitution of the Republic of Korea (ROK-pronounced ROCK). On July 16, the Assembly elected Rhee president of South Korea. On Aug. 15, 1948, the government of South Korea was formally inaugurated and the U.S. Military Government in Korea ended. On Aug. 24, President Rhee and LTG Hodge signed an interim military agreement to be in effect until the U.S. withdrew its troops. That withdrawal began on Sept. 15, and the U.S. recognized the new Republic of South Korea on Jan. 1, 1949.

It was also on that date that the U.S. Army's 5th RCT was formed in Korea from elements of the 7th Infantry Division. Members of the 32d Infantry Regiment were transferred to the new command. The 48th FAB became the RCT's 555th FAB. The 72d Engineer Combat Battalion (ECB) became its 72d Engineer Combat Company (ECC). The 7th Mechanized Reconnaissance Troop also went to the 5th. The regimental combat team was sent to Hawaii on June 29, 1949. At about the same time, the 7th Division was sent to garrison Hokkaido, Japan. USAFIK was deactivated at midnight on June 30, 1949.

CHAPTER TWO — The Development of the North and South Korean Armed Forces

The North and South Korean armed forces are ultimate examples of an offensive military instrument (the North) and a defensive military instrument (the South). Only in their Coast Guards do we see that both nations designed them to protect their shorelines from smugglers, small raids and the like.

The North Korean Armed Forces

Japanese police maintained order, generally, in the north, until the Soviets arrived. Soon after their arrival, local Communist police or security organizations, such as the People's Guards and Red Guards, sprang up. These soon gave way to the Peace Guardians, a province level police force. Centralized control of the provincial police was quickly established by the Department of Public Safety. On Sept. 25, 1945, Kim Il Sung and a group of Soviet-trained Koreans landed at Wonsan. These people, formerly guerrillas against the Japanese, were assigned as advisers to provincial governments. Their mission was supervision of the police forces of the provisional police bureaus.

The Central Party School of Police Officials, begun in January 1946, tightened the Communist Party's control of the police. In 1945, the Pyongyang Military Academy was organized. Academy graduates went into the Constabulary. In March 1947, three more similar officer training schools were set up. The four academies then turned out officers for the Peace Preservation

Officers' Training Schools. These "schools" masked the North Korean armed forces.

In 1946 the North organized a Railway Constabulary, independent of the Department of Public Safety. Its principal mission was to receive officers and men of the Volunteer Army and new recruits. Both the Peace Preservation Officers' Training School system and the Railway Constabulary then became part of the security forces of the Department of Public Safety (later the Department of Internal Affairs). During 1946, officers and enlisted men who had been members of the Korean Volunteer Army in Manchuria were released to enroll in the Korean Railway Constabulary.

The Soviets began arming North Korean forces in December 1946, Some of this equipment came from Soviet troops who were returning home. In 1947, Russia began providing arms in exchange for foodstuffs from North Korea.

The Soviet army in Korea also provided early training to the Koreans. By December 1946, North Korean training units had Soviet officers permanently assigned to them as advisers. Nearby Russian army garrisons provided special training cadres.

A major campaign was launched in 1946 to recruit men into the armed forces. North Korean Labor Party members were urged to enlist. Men with previous military service in the Japanese Army, or who had been trained by the Japanese as policemen, as well as those who were former members of the Korean Volunteer Force or of

other Chinese Communist trained forces, all were inducted into the armed forces. Police force volunteers also were transferred wholesale into the nation's new "security" formations. There was also a general conscription of men between the ages of 18 and 35.

North Korean, Chinese Communist and Soviet military leaders arranged for Soviet-trained North Korean troops to be employed with the Chinese Communist Army. As a result, in March and April 1947, over 30,000 North Korean troops, equipped with Soviet arms, were moved to Manchuria.

The true goal of the Peace Preservation Officers' Schools was to organize, equip and train a national army. The mask was lifted in September 1947 with the organization of the Department of Military affairs. At the same time, the 1st, 2d and 3d Peace Preservation Officers' Training Centers became the People's Army's 1st and 2d Division and the Independent Infantry Brigade. However, the North Korean Government did not announce the activation of an armed force under the title "People's Army" until February 8, 1948. That year, too, the Department of Military Affairs became the Ministry of National Defense.

The overall strength of the People's Army at the time was about 30,000. In addition, there were approximately 170,000 trainees, including members of the Police Constabulary, Fire brigades and Coast Guard.

The Independent Mixed Brigade became the

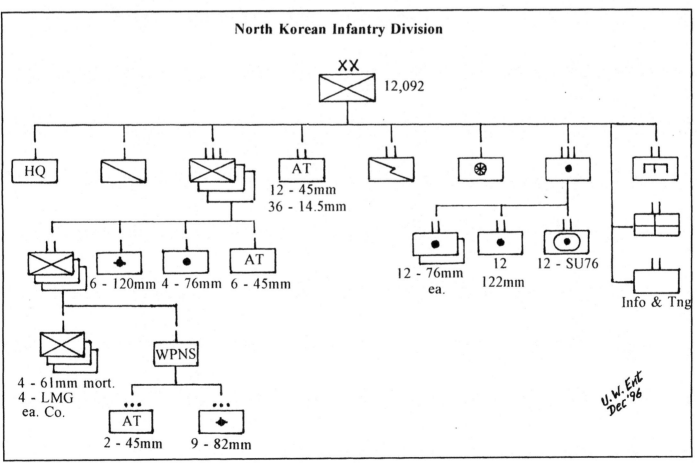

North Korean Infantry Division

The North Korean Army

1st Div. (20, 22, 24 Regts)	11,000	766th Ind. Inf. Unit	3,000
2d Div. (4, 6, 17 Regts)	10,838	12th Motorcycle Regt	2,000
3d Div. (7, 8, 9 Regts)	11,000	105th Armd Bde (107, 109, 203	
4th Div. (5, 16, 18 Regts)	11,000	Armd Regt, 206 Mech Inf Regt)	6,000
5th Div. (10, 11, 12 Regts)	11,000	1st Bde, Border Constab	5,000
6th Div. (13, 14, 15 Regts)	11,000	2d Bde, Border Constab	2,600
7th Div. (1, 2, 3 Regts)(Later		3d Bde, Border Constab	4,000
redesignated 12th Division)	12,000	5th Bde, Border Constab	3,000
10th Div. (25, 27, 29 Regts)	6,000	7th Bde, Border Constab	4,000
13th Div. (19, 21, 23 Regts)	6,000	Army, I & II Corps	6-7,000
15th Div. (45, 48, 50 Regts)	11,000		

TOTAL: 137,438

To that, add these:	122mm Artillery Regt	1,300
	603d (83d) Motorcycle Rcn Bn	3,500
	Engineer Bde	2,500
	Signal Reg	1,000
	Guerrilla Command	2,500

TOTAL: 10,800

GRAND TOTAL: 148,238

3d Division in Oct. 1948; the 4th Division was formed in late 1949. At the same time, the Chinese Communist 164th and 166th Divisions, made up of Koreans, became the nucleus of the 5th Division, formed in August and the 6th Division, organized in July. The 7th, later redesignated the 12th, was formed from veterans of the Chinese Communist 15th and 156th Divisions. A tank battalion, organized in the fall of 1948, was expanded into a regiment by May 1949. It eventually grew to be the 105th Armored Division. Finally, the 10th and 15th Divisions were organized in March 1950 and the 13th in June of that year.

On the eve of the Korean War in late June 1950, the North Korean People's Army(NKPA) or *In Min Gun*, had between 150,000 and 180,000 men. Right after hostilities began, the 1st and 3d Border Constabulary Brigades, which had been follow-up troops in the invasion of South Korea, were redesignated as the 8th and 9th Divisions, respectively. The North Koreans also had Russian-trained pilots, aircraft mechanics, tankers and tank maintenance personnel.

The North Korean Infantry Division was authorized 12,092 personnel. Only the 7th was at that strength. The structure followed closely that of the WWII Soviet Rifle Division. On the left are the estimated North Korean strengths at the start of the Korean War.

The North Koreans had a total of 150 T-34

Constabulary Group Training with 81-mm Mortar at the Korean Weapons School, Taegu. (Source: Page 31, Military Advisers in Korea: KMAG in Peace and War, Sawyer, U.S. Government Printing Office, Washington, D.C., 1962)

Korean police arrest a Communist rioter in Seoul. (Source: Page 74, Military Advisers in Korea: KMAG in Peace and War, *Sawyer, U.S. Government Printing Office, Washington, D.C., 1962)*

tanks, 120 of which were in the 105th Armored Brigade. The three-tank regiments each had 40 tanks, each with three medium tank battalions of 13 tanks each. A tank battalion consisted of three tank companies of four tanks each. Company, battalion and regimental commanders each had a personal tank. Tank crews had five men. The brigade was expanded to the 105th Armored Division at the end of June 1950.

One hundred and fifty tanks does not seem like many, but Korea, chopped up by steep mountains, narrow valleys and rice paddies, is poor tank country. The North Koreans knew that the South had no tanks or effective antitank weapons and did not expect to confront U.S. troops. The T-34 was one of the better tanks to emerge from WWII, with a low silhouette, good armor, a wide tread and a good gun. Characteristics of the T-34 are in a Chapter Note.

The North Korean air force in June 1950 numbered 2,000 men, with 140 aircraft. Of these, 40 were Yak propeller-driven fighters and 70 propeller-driven bombers. The Coast Guard contained 13,700 men, the Marines 9,000 and the internal security establishment 34,000.

The South Korean Armed Forces

The Republic of Korea Army evolved from the ROK 15,000-man Constabulary. On Nov. 13, 1945, the U.S. military government established the Office of the Director of National Defense, with jurisdiction over the Bureau of Police and a new Bureau of Armed Forces. This bureau was to oversee the Army and Navy departments.

The ROK armed forces first were envisioned to consist of an army of one corps with three divisions, and an air force with one transport and two fighter squadrons. The Army Air Force would total 45,000 men; the Navy and Coast Guard would have another 5,000. The projected national police force would number 25,000. The U.S. State-War-Navy-Coordinating Committee (SWNCC), back in Washington, concerned that the Soviets might misunderstand, recommended that implementation of the plan be postponed until after a joint U.S.-USSR commission on establishing a unified government had met.

An alternate plan, establishing a 2,500 man police reserve then was adopted. This plan (named BAMBOO) envisioned one company of 225 enlisted men and six officers being stationed in each province. The company would essentially be an infantry company, without mortars and the like. A U.S. training team of two officers and four enlisted men would be sent into each province to select activation and training areas and begin recruiting and organizing. Gradually, the company would be expanded into a second and a third, forming a battalion. The expansion was expected to continue until there was a regiment of police in each province.

By April 1946, this national constabulary numbered somewhat over 2,000 men, armed with WWII Japanese rifles. U.S. LTC John T. Marshall was the first American Chief of Constabulary. His staff included Lee Hyung Koon, former Korean colonel in the Japanese Army, as an "adviser." In January 1946, 16 lieutenants from the deactivated 40th Division were added to his staff. These officers were sent out in pairs to the provinces, along with an American of Japanese descent, to organized the regiments.

The South Korean Coast Guard

A coast guard existed under the Japanese. Coincident with the establishment of the Constabulary, the Americans helped to reform the coast guard. On Jan. 14, 1946, the Military Government transferred it to the jurisdiction of the Director of National Defense (first headed by BG Lawrence E. Schick, then Colonel Arthur S. Champeny). Recruiting began the next month. Both qualified personnel and equipment were scarce, as were qualified advisers. Fifteen U.S. Coast Guard officers and enlisted advisers arrived from the U.S. in September 1946. However, in July 1947, the U.S. Treasury Department, under which the U.S. Coast Guard operates, protested the prolonged assignment of these men overseas. Finally, in mid-1948, arrangements were made to employ retired Coast Guard officers as advisers to replace the active duty men. Both the Constabulary and Coast Guard were activated Jan. 14, 1946.

A Bureau of Police managed the National Police force. In March 1946, this Bureau was removed from the office of the Director of National Defense and became a separate organization.

Development of the Constabulary

In September 1946, CPT James H. Hausman was transferred to the Bureau of Constabulary in Seoul and, shortly thereafter, directed to begin building up a Constabulary headquarters and to accelerate the entire program. BG William L. Roberts (Ret.), first chief of the Korean Military Advisory Group, once wrote to GEN Orlando Ward, Chief of Military History: Hausman "had more to do with the... arming, equipping, moves, expansions [of the Korean Constabulary] than anyone else."

Hausman was faced with too few advisers and a large geographic deployment of Constabulary units. In one case an adviser had to drive a circuit of 350 miles through the mountains to reach all the units under his supervision. The Constabulary trained seven days a week, including classes at night for Korean officers and noncommissioned officers (NCOs). Some advisers also conducted additional classes in English.

Training was restricted by the lack of adequate numbers of advisers as well as by the type of training which was permitted. Since the Constabulary was a police reserve, training was restricted to the use of small arms, basic drill and internal security methods.

The advisers, believing that the Korean Constabulary might eventually become the Korean Army, used their own initiative to further training. Where U.S. troops were close by, advisers borrowed American weapons and enlisted men — sometimes a whole squad — for demonstrations. As a result, Korean soldiers did receive some training with M1 rifles, mortars and machine guns months before these weapons were issued to them.

The Constabulary's training often included actual experience in quelling civil disorders and combat with guerrillas. These actions taught them valuable lessons in the importance of control in military operations and the principals of fighting in towns. During one operation in late 1947, the unit advised by LTC Clarence C. DeReus combined the tactics of a raid with those of a night attack.

Since there was a shortage of American advisers, Korean officers who had had military experience under the Japanese or Chinese often took over, sometimes employing methods in conflict with U.S. doctrine. But their influence had a positive side. In field operations they were not bound by roads and were satisfied with horses or human carriers. This attitude proved advantageous in the coming war.

The Soviet Union and the U.S. failed to agree on a reunified Korea with a single government, although they negotiated on the matter for some two years. In the meantime, anticipating the eventual establishment of Korean independence, the U.S. military set up a South Korean interim government in May 1947.

Then began the exploration of how and in what form the Korean armed forces should be developed. North Korea announced the establishment of the NKPA on Feb. 8, 1948. In March the U.S. revealed support for a South Korean Constabulary of 50,000 men.

On April 8, the Department of the Army ordered that a South Korean armed force be organized, equipped and trained for internal security and defense. The American government was fearful that the South Koreans would use their armed forces against the North and embroil the U.S. in a war. As a result, the ROKA was pitifully armed and equipped to defend itself against the onslaught of the NKPA in June 1950.

As previously noted, both the U.S. 6th and 7th Divisions now became more deeply involved in training the South Koreans. Constabulary troops received valuable training in the use of American machine guns, 60mm and 81mm mortars, 57mm antitank guns and the 105mm howitzer.

The Revolt at Yosu

As U.S. troops left Korea in late 1948 and early 1949, they gave some of their equipment to the ROK military. In 1948, the South Koreans expanded the Constabulary from nine to 15 regiments in five brigades. On Oct. 19, the mutiny of the ROK 14th Regiment at Yosu put the fledgling government and Army to the test.

The revolt was touched off by an order assigning the 14th to the island of Cheju-do to help quell disorders there. The regiment had been issued U.S. M1 rifles, but had retained its Japanese rifles as well. A number of Communists among the regiment's NCOs had planned an uprising and were going to use the extra rifles to arm sympathetic people in nearby villages. A second order directing the regiment to move at once caused the Communist leaders to start the rebellion before they had planned. They incited anti-police sentiment among the troops, and the men of the 14th attacked to seize the town.

As the rebellion spread, loyal Constabulary and police units were rushed in from nearby districts. BG Song Ho Seung, Chief of the Constabulary, was placed in command. CPT Hausman and seven other advisers were sent to assist Song, but the seriousness and scope of the revolt grew. Two American officer advisers were captured by the rebels, but escaped. Finally, COL Hurley E. Fuller was sent to take over as senior adviser on the scene.

Led by CPT Hausman and CPT John P. Reed, part of a Constabulary regiment counterattacked. With the help of reinforcements, the loyalist forces drove the dissidents back into Yosu in four days. In two days of savage fighting, the rebellion was ended. Many of the mutineers slipped off into a guerrilla life in the nearby Chiri-san mountains.

As a result of the Yosu revolt, Communists were purged from the Constabulary; over 1,500 were identified and discharged from the service. The 14th Regiment was abolished and its colors burned. All units having the number 4, either alone or in combination with other numbers, were redesignated, and the use of that number was abandoned from then on.

Captain Hausman (Source: Page 41, Military Advisers in Korea: KMAG in Peace and War, *Sawyer, U.S. Government Printing Office, Washington, D.C., 1962)*

Growth of the Armed Forces

The ROK government set up the Departments of National Defense, Army and Navy on Dec. 5, 1948. BG Lee Hyung Koon became the first ROK Army Chief of Staff. At the same time all ROK Constabulary brigades became Army divisions and 14 Army branches were created. By March 1949, the ROK Armed Forces totaled some 114,000: 65,000 Army; 4,000 Coast Guard and 45,000 National Police.

As American occupation troops left Korea, they provided carbines, helmets, field packs and a six month supply of carbine ammunition to equip an additional 15,000 men in the ROKA. Additional arms and vessels were given to the Coast Guard. Small arms support and ammunition for a 35,000-member National Police force also were provided. In addition, a six-month stock of maintenance supplies was made available to all Korean security forces.

American soldiers helped train ROK soldiers in tactics and in the use of the weapons and equipment they were about to receive. Military advisers no longer had to make their own private arrangements with nearby units to borrow equipment and demonstration troops. The 5th RCT presented squad, platoon and company attack and defense demonstrations. Battalion demonstrations were staged for ROK officers and NCOs.

Role of KMAG.

When USAFIK received orders on April 2, 1949, to prepare to withdraw from Korea, the Military Advisory Group was instructed to expand its organization. Following discussions, recommendations to Department of the Army, and further refinement, KMAG came into being July 1, 1949. Its initial strength was 186 officers, one warrant officer, one nurse and 288 enlisted men. American military advisers already had been hard at work. KMAG would continue in an advisory capacity well into the Korean War. It is difficult to overestimate the value of these men in first, doing all they could under many handicaps, to train and advise their charges, then to share with them the test of battle, the frustration of a fighting retreat, the determination of a stubborn and successful defense and the joy of victory in breaking out of the Perimeter. They were indispensable to the ROK Army.

KMAG would operate under the control of the American ambassador, John J. Muccio. In December, KMAG's authorized strength was set at 181 officers, seven warrants, a nurse and 283 enlisted men.

Since duty with KMAG was not popular, the tour was short — only 18 months for those without dependents, two years with dependents. KMAG personnel also were paid an additional $90 per month to defray the costs at the mission-operated commissary, the only source of groceries for all Americans. Medical and dental care were provided by a small dispensary at the KMAG main base, Camp Sobinggo, near Seoul. Serious cases went either to the nearby Seventh Day Adventist Hospital or to Japan.

KMAG was organized to support six ROK divisions. When the ROKA formed eight, KMAG had to juggle its people to cover the added divisions.

The men of KMAG worked long trying to build the ROK armed forces. They were hampered by the necessity of keeping troops along the 38th parallel after American forces had gone, lack of proper training sites and the ever-present cultural and language problem. In addition to troop field training, they helped organize and run a series of schools for officers and NCOs.

The small advisor group was scattered all over South Korea. KMAG had to depend upon radio networks to communicate with its men in the field. By the end of 1949, two nets were in operation.

Beginning in mid-1948, some Korean officers attended courses at the Infantry School, Ft. Benning, GA, and at the Field Artillery Training Center, Ft. Sill, OK. In April 1950, a small group of ROK officers were sent to Japan to observe the administration and training of American units.

The ROK Air Force

The development of the ROK Air Force was stymied, first, because KMAG included too few Air Force advisers, and second, because the ROK had insufficient equipment to warrant such a force: 10 A-6 training planes. KMAG recommended that 40 F-51 fighters, 10 T-6 trainers and 2 C-47 cargo planes, plus supporting signal equipment, be allocated to the ROK Air Force in fiscal year 1950. By June 25, 1950, the Air Force had only 1,865 personnel, 10 T-6 trainers and some light liaison aircraft, but no combat airplanes.

On the eve of the war, the ROK infantry division was somewhat smaller than that of the NKPA. But it was woefully lacking in artillery and mortar support, with no tanks, no medium artillery, no heavy mortars, no recoilless rifles and no effective antitank weapons.

When the war began, the ROKA numbered about 98,000 men — 65,000 combat and 33,000 HQ and service troops. This chart (extracted from *South to the Naktong, North to the Yalu*) shows the combat division strength on June 1, 1950 (see page 24).

This force had 89 serviceable 105mm M3 howitzers, 114 57mm antitank guns, 22 M-8 armored cars equipped with 37mm guns and 15 halftracks.

The following chart graphically shows the disparity in organic artillery and mortar support between the NKPA and ROKA divisions (See page 24).

In spite of being inferior in combat-experienced personnel, training and armament, the ROKA did a remarkable job of slowing the enemy until the U.S. could intervene. They fought many vicious battles with the North Koreans, inflicting heavy casualties. At times, ROK soldiers made human bombs of themselves to destroy enemy tanks. The ROKA never has been given credit for what they accomplished in those early days of the war.

Chapter Notes:
P. 21 The T35/85 medium tank was armed with one 85mm main gun and two 7.62mm machine guns, one of which was fixed in the hull and the other one coaxial with the turret-mounted main gun. The tank weighed 35 tons had 3 inches of maximum armor and had a maximum speed of 30 MPH. Cross-country, this was reduced to 15 MPH. Maximum range of the main gun was 5,716 yards. It could penetrate up to 4.2 inches of armor at 500 yards. The tank carried 55 rounds of 85mm ammunition and 2,745 rounds of 7.62mm machine gun ammunition. (Source: Footnote, p. 12, South to the Naktong.)

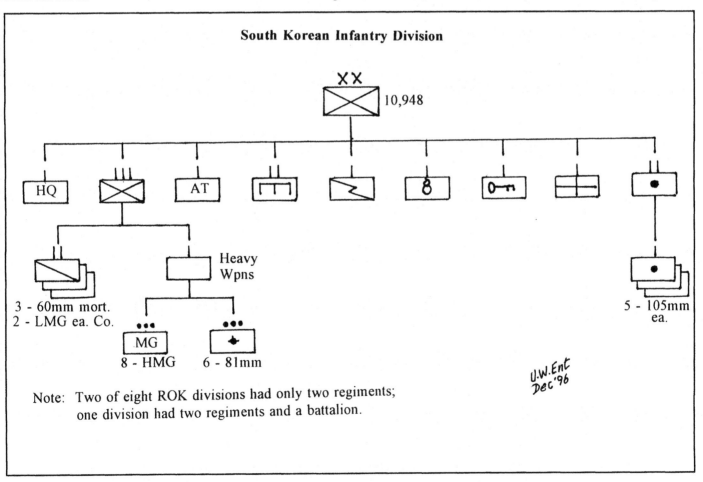

South Korean Infantry Division

XX
10,948

HQ   AT   Heavy Wpns

3 - 60mm mort.
2 - LMG ea. Co.

MG
8 - HMG   6 - 81mm

5 - 105mm ea.

U.W.Ent Dec '96

Note: Two of eight ROK divisions had only two regiments; one division had two regiments and a battalion.

Organization of the South Korean Army

1st Div. (11, 12 13 Regt.	9,715	6th Div. (7, 8, 19 Regt.	9,112
2d Div. (5, 16, 25 Regt.)	7,910	7th Div. (1, 3, 9 Regt.)	9,698
3d Div. (22, 23 Regt.	7,059	8th Div. (10, 21 Regt.)	6,866
5th Div. (15, 20 Regt; 1st Sep. Bn.	7,276	Capital Div. (2, 12 Regt.)	7,061
17th Regt.	2,500	**TOTAL: 64,697**	

Artillery and Mortar Support

	NKPA			**ROKA**	
No.	Type	Range/Yds	No.	Type	Range/Yds
12	122mm How M1938	12,904	15	105mm How M3	7,250
24	76mm Gun M1942	14,545	12	81mm Mortar M1	3,290
12	SU 76mm SP Guns	12,400	ROKs had nothing more		
12	76mm How M1927	9,143			
18	120mm Mortar M1938	6,564			
81	82mm Mortar M1937	3,400			

(Note that the NKPA division had 60 heavy weapons which outranged the heaviest artillery of the ROK division.)

In summation, the NK and ROK armed forces are compared below:

	NK	ROK
Army	150,000	98,000
Air Force	2,000	1,865
Marines	9,000	3,000 (Est.) One 3-bn regt.
Coast Guard	13,700	6,145
Nat. Police/Scty Forces	34,000	48,273
Combat aircraft	110	None
Tanks	150	None
TOTAL PERSONNEL:	**208,700**	**157,283**

PART TWO

INVASION!

Delaying action in successive positions is based on limited resistance on a position, with the intention of renewing this resistance in successive positions if necessary. This defense on each position must force the enemy to early deployment and to time-consuming preparations for battle. Combat is ordinarily broken off in each position before troops become closely engaged.

U.S. War Dept. FM 100-5 Field Service
Regulations OPERATIONS, June 15, 1944

CHAPTER THREE — Cross-Border Assault and Fighting Retreat

North Korea's Motivation to Invade South Korea

What motivated North Korea to invade the South on June 25, 1950?

The answer lies in a number of factors, including:

1. All U.S. military forces had left South Korea in 1949, leaving only a small military advisory group.

2. The North Korean government believed that their armed forces were far superior to those of the South.

3. Both Kim Il Sung in the North and Syngman Rhee in the South had vowed to reunite Korea. There had been numerous border clashes, some of which involved entire regiments on both sides. Kim Il Sung, by attacking first, would preempt any ideas Rhee may have had of attacking the North.

4. U.S. governmental and military leaders had announced that Korea lay beyond the sphere of American interest in the Far East. Korea was not of political nor military value to the U.S.

5. There was a sizable pro-Communist guerrilla movement in the South, which North Korea believed reflected the feelings of many South Koreans.

6. Kim convinced Josef Stalin, leader of the Soviet Union, that he could win a quick victory over the South and reunite Korea as a Communist state.

The third factor, a preemptive strike, is demonstrated by ample evidence that both Kim and Rhee wanted a single Korea. Each envisioned a united Korea under his own leadership, vowing as much in speeches.

As early as 1947, the U.S. Joint Chiefs of Staff had reported to the president that "from the standpoint of military security, the U.S. has little strategic interest in maintaining the present troops and bases in Korea." When asked in early 1949 for advice from the JCS on the possible effects of withdrawing from Korea and the best time to complete that withdrawal, GEN MacArthur responded in part, "In the event of any serious threat to the security of Korea, [American] strategic and military considerations will force abandonment of any pretense of active [U.S.] military support."

Secretary of State Dean Acheson made it clear in a speech to the National Press Club on Jan. 12, 1950. He stated that the American "defensive perimeter" included the Aleutians, Japan, the Ryukyus and the Philippines. Neither Taiwan nor Korea were included in this perimeter. They were among "other areas" in the Pacific and, said Acheson, "no person can guarantee these areas against military attack." If they were attacked, he said, "the initial reliance must be on the people attacked to resist it and then upon the commitments of the entire civilized world under the charter of the United Nations."

The withdrawal in 1949 of all U.S. troops from Korea, along with such offical U.S. statements that Korea was outside the American perimeter of strategic interest, gave the North Korean government a fairly clear indication that it could invade South Korea with impunity. As for the U.N., the war would be over before that ponderous body could react.

The ROK military fought dozens of battles with guerrillas in 1949 and 1950. The North also believed that a number of South Korean soldiers could be subverted, perhaps even induced to surrender or change sides. The Yosu revolt in October 1948 and the defection of two ROK battalions during a border clash near Kaesong on May 3, 1949 were indicators to the North that the ROK military might be shaky. These incidents, a number of riots and demonstrations, and other indications of dissatisfaction with the Rhee government convinced Kim Il Sung that an invasion would precipitate a revolt in the South.

Nikita Khrushchev reported in his memoirs that Kim discussed plans to attack South Korea with Joseph Stalin near the end of 1949 and possibly again in early 1950. Stalin liked the idea, but wanted Kim to return with more concrete plans, which he did. Mao Zedong was also consulted, and eventually concurred with the idea. Kim's contacts with Stalin and Mao, both in person and by correspondence are detailed in Chapter 5 of *Uncertain Partners: Stalin Mao, and the Korean War*, by Sergei N. Goncharov, John W. Lewis and Xue Litai, Stanford University Press, Stanford, CA, 1933.

There is little doubt that North Korea would not have embarked on this war without assurances of support from Russia and/or Communist China (the People's Republic of China). The USSR supplied the North Koreans with arms and equipment during the war, but principal backing came from Communist China.

All the principal elements favored the North Korean decision to strike swiftly and decisively, overwhelming the ROKA at or near the 38th parallel, then sweeping south in multiple columns to Pusan.

The South Korean Plan of Defense

The South Koreans and KMAG advisers never doubted that North Korea would eventually attack the South — the question was when. The site was dictated by the natural avenues of assault into South Korea (avenues of approach), from west to east:

1. The Kaesong-Munsan-ni-Seoul route.

2. The Uijongbu corridor to Seoul. Two routes converged from the north on this corridor, one via Chorwon, Yonson and Tongduchon-ni, the other from Kumwha through Pochon.

3. One route from Hwachon through Chunchon, and another from Inje, converged at Hongchon far south of the 38th parallel in north-central South Korea.

4. Finally, there was the east coast route leading through Kangnung to Samch'ok, almost 50 miles south of the parallel.

5. Isolated in the west was the Ongjin peninsula. While not of much strategic value, it had to be captured to eliminate its use in any counterstroke.

The ROKA was deployed across each of these avenues. The 17th Infantry (COL Paik In Yup) was on Ongjin. The 1st Division (COL Paik Sun Yup, brother of Paik In Yup) was responsible for the Kaesong approach, with its 12th Regiment (COL Chun Sung Ho) in and around the city itself. The 13th Regiment (COL Kim Il Yul) guarded the eastern part of the division's sector. The 11th Regiment (COL Choi Kyung Nok) was in reserve northwest of Seoul.

The 7th Division (BG Yu Jae Hung) covered the two roads leading to Uijongbu. In the center, the 6th Division, commanded by COL Kim Chong O, held Chunchon and the road from Inje. The 8th Division's 10th Infantry Regiment held the coast road, while one battalion of its 21st Infantry Regiment was stationed in the coastal town of Samchok. The 8th, commanded by COL Lee Jung Il, had only two regiments.

In reserve were the Capital Division (less the 17th Regiment, which was usually affiliated with the division) at Seoul. The Capital Division was largely a "palace guard" command and had no organic artillery. The 2d Division (BG Lee Hyung Koo) was centered at Taejon; the 3d, (COL Yu Sung Yul), which had but two regiments, was near Taegu; the 5th (MG Lee Ung Joon) in the vicinity of Kwangju in southwest Korea, and the cavalry regiment. BG Lee Joon Shik took over command of the 3d Division on July 10.

The Army reserve's priorities, in their order, were to counterattack, reinforce the 1st and 7th Divisions, reinforce the 6th and 7th Divisions, and to suppress guerrillas in the interior of the country.

North Korean Invasion and South Korean Resistance

June 24-25, 1950, was a weekend, so many South Korean soldiers along the border were away on passes. Only four regiments and a battalion were actually in defensive positions in the pre-dawn hours of June 25. Consequently, there were only initially about 10,000 to 11,000 men to oppose the North Korean onslaught.

(Henceforth, all North Korean military units will be italicized in the book. All strength figures are approximate.) The NKPA, divided into the *I Corps (1st, 3d, 4th and 6th Divisions and 105th Armored Brigade)* and the *II Corps (2d, 5th and 7th Divisions, 766 Independent Unit and 17th Motorcycle Regiment)* was deployed thusly:

Ongjin — *3d BC Bde* and *NK 14th Regt (6th Division)* of 6,500 vs. ROK 17th Regt of 2,500. Actually, only one battalion of the 17th was on line at the time.

Kaesong-Munsan — *NK 1st Div, 6th Div (minus the 14th Regt)* and *203d Armd Regt* of 20,000 vs. ROK 1st Div. of 7,200. Half of the reserve 11th Regiment was on weekend pass and was not immediately available.

Routes to Uijongbu — *NK 4th* and *3d Divisions* and *105th Armd Bde (minus 203d Armd Regt)* of 26,000 vs. ROK 7th Div. of 9,600.

Hwachon- Chunchon — *NK 2d Div.*

Inje-Hongchon — *NK 7th Div.* (Both the *2d and 7th Divisions)* of 23,000 vs. ROK 6th Div. of 9,000.

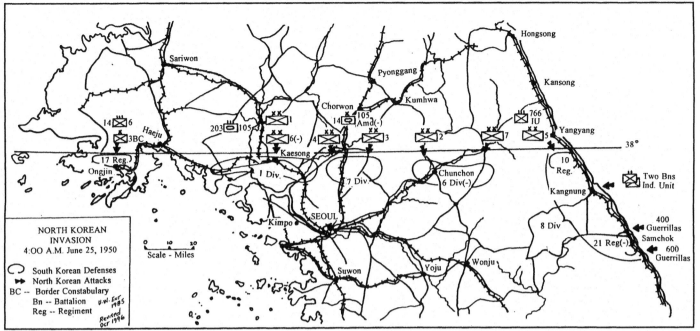

Map 4 (Source: Uzal W. Ent)

East Coast Road — *NK 5th Div, 766th I.U.* (regimental-sized command) and *17th Motorcycle Regt.* of 16,000 vs. ROK 10th Regt. of 2,400.

The Korean monsoon had begun. Scattered, heavy rain swept along the 38th parallel in the early hours of June 25, 1950. The North Korean attack began with heavy small-arms fire from the *3d B.C. Brigade* on a battalion of the 17th Regiment on the Ongjin peninsula.

At about 4 a.m. local time, heavy artillery and mortar fire began to fall on the ROKs, continuing for more than an hour. Initially shocked, the defenders recovered and began to return fire. As dawn broke at about 5:30, the *14th Regiment* attacked through the *Border Constabulary* and soon overwhelmed the ROK battalion. Remnants of the unit fell back. The ROKA sent two Landing Ship Tanks (LSTs) to join the one already at Ongjin. COL Paik managed to evacuate about 1,700 men and their equipment; another 750 were lost to the enemy. By 5:30 p.m. on June 26, the enemy had complete control of the peninsula.

The city of Kaesong is the ancient capital of Korea, just 2,000 meters south of the 38th parallel. The city had no tactical nor strategic value and was completely dominated by North Korean constabulary units on Songak-san, overlooking the town. In this area the only real defensive position south of the 38th lies along the south bank of the Imjin River, about 11 or 12 miles east and southeast of Kaesong. COL Paik Sun Yup hoped to deploy his 1st Division along this river and stop the North Koreans. Paik was then only 29 years old, about the age of a rifle company commander, but he fought his division in a superior manner in the next week. A career ROK officer, he eventually rose to be Chief of Staff of the Republic of Korea Army. He was highly regarded by U.S. Army officers. Because "paik" means "white" in Korean, COL Paik was affectionately known as "Whitey" Paik by these officers.

Paik's 12th Regiment was deployed in and around Kaesong; the 13th was near Munsan-ni,

along the Imjin, and the 11th (what there was of it present for duty) at Susaek, closer to Seoul.

When the war started, COL Paik was attending a course at the Korean Infantry School. In his absence, the 11th Regimental commander, COL Choi Kyung Nok, was acting division commander. Paik was living at home while attending the school. At 7 a.m. on June 25, his G-3 called on the telephone to inform him that the North Koreans had invaded. The colonel immediately tried to get to ROKA HQ. Unable to find a taxi, he finally stopped a passing jeep. Seoul's people were, as yet, unaware of war. The streets were deserted and church bells rang, calling parishioners to worship.

Unsure if he was to resume command of his division, Paik asked the Army Chief of Staff, MG Chae Byong Duk. "Get to your division now!" was the response. Paik rounded up KMAG division adviser LTC Lloyd H. Rockwell at his quarters. With Rockwell driving a KMAG jeep, the two stopped to pick up COL Choi, then hurried to 1st Division headquarters at Susaek.

Upon arrival at Susaek, COL Paik was briefed by his staff. The news was grim. Communication with the 12th regiment at Kaesong was out, the 13th near Munsan was heavily engaged with the enemy and only about half the reserve 11th Regiment was present for duty. The remainder were away on pass, as a result of the lifting of an alert order by ROKA headquarters a few days earlier. Obviously, the 11th would be of little help until more of its men could be rounded up and returned to the regiment. Faced with all this disheartening news, COL Paik wrote later that all he could think of was, "What a hell of a mess this is."

But he wasted no time in organizing a small tactical staff to accompany him to the division's forward command post (CP). From the top of a hill above the CP, COL Paik could see all across his division's front. The whole area seemed under intense artillery and mortar bombardment, which kicked up clouds of smoke and haze. He found that there was no communica-

tion with the 7th Division to the east of his 1st. At this critical juncture, COL Rockwell was ordered by KMAG to return to Seoul. COL Paik was both hurt and angered. Just when he and other ROKA commanders needed help most, the U.S. was pulling out all advisers. KMAG had seen to all ROKA logistical supplies and equipment; without them, he felt, the ROKs were left empty-handed.

As time passed, Paik discovered that the 13th Regiment was holding the division right flank, though heavily engaged. and that the 11th, now with most of its men, was moving into defensive positions east of the Imjin, centered on Munsan-ni.

The railroad from Kaesong to Seoul passed over a bridge on the Imjin at Munsan. The colonel wanted to destroy the bridge, but felt compelled to await the return crossing of whatever was left of the 12th Regiment. Finally at about 3 p.m., regimental commander COL Chun Sung Ho and 30 or 40 men made their way across the bridge. Chun had been wounded and was evacuated. In another hour only a few more men escaped. Finally, when the enemy was almost to it, he gave the order, "Blow the bridge!" Nothing happened; evidently shell fragments or something had severed the fusing cord. A violent gun battle ensued for possession of the bridge.

The North Koreans were halted there, but a tank column entered the 13th sector to the north. Fire from 57mm antitank (AT) guns and 2.36-inch rocket launchers had no effect on the enemy's T-34s. The rockets failed to penetrate the armor and the 57s had no armor-piercing ammunition. This, coupled with the fact that ROK soldiers had never seen a tank in action, contributed significantly to what COL Paik called "T-34 disease": As soon as the men heard the word "tank" they were terrorized.

A few courageous soldiers of the 13th Regiment made human bombs of themselves and succeeded in destroying some tanks, preventing the North Korean armor from getting through the regiment's lines that day.

27

KMAG group leaving Seoul. (Source: Page 129, Military Advisers in Korea: KMAG in Peace and War, Sawyer, U.S. Government Printing Office, Washington, D.C., 1962)

Late in the day, the 1st Division received welcome reinforcements when the demonstration battalions from the Korean Military Academy and the Infantry School arrived by train. They partially offset the loss of the 12th regiment.

CPT Joseph R. Darrigo and 1LT William E. Hamilton shared quarters in a house just northeast of Kaesong at the foot of Songak-san. On June 25 Darrigo, assistant adviser to the ROK 12th Regiment, was alone; Hamilton had gone to Seoul for supplies. At about 5 a.m., Darrigo was awakened by an unusually heavy artillery barrage on Kaesong. Soon shell fragments were hitting his house. He jumped from bed, pulled on a pair of trousers and grabbed a shirt and his shoes. Meeting his houseboy, the two climbed into his jeep and sped into Kaesong, where they were fired on by the enemy. The North Koreans had entered town in an estimated 15-car railroad train. Leaving Kaesong, Darrigo reached Munsan-ni and joined COL Paik.

The main North Korean assault on the 25th came from the *NK 3d* and *4th Divisions*, supported by the bulk of the *105th Armd Brigade*. The *4th Division,* with about 40 tanks of the *107th Armd Regiment*, struck straight south from Yonchon toward Uijongbu while the *3d Division*, supported by another 40 tanks of the *109th Armd Regiment* attacked along the Kumwha-Uijongbu road.

The ROK 1st Regiment (7th Division) faced both columns and lost heavily. Behind it at Pochon, on the road from Yonch'on, was the 7th Division's 9th Regiment. Further south on the Kumwha road at Tongduch'on-ni was the 3d Regiment. By 8:30 a.m. BG Yu Jae Hung's 7th Division was hard pressed by the converging enemy columns. Although it inflicted heavy casualties on the North Koreans, the 7th could not stop their advance.

In the rear, two Yak fighters strafed Seoul's main street. Other enemy aircraft were reported to have attacked Kimpo Airfield. That afternoon more enemy planes again flew over Kimpo and Seoul.

In the Chunchon sector, North Korean plans called for their *2d Division* to drive down and seize that town by afternoon of the first day. Meantime, the *NK 7th Division* was to attack Hongchon, more than 20 air-miles southeast of Chunchon, which the ROK 7th Regiment (6th Division) defended. Another regiment of the division was to the east of the 7th. The reserve regiment and division HQ were at Wonju, 45 miles south of the 38th parallel.

The *4th* and *6th Regiments* of the *NK 2d Division*, began their attack on the ROK 6th Regiment early in the morning of June 25. Heavy ROK artillery fire and the stubborn resistance of the ROK 6th halted the enemy, who now committed their reserve, the *17th Regiment.* The ROK 6th, unlike many other ROK formations, had all its men present because it had not granted passes. All battle positions were fully manned.

The ROK reserve regiment arrived late in the day to reinforce the beleaguered 6th. The failure of the *2d Division* to capture Chunchon forced the enemy to direct its *7th Division* to that area. The division arrived there on the evening of June 26. The *7th* brought some tanks with it, but the ROK 6th Division continued to stubbornly hold off both enemy divisions. Only when ordered to withdraw by ROKA HQ on June 28 did the 6th give up Chunchon, withdrawing in good order with its weapons and equipment.

The enemy paid dearly for the town. The *NK 6th Regiment* lost over 50 percent of its men. The *2d Division* suffered 40 percent casualties and lost seven SP guns, two 45mm AT guns and a number of mortars. The *NK 7th Division* also took many casualties, but not nearly as many as the *2d.*

The ROK 10th Regiment (8th Division) on the east coast was attacked early on June 25. No U.S. advisers are reported to have been with the 10th at the time. However, MAJ George D. Kessler was at Samchok with the headquarters of the 8th Division's 21st Regiment. Only one battalion of the 21st was there, as previously noted. However, the regiment's mortars, 57mm AT guns and heavy machine guns were all at Samchok.

MAJ Kessler was awakened at dawn and informed of the North Korean attack on the 10th Regiment. About the same time, Korean police told him that enemy troops were landing at points north and south of Samchok. Driving quickly to a hilltop near Mukhojin-ni, Kessler and the commander of the 21st Regiment discovered junks and sampans lying offshore and several hundred men on the coastal road. They found a similar

KMAG G-2 Advisor briefs ROK engineer platoon about to set out on a reconnaissance patrol. (Source: Page 157, Military Advisers in Korea: KMAG in Peace and War, Sawyer, U.S. Government Printing Office, Washington, D.C., 1962)

Major General Paik Sun Yup. (Source: From Pusan to Panmunjon, *Paik Sun Yup, Brassey's, 1992)*

situation south of Samchok. When they got back to the town, they discovered ships circling offshore prior to landing more men. ROK AT guns sunk two enemy boats and the North Korean naval force withdrew from Samchok.

MAJ Kessler did not realize then that a full-scale invasion of South Korea had taken place, since the North often tried to infiltrate guerrillas. The enemy had managed to successfully land 400-600 men below Samchok. This force made its way inland to become guerrillas.

Meantime, unfortunately undetected and unopposed, two battalions of the *766th Independent Unit* landed at Kangnung, between the 10th Regiment in the north and Samchok. The remainder of the *766th*, with elements of the *NK 5th Division*, pressed the ROK 10th Regiment.

Back on the 1st Division front, the enemy continued to build pressure on June 26. A counterattack in the Munsan area by the ROK 11th Regiment and the demonstration battalions failed. Late in the day the North Koreans broke through and seized Munsan. COL Paik realized that he could hold no longer along the Imjin. He also learned that the ROK 7th Division on his right had withdrawn, exposing that flank. He therefore decided to withdraw to another line just west of Seoul.

As Paik's men began to execute the withdrawal, MAJ Michael Donovan, KMAG adviser to the 12th Regiment, came to Paik's CP with the news that KMAG advisers were returning and that the ROK Army was planning a counterattack by five regiments in the 7th Division sector to the east. The 1st Division's mission in support of the impending counterattack was to hold its present positions. This meant holding at all costs.

By dawn on June 27, the ROK 1st Division was deployed on the line it must hold. Two more battalions had reinforced the division, one from the 15th Regiment and one from the 20th Regiment (both from the ROK 5th Division). The enemy attacked Paik's

division that day, without success. Late that night, he received orders from the South Korean Army Chief of Staff, GEN Chae Byong Duk for his division: "Fight to the death in [your] present positions."

The South Korean high command, realizing that a full-scale invasion was taking place, began moving reserves forward by mid-afternoon of June 25. Elements of the 5th Regiment and part of its parent 2d Division headquarters left Taejon at 2:30 p.m. that day. The 22d Regiment, 3d Combat Engineer Battalion and the AT company of the 3d Division were sent north from Taegu that night. By dark, parts of the 5th Division also were started for the battle area from Kwangju.

GEN Chae was determined to launch a counterattack in the Uijongbu corridor on the morning of June 26, with the 7th Division on the left of the highway and the 2d Division on the right. He moved the 7th from their defensive positions on the Pochon road west to an area near Tongduchon-ni. The 2d Division was to take over the positions vacated by the 7th.

Chae overruled the 2d Division commander's strenuous objections to the plan. BG Lee had only two battalions available. He would have to attack piecemeal as the rest of his division arrived. Lee asked that the attack be delayed until his command could be assembled. CPT Hausman, who was with GEN Chae, supported Lee, without success. The 7th counterattacked as scheduled, but the two battalions of the 2d remained in their defensive positions. GEN Lee made no effort to attack with them.

BG Yu's 7th Division met with initial success against the *NK 4th Division* north of Uijongbu. But the enemy *7th Regiment (NK 3d Division)*, led by a column of tanks, attacked through the two 2d Division battalions and seized Uijongbu. As a result, the 7th Division had to halt its attack and withdraw south of the town. By the evening of June 26, the *NK 3d* and *4th Divisions*, supported by most of the *105th Armd Brigade*, had control of Uijongbu and were preparing to continue their attack toward Seoul.

On the morning of June 27, ROKA HQ had displaced from Seoul to Sihung-ni, some five miles south of Yongdungpo, without informing KMAG headquarters. COL William H. S. Wright of KMAG persuaded GEN Chae to return to Seoul. Both the ROKA HQ and KMAG were back in the city by 6 that night.

Fighting on June 27 north of Seoul were disjointed, uncoordinated, and largely unsuccessful actions by the ROK 7th and parts of the Capital, 2d and 5th Divisions. Marshal Choe Yong Gun, commanding North Korean troops, broadcast a surrender appeal to the people of Seoul. The civilian population began to flee the city in ever increasing numbers.

The ROKs had planned and rehearsed roadblocks and demolitions to impede invaders. Panic caused by the T-34 tanks was so great that demolitions were not set off, roadblocks not manned and obstacles not covered by fire. However, LTC Oum Hong Sup, ROK Engineer School Commandant, with a scratch force of men armed with pole charges and demolitions did knock out four T-34s at a mined bridge on the Uijongbu road north of Seoul.

The *9th Regiment, NK 3d Division* reached the suburbs of Seoul about 7:30 p.m. on June 27, but was driven back temporarily by heavy fire. Less than two hours later an enemy tank

DC-54 Military Transport Plane on fire. (Source: P. 24, Korea, *1950, Chief of Military History, Washington, D.C., 1982)*

and infantry platoon entered the Secret Gardens of the Chang-Duk Palace. Korean police destroyed the tank and drove off the infantry. A company of ROKs dug in on South Mountain in the city and fought to the last man.

The Han River bridges had been packed with explosives and ROK engineers prepared to blow them up. MAJ George R. Sedberry Jr., the G-3 adviser to the ROK Army tried to persuade the ROK Deputy Chief of Staff, GEN Kim Paik Il, to hold off destroying the bridges until ROK troops, equipment and heavy weapons could be sent south across them from Seoul. There had been an agreement between GEN Chae and KMAG that the bridges would not be blown up until enemy tanks reached the street on which the ROK Army headquarters was located.

GEN Chae was then somewhere south of the Han, having been sent there over his protests, and not available to ensure that this agreement was met. Kim said he had orders from the Vice Minister of Defense to destroy the bridges at 1:30 a.m. on June 28. The pleas of GEN Lee of the 2d Division finally persuaded him to delay. He ordered the ROK G-3, MG Chang Chang Kuk, to drive to the river and halt the bridge blowing. Unfortunately, because of the heavy stream of refugees and traffic, he arrived too late. At 2:15 a.m., in a spectacular orange-colored explosion, two spans of the Han highway bridge were blasted into the waters below. Between 500 and 800 people died. Thousands more were injured. The 1st Division, as well as sizable portions of the 7th and elements of the Capital and 2d Divisions, were also cut off west of Seoul when these bridges over the Han River were blown up.

Keyes Beech of the Chicago *Daily News* was in the rear seat of a jeep being driven by Burton Crane, New York *Times*. Frank Gibney, of *Time* magazine, was in the seat next to Crane. They were headed south in the middle of the bridge when the whole column stopped. Mr. Beech, in his book, *Tokyo and Points East*, describes what happened: "Then it seemed the whole world exploded in front of us.... Silhouetted against the flame was a truckload of Korean soldiers. The truck was lifted into the air. I felt our jeep in motion — backwards."

Both Crane and Gibney had been badly cut by flying glass from the shattered windshield. The three men believed that an enemy tank had caused the damage. No tank fire followed, the bridge burned and wounded Koreans called for help.

They decided to try to work the jeep across the ruins of the bridge. Gibney took the wheel and Crane occupied the front passenger seat. Beech started to walk ahead of the jeep and around the remains of the truck, but stopped abruptly. "Standing on the jagged edge of the bridge, I was looking down 75 feet below into the black waters of the Han," he said.

The three men abandoned the jeep and walked back to Seoul. They made their escape across the Han on a raft a few days later.

The premature destruction of the Han bridges was a major blow to the ROK Army. The 1st Division, as well as sizable portions of the 7th and elements of the Capital and 2d Divisions were trapped north of the river. The bridge could have remained in service for at least another six to eight hours, enabling the South Koreans to evacuate men, weapons and equipment. As it was, thousands of troops, as well as the artillery, heavy weapons and equipment of the cut-off divisions were lost.

Although mistakenly strafed by U.S. aircraft, COL Paik managed to bring about 5,000 of his men across the river. GEN Yu escaped with about 1,200 men and four machine guns of his 7th Division.

Disorganized but bitter ROK resistance delayed North Korean entrance into the center of the city until early afternoon of June 28.

In the first four days of the war, the *NK 3d and 4th Divisions* lost about 1,500 men. Of these, 1,112 were from the *4th Division*, which had fought the ROK 7th Division north of Uijongbu. On July 10, Kim Il Sung cited both the *3d and 4th Divisions* by conferring on them the honorary title "*Seoul Division*." The *105th Armored Brigade* was concurrently raised to division status and given the same honorary title.

Some of the first Americans to volunteer for Korea were CPT Frank J. McCabe, two other officers and 34 men of the 507th AAA AW Bn. Known as Detachment X, this element of automatic anti-aircraft weapons, with their four quad-.50 caliber vehicles, was placed to defend Suwon Airfield from enemy air attack. On June 29 these men became the first U.S. Army troops to fire on the attacking North Koreans. On that date, the detachment shot down one of four enemy planes attacking the airfield. Another enemy plane crash landed after having been hit by their fire. That night, the detachment drove off another enemy air attack.

By the end of June, the ROK Army was badly battered. MG Kim Hong Il, now commanding what was known as the "Sihung District Combat Headquarters" also was charged with defending the Han. For this he had what was left of the 1st and 7th Divisions, parts of the 5th at Yongdung-po and elements of the Capital at Inchon. To the west, near the confluence of the Han and Pukhan rivers, were the remnants of the 2d Division. The 6th Division, still intact, was withdrawing south of Ch'unch'on toward Wonju, while the 8th from the east coast (also intact) was moving inland and south. The ROK 3d Division's 23d Regiment was at Ulchin on the east coast, 65 miles north of P'ohang-dong, with the mission of blocking any North Korean move down the coastal road.

On June 30, American planes dropped U.N. leaflets in South Korea encouraging ROK soldiers to "Fight with all your might.... We shall support your people as much as we can and clear the aggressor from your country."

GEN Kim's defensive effort was thwarted from the start. Elements of the *NK 6th Division* crossed the Han west of Seoul late on June 28 and seized Kimpo Airfield the next day. On June 30, after a night of intense artillery bombardment, the *8th Regiment, NK 3d Division,* crossed the Han near the Sobbingo ferry. But the enemy did little more than secure a foothold, not even attempting to occupy the large suburban Yongdongpo industrial complex.

By this time, the U.S. had become involved in the Korean War. BG John H. Church, heading a GHQ Advance Command and Liaison Group (ADCOM), was on the Han River scene. Church directed GEN Chae to counterattack the North Koreans, but heavy enemy artillery fire prevented this.

On July 1, the *NK 4th Division* made the enemy's main river crossing at Yongdung-po. The ROKs fought hard for the complex, but by 8 a.m. on July 3 it fell to the enemy. The *NK 4th Division* lost over 2,000 men in the battle.

Also on July 3, the *NK 3d Division* finished crossing the river and the *NK 6th Division* reached the outskirts of Inchon. That night a North Korean battalion with six tanks entered the city. On July 4, the *3d* and *4th Divisions*, with ample tank support from the *105th Armd Bde*, were ready to drive south toward Suwon.

By July 1, 1950, the South Korean Army had lost some 40 percent of its men and much of its artillery and mortars. It could account for only about 54,000 of its original 98,000 men. Untold thousands of men, plus the artillery, mortars and other heavy equipment of both the 1st and 7th divisions were lost, due primarily to the premature destruction of the Han Bridges. The artillery alone amounted to 30 105mm howitzers — guns which could have been put to effective use against the enemy's river crossings. The loss represented 33 percent of the entire ROK field artillery capability.

Although the *In Min Gun* had been successful, the ROK Army had not just given up. They had fought many hard, bloody battles, often making the enemy pay heavily for their victories. The disintegration of the ROK 1st and 7th Divisions was not due to poor or irresolute division leadership. On the contrary, both commands fought well. The ROK 6th and 8th Divisions also acquitted themselves honorably. The force of the enemy onslaught was, in truth, too heavy and too swift to counter effectively. The abortive counterattack in the Uijongbu area actually hastened the demise of effective resistance along this, the principal avenue into South Korea and Seoul.

Given the weight of North Korean forces along each avenue of invasion, the intervention of more than a single division would have been required in order to blunt the North Korean assaults. Further, the South Korean high command played into the enemy's hands by allowing a liberal weekend pass policy. The additional troops, in position or in reserve, certainly could have helped slow the North Korean advance. Even so, given the ferocious and terrible battles along the Pusan Perimeter a few weeks later, it is doubtful that the successful commitment of all of the ROK 2d, 3d, 5th and Capital Divisions would have been sufficient to halt the invaders, no matter how stubbornly or how heroically they resisted.

Though initially cowed by the T-34, they learned to deal with that threat as best as they could. The ROK Army should never be condemned for their conduct in the early days of the war. With so many factors against them, they often did better than could reasonably have been expected. Their efforts slowed the North Koreans long enough for U.S. forces to arrive in strength. For that they should be praised and the people of South Korea should be eternally grateful.

CHAPTER FOUR — Task Force Smith

The United States Enters the War

On June 27, 1950, President Harry S. Truman announced both the U.S. and UN responses to the North Korean invasion of South Korea:

"The Security Council of the United Nations called upon the invading troops to cease hostilities and to withdraw to the 38th parallel. This they have not done, but on the contrary have pressed the attack. The Security Council called upon all members of the United Nations to render every assistance to the United Nations in the execution of this resolution.

"In these circumstances I have ordered the United States air and sea forces to give the Korean Government troops cover and support"

GEN MacArthur made a flying visit to Korea, concluding that the immediate introduction of American ground troops was necessary. In his report to the Pentagon (received there about 3 a.m., June 30) MacArthur stated:

"The only assurance for the holding of the present line, and the ability to regain later the lost ground, is through the introduction of U.S. ground combat forces into forces into the Korean battle area."

He proposed moving a U.S. regimental combat team (RCT) at once to Korea, followed by a "possible one to two-division strength [force] from the troops in Japan for an early counter-offensive."

Within two hours of the receipt of MacArthur's request in Washington, Truman approved sending a regiment to Korea. Before noon that day, after meeting with State and Defense Department officials, he approved deploying two divisions from Japan to Korea. and a naval blockade of North Korea.

MacArthur immediately directed LTG Walton H. Walker, Eighth Army commander, to order the 24th Infantry Division to Korea, because it was the closest division to Korea. MG William F. Dean commanded the 24th. Dean was then 50 years old, youngest of the division commanders in Japan and the only one of them to had ever commanded a division in combat. Having been stationed in Korea in 1947-48, he was familiar with the country and its people. During WW II, Dean had been assistant commander, then commander, of the 44th Infantry Division. He led it well.

The evening of June 30, GEN Dean received orders to attend a conference in Tokyo. He started for the airfield at Itazuke, but was intercepted by an officer who had new orders: Return to HQ and await further orders. The new orders arrived at midnight. Dean was to go to Korea as commander of his division and over-all commander of a land expeditionary force. At that time, June 30, the entire 1/21 Inf., plus attachments from Heavy Mortar Co. (HM Co.), medics and M/21 Inf. were preparing to move to Itazuke Air Base for airlift to Korea. Eighth Army Operations Order 2 (OPORD 2) also directed that a task force of two reinforced rifle companies, with

a field artillery battery, be flown at once to Korea and report to BG Church.

The 24th numbered only 11,242 men. The three regiments of the division each had only two battalions. The 21st and 34th were on Kyushu; the 19th was at a training area on Honshu.

To bring the 24th Division up to a reasonable strength, 2,108 men were taken from other divisions in Japan, plus 2,615 more from other sources. The number of men taken from the 1st Cavalry Division is typical: 15 officers and 732 enlisted men.

The Formation of Task Force Smith

Dean chose LTC Charles B. (Brad) Smith to lead the task force. Smith was the 34-year-old commander of the 1st Battalion, 21st Infantry Regiment (1/21 Inf.). He was a 1939 graduate of West Point, and an infantry company commander in Hawaii at the outbreak of WW II. GEN Dean thought highly of LTC Smith. "He had a fine World War II record... and was a natural leader," he wrote. BG George B. Barth, on loan from the 25th Division to command the 24th Division Artillery in the absence of the commander, who was on leave in the U.S., also had a high opinion of LTC Smith. "He was my man from the minute I saw him.... His quiet confidence gave the assurance that his men would give a good account of themselves...."

LTC Smith had just finished an alert period with his troops and was exhausted. He literally collapsed in bed at 9 p.m. on the June 30, only to be shaken awake by his wife a few hours later. COL Richard W. Stephens, his regimental commander, was on the phone. "The lid has blown off!" declared Stephens. "Get on your clothes and report to the CP."

COL Stephens then contacted other commanders of the 21st for officers and enlisted men to bring Smith's task force up to strength.

It is difficult to be certain of the number of men with Task Force Smith (TF Smith), or to account for them by name. The 1/21 Inf. adjutant 1LT Russell W. Bertholf Jr. wrote that "I had little confidence in the accuracy of the rosters prepared. Things were happening too fast." The rosters were lost at Osan when the field desk they were in was abandoned.

When he got to the CP, Stephens ordered Smith to take companies B and C (both understrength), with a command group, to Itazuke Air Base; they would fly to Korea immediately.

LTC Smith went ahead to Itazuke. TF Smith, when assembled, included one half the battalion HQ, companies B and C, one half of the Communications Platoon, a composite 75mm recoilless rifle platoon (RR plt) (two guns each from Companies D and M) and a platoon from the Medical Co., 21st Infantry. Between them, the rifle companies had six 2.36-inch rocket launchers (also known as "bazookas") and four 60mm mortars. Each rifleman had 120 rounds of ammunition and two days C-rations.

The force numbered 440 men, 406 of which made it to Korea the next day. The artillery portion of TF Smith originally numbered 108 men and included half of HQ and Service Batteries, Battery A, 52d FAB (A/52 FAB), six 105mm howitzers and 73 vehicles. LTC Miller O. Perry, commander of the 52d FAB, commanded this contingent. The artillery traveled independently from the infantry. Perry was a 1931 graduate of West Point. He served in the Artillery Section, HQ, U.S. First Army, during WW II.

In addition to Smith, about one-third of his officers had WW II combat experience. Almost half the NCOs were WW II veterans, but not all of these had seen combat.

MAJ Floyd Martin was Smith's executive officer (XO). 1LT Charles R. Thomas, a combat veteran of the 34th Infantry Division in Italy, commanded Co. B and CPT Richard Dasher, a WW II veteran with "combat savvy," Co. C. LT John J. Doody, from C Co., was detailed to take charge of the 4.2-inch mortars. Doody was a 1948 graduate of West Point. Before attending the Military Academy he had been in a Naval training program. CPT Pierre Kirby was Dasher's XO. He was a Transportation Corps officer, assigned to the 21st at Camp Woods, Kumamoto, as part of a program which required all regular officers to serve two years with a combat arm.

B Co. platoon leaders included 2LT Jansen Cox, 2LT Carl Bernard and 2LT Ollie Conner. Conner was from Co. I of the 21st and Bernard from Co. L. LT John A. Fox was the Co. B XO.

Carl Bernard was an enlisted combat veteran of the Marines during WW II, honorably discharged in 1946. A short time later he enlisted in the Army and became a paratrooper, where he learned how to load troops, weapons, vehicles and equipment onto aircraft. In March 1949, he graduated from OCS at Fort Riley, KS and was sent to Japan later that year. When loaned to LTC Smith, all he was supposed to do was help ensure that the Task Force's vehicles and equipment were properly loaded and lashed down. Recognizing that he had a good, experienced man, Smith added him to the Task Force and gave Bernard command of the 2d Rifle Platoon of Co. B.

The platoon leaders of Co. C included 1LT Philip Day, 2LT Harold Dill, 2LT Robert A. Nieman and 1LT William E. Wyrick.

Day was a 1948 West Point graduate, assigned to the 21st in August of 1949. Day's outfit had been undergoing a series of alerts for several days before June 30. He was at home when CPT Dasher phoned to order him back to the company. Day left his wife, who had arrived in Japan in April and was now expecting a baby. He next saw her and the baby a year later.

LT Dill was in Army basic training when WW II ended. He went on to airborne training at Fort Benning, GA. Dill left the Army in 1947, but reenlisted in 1948. He received a direct commission as a 2LT of Infantry (his choice) Jan. 25, 1949, joining the 21st in Japan that summer.

LT William E. Wyrick had also been in the Army for a time. He had been in Japan in 1945-

46. Before being assigned to the 21st Infantry in the late summer of 1949, he had spent the previous nine months in Japan as a member of the Military Government Team in downtown Kumamoto.

On Saturday evening, June 30, Wyrick was in his quarters. He and his wife were playing cards with another couple when the company first sergeant called him on the phone with the words, "Lieutenant, you better get down here in a hell of a hurry!" Wyrick thought it was a barracks fight. CPT Dasher met him at the orderly room door and demanded to know where his bag was. "What bag?" Wyrick responded. Dasher told him they were going to Korea and gave him 15 minutes to go home, pack and return.

When Wyrick returned to the company, C-rations and ammunition were being issued to the men. Dasher ordered the men to leave the barracks "like for inspection." Wyrick remembered that the company area "looked as good as I had ever seen it" when the unit pulled out for Korea.

LT Robert A. Nieman was a young and inexperienced Infantry officer.

CPT Edwin L. Overholt, MD, 27, the task force surgeon, was "drafted" for the job. He had been the physician assigned to care for the 700 Americans evacuated from Inchon at the start of the war. On June 30, he "was sitting in the Officer's Club about 10 o'clock in the evening [when he] received a call" to report in full gear at 6 a.m. the next day to Itazuke Air Force Base. He was able to scrounge up everything he needed except combat boots. "In a driving rain, I was jeeped over lousy roads to the air base.... I met for the first time the medics of [the task force] on our transport plane." He got boots when one of the men gave him his spare pair.

TF Smith assembled in the rain and departed for Itazuke Air Base at 3 a.m. July 1. Because of the driving rains and narrow Japanese roads the 75 mile trip took five hours. They arrived at 8:05 a.m. where GEN Dean met LTC Smith and issued him this order:

"When you get to Pusan, head for Taejon. We want to stop the North Koreans as far from Pusan as we can. Block the main road as far north as possible. Contact GEN Church. If you can't locate him, go to Taejon and beyond if you can. Sorry I can't give you more information. That's all I've got. Good luck to you and God bless you and your men."

Only six C-54 planes were available to fly the task force to Korea. The first plane took off at 8:45 a.m. The first two planes to arrive over the small Pusan runway were unable to land because of dense fog, and both returned to Japan. Smith, who was on the second aircraft, was unable to get back on a plane until the 10th flight - some time between 2 and 3 p.m. LTC Rollins S. Emmerich, with a few other KMAG officers and a crowd of South Korean civilians met the first planes when they landed about 11 a.m. Some of the task force, including Co. C, did not fly out of Itazuke until July 2.

Up to this point, neither LTC Smith nor his men had any information about the enemy. In short, TF Smith had been told nothing. From GEN Dean on down, no one knew what to expect. The troops were never oriented on the North Korean soldiers, weapons, or anything else. They entered combat completely ignorant of what to expect, deluded into believing that the whole affair would be over in short order.

BG Eugene M. Lynch, Walker's pilot in Korea, put his finger on the mentality prevalent among many senior U.S. officers at the time when he said, "They always talked about the last three or four weeks of the war [WW II]; how we ran roughshod over everybody. These guys thought, 'Boy, this will be a piece of cake.'" False attitudes like this so deluded the young soldiers that it was almost criminal.

The greeting which they received from joyful South Koreans as they bounced along over 17 miles of dirt roads in a variety of commandeered vehicles to the Pusan railway station was a deceiving boost to the soldiers' morale. People lined the streets, cheering and waving. Banners, flags, posters, etc. were everywhere. Korean bands gave the task force a rousing sendoff from the railway station at 8 p.m. that day. (Some of the task force had departed much earlier in the day. There were no bands for them.)

Prompted by this reception and the false belief in a short, heroic, but bloodless adventure, the men believed that the North Koreans would back off once they discovered that the U.S. had sent ground troops into the war. LT Day wrote to historian David Detzer: "We thought they'd back off as soon as they saw American uniforms." He also remembered someone asking him, "Do you suppose the North Koreans will attack... really come and attack American troops?"

LT Doody said, "I regarded the episode as an adventure that would probably last only a few days."

Carl Bernard, in an article appearing in the June 24, 1951, issue of the *Washington Post*, stated, "We were all calm and confident when we loaded on planes July 1.... We were regular soldiers and we were trained for this. We were under strength and we were short of equipment, but we were not fat and lazy from Japanese occupation duty, as some people said."

Howard A. Stevens, who was then a young soldier in HQ Battery, 52d FAB, wrote that his reaction to being ordered to Korea was that he "couldn't wait to get there. Everyone was excited about going." Stevens was LTC Perry's driver for TF Smith.

1SG Billy M. McCarthy was the task force sergeant major. He was a WW II veteran of the 21st Infantry where, he wrote, he "was the transportation of the base plate," carrying the base plate for an 81 mm mortar crew. McCarthy had been in Japan since Fall 1945. He served for a time with Co. H, 21st Infantry. In late 1949 he was returned to l/21 Inf. and appointed acting battalion sergeant major.

McCarthy remembered the train ride from Pusan to Taejon. "[W]e were loaded on railcars that were eventually packed with troops and personal equipment. The cars were suffocatingly hot and when we opened the windows to get some air, we were treated to sulfur fumes, train smoke and the wonderful smell of 'honey'"

As some of the Task Force boarded their train, many of the men saw a number of boxcars on a siding, filled with ROK wounded, some of whom seemed badly hurt. There appeared to be no medical personnel to help them. As Wyrick put it, "medical personnel were conspicuous by their absence." As their train proceeded toward Taejon, the men saw more cars on sidings, filled with wounded ROK soldiers. These sights suddenly made them realize that they were going into battle, where they, too, could be killed or wounded.

LT Day recalled that, while the Task Force train waited to pull out, a train from the north pulled into the station. It was literally covered with people, including many wounded ROK soldiers. "My God," he thought, "maybe there was a real war going on!"

The first train arrived in Taejon at 8 a.m. on July 2. LTC Smith was met by LTC LeRoy Lutes, of Church's ADCOM staff. Lutes escorted Smith to Church's CP. Church's instructions to Smith were as short as Dean's — and they included not one word about the ROK nor the North Korean situations.

Pointing to the map, Church said, "We have a little action up here. All we need is some men up there who will not run when they see tanks. We're going to move you up to support the ROKs and give them moral support."

Smith asked permission to go forward and reconnoiter for a suitable defensive position for his little force. Neither Smith nor Church had any idea where that position would be.

Taking his principal officers and selected staff with him, the colonel began driving north on the road toward Seoul, meeting thousands of civilian refugees fleeing south. Five different times they stopped at potential defensive sites, but drove on to find a better one farther north. Finally, 80 miles from Taejon, he found the best position, just a little over 2 miles north of the town of Osan. At that point, the road north runs through a saddle and descends into a long valley running to Suwon, 8 miles to the northwest. From these low hills, none more than 125 meters high, one could see all the way to Suwon and defend both the road and nearby rail line.

Smith chose the position because of these factors and because tanks could not negotiate the steep slopes in front, nor attack into his hills from the rear due to rice paddies. The tanks could shoot at his men, but they couldn't overrun the position. His infantry front would be a mile wide.

While Smith and his party were on these hills, a flight of enemy fighters flew over, ignoring the little group of men below. After issuing defense orders to his officers, LTC Smith and his command group headed back to Osan, arriving there well after dark.

While Smith was on reconnaissance, the remainder of his task force, including LTC Perry and the 52 FAB contingent, were on the way to Taejon. The last of his infantry arrived there between 2 and 3 a.m. When Smith returned, Church approved his plan, but ordered him to take part of his force to Pyongtaek and part to Ansong, 15 miles south and 20 miles southeast, respectively, of Osan.

LTC Smith asked for antitank mines for the task force, only to discover none were available in Korea. His men were loaded on trains and set out, Co. C to Ansong and Co. B to Pyongtaek, 12 miles apart. Task Force CP was at Pyongtaek.

Harold Dill's Co. C platoon of about 25 men (15 short of authorized strength) dug in after dark on a roadblock outside of Ansong. Wyrick's platoon, only 18 men, also was deployed as a roadblock. He also had a CPL Rashel and a PVT Madey from Co. A. He recalls being called into Ansong for conferences a number of times. During one of these trips, he saw "a map of Korea posted on a 'bulletin board.' I was able to get one of the Koreans to point out Ansong, Taejon and Seoul on the map," he wrote. "This information would prove valuable later."

July 3 was a day of air attacks by U.S. and Royal Australian fighters against ROK and U.S. troops.

Joseph Langone, a member of Co. B, had enlisted in the Army May 10, 1948, at 18 because he wanted to be a professional soldier. He remembered training in Japan as "excellent," adding, "We trained continuously and it was tough training.... As far as being fat and lazy... I have read from people who have written about the Korean War..., I think it was ridiculous. We trained hard and were in tough physical [and] mental condition and ready to go into battle...."

Langone witnessed six strafing runs on a ROK ammunition train at Pyongtaek. The aircraft fired rockets and machine guns into the six-boxcar train, blowing it up, demolishing the station and shooting up parts of the town. Many civilians were killed in the attack.

Langone's company had just finished digging in when they "noticed a group of aircraft... bombing and strafing probably 2 or 3 miles away," he wrote. Then "these aircraft came over our position and... got up, up into the sun where it was difficult to see them.... They came in strafing our position.... The only insignia I saw was something like a bullseye. I know it wasn't American aircraft." Langone also stated that he was strafed by "friendly" aircraft the next day, too.

Obviously, pilots had been directed to attack "targets of opportunity." There were no forward air controllers, nor any other ground-to-air coordination at this stage of the war. As a result, on July 3, in addition to the mistaken and very costly air attack on the ammunition train, U.S. aircraft strafed a ROK truck column near Suwon. The ROKs shot one plane down, forcing the pilot to land at the Suwon Airfield, where he was promptly captured by the ROKs. One KMAG officer said he was attacked at Suwon five times that day by "friendly" aircraft. American planes hit gas and ammo dumps, trains, motor columns, Suwon airstrip and Korean Army HQ.

That afternoon four U.S. jets struck Suwon and the Suwon-Osan highway. They destroyed buildings, set gasoline afire and injured civilians at the railroad station. On the highway, they attacked and burned 30 ROK trucks, killing 200 South Korean soldiers. An angry GEN Church protested to the Far East Air Forces (FEAF), asking that air action be confined to the Han River bridges and northward. FEAF complied.

The infantry soldiers of TF Smith had no real rest since leaving Japan, either preparing to move, moving, digging in, or moving again since their arrival. By July 4, when the infantrymen reassembled at Pyongtaek, they were getting bushed. The artillery contingent joined them there that day.

Field artillery support for TF Smith came from B/52 FAB. LTC Miller O. Perry and a small contingent from HQ and Service Batteries also were part of this element. At first the plan was to airlift the artillerymen, without their howit-

zers, to Korea. There they would pick up light 105mm howitzers normally used by airborne units. They would be limited to jeeps in the airlift, which would have to be used in tandem to move the guns. "By noon July 1st, the 52d FA Bn (-) was ready to go," GEN Perry wrote. Heavy rains had closed the airfield at Pusan. As a result, the plan was changed. Able Battery took their own guns and trucks and loaded out on a Landing Ship Tank (LST) from the port of Fukuoka.

Loading the trucks onto the LST was "quite slow," wrote Perry. "The Japanese LST crew knew no English and the artillery personnel knew little Japanese," he continued. "Equipment had to be tied down with chains attached to rings in the deck of the ship." The battalion had never trained to load out on a ship.

LTC Miller's staff included Assistant S3 CPT Carl Simpson and Adjutant CPT Ambrose Nugent, who volunteered to be the liaison officer with Smith. CPT Richard Hooper commanded HQ Battery, assisted by 2LT Isadore Peppe, Battalion Communications Officer. Battery A was commanded by 1LT Dwain Scott. Battery officers included 2LT James Thompson, forward observer and 2LT Bruce Haney, motor officer.

The 12-hour sea voyage was uneventful. They arrived in Pusan late on July 2. The next day, two trains took them on to Taejon, where GEN Church ordered LTC Perry to join Smith at Pyongtaek. At some of the stations along the way "small bands played music and the school children had been let out of school and waved flags," Perry recalled. About 9 p.m. the artillerymen proceeded by train, but had to detrain at Songhwan-ni because of the destroyed railway station at Pyongtaek. The unit completed the last six miles of the journey in their own vehicles. Artillery forward observers joined the two rifle companies on July 4.

Co. C, at least, found some Korean beer with which to celebrate the July 4. Otherwise, the day passed without much special notice by the task force.

While TF Smith was assembling in Korea and moving up for defense, GEN Dean was having difficulty getting to Taejon. Clay Blair, in *The Forgotten War*, writes that Dean first tried to get to Pusan in a four-engine C-54, but could not land because the dirt field had been so cut up by the planes carrying TF Smith. He returned to Japan, changed to a smaller C-45. Because he had to use the smaller aircraft, he had to leave his jeep and other equipment in Japan. Taking off from Pusan, they tried for Taejon, but the pilot said the field was too small for the C-45. Back to Japan he went again. Fog covered South Korea, but Dean was determined this time, and he finally landed at Taejon at 10:30 a.m. on July 3.

That afternoon, MacArthur appointed Dean commander of the United States Army Forces in Korea. (USAFIK) effective at one minute after midnight July 4. Dean appointed Church as his deputy commander. Most of Dean's USAFIK staff came from ADCOM, with a few others from KMAG. But his own division staff was scattered. His Intelligence Section (G2) was at Taejon; Operations (G3) at Pusan and his G1 (Personnel and Administration) and G4 (Logistics) elements were still back in Japan.

GEN Dean met his acting division artillery commander, BG George B. Barth on July 4. GEN Barth was a Field Artillery officer, but had WW II combat experience as commander of the 90th Division's 357th Infantry. Later, he served as Division Chief of Staff. Barth wrote that he was much impressed with Dean's decisiveness, determination and leadership. He also noted that Church appeared calm, although Barth was sure that he had no such inner feeling.

The Task Force Moves Into Position

Dean sent Barth to direct LTC Smith, then at Pyongtaek, to "take up those good positions near Osan you told GEN Church about." Barth departed from Pyongtaek by jeep about 3 p.m. on July 4. Smith made a last reconnaissance that day, this time with LTC Perry, who selected his artillery positions.

Shortly after midnight, in the rain again, TF Smith began moving from Pyongtaek to their defensive positions north of Osan. They traveled in commandeered Korean trucks and other vehicles. The Korean drivers deserted when they discovered that the convoy was headed north. American soldiers took over and the column continued.

"The medics were last in the transport line," wrote Dr. Overholt. "The lead truck which I was in became overheated and we had to repeatedly stop to fill the radiator with water. Because of this difficulty, we were at least an hour behind the two companies of infantry." The doctor, who was on the last reconnaissance with Smith, had marked with white gauze where the medics should leave the road to go to the site he had selected for the aid station, on the reverse slope of the large hill occupied by Co. C and most of Co. B. He also marked the route across the rice paddies into the aid station. The doctor should have had a Medical Service officer (an administrative officer) to assist him in setting up and organizing the station. However, Smith had assigned that officer (1LT Raymond "Bodie" Adams) to other duties. Adams would have been a great help, since the medical unit did not know Overholt and were at first reluctant to follow him to the station. But he eventually assembled them and set up the site. By 6 a.m., Overholt had litter teams out to the rifle companies and the aid station was operational in a "lean-to tent," covering a muddy 12-foot-square dugout deep enough to protect from enemy fire.

From Osan the railway and road ran close together until the land began to rise into hills. At this point, the railroad bent eastward away from the road then split into two single lines to pass over the low ground between hills on the ridgeline. At that point, the highway and rail line were about a mile apart. LTC Smith placed a platoon (Cox's) of Co. B to the left of the road, with the other two platoons (Conner and Bernard) of that company on the forward slope of Hill 117. To the right of Co. B was Day's platoon of Co. C. Next was that of Wyrick. Part of his platoon faced north, with the remainder facing east on a refused flank. Dill's platoon was dug in behind Wyrick's, on a finger facing east, further refusing this flank.

At least one 75mm RR rifle was emplaced in

Co. B's sector, overlooking the road. Two others were between the platoons of Day and Wyrick. (See Chapter Note on the number of 75s with TF Smith.) The two 4.2-inch mortars were placed 400 yards behind the center of Co. B. Under command of LT Doody, the mortar crews consisted of one private from the Mortar Co., plus an NCO and 4 or 5 men from B/21. Smith's CP was on the reverse slope of Hill 117.

Most infantry vehicles were parked along the road just south of the saddle, while those of the artillery were concealed behind buildings and in yards north of Osan. In addition to the six HEAT (High Explosive Anti Tank) rounds, the artillery had about 1,200 rounds of HE ammunition.

When finally dug in north of Osan, TF Smith had a total of 540 soldiers. The infantry numbered 17 officers (O) and 389 enlisted men (EM); the artillery 9 O and 125 EM.

The Battle

July 5 began with rain, and it continued during the battle. At first light, GEN Barth inspected Smith's position, noting it was "on strong ground but pitifully weak in numbers." He then left for the artillery position.

Shortly after Barth left, LTC Smith was at an observation post atop Hill 117. About 7 a.m., he saw movement on the road from Suwon. Thirty minutes later, a tank column could be seen on the road, headed for his position. Eight tanks were in the lead, a break, then more tanks. When they reached a point 4,000 yards from the artillery, and about 2,000 yards from the infantry line, a forward observer called in a fire mission. At 8:16 a.m., the first American shells fell on the North Koreans. Although some hits were scored, the tanks continued towards the dug-in infantry.

GEN Barth had arrived at the artillery position when the first fire mission came in. He left almost immediately for Pyongtaek to advise the newly arrived 34th Infantry.

Perry had emplaced one howitzer as an antitank gun 1 1/2 miles south of the top of Hill 117. The gun could cover almost the entire 1 1/2 miles. Unfortunately, it had only six HEAT rounds, one-third of the total HEAT rounds available to the entire 24th Division. The remaining four guns of the battery were located about a mile and a half behind the AT howitzer and 150 yards to the left (west) of the road. It had been necessary to use two jeeps in tandem to get the guns into position over the narrow trail from the road. One howitzer had been left at Pyongtaek because of a problem with it.

Volunteer artillerymen from the HQ and Service Battery contingents under LT Peppe formed four .50-cal machine gun teams and four bazooka teams to reinforce the infantry line. Nineteen-year-old Robert Fitzgerald was one of the artillerymen-machine gunners. He wrote that he didn't recall volunteering so much as being "volunteered." He and another man were the crew of a gun emplaced on the left of the road in Co. B's position.

Joseph Langone was with Cox's platoon of Co. B to the left of the road. They had moved into position shortly after midnight on July 5. "It was raining and it was cold and miserable," wrote Langone. "By the time we finally got ourselves dug in, dawn started to break. I was look-

ing to the front.... We were laying there waiting for the [enemy] soldiers and for the war to start. To be perfectly honest, I didn't believe that they were gonna come. The first thing I saw was a tank and then I saw another tank and another tank, and the tanks kept coming. In addition to the tanks, the infantry started to come. There was some artillery fire coming in and some mortar fire coming in and we started to fire back from our positions."

In a 1951 interview, LT Bernard said, "It was raining to beat hell the morning we dug in north of Osan. We were in pretty good spirits, though, considering that we ran into the more-than-half-rock soil of Korea for the first time. Some of the 17th ROK Regiment fell back through us and told us stories of the tanks the North Koreans were using, but we paid no attention to them. We figured they were not regular soldiers and had not fought tanks before"

Philip Day "didn't think there would be any enemy action. Even at the last moment.... We were very surprised the next morning... to look out in a rain and see...tanks coming down the road toward us.... The battle started very early in the morning in a rain storm. We were very tired and had been up all night.... I think I counted 33 tanks. We couldn't believe our eyes. What the hell was going on? The first thing I knew, our artillery... started shooting out at them. They hit a couple.... They came down the road and got very close.... They stopped for awhile and shot a few rounds and finally... drove down the road and went right through us. They didn't get off the road...."

When SFC Loren Chambers saw the tanks, he dryly observed to Day, "Those are T-34 tanks, sir, and I don't think they're going to be very friendly toward us."

LT Dill wrote that he "counted 33 T-34 tanks lined up on the road and deployed astride the road north and northwest of the Task Force's position. Because of the rain, low cloud cover and the resultant reduced visibility it was impossible to employ aircraft against what would have made a near-perfect target." (See Chapter Note.)

Early in the morning, Dill observed a small group of the enemy moving along the railroad tracks to his front. They appeared to be a patrol trying to fix the flanks of the task force. After satisfying himself that they were not stray South Koreans, he took aim at the member of the group who appeared to be the leader and dropped him with one shot from his carbine. The remainder ducked for cover. This may well have been the first U.S. small-arms round fired in the Korean War.

Wyrick's platoon had easy digging in the rain, in contrast to the problem with rocks that Bernard's men had. Since there were few trees and little vegetation, Wyrick's men had little trouble clearing fields of fire. At first light, he checked his platoon sector, making some adjustments to foxhole camouflage. From his own foxhole he could look down on the railroad and up the main road towards Suwon. He could also see the northern entrance to a tunnel, through which one of the rail lines ran. Wyrick's platoon radio was not working, but he had communication with the company CP by sound-powered telephone.

"After good daylight," Wyrick wrote, "one

of my men observed a small group of men, dispersed like a patrol, moving by leaps and bounds southeast along the railroad tracks.... I requested and received permission to fire on them. They were engaged with the platoon's .30-cal machine gun. We fired 10-15 rounds; they took cover and were not seen again.

"A short time later," he continued, "we saw tanks coming down the road from Suwon.... Surface visibility was good for several miles. We could see artillery rounds bursting around them. There was a 75mm recoilless rifle in the platoon area to my left, which fired several rounds at the tanks. The 75's position received return fire from the tanks." This was the only incoming fire his platoon experienced in its initial position. As the tanks closed on Co. B's position, Wyrick could no longer see them.

Robert Roy, then a PFC, was part of the crew of the 75mm recoilless rifle that Wyrick mentioned. By June 1950, he had been in Japan about a year. "At 2 a.m. on July 1, 1950, came the big surprise. The [barracks] lights were abruptly thrown on by our first lieutenant, who told us to get all our combat gear together, leaving personal items in foot lockers." They were going to Korea.

Roy's gun and crew, under CPL Bond, were located on the right of the road, where they "set up a position to have a good field of fire at the pass," Roy wrote.

"At approximately 8 a.m. we started to open cans of C-rations.... We had a view of the road ahead... for about 2 to 3 miles. Around the mountain came the first T-34 tank and we started counting. Artillery shells began bursting on both sides of the road. We dropped our C-rations.... We were amazed at the speed at which they rumbled down the road, some distance between them. At a count of 30 or so we fired the first direct fire on the enemy in this new war. Our field of fire was limited and the tanks flew past us with the shells hitting behind them, or bouncing off." Roy's "eye never left the sight [of the gun], except at the recoil," he wrote. "They went out of sight and reappeared in the pass, between the two hills, and then came out behind us."

The gun crew moved the 75 so as to "fire on them as they went down the road [to the rear]. We fired one round that was short and we saw the turret of the tanks turn and fire. [The tank round] was short but, from the backflash of our weapon when it fired he [the enemy] knew our exact position." Before Roy's crew could get off another shot, the tank fired again. "It hit directly in front of us, so close that we were all [temporarily blinded and deafened] by the explosion...[and] concussion." The men were struck by dirt and rocks kicked up by the exploding tank round. Roy and his comrades "quickly in our shocked state of numbness... stumbled, half-rolling, over the other side of the hill."

The rifle remained in position, but the men saw that the tank was waiting for them to reappear. After several minutes, the T-34 crew, apparently thinking they had knocked out Roy's gun, went on their way south on the road. Soon afterward, orders came to move the 75 across the pass to cover the rear of the position in case the tanks turned to attack. To top it all, Roy recalls, "We had no [antitank] shells that could [have] pierced their [T-34] armor."

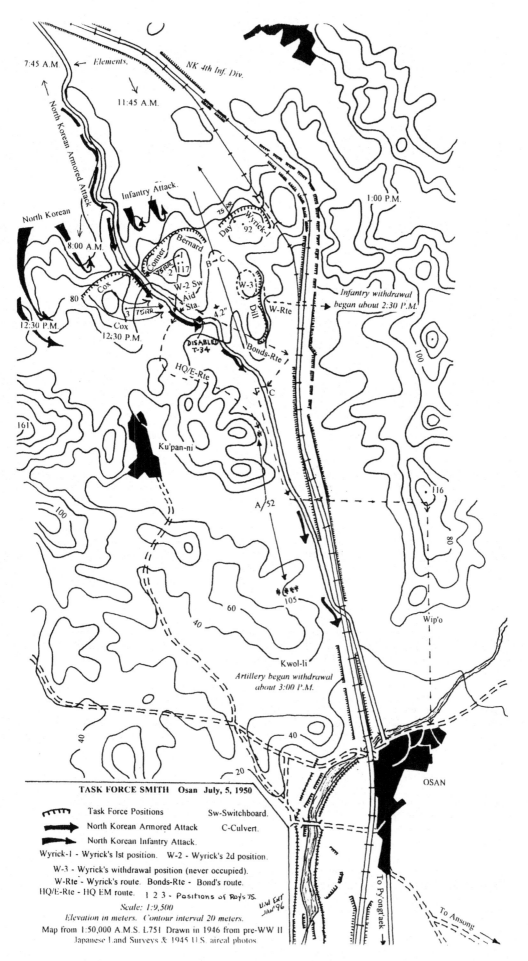

7:45 A.M. ← Elements,

NK 4th Inf. Div.

11:45 A.M.

North Korean Armored Attack

Infantry Attack.

1:00 P.M.

North Korean

8:00 A.M.

75 RR
Day
Wyrick-1
·92

Bernard
Conner
·1
75 RR
2
117
B—C
W-3

Cox
80
W-2 Sw
Aid
Sta.
4.2"
Dill
W-Rte

Infantry withdrawal
began about 2:30 P.M. →

12:30 P.M.

Cox
12:30 P.M.
3 75 RR

DISABLED
T-34

Bonds-Rte

100

HQ/E-Rte

C

161

Ku'pan-ni

116

A/52

80

100

105

60

40

Wip'o

40

Kwol-li

Artillery began withdrawal
about 3:00 P.M.

40

20

OSAN

TASK FORCE SMITH Osan July, 5, 1950

Task Force Positions   Sw-Switchboard.

North Korean Armored Attack   C-Culvert.

North Korean Infantry Attack.

Wyrick-1 - Wyrick's 1st position. W-2 - Wyrick's 2d position.

W-3 - Wyrick's withdrawal position (never occupied).

W-Rte - Wyrick's route. Bonds-Rte - Bond's route.

HQ/E-Rte - HQ EM route. 1 2 3 - Positions of Roy's 75.

Scale: 1:9,500

Elevation in meters. Contour interval 20 meters.

Map from 1:50,000 A.M.S. L751 Drawn in 1946 from pre-WW II
Japanese Land Surveys & 1945 U.S. areal photos

UM ENT
JAN '96

To Pyong'taek

To Ansong

Map 5 (Source: Uzal W. Ent)

LT Day and the crew of the other 75 moved to get a clean shot. This crew included a CPL Denton. In their eagerness to engage the tanks, they placed the gun on the forward slope of the hill. The backblast from their first round blew a hole in the hill to the gun's rear, covered the crew with mud and dirt, and jammed the weapon. They quickly cleared the gun and moved it to a better position. "I swear we had some hits, but the tanks never slowed down," Day recalled. "More of the tanks began shooting at us.... One blast knocked me and the gun over backward. I began bleeding from my ears." He didn't know what happened to the other crew members.

SGT Donald M. Pugh commanded one of the 75s. Pugh expended all his 75 ammunition, scoring hits, but without stopping one tank. One of his men was killed and another wounded in the tank battle.

Some tanks had been hit by recoilless rifle and artillery fire, without apparent damage. As the T-34s began entering the infantry positions, rocket launcher teams began attacking them. One of the most notable attackers was LT Ollie Conner. He crawled down the hill into a ditch along the road, then worked his way along the ditch until he reached the rear of one of the tanks, where the armor was thinner than on the front of the vehicle. He was only 15 meters from the tank. Conner's first round burned out against the T-34 without effect. Quickly he loaded and fired again, without effect. He finally stood up to get a better view. Conner fired 22 rockets against T-34s that day. Several rounds failed to detonate properly on impact, but he was credited with disabling two tanks. The launcher ammunition was at least five years old and had been in storage. Some, if not all of it, had deteriorated.

Lieutenants Cox and Bernard also directed bazooka teams against the tanks, with no apparent effect.

LT Doody, observing the launcher team attacks, exclaimed, "It was heartbreaking to watch those men firing point-blank and doing little damage. Rockets hit the tanks in the tracks, turrets and bogies, and still they couldn't stop them!"

One man who did not see the enemy tanks rolling toward the Americans was PFC Earsel Bonds. He had been in Japan for over a year and a half before the Korean War, first with the 1st Cavalry Division, then in the Communications Platoon, HQ. Co., 1/21st Infantry. He was an experienced switchboard operator. He recalled that his platoon was well trained because of the efforts of SGT John T. Hawkins, a WW II veteran. Hawkins, Bonds recalled, "knew everything about everything we had to work with. He taught us."

Bonds was tapped to accompany TF Smith as a switchboard operator for the CP. When they arrived on the Task Force position, he and his comrades dug in the switchboard. All they had to protect it from the rain was a poncho. If the switchboard got wet, it would short out and communications would be lost. The Communications Platoon laid telephone wire out to the companies and the artillerymen laid wires from the gun position up to Bond's switchboard. Unfortunately, there were two critical problems with the wire. First, this was commo wire which had been used in training over and over again. It had been

Some of the first U.S. troops to arrive in Korea. (Source: P. 41, Pictorial History of the War in Korea, Veterans of Foreign Wars, 1951)

spliced and respliced so many times that it was of doubtful value. Second, the wire was just laid on the ground and across the road, instead of buried in a shallow trench. Even if it had been buried a few inches below the surface, it would have had some protection, even from tank treads. Because it wasn't protected, it was broken by artillery and mortar fire and chewed up by the tanks.

In the hole, operating the switchboard under the dubious rain protection from the poncho, Bonds heard someone call out that tanks were coming. From his position on the reverse slope of the hill, he couldn't see the T-34s until they rounded a bend in the road. Then, "I could look right down into the tanks," he recalled. He realized that the switchboard was not dug in deep enough. When they had first dug the hole, they had hit solid rock about two feet down and stopped digging. Between the passage of the first group of eight tanks and the arrival of the next, Bonds and his companions managed to get the hole a little deeper.

LT Bertholf discovered 10 or 12 wooden boxes stacked by the side of the road, with Japanese or Korean printing on the sides. He had no way to open them and did not know what they contained : "Some kind of ammunition or explosives," he wrote, "maybe even mines." He thought they could be used to slow the tanks so "the 75mm gunner might get a telling shot... at a stationary target." During a lull between the passage of one group of tanks and the next, he and a soldier whose name he never learned "positioned several of the boxes across the road simulating a mine field pattern. Our B Co. 'spotter'... warned us of more tanks." The lead tank stopped abruptly, then jockeyed some as the tank com-

mander tried to decide what to do. The 75mm recoilless rifle scored a couple of hits on the tank. The HE ammunition had no apparent effect; they had no AT ammunition. Then the tank rolled over the boxes. One of them burned, nothing more. "Our feeble effort to make some kind of difference came to naught," Bertholf concluded.

Some time after the tanks passed through, MAJ Martin ordered Bonds and others to move the store of Task Force spare ammunition to a better location. They took the ammo from a storage area at the bottom of the hill and brought it all forward. All the while, they were under enemy mortar fire.

When the first two enemy mortar rounds landed in the CP area, "I...remember two soldiers' heads popped up from adjacent fox holes like wild-eyed prairie dogs," Bertholf wrote. "I shouted to them that 'Now you know what incoming sounds like....' I really don't think my admonition was needed."

By 9 a.m., the entire tank column had moved through the infantry positions. Their treads chewed up the commo wire, and with their guns, they destroyed most of the American vehicles parked beside the road. In the hour it took them to pass through the infantry, the tanks had killed or wounded about 20 of Smith's men.

Some of the artillerymen had been assured by the infantry that the tanks never would get back to their position. Now, a forward observer informed them that the tanks had broken through.

As the column approached the lone 105mm howitzer being employed as an AT gun, the artillerymen opened fire, damaging the two lead tanks. The two moved aside to make way for those that followed. One of the damaged tanks caught fire. Two crew members came out of the turret with their hands up. A third jumped out and fired into a U.S. machine gun position with a burp gun. He killed the assistant gunner, but he and the other two tankers were cut down in turn.

The third tank in line knocked out the howitzer, wounding one of the crew. The HEAT ammunition had accounted for two enemy tanks.

The tanks next engaged the remainder of the battery, without effect. Just south of the knocked out AT howitzer, the T-34 column stopped behind a small hill. Then, one by one, with hatches closed, they rushed down the road. Some fired their main guns, others just machine guns. The tankers apparently had not located the battery, for they fired aimlessly on both sides of the road. At ranges from 300 to 150 yards, the artillerymen returned fire, their HE rounds bouncing harmlessly off the tanks. One T-34 pulled off the road and appeared to be ready to overrun the battery, then drove on south toward Osan.

The artillery already had three bazooka teams in position along the road when the tanks appeared. LTC Perry and SGT Edwin A. Eversole each headed two more. The Perry and Eversole teams were caught in the rice paddies by the first tank. Eversole's first rocket bounced off the tank's turret. Suddenly, he recalled, that tank looked to him "as big as a battleship." The T-34 then fired its 85mm cannon, blowing down a telephone pole, which fell across the drainage ditch Eversole had jumped into. He was unhurt. Then a 105 howitzer round damaged the third tank's tracks. Other tanks in the group went on. Except for the AT howitzer, the U.S. battery was undamaged to this point.

Perry took an interpreter, CPT Seung Kook Yoon, and cautiously approached the damaged tank. When he received no response from his call for the crew to surrender, he ordered the artillery to destroy it. Three artillery rounds hit the tank. Two men jumped from it and into a nearby culvert. Perry sent a squad of men to kill the two enemy soldiers.

LTC Perry was wounded in the leg by small arms fire some time in the engagement with these first tanks, but refused evacuation. Hobbling about, or sitting against a tree, he gave orders in preparation for the appearance of the next group of tanks.

About 10 minutes after the first group of T-34s had disappeared on the road to the south, more came into view from the battery position, "a string of them," as Eversole said. They moved along, one, two or three at a time, seemingly without organization.

The sight of a new batch of tanks caused some of the gun crews to take off. Officers and senior NCOs took over the guns and began to fire on the advancing T-34s. This good example and strong leadership from LTC Perry, 1LT Dwain L. Scott and others soon got the men back to the guns. The artillery again could not stop the tanks, although it disabled another one in front of the battery position. Some of the tanks had a few infantrymen riding on them. Most were already dead; more were killed or blown off by the artillery. Bodies slowly jolted off onto the road as the T-34s rolled along.

Tank fire hit a building near the guns and an artillery ammo dump close by. About 300 artillery rounds in the dump began to explode. By 10:15 a.m., all the tanks had passed the artillery, headed for Osan. The entire *NK 107th Armored Regiment* had gone through TF Smith. Four of the 33 tanks had been knocked out and three others damaged.

Casualties among the artillerymen were remarkably light. One man had been wounded at the forward howitzer. Perry and his driver, Howard A. Stevens, were the only casualties at the battery site. Stevens, only 18, was hit in the hand by tank round fragments. His wound kept him out of battle for 10 days.

While the artillerymen were battling the tanks in the rear, the infantry remained in position. When the last of the T-34s passed south of the artillery, an uneasy quiet prevailed over the battlefield. To his front, Smith could see for miles. The road to Suwon was deserted. It continued to rain and the men dug in a little deeper. Smith had been promised air support, but the rain and low clouds prevented this.

About an hour after the tanks had passed the artillery, LTC Smith saw movement several miles north on the Suwon road. Slowly, a column of trucks, led by three tanks and followed by marching infantry, took shape. Smith estimated that the column was 6 miles long. He was looking at the *NK 16th* and *18th Regiments,* some 4,000 men of the *4th Division.* The way these troops were moving, it seemed doubtful that they knew the Americans were there. NK Sr. COL Lee Hak Ku was captured later in July. When interrogated, he said that it came as a complete surprise to the North Korean soldiers that the U.S. had entered the war.

It took the enemy column about an hour to get within good artillery and heavy mortar range of the Task Force. When it came within 1,000 yards of the defenders, Smith opened up with mortars and .50-cal machine guns. The barrage was devastating. Trucks burst into flames, men were blown into the air or jumped from the vehicles into roadside ditches. The tanks moved to within 200-300 yards of the dug-in infantry and began to rake the defenders with cannon and machine gun fire.

"The trucks closed bumper to bumper as far as the eye could see," Wyrick said. His assistant platoon sergeant, SFC Loren Chambers (who had been with Day earlier that morning) got on the platoon phone and asked for 60mm mortar fire on the trucks and troops. The conversation, according to Wyrick, went something like this:

"Won't reach that far," came the reply to Chambers.

Chambers shouted back, "How about the 81s?"

"They didn't get here."

"Well, for Christ's sake, throw in some 4.2s!"

"The 4.2s can't fire," was the answer.

"What about the artillery?" asked Chambers.

"No communications."

"How about the Air Force?" he queried.

"They don't know we're here," came the response.

"Then, damn it, call the Navy!" shouted the exasperated Chambers.

"They can't reach this far."

"Well, for Christ's sake, send me a camera then," he said. "I don't want to miss this completely!" (Another version is: "Send me a camera, I want to take a ____ picture of this.")

Chambers had been wounded five different times during WW II. Shortly after asking for the camera, he was wounded again. He eventually earned five more Purple Hearts and a battlefield commission before being rotated home from Korea.

"Finally, we could see movement, both trucks and dismounted men," Wyrick continued. "We could hear Co. B coming under attack."

PFC Langone also watched the approaching enemy column. Enemy infantry dismounted, perhaps 1,000 men in all. They dispersed to the left and right of the road. While some of the enemy engaged the Americans from the front, the remainder began outflanking the position from both sides. Enemy mortar and artillery fire began falling on the two rifle companies, creating casualties and knocking out weapons.

"The infantry was moving up on the left...and toward our positions," wrote Langone. "One of our sergeants told us to wait a few minutes before we opened up.... When they got within maybe 200 yards... maybe even less, we started to fire at these North Korean soldiers.... The Koreans kept moving in on us and getting closer and closer...."

Fitzgerald and his assistant gunner also opened fire on the attacking enemy. "I'm pouring rounds into them.... I could see some of them dropping.... I could hear bullets zinging past my head, I could see bullets kicking up the dirt in front of me, I could see mortar rounds coming in, exploding on the hill in front and off to the side.... They were pouring a hell of a lot of fire into us."

Co. B stopped the frontal assault. But the North Koreans outflanked Smith's left, ascending a hill mass from which they could dominate the position to the left of the road manned by Cox's platoon. This was at about noon. Smith ordered the platoon to new positions to the right of the road, facing west. This presented a refused left flank and tightened the infantry perimeter. The enlisted men of his battalion HQ group also were employed along this flank to augment the infantry.

When ordered to withdraw, about 12:30 p.m., "we scooted across the roadway and headed for the next hill," wrote Langone.

Billy McCarthy was among the HQ contingent. He saw the redeployment of the Co. B platoon. "I was impressed by their orderly movement, while under direct fire."

When his platoon got across the road, PFC Langone dropped down beside CPL Florentine Gonzales. "CPL Gonzales was mowing those Korean soldiers down," recalled Langone. He thought Gonzales killed 44 enemy soldiers himself. "He was killing them and they kept on coming, almost like a banzai attack. They were coming across [the] rice paddy. He kept shooting and shooting and they kept falling and falling, stepping over each other.... I said 'Geez, how... can you stop people like this that don't care for their lives.' They got close at times but never really overran us." Gonzales stuck with his gun, although wounded, and was captured by the enemy later that day.

PFC John Crespo, a young Co. C 60mm mortarman, had the bipod of his mortar shattered by shell fragments. SFC Calvin Patterson, Weapons Platoon Sergeant, was struck in the neck by fragments. He refused evacuation and stayed with the 60s until they ran out of ammunition. "We won't get out, anyway," he said. When the mortars ran out of ammunition, he led his men, including Crespo, as riflemen. After the battle, Crespo was reported missing in action. He ended up a POW.

Vern Mulligan of Co. C killed six of the enemy that day in a close-in firefight. He and Gonzales each were awarded the Silver Star for their actions.

McCarthy and the battalion enlisted staff were positioned overlooking what they believed was a deserted enemy tank. It had thrown a track. "While I was watching the vehicle," he wrote, "the turret moved and the occupants appeared to be looking for targets. Someone hit the tank with a rifle grenade and the hatch popped open. A soldier climbed out... with a submachinegun and attempted to flee. Our S-4 Sergeant [SGT Martin] yelled for him to surrender. The man turned and fired a burst in Martin's direction and Martin dropped him in his tracks."

McCarthy and some others checked and discovered the tank was empty. When they inspected the dead man they "were surprised that he was not a Korean, but a blond Caucasian [with] the shoulder tabs of a Russian Master Sergeant. Someone pulled off the tabs and promised to give them to someone in Intelligence if and when we got out of the mess we were in." No mention of this is made in the official U.S. Army history, nor did 1SGT McCarthy know what became of the insignia.

"From time to time," McCarthy wrote, his men "would receive fire from the left flank," but it didn't seem to be aimed.

When LTC Smith decided to tighten his perimeter, LT Wyrick's platoon on the task force right flank was moved to a new position facing generally south. His men found this ground difficult to dig into, but they worked, under enemy mortar and artillery fire, to prepare foxholes. Wyrick was able to dig down about 2 1/2 feet during the time he occupied this position. At that time, he recalls, his men still had all their equipment, including gas masks.

As the battle developed, Dr. Overholt's tiny aid station became inundated with casualties. Although he was an experienced physician, nothing ever had prepared him for this.

"A broad spectrum of wounds quickly found their way to my aid station, where we feverishly worked in the pouring rain. The canvas shelter was not protective in the drenching rain and equipment and supplies were very inadequate for the number and severity of wounds," he wrote. It rapidly became a desperate medical situation.

"The roads behind me where I had positioned trucks to evacuate the wounded to the rail station were commanded by [enemy] tanks. The severe cases had to stay in the aid station," he continued. He directed the walking wounded "east across the rice paddies," hoping "they would find assistance to the rear. There was no alternative."

LTC Smith moved about, observing and directing. Soon after he had brought Cox's platoon across the road and tightened his perimeter, enemy mortar and artillery fire increased and machine gun fire started to come from the hill to Smith's right flank. His little force was now being assailed from both flanks.

In their new sector, generally behind Co. B and facing south, Wyrick's platoon had no enemy in sight to take under fire. All they could do was dig their foxholes and hope that an enemy mortar or artillery round did not find them.

A disabled tank on the side of the road near the 4.2" mortar position intermittently fired a machine gun, without much effect. Some GIs tried unsuccessfully to knock it out.

Co. C's 60mm mortar section fired in support of Co. B. The mortar section was just behind Wyrick's foxhole and he could hear SFC Patterson giving fire commands. "It was really frustrating — enemy shells were falling in my position, I could hear our sergeant giving fire-adjustment commands, I could see the North Korean tank firing in our general direction, but there was nothing against which I could direct my platoon. I wanted desperately to fire my weapon at the enemy, but there wasn't a target in range of my carbine."

About 2:30 p.m., Smith realized that his infantry was in danger of being cut off and destroyed if it didn't withdraw. LT Bertholf was with LTC Smith at the time, and recalled the colonel saying, "I'll probably regret it the rest of my life, but I'm going to have to order a withdrawal." As Bertholf wrote, "It was the only possible decision and precluded the complete destruction of the Task Force." Smith wanted to execute a daylight withdrawal while in heavy contact with the enemy, a very difficult maneuver to execute under the best of circumstances, and his troops had never had the opportunity to practice it during training. There was no alternative. He envisioned that Co. C would withdraw first, find a suitable position, go into it and cover the withdrawal of Co. B.

"Around 2:30 p.m.," wrote LT Wyrick, "I was called to the company CP.... LTC Smith was there. So was LT Dill." Dill and Wyrick were ordered "to a ridgeline east-south-east" of their present positions to "form a delaying force to cover the withdrawal of other units. LT Dill would be one the left and I would be on the right."

Wyrick went back to his platoon and called the platoon sergeant, MSG Walter E.Henson, and the squad leaders together. He outlined the situation and pointed out the flanks of the new position. He instructed MSG Henson to move the platoon, with its weapons and equipment, to an easily identifiable spot on the new position. "I will join you there," he concluded.

During much of the fight, LTC Perry's artillery could not help with supporting fire. Wire communication was out and the infantry radios failed. Perry tried a number of times to lay new wire, but his wire parties always were fired on. Finally, he sent another party forward, telling them to avoid the area where other teams had been fired on.

The Withdrawal

Almost from the start, the withdrawal plan began to fall apart, due chiefly to enemy machine gun and rifle fire, and partly to a breakdown in communication and coordination within infantry units.

For example, when LT Wyrick completed his reconnaissance and moved to the hill where he expected to meet his platoon, it wasn't there. His platoon sergeant became a POW, so he never learned why the unit had not gone to the delaying position as ordered. Instead, his men had left, heading south with "the main body." Wyrick was left by himself.

LT Dill said he never got the actual withdrawal order. "Consequently," he wrote, "what was left of my platoon was cut off and isolated. There were nine men, as I recall. When I realized that the remainder of the company had moved south, I started to pull out too."

LT Bernard had no idea that a withdrawal was in progress until he sent a runner to the company CP. The man returned to tell him that the CP was deserted. Bernard confirmed that the entire position was just about deserted, then gathered up his eight or 10 men, plus another 12 from the reserve platoon of Co. C, probably from Wyrick's platoon. He eventually had about 25 men with him, and was the only officer. Late that afternoon, they ran into LT Fox. "Fox was alone and he had a map with him," Bernard recounted. "He had been a prisoner of the Japanese during World War II, but he wouldn't come with us because we had too many people. He was going back alone. He got captured and spent another two years [as a POW]." LT Bernard broke into a school and tore a map out of a book, but it proved of little use to him. It did not have the roads on it where he was located.

During Bernard's escape, he had some wounded with him, including a sergeant who was in bad condition. Bernard gave a Korean farmer his new Longine wrist watch and a note. The note stated that the American medical unit to whom the farmer delivered the sergeant was to pay the Korean $100. The sergeant got to Pusan in a Korean fishing boat.

On the second day after the battle, Bernard divided his group, sending eight men off with a capable and impressive young man who, he later discovered, was a private. The private's group also made good their escape.

Wyrick decided that he should attempt to get away. He moved to the east side of the ridgeline, where he met several men, not from his company. "I told them to stay with me," he wrote. They moved a short way to the west edge of a large rice paddy. He knew the North Koreans were south of them, so he decided to go east toward the railroad. Rice paddies that time of year were filled with water and deep mud. As the lieutenant put it, "you could sink in over your knees" trying to cross one of the paddies. So they began running along the dikes separating each paddy. When Wyrick started across, a machine gun on the high ground to his left opened fire. "The bullets hit all around me. I ran as fast as I could along the wet, slippery dikes until I reached the railroad."

He had become separated from the men he had been with, but just over the railroad embankment he met LT Raymond Adams of the medical platoon. Adams had been a pitcher and captain of the regimental baseball team. Some time during the withdrawal he destroyed an enemy machine gun and crew with a 40-yard grenade throw. The gun had caused a number of casualties among the retreating Americans.

Wyrick and Adams teamed up. They could see Americans going up and over a ridge due east of them, and decided to head east themselves. The two men helped one another to the top of the ridge, all the while under enemy fire.

"LT Adams and I assembled a real mixture of people in the first mile or so east of the ridge. There were 30-35 from B, C and D Companies, Chaplain Hudson, Dr. Overholt and several medics," Wyrick said. Neither the doctor nor chaplain were in good physical condition. "At times," Wyrick said, "it looked as if they were actually 'carrying' each other."

Dr. Overholt recalled that after two hours of fighting, it was obvious that LTC Smith had to withdraw. Overholt got this word when a lieutenant "came running over the hill and stopped in his tracks when he saw the aid station surrounded by seriously wounded. 'What the hell are you doing here?'" he yelled. The doctor told him off. Overholt was going to stay with the wounded, but North Korean soldiers fired at the medics, although they wore red cross markings and were not armed. As he knelt beside several badly wounded soldiers, "one looked at me and [told] me that all was lost and to get the hell out of there," Overholt recalled. That's when he and the chaplain made a break. The North Koreans "were more interested in the equipment and wounded left behind," Overholt wrote. Overholt treated wounded GIs along the way out as best as he could.

PFC Max E. Meyers and CPL Ernest A. Fortuna, both of the medical detachment, remained with the wounded. Both were captured and were repatriated at the end of the war.

Wyrick didn't have a map, but he had a good sense of direction. He organized the column, with the wounded and those without weapons in the center and those still armed at the front and rear. The little group then set off for Ansong.

They came upon a KMAG engineer, CPT Willis C. Corder, and one or two sergeants who had been visiting Wyrick's battalion when the enemy attacked. The lieutenant tried to get the captain to take charge, without success. The captain said he was not an Infantry officer.

Later, they met some South Korean soldiers who joined the group for a time. A little while later, the KMAG officer disagreed with Wyrick on the direction which should be taken and the KMAG people left. The South Koreans also departed about the same time.

Wyrick's group trudged on. The men were hot, tired and hungry. The column stretched out longer and longer. Men ran into fields along the road to dig up vegetables. It became increasingly difficult to keep them moving. Men even drank from the paddies. The soldiers all had been awake now for almost three days. They stopped for 10-15 minute breaks every 30 to 40 minutes. By 9:30 p.m., the exhausted men were stopping even more frequently, then falling asleep.

Wyrick himself fell victim to this. "Suddenly I woke up," he wrote. "I was flat on my back and it was raining.... I was alone." Quickly, he rolled off the road and concealed himself. He sorted things out in his mind, then decided to head south on low ground at night and hide on a ridge during the day. It was about 2 a.m.

He set out, "keeping my carbine at the ready." An hour and a half later, he was challenged by a Korean policeman. Wyrick knew only three Korean words. Luckily, one of them was enough to

identify himself. He responded "Megook," to the challenge. ("Megook" meant "American" in Korean.) At the police station, he met CPT Dasher, LT Day, 1SG Godby and others from his company, 65 men in all. There, he had his first food since before the battle, "balls of rice... about the size of a baseball, wrapped in... a leaf and a fig or plum on the inside. It was very, very good."

LT Dill began his withdrawal with nine men. "I lost some men early on and picked up some [others], including a first lieutenant from the 52d Field Artillery Battalion who had removed his insignia of rank." Dill, and his men headed south, eventually getting away from the North Koreans. He had a compass, but no map. "Just keeping the men moving, without food and little ammunition, became a chore!"

They walked south for six days, hiding at night. "Not one of my soldiers threw away clothing, equipment or ammunition.... I was proud of [them]." Finally, they saw a U.S. 2 1/2-ton truck, which Dill waved down. He wrote, "I received a Silver Star for my exploits.... A million mosquito bites and a fair case of dysentery. That lasted so long that when I was cured... I didn't know what to do with my spare time."

Philip Day and his platoon sergeant, MSG Harvey Vann, had positioned the platoon in two-man foxholes. Day controlled half the position and Vann the other half. The two men were close enough to call back and forth. Vann was a WW II veteran of the 1st Infantry Division (The Big Red One). He was then about 40 and tough, but cool in battle. Day's platoon also had hit rocky ground when digging in. Soon after the battle started, they started taking casualties. Vann saw that the wounded were evacuated for medical attention. Day recalls being given a withdrawal order. CPT Dasher said something like: "We're going to fall back. Start with 1st Platoon, 2d Platoon, then 3d. I want you up on those hills right behind us there. And cover for each other." This tracks with what Wyrick remembered — a planned, phased withdrawal.

Shortly after giving the withdrawal order, LTC Smith, having no communication with the artillery, went back to inform LTC Perry that the infantry was leaving. Descending the reverse slope of the hill mass, Smith followed the railroad tracks back until he was due east of the battery position. Heading west from that point, he ran into the wire party. He and the wiremen returned to Perry. Smith was surprised to find the artillery operable and only Perry and two others wounded. He quickly briefed Perry. There was no way to take the guns out in a hurry, so the artillerymen took the sights, breech locks and aiming circles. Perry, Smith and the artillerymen drove into Osan. As they rounded a bend near the southern edge of town, they spotted three North Korean tanks. Their crews were standing around smoking cigarettes. The artillery column quickly turned around and, without a shot being fired, drove back to the north edge of Osan. There they turned onto a little dirt road to the east, hoping to get to Osan. They soon came upon men from the infantry. Some of these men were without headgear, others with no shirts and some had taken off their shoes to get through the paddies. The artillery vehicles picked up about a hundred of these men and made it safely to Ansong.

LT Bertholf was among these men. When the

withdrawal order had been given, he and some of the CP personnel moved off Hill 117 into the valley and rice paddies. They received some enemy small arms fire from the east, "but I didn't see anyone get hit," he wrote. "I soon came across Brad Smith and a small group," he continued. Smith told Bertholf "to keep as many troops together as possible and continue southward." Smith himself went in search of the artillery to inform them of the withdrawal. When Bertholf and the men with him first saw U.S. vehicles moving to the east out of Osan, they thought the enemy had captured the artillery trucks. "We saw a ring-mounted .50-cal machine gun swing in our direction," Bertholf recalled. "Fortunately, mutual recognition was established and we made a dash for the vehicles."

Day began to pull his platoon out, executing the withdrawal plan, he thought. "We started pulling back and they [the enemy] were up on those ridges and... were... picking us off, shooting in mortars."

His men and others pulled back about 500 yards to the position designated by CPT Dasher, but did not dig in. Day believed they were there about half an hour. Disorganization began to set in as casualties mounted. Dasher ordered another withdrawal and led them out. "We had wounded with us," Day continued. "Generally we put a guy on each side of a wounded man."

About this time, SGT Hawkins of the Commo Platoon was hit in the neck. "He had blood running down his neck. I thought, 'My God, he's dying,'" Day concluded. But Hawkins didn't die; he survived the war.

MSG Vann did not leave with the platoon. "I'm too old to go racing across rice paddies," he told Day, "so I'll stay here with the wounded." Vann stayed and was captured. He died in a North Korean POW camp.

"I saw very few people throw their weapons away. There was no panic," Day said, but "some men had taken off their boots to go faster through rice paddies and others had lost their helmets."

"We stuck together and trusted our lives to CPT Dasher.... Old Dasher got us out of there," Day recalled. The captain had no map but kept the men moving. They stopped once when they found some potatoes and rice. The next morning, they came upon a unit of the 34th Infantry at the town of Ansong.

The battalion HQ got the word to withdraw about 2:30 p.m. Billy McCarthy and operations sergeant SFC Johnson teamed up. Johnson had a map. They crossed the road and took to the hills, heading south, keeping the road in view on their right (west). Their group had about 30 men of different units, including some walking wounded. They saw the 52d FAB "trucks disappear down the road and [momentarily] felt deserted."

They were spotted and fired on by a North Korean patrol. Ducking down, the men waited 15 or 20 minutes. The enemy patrol moved on.

About 10 p.m., they entered a village and were fed by the inhabitants. The soldiers fell asleep. About midnight, the village leader woke them up and warned of North Korean tanks in town. McCarthy and his party moved off hastily. The next day, about mid-afternoon, they came upon a 34th Infantry position. As they entered the 34th Regiment's lines, a lieutenant colonel looked at them and shouted, "Get out of here, you'll demoralize my men!" McCarthy admits they "were a sorry sight... torn clothing, many minus weapons and helmets, and of course, filthy...." They got to Taejon the next day.

Robert Roy remembered that during the withdrawal "the situation became chaotic.... The air around us was filled with the sounds of bullets. Some infantry were firing at the North Koreans while others were heroically and with disregard for themselves were carrying wounded on their backs. Many did not make it." His group of about 28 made good their escape.

Joseph Langone and a SSG Eckstedt left together when the withdrawal order came. "It was extremely harrowing... the Koreans... were shooting down on us." The enemy turned an abandoned American machine gun on the men. Langone and others crawled through rice paddies and "across bodies to get out."

"The intensity of the fighting was unbelievable," Langone continued. "The bullets were zinging at us... you could here the cracking of the bullets and ricochets of the machine gun.... There were so many dead people and so much fighting, it was miraculous that we even got out of there." A master sergeant with them ordered the men to throw away their weapons and grenades. The soldiers were skeptical. The sergeant told them that they would be killed by the enemy if caught with a weapon. The men then disassembled their weapons and threw them in different directions. Langone, "being the trained infantryman, did not think I should be doing this." He kept two or three grenades. Shortly, Langone's group of about 25 to 30 men ran into two Korean men, dressed as civilians, who offered to guide them to safety. It seemed to Langone, though, that they were heading north, not south. When the group spotted a South Korean patrol looking for survivors of the task force, the two "guides" left in haste.

The 17-year-old Earsel Bonds recalled about 10 stretcher cases at the aid station as he got the order to pull out. (Other sources state that there were eventually 30 litter cases at the aid station.) Bonds destroyed the switchboard with a thermite grenade. Upon leaving, he also noted a large, dead North Korean soldier near a knocked-out tank.

Bonds, SGT Hawkins and a man who had helped move the ammunition began running across a rice paddy under enemy machine gun fire. When they got about halfway across, the man was shot in the neck. "I stopped at this guy and he just couldn't talk, bubbling blood coming out everywhere.... I told SGT Hawkins that there was nothing we could do for him."

Bonds and others reached a culvert, crawled through it to cross the road and headed for the railroad tracks. He joined SGT Johnson and MSG John W. Finley (Co. D), who were part of the McCarthy-Johnson group. When he joined them, Bonds said the men in the group had their "weapons and everything." SGT Johnson, according to Bonds, told the men to break up in small units, disarm and make our way south, the best we could.... So, we did.... I disassembled my carbine [and] threw it in different directions."

Langone and Bonds must have been in the same group, since both report that a sergeant gave the group the same order.

One of the men tried to break his carbine by hitting it against a concrete post. The carbine discharged, wounding him in the leg. The men traveled in the hills. The next day they took onions and raw potatoes from nearby fields. At another place, they obtained some cooked rice from a Korean woman. They, too, drank from the paddies. Exhaustion overcame them. "We were so tired, we would be walking along rice paddies and just fall in. When you hit the water, [it] would wake you up," Bonds recalled.

On July 7, an American plane made a strafing run at Bonds' group. Later, two rounds of American artillery fire landed near them. Finally, they reached lines of the 34th Infantry. Bonds was overjoyed. In his enthusiasm, he said, "Boy, come here and I will kiss you!" The man from the 34th he spoke to was offended. "What the hell is wrong with you guys?" he asked, indignantly. The men were taken back and treated to a breakfast of powdered eggs. "They tasted pretty good," Bonds recalled.

LT Bertholf wrote that he made it his "main mission to beg, borrow or steal rations for our troops.... The 34th Inf. personnel were quite willing to share and I loaded as many rations as my vehicle would hold and got back to Ansong about daylight...."

Bob Fitzgerald's story did not have this happy ending. When the order came to withdraw he and others crawled through a rice paddy, then ran, zig-zag, through a plowed field, bullets kicking up dirt all around them. The North Koreans were firing at the fleeing Americans from the abandoned positions. Fitzgerald and his companions wandered in enemy territory for 18 days, traveling by night, getting food from fields or from friendly Koreans. At daylight one morning, they ran across a Korean man and woman who assured them that there were no North Koreans ahead.

One of the officers decided it was safe to travel during the day. A short time later, when the group was about halfway across a rice paddy, they were halted by a voice calling, "Come back! Come back!" They turned to see a whole line of well-armed enemy soldiers along the edge of the paddy. Fitzgerald and his comrades became POWs. He was exchanged in August 1953.

LT Jansen Cox and 36 men were captured on July 6 southeast of Osan. CPT Ambrose H. Nugent, 52 FAB, also was among the POWs. In all, the North Koreans said they had captured 72 Americans from the 1/21 Infantry and 52 FAB.

By July 7, LTC Smith was able to assemble 250 survivors of his command at Chonan. He had lost 156 men. The artillery had 31 men unaccounted for. One or two more survivors of TF Smith made good their escape over the next few days, but total losses in killed, wounded and missing came to some 185 men. The *NK 4th Division* admitted to 42 KIA and 85 WIA at Osan. Best estimates put their tank losses at four destroyed and two or three damaged.

What had TF Smith accomplished?

The Task Force had faced the entire *107th Armored Regiment*, plus 2,000 men or more from the *NK 16th* and *18th Infantry Regiments*. Given their shortcomings in AT weaponry, artillery, faulty AT ammunition, failure in communications, lack of training in withdrawal tactics and the psychological shock of actually being attacked by a determined enemy, TF Smith did a remarkably good job in delaying the advance of the *NK 16th Division*. True, the *107th* punched through, but then had to slow up because they had no infantry or artillery support. What impact the seven-hour delay which TF Smith won is difficult to fully assess, although it was significant. Here are two of the results:

1. Infantry elements of the *4th Division* were moving in a combination motorized and foot column. If the column hoped to stay close together, it had to travel about 3 MPH, or about 20 miles in seven hours, including breaks for the marching men. Unopposed, they could have been almost to Chonan, about 25 or so miles south of Osan.

2. The 1/34 Infantry arrived at Pyongtaek about 5 a.m. on July 5 and went into position two miles north of town. Pyongtaek is some 15 miles south of Osan. Without the intervention of TF Smith, 1/34 Infantry would have been hit by the *107th Armored Regiment* about mid-morning and the *4th Division* about noon that day. Because of TF Smith, the enemy did not come upon 1/34 until dawn on July 6.

A third possibility is if the North Korean motorized column had pressed on, leaving the walking infantry behind. Had that happened, 1/34 Infantry could have been under a tank-infantry attack about mid-morning on July 5.

Under any scenario, the enemy would have been that much closer to completely out-flanking the ROK and U.S. forces. The sacrifices of TF Smith were not in vain.

What might have happened if TF Smith had been able to stop the tank column north of their defensive position?

First, the commander of the *4th Division* would have learned hours earlier that there was opposition ahead, because the tank column would have blocked the road south of Suwon. Next, the full force of 30 85mm tank guns could have been turned against the task force infantry foxholes, with terribly bloody results. Third, the enemy commander, with an earlier alert to this impediment to his advance, could have more quickly deployed his artillery and heavy mortars and taken both the infantry and artillery elements of TF Smith under heavy fire much sooner. The combination of direct fire from 30 tanks and the indirect fire of the artillery and mortars of the bulk of an enemy division would have devastated the task force. Finally, again because of the early warning, the enemy commander could have begun deploying his infantry, developed a feel for the extent of the opposition and begun envelopments of the task force position hours before he did. In short, TF Smith may well have been totally lost, without having accomplished the delaying action they did, all if they had stopped the tanks forward of their positions.

As one of the survivors of TF Smith observed, many of the North Korean soldiers were more interested in abandoned American equipment and the wounded in the aid station than in shooting at the retreating soldiers. Had the enemy made a concerted, coordinated effort to shoot down or chase the U.S. soldiers, far fewer would have escaped. GEN Eugene M. Lynch made this same point in conversations with Carl Bernard years after the battle.

As to the sergeant's orders to his men to disarm, such an order never should have been given. One armed enemy can easily overpower many unarmed men. It is a soldier's duty to retain his weapon and fight, or to escape with his weapon to fight another day.

Postscript

On the infantry positions of TF Smith, enemy soldiers surveyed the carnage. Many dead Americans lay here and there, mouths open in death. John Toland, in his *In Mortal Combat*, records that one North Korean soldier laughingly remarked,

"The Americans are still hungry, even though they're dead. Here have some earth to eat." With that, he threw a handful of dirt into each mouth, to the amusement of his comrades and onlooking villagers. One wonders if that North Korean soldier himself "ate dirt" some time in the battles to come. American soldiers who fought at Osan on July 5, 1950, hope he did.

Chapter Notes:
P. 34 Apparently, a four-gun composite platoon of 75mm recoilless rifles was sent

with TF Smith. Accounts by survivors and magazine articles in possession of the author identify three NCOs as each being in charge of a 75 in the battle. They were Corporals Bond and Denton, both of M/21st Infantry, and SGT Donald M. Pugh, D/21st Infantry. This indicates three 75's at Chonan. However, no one can account for more than two in the battle. The mystery remains.

P. 34 The official history gives the number of tanks as 33. There were eight in the first group, then others, spaced out into smaller groups.

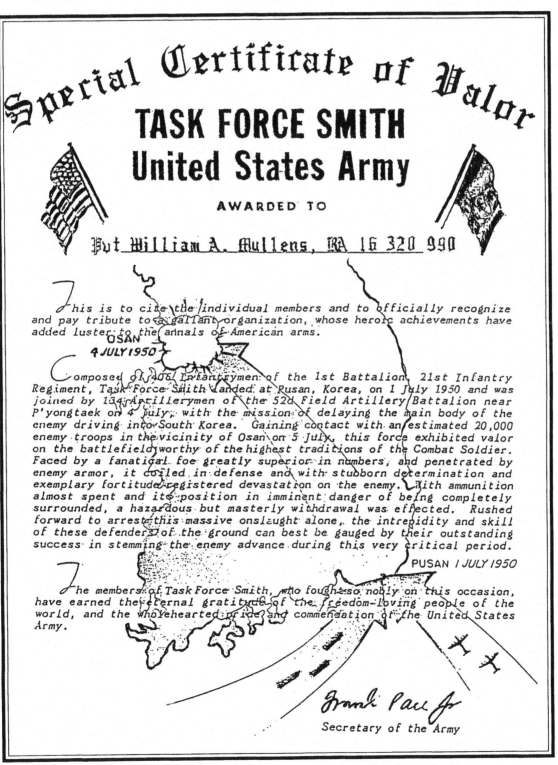

Special certificate awarded to each member of Task Force Smith a number of years after the war.

The 24th Infantry Division

The 7th and 25th Infantry and the 1st Cavalry Divisions each were required to send hundreds of men and a number of officers to help fill up the ranks of the 24th. The experience of First Sergeant George S. Hearn (B/27 Inf.) is typical of what happened in many units called upon to supply men. Hearn recalled, "First sergeants and company commanders went to Regimental Headquarters. From that meeting each company [of the regiment] lost most of its single NCOs [who] went to the 24th Division...."

With the added men, the 24th Division numbered 15,965 troops and 4,773 vehicles. It was still almost 3,000 men short of full war-time strength, primarily because each of its regiments still had only two battalions. In effect, the 24th Division entered combat still short one-third of its infantry strength, one third of its artillery and with only 14 percent of its tanks.

The division had no opportunity to assimilate the over 4,500 new officers and EM. The new men had no opportunity to know the other men in the units to which they were sent. Officers were unfamiliar with other officers, commanders, the staff, or the platoon, company or battalion to which they, themselves, were assigned to lead.

Most of the senior leadership within the division was considered aged for the demands of combat leadership. Of the three regimental commanders, only one, COL Jay B. Lovless (34th Infantry Regiment), had commanded a regiment in combat.

Dean stood six feet tall and weighed about 220 lbs. He was, at heart, a humble man, and had no use for the pompous and the self-important. As Clay Blair put it, "Dean was... a simple, down-to-earth soldier who saw most issues in blacks and whites...." The general preferred to walk rather than to ride in his jeep or a staff car. As a result, the Japanese called him "The Walking General." He was 51 years old. (See Chapter Notes.)

Dean's assistant division commander was BG Pearson Menoher, age 58 (West Point 1915), considered by many to be too old for the assignment. During WW II he had been chief of staff of the XV Corps in Europe. Commanding the division's artillery was BG Henry J. D. Meyer, 50 years old (West Point 1919) and was considered by his superiors to be a "superb soldier." He had commanded the 45th Division Artillery in Europe during WW II, but Meyer was now on leave in the states. BG Barth, as previously noted, temporarily replaced Meyer.

Early in 1950, GEN Walker had relieved the commander of the 24th Division's 34th Infantry Regiment because of its poor performance during its readiness tests. COL Jay B. Lovless, from the IX Corps logistics staff, was named regimental commander in March of that year. Lovless had commanded the 23d Infantry Regiment with distinction in Europe during World War II. At 49, he also was considered too old for regimental command in combat. (See Chapter Note.)

Lovless dug in hard to train his regiment, keeping one battalion in the training area at all times. But, he complained, the training site was "so cut up that it was impossible to conduct a satisfactory battalion exercise." Some of his officers considered the new regimental commander impatient and dictatorial, while others viewed him as being just who they needed to get the regiment on track. Murray Carroll, a young officer of the 34th at the time, wrote that "COL Lovless brought a feeling of stability to the Regiment that was both timely and badly needed. The period of his command was the most effective of any in the year I was in the Regiment."

The 21st Regiment was led by COL Richard (Dick) W. Stephens (West Point 1924). He was 47. In World War II, he was chief of staff of the 30th Infantry Division in Europe, but had never led troops in combat. Some of his officers and EM did not like him. However, COL Philip S. Day Jr., a platoon leader in TF Smith, told an interviewer he considered Stephens as "probably the best regimental commander [in Korea].... He was a tough S.O.B.... He was a smart guy who knew the enemy... the ultimate professional. He knew how to fight a war." COL Harry J. Maihafer, who was another young officer of the regiment, in a June 13, 1996 letter to the author, wrote that Stephens was "highly respected and even loved... including yours truly." Stephens' XO, LTC Charles F. Mudgett wrote to Clay Blair that Stephens was "unconventional in many respects" and a "real character." He was "outspoken in his relations with seniors," and "loved his evening martinis." His men knew Stephens as "Big Six." (See Chapter Notes.)

Keyes Beech, an enlisted veteran of the Pacific war before becoming a correspondent in Korea, wrote in *Tokyo and Points East*, that Stephens "fought with grace and ease in trying situations."

COL Guy (Stan) Meloy commanded the 19th Regiment. He was 47 and a 1927 graduate of West Point. In WW II, Meloy had been the chief of staff of the 103d Infantry Division, and retired in 1963 as a four star general.

Plans and Orders.

Eighth Army Operations Order No. 2 (OPORD 2), July 1, 1950, confirmed a previous message, and included orders to the 24th and 25th Infantry and 1st Cavalry Divisions. Key provisions are outlined below:

24th Infantry Division, with attachments:
On July 1 move TF Smith by air to Pusan. The remainder of 24th Infantry Division move by water to Pusan at once, and establish a base for early operations. Upon landing the division was to immediately send a delaying force north to contact and delay the enemy advancing south from Seoul toward Suwon.

25th Infantry Division:
The division was to move a regimental combat team to Kyushu, and take over the occupation and evacuation mission of the 24th Infantry Division.

1st Cavalry Division (Inf):
Intensify security of Totsuka radio station, and prepare five movement plans. The first, to lift one battalion combat team (BCT) to Korea by air. Next to move the Division HQ and support troops by air to Korea; third, movement of the entire division by water; fourth, airlift a part of the division, and; fifth for an RCT to make a tactical amphibious landing.

This order also created USAFIK and appointed MG William F. Dean its commander. The order also directed that the 24th Division be brought up to TO&E strength.

Eighth Army OPORD 2 clearly spelled out the 24th Infantry Division's mission in Korea: The Division was to advance north, contact the enemy and delay their advance south from Seoul. But by the time that TF Smith from the 24th Division could begin to execute the order, the enemy was already in Suwon, poised to continue its drive south.

It is important to note that, under GEN Dean and USAFIK, the 24th Division's mission remained the same: Delay the enemy. With the troops he had available and the fact that they arrived in Korea over a period of days, Dean was never able to muster his command as a division — or even close to it. As a result, the 24th Infantry never fought as a division until the first battle of the Naktong Bulge, beginning Aug. 5, 1950.

Few historians have recognized that the mission assigned to the 24th Division when it went to Korea was to move north, contact the enemy, then fight a delaying action; that the 24th Division could not be assembled, as a division, in order to carry out this mission, and; that GEN Dean had no choice but to commit battalion elements of his command as each of them became available.

Dean, in attempting to accomplish his delaying mission, employed under strength battalions, because that's all he had, where even a full strength regiment would have been hard-pressed to delay the enemy. As a result, the division was committed to battle almost a battalion at a time, and was chewed up in the same way. Dean acted in a very aggressive and positive a manner, based on his evaluation of the enemy situation, his mission, the weather, terrain and the troops he had available. Given all the shortcomings with which the men of the 24th Division were faced, they did a remarkable job.

The division was deployed on the extreme left flank of the U.S.-ROK force. There it fought a series of ferocious delaying battles, suffering frightful losses in the process. Not only did it delay the North Koreans, the 24th Division prevented the *NK 3d* and *4th Divisions*, reinforced by the *107th Armd Regt*, from sweeping around the left flank of the U.S.-ROK defenders. Had the enemy successfully executed this end run, the war could have been lost before the end of July 1950. The division never stopped the enemy and never "won" a battle, but their bitter, frustrating struggles in July, along with the ROK Army's own stubborn delaying battles, contributed significantly to the future success of the U.S. and ROKs. It bought just the right amount of time for American troops to get to Korea, in the strength needed, to form and defend what became known as the Pusan Perimeter.

The 24th Division's tribulations in these early battles has led to some controversy, including charges that some leaders made mistakes or failed to lead properly; faulty disposition of troops; cowardice of some men; troop panic; abandoning or throwing away equipment and weapons. In short, the officers and men of the division have been accused of every mistake and misdemeanor one could find in an untrained, undisciplined collection of men.

Leadership within the 24th Division made some mistakes and a few leaders failed to lead, in some of their battles. Troops were deployed to face the enemy based on the best information available to the commander at the time, and consistent with the command's delay mission; that some of these deployments proved faulty is possibly true. A very few men did prove to be cowards, but their numbers were minuscule. Overpowering fright and flight overcame some individuals and the remnants of a few squads or platoons. There is little evidence that an entire company "bugged out" without orders, and none that any battalion ever did.

Some men abandoned weapons and equipment. Unfortunately, abandoned radios and weapons were employed by the enemy to their advantage against U.S. troops later on. To their credit, the artillerymen with TF Smith rendered their artillery pieces unusable to the enemy by removing the sights and breech locks and taking the aiming circles with them. It is a military rule, that if weapons or equipment must be left behind they (or it) must be destroyed or otherwise rendered unusable to the enemy.

It is obvious, from an operations order recently discovered in the National Archives by MAJ Lacy Barnett, USA, Ret., that GEN Dean sent Barth out on July 4 with more instructions than to be his (Dean's) representative or his "eyes and ears." (See Chapter Notes.) This is the order (see above right).

COL James W. Snee was GEN Dean's 24th Division Operations Officer (G3). Although dated 062100 July 1950 (9 p.m., July 6, 1950), it may not have been written on that date. Written orders were sometimes prepared after the fact for record purposes.

GEN Barth had command authority over the 34th Infantry and the 52d and 63d FABs, but neither he nor Dean ever told anyone verbally or in writing that a TF Barth had been formed. None of the commanders of organizations composing the task force ever recalled such a formation. Barth violated military protocol by giving orders directly to Ayres without going through the regimental commander. Apparently, at the time, he felt it necessary to do this. The general did inform COL Lovless of his orders to the 1st Battalion, but left the regimental commander confused. At that point, Lovless thought Barth had taken command of the regiment. By virtue of being acting division artillery commander, Barth could give orders directly to the two artillery battalions.

Both generals failed to inform the commanders concerned of the command arrangement, creating unnecessary and unfortunate confusion, particularly in the 34th.

The 34th Regiment began arriving in Pusan by ship late in the afternoon of July 2. Regimental equipment (trucks, jeeps, etc.) arrived in two LSTs the next afternoon.

Lieutenant Murray L. Carroll was then assigned to the Regimental S4 (Supply) Section. Carroll had WW II combat experience in the Pacific and earned a regular Army commission as a distinguished graduate from ROTC, University of Wyoming. Arriving in Japan in late Summer 1949, he was given command of the 81mm mortar platoon, Co. D, 34th Infantry Regiment. He wrote that he inherited "four badly worn and poorly maintained 81mm mortars and sights." The company had no radios and few field telephones. The telephone wire had been spliced, taped and repaired repeatedly. There were no firing tables nor aiming stakes for his mortars. He got some firing tables from civilians working in an Eighth Army ammunition repacking facility and had a Japanese carpenter make aiming stakes, including some with wooden bases for use in the barracks during inclement weather. He fostered competition among his men by awarding the best gun crew slots to the most proficient men. The company XO arranged for the mortar and recoilless rifle platoons to conduct live firing exercises at targets set up on a small island near Sasebo. The training, although very basic, paid off. His platoon scored high in tests administered in late 1949.

In 1950, Carroll was transferred to the newly-formed 4.2-inch (Heavy Mortar) company. But so much of his time was consumed as trial counsel that he was finally transferred into the Regimental HQ S4 Section. He recalled that the Eighth Army Command Inspection of February 1950 found 90 percent of the regiment's weapons "unfit for training." Yet, these were the very weapons which the regiment took into battle in Korea.

When the regiment's vehicles arrived in Pusan, they were loaded onto flat cars. Having no standard tie-down equipment, rope or cable, the 34th had to use Korean rice straw rope.

On July 3, the regiment numbered some 1,981 men. The 1st Battalion aggregated somewhat over 600. The 3d Battalion numbered about 640. The Regimental Headquarters and Headquarters Company (HHC), Heavy Mortar, Service and Medical Companies totaled almost 600 officers and EM.

Appleman, in *South to the Naktong*, wrote that early on July 5, at Taejon, GEN Dean told COL Lovless that LTC Harold B. (Red) Ayres (from 2/27 Inf) had just been flown in from Japan and placed in command of 1/34 Inf at Pyongtaek. Lovless had never met Ayres, who was an experienced WW II battalion commander.

It is possible that Dean did tell Lovless that Ayres would be arriving to take over 1/34 Inf. and that Lovless did not know Ayres, but not on July 5. According to records, Dean gave LTC Ayres command of 1/34 July 4 and Ayres was in Pyongtaek by the end of the day. He did not fly to Korea, but traveled by Japanese ship with el-

---

SECRET

062100 July 1950
(Confirmation of oral order
by Gen Dean to Gen Barth
on the ground)

Operations Order
Number 1

Task Force Barth
34th Inf
52d FA Bn
63rd FA Bn

1. a. See overlay. *(Not available)*
   b. See overlay. *(Not available)*

2. Unchanged.

3. Elements 1st Bn 21st Inf continue to hold present positions until ordered to withdraw. Task force will withdraw to the west Patrols and road blocks will be established on road leading to west from present positions.

   a. 21st Inf (-) now enroute by rail will defend in the general vicinity.
   b. 1st Bn 21st Inf will reorganize and re-equip in Taejon area.

SNEE
G-3

SECRET

ements of the 21st Infantry. They arrived in Pusan the morning of July 4. He reported to COL Lovless there, who told him to report to GEN Dean in Taejon. Ayres flew from Pusan to Taejon. Dean told him that he was relieving LTC Lawrence G. Paulus as commander of 1/34 Inf and that Ayres was to take command of the battalion. Paulus was to remain with Ayres for the time being. LTC Paulus was another victim of an Army "directed assignment." His branch was Coast Artillery, not Infantry.

Ayres recalled that Dean then said, "I think you can get as far as Pyongtaek, but go as far as you can. Your mission is to delay the North Korean advance and to try to stop the ROKs from retreating." The COL recalled no mention by Dean that Ayres was to stop at Pyongtaek, that the town was any more important than any other town or place, or that Dean thought it was a strong position.

But Dean did have a plan. Two roads came down the western part of Korea in the 24th Division's sector. The first of these, and the main highway in the west, passed through Osan, Pyongtaek and Chonan southward to Kongju. The second road paralleled the first, but seven to ten miles further east, entering Ansong. Here, one road turned west to Pyongtaek, another ran generally eastward toward Chungju and a third headed south then eastward.

Just north of Pyongtaek an arm of the sea came almost to the highway. Actually, a small river, the Chinwi-chon, meanders in the area. A giant loop of this river does come within about three miles of the west side of the road. Dean thought that the sea would protect the left flank of a force defending in that area. The "sea" was really the Chinwi-chon, which widened, or narrowed, as the tides from the nearby sea flooded or ebbed. Ansong was flanked on its right (east) by mountainous terrain. He reasoned that these mountains would minimize flanking problems on the right of a force defending near Ansong. Therefore, the general decided to employ 1/34 Inf. at Pyongtaek and 3/34 Inf at Ansong. At the time, Dean believed that TF Smith would "still be out in front to blunt any enemy attack along the main road before it even touched this line." In fact, TF Smith had already been defeated and scattered on July 5.

There would be no "line." Ansong and Pyongtaek are about 10 air miles apart. No two full strength battalions could possibly establish a defensive line over that distance. Two full regiments, or more, would have been needed, but Dean had to work with two under strength battalions to delay as best as they could.

COL Lovless protested this fragmented commitment of his regiment, saying that he would be much more effective if he could assemble his command. Dean and Lovless got into a spirited "discussion." Dean, finally exasperated, ordered, "I want a battalion up there!" That ended the conversation.

Pyongtaek (1/34 Inf, 5-6 July)

When Ayres received his orders, Dean told him to take Paulus along. Ayres went to the train station at Taejon where his battalion was preparing to go north. Leaving Paulus to bring the battalion up by train, he took a few jeeps, the

battalion S2 and S3 and an NCO from each company to act later as guides, and headed out to find a defensive position. At the time, Ayres had not decided on setting up at Pyongtaek. When he arrived in the town, he found the railroad leading north was damaged. This precluded moving his battalion any farther by rail. Further, he had only about an hour of daylight left in which to find a battle position, which he did.

The battalion arrived in Pyongtaek about 3 a.m. on July 5, according to Ayres. The Army's official history states about 5 a.m. Guides took each company to its position. Co. A occupied low hills to the left of the road, a little over a mile north of Pyongtaek. One platoon extended the company front eastward. A 17-man roadblock with a machine gun and three bazookas, under LT Herman L. Driskell (1st Platoon), covered the rail line and road from Osan. B was on a low hill mass across the rice paddies east of Co. A. Co. C was in reserve astride the road and rail line to the rear of the other two units. The Battalion CP was in a nearby schoolhouse. Everyone was in position before daylight. But the battalion had no tanks or artillery support. It had a few 4.2-inch and 81mm mortars, one 75mm and two 57mm recoilless rifles. The 4.2s had very little ammunition. Each rifle company had about 140 personnel.

In briefing his unit commanders, Ayres stressed maintaining morale and alleviating anxiety in the men. "I further stressed to them the lack of intelligence we had reference the enemy," he wrote. Ayres also wrote that he did not assert that the enemy was inept or that there would be no difficulty stopping them, as Russell A. Gugeler wrote in his *Combat Actions in Korea*.

William Caldwell recalled a briefing along the lines Gugeler wrote about. In an interview for Clay Blair, he said, "We had an Eighth Army liaison officer [assemble] all the battalion officers in one car of the train and briefed them.... He explained... that he had been in Seoul when the North Koreans attacked.... But he now felt very confident and comfortable that as soon as the flag and troops of the United States Army were in position, that it would stop this sort of rabble organization of the North Korean Army. He said they were filled with a group of young soldiers, many of them teenagers, often without weapons, who were ill-trained and didn't have much combat capability. I remember... how incongruous this remark seemed... due to the fact that he had barely escaped with his life from the North Korean attack."

Meantime, LTC David H. Smith's 3/34 Inf moved into position at Ansong and COL Lovless established his CP at Songhwan-ni, 6 miles south of Pyongtaek on the main road and rail line. There was no radio or wire communication between battalions nor between the regimental CP and the battalions. Communication would have to depend upon jeeps and men.

GEN Barth arrived at 1/34 Inf CP on July 5 and filled Ayres in on the situation concerning TF Smith and the enemy tanks which had broken through. Barth ordered Ayres to delay the enemy but not let his "battalion suffer the same fate as Brad Smith's...." As Barth wrote, "We could not afford to sacrifice a second battalion at this time." If the 1/34 Inf were lost, the enemy

could have run almost unimpeded on to Chonan and beyond.

Patrols armed with bazookas were sent out on July 5 to find the enemy. LT Charles E. Payne, 1st Battalion S2, had earned a battlefield commission in WW II. He volunteered to lead several three-man bazooka teams forward to engage any enemy tanks they found. Each launcher had about three rockets. Payne believed that they could stop the tanks by hitting them in the treads.

The teams headed north by truck in the rain, passing refugees and ROK soldiers heading south. At a point near the village of Sojong-ni, about two miles or so from the battalion's position, they spotted tank tracks in the mud. The trucks stopped and the men dismounted. About the same time, a South Korean soldier rode by on a horse, shouting, "Tanks! Tanks! Go back!"

Robert L. Witzig and PFC Kenneth Shadrick of Co. C, were among the volunteers. Witzig had been in the Army about two years. He wrote, "We were cold and wet [when we] made contact with three or four T-34 tanks on a rail trestle.... We did knock the tread off one [that] was coming over the railroad trestle. I believe we fired about twelve rounds but Private Shadrick was killed by machine gun fire and we returned to our positions."

LT William B. Caldwell, III, a platoon leader from Co. A (West Point 1948) had been with the 34th almost a year before the Korean War. He felt that his unit trained hard. It had been at a major training area at Onobaru, Japan when the war started. Witzig and Shadrick were in some teams which he led. His recollections of the encounter with a T-34 are similar to Witzig's.

Caldwell and Payne employed four launcher teams in a semi-circle facing the stranded tank. The T-34 had use of its main gun and machine guns. Caldwell used a system of signals to direct fire on the tank. One team would fire a rocket and duck down. As the tank's turret turned to engage that team, another bazooka team would pop up from a different spot and fire. The men engaged this tank and possibly others in this manner for about 45 minutes but no tanks were destroyed; the rocket ammunition was faulty.

PFC Alfred Beauchamp and PVT Joseph P. Krahel also were part of the bazooka force. Beauchamp recalled that he fired the first rockets at the stalled tank, eventually scoring two hits. He would fire and move back, let the tank fire, then move up for another shot.

While the Payne-Caldwell force was engaging the T-34, a group of war correspondents, including Roy McCartney of Reuter's and Marguerite Higgins of the New York *Herald Tribune*, drove up to observe the battle. Higgins watched the action through field glasses. "I could see a blond American head poke up out of the grass," she wrote in her book, *War in Korea*. "Flashes from the tank flicked the ground horribly close, and I thought I saw him fall." Higgins had witnessed the death of PFC Kenneth Shadrick.

Caldwell believed that the correspondents' movements had attracted the tanker's attention. He said, "As I signaled one of my teams to get up, [I did not realize] that the correspondents had already exposed themselves behind the team.... The enemy tank was moving toward the area where he had spotted the correspondents.... As that rocket launcher team stood up to take its aim, a soldier was immediately shot. That was Private Shadrick.... It was at that instance that I realized fully that the things to come were going to get worse."

Caldwell informed his company commander that they were unable to stop the tanks; "that our ammunition was no good." The patrols and bazooka teams were ordered to return to the battalion position about 4:30 or 5 p.m.

That evening, GEN Dean drove to Pyongtaek. He had no word from TF Smith, but the appearance of tanks south of Osan led him to believe the worst. After a short visit, he returned to Taejon. Shortly after Dean left, the first TF Smith survivors arrived in Pyongtaek. Then LTC Perry came in from Ansong and reported to Barth. Based on this report, Barth and Ayres decided to destroy a highway bridge just north of town. The general left Pyongtaek for Lovless' CP about 1:30 a.m. The bridge was destroyed at 3 a.m.

July 6 dawned foggy and misty. LTC Ayres came forward to an observation post in the A Co. position. The company was commanded by CPT Leroy Osburn, a 20-year Army veteran, with 12 years as an enlisted man. He had commanded an infantry company in Europe during WW II. The men of the company were dug in two-man foxholes. All the holes were partially filled with water from the rain.

SFC Roy F. Collins was in LT Robert R. Ridley's 2d Rifle Platoon. Collins was a veteran of the 11th Airborne Division during WW II. He had been with Co. A only since late on July 4, having been sent with others from the 35th Regiment (25th Division) to reinforce the 34th.

About 4:30 a.m., Collins ordered his men to break out their C-rations and eat breakfast. It boded to be a miserable day, cold, foggy and raining. Collins had consumed about half a can of beans when he heard the unmistakable noise of approaching tanks. Through his binoculars he could see in the fog the faint images of enemy soldiers and the outlines of two tanks. They were stopped about 1,000 yards out, where the bridge had been blown. Infantrymen went around the stopped tanks and continued to march forward, fanning out into the rice paddies.

Just before Collins heard the approaching tanks, CPT Osburn was talking on the telephone to LT Johnson, commanding Co. B. Both officers detected approaching foot soldiers through the fog and mist. "It was several minutes later before we observed the first tank," Osburn wrote.

LT Caldwell was in the Able Company observation post (OP) at the time. He was looking through his field glasses. LTC Ayres was nearby. Caldwell saw men moving along the road in the morning mist, in files along each side of the road.

"I told the battalion commander it looked to me like the 21st Infantry, whom we had been told were withdrawing... seemed to be coming down the road to our front," said Caldwell. "It was exactly the formation we would have been in, with a point, the advanced party, the main body, and then the tanks...."

He handed the glasses to Ayres. Looking for himself, Ayres exclaimed, "Hell, that's not Task Force Smith — it's the whole damn North Korean Army!"

"The troops started going parallel to our position... and just kept coming," Ayres wrote. "They got completely outside our flanks coming toward our position...." He called in 4.2-inch mortar fire through CPT Spalding, from the heavy mortar unit. Spalding was with Ayres in the OP. After one round of white phosphorous, Ayres made a fire adjustment and was right on target. Several enemy vehicles were set on fire. (See Chapter Note.)

Both Collins and Ayres recalled that there were 13 tanks in the enemy force, but they were halted by the blown bridge.

The mortar fire brought answering enemy tank fire. Collins and some others ordered the men to begin firing on the approaching enemy infantry. A two-man outpost of Co. A came under enemy small-arms fire. One of the men escaped under fire. The other, PFC Patrick Gallagher, stayed in the hole and was never seen again.

Down in the valley near the road, LT Driskell's men could hear all the firing, but because of the railway embankments, could not see the enemy soldiers or tanks. MSG Zack C. Williams and PFC James O. Hite were near one foxhole in the valley. Private Hite watched an enemy shell explode on the hill, then another. He thought they were short rounds from friendly artillery or mortars. Williams, a combat-experienced man, said, "It's no short, it's an enemy shell." Both men quickly slid into their water-filled foxholes.

MAJ John J. Dunn was S3 of the 34th Regiment. An enlisted man prior to WW II, he had combat experience. Dunn was asleep in the regimental CP when he was awakened about 3 a.m. on July 6 to find the HQ in a state of excitement. News had arrived that TF Smith had been overrun. Since the CP had no communication with 1/34 Inf., he asked Lovless for permission to go to Pyongtaek in order to determine the situation. His operations sergeant volunteered to go along. Before departing, Dunn asked Lovless if he had any instructions for Ayres.

"He [Lovless] spread a map on the table," wrote Dunn. "He told me to tell COL Ayres to hold as long as he could but not to lose the Battalion and then to fall back to a position in the vicinity of Chonan, which he pointed out on the map.

"To be certain there would be no misunderstanding I asked him to repeat his instructions. He repeated the same instructions," Dunn wrote.

Just before arriving at the 1st Battalion CP, Dunn met about ten survivors of TF Smith going south without weapons or shoes. They could tell him nothing. He arrived at the CP shortly after daylight, where he met the Battalion XO, MAJ Leland R. Dunham. He learned that LTC Ayres was out inspecting positions. Dunn looked for Ayres for about 40 minutes then returned to the CP. He found Ayres there. The colonel told Dunn that he had stopped the enemy in front of his position but that "heavy enemy flanking columns were moving around both flanks." Ayres was receiving constant telephonic updates from his forward companies. With the enemy flowing around both flanks, Ayres thought he could hold out one more hour. Then Dunn gave him Lovless' instructions. Dunn "told him that the decision as to when to fall back was his, but that in [Dunn's] opinion, one hour would not help...and might put him in an impossible situation," said Dunn. "He picked up the phone and gave the order to withdraw."

In later writings and statements, Osburn and Ayres give the impression that the colonel ordered the battalion to withdraw very soon after sighting the approaching North Korean tank-infantry column. However, Collins, Caldwell and Dunn recalled that the withdrawal order came after the forward companies, particularly Co. A, had engaged the enemy infantry with small arms. The little 4.2-inch mortar ammunition available was soon expended. There apparently was no ammunition for the recoilless rifles and very little (a hundred rounds or less) for the A Co. 60mm mortars.

Collins recalled that actually seeing enemy soldiers attacking seemed to shock some of his men. Many of them could not believe that they were actually at war. He ordered his men to fire, and began firing his carbine, but he had only 50 rounds of ammunition. Gradually, the company's fire built up, but some weapons wouldn't work; others had to be hand-cocked. Collins claims that a third of the individual weapons in his platoon were defective. During the withdrawal, he gathered up the defective weapons in his platoon and threw them down a well. CPT Osburn said that if he had known of this he would have court martialed Collins, since he didn't think the sergeant was qualified to determine which weapons could not be repaired.

Collins said that the machine gun with his platoon fired two boxes of ammunition, then jammed. The enemy kept advancing. "You could close your eyes and hit something," he said.

He believed that after about a half hour he noticed part of Co. B withdrawing. About the same time, CPT Osburn ordered the withdrawal of Co. A, with the 2d Platoon covering the initial movements. Caldwell said that they fought for "several hours" before pulling out.

When he got the order to pull out, Osburn assembled his platoon leaders and gave them the withdrawal order. This would be another daylight withdrawal while in a heavy battle with the enemy. Ayres had directed a withdrawal by companies; companies would withdraw by platoons.

In a letter to the Army Chief of Military History, dated January 21, 1952, CPT Osburn gave this account of the withdrawal. "COL Ayres informed me prior to leaving the hill that he would have Company B pull back on the opposite side of the road.

"At approximately 0700 hours [7 a.m.]... I gave the order for the second, third and fourth platoons to withdraw under the command of Lt Caldwell. I remained on the hill with the First Platoon until approximately 1000 hours [10 a.m.], when the enemy was coming up the forward slope of the hill.... The only way out was through 2,000-3,000 yards of rice paddies which was [sic] about waist deep in water and mud. The whole distance from the hill to the village [of Pyongtaek] was under fire from the tanks." Osburn, with the First Platoon, less that portion with Driskell on the roadblock, stayed on the hill "until we could see the whites of their eyes," Osburn said. LTC Ayres wrote that the withdrawal "took all day to complete and close in Chonan by dark on July 6."

Co. B pulled out first, followed by A. Collins' account of the withdrawal is at variance with CPT Osburn's, who claimed that when A Co. withdrew, the First Platoon left first. A note in the transcript of his Aug. 4, 1951 interview states that "the Weapons pulled out first.... Then the First Platoon. Once the First Platoon had left, the Third Platoon followed, moving around the left side of the hill. The Second Platoon was the last to leave." Up to this point, the withdrawal had been orderly. Then, according to Collins, an enemy machine gun fired on the last few squads as they topped a little ridge. Then Collins said, it was "like a bunch of wild cattle running." Some men had discarded everything except weapons and ammunition. Some left their ammunition belts, and one or two left their weapons, according to the sergeant. Only Collins and two or three other NCOs kept their packs.

Richard F. Warner was with the 4.2-inch mortar unit supporting Ayres battalion. He had been one of the men sent from the 27th Infantry "Wolfhounds" to reinforce the 34th. Warner and a number of other men, including several other former "Wolfhounds," were put on outpost duty. Warner wrote, "Two North Korean soldiers came at me firing burp guns. I was scared, but I knew it was me or them...." The outpost never got the word to pull out. "When we got back to the company position they were gone.... We destroyed the four 4.2-inch mortars left behind." Warner and his comrades were missing for three days. When they got back, the company commander said he had sent a runner to notify them of the pull-out.

CPT Osburn, with the First Platoon still in position, was not present with the other platoons when the enemy machine gun opened fire on Collins and his men. However, as the men got behind the hill, the officers and some NCOs started sorting them out. By the time Co. A got to Pyongtaek, order had been restored.

In Pyongtaek, Co. A found an abandoned jeep, which they managed to start. All the unit's machine guns, mortars, bazookas and BARs (Browning Automatic Rifles) were put into the jeep trailer. Then someone observed some wounded trying to make their way along the road to the village. PVT Thomas A. Cammorero and another man volunteered to go back for them. The other man grabbed a BAR from the trailer, loaded it, and, with Cammorero at the wheel, they took off - with all the unit's crew-served weapons. Neither the jeep nor the men ever returned. (See Chapter Note.)

Osburn, with men of the First Platoon, rejoined the unit just south of Pyongtaek. From there on he conducted an orderly march toward Chonan, eventually borrowing three ROK trucks to shuttle his men. The bulk of 1/34 Inf. was ahead of Osburn's unit. There is no evidence at all to indicate that it had anything but an orderly withdrawal and march to Chonan. Only Able Co. was subjected to heavy enemy fire, and that only until it reached Pyongtaek.

The official Army history states that the road between Pyongtaek and Chonan was littered with discarded equipment and clothing, inferring that this was from Ayres' battalion. But the men of the 34th also noted the abandoned equipment and clothing. It is, therefore, more likely that it had been discarded by ROK units, which a few days earlier had retreated along this same route.

Co. A lost 13 WIA and 27 MIA at Pyongtaek; Co. B 5 WIA and 6 MIA. Among Able's MIA

were LT Driskell and about 10 men who stopped to administer first-aid to a wounded man.

Osburn's unit was the last of the battalion to arrive near Chonan. There Osburn was met by LT Charles Payne and directed into a defensive position, "where we prepared,... a good one.... I had telephone communications with each platoon and adjoining companies," Osburn remembered.

Some historians have claimed that some men in Co. A were without shoes, others without weapons. To these assertions, Osburn wrote, "If there had been men without shoes and rifles, I would have known as I checked each position not one, not two, but at least a dozen times."

Discussion of Pyongtaek.

It is difficult to obtain a clear picture of the action at Pyongtaek, or even the sequence of some events. The Office of the Chief of Military History (OCMH) contacted CPT Osburn during the research for Gugeler's *Combat Actions in Korea*. The captain responded with two letters. OCMH also conducted interviews of SFC Collins, MSG Zack Williams and SFC Beauchamp. However, the office never sent Osburn a draft of the chapter, as it promised. In addition, although they were all still in the Army and available for interview, neither Gugeler nor anyone else from OCMH tried to contact LTC Ayres, LT Payne or LT William Caldwell. Had they done so, much of the controversy and innuendo now surrounding the Pyongtaek action could have been avoided. The reputations of the officers and enlisted men who fought there have been tarnished for more than 40 years because of this oversight. (See Chapter Notes.)

OPORD #2 clearly gave GEN Barth command authority over the 34th Regiment. Apparently, no historian writing about Pyongtaek and subsequent early actions of the 34th knew of the existence of this order nor of TF Barth. Also, many of them did not have access to letters and statements from Ayres, Caldwell and Payne, subsequently obtained by MAJ Barnett in his research and made available by him to this author.

This material indicates that Clay Blair's account of Co. A's withdrawal in *The Forgotten War* is in error. He wrote: "Red Ayres could not prevent a disgraceful bugout in the 1/34 and its 'covering' force, the reserve L Company. When the withdrawal order reached company level, discipline broke down.... Under increasingly heavy fire the Americans fled the battlefield, many leaving behind all their heavy weapons, rifles and carbines."

There was not a "disgraceful bugout in the 1/34." Evidence indicates that only Co. A was subjected to intense enemy fire as it attempted to break contact, much from tanks, which the company could not possibly have counteracted with the weapons it had. Further, once the men left their foxholes, they were completely in the open, many struggling hip-deep in the mud and water of rice paddies. The enemy, too, already had flanked the position. Order was restored in the unit on the road to Pyongtaek. There is nothing to support anything but an orderly withdrawal by the remainder of the battalion. As for Co. A, it marched from there to Chonan without incident.

Co. L belonged to the 3d Battalion: LTC Ayres had no authority over that unit. Further, the action by Co. L occurred on July 7, not July 6. On July 7, Ayres' battalion was dug in just south of Chonan.

T. R. Fehrenbach's account in *This Kind of War* also contains many inaccuracies, according to other evidence. For example, he states that Ayres characterized the enemy as poorly trained, with only half having weapons, and that the 1/34 would have no difficulty stopping them. Untrue. LTC Ayres, in an April 7, 1989 letter to Lacy Barnett, wrote: "In Gugler's book [*Combat Actions in Korea*], it is asserted that I briefed my company commanders on 4 and 5 July [1950] and told them that the North Koreans were inept. That is not true. I stressed the maintaining of morale and alleviating anxiety. I further stressed to them the lack of intelligence we had reference the enemy." The only record of such a briefing was by William Caldwell in an interview for Clay Blair mentioned previously, in which he asserted that it was given by an "Eighth Army liaison officer."

Fehrenbach and Gugeler also are both specific about the amount of ammunition each man carried, but no other contemporary account backs this. Fehrenbach states that the Weapons Platoon dug in "only three 60mm mortars," and that it also had one 75mm recoilless rifle. U.S. Army Tables of Organization and Equipment of the time authorized a rifle Company Weapons Platoon only three 60mm mortars and three 57mm recoilless rifles. The 75 mm recoilless rifle was organic to a battalion weapons company, and 1/34 did not have a full complement of 57s. The 2.36-inch bazooka had been substituted for many of them.

Fehrenbach and others accept Collins' statement in his OCMH interview that he ordered the men to fire as soon as the enemy infantry began to deploy. The morning was foggy and misty, therefore vision was poor. All accounts indicate that the enemy was 1,000 yards away. Infantrymen do not take an enemy under fire at 1,000 yards. Rifle and machine gun fire is not effective beyond 500-600 yards. Further, in a March 10, 1989, letter to Lacy Barnett, Osburn refutes Collins entirely concerning the men of A/21st Inf. firing on enemy troops in this battle: "SGT Collins' statement about men not firing is false. He states that a full 15 minutes passed before any volume of fire was built up. This is unbelievable to me as no order to open fire had been given by me or anyone else to my knowledge.... It is not the Infantry School solution to fire M-1s and carbines at ranges greater than 600 yards. It is possible that SGT Collins did not know this. His statement that the enemy advanced to within 200 yards of the hill is false. The only movement made by the North Korean infantry was to our flanks."

Ayres, in an April 7, 1989 letter to Lacy Barnett, supports Osburn, when he wrote: "When I left the MLR [Main Line of Resistance], the North Koreans were still a good 1,000 yards away and we had not fired a shot. They did not advance directly toward us but did advance to our flanks."

Fehrenbach (Page 114, *This Kind of War*): "The Weapons Platoon, hearing Osburn's shout, immediately got up and moved to the rear," and

"The running men tore past Osburn, and some of the men with him began to run too." There is no evidence to support these statements and there are many other discrepancies in the Fehrenbach narrative.

LTC Ayres' leadership also has been questioned by some historians. LTC Ayres was a highly-respected officer with much combat experience, having commanded three different battalions in WW II — the first when he was only 26. He was 31 when given command of 1/34. Payne called Ayres "a fine man, taught me a lot about being cool in combat...." Caldwell said that the colonel "was the most outstanding, the coolest and the best battalion commander that I have ever seen." Caldwell retired as a lieutenant general in 1980. He was a brigade commander in Vietnam and later commanded a division in Europe. Dunn wrote that Ayres "was a brave, outstanding combat leader — one of the coolest men under fire I have ever seen."

At Pyongtaek, LTC Ayres did not act in haste when he withdrew his battalion. Since the enemy had already flanked his position, Ayres' action was timely and effective. Only the last unit out suffered appreciable casualties. He moved his command directly to Chonan, as instructed by COL Lovless. This was the last order he received. Coming from his regimental command, it superseded previous instructions from GEN Barth. In his 1955 manuscript, Barth does not write that he ordered Ayres to delay on successive positions, but, in a 1952 article of *Combat Forces Journal*, Barth states that was part of his orders to Ayres.

Chonan (3/34 Inf. 6-8 July)

When Barth left Ayres' CP he headed for that of COL Lovless in Songhwan-ni, arriving about 2:30 p.m. on July 6. He found the CP in process of moving to Chonan. He briefed Lovless on the situation as he knew it, and his instructions to Ayres. He also should have clearly explained the command arrangement to Lovless. Barth then left to reconnoiter delaying positions near Chonan, but he failed to invite COL Lovless to accompany him.

After reconning, Barth went back along the railroad and stopped at a station where he called Dean on a civilian telephone, using his interpreter to get through. The stationmaster at Taejon sent for one of Dean's staff officers. This was the only way Barth could communicate with Dean at the time, since there were no U.S. Signal Corps units available to them for long distance communication. (See Chapter Notes.) Barth made arrangements for the newly-arrived 63 FAB to detrain at Chochiwon and move forward in its own vehicles.

Troop trains, carrying Companies A and D and the remainder of HHC, 1/21, arrived in Chonan the morning of July 6. GEN Barth ordered the command into defensive positions 2 miles south of town.

Early the afternoon that Barth returned to Chonan, he was surprised to find 1/34 retreating through town. He found Lovless, who reported that Ayres had found it necessary to withdraw from Pyongtaek. Barth ordered 1/34 to join the 21st Infantry and extend the defensive position south of town. He also ordered Lovless to move his 3d Battalion from Ansong to Chonan by

motor. Barth then sent his aide to report the situation to GEN Dean. (See Chapter Notes.)

About 4 p.m., GEN Dean learned from Barth's aide that the 34th was now south of Chonan. He was furious, having expected that 1/34 would remain longer at Pyongtaek, and because 3/34 had left Ansong without a fight. Barth obviously did not instruct his aide to inform Dean that he, Barth, had ordered 3/34 out of Ansong. Dean also was unaware of Lovless' orders to Ayres to withdraw to Chonan.

Dean rushed to Chonan, where he presided over a very uncomfortable meeting in Lovless' CP. He demanded to know who had authorized the retreat from Pyongtaek. No one said anything; neither Barth nor Lovless spoke up. Finally, Ayres said that he accepted responsibility. Dean was so angry that he seriously considered ordering the regiment north at once, but feared an ambush. Lovless said that if he had known the situation at Pyongtaek he would have ordered the withdrawal of 1/34. (See Chapter Notes.)

Dean finally settled for sending one company north the next day to gain contact with the enemy. Barth stayed at Chonan that night and returned to Taejon the following morning.

The 3/34 arrived in Chonan from Ansong the afternoon of the July 6. Lovless ordered Love Co. and the Regimental Intelligence and Reconnaissance Platoon (I&R Plt) to make a reconnaissance the next morning. By that time, both battalions of the 34th, plus what was left of 1/21, were digging in south of Chonan. LTC Robert Dawson's 63 FAB and elements of the 52d were preparing to back them up with artillery support.

Co. L and the I&R Plt started out at 8:10 a.m. on July 7. Chonan was deserted, except for some South Korean police. With the I&R Plt in the lead, the force moved forward, passing masses of South Koreans moving south. Men on the point observed enemy soldiers on high ground where the road dipped out of sight. The point continued advancing and the enemy kept withdrawing. About four or five miles north of Chonan the I&R Plt came under enemy mortar and small-arms fire, stopping the advance shortly after 1 p.m.

About 10 a.m. that day, COL Robert R. Martin appeared at Lovless' CP. He was in garrison attire — soft cap, low-cut shoes and khaki uniform. He had no weapon, steel helmet or other field gear. Dean had asked FEAF HQ for Martin to command one of his regiments. They were good friends from the 44th Division in WW II, and Dean had great confidence in him. The colonel had come from the 24th Division CP, where he had been for over two days. In his comments to Appleman, Forrest Kleinman, a member of the Division G3 Section, wrote that COL Martin was at that CP "for at least 30 hours before he was assigned to the 34th Infantry Regiment. He spent this time in close study of the tactical situation. I know, because he was looking over my shoulder in the G3 Section much of the time." Kleinman retired as a lieutenant colonel.

Martin remained with Lovless for the remainder of the day. Before noon, they observed many armed men moving south on the hills to the west. An interpreter said they were South Korean soldiers. About this time, Lovless received a message from Dean. It read:

"Time filed 1025, date 7 July 50. To CO 34th Inf. Move one Bn fwd with minimum transportation. Gain contact and be prepared to fight delaying action back to recent position. PD air reports no enemy armor south of river. CG 24D"

Lovless immediately moved the 3d Battalion up behind Co. L.

Shortly after the I&R Plt was attacked, some time after midafternoon, an artillery officer reported to Lovless that he had one gun available. Lovless had him emplace it about three miles north of Chonan in a position to place direct fire in front of Co. L.

Now a liaison plane came over and dropped this message to Lovless:

"To CO 34th Infantry, 1600 7 July. Proceed with greatest caution. Large number of troops on your east and west flanks. Near Ansong lots of tanks (40-50) and trucks. Myang-myon large concentration of troops. Songhwan-ni large concentration of troops trying to flank your unit. [Sgd] Dean."

Lovless ordered LTC David Smith to withdraw his 3/34 to Chonan. Then he and Martin drove to the 1/34 CP to inform LTC Ayres of the situation north of Chonan. Upon arrival they met BG Menoher and GEN Church. Menoher handed Lovless the order from Dean relieving him of command of the 34th and directing that he turn it over to COL Martin. At the same time, he gave Dean's order to Martin directing that he take command of the regiment.

The withdrawal of 1/34 all the way to Chonan without his sanction and the withdrawal of 3/34 from Ansong gave Dean the reasons he needed to give Martin the regiment. Lovless gave Martin his pistol, pistol belt, canteen and first-aid kit, and left the CP. This occurred about 5 p.m. (Appleman states 6 p.m., and 5 p.m. as the time 3/34 went back into Chonan after their retreat, but that happened after Lovless was relieved.)

Meantime, MAJ Dunn had gone forward to the 3d Battalion. After the I&R Plt had contacted the enemy, 3/34 began moving into defensive positions on high ground astride the road. Dunn was standing in the road talking to the battalion commander, LTC David Smith, when the I&R Plt leader drove up in his jeep. Although he wasn't hit, there were bullet holes in his clothing and canteen. His platoon had been ambushed in a small town about a half mile to the front. The platoon had withdrawn, but three of his men were still there, along with about 40 enemy soldiers.

MAJ Dunn told LTC Smith that he would go forward to check the situation and asked permission to use Love Co., if needed. Smith assented. Dunn went forward and found the unit stopped on the road. He ordered the company mortar section into a firing position and directed the company commander to move his unit off the road to the right and deploy for an attack, then pointed out the direction of attack to the commander.

While the company moved into position a jeep came from the direction of the village with MAJ Boone Seegers, 3d Battalion S3, and three or four men. He had found the missing men, confirmed by the platoon leader.

Dunn called off the attack. He instructed the company commander to fall back to a position about a half mile forward of where the remainder of the 3d Battalion was digging in, and to deploy on the high ground on both sides of the road until the battalion position was organized.

"He got his company back on the road and just started back when we were fired on by a group of enemy off to our right (west) flank," Dunn wrote. He estimated that there were only 10 to 30 enemy. The entire company began firing. "They were green kids," Dunn commented. He got the officers and NCOs to keep the men moving and started into position. These men then began firing over the heads of those still coming down the road. It took several minutes to get this wild firing "in all directions" stopped.

But, "as the last of the company was going into position, mortar fire began falling," Dunn recalled. "It came from the rear, so it was our own."

The major went back to investigate and found that the battalion had pulled out. He could find neither the CO nor XO, but located Seegars. Seegars didn't know why the battalion was pulling back, but said that the order came from the rear and he didn't know who had given it. (There was no radio or wire communication between the battalion and regiment.)

MAJ Dunn finally found LT Minietta, who told him that COL Lovless had been relieved by COL Martin. Approaching the regimental CP, Dunn met Lovless coming out. He started to explain the situation, but the colonel told him to go inside and explain it to the general. Dunn went in and outlined the situation. He said that the 3d Battalion was abandoning one of the best defensive positions he had seen. Dunn also told the general that he couldn't find the battalion commander. A colonel "asked me if the Regiment would take orders from me," Dunn remembered. "I said 'Yes.' He then said, 'Put them back on that position.'"

The colonel was Martin, who failed to inform Dunn that 3/34 had been ordered to withdraw to Chonan because enemy troops had been spotted on both of their flanks. It is doubtful if Dunn would have taken some of the actions that he did, had he been properly briefed by COL Martin.

"The road was jammed with retreating infantry, artillery and service troops. I succeeded in turning the whole column around and headed them back north," Dunn wrote. He took Seegars, commanders of the two leading rifle companies, and a jeep-load of guides and went ahead. They were about a half mile ahead of the leading elements of the battalion and about the same distance short of the positions Dunn wanted to occupy, when his jeep group was fired on from both sides of the road. A number of men were hit, including Dunn, Seegars and LT Walter P. Meyer (Lovless' son-in-law as of July 1). Everyone jumped into roadside ditches. Dunn had been hit three times, one bullet passing through his jaw, severing an artery. A jeep driver dragged MAJ Seegars, who also was badly wounded, into the brush and bandaged him. The unhurt officers, wrote Dunn, "did absolutely nothing to aid the wounded."

As soon as the firing began, the leading company deployed and returned fire but did not ad-

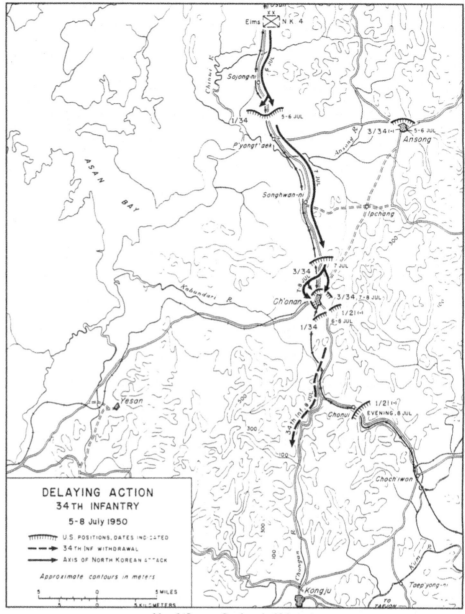

Map 6 (Source: South to the Naktong)

vance, simply forming a skirmish line and returning fire for about 20 minutes.

Dunn crawled out of the ditch. "From the position I was in on top of a knoll," Dunn wrote, "I had a clear view of the whole scene. There were not more than 30 or 40 enemy in the whole area.... I could hear [our] officers shouting instructions and could recognize our men as they moved up on the line. They could easily have walked right through the scattered enemy.... I was thoroughly disgusted.... It bordered on cowardice. To think that a regular American unit commanded by professional officers, outnumbering the enemy... in manpower and... in firepower would abandon their own people and leave the field in possession of a few trained monkeys was nauseating. They were... familiar with the situation in my group because one of the captains who was with me ran [back] saying he was going for help." MAJ Dunn was captured by the enemy. Their main body did not arrive for two hours after the American company had left. MAJ Seegars bled to death.

Edward Arendell was drafted into the Army in 1944. After the war he could not find a job, so

he re-enlisted. In 1950 Arendell was a trained Infantryman and an NCO. His company (HC, 3/34) was moving forward on the road when the 1SG fired on something about 100 yards to the front, starting a storm of firing at his unit. "We... were pinned down in this rice paddy with all this confusion and sudden engagement. Nobody knew who was where," he wrote. Arendell wrote that he wondered where the line [rifle] companies and officers were. Amid the confusion, his unit was ordered to retreat.

As 3/34 pulled back, not everybody just left the field. SGT Joe Baushmein was wounded. Henry G. Leerkamp, an NCO in Co. L with over 10 years service, commandeered a jeep to evacuate him. As 3/34 retreated, Leerkamp recalled SGT DeLaRosa, the last man out from Co. I, walking backward firing his BAR.

Matthew R. Thome was a 2LT in King Co. During WW II, he had been a Marine NCO and had combat experience. His unit held the high ground north of Chonan to cover the retreat of Co. I.

The 3/34 withdrew to Chonan in confusion.

The battalion XO, MAJ Newton R. Lantron, stood in the middle of the road with his pistol drawn, stopping the disorderly retreat. He, LT Herbert Marlatte (CO, Co. L), 1LT James C. Little and some other officers and NCOs restored order. South of Chonan, COL Martin ordered LTC Smith to return to Chonan and defend it.

Unable to find the commander of K Co., the battalion commander placed LT Thome in command of the unit. When orders came to return to Chonan, he and 17 men piled into a jeep and trailer and headed back. "A T-34 on our left rear opened fire," he wrote. Six men were killed and six others wounded, including Thome. All 12 men were returned to U.S. positions and the wounded were evacuated.

When the battalion redeployed in Chonan, part of it was placed along a railway embankment west of Chonan and on the northern edge of town. The concrete platform at the railroad station was organized as a strong point. A secondary road running from the northwest was sown with antitank mines.

Discovering that some 3d Battalion mortars and other equipment had been left behind when it retreated, COL Martin led a patrol from the regimental headquarters company out to retrieve the abandoned materiel north of Chonan. Murray Carroll was a member of the patrol. "We [recovered] some of the equipment," he wrote, "[but] ran into heavy resistance north of town."

Men of 3/34 spent a nervous night in Chonan, and there was some indiscriminate small-arms firing. Fred Hollister, a warrant officer and Regimental food service officer, wrote that one of the cooks in the Service Co. was accidentally killed by a frightened guard. Hollister was a nine-year Army veteran trained in food service and supply. He remembered that COL Lovless was still with the regiment, although by then did not command it.

Arendell wrote that his company "got a lot of incoming mortar and tank fire." Wounded men were brought to a location near his position but were not evacuated farther that night, although the 1SG tried to get the officers to do so.

In L Co., the men became jumpy and started to fire their weapons. Being near the railroad, some of their bullets hit the rails and began to ricochet in all directions. This created the illusion that enemy soldiers were firing back. "It wasn't long before the whole line started to open up," wrote Jose Leyba, of Love Co. Finally, officers and NCOs got the firing stopped, but the men had shot off so much ammunition that more was needed. Leyba and some others went back for a resupply and were caught in a 120mm mortar barrage. Most of the rounds exploded harmlessly in rice paddies. After obtaining the ammunition and distributing it to the men, Leyba discovered that he had been slightly wounded in one arm. He stayed with the unit. The enemy fired mortars on the dug-in Americans all night.

At least part of 3/34 were not firing at shadows. A column of North Korean tanks and infantry approached Chonan from the east. About 8 p.m., a battery of the newly-arrived 63d FAB began to fire HE and WP at the advancing enemy. Two T-34s were reported destroyed. It appears that the first enemy infiltration of Chonan began just before midnight.

Some time after midnight, COL Martin and about 80 men with him were reported cut off in Chonan by regimental XO, LTC Robert L. "Pappy" Wadlington. He also relayed to GEN Dean that ammunition stocks were low and asked for instructions. Dean told him to fight a delaying action and to get word to Martin to bring his force out under cover of darkness. Two hours later, Martin had returned and the supply road to Chonan was again open.

Before daylight, COL Martin returned to

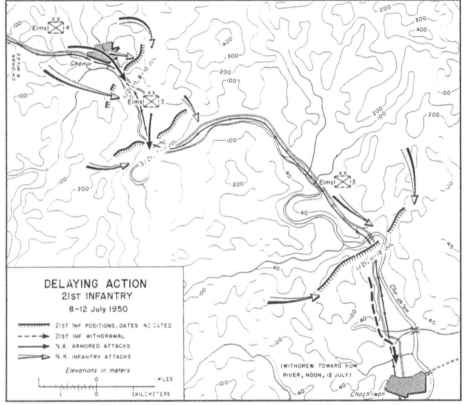

DELAYING ACTION
21ST INFANTRY
8-12 July 1950

21ST INF POSITIONS, DATES INDICATED
21ST INF WITHDRAWAL
N.K. ARMORED ATTACKS
N.K. INFANTRY ATTACKS

Elevations in meters

Map 7 (Source: South to the Naktong*)*

South of Osan on 4 July, PFC Kenneth Shadrick crouched beside his gunner, loaded the 2.36 rocket launcher and stepped away from the back blast. At 1620 in the midst of a torrential downpour, Shadrick was struck in the chest by a burst of machine gund fire. He died seconds after. The 24th Division infantryman was the first American soldier killed in combat during the battle for thew invaded South Korean republic. (Source: 24th Forward *A Pictorial History of the Victory Division in Korea, Tokyo, 1953)*

Chonan. About daylight, a 2 1/2-ton truck-driver enroute with ammunition spotted a T-34 approaching Chonan on the road from the northwest, with other tanks following. They passed over the mined road without detonating a single mine. Either the mines had not been properly armed, or they had been removed by enemy soldiers. The driver turned his truck around and escaped.

Arendell described the oncoming enemy this way: "What we saw was not a friendly sight. Immediately to our front were tanks with soldiers along with them. They started intense firing and advancing upon us."

Henry Leerkamp recalled that his unit was "hit hard — tanks and small-arms fire." He went to check on his men early in the morning and was cut off and captured about noon. The enemy "beat us to the ground, tied our hands with communications wire and marched us north. Could see wounded men shot and bayoneted around us." (See Appendix A for a discussion of American POWs and MIAs, as well as more on Leerkamp and others as POWs.)

Jose Leyba wrote that at about 10 a.m., "I never saw so many enemy tanks coming toward us... firing their cannon... while their infantry were lying back behind their tanks." American artillery began falling on the enemy tanks and infantry, breaking up the attack. When the tanks faltered, "our men started to holler like wild men, and quite a few of us jumped out of our foxholes to chase their infantry as well," Leyba wrote. Robert Lee leaped onto one tank and tried to destroy it with grenades. Leotis E. Heater did set one tank on fire with five grenades. Leyba recalled that they fought all day. "We were proud of ourselves. Our commander was also very proud of the way we handled ourselves."

About five or six enemy tanks did get into Chonan at about 6 a.m., firing on the railroad station, a church, a number of buildings believed to contain U.S. soldiers, and every vehicle in sight. These tanks and enemy infantry cut off two rifle companies of 3/34.

LT Little, a battalion staff officer, led a bazooka team hunting for these tanks. With the team and a grenade launcher, he is credited with destroying two T-34s. He then organized the leaderless platoon he found himself with and fought off the enemy until ordered to withdraw. During the pullout, he personally destroyed an enemy machine gun holding up the movement. He and his men then withdrew in good order.

COL Martin met his death in Chonan about 8 a.m. He had obtained a bazooka and stationed himself in a shack along the main street. SGT Jerry C. Christensen, of the Regimental S3 Section, acted as his loader. Martin intended to fire into the side of tanks which had entered the left rear of the regiment's position.

A tank appeared in the street and aimed its gun at the shack. Martin and the tank fired at about the same time. Martin was blown in two. One of Christensen's eyes was blown from its socket. He put the eye back in and it functioned all right. Christensen was captured at Taejon and died as a POW on Dec. 10, 1950. He gave MAJ Dunn this account of Martin's death in POW camp.

More enemy tanks got into Chonan, along with more North Korean infantry. The situation was becoming desperate for 3/34. A continuous WP screen allowed many of the men to escape. Arendell recalled that at some point just before his unit escaped, the enemy just quit firing. When Leyba's Co. L had to pull out, they left "our wounded fall into enemy hands. I and others [witnessed] the enemy tie our men's hands behind their backs and shoot them in the head," he wrote. "This made me a very rough fighter.... I couldn't kill enough of them."

Robert L. Hysell had enlisted in the Army in 1948 at the age of 16 because there was no work available. He was a trained combat medic with L/34. When he learned he was going to Korea, his reaction was to ask, "Where the hell is Korea?" He summarized his recollections of Chonan: "We medics risk[ed] our asses to get to a wounded man to patch him up only to have some lieutenant or captain have us leave him [to become a POW or be killed]. What a hell of a sad thing to do." (See Chapter Notes.)

When the 3d Battalion assembled south of Chonan, only about 175 men could be accounted for. A few more came in over the next several days, including one 1SG with eight or 10 men. Morning reports indicated 37 WIA and 45 MIA. Most of the MIA were later found to have been killed. The enemy claimed to have captured 60 men.

The battalion commander, LTC Smith, was physically exhausted and was evacuated a few days later. "Pappy" Wadlington now commanded

105mm howitzer in action, firing almost point blank against the enemy. (Source: P. 47, Pictorial History of the War in Korea, Veterans of Foreign Wars, 1951)

4.2-inch chemical mortar, in action. (Source: P. 42, Korea, 1950, Chief of Military History, Washington, D.C., 1982)

U.S. M-24 Light Tank in action south of Ch'onan. (Source: P. 43, Korea, 1950, Chief of Military History, Washington, D.C., 1982)

the regiment. He appointed MAJ Lantron to lead 3/34.

Leerkamp had served previously with Lantron. He wrote that MAJ Lantron "carried himself well and was a model officer.... He delegated authority but kept his hand on all units." At Chonan, Leerkamp credits Lantron with stopping a rout of the 3d Battalion, but was critical of COL Martin, who he wrote, "instead of assembling his officers to restore some order, chose to get a bazooka and go tank-hunting. He was promptly killed... leaving the regiment without a leader again."

SGT Charles W. Menninger, 3d Battalion Operations Sergeant, a combat veteran of the 3d Infantry division, felt about the same way. He criticized both communications and leadership, and said that NCOs were left in the CP while officers were out doing what enlisted men were supposed to do. In reference to the lack of leadership, he also gave COL Martin's tank-hunting instead of directing his troops as an example.

The 34th was in bad shape after Pyongtaek and Chonan. Two regimental commanders were lost within three days, one to relief and one to death. Other leaders, such as LTC Smith and majors Dunn and Seegers were gone, as were many other officers killed, wounded or trapped in Chonan. The enlisted men were mentally and physically exhausted.

Many historians, prompted by early writings about the war, have concluded that the 34th wouldn't fight. But the 1/34 at Pyongtaek and 3/34 in Chonan placed the 34th into situations where they could not possibly have been successful. The problem was not the men; the fault lay with leadership, including the loss of positive leaders (such as MAJ Dunn) at critical times.

Ayres had been skeptical of Martin at their first and only meeting. COL Martin came into Ayres' CP on the night of July 7. He introduced himself and said that he had taken command of the 34th. Then Martin said, "We are going to fight. The next time we withdraw, we will withdraw 100 yards and then we are going to stand and fight. We will withdraw another 100 yards when forced to and fight again." To Ayres, "he sounded like Custer." LTC Ayres knew something about withdrawal techniques. Just before the Korean War started, he and LTC Gilbert Check, CO of 1/27, had given a class to regimental officers on withdrawal actions. When Martin left the CP, Ayres just looked at his officers there and said, "no way" to Martin's withdrawal tactics.

Perhaps COL Martin did wrong by going into Chonan not once, but twice. In retrospect, it seems that he would have been better occupied in establishing communications between his headquarters and his two battalions, even if by a system of couriers, and of informing his staff and the two battalion commanders of the situation and his intended course of action for the regiment. There is no question that COL Martin was an aggressive and brave man, but he should have been leading the regiment, not tank-hunting.

LTC Waddlington was about 50 years old, by Marshall's and Ridgway's standards, too old to command a regiment in combat. COL Stephens, 21st Regimental commander, had little regard for the 34th Regiment, and wrote to Appleman that Waddlington "was too weak for the job." But Dean praised Wadlington's performance, writing, "Pappy lived up to all my expectations.... He kept his outfit in hand and fought a stubborn delaying action back to the Taejon perimeter...."

The *16th* and *18th Regiments* and part of the *105th Armd Division* battled the 34th at Pyongtaek and Chonan.

Chonui and Chochiwon
(21st Inf., 8-12 July)

On the morning of July 8, GEN Walker flew into Taejon. He told Dean that the Eighth Army was on the way to Korea. Together, the two men drove up to the last hill south of Chonan and witnessed the remnants of 3/34 escape from the town.

South of Chonan the road splits, with the main highway and rail line running southeast to Chochiwon, and the other road going almost due south to Kongju and the Kum River. Dean ordered the 34th to delay on the Kongju road and the 21st to delay on the Chochiwon road. Both roads converged on Taejon beyond the Kum, and both had to be defended.

As the 34th headed south in the late afternoon of July 8, North Korean soldiers could be seen on the ridges paralleling its march.

COL Stephens arrived in Taejon with a trainload of his 21st Infantry before noon on July 7. He reported to GEN Dean and received orders to delay along the Chochiwon road. The 21st found mass confusion at Chochiwon. Train manifests and schedules were nonexistent. Supplies for the 24th Division and ROK troops to the east arrived mixed together. Train engineers balked at traveling forward, and guards had to be provided to make them move.

COL Stephens placed LTC Carl C. Jensen's 3d Battalion astride the highway 6 miles north of Chochiwon. He positioned A and D companies of 1/21 in a blocking position somewhat over a mile north of the 3d on a ridge just east of Chonui. Chonui lies about 12 miles below Chonan and 3 miles south of the Kongju fork.

GEN Dean's OPORD 3, dated 9:45 p.m., July 8 essentially confirmed his earlier orders. After delaying the enemy back to the Kum River, the order directed that both the 21st and 34th regiments "Hold river line at all costs. Maximum repeat maximum delay will be effected." The 19th Regiment was ordered to send one of its two battalions from Kumchon to Taegu and the other to protect the Yonil air strip. This regiment also was to contact ROK troops at Yongdong and be prepared to reinforce them with a battalion.

A 105mm field artillery battalion was attached to each of the regiments and one battery of 155mm howitzers from the 11 FAB was placed in direct support of the 21st Infantry. Under this order, each regiment would have more artillery support than ever before. The 21st also received the support of Co. A, 78th Heavy Tank Battalion (actually M-24 light tanks). This is the first time that any infantry element of the division would have U.S. tank support.

A notation on the bottom of a copy of this order states that it was never issued "due to rapid change in situation," but most, if not all, instructions contained in the order were implemented. Dean also made it clear in messages to Stephens that the 21st must hold at Chochiwon in order to cover the left flank of ROK forces to the east until they could withdraw.

It was obvious that Dean wanted to stage a determined battle along the Kum River, the last natural obstacle before Taejon. Taejon, aside from being a major city, was militarily significant as a highway and rail hub. Major highways ran south and east from the city. Capture of Taejon placed the North Koreans in position to attack generally eastward through Yongdong and Kumchon, south through Kunsan all the way to Hadong and Chinju. Lateral roads off this main north-south route led eastward, outflanking all U.S. and ROK forces then in Korea. In short, Taejon represented both a tactical and, potentially, a strategic prize for the enemy.

Part of 1/21, comprising about 500 men of A and D companies plus replacements for B and C, was emplaced in a three-quarters of a mile front on a low ridge 500 yards east of Chonui, and a higher hill 800 yards south of town. Rice paddies lay between Chonui and the ridge line. The road and rail line ran between the ridge and hill to the south. Another hill further west dominated the left flank, but 1/21(-) had too few men to occupy it. (A minus sign in brackets behind a unit designation means that the command is not compete.)

CPT Charles R. Alkire of 3/21 commanded a forward blocking position at Chonui. On the morning of July 9, COL Jensen (CO, 3/21) began registering his 4.2-inch and 81mm mortars, and engineers blew bridges forward of Chonui. By noon, enemy tanks were reported moving south from Chonan.

In midafternoon, Alkire saw from his forward position 11 tanks and 200-300 enemy infantry to his front. Ground-air coordination had finally been established in the 24th Division. Rainy, overcast skies, which had prevented the employment of aircraft against the enemy even before the TF Smith battle, finally cleared. Alkire called for an air strike. LT Oliver Duerksen, USAF, heading the Tactical Air Control Party (TACP) with the 21st, brought in a flight of F-80 jets. Artillery also took the tanks under fire.

By this time, enemy infantrymen could be seen running from house to house in Chonui. They were taken under fire by 4.2-inch and 81mm mortars. Columns of black smoke rose from northwest of town

Near dusk, COL Stephens arrived at the 1/21 CP and stayed overnight. LTC Brad Smith, the 1/21 commander, together with others of his task force, had not yet rejoined the regiment. Stephens, no doubt, opted to be with 1/21(-) at this critical time in the absence of Smith. Further, it was obvious that this element of the regiment soon would be engaged. Enemy patrol activity portended an attack against his 1st Battalion on July 10.

July 10 dawned with a heavy ground fog, blanking out visibility. At 5:55 a.m., enemy voices could be heard on the left, followed by firing from that direction. Some men near Stephens began firing blindly into the murk. He quickly stopped them. Enemy mortar fire began falling on the defenders at 7 a.m.

LT Ray Bixler's platoon of Able Co. held the hill of the left flank. Judging from the volume of fire and shouting coming from Bixler's position, it was apparent that he was facing the main enemy attack. They were coming down onto him from a higher hill to his left. Mortar fire broke up this attack.

Meantime, an enemy force slipped around the battalion's right flank and assailed the 4.2-inch mortar position, while tanks drove out of Chonui and through the battalion lines. Because of the fog, the defenders could hear, but not see, the tanks.

When the fog lifted at 8 a.m., Chonui was still burning. Four T-34s entered the town from the north. Stephens called for an air strike. About the same time, the enemy tanks in the rear began firing in support of their infantry's attack on the mortar site. By this time in the battle, all communication with the heavy mortars was out. The enemy overran the mortar position, causing the battalion to lose critical 4.2-inch mortar support. The artillery, further to the rear, continued to fire.

About 9 a.m., enemy infantrymen attacked from Chonui in a frontal assault against the 1st Battalion's center. Artillery fire turned them back. Then T-34s came out of town and raked the U.S. positions with machine gun fire.

A little after 11 a.m., the North Koreans made another determined attack on Bixler's platoon. The enemy could be seen closing in on his position. At 11:25, the lieutenant radioed COL Stephens for reinforcements, saying he had heavy casualties and requesting permission to withdraw. Stephen refused and called in an air strike instead. The planes temporarily stopped the enemy, but as soon as the planes left, they attacked Bixler again. He called Stephens for the last time at 11:35 a.m. to report that he was surrounded and that most of his men were casualties. The enemy overran Bixler's position, killing most of the men.

During the air strike, survivors of the mortar and recoilless rifle positions scrambled up the reverse slope of the ridge and joined the infantry in the center of their position. About 11:32 a.m., friendly artillery fire began to fall on the hill. Artillerymen, observing figures running up the backside of the ridge, thought that the enemy had overrun the battalion. The battalion's artillery forward observer's radio had gone out. Stephens called his regimental CP on his radio, but could not get the firing stopped.

By 11:40, the 1st Battalion was in a precarious position. The left flank platoon had been crushed. Enemy tanks and infantry were in its rear, having destroyed the heavy mortar platoon. And, even before the friendly artillery began to fall, some men on the battalion's right flank had begun to leave their foxholes.

"Get those high priced soldiers back into position!" Stephens shouted. CPL Richard Okada, from Hawaii, was able to stop a few men and form a small perimeter.

By 12:05 p.m., Stephens realized that the remnants of the battalion on the ridge would have to retreat. On his signal, the men ran from their foxholes, through an orchard and into the rice paddies beyond. As they ran, two U.S. jets strafed them but caused no casualties.

Co. A lost 27 wounded and 30 missing out of 181 men. Co. D lost 3 KIA and 8 MIA. Heavy Mortar Company (HM Co.) lost 14 men. In all, about one-fifth of the men there were lost.

As soon as he got back to the 3d Battalion, COL

Stephens ordered LTC Jensen to counterattack to regain the lost ground. Jensen's battalion took the ridge, but was unable to retake Bixler's hill. Co. L found about 10 men from A and D who had been pinned down by fire, and the three groups came out at midnight. Jensen's men discovered the bodies of six men from the HM Co. who had been ambushed and killed by enemy infiltrates early in the day. LT Carl Bernard remembered that white engineer tape had been placed to mark the location of their bodies. He wrote that the engineer tape "struck those of us who passed the bodies during the counterattack as perhaps slightly unreal." One of the ambushed men had managed to escape, and the entire episode had been witnessed by an American officer who was farther back.

In tank action on July 10, U.S. tanks knocked out a T-34. Two American tanks were lost. The tank main gun requires recoil oil to operate properly. COL James W. Snee (West Point 1934 and Division G3) said that this oil had been on back order for two years prior to the Korean War. Lacking the oil, the guns had never been fired. At Chonui, they were fired by lanyard. This "promptly blew off the tank turrets," Snee told Clay Blair.

The enemy did suffer heavy losses that day, however. Late in the afternoon, an F-80 dropped below the clouds near Pyongtaek. The pilot discovered 200 or more enemy trucks, tanks and other vehicles on the road. Every available B-26 bomber, F-80 and F-82 fighter was sent to attack this huge target. Although the results reported (117 trucks, 38 tanks, seven half-tracks and a large number of enemy soldiers destroyed) were probably exaggerated, there were considerable losses. Enemy prisoners later confirmed that artillery and air attacks north of Chonui destroyed 20 of their tanks, a severe blow to the North Koreans.

As Appleman points out in his book, close air support in the early days of the war was furnished by U.S. Air Force, Navy, Marine and Australian aircraft. By July 5 a Joint Operations Center (JOC) for the FEAF was in Taejon, moving to Taegu on July 14. By July 19 a virtually complete tactical air control center was in operation in Korea. The Advanced Headquarters, Fifth Air Force opened at Taegu on July 20..

Six TACPs operated with the 24th Division in the early days. Later, similar air control parties were sent to each ROK division and corps and an air liaison officer joined each ROK corps as an adviser.

Soon after the war began, the Air Force began using T-6 trainer aircraft equipped with VHF radios for contact with TACPs and fighter aircraft and an SCR 300 radio to contact front line ground troops. T-6 pilots began using the call sign "Mosquito," causing these aircraft to be known as Mosquitoes. These aerial controllers — a pilot and a ground force observer in each plane — could more quickly and accurately bring aircraft in on a strike than the TACP by itself.

The three best close-support aircraft were the Marine F4U Corsair, the Air Force F-51 and jet F-80 "Shooting Star." The Corsair and F-51, being slower than the jet, usually spent more time on station and often were more accurate in their bombing and strafing runs than the faster jet.

On July 8, Dean wrote a letter to MacArthur, saying, "I am convinced that the North Korean Army, the North Korean soldier and the status of training and the quality of his equipment have been underestimated." He also addressed the shortcomings of the two battalion regiments of the 24th Division: "The... regimental organization with which we are operating does not lend itself to effective combat.... Recommend that infantry battalions be sent to bring all regiments of the 24th Division up to regular organization."

The American soldiers urgently needed 3.5-inch rocket launchers, as well as HEAT artillery ammunition, 90mm guns and more powerfully armed tanks to stop the T-34s.

Chochiwon (3/21 Inf. 10-12 July)

When the 3d Battalion returned from the ridge east of Chonui, they found enemy soldiers in some of their positions. It took King Co. an hour to eject the North Koreans from its old position.

On July 10 in an 8:45 p.m. message to COL Stephens, Dean suggested he withdraw his 3d Battalion, but reminded the colonel that the loss of Chochiwon would mean that the ROKs would loose their MSR. An hour later, Dean authorized falling back 4 miles to the delaying position 2 miles north of that town. But, he admonished, "Hold in your new position and fight like hell. I expect you to hold it all day tomorrow."

Meantime, Smith's B and C companies had received 205 replacements. The 1/21 was re-united and re-equipped as a complete battalion at Chochiwon on July 11 and was dug in astride the highway two miles north of town.

Four miles away, Jensen's 3/21 was attacked shortly after 6:30 a.m. Within minutes, four enemy tanks got through the battalion minefield, and concealed by morning fog, moved into the American defenses. At the same time, enemy mortar fire hit the Battalion CP, destroying the communications center, the ammunition supply point (ASP) and creating heavy casualties. About 1,000 North Korean infantry enveloped both flanks of the battalion. Failure of communication prevented observers from calling in defensive mortar and artillery fire. The enemy attack was well coordinated, with a frontal attack to pin the defenders in position, supporting fire to keep the Americans in their holes, and troops moving around both flanks in a double envelopment. Not only were communications to the rear cut, but enemy soldiers in rear areas prevented the evacuation of wounded and the resupply of ammunition. The men fended off the enemy the best way they could, and many close, bloody, individual battles ensued.

PVT Paul R. Spear was a member of K Co. When an enemy machine gun began firing into the unit CP, Spear, firing his a pistol, charged the machine gun. Although seriously wounded in the action, he jumped into the gun position with his pistol empty and chased the enemy gunners away.

CPL Charles E. Kinard was a squad leader with the 2d Platoon of Love Co. His squad held their position on the company front until 10:30, repelling every enemy attack. During the withdrawal, Kinard was hit in the shoulder by a rifle bullet. He and a CPL Bunting were sent to the rear for treatment. When they got to the bottom of the hill, enemy tanks blocked further movement. The two men remained hidden until dark. While attempting to get through enemy lines, they were detected. Bunting was killed and Kinard was captured. One of the enemy soldiers pushed a C-ration can opener into Kinard's wound. Without medical treatment, he and other prisoners were marched all the way back to Seoul. There, he and another soldier were taken to the Han River. When guards killed the other man, Kinard jumped into the river and escaped. Evading the enemy, he made his way south, eventually reaching the lines of HM Co., 19th Infantry.

LT Elmer J. Gainok commanded the weapons platoon of King Co. The platoon had only two 60mm mortars, and no 57mm recoilless rifles. His platoon sergeant and a number of his men were killed while he and a messenger were at the company CP and M Co. mortars. Gainok and the messenger were returning to the platoon when they were fired on by a T-34. A machine gun bullet hit the messenger's helmet, grazing his head. He exclaimed, "Sir, I'm wounded!" Gainok made a quick examination and determined that the man had been grazed. "Sir, my ass," Gainok replied, "let's get the hell away from here."

They were fired on again and became separated. Gainok didn't get back to his platoon until that night. No matter where he turned, enemy mortar and artillery fire seemed to follow him. At one point an enemy bullet, strangely, hit his belt buckle as he laid on it atop a rice paddy dike.

By July 10, LT Bernard had returned to L/21 and resumed command of 1st Platoon. That morning the artillery forward observer (FO) was with Bernard in the unit's OP, but his radio wasn't working and he had no wire communication. Bernard recalled that they "had many fine targets, but no way to get artillery fire on them."

The last organized position in Love Co. was manned by Bernard's platoon. CPT O'Dean T. Cox, company commander, ordered the 2d Platoon to withdraw to Bernard's location about two hours after the battle started. At about 11 a.m., Cox told Bernard to hold for another 15 minutes. Cox, with his radioman, runners and several riflemen, went back to establish a blocking position to cover Bernard's withdrawal. By this time his platoon was spread out on the reverse slope of the hill. Cox and his party disappeared. They, along with the Battalion S1, LT Cashe and S3, LT Lester all were listed as MIA.

Bernard pulled his men back. "By the time I reached our rearmost position. I ran into a number of our men exhausted by the road," he wrote. A machine gun blocked their escape for a time, but was knocked out. Bernard was hit by mortar fragments, struck in a bone at the base of his spine and knocked down.

After that "most of the men were too funked out to go on." One master sergeant told Bernard, "Lieutenant, you'll have to go on. I'm too beat up; they'll just have to take me." The sergeant was not wounded, but like many of the men by the side of the road, he would not try to escape with LT Bernard.

The battalion commander, LTC Jansen, and his S2, LT Leon J. Jacques also were killed. Al-

most 60 percent of the battalion was lost and 90 percent of the men who did escape were without weapons, helmets or ammunition. A total of eight officers and 142 men fit for duty from the battalion were formed into a provisional company. By July 15, however, 322 of the original 670 men had returned to duty.

Appleman wrote that the 21st lost enough weapons and materiel to outfit two infantry battalions and individual and organic equipment and clothing for 975 men.

The NK 3d and 4th Divisions had followed the 21st and 34th Regiments. The 3d attacked the 21st while the 4th turned toward Kongju and the 34th.

Late on July 11, GEN Dean instructed Co. A, 3d Engineer Combat Battalion (A/3 ECB), to prepare all possible obstacles to help defend the Chochiwon area, and if necessary, cover the withdrawal of the 21st. He also ordered the 19th Infantry and 13 FAB to go to Taejon from Taegu and Pohang-dong.

The 1/21 was still in position north of Chochiwon on July 12. An enemy patrol approached Co. C at dawn while other members of the battalion detected North Koreans on both flanks. About a battalion of enemy infantry, supported by artillery, attacked Smith's left flank about 9:30 a.m. Shortly, this grew into a general attack by an estimated 2,000 enemy soldiers.

By noon, COL Stephens knew that his understrength 1st Battalion, now composed of new and untried soldiers, would have to retreat. He sent this message to Dean:

"Am surrounded. 1st Bn left giving way. Situation bad on right. Have nothing left to establish intermediate delaying position am forced to withdraw to river line. I have issued instructions to withdraw."

The 1st Battalion withdrew by companies, one at a time, and was loaded on trucks near Chochiwon. While this was going on, enemy artillery bombarded the regimental CP. However, there was no pursuit, and by 3:30 p.m. the 21st Regiment was on the south bank of the Kum River astride the highway near Taepyong-ni. About 325 men of the Regiment (64 from 3/21 and the balance from 1/21) occupied the new position.

Suchon-ni (1/34 Inf, 8-12 July)

The 1/34 was not engaged at Chonan on July 8, but was hit by some enemy artillery late in the day. Shortly thereafter, it was ordered to retreat toward Kongju. The battalion moved into another delaying position just over 3 miles north of the town; Kongju is situated a half-mile or so south of the Kum River.

By midafternoon of July 9 the battalion was dug in on both sides of the road and had received an issue of rations and ammunition. Able Co.'s Weapons Platoon was issued one 60mm mortar. The men were told that another division (the 25th) was on its way from Japan. B Company was on a low ridge to the left and flanking the road. Somewhat over 1,200 yards away, across intervening rice paddies and a stream, was Co. A. The ridge it was on rose from the paddies east of the road to Hill 194, about 3,000 yards to

the north. The 3d Platoon was placed astride the road facing generally north. The 2d Platoon was higher on the ridge, with its left flank near the road and its right a few hundred yards short of the top of Hill 194. The surviving 10 members of the 1st Platoon were on Hill 194. The Weapons Platoon was more or less behind the 2d Platoon. The entire company was facing generally northwest. Elements of the 63d FAB (105mm) were in position to the rear in support of the battalion.

July 10 and 11 passed without incident. The sun came out and the men had their first opportunity to dry out and get a little rest. On July 12 the 81mm and 4.2-inch mortars were registered and more ammunition was issued to the troops. About 5 p.m., the tranquillity was broken by the explosion of an enemy artillery or mortar shell. The initial enemy infantry attack hit the right flank of Co. A's 1st Platoon on Hill 194. Since the platoon's orientation was to the northwest rather than to the north, the attack was devastating. Five of the 10 men fell at the start of the fight. The others escaped down the hill toward the 2d and Weapons platoons.

SFC Edwin E. Knight, 2d Platoon guide, checked on the sudden burst of fire on Hill 194. He saw a flag where the 1st Platoon had been. "That's a North Korean flag!" he shouted. By this time, about 20 enemy soldiers were atop the hill. A number of them began sliding down the hill toward the right flank of the 2d Platoon, shouting and firing as they came. Since the men of the 2d Platoon were all faced the wrong way, they had to leave their foxholes to meet this attack. Very soon, they began to pull out and down the hill toward the 3d Platoon. The 3d Platoon and Co. B, across the valley, brought the enemy under heavy fire to cover the 2d Platoon's retreat. Platoon leader LT Ridley and five men withdrew together. Three others, CPL William J. McLafferty and PFCs Lawrence E. Perry and Patrick J. Gallagher, carried SFC Knight, who had been hit in the hip. Enemy fire lashed across the ridge after the retreating men. Perry was hit in the stomach by a bullet. As the 2d Platoon cleared the intervening ground, the 1st and Weapons platoons and Co. B poured out a heavy volume of fire, stopping the enemy. Second Platoon survivors climbed back up the hill and joined the rest of the company in a stubborn defense. The men, for the first time in the war, had plenty of ammunition. A small-arms battle continued until after dark.

About 2:30 a.m., LT Henry L. Oppenborn Jr. walked along the line whispering to his men to get ready to withdraw. The NCOs quietly assembled them. Stealthily, the battalion gathered in groups and moved silently southward, concealed in the shadow of a hill cast by dim moonlight.

In this way the battalion successfully extricated itself and dug in on the south bank of the Kum River just outside Kongju, where it was joined by the 3d Battalion. LTC Ayres and his battalion had done a masterful job in holding off the enemy and then in executing an undetected night withdrawal.

Four light tanks of the 78th Tank Battalion (78 Tk Bn) had been in the battle. Two were lost to enemy artillery and mortar fire. Another was destroyed by enemy infantry when it went to the aid of a litter jeep which had been ambushed. Co. D, 3d ECB prepared demolitions along the road to delay the enemy's pursuit. Love Co. of the 34th outposted the north bank of the river for about 600 yards. The bridge was rigged with explosives. Dean had ordered it blown "only when the enemy starts to cross."

Clay Blair in his *Forgotten War* wrote: "The Americans had achieved little in this piecemeal and disorganized waste of precious lives and equipment. At most they delayed the NKPA a total of three, possibly four days. Notwithstanding Army claims to the contrary, these delays were not in any way decisive to the American forces and might well have been matched at less cost by a consolidated and cohesive defense behind the Kum River."

There is no doubt that assembling the 24th Division, or the 21st and 34th Regiments, along the Kum would have presented a more solid defensive posture. But the mission of the 24th was not to select a defensive line. The mission was to delay the enemy as far forward as possible. GEN MacArthur in *Reminiscences,* wrote: "The immediate necessity was to slow down the Red advance before it enveloped all of Korea. My only chance to do this was to commit my forces piecemeal as rapidly as I could get them to the front...." The front was not along the Kum at that time, it was 60-70 miles further north near Suwon.

If the enemy had been allowed to march south from Suwon, unimpeded, they could have easily reached the Kum by July 8. A motorized or mechanized column, unchecked, could have made the trip in about a day, reaching the river July 6. Friendly air was no factor until the rainy, overcast skies cleared on July 10. U.S. aircraft would have been no deterrent to such a rapid advance. The 24th barely would have been deployed along the Kum by July 6, and even if it had been, the North Koreans were advancing with their *3d* and *4th Divisions* in that sector, followed by the *6th*. One of their divisions, or one with elements of another division could have pinned the 24th Division at the Kum while the remainder of their force easily slipped around the western flank on an unimpeded race south and east toward Pusan. Remember, this scenario would have taken place between July 6 and 8. A battle by the 24th along the Kum River, even if they held for four or five days, would not have prevented the enemy from this flanking movement. There were no organized ROK units in the area to face such a movement.

What if the enemy had not tried the flanking movement described above, but concentrated on breaching the Kum River? Even if Dean would have had all three of his regiments, they actually equaled only six battalions. Realistically, he would have been able to present only a five-battalion front, making his whole position easy to outflank. Further, at this stage, he still had no effective way to stop the T-34. His field artillery equaled only two battalions of 105mm howitzers and two batteries of 155mm howitzers. When the enemy outflanked his position — and they would have — there easily could have been a debacle, as the remnants of the division attempted to extricate themselves, battling the enemy from the front, flanks and rear.

Perhaps some of the delaying actions by the 21st and 34th Regiments could have been more effective. The purpose of delaying actions is to make the enemy stop, deploy, fight, then reassemble, to buy time. Inept as some of delaying battles may have been, they achieved the mission. They fought a series of a half a dozen or so battles with parts of two enemy divisions and lost every engagement, but won the most critical element — time!

Two very significant events occurred during this phase:

1. Thousands of ROK soldiers streamed through these delaying positions. In the rear they were sorted out. Units, battalions and regiments were reconstituted and sent back to reinforce ROK divisions fighting in the central mountains. Without this infusion of troops, those divisions would have been defeated.

2. Two regiments of the 25th Infantry Division were deployed to Korea. The third regiment arrived on July 15. One regiment, the 27th, could have been deployed into battle on July 10, if necessary.

The four battalions of the 21st and 34th Regiments, therefore, did not sacrifice in vain.

The ROK Army Delays the Enemy

The U.S. 24th Infantry Division, by moving up to delay along the highways near the west coast of Korea, assumed responsibility for that flank during the ensuing delaying actions executed by U.S. and ROK troops. The ROKs were responsible for the central and eastern fronts, where they gave ground grudgingly, often inflicting heavy losses of men and equipment on the enemy.

The ROK front covered three avenues leading south, two in the mountainous central Korea. The western avenue follows the road from Wonju almost due south through Chungju, Mungyong and Sangju to Kumchon. Farther east, also beginning at Wonju, a road leads slightly southeast via Chechon, Tanyang, Yongju, Andong and Uisong to Yongchon. The third avenue is the east coast road Ulchin-Pyonghae-ri-Yongdok to Pohang-dong.

A high east-west branch ridge system of the Taebaek Mountains crosses the first two avenues. Mungyong and Tanyang lie in two passes over this ridge system. South of this rugged obstacle are the towns of Sangju, Hamchang, Yechon and Yongju. These towns could be used as jumping-off points for attacks southward toward Taegu, or from Yongju, the enemy could drive south through Andong to Yonchon. The capture of Yongchon would place them astride a corridor between Taegu and Pohang, or into the Kyongju corridor south to Pusan.

As the 24th Division entered the fray, the ROKs were still reeling from the first battles, but were striving hard to get organized and present a more cohesive defense. From west to east the ROK Army consisted of the 17th Regiment, 2d, Capital, 6th and 8th Divisions, with the 23d Regiment (3d Division) on the coast. The 2d and Capital Divisions were in name only, having sustained very heavy losses. The other commands had suffered losses but were pretty much intact.

In early July the ROK high command acti-

vated the I Corps Headquarters, under MG Kim Hong Il. This headquarters would facilitate command and control of ROK divisions.

About July 5, the ROKs cut off an enemy regiment at Ichon, about 30 air miles southeast of Seoul, and destroyed or captured a number of mortars and artillery pieces. Near the same date, on the Yongin road further west, the ROKs virtually destroyed another enemy regiment.

While GEN Dean moved the 34th into positions at Pyongtaek and Ansong, MG Kim ordered the 1st ROK Division, about 2,000 men at the time, to march from Chochiwon, where it had assembled, northeast to Umsong. This town is about 20-25 air miles east and slightly south of Ansong. COL Paik got his men on the road at once.

By July 8, Paik's 1st Division had begun to gain strength. From a low of 2,000 men when it had begun its retreat, it had grown to 5,000, but it had no artillery nor heavy weapons and was physically exhausted. These men had walked, not ridden, wherever they had to go. At Umsong, Paik was to replace the ROK 6th Division's 7th Regiment. Because of the poor condition of the 1st Division, the 7th Regiment remained. (The 7th had soundly defeated one enemy thrust earlier in the month.) The two commands fought as one until ordered to withdraw. GEN Paik recalled that, because of recent successes against the North Koreans, the morale of the ROK 6th Division was "sky high."

On July 9, the ROK Capital Division, with some ROK police, ambushed a battalion of the *2d Division,* capturing four artillery pieces and 27 vehicles. The Capital Division held their ground for three days before being outflanked in the west by the fall of Chonan and Chonui.

The *2d Division* had been badly battered and its men neared exhaustion, but its commander allowed it no rest. After capturing Chinchon, he drove his men on toward Chongju. Near the town, ROK artillery blasted advance units, inflicting an estimated 800 casualties. The 24th Division's loss of Chochiwon, just 12 miles to the west, forced the Capital Division to withdraw.

On July 12, the ROK 17th Regiment commanded by Paik's younger brother, COL Paik In Yup, distinguished itself by ambushing elements of Park Song Chol's *15th Division,* inflicting heavy losses. For this, every man in the regiment was promoted one grade.

Farther east, the ROK 6th Division fought a successful delaying action against the *NK 7th.* In the first few days of the war, the 6th killed or wounded some 400 members of the *7th* and destroyed a number of their tanks. On July 7, the North Korean High Command relieved the commander of the *7th Division,* MG Chon U, because his division was behind schedule, redesignated the *7th Division* as the *12th,* and activated a new *7th Division.*

Three days later, the North Korean leadership sacked LTG Kim Kwang Hyop as commander *II Corps,* headquartered at Hwachon. He was deemed inefficient because his corps, operating in the central mountains failed to maintain its schedule of advance. LTG Kim Mu Chong took his place. The rugged terrain and obstinate opposition by the ROKs should be credited with destroying the corps' timetable.

By July 12, the ROK 6th Division was defending the Mungyong area, while the 8th was near Tanyang. The *NK 1st, 13th and 15th Divisions*, supported by the *109th Armd Regt*, drove for Mungyong. The *12th* and *8th Divisions* made for Tanyang.

The high, almost trackless Taebaek Range effectively cut the narrow coastal region from the rest of the country, creating a separate area of operations. The *NK 5th Division* and *766th Independent Infantry Unit* drove down the coastal road. Between Tanyang and the coast roamed 2,000 to 3,000 North Korean guerrillas, but they proved to be of little value to the enemy.

By mid-July, the enemy finally dislodged the ROK 6th Division from the Mungyong area and flanked the ROK 8th Division out of its Tanyang position. Meantime, the *11th Regiment (5th Division)* had moved inland. It set out on an eight-day, 175-mile march, as Appleman describes, "through some of the wildest and roughest country in Korea." At Chunyang it fought a pitched battle with part of the ROK 8th Division, which was withdrawing from the Tanyang area. The regiment then turned east, joining the remainder of the division at Ulchin about July 10. The *5th Division* had lost some 1,800 men in their advance to this point.

Appleman makes a good point in *South to the Naktong*, when he states that one of the North Koreans' major tactical mistakes of the war was their failure to move rapidly down the coastal road. He is probably correct in concluding that a fast-moving column could have reached Pohang-dong within two weeks after the war began. The *5th Division* did dissipate its strength and wasted time sending formations into the wild, desolate Taebaek Range. The division commander was apparently overly concerned about his flanks and rear. Once at Pohang-dong, the *5th Division* would have been in position to drive down on Pusan. Before July 9, when the first elements of the 25th Infantry Division began arriving in Korea, neither the ROKs nor the U.S. had sufficient troops near enough to the Pohang-dong-Pusan corridor to seriously delay the *5th Division*.

Only the ROK 23d Regiment faced the *5th Division* and *766th Independent Infantry Unit*. The 23d was commanded by "Tiger Kim," COL Kim Chong Won.

GEN MacArthur ordered Dean to send troops to halt the enemy and protect COL Robert Witty's 35th Fighter Group at Yonil, 5 miles south of Pohang-dong. Dean sent 3/19. The battalion arrived at Yonil on July 8 and an antiaircraft battery the next day. Simultaneously with these deployments engineering equipment was sent by LST to improve and extend the Yonil air strip. The 3d Battalion, 19th Regiment, even with the antiaircraft battery, could not have slowed the *5th Division* significantly if it already had been near Pohang-dong at the time.

As more pressure from the *5th Division* was brought to bear on his regiment, "Tiger Kim" called for reinforcements. COL Emmerich, the ROK 3d Division adviser, immediately requested ROK Army to send the 1st Separate Battalion and the Yongdungpo Separate Battalion to Kim's aid. The two battalions were engaged in anti-guerrilla operations in the Chiri Mountains of southwest Korea. The ROK Army sent the two

commands to Kim. Although lightly armed with Japanese rifles and carbines, they provided a welcome additional 1,500 men.

The 23d, near Pyonghae-ri, appeared to be slowly crumbling. CPT Harold Slater, the regiment's adviser, so informed COL Emmerich. Emmerich and the 3d Division G3 immediately started forward. At Pohang-dong they discovered the regimental XO setting up a rear CP, and ROK soldiers in the town. They all were ordered summarily back north to Yongdok.

U.S. naval and air forces, plus USAF fighters from Yonil, all pounded the *5th Division*. This almost-constant bombardment, and a landslide caused by monsoon rains, all helped to slow the enemy. But the 23d Regiment's CP withdrew into Yongdok on July 11. The 3d Division commander, now in Pohang-dong, ordered his military police to shoot any ROK troops caught in town. On July 12, BG Lee Chu Sik arrived to take command of the division.

The *5th Division* entered Pyonghae-ri on July 13, just 22 miles north of Yongdok and 50 miles from Pohang-dong. The *5th Division's 10th Regiment* then moved westward into the westward into the mountains toward Chinbo, outflanking Yongdok. A fight for that town was not far off.

Chapter Notes:

P. 42 MG William F. Dean, commanding the 24th, was commissioned from ROTC in 1923. In World War II he became the assistant division commander of the 44th Infantry Division in Europe, ending the war as division commander. In 1947-48, he was both military governor and deputy to GEN Hodge in Korea, then commander of the 7th Infantry Division in Japan. He served as GEN Walker's chief of staff from May to October 1949. When the command of the 24th Division opened, he asked for the job, and Walker gave it to him.

P. 42 The concept that regimental commanders should be no older than 45 came from a recommendation by GEN George C. Marshal during WW II. GEN Matthew B. Ridgway, the U.S. Army's deputy chief of staff for administration at the beginning of the Korean War, visited the U.S. Eighth Army in early August 1950, and stated that "some" regimental commanders were "very poor, being too old and lacking combat experience and aggressiveness." COLs Richard C. Stephens, 47, and Henry G. Fisher (35th Inf.), 50, were "old" by Marshall's and Ridgway's standards, but both were proven outstanding regimental commanders in Korea by their records.

P. 42 "Big Six" was derived from his radio call sign. At the time, "Six" referred to the commander and "Five" to the XO. "Able Six" would be the CO of Co. A; "One Six" would be the platoon leader of A company's 1st Platoon.

P. 43 MAJ Barnett has devoted over 10 years to the serious study and research of actions by the 24th Infantry Division and 34th Infantry Regiment during the early months of the Korean War. He sent a copy of this OPORD to this author, confirming that GEN Dean already had given GEN Barth oral orders and that TF Barth had been established, consisting of the 34th Infantry and the 52d and 63d FABs.

P. 45 White phosphorous was also known as WP or Willie Peter.

P. 46 The Browning Automatic Rifle was a gas-operated, shoulder-fired weapon weighing 16 pounds, with a 20-round magazine and a rate of fire of 500 rounds per minute. It also could be fired from a bipod. It was commonly called a BAR. The Army's nine-man rifle squad was authorized one BAR; the Marine 13-man rifle squad was authorized three.

P. 46 Lacy Barnett provided this author with copies of correspondence and tape transcripts from all the officers and enlisted men quoted in this account of 1/34th Inf. at Pyongtaek, including the OCMH notes on its interviews of Collins, Williams and Beauchamp. Detailed references are in the Sources and Acknowledgments section of this book.

P. 47 To their surprise, many U.S. soldiers found the Korean telephone system in operation in these early days. More than once, Americans used Korean telephones when all other communication was out or unavailable.

P. 47 In his 1955 monograph, GEN Barth wrote, "Ayres may not have understood that to gain time he must defend on the first available position from which he could physically block the tanks by demolitions." Ayres apparently had no such understanding, because the last order he received from Lovless was to move directly to Chonan. Further, 1/34 had no demolitions with which to create a roadblock. Ayres wrote: "If demolitions were to be placed, I don't know where I would have gotten them."

P. 47 It is obvious that GEN Dean had little understanding of the strength and disposition of the enemy opposing his isolated battalions. Apparently because an arm of the sea came up near Pyongtaek, he considered it a strong position; the Army official history states that Dean "placed great importance on holding the Pyongtaek-Ansong line"; Barth characterized it as "weak." Ayres wrote that "GEN Dean did not tell me to establish positions at Pyongtaek — he merely ordered me to do so as far north as possible.... It was my sole decision to establish the position in the Pyongtaek area, primarily because the trains could not carry the troops any farther since the tracks were gone."

As the terrible ordeal of the 24th Division unfolded, it seemed apparent that GEN Dean never fully grasped how badly outnumbered, outgunned and outmaneuvered he really was. He had little, if any, way to obtain decent information about the enemy. Further, the forces he had available were too weak. The enemy could maneuver them out of position every time.

P. 50 It is a hell of a sad thing to do. The Marines had — and have— a doctrine that their dead and wounded will not be left behind. The Army then did not stress such a policy. Some Army units and commanders followed the same code as the Marines in this regard; others did not.

CHAPTER SIX - Walker Takes Command

U.S. Perception of the Threat and Its Reaction

American leaders, and the heads of many western nations believed that the North Korean invasion of South Korea was merely the opening of a global push by Communist nations led by the Soviet Union. U.S. military planners, therefore, had to consider global commitments. But the American military had been "Johnsonized," a derisive term referring to the efforts of Secretary of Defense Louis A. Johnson to reduce the size and composition of U.S. military forces. Postwar national budgets had slashed military appropriations, leading to the retention of unfit military weapons, equipment and ammunition stocks, lack of spare parts for equipment repair and maintenance, reduced strength formations and a lack of urgency in training. Secretary Johnson, implemented, if not led, these budgetary slashes and was generally considered an enemy by many top U.S. military leaders.

To meet global commitments, the U.S. Army had 10 divisions. Four were in Japan, one in Europe and five in the United States. In addition, there was the 29th RCT in Okinawa, 5th RCT in Hawaii, the 3d Armd Cav. Regt (ACR) and the 14th RCT. The Army totaled 591,000 men of 630,000 authorized. The projected budget at the start of the Korean War would have cut the authorized force to 611,000, eliminating one division in Japan. The Air Force, Navy and Marine Corps almost were equally low in strength, equipment, weaponry and appropriation money.

With this dearth of force, America found itself hard put to meet what it conceived as a world-wide Communist threat, preventing Army leadership from going all-out to support MacArthur's requests for troops, weapons and equipment. In order to meet perceived requirements in Europe and Asia thousands of individual reservists were called to active duty. On Sept. 1, 1950, four National Guard divisions (28th, 40th, 43d and 45th Infantry Divisions) and two Guard RCTs (196th and 278th) were called to active duty. Two more Guard divisions, the 31st and 47th, were activated in January 1951.

In Japan, GEN MacArthur had to balance the defense of Japan and the Ryukyus with providing sufficient combat power to halt, then turn back, the North Koreans. He soon realized that much more than the 24th Infantry Division would be needed in Korea; his woefully under strength command was unable to do the job by itself. MacArthur waged an almost-continuous campaign with the Joint Chiefs of Staff (JCS) for men, weapons and equipment. His efforts paid off in the rapid deployment of a Marine Brigade, the 2d Infantry Division and the 5th RCT, as well as reinforcing artillery, armor and a variety of other combat support and service support battalions and companies.

His immediate concern in early July was the command and control of forces sent to Korea from Japan and the United States. By July 6, he had decided to send the Eighth Army to Korea, under LTG Walton H. Walker.

GEN Walton H. Walker

GEN Walker, a native of Belton, Texas, graduated from West Point in 1913 and briefly commanded a battalion in World War I. During World War II he commanded XX Corps in GEN George S. Patton's Third Army. Patton called him "my toughest son of a bitch" — high praise from Patton.

Walker's short stature and barrel chest belied the hard, courageous and superb fighting general that he was. His stature and pugnacious temperament combined to earn him the nickname "Bulldog." His skillful formation and defense of the Pusan Perimeter bought the time necessary to launch the Inchon landing, leading to the expulsion of the North Korean Army from South Korea. In Hoyt's *The Pusan Perimeter*, he states that "GEN Walker was the real unsung hero of the Korean War."

Walker carried a .45-cal automatic pistol and a repeating shotgun in the jeep he used to dash around the battle area. "I don't mind being shot at," he once said, "but these bastards are not going to ambush me."

GEN Walker led the Eighth Army with uncommon ferocity, meeting every enemy thrust with an iron-willed determination to win. He skillfully utilized his meager reserves and employed threats, coercion and exhortation to stiffen American and ROK leadership. He absolutely refused to give up one inch of the Perimeter without a desperate struggle. It was this short statured, rather rotund and unimposing looking man, whose powerful leadership and consummate tactical skill won the battle of the Pusan Perimeter.

BG Eugene "Mike" Lynch, Walker's pilot in Korea, probably spent more time with the man than anyone, including his aides. Here are some of his recollections of Walker: "Walker was the most down-to-earth, honest, straightforward guy you could ever meet." And, "if you ever want to go to war with a guy, go with Walker.... You guys were lucky you had him."

COL William A. Collier wrote, "I probably knew GEN Walker better than any other individual in Eighth Army.... [He] was not only a soldier's soldier, but... a battlefield leader as opposed to a command post commander."

In short, Walton H.

Walker was the right man, at the right place, at the right time.

On July 6, Walker contacted COL William A. Collier at Kobe and told him that Eighth Army was taking over in Korea and that he wanted Collier to go to Korea as soon as possible to set up a forward CP. COL Eugene M. Landrum, then Eighth Army Chief of Staff, would remain in Japan for the time being. Collier would be Combat Chief of Staff until Landrum could take over.

Collier flew to Korea on July 8. He found Taejon unsatisfactory for the Army CP. He knew most other South Korean towns were too small and lacked proper communications for the CP. The only place that might work was Taegu, which was the hub of a road net, had rail service and had a cable relay station of the old Tokyo-Mukden cable system. There, Collier found the relay station in operation and a large compound of school buildings right across the street. He quickly made arrangements with local officials for their use, then called COL Landrum. At 1 P.M. July 9, an advance party opened Walker's CP in Taegu.

In 1948 and 1949, Collier was Deputy Chief of Staff, then Chief of Staff, of U.S. Army Forces in South Korea, and was well acquainted with the country. "Gene" Landrum's career had been up then down. At the beginning of WWII, he was a full colonel and a division chief of staff.

LTG Walton H. Walker leaving 25th Division Headquarters. (Source: Battleground Korea - 25th Division in the Korean War*)*

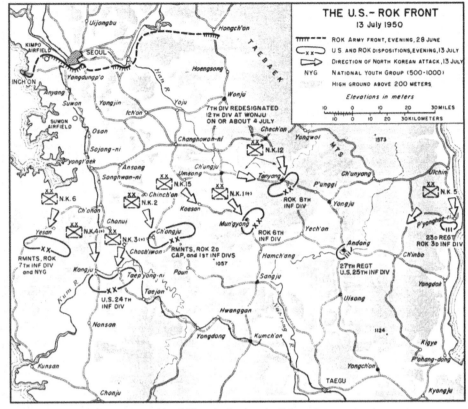

Map 8 (Source: South to the Naktong*)*

He commanded one division in the Pacific well, but did not do well with another division in Europe. Although he attained the rank of major general, after the war he was reduced to colonel and became Walker's G-1, then Chief of Staff in Fifth Army. When Walker went to command Eighth Army in Japan, COL Landrum went along to become its Chief of Staff. At the outbreak of the Korean War, he was 59. Landrum retired in January 1951, at which time his WWII rank of major general was restored to him.

GEN Walker assumed command of the Eighth United States Army in Korea (EUSAK) at 12:01 a.m., July 13, 1950, arriving Korea that afternoon to stay. The following day he issued Letter of Instruction No. 1 to all division and separate unit commanders in Korea. The text of the letter follows:

1. Circumstances have imposed a temporary strategical defense upon this Army. The offensive will be assumed at as early a date as possible.

2. Pending the initiation of the counter offensive it is desired that every unit within its own sphere seize every opportunity to employ aggressive offensive tactics and methods.

3. Counterattack will be utilized by all units from squads upward to keep the enemy off balance, to improve positions, and regain lost ground.

4. Extensive and aggressive patrolling will be conducted in order to maintain contact, conduct reconnaissance and to harass the enemy.

5. Road blocks, mine fields, demolitions and other obstacles will be utilized to the maximum, to disrupt enemy advance in order that he can be attacked with advantage.

The letter was signed personally by GEN Walker. To the soldier, the "desire" of a commander is the same as an order.

On the 14th, BG John H.Church, who had commanded a GHQ advance command and liaison group in Korea, returned to Tokyo. Four days later he was promoted to major general.

Walker's command initially consisted of about 18,000 Americans and 58,000 ROKs. The addition of the 25th Infantry and 1st Cavalry Divisions would more than double the American contingent. A few days later, through President Syngman Rhee, all ROK forces were placed under MacArthur's command. Walker, by extension, directed the ROK Army through its own Chief of Staff, GEN Chung Il Kwon.

Contact in the ROK Army was made through U.S. Army KMAG officers. At the time, MAJ James W. Hausman was the American liaison officer to the ROK general staff. Lynch accompanied GEN Walker on his first visit to ROK headquarters, where he went to see MAJ Hausman. Facetiously, Walker asked him, "Are you the guy I have to see to move the Korean Army?"

Logistical Shortfalls and Considerations

Most of the shortcomings of the units, equipment and weapons in Japan already have been discussed. In addition to large numbers of unserviceable rifles, carbines, and 60mm mortars, there was a universal shortage of radios, radio batteries, spare machine gun barrels, rifle cleaning rods and cleaning oil. There were few trip flares, hand grenades and 60mm illuminating rounds. Even the available illuminating rounds and 2.36-inch rocket rounds included many duds.

Through the Pusan Perimeter campaign, rifle ammunition was sometimes issued to rifle companies in 20-round cardboard boxes. The company then had to hand-load the ammunition into eight-round clips for the M1 rifle. Machine gun ammunition was sometimes issued to companies in old WWII web belts, to which the rounds had corroded fast. If used, this caused the machine gun to malfunction, so the rounds had to be removed from the web belt, hastily cleaned and reloaded into a metal link belt. At times in this period of the war, other ammunition, particularly 81mm mortar and artillery ammunition, was also in short supply. The shortage of artillery ammunition was never more severe than at the time of the breakout (mid- to end of September).

Vehicles which wouldn't start also went to Korea, in some cases being towed aboard LSTs. Primitive Korean roads destroyed tires and tubes at an alarming rate.

The first months in Korea were "war on a shoestring." The reclamation of WW II materiel was speeded up dramatically in Japan to meet demands, with certain weapons modified to meet the new requirements. The M4A3 tank was refitted with a high-velocity 76mm gun; the 105mm howitzer carriage was modified to allow a higher angle of fire to clear Korean hills and mountains; and the M15A1 half-track was converted to a T19, mounting a 40mm gun instead of the old 37mm.

Critical supplies were airlifted from the U.S. to the Far East, including weapons, ammunition and combat rations. Eventually, all the C- and B-rations left over from WW II were sent to Korea.

GEN Walker was well aware of all the shortcomings and problems. Rather than complain, he tried to overcome them, and expected his subordinates to do the same.

Slowly, the logistical situation corrected itself and organization replaced the frantic early efforts. Even so, some of ammunition problems still existed in September.

Aside from airlift into relatively small airports, the only points of entry into Korea were Pohang-dong and Pusan. Pohang was not a satisfactory port; it soon became a battleground. Pusan was a good port, where 24 deep-water ships and 14 LSTs could be accommodated at once. The lack of skilled workers and heavy unloading equipment kept the potential 45,000 ton daily discharge rate to about 14,000 tons.

Good Japanese-built rail lines ran north, west and northeast from Pusan, proving invaluable to logistical and troop transport efforts. Roads were another matter. Most were less than two lanes, constructed of dirt or dirt and stones. The best roads were 18 feet wide, narrowing to 13 feet or less at bridges and bypasses. Secondary roads were barely one lane wide, while others were hardly more than a cart track. When the weather was dry, vehicles traveling these roads kicked up huge clouds of dust which blocked out the vision of any following driver. The rains turned all but the best dirt and gravel roads into lanes of deep mud. Adding to these difficulties, many of the roads followed old foot paths or cart tracks and contained sharp turns and grades up to 15 percent. Most road and rail lines were oriented north-south, with few east-west connections.

MacArthur's Requirements

Almost from the start, MacArthur visualized stopping the enemy somewhere in the south, pounding him with air power, blockading North Korea and hitting him with an amphibious attack in the rear. To do this he needed more troops, artillery, armor and equipment.

By July 5, he sent a request to the States for the 2d Infantry Division, an RCT from the 82d Airborne Division; the 2d Engineer Special Brigade; an AA battalion; 18 tanks and personnel, 700 aircraft, three medium tank battalions; personnel to operate a variety of landing craft; and a Marine RCT, beach group and two air squadrons with an air group echelon. He also requested authorization to expand all existing heavy tank companies in his command to battalion strength.

In response to a JCS request to furnish his estimate of what he needed, MacArthur said, on Aug. 7, said that he needed four to four and a half full infantry divisions; one Abn RCT, with necessary airlift; one Armd group with three medium tank battalions and reinforcing artillery and service units.

He also reported that 30,000 reinforcements would allow him to put this force into Korea without endangering the security of Japan. He told the JCS that, "It is now apparent that we are confronted...with an aggressive and well-trained professional army equipped with tanks and perhaps other ground material quite equal to, and in some categories superior to, that available here." MacArthur rated enemy leadership as "excellent."

Reinforcing B-26 and B-29 bombers were already on the way, as well as some of the F-51 and F-80 fighters he so urgently needed for close-air support.

On July 10, MacArthur requested four heavy tank battalions, 12 heavy tank companies, 11 infantry battalions, 11 105mm howitzer battalions and four antiaircraft automatic weapons battalions (AAA AW), minus four batteries. These represented the unit shortages in the four divisions in his command.

On July 12, Walker asked for infantry from the 29th RCT on Okinawa. The next day, MacArthur ordered the shipment of two battalions of the 29th to Korea.

Walker's Plan of Defense

Before GEN Walker took command in Korea on July 13, GEN Dean and the 24th Division were governed by orders from MacArthur in Tokyo, through his Chief Of Staff, MG Eugene Edward (Ned) M. Almond. When Walker took over in Korea, he too, had to go through Almond to get to MacArthur.

Walker was responsible for halting the North Koreans somewhere. Aware of the terrain in southeast Korea, he began planning the deployment of his forces to accomplish this mission.

He directed COL Allan MacLean to start looking for some place where he could establish a reasonable defense line. MacLean (West Point 1930) had served as Chief of Operations in HQ, European Theater of Operations (ETO) during WWII. In 1949-50 he commanded the 7th Infantry Division's 32d Infantry Regiment. In 1950 he was reassigned to the Eighth Army's G3 Sec-

tion. Later, he commanded the 31st Regiment, also of the 7th Division, and was killed in action Nov. 29, 1950.

MacLean, in company with Walker's pilot Lynch, began reconnoitering for a suitable defense line, finishing their work by July 12. Army Chief of Staff GEN J. Lawton Collins, was visiting Walker then. Walker outlined to Collins what he had in mind: "There are a lot of refinements to be done," he said, Lynch recalled, "[but] basically if I could get in behind that river [Naktong] without losing anybody, with what's coming, I think I can do pretty well."

His final plan envisioned a defensive line from the Chosen Strait in the south, north to the Naktong, then northward along the east bank of that river to near the town of Naktong-ni, then generally east through rugged mountains to the Sea of Japan. The Naktong is a winding, looping river, forming a water obstacle of from 200 to 350 meters wide and varying from about three to six feet deep. The speed of its current was slow enough not to be a major factor in river crossing operations.

To systematically occupy the envisioned line, Walker knew he had to continue delaying the enemy with the ROK Army, the U.S. 24th and 25th Divisions and the soon-to-arrive U.S. 1st Cavalry Division. He then had to move the U.S. divisions into positions extending south along the Naktong to the Chosen Strait. At the same time ROK divisions had to move into their defensive positions along the northern front in the mountains to the sea.

To execute the delaying phase of his plan, he wanted to deploy the 25th Division in the Hamchang-Andong area, with the ROK 17th Infantry on its left and ROK divisions on its right all the way to the Sea of Japan. South of the ROK 17th Regiment, he planned to have the 1st Cavalry take over for the beat-up 24th Division east of Taejon. The 24th would withdraw through the 1st Cavalry and redeploy east of Waegwan, with the Naktong to its rear. The 1st Cavalry then would fight a delaying action back to the Naktong. As the Cavalry approached the river, the 24th would slip back to the east shore of the Naktong and south of the Cav. The 1st Cavalry would halt and also defend the east bank of that river.

By this time the 25th Division was expected to have delayed back to near Naktong-ni. In that area, the division would pass through ROK defenders dug in on what Walker hoped to be part of his perimeter. The 25th would then swing south of the 24th, covering the southern flank of the Eighth Army from the confluence of the Nam and Naktong rivers to the Chosen Strait. When the 2d Infantry Division arrived, it would take over much of the southern sector. The other American divisions on the Naktong front would narrow their frontages to make room for the 2d. The Marine Brigade, plus the equivalent of an Army regiment, would constitute the Eighth Army reserve.

The ROK Army would defend the northern flank of the Perimeter through the rugged Taebaek Mountains to the Sea of Japan. American divisions on the Naktong flank would have much longer sectors to defend than the smaller, less well-armed ROK divisions.

GEN Walker believed that a force of 28 in-

fantry battalions, backed by six more in reserve, could hold the Naktong front to the sea. The projected deployment from north to south on the Naktong line was to be 1st Cavalry, 24th, 25th and 2d Infantry Divisions. The three-battalion Marine Brigade, although short three rifle companies, and three Army battalions, taken from one or more of the divisions, would constitute the reserve.

When this plan was being developed, the projected battalion count showed that the four U.S. divisions should provide 28 battalions, and the 29th Infantry, 5th RCT and Marine Brigade an additional eight, for a total of 36. When the plan had to be executed in early August, Walker did not have 34-36 battalions; he had closer to 22 battalion-equivalents; 18 or 19 from the divisions, and four from the 29th Infantry, 5th RCT and Marine Bde. (See Chapter Notes.)

GEN Walker wanted very much to bring the 1st Cavalry, 24th and 25th Divisions up to their proper number of infantry battalions, and needed eight battalions to do this. He had planned to allow the two battalions from the 29th some training time, then assign them to the 27th and 35th Regiments to round out the 25th Division. Upon arrival in Korea, the 5th RCT would furnish three more battalions for either the 1st Cavalry or 24th Infantry Divisions. The remaining three battalions would come from the U.S. But he was unable to execute this plan, except for the two battalions of the 29th; 1/29th was attached to the 35th on Aug. 6 and 3/29 was attached to the 27th on Aug. 7.

Walker faced the task at hand. By having far fewer infantry battalions than he planned, the general was at a major disadvantage along the Naktong front. The need to deploy American battalions on the northern front to help the ROKs during the campaign would complicate matters. ROK divisions remained smaller than those of the U.S. and still had no organic tanks, fewer heavy mortars and about one-fourth the organic artillery support of an American division; the North Korean division was authorized up to 60 artillery pieces and heavy mortars, all of which outranged anything in the ROK division, and had tanks to support many of their attacks on the ROKs. The ROK Army also was short of reserves, being hard-put to keep their active divisions up to strength. Over the next few months, the northern front became so critical at times that the ROK Army was forced to commit newly-formed and untrained battalions and regiments to plug gaps and shore up defenses.

Arrival and deployment of the 25th Infantry Division

The 25th Infantry Division deployed to Korea July 10-15; the 27th Infantry (Wolfhound) Regiment on the 10th; the 24th Infantry (Golden Eagle) Regiment, the only regiment from Japan which had all three battalions, on the 12th; and the 35th Infantry (Cacti) Regiment between July 13-15.

COL Horton V. White (West Point 1923) commanded the 24th and COL Henry G. "Hank" Fisher (West Point 1923) the 35th. LTC John H. "Mike" Michaelis (West Point 1936) assumed command of the 27th as it landed in Korea. The former 27th commander, COL John W. Childs,

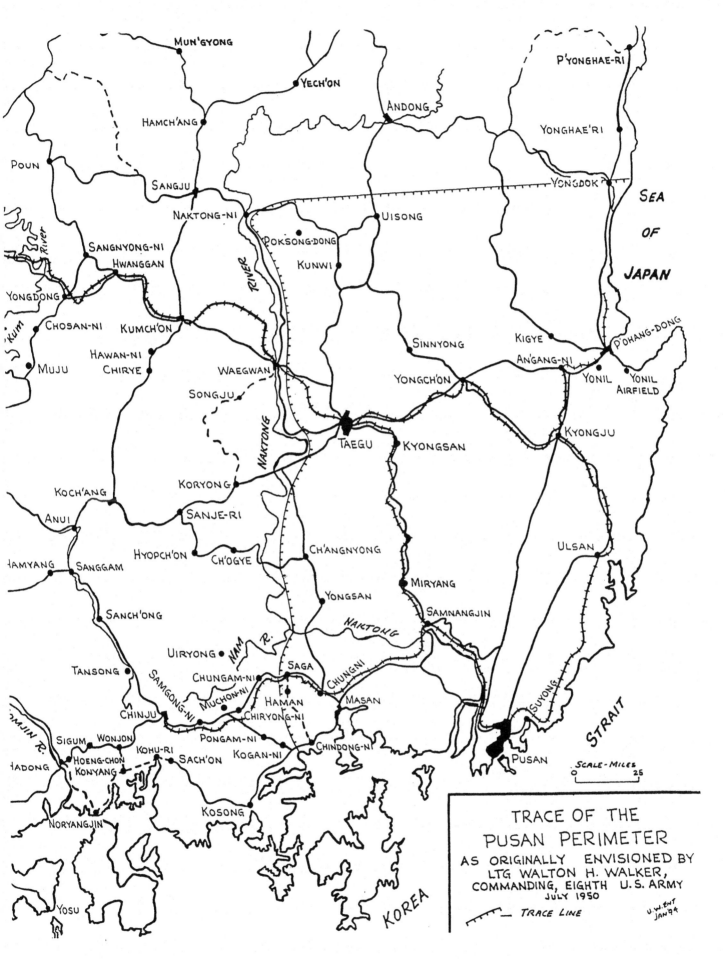

MUN'GYONG

YECH'ON

P'YONGHAE-RI

HAMCH'ANG

ANDONG

YONGHAE'RI

POUN

SANGJU

YONGDOK

SEA

NAKTONG-NI

UISONG

OF

POKSONG-DONG

JAPAN

SANGNYONG-NI

River

KUNWI

HWANGGAN

RIVER

YONGDONG

Kum

CHOSAN-NI

KUMCH'ON

SINNYONG

KIGYE

P'OHANG-DONG

HAWAN-NI

AN'GANG-NI

MUJU

CHIRYE

WAEGWAN

YONGCH'ON

YONIL

YONIL
AIRFIELD

SONGJU

NAKTONG

TAEGU

KYONGSAN

KYONGJU

KOCH'ANG

KORYONG

ANUI

SANJE-RI

ULSAN

HYOPCH'ON

CH'OGYE

CH'ANGNYONG

HAMYANG

SANGGAM

MIRYANG

YONGSAN

SANCH'ONG

NAKTONG

SAMNANGJIN

UIRYONG

NAM R.

SAGA

TANSONG

CHUNGAM-NI

CHUNGNI

SUYONG

SAMGONG-NI

MUCHON-NI

HAMAN

MASAN

CHINJU

CHIRYONG-NI

SIGUM

WONJON

PONGAM-NI

KOGAN-NI

CHINDONG-NI

STRAIT

HOENG-CHON

KOHU-RI

SACH'ON

PUSAN

HADONG

KONYANG

SCALE-MILES

0   25

NORYANGJIN

KOSONG

TRACE OF THE
PUSAN PERIMETER

AS ORIGINALLY ENVISIONED BY
LTG WALTON H. WALKER,
COMMANDING, EIGHTH U.S. ARMY
JULY 1950

YOSU

KOREA

TRACE LINE

U.W.ENT
JAN'94

was appointed 25th Division Chief of Staff. Childs (Georgia Tech 1921), at 50, was considered by some too old to command the regiment in combat.

The 24th RCT was a throwback to the post-Civil War days, when two regiments of cavalry (9th and 10th) and two regiments of infantry (24th and 25th) were formed, composed of black enlisted men and white officers. Segregation in the Army continued from then on. As the years went by, a few black officers were appointed to lead some black units.

On the eve of the Korean War all black soldiers in combat units in the Far East were assigned to the 24th RCT. The RCT consisted of the 24th Infantry Regiment, the 159th FAB, 77th Engineer Combat Company (ECC) and an MP company — all black enlisted men and about 90 percent white officers.

It is generally believed that President Truman ordered the integration of black and white soldiers in 1948. His Executive Order 9981, dated July 26, 1948, directed a policy of equal treatment and opportunity "in the armed services without regard to race, color, religion or national origin." It also created an advisory committee in the military on equality of treatment and opportunity.

Integration was about to begin in 1950, prior to the Korean War, but it did not happen until 1951, when the 24th RCT went out of existence and its soldiers transferred to other commands.

When the 25th Division arrived in Korea, its commander, MG William B. Kean, his Division Artillery commander (BG Barth) and all three of his regimental commanders were West Point graduates. Only Barth and Michaelis had WW II battle experience.

GEN Kean "missed" WW I, but in 1939 he was assigned to the personnel section of the Chief of Infantry, War Department G1 Section, working for Omar Bradley. Bradley, who once called Kean "Captain Bligh," remembered him as "a hard taskmaster and a perfectionist, curt and abrasive with his underlings, but an able, professional infantryman."

In Europe, he was chief of staff, first with the II Corps, then of First Army. When Bradley became commander of Twelfth Army Group, Clay Blair wrote, Kean, "at Bradley's request, remained First Army chief of staff, partly to keep a fire lit under its conservative, low-key commander, Courtney H. Hodges." After the war, in 1948, then-Army Chief of Staff Bradley gave Kean command of the 25th Division in Japan and promoted him to major general. The 25th Division Artillery XO, COL William W. Dick, rated Kean a top division commander.

BG Vennard Wilson (Tulane 1917) had been the Assistant Division Commander since 1948. He was a WW I veteran and commanded an independent cavalry group (106th) in Europe in WW II. GEN Barth wrote that because he was so unassuming, not many people realized how good he was. Barth considered him excellent with infantry and an expert armored tactician.

Michaelis enlisted in the Army in 1932. He had a distinguished WW II combat record, commanding the 502d Parachute Infantry Regiment until wounded in Holland. When he recovered from his wounds he was appointed Chief of Staff of the 101st Airborne Division.

After the war, Michaelis served on the War Department General Staff, including two years as senior aide to Army Chief of Staff Dwight D. Eisenhower, who considered him one of one of four Army lieutenant colonels "of extraordinary ability." (See Chapter Notes.)

When the Korean War started, LTC Michaelis was a member of the Eighth Army G3 Section. Some people referred to him as "The Fair-Haired Boy of Eighth Army." But Michaelis was a professional, vitally interested in training and teaching the officers and soldiers whenever he could. Here is an example of that interest:

In early 1950, Michaelis was appointed chief umpire for some tactical exercises at Mt. Fuji. He assembled all the young lieutenant platoon umpires the day before the exercises and took them on a tactical walk across the two-company front to be used in part of the exercise. As the group made its way across this terrain, Michaelis stopped it in each company position. At each stop, he had the officers reconnoiter and select platoon, squad and crew-served weapon positions. Then he reassembled the officers and asked them for their solutions, always asking, "Why there?" Then he told the officers how he would have organized each position, and why he had selected the ones he did. Here, Michaelis took advantage of an opportunity to instruct and train, as few staff officers and commanders did.

Michaelis looked like a soldier, handsome, young and charismatic. In Korea he was friendly with the press and made good copy. Michaelis seemed to draw correspondents like a magnet. But not everyone thought highly of him: One of his young staff officers once referred to him as a "phony baloney." That officer soon was sent to a rifle company.

Michaelis was a hard-charger, an aggressive, tenacious fighter, with great initiative. His division commander could count on him and his regiment. He made sound decisions and did not panic in a crisis. He had two good battalion commanders in LTC Gilbert Check and LTC Gordon E. Murch, plus a number of solid company commanders. The 27th, luckily, retained these superior leaders. This continuity in good leadership reflected in the regiment's performance in battle. Some other regiments were not so fortunate; their men suffered as a result.

COL Horton V. White, commanding the 24th, was a member of the Sixth Army G2 Section in WW II. He had planned and carried out the liberation of 500 American POWs in the Philippines in 1945, retiring on disability as a colonel in 1954. LTC Charles M. Bussey, commander of the 77th ECC in the 24th RCT, wrote that White was "a very fine officer and an outstanding peacetime garrison commander, [but was] too old and frail to lead troops in combat." White knew this, too. He once confided as much to Bussey, but told him he would carry on as regimental commander until ordered to another assignment.

COL Henry G. "Hank" Fisher, White's West Point classmate, commanded an infantry regiment in Europe during the WW II. He was about the same age as White, but was in far better physical condition. Fisher was given command of the 35th Infantry in 1948, remaining in command until 1951. Sidney B. Berry (West Point 1948), an officer in the 35th (who retired as a

LTG), wrote that Fisher "was a superb commander. He trained hard in Japan and led us well in Korea. Many of us are alive today because of 'Hammering Hank' Fisher's demanding training and the effective leadership and skilled tactical fighting abilities in Korea."

Based on interviews with officers who knew COL Fisher, Appleman wrote that he was "calm, somewhat retiring,...possessed of a strong, compact body," and "was a fine example of the professional soldier." He knew exactly "the capabilities of the weapons used in an infantry regiment and was skilled in their use," as well as being a "technician in the tactical employment of troops," Appleman continued. Fisher, unlike Michaelis, was "quiet" and "did not court publicity."

The division's mission was to block the enemy advance south from Chung-ju and to defend the Yonil airstrip. On the 12th, the 25th Division CP opened at Yongchon, midway between Taegu and Pohang-dong. The same day, the 27th went to Uisong, 35 miles north of Taegu, moving the next day to Andong. From positions overlooking the railroad, men of B/27 watched trainloads of refugees heading south. Men, women, children and old people were in and on every boxcar, flatcar, passenger car, engine tender and even the engine itself. People hung onto the sides of the cars, atop the boxcars and on the front "cow catchers" of the engines. They didn't know where they were going, but knew it was away from the North Korean Army.

The 24th was initially sent to the Kumchon area and the 35th to a reserve position near Yongchon. The three regiments remained in the Andong, Kumchon and Yongchon positions from July 15-20.

Arrival and Deployment of the 1st Cavalry Division

Meantime, the 1st Cavalry Division began to arrive. MacArthur had planned to employ the 1st Cavalry to land in rear of the enemy, while a combined U.S.-ROK force counterattacked from the front, but events overtook this plan. The division was directed to make an amphibious landing at Pohang-dong, freeing Pusan to land supplies and reinforcements; placing a large force initially at Pohang, giving added protection to Walker's right flank; and putting the 1st Cavalry in position for a rapid move westward to the aid of the 24th Division. The landing was to take place July 18.

The 8th and 5th Cavalry Regiments made unopposed landings at Pohang on the appointed day. The follow-up 7th Cavalry and 82d FAB were caught by Typhoon Helene and kept at sea until July 22.

On July 19, the 5th Cavalry started toward Taejon; the 8th Cavalry followed by rail and motor the next day, stopping at Yongdong that evening. On July 22 the 8th Cavalry relieved the 24th Division's 21st Infantry at Yongdong. At that time, the 1st Cavalry assumed responsibility for delaying the enemy along the Taejon - Taegu corridor back as far as the Naktong River.

At Taegu, Walker conferred with MG Hobart R. Gay, commanding the Cavalry Division. Lynch recalled telling Gay to protect

Yongdong, remembering that there were no friendly troops behind him. Walker told Gay he must keep a supply route open, because troops could live without food but couldn't last long without ammunition. Lynch said that Walker also admonished, "For Christ sake, watch what the hell you're doing. Don't get caught up in this thing. These guys can fight and they'll envelop you. If you don't know how the hell to pull back when you have to pull back, you're going to be chopped to pieces. It's a whole different war."

After the conference, a news correspondent came up and asked, "Well, GEN Walker, now that you've got the 1st Cavalry here, are you going to counterattack and knock these guys out of here?" Walker and Lynch exchanged glances. Walker's face was totally expressionless.

"He turned around," Lynch said, "and looked this guy up and down... then he looked at me and said, 'Come on, Mike.'" The general, without answering the correspondent, climbed into the plane. "GEN Walker," said Lynch, "you're not going to be popular with these guys."

Walker looked at Lynch and responded. "Let me tell you something.... There is no way you can give an intelligent answer to a dumb question!"

Meanwhile, GEN Gay joined his troops and his artillery commander, BG Charles D. Palmer, at Yongdong. There, COL MacLean, from Eighth Army G3, wanted to position one battalion 4 miles northwest of Yongdong, south of the Kum River, covering the main avenue along the Taejon-Taegu highway. Another battalion was to be posted 2 miles southwest of Yongdong to guard the Chosan-ni-Muju-Kumsan road. Palmer protested to MacLean because he felt that each battalion could be cut off and destroyed by the enemy. He wanted to position the Cavalry Division on ridges east of Yongdong and allow the 24th to pull back through it. Gay agreed with Palmer, but Eighth Army confirmed MacLean's instructions and the two battalions of the 8th Cavalry Regiment were emplaced in accordance with those orders. GEN Gay deployed the 5th Cavalry Regiment east of Yongdong in a blocking position.

MG Hobart R. "Hap" Gay (Knox College 1917) was 56 at the outset of the war. During a polo game in 1929 he was blinded in one eye, forcing his transfer to the Quartermaster Corps. In 1941, Patton appointed him Chief of Staff of the I Armored Corps, then Seventh Army and finally, Third Army. He was replaced, at Eisenhower's insistence, because Eisenhower did not think he was forceful enough to represent Patton at other high headquarters. Patton retained Gay on his staff to oversee certain staff functions. He did so well that Patton not only succeeded in having him restored as Chief of Staff, Eisenhower promoted Gay to major general for his outstanding staff work. Walker and Gay, serving with Patton at the same time, became good friends. In 1949 Walker arranged for Gay to take command of the 1st Cavalry Division.

The 1st Cavalry Division's Assistant Division Commander (ADC) was 54-year-old BG Frank A. Allen, Jr. He, too, had been a cavalryman and tanker. Allen became Eisenhower's public relations man at Supreme Headquarters,

Allied Powers, Europe (SHAPE), and was a Pentagon lobbyist after the war.

The Division Artillery commander, BG Charles D. Palmer (West Point 1924) was then 48. During WW II he had been Chief of Staff of the 2d Armored Division, then of VI Corps in Europe. Later in 1950, he would succeed Gay as 1st Cavalry Division commander. Palmer and his older brother, Williston B., both retired as four-star generals, the only brothers in U.S. history to do so.

COL Ernest V. Holmes, division chief of staff (West Point 1925) was an artilleryman. Most of his WW II service was in Hawaii. He retired as a brigadier general in 1955 on physical disability.

The 5th Cavalry Regiment was led by COL Carl J. "Rosie" Rohsenberger. He was almost 56 — considered an advanced age for combat command. Further, he was very hard of hearing. But, "Rosie" had worked his way up the ranks from private and was considered a fighter.

Forty-nine-year-old COL Cecil W. Nist (West Point 1923) commanded the 7th Cavalry Regiment. His forté was military intelligence, having been G2 of XXIV Corps 1944-45 and G2 of U.S. Army Forces, Korea in 1946. After commanding the 7th Cavalry in Japan and Korea, he returned to Japan. In 1953 he became G2 of Second Army and retired in 1954 as a colonel.

The 8th Cavalry was led by COL Raymond D. Palmer (VMI 1924), age 49. (No relation to BG Charles D. Palmer). Raymond was also on Patton's staff during World War II. His regiment would be the first of the Cavalry Division to meet the enemy in battle.

Not one of the senior commanders of the 1st Cavalry Division had any experience leading troops in battle. They would learn "on the job" or be replaced.

Unfortunately, after WW II, division and even regimental commands were often given to officers as "rewards" for long and faithful service. Most of these officers had splendid records as staff officers at various levels, but had little or no battlefield experience. Some of the divisions and regiments that first deployed to Korea went into battle with inexperienced commanders, and soldiers often suffered as a result.

All three U.S. divisions in Korea, together with the ROKs, continued to delay through the end of July and the first days of August.

The ordeal of the 24th Division was not over; the Kum River and Taejon were yet to come. For the 25th Infantry and 1st Cavalry Divisions, it would be places like Hwanggan, Yechon, Hamchang and Yongdong. Once the Naktong River was reached, it and the mountains north of the Taegu-Pohang-dong corridor would have to be held at all costs. At that point the war passed from delaying the enemy to stopping him.

Chapter Notes:

P. 58 This chart depicts the projected battalion count:

Division	Battalions
1st Cavalry	6 battalions (authorized 9; short 3)
24th Infantry	6 battalions (authorized 9; short 3)
25th Infantry	7 battalions (authorized 9; short 2)

2d Infantry	9 battalions (From U.S. 9th Regt arrived 31 July; 23d Regt 4-5 Aug.; 38th Regt 19 Aug.)
Regiments	
29th Infantry	2 battalions (From Okinawa. Arrived 31 Jul.)
5th RCT	3 battalions (From Hawaii. Arrived 31 Jul.)
Marine Bde	3 battalions (From U.S. Arrived 2 Aug.)
	36 battalions

This chart depicts the actual battalion-equivalents in August, when Walker's plan had to be executed:

Divisions	Battalion-Equivalents
1st Cavalry	5 battalion-equivalents (plus or minus)
24th Infantry	3-4 battalion-equivalents (plus or minus)
25th Infantry	5 battalion-equivalents (plus or minus)
2d Infantry	5 battalions (One from the 9th Regt. was on the northern front and the 38th Regt. did not arrive until Aug. 19)
Regiments	
29th Infantry	0 (Less than a battalion-equivalent.)
5th RCT	2 battalion-equivalents (plus or minus)
Marine Bde	2 battalion-equivalents (plus or minus)
	22 (plus or minus)

** Battle losses had reduced most of these commands to roughly the battalion-equivalents shown.

P. 61 After the war, Michaelis had been reverted to lieutenant colonel. This was not unusual. Hundreds, if not thousands, of Regular Army officers were promoted one or more grades during WW II. They all knew that they had "permanent" and "temporary" grades and that, after the war, they could be required to return to their lower permanent grade.

Deployment of the 24th Infantry Division to Defend the Kum River

By July 13 the three infantry regiments of the 24th Division totaled 5,496 men. The 21st, with 1,100, was little more than the equivalent of one battalion; the 34th, with 2,020, equaled two battalions. The untried 19th had 2,276 troops. Because it was so badly battered, Dean ordered the 21st back to the vicinity of the Taejon airstrip for refitting and replacements. He now tried to delay elements of the *3d* and *4th Divisions* along the Kum River with the 19th and 34th Regiments, just four battalions

The 19th Infantry was moved from Taegu to Taejon on July 11, then on to the Kum to relieve the 21st Infantry, which took place on the morning of July 13.

Dean placed the 34th Infantry on the left and the 19th Infantry on the right. The 21st Infantry, with A/71st Tk Bn, from the 1st Cavalry Division, attached, and the 26th AAA Battalion were in division reserve near the Taejon airstrip.

The 3/34 was deployed along the Kum at Kongju. The 24th Reconnaissance Company (24 Recon Co.) screened the regiment's left (west) flank along the river for over 5 miles. Not including the Recon Co. area, 3/34 had a 4-mile river frontage. The 63 FAB was emplaced somewhat less than 3 miles back along the road from Kongju, the village of Taebong on later maps. The 1/34 was at Yongsong, about two miles farther south along the same road.

The 1/19 Inf. was at Taepyong-ni, with E/2/19th about 5 miles to the east, screening a 5 mile stretch of river eastward to the boundary with the ROK 2d Division on the 24th Division's right flank. A platoon of G Co. covered a potential river-crossing site about 3 miles west of Taepyong-ni, and the regimental Intelligence and Reconnaissance Platoon (I&R Plt) outposted 3 more miles of the river west of G's platoon. In air miles the 19th's sector was 15 miles wide, but the river frontage was 30 miles or more. The 2/19 (-Co. E and a platoon of G) was in reserve about two miles south of Taepyong-ni.

In all, the 1/19, 3/34, E/2/19, the Recon Co., the platoon of Co. G, and the I&R Plt could not have numbered over 2,000 infantrymen, on a frontage of 34 miles along the Kum River.

The Kum River represented the first major water obstacle to the North Koreans after they crossed the Han further north. The Kum flows generally south from its source in the mountains of southwest Korea, forming a giant loop north, east and southeast and 8-12 miles from Taejon. At Taepyong-ni the Kum was 200-300 yards wide, with banks 4 to 8 feet high. The water was 6 to 15 feet deep, with a current of 3 to 6 MPH. Sand-bars, wide bends and channels that shifted back and forth from the center characterized the river in this area. In 1950 two roads crossed the Kum toward Taejon, at Kongju and Taepyong-ni. The Seoul-Pusan railroad crossed the river 8 air miles north of Taejon and 9 air miles east of Taepyong-ni then headed south to Taejon.

Taejon, itself, was important for the road system which radiated east, south and south-west from it. There, too, the rail line split, the main line running east to Taegu, then south to Pusan. The other branch angled west, southwest, then south, with sub-branches serving Chonju, Kwangju and other locales in southwest Korea. It then turned east near the southern coast through Sunchon, Chinju and Masan, to rejoin the Taegu main line 25 or 30 miles north of Pusan.

The *NK 3d* and *4th Divisions* had both suffered heavy casualties. The *4th Division*, for example, was estimated to have between 5,000 and 6,000 men, 20 tanks and 40 to 50 artillery pieces. The *4th* was destined to attack the 34th and the *3d* would attack the 19th.

The Intelligence Section (G2) of the 24th Infantry Division issued Periodic Intelligence Report #2 (PIR #2) at 8 p.m. on July 13, covering the period from 6 p.m. on July 12 to 6 p.m. July 13, disclosing that the enemy was moving along roads toward Kongju; that groups of men varying in number from 10 to 50 had crossed the Kum River at three different points and that 41 tanks, a number of SP guns (SU 76) and artillery also were moving toward Kongju. 2LT Bai Jun Pal, a North Korean officer, was captured just before this report was issued. He said that the *793d Tank Battalion* was then at Umsong, and that the *16th Regiment* had been ordered to capture Kongju. The G2 ended the report by stating that the enemy's most likely course of action (C/A) would be to "Hold front and make wide envelopment of left flank; cross the Kum River and cut off 34th Inf from behind." His prediction was very accurate.

The *N.K. 4th Division* Flanks the 34th Regiment

The 3/34 had L, I and K Co.'s on line in that order, from west to east for about 2 miles along the river, just north of Kongju. The 81mm mortars of Co. M were behind them. The 63 FAB and 1/34 remained in their respective positions further south.

Communication within 3/34 was worse than ever. Telephone wire was unobtainable, and the wire used on delaying positions could not be retrieved when the pull-out had come. In Co. L, the CP could communicate with only one squad by sound-powered telephone. That squad, therefore, became the company's lookout. Company commander 1LT Archie L. Stith unsuccessfully tried to obtain a working radio at battalion headquarters, since his only communication with battalion was by messenger. Radio batteries were almost unobtainable.

D/3 ECB blew the steel truss bridge in front of Kongju at 4 A.M. on the 13th. The enemy set up a machine gun across the river a few hours after daylight, 700 yards in front of the 34th. A T-34 appeared on high ground north of the machine gun. The enemy began shelling Kongju that afternoon.

Roy Appleman writes in *South to the Naktong* that both the Regimental S2 and S3 were now evacuated because of combat fatigue, but morning reports for the regimental HHC do not substantiate this. One junior officer was evacuated as a non-battle casualty during this period. That night, the 40 men who were in Co. K were evacuated to Taejon, because their mental and physical state was such that they were deemed liabilities in combat. That left just two under-strength rifle companies on line. Wadlington estimated the two units together had only about 104 men.

LT Murray L. Carroll, of the 34th Regiment's S4 Section, knew that the supply situation was critical, particularly regarding food and ammunition. He had preceded the regiment back to Kongju, where his supply group was met by LTC Dixon, the Division G4. "He made a complete review of our supply picture," wrote Carroll. LT Carroll went back to Taejon with Dixon, who explained to division special staff officers what was needed. Division trucks would carry the supplies forward. "The Division Ordnance Officer informed me," Carroll wrote, "that he could not possibly do anything until the next day... his troops were still setting up cots, etc." Carroll added that he seriously considered killing this very stupid Ordnance officer on the spot. LTC Dixon intervened, telling Carroll to get some rest while he (Dixon) had the needed ammunition and supplies assembled. At 2 A.M. the next day, Carroll was able to return to the regiment with the much needed ammunition, rations and other supplies.

James A. Jones joined Co. I of the 34th as a replacement. James was a combat veteran of WW II and had been a member of the 27th Infantry in Japan, with the rank of Staff Sergeant (SSG). He joined I Co. at night on the Kum River and was assigned to take over a rifle squad. "It was pitch dark and all you could see were dark objects," he said. "I wasn't even told how many men I had, much less where they were... . [I] knew better than to go roaming around under these circumstances... . So I found me a place and dug in and [waited] for daylight. This turned out to be a smart move, because some time later in the night a shot rang out... one of the men had killed one of our own... [a] J. Jemete."

CPT Melicio Montesclaros, of the 19th, visited I/34 and told them that there was a 2-mile gap between the company and his left flank position of the 19th. (See Chapter Notes.) As daylight came on July 14, men of the 34th heard enemy tanks in the village across the river. By 6 a.m. Item Co. was under flat trajectory fire, possibly from tanks. It was believed that their target was the mortar position behind the company. At the same time, air-burst artillery rounds exploded above Love Company, but too high to be effective. Then L Co. observers reported about 60 North Koreans crossing the river in two barges 2 miles to the south. Between 8 and 9:30 a.m., they estimated that 500 enemy soldiers crossed at that site. This was part of the *16th Regiment (4th Division)*.

A spotter plane from the 63 FAB also reported enemy crossings at about the same time and same location. The artillery battalion S3, MAJ Charles T. Barter passed up firing on the crossing in favor of larger targets later on. A platoon of A/11

FAB (155mm) did fire briefly on the crossing site but, when a YAK fighter chased the spotter plane away, they ceased firing.

LT Stith couldn't find the machine gun and mortar sections supporting his company. His L Co. was receiving ever-heavier, ever-more-accurate enemy mortar and artillery fire. Stith felt that his position had become untenable. Just before 11 a.m. he ordered the unit to withdraw from their positions, and he went in search of the 3d Bn CP. He finally found it at Nonsan, 20 or more miles south of Kongju, and told the battalion commander, MAJ Lantron, what he had done. He was summarily relieved of command, and Lantron threatened him with court-martial.

When L Co. came through the 63 FAB positions, SGT Wallace A. Wagnebreth, a platoon sergeant of the unit, told an artillery officer about the enemy river crossing. Wagnebreth said the artillery officer showed little interest.

Destruction of the 63 FAB

The 63 FAB was in position three miles from the river, with batteries were in a north-south line (A, HQ and B in that order) over a distance of about 500 yards along a secondary road near the village of Samyo (or Samgyo), recalled Art Lombardi, an officer in Battery A. The road was bordered by hills covered by scrub pine. LT Lombardi was a parachute field artilleryman in WWII, and had combat experience as a gun captain, chief of section and first sergeant. He retired in 1978 as a COL.

The 63d had little respite since first going into action on July 7 near Chonan, Lombardi recalled. Able Battery's FO with the 34th was killed that night — the first casualty for the 63d. From July 7-11, the battalion had been shooting and moving continuously.

On July 11, the battalion had been just north of the Kum River, where it had fired the last of its ammunition and withdrawn, on order, to these positions near Samyo. The men were physically and mentally exhausted. Like most of the other American soldiers who came to Korea at the time, the monsoon heat and chronic dysentery which affected almost everyone was extremely enervating to them.

The battalion was in communication with the 34th CP near Nonsan, but not with the infantry, nor the FOs with them on the Kum River. This severely reduced the effective use of artillery support for the front-line infantrymen. LTC Robert H. Dawson had commanded the 63d until July 13. That day he was evacuated to Taejon because of illness. MAJ William E. Dressler was now in command.

The 63d had outposts on the hills near the battery positions. About 1:30 p.m. on July 14 one of the outposts reported the enemy approaching its position. It was told to hold fire; the approaching men might be friendly soldiers. They were not. The enemy captured the OP and its machine gun. They turned the gun on HQ. Battery, beginning the enemy's attack on the 63 FAB. These were troops of the *16th Infantry*.

The first attack on Able Battery came from the northeast. "They came swarming across a rice paddy," Lombardi wrote. "Fortunately, the ground attack was preceded by a mortar barrage. This provided the... defense the time to react." Men of the

battery opened on the attackers with small arms fire. Faced with this resistance, the enemy withdrew to near-by foothills, but mortar fire continued to fall into the battery position.

"The second attack came... more from the east... within minutes of the first attack," Lombardi wrote. This second attack would have overrun the battery "had not an enemy mortar round made a direct hit on a fully-loaded ammunition truck... in the center of the battery position." The exploding artillery ammunition halted the enemy short of the battery area.

Mortar fire, combined with that from the captured machine gun, swept over HQ Battery while Battery A was under attack. The first mortar round destroyed the headquarters switchboard, cutting telephone communications to the two firing batteries. The medical section, the CP radio truck and another truck laden with ammunition all were hit in rapid succession. Exploding artillery shells added to the destruction and chaos in HQ Battery.

"Immediately after the first attack," Lombardi continued, "the battery commander recognized that the position was untenable and made the decision to evacuate the position on foot." The road was in control of the enemy. "His instructions to me before leaving the area was to destroy the guns and to then leave. Remaining with me were two men."

CPL Lawrence A. Ray and PVT Fred M. Odle were members of Battery A. CPL Ray, though twice wounded, manned his BAR until a mortar burst wounded him again and knocked him unconscious. When he regained consciousness he crawled into a ditch. There he found 15 other artillerymen, all weaponless. The group escaped south. On the way, they discovered the body of the A Battery commander, CPT Lundel M. Southerland.

Meantime, LT Lombardi and his two men sought shelter from shells exploding in the ammo truck in deep foxholes to the rear of the gun positions. They remained there for several hours. When most of the rounds from the truck had exploded, Lombardi checked the gun positions. "No live crewmen were present," he wrote. "The tires of the howitzers were burned.... I smashed the sights." Enemy bodies dotted the rice paddies in front of the battery area, the result of the first attack. It was now late afternoon. The lieutenant knew that the enemy soon would enter the position, so he and his two men began to withdraw. They had gone scarcely a hundred yards when they discovered the bodies of CPT Southerland and his men.

Enemy machine gun fire cut off the men in a building housing the Fire Direction Center (FDC). The men slipped out into a dugout, then a ravine, and escaped to Service Battery, farther south.

The enemy attacked Baker Battery with some 400 men about 2:15 p.m. They opened fire with machine guns into the battery's rear. The BC, CPT Anthony F. Stahelski, responded with two of his machine guns. Enemy mortar fire then began to fall, hitting two howitzers, a radio jeep and a 2 1/2-ton prime mover. Then a group of South Korean cavalry intervened, attacking west into the enemy. The confusion was so great that no one recalls what resulted from this charge. When CPT Stahelski gave the battery "March

Order" at 3 p.m., it was impossible to retrieve the artillery pieces. The men escaped on foot.

The 63 FAB lost all 10 of its howitzers. In addition to the five guns lost by Battery A, two of the five in Battery B were destroyed by enemy mortar fire, and before they withdrew, the battery members removed the firing locks of the other three. Appleman wrote that the Battery A guns fell to the enemy intact.

As noted above, some men arrived at Service Battery before that unit withdrew. Remnants of the battalion assembled at Nonsan. The next day a count showed 11 officers and 125 EM missing. Among these were MAJ Dressler and CPL Edward L. McCall. Their bodies were found in a common foxhole almost 2 1/2 years later.

LT Lombardi, the only surviving officer of A/63, was given a howitzer a few days later. "There were only enough men to man one [gun] section," he wrote. He and the gun crew were attached to the 11 FAB. That howitzer was lost at Taejon.

GEN Dean's Operations Instructions No. 3, issued on July 14, directed the 34th to "hold Kongju with not to exceed one (1) BCT [Battalion Combat Team]." The regiment also had the mission of preparing delaying positions "along main routes leading south from Kong-ju." To accomplish that, LTC Wadlington left his CP at Ponggong-ni early on July 14 to reconnoiter the Nonsan area for likely delaying positions. He returned to his CP in midafternoon. Some time between 3 and 4 p.m. he was informed by an escaped member of the 63 FAB that the battalion had been overrun. He immediately ordered LTC Ayres to counterattack north with the 1/34 to recover the ground, howitzers and surviving artillerymen.

1/34 Attack to Recover 63 FAB Positions

LTC Ayres wrote to Roy Appleman Oct. 3, 1952, stating that his battalion was "in a defensive position some 6 miles southwest of Kongju. My instructions from the regimental commander were to protect the east flank of the regimental zone and be prepared to move anyplace in the zone on order." Ayres formed his battalion into a perimeter astride the road and "sent small detachments to outpost the Kum River and give early warning of any enemy movement." LTC Ayres wrote that his battalion was about 2-3 miles from the 63 FAB, but that he had heard no small arms firing from that direction. He was out of his CP much of the time.

While Ayres was out of his CP, 1LT Herman W. Starling, 63 FAB Communications Officer stated that he went to the CP of 1/34 about 2 p.m. and reported to an unnamed officer that the 63d was under attack and asked for help. Starling's report and request for help never got to Ayres nor to any of his principal staff.

The first word Ayres claims to have had of the attack on the 63d came from regiment, when LTC Wadlington ordered him "to attack and save any men or equipment in the area — this was about three in the afternoon," LTC Ayres recalled. "Wadlington also told me that if we succeeded by nightfall we were not to continue but were to withdraw. He stressed the fact that we were not to be cut off up there after dark."

The 1/34 moved out in a column of companies on this mission about 5 p.m. with Co. C leading. The battalion "ran into intense small arms fire from the high ground overlooking the position," Ayres wrote. "We were able to take out a couple of wounded men and a couple of jeeps. We looked for other men but found none; we also tried to start some of the vehicles but were unsuccessful. The small arms fire continued to rake the road and low ground as we attempted to move around the area. I was with the lead company and just after dark I ordered a withdrawal.... . The orders received from the regimental commander were sound... . We had searched the area for men and to risk a battalion to recover equipment would have been silly." Returning to its former position, 1/34 loaded onto trucks and drove south toward Nonsan.

Item Co., 34th stayed on its positions along the Kum by itself. Enemy mortar fire fell near the position until about noon. Shortly thereafter, enemy artillery fire from across the river took up the bombardment. LT Joseph E. Hicks, acting company CO, tried without success to find Co. L and the 3d Bn CP. Some men from the Heavy Weapons Co. told him that there were enemy roadblocks in his rear, cutting off the unit. Except for the shelling, the company was left alone by the enemy. Under orders, Hicks led the unit in withdrawal at 9:30 that night. The unit rejoined the regiment, which took up positions east of Nonsan early on July 15. The *N.K. 5th Regiment* captured Kongju.

Before the end of the day on July 14, the enemy's *4th Division* was across the Kum River in force, threatening the 19th Infantry's left flank. On July 15 the 24th Division called in air strikes to destroy the guns and equipment left behind by the 63d.

The 34th Regiment, at Nonsan, was well south of any part of the 19th. At 4:30 p.m. Dean, trying to make the best of the situation, sent this message to the 34th:

"Hold everything we have until we find out were we stand - might not be too bad - may be able to hold - make reconnaissance - may be able to knock these people out and reconsolidate. Am on my way there now."

He briefed the 21st Inf. commander, COL Stephens on the situation. "We must coordinate so that the 19th and 34th come out together," he told Stephens, and asked the COL to come to the Division CP to discuss his plans.

Some of the *4th Division* crossed the Kum at Kongju on July 15, harassed by U.S. air strikes, which destroyed some of their boats and killed or wounded a number of their men. Only two tanks were spotted south of the river. Enemy armor crossed later on — either after dark or the next day.

The 19th Infantry vs. the *N.K. 3d Division*

The 19th Infantry (Rock of Chickamauga) Regiment had not yet been committed to battle. GEN Dean had served as a captain with the 19th in Hawaii in 1936.

LT Robert G. Fox recalled his landing in Korea and move forward to Taegu. Fox was a March 1949 graduate of OCS. He was an enlisted man in the airborne infantry in WW II,

and later in military intelligence, and now a military police officer, commanding the MP detachment attached to the 19th Infantry. When the regiment landed at Pusan, the Korean stevedores refused to unload the ships, Fox recalled. "The American troops, plus the Japanese crews ended up unloading the ships," he wrote.

When the unloading was completed, COL Meloy assembled the officers, outlined the plans and issued map overlays. After the briefing, he turned to LT Fox. "Fox," he said, "I want you to take your six tanks and 24 MPs to Taegu. You are the advance element. Set up regimental headquarters when you get there."

Meloy grinned as he gave this order. There were no tanks. Fox had six jeeps and 24 men. All the officers "broke up laughing," Fox wrote, but the remark broke much of the tension they felt confronting the unknown of impending battle. LT Fox could not remember much after the trip to Taegu. He was severely wounded soon after that and evacuated to Japan.

On the Kum River, the main defensive force of the 19th, the 1st Battalion, was astride the Seoul-Pusan highway where it crossed the Kum River at Taepyong-ni. Co. B overlooked the river west of the road on a front of just over a mile. The 1st Platoon of Co. B, dug in behind a dike, tied in with Co. A on its right. Co. A was east of the road and Taepyong-ni on a 1 1/2 mile front. One of its platoons was a mile south of the Taepyong-ni area on a 500-foot-high hill mass. Co. C (CPT Henry T. MacGill) was three miles east of the town on the battalion's right flank, atop Hill 200 overlooking the river, covering just under a mile of riverfront. On a river frontage of about 30 miles, only about four miles were occupied in strength. Huge gaps — measured in miles — existed to the battalion's left and right and outposts and OPs (observation posts) of the regiment further along the river.

Engineers destroyed the highway bridge over the river on July 13, and the railroad bridge further upstream at Sinchon on July 15.

CPT Melicio Montesclaros commanded the platoon of Co. G, the I & R Platoon (about 70 men), a platoon of engineers and a battery of artillery, all screening the western-most 3 miles of the regimental sector. CPT Upham's E/19th Inf. screened an area of over 6 miles along the river in the east, where the 24th Division right flank and the ROK 2d Division's left flank joined.

The CP of 1/19 (LTC Otho T Winstead) was at Kadong, a village on the road about a mile south of the river. The regimental CP was another mile farther south on the road at Palsan. LTC Thomas M. McGrail commanded 2/19. His battalion, less Co. E and a platoon of G, constituted the reserve and were just south of Palsan. Co. F was west of the road and G(-) was to the east. Part of the 4.2-inch (Heavy Mortar or HM Co., CPT Elliot C. Cutler Jr.) was just east of the road in rear of the platoon of Co. A on the hills. Another element of HM Co. was located a little over a mile south of Co. C.

Three artillery battalions supported the 19th - the 52 and 13 FABs (105mm) and the 11 FAB (155mm), each with two firing batteries. LTC Charles W. Stratton's 13 FAB coordinated the firing of all three battalions. The 52d was along the road near Tumanni, just south of 2/19. The 11th

and 13th were another mile further back; the 11th on the left and the 13th on the right of the highway. Four M-24 light tanks from A/78 Heavy Tank Battalion and a few quad-.50s from the 26th AAA AW Battalion were attached to the 19th.

In spite of air strikes, the enemy built up armor opposite 1/19. Dug-in T-34s began firing directly into the regimental sector at 1 p.m. on July 14. Eleven dug-in enemy tanks were spotted firing as artillery. Weak enemy efforts to cross the river at Taepyong-ni were easily halted by the defenders. Then came the news that the 34th Infantry had withdrawn from the Kongju area under GEN Dean's orders.

At midnight, GEN Dean issued Op Instr #4. The 34th was to withdraw and occupy new positions; the 19th was to remain and defend in place. The 21st was to prepare to counter-attack north from the vicinity of Taejon east of the railroad "in a northerly direction." Service support elements of the division were ordered back to Yongdong or Kumchon.

At 7 a.m. on July 15, the 19th's I & R Platoon reported an enemy river-crossing attempt, but the platoon's machine guns and air strikes stopped them. Shortly after, a patrol from the platoon trying to contact the 34th Regiment engaged the enemy while in the 34th's former sector.

COL Meloy realized his left flank was in danger. He sent LTC McGrail with the remainder of Co. G, a platoon of machine guns, an 81mm mortar section, two tanks and two quad-.50s to reinforce the left. B/13 FAB was directed to support this force, known as Task Force McGrail. Dean knew that Meloy would have to deploy troops to protect this flank.

At 6 a.m. on July 15, the 21st Infantry began moving to Okchon, 10 miles east of Taejon. The 1/21 numbered 517 men; 3/21, consolidated as K and M Co.'s (132 men) was attached to 1/21. The regiment also had a provisional formation of 466 troops. With some 1,100 men, it was a shadow regiment, at best.

Strengths of companies, battalions and regiments did fluctuate. Replacement troops came in during these first weeks, but were lost an alarming rate. As a result, none of the regiments or other major formation of the 24th Division could substantially increase its present for duty strength.

The mission of the 21st near Okchon was to protect the Division's rear area from penetration out of the ROK sector to the east. The regimental line was established about 5 miles east of Taejon and somewhat less than 2 miles east of one highway and one railroad tunnel. The 21st occupied some of the highest ridges in the area, but its lines did not control the tunnels.

The 21st did control a secondary road leading south from the Kum. Engineers prepared the tunnels for demolition. The enemy never achieved a breakthrough in the ROK sector, but locating and leaving the 21st in this area effectively took them out of the forthcoming battle for Taejon.

Meloy prepared to repel any enemy attempt to cross the river on the night of July 15. His artillery and mortars fired into villages and other known or suspected enemy assembly points. Air strikes also were called in, and the villages were consumed in flames.

Enemy POWs later confirmed that the air strikes severely impeded North Korean preparations for a crossing. Tanks, heavy mortars and artillery pieces moved in peril of being destroyed. The morale of the *3d Division* nose-dived. Political officers told the men that, once Taejon was captured, the Americans would surrender and they would have a long rest.

2LT Charles C. Early, commanding 3d Platoon, B/19, spotted nine T-34s rounding a bend in the road across the river, about two miles away. It was just getting dark. He telephoned a report to his company commander. Three of the tanks pulled off the road, traversed their guns and began firing toward Early. Most rounds passed overhead. Battalion called for an air strike. Two planes responded, causing all the tanks but one to hide in nearby woods. The lone tank was destroyed. When the aircraft left, enemy infantry were brought to the north bank of the river in trucks.

Some of the enemy waded into the river, while others ran out and jumped off the end of the destroyed bridge, trying to swim across, but battalion recoilless rifle and machine gun fire thwarted this attempt. Elsewhere, some of the enemy did cross under covering tank fire.

Meanwhile, Co. C, on Hill 200, repelled three crossing attempts in their sector. During this action, two 81mm mortar rounds fell short, destroying two of the company's 60mm mortars and broke the base plate of the third. Improvising a base plate, CPL Tabor fired some 300 mortar rounds while holding the tube in his hand.

These first enemy attacks were mere probes. An enemy plane flew over the battalion at 3 a.m. on July 16 and dropped a flare, signaling the main attack. Enemy guns of almost every type opened fire. Meloy likened the intensity of this bombardment to the heaviest he had experienced during WW II, when he was a division chief of staff.

As their mortars, artillery and other weapons raked American positions, the North Koreans swarmed to the attack; some waded or swam, others utilized boats and rafts. The Americans met the attackers with every weapon available.

A 155mm howitzer of the 11 FAB was firing flares over the river on call. In the midst of the enemy's attack, 1/19 called back through regiment for a slight adjustment of fire. Misunderstanding the request, the artillerymen shifted the howitzer to an azimuth which required moving the gun trails. As a result, there were no howitzer flares over the crossing area for quite some time. The 1/19 commander, LTC Winstead, later said this mistake and the loss of flare support was more damaging to his battalion's defense than anything else.

The 1/19 pretty much thwarted the North Koreans in their sector. But about 4 a.m., the enemy found and exploited the huge gap between C and E Co.'s. They struck C's 1st Platoon on the right flank finger of Hill 200. The platoon leader, LT Thomas A. Maher, was killed just after telling LT Henry T. McGill, "We're doing fine." The enemy overran the platoon in their fourth assault. The platoon sergeant and about a dozen others managed to escape. Charlie Company consolidated what was left of the unit on the middle finger of the hill and stood fast. Meantime, the enemy exploited the gap they had found by moving into rear areas and attacking the 4.2s, CPs, and the like.

While the enemy probed across the river on the battalion's right, the North Korean main crossing apparently took place between Co. B's left flank and the G Co. platoon several miles downstream. At first light, Baker Co. spotted about 300-400 enemy soldiers on high ground to the southwest, well into the left rear of the battalion. The enemy crossing was still in progress as groups of 25-30 men, holding their weapons and equipment overhead wadded neck-deep across one of the ferry sites.

COL Meloy, from his OP, also could see the crossing site, but not much more. Both Co. B and Meloy called artillery fire onto the crossing. Meloy's artillery liaison officer (Ln O), CPT Monroe Anderson, who was with Co. B, noted that some of the North Koreans moved south after crossing the river while many more remained on the hills and ridges camouflaged with small trees and shrubs. LT Early, concerned about a possible enemy attack on the rear of his platoon, moved to a better spot from which to observe the North Koreans. For an hour, he watched the enemy move south past Baker's left.

By 6:30 a.m., LTC Winstead reported to Meloy's headquarters that both his CP and the HM Co. were under attack and that the center of the battalion was withdrawing. The enemy's persistence at and near the bridge had paid off. By 8 a.m. they had overrun part of Co. A, the platoon of Co. B along the dike and on the high ground at Kadong-ni. Baker's weapons platoon leader, LT John A. English, saw the platoon being overwhelmed. Throwing off his helmet, he ran down the hill, jumped into a small stream between him and the platoon and swam across to it. He succeeded in leading out 14 survivors.

MSG Jack Y. Buff was in 1/19 at the time. A nationally-known marksman with both the M1 rifle and .45-cal automatic pistol, Jack first engaged the enemy with his rifle. As they got closer, he switched to his .45, until captured. Jack was murdered by the enemy about Nov. 6, 1950.

COL Meloy already had taken action to consolidate his regiment and reinforce his reserve by recalling TF McGrail. About 4 a.m. the 2/19 S2 sergeant, SFC Joseph McKeon, was sent to bring G Co. back to the regiment. During WW II, SFC McKeon had been in what later became known as "Long Range Patrolling" — behind enemy lines. He and a jeep driver set out. McKeon insisted that the driver raise the windshield on the jeep before they left. Down the road, the enemy had strung wire across the road at the height where it would have caught the men seated in the jeep about neck level. If the windshield had not been up, he and the driver would have been killed. Shortly thereafter, all jeeps were fitted with a 6 to 8-foot boom, attached at right angles to the front of the jeep, effectively disposing of wires strung across roads and trails.

Upon arrival at G Co. (CPT Michael Barszcz), McKeon found LTC McGrail and CPT Montesclaros and relayed COL Meloy's message. Soon thereafter, 2LT Robert E. Nash, 2/19 S4, appeared with a number of trucks. "I can only surmise," wrote McKeon, "that he and I had been given the same mission."

Nash had been on his way from the rear with a resupply of ammunition when he was stopped by heavy enemy fire about three miles south of the regiment's rear. He managed to get through

to COL Meloy on the phone. Meloy ordered him to find McGrail and bring "G and H Co.'s to break the roadblock." At about the same time, the COL was informed that the 13 FAB was under attack.

While SFC McKeon was on his mission to TF McGrail, colonels Meloy and Winstead scraped together a counterattack force from members of the 1st Bn HQ and regimental HQ Co. All available officers, clerks, cooks, drivers, mechanics and the security platoon, reinforced by a tank and a quad-.50, counterattacked. The enemy was driven from the high ground at Kadong-ni by 9 a.m. CPT Cutler, with a patrol from his company, swept the village and rice paddies to its front. They found the village empty, but got two of the enemy in the paddies.

MAJ John M. Cook (XO, 1/19) and CPT Alan Hacket (S1, 1/19) were among those killed during this battle. CPT Wayne B. Macomber (S3, 1/19) was captured and died in a POW camp in July 1951. A number of the enemy, impressed by this determined assault, recrossed the river. Meloy believed he had thrown the North Koreans back and that his regiment was in pretty good shape. He notified GEN Dean, saying he could hold on until dark, then fall back to another delaying position closer to Taejon.

There were too many North Koreans in the 19th Infantry rear areas. Winstead reported them behind his lines. This, along with the attack on his artillery and Nash's report of a roadblock three miles south, convinced Meloy that the regiment would have to fight its way out.

The colonel called for the first air strikes since mid-morning. Accompanied by his S3, MAJ Edward O. Logan, he went to investigate the situation at the roadblock at about 11 a.m. Before leaving on the reconnaissance, Meloy gave instructions to Winstead concerning a night withdrawal by 1/19.

The enemy which established the roadblock had come through west of Baker Co. Some North Koreans turned off to engage the only available regimental reserve, Co. F, while the remainder either attacked the artillery positions or helped form the roadblock.

Buford Goff was a member of Co. F., having served with the Arizona National Guard. He was in Japan with F/19 when the Korean War started.

There, near the Kum River with Co. F, 17-year-old Goff was a radio operator, armed with the type of sub-machinegun called a "grease gun." It was called this because it resembled the grease gun used to lubricate vehicles. The first night in position "was very quiet," he said, but "so dark - - there was no moon." He went on, "I'd never experienced combat.... The unknown, the uncertainty, every whisper, every crack of a leaf... it's just startling, you don't know what to expect.... I do remember that just at the crack of dawn... the [enemy]... opened up with mortar, artillery, automatic [weapons] and the screeching of bugles... .It was one more hell morning... "The company had a number of casualties, "but it [the enemy fire] stopped as abruptly as it started."

LTC Perry (52 FAB) looked out from his CP near Tuman-ni about 10 a.m. to see a long file of North Koreans dressed in white clothing move over a ridge two miles to the west and disappear southward over another hill. He had Able Battery fire on them and notified the 13 FAB south of him of the approaching enemy. A group of the enemy, in regulation North Korean Army uniforms, began to attack Baker Battery with mortar fire, killing the battery commander and first sergeant almost immediately. 1LT William H. Steele, battery XO, took over and directed the defense of the battery position.

In the first months of the Korean War, enemy soldiers often dressed in the white clothing of civilians in order to infiltrate U.S. and ROK lines and to mingle with the masses of refugees fleeing south. Once behind American or ROK lines, these soldiers left the refugee column and slipped into remote mountainous areas of the south, from which they attacked individual vehicles, convoys and rear area installations. Often, these enemy troops slipped through the lines, then coordinated their assaults with North Korean offensive operations. Attempts to screen refugees to detect infiltrators were only partly successful because of the huge number of refugees.

Having recovered from his wounds while with TF Smith, Howard A. Stevens rejoined the 52 FAB on July 15. He recalled that the North Korean attack on B Battery began about 1 p.m. "COL Perry rounded up all the HQ personnel he could find," Stevens wrote, "and we attacked the North Koreans. I was with COL Perry and he was doing everything; directing fire here and there. We finally got some... tank support along with some infantry [from the 19th] and pushed the North Koreans up in[to] the hills."

Before noon, the enemy began establishing a roadblock about 800 yards south of the 52 FAB position, below Tuman-ni where the road made a sharp bend. There was a narrow pass at this point with a steep 40' embankment and drop-off to the small Yongsu River on the west side of the road, and a steep hillside on the east. There was no way that a vehicle could bypass the area. As the day wore on, the enemy extended and strengthened their hold on the road at this point. Vehicles and men piled up at the block.

COL Meloy might have anticipated the enemy getting into the rear area and onto his MSR, but with the troops he had available and his mission to defend the river, he had nothing with which to oppose such a move.

The 11 and 13 FABs were about a mile south of this point. Although both battalions were subjected to long-range fire and, by 11 a.m., had lost communication with their FOs, they continued to fire on the Kum River crossings.

Meloy and Logan found complete disorganization at the roadblock. Some men were returning desultory fire in the general direction of the enemy. No one was in charge. COL Meloy set about organizing troops to attack the roadblock when he was shot in the calf of one leg. He turned over command of all troops along the Kum River to LTC Winstead.

MAJ Logan contacted GEN Dean about 1 P.M. The G2 Journal recorded: "COL Meloy hit in calf of leg. Winstead in command. Vehicles badly jammed. Baker Battery is no more. Will fight them and occupy position in rear. Both sides of road. Vehicles jammed. Taking a pounding in front. Air Force does not seem able to find or silence tanks." Other reports indicate B/52 FAB was still "alive."

Dean responded that he was preparing a force to break the block but that he could not get there until about 3:30 p.m. He directed the 19th to withdraw immediately with as many personnel and as much equipment as possible. Right after this, the regiment's radio truck was destroyed by enemy fire, ending all communication with division. Winstead directed Logan to try to knock out the roadblock and get someone through to the approaching relief force. LTC Winstead went back to his 1st Battalion, where about 1:30 p.m., he ordered it to withdraw. He was killed some time afterward.

CPT Cutler, HM Co., wrote, "When the withdrawal order was received we attempted to torch the heavy mortars but only succeeded in getting one of the men burned. So we contented ourselves with removing the sights and commenced withdrawal along the road to the rear."

As 1/19 started to pull out, some companies or platoons were in their original positions while others had been forced back by enemy pressure. In Co. C, incoming mortar fire pinned men in their foxholes, and unit officers had trouble getting them out to withdraw. CPL Jack Arawaka's machine gun blew up in his face. Although deafened, nearly blind and wounded at other places on his body, he picked up a BAR and continued fighting. He was still firing from his foxhole when company survivors left Hill 200.

Part of the company left under 2LT Augustus B. Orr. They came upon a group of enemy soldiers lying partly covered by the water of a rice paddy, apparently dead. Orr noticed one, clutching a hand grenade, send up bubbles and open his eyes. The enemy soldiers were pretending to be dead, intending to kill Orr and his men once they had passed. Instead, Orr and his men shot and killed all the enemy soldiers.

Able and Baker Co.'s preceded Charlie Co. down the road in withdrawal. Co. C's move toward the road flanked a body of enemy troops, who promptly ran back toward the bridge. As the company began moving along the road, it was taken under fire by an estimated six enemy machine guns from a hill east of Palsan-ni. The company scattered; the men made their way out the best way they could. Some of the escapees saw American wounded in the ditches along the road, being tended by valiant medical aidmen who stayed behind with them.

F Company's left front, left flank and left rear were now under heavy enemy fire, as it covered the withdrawal of Co. B.

Almost-complete disorganization still prevailed at the roadblock. Enemy machine guns raked the area. A number of attacks by small groups of men all came to naught. One was aborted when a flight of four F-51s attacked the hill. Another, led by LT Lloyd D. Smith (81mm mortar platoon, D/19) and another officer also crumbled as men were killed or wounded or just dropped off along the way.

Harold Stevens, of the 52 FAB, was at the roadblock. "All vehicles were bottled up bumper to bumper (approx. 80)," he wrote. "We were told a machine gun along with some infantry were zeroed in on the road... A LT from the infantry was asking for volunteers to knock that machine gun out so we could move these vehicles along with the wounded... and get this stalled column out. I went along with this group

of artillery and infantry guys. We numbered about 40... ." The men thought they were going against an enemy machine gun and about a platoon of men. "I did not know any of these group," Stevens continued. "But I was next to a guy named Charlie (forgot his last name)." The plan was to go along the road until they came to the roadblock, then go up into the hills "knock out the machine gun and drive off the North Koreans."

"We found the roadblock [about] 2 miles... from our artillery position... .One ambulance and two jeeps [were] all shot up and one three-quarter-[ton] truck upside down in the ditch... .It was apparent that this was [the] kill zone... ."

Two volunteer scouts led the group up the hill on the right of the road heading south, planning to take the enemy in flank. The scouts were about 20 yards forward of the main body. It was about 3 p.m.

"I was near the end of the column when all hell broke loose — we [had] walked right into their positions. We shot it out for about 15 minutes. But all our guys were dead or wounded," Stevens wrote. "I jumped up with Charlie, and ran over a little knoll right into two North Koreans. The first one opened up with his burp gun. Charlie took 5 or 6 rounds in the chest... and I got hit in the left leg." Stevens killed the two North Koreans. Charlie was dead. Stevens' M1 rifle had been malfunctioning so he took Charlie's and ran from the ambush area. It was now dark. "I was so tired I couldn't think properly. I laid down for a short rest and awoke with a sharp pain in my kidney area." Five enemy soldiers were standing over him; Stevens became a POW.

From time to time, men tried to push vehicles out of the way to allow others to pass, but each time the road was temporarily cleared, enemy machine gunners raked the area, creating more casualties and destroying more vehicles, blocking the road again. Air strikes had no effect on the enemy roadblock. Two light tanks at the block also were unsuccessful in knocking out the enemy guns. Further, Fox Company was almost completely surrounded and could not attack south against the roadblock, as ordered.

MAJ Logan tried to determine the extent of the roadblock and locate a by-pass. About 2:30 p.m., he put CPT Edgar R. Fenstermacher in command at the roadblock. Taking 20 men, Logan moved to the east, then south. Some two hours later they came into the position of the 13 FAB. The battalion was beginning to withdraw to the south. Within a few minutes, GEN Dean appeared with two light tanks, two quad-.50 and two 40mm gun AA vehicles.

Nash had run the roadblock on his way to find McGrail, but his jeep was destroyed by enemy fire. He borrowed another from the 13 FAB and got to McGrail's CP at Sangwang-ni. After delivering Meloy's message, the lieutenant drove back to the Taejon airstrip for trucks in which to move McGrail's men. The ADC, BG Menoher, had to order the trucks be given to Nash for the mission. When SSG McKeon met Nash in the G Co. area, Nash was returning from Taejon with trucks to transport the company. McGrail had gone on ahead to the 13 FAB CP to await the arrival of his infantry and the armor and AA vehicles Dean had promised.

Logan briefed Dean on the roadblock situation and offered to lead the attack to break the block. Dean told him to go south instead, and form a new position west of the Taejon airfield. LTC McGrail was ordered to lead the roadblock attack. As Dean and Logan stood on the road in conversation, five jeeps careened down the road toward them. In the lead jeep was LTC Homer B. Chandler (XO, 19th Inf.). The other jeeps were filled with wounded, many of whom had been hit again by enemy fire as they dashed through the roadblock.

The relief column started forward, one tank leading, followed by the AA vehicles. The remaining tank brought up the rear. About a mile north of the 13 FAB position enemy machine gun and light antitank fire tore into the column, killing and wounding the soldiers on the AA half tracks. The column was halted on a straight stretch of road. Two vehicles returned fire as the infantry jumped into roadside ditches. McGrail, too, dove for cover, noting the wreckage of COL Meloy's and Logan's jeeps. The four AA vehicles soon were destroyed by enemy fire, and 90 percent of the men in these vehicles became casualties. LTC McGrail managed to crawl back along the ditch and out of enemy fire. The relief column had been stopped within 400 yards of the remnants of the 19th Regiment on the other side of the block. Tanks fired into the roadblock until about 4 p.m., when they used up all their ammunition.

All this while Joseph McKeon was trying to return to the 19th. As he approached the turn in the road, just north of the town of Yusong, to take him back to the regiment, "A figure stepped out from the side of the road holding a hand up in the air," McKeon wrote.

It was BG Menoher. He told McKeon, "You can't do any good up there, so pull over into that schoolyard," pointing to a nearby building.

Just at this time, CPT Barszcz arrived with G Co. CPT Montesclaros had stayed behind with the I & R Platoon and some engineers. They blew craters in the road, then withdrew. GEN Menoher first ordered Barszcz to deploy his company along the riverbank in Yusong, but then directed him to lead the unit forward to the roadblock. Barszcz "hadn't gone far when [a small convoy of vehicles led by a 2 1/2-ton truck] came racing down the road.... They started yelling something about 'the Gook tanks are coming.' Barszcz swung his vehicles sideways in the road," McKeon wrote, "and had his troops... deploy.... When... nothing happened, he reloaded and started north again." Appleman states that G Co. was afoot.

Meeting GEN Dean a short time later, CPT Barszcz was ordered to try to break the roadblock from the south. Six miles north of Yusong and two miles below Tuman-ni, George Co. came under long range fire. The captain then was ordered to move along the high ground to the left of the road toward the enemy, believed to be about a half mile ahead. The unit suffered a number of casualties while climbing the hill. It was dusk when they arrived at the top. The company dug in for the night, but then were summoned to return to the road and withdraw.

The roadblock now covered about a mile and a half on a hill mass overlooking a straight stretch of road between the curving pass southward to another sharp curve.

Many troops did not come south as far as the roadblock, but broke off in small groups into the hills and made their way southward toward Taejon.

Cutler and his unit came to where the vehicles were held up by the roadblock. There, he met COL Meloy. "He directed me to form a rear guard out of the Heavy Mortar Co.," wrote Cutler, "so we took position along a low ridge in front of that place. After a while the motor column took off down the road. And then the remaining 1st Bn troops [there] departed across country. After a respectable pause we followed the route of the foot column and reached Taejon the next morning [July 17]."

About 6 p.m. staff officers put the wounded COL Meloy into the last remaining tank. It rammed through the jam of disabled trucks to freedom, followed by about 20 other vehicles, then enemy fire closed the block for good. A few miles beyond the roadblock the tank stopped because of mechanical failure, and COL Meloy ordered the tank destroyed. Tank commander LT J.N. Roush dropped a thermite grenade into it. All the vehicles that had followed the tank sped on by. None stopped. Co. G came upon Meloy and the tank crew. Someone finally returned from Yusong with a truck and evacuated the COL and the other wounded with him.

About 7 p.m., CPT Fenstermacher ordered the men with him at the roadblock to escape cross-country to Taejon. There were about 500 men there at the time, many critically wounded. The severely wounded and others incapable of walking were put on litters. Fenstermacher and a party of men poured gasoline on the vehicles, about 100, and set them on fire. The captain was shot and wounded in the neck at this time. About 9 p.m. the last of the men at the roadblock moved into the hills east of the highway, bent on escape.

A mixed group of infantrymen, engineers, medics and headquarters personnel, about 100 men in all, took some 30 wounded with them, including some on litters. Forty men acted as litter bearers, but some of the bearers abandoned their litters. The few men who reached the hilltop with the seriously wounded decided that they could take them no farther. Chaplain Herman G. Felhoelter and the medical officer, CPT Linton J. Buttrey, remained with the wounded. When the enemy could be heard approaching, Chap. Felhoelter convinced CPT Buttrey to try to escape. He did so, but was badly wounded in the effort. The North Koreans murdered all the wounded left behind, as well as Chap. Fehoelter, as he prayed over them. The fate of CPT Fenstermacher is unclear. It is probable that he was with the wounded and was killed with them.

Only G and E Co.'s of the 19th escaped unhurt. On Meloy's orders, G dug in at Yusong for the night.

The NK 3d Division did not employ tanks south of the Kum River on July 16. A few American tanks supported the 19th, but their performance generally was not good. Once, two tanks with Logan at the roadblock refused to go around a bend in the road to engage the enemy unless accompanied by infantry. Later, both tanks charged through the roadblock on their own, without orders. At one point, an officer asked GEN Dean if there was anything he could do to

help. "No thank you," Dean replied, "unless you can help me give these tankers a little courage."

The regimental headquarters and 1/19 lost almost all their vehicles. The 52 FAB saved only one of nine howitzers and three vehicles. Of about 900 men of the 19th on the river line, only 434 were present for duty in Taejon the next day. The 1/19, plus the regimental headquarters, Service, Medical and HM Co.'s went into the battle with 34 officers. Only 17 survived; 13 were killed and four MIA. Co. C lost 122 men of 171; 1/19 338 of 785 men; 2/19 86 of 777; 52 FAB 55 of 393 and regimental headquarters 57 of 191 men. In all, 650 men of 3,401 engaged were lost — 19 percent . Only the 11 and 13 FAB got away without loss of weapons or equipment.

Co. B, 34th Infantry, relieved G/19 at Yusong on July 17, just 5 miles northwest of Taejon. That afternoon, the 19th Infantry moved into Yongdong, almost 30 miles east of Taejon, to refit.

Once again, at the Kum River battle on July 16, U.S. forces fought without adequate troops for the front assigned and a grossly inadequate reserve. The enemy was able to exploit the situation by executing a double envelopment, then setting up a powerful roadblock in rear of the defenders. The reserves available to COL Meloy were insufficient to meet and defeat the threat. The commitment of these short-handed regiments to defending extended frontages of from 4 to 30 miles was, at best, a series of "forlorn hopes." (See Chapter Notes.)

COL Min Sik Ki on the Kum River

Before the war, COL Min Sik Ki was the principal of the Seoul Infantry School. The staff, faculty, students and school troops soon went as replacements to ROK divisions. COL Min then was ordered to reorganize the ROK 7th Division in Cholla-Pukto, South Cholla Province. Before July 15, he had assembled 10,000 men, training them to fight with their fists while waiting for guns and equipment. His troops were at Kunsan, Iri and Chonju. Kunsan is on the west coast where the Kum River empties into the Yellow Sea. While the U.S. 24th Division faced the *NK 3d* and *4th Divisions*, their *6th Division* moved on line to their right in order to move south near the Yellow Sea. COL Min retained 700 select men to stay with him to face the *6th*, sending the others back toward Pusan.

He and his men, with some ROK policemen, defended the Kum River from Kunsan to Hamyol. They destroyed all the boats and rafts and forced the enemy to spend much time trying to cross the river, which is very wide in this area. Min recalled that he and his men fought a big battle with the enemy before relinquishing Kunsan, and confronted the enemy in stiff contests later near Hamyang and Chinju before the Perimeter was finally organized.

Battle at Yusong

The enemy left B/34 alone on July 17. Two platoons of the company manned the forward edge of the perimeter, with the 3d Platoon protecting the rear. It was dug in on a small hill adjacent to a Korean schoolhouse. SFC Robert W.

Moser was a rifle squad leader with the platoon; SSG Brennon was his assistant. He recalled that a LT Bryant commanded the platoon.

Moser had come to the 24th Division in 1948. Previously he had been a member of the 82d Airborne Division. In the 24th he was assigned to B/19 — the 24th Division Honor Guard, commanded by CPT Barszcz. Then he transferred to the 7th Division in Hokkaido. On July 2, he, SSG Brennon, SFC Slaik and a machine gunner were sent to the 24th Division. He joined Co. B/34 south of Chonan on July 7.

July 17 was quiet, except for some North Korean patrols. Early on July 18, Moser noticed an enemy patrol marching down the road behind their position and approaching Yusong. He ordered his BAR man to fire. The weapon would not fire. However, when the patrol returned later in the day, the platoon was waiting for them. The 3d Squad was positioned in a rice paddy adjacent to the road. Platoon fire wiped out the enemy patrol.

Then part of the *5th Regiment, 4th Division*, with a supporting tank company, attacked Co. B. "The main NKF [North Korean Forces] attack was proceeded by a heavy artillery preparation," Moser wrote. "We were well dug in and casualties were light. LT Bryant was wounded and evacuated. He gave me his binoculars... . I watched the attack begin. T-34s came around the cut in the ridge about 1,000 yards northwest of our position. They fired a few rounds, [hitting] our position." Then Moser saw what he believed to be a battalion or more of the enemy standing on a ridgeline. Many were smoking. "They moved down the hill in line as skirmishers," he wrote. "We had a machine gun... on the military crest, and he gave a good account of himself... . I thought our firing was uncoordinated, [and] if we would have had another machine gun at the paddy level we would have done much better."

On July 18, LTC Ayres saw from his CP large numbers of enemy troops assembling northwest of Yusong. These were possibly the same troops which Moser spotted. Ayres called artillery fire on them, with good results. GEN Dean somehow managed to visit Yusong the day of this fight.

On July 19, as the enemy attacked Co. B frontally, SFC Moser saw some of them moving around the company's left flank. "The action at Yusong got hot and heavy," wrote Ayres. "Both front-line platoon leaders were wounded... the NKs had flanked the position. The two front-line platoons were cut off from Yusong and fire began to come into the B Co. CP [killing] one man... . Casualties were heavy in the platoon defensive areas." Accordingly, Ayres obtained permission to withdraw the unit.

"We had no reserve to counteract [the enemy flanking movement] and... were overrun," Moser continued. "We received orders to evacuate the position. One group with me and SSG Brennon withdrew... through the schoolhouse complex [and] crossed the road to the paddy. We used the elevated road as cover to pull back through Yusong... ." The company reassembled and withdrew behind the Kapchon River and into a reserve position near Taejon.

While B/34 was at Yusong, LT William B. Caldwell was ordered to take out a platoon-strength combat patrol. He recalled that the pla-toon traveled some 15 miles, encountering a North Korean patrol. Caldwell ambushed the enemy, killing them all. SFC Roy Collins was with that patrol. He said that the Americans lost 2 KIA, 2 WIA and 3 MIA in the fight. Caldwell retrieved his dead and wounded and returned to his lines. Since he was unable to capture any of the enemy, he was unable to obtain any information.

Taejon
The North Korean Plan

LTC Ayres wrote that, on July 19, he saw "large groups of NKs assembling, artillery going into position, and trucks on the road. All of these indications of attack were taking place in the draw northwest of Yusong." He stated that he called artillery and air strikes in on these enemy concentrations.

In spite of artillery and air strikes, by the 19th, the *NK 3d* and *4th Divisions* were in position to attack Taejon. The *4th* was somewhat closer to the city than the *3d*. The *NK 2d Division*, on the left of the *4th*, also was to take part in the attack in the Taejon area. However, the ROKs, particularly the Capital Division, had inflicted crippling losses on the *2d*. As a result, it was unable to advance far enough to participate in the forthcoming battle. The North Korean plan had been for the *4th Division* to flank Taejon on the west, the *3d Division* to drive on the city from the north and the *2d* to outflank it from the east. In short, a three-division offensive, featuring a double envelopment. This would have been the equivalent of a corps operation. The *2d, 3d* and *4th Divisions* were part of LTG Kim Ung's *NK I Corps*.

GEN Dean's Plan

The three regiments of the 24th Division now resembled the strength of three battalions. The men were physically and mentally beaten; morale was low. Dean, too, was almost worn out. For two weeks he had faced one crisis after the other without letup.

On July 14, COL Beauchamp (West Point 1930) arrived to take command of the 34th Regiment. HHC, 34th Infantry Morning Report, dated July 16, states that COL Beauchamp was "assigned and joined" effective July 14. His assumption of command order was effective July 14. Beauchamp, at 42, was the youngest regimental commander then in Korea, and had the least experience with troops. He had requested troop command, but didn't get it until assigned to the 32d Infantry Regiment in Japan in March 1950. When COL Martin was killed, Beauchamp was tapped to replace him. Upon arrival in Korea, the COL set up his CP at the Taejon airport northwest of the city.

MAJ William T. McDaniel came with Beauchamp to be his S3, replacing MAJ Dunn, then MIA. McDaniel (West Point 1941) had been a combat liaison officer with the Chinese Army in Burma in 1943-44. He was captured by the North Koreans on July 20, 1950, and was murdered by his captors Oct. 20, 1950.

GEN Dean consolidated all the surviving 105mm artillery into a composite battalion. The 11 FAB (155mm), still in reasonable shape, remained as an independent artillery battalion. He concentrated all this artillery at the Taejon airstrip. Dean sent his headquarters back to Yongdong, 28 miles southeast of Taejon, but retained one aide, LT Arthur M. Clarke; CPT Richard A. Rowlands, Assistant G3; CPT Raymond Hatfield, Transportation Officer and Assistant G3 and two drivers. CPT David Bissett was instructed to establish an office for Dean at Okchon in the 21st Regiment's CP, to provide contact with his right flank regiment and give him a place to rest at night.

A hill and ridge mass rises along the east bank of the Kapchon River about three miles west of Taejon. The hills and ridges range in height from about 120 to 199 meters. The road from Kongju to Taejon, the main Seoul-Pusan highway, skirts the ridge system on the north, while the Nonsan-Taejon road runs through a pass two miles to the south. Dean had envisioned using this hill-ridge system for a two-regiment defensive system somewhat over four miles long to protect Taejon, known as the Yusong Position. He intended to emplace the 19th Infantry on the northern end of the ridge protecting the Kongju Road, and the 34th further south to guard the Nonsan Road. From these positions the two regiments could fight another delaying action. However, after the Kum River battle, the 19th was no longer combat effective as a regiment. Dean now had only the 34th immediately available for his projected delay.

Discussion of the Plan for the Relief of the 24th Division by the 1st Cavalry Division

On the morning of July 18 GEN Walker visited GEN Dean in the 34th Infantry CP outside Taejon. The exact nature of the conversation has been a matter of controversy ever since. Walker briefed Dean on the arrival of the 1st Cavalry Division and his (Walker's) general plan for the future employment of both the 24th and 1st Cavalry divisions. He told GEN Dean that he needed two days to bring the 1st Cavalry from Pohang into position in the Yongdong-Kumchon-Taegu area. What is at issue is whether or not Walker envisioned the Cavalry relieving the 24th Division at or near Taejon.

As of July 19 the 24th Infantry Division's 19th RCT was positioned northwest of Yongdong; the 21st RCT was occupying a ridgeline somewhat over three miles east of and facing toward Taejon; the 34th RCT occupied positions along the Kapchon, covering the Kongju road and other positions near Taejon.

The Eighth Army War Diary for July 19, 1950, states that the 1st Cavalry Division was to concentrate in the Taegu-Yongdong-Kumchon area. Army G3 published an Operational Directive, confirming oral and fragmentary orders which had been given during the period. Under this directive, the 1st Cavalry Division was to move to assembly positions in the Taegu-Kumchon-Yongdong area, prepared to relieve the 24th Division on order. The 24th Division was to secure the airfield at Yonil and port of Pohang-dong with not to exceed one RCT; to be prepared to block enemy movement south and east; to maintain contact with ROK forces; and, when relieved, to revert to Army reserve. Effective on July 20, A/71st Hvy Tk Bn was relieved from attachment to the 24th Division and returned to the 1st Cavalry. This company was part of the Cavalry Division's organic tank battalion.

This war diary entry infers that the Operational Directive was to be implemented immediately. The 1st Cavalry remained in the same areas it had been ordered to concentrate on July 18. It was not ordered to move to Taejon. The diary's summation of the order to the 24th Division directs it to send an RCT to the Yonil-Pohang area and returns the attached tank company to its parent 1st Cavalry Division. The company had been further attached to the 21st Regiment before and during that battle. The 21st Infantry's Unit Reports list the tank company as an attachment. Like the 21st, it was destined not to play any part in the battle.

Attaching and detaching elements of one command to and from another is common, and can take place at any time. The implication is that the tank company would revert to its parent 1st Cavalry Division at about the time the 24th Division passed back through the Cavalry. At the time of passage, the Cavalry Division would take over the front in the Yongdong Kumchon area. Another factor supporting the position that the 24th was to pull back through the 1st Cavalry in the Yongdong-Kumchon area is that combat power, in this case a tank company, is not normally taken from a forward command in battle or contact with the enemy.

Appleman, in trying to sort out what was said or implied, obtained letters from Collier, Landrum, Beauchamp, Arthur M. Clarke (Dean's aide) and Layton C. Tyner, one of Walker's aides. He also interviewed COL Beauchamp, who heard part of the Walker-Dean conference, and LTC Paul F. Smith, Combined Operations G3, EUSAK, in July 1950. Appleman wrote that Walker stated "he would like to hold Taejon until the 1st Cavalry Division could move up to help in its defense or get into battle position alongside the 24th Division... . [Walker] said he needed two day's time to accomplish this." Walker then returned to Taegu and "informed COL Landrum that he had told GEN Dean he needed two day's delay at Taejon to get the 1st Cavalry up and into position," Appleman continued. Walker expressed every confidence in Dean, whom he characterized as "a fighter who won't give an inch if he can help it." He told Landrum that he gave Dean the latitude to abandon Taejon earlier if necessary and that Walker would back his decision.

Dean took Walker's instructions to mean that he should delay at Taejon through July 20. But BG Eugene M. Lynch (Ret.), Walker's pilot, in a series of interviews by Lacy Barnett (April 22-24, 1992) asserted, "Walker wanted Dean to keep the enemy from advancing beyond Taejon for two days... . Walker assumed the 24th would be out of the city before dawn on... [July] 20."

MG Beauchamp (his retired rank), in his 1984 interview by Clay Blair said that if he could have done anything different in Korea, "I would have withdrawn from Taejon the day before [July 19] I did [July 20] and I could have too. It was my own fault... . I could have pulled out one day earlier because I had accomplished what GEN Walker had wanted me to do"

In a letter to MAJ Lacy Barnett, dated March 27, 1986, MG Beauchamp reveals a meeting which he had with GEN Walker on the morning of July 18, 1950. He wrote that Walker "directed that I hold the Taejon road network for three days and deny its use to the enemy. This turned out to be one day too long. GEN Dean was not present during this visit.... No one ever mentioned to me that the 1st Cav. Division was to relieve us at Taejon. GEN Dean did say to me during the fighting on July 20, that a battalion of the 21st Infantry was coming to the Taejon area to support our withdrawal. It was my plan to withdraw on the night of the 20th and I'm sure my Battalion Commanders understood that."

If, as MG Beauchamp writes, GEN Walker ordered him to retain the Taejon area for three days, it sheds some light on why he may have ignored two recommendations from LTC Ayres on July 19 that they withdraw from Taejon that night. Neither colonels Ayres nor McGrail ever indicated that they were apprised of those orders, although they may have been.

The Battle of Taejon, July 19

Taejon was, at the time, the sixth largest city in South Korea, the center of road and rail lines as well as of commerce. Large rice paddy areas were located north and west of the city. An airstrip was situated on a low plateau about a mile and a half northwest. The Taejon River flowed northwest, one arm through the city and another to the east, with the two arms rejoining just north of town. Somewhat over a mile farther north, the Yudong River, situated west of the city, flowed onto the Taejon, which then rolled on into the Kapchon. The Kapchon is a tributary of the Kum. A railroad station and rail yards lay on the east side of Taejon. A road coming south from the Kum River ran along the railroad, entering the northeast corner of the city.

Two roads exited the southeast corner of Taejon, one eastward toward Okchon and the other south to Kumsan. The railroad more or less paralleled the Okchon road. Somewhat over 2 1/2 road miles east of Taejon were both a highway and a railroad tunnel.

Beauchamp positioned 1/34 along the Kapchon River, covering the Kongju road. The battalion covered a front almost two miles wide, based on Hill 138, including a few hundred yards occupied by 1st Platoon, B/34, when that unit returned from Yusong. Co. A overlooked the Kongju road south along the Kapchon for some 1,220 to 1,400 yards. Charlie carried the line another 1,300-1,400 yards further south along the river. Upon its return from Yusong, Baker Co., minus the 1st Plt, was assembled on high ground centered behind the two front line companies. Battalion headquarters personnel were on high ground just north of B Co. The battalion CP was in a small village in a valley behind the front lines and generally between the headquarters personnel to the north and Co. B (-) to the south and about 1/2 mile from the river.

One platoon of Item Company manned a road and rail block three miles north of Taejon. The remainder of the company was on a low ridge astride this road and just north of the city. A platoon of Love Co. manned a similar block at the bridge where the Nonsan road crossed the Kapchon. The 3/34 (less roadblocks) occupied a low ridge just east of, and facing, the Taejon airfield. All available artillery was concentrated near the airfield, in position to support the infantry in any direction. The 24th Recon Co. was located at Kumsan, 20-odd miles south of Taejon.

The 21st Infantry was stretched across four miles of high ridges three to four miles east of Taejon, covering the Okchon road and the division's right flank. The regimental line was over a mile east of the highway and railroad tunnels on this road. These tunnels would become the choke points which the enemy later used with a road block that covered more than a mile of the highway with murderous fire.

After his conference with Walker, Dean returned to his Yongdong CP and took action to shore up the defense of Taejon. He ordered 2/19 back to Taejon from Yongdong and Btry A, 13 FAB to the Taejon airstrip from Okchon and released the 24th Recon Co. to COL Beauchamp. He envisioned the COL employing the unit to screen the southern flank, including the Taejon-Kumsan road.

GEN Dean also reviewed the role of the 21st Regiment with COL Stephens. The regiment was to keep open the withdrawal route east out of Taejon. Stephens told Dean that his regiment was already astride that road and on the hills nearby, and asked Dean if he should move them. The GEN said no, because he was concerned about an enemy penetration from the east through the ROK troops. Dean directed that the 21st remain in place but patrol the area north of the Taejon-Okchon road and send periodic patrolling over the road itself.

At 7:30 a.m. on July 19, six YAK fighters made a strike on the railroad bridge two miles northwest of Okchon in the 21st Regiment's sector. They dropped four bombs, one of which struck and damaged the bridge. However, B/3 ECC had the bridge repaired and ready for traffic by noon. The YAKs also strafed the regimental CP and dropped surrender leaflets signed by three officers and three NCOs who had been captured at Osan.

LT Murray Carroll was with a convoy of trucks headed for Yongdong when the YAKs made their runs on the bridge. The convoy was caught on the road in a steep, narrow canyon, with a river midway through. There was no place to run or hide. The vehicles and men would have been "sitting ducks," but the YAK pilots ignored Carroll's trucks and went after the bridge.

Four other planes strafed the Taejon airfield. Two enemy fighters were shot down near Yusong by Btry A, 26th AA Battalion, supporting 1/34.

After July 19, enemy fighters all but disappeared from the skies. Thereafter, almost all enemy air attacks were of the "Bedcheck Charlie" type — single aircraft flying over some area, dropping one or two ineffective "bombs" and scooting for home. This was because between July 17-20, USAF and carrier pilots concentrated on destroying the North Korean Air Force. In those few days, they shot down six YAKs, destroyed 32 enemy fighters on the ground and damaged seven more. On July 19, the Air Force also bombed and burned known and suspected enemy concentration sites west and southwest of Taejon.

The enemy made partial repairs to the Kum

River bridge at Taepyong-ni and used it to hasten forward tanks and artillery. The *4th Division* split up to attack Taejon from the west in two columns. The *16th* and *18th Regiments, Artillery Regiment* and most of the tanks went south to Nonsan then turned east toward Taejon. The *5th Regiment*, with a tank company, headed for Yusong.

The Recon Co. arrived in Taejon at 10 a.m. on July 19. COL Beauchamp sent its 2d Platoon (39 men) southwest along the Nonsan road. At 10:30 the platoon was ambushed three miles west of the Kapchon and withdrew back to the L Co. roadblock on the east shore of the river. The remainder of Co. L moved up to reinforce the roadblock.

Dean, meantime, had gone to Okchon. About 10 a.m. he started to worry about the 34th at Taejon, so he returned to the city and remained there.

McGrail's 2/19 arrived in Taejon shortly after noon and by 1 p.m. was ready to move out of the railroad station. He received orders for the battalion to attack down the Nonsan road to relieve L/34, now being pressed hard by the enemy.

The 2/19 attacked astride the Nonsan road, with Co. F on the north and Co. C on the south. GEN Dean was there, directing the fire of two tanks in support of the attack. As F attacked, they thwarted an enemy attempt to envelop l/34's right flank. At one point, Co. F men raced the enemy to critical high ground, took and held it, throwing the enemy back. Co. F then occupied positions along the Kapchon north of the Nonsan road and Co. E dug in south of it. The battalion front stretched about 1 3/4 miles along the river. Co. G was in reserve on a hill about a mile behind E. There was a gap 1 mile wide between 3/34 on the Kongju road and 2/19 to the south on the Nonsan road.

Buford Goff, a radio operator in Co. F, dug in with comrades on the newly-won position. Late in the day, one of the company's lieutenants was badly wounded in the shoulder. Buford was detailed to help the officer to the aid station. Shortly after he returned to the company, Goff was with the first sergeant near the top of the hill. SGT Romeraz, a machine gunner on the forward slope, was hit in the chest, arms and legs by enemy automatic weapons fire. Goff volunteered to go forward to rescue the sergeant. Handing his "grease gun" to the first sergeant, the young soldier crawled down the hillside, covered by small arms fire from the company. "I rolled under SGT Romeraz and he screamed with pain," said Goff. "I had no morphine to give him, nothing of first aid to give him. I rolled him onto my back and belly crawled to the top of the hill — between 20 and 50 yards, over the crest of the hill to where the company aidman came in and took it from there... ." He then went back and retrieved the machine gun and ammunition.

That evening, he happened to look back to a large rice paddy in rear of the position. "There was a Korean woman in white, 100 yards away with a mirror, signaling up the mountainside... . A reply signal was flashed back to her. Artillery came in — three quick rounds." She was still standing in the rice paddy when I grabbed another man's M1 and shot and killed her," Goff wrote.

Just before noon, Appleman wrote, the enemy began shelling the airstrip with counterbattery fire from the north and northwest, increasing in intensity during the afternoon. Dean told CPT Bissett that the fire was as heavy as he had ever seen in one day in Europe during WW II.

Included in the artillery at the Taejon airstrip was A/11 FAB (155mm), B/13 FAB (105mm) and a battery from the 63 FAB, also 105mm.

2LT Ernest P. Terrell was an officer in A/11 FAB, assigned there in January 1950. They underwent howitzer and FDC (Fire Direction Center) training almost every day at their base in Camp Hakata, Kyushu. Ernest was the battery motor officer, responsible that unit vehicles were in running condition. But Battery A had the same problems which plagued all other units in Japan — it was "at the tail end of the Far East supply line," as Terrell put it. "I worked the maintenance personnel in two shifts each night and day of the week Monday thru Saturday and sometimes on Sunday just to keep enough vehicles running for training," he wrote.

A few weeks before the Korean War started, the battalion underwent an Eighth Army Inspector general (IG) inspection. It was the only command in Division Artillery (Div Arty) inspected. "For three months prior to the inspection our Battalion received all the efforts of the Division... Ordnance, Quartermaster, Engineers, etc." he wrote, "in an attempt to get all our equipment in tip[-top] shape." But the inspectors declared all of the battalion howitzers "and about 90 percent of small arms and crew served weapons to be 'Combat Unserviceable,'" he continued. "That was the equipment we took to Korea."

The battery first saw action at the Kum River, then moved several times until emplaced at the Taejon airstrip, from which it began firing on the morning of July 19. Three or four YAK planes appeared, Terrell recalled, but were driven off by F-51 fighters.

All the batteries of U.S. artillery at the airfield were out in the open, easy targets for counterbattery fire. Soon after they started firing, enemy counterbattery began to fall in and near the gun positions, continuing all day.

2LT Ellsworth "Dutch" Nelsen was the XO of B/13 FAB at Taejon. Artillery gun positions were very hard to find during the Summer in Korea at the time. "Every bit of ground that is usable is, indeed, used — and mostly for rice paddies," he wrote. "Once in a while we could find a cotton or soybean field, and schoolyards were also fine if we could find one." Often, however, they just had to "drop trails and fire from the road... itself." At Taejon, he recalled, they were out in the open. The enemy could easily see them and direct counterfire without difficulty. B/13 was at the north edge of the strip. Right after dawn, the battery began to fire from that position.

"The enemy fired counterbattery with 76mm howitzers," he recalled. The fire set one of several nearby quonset huts aflame, one containing ammunition. But the battery all but ignored the enemy 76 fire. Then, as Nelsen described it, they heard a deep "Boom! Boom! Boom!" Enemy 122mm howitzer counterbattery fire began to fall on the Americans. One round landed between the trails of a battery howitzer, badly damaging

it, but the battery kept firing. Near nightfall, the unit pulled out, one howitzer at a time, until the entire battery had displaced to a new position on the southwestern edge of Taejon.

Terrell's A/11 FAB also lost a howitzer to enemy fire. "About 1500 (3 p.m.) my number 2 howitzer received a direct hit, wounding half the gun section and demolishing the howitzer," he wrote.

About dusk, Terrell's battery received two or three 3.5-inch bazookas, but had no time to bore sight or test them. His battery also displaced one gun at a time, normal in a combat situation when the battery continues to fire as it displaces.

"It was almost daylight [July 20] when I got the last howitzer laid in the new position," Terrell wrote. Then he discovered two T-34s approaching along a road to the right of the battery position. None of the howitzers was in a position to fire on the enemy tanks. Ernest "grabbed a CPL Walker" (the battery's best marksman with the old 2.36-inch launcher) "and got three rounds of ammo and I loaded while he fired." One round was short and one was over, but the rocket fire drove the tanks away. In escaping, one of the tanks backed over and destroyed a battery trailer. Terrell wrote that he then moved two howitzers to cover the two roads leading into the battery position, which fired on enemy tanks from time to time during the day, but scored no hits. He wrote, however, that aerial observers credited indirect fire from A/11 FAB with "knocking out five to seven T-34s on the outskirts of the airstrip on July 20."

In the early afternoon Terrell's BC [Battery Commander]went on recon for another position south of Taejon, taking the only map with him.

On July 20, LT Nelson was ordered to take two 105mm howitzers to a hill about 1,000 yards forward of the battery position to engage T-34 tanks. Nelsen protested the order in vain; the battery had only four workable howitzers. He detailed two gun sections and their guns to accompany him. Some of the men grumbled about what they thought to be a raw deal, but he told them to shut up.

Nelsen went to the top of the hill, where an infantryman pointed out one tank hiding in the shadow of a building and another backing into a stand of bamboo. There was supposed to be another tank, but the infantry had lost track of it.

The lieutenant and his men manhandled one howitzer to the top of the hill, planning to fire one HEAT round at each tank, then withdraw. However as the howitzer reached the hill's crest, a tank round hit it dead on the yoke. "The gun jumped about eight feet in the air," Nelsen recalled, "and recoil oil spewed out." He and his men began running down the hill. Realizing that he shouldn't be doing that, he stopped, and so did his men. They went back up the hill to salvage parts from this howitzer to patch up the one damaged earlier by 122 fire.

Enemy mortar fire now fell onto the hill, and Nelsen and his men hit the ground. Glancing to one side, he discovered that he was right next to the spot where a round had just landed, and quickly moved. More rounds landed. This time a large mortar fragment broke his bayonet and scabbard in two and lodged in his leg. An infantryman observed that but for the bayonet, the fragment might have severed Nelsen's leg.

The shard was removed and his leg sewn up at an aid station. As he sat there, a man came by passing out .45-cal automatic pistols. "What's this for?" Nelsen asked.

"We have a train going out with the wounded," responded the surgeon. "We're going to blast our way through. Do you want to be evacuated?"

Ellsworth thought that with a cane or something he might be able to hobble around. His battery was still firing nearby. "No," he responded. Finding a cane in the aid station, he hobbled back to the battery and later withdrew from Taejon with it.

David Livingstone Moffatt was a member of the 1973d Airways and Air Communications Squadron (AACS Sqdn), USAF. At the time he was based at the Taejon airstrip. AACS provided communications, navigational aids and flight services for the Air Force. One day, Moffatt was sitting on rice straw mats in an old half-filled "honey pit" at the end of the runway. He and his lieutenant were using a pair of radios to talk down C-47s for landings. One C-47 was hit by mortar fire as it landed and turned at Moffatt's end of the runway. The plane began to burn. "Four bodies bail out — three came my way," Moffatt wrote. "One, with a perfect baseball slide... ends up alongside me and the other two slide in head first... in knee-deep 'you know what.' The upright gentleman... says, 'How you doing, Sergeant?' 'Fine, Just fine, Sir.'" Moffatt noted, "'Tis a general I'm speaking to." The other two men were civilians. The general never was identified.

The mortar fire ceased and all was quiet — until the C-47 blew up! The general, "cool as a cucumber, mutters a few unkindly words" about the enemy, Moffatt wrote. "Then with a hard pat on the back, with a good word or two," the general jumped out of the hole and made his way across the strip. The two civilians, covered in human waste from the dive into the hole, follow the general "in stunned and silent dread and consternation," as Moffatt put it.

At 2 p.m. on July 19, LTC Ayres recommended to COL Beauchamp that the 34th Regiment withdraw from Taejon that night. Ayres' Baker Company was then engaged in a heavy battle near Yusong, as previously described. Ayres himself had seen large groups of enemy infantry and tanks assembling near Yusong on July 18 and 19. "I reported that an estimated division was facing the two understrength battalions on the line," he wrote. He also believed "that if an attack was launched around the flanks Taejon and everything in it would fall." He thought that Co. B at Yusong had deceived the enemy, but they (the enemy) "now had had plenty of time to build up for a major attack and had a good idea of our defensive dispositions." He wrote, "I based my recommendation on combat experience and personal observation." LTC Ayres also wrote that history would record that the enemy launched a coordinated corps attack against Taejon. He was close.

The North Koreans attacked on July 20 with their *4th Division* and part of the *3d*. The *NK 4th Division's 5th Regiment*, reinforced, struck Ayres' battalion. Ayres' analysis of the situation and the enemy's probable course of action were correct. His recommendation should have been adopted and executed by Beauchamp.

COL Beauchamp told GEN Dean he felt that he could hold Taejon for one more day. He moved his CP into Taejon after dark on July 19 and concentrated all artillery on the south edge of the city. The main Ammunition Supply Point (ASP) was established in the Taejon rail yards.

In a letter to Appleman, LTC Ayres wrote, "At dark I instructed my motor officer to move the transportation into Taejon. I retained one jeep per rifle company, two jeeps in D Co., the radio vehicle and one command vehicle."

The men on the right of F/19 heard noises on their right flank in the night, indicating that the enemy was moving into and through the gap between them and 1/34. The night was fairly quiet. Passing showers settled the dusty roads and streets around and in Taejon.

At 10 p.m. Ayres heard "the rumble of tanks... . from our right." He sent out patrols, "but subsequent events prevented their rendering a report," he wrote. Ayres called COL Beauchamp about the time he heard the enemy tanks and again recommended withdrawal. "I stated that I thought Taejon was being surrounded. This was the last conversation I had with regiment prior to the attack."

Just prior to midnight, an enemy unit was reported six miles south of Taejon on the Kumsan road. 1LT George W. Kristanoff and nine men of Recon Co. went on a jeep patrol to check. Six miles below the city they were halted by an enemy roadblock. Kristanoff reported the block, then contact was lost. A platoon of Recon Co. was sent out about 3 a.m. on July 20 over the same route. It, too, was stopped by the roadblock. The men saw the bodies of men from the earlier patrol and their four wrecked vehicles. At 2 a.m. a jeep was reported to have been ambushed on the Okchon road.

All these reports — from LTC Ayres, LT Kristanoff, the follow-up platoon patrol, the Okchon road ambush and the noises which the 1/19 heard between them and 1/34 — pointed to one fact: The enemy was rapidly investing Taejon from all sides. Dean said afterward that he did not know about the Kumsan roadblock and had dismissed the Okchon road incident. COL Beauchamp at least should have received reports of these incidents, as well as the tanks which Ayres had reported to him; it is not known if he was informed of enemy activity between 1/34 and 2/19.

The Battle of Taejon, July 20

LTC Ayres left his OP at dark on July 19, leaving his S2, LT Payne, and part of his section to man it. "Shortly after 0300 (3 a.m., July 20) he [Payne] reported into my CP," LTC Ayres said, "stating that the NKs had overrun the OP and had penetrated the MLR (Main Line of Resistance)." Ayres continued, "Another report came in that tanks had appeared on the right." Flares were popping overhead and small arms fire could be heard to the front and right near Co. A and a platoon of Co. B, but there seemed to be no action in the C Co. area. "They pushed up... the draw and hit my HQ Co., D Co. and Heavy Mortar Co."

Wire communication between 1/34 and the regimental CP went out during the night. Twice crews went out to restore the line, but were turned back by infiltrators. Two messenger jeeps with armed guards also tried to get through, but only one made it.

"Extremely heavy shelling began falling on our positions before dawn," recalled LT Caldwell of Co. A. "The enemy attack force was supported by tanks and a great number of infantrymen. Fighting during the early morning hours [was] extremely heavy. Casualties [were] high on both sides." Caldwell lost communications with the company CP. He suspected the company could no longer communicate with battalion. "From my position, I could observe small-arms fire... in the vicinity of the Bn CP... . The 1st Bn positions were overrun... ."

SFC Collins (Co. A) related that SGT Williams was on an outpost when he saw enemy soldiers coming over the top of a hill to his right in three skirmish lines, about 300 yards away. Looking to his left, he saw others there "just boiling over the hill." Williams raced back to the battalion CP and reported to LTC Ayres. Ayres recalled that several men reported news of the attack. "They were excited and in an effort to calm them down I tried to lessen the seriousness of the situation... ."

CPT Osburn wrote, "At daylight 20 July the North Korean army launched an armored attack. Approximately six [to] eight tanks with infantry troops riding and alongside their tanks. They hit with such force and speed we could not even slow their approach." Osburn received a call from the Battalion XO, MAJ Dunham that the battalion CP was displacing to the rear, but that Osburn's unit was "to hold position until [he] heard from [Battalion]." Osburn never received any more messages from the battalion headquarters. His unit "remained on position for several hours.... " Osburn continued. He could see the road, airport and city of Taejon. "I watched the tanks roll into Taejon and literally blow it to hell," he wrote. About 11 a.m., he withdrew Co. A toward Taejon, picking up men from other Co.'s along the way.

SFC Moser's platoon of B/34 was on the right of the front line. "We remained in position until about 0430 (4:30 a.m.), then moved out north on a trail that was at the base of a hill," Moser wrote. "My squad was [on the] point.... As we closed on the main road I noticed that troops and tanks were moving south. I halted the column. A lieutenant came forward and told me to hold." The lieutenant left and never returned. Moser's squad was at the edge of a rice paddy which extended to the road over which enemy tanks and troops were traveling. Realizing that his men were in an exposed position with coming daylight, SFC Moser ordered his men up the ridge to the left.

"We started to draw fire from... the road," he wrote. He discovered he and his men were all alone; the rest of the company had already started toward Taejon across the paddies to his rear. He and SSG Brennon provided covering fire for the squad. "We were taking casualties and had to move fast," he recalled. A party of enemy soldiers gave chase. Moser was hit in the hand and SSG Brennon also was wounded. They made their way to what Moser described as "a CP location." There he was ordered by a warrant officer "to take command of a small group of stragglers... [and] take to the hills and head for Pusan. I did not notice other personnel at the CP."

2LT George W. Wilcox was the platoon leader of the 75mm recoilless rifle platoon, D/34 at Taejon. On July 19, his 75s were in support of LT James Bryant's outpost from Co. B. The OP caught harassing small-arms and mortar fire all day, and Bryant was wounded. The OP captured one enemy soldier, who said he had been sent to reconnoiter a route for tanks to Taejon. The OP withdrew to the east bank of the Kapchon at 1 a.m. on July 20. The 4.2-inch mortar position received point-blank enemy tank fire some time afterward and displaced across the ridgeline to the vicinity of Co. D and the battalion HQ Co. At 5 a.m. his unit, along with elements of the 4.2-inch mortar company and 1/34 headquarters, began pulling out of position. Wilcox thought there were about 200 men in the group.

PFC Edgar (Sinnett) Pawelczyk's 81 mortars were behind Co. A. "When the attack came we fired... 'till the barrels were red hot and everyone in the platoon began to fire at the high ground in front of us. When the orders came to [withdraw] we took off for a big mountain southwest of [Taejon]," he wrote. They passed an abandoned 4.2-inch mortar position. Some of the mortars were still there and a few of the 81 mortarmen stopped long enough to fire off some rounds from the abandoned 4.2s. Pawelczyk was carrying the tube of an 81mm mortar. When they got to the top of the mountain, CPT Sidney Marks, Pawelczyk's company commander, told him to destroy the tube.

The last message LTC Ayres got out over his radio was sent about 3 a.m.: "Tanks have penetrated my position and are headed your way." The operator at regiment acknowledged receipt of the message. Ayres tried, unsuccessfully, to contact his rifle companies.

About 4 a.m. bullets began hitting the house Ayres was using as a CP, and soon it was under heavy small-arms fire from two directions. His battalion had been overrun. "We were pushed out of our positions... by the North Koreans," said LTC Ayres. "I really did not give an order to withdraw — we were forced out."

Ayres described pulling out of his CP: "With the help of my S3 [MAJ Cooper] we cleared the CP... with bullets kicking at our heels (no exaggeration...)." Men from A, B and D Co.'s also had begun to pull out. Ayres and his officers collected all the men they could, but many soldiers became separated from their units and moved to the rear in small groups.

"I went back along a valley," said Ayres, "and saw some tanks between my position and... Taejon." He and the men with him went into a river bed and stayed there for a while, where he collected about 200 men of the battalion and they proceeded into the hills just outside Taejon. Ayres planned to head southeast, cross the bridge over the Yudong-chon, behind 2/19 and head into Taejon. About 7 a.m., just before reaching the bridge, the colonel saw F/19 engaged in a heavy fire-fight. As he watched, men of 2/19 began pulling out, headed for Taejon. "It appeared they were greatly outnumbered," he recalled. "The NKs were swarming over the hills."

The bridge had come under heavy enemy fire, so Ayres and his men waded across the river and moved onto a hill overlooking Taejon. LTC Ayres turned the 200 men over to his XO, MAJ Leland R. Dunham, and told him to move down on the road and set up a blocking position. Ayres took with him MAJ Cooper, CPT Spalding (CO, HM Co.); a sergeant; a runner; radio operator; his interpreter, MAJ (or Mr.) Seoul; *Time* Magazine correspondent Wilson Fielder, and two others. They headed for Taejon to find COL Beauchamp. Ayres had no radio communications.

Ayres and his party proceeded about 400

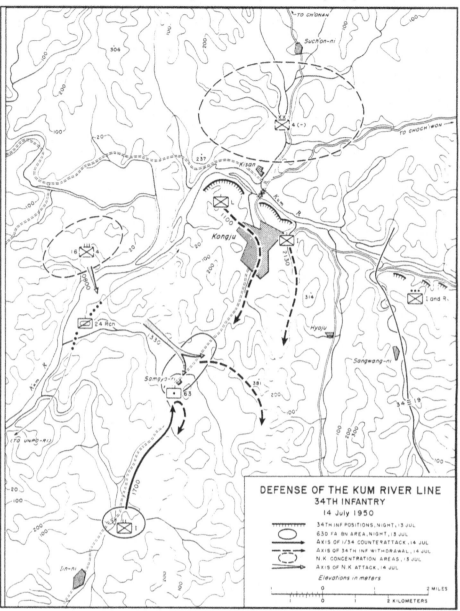

Map 10 (Source: South to the Naktong)

Combination Gun Motor Carraige M15A1 moving into position along the Kum River, 15 July. This weapon carried a 37mm gun and two .50 caliber machine guns. (Source: P. 48, Korea, 1950, Chief of Military History, Washington, D.C., 1982) (See Chapter Notes.)

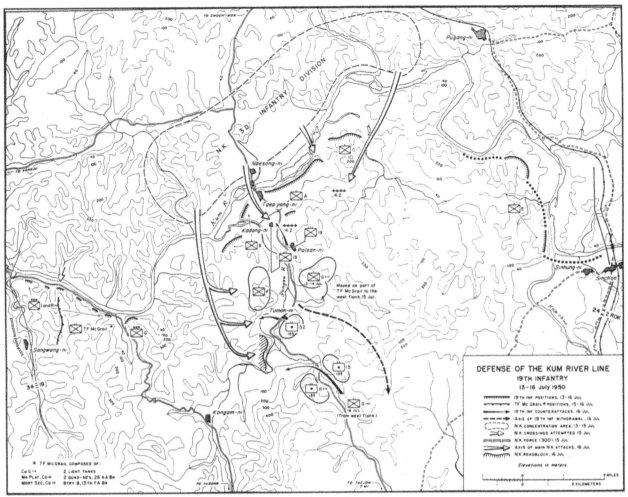

Map 11 (*Source:* South to the Naktong)

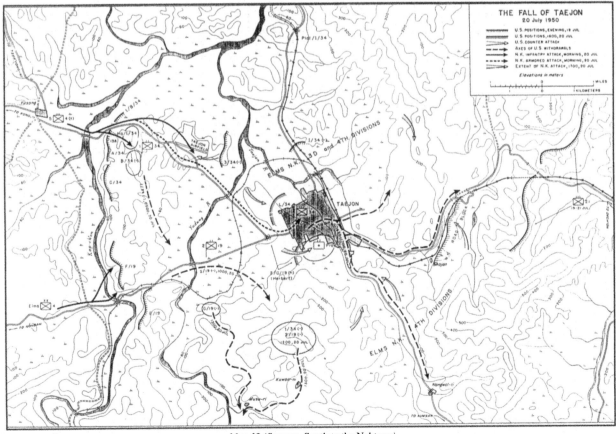

Map 12 (*Source:* South to the Naktong)

LT Elmer Gainok, Amherst, Ohio, extreme left with hand pointing, briefs platoon on their new defensive positions on the south bank of the Kum River. (Courtesy of Dr. Elmer Gainok, K & L/21 Infantry)

3.5" M30 Rocket Launcher (superbazooka) on a battlefield, 20 July. This launcher weighed fifteen pounds, designed for use against ground targets, is a two piece unit for carrying purposes. (Source: P. 57, Korea, 1950, *Chief of Military History, Washington, D.C., 1982)*

Troops of the 19th Regiment escaping through Taejon's residential district, caught by volleys of automatic weapon fire from the rooftops. (Source: 24th Forward *A Pictorial History of the Victory Division in Korea, Tokyo, 1953)*

yards from the road when they stopped at about 2 p.m. Leaving Spalding and the others, Ayres, Cooper and Seoul went into a nearby village in search of food. While talking to a woman there, they saw some North Koreans approaching on a nearby path, and took shelter in nearby thorny bushes. They were trapped there the remainder of the day, surrounded by 30-40 enemy soldiers, and heard shots from the direction which they had come. Spalding and the men with him had been discovered by the enemy. All were killed, except Spalding, who played dead.

When wiremen reported that they could not get through to restore communications with 1/34, COL Beauchamp decided to see for himself. At the Nonsan-Kongju road junction just a half-mile west of Taejon, he came upon an enemy tank. Just as the tank's machine gun fired, Beauchamp dove out of the jeep. He was grazed by one bullet and his jeep was set on fire. The driver was unhurt. Crawling back about a hundred yards, he found a 3.5-inch bazooka team from C/3 ECB. The team destroyed the tank and captured the crew, then took position at the road junction. Later in the morning, this team, plus one from 24th Recon Co., destroyed two more tanks coming from the airstrip, the first three "kills" scored by the 3.5-inch rocket launcher in Korea.

Jose E. Leyba of L/34 had been one of the men selected to train with the new 3.5. He was enthusiastic about the weapon. "We couldn't get back to our units fast enough with the good news" that this bazooka could knock out the T-34. "Believe me, this helped our morale quite a bit... ."

"When we reached Taejon, I Co. [34th Regt.] was deployed along a small ridge almost due north just outside the city," said James A. Jones. "I don't think all of us dug in... digging into that ground was like digging through concrete." They ran patrols east and northeast through July 19. Rumors had it that American tanks would be arriving soon. "So when a column of tanks came into view from the northwest on [July] 20th some of the guys began to get excited," Jones continued. The men thought that American troops were off in that direction and the tanks didn't have infantry troops with them. But "when they got closer I realized something was wrong. The outside of the tanks were too empty."

Jones was a WW II combat veteran of Europe. "I knew they were supposed to be a case of C-rations, duffel bags and GI shorts hanging out to dry if they were American," he explained. Jones and his comrades "laid low." The tanks were 200 or 300 yards away and on higher ground. When the first tank drew about even with the left of Item Company's position it began to fire into Taejon.

The company now had a 3.5-inch rocket launcher team. Jones recalled that they had only three rocket rounds. Item's team closed in on the last T-34 and knocked it out, using all three rounds to do so. Four tank crewmen crawled out of the escape hatch in "the bottom of the tank and ran along a ditch on the opposite side of the road from us until they were about 500 yards away then got up on the road," Jones recalled. "This was a big mistake. We had a BAR man who slept all the time but he was one hell of a shot." Someone woke him up. "When the North

Koreans hit the road it was all over. He laid down three or four bursts and got all four of them. It didn't take him very long and he was asleep again," said Jones.

Co. I remained in position. Communication with the rear was poor, but in midafternoon the unit was ordered to withdraw from Taejon. The first order was for it to be the rear guard in the city, but that order was changed soon after: They would lead instead.

Some time after he returned to his CP, COL Beauchamp was told by one of his staff officers that 1/34 reported they were in good condition. The enemy may have captured Ayres' radio jeep and sent this false report.

After daylight on July 20, COL Beauchamp ordered 3/34 to attack into the gap between 1/34 and 2/19, although by this time, 1/34 was no longer in position; it already had been displaced by the enemy. K and part of M Co.'s began the attack, but ran into six enemy tanks and a battalion of infantry, stopping the attack and scattering some of the troops. SFC Robert E. Dare (Co. K) heroically lost his life directing, then covering, the withdrawal of the unit's advanced platoon.

About 9:30 a.m., MAJ Newton W. Lantron, CO of 3/34, left his CP and was not seen again. Lantron told MAJ Lacy Barnett in a telephone conversation on April 12, 1992, that he didn't recall specifically why he left the CP, but it was in connection with his duties and responsibilities as commander of 3/34. He said he couldn't get back because the enemy blocked the way. He evaded the North Koreans for two or three days before being captured and taken to Taejon. In the same conversation, Lantron said that 3/34 did not have a clear mission nor any clear withdrawal instructions on July 19-20. "It was a matter of acting and reacting as the situation developed; it was very frustrating," he said.

When MAJ Lantron was discovered missing, CPT Jack E. Smith was appointed to take command of 3/34. LTC Wadlington made the appointment about 11 a.m., when he visited the 3d Battalion. About noon, CPT Smith received orders to withdraw 3/34. He got the battalion loaded on trucks and drove to the regimental CP, as ordered. There, he was directed to provide security for the regimental CP and to provide "cover for the recovery of a battery of 155mm howitzers." Sending the rest of the men on in trucks, Smith remained with Co. L to protect the CP.

The *NK 5th Regiment* captured the Taejon airfield by 4 a.m., but neither Beauchamp nor Dean knew this. Some enemy tanks and infantry actually entered Taejon before dawn.

While the 3/34 counterattack was being halted by the enemy, Beauchamp was telling Dean that 1/34 was holding, based on the false radio message. Beauchamp did not know then that 3/34 had been stopped, so matters seemed to be in hand. In fact, they already had lost the battle. GEN Dean directed COL Beauchamp to plan a withdrawal, to take place after dark on July 20 over the Okchon road through the 21st Infantry.

"At the crack of dawn, July 20... all living hell broke loose," said Buford Goff. "I have no idea of how many men were lost in our company... . I saw men falling back running from

A 34th Regiment BAR-man street fighting in the outskirts of Taejon. (Source: 24th Forward A Pictorial History of the Victory Division in Korea, *Tokyo, 1953)*

Taejon, about 11 A.M., July 20, 1950. CP 3/34 near Taejon airstrip. The three on the right were captured by Donald L. Luedtke and another man from HQ. 34 Infantry. Photo by Dan Cavanaugh. (Courtesy of Donald L. Luedtke, HQ. 34 Infantry)

the lines... . The first sergeant stood his ground trying to keep our company together... an almost impossible task... . A mortar round landed extremely close to me; it knocked me out. I was left for dead. My left eardrum was pierced. I had shrapnel in the right side of my head." It was dusk when he came to. "North Koreans were everywhere. I laid as still as I could and under cover of dusk, I crawled to the nearest rice paddy... not far from where the CP had been." There, Goff was captured, stripped and beaten unconscious. He regained consciousness in an old compound containing about 20 other American POWs. All had been stripped naked, including dog tags, rings, watches, clothing and shoes.

The 2/19 experienced alerts and alarms the night of July 19-20 and a false report even was received in Taejon that the battalion had been overrun. Co. F was hit very hard at daybreak and was forced back about 200 yards; Co. E remained in position.

When the party of men from 1/34 with MAJ Dunham reached the road in rear of 2/19, the MAJ conferred briefly with LTC McGrail. McGrail said that he had reports that enemy armor had cut the Nonsan road to Taejon in his rear.

LTC McGrail had received this information soon after daylight from men who dashed into his CP east of the Yudung bridge in a jeep. The men reported three T-34s at the junction of the Kongju-Nonsan road, not knowing that the tanks already had been knocked out. They also reported three more tanks approaching the junction on the Kongju road. Parts of Taejon were afire and the sounds of explosions and gunfire came from the town.

LTC McGrail ordered 2LT Robert L. Herbert to take his 2d Platoon of Co. G and open the road to the city. Enroute to the junction, Herbert came upon a bazooka team and persuaded them to accompany his platoon. He also passed part of B/34 unit filling their canteens from a streambed. At the road junction, he found two tanks burning and another which had been destroyed earlier.

1LT James C. Little and a reinforced squad from the 34th Infantry, armed with two bazookas, already manned a roadblock at the junction. Herbert's platoon joined Little's block. The wrecked vehicles of HM Co., 34th Infantry, littered the road to the airstrip. A mile north on this road stood three T-34s. Shortly, elements of H/19 passed by on their way to Taejon.

Soon after Herbert left on the road-opening mission, McGrail lost contact with the 34th Regiment's CP. He knew from MAJ Dunham that 1/34 on his north flank had been overrun and that his own F Co. had pulled back. The consensus of McGrail's staff was that the road back to Taejon had been cut by the enemy. Around 11 a.m., CPT Montesclaros, 2/19 S3 Section, volunteered to try to get to the regimental CP in Taejon for instructions. He found the road open all the way. Meeting GEN Dean as he entered the city, Montesclaros reported to him, giving the current situation of 2/19, and asked for orders. GEN Dean patted the captain on the back and said, "My boy, I am not running the show, Beauchamp is." He then led Montesclaros to the 34th CP. COL Beauchamp was not there, but a regimental staff officer gave the captain written orders for 2/19 to withdraw to the western edge of Taejon.

GEN Dean's remark to CPT Montesclaros was true. COL Beauchamp was the tactical commander at Taejon; Dean was the overall commander of the 24th Division. He was in Taejon because that was the most critical point of action at the time.

When Montesclaros got back to the 2/19 CP it was deserted and he couldn't understand what had happened. Starting back to Taejon, he returned to the CP site again, but he could find no living soul. All was eerily quiet. On his return to Taejon he came upon E/19. He instructed the commander to go into position right there. As he entered Taejon for the second time, the captain met 1LT Tom Weigle (S2, 2/19). Weigle told him that McGrail had set up a new CP on a high hill south of the road, pointing it out. Montesclaros set out for the site. Forty-five minutes later he reached the place to find no CP, no battalion commander. The few men who were there had no idea where the CP or McGrail might be.

As Montesclaros turned to go back to Taejon, he met LT Lindsay and Co. E, climbing the hill. The enemy had overrun their position on the road. About a battalion of the enemy could be seen on the road marching in a column of platoons toward Taejon, and a T-34 was moving west on the road out of the city. At sight of the tank, the enemy soldiers scattered for cover, not knowing it was one of their own. Montesclaros decided to stay with Co. E.

Believing the battalion to be cut off, LTC McGrail had moved his CP to high ground south of the Nonsan road. He could only notify Co. E to withdraw before his radio failed. Just before Montesclaros returned, McGrail moved his CP to Poman-san, south of Taejon, a mountain rising to a height of 1,488 meters.

The two forward Co.'s of 2/19 (E and F) both were gone from their positions by late morning. Only G Co., the battalion reserve, was still dug in behind the former front line. Just after daylight on July 20, G's commander, CPT Barszcz, had sighted two T-34s entering Taejon two and a half miles away, and reported this to the battalion CP. Just before noon, 2/19 S3, CPT Kenneth Woods, came to Co. G and instructed Barszcz to take his company and join the 1/34 elements which had passed earlier, and to withdraw with them. George Co.'s 3d Platoon was to be the last element out, following the Weapons (4th) Platoon, but the 4th's 60mm mortar section still was firing at the time to leave. The Weapons Platoon leader asked the 3d Platoon leader to go on ahead; the 60s still had some ammunition to fire. The whole section, an officer and 18 EM, fell to the enemy.

By 1 p.m., there was no organized resistance west of Taejon, except for the little roadblock at the Kongju-Nonsan road junction. Most of the survivors of 1/34 and 2/19 bypassed Taejon to the west and headed into the high mountains south of the city. Neither battalion received any orders from regiment or division to enter Taejon. They were "on their own." Both commanders could see fires raging in the city and hear gunfire and explosions. LTC McGrail believed his battalion was cut off from the city. If what CPT Montesclaros saw from the mountain shortly after noon on July 20 was any indicator, by that time 2/19 was cut off from Taejon. The 1/34, elements of which passed west of Taejon earlier, also were subjected to enemy attack short of Taejon. Further, the enemy claimed to have taken the Taejon airstrip by 4 a.m., an area just to the rear of 1/34 positions on the Kapchon River.

It also is known now that elements of both the enemy's *3d* and *4th Divisions* had infiltrated east and south of Taejon as early as July 18, and had strengthened their hold on many exits from the city by the night of July 19. The counterattack by the 3/34 on the morning of July 20 was stopped cold by the enemy, almost before it started. A city even partially occupied by an enemy is a deathtrap to withdrawing troops. All advantages lie with the force already in battle configuration. Considering these factors, it should not be uprising that the bulk of 1/34 and 2/19 went south and not into Taejon.

The sequence of events and the time each

Machine gun positions. .30 cal Browning Light machinegun M1919A6 (top); .50 cal Browning machine gun M2 HB (bottom). As rear guard troops left Taejon on 20-21 July, defensive positions were set up southeast of Taejon. (Source: P. 62, Korea, 1950, Chief of Military History, Washington, D.C., 1982)

took place in Taejon on July 20 is difficult to sort out. Records of events were lost and there is almost nothing more to rely upon than the recollections and experiences of survivors.

The first enemy tanks entered Taejon from the airstrip about dawn on July 20. There is no evidence that bazooka teams of 1/34 had engaged these tanks. SGT Williams came from one of these teams to report to LTC Ayres.

Enemy Tanks and Infantry in Taejon

Evidence that the enemy had troops in Taejon on July 19 is borne out by the experience of Jose E. Leyba (L/34). That evening, Leyba was ordered to take a patrol out to contact the enemy. "Before we hit the outskirts of Taejon, we were able to make contact. None of us thought the enemy was that close behind us." Leyba's patrol fired on the enemy and he reported the contact; his men then disengaged without loss.

The Listening Post (LP) on the outskirts of Taejon, manned by Edward N. Arendell and two other men from HHC, 34th, also made contact. "Three times during the night I went back and informed the S2 and S3 that tanks and men were moving through us," he wrote. "You could hear them everywhere." The LP was withdrawn just before daylight, and Arendell returned to his duty in the S4 Section.

PFC Donald L. Luedtke had been on radio duty almost all night on July 19-20 in the 34th CP, in a school compound just north of where the Nonsan road entered Taejon. "About dawn, I was given a walkie-talkie 300 radio and told to try to get in touch with a patrol; I was given no other information," he wrote. He couldn't make radio contact with the patrol, so he walked a short distance down the road to the west of the headquarters. "Here came a half track at full speed," wrote Luedtke. "About 500 yards behind it came a tank and about 100 yards behind it came another tank. The lead tank had Koreans hanging all over it. I stood alongside the road and they all went by me. I thought the tanks were South Korean.... I came running back to HQ and most of the people there were asleep." At this point, the South Koreans still had no tanks of their own.

The half track turned north and the tanks went south at an intersection tree or four blocks east of the CP. "The men in the half track stopped and began firing at the rear tank with their quad-.50s and 37mm guns," Luedtke continued. "All they did was rattle the hatches. From that time on in Taejon, the shooting never stopped."

LT Arthur M. Clarke was an aide to GEN Dean. His notes on July 20 contain the following: "Awoke at 0530 [5:30 a.m.] to the tune of small arms fire." He and the general started out about 6:30 a.m. toward the junction of the Kongju-Nonsan road. Two burning T-34s were near this intersection. The lieutenant saw another tank about 1,000 yards away. GEN Dean guided a 3/4-ton truck mounted with a 75mm recoilless rifle into a position to take the tank under fire. "The 75 failed to hit the tank with its four or five rounds, and withdrew," Clarke continued.

About 10 enemy tanks entered Taejon beginning just after daylight on July 20. Eight T-34s were destroyed by the recently acquired 3.5-inch rocket launcher and two more by direct artillery fire. Confidence in the 3.5 was such that a number of officers and enlisted men went "tank hunting." Some men even went after the T-34s in Taejon with the old 2.36-inch launcher, but there is no evidence that they scored any kills. (See Chapter Notes.)

A number of men experienced or witnessed tank actions and others were members of "tank-killer" teams. (There may be some duplication in the following narratives, because some of these men may have been involved in or witnessed the same action, but from different perspectives.)

CPT Clarke, Dean's aide, wrote, "About 0830 (8:30 a.m.), a tank passed between the 34th CP and Artillery Area at a distance of approximately 200 yards from the CP. Tracked the tank to the burning tanks, but could not locate its position."

60mm Mortar (Courtesy of Edward N. Arendell, HC, 34 Infantry)

Browning Automatic Rifle (BAR) (Courtesy of Edward N. Arendell, HC, 34 Infantry)

PFC Luedtke apparently was nearby when Dean went after this tank. He recalled that, when the tank neared the CP, "It did wake everyone up. GEN Dean came running out of the HQ building and immediately began looking for a bazooka team. He posted a couple of guys with a bazooka along the road ditch in case any more tanks came in, and sent some people after the tanks... and told the rest of us to dig in."

"The tanks that came by regimental headquarters had moved into the center of town," LT Carroll wrote, "and the infantry they were carrying had spread out and established sniper positions on most of the major streets." More T-34s got into Taejon, but ignored the regimental CP. Instead, two tanks attacked the 34th Service Company compound in a schoolyard in the southwest corner of Taejon, where the regimental kitchen area and motor pool were, as well as the kitchens of 2/19. About 150 men were in the compound when the two T-34s opened fire with their main guns, killing several men, destroying vehicles and setting an ammunition truck on fire.

After making a recon run south to Chonju and back, SSG Joseph McKeon had pulled his vehicles into the Service Company compound. A well-built bridge crossed a large canal-like ditch behind the compound.

"On the morning of the 20th,... a T-34 came clanking across the bridge adjacent to the schoolyard.... About the same time [a] T-34 which had gone down to the corner intersection with the road out of Taejon, turned his turret," McKeon wrote, "and fired a round into the compound.... It hit a 2 1/2-ton truck loaded with drums of gasoline and it caught fire." The burning truck was in the middle of the motor park and would have set the other vehicles afire. "But one young fellow came running out, jumped into the truck," drove it to the schoolyard entrance, crashed the gate," then bailed out... and let it" cross the street and smash into a building on the opposite side. "By this time," Joseph wrote, "the truck was fully engulfed in flames and soon the houses... [there] were burning too."

SSG McKeon and his I & R detachment left the compound to find his battalion CP. Recon Company sent bazooka teams, with gunners PFC Jack E. Lowe and CPL Robert B. Watkins, after the two tanks which had attacked the Service Co. compound. The T-34s next attacked two Medical Co. jeeps, wounding two men and killing the rest. A tank ran over one of the wounded men as he lay helpless in the street. A bazooka team hit one tank, bouncing it off the ground, but the T-34 moved on to the railroad station where its gunnery started fires and destroyed supplies and equipment. There it died, with a track knocked off. Riflemen then killed the tank commander. A rocket blew a 3-foot-square piece of armor off the front of the second tank. A third tank was destroyed after a rocket round penetrated the top of its turret.

GEN Dean, Clarke and the general's interpreter, Jim Kim, made another foray, stalking a T-34 near the old dependent housing area, with M1 rifles, a .45 automatic pistol and two hand grenades. As the party approached within about 75 yards of two T-34s, they were driven away by machine gun fire. In returning to the CP, they retrieved two abandoned jeeps. At 10 a.m., they went out again, this time with a bazooka and gunner. As they approached the road leading to the Taejon airstrip, the two tanks were still there. The tanks began to move, and the launcher gunner quickly fired at a range of 150-200 yards. The round — the only one he had — fell short. The disappointed group returned to the CP.

The Regimental S4 Section began to establish an auxiliary ASP. About 8 a.m., Edward Arendell was sent to the Taejon railhead for ammunition for this ASP, but he had to find the railhead first. "By this time you could hear fighting all over the city," Arendell recalled. "We were fired on numerous times." When he and his companions arrived at the railhead, Arendell wrote that the officer in charge was so "shook up" that they had to find the ammunition themselves.

LT Carroll also helped to establish the new ASP, using his jeep and trailer to haul ammunition from the railhead. On each trip, "as I crossed the Taejon River bridge I came under machine gun fire," recounted LT Carroll. "There was a T-34 half-hidden just off the next bridge down.... Probably the only reason they didn't use their 85mm gun was that they didn't want to damage the bridge." The Division Transportation Officer, CPT Hatfield, was preparing the ammunition train to leave Taejon, so it was imperative that Carroll continue moving ammunition to the new ASP. While he worked, several officers of the 34th headquarters, including MAJ McDaniels, borrowed a 155mm howitzer from the 11 FAB and moved it to the edge of town on the Nonsan road. There, they knocked out one tank with the howitzer, but fire from other T-34s drove them away.

Around noon, a 3.5-inch rocket team from 3 ECB hunted down and destroyed another T-34. "At 1215 a tank rattled by the CP," wrote Clarke. GEN Dean, Clarke, CPT Rowlands and some others followed this tank. LT Carroll, having made several ammo runs, went along to help provide covering fire. At first they had no rocket launcher, but were soon joined by a team from 3 ECB. Clarke carried a bottle of gasoline he intended to throw onto the tank to set it afire. The group spent about an hour trading shots with snipers and hunting down the T-34. About 2 p.m., GEN Dean, the two-man bazooka team and two or three riflemen entered a business building and went to the second floor. There, directly below a window, was the tank, with its gun tube no more than twelve feet away. LT Clarke, Carroll and some others "covered the street corners and adjacent buildings," wrote Carroll. Clarke placed himself "by the corner of the building in front of the tank to use [his] Molotov cocktail on it if it began to move," wrote the lieutenant. "The first [rocket] round hit the tank, and the occupants began to scream and moan." Two more rockets were sent into the tank, setting it ablaze. GEN Dean and his group withdrew and paused to watch the tank burn. They returned to the CP about 2:30 p.m.

GEN Dean, in his comments on *South to the Naktong*, told Appleman that he personally went after enemy tanks in Taejon to inspire his men to become tank-killers. Since communication was so poor and he was still the leader of the entire 24th Division, if not the tactical com-

mander at Taejon, he should have remained in or near the CP of the 34th Regiment. The team, with its supporting riflemen, could have knocked out the tank without Dean. GEN Dean seemed to realize this later, writing in his own book that "very few of the things I did in the next 24 hours could not have been done by any competent sergeant... ."

Not every 3.5-inch rocket launcher team was successful. One team with 2LT Spero W. Calos (HQ/34) had gone to the roof of a building in Taejon to "ascertain the situation," as he put it. The bazooka gunner proudly carried a pearl-handled pistol. "Everyone in the unit associated him with this pearl-handled pistol," wrote Calos. "A T-34... came toward the building.... The lad's number-two man loaded the bazooka and the lad fired at the tank. He missed." The number-two man moved to another position, but the gunner remained kneeling at the spot where he had fired. "The turret-gunner of the T-34 immediately spun his turret around and fired," Calos continued. "The lad, still kneeling... caught the tank projectile full blast,... and it detonated upon him, leaving meager traces of splattered blood, flesh, wearing apparel, equipment, etc. Had it not been for the pearl-handled pistol, you would have never known who it was."

Maurice R. Slaney was a member of Service Co., 34th Regiment, at Taejon. When the North Koreans invaded South Korea, he believed "The main feeling was 'Who cares.' It was Korea and we were in Japan."

About noon on July 20, Slaney, with three other men he identified as Stevens, Griffe and Graham, formed a bazooka team using the 2.36-inch model with eight or 10 rocket rounds. "We saw two T-34s about a block away and we ran into a house and up to the second floor. We had been told the armor on top of the T-34 was thin and we could get it that way." But there was another tank nearby, unnoticed by the men. That tank "put an 85mm shell right into the room we were in," Slaney recounted. "Strange thing. I believe I was the closest one to the explosion. Yet I was just wounded with fragments in the head, body and legs. And blown out of the room too. The others were killed outright." Slaney was evacuated to Japan.

LT Carroll recalled that LT Freddy Abt (HM/ 34), whom he knew, was a bazooka gunner that day. Abt once fired his launcher from inside a building. "The back-blast from the rocket blew out the back wall and stunned him and the 3.5 crew," Carroll wrote.

PFC Luedtke was busily digging his foxhole back at the 34th CP compound. "When someone started hollering tanks.... I dived into my foxhole; the only thing that fit was my head and chest," recounted Luedtke. Two enemy tanks were about 30 feet from him when they let loose with their cannons and machine guns. "I was positive I was a goner," Luedtke declared, but the tanks were too close to depress their guns to fire on him. Then a friend of his from L Co. suggested that they go after the tanks. The L Co. man said they would sneak up on the T-34s and throw grenades down the hatch "or some other place that might do the job." He and his friend worked their way close to the tanks, "but someone got them with a bazooka, which was fine with me," declared Luedtke.

A little later they were hiding behind a house from which they heard Korean voices. Luedtke and his friend decided to capture the Koreans. He and the L Co. man fixed bayonets; the L Co. man slid the door open, covered by Luedtke. They found three unarmed Korean men in civilian clothes. "They tried to tell us they were South Koreans," he wrote, but he and his friend didn't buy that. They marched the prisoners back to the CP, where South Korean police coerced "confessions" from the captives. It was about noon. He recalled that the CP had no communication with either 1/34 or 3/34. "Almost every one was mixed up — not much unit organization," he wrote, "no one seemed to know what was going on. . . ."

During the withdrawal from Taejon, enemy tanks were no longer a factor. Rather, concentrated small arms and machine gun fire created deadly gauntlets through which trucks, jeeps and other vehicles had to run, and many vehicles were destroyed, effectively blocking one street after the other.

After his bazooka team destroyed the T-34 in downtown Taejon, GEN Dean returned to the CP and joined COL Beauchamp. Both officers, ignorant of the rapidly deteriorating situation, believed they were in control, but Dean now decided they should withdraw from Taejon during daylight. Appleman gives the time of this order as about 2 p.m. Beauchamp sent runners with written orders to 1/34 and 2/19, but neither battalion could receive this order, having pulled out of position. The 3d Battalion, 34th, along with other units in Taejon, got the order about 3 p.m. The planned order of march out of Taejon was 3/34, artillery, Medical Company, 34th Command Group, 2/19 and 1/34.

After lunch, Dean went to the TACP, located at the end of the CP building. Friendly aircraft were overhead, but apparently were not attacking. TACP reports were being ignored by the 34th CP, which seemed to be in disarray. Dean himself called in several strikes on enemy artillery and tank concentrations.

A platoon of tanks from Co. A, 71st Heavy Tank Battalion, 1st Cavalry Division, arrived in Taejon about this time. A/71 Tk Bn was attached to the 21st Infantry. The platoon leader reported to the general, who was surprised to see him. The young lieutenant said that he had been sent there to escort vehicles out of Taejon as requested by the 34th Regiment. He had been startled to see the smoking hulks of T-34s in the center of the city.

Some time between 3:30 and 4:30 p.m. the Cavalry tankers escorted the first group of vehicles out of Taejon over the road to Yongdong via Okchon.

Appleman, in *South to the Naktong*, points out a number of incidents which took place before noon on July 20. Dean and Beauchamp seemed to have misinterpreted their significance.

The first of these was a telephone call from an artillery observer who demanded to speak to the senior officer present. Beauchamp took the call. The observer said that a large column of troops was approaching Taejon from the east, and that he was positive that they were North Koreans. To Beauchamp, that meant the Okchon road, and the 21st Infantry, an impression he gained from his conversation with GEN Dean, who had indicated that the 21st would cover the withdrawal from Taejon. COL Beauchamp thought the 21st was moving forward to provide this cover. What Dean had meant was that the 21st was to cover the withdrawal from its Okchon positions, keeping open the road from Taejon. Beauchamp told the observer that the troops were friendly and not to fire on them. Appleman believed that these troops were actually on the Kumsan road southeast of Taejon, which is quite possible.

Late in the afternoon, shortly after the Cavalry-escorted convoy had departed, GEN Dean received a report from an aerial observer that a truck column of about 20 vehicles was moving north on the Kumsan road. Dean checked with the 34th Infantry's S3 and was told the vehicles were from the 24th Recon Co. The general believed the column actually was one of enemy vehicles, but elements of the Recon Co. did enter Taejon from that direction at about that time.

LTC Ayres earlier had seen movements of large bodies of enemy troops, but he was in no position to report to the Taejon CP at that time.

Escape of 1/34

MAJ Dunham (XO, 1/34) took his 150 or so men to establish a roadblock on the Kumsan road to protect Taejon's rear. On the way, they had one fire-fight with what they believed were guerrillas. Moving on, the party entered a draw at Kuwan-ni, about 2 1/2 miles south of Taejon. The enemy fired down into the Americans from nearby hills, wounding the major and creating other casualties. CPT Sidney M. Marks, a WW II paratrooper and CO of Co. D, took charge of the group. Marks had been a company commander with the 101st Airborne at Bastogne, and later commanded a brigade in Vietnam, retiring as a MAJ GEN. William B. Caldwell, then a platoon leader in A/34, said that Marks "was probably one of the outstanding leaders... that we had in the Army." Caldwell retired as a lieutenant general.

Edgar Pawelczyk was with this group. He recalled they split up just before the major was hit. CPT Marks led one element along the ridges, while MAJ Dunham descended into the valley with another. Pawelczyk started to follow Dunham, "when I heard the captain yell 'All Co. D follow me,'" Edgar wrote. He turned and followed Marks up the hill.

The enemy was in force between Marks' group and Taejon and could be seen south of the city. It was decided to head south, then east. "With this group of 200-plus people, the five officers and [the] wounded we headed south," said Caldwell.

"CAPT Marks took the lead column and went west into the valley," recalled LT Wilcox (D/34). There, they met other elements of 1/34 — CO of Co. C, CPT Jess Portman with 15-20 men; CPT Osburn (A/34); LT Johnson, CO of Co. B, with several men and CPT Barszcz, of the 19th, with a small force.

"We found a road running north and south," wrote CPT Osburn. "The South Korean civilians had evacuated, which placed us in a vacuum [between enemy and friendly lines]."

The combined party marched south all that night, taking breaks along the way. "SGT West had two cans of wet rations and about a dozen of us got about half [a] spoonful," recalled PFC Pawelczyk. At about 10 a.m. on the 21st they reached Kunsan. Here, some men headed northeast toward Yongdong, while those from 1/34 continued south. It was possibly in Kunsan that Pawelczyk and a few others obtained some rice balls "and raided a watermelon patch... . Our water was scarce so we drank from the streams," he wrote.

Friendly Koreans reported enemy soldiers on both eastern and western flanks of the group. Men went into fields along the way to dig up and eat raw vegetables. Caldwell said that he saw some officers in the force who failed to do their duty, and, in his opinion "did not deserve to wear the rank which they had on their collar." But he believed that "had it not been for CAPT Marks, the group" would never have escaped.

Marks and others had organized the group, but for three days they progressed "at a snail's pace," as Caldwell put it. After the fourth day, Marks had the force put out security and he and LT Caldwell, both "in super physical condition," went ahead to reconnoiter. The following morning the two officers came to a ROK Corps headquarters. At first the corps commander refused to help. but when CPT Marks pointed out that refusal might cause an international incident, the general relented and provided three trucks to shuttle the captain's men to the corps CP. While there, Marks got through to Eighth Army HQ, and was told that the Army couldn't help him.

As the exhausted men arrived at the ROK Corps CP, they were taken to a schoolhouse and fed tomatoes, rice, eggs and potatoes. Marks and his men then commandeered a ROK boxcar train and went down to Yosu. At Yosu, they obtained about 300 eggs and hard-boiled them in the old engine's boiler. There was no water to drink, so the troops washed the eggs down with one bottle of beer per man and one pint of saki (rice wine) per platoon. "This was the first purified liquid that the men had in the course of these five days," said Caldwell. Next, they commandeered a boat and sailed on to Pusan. At Pusan they were met by an Eighth Army representative. After spending the night in a schoolhouse, they were outfitted with new weapons and equipment, and were sent the following day to rejoin the 34th.

LTC Ayres, MAJ Cooper and Seoul waited in hiding until dark on July 20, then crawled away and got onto a path. "After that we traveled west... for a few hours along a narrow path," Ayres recounted. "It was moonlight and we could see fairly well. All of a sudden, there was a large square rock on the right of the path" with some Koreans nearby. The enemy soldiers saw Ayres and his party. One of them jumped on top of the rock and started yelling and waving his arms. Ayres shot him with his pistol, then he, Cooper and Seoul ran. Ayres became separated from the other two. On July 21 he joined a group of civilians walking along the road. "Suddenly, one of them patted me on the back and in perfect English told me that I should not be with them because there were North Koreans in the area." The colonel took the man's advice and left the group. For three more days he traveled on, picking up another American soldier here and there until he ran across some men from 2/19. There were between 100 and 200 men with him when they finally regained 24th Division lines. Shortly afterward, MAJ Cooper and Seoul came in on a Korean cart. Once back in Yongdong, LTC Ayres rounded up all the men of his battalion he could find and began reorganizing.

Withdrawal from Taejon

Back at Taejon, early in the afternoon of July 20, LT Herbert's platoon sergeant pointed out to him a large column of troops on high ground west of the roadblock. Herbert soon decided they were enemy — about a battalion. The enemy approached to about 600 yards of the block, stopped and observed. Shortly, a runner from a 155mm howitzer battery a little distance behind the position arrived to ask about the situation. Herbert went back with the man to talk to the BC. The howitzers were placed to fire in three different directions, but none to cover the area forward of Herbert's roadblock. The BC told Herbert that he could not change direction of the howitzers without the authority of the battalion S3. That officer, in a telephone conversation with Herbert, refused to approve the change.

While Herbert was trying to get artillery support, the enemy facing the roadblock began to shell both his position and that of the artillery battery, producing both infantry and artillery casualties. In response to a runner-delivered message from the lieutenant, a scratch force of 50 men, under LT William Wygal (S2, 2/19) was sent to reinforce him. The combined force held off the enemy.

GEN Dean, watching the fight, thought that this was 2/19, not just a small roadblock. The troops seemed to be holding their own. He returned to the CP to discover that COL Beauchamp was not there, and no one knew where he had gone. He had not been seen since 3 p.m. LT Murray Carroll also returned to the CP about this time. "Everything was becoming chaotic and disorganized," he wrote, "and there was an underlying feeling that we had stayed too long." Carroll made another trip to the rail yard for ammunition. When he returned to the CP he discovered that a "truck-load of mail came in from Yongdong!" The driver reported sniper fire just outside of Taejon.

LTC Wadlington had been in and out of the 34th CP all morning. He was unaware that withdrawal orders had been issued, nor did he know the whereabouts of Beauchamp. LT Walter Sas, of the I & R platoon, later came in and reported seeing the colonel headed toward Yongdong (on the Okchon road).

COL Beauchamp, apparently without informing anybody of his intentions, left the CP in his jeep about the time that the first convoy was forming to leave Taejon. He drove along the withdrawal route to the southeast edge of town, where he found four tanks of the 24th Recon Co. and ordered them to remain and defend the area and the Okchon road. As he started back into Taejon, he looked back to discover the tanks leaving their positions. He turned around and ran them down on the Okchon road, braving sniper fire to do so. Climbing a nearby hill, he discovered many groups of North Koreans heading for the Okchon road from the south, and he knew the enemy already had the withdrawal route under fire.

The colonel decided to organize a force to defend the critical pass 4 miles east of the city. Taking the two Recon Co. tanks he had with him, Beauchamp put them into position, then commandeered some passing quad-.50 half tracks to add to the force. Some artillery vehicles passed through on their way to Okchon. Then what appeared to be an infantry company passed through. The colonel tried to wave them down, but the commander just waved back and kept on going.

As to the identity of the company, I/34 was to "lead" at least one convoy element out of Taejon. It has not been established when that unit left the city. The 24th Division War Diary 192400K to 202400K July (midnight July 19 to midnight July 20) states that 3/34 and part of the field artillery cleared through the tunnel without a great deal of interference at 1 p.m. Enemy forces then established a strong block, preventing any more troops from getting through so easily. The diary also noted that the 24th Recon Co. arrived in Yongdong at 6 p.m. on July 20.

GEN Dean had ordered the Recon Co. to escort medical units and wounded out over the Okchon road. "We executed this order from GEN Dean, knocking out the roadblock on the outskirts of Taejon and effecting the escape of the medical units," wrote LT William F. Coghill (West Point, 1947; XO, 24th Recon Co.). Given previous evidence, the unit which passed him may have been the Recon. Co., under Dean's orders to escort medics and wounded out of Taejon. However, William Coghill has no such recollection. "I vaguely recall encountering a senior officer at a bridge while we were exiting Taejon," he wrote. "He was standing there with a carbine shooting the electrical lines near the bridge... . I do not recall us being flagged by an officer of the 34th Inf... .." At Yongsan, in August 1950 he was badly wounded and lost his left leg.

Enemy fire built up little by little along the pass to the tunnels. At about 4:30 p.m., COL Beauchamp saw a train halted by enemy fire at the railroad tunnel. He was under the impression that the 21st Infantry was supposed to cover the withdrawal route. Getting into his jeep, he drove through to the CP of 1/21. The 1/21 Journal states: "1812 hours [6:12 p.m.] COL Beauchamp arrived at command post." From there, Beauchamp phoned GEN Menoher, who was at the 21st CP. He ordered Beauchamp to come to Okchon and give a detailed report.

The train which COL Beauchamp saw was probably the one which CPT Hatfield sent out toward Yongdong. He had tried to get this train out in midafternoon, only to discover that the Korean crew had taken the locomotive and fled south. Dean called the division CP for another engine. One was dispatched from Iwon-ni, 15 miles south of Taejon. The locomotive's tender was punctured by enemy fire enroute to Taejon. Hatfield waited at the sniper-infested yards of the city. As the engine pulled into the station, it was hit again. The engineer told the captain that the locomotive was so damaged that it couldn't pull the train.

To Hatfield's amazement, the engineer threw the train in reverse and backed quickly southeast out of the yard. The engineer was killed at the tunnel when enemy fire and grenades struck

the locomotive. Although wounded, the fireman got the train through to Okchon. Dean was told of this incident and called for another locomotive. At 5 p.m. he was informed by phone that another engine was being sent, under guard. Hatfield dutifully stayed at the yard in Taejon and was killed waiting for the locomotive that never came. The next morning American aircraft destroyed the ammunition and supplies remaining at the Taejon rail yard.

Once again, the leadership of the 34th, or what was left of it, in Taejon (and now elements of the 19th, plus supporting artillery at Taejon) fell to LTC Wadlington. He issued instructions them to withdraw from the city.

He recalled the 3d Platoon, 24th Recon. Co. from a position it occupied a few miles south of Taejon on the Kumsan road, which the enemy had left alone. As the platoon withdrew it was fired upon by a machine gun near the railroad station. PVT James H. Nelson knocked the gun out with a .50-cal machine gun mounted on a 2 1/2-ton truck. By this time, CPT Jack Smith, acting CO of 3/34, had L Co. deployed to defend the regimental CP and had sent the rest of the battalion on to join a convoy.

Herbert's roadblock remained in place. The 155 howitzer battery left. Enemy troops moved in on Herbert's position and the battery site when he pulled his men out to join the withdrawal.

Over in A/11 FAB the artillerymen had been observing "a steady stream of people in civilian clothing walking" over a ridge about 500 meters from the battery position, wrote Terrell. "About 1500 (3 p.m.), we started receiving heavy small arms and machine gun fire from that ridge." The battery continued firing missions, even though the enemy fire became heavier. About an hour later, "I received a call from a lieutenant colonel from Div Arty... . He told me to evacuate the position, leave the howitzers and equipment and just get the battery personnel on wheeled vehicles and leave Taejon," Terrell wrote. He informed the colonel that he could get everything out, although it might take time.

"We weren't going to leave the equipment. He then gave me a direct order to leave the equipment and get the men out of Taejon," Terrell continued. He loaded the men up and went into Taejon, where they were caught in what he described as "a horrendous traffic jam." GEN Dean's aide came along and told him to report to Dean. The general asked Terrell if he could get the howitzers out if protected by infantry support, and Terrell responded that he could. Dean told him to get his men and to meet the infantry contingent back at the battery position.

Terrell returned to the stalled convoy, selected 12 or 15 men to accompany him, and directed the remainder of the battery to continue south out of Taejon to try and rejoin the battalion.

"Our infantry did an outstanding job in drawing a lot of enemy fire off of our operations and we [had] no casualties," Terrell related. "The 12 men and I got all five howitzers (one at a time) and the rest of the equipment out of the position." (See Chapter Note.)

Terrell was unaware of McDaniel; all he knew was that some "infantry" were keeping the enemy occupied while he and his men from A/ 11 FAB retrieved all five howitzers of their battery. The howitzers were subsequently lost dur-

ing the withdrawal, but none of them were left in the battery position at Taejon.

Terrell led the five M-5 tractors pulling the five 155mm howitzers through Taejon. "The town was ablaze," he wrote, "and... snipers [were] shooting from... windows." His 3/4-ton truck was disabled by this fire and was pushed aside by the first tractor. The artillerymen loaded infantry and engineer wounded onto the tractors and moved out again, while Terrell rode hanging onto the side of the vehicle.

His little convoy took the wrong road and was attacked by enemy "burp guns," mortars and machine guns. The lead tractor, with Terrell on it, crashed into one of the numerous trees lining the road out of town. No one was hurt, but the tractor wouldn't restart. The wounded were transferred to the remaining tractors and the unit started out again, with Terrell hanging onto the side of this tractor, too. A mortar round exploded beside it, wounding him. "I felt like I had been hit in the left arm and shoulder by a baseball bat," he wrote, "but I hung on the side... . I found I had been hit by numerous small fragments from the mortar round but it really wasn't serious."

Back at the 34th CP, word came that the enemy had destroyed a number of trucks, blocking the street at the southeast edge of town. Fires could be seen and firing heard from that quarter. Dean sent a message in the clear to Division headquarters ordering armor to be sent; that there was a roadblock on the eastern edge of Taejon. There is no evidence that any action was taken to try to carry out this order.

Unable to get any information from panic-struck South Korean officials about an alternate northward route out of Taejon, Dean returned to the CP. Since Beauchamp was not present, he ordered Wadlington to close the CP and withdraw. Enemy artillery and mortar fire fell into the city, one round striking the 34th Infantry's medical collecting station, wounding 10 men.

LTC Wadlington led the convoy with two jeeps with five men in each. MAJ McDaniel was at the end of the column. Dean told Smith to keep Co. L in position for 45 minutes then withdraw. At 5:55 p.m., GEN Dean drove out the gate of the CP, conferred briefly with Wadlington and other senior officers, and instructed them to clean out any snipers that stopped the convoy. The large main convoy started a few minutes after 6 p.m. Parts of the city were aflame, and some of the buildings along the route were afire. Dense clouds of smoke sometimes blinded drivers. The convoy paused once while a burning ammunition trailer and telephone poles were removed from the street.

Herbert and his runner were in the seventh or eighth vehicle in the column, a 3/4-ton truck, with the remainder of his platoon near the end of the convoy. About three or four vehicles from the end was SFC Joseph S. Szito, with elements of Co. H, 19th Infantry. As the convoy proceeded, other vehicles joined the end of the column. As the convoy gained a wide street, heavy enemy small arms and machine gun fire swept the column. Wadlington and the men from the lead jeeps jumped out and returned fire. In a few minutes enemy fire slackened. The colonel then had the second jeep take the lead while he watched part of the convoy go by. In trying to overtake the head of the column, his jeep took some wrong turns, ending in a dead end schoolyard. Destroying the jeep, he and the men with him headed into the hills nearby.

The convoy moved rapidly through the city under enemy fire all the way. LT Carroll, George Reed, regimental motor officer, and Al Thomas were in the S4 jeep. Reed was driving, Thomas in the passenger seat and Carroll in the back. "The major portion of the city seemed to be on fire now," said Carroll. "Burning debris was falling in the street.... . Al and I were keeping up a steady fire on both sides of the street." At an intersection they saw a 24th MP jeep overturned and burning, with two MPs lying dead nearby.

A 2 1/2-ton truck smashed into a building at one intersection, almost blocking the road. The first part of the convoy, about 50 vehicles, took a wrong turn through an underpass of the railroad and ended up in the same schoolyard as LTC Wadlington. LT Wygal, LT Herbert and his runner were in this group, but not his platoon. Abandoning the vehicles, the approximately 125 men in this party, led by an artillery major, went into the hills. During the night, about half the men stopped for a break, while 60 others with Herbert and Wygal kept going. The group that halted was attacked by the enemy, and all either were killed or captured. The Wygal-Herbert party gained 21st Infantry lines on July 22 without incident. Herbert's platoon was not so fortunate — only seven of them got out, five of whom were wounded.

When Carroll's jeep made the turn under the underpass, he discovered that the convoy ahead of them had gone in the wrong direction. "We made sure that the vehicles behind us saw the turn we made and kept with us," he wrote. Once out of town, enemy fire on the column got heavier. "A BAR man jumped up out of a ditch along the road... and [we] pulled him aboard." The man was from the 19th, and he sat on the hood of the jeep firing his BAR. They passed burning vehicles and dead bodies along the road.

Vehicles behind them were knocked out and set on fire. "One stretch along a rice paddy was like a shooting gallery," Carroll wrote. "The trip through the tunnel and defile was a nightmare. The small-arms fire continued to increase in intensity, with mortar fire added to it." But Carroll, the men with him, and his jeep made it through to a detachment of the 3d Engineers on the road commanded by CPT Yancy Bivings. They were directed to an assembly area, where COL Beauchamp arrived about 10 p.m., Carroll recalled.

LTC Wadlington and his group started out in the hills, but the men were so exhausted that he moved to low ground. A quartermaster officer was brought to them late in the afternoon by friendly South Koreans "That made two officers in the group," wrote Wadlington to GEN Dean on July 1, 1954. He was commenting on Appleman's manuscript of *South to the Naktong*. "[An] NCO and I walked at the head of the column with three men acting as a point about 200-300 yards ahead of the column. There was no flank security — men were too exhausted to continue cross country," he continued.

LTC Wadlington said that there was one NCO with the group who was very helpful to him, perhaps SFC Szito. Also, Szito may have been among a small group of men which the colonel

recalled joining his late in the afternoon. "There were no Koreans with us at any time," he wrote. "A raft was built on my orders... as some of the men could not swim and others were too exhausted... ." One man ... drowned. He "was too exhausted to even hold onto the raft as he was ferried over no more than 30 feet of deep water." Finally, wrote Wadlington, "The total number of men in our group was not over 30 when we got into the lines of the 21st Inf."

When the part of the convoy SFC Szito was in was stopped by knocked-out and burning vehicles and heavy enemy machine gun fire on the road, he set up a 60mm mortar in a ditch and lobbed 24 rounds on a group of enemy on the hill south of the road. Then he manned an 81mm mortar and laid down a screen with 30 smoke (white phosphorous) rounds, then fired an additional 30 or 40 rounds of HE against enemy mortars. But enemy fire continued unabated. At about 8:45 p.m., the surviving vehicles behind this block were burned by the men and then they headed into the hills. SGT Scoggins, Co. H Machine Gun Platoon, fired at the enemy from an exposed position on a rock as the troops moved up the slope. A man about three feet forward of Szito was hit in the head.

Szito gained shelter on the hill, until driven away by enemy mortar fire about dark. He joined a column of about 40 men led by a South Korean colonel who had a police dog with him. Szito indicated that two other South Korean officers were with this group. When the party came upon an enemy soldier, the colonel engaged him in conversation while one of the officers slipped up behind the North Korean and killed him with a knife. The Korean officer returned and told the group that they would be unable to cross the bridge a short distance away because the enemy was there. The group then rested in place. Szito dozed off. When he awoke about 3 a.m., the Korean officers were gone. Scoggins then volunteered to go ahead for help from U.S. tanks. He found no tanks, but eventually made it into friendly lines. Szito took charge of the group. Shortly after daylight they set out to the northeast. Three North Koreans gave chase, but after about an hour, gave up.

About 11 a.m., Szito's group came upon a party of 40 men, including the first sergeant, a platoon sergeant and several others from Co. H. The combined force continued northeast until they overtook another group of about 60 more men about 1 p.m. SFC Szito claimed that LTC Wadlington was in this group. Szito's account of what happened from that point does not agree with that of LTC Wadlington, recounted above.

Szito claims that he, not LTC Wadlington, led the combined group from then on. He also averred that the colonel, LT Paul F. Regan (CO, H/19), and another officer stayed in the center of the column and took no leadership role. The sergeant also indicated that the group included seven wounded men, including a PFC Petry and a SGT Goodson. Along the way a railroad handcar was found and the wounded placed aboard. Six men, led by SGT Justice, "pumped" the car to safety in friendly lines. Szito said that 18 men became separated during a break at night, but made it on their own to safety.

The sergeant then told the interviewer that at a river they came to, the men built a raft for the

colonel because he could not swim, and sent him across first. He then said that Wadlington went on ahead, not waiting for the others to cross. A few miles beyond the river, the party entered 21st Infantry lines. Szito said there were 103 men in the group.

The two accounts cannot be reconciled, but the lack of leadership by Wadlington which Szito claims does not square with his previous actions, nor his conduct later on. The colonel's leadership and his conduct before and after Taejon always were exemplary. Since Wadlington had written that he had been swimming since the age of 5, the raft did not have to be built specifically for him, as Szito declared. (See Chapter Notes.)

Edward Arendell and his driver, Henry Martin, were returning from the rail yard with a load of ammunition when, to their amazement, GEN Dean stepped out in the street and stopped them. "He was stopping all vehicles," Arendell wrote. "He said get in line with the other vehicles and prepare to move out on command... ." Finally, the convoy started off and the enemy took it under fire. "Small-arms fire was coming from every direction," Arendell recalled. Many times the convoy halted while damaged or wrecked vehicles were pushed aside. "We picked up wounded men," Arendell continued. "Our truck was hit with small-arms fire. Two of the outside dual tires were shot out... . During this ordeal I saw colonels and lieutenant colonels directing fire on the enemy... . We fought through this enemy gauntlet until some time during the night." Arendell and his truck, though damaged, got through. Finally, Edward wrote this: "Why did the units of the 24th sit and let the enemy close all about them before any action was taken?"

Meantime, SSG McKeon and his men, after dropping the sick man off at the aid station in the Taejon railroad station, drove back into town. There, in conversation with GEN Dean, McKeon was advised to try to rejoin his unit. He searched in vain, then returned to the railroad station. "The fire [from blazing buildings and vehicle hulks] was now becoming rather general," he wrote. So he left Taejon. "I cautioned my drivers to wait until the vehicle in front of them had gone into the smoke, then to floor the gas pedal and keep on going until they came out the other side. There was to be no stopping for anything part way through." They made it out of Taejon and were starting up a grade when they came under fire from the crest of a hill to the front. A number of McKeon's vehicles had machine guns mounted on them, and some of his men returned fire with these guns. "[W]hile they laid down protective fire, the rest of the vehicles made it up the hill," McKeon wrote. "Here they stopped and laid down protective fire for the other vehicles to join. There was a lot of firing going on... ."

"Approximately 1900 or 1930 (7 or 7:30 p.m.) we started our departure from Taejon," wrote LT Clarke. "Drove through streets infected with snipers, machinegun nests and burning gasoline. Outside Taejon the GEN [Dean] stopped his jeep... and loaded [some wounded] on board." The general waved on his jeep and the escort jeep, containing Clarke and more wounded. Shortly, Clarke was also wounded when they hit another roadblock. There was a disabled truck ahead of the jeeps and the area was under enemy machine gun fire. "At this point," continued Clarke, "the general arrived on a prime mover of an artillery piece. The general jumped into the ditch and I followed close behind." GEN Dean, LT Clarke and others with them were able to hide until nightfall.

At about 9:30 p.m. they left their hiding place, crossed a bean patch and headed into the hills. About 50 minutes later, CPT Rowlands went ahead with 12-15 men. GEN Dean, Clarke and four or five others stayed behind with a badly wounded, delirious soldier, who drank all the water and wanted more. About midnight Dean wanted to go for water, but Clarke dissuaded him, saying that the enemy might be trailing them and that there was probably water further ahead. About 1:15 a.m., Clarke was proceeding when he discovered that no one was following. He went back and found five men asleep on the ground — but not the general. He had gone for water, said one of the men. Clarke waited until about 3:15 a.m., then set out with the five men. The general never returned. He had fallen down an embankment, knocking himself out. Now alone, he wandered in enemy territory for 36 days. On Aug. 25, two South Koreans, pretending to be friends, led him into capture by the North Koreans. The two men who betrayed him later were caught and executed by the South Korean government.

LT Terrell's path crossed that of GEN Dean again. About 6 miles out of Taejon, as Terrell remembers it, they came to a house next to a bridge over a dry creek bed. "I saw GEN Dean's wrecked jeep near the front of the house and he was laying on the ground beside the jeep," Terrell wrote. He jumped off the tractor and discovered that Dean was apparently alone and unhurt. Terrell offered him a ride on the tractor. The general declined. It was already too crowded with wounded, but he urged the lieutenant to go on with the vehicle. "I couldn't leave him there alone," wrote Terrell, "so I told the driver to go on... . (We didn't know it at the time, but there were no more North Koreans south of the road to Yongdong)," he continued, "and the tractor that I tried to get GEN Dean to ride was the only [one] to make it to Yongdong."

He and Dean crawled behind the house, where they found the general's aide, CPT Clarke, and five or six other men. By nightfall, another "15 or so soldiers" had joined the little band. They headed west toward a ridge to get away from the road. Terrell recalled crossing a "dry [his emphasis] river bed then moving up to the top of the ridge. At this point," Terrell recounted, "GEN Dean insisted on going back... to the river... to get some water and left us. Some of us waited on... that ridge until dawn... before we continued our march."

After traveling another night with this group, Terrell and some others "went back to the road," he wrote, "stole some food and Korean clothes and mixed with the refugees traveled South... [ending] up on the 24th or 25th of July [in] the lines of the 8th Cavalry Regiment."

Stewart Sizemore, of D/34 was in a party of 10-12 men trying to escape Taejon. "There were columns and columns of vehicles that were burning with bodies in them," said Stewart. He had two friends who worked in the battalion radio truck. "As I was going through the town I saw them. They were both dead in a truck sandwiched

in with the rest of them... . The Division Clearing [Company — a medical unit]... was another catastrophe. The enemy got behind them and just destroyed everything. I'm sure they weren't out [to take] any prisoners... ."

LT Spero Calos wrote, "The noose was getting tighter [in Taejon], the avenues of escape fewer and the presence of the enemy even greater... . As we departed the city, parts of it were going up in flames... . Had it not been for a 2 1/2-ton truck that I boarded and managed to navigate through the city and around road blocks and traffic jams, we too, would have had to cross the mountains... afoot... . The exodus out of Taejon was frightful, horrendous and costly."

Co. I, 34th Inf. led one convoy element out of Taejon. American troops fired back at the enemy as the trucks rolled out of the city. "We were shooting from both sides of the truck as the driver wove his way through the streets," said James Jones. "It's a good thing he knew where he was going otherwise we wouldn't have made it out of town. The North Koreans were shooting at us from all sides but it was hard to see them... ." First, there was obscuring smoke from burning buildings and vehicles; then the trucks bouncing "up and down like a wild horse." Third, the enemy was using smokeless powder, making it almost impossible to detect the sniper's location. "I never saw any of the enemy," Jones said, "until we got out in the open; and even then you couldn't fire an accurate shot. So we fired in their general direction... . It was one hell of a ride. Too bad we don't have it on film, it would make a movie better than any of John Wayne's westerns."

There were casualties on Jones' truck. "I felt something like a light slap just below my belt on the left side," said Jones. The man next to him, N. Eggers, yelled, "I'm hit!" Eggers was laid on the floor of the truck, where someone tried to help him. Jones found a sliver or metal shaving clinging to his trousers. Had he been turned to the right to fire instead of the left, he would have been hit instead of Eggers. The truck got through to the lines of the 21st Regiment, and the wounded were removed. "The rest of us just sat on the trucks too damned tired to dismount," he wrote.

Enemy mortar fire joined the small-arms and machine gun fire raking vehicles trying to negotiate the Okchon road. The lead vehicle of one group was hit by a shell and began to burn. A half-track pushed it to the side of the road. For some, the firing was so fierce that they jumped into nearby ditches. At places, North Korean soldiers rose from nearby rice paddies to spray the column with burp gun fire.

Between the vehicles destroyed by the enemy and those set afire by the Americans, the road was littered with wreckage of the first convoys, making it almost impossible for following elements to get through. As it grew late in the day, men from those following trucks jumped from their vehicles into roadside ditches and waited for darkness, an estimated 250 men.

"About 1600 (4 p.m.) the motor officer of the 34th told me to join the regimental train for a dash out of town," said 2LT Ralph C. Boyd, a truck platoon leader with the 24th Quartermaster Company (QM Co.) The motor officer told Boyd that the 21st had cleared the road.

He was mistaken: The 21st had no control over the Okchon road except where it entered its lines two miles or more beyond the highway, and the railroad tunnels which were the choke point of the enemy's roadblock. By the time Boyd and his convoy got out of Taejon, the enemy had established a 1 1/2-mile-long gauntlet running west from the tunnels. The lieutenant was in the convoy which came upon the wreckage-strewn highway. Three of his drivers were wounded, but all stayed with their vehicles. But his convoy was stopped by the wreckage, it was not long before all 150 vehicles also were knocked out.

When darkness fell, LT Boyd looked for a senior officer to take charge of the 250 or so men there. He found a chaplain and a Medical Service officer (an administrator, not a doctor). So Boyd organized the people the best way he could. "I located six vehicles which we could operate: A full-tracked artillery prime mover, two half tracks, two 2 1/2-ton trucks and a jeep," Boyd recounted. He had the prime mover clear the road and loaded the seriously wounded on the other vehicles. All the men who could walk moved along the ditches. "Occasional machine gun and small-arms fire came near our column," Boyd said, "but I had warned the men not to fire back. I believed that we would be harder to locate... and... that the enemy might think us part of their own force." The little column moved along without much difficulty. Boyd decided to go around the tunnels by using a bypass. Being very tired, the lieutenant climbed onto the prime mover with SGT Richardson.

"Near the first tunnel a machine gun opened fire on our column," Boyd continued. "Three rounds tore into Richardson's right arm and one creased my knee." Both men were knocked from the prime mover. Boyd was knocked unconscious when he fell on some large rocks. When he came to all was quiet — the trucks and men were gone. He got up and literally ran 2 1/2 miles into the 21st Infantry lines. Scorning medical attention, he jumped from the ambulance he was put into, "hitched a ride to division... and reported to the G4." He then went on and reported to the G2 what "he had seen during the previous day and night." Only then did he check into the medics for treatment. LT Boyd's platoon lost all their trucks, and five or six of his men were wounded, but none were killed. SGT Richardson escaped. Boyd was awarded the Silver Star for organizing and leading the remnants of the column to safety.

Robert Moser, of B/34, with his small group of men, climbed a steep hill south of the CP where he had met the warrant officer. From the hill, "I surveyed conditions in Taejon," Moser wrote. "Parts of the town were burning [and] vehicles bumper to bumper seemed held on the road heading east (the Okchon road). There were T-34 tanks in town... ." When Moser and his party reached the top of the hill, they headed south, following the ridge's crest. Although fired on from time to time, his group moved about five miles without much interference. At that point, they descended, Moser wrote, "to a valley floor to the east and traveled south along the road." Coming upon an engineer detachment at a bridge, "we traveled south on their 2 1/2-ton trucks. Picking up stragglers along the way, we were finally commanded by an Infantry captain of the 3d Battalion, 34th Infantry." At Chinju the men boarded a train for Pusan. Along the way, Korean women fed them — the first food they had since Taejon. At Pusan the wounded were sent to Japan and the others went back to their units.

There were many acts of bravery and self sacrifice during the withdrawal from Taejon, such as those by PVT Charles T. Zimmerman and SGT George D. Libby, both of C/3 ECB. Zimmerman's jeep was destroyed by a mortar round and he was wounded. The enemy then fired at his group. In addition to his first wound, Zimmerman was struck by 11 more bullets. In spite of this he killed five of the enemy and destroyed two machine guns.

SGT Libby already had twice risked his life at the roadblock by running out onto the fire-swept road to pull wounded men to safety, then returning enemy fire with his carbine. An artillery prime mover came along, towing a 105mm howitzer. Libby placed a wounded man on the truck and stationed himself as a human shield for the driver. "You're crazy, bud!" declared the driver.

"Maybe so," Libby responded, "But you're the only guy around here who can drive this thing."

SGT Libby was struck again and again by enemy bullets, but he clung to his position shielding the driver until they were out of enemy range. He then collapsed and died. For his unselfish sacrifice, SGT Libby became the first soldier of the 24th Infantry Division to be awarded the Medal of Honor.

James H. Griffin was wounded for the first time trying to get out of Taejon. He was a member of HHC, 2/19. At the time of the battle, he had been in the Army four years, almost to the day. Unlike most of the soldiers sent from Japan, he had been stationed in Korea before and was familiar with the country. Griffin used this knowledge to help him elude the enemy and escape to friendly lines. He was wounded again on the Naktong River.

The Odyssey of PVT Donald Luedtke

"Our radio truck," wrote Luedtke, "was four vehicles behind GEN Dean's jeep" as they began moving through Taejon to escape. "We started taking sniper fire. We'd bail out of our vehicles and shoot in the places we thought it was coming from, then we'd get in our vehicles and try to keep moving." Donald Onion, one of Luedtke's friends had climbed aboard the one behind Luedtke. He did not make it.

"We got to a place where the buildings were burning on both sides of the street. It was an inferno — two enemy tanks were burning.... GEN Dean... pulled off [t]o the side of the street," Luedtke continued. A number of vehicles, including Luedtke's, made a dash through the smoke filled street and most of the fire, when the driver of his truck, CPL Yantz, was shot just under one eye. The bullet went on through to hit the man next to him in the shoulder. Luedtke and others jumped from the vehicle and returned fire. Yantz was "slumped onto the steering wheel bleeding from his nose, mouth and both sides of

his face," Luedtke recalled. A few vehicles made it through. Luedtke and others jumped on a passing vehicle and rode until it stopped. Many men were shot down, but Luedtke finally made his way to the head of the convoy in this manner.

Out on the open road, the surviving men and trucks were caught in a cross-fire from a creek bed to the west and other enemy on a ridge line to the east. George Taylor (L/34) crawled up to Luedtke with a 3.5-inch bazooka. The two men fired the launcher into some houses where they thought the enemy might be, and discovered the enemy up on the ridge. Luedtke fired his carbine on full automatic at them, while lying partly on the road. A slug from return fire "hit the ground... in front of me," he wrote, "and ricocheted and hit the guy next to me" in the calf of his leg. Luedtke patched the man up. He could see enemy all around and some of the men with him were talking surrender. "Everyone was looking for leadership," he wrote.

LT James C. Little came along shouting for the men to get in the vehicles and move out. Men piled into a jeep, Luedtke helping the man with the calf wound. "I could hear the dull thump of slugs hitting, and the screaming and moaning of guys getting hit," he wrote. The jeep turned over in a ditch. Luedtke ran across the road to the east, about 50 yards up a sandy knoll, and jumped into an abandoned foxhole. Enemy bullets kicked up dirt all around him. Three men ran by, one of them the man with the calf wound. Luedtke started to crawl out of the hole on his stomach as bullets struck all around him. "One hit directly under my face, momentarily dazing me." As he rose to a squatting position, a bullet struck him near the base of his spine, plowed through his thigh and pushed the skin outward on the front and lodged there. "I got up limping, not able to see out of my left eye and bleeding from my face and mouth," he wrote. He caught up to the three men who had run past him. They got to a position about 20 yards from an enemy machine gun and a number of enemy soldiers and there remained hidden.

About 10 p.m. the men started south, Luedtke well in the lead. At the top of a knoll, an enemy soldier shot at him but missed. The men ducked around the enemy foxhole and kept going. They continued to travel east then south, "when suddenly about 100 feet from us, two people came into view," said Luedtke. The two figures also stopped. Luedtke was ready to shoot, but discovered, in time, that it was a lieutenant and CPL Yantz, the wounded driver. Yantz "was quite weak from loss of blood and his eyes were swollen shut," Luedtke recalled. "So we put a man on each side of him... and we headed southwest toward the mountains." None of the men had any water, but they came to a little wash and drank from that. Later, they eluded an enemy patrol, then skirted an area where a battle was in progress.

They climbed near the top of a mountain, where they found a stream. Luedtke, Yantz and the man with the calf wound all needed water and a rest. After resting a time, the lieutenant suggested that they move on. Luedtke, Yantz and one of the unwounded men went to get another drink of water before going on. While they did so, the officer and two men left them.

Luedtke and the two men with him struggled

on by themselves, finally moving into the valley where it was easier to travel. There they found a stream and drank again. When Luedtke said that they should go back up into the hills, the unwounded man balked. "I reminded him of our vow not to surrender; he said he wouldn't; he'd shoot it out with them. I pleaded with him that I needed his help, but to no avail.... So I left him there."

He led the blinded Yantz by the hand up the mountain. At about 3 a.m., they eluded another enemy patrol. His leg was getting difficult to move. Once they came upon about a dozen Korean civilians near a house. After watching them for a time, Luedtke and Yantz approached the Koreans. The people didn't seem to want Americans around, so the two men got away as quickly as possible.

Later, they met an old Korean man, who pointed to the top of a nearby mountain. Following him, they found South Korean police digging in. After resting, Luedtke and Yantz returned to the road below, following it to a village where they met a number of GIs, some of whom were badly wounded. The villagers helped all they could. There, Luedtke told Yantz to go on with the group. Using a stick for a crutch, Luedtke hobbled along. "I got accused of looking like Rip Van Winkle," he wrote. Finally, he could go no farther. He and two other men stopped at a village where they found another wounded soldier, but the town looked suspicious, so the four injured men set off again, coming across four more GIs — three of them badly wounded. The four having the worst wounds were put into a house, with the others' promise to try to get help.

Luedtke rode in an oxcart for about a mile, after a soldier "persuaded" a Korean farmer at gunpoint. Late on the afternoon of July 21, they came upon a man from the 34th radio section. About 2:30 p.m., they stopped at a Korean house where they were fed — their first food since the evening of July 19. The Korean took the men by cart to a larger town, where they met a captain from the 34th.

The captain had sent some men ahead, who had made contact with the 1st Cavalry Division. The division sent out a patrol to rescue Luedtke and those with him, but refused to go on to rescue the men who had been left in the house since it already was five miles into enemy territory. Luedtke finally was operated on the 23d and the bullet was removed from his leg.

The Rear Guard

CPT Jack Smith, with L/34, was left in Taejon as a rear guard. GEN Dean told him to give the motor column a 30-45 minute start before withdrawing the company. The captain thought they began their withdrawal about 5 p.m. "I remained at the CP until L Company had cleared, checking the area to make certain that we didn't leave anyone behind," Smith wrote. He became separated from the company, but managed to get out of town to the south. The Kumsan road south of Taejon "was littered with trucks, howitzers and men; roadblocks were covered by automatic fire." Smith managed to assemble about 150 men — 50 of them wounded — a tracked prime mover, two 2 1/2-ton trucks and four jeeps. His party included engineers, artillerymen, men from both the 34th and 19th Regiments, regimental headquarters and other units. "We fought our way through the road blocks [about 7 miles] and cleared the last one just prior to dark.... We were not capable of getting into another scrap," he continued, "no food to speak of, very little ammunition and about 50 percent of the force wounded."

Smith and his band continued south to Chinju, where he was able to contact Pusan, and a hospital train was sent to pick them up. The captain then joined LTC Wadlington and returned to the 3/34.

Jose E. Leyba was with the L/34 rear guard in Taejon. When orders came to pull out, the men loaded on trucks and started out. Soon, they were assailed by enemy machine gun and small-arms fire from all sides. The GIs returned fire from the trucks as the unit convoy tried to get out of the city, but the column was blocked by knocked-out trucks and a number of men were wounded. Two men of Leyba's squad — Frank Coronado and a man named Duran — both were hit in the legs. "We started to unload and take cover," Leyba wrote. "We could see the outline of the enemy firing at us. I helped bandage some of the wounded, and the walking wounded started to follow me toward the front of the convoy so we could get out of the city." He noted that the enemy was firing from a hilltop to his right, and spotted a half-track mounting dual 40mm guns. "I climbed aboard with the idea of knocking out [the enemy] that were raising hell with our men." He couldn't get the guns to fire; apparently the half-track motor had to be running to power the gun mechanism.

Leyba and the men with him moved forward a little farther, until they came upon an enemy tank. He commandeered a bazooka from a man who didn't know how to fire it. With one shot, Leyba set the tank on fire. The group then climbed a nearby hill, where he and a couple of others reconnoitered ahead, running into some more American soldiers. Although there was a lieutenant present, Leyba found himself leading the combined group. As they started down a slope, "the men heard the enemy below us, and before I knew it they all bugged out on me and headed back up the hill," he wrote. As it turned out, the enemy patrol also ran off when they heard the Americans. Leyba was now by himself. Although dead tired, he forced himself to keep moving before daylight.

About dawn, he spotted a bridge, where he planned to hide during the day. There he came upon a man from the 21st, and they almost shot one another at first. The two soldiers rested under the bridge for awhile, then climbed to the top of a nearby ridge and decided to lie low. "It wasn't long before I [observed] movement to my right flank," he wrote. Before I knew it they stood up, and one was facing me no more than 30 yards away... ." Leyba made ready to fire when "one of the other guys started to cuss out his friend in... English. I stood up and hollered 'GIs?'" The American soldiers were startled. One of them was Japanese-American, and Leyba had first taken him for an enemy soldier dressed in a U.S. uniform. After some C-rations and a nap, Leyba began to walk on the road. After about a mile a jeep stopped next to him. "It was GEN Gay from the 1st Cavalry Division," noted Leyba. He told

the general that he was with the 34th Infantry. Leyba rode about 10 miles with the general, then made his way back to the 34th, where he discovered that he was the ranking survivor of his platoon.

Too Little, Too Late — The Attack that failed

In the 21st CP at Okchon, COL Beauchamp briefed GEN Menoher about the enemy roadblock building up at the two tunnels on the Okchon road. Menoher directed Beauchamp to take a platoon of M-24 light tanks which were at the CP and the rifle company which had come through the pass with him and go back, take and hold the pass.

As James Jones and his comrades sat exhausted in their trucks after running the Okchon roadblock, "COL Beauchamp came along and started asking for volunteers to go back and try to break the roadblock so that other troops could get out," Jones recalled. "As tired and beat as we were, many of us volunteered while some of the troops remained on the trucks. I couldn't believe what I was hearing... he's asking instead of ordering. I don't think I was any better off physically than any of the rest but I had rather been dead than to have stayed on a truck under those conditions."

COL Beauchamp managed to assemble about 60 infantrymen. It was dark by the time they started approaching the pass. One of the tanks struck a mine and an enemy soldier electronically set off several more.

"They threw several rounds at us, most of them hitting the side of the hill beside us. We could and should have done more than we did," Jones wrote, "The resistance wasn't that stiff in my opinion... there was a lack of leadership. We were a bunch of volunteers with no leader... . I don't know who made the decision to pull back or why. Maybe we did some good, because I heard later that we caused enough commotion to allow some troops to get out."

At the pass, COL Beauchamp saw the bodies of the engineers he had left to defend the area. The two tanks and AA half-tracks had disappeared.

Jones had another close call in this action. "I felt another one of those slaps which was a little harder. This time my right hip." His right rear pocket had been torn off by a piece of shrapnel, tearing the skin on his upper leg. "It turned out to be minor and in those days you didn't run to the medics for small things. If you could walk you could fight."

Escape From Capture

After CPL Bufford Goff (F/19) was captured on July 20, he and the other captives with him were not fed for several days and not allowed to talk to each other. The North Korean interrogator spoke perfect English. Goff remembered an older POW, about 35. "[The] officer asked him a question and the man spit in his face. A guard jumped forward and thrusted him in the gut with a bayonet," killing him, said Buford.

A few nights later, "we overpowered our guards, killing as many as we could with mud bricks, clubs, anything we could get and we left

and scattered in all directions," Goff recounted. "I escaped to the mountains. I hid during the day and tried to travel at night... . I saw an engineer truck.... I was tempted to wave to them but saw a Korean man coming up the hill about 100 yards from me." The Korean man either stepped on a mine or was blown up by a charge of explosives. Goff didn't wait to investigate. He took off and wandered several more days, finally mixing in with a group of Korean refugees. In this way he made his way back to U.S. lines and rejoined his unit. He refused to be checked by the medics. "I said I wanted to stay in the company," he explained.

A few days later, he and some friends were listening to a North Korean broadcast on an old radio. A woman came on the radio and read off a list of men captured at Taejon, including CPL Goff of Co. F, 19th Infantry. She said they had been tried by people's court and executed for crimes against the Peoples Republic of North Korea.

Taejon in Retrospect

Appleman, in *South to the Naktong,* wrote that the enemy's highly successful envelopments of U.S. positions at the Kum River and Taejon were "excellent examples of this type of military tactic," and the enemy was numerically superior. But the enemy maneuvers were not unusual nor remarkable; that is what could be expected under the circumstance.

GEN Walker told GEN Dean he needed two more days to deploy the 1st Cavalry Division; that the 24th Division was to hold Taejon two more days. But he wasn't specific enough. Dean believed he meant through July 20. However, the consensus now is that he meant the remainder of July 18 and 19 and that the 24th should withdraw the night of July 19-20. Since he didn't specify the date a question remains.

The principal mission for the 21st Infantry was clear: Cover the division's right flank adjacent to the ROK sector against any enemy attack from that quarter. Dean and Stephens discussed withdrawal from Taejon over the Okchon road after the Walker-Dean conference. GEN Dean wanted the Taejon-Okchon kept open so troops coming out of Taejon would not have to fight their way through roadblock(s). COL Stephens later wrote that he asked Dean if he should move his regiment, already deployed on high ground over two miles east of the road and railroad tunnels. Dean, concerned about his right flank, directed the 21st (which had A/71 Tk Bn attached) to remain in place but to patrol a secondary road to the north and the Okchon road. There is no record of any discussion about the 21st providing relief or roadblock-breaking forces.

COL Stephens wrote that he had patrols on the Okchon road all day on July 20, but he and his staff were ignorant of what was happening on that road until COL Beauchamp got through the developing roadblock and telephoned GEN Menoher at the 21st CP some time after 6 p.m. Then GEN Menoher ordered Beauchamp back to the 21st CP to render a fuller report, wasting several hours that could have been used to reduce the roadblock in daylight. (See Chapter Notes.)

BG Charles B. Smith (then LTC commanding 1/21) stated in a letter to MAJ Lacy Barnett (June 26, 1986): "We did not patrol the road to the front [toward Taejon] since we had good observation from the hills for several miles."

Except for Hunnicutt's patrol, there is no record of patrols from any other element of the 21st Regiment nor by any of their attachments. The I&R patrol was the only patrol made on the Okchon road that day.

The 1/34 and 2/19 on the high ground west of Taejon were on the most defensible terrain in that quarter. Adding part or all of the 21st would have marginally strengthened Taejon defenses, but the regiment was too under strength to have made a difference. Deploying that command so that not even a part of it could be assembled to counter enemy blocks on the Okchon road was a mistake. The attached tank company — a powerful force —apparently was not utilized for any purpose, except when a platoon was dispatched to escort a convoy from Taejon, and another almost at dark, to support COL Beauchamp's abortive attack.

COL Beauchamp did not employ the 24th Recon Co. to the best advantage. It could have been employed better as a company along the Kumsan road, not just one platoon at a roadblock, and provided him with more information about the enemy south of Taejon. Later in the day, the colonel saw groups of the enemy heading toward the Okchon road from the south.

Communications between Beauchamp's CP in Taejon and 1/34 and 2/19 was not too good, and the enemy cut wire communication with 1/ 34 early in the battle. Neither battalion received any orders from Beauchamp during the battle leaving them in effect, on their own. It was Beauchamp's responsibility to maintain communication — wire and radio — with the forward battalions. He vainly sent out wire parties toward 1/34, but he did have radio contact, as demonstrated by the enemy's false message using the captured 1/34 radio truck. LTC McGrail tried to get word from Beauchamp's CP by sending CPT Montesclaros back to Taejon. He also sent LT Herbert's platoon back to clear the road to Taejon, because he had neither radio nor wire communication with the CP there.

On July 19, road and other communication between Taejon and Okchon was no problem. On July 20, apparently the only means of communication between the two points was via the Division CP in Yongdong. On that day, Dean and the 21st could talk by phone to Yongdong, but not to each other. Information could have been relayed through Yongdong, albeit at a slower rate. There is no evidence that the 21st relayed any information to Taejon. Beauchamp would have been interested in knowing 200 enemy were in his rear, or that there were enemy tanks on the Okchon road, both observed by the 21st Infantry. Although Beauchamp was no longer in Taejon at 4:45 p.m., LTC Wadlington and GEN Dean would have been interested to know about the 21st Regiment's I & R report of snipers on the Okchon road, since they were in Taejon until about 6 p.m. that day.

No record exists that the command in Taejon received any information, either from the 21st, relayed through Division Headquarters at Yongdong, or from Yongdong, which had a significant bearing on combat operations at Taejon.

Another very significant failure was in inter- and intra-battalion communications and from Beauchamp's CP to the forward battalions, the most important factors in the failure of the two commands to operate, then withdraw, in a unified, orderly and organized fashion.

Lack of communication deluded Beauchamp and Dean so long about the true tactical situation that when they realized how bad things were, it was too late. The lack of communication also prevented them from notifying subordinates and organizing a fighting withdrawal.

In addition to an almost total collapse of communication the defenders of Taejon also suffered a loss of key leadership at critical times, causing the loss in command and control of units, battalions and eventually the entire force defending Taejon, in and outside the city.

LTC Ayres lost control of his battalion early in the battle. When F/19 collapsed, LTC McGrail was unable to retrieve the situation and much of his battalion withdrew in disarray. MAJ Lantron, 3/34, was lost just when his battalion was to make a critical counterattack.

The lack of effective leadership complicated matters in the city all during July 20. GEN Dean, COL Beauchamp and his XO, LTC Wadlington, all were in and out of the CP all day. It is normal for a commander to be out of his CP, but it is essential that the commander inform someone in the CP that he is leaving, his expected itinerary, and when he expects to return, especially when communication is bad. Apparently, neither MAJ Lantron, GEN Dean, COL Beauchamp nor LTC Wadlington kept their CPs informed of their itineraries..

When a commander leaves his CP, someone is left "in charge." Normally, LTC Wadlington as XO would have had that role when Beauchamp was away.

In cases where the commander cannot be located, the senior staff officer in the CP should have authority to make decisions and issue orders, but there was no such arrangement at Taejon. Both Beauchamp and Wadlington were out of communication with the CP at the same time at critical times during the battle, leading to confusion and loss of vital time. When COL Beauchamp continued along the Okchon road, he abdicated command at Taejon — a bizarre situation. He couldn't be found when it was time for his CP to vacate the city.

GEN Dean later wrote that he was in Taejon to stimulate the "fighting spirit of the 34th... and attached troops in the city," as an example to ROK leaders, to give confidence to ROK forces and to see "what kind of fighter the North Korean was." It was not until he tried to get out of Taejon that he realized the extent of the enemy's envelopment of the city.

The general's reasons are difficult to understand. First, the one battalion of the 34th on the line at Taejon was commanded by LTC Ayres, who had more combat experience than any other senior commander or staff officer in the 24th Infantry Division. If the 34th seemed in disarray, Dean had contributed to that by relieving COL Lovless even before that officer had the opportunity to command the regiment. GEN Barth had been giving all the orders to the regiment and its battalions when Lovless was relieved. Second, there were no ROK leaders nor ROK troops at Taejon. Third, it seems odd that after two weeks of unremitting, hard combat by elements of his division, GEN Dean would not already have formed a fairly accurate concept of the kind of fighter the North Korean was.

There were only two valid reasons for Dean being in Taejon: First, because that is where he expected the principle battle for the 24th Division to take place; and second, to support COL Beauchamp, who had just taken command of the badly-battered 34th Infantry.

The general's influence at Taejon was minimal. He absented himself from the CP and out of communication, a number of times on tank-hunting expeditions.

Each of these officers did what he believed he should be doing at the time. But there were serious breakdowns in command, control and communications, all of which made the defeat at Taejon that much worse.

Not one successful effort to extricate significant numbers of troops, or to attack through a road-block, was led by anyone higher in rank than a captain, except for the company which came out with COL Beauchamp. All senior commanders and field-grade officers were taken out of leadership roles by circumstances. Some officers and NCOs abdicated their leadership responsibilities, but a number of other NCOs and junior officers demonstrated remarkably good judgment and leadership under the most adverse conditions.

24th Division losses at Taejon

The Division had 3,933 men engaged, 1,150 of which became casualties. Reports listed 48 KIA; 228 WIA and 874 MIA. Most of the MIA were killed, either in battle or murdered by their captors at the time of capture. The L/34, the rear guard, lost 107 of 153 men present.

This chart shows the losses of some of the major commands at Taejon:

Command**	Casualties	Percent
HHC, 34 Inf.	71 of 171	41.5
1/34	203 of 712	28.5
3/34	256 of 666	38.5
2/19	211 of 713	29.5
C/3 ECB	85 of 161	53.0
A/11 FAB	39 of 123	31.7

** Figures for 13 and 63 FABs and MP Co. were not available.

Equipment losses were crippling. Only B/13 FAB, B/63 FAB and I/34 escaped with most of their equipment. The 34th Regiment had barely 35 operational vehicles after Taejon. The QM Co. lost 30 of 34 trucks. A/11 FAB lost all five of its 155mm howitzers. Since July 5, the division had lost 31 105mm howitzers and five 155mm howitzers.

Losses in Key Leadership within the 24th Division, July 5-22, 1950

The division had lost severely in senior commanders and staff officers, materially eroding leadership and battle efficiency, culminating in the loss of GEN Dean.

The 34th was hardest hit, losing four regimental commanders in nine days. The first, COL Lovless, was relieved on July 7. The second commander, COL Martin, was killed on July 8, after about one day; LTC Wadlington, the XO, assumed temporary command. COL Beauchamp took command of the regiment a few days before Taejon. The 34th also lost two S3s, Majors Dunn (WIA/POW) and McDaniel (POW). The 1/34 lost their XO, MAJ Dunham (WIA/POW). The 3/34 lost two battalion commanders, LTC David Smith (NBC) and MAJ Lantron (MIA/POW), and the S3, MAJ Boone Seegers (KIA).

The 19th lost their XO, LTC Chandler (WIA). The 1/19 lost battalion commander LTC Winstead (KIA) and the 3/21 two commanders, LTC Pryor (NBC) and LTC Jensen (KIA). The 63 FAB lost two commanders, LTC Dawson (NBC) and LTC Dressler (KIA).

The Enemy

The *NK 4th Division* enveloped Taejon from the west and south with the *16th* and *18th Regiments*. Strong elements of the two commands also set up roadblocks on the Okchon road. The division's *5th Regiment* attacked 1/34 shortly after midnight on July 20, capturing the airfield by 4 a.m. The *16th* and *18th Regiments* traveled light, no trucks or artillery.

The *3d Division* enveloped the city from the north and northeast. The first tanks to enter Taejon were from the *107th Tk Regt.*, attached to the *4th Division*. Those which entered later were probably from the *203d Tk Regt.*, attached to the *3d Division*. As previously noted, the *NK 2d Division* was supposed to participate in this battle but was delayed by stubborn ROK resistance.

Losses among North Korean infantrymen were probably relatively light. But they lost between 15 and 20 tanks (at least eight to the 3.5-inch rocket launchers in Taejon, two more to artillery and the remainder to air attack). The *4th Division* also lost 15 76mm guns, six 122mm mortars and 200 artillerymen. (See Chapter Notes.)

At noon on July 22, the 24th Division, then totaling 8,660 men, passed through the 1st Cavalry at Yongdong-dong. In two and a half weeks, it had been forced back a hundred miles by two enemy divisions, suffering 30 percent casualties. Over 2,400 men were MIA, a good number of which actually were dead.

Chapter Notes:

P. 62 COL, Ret., Montesclaros, in a telephone conversation with the author on April 21, 1994, said that he did not remember this — not that it wasn't true.

P. 67 GEN George Washington called the detachments of men sent ahead to remove abatis in the storming of Stony Point, NY July 16, 1779, "Forlorn Hopes." From time to time ever since, the term has been applied to forces which will probably be defeated, or actions which will probably be lost.

P. 72 The anti-aircraft half track armed with a 37mm or 40 mm had two .50-cal machine guns, not four, which fired in the same direction as the 37 or 40.

P. 77 During World War II, the Russians, often lacking proper antitank weapons, used bottles filled with gasoline to set enemy tanks on fire. A rag or piece of rope was stuffed into the top of the bottle. The objective was to approach a tank from the side, rear or above, light the wick and throw the bottle onto the tank. No matter where it landed, the gasoline was immediately ignited, spewing flames over the tank. The best point of attack was the tank's rear deck, where the engine was located. This crude but effective device was named "Molotov cocktail" for V. M. Molotov, the Soviet Union's Foreign Minister at the time. Why this "field expedient," well-known to WW II veterans, wasn't used in the early days of Korea is unknown.

P. 77 The 2.36-inch rocket launcher was developed by the U.S. about midway through WW II as an antitank weapon. In 1943, one of its designers resigned because he believed that this AT launcher was too small to destroy German tanks. This was confirmed in Sicily when rocket launcher gunners of the 82d Airborne Division were killed by the tanks they were attempting to stop with the new weapon. GIs in Europe preferred the German Panzerfaust. It did kill tanks, albeit from the short range of 50 yards.

The 2.36-inch launcher's HEAT round was supposed to penetrate 5 inches of armor plate, blowing a hole 1/2-inch in diameter, splattering hot metal particles into the interior to kill or wound the crew, set off ammunition, and possibly set the tank afire.

By 1949, the 3.5-inch rocket launcher, a much more powerful antitank weapon, had been developed. This launcher's HEAT round could penetrate approximately 11-inch of homogeneous armor plate, making a half-inch hole, blowing white-hot metal from the interior of the tank's armor throughout the crew compartment. Maximum range was 960 yards, and it could destroy every type of tank then in use.

Because the old 2.36-inch launcher included WP ammunition, some Marine units carried both types of launchers in Korea. They used WP against enemy infantry and to mark targets for other weapons or air strikes.

The new launcher was being used in training in the U.S, but there were none in Japan or Korea. A few of them with the ROKs and Americans at the beginning of the war easily could have decimated North Korean armored units. A small number of 3.5s were flown to Korea and first used by the 24th Division at Taejon. After that, the T-34 lost its mystique and repeatedly fell prey to resolute 3.5-inch rocket launcher gunners.

For unknown reasons, although available in the U.S., it was not in the hands of soldiers in South Korea, Japan and Okinawa before the Korean War started.

References:

FM 23-32, Rocket Launchers, Dept. of the Army (DA), Nov. 1949. Pp. 20-22 and Change 2,

FM 23-20, 3.5-inch Rocket Launchers, Nov. 1949. P. 6.

The National Guard Basic Manual, DA, 1948. P. 481.

The United States Army in World War II, European Theater of Operations, The Lorraine Campaign, H. M. Cole, DA, 1950. P. 603.

GEN James M. Gavin, USA, Ret., On to Berlin: Battles of an Airborne Commander, 1943-946, Viking Press, NY, 1978. Pp. 51-51; 223.

Address by COL Carl Bernard (21st Inf), USA, Ret., to 24th Div Assn., 1985.

GEN Bohn transcript, reference Marine employment of the 2.36-inch launcher.

P. 80 Appleman credits MAJ McDaniel (34th Infantry S3) and personnel from the 34th CP with leading this effort. Appleman wrote that a lack of tractor drivers prevented taking all of the howitzers out, that those left behind were rendered inoperative.

P. 81 It is difficult for this author to believe everything which interviewer Martin Blumenson claims SFC Szito said or did. The record of this interview is not verbatim, but a narrative composed by Blumenson.

P. 84 In a telephone conversation with the author on June 20,1994, LT George Hunnicutt said he could recall only one patrol toward Okchon on July 20, 1950, made late in the day by a squad with three machine gun jeeps from his I & R platoon. It received enemy sniper fire as it approached the railroad tunnel, fired back, then returned to base. He said that the platoon made no earlier patrols because it did not have time after arriving in Okchon.

P. 84 Fortunately for the Americans, the North Koreans completely misused their tanks at Taejon. They did not use them in organized tank-infantry teams, with infantrymen accompanying each tank to secure buildings and other areas along the way, and protecting the tanks from anti-tank fire. As a result, their losses to the new rocket launcher were high — most were destroyed by noon on July 20. The tanks seemed to roam about in ones and twos without any coordination or common mission.

CHAPTER EIGHT — First Battles - 25th Infantry and 1st Cavalry Divisions

The ROK Army Battles on the Northern Front

By July 13, the enemy's *5th Division* slowly closed in for a final attack to take Yongdok, where a key lateral road came over the mountains from the west. The ROK 3d Division defended the town. The bridge at Yongdok either had to be held or blown up, so it was rigged with explosives for the latter contingency.

An enemy captive revealed a North Korean plan to destroy a bridge near Angang-ni on the Taegu - Pohang-dong road and to destroy both ends of the Chongdo railway tunnel between Pusan and Taegu. The loss of the tunnel would seriously impair logistical support of combat troops in the area. Two platoons of ROK troops, with two U.S. officers, were sent to protect the tunnel.

COL Allen MacLean, of the Eighth Army G3 Section kept in constant contact with COL Emmerich, KMAG Adviser to the ROK 3d Division. On July 14, BG Lee Chu Sik, commanding the ROK 3d Division, wanted to move his CP to Pohang-dong and withdraw his troops south of Yongdok. COL Emmerich told him that couldn't be done; the coastal road had to be held at all costs.

The ROK 3d Division was supplied by large fishing boats traveling up the coast from Pusan. Plans were made to establish a railhead at Pohang-dong to augment this support. The coordination of mortar, artillery, naval gunfire and air support would be critical in the forthcoming battle. CPT Harold Slater, KMAG G-3 advisor to the 3d Division, was placed in charge of this center, assisted by CPT Airsman. The 3d Division had three batteries of 75mm pack howitzers, of four guns each, and one battery of 105mm howitzers.

Under constant pressure, the ROK 23d Regiment finally gave way on July 16. COL Emmerich reported to Eighth Army: "Situation deplorable, things are popping, trying to get something established across the front. 75 percent of the 23d ROK Regiment on the move south."

KMAG advisors threatened and shot into the air, trying to stop the retreat. A straggler line, set up by the division commander, also was unsuccessful, and the enemy seized Yongdok on July 17. That day, Battery C, 159th FAB (from the 24th RCT, 25th Inf. Div.) entered the fray, but the battle for Yongdok went on for three more weeks. The town changed hands several times. On July 18, the ROKs counterattacked at 5:45 a.m., supported by naval gunfire. They drove the enemy three miles north of the town. On July 19, the enemy charged down and threw the South Koreans out once again. In a conference at Yonil on July 20 with generals Walker, Partridge and Kean and colonels Emmerich and Robert Witty (commanding the 35th Fighter-Interceptor Group), COL Emmerich presented a thorough briefing on the situation. GEN Walker directed that the ROK 3d Division re-take Yongdok. The ROK division commander balked, but was ordered by ROK headquarters to comply with the order.

The 40th Fighter-Interceptor Squadron became operational at Yonil on July 20 and four American destroyers (*Higbee, Mansfield, DeHaven* and *Swenson*) and the British cruiser *Belfast* would support the ROK effort.

The second battle for Yongdok, begun on the morning of July 21, was a close-in, savage fight. Accurate enemy mortar and artillery fire created heavy ROK casualties. The concentrated heavy bombardment of artillery and naval gunfire churned the area from Kanggu-dong to about two miles north of Yongdok into a smoldering ruin. Vegetation was blasted down and every village razed to the ground.

The enemy, too, suffered terrible casualties. The U.S. cruiser *Juneau*, which also was supporting the ROKs, alone was credited with killing 400 North Korean soldiers. In the end, the enemy held Yongdok, but it was a hollow victory. They were virtually trapped in the grip of what Appleman described as "pulverizing artillery and mortar fire, naval gunfire and almost continuous air strikes." Enemy attempts to flank the ROKs by swinging inland led to more heavy North Korean casualties. On July 24 the enemy lost 800 men to artillery, mortar and naval gunfire. Naval gunfire and air strikes trapped another enemy battalion, almost wiping it out in a maelstrom of bomb and shell fragments, rockets and strafing machine guns.

By July 24 too, the ROK 22d Regiment, plus 500 men of the ROK naval combat team and its engineer battalion, had arrived in the Yongdok area. All the ROK troops there were organized into a new ROK 3d Division.

Walker had used a succession of U.S. battalions to protect the Yonil Airfield, starting with 3/19 on July 9. Then, in turn, came 2/27, 1/35 and 1/7 Cav. The 1/7 Cav was reinforced with a platoon of 4.2 inch mortars,

The 2d Battalion, 35th, was in the Pohang area July 14-15, with 2/35 occupying a ridge. PFC Earl Miller and PVT Howard Mattice of Co. G were sent forward on a finger of the ridge about 75 yards beyond the main line. They had an SCR 536 radio, called a "walkie-talkie" by the troops, to report back any enemy movement. About 9 a.m. the next morning, "I heard police whistles," Miller wrote. Looking toward the bottom of the ridge, he saw "approximately 150 North Koreans lined up to attack. I called the company CP on the walkie-talkie." CPL Olivas of the 60mm mortar section came on the radio and told Miller he was going to fire a ranging round of WP. The first round "landed about 100 yards behind the enemy," Miller continued. Miller had the mortars drop 50 yards and fire again. This round landed about 20 yards behind the enemy. "I told him to drop ... another 25 yards and fire for effect... . We put 15 or 16 mortar [rounds] into the air before the first one hit the ground."

The rapidly falling mortar rounds confused the enemy. "It seemed [that] ... no matter which way they turned a mortar round was hitting in front of them," Miller wrote. One round exploded next to an enemy wheeled machine gun, knocking the gun over and wounding the three soldiers with it.

In a 4 1/2-hour battle, three men of G/35 were wounded, Miller wrote, and the bodies of 25 or 30 enemy soldiers lay at the foot of the ridge. About 8 a.m., Miller and Mattice were withdrawn to the unit's main line. Neither man had been injured in the fight.

Back at Yonil, the 1/7 Cav, with the attached heavy mortar platoon took up positions on July 22, relieving 1/35 Inf.

LTC Peter Clainos (West Point 1933) commanded 1/7 Cav. His combat experience in WW II probably influenced GEN Gay to often employ Clainos' battalion as division reserve during the Naktong battles. The 1st Battalion was directed to support the ROKs by fire only, but on July 23, the enemy surrounded the 81mm mortar platoon of Co. D, precipitating close-in fight. Aside from this, the battalion did not have much action. Clainos was able to rotate companies on a hilltop from which the men could see fighting and "get the smell of gunpowder." He recalled that "this gradual initiation into combat" was invaluable training and built confidence. The 1/7 Cav was replaced by the 21st Regiment, 24th Division on July 24.

The ROKs prepared for another attack to retake Yongdok on the 27th. During the night of the 26th, ROK troops captured 17 machine guns but only eight prisoners.

The attack began at 8:30 a.m. on July 27 with artillery, mortar and naval gunfire, followed by air strikes. Applying unremitting pressure and more heavy artillery, mortar, naval gunfire and air strikes, the ROKs finally retook Yongdok at 6 p.m. on Aug. 2. Prisoners reported that the *NK 5th Division* had suffered 40 percent casualties.

As Appleman points out, the battle at Yongdok was the only success story in all of Korea. It was due to overwhelming American firepower and terrain which restricted the enemy's ability to maneuver.

While this protracted and savage battle for Yongdok was in progress, an equally gory clash was taking place further west in the mountains between the *NK 12th Division* and the ROK 8th. The *12th* had crossed the Han at Tanyong and began advancing through Yongju to Andong. On July 21, the ROK 8th attacked the *12th Division* between the two towns. While the two divisions were locked in fierce fighting, the *NK II Corps* ordered the *12th Division* to turn and capture Pohang-dong by July 26.

There are about 75 air miles between Yongju and Pohang but it would be much farther by the trails which the *12th Division* would have to traverse. Trying to meet the deadline, it resumed marching during daylight as well as at night.

Bitterly opposed by the ROK 8th Division, the *NK 12th* pressed slowly forward. After a five-day fight, it wrested Andong from the stubborn ROKs on Aug. 1. The North Koreans claimed to have killed 1,500 ROKs and captured 1,200 more, along with six 105mm howitzers, 13 automatic weapons, 900 rifles and a great number of vehicles.

As the ROKs battled the enemy, giving ground usually only after a bitter, bloody contest, it also was reorganizing itself. On July 24 the ROK Army reorganized into two corps (I and II) and five divisions. I Corps had the 8th and Capital divisions; II Corps controlled the 1st and 6th divisions. The 2d Division was deactivated and its troops absorbed into the 1st. The ROK 3d Division, because of its isolated position on the east coast, was placed directly under ROK Army headquarters.

The ROKs lined up in the north as follows: 3d Division east coast; I Corps (CP at Sangju-briefly at Andong) with the Capital and 8th divisions. West of the 8th Division were the 6th and 1st divisions (east to west) under II Corps (CP Hamchang).

After reorganizing and absorbing a large number of conscripts, the ROK Army numbered 94,570 troops, but only 85,871 were "effectives," with 8,699 wounded and nonbattle casualties carried on the rolls. (See Chapter Notes.)

GEN Walker ordered the 25th Division deployed north of Sangju to assist the ROKs in preventing the enemy from moving into the upper Naktong valley. Sangju is the site of a major crossing of all roads in this mountainous part of Korea, situated south of the Mungyong plateau and held a commanding position in the Naktong valley. The town was filled with refugees streaming south and retreating ROK troops. As the 25th Division began deploying in the area, the ROKs and North Koreans already were battling for the Mungyong plateau.

E/24 Infantry - Sangju Area, July 16-20

Co. E, 24th Infantry, was moving forward toward some mountains near Sangju about July 16. As the unit approached a village, SGT Joel T. Ward moved his squad off the road and began to cross a rice paddy toward it. "We received machine gun fire as we got to the middle of the rice paddy," he wrote. Taking shelter behind a paddy bank, the squad worked its way back to the road. "As I got to the road. I told my men to pause. Then I gave the order to dash across the road all at once." he continued. The squad ran safely across the road and into a Korean shack. Once the men were safely in the shack, they systematically set the village on fire with tracers.

"Two days later, we advanced again all day," Joel recalled. "That night we were attacked by T-34s. Three tanks were hit...and disabled. We shot any and everything that moved."

The next day, they moved out again and that night, the unit was hit by artillery fire. "Those who didn't have a foxhole dug one in a hurry," Ward remembered. On the following day, about July 20, with Ward's squad, accompanied by a Korean interpreter, still as point, the company moved out. Shortly after starting, Ward's men came "face to face with about 100 men in a column of twos coming toward us," he wrote. "We were well ahead of the company." The platoon leader, LT Leonard Preston, came forward, and he and interpreter talked to members of the column. The interpreter said they were South Korean, and they were dressed in U.S. uniforms and carrying M1 rifles.

Preston told Ward, "I don't like it. Be on your toes." Ward's squad came to a bridge, then "all hell broke loose behind us and a machine gun opened up in front," Ward recorded. "LT Preston

got hit and his leg wouldn't function. The men dove for cover behind the bridge and nearby dike." Ward determined that only the lieutenant had been hit. The squad, carrying LT Preston, worked its way back along the ditch. The officer, although in pain, asked about the other men. Ward assured him "everyone was OK." Artillery was brought in on the enemy, Preston was evacuated and the squad worked its way to the opposite side of the road and up a small hill. The column of enemy soldiers was wiped out when they began to fire on Co. E. The unit dug in for the night, and the next day, Co. E was ordered to begin what would be a succession of withdrawals, culminating in the Pusan Perimeter.

Yechon - July 19-20

On July 19, the enemy captured the town of Yechon, about 22 air miles northeast of Sangju. GEN Walker ordered GEN Kean to retake the town. Kean designated COL White's 24th Regiment for the task. COL White tapped his 3d Battalion (LTC Samuel Pierce Jr.)

The 3/24, with Battery B, 159th FAB, a heavy mortar platoon, 3d Platoon, 77th ECC and a detachment of the 25th Signal Co., set out on the mission. About a mile short of Yechon the battalion encountered heavy enemy machine gun, mortar and rifle fire. LTC Pierce deployed his three rifle companies south and west of Yechon. King Co. (1LT Jasper Johnson), with LT Chester Lenon's platoon of the 77th ECC, got into the town. The remainder of the battalion failed to take a ridge on the left overlooking Yechon, and the attack was called off at 9:30 p.m. due to darkness.

Tom Lambert of the Associated Press witnessed the battle on the 20th. From a soy-bean patch on a hillside, he watched two enemy companies try to flank the village under a barrage of artillery and mortar fire. This is a synopsis of his dispatch to the AP:

West of Lambert, small groups of U.S. soldiers ran across the rice paddies. A machine gunner moved doggedly up a slope, with his gun, into a grove of trees, soon adding its fire to the battle. Members of 3/24 were now in Yechon, firing as they advanced, warily inspecting each mud house. Suddenly, enemy mortar fire began falling, but the men moved on into the village. Part of the town was afire. An air strike was called in on the enemy, while some Americans dodged back and forth across a ridge to avoid the airplane's line of fire. Then the two flanking enemy companies came under heavy mortar fire. The battalion commander withdrew his men from Yechon.

The following are recollections and experiences of some of the men who took part in this attack:

CPT Jasper Johnson recalled that his King Co. had a fight at Yechon that day and that the unit got into the town. He confirmed that the enemy on nearby hills prevented the company from staying in Yechon overnight. Co. K was directed to withdraw and LTC Pierce ordered a battalion attack for the next morning.

LT Chester Lenon's 3d Platoon, 77 ECC, accompanied Co. K toward Yechon on July 20. CPL LaVaughn E. Fields commanded the

platoon's 2d Squad. The platoon mission was to take and clear a small village about a mile west of and on the road to, Yechon.

"This was our first shot at live combat," he said. "We ran into a lot of women and children screaming and hollering; they were scared and we were scared along with them." There were no enemy soldiers in the village. The platoon swung to the left (west), with the squads on line 3-2-1, from left to right.

As CPL Fields topped a small knoll, he saw the enemy to his front. Further to his left was a larger hill (Hill 122). "There were many of them," he said of the enemy. They were dressed in white, trying to disguise themselves as civilians. "Some working in the field, some not.... There were about 15 or 20 of them in a line, which was odd for Papa-san to be in this kind of formation. On my far left [Hill 122]...we heard an automatic weapon open up ... . He began to rain hell on that area. The line of Papa-sans...all hit the dirt. This told us that they were soldiers and not civilians.... The machine gun began to chop them up." (See Chapter Notes.)

The enemy responded with a heavy concentration of mortar fire. PFC Curtis Womack of Fields' squad had a red towel around his neck. Fields yelled out, "For God's sake, take the towel off, you're a human target!" As he said the word "target," a mortar round landed between Fields and Womack. The corporal was unhurt, but Womack was hit three places in the head. "He screamed," said Fields, "[and] blood scattered everywhere. I told him to get down — he was standing up hollering." Fields tackled the wounded man, carried him back to an irrigation ditch and called for a medic. "OK," someone called back.

"At this time, mortars began to fall heavily," Fields continued. "I looked up and saw him [the medic] disintegrate. I swallowed; sweat came into my mouth. I didn't know what to do. I had never seen this before." He turned his attention to getting Womack to safety.

Fields wrote that he "pushed, shoved and dragged him 'till I could show him the trucks and told him to get the hell out of there." Still shaken by the severe wounding of PFC Womack and of seeing a man blown to pieces, he returned to the squad. The medic was killed was Eldridge Gamble.

While all this was transpiring, LT Lenon took some men to knock out an enemy machine gun. "We were being held down by machine gun fire," Lenon recalled, "and I got permission to take two or three men...and see if we could get this machine gun out.... We got it out of action and then our troops were able to move into the town...."

Co. L had followed King Co. with CPT Bradley Biggs commanding. "Just south of Yechon," he wrote in a letter to Clay and Joan Blair (*The Forgotten War*) on October 20, 1986, "we attempted to move through a village but were brought under mortar fire.... Untrained in house-to-house fighting, we had no knowledge of what to do in the village" CPT Biggs sent LT Oliver Dillard's platoon to the left and LT Sergeant's northward on the right side of the road. "With the second platoon and field artillery observer," he continued, "we attempted to move through the village with the help of a P-51 [F-51] which

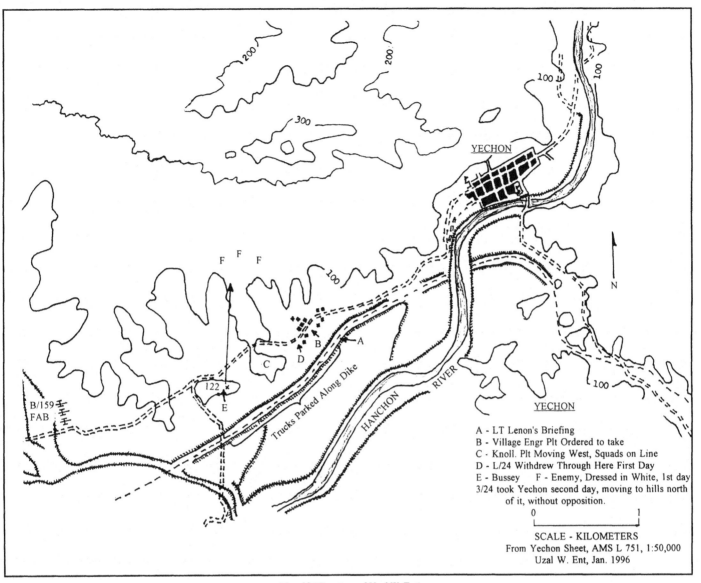

YECHON

YECHON

A - LT Lenon's Briefing
B - Village Engr Plt Ordered to take
C - Knoll. Plt Moving West, Squads on Line
D - L/24 Withdrew Through Here First Day
E - Bussey   F - Enemy, Dressed in White, 1st day
3/24 took Yechon second day, moving to hills north
    of it, without opposition.

SCALE - KILOMETERS
From Yechon Sheet, AMS L 751, 1:50,000
Uzal W. Ent, Jan. 1996

Map 13 (Courtesy of Uzal W. Ent)

was strafing the village and beyond. The mortar fire came at us too heavily and rather than be trapped in a village where snipers and ambushers were prevalent, I ordered the central platoon out of the town [and] across a rice paddy...." North Korean mortar rounds followed the withdrawing unit, but exploded harmlessly in the muck and water of the paddy. The company took up positions on high ground near the battalion CP.

While the fight for Yechon was in progress, the first mail for the 77 Engineers came through to the unit CP. CPT Bussey, not knowing that there was a battle at the town, gained permission from the 24th Regimental XO, LTC Roberts, to take mail up to Lenon's platoon. Bussey jeeped forward in search of his platoon, and came to a halt behind the last vehicle of the parked convoy which had brought 3/24 to Yechon. Ahead he could hear the noise of battle for the town.

"The village of Yechon was cradled deep in a buttonhook mountain, which nearly ringed it," Bussey wrote in his *Firefight at Yechon*. "The enemy had fallen back, climbed part way up the mountain, and was raining fire down on the town."

The levee on which the vehicle column was parked was too narrow to turn the trucks around, so if any of the rear vehicles were destroyed the

entire column would be trapped. Bussey judged by the volume of fire that the enemy force was about all a battalion could handle.

North of the rear of the column was a hill several hundred feet high. Bussey climbed the hill and studied the vast rice paddy area to his front, stretching toward Yechon to the east and the mountains to the north. About a thousand yards to the north he saw a large body of men, dressed in civilian white, come out of a defile and head in his direction. He scrambled quickly back down the hill, rounded up about a dozen drivers and others near the vehicles and had them carry a .50-cal machine gun and mount and a heavy water-cooled .30-cal machine gun up the hill, plus all the ammunition they could carry in two trips. Bussey spotted the guns 25-30 yards apart. He and his driver, CPL Pinckney, manned the .50, while two infantrymen manned the .30. Bussey sent an infantry sergeant and half a dozen men back to the trucks for more ammunition.

The captain fired a burst from the .50-cal machine gun over the heads of the oncoming column of men. They all "hit the dirt." A leader blew a whistle and signaled some of the men to flank Bussey's position. Bussey and the soldiers on the .30 caliber machine gun began to rake the enemy

with fire. The North Korean leader and those near him crumpled "like rag dolls," Bussey wrote.

Very soon, accurate enemy mortar fire began falling all around the captain and his men. The assistant gunner on the .30 was killed and the gunner badly wounded. Fragments from bursting mortar rounds flew in all directions, as round after round fell on the ridge, trying to destroy the machine guns. Bussey was struck twice by fragments; once in the right wrist and again in the cheekbone, causing him to spit blood. Then his .50-cal froze — it would no longer fire. Quickly, he moved to the .30, moved the dead assistant gunner aside and had the wounded gunner feed the gun with his good arm. The other had been shattered by mortar fragments. The two men continued to pour deadly machine gun fire on the hapless enemy below.

"Finally there was no more movement," Bussey wrote, "and the carnage ceased. There was nothing left to kill. The gentle breeze of early evening bathed us all."

He rounded up some of the men from the trucks and they went out into the paddies. "We counted the enemy dead. In that plain there were 258 dead men in large and small pieces. The rice paddies were now crimson and green. I was sick, sicker than I'd ever been in my life.... I climbed the hill again and took a final look at that valley. The valley of death."

It was after dark when CPT Bussey returned to his company. He was haunted by the scenes of that day for many years afterward.

After hearing Bussey's driver describe what had happened, the 77th's first sergeant, Roscoe C. Dudley, interviewed witnesses to confirm the facts and them submitted a written recommendation that CPT Bussey be awarded the Medal of Honor. 1SG Dudley, now deceased, confirmed that he took this action in a July 15, 1986, sworn affidavit.

While 1SG Dudley was assembling data to support his recommendation, MG Kean visited the 77th, awarding Bussey a Silver Star as "a down payment" on a higher award later. The paperwork for the Medal of Honor disappeared, and CPT Bussey never received that award. (See Chapter Notes.)

LTC Pierce, determined to seize and hold Yechon, issued orders to renew the assault the next day. The plan was for Co. L to make the main attack into Yechon while Co. I occupied the high ground on Co. L's route of advance, screening that flank from the enemy. Co. K would follow Co. L, clearing any pockets of resistance by-passed by Co. L. CO. M (Heavy Weapons) attached half of the Machine Gun Platoon to Co. L and half to Co. K.

An artillery preparation was fired on Yechon just before the July 21 attack. At 4 a.m., with 1LT Oliver Dillard's platoon in the lead, Co. L crossed the LD in a column of platoons. The attack was executed "by the book." His unit "may have received a few enemy rounds," Dillard recalled, "but nothing to concern me about the safety of my men. "Co. I came up on the left of L, according to plan.

CPT Biggs wrote that Co. L moved "to within 100 yards of the outskirts of Yech'on where we came under fire from two positions. One a machine gun nest in a hut in an open field, which I took under fire with a .50 cal mounted on my jeep." He silenced the enemy gun. After that, he recalled "some slight mortar...and sniper fire from a heavily wooded area on the hill. I ordered the lead platoon to strike out at the trouble, running.... I ordered LT Sergeant's platoon to go back down along the river bank, securing the breech and assuming his old platoon position [of the previous day's attack.] The rest of us kept at the double through the town, firing at whatever fired at us." The enemy fled, some right into Co. I. Co. L secured Yechon, and the battalion went on to occupy the hills north of town.

If Yechon failed to be regarded as a major battle, it was, as Lyle Rishell remarked in his book, *With a Black Platoon in Combat*, "a symbolic victory for U.S. ground troops...."

After the battle of Yechon, the 24th Regiment turned the area over to the ROK 18th Regiment of the Capital Division.

The Misfortune of Co. F, 35th Infantry - July 22

The 25th Division had to protect two main avenues to Sangju in order to secure the town: The main road running south from Mungyong through Hamchang to Sangju 15 miles farther

south, and a secondary road farther west, which came south through the mountains, then east to Sangju.

The 2/35 blocked northwest of Hamchang, supported by a platoon of tanks from A/79 Tk Bn and A/90 FAB. The 1/35 was farther south and west, supporting the 27th Regiment. The 24th Regiment defended the secondary road west of Sangju.

The 2/35 was deployed on a hill south of Mungyong along the south bank of a stream flowing past Sangju and emptying into the Naktong. A ROK battalion held the front line just north of the stream. Co. F was sent across the stream and inserted in the center of the ROK battalion. BG Vennard Wilson, 25th Division ADC, had insisted on this despite vehement protests by COL Fisher and the battalion commander, LTC John L. Wilkins. The two commanders did not want this inexperienced company to depend on ROK stability in its first battle. There was a small hill behind the F Co. and ROK positions, north of the stream. The stream was a raging torrent, swollen by heavy rains, with current so swift that large boulders were rolled along downstream.

The enemy attack was supported by T-34 tank fire. Jack Gates of Co. F was ordered by his platoon sergeant to withdraw. Just after he left his foxhole, it took a direct hit from a T-34. "Then the North Korean infantry came and pushed us off the hill," Gates wrote. "We were trapped by the river; had to swim [it] while they were shooting at us."

William F. McCafferty was a member of Fox Co. in its first battle. "We held most of the day," he wrote, "then started withdrawing in the afternoon. As I started down the hill a sergeant told me to go up the trail to the right and another guy to go up the trail to the left. and lay down cover fire for the withdrawal. I fired my rifle 'till I had two clips left. I called to the soldier on the left." There was no answer and McCafferty couldn't find him, so he started down the hill alone.

About half-way down he found a middle-aged, unwounded soldier standing on the trail. McCafferty tried to get the man to go with him. While they conversed, McCafferty could see his comrades trying to get back across the swollen stream. "One was hit and started splashing in the water [while] being washed downstream," McCafferty wrote. Another man was struck "and he jerked around like he was trying to shake the bullet out of his body." McCafferty could not get the soldier on the trail to come with him, so he started down the hill by himself, and was shot in the leg. About the same time, he saw another man hit trying to cross the stream. "He started to make strange noises like a seal or dog barking," McCafferty continued, and was "washed down the river."

Two officers and an NCO tied a pair of twisted telephone wires around their bodies and attempted to swim to the opposite side and fasten a line, but each in turn was swept downstream a hundred yards or more, where they stumbled ashore on the same bank from which they started. Some men drowned trying to escape across the rushing stream. A platoon of tanks stopped the enemy and most of Fox Co. eventually escaped. McCafferty and four or five others took shelter and waited for darkness. Just before dark, a ser-

geant came back and led them to safety. Co. F lost 6 KIA, 10 WIA and 21 MIA.

On the morning of July 23, five T-34s crossed the river heading for Hamchang. The 90th FAB knocked out four of them and the fifth was destroyed by an air strike after it turned back across the river.

The 2/35 executed a series of withdrawals, under orders, through the end of July, falling back some 30 miles on the Sangju front.

The 24th Regiment on the Sangju Front - July 22-30

The 24th Regiment had taken over the front from the ROK 1st Division and the 27th Infantry had relieved the ROK 2d Division. Remnants of the 2d Division were absorbed into the 1st. ROK troops on the Hamchang front destroyed 11 T-34s and captured another between July 24-27. By the 24th, the U.S. 25th Division held the old sectors of the ROK 1st and 2d Divisions from Sangju westward to the Seoul-Taegu highway.

On the same day that F/35 experienced its first battle, 2/24 and elements of the ROK 17th Regiment were moving into the mountains northwest of Sangju. Co. E of the 24th led the battalion along a dirt road into a gorge, with steep mountains on both sides. Without warning, an enemy light mortar and one or two machine guns fired on the company. The men scattered into roadside ditches. ROK officers tried to get the company deployed to the left and right for an envelopment, but were misunderstood. Soon concentrated enemy rifle fire caused both E and F companies to hastily withdraw.

CPT Roger S. Walden, a WW II paratrooper, commanded Co. F, following Co. E. Behind Co. F was the battalion command group, followed by G and H, enroute to an assembly area for a forthcoming attack. "The situation was very vague...," Walden wrote. "Suddenly E Co. came under heavy machine gun fire.... Our radios didn't work, nor did our SCR 300s to Battalion...." Walden moved forward to assess the situation. As he did so, his first sergeant "freaked out," he recalled. Walden had to go back, appoint another NCO as first sergeant, then return to the head of his company. By that time, the regimental and battalion commanders had discussed the situation and ordered the battalion to withdraw. "This was done in an orderly manner," Walden declared, " and not as Appleman describes in...*South to the Naktong*...." (See Chapter Notes.)

During the Sangju operation the 64th FAB was placed in general support of the 24th Regiment. Cleo O. Bell was an F.O. with G/24 in a blocking position. It was to be his first battle. A North Korean force with tanks was approaching from the northwest toward Sangju. Cleo established his OP about 50 yards from the crest of a hill. Co. G was dug in from the base of the hill and up slope to cover the road and a bridge about a quarter mile to the northwest. He registered his battery and settled in for the night. "At first light, flares and heavy weapons fire signaled a North Korean attack from hills across the road," he wrote. Bell called in fire from his battery. The 24th remained in position until friendly artillery ceased firing. The battery had to quit firing in order to repel a North Korean infantry attack on its position.

Shortly afterward men of Co. G beat a hasty retreat "past my OP to safety beyond the crest," Bell recalled. The G Co. commander came by and told Bell that he'd better pull out, too.

"I sent my radio operator and my recon sergeant first and followed in a minute or two," he recounted. "The forward slope was under heavy machine gun fire at this time." The radio operator was killed and the enemy cut the road to the rear. "I gathered 8-10 riflemen and kept to the hills parallel to the road," Bell wrote. Later that day, he and the riflemen reached friendly lines.

Between July 22-30, the 24th slowly withdrew. On July 24, LT Rishell took a recon patrol to within about two miles of Poun, capturing an enemy 57mm field piece in the process. On July 25, 3/24 engaged in a heavy firefight to the right rear of 1/24. The enemy had bypassed the 1st Battalion to get to the 3d. Co. B counterattacked through Co. I on July 26 and took a hill from the enemy. Division headquarters then ordered a withdrawal, characterized as "organized" in Rishell's memoir.

For the next few days units, of the regiment withdrew on successive positions. "This worked well until one of the units was attacked, or until it was flanked by the enemy," Rishell wrote. Then counterattacks were made to try to restore the line, one on July 28, when 1/24 attacked to relieve pressure on the 2d Bn.

Before the Perimeter, most battles were fought by individual U.S. battalions with open flanks. The defenders had no barbed wire, no AP mines, no flares or sandbags with which to enhance any defensive position. In almost every case, the defenders were attacked frontally, while other enemy troops flanked the position and attempted to cut off the defenders. Before establishment of the Perimeter, a reserve rarely was available large enough to relieve the defenders. Almost without exception, withdrawal was their only salvation.

This constant pressure on the 24th was wearying and demoralizing to the men. They were unhappy and frustrated by the moves from one position to another and the lack of support in troops and supplies. They were physically and mentally exhausted.

Rishell's platoon was in position on July 31 when he was ordered to withdraw commencing "at dark and no later than 2130 hours [9:30 p.m.]." Earlier that day, 1LT Leon A. Gilbert, commanding the company, withdrew from an outpost with about 15 men. Although ordered by COL White and other senior officers to return to the outpost, Gilbert refused. The senior NCO took the men back to the position. Gilbert was court-martialled and sentenced to death. President Truman commuted the sentence on Nov. 27, 1950, to 20 years hard labor, dismissal from the service and forfeiture of all pay and allowances.

Lyle Rishell takes issue with authors who denigrate the entire 24th Infantry Regiment. Often, they have condemned entire battalions and the regiment for the actions of a few men, a platoon or company. The 24th Regiment withdrew through Sangju on the night of July 31, covered by 1/35 Inf. In 11 days of action the 24th lost 27

KIA, 293 WIA and 3 MIA, a total of 323 battle casualties.

Strength of the U.S. Eighth Army - July 19

With the 1st Cavalry and 25th Infantry Divisions in Korea, the Eighth Army numbered somewhat over 39,000. General HQ, Far East Command G3 Operations Report 34, dated July 19, 1950, gave these totals:

Eighth Army HQ, Korea	2,184
KMAG	473
1st Cav Div.	10,027
24th Inf Div.	10,463
25th Inf Div.	13,059
Pusan Base	2,979
ADCOM	163
Misc. Personnel	91
TOTAL:	39,439

Of this number, 33,549 were in combat divisions, with a combined total of no more then 57 rifle companies, 18 in the 1st Cav and 24th Divisions and 21 in the 25th Division, averaging no more than about 160 men each. Therefore, the front line rifle companies of the three divisions probably totaled fewer than 10,000 men.

Yongdong - 8th Cavalry Regiment - July 23-25

On July 22, when the 8th Cavalry relieved the 21st Infantry (24th Division) in the Yongdong area, the 1st Cavalry Division had the responsibility of blocking the enemy along the main Taejon-Taegu corridor. Under Eighth Army orders, but contrary to GEN Gay's wishes, the 8th Cavalry was split to cover two widely separated approaches. The 1/8 Cav was on the Taejon road northwest of Yongdong, while 2/8 Cav was deployed two miles southwest of Yongdong on the Chosan-ni-Muju-Kumsan road. The two battalions were separated too widely to support one another, and could easily be outflanked and beaten. Gay had positioned the 5th Cav to block east of Yongdong.

On July 23, the *7th* and *9th Regiments, NK 3d Division*, began their attack against the 8th Cavalry Regiment. During the morning 1/8 Cav destroyed three T-34s with 3.5 inch rocket launchers, but later in the day the enemy got through southwest of Yongdong and established a roadblock a mile and a half behind the 2d Battalion. The 1st Battalion was being fiercely attacked from the front northwest of town.

This was to be Donald Summers' (C/8th Cav) first battle. His outfit was "dug in on both sides of the road on a natural ridge line extending east and west," he wrote. Shortly after elements of the 24th Regiment passed through the position, the enemy attacked. "We were being shelled by T-34 tanks and the NKPA were behind.... Our artillery and 3.5s stopped several tanks.... The NKPA tried several frontal assaults but we stopped them."

Four times the next day, three U.S. tanks tried to break the block behind 2/8 Cav. The commander of the 2d Battalion, LTC Eugene J. Field, was wounded at the roadblock. The 1/5 Cav and

the 16th Recon Co. were sent to try to reach 2/8 Cav, but by noon, enemy infiltrators were attacking the 99th and 61st FABs, which had been supporting the 2d Battalion.

On the northwest road, 1/8 Cav, supported by quad-.50 and 37mm fire from A/92 AA/AW Bn and the 7 FAB, managed to repel the enemy.

By July 25, there were so many enemy troops behind the two battalions of the 8th Cav that it became necessary to withdraw the regiment. The 1/8 Cav (LTC Robert W. Kane), northwest of Yongdong, got out in an orderly withdrawal, covered by HM Co. and two batteries of the 77 FAB (LTC William A. Harris). When the mortar company lost their mortars, they continued to fight as infantrymen.

Southwest of Yongdong, 2/8 Cav called in artillery fire so close that four U.S. soldiers were wounded by it. Before dawn, the battalion attacked the roadblock, briefly opening it at 4:30 a.m. on July 25, but the rear of the column, which included F/8, the 16th Recon Co. and 1st Plt, A/71 Tk Bn, was cut off. Seven of 11 tanks failed to get through the block and were abandoned. A group of 219 men, primarily from the Recon Co. and F/8, made their way out on foot.

Joseph M. Christopher was with F/8 Cav southeast of Yongdong as an ammo-bearer for 60mm mortars. It was raining when his unit set out for Yongdong on July 21. They arrived on the assigned position after dark and dug in. "The rain had stopped and the stars were out," Christopher wrote. On July 22, he and a number of other men were detailed to screen refugees coming through the lines.

The enemy made contact with 2/8 Cav on the 23d, but Christopher's outfit was in reserve and not engaged.

"That evening the platoon leader instructed us that we were surrounded," Christopher recalled. "Later the platoon sergeant, CPL Hewins...told us we would withdraw about 0300 hours (3 a.m.) and...would not take the mortars." The plan was for about half the battalion to attack through the roadblock, while Co. F, with tanks, would attack from a different direction.

In the early hours of the next day, the company moved out. "At the bottom of the hill we joined...eleven M-24 tanks," he wrote. Co. H (Heavy Weapons) was already on the road with the tanks. "There was no sneaking out silently," Christopher observed. He could see gun flashes at the head of the column. Young Christopher was walking close to a tank when it fired its main gun; after that, he stayed away from the tank.

"I saw a medic on a porch [of a burning building] working on someone," he recalled. "I stopped, and he shouted [for me] to shoot the Korean nearby getting to his feet. I shot the [Korean] man twice with my carbine and moved on."

The column that Christopher was with made a wrong turn in the dark. He was near the rear of the unit. "Suddenly machine gun fire came flying by," he wrote. The men jumped off the rice paddy dikes they were traversing into the water and stinking muck of the paddy, itself. A number of men were hit and PFC Lee Simpson was among those killed. The men at the head of the column caved in and came back through Christopher's area, but the company commander, CPT Terry Field, finally got matters sorted out.

Yongdong, southeast of Taejon. Units and equipment dispersed (foreground); note artillery bursts (center background). The numerically superior enemy, emplaced in the rugged hills around the town forced the U.S. Army to withdraw on 26 July. (Source: P. 68-69, Korea, 1950, Chief of Military History, Washington, D.C., 1982)

The company made its way through enemy lines and rejoined the regiment a few days later.

West of Kumchon - 2/7 Cavalry - July 26-27

While the 8th Cavalry was engaged outside Yongdong, the headquarters and 2d Battalion, 7th Cavalry went into position west of Kumchon. On the night of July 25-26, under the impression an enemy breakthrough had been achieved in the sector of the 27th Regiment (25th Division) defending a nearby road, the 7th Cavalry headquarters and 2/7 Cav began to withdraw. The withdrawal became disorganized.

CPL Marvin C. Daniel, of Co. E, recalled some of what happened to his unit. "We had just moved into position as it was getting dark. We were digging in on the left side, having a road to our left with a steep incline descending to the road. There was a minefield on the opposite side of the road.... [It] seemed to be in excellent position to defend the hill. I was a 17 year old gunner on a 2.36 rocket launcher with two ammunition bearers. I could hear the communication from the Weapons Co. Commander to battalion. It was approximately 11 to 12 midnight and I heard battalion give the order to pack up and move out.... The company commander told the radioman to get confirmation of the order and to tell them we were set up and in good position to defend the hill."

Daniel continued, "Approximately five minutes passed while he was waiting the confirmation, and we began to take heavy small arms fire from every direction. So part of the company heard the order, but not the second confirmation that was requested. I began to move around the face of the

hill...and there was... [a] 2d LT and Sergeant First Class and another Private.... We began to move around the hill, which was very steep.... I was on the low side of the men, towards the road. I began to slide down the hill toward the road, and the small-arms fire was very intense.... [It] was hitting right at my feet with dirt and rocks flying up around my face. Every time I tried to take a step up the hill, I continued to slide down the hill farther. I was unable to gain any footing and I could hear the North Koreans yelling as they fired at me, 'Die, GI! Die, GI!'"

Daniel finally grabbed a tree root, stopping his slide toward the road. He then put the launcher together, and used it as "walking stick" to help him climb back up the hill. The officer told the men not to return the fire because it "would give away our position." The enemy tried to cut off the company, and the men ran a gauntlet of fire to escape. Daniel wrote that the North Koreans "were chasing us and firing at us." The chase ended by daylight, he wrote. "I ran so far and was so exhausted that I sat down and began to slide down the hill." The men made contact with other friendly troops on the road. CPL Daniel credited his 2.36-inch rocket launcher for saving him that night. "I...believe that although it was never fired that night, and used as a mountain stick, it helped to save my life."

During the night, a T-34 tank was reported to be heading to the rear of the regiment; Co. H CP was under enemy fire. Edward L Daily wrote "We received no orders to withdraw, and all hell was starting to break loose as firing from everywhere along the road was directed at the 2d Battalion." In his *The Legacy of Custer's 7th U.S. Cavalry in Korea*, Daily writes that 2/7 Cav was, in fact, moving to the aid of the 8th Cavalry when

a combination of heavy enemy fire and a road clogged with "masses of refugees," ROK soldiers, "24th Infantry Division [troops] and our 7th Cavalry Regiment" caused the dissolution of organization and precipitated the hasty pullout. He called it a "confusing and disorganized mess" which led to "chaos and panic." In addition to the inexperience of the troops, he wrote that the loss of experienced NCOs and officers to fill the 24th Division was another factor contributing to the chaos.

SFC Harold Blanc, H Co. commo sergeant, recalled that the unit was on the way to help the 8th Cavalry, but the road was so clogged with refugees, ROK and American soldiers going the other way, "there was no way for our unit to progress forward as ordered." As darkness fell, a T-34 began firing. "The projectiles looked like tracers or balls of fire," Blanc remembered. Hordes of refugees caused confusion and panic, and impeded the movement of Co. H before it starting to withdraw in disorder, "PFC Bob Alicea and I were ... the last troopers to leave...."

The How Co. commander, CPT Melbourne C. Chandler, did get some order out of chaos, assembling many of the 2/7 Cav men and leading them out of danger, but he was very angry. "I will tell you this," he declared to his men, "from now on Co. H will not become disorganized! We came to Korea as a fighting unit and that's the way it will remain!"

The 2d Battalion left behind a switchboard, an emergency lighting unit, 14 machine guns, nine radios, 120 M1 rifles, 26 carbines, seven BARs and six 60mm mortars. The next day, a party of men in vehicles went back and recovered some of the abandoned weapons and equipment.

While 2/7 Cav was engaged, the *7th Regiment, NK 3d Division* started a flanking movement to the southwest through Chirye, then northeast against Kumchon. The night of July 26-27, elements of the *3d Division*, with four tanks and an infantry force, drove hundreds of refugees ahead of them and attacked elements of the 1st Cavalry Division east of town.

1st Cavalry Division Plans - Counterattack and Withdrawals - July 27

On the morning of July 27 the 5th Cav was in position to the left rear of the 7th Cav, and the 27th Inf (25th Div.) was on the 7th's right. The 77th FAB supported the 7th Cav, with individual guns in the batteries laid on separate azimuths to cover the 270-degree perimeter. If artillery fire had to be concentrated, it was necessary to move the trails of other pieces in the battery. On the 28, the enemy penetrated the right flank of 2/7 Cav, and tried to turn both flanks of 1/7 Cav without success.

A conference was held in the CP of the 7th Cavalry on the morning of July 28 to plan for counterattacks and withdrawals. Since the 27th Infantry was involved, LTC Michaelis, commanding the "Wolfhounds," attended the meeting. GEN Frank Allen, ADC, 1st Cavalry Division, laid out the plan:

8th Cav: Move forward; one battalion on the forward ridge and one battalion behind the 27th, to occupy critical ground on their left.

7th Cav: Hold present positions. 1st Bn attack to close the gap between 7th Cav and 27th Inf.

27th Inf: Plan to withdraw through the 1st Cav Div.

GEN Gay, concerned about the enemy on both flanks and threatening the division's rear areas, worried about the 27th Infantry's ability to hold and ordered a withdrawal that day. The meeting that morning, plus the heavy fighting which the 16th Recon Co. had at Chirye during the day, added weight to his concern.

Chirye - 16th Recon Co. - July 28

That morning, LT Lester Lauer led a platoon-sized patrol from the 16th Recon Co. through Chirye. Later South Korean police told Lauer that a North Korean battalion was in Chirye, but by that time, Lauer's patrol was beyond the town. He radioed to Recon Co. C.O., CPT Charles V. H. Harvey, telling him of the enemy reported in Chirye and asking for instructions. CPT Harvey took a platoon and 14 South Korean policemen, and went to the lieutenant's assistance. At the edge of Chirye, the force surprised and killed three enemy soldiers, then drove on through the town. At noon, the two platoons joined forces.

Cautiously re-entering Chirye, the column came upon a partially-built roadblock where an estimated platoon of enemy opened fire. CPT Harvey ordered the column to smash through, and an M39 vehicle pushed a Korean wagon out of the way. The M39 and one jeep got through, but enemy machine gun fire disabled the next vehicle in line. With that, several hundred enemy closed in on the trapped men. The patrol fought its way to the south end of town and set up its three 81mm mortars. Although wounded four times and bleeding badly, CPL Harry D Mitchell continued to fire his mortar until it ran out of ammunition. Early in the battle, CPT Harvey was struck in the hand by a bullet, then a machine gun hit him in the neck, severing his jugular vein killing him in a few minutes. His last order was for the patrol to withdraw.

Abandoning the vehicles and heavy equipment, three officers and 41 EM escaped to a nearby hill. Walking all night, the group reached 1st Cavalry lines the next morning, a trek of 35 miles. Co. losses were 2 KIA, 3 WIA and 11 MIA.

With 2/7 Cav - July 29-31

At 4 a.m. on July 29, H/7 Cav came under heavy tank and mortar fire, with the tanks concentrating on H/7's 81mm mortar position. When he heard the tanks approaching, mortar platoon leader 2LT Robert Wood sent SFC Harold Blanc to notify 2/7 Cav. SFC Blanc and LT Wood had known one another since 1948 at Ft. Dix, NJ. Blanc left his foxhole, which he shared with PFC Marvin Hoffman, and delivered the message to the Bn C.O., MAJ Omar Hitchner.

"Upon my return to Co. H," Harold recalled, "I could see the fire belching out of the tubes of the 81mm mortars.... Then, suddenly, an enemy

tank round burst in a tree... [killing LT Wood] and nearly wiping out the entire...platoon...." PFC Hoffman was killed by mortar fragments. Had Blanc not been sent to deliver the message, he also would have been killed or wounded.

Ed Daily had been promoted to sergeant the day before this action. He and PFC Ray Scarberry manned a heavy water-cooled .30-cal machine gun, attached from Co. H to Co. E. To his left was another "heavy," manned by SFC William Brown and PVT George Vernon. "With our machine guns firing at maximum potential...two waves of the enemy attack were repelled," wrote Daily, but his ammunition was almost gone and the gun was getting too hot. Suddenly, SFC Brown and PVT Vernon leaped from their foxhole with fixed bayonets "screaming 'GARRYOWEN' at the top of their lungs." The startled enemy dropped their weapons and started to run. Brown and Vernon killed 12 and wounded about 25 others with rifle fire and the enemy's own grenades.

Soon after this, CPT Chandler ordered Daily and his machine gun squad to accompany him to an adjacent ridge. The captain directed Daily to dig his guns in and to provide good fire support while he moved forward to a position from which to direct air, artillery and mortar support. Chandler went forward, while Daily and his men poured machine gun fire out to keep the enemy pinned down.

CPT Chandler directed fire into enemy concentrations from his exposed position. Everything from company mortars, 105mm howitzers of the 77th FAB to F-51 fighters rained fire on the enemy.

"Suddenly I saw Captain Chandler fall to his side and I thought he had been hit by enemy fire," Daily wrote. He rushed forward to Chandler: "He was laying on his back with blood all over both legs and his fatigue uniform. I asked 'Captain, sir, have you been hit?' He looked at me and said, 'There's nothing wrong with me, now get the hell out of here and back to your position.' I answered, 'Yes, Sir!' I ran back to my position and squad."

Chandler had been wounded, but refused medical treatment. The enemy was beaten off with heavy losses. The battle, as so many in the first months of the Korean War, was fought in oppressive 100 plus-degree heat and high humidity. Korea had no jungles, but negotiating its steep valley ridges and hills in these extremes was very debilitating.

That night, the enemy loosed heavy barrages of mortars and artillery onto 2/7 Cav and began probing attacks before dawn. LT Marvin Goulding dashed up to SGT Daily and ordered him to displace his squad. As daylight came, enemy artillery and mortar fire increased in intensity.

Daily and his men followed the lieutenant. "Suddenly a mortar round hit very near us," wrote Daily, "which sent me tumbling over the top of him." As the dirt and dust cleared, Goulding asked, "Are you OK, SGT Daily?" Daily was unhurt, but one of his ammo bearers, a young private, was killed by the blast. Daily recalled that the man was a recent replacement, and he didn't even remember his name.

Goulding, Daily, his crew and gun made it to LT John C. Lippincott's 3d Platoon of Co. F.

Lippincott needed machine guns to suppress enemy fire so his 3.5 inch rocket launcher team could get close enough to knock out two enemy tanks firing at his platoon from a railroad position nearby. Daily was expected to provide this fire, as well as support for the platoon when it received orders for a planned withdrawal. Lippincott sent Daily and his crew to the summit of a hill to the right of the road which the 3d Platoon was defending. Reaching the top of the designated hill, Daily found it "an excellent location.... Not only did it offer enfilade fire in respect to the road, but plunging fire as well." Soon he was providing Lippincott with welcome and effective machine gun support. However, the rocket launcher team never arrived, apparently because of a shortage of ammunition.

Donald D. Down was a BAR-man with F/7 Cav. The company was on the left flank of the battalion position on July 30-31. Enemy tanks took the unit under fire. About 1 a.m., squad leader CPL Alfred Clair, assistant squad leader CPL Ralph Bernotas, Down and PVT Alzondo Berryman went after tanks. "Berryman was the Co.[Co.] sniper and carried his rifle," Clair wrote, "Bernotas carried the bazooka, I carried the rockets — three on a back pack and a fourth in my shirt. Like Down, I also had a BAR." They "went down the right side of the railroad tracks...[and] finally got even [with] the tanks," Down wrote. Enroute to the enemy tanks, the four men passed close to enemy soldiers moving to attack their company.

Down and Berryman stayed at a culvert along the tracks to cover Clair and Bernotas. These two men took the bazooka and a BAR, crossed the tracks and headed for the tanks. "All hell broke out," Donald continued. "Machine gun fire - tanks firing their main guns. Then we heard an explosion near the tanks. All firing stopped for...maybe ten minutes.... Then it started up again." Stray shots ricocheted off the walls of the culvert. When the two corporals had not returned by daylight, Down and Berryman started to return to F Co., but they had forgotten the password. Fearing they might be mistaken for the enemy, the two men took shelter in a railroad station house until they heard voices from their mortarmen giving fire commands.

Corporals Bernotas and Clair had moved toward the muzzle flash of a T34. Bernotas had the 3.5 ready to fire. His first round was short.

"I elevated my sights and reloaded a second shell," he recalled, "and waited.... When the tanks resumed firing, I squeezed off another round.... The tank...exploded and continued to burn and explode throughout the morning." The two men started back to their unit, when they encountered an enemy machine gun, which they knocked out with a grenade. Bernotas had one more shot at a tank with his launcher, but had set the sight too high and "missed the sitting duck," he lamented. "I almost cried because it was such an easy target."

"My heart sank when I saw the miss," Clair recalled. "That 85mm on the tank was traversing to shoot at us. We were running in water, and I'm sure the water took the blast and saved us. We passed a bend in the tracks and got safely out of sight of the tank."

These men all belonged to 2LT John Lippincott's 3d Platoon, F/7 Cav. Lippincott remembered the battle of 30-31 July as "one of the toughest fights."

CPT James T. Milam, commanding Co. E., accounted for 34 enemy dead. He led a patrol into enemy territory, destroying a machine gun and killing 7 more of the enemy. Fox Co.'s LT John O. Potts rendered aid to a wounded man while under heavy enemy fire. PVT Willis Monington of the same unit maintained telephone communication for the company by repeatedly repairing broken wire throughout the battle. Then there was CPL Chester L. Hart (HHC, 2/7 Cav), who rescued a wounded soldier in a hail of enemy small-arms and machine gun fire.

Gerald Gingery, assigned as a cook in H/5th Cav, suffered heat stroke shortly after his outfit got to Korea. He was evacuated to a hospital in Pusan because medics at the aid station could not stabilize his blood pressure. After about ten days, he was sent to a replacement unit. The second day there, he went AWOL and went back to find his old unit. He got a ride on an ammunition truck, which took him forward and dropped him off. Gingery headed north on the road. Entering a town, he saw what he thought to be enemy at the other end. Soon, these soldiers fired on him and Gerald "headed south as fast as the legs would go," he wrote.

He finally rejoined Co. H, "dug me a hole and settled in for the night," as he put it. The company was attacked by a large force that night and "all cooks, clerks and supply people were rushed up front to plug the gaps, me included," he recalled. The company suffered many casualties, including Gingery's "best buddy," Bobby Jones, who was killed.

27th Infantry on the Poun - Hwanggan Road - July 22-29

The 27th Infantry Regiment was inserted on the Poun-Hwanggan road to oppose elements of the *NK 2d Division*, which were moving to the northwest of the 1st Cavalry Division, threatening to advance from Poun to Hwanggan, about 10 miles east of Yongdong.

The regiment moved into an assembly area at Hwanggan the night of July 22-23, while the 24th Regiment dug in west of Sangju and the 35th (less its 1st Battalion) moved into positions south of Hamchang to protect the northern area of the division sector. The 1/35 was still at Pohang-dong, and the 27th relieved elements of the ROK 2d Division.

The 1/27 (LTC Gilbert J. Check) took position on hills astride the road just north of the village of Sangyong-ni, on the road to Poun. At 5 p.m. that day the last of the ROK 2d Division passed through the battalion.

Co. B was on the right of the road and A on the left. Co. C was angled to the right rear of Co. B, to refuse the battalion's right flank.

The three rifle company commanders, CPT Logan Weston, Co. A; 1LT Gordon C. Jung, Co. B and CPT Alfred S. Burnett, Co. C, all were combat veterans of WW II.

Co. B was deployed generally to the right of the road, with the 3d Platoon on the road, the 2d Platoon forward on a ridge nose jutting forward from the main line. The high point on this nose was a knob — Hill 170. The 1st Platoon was to

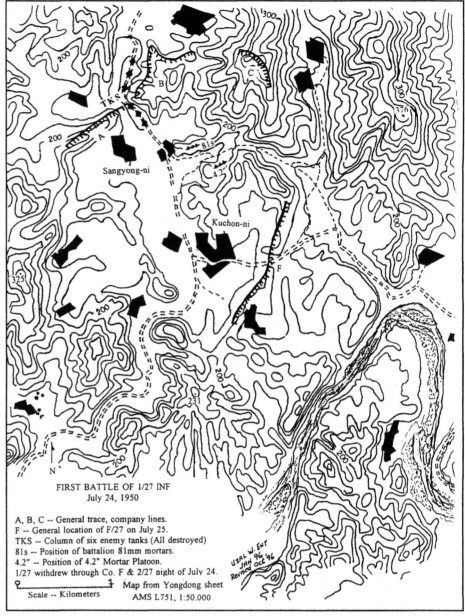

FIRST BATTLE OF 1/27 INF
July 24, 1950

A, B, C -- General trace, company lines.
F -- General location of F/27 on July 25.
TKS -- Column of six enemy tanks (All destroyed)
81s -- Position of battalion 81mm mortars.
4.2" -- Position of 4.2" Mortar Platoon.
1/27 withdrew through Co. F & 2/27 night of July 24.

Scale -- Kilometers

Map from Yongdong sheet
AMS L751, 1:50.000

Map 14 (Courtesy of Uzal W. Ent)

the right rear of the 2d, along the main ridge, facing generally north. The 1st Platoon Leader originally deployed his men near the bottom front of the hill to achieve grazing fire, remembering its importance from his Infantry School training. Shortly after the men began to dig in, he decided to move them part way up the hill, so they could obtain a better view of the low ground to the front. But even this was a mistake. The platoon should have been deployed along the military crest — just below the actual top of the hill — or even on the reverse slope, as it turned out. Twelve men of the platoon, one-third of its strength, were lost the next day. All 12 were on the right flank of the platoon, where the line was bent back along the ridge to refuse that flank. Evidently, the enemy had a vantage point from which they could cover that part of the foxhole line with very accurate machine gun and mortar fire. The platoon leader never again made such a mistake. (See Chapter Notes.)

COL Check was unable to obtain any information from the withdrawing ROKs, so he sent out a 30-man patrol that night under 1LT John

A. Buckley of Co. A. The patrol departed about 10 p.m. and went about a mile north on the road. Buckley deployed half the patrol in each side of the road and waited.

Harry Leonard, CPL Della Vecchio and CPL Poole were members of the patrol. Leonard recalled, "About 12 that night we could here them coming.... They had three or four men about a hundred yards ahead. [The men] were talking and laughing. We let them go through." The main body came marching down the road four abreast. When the enemy column approached his position, LT Buckley fired the first shot. "There was no way you could miss," Leonard wrote. "We had two BARs, carbines and M1s. How many we killed I would not guess, but they were laying everywhere. The enemy panicked." Buckley gave the order to pull out, but some T-34s had arrived on the scene, preventing the patrol from reuniting. Buckley returned to Co. A with most of the patrol about 4 a.m. on July 24.

Leonard and two other men went into the paddies on the right of the road then climbed to higher ground. They stayed hidden all day, but could see the "North Koreans and their tanks and artillery set up on the road and start shooting toward our lines," he wrote. The men could hear U.S. troops returning fire. "Our troops were giving a good account of themselves," Leonard recalled. That night, the three men set out again, following a ridgeline all night until about an hour after daylight, when they were fired on. "We could see that they were our troops," he wrote. "[We waved] but they kept on [firing]. Then I thought of my red hair. I took my helmet off and waved my hair and they ceased firing." The three men had reached the lines of E/27. Leonard recalled that after he and his two comrades came in, three men of the patrol remained missing.

The ferocity of fire by Buckley's patrol apparently caused the enemy to believe it had run into a main defense line, and they stopped for the night.

A BAR of B Co.'s 1st Platoon was sighted to fire across the front of the right flank of the 2d Platoon. As daylight came on July 24 the whole area was covered by dense ground fog. The BAR-man charged with covering the 2d Platoon's flank strained to see through the fog. Suddenly, he spotted the dim figure of a man running toward the 2d Platoon's line. He fired a quick burst from his BAR and the figure crumpled. Later it was discovered that he had killed a member of the 2d Platoon, who had served as a listening post. The 2d Platoon had failed to notify the 1st that they had any men beyond their lines, so the first KIA in B/27 was a man shot down in error by a comrade.

Shortly after this incident, about 6:30 a.m., enemy infantry attacked the 2d Platoon, under cover of the fog. Enemy mortar and machine gun fire supported the attack as soon as the sun burned off the mist. Tanks joined in, firing their main guns and machine guns. The 2d Platoon often grappled hand-to-hand with the enemy infantry. This battle went on all day, but the 2d Platoon repelled every attack.

CPL Earl H. Demage was with the 2d Platoon that day. He recalled PFC Bennie Sutton, from Co. D, and the water-cooled .30-cal machine guns he had set up nearby. "He and his two guns did a helluva lot of fighting that day," Demage remarked. "He saved my skin more than once that first day."

Enemy mortar fire drove an 81mm mortar OP from their position in the 1st Platoon's area. The hills occupied by 1/27 were bare of trees or shrubs, so the enemy easily could see the dirt thrown up around the foxholes. This may have contributed to their ability to drive off the OP and to create such carnage on the 1st Platoon's right flank.

An enemy column of six tanks approached along the road, firing as it came. Air strikes destroyed three tanks, but also hit a U.S. 3/4-ton truck, killing 2LT Trevor J. Perry of the Medical Co.. He was the only officer of the regiment killed that day. Rocket launcher teams accounted for the other three tanks.

"About 3 p.m. three tanks came down the road and passed one of my platoons," LT Jung was quoted in Tom Lambert's July 25, 1950 dispatch to the *Los Angeles Examiner*. "They went past my command post about 75 yards away."

The company had a combination of 2.36 and the new 3.5 inch rocket launchers, but the 3.5s had only three rounds each. CPL Claron Grigsby, acting supply sergeant of Co. B, grabbed one of the new bazookas and ran to a hillside overlooking the road. When the lead tank got to within 75 yards of him, Grigsby fired. "I hit him on the left side in the center," said Grigsby. "I hit him again right under the gun. I missed him with my next shot, but got him with my last one.... There was no more fire from that tank...."

One of the tanks began firing into one of Baker's platoons. SGT Miner Dixon jammed the T-34's turret with one shot from a 3.5 inch launcher. LT Jung, observing Dixon so near the tank, thought, "There goes Dixon. The sergeant thought to himself, "There went Dixon."

Two tanks penetrated as far as HM Co., commanded by 2LT Bertram Bishop. By this time, the mortars had been firing so fast that they had run out of ammunition. Bishop and MSG Robert Clark evacuated the mortarmen, except SSG Ralph Bevins, a Marine combat veteran of Bougainville, Guam and Iwo Jima; PFC Warren G. Bender and PVT Robert Starling. These three men fired at the two tanks with their M1 rifles for about a half hour. "I fired a whole bandoleer...at them," said Bevins. "The two tanks would spray our holes with their .50- caliber machine guns, then we'd get up and shoot back...." An air strike finally destroyed both tanks.

SSG John York, platoon sergeant of the 1st Platoon and a WW II combat veteran, took the platoon's rocket launcher over to the road to help, but the tanks had either already passed or had been knocked out by other teams.

During Baker's stand, MSG Moryl, platoon sergeant of the 2d Platoon, returned once to the company CP for more ammunition. All he could get was "ammo in cartons of 20 rounds," recalled 1SG George Hearn, "that had to be loaded in 8-round clips" for use in the M1 rifle and as issued by the Division's ASP.

The 27th Regiment's historical report for July 1950 states that M1 rifle ammunition was in critically short supply, with each rifleman having only 80 rounds. There also was a shortfall of 4.2 inch mortar ammunition. The shortage of rifle ammunition was corrected before the regiment went into battle, but not that of the mortar ammunition. Other critical shortages in the regiment were in medical personnel and equipment and spare parts for weapons. The Medical Collecting Station was manned by only four men; instead of 18. The shortage of medical personnel was so bad that as the Medical Co. report for July stated "drivers, cooks and technicians on duty in the Collecting and Battalion Aid Stations volunteered to go forward to assist in evacuation and treatment of the wounded. Since there was a great shortage of litter bearers, litter jeeps often went forward to Co. CPs to evacuate the wounded." Rifle company soldiers, too, helped to carry out the wounded. One medical aidman was supposed to be attached to each rifle platoon, but personnel shortages in the Medical Co. prevented this. Often medics had to provide aid to more than one platoon.

Able Co. had an outstanding rifle marksman in MSG Philip File IV, a combat veteran of Guadalcanal, New Georgia, Arundel, Kolombangara and Luzon. He was training for the Far East Command Rifle matches when the Korean War started.

From his foxhole, he could see the enemy attacking Co. B, as well as into the area behind the North Korean assault troops. They "strolled around in a casual fashion behind the assault troops," he wrote. "They were setting up a mortar behind a hillock across the road from me. I figured the range at about 500 yards." File's rifle was the one he had been practicing with for the rifle matches, so he knew the sight settings required for every range out to 600 yards. Setting the sights, he began to pick off the enemy's mortarmen. "I concentrated in making things uncomfortable for the mortar crew. It was several hours before they could get a round off," he wrote.

An enemy tank came up and File's position was pointed out to the tankers. "The first round hit the rock I was lying on," he recalled. File was not hurt, but CPL Donald Durst, near him, lost a leg below the knee. Durst was evacuated, only to be killed when his truck was hit by the air strike which killed LT Perry later in the day.

File and his companions saw more tanks coming down the road and through Co. B. "All we could do was harass the foot soldiers with rifle fire," he lamented. File observed one 2.36 inch launcher team attack one tank without success; the rockets just bounced off the tank. Then "a lieutenant [ran] across the open field in the face of machine gun fire from the tank, leading a carrying party. They ran across the road and up the hill and delivered a brand new 3.5 [inch] rocket launcher and rockets," File continued. The team assembled the launcher and the gunner knelt with the weapon on his shoulder. The loader, in his nervousness, dropped the rocket. It rolled down the hill and onto the road in front of the tank. The loader scrambled down the hill, retrieved the round, ran back up the hill, loaded it into the launcher "and sat back with a pleased grin on his face," File wrote. The gunner's first round disabled the tank.

The enemy never pressed an attack on Co. A, but concentrated on B and Co. C, to B's right flank. "At one time," wrote File, "we could see steel flash in the sunlight when C Co. fixed bayonets and drove the enemy from the hill."

File may have seen a team ordered out by CPT Weston. Frank L. Sandell recalled, "LT Buckley...[ordered] a rifle squad and a bazooka launcher team down to the roadway where there was a cut in the road.... The team...was led by [SFC] Taylor.... They successfully knocked out the right track of the tank, disabling it...." The disabled tank slewed sideways, blocking the road and preventing following tanks from advancing. Rice paddies at that time of year were filled with water, keeping the tanks from going around the flooded paddies.

CPT Weston was commanding Co. A, and was with the rifle squad and bazooka team which Sandell saw. Weston was trying to get artillery fire on the enemy when the tanks appeared and began firing into his CP. At about the same time, a jeep arrived with new 3.5 inch bazookas and some men who had received orientation on its use that morning. Weston grabbed an M1, and with the team and some riflemen, crawled about 250 yards through the paddies "to a drainage ditch where we found cover about 25 yards from the lead tank," he wrote. His launcher team had three rockets. "The first rocket knocked the track off the lead tank. The second rocket hit the bogie on the third tank. The second tank was bottled up between the other two...but began to rotate its turret toward [us]," Weston recounted. "We fired the third rocket at the turret, but overshot our target."

The captain sent one of the men back for more rockets. Unknown to him, the man was cut down by enemy machine gun fire. Weston and the rest of the men peppered the tank with rifle fire to keep it buttoned up, but the other two tanks began to rotate their turrets, searching through their periscopes for Weston's location. "Using our M1 rifles," he wrote, "we shot out the periscopes as fast as [they] could replace them." The captain had three rifle grenades, which he fired at the first tank, while he had the men with him "fired their rifles directly into the barrel until the gun stopped searching."

Meantime, the third tank located their hiding place. "Its main gun fired directly into our position," killing the three men with Weston, destroying the launcher and deafening him. "One of the men fell right on top of me," Weston continued. "He had been cut in half. I held him in my arms, looking into his sky-blue eyes, watching them turn a smoky gray," as he died. Weston then sprang onto the first tank just as the turret hatch opened. He quickly threw in two grenades, killing the crew. He also killed the crews of the other two tanks as they tried to escape from their vehicles.

CPT Al Burnett in Co. C recalled that his unit numbered 142 EM and four officers when it went to Korea, about average for rifle companies in the 27th at the time. Full strength was 205 EM and six officers. The full impact of war had not set in on the men of Charlie Co. "I remember the difficulty I had...in getting the men to dig a fox hole to the proper depth," he recalled. "They...had not yet learned the first rule for survival in the defense, which is a well-constructed emplacement from which to fight," Burnett wrote. The first enemy artillery rounds falling into the position solved the problem; "the dirt flew," Burnett recalled, as the men dug in deeper.

"First came a very heavy and accurate mortar and artillery barrage, which lasted for about 30 minutes," Burnett wrote about the start of battle on July 24. "Then the enemy infantry began moving forward in waves.... They came up every gully and crevice in the ground.... Our men did a wonderful job...and fought until their ammunition was exhausted... then braved the intense fire to bring up more." He too, saw enemy tanks get behind companies A and B. Then an air strike came in. "Those P-51s [F-51s] were about the most welcome sight I ever saw," he recalled.

Richard S. Majcher of Co. C recalled that his M1 rifle already was about worn out when he went to Korea, but it was the only weapon he had in this first battle. "In the first fire fight the front sight fell off," he wrote.

The combination of accurate and deadly enemy mortar and artillery fire and the enemy tank breakthrough made the area to the rear of the front line companies almost as dangerous as on the front.

"The first 120 mortar shell hit the 81s as they were putting out additional aiming stakes," wrote Cressie Johnson of Co. D. Strangely, too, the 4.2 inch mortars were on the forward slope of a hill, forward of the 81s. 2LT Bertram Bishop, the unit commander, had to hastily displace these heavy mortars when the T-34s came into view in the rear area. The 81mm mortars displaced later in the afternoon. Johnson recalls PFC Norron of Co. D firing two rocket rounds at a tank. Both rounds bounced off the tank and exploded in the ditch.

2LT Posie Starkey and his platoon sergeant of the Battalion Pioneer and Ammunition Platoon (P&A Plt) "were dug in the paddy across from the aid station," Starkey wrote. "From the number, color and direction of tracers and black smoke from exploding 120mm mortars and 122 howitzer rounds, I could tell the rifle companies were catching hell." In addition to the aid station across the road from his foxhole, Starkey recalled that a number of ammunition trucks were parked there too. "After T-34 tanks penetrated [we] received tank and machine gun fire [in addition to 120mm mortar and 122mm artillery fire]." While he and others moved the ammunition trucks behind a protecting hill, they came under long-range 76mm SP fire. He wrote, "I didn't comprehend how bad the battle was until later."

Lewis Millet was a lieutenant in the 8th FAB at the time. During the battle, he was sent with a patrol from artillery to make a security sweep. Returning, he passed Battery A, in the process of firing a mission when enemy counter-battery fire fell on the position. Millett grabbed a piece of Korean pottery and, using it as a kind of tambourine, walked up and down among the gun crews chanting an old Salvation Army ditty, "Put a Nickel on the Drum, if You Want to Be Saved."

Millett's version went something like this:

C'mon, you drunken bum, put a nickel on the drum,
Put a nickel on the drum and you'll be saved.
For it's S-A-V-E-D for the ways of S-I-N.
Put a shell in the gun and you're IN!**

** From a notation which Millett made on an undated letter to 1SG Lewis Michelony, USMC, Ret. Michelony was researching for John Toland's book, *In Mortal Combat.*

Millett's bizarre display and his little ditty heartened the gunners. They grinned and stood to their howitzers, pumping out round after round. Crewmen were killed and others wounded by incoming fire, but the battery never diminished its fire.

"SGT Tribble [8th FAB] was a casualty the first day of fighting.... "Enemy shell... fragments caught him and two of his men," wrote CPT Joseph W. Terman to his wife, Leota, on July 30, 1950. He was referring to the July 24 battle near Sangyong-ni. The 8th FAB was firing in support of 1/27th Inf. "Have no doubt about it," he continued, "the fight over here is a toughy. I've been under more fire any one day here than I was in the whole Philippine campaign."

Back in Co. B's sector, the unit held its own all day. A number of medics were reported wounded in the 1st Platoon's area. At the time, few units had sound-powered telephones or small radios for communication between the platoon CPs and individual squads. As a result, the platoon leader could not know what was happening all along his front. To alleviate that problem in the 1st Platoon, the platoon leader decided to go to the right flank to determine the situation. Arriving behind the hill where the platoon's flank was refused, he called the names of a number of men who were dug in on the forward slope, but there were no answers.

Not realizing it, he had worked his way onto a wide, flat, open space, devoid of any vegetation. Naturally, the enemy spotted him and began to snipe with 60mm mortars. When the first rounds landed, he fell to the ground, feigning death. Then he heard a voice calling from his rear, "Are you hit, lieutenant?" Lying there, he looked over his shoulder to see a medical aidman, ready to dash out in the open to his assistance. "No, I'm OK," he shouted. "Go back, I'm OK!" The lieutenant, not hearing any sign of life from the forward slope of the hill, remained on the ground until the mortar fire ceased, then got up and ran off the flat area. It was later discovered that, one by one, the men in this area had been killed or wounded, with no word of this debacle ever reaching the platoon CP.

The North Koreans pressed 1/27 hard all day, without success. LTC Michaelis was able to send this message at the end of the day: 7: 24 P.M. Reds have been repulsed. We are still in position. Six tanks destroyed within our position.... Am pulling in my perimeter slightly to tighten up for the night.

After dark, under orders, 1/27 executed a calm, quiet, orderly textbook withdrawal through 2/27. Both Michaelis and Check expected the enemy to envelop the 1st Battalion if it remained where it was. The 2d Battalion was deployed along north-south ridges east of Kuchon-ni astride the road somewhat over a mile behind the area formerly occupied by the 1st Battalion. Co. F was north of the road.

"We had a clear field of fire in front of us down through the valley," wrote CPL Glenn V. Ellison, of F Co. Ellison had come from the 32d Infantry, 7th Division, joining the company at Pusan.

Early on the 25th, obviously unaware that 1/27 had withdrawn, two enemy battalions swept down on the deserted 1st Battalion position in a double envelopment. The maneuver brought hundreds of North Korean soldiers out in the open forward of 2/27. American machine guns, rifles, mortars, artillery and tanks literally rained fire on the surprised and shocked enemy troops. Ellison describes the fury of firing and explosions as a "deafening roar." He continued, "I fired clip after clip through my M1 rifle.... They didn't know what hit them."

The enemy did pay dearly for its mistake, and remnants of the attacking force withdrew in confusion. About 30 prisoners were taken. After regrouping, the North Koreans came on again that afternoon, this time trying to outflank 2/27. LTC Michaelis ordered a general withdrawal of the regiment to high ground near Hwanggan, which began at about midnight, while Co. F, supported by nine tanks from A/79th Tk Bn, fought off an enemy attempt to crush the battalion (and regimental) right flank. Enemy mortar and artillery fire fell into 2/27 at the rate of eight to ten rounds per minute, but Fox Co. and the tanks held off the enemy.

During the withdrawal of 1/27, MSG File and two men from Co. A had been left behind to cover the unit's pull out. "Things were quiet for over an hour and the sounds of the battalion withdrawing tapered off ..." wrote File. Then there was complete silence. "A noise on the hill above alerted us. Men came stumbling down to the road." It was a platoon of E/27, which then moved on down the road, following 1/27.

A wrecked U.S. jeep was on the road near File's position. "I knew it would attract the curious," he recalled. Shortly, a lone enemy soldier appeared and walked around the jeep, then called softly. Two more enemy soldiers came up and the group inspected the jeep. When the three got on the side of the vehicle nearest File, he dropped them all with three quick shots from his M1. With that, he and his two companions legged out of the area, catching up to the battalion about daybreak.

The next day, July 26, 1/35 Inf came up on the 27th Regiment's right flank, relieving the pressure from that direction. However, on July 27, the enemy struck hard at the regimental left flank, exploiting a gap between the 27th Infantry and 7th Cavalry Regiments. The North Koreans smashed into C/27, precipitating a hard fight for one mountain peak that changed hands three times.

Co. B was on C's right flank, in a perimeter of their own on high ground overlooking a valley to the front. A stream ran along the base of the hill on the unit's right. The 2d and 3d Platoons occupied the forward slopes of the ridge, with the 1st Platoon deployed to protect the rear.

Co. C bore the brunt of enemy attacks in the 1st Battalion sector on July 27. Both Easy and George companies of the 2d Battalion repelled enemy probes that day.

On the evening of July 27, a man in Co. B's 1st Platoon, broke his glasses, and could not see. The only person in the platoon who knew the location of the battalion aid station was the platoon medic. The platoon leader told the medic to leave his aid kit and guide the man with the broken glasses back to the aid station, and return the following morning.

About daylight on July 28, men of Co. B saw trucks loaded with troops appear on the valley road in the distance. As they watched and tried to get artillery fire on this target, the trucks stopped, the enemy troops dismounted and ran into the hills. Soon afterward, Co. C came under heavy attack again. The enemy tried to deceive the Americans by dressing in U.S. uniforms. The North Koreans finally drove the men of Charlie Co. into Baker's perimeter. There were now almost twice as many men in B's position, but with foxholes for only half of them. Soldiers from C tried to squeeze into Baker's foxholes, and B company men tried to make room for them.

The enemy systematically began to pound Co. B with 120mm mortar fire. Three or four rounds fell, with a pause as the enemy mortarmen adjusted their sights, then three or four more rounds. The explosion of every mortar shell killed or wounded more men. Men who could not find shelter in foxholes just lay on the ground. Some of the rounds fell into foxholes, killing the occupants. The two units were unable to respond.

Most of the enemy mortar fire fell on top of the ridge where most of Co. B was located. The 1st Platoon seemed relatively safe from the bombardment. With the aidman's medical kit in his possession, their platoon leader went forward where the 120mm rounds were falling. Between salvos he hunted for wounded to treat. At one point, a round seemed to have detonated near a foxhole. The lieutenant ran to the hole and looked in. Both occupants were dead; one with a hole in the base of his skull, the other with his lower jaw blown off, exposing his throat. Blood welled up and dripped from the gaping hole as though his whole body was filled with blood.

After another salvo, the young officer found a man lying on his back with a shell fragment hole about an inch in diameter in the outside of his upper left leg. Lying at right angles to the man and downslope just below him, the lieutenant used his own belt (a mistake) to apply a tourniquet, then began to bandage the wound. In the meantime, orders had come for the two units to withdraw. As the members of his platoon came by, the officer told them to go on; he would follow shortly.

Soon, there was no one left on the hill but the lieutenant and the wounded man. Four more 120 mortar rounds came in and exploded. The wounded man grasped his right thigh, shouting, "I'm hit!" A quick inspection revealed that a tiny sliver of metal driven into his right leg. The lieutenant pulled it out. As soon as the wounded man was bandaged, he jumped up, grabbed an M1 with a missing sight lying nearby and began to run down the hill. The officer grabbed up his carbine and aid kit and ran after him. The men crossed the stream at the bottom of the hill and headed south. They soon passed a warrant officer and a BAR-man, firing on the hill they had just left. In spite of his wound, the man almost outran the officer.

The two rifle companies had heavy losses. Co. B lost 26 men (7 KIA, 18 WIA, 1 MIA); Co. C lost 29 (9 KIA, 19 WIA, 1 MIA). Among the wounded was Co. B's 1SG Hearn. Co. C now was reduced to about 60 men and B to about 85.

LTC Michaelis sought and received permission to withdraw the 27th through the 1st Cavalry Division. Before dawn on July 29, the regiment withdrew to a position about a mile east of Kumchon. That afternoon the regiment was ordered to Waegwan as Eighth Army Reserve. The 5th Cav also was withdrawn, leaving the 7th and 8th Cav on line.

For some men of the 27th and 35th, recollections of the first days of combat can be sorted out by day and date, but some recollections are not that easily identified.

CPL Jim Trumble of Easy Co. wrote that in the first few days of the war, "Easy Co. discovered it could make a difference. I believe that this feeling of a sort of quiet confidence came about for two reasons. First, Easy Co. had a double dose of 'errant' garrison troops (including men already in the unit and those transferred in from the 32d Inf.) Second, we were fortunate in having good leadership from officers and noncoms." The company commander, he described as "a calm, level-headed officer with a common-sense approach to getting the job done."

On July 25, Trumble was dug in with other members of a 3.5 inch rocket launcher crew, when the enemy "landed four rounds within twenty feet of each other right in the middle of our position," he recalled. "PVT Monohans, my gunner, was killed. Another man's arm and leg were broken and I got some shrapnel in my back and left arm."

Then-PVT Glenn E. Berry of CPT LeRoy E. Majeski's Co. G, 35th Infantry wrote, "It was a dark, overcast night and we could see very little, so had to rely a lot on sound. We began to hear rustling sounds to our front, then to our flanks, then everything would be quiet — [then] we would hear more noises." Once in a while a jittery rifleman would fire, setting off firing by other men, but when they realized that the enemy was not firing back, the men quit shooting. "Then we began getting an occasional round of sniper fire, then another from a different direction," Berry continued.

It was late July 1950 and the enemy was firing occasional shots to get the Americans to reveal their positions and the location of machine guns and BARs.

"Suddenly, we were attacked," Berry wrote. "They came with rifle fire, grenades and making a lot of noise, yelling and firing and bugles sounding in the rear. The battle lasted only a few minutes and they withdrew.... An enemy soldier lay...dying just a few feet in from of my foxhole." Before he died "he lay there and screamed and moaned and mumbled in his foreign tongue. It was something that this 18 year old soldier will never forget. Then there was silence."

Then it started all over again — single sniper shots, "then a little more fire. Then here came the attack," Berry recalled. "There were more this time and they fought longer and harder. The rifle fire, grenades...the noise and the bugles. Then, as fast as they came, they withdrew. This went on all night...each attack a little longer, fiercer, then they'd disappear.

"When the sun came up the next morning they were out of sight, and they'd taken all their dead and wounded they could take with them. Then it came to us — this was our first real battle... [and] we had very few casualties. We'd won our first fight.

"I was having my first real test of manhood and my ability as an infantry soldier. I felt I had passed the test," he wrote. During future battles he "was nervous and scared, [but] I never let this fear control me...."

Berry also wrote that during the early days in Korea the men had to contend with worn out rifles, bad ammunition and grenades which failed to explode.

On July 29, 1950, 1/35 Inf was ordered to withdraw. Roy N. Fomby was then a member of Co. C. He recalled that the orientation he got from his Platoon Sergeant Mills when they got to Korea was one sentence: "We are here to kill these bastards...."

"We had retreated about a mile when we saw soldiers," wrote Fomby. "Battalion said they were South Koreans .... They opened fire on us," killing "CPL James White in my squad." Later in the war, Fomby was slightly wounded but stayed with the unit.

On July 30, GEN Gay sent 1/5 Cav, along with 3/21 Inf on loan from the 24th Division, backed by the 99th FAB, to Chirye. The force got into the town, but the enemy retained the hills dominating it. Heavy enemy artillery fire the next day forced the Americans to withdraw to positions northeast of town. The enemy's *8th*

Regiment now joined its *7th Regiment* at Chirye, meaning the bulk of the *NK 3d Division* had gained the southern flank of the 1st Cavalry Division.

The *NK 3d Division* closed in on Kumchon on July 31. A squad of enemy infiltrated the 8th ECB CP about daylight, killing five men, including the Battalion XO and wounding five more. This CP was barely 1,000 yards from that of the Cavalry Division. Enemy troops also attacked the 7th Cavalry, losing a reported 13 T-34s, with six others set afire.

The end of July 1950 was the beginning of the transition from delay to defense for the ROK and Eighth armies. The Naktong had been reached, and there was no other comparable defensive obstacle between that river and Pusan. The 24th Division had lost heavily in executing their delaying mission, as had the South Koreans.

Casualties

In addition to the casualties of the 24th Division mentioned earlier in this narrative, the 1st Cavalry and 25th Infantry Divisions together suffered over 158 KIA, 993 WIA, 471 MIA, and several hundred non-battle casualties. The 27th Infantry reported 53 KIA, 221 WIA, 49 MIA and 90 NBC between July 19-30. In the same period, the 24th Infantry lost 27 KIA, 293 WIA and 3 MIA. There are no figures for NBC in the 24th. Total losses for the 1st Cavalry Division in their first 10 days of battle were 78 KIA, 419 WIA and 419 MIA, with no figure for NBC. Using these partial figures as a basis, it is safe to say that each division lost over 1,000 men during the last 10 days of July 1950.

Enemy casualties were much higher. The *NK 15th Division*, which fought ROK troops and the 24th RCT, lost close to 5,000 men in the same period. The losses in the *NK 2d and 3d Divisions*, which had engaged elements of the 1st Cavalry and 25th Divisions, numbered between 2,000 and 3,000 each.

Chapter Notes:

P. 88 This table, based on Table 2, South to the Naktong, depicts a breakdown of ROKA strength on July 26,1950 (see chart below):

P. 88 In the first weeks of the Korean War, the enemy often dressed its men in civilian clothing to mingle with the thousands of refugees streaming south, making it almost impossible to screen out all the soldiers. The civilians, afraid of being killed later by these infiltrating enemy soldiers, did not betray them, allowing thousands of North Korean soldiers to gain friendly rear areas, set up roadblocks and act as guerrillas. They directed the very accurate mortar or artillery fire that landed suddenly in rear areas. More than one woman was detected carrying ammunition or directing fire for the enemy. When caught, these collaborators were summarily executed.

P. 90 David Carlisle, believing that racism was involved, launched a campaign a number of years ago, through official channels, to have the Silver Star upgraded to the Medal of Honor.

P. 90 Appleman stated that Co. E and F "began withdrawing in a disorderly manner." And that the regimental commander "found the battalion coming back down the road in disorder and most of the men in a state of panic."

P. 90 Edwin P. Hoyt wrote these untruths in The Pusan Perimeter: *"The men of the 25th Division said their regimental theme song was the 'Bug-Out Blues,'* and *"They bugged out of Cho'nan, Chongju, Taejon, Yongdong and Chirye." There was no Division official or unofficial "theme song," and troops did not "bug out' of those towns.*

Hoyt, Max Hastings, Joseph C. Goulden, T. R. Fehrenbach and others all reiterated in one form or another what was first written by Roy Appleman in South to the Naktong, North to the Yalu. *Appleman's book remains the most authoritative work on the U.S. Army's operations during the first five months of the Korean War. However, recently declassified material and other sources have indicated, and at times proven, him to be wrong in some instances.*

Relying on Appleman, many authors have perpetuated his mistakes, as well as his slanted presentation of both the 34th and 24th Regiments. Some have tarnished the record further. Goulden, in his Korea The Untold Story of the War, *wrote "The appearance of a 24th Regiment patch on a uniform would bring jeers from other units." He didn't know what he was talking about. The 24th Regiment had no "patch;" regiments had crests — metal devices — which were not usually worn on combat uniforms. As for the 24th at Yechon, only Clay Blair, John Toland and Tom Lambert go beyond Appleman's narrative. Blair and Toland include input from soldiers; Lambert (AP) wrote as an eye-witness.*

P. 94 This officer requested his name not be given.

ROK Army, July 26, 1950

Total Assigned	94,570	HQ, ROK Army	3,020
Effectives	85,871		
Wounded and NBC	8,699	3d Div (1st Cav, 22, 23 Regts)	8,828
		ROK Troops	11,881
HQ, I Corps	3,014	Replacement Training Command	9,016
Chonju Training Command	8,699		
Capital Div (1, 17, 18 Regts)	6,644	Kwangju Training Command	6,244
8th Div. (10, 16, 21 Regts)	8,864	Pusan Training Command	5,356
Corps Combat Troop Total	15,508	Combat Troop Total, Under ROK Army HQ	8,828
HQ, II Corps	976	Combat Troop Total Entire ROK Army	*37,665*
1st Div. (11, 12, 15 Regts)	7,601		
6th Div. (2, 7, 19 Regts)	5,727		
Corps Combat Troop Total	13,328		

(NOTE: Of the 85,871 effectives, the five combat divisions — the part of the army doing the actual fighting — totaled only *37,665*; roughly equaling three divisions, not five.)

PART THREE

DEFENDING THE PERIMETER

The two primary forms of defensive operations are mobile and area defense....
Mobile defenses orient on the destruction of the attacking force by permitting
the enemy to advance into a position that exposes him to counterattack by a
mobile reserve. Area defenses orient on retention of terrain by absorbing the
enemy in an interlocking series of positions and destroying him largely by fires.

U. S. Army Field Service Regulations, 1993

The *NK 4th* and *6th Divisons'* End Run

As the 24th, 25th and lst Cavalry Divisions were fighting other North Korean divisions in the Yongdong area, the *NK 6th Guards Division* moved south close to the west coast, attempting to outflank the Americans and ROKs and slip into Pusan. (The honorary "Guards" title was bestowed on the division after its capture of Inchon on June 30.) About July 11, Eighth Army "lost" the *6th*. Enemy prisoners of war and other sources subsequently revealed the division's movements: On July 13 it had moved out of Yesan in two columns, crossing the lower Kum River on July 16, and seized the port of Kunsan about July 19. After reuniting at Chinju, 30 miles south of Kunsan, the division departed there for Kwangju about July 20 Arriving there on the 23d, the *6th* split into three regimental columns: The *13th* headed for Mokpo on the south coast; the *14th* made for Posong; the*15th* moved southeast, via Sunchon to Yosu, also on the south coast.

Meeting little resistance from only a few hundred survivors of the ROK 7th Division, some ROK marines and a few local police units, the division reassembled at Sunchon about July 25 and prepared for its final drive on Pusan, just ninety miles away. The command was in poor logistical shape, particularly in rations; half rations were usual, but sometimes there were none at all.

GEN Pang Ho San, *6th Division* commander, exhorted his troops on the eve of their advance on Chinju: "Comrades, the enemy is demoralized. The task given us is the liberation of Masan and Chinju and the annihilation of the remnants of the enemy.... The liberation of Chinju and Masan means the final battle to cut off the windpipe of the enemy." (Quoted from Appleman, p. 211)

The *6th Division* was now reinforced by the *83d Motorcycle Regiment,* originally from the *105th Tank Division.* (See Chapter Notes.) Although bitterly opposed by the few ROKs who could be mustered, the *6th* seized Chinju by Aug. 1. The *13th Regiment* remained in that city, while the other two moved on to Sachon and Kosong on July 2, where elements of the division were confronted by parts of 2/19, 1/27 and the remnants of the 3/29.

The enemy's *4th Division,* after Taejon, also began to move southward, opposed by meager local police units. On July 22, elements of the division were at Nonsan. Intelligence reports indicated that the command was moving to the south. Aerial reconnaissance was maintained over southwest Korea to try to pick up and track elements of these two enemy divisions. The lack of armor prevented long range tank recon to supplement the air. Heavy overcast skies on July 21-22 allowed the enemy to use the roads during daylight hours to move forward rapidly without concern of detection, but aerial recon on July 23 confirmed an Eighth Army G2 estimate that elements of one enemy division were in southwest Korea moving at the rate of two miles per hour, were swinging east to get behind the Eighth Army's left (west) flank, and would reach the Anui-Chinju are in the Chiri mountains by July 25.

To slow or stop this threat, GEN Walker had no alternative but to commit the badly- battered 24th Infantry Division. He directed his Chief of Staff, COL Landrum, to ensure that the Fifth Air Force made a major effort against these enemy forces.

At noon on July 24, he called GEN Church, the newly-appointed commander of the 24th Division, to headquarters in Taegu. There, he gave Church the bad news: "I am sorry to do this, but the whole left flank is open, and reports indicate the Koreans are moving in. I want you to cover the area from Chinju up to near Kumchon." This was an area 65 air-miles wide in the remote Chiri Mountains.

Both Church and the 24th Division were unfortunate. The general had been appointed commander on July 23 and the command had been off the line just one day, with no opportunity to receive replacements or re-equip. Somewhere between 60 and 70 per cent of the division's equipment needed replaced. Church was not a "Walker man"; he had been appointed by MacArthur, without consulting Walker.

Church was no stranger to combat, having commanded a regiment at Anzio during WW II, but now he was 58, frail and in ill health. He and his battered 24th Division were facing a daunting task. By midnight of July 23, the 19th Infantry was enroute from Kumchon to Chinju. Walker's verbal orders were formalized at 5 p.m.on July 25 when Eighth Army ordered the 24th (less the 21st Infantry) to defend the Chinju area.

Reports to Eighth Army indicated concentrations of enemy troops as follows: Mokpo, 10 tanks, 500 infantry; Namwon, 26 trucks, 700 troops; Kurye, tanks, trucks and 800 troops; Hadong (500 soldiers battling South Korean police).

At 6 a.m., July 25, COL Ned D. Moore replaced COL Meloy as commander of the 19th Infantry at Chinju. At 3 p.m., the regimental headquarters and 3d Bn arrived there. LTC Tom McGrail was back in command of 2/19, and LTC Robert L. Rhea's 1/19 remained on the Kumchon road north of Chinju. COL Rhea placed his Co. A at Anui, where a road came in from the west, and deployed the rest of the battalion 8 miles south at Umyong-ni (also known as Sangan or Hwansan-ni), a major road junction east of Hamyang. Together, the two battalions of the 19th totalled only about 600 men.

On July 26 the 34th Regiment moved to Kochang; 24th Division headquarters and division troops moved to Hyopchon, 12 air miles west of the Naktong and more or less in the center of the 24th Division 's huge sector.

While the 24th Division, followed by the 25th and 1st Cavalry Divisions fought these early battles, help was on the way in the form of two battalions of the 29th Regiment from Okinawa; the 5th RCT from Hawaii; the 1st Marine Provisional Brigade from California and the 2d Infantry Division, from Washington state, plus newly-formed armor and other special formations. These were massive reinforcements, if the troops in Korea could "hang tough."

Deployment of the 1st and 3d Battalions, 29th Infantry to Korea

The first reinforcements to arrive were 1/29 and 3/29 from Okinawa. The original plan was to train the two battalions in Japan for six weeks. Within days, this was changed. MAJ Tony J. Raibl, XO of 3/29 had been sent ahead to Japan, where he learned on July 20 that the two battalions of the 29th would not stop in Japan, but continue to Korea.

On July 15 Far East Command issued orders for the 29th to prepare two of its three battalions for deployment. Men were taken from the regiment's 2d Battalion to help fill the 1st and 3d Battalions, destined for Korea. On July 20, the *USS Walker* docked at Naha, Okinawa, with about 400 recruits aboard. These men all were assigned to the 1st and 3d Battalions, issued weapons and equipment and taken back to the docks. They filled the two battalions to full strength. These recruits added only to the morning report strength and contributed little to the combat effectiveness of the two commands. In fact, these men being untrained for hard combat, often were more a liability than an asset.

MAJ Raibl next was told that the battalions would have 10 days of "intensive field training" near Pusan. When he arrived in Taegu on July 22, Raibl had an extensive conference with GEN Walker. As a result of this meeting, the major understood that the battalions would have three days at Pusan to draw equipment, zero and test-fire weapons.

But when the two battalions unloaded at Pusan on the 24th, they were rushed to Chinju and attached to the 19th Infantry Regiment. They were allowed no time for anything. Rifles were not zeroed-in, nor crew-served weapons test-fired. Some weapons, such as the newly-issued .50-cal machine guns still were in cosmoline. The perilous tactical situation on the southern front virtually dictated that these two commands be rushed there at once, otherwise the decision to rush the 29th into combat in this fashion would have been criminal. As it was, both commands suffered crippling losses in their first battles.

Possibly contributing to the troubles of both battalions was the fact that both of their commanders were new to their commands, and neither had any combat experience. LTC Wesley Wilson (West Point 1929), then 43, commanded the 1st Battalion; LTC Harold W. Mott commanded the 3d.

On the afternoon of July 25, the two commands arrived at Chinju. That evening, 3/29 was ordered to take Hadong, a road junction town 35 miles southwest of Chinju.

The impetus for seizing Hadong came from MG Chae Byong Duk, former ROK Army Chief of Staff, who was then in Chinju. He told COL

Moore that Hadong controlled the western avenue into Chinju; it was important to have the town. GEN Chae volunteered to accompany the battalion as advisor and interpreter, and COL Moore assented. Reportedly, the nearest North Koreans were an estimated 500 troops moving on Hadong.

Debacle at the Hadong Pass - 3/29 Inf - July 27

The battalion began a motor march to Hadong at 12:30 a.m. on July 26. LTC Mott and MAJ Raibl expected the command to be in the town before daylight, but an impassable ford required a detour. The road was narrow; vehicles slipped into rice paddies and had to be pulled out.

Shortly after daylight, a truck containing 15 or 20 badly-wounded South Koreans came by, reporting themselves to be survivors of a force of some 400 local militia which had attempted to defend Hadong. The town was already in enemy hands.

LTC Mott took the battalion on to the town of Wonjon. There, the men had breakfast while Mott and Raibl conferred. Since there was no radio contact with Moore, Raibl was sent back to report the latest information and to obtain further orders.

Relaying the South Koreans' report to COL Moore, the major asked that 3/29 be permitted to dig in west of Chinju to defend the Hadong road. At the conclusion of much discussion, Moore ordered the battalion to seize Hadong. Raibl had considerable misgivings about this because he did not believe that the battalion could accomplish the task, but he returned to Wonjon a little after noon and briefed Mott.

Mott got his command back on the road, arriving about dusk at the village of Hoengchon, which was on a sharp bend in the road just 3 miles short of Hadong.

The Air Force TAC radio, which was to call in air strikes and maintain contact with Chinju the next day proved defective. It could communicate neither with Chinju nor the aircraft.

The Battalion S2, CPT William Mitchell, his driver, John R. Toney, PVT James W. Yeager and a South Korean policeman as interpreter, went on a recon patrol that night. Moving into a valley, the captain questioned a farmer through the interpreter. "This old man told us there was going to be a big battle," said Yeager. While the questioning was going on, Yeager noticed the glow "like fireflies"of cigarettes in the darkness nearby, he recalled. During the patrol, they noticed men, all in white clothing, along roadside ditches. These men offered no information, but left the patrol alone. "The farmer told us there was a large force of North Korean regulars in the area," Yeager continued. The patrol returned safely about 2 a.m. and reported what they had seen and heard.

The battalion departed Hoengchon about 8:45 a.m. on July 27. The order of march was Co. L (CPT George F. Sharra), with elements of the Heavy Weapons Co. (Co. M); battalion command group; Co. K (CPT Joseph K. Donahue); Co. M (-) (CPT Hugh P. Milleson) and Co. I (1st LT Alexander Makarounis). CPT Sharra, with the lead company, was a seasoned rifle company commander from WW II.

Co. L approached within about 1,000 yards of the top of the Hadong pass. Sharra saw a group of 10 to 12 North Koreans move through the pass and start toward the Americans. The 75mm recoilless rifle platoon fired its two weapons, but the rounds were high. The enemy patrol scurried back over the pass. The captain ordered his unit forward. They reached the top and deployed on both sides of the pass at about 9:30 a.m. An air strike was scheduled to hit Hadong at 9:45.

The road snaked along the southern flank of a high ridge, climbing toward the pass, then fell toward Hadong 1 1/2 miles to the west. On the right (north) of the pass was a high peak overlooking the road; to the south was a hill, plus large paddy areas, extending to the Sumjin River.

LTC Mott, his S3, CPT Robert M. Flynn, William Mitchell, S2, the Assistant S2 and others of the command group, accompanied by GEN Chae and his party, moved quickly up to the pass. CPT Sharra pointed out a large group of people moving around on high ground far to the north. Glancing in that direction, Mott said, "Yes, I have K Co. moving up there." Raibl, at the rear of the battalion, was summoned forward to join the colonel. This large group of officers in the pass worried Sharra. He prudently moved over to the left and got onto the ground next to one of his light machine guns.

When Raibl arrived at the pass, he noted that Co. L had two platoons on the left of the road and one on the right. King Co. was moving up on higher ground farther north (right).

Mott and the others detected an enemy column of soldiers marching toward them with files of men on either side of the road. The North Koreans seemed to be unaware of Americans in the pass. Sharra ordered his machine gunner to hold fire.

MAJ Raibl and GEN Chae stood in the pass watching the approaching troops. Some of the men appeared to be in U.S. fatigue uniforms while others were in the North Korean mustard brown attire. GEN Chae, unsure of who they were, allowed the column to get within a hundred yards. At that point, he called to them in Korean. Without responding, these soldiers dove for roadside ditches. CPT Sharra estimated the enemy at about a company. His unit machine guns opened fire on the North Koreans.

Their fire and enemy machine gun, mortar and small-arms fire started at almost the same time. The enemy guns swept down the road. One of the first bursts killed GEN Chae instantly and wounded MAJ Raibl. As Chae's aides carried him back to a vehicle, Raibl rolled down an embankment. LTC Mott, Mitchell and the Assistant S2 also were wounded by these first rounds of enemy fire, which also destroyed several vehicles, including the TACP jeep and radio. CPT Flynn was one of the few members of the command group who was unhurt. The loss of key leaders would continue as the battle developed. The battalion never had a chance.

Very soon after the battle started, U.S. aircraft flew back and forth over the area, but of course could not contact the TAC. After a number of passes, they left without making an attack. All the while, enemy machine gun, mortar and small-arms fire raked the area. Raibl, hit again by mortar fragments, went down the hill in search of an aidman.

LTC Mott only had been creased across the back by a bullet. He was now just below the pass, helping to unload ammunition. A box dropped, breaking his foot, so a soldier prepared a foxhole for him. During the ensuing battle, everyone around him was killed, wounded, or had retreated.

Sharra recalled that the regimental surgeon found Mott and brought him to the aid station. Sharra said that Mott told him to get the battalion started along the road and that he (Mott) would send a messenger back with instructions where to stop. CPT Sharra saw to it that the wounded were evacuated by vehicle and stayed until "every soldier I could see was gone."

"I was on the back of the second jeep [of the battalion] convoy," wrote PFC William Molton, of Co. M. "As the lead jeep was almost at the crest of the hill the North Koreans were waiting for us. We were caught in a crossfire. I think all on the first jeep were killed and as far as I know I was the only one to get out from the second jeep. " After the battle, Molton was in enemy territory for three days before getting back to American lines.

Charles L. Dawson, also of Co. M, was "on the left of the pass when it started," as he put it. He didn't know where the machine gun fire was coming from, but he knew that GEN Chae had been hit and that the air controller's jeep and radio were knocked out.

Privates Jim Yeager and John R. Toney were in the third jeep, followed by the Air Force air controllers. The next vehicle was a 3/4-ton truck mounting a .50-cal machine gun. The Air Force officer was dressed in "suntans," the normal garrison uniform, Yeager recalled. When the convoy stopped, the officers went forward in a group. "Then all hell broke loose," James said. He and Toney "piled out on the right side into a ditch.... I told Toney we better get away from the road before they start dropping 120 mortars on us" Before they could move, a master sergeant ordered the two men up the hill. They had gone barely 50 yards when their jeep was blown up.

"We went on up to the military crest," Yeager continued. "There was a squad just out on the flat ground in front of the pine trees. All were dead — shot to hell. You could see where they had been hit by machine gun fire." Yeager had a carbine which he had "appropriated" when he had been transferred into the battalion headquarters. It apparently wasn't assembled properly and kept falling apart. Yeager took the M1 rifle from a dead sergeant and began firing toward the enemy. An officer yelled at him to "attack that hill." Yeager called back to get a mortar or something up to knock out the enemy machine gun first. Several men with a 60mm mortar, made their way forward. They fired two rounds, which went over the enemy gun and into a friendly company. Then a man came forward with a bazooka and two rocket rounds. Yeager and some other men marked the location of the enemy machine gun by rifle fire. The bazooka-man fired. "His first round...gooks, [and] mud went up in the air," Yeager recalled.

He and the men around him fought all day on that hill. A BAR-man joined them during the fight. More ammunition was brought up and some of the men reloaded M1 clips and BAR magazines while others kept up the fight. "One guy came up and couldn't even load his weapon. I said 'Where in the hell have you been?' He said 'I was in the GHQ for three years and they extended me.' He was scared." Yeager showed him how to load his rifle.

About dusk, most of the firing had stopped. Yeager checked the area with binoculars. He and the men with him appeared to be surrounded. His group numbered about 15. They loaded up on bandoleers of ammunition and came off the hill. But first, Yeager dug a small hole, laid a grenade in it then carefully placed a BAR over the grenade and pulled the pin. Whoever picked up the BAR would be killed or injured by the grenade.

When they got off the hill "there were dead up and down the road.... All I saw were dead American troopers," Yeager recounted. He rigged another booby trap by placing a grenade with the pin pulled under the hood of a 3/4-ton truck.

The group dove over the bank and into the rice paddies, with the enemy chasing them. The Air Force officer, a captain, was with Yeager's party. After running up a ridge, the whole group were sprawled out lying down, or on their knees to rest, "panting our guts out," Yeager recalled. A man named Blackwell (or PFC Remus M. Blackwood, HC,3/29), the captain and Yeager, were toward the front, with the captain on his knees. A shot cracked, the officer moaned and fell dead, shot in the heart. Yeager, lying next to the captain, was concealed by scrub pine. "I killed all three of them [the enemy] before they could get off another shot. (Good old M1!) My father had taught me well," wrote Yeager. "They had run into a deer hunter from Colorado." He pumped 16 rounds into the three enemy soldiers as fast as he could fire and reload.

The firing scared off his comrades, who ran from the scene, leaving Yeager, Toney and Blackwell. They watched as enemy machine gunners shot up eight Americans trying to escape across a rice paddy below. He and Toney then went down the hill to a Korean graveyard, which was their undoing. Two enemy soldiers jumped up in front of them, armed with burp guns. Yeager turned to speak to Toney and discovered what seemed to be a whole platoon of enemy behind them. Yeager took off his helmet, in which he had a map, and "gave it one hell of a kick," he said. "I knew that if they caught me with a map...they would figure I was somebody important." (See Chapter Notes.)

He and Toney were marched down the road. Yeager managed to get his watch, two rings and his dog tags into one of the pockets of his fatigue trousers. He also had a carbine bayonet stuck into his boot. The enemy took the bayonet, but did not discover his watch, rings and dogtags. (See Chapter Notes.)

Yeager and some other prisoners were marched back into Hadong with their arms raised. When they got into Hadong and could lower their arms, he discovered that he had a rifle grenade launcher in one pocket. He was tempted to hit a guard with it. Instead, one of the guards took the launcher and hit Yeager with it.

(The experiences of Yeager and some other POWs, are contained in an appendix.)

"I was assigned to a .30-caliber light machine gun as an ammo bearer," wrote John L. Kirby. In this, his first battle, he recalled, he was "scared as hell."

When the officers went forward, Kirby's gun crew was ordered to set up to the left of the road on a little rise of ground. They started to dig in. Kirby, as an ammo bearer, was preparing a foxhole a little way behind the actual gun position. "The next thing I can remember," he wrote, "is looking at my M1 rifle and wondering what had happened. My rifle was in pieces and my cans of .30-cal machine gun ammunition were all around me." To his front, the gunner and assistant were dead and the gun destroyed. He guessed that a mortar or artillery round had done the damage. "The next thing I remember," he continued, "was fire hitting all around me and a...guy named Santos calling for help. "He was hit through the left side just below the heart."

Kirby helped Santos, and the two, both now unarmed, made their way toward "a very bad foul-smelling stream." Enemy soldiers gave chase. Kirby and Santos jumped into the stream and swam across "as quickly as we could — all the time under heavy fire." They got across, ran to the road, where he, Harkin Summers and some other men stopped a truck and escaped from the ambush area.

Neal Vance, with Co. L, was on the left of the road. When the remnants of the unit pulled out, he skirted the hill south of the pass and made his way back to vehicles farther to the rear on the road. His friend, PVT Eddie Payne, was killed, along with PVT Richard H. Klase.

2LT J. Morrissey's 1st Platoon of Co. L was on the north side of the road. The enemy came in on his right, between his platoon and Co. K, which was trying to climb the hill farther up. Two men were bayonetted, but the platoon held in spite of other heavy losses.

South of the pass, CPT Sharra and the 2d Platoon fired in support of the 1st. Sharra only could communicate with his platoons by voice, but he, his officers and NCOs led the unit superbly. Half the men were young recruits who had been assigned just days before. Co. L stood fast and fought, killing and wounding many of the enemy.

While all of this was taking place, CPT Flynn had moved back from the pass in order to hasten forward the remainder of the battalion. Finding part of K and M companies, he ordered a platoon of K to attack up the hill to the right of the road. After conferring briefly on the radio with King's leader, CPT Joseph Donahue, Flynn moved on down the road and saw to it that the wounded, including MAJ Raibl, were evacuated to Chinju.

Locating LT Makarounis (Co. I), he ordered the unit forward to fill the gap between L and K. He sent a platoon of L, under MSG James A. Applegate, into the paddies south (left) of the road. He believed it would be covered by the dikes in crossing the large paddy area toward the enemy-held hill.

Nine days before Hadong, Louie M. Hollis had been a file clerk in the 3d Battalion headquarters. He "was handed a rifle and told to report to K Co. just before we boarded ship for Pusan," he wrote.

As Co. K approached the Hadong pass behind L, Hollis describes what he saw. "There was a large valley of rice paddies with a river running through it and a bridge as the road went on through a pass between two mountains." As his unit moved forward it began to take enemy small-arms fire, and the men dove for cover. A particularly deadly enemy machine gun was destroyed by one of the unit's rocket launchers.

After the launcher had disposed of the machine gun, Hollis and others of King Co. moved out. "We...moved along the bank of the road to the river and under the bridge," wrote Hollis. After crossing they, "started up a steep bank, when a sniper began firing." Borrowing Hollis's rifle, his lieutenant fired up into a tree. Then "we raised up and began to climb the bank," Hollis continued. "He was about four feet in front of me and about a foot to my left. I heard an explosion. My head was down and facing his back. I saw his shirt blow back between his shoulders as the bullet hit him dead center. He slid down to his knees but got up again shaking his head and we both charged on up the bank. I never saw him again."

Hollis then became an ammo bearer for a 60mm mortar, but enemy artillery soon zeroed in on the position. The men frantically tried to dig in. "About that time," Hollis went on, "someone said we were ordered to pull back off the hill. As we looked around it seemed everyone was gone."

By this time, the enemy were all around the men in the pass and valley behind it. Machine gun fire "was coming from all directions," Hollis recalled, "and we were sitting ducks."

Hollis made ready to run to the river, when he heard someone crying for help. It was a corporal who had been shot in the leg and was bleeding badly. Hollis helped apply a heavy gauze bandage to the wound, then went on. At the river he discarded his helmet and boots and jumped in, with enemy bullets following him. From the river he got into a rice paddy, trying to make it to a ridge beyond. He came across the bodies of two dead GIs. "I ran as fast as I could and dove down in the water and mud. There was a small dike...just [high] enough to get my head behind," he wrote. But soon his legs cramped up and he had to jump up and run. "I could hear bullets hitting the rice paddies...and when I dropped behind a little dike a bullet hit in front of my face knocking mud in my eyes." He cleared the mud from his eyes and ran for a line of bushes at the foot of the hill, climbing over dead American soldiers to get there. The enemy, believing he had been killed when he dove into the paddy, quit shooting.

Climbing the hill, he ran into a North Korean patrol. In trying to escape, he stepped onto a sharp shell fragment which split his foot wide open. Thinking he had escaped, he lay down to drink paddy water, which "looked a little clear." While in this act, he was captured by half a dozen enemy soldiers. Enroute back to the road, they tried to get Hollis to call out to other soldiers to surrender, but he refused. On the road were about a dozen other prisoners. The North Koreans took their watches and rings. All Hollis had was his high school ring. An enemy soldier took it from him, looked it over then tossed it into the paddy.

Manuel V. Cabrera, of K/29, was anxious to get into combat. At Hadong an enemy bullet went between his fingers, but did not hit him. Later in the day, he was slightly wounded in the neck by a shell fragment while taking wounded down the hill to cover under a 2 1/2-ton truck. He especially remembered at Hadong that some U.S. hand grenades failed to explode. After Hadong, he said he the other survivors of the battle developed a great hate for the enemy.

Frank F. Byrne turned 23 in June 1950. During WW II, he had been a member of the U.S. force invading Okinawa. Now, in 1950, he was a squad leader in K/29. His five-man squad included three athletes, for whom athletics obviously took precedence over training. As a result, only two riflemen were available for training each day.

He recalled at Hadong, the outfit was "a partially trained straight leg infantry battalion, with NO support, carrying weapons left over from World War II that we had never fired, 48 rounds and a grenade." Each rifleman also had a bayonet. (See Chapter Notes.)

On the approach to Hadong, the road made a perfect U. Byrne was toward the rear of Co. K. "I happened to look across the rice paddies and could see the point man," he wrote. "As I made the right turn, ALL HELL BROKE LOOSE! I HAVE NEVER HEARD SO MANY AUTOMATIC WEAPONS FIRE AT ONE TIME, from every direction." (Capitalization and underlining are as Byrne wrote it.) Bullets chipped away at the rocks next to him, and Byrne dove into a drainage ditch. "Then the mortars came in like rain," he continued. When the mortar fire slackened, he crawled forward to get his men to move up and join the remnants of the main force. "When I crawled over to them I realized they would never move again!" He and some other survivors managed to assemble. Officers and NCOs tried to set up a defense "but we were outgunned and outnumbered too much," Byrne recounted. "The order was passed to save yourself," he wrote. He slipped into a drainage stream at 4:20 p.m. — at least that's when his non-waterproof watch stopped.

He and a number of others evaded capture, eventually making their way to the coast, where a South Korean gunboat took them back to Pusan. (See Chapter Notes.)

Charles Dawson was near one jeep when it was hit. "Jeep parts flew everywhere," he said. While Dawson went back to a 3/4-ton truck for ammo, his 75mm recoilless rifle was knocked out. The sergeant formed the men up at the bottom of the hill. "More artillery and mortars came in.... "It was absolute chaos. There was small-arms fire all around, Dawson continued. He went up into the pass, where he was pinned down by a sniper, but Dawson had thrown himself down on an ant hill. Soon, "these ants got into my clothes and were torturing me.... So I jumped up and off the side of the hill, figuring it was a ditch. Instead, I fell about 10 feet...into a rice paddy. I went down to my knees in mud...."

Shortly, a lieutenant came by and ordered Dawson and five other men with him to go up on the ridge to the right of the pass. The men obeyed and fought there until ordered out. When Dawson got back to the bottom of the hill, he found himself alone. Dead GIs and knocked out vehicle littered the road to the rear. Across the valley in the rice paddies, other American soldiers were being shot down by enemy fire. See-

ing the slaughter in the paddies, he thought, "'Hell, I can't go that way.' I was confused about which way to run," he said.

Finally, Dawson did cross the paddy and gain the ridge beyond. Strangely, as he climbed the mountain he was not shot at, although he could see enemy soldiers behind him and other GIs being shot down as they, too, tried to cross the paddy. He ran along the ridge and down to the Sumjin river. Discarding clothing and equipment which would impede him, he swam across the river and hid in the weeds. Soon, two other soldiers came by. All they had on were their undershorts, having discarded everything else. More soldiers assembled as they moved along, including a badly-wounded sergeant and a lieutenant. The sergeant was too badly hurt to lead and the lieutenant didn't want to, so the sergeant told Dawson, "You do it."

Frank Myers (Co. I) was in this group. He and Dawson cared for the sergeant, who begged for a drink. The NCO was fatally wounded, so they gave it to him. Myers and Dawson gently laid him down along the stream. "He had a hole in his side," said Dawson, "One side of his face was shattered and he had a third shot in his back" and was bleeding badly.

For three days Dawson's party worked their way back to Chinju. None of the men had shoes or boots. At the aid station, the surgeon told Dawson, "There's nothing wrong with your feet. Don't waste my time." Dawson angrily replied, "I didn't come in here because there was something wrong with my feet, I was ordered to come in here." He was given a shot of whiskey and told to go find his unit.

When LT Alexander Makarounis's Co. I, 29th Infantry boarded the *Tagasaka Maru* bound for Korea, it numbered six officers, one warrant officer and 205 EM — a full-strength rifle company. But, as Makarounis pointed out in a March 1951 story in *Argosy* magazine, the "new men were mostly just kids, 18 or so, and they'd landed on Okinawa from a stateside troop transport in the morning, got a new issue of clothes in the afternoon, and by evening were on the *Tagasaka Maru*."

LT Makarounis recalled that when the firing began at Hadong, the column halted, but no word of what was happening came back to him. A lieutenant and two enlisted men from M Co. finally came by and told of a big battle n progress ahead. Makarounis called battalion on the radio, asking for a mission. He was told to wait. Five minutes later he called again and again was told to wait.

Soon after the second call, the Battalion Assistant S3, CPT Hacker came by and told the lieutenant to move the company forward a little. With LT Chamberlain's platoon in the lead, the unit advanced about 100 yards. At that point, the lead platoon came under intense mortar and machine gun fire.

Makarounis began to make a reconnaissance, but mortar fire intensified and he was struck high in the center of his back by a mortar fragment. He didn't take the wound seriously.

"I was a private in the first squad and fourth man to the rear," said Frank Myers. The company was moving forward in a column of twos, with a file of men on each side of the dirt road which was climbing uphill at that point. It was

about 100 degrees , and very humid. To the left, a steep embankment dropped off to a river. The leading companies of the battalion already were fighting the enemy ambush.

"As we reached the apex of the hill and made our first appearance," Myers continued, "we got a shower of small arms fire from the hill followed by mortar fire." Two I Co. men were hit. Myers and some other men went out and brought one of the wounded back.

LT Makarounis sent part of the company to a hill on the right and ordered the remainder, including Myers, to the left side of the road. There they were ordered to dig in. Myers moved to the left, removed his pack and began to watch the battle ahead through the scope on his sniper rifle. He saw many GIs being hit by enemy fire, and enemy soldiers, heavily camouflaged with bush branches, on the hill opposite. Enemy fire also struck a number of American vehicles, setting them afire. "I saw a jeep speeding down the road. The driver got shot and the vehicle rolled over and over.... It killed all the men in the jeep," Myers said. (See Chapter Notes.)

Enemy small-arms, machine gun and mortar fire peppered Co. I. About this time, CPT Flynn arrived and told Makarounis to move his company forward in support of the hard-hit Co. L.

To get to the beleaguered Love Co., Co. I would have to cross an extensive rice paddy. Makarounis sent a platoon to the left, then moved more men to the left. "There was a hill on the immediate left," Myers recalled. "We came down and across the rice paddies, across the ditches and across the draw." companies K, L and most of M were on the hills ahead and under heavy fire from front and flank.

The first two men from Myers' squad who tried to cross the paddy were hit — one in the face and one in the shoulder. They managed to help one another back to shelter. Then enemy fire on this part of the paddy stopped. The company commander wanted the platoon to cross the paddy. Myers argued with him, then furious with LT Makarounis, got up and ran across the paddy without stopping, flopping down in a draw on the other side, in a stand of trees near a waterfall. Looking back, he saw several other men coming to join him. Then more of the company started across. "As they reached the center of the rice paddy there is a tremendous amount of enemy fire coming in on them.... [The bullets] hitting the water like hail.... It was massive small-arms fire power." This devastating fire created total chaos. "Some [men] were bleeding and had their shirts off. Some were pulling back. Some were panicked and crying.... It was so unreal," said Myers, "that it was difficult to believe what was happening."

Myers picked up three grenades to add to the two he already had. He also had five bandoleers of M1 ammunition (240 rounds) and his bayonet. He waited, in vain, for men from Co I to join him. Only CPL Pratt and PFC John L. Napier were there, just below him on the hill, when both large and small sized mortar rounds "came in and plastered the whole hill," he recalled. Then a voice called out from below, "Make an orderly withdrawal!"

During a lull in the mortaring, LT Makarounis had stepped up onto the road, where the HC First Sergeant met him. The first sergeant said, "Sir, the battalion commander wants you to withdraw." "Which way?" asked the lieutenant. "I don't know, sir," the NCO replied. "I wasn't told." Enemy fire was all around; many of the vehicles forward and to the rear of Item Co. were disabled or in flames.

Makarounis decided to withdraw through a nearby rice paddy. The paddy, like most in Korea at the time, was divided into rough squares by low dikes. He thought that by moving from the protection of one dike to the other, the unit would be able to move to a creek close by to the rear.

He shouted orders to Chamberlain and notified the other platoons by messenger. He sent the company headquarters on their way under the XO, LT Wampler. As he waited for his platoons, Makarounis saw that the enemy had turned machine gun fire on the creek. One man began running across a paddy in fear. He was cut down as he stepped over one of the dikes.

The order to withdraw angered Myers. He called out, "Let's go get the bastards!" With that, he moved up the hill, where he came upon PVT James W. Yeager, of the Battalion HC. He and some others were fighting the enemy. Myers talked briefly to Yeager. Looking back, Myers saw five men shot down be enemy fire, the last three by a machine gun just up the hill from his position. Turning, he ran up the slope toward the gun. He was headed for some bushes, when they parted and took off. They were enemy soldiers using bushes as camouflage. Myers fired at the retreating enemy. Near the top of the hill he threw a grenade, then another as he reached the crest. Some enemy soldiers came at Myers from his right rear, and Yeager drove them off with well-placed shooting.

"I then went after the gun that was shooting at us.... "I threw a grenade at it," Myers said. There were enemy soldiers all around. Lying there, he fired clip after clip at them. Below, he saw a North Korean officer trying to organize a group of enemy soldiers to go back up the hill. Myers fired, dropping the officer. To his right, a group of enemy were dragging a wheel-mounted machine gun up the slope. He took them under fire and the machine gun rolled down the hill.

The North Koreans now circled the hill to his left and rear. Some of the enemy tried to retreat from GI fire, but their officers chased them back up. An enemy bullet smashed the butt plate of Myers' rifle. Even so, the enemy was not firing much on the hill.

Enemy mortar and machine gun fire still pounded the rice paddy behind him, and enemy troops were in every direction. He moved back to the rear of the hill. Some GIs began to fire at him until he waved to them. Returning to the bottom of the slope, Myers discarded his damaged M1 and picked up another weapon. On the way down, he saw a medic treating the wounded while under fire. "I yelled at him to get the hell out of there," said Myers. "He didn't answer. That guy was really brave."

Most of L Co. was pinned in the paddy, or so it seemed to Myers. As he got out into the paddy, "something like a big hand told me to get down," he recounted. "Just as I did, four big mortar shells came in and landed about 15 feet from me. Blew my helmet off and knocked me down, but not a scratch did I get." As he sat there, an enemy bul-

let went through one trouser leg. Looking for the sources of the shot, he saw the foot of an enemy soldier hiding in a tree. Grabbing a carbine, he killed the man.

Reaching LT Makarounis, Myers advised him to use a nearby ditch and go to the right. Myers said that the officer did not take his advice.

About this time, CPL Richard L. Wilson, who had been sent with the message for the Weapons Platoon returned to report to Makarounis that he couldn't find them. They were gone from where he had left them.

LT Makarounis joined his other platoons when they came by. Enemy fire raked the paddies and creek, leaving many dead and wounded. Medics wearing red-cross arm bands seemed to be special targets to the enemy. The practice of identifying medical personnel by such armbands and ambulances by large red crosses on a white field was stopped soon after this battle.

Makarounis got into the creek, meeting SFC Applegate. The two men, trailed by a number of other survivors, waded waist-deep along the creek while under machine gun fire from three directions.

Finally the officer and NCO decided to extricate the group by fire and movement. Applegate led with about 30 men, firing toward the enemy. The M1 rifle fire which they were able to muster was pitifully inadequate. They had no machine guns or workable BARs, but Applegate and most of the men with him escaped. The lieutenant, with about 40 more men, was pinned behind paddy dikes. Ten men were behind one dike with Makarounis. He glanced at his watch at 4 p.m.; darkness, and a chance to escape, was over five hours away.

Later, the firing stopped, and everything became quiet. Then he heard a whispered voice.

"Lieutenant." Then again, "Lieutenant."

"Yes," replied Makarounis, "What do you want?"

"Nothing, sir. I just wanted to know if you were there," responded the same voice. This happened several times more, from different quarters.

Later, cautiously peeking over the edge of his dike, Makarounis saw many enemy soldiers coming together from the east and south. He slowly lowered his head. Some time later, machine gun fire started again and Makarounis was hit. "Like somebody hitting me in the back — once, twice, three times, four times. Like that," he said. He spit to see if there was any blood, but none came from his mouth. His back was bleeding.

He stole another glance over the dike. Just in front of him he saw GIs with their hands in the air, surrounded by the enemy. He and the others in the paddy struggled to their feet, the unwounded and less seriously wounded helping each other and those who were more badly injured. PFC Harding, although wounded himself, helped Makarounis to his feet. Then the two of them gave a hand to PVT Donald M. Frasher (Co.I), who had three wounds.

Enemy soldiers took their watches and rings and had the men remove their shirts. It was then that Makarounis discovered one very large hole and a smaller one in the back of his shirt, and blood all over it. Then he discovered his messenger, PVT Gardner (PVT James D. Gardner?),

whose left arm was shattered and who had sustained other wounds in his cheek and back. "Lieutenant!" he shouted. "Lieutenant! Help me!" But Makarounis was hustled away, along with other prisoners capable of walking. He looked back, heartsick, but helpless. Harding said, "Come on, lieutenant." That was the last he saw of Gardner.

About 75 American POWs were assembled, men unhurt, men helping others who were injured. At some point, a man named Allen (John F. Allen, M/29?) came by "with a pile of GI bandages," which he distributed. It was then that Makarounis discovered that one of his back wounds was the size of a silver dollar; the other a bit smaller.

The badly-wounded Frasher, had found the lieutenant's wallet in the rice paddy. He passed it forward in the column of prisoners to Makarounis, "with his compliments." Makarounis was overwhelmed by this act of a seriously, maybe fatally, wounded soldier.

Shortly thereafter, the prisoners were separated into three groups: Unwounded, walking wounded and those who couldn't walk at all. Makarounis and the other walking wounded were loaded onto 29th Infantry jeeps. The unwounded marched, and those who could not take care of themselves were murdered by North Korean soldiers.

Enemy soldiers marching along the road past the jeeps filled with GI POWs tried to hit the Americans as they went by. Makarounis and about 30 other wounded men were placed in a large room of what appeared to be a school building.

PFC Sylvester J. Vulturo, the I Co. baker, was with Makarounis in this room. Although wounded himself, Vulturo took care of the officer. A Korean medic came by and swabbed both of Alexander's wounds and put a bandage on the largest one.

2LT Clyde A. Fore led the 3d Platoon, I/29, at Hadong. He recalled that the men of the 3d Battalion were told that there were about 300 poorly-armed "communist partisans" in Hadong. When confronted by heavy machine gun, small-arms, mortar and artillery fire, the men realized that the report was untrue.

The recon patrol the night before the battle confirmed that North Korean regulars were in the Hadong area. Obviously, this information was never disseminated to the troops.

Fore recalled a YAK fighter flying over his platoon late on the afternoon of July 26. His platoon was on the flank of the battalion during the march. The YAK flew so low, Fore wrote, that he had eye contact with the pilot. The troops did not fire at the plane and it flew away.

At Hadong, LT Fore was wounded and suffered concussion from a 120mm mortar round. In addition, he had 13 bullet holes in his clothing and two rounds hit him. One glanced off a metal button and the other was a spent round. Only eight of his 52-man platoon were still with him at the end of the battle, and six of them were wounded. His platoon had been ordered up into the pass to protect the battalion's left flank and to recapture 75mm recoilless rifles which had been overrun by the enemy.

He knew that he and his men could not follow the other survivors of 3/29. He and LT

Wright, a WW II veteran, gathered up about 30 or 40 men. All but 12 were wounded. They made their way south, pursued by the enemy. They made contact with two ROK Navy patrol boats. Technically, as the senior officer, Fore was in charge of the party, but his wounds and concussion caused "cobwebs" in his "battered head," as he put it. Fore wrote that Wright "was the will power of the group" when Fore's concussion caused him to become fuzzy-headed. He and some of the others had seen the enemy killing American wounded, which infused the men with a renewed will to escape. Fore proudly wrote, "We didn't lose a soldier enroute!"

When they reached the sea, Wright and a few others searched the coast and discovered a ROK Navy boat. "He returned 'bout 10 minutes before several hundred NKPAs would have reached the WIAs (and me)," Fore wrote.

The men were loaded on two ROK patrol boats, and the last boat backed out to sea, firing at pursuing enemy soldiers. Fore made it back to Pusan, then to the Osaka Hospital.

"In June of 1950, I departed from Oakland, California for...assignment to Okinawa," wrote PFC John Napier. "I thought that [it] would be an uneventful eighteen month overseas tour.... I was eighteen...."

Napier was one of the newly-arrived 400 men who were assigned to the two battalions of the 29th just before they sailed for Korea. He was assigned as a rifleman in LT Fore's 3d Platoon, Co. I.

When the battalion was ordered to take Hadong, Napier recalled that the men were told they would face "a guerrilla force of civilians, which would be armed with pitchforks, knives, etc. (but no weapons). We were issued a certain amount of ammunition and told there was no more...once we used what we had," he wrote. "We would have to fight with bayonets and hands."

Napier wrote that the North Koreans sprang a trap on the battalion and "closed the circle around us.... My platoon sergeant was in touching distance of me when he was killed.... The bullets were falling like rain into the rice paddy we were in.... It was literally hell."

During the withdrawal, Napier was wounded as he tried to run across a road. "The mortar round went off close to me and knocked me back down in the rice paddy...." He lay there on his stomach for about three hours, but was conscious. "The North Koreans would be over me talking and would poke me with their rifle butts...." On three occasions enemy soldiers came by and left him for dead.

After dark, he hobbled and crawled to a Korean farmer's house, but the farmer was too frightened to help him. About three hours later he was captured while trying to get away from a North Korean patrol. The enemy soldiers took all his personal belongings and stripped him to his shorts. The rest of the night they beat him and indicated that they were going to kill him. On July 28 he was taken to a church in Hadong, where he joined other POWs.

Let us now return to Frank Myers.

Myers and a few other men of the unit continued to engage the enemy with any weapon they could seize, working their way into a stream and letting the current carry them downstream.

Eight or nine men were with Myers, a few with weapons. Leaving the stream, he crawled up another hill, where he came across an enemy wearing GI boots. With no time to pull the pin, Myers hurled a grenade at the man, hitting him in the chest. The enemy soldier fired a shot, but missed Myers, who grabbed the rifle and beat the North Korean over the head with it.

He could see the enemy taking GI prisoners, but Myers and a number of men reached a river which was about 100 feet wide, jumped in and crossed it to a small village. There they met some other survivors. Myers, a man who he believed to be an officer, and one or two others began discussing how to get away. "About 15 guys ran ahead of us," he recalled. "Then a machine gun opened up on them when they got about 100 yards ahead of us.... They disappeared."

Wounded were everywhere. Up the trail from the village was a soldier with blood pumping out of his back. Myers put his first aid packet on the wound, but the man was dying. He looked up at Myers and asked, "Could you please tell my Mom and Dad that I will be OK and that I love them?"

Moving with Myers and his party was a corporal with a wound through his side and another soldier who had been shot by an enemy bullet through the face, head, throat and nose. The others took turns helping wounded along; the group had about 20 weapons among them.

Near dark, Myers borrowed a carbine from a corporal and moved up a hill to the left, where he had seen three enemy soldiers. Getting to within about 30 yards of them, he took careful aim and fired three shots. Two of the enemy fell and the other just disappeared. Myers got up and ran away as fast as he could, soon rejoining his party in a wooded area. Some of them were smoking. He told them to snuff out the cigarettes because the enemy was all around and could see the glowing tips. An American patrol of two or three jeeps came along. The wounded were loaded on them and the vehicles sped away.

At daylight, Myers and three other men found themselves on a hill overlooking a village. Three enemy motorcycles and some captured GI trucks pulled into the village. Enemy soldiers dismounted and began to splash around in the water of a nearby stream. The four Americans took the enemy under fire, blasting away until out of ammunition, "then [we] ran like hell out of there," Myers said. Late that day (July 28), Myers and his companions arrived in Chinju.

Only LT Morrissey's 1st Platoon of Co. L, on the north side of the pass, did not get the word to withdraw. The remainder of the unit loaded on trucks and, at midafternoon, headed for Chinju.

On the way, they met B/13th FAB, which was supposed to have provided 3/29 with artillery support during their attack on Hadong. The battery had started for Hadong at 8 a.m., moving along slowly, stopping frequently to recon. As a result, 3/29 never had any artillery support. The battery now turned around in the road and headed back to Chinju. In the unit's haste, it abandoned a 105mm howitzer and four 2 1/2-ton trucks, which had gotten stuck in rice paddies.

Mott also radioed CPT Flynn, near the top of the pass, telling him to withdraw everyone still on the hill. Flynn notified Morrissey, who was

still holding the right of the pass. The lieutenant, one wounded man and 11 others were all that remained of the platoon. The Air Force captain, killed in trying to escape, had fought all day as a rifleman. So, too, had CPT William Mitchell, the S2.

Flynn saw to it that Morrissey's men were loaded on trucks and sent off, but his own jeep wouldn't start. Looking back, he saw a large body of enemy, about a battalion, swarm over the pass. Flynn and other elements of 3/29 negotiated paddies and the stream under enemy mortar and machine gun fire. He and about 20 men reached lines of the 19th Infantry the following afternoon.

Co. I's SGT Applegate, after leaving Makarounis, finally assembled 97 men and led them to the coast, where they were rescued by a South Korean fishing vessel at the town of Noryangjin, 5 miles south of Hadong.

Robert W. Mildenberger, of Co. M, although wounded that day, was luckier than many of his comrades from the unit. "I was wounded," he wrote, "and was taken by the South Korean advisers [some of GEN Chae's men]. I was put on a small boat and taken down a river and picked up by a larger boat and taken to a hospital in Pusan and then to an Army hospital in Osaka, Japan."

On the morning of July 27, CPT Michael Barszcz was ordered to take his company (G/19) on a motorized patrol from Chinju along secondary roads north of Hadong. He had 78 men available for the mission. During the morning, his unit covered about 14 miles of road northeast of Hadong, without signs of the enemy. That afternoon, he returned to the main Hadong-Chinju road near the village of Sigum, some 12 miles east of Hadong.

While here, an officer and about 50 men from L/29 came by, claiming they were the only survivors of the unit. Most were without clothing, except shorts and boots. The group had only two weapons, an M1 rifle and a .45 automatic pistol. Barszcz took the two weapons, put the men on two trucks and sent them back to Chinju. The men had explained their condition by saying that they had to discard weapons and equipment in order to swim a river and wade through water filled rice paddies.

CPT Barszcz was unimpressed. "In my opinion, a soldier without a weapon in combat is a deserter. This opinion I expressed to them...." Barszcz' opinion did not go down well with the men of L he confronted. They felt that they had fought hard, had withdrawn only on orders and had borne a terrible ordeal just to escape.

The captain, expecting more stragglers from Hadong, deployed his company astride the road. He sent a message back with the L Co. survivors, telling what he had done and asking for orders. Co. G stayed there until 4 a.m. on July 28, when CPT Montesclaros came up with trucks and took it back to positions in the hills west of the Nam River, 4 miles from Chinju.

MAJ Raibl and other wounded arrived in Chinju early in the afternoon of July 27. They reported that the 3d Battalion was fighting well. As a result, COL Moore thought things were going well at Hadong. Reports from survivors later on gave a truer picture of the disaster.

The battalion had gone into action at Hadong

at about full strength — 900-925. The next day, July 28, 354 personnel, including some walking wounded, were present for duty. A North Korean soldier captured later said that the enemy captured about 100 Americans at Hadong. CPT (later MAJ) Sharra told Appleman that the bodies of 313 U.S. soldiers were recovered in and near Hadong in September 1950. These figures account for 767 men of the battalion.

Almost all the battalion crew-served weapons, communications equipment and individual weapons were lost, as well as about 30 vehicles.

On July 28, all remaining personnel from 3/29 who were fit for duty were organized into Companies K and L. The following day, Co. K was attached to 2/19 at Chinju and Co. L was attached to 1/19, 2 miles south of town.

Three key factors led to the catastrophe which befell 3/29 at Hadong:

First, the battalion fell into a true ambush. Only Co. L, at the pass, was able to deploy as a unit. Companies K and I were never able to fight as cohesive units.

Second, key leadership was lost in the battalion almost from the start. As the battle progressed, more leaders also fell. The recollections and experiences of survivors support a scene of chaos and disorder from about noon at Hadong, but battalion leadership had broken down hours before that time.

Third, the influx of many men from other elements of the 29th had an adverse effect on the command. The 200 troops right off a troopship, many just recruits, actually were a hazard to the command.

Another factor, never before emphasized, was that the battalion had no artillery, armor or air support. Why B/13th FAB was not hurried into position to support the battalion has never been explained. There apparently were no tanks available to support the battalion. The lack of air support was due to the loss of the air controller's radio and their being no other means of communication with aircraft. The battalion also had no communication with COL Moore so it might report the situation.

The 3d Battalion, 29th Infantry never had a chance at Hadong.

Movements of the *NK 4th Seoul Guards Division* - July 23-28

As the *NK 6th Guards Division* made a wide sweep to flank the U.S. Eighth Army, the *4th Seoul Guards Division* moved to execute a parallel, but closer envelopment. On July 23, after receiving about 1,000 untrained replacements, the *4th Division* moved south from Taejon toward Kumsan. There, it received another 1,000 virtually untrained replacements on July 24-25 and headed southeast toward the Kochang-Anui area. The division reportedly left a supporting tank regiment at Kumsan. Elements of the *4th* attacked Anui on July 27. On July 28, American intelligence correctly reported that the elements of one enemy division were probably in the Chinju area and major portions of another were near Kochang, but erroneously identified the enemy division on the Chinju-Masan axis as the *4th*. It was the *6th*. (See Chapter Notes.)

Sending the *4th* and *6th Divisions* (the latter reinforced by the *83th Motorcycle Regiment*) on

a deep flanking movement was probably a North Korean mistake. A shallower, more concentrated envelopment would have had a good chance of crushing the Eighth Army's left flank, cutting it off from resupply via Pusan, and leading to its defeat. Elements of the 24th Division, plus the two battalions of the 29th, arriving in Pusan on July 24, were probably too weak to prevent this and to defend Pusan. It is very likely that the enemy could have seized Pusan before the 5th RCT, Marine Bde and advance elements of the 2d Division arrived. The time which it took the *NK 6th Division* to make the wide swing took it out of contact and battle long enough for the Americans to react by sending the 27th Infantry, then the entire 25th Division to the extreme southern flank near Chindong-ni, and finally building up this force with the 5th RCT and Marine Bde.

As of July 27, the 34th Regiment, with about 1,150 men; about 350 men in each of its two battalions defended Kochang, which lies midway on the road between Kumchon and Chinju. A road runs eastward from the town vias Kyosen,

across the Naktong, to Changnyong. The latter town lies on one of the two main roads running south from Taegu.

Early on the afternoon of July 27, LTC Wilson's 1/29 relieved LTC Rhea's 1/19 at Umyong-ni. The 1/29 had no armor, artillery or air support, the same situation as with 3/29 at Hadong. A supporting 4.2 inch mortar platoon had only two rounds of WP ammunition. The only communication between Wilson and Moore's CP were jeep messengers travelling a 35-mile road between the two.

Early the same afternoon, LTC Rhea guided B/29 (1LT John C. Hughes), reinforced by about 35 men from Co. D, from Umyong-ni to relieve A/19 at Anui. But A/19 was in a small-arms fight with the enemy, delaying relief. Rhea returned to Umyong-ni, leaving orders for Co. A to follow as soon as possible. He expected they would be along shortly, but waited five hours at Umyong-ni. The company failed to arrive and reconnaissance showed that the road to Anui was cut by the enemy. The colonel left for Chinju with the rest of the battalion just before dusk.

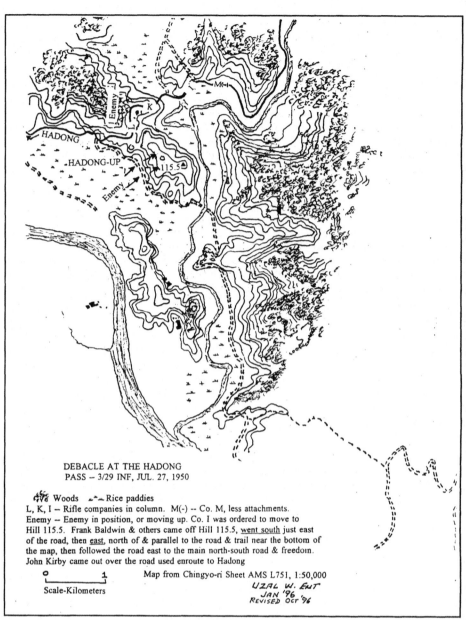

DEBACLE AT THE HADONG
PASS -- 3/29 INF, JUL. 27, 1950

Woods   Rice paddies
L, K, I — Rifle companies in column. M(-) -- Co. M, less attachments.
Enemy — Enemy in position, or moving up. Co. I was ordered to move to
Hill 115.5. Frank Baldwin & others came off Hill 115.5, went south just east
of the road, then east, north of & parallel to the road & trail near the bottom of
the map, then followed the road east to the main north-south road & freedom.
John Kirby came out over the road used enroute to Hadong.

Scale-Kilometers 0   1   Map from Chingyo-ri Sheet AMS L751, 1:50,000
UZAL W. ENT
JAN '96
REVISED OCT '96

Map 15 (Courtesy of Uzal W. Ent)

At Umyong-ni, LTC Wilson had sent his S2, 1LT Sam C. Holliday, to contact the ROKs at Hamtang, and the Assistant S2, 2LT Frank Iwanczyk, with two jeeps to contact the 34th Infantry at Kochang.

Iwanczyk's two jeeps kicked up heavy clouds of dirt and dust as they travelled along, causing the second jeep to keep well behind the fist. A mile beyond the Anui crossroads, an enemy machine gun hidden in a building at a turn in the road ambushed the first jeep, and all four occupants fell dead from the wrecked vehicle. The second jeep skidded to a halt and the men leaped into the roadside ditch. All was quiet for several minutes. Then seven or eight enemy soldiers came down the road, past the first jeep. Approaching the second, they shouted and began to run toward it. PVT Sidney D. Talley rose up, firing his M1. Two North Koreans fell dead. The three other Americans now also began shooting, driving the enemy away.

One of the GIs jumped into the jeep, turned it around, and the others scrambled aboard. They sped back to the Anui crossroads, telling Co. B about the ambush, and repeating their story at the battalion CP.

Meantime, LT Holliday had found almost 600 men of the ROK 7th Division and 150 ROK Marines at Hamyang. He then was sent toward Anui in a jeep with three other men, but they were ambushed 2 1/2-miles short of the town. The jeep was destroyed and one of the men was wounded in the chest. Holliday covered his three men's escape with a BAR, then followed them.

After being relieved at Anui about 4 p.m., A/ 19 started south to join the rest of the battalion. A mile out of town it came upon a firefight between enemy and ROK troops. Enemy fire destroyed six vehicles, and the unit destroyed the others. They started on foot over the hills toward Kochang and 34th Infantry lines, leaving heavy equipment behind.

The following morning 64 GIs and 60 ROKs came into 34th Infantry lines. Why A/19 did not go back to Anui and join B/29 is unknown. A rifle platoon of that unit was on a roadblock along the Anui road. (See below.)

Anui - B/29 - 27-28 July

In all, LT Hughes had 215 men in his B/29, including the 35 men attached from Co. D. MSG Connoly Byrd led the D Co. contingent. Co. B, with the men from D, was initially deployed on high ground west of Anui. The enemy attacked with superior forces from three sides, putting the Americans in desperate battle from the beginning. By nightfall on July 27, Co. B had been forced back into the town. Hughes planned to withdraw to high ground across the Nam River east of town. Two officers and 16 EM got across the river before enemy machine gun fire cut off the rest of the unit. These 18 men tried to help the others break out, finally, giving up and making their way through the hills to the 34th near Kochang.

Harold L. Gamble was a combat medic with B/29. The cut-off men held out in Anui until midnight, when survivors escaped through the hills. About half of the 215 men were KIA or MIA. Gamble wrote that Hughes lost 117 KIA and 14 POWs. 2LT Dennis Nicewander, D/29,

said only "one or two of my men came back, the others having been killed or captured."

Darold Freeman was a demolition specialist in 1/29 at Anui. He wrote that after Anui, he "wandered around in the hills for a few hours, met up with four members of my company...." A few hours later, they joined the battalion headquarters company, which was withdrawing to Sanchong. "Again, we ran into an ambush and told to 'scatter into the hills.' Hiding during the day and moving at night the five of us were able to find [what was left of] our company two days later."

2LT Frank L. Griffin's 1st Platoon, A/29th Infantry, reinforced with machine guns, mortars a 57mm recoilless rifle and machine gun jeeps, manned a roadblock on a knob on the right side of the Anui road. "That gave us a commanding view of the road," Griffin wrote. "That night a continuous bombardment and heavy weapons firing could be heard from the Anui area." Griffin reported this to LT Leonard Becicka, his company commander. Becicka told Griffin to keep his "eyes peeled on the road and the high mountains to the right of my position, to hold my position, and that the remainder of the company would be enroute to reinforce me very shortly. Midmorning...four or five soldiers came in to our position who had been in Anui." Two were from Co. B, two from Co. D and one from the 19th Infantry. "All were quite shaken," Griffin wrote, "half clothed, and no weapons." These survivors reported everyone dead at Anui and that "thousands" of enemy soldiers were headed toward Griffin. The men were given food and medical attention then sent to the rear.

About that time a Korean colonel came into Griffin's position and reported that most of the defenders were in fact dead, and that a large force of enemy troops was headed his way. "About noon," Griffin continued, "on a very high ridge line we observed a long line of what we believed to be NK troops and horse-drawn artillery moving perpendicular to my front toward the Battalion assembly area." Griffin figured these troops to be about 2,000 yards away. He reported this to his CO and was told to stand fast, that Co. A was on the way. When the unit arrived, it "came under fire from the Anui road," he related, "and at the same time we began to receive indirect fire in and around my blocking position." Griffin's platoon was relieved and ordered back to the main Battalion position, covered by the remainder of Co. A. Shortly after the whole company returned to this position, LTC Wilson "looked me up, shook my hand, and told me he was proud of the job we had done...." Griffin wrote.

Although LTC Wilson did not know the situation at Anui, he knew that enemy forces were between his 1/29 (- Co. B) at Umyong-ni and Anui. Twice he tried, unsuccessfully to send help to Co. B.

Enemy troops in the area were from the *NK 4th Division*. Turning south at Anui early on July 28, these troops moved toward 1/29, east of the Nam River, and COL Min Ki Sik's ROK force on the west. Mortar fire turned the enemy back east of the river, and the timely arrival of some ROK marines prevented a possible defeat of COL Min's force west of it. The enemy withdrew. Wilson learned the fate of his Co. B from North Korean prisoners.

LTC Wilson discovered that the enemy was

flanking his battalion and heading for Chinju, so after dark he withdrew the battalion. On July 30, as ordered by COL Moore, 1/29 finally deployed in defensive positions near Sanchong, 20 miles north of Chinju. COL Min's ROKs continued into Chinju.

Kochang - 34th Infantry - July 29

"The move to Kochang...was accomplished with no problems," wrote LT Murray L. Carroll of the 34th Regiment. "We were told that Koch'ang would probably remain quiet, and we could continue to rebuild there."

Carroll was in charge of one section of the convoy enroute to Kochang. "We met GEN Walker...and he chewed me out unmercifully about the men not having on their fatigue jackets and helmets," Carroll continued. "When I was able to get a word in edge-wise — not easy with God, GEN Walker or GEN MacArthur...I explained...that the men...did not have jackets. The same with helmets, and...that some didn't have pants or shoes either. (One driver,...[who] wore size 15 boots...had been driving bare-foot for two weeks. His feet were blistered from the hot steel floor plate of his...truck.) GEN Walker inspected the trucks, growled and got back in his jeep." That night, trucks brought up fatigues, boots, helmets and helmet liners for the men.

Carroll wrote that at Kochang they found a number of civilians, including women and children, who had been killed "execution style, hands and feet bound. The Police Chief [blamed it on] guerrillas, [but] some civilian told us that...the Police Chief and his men had done it...." The dead civilians were alleged to be Communist sympathizers.

Kochang lies in a 2 1/2-mile north-south oval valley. The 34th was deployed in a horseshoe configuration, with a reinforced platoon of Co. I on a roadblock 4 miles north of town on the Kumchon road, the remainder of the 3d Battalion on hills blocking the Anui road 2 miles west of town and the 1st Battalion about the same distance out on the Hyopchon road to the east. HM Co. manned the north edge of town. Battery A, 13th FAB, with five 105mm howitzers, was located 2 miles southeast of the town.

The 34th Infantry had no time to regroup or re-equip. The regiment had no switchboard and few radios, and was short on mortars, bazookas and machine guns. As LT Carroll pointed out, many men were without complete uniforms and helmets. Most had retained their entrenching tools and every man had his individual weapon.

Just before nightfall on July 28, enemy vehicles began to pile up beyond the 34th Infantry roadblock on the Anui road west of Kochang. Artillery was brought in on this target until full dark. COL Beauchamp moved his two battalions nearer town for a tighter defense.

Early in the evening, Beauchamp was ordered to report to GEN Church at the 24th Division CP in Hyopchon, where he told Church that he planned to withdraw 3/34 to a position 3 miles southeast of Kochang. Church disapproved; Beauchamp called his CP and halted the move. When he returned to the town at 3 a.m., all was quiet.

An hour later, the enemy made two night attacks. The first cut off Co. I in the north. The other, also from the north, thrust south across the road east of Kochang into the 1st Battalion. The battalion held, but began falling back without orders toward its secondary position 3 miles east of Kochang. Beauchamp stopped the battalion on the road.

Before dawn, the 3d Battalion also fell back through Kochang without orders. Co. I was left isolated north of town. Although the battalion ran a gauntlet of fire for about a mile, darkness kept casualties small. The 1/34 rescued all but one platoon of Co. I shortly before daylight; the men of that remaining platoon were either killed or captured.

For PFC Leonard F. Korgie, Kochang was his baptism of fire. When the war started, Korgie was a military policeman and corporal of the guard, HQ Det. #1, Sugamo Prison, Tokyo, the prison housing Japanese war criminals.

He and about 250 other MPs were told they would go to Korea as an MP POW escort unit. At the Yokohama Replacement Depot, they were assigned as replacements to infantry units. Korgie went directly from Japan to L/34 at Kochang. Here are his recollections of Kochang, as a member of Co. L, 34th Infantry:

"We had a U-shaped perimeter with open flanks.... It was early morning. I glanced across the valley to the opposite hill.... All the vegetation on that hill was sliding down into the valley. The North Koreans camouflage revealed only movement. (See Chapter Notes.)

"They opened fire all at once — it was deadly," he continued. "This was my baptism of fire. I jumped into the foxhole and started firing back. Their bullets were kicking dirt in my face. I was stunned — so this is combat! It was also survival. All our guys opened up. We had no leader on the spot." The platoon leader and two men had gone on a recon early in the morning and never came back.

"It was withering small arms [fire] going both ways all day with different levels of intensity. A happy kid ran up to my foxhole [with] a bullet hole through the palm of his hand.... He had me light a cigarette for him and put it in his mouth — just like in the movies. He knew he had a million-dollar wound." (A wound bad enough for him to be sent to a hospital, but not fatal, and never have to return to combat again.)

The enemy attacked the unit from the front, while others started enveloping the position. Some enemy soldiers got behind Korgie's company "and started picking off our guys. Some GIs up the hill eliminated that."

But the North Koreans came on. As they neared the top of the hill Korgie was on, "we called for artillery and mortars," he wrote. "There was none — it was lost at Taejon. The Air Force never showed. We were on our own and about to be overrun. That was a helpless feeling."

About 4 p.m., orders came to pull out. "We executed in an orderly way and brought out our dead and wounded. I was surprised — a motley group of replacements and the remnants of the 34th; necessity and survival molded us into an effective fighting force. I weathered my first day of combat quite well...."

Battery A, 13 FAB came under enemy attack from a ridge about 500 yards to the east. Many members of the battery, plus two infantry squads

which were to provide security, spooked. Someone yelled, "Run for your life!" The BC thought the battery had been overrun. The XO said that men had just "taken off," although he had ordered them to their foxholes when the firing began. MAJ Leon B. Cheek, artillery battalion XO, was awakened by the firing. After hearing the reports of the BC and battery XO, he put a stop to the wild shooting around him. Cheek rounded up the prime mover drivers and a dozen men from the battery. A BAR-man and three riflemen from the infantry contingent volunteered to cover the artillerymen as they pulled out the howitzers. Cheek put the four men into firing positions, where they quickly suppressed the enemy fire from about a squad of North Koreans. Under MAJ Cheek's direction, the battery's ammunition and equipment were loaded up and the guns hitched to the prime movers, and the battery displaced to the east.

On July 29, the 34th withdrew to positions near Sanje-ri on the Hyopchon road, 15 miles east of Kochang. Here the 34th and attached engineers destroyed all the bridges and created a number of landslides across the road by demolition charges. The destruction of bridges forced the *NK 4th Division* to leave its artillery at Kochang; only mortar fire supported it from then on as it advanced to the Naktong River.

Alarmed by the enemy's advance in this area, GEN Walker sent the 2,000-man ROK 17th Regiment to take positions with the 34th. This regiment began to deploy on each flank of the 34th at 2 a.m. on July 30. Walker also sent 1/21 from the Pohang area to defensive positions west of Hyopchon, behind the 34th.

COL Beauchamp wrote this to MAJ Barnett on Mar. 27, 1986, regarding the 34th Regiment's delaying action from Kochang to the Naktong River: "The Regiment occupied successive delaying positions over a period of several days. I felt the units handled themselves well, considering what they had been through and without replacements of either men or equipment.... The Regiment again accomplished its assigned mission." The 34th received some replacements, as evidenced by Leonard Korgie. But those it received were few and did not bring squads or platoons near authorized strength. The regiment remained as starved for personnel as before.

Finally on July 31 Eighth Army correctly identified the locations of both the *NK 4th* and *6th Divisions*, concluding that the *6th* was headed for Pusan via Masan.

GEN Walker's Plan to Move Communications Equipment from Taegu to Seoul

When Eighth Army Headquarters was established at Taegu, with it came very sophisticated and almost irreplaceable communications equipment, and a host of administrative personnel and their equipment. As the enemy slowly forced U.S. and ROK forces back, Walker became concerned about this communications equipment.

GEN Walker planned to use the Naktong River to anchor his western flank. Not having enough troops available to establish a position or area defense along the Naktong, even with those due to arrive soon, he contemplated em-

ploying a mobile defense along the river. To do this, and to ensure he could reinforce the northern front when the situation warranted, he needed to have roads uncluttered by vehicles on administrative missions. Therefore, he prudently planned to displace certain administrative personnel and functions back to Pusan. His CP, the facility from which he would direct the battle, would remain in Taegu. He had no intention of withdrawing the Eighth Army CP to the vicinity of Pusan. GEN Landrum, COL Collier and COL Albert K. Stebbins (Eighth Army G4 at the time), wrote Appleman that Walker had not discussed this with his staff.

When Walker outlined his plan to GEN Almond for transmittal to MacArthur, Almond said that he personally thought the contemplated move would have a bad effect on both the Eighth Army and the ROKs. It might lead them to believe that Eighth Army could not stay in Korea and could be the forerunner of a great disaster.

Eugene M. Lynch, Walker's pilot, was present with GEN Walker during this telephone conversation.

"Walker said he was pulling the administrative elements of his Army the hell out of Taegu," said Lynch, "and putting them back down to Pusan. Why? Because all of the road traffic that was tying up those roads was administrative, not tactical in nature, and he had to clear his interior lines in order to fight a mobile defense within the perimeter. He finally told Ed Almond, who went to MacArthur and said that Walker was losing his nerve. Walker had made the greatest tactical decision of those first days and here is an idiot like Almond who didn't even understand what it was all about.... Walker had to fight the battle and then try to teach the principles to Almond who was trying to fight it from Tokyo...."

GEN Almond relayed the "substance" of this conversation to GEN MacArthur, strongly recommending that MacArthur fly to Korea the next day to talk with Walker. After mulling the matter over in his mind for about half an hour, MacArthur decided to visit Walker, and arrived at Taegu at 10 a.m. the next day.

MacArthur, Walker and Almond met for an hour and a half; no one else was present. Although MacArthur did not mention Walker's request and did not criticize him, he stressed that the Eighth Army should stand its ground; that withdrawal must cease. After lunch, he said that Korea would not be evacuated; that there would be no Dunkirk. He praised the U.S. 24th and ROK Capital divisions.

This conversation must have been disgusting to Walker. He never had any intention of giving up Korea. He was determined to stop the enemy and eventually, launch a counterattack. He needed MacArthur's support and backing, not admonitory visits which wasted everyone's time.

Except when GEN MacArthur flew to Korea to talk to GEN Walker, the two never had a commander-to-commander relationship. Walker could never establish a personal relationship with MacArthur; his calls and messages to MacArthur were filtered through Almond, often leading to telephonic arguments between Walker and Almond. (See Chapter Notes.)

Walker was unhappy with the situation in Korea in late July 1950. Both the 1st Cavalry and 25th Divisions still were trading space for time. After MacArthur's visit, Walker knew that he had to take action to try to stop this rash of withdrawals if he expected to make a stand along the Naktong. He knew it was imperative that he make clear to the troops exactly what he and MacArthur wanted: That they must stop withdrawing, halt the enemy, then defeat him.

Based on notes made at the time, Appleman wrote this undisputed version of what Walker said, when addressing the staff of the 25th Division on July 29:

GEN MacArthur was over here two days ago; he is thoroughly conversant with the situation. He knows where we are and what we have to fight with. He knows our needs and where the enemy is hitting the hardest. GEN MacArthur is doing everything possible to send reinforcements. A Marine unit and two regiments are expected in the next few days to reinforce us. Additional units are being sent over as quickly as possible. We are fighting a battle against time. There will be no more retreating, withdrawal, or readjustment of the lines or any other term you choose. Every unit must counterattack to keep the enemy in a state of confusion and off balance. There will be no Dunkirk, there will be no Bataan, a retreat to Pusan would be one of the greatest butcheries in history. We must fight until the end. Capture by these people is worse than death itself. We will fight as a team. If some of us must die, we will die fighting together. Any man who gives ground may be personally responsible for the death of thousands of his comrades.

I want you to put this out to all the men in the Division. I want everybody to understand that we are going to hold this line. We are going to win.

GEN Walker talked to other division commanders at the time in the same vein, but did not address their staffs.

Word of the "stand or die" dictum quickly reached the troops. Some scoffed at it as being unrealistic, since there was no "line" to start with. Others believed that it meant they were to hold where they were at all costs. COL Fisher of the 35th Infantry said that he and his troops were heartened by these tough words. Actually, Walker was referring to situations where troops left positions before being threatened by encirclement by the enemy. In reality, over the next three or four days, there would be more withdrawals until he had the Eighth Army behind the Naktong River.

The Fall of Chinju - 19th Inf and 3/29 -July 31

On July 28, 1/29 (less Co. A) arrived in Chinju and was ordered to form a blocking position about 10 miles south of the city. LTC Rhea moved to the vicinity of Kuho-ri, 2 miles west of the Sachon airfield. There he deployed the 200 riflemen of his battalion astride the secondary road approach from Hadong.

LTC McGrail's 2/19 deployed in positions on hills astride the Chinju-Hadong road just west of the Nam River. Elements of 3/29 and a number of ROK troops also were in and near Chinju. Intelligence reported an estimated two enemy regiments, reinforced by tanks, in the Hadong area.

F/19 manned a roadblock about 6 miles west of Chinju. Late on the morning of July 29, an enemy column led by three motorcycles approached the position. There was little fire from Co. F, and artillery called in was inaccurate and ineffective. The unit then withdrew to the main battalion position, just west of the Nam River and 4 miles from Chinju. An air strike temporarily halted the enemy column.

Early on July 30, the enemy slipped around the northern (right) flank of 2/19 and cut the road running northwest out of Chinju to the 1st Battalion.

CPT Barszcz' Co. G was dug in west of Chinju, across the Nam River. He reported sighting at least 800 enemy soldiers moving across his front. These soldiers ignored U.S. small-arms fire. He called for an aerial observer, who was unable to detect the enemy because they were wearing foliage camouflage. While the airplane was overhead, the North Koreans simply squatted down and remained motionless. Barszcz called in artillery fire, but after about 20 rounds, it ceased, due to a shortage of artillery ammunition. Rain and overcast skies also restricted efficient aerial observation of enemy movements that day.

On the afternoon of July 30, 1/19 withdrew across the Nam River to positions 2 miles west of Chinju. G Co., on the left flank, had no physical contact with the rest of the battalion.

The strength of the 19th Infantry as of July 30 was given in the regimental report as 1,895; 300 men in the 1st Battalion and 290 men in the 2d. COL Moore gave 1,544 as its strength, including replacements of 175 on July 28 and another 500 on July 30. The still disorganized 3/29 reported 396 men. ROK forces, known as Task Force Min, numbering 1,249 soldiers, arrived in Chinju on July 30 and 31. These numbers do not include the field artillery. It is known that the 13th FAB received somewhat less than 100 replacements on July 30. There are no total figures for the artillery.

COL Moore directed that the 500 replacements received on July 30 be sent forward at once to help the units which then were engaged with the enemy. About 150 of these replacements arrived at 1/19 just before dark and LTC Rhea assigned them at once to companies.

LTC Forrest Kleinman, then S3, 1/19, recalled the battalion received 100 black replacements about this time. The trucks carrying these soldiers came under machine gun fire. Kleinman wrote that he sent these replacements to the nearest foxholes in the battalion's horseshoe-shaped position. "Each squad got one or two to help in the all night fight," he wrote.

The 2/19 also received about 150 replacements, who arrived at their assigned units about dusk. A number of replacements for both battalions were killed or wounded before they reached their unit of assignment. CPT Barszcz almost had begged the battalion XO not to send the replacements forward in the midst of battle, to no avail.

That night, the enemy moved in on George Co.; a number of them were killed inside the unit's position. Hard pressed, out of communication with battalion headquarters, and with friendly artillery fire falling near, Barszcz tried to slip his unit to the right and join the rest of the battalion, but the enemy was in force on the road.

Slipping around near midnight, the men of Co. G crossed the road to the north and concealed themselves in scrub brush for two or three hours. While there, they observed several troop-laden enemy tanks clank by, heading for Chinju.

Beginning with an artillery preparation about 2:15 a.m. on July 31, the enemy concentrated their principal attacks against Easy and Fox companies, with the main thrust against Fox. Whistles signalled the enemy infantry attack on the two units about 3 a.m. Co. F was heaviest hit; by 5 a.m., it was in serious trouble.

Soon after, the enemy broke through Fox Co. Part of H, the Heavy Weapons Co., was behind Co. F. One of Fox's platoons came off the hill, followed by enemy soldiers. A platoon of How Co. fired into the oncoming intermingled group of U.S. and enemy soldiers, but soon withdrew too. Part of F Co, ran into the positions of Co. E. LTC McGrail stopped Co. H and placed it as security around the battalion CP. Elements of E and F companies pulled back to Chinju about daylight.

During this battle CPT Barszcz was ordered to move back to Chinju. The company moved north then east, picking up wounded and unwounded members of E, F and H /19 and K/29. Daylight found Co. G and these stragglers a couple of miles north of Chinju. By the time Co. G joined the remainder of 2/19 east of Chinju at about noon, it had suffered 40 casualties, however, it was able to bring 20 wounded out with it, 10 on litters.

The 1/19 occupied what Appleman described as "a strong defensive position " on hills "overlooking the Sachon-Chinju road near its juncture with the road east to Masan." This was south of the Nam River and 4 miles from Chinju.

Just before nightfall on July 30, the men of 1/19 saw the enemy going into position to their front but were not allowed to fire on them. A ROK Marine battalion was supposed to attack across their front, but the attack never took place. The enemy were from the *NK 15th Regiment*. That night the *15th* tried and failed to infiltrate lines of 1/19, supported by mortar and SP fire. Before dawn, they drew off and apparently headed northwest.

Shortly after daylight on July 31, COL Moore ordered LTC Rhea to move his battalion eastward about 10 miles and take up defensive positions at the Chinju pass. The 1/19 moved without encountering the enemy, and was in position before nightfall.

Enemy mortar, machine gun and small-arms fire fell into Chinju shortly after daylight, and continued as COL Moore pulled his CP out of the town and the 13th FAB (- Btry A) and B/11th FAB displaced to the east. Enemy infiltration began about 6 a.m. in the western edge of town. In addition, six enemy armored vehicles, believed to be three tanks and three SP guns, also were in Chinju, firing at the Americans.

Moore kept his CP in Chinju until about 8 a.m. MAJ Jack R. Emery (S4, 19th Inf.) sent the last of five trains containing 19th Infantry supplies out of town at 7:45 a.m. The trains totalled 25 cars.

Included in Chinju city's fire fighting equipment was a 1939 Reo hook and ladder fire engine. Some of the wounded from the 19th Infantry were loaded onto it, then the firemen climbed aboard and the engine left town, recalled Robert A. Spangenberg.

Spangenburg was a member of the Regimental Medical Co. He, PFC Walter Horn, PVT George Gilbert and PFC Albin Harp (from the 29th Infantry) became separated from their units and wandered for almost a week behind enemy lines. PVT Harp said, "I must have walked 50 miles...with a Korean guide before I reached this place." In describing the battles, he said "I come from Harlan, KY. That's what they call bloody ground. If anybody ever tells me that's bloody ground again, I'll laugh in their faces. I know what bloody ground is now. The North Koreans came at us by the hundreds, screaming and firing machine guns." PVT Gilbert said he walked at night until he met a Korean who helped him, scouting ahead while Gilbert stayed hidden. The Korean would come back and lead him a little farther. "I would take cover and he would walk ahead again," he wrote.

On the whole, the withdrawal from Chinju was orderly but slow. American and ROK soldiers, refugees and animal drawn carts intermingled along the streets of the town. Enemy fire made the main highway bridge over the Nam south of town unusable. The 2/19 went north and assembled at Uiryong. The regimental CP headed east, crossing the Nam River about 3 miles northeast of Chinju, then took the Masan road to the village of Chiryong-ni. This town was a mile beyond the Muchon-ni-Masan road fork. The artillery and 3/29 went to Uiryong, then eastward to Komam-ni (Saga), arriving shortly after noon. An air-dropped message from GEN Church sent the five 105mm howitzer B/13 FAB and the eight 155mm howitzers then assigned to B/11th FAB to positions at the Chinju pass to support 1/19.

On July 29, Frank Myers (I/29) found himself with men from the 19th Infantry, along with some others from the 29th, led by a master sergeant. Myers and the others observed the enemy arrive in trucks in the valley to their front. On his own, Myers moved out on a ridge about a half mile forward of U.S. lines where he could better observe the enemy through the scope of another sniper rifle he had obtained in Chinju.. A man came forward from American lines to get Myers, but he refused to leave his position, and sent the man back to ask for an air strike. Shortly, F-51s and Corsairs did attack the enemy.

Myers said he had a BAR blow up in his face at Hadong, swelling his right eye shut. He fired left-handed at enemy soldiers as they ran from the strafing planes, dropping three or four. Toward dark, Myers returned to the lines, where he met two other soldiers. He recalled their names as Whitey and Ford. Under the master sergeant's instructions, the troops set out grenade booby traps and trip flares.

After dark , enemy artillery began falling; U.S. artillery responded, driving off an enemy patrol. A quad-.50 fired across the valley at the enemy. Some time after 10:30 p.m., enemy infantry attacked in force. American artillery fired flares and "we saw a real sea of people," he wrote. In a bitter grenade and close-in small-arms battle, the enemy was driven off. Whitey and Ford took off and were shot for enemy soldiers by the master sergeant. Myers said he grabbed

the sergeant's weapon from him and told him to get off the hill.

About this time, an officer who Myers later identified as CPT Barszcz and an MP came up. Myers explained to the captain what had happened. Barszcz asked him what he would do if he were in charge. Myers replied that he would create the impression that they were staying, but actually pull out before dawn.

Myers' party beat off another attack about 11 or 11:30 p.m., and an even-heavier one at 4 a.m. on July 30. American artillery fired air-burst rounds at the enemy. But the enemy attack was too much; Myers and his men ran down the hill and made for the river as the enemy swept over the crest. As daylight became stronger, U.S. artillery fired flat trajectory WP rounds into the enemy, joined by 81mm mortars and air strikes. (See Chapter Notes.)

The enemy was stopped and the Americans dug in again. Myers' party now numbered about 50 or 60 men.

"Late in the afternoon," he wrote. "I observed a column of enemy soldiers dressed in white farmers' clothing, coming down from one of the mountainsides...west of the river. The group consisted of two to three hundred enemy...." He assembled about 20 men and took them toward the river, intending to fire on the North Koreans when they got closer, ensuring maximum casualties.

Just then a major ran up, ordering Myers not to "kill those innocent farmers," and instructed him to get his men back up the hill. Myers argued with the major in vain, when the major ended the conversation by threatening him with court martial.

The white-clad enemy moved on into the rear of the American line. About dusk, enemy 120mm mortar fire fell into the position, creating a number of casualties. American mortars responded. Some of the wounded were loaded onto an ambulance and a jeep, which were ambushed soon after departing. The jeep escaped, badly damaged. The passenger in the right seat had the side of his face blown off and the driver had been shot in the chest. "He was crying," Myers wrote, "saying that they had been ambushed by a bunch of farmers in white clothes [and] that everyone in the ambulance had been killed"

Apparently he was the major's driver. When he heard the driver's story, the officer was filled with remorse and apologized for not believing Myers earlier in the day.

Myers called on a nearby quad-.50 half track crew to bring the enemy under fire. The track backed down the road, shot up flares and discovered a concentration of the enemy. With the aid of flares, the crew opened up. "The slaughter [of the enemy] lasted maybe ten minutes," Myers wrote.

He was taken into Chinju with a badly sprained and extremely painful his ankle. As he rested in the aid station, word came that "we were being surrounded and overrun. I...sprang up and grabbed a rifle. I ran outside and up a street toward the firing," he wrote. Several other armed GIs were with him.

Suddenly at an intersection, they ran into about six of the enemy. "It was fairly dark and I was startled," he continued. "I swung to fire and lost my balance and fell to the ground." A North

Korean slashed at him with a bayonet, grazing the right side of his leg. A GI behind Myers killed this enemy soldier and several others. "I fired from the sitting position at several as they ran...dropping several more," Myers wrote. Returning to the aid station, he helped take wounded to the train station and load them onto a train.

At daybreak on July 31, the wounded-laden train was still in the station when a large number of the enemy started to charge across a nearby rice paddy toward it. "We started firing out of the train," Myers wrote. "One of our group...hobbled off his bunk and told the engineer to get going or he'd kill him...." The engineer started the train without argument. Soon after, more enemy fired on the train, but it successfully escaped from Chinju.

Some time during the trip, Myers passed out. When he awoke, "I was in a clean white room in fresh clean sheets — the morning sun was bright.... A pretty lady in a white dress [came by]. I asked 'Where are Mom and Dad, am I in heaven?' For a moment I thought sincerely that I was," he said. "After all, I had just been through hell."

SGT Lawrence P. Martin, of HQ/3/29, was not so lucky. He was captured at Chinju; he and a buddy, CPT Carl M. Anderson, later escaped from their captors.

1LT Samuel R. Fowler, MSG Bryant E. W. Shrader and 13 other enlisted men with three M-26 Pershing tanks remained in the part of Chinju south of the Nam River.

About first light on July 31, LT Fowler went to COL Moore for orders. Moore responded that if the North Koreans overran the 19th Infantry northwest of Chinju and Fowler could not get the tanks out under their own power, he was to destroy them and pull his men out by truck. The lieutenant telephoned Masan and apparently discovered that flatcars were on the way. He decided to stay.

The firing in Chinju all but stopped. A passing ROK soldier reported that few ROK soldiers were still in town.

About 1 p.m., AP correspondent William R. Moore showed up and recommended that Fowler investigate a group of soldiers coming up the railroad track. They proved to be about a platoon of North Koreans. The tanks opened fire with their .30- and .50-cal machine guns, and the enemy responded with small-arms fire. Fowler was hit in the left side by a bullet. Tank fire killed or wounded most of the enemy. Placing Fowler in one of the tanks, his men started the three machines east on the road to Masan.

A blown bridge two miles down the road stopped the tanks. The men removed Fowler from his tank, made a litter for him and prepared to escape on foot. The lieutenant first ordered the men to destroy the tanks by dropping grenades into them. As three men started for the tanks to do this, the enemy fired from ambush. Several men got under the bridge with Fowler. Only MSG Shrader was left on a tank, and he returned fire with the .30-cal machine gun. A North Korean soldier called out in English for the men to surrender.

Shrader stopped firing, started the tank and drove close to one of the other tanks. He took six men on board through the escape hatch and drove back toward Chinju. He stopped at the bridge over the Nam River, where the overheated engine stopped, this time for good. The seven men dashed into nearby bamboo thickets. Shrader and his party eventually entered the lines of the 25th Division west of Masan. Most of the men back at the bridge were killed, one or two captured. One of the captured, PFC Carl Anderson, said he recognized the bodies of Fowler and Moore floating in the stream with some others.

The 1/29 was at Sanchong on July 31, unaware that Chinju, 20 air miles to the southeast, had fallen and that the 19th Infantry had moved to the east. Then local villagers suddenly left, a certain indication that the enemy was nearby. LTC Wilson drove south to a roadblock he had at Tansong, 10 air miles from Chinju. As he talked with the roadblock platoon leader, LT Frank L. Griffin, some 700 refugees came by, confirming that the North Koreans were not far behind.

LTC Wilson returned to his CP and sent the battalion's heavy vehicles out under the leadership of his XO, MAJ Charles E. Arnold. The column travelled south to Tansong, then eastward over a mountain trail toward Uiryong. The trail was passable only to jeeps, until Arnold's men and local Korean civilians widened it to allow passage of all trucks. All the vehicles got through to Chungam-ni, except one that broke through a jury-rigged bridge and had to be left behind.

The 1/29 started south from Sanchong at 5 p.m. About an hour later a liaison plane flew over and dropped a message, reading, "Yesterday you were ordered to report to the concentration area of Haman. What are you doing here?" LTC Wilson was astonished; this was news to him. Haman was 35 miles away by air, but far more by road and trail.

He marched the battalion on to Tansong. There, a ROK naval lieutenant came up and informed the colonel that Chinju had fallen and that U.S. troops had withdrawn to the east. He also said that the enemy was only 7 miles away and would get there that night. Wilson eventually believed the ROK officer. He consulted with his staff, then ordered the battalion to head over the mountains to Haman.

The troops left behind all their personal effects; the few sick and injured were placed on jeeps, which with their trailers, also carried all the battalion crew-served weapons and radios. They marched until 2 a,m., then halted just beyond Masang-ni. At Masang-ni was located the last north-south road which the enemy from Chinju could use to intercept them. By the time the battalion halted, a number of refugees had joined the column.

An hour or so after the battalion set off the next morning, they were met by MAJ Arnold and trucks to take them the rest of the way.

By the end of July the *6th Division* was poised for one last drive to seize Masan and Pusan.

As the North Koreans closed in on Chinju, GEN Walker sent GEN Church his only reserve, the two-battalion 27th Infantry from Waegwan, where it had been for just one day.

LTC Michaelis of the 27th was ordered to report to GEN Church at the 24th Division CP in Changnyong. Taking his S3, CPT Earl W. Buchanan, Michaelis left at once (July 31), leaving his XO, MAJ Arthur Farthing, to bring the regiment. When he arrived at the 24th Division CP later that morning, GEN Church was absent. BG Pearson Menoher, assistant division commander, arranged for Michaelis to meet Church that night at the little railroad and crossroads village of Chung-ni, 4 miles northeast of Masan. The regiment reached Changnyong in early afternoon, heading toward Chinju.

Late on July 31, 1/19 with its supporting artillery occupied the Chinju pass. Four miles east of the pass, at the tiny village of Muchon-ni, the road forks. The north fork goes north and east via Chungam-ni and Komam-ni, then swings south to enter Masan from the north. The other fork curved south through Kogan-ni and Chindong-ni, entering Masan from the south. Between the two looping routes lay the high mountain mass of Sobuk-san — later to be known as "Bloody Sobuk."

It was about midnight July 31-August 1 when GEN Church, LTC Michaelis and COL Moore met in the Chung-ni railroad station. COL Moore briefed GEN Church and LTC Michaelis on the 19th Infantry's situation. Church filled in the two colonels on the division situation, pointing it out on a map he had spread out on a table. Then he gave his orders.

The 1/19 would retain its blocking position west of the Muchon-ni road fork (the Chinju pass position), while the 27th established a defensive position at a pass 3 miles west of Chungam-ni on the northern Masan road. Once the 27th was in position, the 19th was to pull back through it and go north. "The south along the coast looks all right, right now," Church said. "The best intelligence we've got says they've got no strong forces down there. But I don't know...." He stressed that as long as they held the road junction, the enemy was blocked to the south.

Moore returned to his CP, located about a mile east of Muchon-ni. Michaelis waited in the rain for his regiment which arrived about 3 a.m. on Aug. 1. He sent it on to dig in on the hills beyond Chungam-ni, 15 miles to the west.

Shortly after daylight, LTC Michaelis, along with his two battalion commanders, LTC Check and Murch, his S3 CPT Earl W. Buchanan and some other staff officers, set off to recon positions at what became known as "The Notch," a pass a few miles southwest of Chungam-ni. As they began planning their defense, shortly after daylight, CPT Elliot C. Cutler, Acting S3 of the 19th, arrived. He, too, was reconnoitering for potential defensive positions, and already had identified four likely sites between Muchon-ni and the Notch. He told Michaelis that the Notch was the best of the four, then returned to the 19th CP, believing that the 27th would occupy the Notch position.

Michaelis evidently deduced from his conversation with Cutler that the 19th was about to withdraw, allowing the enemy access to the southern route to Masan. Michaelis went back to the 13th FAB's CP just west of Chungam-ni and called Moore on the phone.

COL Moore told LTC Michaelis that the 19th could not hold in its present position and would withdraw to the Notch. Michaelis responded that it then would be necessary to block the southern route to Masan to prevent the enemy from driving on Pusan along that avenue. He recommended that the 19th attempt to hold at the Notch, while the 27th moved down through Masan, then west on the southern road to a point near the village of Chindong-ni. Michealis told Appleman that Moore agreed to this. Moore told Appleman that he did not recall the conversation at all. MAJ Jack J. Kron, then XO, 13th FAB, heard Michaelis' end of the conversation, and confirmed the Michaelis version in an interview with Appleman Aug. 1, 1951.

LTC Michaelis then tried without success to contact both the 24th Division and Eighth Army for approval of his plan. It was almost noon, and timely action was vital. Convinced that this was the correct course of action, he ordered the 27th to head for Chindong-ni although he had no approval from any higher headquarters for this action.

When he got to Masan, Michaelis came upon the newly-arrived advance CP of the 25th Division. From there, he again tried unsuccessfully to contact GEN Church at the 24th Division CP. Then he tried calling Eighth Army again. This time he reached the Chief of Staff, COL Landrum. He listened to Michaelis' proposal, approved it and told him to continue trying to contact Church. Landrum briefed Walker when he returned to the Army CP later in the day. The Eighth Army G3 Section informed Church of the 27th Infantry move and the new troop deployments west of Masan.

LTC Michaelis halted his regiment at Chindong-ni the afternoon of Aug. 1. He and his two battalion commanders, Check and Murch, went forward to some hills near Kogan-ni to confer with GEN Church, who had just arrived. Church ordered Michealis to deploy a battalion on the Kogan-ni hills. One battalion of the 27th and one from the 19th were to conduct an attack the next day toward Chinju, meeting at the Muchon-ni road fork. Each battalion would have a medium tank platoon attached to it. Attack time was to be 6 a.m., Aug. 2.

The 2/27 occupied the Kogan-ni position, about 7 miles west of Chindong-ni. Co. E was deployed astride the road at Pongam-ni, 3 miles farther west. The 1/27 went into an assembly area behind 2/27, and the regimental CP was established in a schoolhouse at the base of a high hill mass at Chindong-ni.

Meantime, COL Moore had ordered 1/19 to move from the Chinju pass directly back to new positions at the Notch. The battalion arrived in an assembly area 2 miles short of the Notch about 2 p.m. LTC Rhea remained at the pass with an M20 armored car as a rear guard. About an hour after the battalion withdrew, two North Koreans approached the rear guard in a captured American jeep. Rhea's group killed the enemy soldiers, recovered the jeep, then withdrew to the Notch. There, Rhea was ordered to reconnoiter the area before emplacing his battalion, so it was evening before he actually received orders to deploy his command at the Notch.

Forrest Klienman (S3, 1/19) described the Notch area this way. The mountain "was king of all the ground as far as the eye could see," he wrote in the January 1961 issue of *Argosy* magazine. "It loomed against the sultry sky like a gigantic oriental dragon guarding the way to Masan and Pusan. Near the rump of its horny spine was a deep notch where the road from Chinju wiggled up and over. A long railroad tunnel pierced its tail. Elsewhere, its hide was scaled with gnarled trees and brush." In truth, the massive mountain stretched north of the Notch for about 5 miles rising to a series of peaks ranging from 456 to 591 meters.

The entire 19th Infantry on Aug. 1 amounted to only 1,273 personnel. The untested 1/29 had a reported strength of 745 and its battered sister 3d Battalion only 317. The entire force totalled 2,335 men in four battalions.

The defense order was oral, wrote Kleinman. The 1/19, at about half strength, would occupy the notch and the ridge to the north. A provisional ROK battalion (LTC Oh) of COL Min's command would extend the line from just south of the Notch southwest along the ridge. The 2/19 was in reserve. Late in the afternoon, 1/29 arrived at Chungam-ni.

Kleinman recalled that the 1/19 officers were oriented about the defense plan using a terrain sketch which had been hastily drawn on a piece of a C-ration case. "On paper, the plan looked pretty good," he wrote.

"It was only about 1400 (2 p.m.) when the head of the column toiled up to the Notch," Kleinman continued. "The men were thoroughly exhausted." Although, by this time, they were carrying only the items essential to an infantryman, weapon, ammunition, helmet, canteen, bayonet and entrenching tool (and some a poncho or raincoat), "it took every spark of leadership and drive that the weary officers could summon to keep the men moving up, up, up the spine of the ridge." These soldiers had been fighting or moving now ever since Taejon, without pause. They were mentally and physically exhausted, but they finally got into position. That evening, the ROK battalion moved in on 1/19's left.

The 1/19 and ROK battalion were deployed as follows: A/19 on the right of the line, north of the Notch, with Co. B to its left. Co. C (- one platoon) carried the line to the Notch. One platoon of Co. C was south of the Notch. The ROK battalion was farther southeast, covering the left flank and overlooking a railroad tunnel. Two batteries of the 13th FAB were in support. Just before dawn, the enemy attacked the left flank, manned by the ROK battalion. The flank was refused, and the North Koreans were unable to dent it. They bounced from one tight ROK unit perimeter to the next. Finally, as they stretched out farther, using the railway embankment for cover, they exposed themselves to attack from the rear by a ROK unit which had been detached to the far hill. Caught in a deadly crossfire, the enemy was defeated and withdrew in disorder.

The story from the right flank, held by A/19, however, was one of disaster. Under cover of darkness, the enemy climbed up the ridge in front and flank of the company, quietly infiltrating its perimeter. The enemy's close-in dawn assault all but destroyed Co. A; one officer and 40 men were all that escaped. The sheer exhaustion of the men of Co. A nullified "professional knowledge, practical experience, training and even the adrenalin of fear," as Forrest Kleinman so aptly put it.

By dawn, both the 1/19 and ROK battalion were fully engaged all along the line in a furious fire fight. There were no reserves to retake the Co. A positions. Fortunately, the 13th FAB had direct observation on that area. Artillery fire into the enemy produced deadly tree bursts. The en-

emy soon broke and ran down hill in all directions. When Co. B later extended its line into the former Able Co. position, they found many North Korean dead. (See Chapter Notes.)

Often the right soldier at the right place at the right time makes the difference. Such a man that day was MSG Edward (Moose) Hoffman. Hoffman took over a 75mm recoilless rifle when all of its crew became casualties. He skillfully sniped at enemy soldiers trying to crawl forward, some with machine guns. His gun commanded all approaches to the Notch from the center and left front.

His marksmanship created heavy enemy casualties. When an enemy tank came into view, he switched to armor piercing ammunition and scored a hit with his first round. The tank never had a chance to fire. Regimental commander COL Moore crawled up to Hoffman's gun position and promoted the sergeant to lieutenant on the spot.

Stung by Hoffman's success in cutting down their troops, the enemy concentrated on him with mortars and machine guns. Bullets ripped through his clothing, but he stayed with that 75 until the enemy was repulsed. Although his clothing was torn by bullets and he suffered severe concussion, "the medics couldn't find a single scratch on his charmed hide," Kleinman reported.

All of a sudden the battlefield fell silent. Then, over the hill from the rear came the tanks leading 1/29 on its attack. The 1/29 still had over 700 men, and had not yet been worn down like other commands by one battle after the other. COL Moore selected this battalion to make the attack toward Chinju possibly because it was the strongest under his command.

Five M-4 medium tanks of the first platoon, Det. A (CPT James H. Harvey), 8072d Medium Tank Battalion, spearheaded the battalion. LT Donald E. Bernard led this platoon. Four M8 armored cars and an engineer platoon also were attached to the battalion.

When assembled at 5:30 a.m. on Aug. 2, the tanks and armored cars led out, each with five infantrymen from C/29 on board. The remainder of the battalion, mounted on 22 trucks and a number of jeeps followed this armored spearhead. The order of march was Co. C, A, D (less attachments to rifle companies) and Co. B, moving off from Chungam-ni at 6:15 a.m. Thirty minutes later the head of the column passed through the lines of 1/19 at the Notch. LTC Rhea was surprised to see the column. Through some error, he had never received a copy of the order, which had been written and disseminated for this attack.

About 12 or 14 vehicles had cleared the pass and were on their way down the southern slope when the enemy opened fire. The tanks came upon North Koreans crawling up a roadside ditch about 100 yards below the crest of the pass. The tanks clanked slowly forward, machinegunning as they went. Some North Koreans ran into the woods bordering both sides of the road. Hatch open, the lead tank proceeded some 400 to 500 yards down the slope when an enemy mortar round struck it, killing the entire crew. The knocked-out tank blocked the road. As the column stopped, it was swept by the fire of three enemy machine guns which were emplaced

along the road just 200 yards below the crest of the Notch. The 1st Platoon, Co. C virtually was wiped out by this fire as the men jumped off the tanks.

LTC Wilson, farther back in the column, jumped from his jeep and ran forward when he heard this heavy firing to the front. As he reached the crest of the hill, LTC Rhea ran up and shouted, "You better be careful — that ground down by the pond is enemy territory. My men were fighting them when your tanks came by." The attack by 1/29 had run head-on into an enemy force which was moving forward again to attack 1/19 and ROKs.

"We bailed out of those trucks into this big deep drainage ditch on the upper side of the road. It had foliage in it," wrote LT Nicewander (D/29). "We found the ditch was occupied by some North Korean soldiers who had been working their way up using the ditch as cover to attack. Some people actually jumped in on top of them. There was some pretty hectic close combat there for awhile. We lost a few people but we killed all the North Koreans who were in the ditch.... I had 2 men killed and 1 wounded."

PFC Charles L. Watson of the 60mm mortar section of C/29 was one of the 400 men assigned to battalions of the 29th just before they sailed for Korea.

"We moved through the Pass and...got about 300 yards...and the North Koreans opened up on us [from] above and below," he recalled. "They knocked out the armored car and leading tanks.... I was on the last truck [of Co. C] and 3 of us got out of it — my squad leader, first gunner and myself." In the ensuing melee, Watson wrote, some of the men from 1/19 mistakenly fired on members of 1/29. Enemy soldiers and those from 1/29 were intermingled for a time in actual hand-to-hand combat. In endeavoring to help fellow soldiers some men from 1/19 apparently inadvertently killed or wounded members of the 29th. David M. Williams, also of C/29, reported the same thing.

When the column came under enemy fire and stopped, "we dispersed into the ditch to the right of the road," Williams wrote. "We found some enemy soldiers already there. We had to first engage them.... A truck in the convoy had been hit and was spilling gasoline into the ditch," he continued. "We had already dispatched the enemy in the ditch so I saw the danger of a fire if weapons were discharged. I yelled for everyone to get out of the ditch." Jackie Mann of Co. C did not hear William's call and fired his rifle. The gasoline was ignited and Mann suffered fatal burns.

Elements of Co. C and others were ordered to attack the hill on the right of the road to drive the enemy away. When the attackers got to the high ground, they met a unit of the 19th. "They had been firing down on us and across the road and over our head[s] at the enemy on the high ground to our front," Williams wrote.

There, Williams met Jerry Goulett of C/19, with whom he had gone through basic training. During the attack, Williams recalled, "we received fire from three directions and it was later determined that we were getting friendly fire." David's squad leader, CPL Norman Weidy, and PVT Jackie Mann from the squad, were among the casualties that day.

PVT Edward F. Balbi of A/29 was at the top of the Notch. His unit was off its trucks when his squad leader, SGT Baker, came from a briefing and announced that the enemy was going to be hit with an air strike. Two F-51s came over, but instead of the enemy, homed in on the troops at the Notch. "I said, 'You better hunt a hole, because those SOBs are going to strafe us!'" Balbi wrote. "Baker hollered, 'He's right, hit it!' I dived under a truck and our Air Force machinegunned and rocketed us. When I got out from under the truck I discovered my safe haven was a truck load of mortar ammunition."

When the enemy fire stopped the column, Balbi and his companions jumped from their truck into what he called a "barrow pit" — part of the ditch and pond area along the road. There, they found enemy soldiers. "It developed into a fight that lasted the rest of the morning and into the afternoon. When your weapon went empty there was no time to reload; you just used it like a baseball bat — fought with your bayonet, fists, teeth — anything else you could get your hands on. We tried to regroup and withdraw into the 19th's lines but when we did the North Koreans went with us and the 19th opened up, and it was back to the barrow pit for more hand-to-hand combat."

Finally, the enemy was beaten back. Overlooking the road on the right, Balbi recalled was "a hill at least 500 feet higher than us, and we could see enemy activity." Battalion commander LTC Wilson "called our rag tag bunch together," wrote Balbi, "and said we had to take the high ground, He placed SGT Baker in charge of the assault." Co. C joined Co. A in this attack.

"Needless to say," Balbi continued, "we were not in the mood to let the North Koreans get any semblance of the upper hand, so despite our exhaustion and aches and pains we went up the hill in all its heat like a mad hornet." Gaining the top, the men were all hot and thirsty. PVT William Brown said he had seen a spring on the way up, so SGT Baker detailed PVT Balbi to take two volunteers and go back to fill the unit's canteens. "So Brown, I and Red Dixon go clanking down the hill," Balbi recalled. Rounding a curve in some trees, they ran into five or six North Koreans. The three GIs dropped the canteens and ran one way. The equally startled enemy soldiers ran in another direction. The three men soon stopped. "Finally Dixon said, 'We can take those bastards and get our canteens back! I'm thirsty!' Well we spooked them over on the next ridge, filled our canteens, climbed back up the hill, caught the North Koreans in the open and had a turkey shoot," Balbi concluded. As the men began to dig in, a runner from LTC Wilson delivered a message for them to pull back.

Jesus Rodriguez was in the same platoon as Balbi. Rodriguez recalled Platoon SGT Hubert Baker and Platoon Leader 2LT Frank Griffin were ordered to take the high ground. "It was very hot," he said, "and I wanted to travel light so I had gotten rid of my entrenching tool. This is where I learned that you never get rid of your entrenching tool or your canteen." He recalled struggling up the hill in a squad diamond formation. Making it to the top, the unit emerged onto a flat area. "There we were taking fire and people started digging a foxhole.... Here I was with no entrenching tool, but I saw a GI up ahead of me

behind a log. So I ran up and made a dash for him." Throwing himself down beside the prone GI, Rodriguez said, "Hi. Move over." When Rodriguez had dropped down, he pushed the man. "The guy rolled over, he was dead," Rodriguez said. "I took his entrenching tool and...started digging a little pit...and finally [had a hole] that I could get into.... After a while we moved up and we cleared the mountain."

"The next morning," Rodriguez continued, "my squad was selected to go down into the Notch and retrieve the vehicles. SGT Baker led the patrol. "We had a fire fight." After the fight, the Americans retrieved the vehicles. "And we made it back," he concluded.

Nicewander, farther forward on the road, wrote, "We couldn't get up out of the ditch and then the vehicles began catching fire from the machine gun fire. We literally had to release the brake on some vehicles we thought were going to explode and let them roll off the side of the mountain."

Some time during the day, Nicewander was wounded. He was knocked unconscious and was hit by shell fragments in the right hip. "I wasn't really hurt too badly," he wrote, "except my back bothered me. By darkness I was back up on the hill with a compress wrapped around me."

Harold Gamble of the 29th medics wrote, "Our battalion aid station did not make it through the Pass, so we set up in defilade about 100 feet from the Pass on the east side of the road. MSG William Marchbanks (D/29) set up his [two] mortars just across the road from us on the high side with a clear view through the Pass. He nearly burned his mortars out that day. MSG [Frank C.] Plass [a platoon sergeant B/29] set up heavy weapons and recoilless rifles nearby. The battle lasted until late in the afternoon when it began to slack off."

Gamble wrote that an air panel was placed on the slope of Hill 152 above the site of the aid station on the right of the road. "So the Air Force should have been able to clearly see it. Yet they made three passes firing on us."

CPT Robert G. Brown, surgeon of 1/29, wrote that his aid station treated an estimated 120 wounded, and he observed another 60 KIA there. He recalled having treated LT Nicewander for shrapnel wounds of the right leg and hip.

Raymond Reis ran the 1/29 message center. "We became filler personnel, liaison, shotgun — attached to others," he wrote. He also remembered the Air Force strafing the battalion on Aug. 2.

Darold R. Freeman was a PFC in B/29 in this battle. Charles Watson wrote that Freeman was riding the lead tank at the time of the ambush. Miraculously, he survived the battle.

During the battle, some North Koreans in the ditches advanced using captured Americans, their hands tied, as human shields. The battles in the ditches resulted in about 30 GI casualties.

One effect of the ambush was to disorganize and intermingle the companies which were attacked. COL Wilson energetically and forcefully reorganized these units, often at great peril to his own life. He brought B/29, some 62 men, from the rear of the column and placed it on line with 1/19. COL Moore placed himself at the CP of 1/19 at the beginning of the battle and remained there most of the day, directing the defense.

Soon after the ambush of 1/29 was sprung,

fighting erupted all along the front of 1st Battalion, 19th Infantry. Appleman wrote that B/19 started up the slope west of the Notch the previous day, but exhausted from the continuous action over the previous week, stopped short of the crest. The enemy caught most of the company asleep in a pre-dawn attack, killing the unit commander and a number of others and driving the remainder of the company from the hill. This sounds like the same episode Forrest Kleinman ascribed to A/29, as recounted earlier. Appleman also confirms that three U.S. aircraft strafed and rocketed U.S. troops at the Notch that day.

The enemy troops which had displaced the right flank company of 1/19 placed flanking fire down toward the Notch. The attack by C/29, aided by fire from the 13th FAB dispersed this enemy force. However, in the attack C/29 lost 12 KIA. COL Wilson believed that half of these were caused by "friendly fire" from nearby American positions.

There was a gap of about a 1 1/2 miles between the ROKs under COL Min and the left flank of 1/19. Enemy snipers got into this gap and killed five GIs by shots in the back of the head. That afternoon, enemy mortar fire east of the Notch also killed and wounded a number of other men.

Observing troops moving along the railroad toward Chungam-ni, COL Moore ordered part of 2/19 to intercept them. The force proved to be COL Min's ROKs. Fire from both the enemy and U.S. soldiers had forced them to withdraw.

The 3/29 and later B/29 had been sent to fill the gap between 1/19 and the ROKs to the left. Enemy troops tried to slip around the flank again, coming out of the railroad tunnel. A platoon of F/19 charged and drove them back.

As the battle died down in midafternoon, a squad from A/19 patrolled forward of the knocked out vehicles on the road, killing a few enemy soldiers lurking nearby. The squad then set up a roadblock about 100 yards beyond the knocked out tanks. Other soldiers evacuated the wounded and retrieved most of the vehicles. The enemy simply disappeared from in front of the 19th by that evening.

U.S. losses at the Notch numbered about 90, Appleman wrote. This does not square with the letter from CPT Brown, 1/29 surgeon, who wrote that his aid station treated "an estimated 120 wounded" and that he observed another 60 KIA.

Although enemy losses are unknown, there is strong evidence from information obtained later that there were two or more battalions of the *NK 6th Division* in this fight.

Attack of 1/27 Inf - August 2 (See Chapter Notes.)

When some writers try to capsulize events in history, they sometimes distort what happened, sacrificing accuracy to brevity. This appears to be the case with Russell Spurr's *Enter the Dragon*. His description of the attack by 1/27 on Aug. 2 and the fight at the schoolhouse the following morning are not correct. (Pp. 24-33) This author was a member of the attack force and was also at the schoolhouse at Chindong-ni.

This is the true account of the 1/27 attack and the battle at the Chindong-ni schoolhouse:

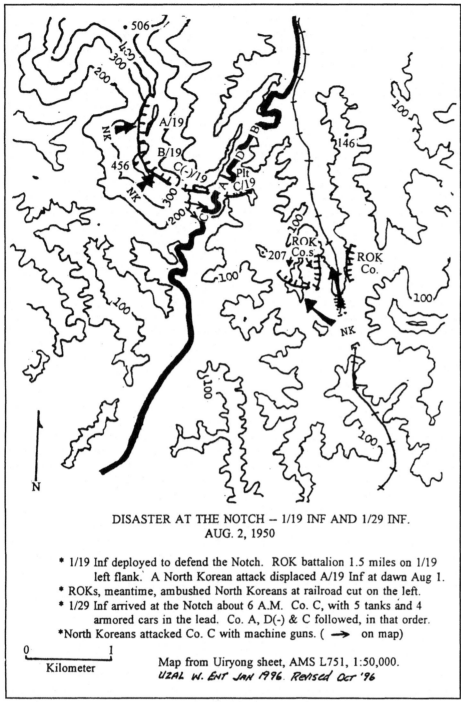

DISASTER AT THE NOTCH -- 1/19 INF AND 1/29 INF.
AUG. 2, 1950

* 1/19 Inf deployed to defend the Notch. ROK battalion 1.5 miles on 1/19
  left flank. A North Korean attack displaced A/19 Inf at dawn Aug 1.
* ROKs, meantime, ambushed North Koreans at railroad cut on the left.
* 1/29 Inf arrived at the Notch about 6 A.M. Co. C, with 5 tanks and 4
  armored cars in the lead. Co. A, D(-) & C followed, in that order.
* North Koreans attacked Co. C with machine guns. (⟶ on map)

0   1
|_____|
Kilometer

Map from Uiryong sheet, AMS L751, 1:50,000.
UZAL W. ENT JAN 1996. Revised OCT '96

Map 16 (Courtesy of Uzal W. Ent)

LTC Check's 1/27 moved out of its assembly area behind Murch's 2/27 at 4 a.m. on Aug. 2. Four M4A3 tanks of 1LT Herman D. Norrell's platoon led the column, with a platoon of A/27 riding the tanks. The remainder of the battalion was mounted on jeeps and trucks, including the remainder of Co. A, with Check's command group following A. Co. B was next in line, followed by D, C and the artillery (A/8th FAB), attached in this case to 1/27. Check expected to meet 1/29 at Muchon-ni.

The column travelled forward a number of miles with no contact. Then the tanks and leading platoon caught an enemy platoon, still asleep, along the road. All but two enemy soldiers were quickly killed by riflemen and tank machine guns; the two survivors were captured. Two small groups of the enemy were surprised and killed in this manner. One of the dead was apparently a paymaster, for he had a satchel full of North Korean money.

By mid-afternoon, 1/27 arrived at the Muchon-ni road fork, where it met and surprised a number of enemy troops. An enemy truck column just had come from the Chinju pass, laden with supplies, part of a much larger enemy truck convoy from Chinju. Many of the trucks were able to escape, but the North Koreans left behind 10 vehicles (2 1/2-ton trucks and jeeps) loaded with food, clothing, ammunition, medicines and other supplies. The appearance of Americans with tanks on the road caused the convoy to beat a hasty retreat. An air strike was called in on it as it sped back toward Chinju.

Of course, the 29th's column never appeared, having been stopped several miles away at the Notch. Check dismounted his troops just beyond Muchon-ni and sent the trucks back to Chindong-ni, since he did not want to risk having them captured. Only the heavy mortar platoon and artillery battery retained their vehicles. With the tanks and Co. A leading, the column set off again. Check sent messengers back to Michaelis, but none got through.

There is a 90-degree turn to the left in the road where it enters the Chinju pass, and the first of a series of high, steep hills which flank the road for miles begin there. The enemy emplaced three 76mm AT guns about 75 yards to the right of the road after it makes that turn to the south. Enemy small arms fire sent the infantry to seek shelter behind the tanks. In quick succession, the second and third tanks were knocked out by the AT guns. LT Norrell's tank, third in line, caught fire, and the lieutenant was wounded. The gunner in the number two tank was killed, and seven other tankers were wounded. Battery A, 8th FAB, quickly notified. The guns were rapidly unhitched, trails dropped on the road and the battery soon silenced the anti-tank weapons and drove their crews away.

There also were infantry casualties. Among these was 2LT Walter J. Scoggin, leader of Co. A's Weapons Platoon, killed instantly by a bullet to the head as he tried to get a fix on enemy positions for his 60mm mortar section. 1LT Bertram Bishop, commander of the HM Co. also was seriously wounded. One of his platoons was attached to 1/27. Bishop had decided to accompany the recon because he had already lost two of his platoon leaders. His company had the reputation of being one of the best, if not the best, in the regiment. When the Heavy Mortar Co. was first organized in 1949, he was appointed commander, although he was only a second lieutenant. All company officers also were second lieutenants.

"I rode the...second tank in the column," wrote Philip File. It was he who manned the tank's .50-cal machine gun when the column came upon the enemy platoon in the ditch. They were soon dispatched, except for two prisoners. The head of the column, he recalled, now began to have "little firefights" about every mile or so.

"In the afternoon the tank I was riding got holed by an anti-tank gun, severely wounding the crew," File continued. He dismounted and engaged the enemy gun crew with rifle fire while others evacuated the wounded tankers. "I directed the third tank to throw a couple of HE rounds up the draw where the enemy AT gun was sited. That flushed the gun crew out and they started running down the nose of the hill to get behind the tanks. They were silhouetted like ducks in a shooting gallery and I picked all seven off with one clip of ammo."

Cressie Johnson from Co. D was attached to Co A. This is what he wrote about the advance: "A first skirmish netted prisoners, a second...surprised about 30 sleeping North Koreans and none got away. Another defense line in a ditch running perpendicular to our road gave the tanks a field day as they pulled up to the end of the ditch and machinegunned all of them to pieces. It was fun to be dishing it out for a change."

The leading tank went around a sharp bend to the left in the road "and an explosion took place with an outbreak of cannon fire. Black smoke poured upward and we worried about the tanks," wrote Johnson. Two had been hit and momentarily knocked out.

"Small arms fire raked the road...and we jumped into the shallow ditch away from the firing source." They then crawled to a position where they could stand up. "[PFC] Harvey (a WW II infantry veteran) dashed past me and hit the ground. Paused and did it again.... I gained a lot of respect for his guts.... I imitated Harvey and soon the rest of the platoon repeated the combat lesson," Johnson continued.

"I now had cover but an enemy tracer from a .52-cal anti-tank rifle [commonly called an "elephant gun" by the GIs] hit a jeep's spare tire and the tire started to burn," Johnson wrote. As he watched, SSG Harold Bemis and a man named Hoak crawled up to the jeep and slowly loosened the burning tire. The two men removed the burning tire and extinguished the flames on the jeep — all while under enemy fire.

"MSG Sheldon took a telephone and a spool of wire and said, 'I won't be back unless they shoot the phone out of my hand,'" wrote Johnson. "In a few minutes he was back...his handset had been shot into two pieces when he brought it up to his ear to call in a fire mission."

When Johnson and another man went to the aid of some wounded, the other man was hit in the helmet by a bullet. It struck the helmet beside his ear, "split about a half inch of the helmet and lodged there," Johnson wrote. Except for some temporary loss of hearing in that ear, the man was unhurt.

"LTC Check...with that thoughtful school teacher way about him...made the cool decisions that saved a lot of lives," Johnson recalled. "I loved and respected that little man and I believe the whole battalion did too."

Frank Sandell of Co. A recalled making contact with the enemy and exchanging gunfire. He did not recall "mortar or artillery fire coming in on us...." LT Gordon Jung, commanding Co. B, the second unit in the column, wrote, "a hillside in front of us exploded with North Korean fire. Bertram Bishop...was hit." But in the ensuing battle, he wrote, "We weren't hurt too badly."

When the AT and other enemy fire halted the column, the infantry farther back headed for nearby ditches and hummocks of ground and scanned the terrain. On the left rose a high ridge; on the right were acres and acres of rice paddies. The 1st and 3d platoons of Co. B were sent up the ridge on the left in order to secure it and bring fire on the enemy across the valley at the ambush site. Meantime, the 2d Platoon, under MSG James R. Wilson, rushed out into the rice paddies, then made a turn to attack the enemy-held ridge from the flank. By this time, friendly mortar and artillery fire had begun to paste the enemy-held ridge.

Soon, the enemy roadblock was eliminated. Volunteer infantrymen took over as drivers of the two tanks which had lost their crews. The advance began again, this time with infantry deployed on the hills on either side of the road. The pace slowed to about 1 to 1 1/2 MPH.

There was some enemy opposition. File was now riding on the lead tank. He manned the vehicle's .50-cal machine gun. "We started getting quite a bit of small-arms fire and some hits

on the tank that seemed to be 20mm," he wrote. "I fired the .50 at targets of opportunity 'till the...crew had no more ammo...."

Some time between 5 and 5:30 p.m. a liaison plane dropped a message to LTC Check. As he "read the contents...I could see his mouth tighten," wrote Johnson. The message read: "Return. Road cut behind you all the way. Lead with tanks if possible. Will give you artillery support when within range."

About 7 a.m. that day at Chindong-ni COL Michaelis was informed by COL Moore that his attack force had been stopped right after it had jumped off. Moore also said that he would be hard pressed to hold his position against the enemy. In late morning and early afternoon, Michaelis also learned that the enemy was on the road behind Check, cutting off his battalion, and that E/27 was in a heavy fight with the enemy. This prompted him to send the message for Check to return a little after 4 p.m.

During the day E/27 at Pongam-ni was attacked by an estimated enemy battalion which had followed Check's column. A 2d Battalion relief force helped the beleaguered unit get back to the main battalion position at Kogan-ni, 3 miles to the east. Other enemy troops ambushed a platoon of A/65 ECB south of Chindong-ni on the Kosong-Sachon road. The platoon lost heavily in men and equipment. These forays proved that the enemy was moving on Masan in strength.

LTC Check got his column turned around, with two tanks leading and two bringing up the rear. First Platoon, Co. B found itself part of the lead elements. In briefing the troops, the battalion XO concluded by indicating that he would be located with the litter jeeps. The men who overheard him, however, took it to mean that he expected a great number of casualties on the withdrawal, so he would be right behind them to pick up the wounded in the litter jeeps.

The head of the column got through without much contact, but the enemy sniped and snarled along the flanks and rear. Soon after the withdrawal started, Check decided to load everyone on all available vehicles to move more quickly. More than a hundred men piled onto the four tanks, while others jumped onto any vehicle or trailer that was close. Artillery fire from 155mm howitzers, the 8th FAB's 105s and HM Co. fell on either flank of the withdrawing column.

Cressie Johnson wrote, "Although we had kicked butt good that day, we were now in trouble with the enemy close in behind us. We piled onto anything we could.... I crawled onto the top of a tractor of ammunition and we ran the gauntlet back down the road...."

PVT Ray Roberts, A/27, led the column out in one of the damaged tanks, hoping that the company could keep it. At one point during the withdrawal, the column was delayed by a road wash-out. Another halt was called by LTC Check so that plasma could be administered to a wounded man. Battalion losses were 21, including 2 KIA. The enemy lost an estimated 250, plus 12 prisoners.

Phil File and two squads of his platoon rode on the last tank. "We seemed to have stirred up a hornets nest with our probe," he wrote. In negotiating the last hill before Chindong-ni, the tank driver accidently stalled the tank. A major in a jeep behind the tank attributed the problem to

the extra weight of the men on the tank and ordered them off. As a result, File and his two squads hoofed it into Chindong-ni long after the rest of the battalion. The regimental XO met File and his men, congratulated them on a fine job and told them to go on the hillock above the schoolhouse and get some sleep. "There was no need to post security," File wrote, since the XO said that "the regimental security platoon was out in front of us. Unknown to me, the security platoon leader thought we were relieving him and he pulled his men out of position and went back to the schoolhouse to sleep." The security platoon was providing close-in protection, not security on a perimeter.

In the dim light of a Coleman lantern, officers of 1/27 crowded into a room of the schoolhouse to be briefed. The companies were to move up and occupy the slopes above the schoolhouse (regimental CP). "What about security?" someone asked. "Don't worry about security," came the reply. "The South Koreans are handling it." One man awake in each squad would suffice. The weary men climbed to the designated positions and prepared for a well-earned sleep. A few took off their boots.

Bullets for Breakfast - Fight at the Chindong-ni Schoolhouse, 1/27 - August 3

Leaders of the *NK 6th Division* knew that U.S. artillery was positioned at the base of a hill near the village of Chindong-ni. They also knew that neither the ROKs nor the Americans were in the Masan area in strength. They had fought American troops to a standstill at the Notch and had met a U.S. battalion entering the Chinju Pass, but had seen it withdraw under pressure heading toward Masan. The North Koreans felt that the force at the Notch could be flanked out of position and that the artillery at Chindong-ni could be destroyed by a dawn infantry attack.

What they did not know was that the 27th regimental CP, service area, 1/27, A/11 FAB (155mm) and all of the 8th FAB were at or near the Chindong-ni schoolhouse at the time.

Marguerite Higgins of the New York *Herald Tribune* and Harold H. Martin of the *Saturday Evening Post* and several officers of the 27th Regimental staff were at breakfast the next morning, Aug. 3. It was a deluxe breakfast of powdered eggs and coffee. Suddenly, bullets slammed in from all directions, sending shards of glass from the windows and splinters from the walls as they punched into the building. A burst from an automatic weapon blew the coffeepot off the table. Then a grenade exploded, and CPT William Hawkes, an S2 officer, was hit in the right hand by a fragment.

Everyone dove for cover as bullets riddled the building. Three enemy POWs were killed. The bullets came down from the hill at an angle through the wall and ripped up floor boards. One after the other, survivors dove out windows and doors. Outside, confusion reigned. Some troops were firing back up the hill, not realizing that other GIs were up there. Michaelis, company commanders and others began to grab some of these soldiers and get them organized. One young soldier "froze" on a machine gun, firing it at U.S.

vehicles and men. A well-aimed shot by an officer winged him and stopped the fire.

Higgins recorded that as she and Martin crouched behind a stone fence, her teeth chattered uncontrollably. Martin, meantime, had his notebook out, taking notes.

Regimental telephones had been pulled from the building and now were located between the stone fence and a radio truck. In the midst of the din of firing, shouts and explosions, division called. LTC Arthur C. Farthing, regimental XO, answered the phone and apologized for not being able to hear too well because of the noise.

Reports came in of more enemy troops assembling in a valley to the north, and that several hundred others had landed on the coast about a thousand yards away.

Michaelis, finally tiring of the chaos, went to the middle of the courtyard and shouted, "Cease firing!" Then, "Let's get organized and find out what we're shooting at." From that moment, the North Koreans lost their initial advantage.

Ernest Smith of Co. B's mess section was trying to light an immersion heater, used to heat water in a 32-gallon can. The stack of the heater was about eight feet high, and from a distance it could be mistaken for a mortar. "All hell broke loose," he wrote. Smith seized his rifle and ran behind the schoolhouse. "There I met [PFC] Hanas [and another man]. They were standing there with a machine gun but no ammunition. I said — and these were my exact words, 'Where the hell is the ammo?' Then we heard a woman's voice say, 'There it is over there.' We turned around... and it was a woman, a white woman. Her shirt was open and her bra was just hanging there.... We had never seen a white woman like that; maybe a Japanese woman but not a white woman." The three young men finally regained their wits, grabbed up some machine gun ammunition, headed for the hill and set up the gun.

"I never saw so many people in a mass confusion in all my life — in a way it was comical — the North Koreans were tripping over each other and running into one another. They looked like frogs in a hailstorm.... Oh, they were in bad shape," Smith wrote. When things calmed down, he returned to the company mess area. CPL Robert B. Clevenger, the unit supply sergeant, came up and gave Smith a big hug, saying, "I thought you were hit." Smith told him what he had done. Then the two men went over to the immersion heaters. Every one was holed over and over again by bullets. Every immersion heater from all the unit mess sections suffered a similar fate. If Smith had just "hit the dirt" there, instead of going with the machine gun team, he most certainly would have been killed or wounded.

Smith looked at Clevenger and said, "'Do you think Eaglebarger [SGT Jewell H. Eaglebarger, the mess sergeant] still wants some hot water?' We laughed," Smith wrote, "and went ahead and prepared breakfast."

CPT Logan Weston, commanding Co A, wrote that his unit was ordered to a "sugar loaf hill north of the school." He recalled that he was told that the battalion was now in reserve and could dig in the "next day after getting a little rest. I took my commo and aid man to the top of the hill, for good radio reception, and grabbed a cat nap."

"At first light I awakened...and...far to the north [saw] a column coming in single file toward us." He tried unsuccessfully to raise either battalion or regiment on the radio, then sent his radioman back to regiment for confirmation of the column's identity. "My messenger came back and said it had to be South Koreans," he wrote. But CPT Weston kept observing this body of men moving closer, counting 76 of them walking on the rice paddy dikes in the valley below. They were being led by a man dressed in white, and looked suspicious to him. Weston sent his messenger back to regiment, and returned with the same response: They are friendly, go back to sleep. By this time, the captain's radio was working, so he called regiment for a third time to report his sighting.

As he watched the approaching men, he saw the man in white receive some kind of payment and step off the dike. His radioman got the same reply from regiment as before — the area was safe. By now, the party of men had reached the bottom of the hill and spread out in a skirmish line.

Weston ordered some of his men up to oppose the advancing skirmishers. He was convinced they were enemy soldiers. Several of them saw him and opened fire. He returned fire, "but one of their first rounds splintered my rifle stock," he wrote, "and cut a muscle and vein in my right arm." But he kept firing from the hip, while more of his company came up on line to oppose the enemy. An aidman applied a compress to Weston's wound. "I then stood up just in time to receive another hit in the right thigh," he continued. "By now my skirmish line was returning fire so I went to the aid station for dressings." After being treated, Weston located a case of hand grenades and dragged it back up the hill with him, using his good left arm.

As he regained his company line, he "saw the head of [one of his platoon sergeants] nearly bisected by a machine gun." Weston, located the enemy gun about 20 yards away and eliminated it with a grenade he threw with his left arm. Then he was shot in the chest, but the enemy had been stopped and he felt that he finally could go to the aid station for good. He was credited with taking out 27 enemy infantrymen and two machine guns that day.

"I was rudely awakened by a nervous young North Korean standing at my feet spraying the ground around me with his burp gun.... I must have been the first American soldier he ever saw. I know for sure I was the last one he ever saw," wrote Phil File. "The sun was already pretty high and on the knoll with me were about a half dozen North Koreans shooting the men still sleeping." File shot them as fast as he could pull the trigger of his M1, "and then started lobbing grenades over the brow of the hill to repel any North Koreans on their way up." At this time, MSG Miller and a man named Marne ran up to join File. "Before they reached my position they were hit by automatic fire — Miller was KIA and Marne...died of wounds. The North Korean who shot them jumped to his feet and started to charge.... I took my time and watched the astonished look on his face when the rifle bullet hit him just above the navel."

As File engaged the enemy, he witnessed CPT Weston firing and being hit and his return-

ing be hit again. "In the meantime, I was having good success," he wrote. File took ammunition and grenades from dead GIs and kept firing and throwing grenades at the enemy.

Co. A's firing line built up as the morning wore on. "The North Koreans on the hillside above us were a nuisance. A lieutenant came up with a .50-cal machine gun on a ground mount...." File pointed out targets to the officer and his gun crew. File got down behind the gun"and fired a couple of bursts to indicate targets. Apparently the lieutenant thought that looked like fun." He took over firing the machine gun, but got off only three or four bursts before an answering burst of enemy machine gun fire badly wounded him. This was 2LT Joe A. Font, a platoon leader of Co.A. Only one other lieutenant was wounded that day, 1LT David E. Kinlaw, 1/27 motor officer.

File now noted that things seemed to be pretty well under control, although he couldn't find any of his men alive. Since he had not eaten for over 24 hours, File decided to go down to the kitchen. "A cook gave me a can of peaches and while I was eating, the regimental XO came upon me. He jumped right on me. 'File,' he demanded, 'what in hell are you doing down here? Get up there where the fighting is!'" With a shrug of his shoulders, File went back up the hill. There, he and an artillery FO spotted trucks 700 to 800 yards away, covered with boughs for camouflage. They apparently had come for the troops which had made the abortive attack on the schoolhouse. "Before the FO could give the target designation to the [artillery] guns, the trucks were loaded...and gone," he wrote. File went about rounding up survivors of his platoon. He had 11 men; less than two weeks before it had numbered 40.

SGT Frank Sandell, 4th Platoon, Co. A, recalled that when the battalion returned to the schoolhouse, Co. A was on the left and Co. B on the right on the hill above the schoolhouse. "Early next morning, August 3, I remember at break of day, I made a check of my squad to see if they were OK and to see what was going on," he said. "To our rear they had set up a mess hall .... I got a whiff of coffee and decided I'd go back and try to mooch a cup.... No sooner did I get back than all hell broke loose" The North Koreans were on up the ridge behind the schoolhouse, above the Americans. "They were firing heavily down upon the schoolhouse grounds." Sandell wrote. He met CPL Mobly, also of the 4th Platoon, and the two men fired back at the enemy for a time, then climbed back up to join their unit. "It was a pretty heavy fight," he said. "We were successful in holding them off."

CPL Johnny Mahan of Co. A recalled that the unit lost a lot of men in the schoolhouse fight. "My platoon — the Second — moved to the hill left of the schoolhouse," he wrote. When Weston was wounded, 1LT John L. Buckley took command of Co. A, having commanded the unit in Japan. Buckley told Mahan to stay with him and the company headquarters. Mahan remembered the fight at the schoolhouse as the worst battle he experienced in three tours in Korea.

Richard S. Majcher (Co. C) recalled that his unit was getting ready for breakfast when the battle started, and seeing Maggie Higgins under a truck.

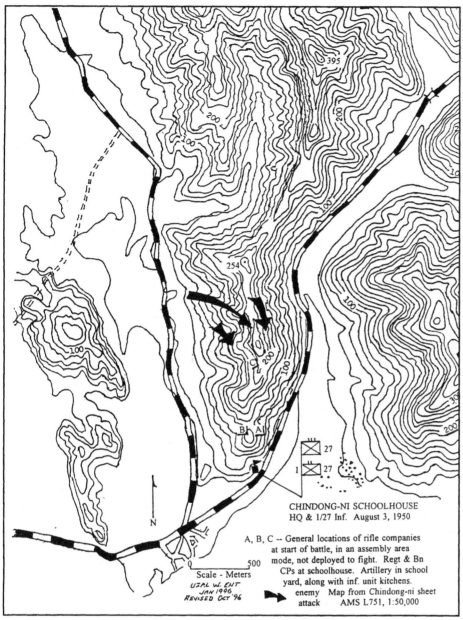

CHINDONG-NI SCHOOLHOUSE
HQ & 1/27 Inf. August 3, 1950

A, B, C -- General locations of rifle companies
at start of battle, in an assembly area
mode, not deployed to fight. Regt & Bn
CPs at schoolhouse. Artillery in school
yard, along with inf. unit kitchens.

▶ enemy   Map from Chindong-ni sheet
   attack   AMS L751, 1:50,000

Scale - Meters
0   500

UZAL W. ENT
JAN 1996,
REVISED OCT '96

Map 17 (Courtesy of Uzal W. Ent)

Hills just above and to the rear of the schoolhouse. The enemy attacked toward the schoolhouse from them. (Courtesy of Cressie Johnson, D/27 Infantry)

"I was sleeping under one of the 2 1/2 ton trucks and was awakened by the sound of burpguns," wrote 2LT Posey Starkey (P & A platoon leader). "The first thing I remember seeing was water spurting from holes in a 32 gallon can with an immersion heater in it. I grabbed a rifle from inside the truck and a bandoleer of ammunition and headed for what I remember as a potato patch on the east side of the schoolhouse." As he ran by the schoolhouse, men and Higgins were "diving out of the...windows. I added to the rifle fire from the group that had assembled on the hill. It included men from headquarters companies and some from the 155mm battery," he recalled. "When the North Koreans withdrew under counterattack from the rifle companies I returned to the schoolyard and began locating others [from his platoon]."

SFC Joseph T. Bass (Co. B) was near the regimental CP when the enemy attacked. He quickly organized 20 men, and on his own initiative took them some 500 yards behind the enemy. Bass, alone, was credited with killing ten of the enemy. The patrol aided substantially in driving the enemy from the vicinity of the schoolhouse. Later, Bass said modestly, "I don't know, I didn't do anything unusual."

SGT Arthur Rogers, mess sergeant for Co. A, was down in the schoolyard with other unit mess sections, busily preparing breakfast when the attack started. He and another man from his section quickly manned a .50-cal machine gun. When they ran out of ammunition, he dashed across 50 yards of schoolyard for more. The other man was killed, but Rogers quickly took over the gun and fired it "in a terrible rage," driving off about a platoon of the enemy.

Co. B was deployed on the lower slopes of the hill behind the schoolhouse. Shortly after daylight, the company area began receiving heavy small-arms and machine gun fire. The 27th Regimental Report for Aug. 3 indicates that the battle started at 7:15 a.m. The startled soldiers awakened, but could not see where the fire was coming from. Some of those who had removed their boots tried to get them back on. One such man in the 1st Platoon was killed by a shot from a .52 cal "Elephant Gun" while trying to get his boots back on. Many of the men scooted down out of the killing zone.

Upon entering the schoolyard where the howitzers were located, one lieutenant from Co. B slung his carbine over his shoulder and went to one of the big guns in the yard. The gun crews all had taken shelter in and between nearby buildings. He called to them to come out and move gun trails so that artillery fire could be delivered on the enemy on the hill above. As he called out, he tugged on one of the trails, unmindful of anything but getting a couple of guns turned to engage the enemy. In spite of his repeated calls for help and cursing, no artillerymen left shelter to assist. Finally, the lieutenant gave up in disgust and ducked between two buildings, but soon was brought back to his duty by a call for the men of Co. B to assemble. He ran to the assembly point, took charge of his platoon, and the company counterattacked up the hill with little trouble.

As the battle raged, mortars, recoilless rifles and 105mm artillery fire began falling on the enemy, who were being driven away by the counterattacking Americans.

117

LTC Augustus T. Terry Jr., commanding the 8th FAB across the road from the schoolhouse, observed a reinforcing enemy battalion approaching from the north in trucks. They were only about a thousand yards away on the Haman road. By the time the trucks stopped and began unloading, Terry's battalion took them under heavy and accurate fire. The survivors scattered.

"Rocky" Roquemore, Regimental Assistant S3, had already been dispatched forward on the morning of Aug. 3. He and a small advance party departed the schoolhouse at first light, enroute to the site of a new regimental CP. As a result, he was a spectator from the new CP site of the schoolhouse battle. He had no radio. Enemy fire "was hitting the road," he wrote, between him and the schoolhouse. "It might have been aimed at the 8th FA battalion emplaced south of the road," he continued. Then he "observed NKVA [North Korean Volunteer Army] infantry try unloading trucks...which the 8th FA took under fire. A .50-caliber [machine gun] at that point would really have raised hell with the enemy — my carbine would not reach [that far]."

Later that day, regiment moved to the new CP, about a mile forward of where it had been.

By 1 p.m., the enemy had been driven away. Patrols counted 400 enemy dead, many where the 8th FAB caught the reinforcing battalion. It was estimated that the enemy lost about 600 soldiers killed, wounded and captured. The 1/27 lost 13 KIA and 40 WIA: total American casualties in the battle were 60.

But the rifle companies of the battalion were mere shadows, like File's platoon in Co. A with only 12 men. The 1st Platoon, Co. B, had three four-man squads, armed with rifles, two BARs a .30-cal light machine gun and a 3.5 inch rocket launcher. Front-line strength of the rifle companies could not have been much over 50 to 60 men each.

In their attack on Aug. 2, 1/27 engaged elements of the *NK 14th* and *15th Regiments (6th Division)*. The 27th Regimental report for August 2-3 states that the *2d and 3d Battalions, 13th Regiment (6th Division)* took part in the schoolhouse attack. (Appleman states two battalions of the *14th Regiment*.) The initial attack was delivered by one battalion; the other was caught by artillery fire while detrucking. The enemy, based on Sobuk-san north of Chindong-ni, used commercial telephone lines. The Americans tapped into the lines and through interpreters, were able to monitor enemy conversations. On the night of Aug. 3, a translator overheard the *6th Division* commander reprimand the commander of the regiment which had attacked at the schoolhouse for losing so many men. The 1/27 Operations Report, Aug. 4-30, 1950, states that the enemy expected to find only an artillery battery at Chindong-ni and requested replacements and artillery support.

Appleman stated that the missions of the *14th* and *15th Regiments* were to cut the Masan road *(14th)* and capture the heights around it *(15th)*. When the *14th* failed to seize its objective, the *15th* did not attack Masan, but infiltrated the high ground southwest of the city.

In their wide swing around Walker's southern flank, the enemy purposely occupied every port from Kunsan to Yosu. It was their intention to use the ports to supply the enveloping force.

Walker believed that if the North Koreans had not been so intent in securing these ports and had driven straight to Pusan, he would have been unable to stop them.

The fight at Chindong-ni, in a way, was pivotal, the "high-water mark" of the North Korean invasion of South Korea. Terrible and bloody battles were yet to come, and the enemy would threaten to break through the fast-developing Pusan Perimeter many times. Another month and a half of fighting on the brink of disaster remained.

Chapter Notes:

P. 100 The 83d called variously "mechanized," "motorcycle" and "motorized," the regiment is referred to as a motorcycle regiment in History of the North Korean Army, *HQ, U.S. Far East Command, Military Intelligence Section, July 31, 1952.*

P. 102 Korean grave sites were unmistakable. Each grave had a mound over it about six or seven feet long and about three feet high.

P. 102 The Army fatigue trousers of the time had an oversized pocket sewn onto the upper outside of each pantleg. One could easily carry C-ration cans, grenades or other bulky items in each pocket

P. 103 "Straight leg" meant that the unit was not airborne.

P. 103 As a footnote, Frank Byrne wrote this: "When I was able to look back on the battle area, I saw the [North] Koreans were not taking any prisoners, ALIVE! Consequently, King Co. of the 27th did NOT either, for the next year I was there." Co. K, 29th Infantry became Co. K, 27th Infantry shortly after this battle, when 3/29 became 3/27.

P. 103 A sniper rifle was an M1 rifle with a scope and special cheek rest, issued to selected expert riflemen

P. 106 The 4th earned the title "Seoul Division" for its part in capturing that city and the addition of "Guards" for the victory at Taejon.

P. 108 A favorite camouflage trick of the North Koreans was for each man to cut a scrub pine bush and hold it in front of him as he slowly crawled along the ground. It was a strange sight to see an entire hill almost covered by slowly moving bushes.

P. 108 Most senior commanders maintain a personal command relationship with their immediate subordinate commanders. Not so with MacArthur. He was aloof, remote and never a hands-on commander, working primarily through staff officers. It is doubtful that he really knew Walker or any other Army commander who was his subordinate in World War II and Korea.

Walker, senior to Almond, with far more battle experience at division and higher levels than he, had to discuss plans with him, but he could not depend upon Almond to be his advocate. Almond was a MacArthur man. On page 36 of The Forgotten War, *Clay Blair writes that GEN John H. Michaelis (CO, 27th Inf. in the Perimeter and late 25th Div. ADC) described the Almond-Walker relationship as "horrible," and that "they just couldn't get along." Blair also quoted COL Thomas J. Marnane, secretary of the Eighth Army general staff, remembering Almond as*

"impossible. Very snotty," and who "gave Walker a bad time."

From his own study of the matter, and the recollections of officers like Michaelis and Marnane, this author is convinced that Almond had little concept of the true situation in the Pusan Perimeter and was unwilling or unable to understand Walker, or represent the Korean situation and Walker's concepts to MacArthur.

P. 110 Air burst artillery employed a proximity fuze, which detonated in the air just above the ground, creating far more shell fragments than a ground burst and causing greater casualties.

P. 112 Mortar or artillery rounds bursting in trees are far more deadly than if striking the ground. In a ground strike, shell fragments go to the side and up. In tree bursts, shell fragments plus hundreds of wood splinters from the tree(s) are hurled in every direction. The wood splinters, often very large, along with shell fragments, can produce far more casualties than a simple ground or air burst. A tree burst acts as a super air, or proximity fuze burst.

P. 113 Appleman refers to this as a reconnaissance in force. However, OPORD 13, HQ, 27 RCT, dated Aug. 1, 1950, is for an attack.

CHAPTER TEN - Forming the Perimeter

Redeployment of the 25th Division

On August 1, the 25th Division (less the 27th Infantry) began moving into new defensive positions south of Sangju. At 3 p.m., GEN Kean received a telephonic order from Eighth Army to move his division south to Samnangjin, on the Naktong to stop the enemy's eastward movement and to be prepared to attack to the west.

The division's advance party moved out about 1 a.m. Aug. 2. GEN Kean and his party left by plane later in the morning, stopping at Taegu to confer with GEN Walker. Walker then changed the division destination to Masan. Kean, using every conceivable method of communication, ensured that all elements of his division, then enroute to Samnangji, were notified of the change.

The division could move by foot and motor from Sangju through Kumchon to Waegwan. From Waegwan the troops would be transported by rail to Masan. But the Sangju-Kumchon-Waegwan road was also the MSR for the central front, and already was heavily traveled. Because of the possibility of hopeless traffic snarls when the 25th began moving south over this road, COL Landrum loaned the Eighth Army G3 every officer he could spare from Army headquarters. These officers were placed at all potential "choke points" along the route.

The movement of the division by rail to Masan was, perhaps, even more complex than the road march. Rolling stock already was in great demand and rail yards along the way were heavily congested. Some units simply commandeered locomotives and rolling stock. Further complicating the use of rail lines were refugees jamming themselves into and onto every available car. They were atop every car and hanging from the sides; they were even on the locomotives and tenders. Rail cars of every description jammed the tracks. The movement of the ROK 17th Infantry to the southwest to assist the 24th Division further complicated matters.

All the division's heavy equipment was loaded onto railroad cars at Waegwan the night of August 2-3. The last of the troops arrived aboard trucks of the 73d Truck Co. at 5:30 a.m. on Aug. 3. By 6 a.m. they were all on their way by train to Masan; the remainder of division equipment departed Waegwan an hour later.

The 25th Division CP opened at Masan at 9:15 p.m. Aug. 2. The 35th Infantry arrived there at 10 a.m. on Aug. 3 and the 24th at 7:30 p.m. When Kean reached Masan that day, he assumed command of all UN forces south of the Naktong River. The 150-mile road and rail movement of the 25th Division was completed in 36 hours.

GEN Walker stated that this "history-making maneuver" saved Pusan, but he also admitted that if the North Koreans had made a strong attack on the Kumchon front while the 25th was passing over the single road through that city, "we couldn't have done it."

Appleman stated that "in recognizing the critical nature of the situation in the southwest and in acting with great energy and decisiveness to meet it, General Walker and his staff conceived and executed one of the most important command decisions of the Korean War."

Reinforcements on the Way

The battered 19th, elements of the 29th and the two under strength battalions of the 27th were then all that faced the enemy's *4th* and *6th Divisions*, the latter reinforced by the *83d Motorcycle Regiment*.

The Army's 5th RCT (COL Godwin Ordway) from Hawaii, arrived in Pusan on July 31. The RCT had three infantry battalions, a tank company of 14 M26 tanks, the 555th (Triple Nickel) 105mm howitzer battalion and the 72d ECC. The artillery battalion had three four-gun batteries. (Six guns was the normal complement for an artillery firing battery.) Many members of the RCT were veterans of the 442d RCT and 100th BCT — both highly decorated Nisei infantry units of WW II. There was also a very close comrade's bond between the infantrymen and the men of the 555th.

July 31 also saw the arrival of the 9th Infantry (2d Infantry Division). The 9th (COL John G. Hill) was one of the oldest regiments in the Army. Its nickname was "Manchu," for its part in suppressing the Boxer Rebellion in China in 1900. Upon arrival in Korea, it was immediately dispatched to Kyongson, 10 miles southeast of Taegu, in Army reserve, along with its supporting 15th FAB (105mm).

The 1st Provisional Marine Brigade, commanded by BG Edward A. Craig, arrived in Pusan Aug. 2, with ground elements numbering 4,984 men. Most of the officers and 65 per cent of the NCOs were combat veterans. Each battalion was short one rifle company, so the command had only six rifle companies.

The preparation and deployment of the 5th RCT, 2d Division and Marine Brigade is addressed in the next chapter.

The 2d Division's 23d Regiment began arriving at Pusan on Aug. 5. Its 1st Battalion was almost immediately placed on a one hour notice for deployment.

By the close of July, Walker realized that he must now pull the Eighth Army behind the Naktong River without delay.

On July 30 the 24th Division's 34th Infantry was near Sanje-ri, guarding the road to Hyopchon and the Naktong; the 21st Infantry (-) crossed the Naktong and went behind the 34th. The 3/21, C/21 and an 81mm mortar section were at Yongdok, on the east coast. The 19th was in the vicinity of Chinju; 3/29 Infantry was near the town and 1/29 northwest of it.

On this date, COL Stephens, commanding the 21st Infantry, claimed in manuscript comments to Roy Appleman in December 1957 that GEN Church orally had placed him (Stephens) in command of both the 21st and 34th Infantry regiments. Stephens, then a general, harshly condemned the 34th. (See Chapter Notes.)

On July 31, the 34th withdrew through 1/21.

COL Stephens wrote that he then moved the ROK 17th Regiment back, placing one battalion on each flank of his regiment and one in reserve. On Aug. 1, the enemy attacked both flanks, but the ROKs threw them back. GEN Church now intended to form a line with the 21st and 34th Regiments and send the ROK 17th Infantry through the mountains to attack the enemy from the rear, but the Eighth Army withdrawal order halted this maneuver.

Diminutive COL Kim Hi Chun, age 28, commanded the ROK 17th Infantry. He was highly respected by ROK officers and enlisted men alike. When he told GEN. Church, "We will stay as long as the Americans," Church could bank on it; the 17th was a very dependable command.

Eighth Army's Aug. 1 operational directive ordered withdrawal behind the Naktong River. The 34th Regiment moved to the vicinity of Yongsan on the 2d. The 21st withdrew across the Naktong on the night of Aug. 2-3, without difficulty, completing the move by 12:45 a.m. Aug. 3. The 14th ECB followed about 3 a.m. The ROK 17th Infantry covered the withdrawal, crossing the Naktong at 6:30 a.m. At 10 p.m. on Aug. 2, engineers blew the Naktong bridge on the Chogye-Changnyong road. The engineers tried to blow the Koryong-Taegu bridge at 7:15 a.m.; the 3d ECB re-rigged the bridge and destroyed it that evening.

The 19th Infantry was relieved by the 35th Regiment in the Chungam-ni-Notch area on the evening of Aug. 3. It then moved northeast across the Naktong to the 24th Division CP at Changnyong, arriving there on Aug. 4. As a result of its fights between July 13 and Aug. 4, the 19th had only 20 per cent of its 1/4-ton trucks, half of its 3/4-ton trucks and about two-thirds of its 2 1/2-ton trucks. Already low in supplies, it was hard-put to obtain individual clothing, hand grenades, 4.2-inch mortar, flares and illumination shells.

The 1st Cavalry Division began moving south from the Chirye-Kumchon area to the east bank of the Naktong near Waegwan, simultaneously with the movements of the 24th Division. Only the 5th Cavalry Regiment, which was heavily engaged, had any difficulty in withdrawing; one battalion was nearly lost. However, by nightfall on Aug. 3, the entire division was across the Naktong except the rear guard. This was 1/8th Cav, blocking on the Song-ju road, southwest of the Waegwan area.

GEN Hobart Gay reserved the decision of when the highway and railroad bridges at Waegwan would be blown. As darkness closed in, thousands of refugees jammed up at the western end of the bridges. Each time the men of the 8th Cavalry started to cross the bridge, masses of refugees surged out onto the bridge behind them. Gay sent the rear guard back, pushing the refugees back to the west bank of the Naktong. The troops tried to run across, but the refugees were again right behind them. Finally, Gay, believing he had no choice, ordered the bridge blown as the last of his rear guard got across.

Untold hundreds of refugees perished when the bridge was destroyed.

The shrinking area occupied by ROK and U.S. troops virtually was overrun by refugees, with some 380,000 crossing into U.S./ROK territory during the middle two weeks of July. This number was increasing at the rate of 25,000 a day, but the destruction of all the bridges over the Naktong materially reduced their flow. The North Korean Army utilized the masses of refugees which jammed the roads to conceal the identities of their soldiers infiltrating U.S. and ROK lines. The sheer volume of displaced people made it impossible to screen them. Although a number of enemy soldiers, and weapons and ammunition concealed in refugee bundles and carts were discovered by friendly troops, hundreds, if not thousands of enemy soldiers made it safely through the lines.

The ROK Army also withdrew behind the Naktong on the night of Aug. 2-3. The ROKs had difficulty disengaging. For example, the ROK 1st Division was locked in a heavy fight with the enemy on Aug. 2. At Andong, the ROK 8th Division's 16th Regiment was engaged in an even more desperate struggle with the *NK 12th Division.*

GEN Walker was upset that some units near the end of July and in early August failed to maintain contact with the enemy. On July 30, he directed all units to maintain this contact; in spite of this, many organizations failed to comply. On Aug. 2 he again issued those orders and directed division commanders to give the matter their personal attention. Later the same day, he reiterated the order and admonished, "Daily counterattacks will be made by all units." He directed commanders to "take immediate and aggressive action to insure that these and previous instructions to this effect are carried out without delay." He concluded by stating that "the counterattack is a decisive element of defense."

The Eighth Army now would make their stand behind the looping Naktong River. Cognizant of the critical situation, GEN Church issued a directive Aug. 4 which was disseminated to every soldier in the 24th Division:

"Defensive and alternate positions must be prepared, routes reconnoitered, intensive patrolling of the river at night, communications perfected, and each individual know his job. There will be no withdrawal, nor need there be any, if each and every one contributes his share to the preparation, and, if attacked, has the will to fight it out here.

"Every soldier will under all circumstances retain his weapon, ammunition, and his entrenching tool. Without these he ceases to be a soldier capable of defending himself. Many of our losses have been occasioned by failure to dig a foxhole when the time permitted."

Other divisions issued similar orders.

The Pusan Perimeter

The air-line distance of the Pusan Perimeter was about 100 miles south-to-north and 50 miles west-to-east. Overland, especially along the looping Naktong River, the actual distance was much longer.

The Naktong formed the western front of the Perimeter, except along the 15 miles south of

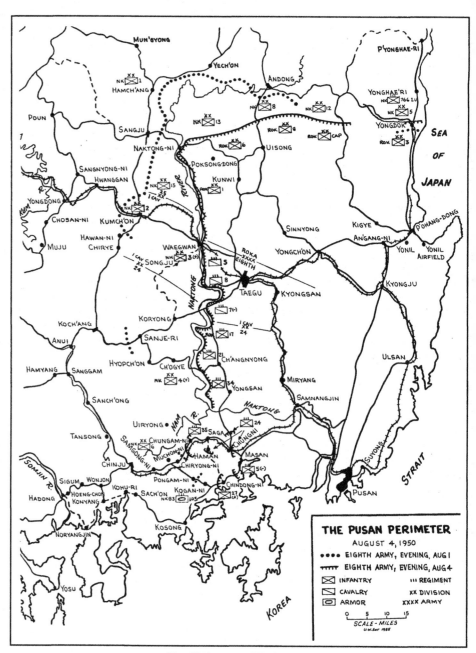

Map 18 (Courtesy of Uzal W. Ent)

the point where it met the Nam River and turned eastward. The southern end of this line rested on the Korea Strait. The northern flank ran from the Naktong north of Waegwan, through the rugged mountains eastward to Yongdok, on the Sea of Japan.

Pusan, the prize for the North Koreans, was at the southeastern corner of the Perimeter. It was only 30 air-miles from there to Masan; 55 to Taegu; 60 northeast to Pohang-dong, and 90 to Yongdok. Taegu, seat of the South Korean government and Forward HQ of Eighth Army, was a bare 10 miles from the Naktong front.

There are a few broad valleys along the Naktong, but generally the terrain is mountainous on both sides of the river. Some very high ridges and peaks lie in the 15-mile stretch of terrain south of the confluence of the Naktong and Nam. The area farther east of the Naktong contains rugged mountains, but the most formidable lie north of Pohang-dong.

Eighth Army hoped to have two reserve

forces available — one near Kyongson, 10 miles southeast of Taegu to support the center and northern fronts, and another near Miryang to back up the Naktong and Masan corridor areas.

Although he had to deploy the 24th Division along the Naktong, Walker knew that it would have to be completely refitted before it could be effective. He also believed that the 25th Division had little offensive capability. The ROKs had just produced 30,000 trainees. He used most of them to bring the five existing ROK divisions up to strength. After that, he intended to use additional recruits to organize new ROK divisions.

A review of the defensive line-up may be in order: Along the northern flank of the Perimeter was the ROK 3d Division anchoring the line on the sea of Japan near Yongdok. To its left (west) was a gap in the lonely, high rugged mountains. Then the ROK Capital, 8th and 6th divisions, from right to left, carried the line to the Naktong River near Naktong-ni. From that point, the Perimeter followed the Naktong River south. with the ROK 1st Division , Naktong-ni to just north of Waegwan; 1st Cavalry Division, covering routes to Taegu from the west; 24th Division south to the junction of the Naktong and Nam Rivers, with the 24th having responsibility for the Nam. The 25th Division carried the Perimeter south through the mountains and valleys to the Korea Strait.

Division frontages along the Naktong were extremely long. That of the ROK 1st Division was over 25 miles long. The 1st Cavalry Division had a river line front of 35 miles, while the 24th Division's was almost 40 miles long. In the south, the 25th Division defended the last 20 miles or so of the Perimeter. Army doctrine of the time called for a division front to be no more than nine miles long and the front of a full-strength regiment to be no more than 10,000 yards. Accordingly, some 13 divisions would have been required to defend this 120-mile front, not the mere four divisions available for the job, none of which was at more than 2/3 strength. Even when the 2d Division arrived in Korea, the Naktong line never could be manned by more than three U.S. divisions.

Since he could not man the Naktong front in sufficient strength to prevent the enemy from breaching the river, Walker adopted a form of mobile defense along this front, depending upon interior road and rail lines to rapidly shift his meager reserves to critical points at just the right time.

At the beginning of August, the 25th Division had the 27th, 24th and 35th regiments on line, in that order from south to north. The newly-arrived 5th RCT and the 89th Medium Tank Battalion were attached to the 25th. On Aug. 6, 1/29 was attached to the 35th Regiment; the following day, 3/29 was attached to the 27th. These battalions from the 29th soon became, respectively 3/35 and 3/27. A ROK force, known as Task Force Min, also was deployed on the division's front, particularly in the 24th Regiment's sector. The Division CP was at Masan. The *NK 6th Division* and *83d Motorcycle Regiment* opposed the 25th Division.

In the 24th Division's sector, the 34th, 21st and ROK 17th Infantry regiments were on line, in that order from south to north. The three regiments of the 24th Division — the 19th, 21st and 34th — still had but two battalions each, and the 19th was in division reserve.

To beef up his very wide front, COL Stephens (21st Inf) deployed seven .50-cal machine gun crews from the 14th ECB along the main battle line. The division CP was at Miryang. GEN Church was ordered to prepare all bridges on the Naktong in his sector for demolition at his order and to destroy all the boats and ferry sites he deemed advisable. The *NK 4th Division* opposed the 24th Division.

Events overtook the Eighth Army plan for the 9th and 23d Regiments (2d Division), just arriving from the U.S., to relieve the 24th Division on Aug. 8.

The 1st Cavalry Division deployed 2/7 Cav., 8th Cav. and 5th Cav., in that order, from south to north along the river. The 1/7 Cav. was in division reserve. The regiments of the Cavalry Division still had but two battalions. The Division CP was at Taegu, ten miles to the center

rear of the front. The *NK 3d Division* faced the 1st Cavalry.

The *NK 15th* and part of the *13th Divisions* opposed the ROK 1st Division, while the remainder of the *13th Division* and the *NK 1st Division* faced the ROK 6th Division. The *NK 8th* and ROK 8th opposed one another east of the ROK 6th Division, while the *NK 12th* and ROK Capital Divisions confronted one another. On the coast, the ROK 3d Division stood against the *NK 15th Division* and *766th Independent Unit (766 IU)*.

The North Korean Army was organized into *I and II Corps*. The *I Corps* had been activated at Pyongyang June 10, 1950 and the *II Corps* on June 12. Corps order of battle was:

> *I Corps: 3d, 4th* and *6th Divisions*. (Later, also the *2d, 7th, 9th and 10th Divisions*)
> *II Corps: 1st, 5th, 8th, 12th, 13th* and *15th Divisions*.

Tank support from the *105th Armored Division* was divided between the two corps.

Although the vast front along the Naktong could not be manned as a continuous line, the Pusan Perimeter finally represented a definitive position which would be defended. There would be no more "delay and fall back." Lost positions would be retaken; the enemy would be stopped and ejected from every penetration. It was now, in fact, do or die!

In addition to the 5th RCT, the 9th and 23d Regiments from the 2d Division and the 1st Provisional Marine Brigade (built around the 5th Marine Regiment), Korea was reinforced by the remainder of the 8072d Medium Tank Battalion. This provisional organization was equipped in Japan with tanks salvaged from the Pacific island battlefields of WW II. On Aug. 7, the 8072d became the 89th Medium Tank Battalion.

Air Support

At the outset of the war, ground-to-air coordination of close-in fighter support for U.S. and ROK troops was poor to none. But, as air power built up and Forward Air Control teams (FAC) became available, close-air support became more and more efficient. However, many veterans of the battles before and during the Perimeter itself recall numerous instances when U.S. or other Allied aircraft bombed and strafed friendly troops — often with deadly, devastating results. The employment of FACs, spotter planes and target marking procedures cut these accidents dramatically. Targets often were marked by white phosphorous mortar or artillery rounds, fired on either flank of a linear target, or at the center of a point target. Similar rounds from other weapons, such as the 2.36-inch rocket launcher, were sometimes used. The 3.5-inch launcher did not have a WP round at this time; one was developed later.

Almost every soldier and Marine who fought in Korea in those early days soon "fell in love with" the fighters that swooped in to their aid one time after another. The Corsair and F-51 aircraft were the favorites because they seemed to be able to stay overhead the longest. Jets appeared too fast to the infantrymen, but they, too, were cheered. In addition to FACs and target

marking by the infantry, the Air Force employed small, unarmed T-6 Texan planes, a WWII vintage training aircraft, with room for a pilot and an observer. Small liaison-type aircraft had been used first in Italy as air-borne spotters, but, at the outset of the Korean War, no aircraft were available immediately to direct tactical air strikes.

Early in the Korean War, FEAF sent to Korea LTC John R. Murphy with nine officers and 35 men, from the 8th Communications Squadron. This advance echelon moved to Taejon on July 5-6 and set up with the 24th Division CP. The Army component, with the men from the 8th Commo Squadron, were to form a Joint Operations center (JOC) to control the employment of tactical aircraft in a ground-support role. However, the combat situation was so confused that the Army did not furnish anyone to man their part of the JOC, and the Air Force officers had to check around the Army's CP to scrounge up likely targets. Very often, the 24th Division G3 could not tell the Air Force where divisional troops actually were. Army liaison aircraft pilots frequently stopped planned attacks because they knew U.S. or ROK troops were in the target area, instead of the enemy. Things just were not working, and vital air support was not getting to the ground troops.

Too often, when the men at the advance echelon did identify a target, communications with Japan to get the mission broke down. The wire circuit back to Japan was not operational about 75 per cent of the time. To offset this lack of communications, BG Edward J. Timberlake, commanding the Fifth Air Force, scheduled F-80 flights out of Japan every 20 minutes during daylight hours. When they arrived on station they were given targets, if any were available at the time. If no close-in targets were assigned, the pilots flew on north between Osan and Seoul and attacked whatever targets they could find for themselves — so-called "targets of opportunity."

Two FACs were sent to Korea on June 28, each with an experienced officer pilot and several airmen to man operate and maintain the party's two jeeps and jeep-mounted AN/ARC-1 radio. Lieutenants Oliver Duerksen and Frank Chermak led these two FACs, from Detachment 1, 620th Aircraft Control and Warning Squadron. The detachment had been formed to train jointly with Eighth Army troops in Japan, so the two parties had some training experience in directing close-support strikes. The jeeps and other equipment they had, were WW II vintage, and not in the best of shape.

The parties were hampered by bad weather and almost zero ceiling during the first days of July. Then Chermak's radio gave out and he had to return to Taejon for another radio jeep. When the weather did clear on the 8th and Duerksen could get F-80s for a strike, he had to remain with the jeep, in an exposed position to direct the attack, since the radio had no remote equipment. This happened very often. Duerksen reported, "Any time that we would be able to get the jeep in a position where we were able to control, we would be exposed ourselves, and the Communists would start laying artillery on us." (Page 80, *The United States Air Force in Korea 1950-1953*.) Further, AN/ARC-1 radios proved too fragile. They literally were beaten to pieces by the terrible roads and trails of Korea.

It took uncommon courage to crouch in the open next to a jeep using a radio to direct aircraft on a close-in attack. The members of Air Force FACs often met the same fate as the soldiers they were trying to help. Some of the early casualties included LT Arnold Rivedal, KIA on July 11. Later that day, LT Philip J. Pugliese and his party were cut off by the enemy as they moved forward to the front lines from a regimental CP in Chochiwon. They destroyed their equipment and tried to escape. SSG Bird Hensley and PFC Edward R Logston from this party were both MIA.

The official history of the Air Force in Korea cited above states that no one knows who finally thought of resurrecting the spotter plane system from WW II to offset the failure of the radio operation. It is believed that COL Murphy asked for an operations officer and five pilots to fly recon missions for his section. LTs James A. Bryant and Frank G. Mitchell brought two L-5G liaison planes to Korea on July 9, modified to accommodate four-channel VHF radios. Unfortunately, the two officers were unable to get the radios to work in the field, but to accomplish their mission, they borrowed rides in two 24th Division L-17s. Bryant was attacked by two YAK fighters, but evaded hits from both of them. Each of the officers called in about ten flights of F-80s that day, calling themselves "Angelo Fox" and "Angelo George." Although the jet pilots did not know that they would be controlled by airborne officers, the missions all were carried out with excellent results. In fact, Murphy thought it was "the best day in Fifth Air Force history." (Page 81, ibid.)

Then, on July 10, LT Harold E. Morris brought a T-6 trainer to Taejon. This proved to be the best aircraft for airborne control missions, because it was fast enough to handle enemy air attacks. On July 11, MAJ Merrill H. Carlton arrived at Taejon to take charge of the airborne control detachment. The usual method of operation in these early days was for the T-6 pilots to receive a pre-mission briefings, then take off and reconnoiter for likely targets. Once a target was spotted, the controller would call fighter bombers to the site. When the controller landed, he was debriefed on what he saw and where. These up-to-date reports helped to update situation maps on the location and disposition of both friendly and enemy troops.

The approaching enemy caused the T-6 operation to displace back to Taegu. On July 15, Fifth Air Force made the nickname legitimate by designating radio calls signs as "Mosquito Able," "Mosquito Baker," and "Mosquito How."

On Aug. 1, the Mosquito unit officially was organized as the 6147th Tactical Control Squadron (Airborne), under MAJ Merrill H. Carlton, based at the Taegu airfield and also known as K-2. Army observers flew in the planes to "spot" targets. Ground commanders soon began regarding the Mosquito plane which flew in their area as "theirs." This proprietary interest came about primarily because the planes adopted radio call signs which helped them identify with the commands they were supporting. For example, the Mosquito operating with the 1st Cavalry Division was known as "Mosquito Wildwest." (See Chapter Notes.)

In time, the ground-air liaison and control of tactical fighter support became more sophisticated and more efficient and the needs at the tactical level were meshed with deep strikes and strategic air operations.

It is doubtful that there is a single infantryman — Army or Marine — who does not owe his life to the airmen of the Air Force, Marines, Navy or allies at least once during his tour in Korea. The author is one of those soldiers grateful to his brothers who flew fearlessly to his aid in many a hard-fought battle. This book would not be complete without recognizing these airmen, and the controllers who brought them in so close and so efficiently.

Air support build-up included more jets and numerous refurbished F-51 fighters left over from WW II, as well as aircraft from the Royal Australian Air Force. (During WW II the F-51 was known as the P-51.)

As Roy Appleman points out, by July 31 U.S.-ROK ground forces were receiving proportionately more air support than did General Omar Bradley's Twelfth Army Group in WW II. Bradley had 28 divisions, supported by 14 fighter-bomber groups. Combined U.S./ROK forces totaled eight divisions, supported by eight fighter-bomber groups.

By the end of July, the U.S. Far East Air Forces (FEAF) had made as many as 400 sorties in a day. (A sortie is one combat flight by one aircraft.) A total of 8,600 sorties had been flown by the end of July. One half of these had been in close support of ground troops, 2,550 in close interdiction, 57 in strategic bombings and 1,600 more in recon and cargo sorties.

Bomber and fighter-bomber targets included the rail center at Wonsan, where lines came into Korea from Siberia; pontoon and railroad bridges over the Han at Seoul; the Chosen Nitrogen Plant at Hungnam; railroad marshaling yards and railroad bridges.

By July 30 the FEAF had 890 planes; 626 F-80 jets and 264 F-51s. But only 525 of these were available for combat.

Aircraft consumed fuel so rapidly and resupply was so shaky that there were times when gasoline terminals in Japan were empty; all aviation fuel was in the forward stations.

The F-80 was armed with six .50-cal machine guns in the nose, plus up to 16 5-inch high velocity aircraft rockets (HVAR). The normal range of the F-80 was only 100 miles, but equipped with wing-tip tanks, that was increased to 225 miles. The F-80 could be armed with two 1,000 lb. bombs, but then it could not carry wing tip tanks. The F-80 was never designed for close-in ground attack. It was a short range interceptor fighter. The principal advantage of the F-80 was that it often could "bounce" the enemy before he could evade the attack; the principal disadvantage was that it could not stay on station very long. All jets except those from the Navy, had to fly out of Japan. Some Navy jets flew from aircraft carriers when those ships arrived.

Most F-51s, on the other hand, operated from bases in Korea and could remain airborne for two or more hours. It was armed with six machine guns in the wings, could carry HVARs and could carry up to 1,000 lbs. in bombs. T-6 Mosquitoes could fly in observation about three hours.

Vought F4U Corsair (Source: P. 95, Korea, 1950, Chief of Military History, Washington, D.C., 1982)

F-51 Mustang Fighter

F-80 Shooting Star jet fighter (Source: P. 261, Korea, 1950, Chief of Military History, Washington, D.C., 1982)

The Never-ending Problem - Replacements

Initially, replacement personnel came from Japan, but that source soon all but dried up. Almost from the beginning, a replacement pipeline started from the U.S. In July, this netted several hundred officers and 5,287 enlisted replacements for Korea. The volume of replacements increased during August and September, reaching 16,000 in October. It had been estimated that 240 personnel could be airlifted to the Far East daily; however during the last 10 days of July the daily average was only 42 officers and 103 EM. The number of replacements was far short of what was needed. Eighth Army monthly replacement quotes were: August, 1,900 officers and 9,500 EM; September, 1,500 officers and 11,500 EM; October, 1,200 officers and 16,000 EM.

The actual supply of replacements was insufficient to keep front line infantry units up to strength. As a result, in September 1950 large numbers of ROK Army recruits were integrated into rifle companies and artillery batteries of American army commands in Korea. The integration of these Korean soldiers, known as KATUSAs (Koreans Attached to the United States Army) actually began in August. These poor souls had received only five days training before being sent to front line units. The 7th Division, in Japan, eventually received a total of 8,625 Korean officers and men. Each division in Korea received 8,300. In all, almost 42,000 Koreans served with U.S. Army divisions in Korea.

In addition to the woeful lack of training, most of the Korean enlisted men had to cope with American food, and American soldiers, who mostly were intolerant and prejudiced against them. U.S. soldiers who had been stationed in Japan for a time could communicate to some degree with the KATUSAs in Japanese and pidgin English. But by August most American soldiers were no longer from Japan. The new soldiers knew no Japanese. Communication between the American and KATUSA was, therefore, deplorable. Consequently, in many units the Koreans were relegated to menial tasks, such as ammunition bearers, and supply carriers. In late October, when U.S. casualties dropped, most of the KATUSAs (at least in the 25th Division) were returned to the Korean Army.

Pusan and Railroads — Logistical Lifeline

Pusan and other Ports

Without a seaport with the capacity of Pusan, it is doubtful that the ROK and Eighth Armies could have been supported logistically. Between July 1 and 31, 1950, 309,314 measurement tons of supplies and equipment came through Pusan, an average of 10,666 tons daily. In the last half of that month, 230 ships arrived and 214 departed, depositing 42,581 troops, 9,454 vehicles and 88,888 long tons of supplies. At the same time, the small ports of Ulsan and Suyong were utilized to receive ammunition and POL (petroleum products) over their beaches from tankers, barges and LCMs.

Air transport shifted more and more to bring critically needed items to Korea, including the new 3.5-inch rocket launchers, with 900 being scheduled daily during August.

The Red Ball Express

Shortly after mid-July a daily combination of railroad-ferry express service was organized to rapidly ship materiel and supplies from Japan to Korea. The Red Ball Express, as it was known started in Yokohama on a rail line to Sasebo, where the cargo was loaded directly aboard ship and sent to Pusan. The Express was inaugurated on July 23, 1950. From that time on, the schedule called for the Express to leave Yokohama at 11:30 nightly and arrive in Sasebo at 5:42 a.m. the second morning afterward. Cargo then was moved directly aboard ship, which departed daily at 1:30 p.m. and arrived in Pusan the next morning at 4 a.m. The Red Ball Express could deliver 300 measurement tons a day to Korea with each shipment taking 53 hours from Yokohama to Pusan.

The Perimeter Rail System

As the enemy advanced into South Korea, the portions of the rail system under friendly control shrank dramatically: On July 1, the UN Command had 1,404 miles of rail track under control; by the end of the month it was a mere 431 miles.

In spite of all the chaotic conditions, effective July 18, U.S. Army Transportation men were able to establish a regular daily schedule of trains to railheads to the front. Two routes were used, the main Pusan-Taegu-Kumchon line, with a branch from Kumchon to Hamchang, and the Pusan-Kyongju-Andong single-track line following the east coast, with a branch line from Kyong-ju to Pohang-dong. By the end of July, the Perimeter had shrunk and trains no longer went beyond Taegu or Pohang-dong.

Fortunately, since Japan had built the railroads in Korea, parts and equipment were easily obtained and shipped in to keep the lines running. As Appleman noted, one of the largest and most important rail purchases from Japan for the Korean railroads was 25 standard-gauge locomotives.

The protection of all railroad bridges and tunnels was made the responsibility of the ROK National Police on Aug. 1, 1950, with armed guards stationed at each of the sites.

Friendly and Enemy Casualties

At the outset, many American units suffered high casualties to heat exhaustion. The rugged Korean hills, devoid of trees and little water, took their toll. Vegetation usually consisted of scrub-type shrubs. The enervating heat and sun felled many men as they clambered up and down the steep hills and ridges. Almost all of these casualties returned to duty in a few days. Yellow jaundice also created a few casualties; these men were returned to Japan for an extended period.

American battle casualties through July 31, 1950 were 6,003: 1,884 KIA; 2,695 WIA; 523 MIA and 901 POW. Total American losses, from all causes, however, were 7,859. Almost 80 percent of these casualties occurred between July 15-31. In that 15-day period, 4,754 men were lost: 1,265 KIA; 2,345 WIA; 971 MIA; 173 POW.

More than half of the total battle losses were in the 24th Division. Reports of the time give these figures for that division, up to Aug. 4: 85 KIA; 895 WIA and 2,630 MIA for a total of 3,610. Most of these MIA were either dead or POWs. (See Chapter Notes.)

ROK losses are difficult to establish because the war destroyed their accounting system. The number of 70,000 battle casualties is given by Appleman as a fair estimate, so total UN losses up to Aug. 5 were about 76,000 men.

North Korean casualties are difficult to assess. MacArthur's headquarters estimated the figure at 31,000 on July 29 and the Department of the Army estimated 37,500. However, based on a study of POW interrogations the actual figure should have been closer to 58,000. MacArthur's headquarters and DA failed to realize that the ROK Army had inflicted great casualties on the enemy during their fighting withdrawal. In a number of battles, the ROKs all but wiped out regiments and even decimated entire divisions. This is yet another instance where the critical contribution of the ROK soldiers to the ultimate success in those early days has been overlooked.

Relative Strengths of Opposing Forces, 4-5 August, 1950

Roy Appleman gives these figures for the *NKPA* as of Aug. 5, as derived from captured documents and interrogation reports (see chart below). The number of tanks actually available

North Korean Peoples Army (NKPA)			
Division	Strength	Division	Strength
1st	5,000	12th	6,000
2d	7,500	13th	9,500
3d	6,000	15th	5,000
4th	7,000	105 Armd (40 tanks)	3,000
5th	6,000	83d Motorcycle Regt	1,000
6th	3,600	766th IU	1,500

is almost impossible to judge; UN aircraft and the 3.5-inch rocket launchers had taken a heavy toll on them. The first tank replacements apparently did not arrive until about Aug. 15, amounting to 21 tanks and 200 crewmen. But the appearance of the 3.5-inch rocket launcher materially reduced commanders' concern about enemy armor. And when the M4A3 and M-26 tanks arrived in Korea at the beginning of August, the enemy's T-34s — what there were left of them — ceased to be much of a factor in battle.

North Korean artillery and heavy mortars also had suffered heavy losses, some due to counterbattery fire and the rest from air strikes. Appleman writes that enemy artillery pieces and heavy mortars had probably been reduced to about one-third of what had been available at the war's outset, probably a fair estimate.

From interrogation reports, Appleman states that "most of the Russian-supplied artillery ammunition used by the North Koreans was four or five years old and verdigris (greenish corrosion which occurs on copper) deposits coated shell casings. There were many misfires and duds." It appears that friend and foe alike had to cope with faulty ammunition.

MacArthur's headquarters reported the troop strength in Korea on Aug. 4, 1950 to be 141,808. Tabulation of these figures is in the chart below.

On the surface it appears that at the front the UN outnumbered the North Koreans 91,524 to 70,000. However, these figures may be deceiving. The rifle elements of a North Korean division accounted for almost 37 per cent of its total strength, whereas the rifle units of a U.S. division amounted to only 30 per cent. This leads to a tentative conclusion that the actual front line strengths of the North Koreans and UN forces were almost even.

UN forces had complete mastery of the air from early July. As a result, air strikes caused a great number of casualties among artillery, mortar and service support elements of enemy divisions — proportionately far more than ROK and U.S. support troops suffered. As the month ended, too, the number of U.S. artillery units increased, some of it 155mm howitzers, which could reach into enemy rear areas. As a result of these two factors, particularly air power, the number of casualties among support type troops in North Korean divisions had to be very high. This, in turn, led to a change in the proportion of combat to support troops. The North Korean division actually was composed of about 40 per cent or more front line troops to 50-60 per cent support.

On the other hand, the bulk of ROK and U.S. casualties were in the rifle companies, and in some instances, certain artillery units. Service support units did not suffer a proportionate number of losses. As a result, the actual percentage of front line troops to support in U.S. and ROK divisions fell below 30 per cent, so at the foxhole level, UN forces did not enjoy any superiority in numbers at all.

Further, because of the very long front neither the ROK nor the American Army had the capability to mass forces at any one point. But because the North Korean Army was on the offensive, it had the initiative. It could (and did) mass troops to gain local superiority of forces, and exploiting every gap and weakness in ROK and U.S. lines to infiltrate large numbers of troops into rear areas, hampering counterattacks.

Because of these factors, many times the North Koreans enjoyed a considerable local numeric superiority over the defenders. As the ROKs or Americans built up counterattack forces and artillery, and air strikes began to take their toll on the North Korean attacking force, the relative combat power swung heavily in favor of the defenders. In almost every case, the enemy eventually was thrown back after suffering terrible casualties.

The leadership of the NKPA must be given credit for its iron-willed determination to win through to Pusan, in spite of horrendous casualties and crippling losses in heavy weapons and equipment. They exerted extraordinary efforts to resupply forward troops and bring forward replacements. Untold thousands of North Korean soldiers died as a result of concentrated artillery fire and the rockets, machine guns, bombs and napalm from UN aircraft; American and ROK troops never had to face such unrelenting bombardment from ground and air.

Chapter Notes:

P. 119 The only documentation to substantiate Stephens' claim of being given command of both regiments is an entry in the 21st Regiment's War Diary; there is no similar entry in the War Diary of the 34th Regiment, nor apparently in that of the 24th Division. MAJ Lacy C. Barnett located some 250 veterans of the 34th Infantry, and none of them recall any orders emanating from then-COL Stephens to the 34th Regiment. If GEN Church did appoint Stephens to command both regiments, he failed to notify COL Beauchamp (34th Infantry) or issue written confirmatory orders. Neither Church nor Beauchamp ever recorded anything to substantiate Stephens' assertion.

P. 122 All airstrips and airfields in Korea had numeric designations, along with the letter K.

P. 123 The figure differences are partly due to the reporting system. Units submitted feeder reports back to clerks or first sergeants. At times, these reports, compiled in battle, were not accurate. Another factor was the regulation that unless the body was recovered or the person was in a medical facility, the man had to be reported MIA. The battle casualty list of 6,003, compiled in a final report on Sept. 30, 1954, is the most accurate.

Troop Strength in Korea on Aug. 4, 1950

Eighth U.S. Army in Korea (EUSAK)	2,933	Recapitulation	
KMAG	452	Total U.S. Forces	59,237
1st Cav Div.	10,276	Total Army	50,367
2d Inf Div.	4,922	Total Marine Bde	4,713
24th Inf Div.	14,540	ROK Army	82,570
25th Inf Div.	12,073		
		Army Ground	
Pusan Base	5,171	Combat Units	41,811
Marine Bde	4,713	Marine Bde	4,713
FEAF (Korea)	4,051	U.S. Ground Troops:	46,524
Other	107		
		ROK Combat	
ROK Army (estimated)	82,570	Strength (Estimated):	45,000
Total Un Ground Troops	91,524		

CHAPTER ELEVEN - Mobilization and Deployment of Reinforcements

Status of the Army and Marine Corps

Because American leadership believed that the North Korean invasion of South Korea might be the opening blow of a global effort led by the Soviet Union, the U.S. was hard-put to muster reinforcing troop units for deployment to Korea. Because of this distrust of the Soviets, the U.S. believed that it had to reinforce Europe, maintain a sizable strategic reserve in America, and send large numbers of individual replacements and major troop commands to Korea.

The Army's General Reserve on June 25,1950 consisted of the 2d Armd Division; 2d Inf. Division; 82d Abn Division; 11th Abn Division (- one RCT); 3d Armd Cav. Regt; 5th RCT (located in Hawaii) and the 14th RCT. These troops, along with combat support and service support units, totaled 360,000. Overseas deployments totaling 210,000 men included about 108,500 troops in the Far East and 80,000 in Germany

The Marine Corps strength at the time was 74,279 — 97 per cent of that authorized. The Fleet Marine Force (FMF) totaled 27,656.

Efforts to Strengthen Commands in the Far East

The Army took action to add third battalions to the regiments in Japan which had but two. For this purpose, two battalions and three battalion cadres were selected from the 3d Infantry division, a full battalion from the 14th RCT, three battalions from the 5th RCT and two battalions of the 29th Infantry (Okinawa). These all were slated to become the third battalions. The two battalions of the 29th arrived in Korea before the end of July and were badly mauled in battle, as we have seen. The Army decided not to break up the 5th RCT, and finally sent it to Korea as a complete team.

Likewise, artillery batteries were drawn from the General Reserve to provide the missing third firing batteries for divisional artillery battalions in Japan. The 2d Armd and 3d Inf. Divisions each provided three 105mm howitzer batteries; two more came from the 14th RCT. The 555th FAB, part of the 5th RCT was to provide three batteries. These 11 batteries were expected to arrive in Korea at only 60 per cent strength and about 40 per cent combat effectiveness.

Eighth Army also was deficient in general support (i.e. back-up) artillery. GEN MacArthur asked for six self-propelled 155mm howitzer battalions, an observation battalion and an artillery group headquarters. The General Reserve contained only 12 battalions of non-divisional artillery — all well below strength; five 105mm howitzer battalions; five 155mm howitzer battalions, one 155mm gun battalion and one 8 inch howitzer battalion. Three 155mm howitzer battalions, the 8 inch howitzer battalion, an observation battalion and the 5th FA Group headquarters were sent to MacArthur.

The T-34 badly out-did the M-24 light tank which U.S. troops took to Korea from Japan, but it was the only tank available to them. To help correct this imbalance, three medium tank battalions (other those already mentioned) were alerted for immediate overseas shipment. These were the 6th (M-46 Patton tanks), the 70th (M-26 Pershings and M4A3E8 Shermans —or "Easy Eights") and the 73d (M-26s). Two of these battalions were from the school troops of the Armored School, Ft. Knox, KY, and The Infantry School, Ft. Benning, GA. The third was from the 1st Armd Division.

The 70th Tk Bn — demonstration troops at Knox — consisted of a headquarters and three tank companies. The headquarters included a platoon of M-24s; two companies had M4A3E8s, (Shermans) from WW II. Each of these tanks mounted a 76mm main gun, plus three machine guns. The tank also had a small metal compartment on the outside right rear, containing an EE8 sound-powered telephone. An infantrymen could talk to the tank commander by means of this phone. The "E8" of the tank's model number denoted a tank with this phone. The third company had Pershing M-26 tanks, mounting a 90mm main gun and three machine guns

Jim Harris was a member of the 70th. The battalion had few veterans of WW II. When the war started, short-timers like Harris were asked to reenlist. All but one of the 13 enlisted, and he later enlisted for the 2d Division in Korea. The battalion was given four days to prepare for shipment to Korea. The 70th, its commander, LTC William Rodgers, recalled, "was nothing more than a paper outfit...of about 200 men.... We did not have a single item of equipment...nothing!" Pershings being used as monuments at Ft. Knox were taken from their concrete pads and used to help equip one unit. Shermans were shipped in from Rock Island Arsenal. Tank parts were flown in to replace worn engines, guns and tracks. Meantime, tankers came in from all over to fill the battalion. As Rodgers said, "nobody knew anybody else. The commander and his men worked for three days and nights without sleep, made the tanks as serviceable as possible and loaded them on flatcars. The deadline was met.

The 6th, 70th and 73d Tank Battalions sailed from San Francisco on July 23 and arrived in Pusan on Aug. 7. The 6th became part of Eighth Army reserve. The 70th joined the 1st Cavalry Division on Aug. 12. The 73d was split up; Co. A to Ulsan guarding the eastern MSR, Co. B to TF Bradley at Kyongju and Kigye and Co. C to the 27th Infantry in the Bowling Alley. In the 1st Cavalry Division, Co. A of the 70th supported the 5th Cav., Co. the 8th Cav. and Co. C the 7th Cav.

A wide variety of troops were needed to support the combat troops already in Korea as well as the projected build-up, including engineer, maintenance, transportation, signal, military police and medical units. MacArthur asked for 200 company-sized service units, but he received about 80 of them, and those only at about 65 per cent strength.

Major Commands

Three major commands were sent to Korea as rapidly as they could be made ready. The first to arrive was the 5th RCT, from Hawaii, which included the 5th Infantry Regiment, the 555th FAB (105mm) and the 72d ECC. It totaled 178 officers and 3,319 EM.

The 2d Infantry Division arrived in Korea in increments; the 9th Infantry July 31, the 23d Infantry Aug. 5 and the 38th infantry Aug. 19. The division was almost at full strength.

The 1st Provisional Marine Brigade arrived in Korea on Aug. 2, including the 5th Marines; A/1st Tk Bn; 1/11 Marines (a field artillery battalion, equipped with twelve 105mm howitzers); A/1st Engr Bn, plus a number of other service support units. There were 4,984 troops, and with air components added, the brigade aggregated 6,534.

The 5th Regimental Combat Team

The 5th Infantry Regiment was activated in Korea on Jan. 1, 1949. Personnel for the regiment and its combat team came from the 32d Infantry Regiment (7th Division); 555th FAB; 72d ECB; 517th Engineer Utility Detachment; 317th Hq, Intelligence Detachment; 371st Ordnance Ammunition Depot; 282d Army Band; 12th Medical Collecting Co. and the 5th Mechanized Cavalry Recon Troop, All of these units were deactivated in Korea, except for the 5th Infantry; 555th FAB;, 72d Engineers, which was reduced to company size, and the 57th Recon Troop. The RCT was ordered to Schofield Barracks, Hawaii. The recon troop was deactivated in Hawaii. The last element of the 5th RCT sailed from Inchon on June 29, 1949. (In his *In Mortal Combat*, John Toland mistakenly refers to the 555th (Triple Nickel) FAB as "all black." He has the 555th FAB confused with the all black WW II 555th Parachute Infantry, deactivated after that war.)

The 5th RCT at Schofield was reorganized and began intensive training. The command already had a good number of combat veterans of the 442d RCT and 100th BCT, highly- decorated Nisei commands from WW II.

"The 5th RCT trained hard in Hawaii," wrote Gene McClure (H/5th RCT). The most important exercise was "Operation Mike," in which the 5th RCT acted as the enemy who had captured the island of Oahu. The 2d Infantry Division from the continental U.S. staged an invasion to retake the island.

Further training continued after this exercise. Then word came that North Korea had invaded South Korea. COL Godwin Ordway Jr., commanding the 5th RCT, assembled all regimental officers in the Post theater and advised them of the attack, and that they were to return to their units and dispel any rumors of the 5th being sent to Korea..

However, the 5th RCT was the designated

Pacific Reserve, and as such, it was only a matter of time before it was ordered to deploy to Korea. The alert came on July 10 and the order followed on July 13.

This order set off a flurry of feverish activity. "All local units were stripped of personnel," said COL James C. Richardson, who was then a lieutenant and Assistant S1 of the RCT. "Many fellows arrived from the States...many of these were raw recruits, [and] many individual reserves volunteered, plus the entire senior ROTC Corps of Cadet class from the University of Hawaii."

When the alert came on July 10, all troops were confined to post. Initially, almost the same sentiment prevailed in the 5th RCT as there had been among the troops in Japan; that this would be a quick war. As Bill Motley (Svc/555 FAB) wrote, "I along with most of my fellow officers and most of the senior NCO's believed this would be a quick 'police action' that could be handled by the troops already in Korea and Japan."

Motley recalled that additional men to fill up the 5th RCT "came from all sorts of units, with little or no training in the jobs to which they were assigned." The shot records of all personnel had to be brought up to date, resulting in many men being given two or more shots for different diseases on the same day. All underclothing was dyed green. Men with automobiles had to sell them. Some men had to square away allotments, make wills and take care of other personal matters. All equipment had to be prepared for shipment, while certain officers and men were placed in charge of packing and crating. Civilian contractors were hired to build crates and packing cases.

Wyatt Logan was first sergeant of B/555 FAB, recently reassigned from the 15 FAB, Ft. Lewis, WA. When the BC, CPT Perry Graves, told him about the North Korean invasion, Logan wrote, "I thought, where in hell is Korea?" A few days later, "We marched the battery over to the Medics, and they gave us every shot in the book. Boy, was the battery ever sick...."

Enroute to Korea, he recalled, "We started giving the 'Cannoneer's Hop' [artillery gun crew training]. What a mess! All jocks, some of whom had never fired a gun." The battery used the ocean trip to Korea "to whip those jocks into cannoneers," he wrote, "which we were able to do."

Each individual driver was made responsible to ready his vehicle for shipboard transportation, Gene McClure recalled. He was a jeep driver. "This included...having the vehicle undercoated for salt water protection, new tires and batteries if needed, new fan and generator belts, new military markings such as the white star and unit markings, jerry cans and tool kits in place and a long list of other such things."

LT Motley was the Service Battery mess officer, motor officer and ammunition train commander. The BC was 1LT Wayne O. Hauck (West Point 1947). Motley, with SGT Henry Awohi, were kept busy transporting artillery ammunition from Kolekole Ammunition Depot to the port. "I was also the unit loading officer," Motley recalled, "designated to coordinate loading of equipment and ammunition with port personnel."

McClure remembered the trip to the Hono-lulu docks. "All the men of the 2d Battalion were loaded into open-top 2 1/2-ton trucks and transported...to the docks...where we immediately boarded a troop ship.... The truck I was riding in slowly pulled alongside a pineapple truck.... The driver of the pineapple truck kept pace with us so that we could reach over with our bayonets and pick a pineapple for a quick snack — a nice send off gesture by that truck driver..."

LT Richardson oversaw packing and crating. The contents of each crate was to be waterproofed and was to weigh no more than 75 lbs., but the Post Engineer said that he had to take certain liberties with the rules. So Richardson and others had to compute the total cubic size of the shipment and figure how many crates 4x4x6-feet would be needed. Of course, many crates that size would contain far more than 75 lbs. The Post Engineer assured Richardson that there was plenty of materiel-handling equipment in Pusan; actually, there was virtually none. As a result, many of these heavy, bulky crates had to be laboriously manhandled onto the docks.

The 5th RCT departed Hawaii July 24 on three ships, the transports *General Buckner, General Mann* and *General Gaffey*.

McClure remembered that "the machine shop on the ship constructed several steel platforms at strategic locations about the ship on which we mounted a few of our own .50-cal and .30 cal machine guns.... I thought [this] was a rather cheap way to go to war.... These guns were test fired several times at sea...."

Buddy Ford was an 18-year-old-ammunition carrier in H Co.'s 81mm Mortar Platoon. "We had good officers and NCOs," he wrote. "Some of the men in the company had been in Korea during the occupation after World War II." His unit was aboard the *General Gaffey*. He recalled the ocean trip to Korea as "an easy nine-day ride.... The seas were calm and occasionally some of us slept up on the deck where it was cooler and less crowded."

Motley recalled that, enroute, the officers were given a Korean war "situation map briefing on deck every morning and afternoon." He remarked that it "would also have been a good opportunity to give some quick 'cramming' on basic artillery lingo, radio security, etc., to the many non-artillery officers and enlisted men transferred into the 555th to fill TO&E slots." Motley also wrote that newly-assigned fillers were given M1 rifle and crew-served weapons training enroute to Korea.

LT Gordon J. Duquemin was having brunch at the Officer's Club when word of the North Korean invasion came in. He was one of sixteen graduates of the West Point Class of 1947 in the 5th RCT, and he had been in Korea in 1949. Duquemin recalled that his reaction to the attack was that he hoped the 5th RCT would get involved. When he learned that the 5th would go to Korea, he thought, "Great — a chance to get into combat — it was my profession," he wrote. "We trained hard in Hawaii [before the Korean War]." Duquemin's experience already included that of a platoon leader and CO in A/5 RCT.

"We trained on the ship — exercised and passed the time talking tactics," he continued, recalling that the transport he was on was the *General Buckner*. "I remember unloading in Pusan early in the morning," Duquemin wrote, "watching some infantry cadre get a quick orientation on the 3.5-inch [rocket launcher]...and given some ammunition. We were issued black-and-white maps with no grid, just town names and contour lines." During the move to Chindong-ni the truck convoy came under enemy artillery fire.

Bill Motley of the 555th experienced some of the same frustration during the unloading of ammunition that Jim Richardson was having in the 5th Regiment. "All the planning and segregating of ammunition during loading was wasted," Motley wrote. "Large nets were lowered into the hold and Korean laborers piled ammunition of all types from all sides into the net. The net was then 'dumped' on the dock." LT Motley and SGT Awohi got the trucks of their ammunition train onto the docks; then the nets were at least dumped into trucks rather than on the dock. The trucks moved from the port area to a point where they were unloaded, the ammunition sorted by type, basic loads made up and reloaded onto the trucks of the ammunition train.

During the unloading, McClure remembered seeing "2 1/2-ton trucks with dead GIs in white mattress covers, stacked like cordwood in their truck beds, and a long passenger train with a large red cross painted on it and many wounded Americans laying on stretchers...and stacked three or four deep...in train car after car."

Most of the RCT was sent to the Hialeah Race Track, outside Pusan. Some men were in the buildings, others in what they described as a bean patch. Eugene Mathews, a veteran of Burma jungle-fighting in WW II, of B/555, FAB, recalled that the guns were placed in firing position. When he learned that his outfit was headed for Korea in 1950, his reaction was, "Well! This is what we are paid for...."

Horace (Andy) Anderson, a squad leader in the 4th (Weapons) Platoon of E/5 RCT and Richard Lewis, Hq Btry/555 FAB recalled the stopover near the race track. "We were assembled in a bean field where we were told to leave our personal bags. We were instructed to make a light pack with change of socks, underwear and an extra pair of pants and shirt, "wrote Andy. Lewis remembered, "We pitched shelter-halfs on top of a dike. The sight of shelter-halfs gave someone the idea of a full-field inspection! Really makes a guy want to fight — spit and polish before combat — just before!"

The 5 RCT battalion commanders were: 1st - LTC John P. Jones Jr., 39; 2d - LTC John L. Throckmorton, 37, West Point 1935; 3d - LTC Benjamin W. Heckemeyer, 39; and 555 FAB - LTC John H. Daly ("Black Jack"), 35, West Point 1936. Throckmorton, known as "Rocky John" by his men, was noted as a cool and brainy officer. He had never commanded troops in combat, but he learned fast, was courageous under fire and was well organized. His battalion did well. Heckemeyer, Throckmorton's classmate at West Point, was a military intelligence specialist. He, too, never had commanded troops in combat. During WW II, Daly served as a staff officer in division artillery and higher commands.

LT James Richardson went to RCT headquarters early on Aug. 2, and found that the CO, XO and entire staff were out and no one knew where they were. "About this time an urgent call came from a general from Eighth Army headquarters, wanting the CO," said Richardson. SGM Bogart took the call. When the general learned that the commander nor any of his staff was present, he asked, "Have you got any officers around there at all?"

"I happened to walk in about this time," Richardson recalled, "and got on the phone, not knowing what was on the other end of it." The general asked where the CO, XO and staff were. "I hemmed and hawed," said Richardson. "Finally, he said 'I need a battalion from Masan. Take action in my name and get your best battalion on the way.'" He also wanted Richardson to report back as soon as the battalion departed. Richardson reflected "for a full 30 seconds," then jumped in a jeep and headed for LTC Throckmorton's 2d Battalion. "This was a battalion that I had served with on the [38th] parallel for some time [during the occupation of Korea in 1949]." Richardson thought it to be the best battalion in the regiment.

"COL Throckmorton immediately began to question me on why the 2d Battalion," Richardson recalled. Finally, to convince Throckmorton, he said, "The general told me to get the best battalion; where the hell do you expect me to go?" This stopped "Rocky John," and he said, "We will be on our way within 90 minutes, Rich."

"So," concluded Richardson, "I guess I could officially state that I gave the 5th RCT their first order into combat." As the convoy carrying 2/5 RCT disappeared down the road, LT Richardson found a telephone and reported to Eighth Army that the battalion was on the way forward.

Meanwhile, LT Motley and SGT Awohi organized their ammo train, consisting of Motley's jeep, Awohi's 3/4-ton, six 2 1/2-tons with .50-cal machine guns and six others without the gun. The train was split in half; Motley had three 2 1/2-tons with machine guns and three without, and Awohi had the same.

While Motley delivered ammunition with his trucks, Awohi would be enroute back for another load. In convoy, the jeep (or 3/4-ton) led, followed by a truck without a machine gun, then one mounting one, alternating this way so that the last truck was one with a machine gun. Each little seven-vehicle convoy had three .50-cal machine gun trucks. The train also had two Thompson sub-machineguns, given to LT Motley by an ordnance civilian at the depot back in Hawaii just before his deployment to Korea.

A "trick of the trade" which his ammunition handlers employed was to turn the outside rows of ammunition boxes on edge in the truck, providing protection for the men from small-arms fire and shrapnel.

LTC Throckmorton established his CP at the base of a long ridge rising to Hill 342 (later known as Fox Hill) and continuing to higher elevations farther to the northwest in Sobuk-san (Hill 738), 2,400 feet high. He sent Co. G directly to Hill 342, while Co. E performed recon patrols in the area and F was held in reserve near the CP.

When orders came for the Caucasian and Oriental members of the 5th RCT to buddy up, Dick Lewis (HHB, 555 FAB) chose CPL

Toshio Uyeda, HC/2/5 RCT. (Courtesy of Toshio Uyeda)

Wellington K. S. Ng. The two men were in the battery Survey Section. Lewis had been with the 6th DivArty in Korea back in 1946-47 and was familiar with the roads and terrain in the Masan-Chinhae area.

Lewis was selected to accompany MAJ Brooks, (XO, 555 FAB), his driver and an interpreter in the first vehicle of the battalion convoy as it moved to Masan. "I was taking the possibility of an ambush quite lightly and the Korean and I had small talk," Lewis wrote. "Maj Brooks was very wary; at every turn and topping the crest of the road [he] crouched with .45 pistol at the ready." As they approached the Chinhae turn-off, Lewis decided to test the Korean. He pointed toward Chinhae and said, "Masan." The Korean, "put it straight," Lewis remarked. At Masan, Lewis was surprised to see the directional signs for the old 53 FAB still in place. The 53d had been stationed in Masan in 1946-47.

West of Masan, the battalion went over a pass and into position south of the road in a valley near Chindong-ni. Able Battery forward, Charlie Battery behind Able, with HQ and Baker batteries next in line in that order. Service Battery was located generally between Btry B and the road.

Lewis and Ng were sent west of the pass where the battalion was to obtain survey information, using a control point which had been established by the 25th DivArty as a reference point. The two men received some small-arms fire from a nearby hill, but they completed their task without injury. Later, while the survey officer was orienting his men, Lewis wrote, "I heard something that was familiar from World War II. Everybody looked at me kind of funny as I got into my foxhole. Quickly, they realized that it was incoming."

While in this position an enemy 120mm mortar round hit the B Battery CP, killing the XO, Lt Stoll; battery officer Lt Mercer, 1SG Headly, the FDC NCO, CPL Stuhand, and WO Gillespie of Svc Btry. SGT Beaullieau, Wire Section; SGT Allman, Gun Section and SGT Matisick, Detail Section all were wounded. Con-

sequently, B Btry was displaced forward to a new location. Three howitzers were placed on the south side of the road and SGT Eugene Mathews' 105 was north of the road near a bridge over a dry stream bed, in an antitank role. All gun sections were alerted to be prepared to fire direct fire if necessary.

Toshio Uyeda was a member of Hq. Co., 2/5 RCT. He was visiting his sister when he heard about the North Korean invasion on the radio. "I was somewhat startled that now I was going to be like John Wayne and the North Koreans were going to catch hell," he recalled.

When his company established their initial perimeter near Chindong-ni on Aug. 2, Uyeda and his foxhole buddy hit rocks as they began digging in. Uyeda looked around and spotted "a grassy area fairly level with two small mounds," he wrote. The two men agreed that, by digging between the two mounds, they wouldn't have to dig so deep. "It was pitch black [at night] but we kept digging — occasionally hitting something solid — but [we'd] pry it loose." They threw these items out of the hole and finally finished about midnight. Early next morning enemy mortar rounds dropped into the company position and the unit's .50-cal machine gun began firing at a hillside about 1,000 yards across the rice paddies. Peering out of the foxhole, Uyeda saw the whole hillside filled with moving bushes — the enemy. That's when he discovered that the things he and his buddy had been prying out of the hole were human bones. They had dug into a Korean grave site!

Before nightfall on Aug. 2, a platoon of G Co. occupied the top of Yaban-san (Hill 342).

The Second Infantry Division

On July 5, GEN MacArthur asked specifically for the 2d Infantry Division, stationed at Ft. Lewis, WA, to be sent to the Far East as soon as possible. On July 8, the division, under command of MG Laurence B. Keiser, was alerted for deployment to the Far East. The original plan, as it was with the 5th RCT, was for the division to garrison Japan. GEN Mark Clark, then chief of Army Field Forces, predicted that the 2d Division couldn't be readied for at least six months. It was short 5,000 men and had experienced a 138 per cent turnover in personnel in the previous year.

Notwithstanding Clark's assessment, the first elements of the 2d sailed on July 17 and its 9th Infantry Regiment attacked the enemy in Korea one month after the first alert.

With the alert, all leaves were canceled, all personnel at school or enroute to other assignments were recalled, and men due for discharge were involuntarily retained in their assignments in the division. Throughout the Army, men due for discharge were involuntarily extended in what became known to them as "The Truman Year."

Hundreds of men from other units at Ft. Lewis were transferred to the 2d Division. Doctors were brought in to bring medical units up to strength in surgeons. At least 1,240 replacements came into the division from these and other sources. As elements of the 2d Division sailed on July 20, another 1,500 replacements, destined for the 7th Division in Japan, sailed with them. Enroute, MacArthur authorized these men also to be allocated to the 2d Division.

Depots throughout the U.S. were tasked to fill divisional equipment shortages and repair unserviceable or marginally serviceable weapons and equipment.

On July 10, COL Charles C. Sloane Jr., commanding the 9th Infantry Regiment, began organizing the 9th RCT. On July 12, COL John G. Hill was named commander of the RCT, but Sloane retained command of the 9th Regiment, a bizarre and unworkable arrangement, corrected later.

More than 1,000 signal items were repaired and made serviceable and 20 per cent of the divisional signal equipment was replaced. Each RCT was provided with a 30-day supply of expendable signal items. The 2d Signal Co. sent wire, radio and photo items to each RCT.

Medical personnel inspected each troop transport and extra serum was stocked on each ship for anyone who had missed getting his shots. MP platoons were organized from the MP Co. for each RCT.

Eleven cargo and 10 personnel ships were loaded in 19 days, along with all the other work attending preparations for deployment.

In addition to getting shots, making allotments, obtaining legal assistance, other processing, packing and loading, the infantrymen, artillerymen, tankers, recon troops and engineers squeezed in all the training possible.

On July 17, 1950, the naval transport USNS *M. M. Patrick* set sail from Seattle with the first contingent of the 2d Infantry Division; the bulk of the 9th RCT, the 2d Recon and 2d QM Co.s The 2d also was known as the "Indianhead Division," for its shoulder patch, the figure of an Indian head with war bonnet. The unofficial name by the Division's membership was "Second to None." On the 18th, the USNS *General C. G. Martin* departed with 3/9 Inf, 15 FAB and more men for the recon and QM companies. The remainder of the division and its equipment were transported in 19 more vessels.

An advance party, under the ADC, BG Joseph S. Bradley, flew into Tokyo on July 25. Two days later, MacArthur decided to send the entire 2d Division directly to Korea, and the Advance Party flew into Korea on July 29. Upon arrival in Korea, the 2d Division was almost up to 100 percent in strength and ordnance equipment. The command arrived in Korea between July 31 and Aug. 20, 1950, mostly by Aug. 4. Dates of arrival of major units were:

July 31 — 9 RCT; lead elements of Div HQ; 15 FAB; 2d Recon and 2d QM Cos. Moved to vicinity of Kyongson.

Aug. 4 — Part of 23d Inf; DivArty HQ; 37 FAB; B/82 AA; B/2 Engr.

Aug. 5 — 1/23 and 2/23 Inf; elements of 2d Med Bn; 2d MP and 2d Sig. Cos.

On Aug. 5, 1/9 Inf, HM Co. and A/15 FAB all were alerted for action in the 24th Division sector. This force moved out on Aug. 6, the day A/15 FAB fired the first rounds of the 2d Division on the enemy. The 38th RCT arrived in Korea Aug. 19.

In the first week of July, William R. Swafford was waiting in Seattle, WA, to be sent to the Far East, when he was sent to Ft. Lewis and assigned to D/9 Inf. In the short time between his assignment to Dog Co. and embarkation for Korea, he received training on the .30- and .50-cal machine guns, the 75mm recoilless rifle and the bazooka. But he recalled, in that short time, he did not get to know the men in the unit. His outfit sailed on the *General Sultan*. "We trained on the ship," he wrote, "firing .30-cal and .50-cal machine guns at balloons dropped overboard."

When the ship approached Korea, "you could smell the odor [of Korea]...well before getting to Pusan," he recalled. The troops disembarked about dark and were put into a large open shed. "I could not sleep that night because of all the noise and several rifle shots," Swafford wrote.

The next day, his unit started to the front on a train. When the train stopped the men had to leave their duffel bags behind and began a foot march from there. Swafford recalled, "At night you could hear artillery and see flashes when the rounds hit the hills."

At one point, the company stopped near an orchard and were sitting on a nearby ridge, eating apples, "when a bullet kicked up the dust a few feet away," he recounted. "Then a mortar round came in (WP) and landed about 30 feet away; no one was hurt...."

The S4 of the 23d Infantry was MAJ Harlos V. Hatter, a combat veteran of the Italian campaign of WW II. When the Korean War started he commanded a battalion of the 23d, but was ranked out of the position by an officer on a DA directed assignment. Hatter was reassigned as the regiment's logistics officer. He wrote that, because the 23d Regiment was not combat loaded aboard ship for Korea, "my regiment had to enter combat without even a full complement of supporting weapons from the three heavy weapons companies, i.e., heavy machine guns and 81mm mortars, buried along with ammunition deep in the hold of the transport ships."

He also remarked on ammunition shortages which U.S./ROK forces experienced at the time. He wrote that "the biggest problem [with supply services] was the shortage of heavy mortar and artillery ammunition." The "shortage of ammunition, especially 81mm...mortar ammunition," sometimes reduced the effectiveness of fire support.

At one point, shortly after his arrival in Korea, MAJ Hatter had to draw 20 2 1/2-ton trucks, heavy machine guns, mortars and ammunition for the regiment, "without so much as a hand receipt." Some of the trucks had no "spare tires, jacks, tools, etc."

When the Korean War started, LT John H. Ramsburg was Assistant S2, 2/23 Inf. He, too, recalled that weapons training, including crew served weapons training from the fantail, continued aboard ship. LTC James W. Edwards, commanding 2/23 Inf, had been stationed in Korea after WW II. He conducted orientation classes, based on his knowledge of Korea, and the battle situation.

John R. Kampershroer was 18 in June 1950, and had just completed an eight-week volunteer course in Marine pipe fitting. About this time, the Navy took over the Transportation Corps ships, "making Army grads useless," he wrote, "and therefore our class almost to a man (or boy) was sent to Ft. Lewis, Washington...for assignment to the 2d Division." Kampershroer went to a rifle company of 3/23 Inf. Disappointed, he asked for a transfer. "A captain at the battalion...looked over my 201 [personnel] file and asked if I'd like to be a medic — Salvation!... I jumped at the chance." Kampershroer's brother had been a sergeant technician in a field hospital in WW II. He envisioned a similar assignment.

He was duly assigned to the 23d Regiment's Medical Co. "I didn't realize that as aidman followed the infantry...[but] didn't carry a gun," he wrote, "instead a medical aid kit with bandages and a scissors."

Kampershroer "was 'Doc' to 42 guys in an infantry platoon of L Company of the 23d — 42 guys that I'd never seen before. I'm sure I must have looked pretty stupid as that's how I felt," he wrote. He lasted in Korea from Aug. 4 to Sept. 16, 1950. Kampershroer recalled that over 30 members of his company were lost as POWs in 1950 — 25 per cent of the unit. Less than half of these POWs lived to be freed in 1953.

Whether they were called Doc, Medic or Corpsman, countless hundreds of these front-line medical aidmen died or were wounded, or sometimes were captured, while unselfishly trying to save the lives of other soldiers and Marines under enemy fire. When men were being wounded and enemy fire was falling thick and fast, these brave men always responded to the call of "Medic!" or "Corpsman!"

"9 July 50 Platoon was notified of alert at 1300 hours by M/Sgt Bishop." This is from the first page of a journal of then MSG Jesse L. Bishop, platoon sergeant, Weapons Platoon, F/23 Inf. With one officer and 19 EM, the platoon was at 50 per cent strength; short two men in platoon headquarters, six EM in the Mortar Section and 12 EM in the 57mm Recoilless Rifle Section.

On July 14 the platoon turned in their three mortars for salvage and drew three new ones the next day, drawing a new 57mm recoilless rifle on July 17. Before shipping out, the platoon lost four men and gained one, according to Bishop's daily journal. Unless he neglected to record other personnel changes, the platoon shipped out for Korea with one officer and 16 EM.

Enroute to Korea, training consisted of films, physical training and classes in map reading and crew-served weapons, including the 60mm mortar. The platoon was administered typhus and cholera shots aboard ship on July 25. All weapons were inspected on Aug. 4, and the ship docked in Pusan the following day. Bishop's platoon unloaded at 7 p.m. and moved into a warehouse for the night. The following day, they departed Pusan by train "and moved north about 30 miles." At this stop, the platoon received twenty-five new men, one of which was medically evacuated two days later.

Between August 6 and 22, the platoon trained, although it moved frequently from one place to another. Bishop became platoon leader on Aug. 20. By this time, the unit was north of Taegu.

PFC James Coulos was assigned to the public information office of the Fifth Army in Chicago when the Korean War started. He became a member of the HM Co., 23d Inf. His unit had a number of men who had never fired the M1 rifle, he recalled. Instruction for them was given on the fantail of the ship, where they practiced shooting at "pieces of wood, balloons, bottles, cans, etc., dropped astern," he recalled.

South Korea "was not all dung-laden rice paddies or scorched and barren hills," he wrote. "I remember the tall grass and trees lining the Bowling Alley. I was so young that it seemed like a beautiful adventure to me."

"I was trained by the company NCOs in the 107th [Infantry Regiment, NY National Guard]," wrote Thomas K. Voorhis, who was commissioned from OCS in Dec. 1942. Voorhis was assistant motor officer of the 38th Infantry when the Korean War began.

"It was my wife's birthday," he wrote. "We were returning from a...trip to Mt. Rainier when we heard the news [about the start of the war]." He had been married less than a year. Although he did not like to leave his new bride, "I accepted the fact," he wrote, that going to war was part of Army life which I had elected to follow."

Enroute to Korea, Voorhis recalled that some men who had served in KMAG oriented them on what to expect in Korea, and its government and history. He, too, recalled inspections, training in weapons firing, indoctrination lectures and films, as well as unit planning meetings.

CWO Fred W. Merten's recollections of preparing for and moving to Korea were much the same as other members of the 2d Division. He was a member of the 38th Infantry at the time. The troops, he recalled, mixed last minute training with "drawing arms and equipment, packing and crating [and] loading and shipping their tanks, trucks and heavy gear."

At dawn of August 19," he continued, "we could see rise from the horizon the bleak and barren coastal ranges of Korea.... It was hot and muggy, with intermittent heavy downpours. The troops either moved in swirling dust or hub-deep mud."

The initial 38th Regimental CP was established in a school building in the village of Chungdae-ri on Aug. 23. A few days later, he wrote, the CP was moved forward to another school building in the village of Sibri-ri, "nestled at the foot of a steep mountain, Hill 289.... We

thought to remain fairly unmolested there. However, some enemy artillery began to drop in on us during the first night. The next day, the CP moved to a draw across the road, where it remained for some time, disturbed only by an enemy SP gun which "would send us greetings regularly every afternoon," Mertens recalled.

When RCTs were formed in the 2d Division in preparation for deployment to Korea, certain separate combat support battalions, such as the 82d Anti-Aircraft Automatic Weapons Battalion (AA/AW Bn) attached their subordinate units to the RCTs. Battery A was attached to the 9th; B to the 23d and C to the 38th. The batteries traveled to Korea on the ships carrying their respective RCTs. Btry A, with a complement of seven officers and 151 EM, sailed July 17 aboard the *General Patrick*. By Aug. 10, the battery was part of TF Bradley at K-3, the airstrip at Yonil. Baker Btry, with seven officers and 133 EM departed July 22 on the *General Funston* and arrived in Korea Aug. 3. By Aug. 13, part of the battery was in battle, supporting a platoon of 1/23 Inf. between Miryang and Yongsan.

The remainder of the 82d (C, D and HQ Batteries) arrived in Pusan on Aug. 16 and proceeded on to Miryang the next day. In a letter to his wife, battalion commander LTC Walter Killilea had this to say about Pusan: "That city is a mess. It is dirty and it smells beyond description. Mean little houses for the most part, built of either flimsy frame construction or an adobe type stuff with part rock walls here and there. Rocks are unmortared — just fitted together. The business and industrial area is of brick and frame construction, but once again incredibly dirty and terribly in need of repair. There are street cars, but how they continue to operate is a mystery.

"Speeding trolleys are the fashion, and as they speed along with parts flapping...it appears they should disintegrate at the next lurch.... [The people] dress poorly, and almost entirely in oriental rather than western garb."

The equipment of the 72d Tank Bn (LTC

Clark Webber) sailed to Korea aboard the transports *Rutgers* and *Joplin*, embarking July 29. Battalion personnel were on the *General Mitchell*, sailing on Aug. 2. The attitude of the men of the 72d was that Korea would be no lark, and they were serious and determined. Although they had not asked for this war, they were "damned well" going to end it, stated the battalion history.

Many replacements came to bring the 72d up to strength; some within 24 hours of sailing. Aboard ship, as with other commands of the division, the new men were integrated into their units, classes were held and weapons fire and inspected.

When the troops arrived in Korea, "the romantic picture of the Orient held by some faded rapidly once the smell of centuries of 'Honey Buckets' came to the nostrils. The smell of filth and decay was everywhere." (Quoted from 72d Tank Bn history.)

Upon arrival, one of the troopers, remembering the recruiting posters which had lured him into the service with travel, adventure, good pay, etc., said, "Okay, I've seen it, let's go home."

The 72d bivouacked for four days just outside Pusan, unloading and servicing equipment, moving to Miryang on Aug. 22. Co. A (CPT Wilfred Pettit) was attached to the 9th RCT and moved to Yongsan the same day; that afternoon 1LT Lock W. Ireland's platoon fired the first shot of the battalion in the Korean War.

2LT Edward B. Quinn, freshly graduated from West Point in early June 1950, found himself assigned to the 72d Tank Bn. He was vacationing in Yellowstone National Park when the war started and found a notice along the road for him to call home. Orders came for him to report immediately to the 2d Division. Quinn said he was one of 42 members of the West Point Class of 1950 assigned to the 2d Division.

Another new officer from the Class of '50 was 2LT John E. Fox, soon to be assigned as a rifle platoon leader in F/38 Inf. He had been a

A view of Puson Harbor, Summer 1950. (Courtesy of John E. Fox, F & G/38 Infantry)

Navy enlisted man toward the end of WW II, but had no training as an infantryman. He was given no opportunity to attend the basic infantry officer's course. (See Chapter Notes.)

What was true of the officers also was true of many of the fillers. Quinn said that half of his unit "had never had a tank ride prior to arriving in Pusan." Although there were many experienced tankers among the NCOs, many of the fillers of the 72d and other units learned on the job, in combat — an expensive way to train.

In the early stages of the war, Quinn reported the lack of skill by both the North Korean and American tank crews (and the status of U.S. equipment) often led to ineffective tank vs. tank engagements. The U.S. crews soon overcame this shortcoming, but the attrition among North Korean crews and huge losses in tanks prevented them from developing appreciably.

Quinn recalled that Co. A, 72d TK Bn, had four platoons; Two of M4A3E8s and two of the newer M-26 Pershings. "These tanks had been painted and cleaned, and painted and cleaned and steam cleaned, to the point that the radios and intercoms were badly rusted and corroded and virtually useless," Quinn said. "We had no on-vehicle tools," he also pointed out.

The principal leadership of the 2d Infantry Division included MG Laurence B. "Dutch" Keiser, 55 (West Point 1917); ADC, BG Joseph Salden Bradley, 50 (West Point 1919); BG Loyal M. Haynes (Knox College 1917), 55, commanding DivArty; COL Joseph M. Tulley (West Point 1916) as Chief of Staff, who encountered difficulties shortly after arriving in Korea and was replaced by COL Gerald G. "Gerry" Eply (West Point 1932), who had been the Division G2.

Due to some foul-up, uncorrected by the Pentagon, the 2d Division had five full colonels assigned to the three regiments. Colonels John G. Hill (West Point 1924) and Charles C. "Chin" Sloane (West Point 1926) for the 9th (Manchu) Regiment; Colonels Paul F. Freeman (West Point 1929) and Edwin J. "Ed" Messinger (West Point 1931) for the 23d Infantry (Tomahawks) and COL George B. "Pep" Peploe (West Point 1925) for the 38th (Rock of the Marne) Regiment.

Keiser appointed Hill to command the 9th RCT, with Sloane commanding the 9th Regiment. Freeman was appointed to command the 23d RCT, with Messinger in command of the regiment. However, in the latter case, Freeman knew GEN Keiser well from previous service and forcefully complained of this unworkable arrangement. As a result, when the RCT got to Korea Freeman remained in command and Messinger became his XO, still a tough assignment.

The First Provisional Marine Brigade

On June 28, 1950, Marine Corps Commandant GEN Clifton B. Cates met with ADM Admiral Forest P. Sherman, Chief of Naval Operation (CNO). During the meeting, GEN Cates recommended that the Fleet Marine Force (FMF) be employed in Korea, and gave Sherman a summary of the strength of the Marine Corps (74,279). However Cates pointed out the Corps' two divisions, the 1st and 2d, would be hard-pressed to field more than one RCT of combat-ready troops with air support.

On July 1, ADM Arthur W. Radford, Commander in Chief, Pacific Fleet (CinCPacFlt), determined that a Battalion Landing Team (BLT) could be loaded in four days and sail in six, and that he could load an RCT in six days and sail in 10.

On July 2, ADM Sherman notified ADM C. Turner Joy, Commander of the Navy, Far East (COMNAVFE) that a Marine RCT could be made available to GEN MacArthur if he desired it. Joy immediately met with MacArthur, and the general enthusiastically accepted.

On July 3, GEN Cates wrote on his calendar: "Attended JCS meeting. Orders for employment of FMF approval." The next day, LTG Lemual C. Shepherd Jr., commanding FMFPac, and his G3, COL Victor H. Krulak, were ordered to Tokyo to confer with GEN MacArthur. Before departing, Shepherd recommended to the CNO that the third rifle platoons be formed in each of the rifle companies of the 5th Marines, and CNO approved.

The 1st Marine Division was stationed at Camp Pendleton, CA at the time. It was a division in name only because it included only one Marine regiment, the 5th, which was well short of war strength. Each of the three battalions had but two rifle companies and a weapons company, instead of the authorized three rifle companies. Even worse, the rifle companies had only two of the three rifle platoons authorized. The action by LTG Shepherd and the CNO corrected the third platoon deficiency, but not that of a third rifle company in each battalion.

Nucleus of the 1st Provisional Brigade, the 5th Marines, went to Korea organized thusly: 1st Battalion: A, B, Weapons; 2d Battalion: D, E, Weapons; 3d Battalion: G, H, Weapons. (See Chapter Notes.)

The 1st Provisional Marine Brigade was a unique and powerful combat force, which included infantry, armor, artillery, engineers, transportation and air support within its organization. No Army command had its own air support, giving the Brigade that advantage. However, when Marine air was available, it came to the aid of Army units with the same speed and efficiency. (See Chapter Notes.)

VMO-6 had the first U.S. helicopter pilots to be formed into a combat service unit. MTACS-2 furnished forward air controllers to the ground elements of the Brigade, called Forward Tactical Air Control parties (FTAC), which performed the same mission as Air Force FACs.

The ground elements of the Brigade, with attachments, numbered 289 officers and 4,785 EM. VMO-6 numbered 15 officers and 63 EM, but is included in the attached personnel. The MAG-33 component added another 192 officers and 1,358 EM. The Brigade totaled 6,624 personnel — 481 officers and 6,143 EM. (These figures are derived from pp. 50-51 and Appendix B - Command and Staff List of the First Provisional Marine Brigade, in the official marine history, *The Pusan Perimeter.*)

The 5th Marines, less attachments, numbered 132 officers and 2,452 EM. Very soon after commitment to battle it became necessary to call for volunteers from many of the Brigade's service support units to replace numerous casualties in the 5th Marines. As one Marine officer put it, they "had to eat their [logistical] tail" to fill up the infantry elements of the Brigade.

Like the soldiers of the Army's 5th RCT and 2d Infantry Division, the Marines of the 1st Provisional Brigade scrambled to get ready for Korea. Assimilation of new men went concurrently with checking, packing and loading equipment, receiving new or additional weapons and equipment, along with bits of training squeezed in whenever possible.

The tank company had trained with M4A3 tanks. For Korea it received 15 of the newer M-26 Pershings with 90mm guns. Company commander CPT Gearl M. English managed to squeeze in one day to fire the 90mm gun. Using two tanks, each gunner and loader had the opportunity to fire two rounds, the only tank firing the men would experience with the 90mm gun until they entered combat.

MAJ Gottschalk was appointed to command VMO-6 on July 3. He had to have his new squadron ready for overseas deployment by July 11,

Jack Wright and Friends (Courtesy of Jack Wright, G-5 Marines)

Marine Commandant GEN Clifton B. Cates in an informal chat with marines about to depart for Korea. PVT David J. bohlke (age 17) is at left. (Courtesy of David J. Bohlke, A-5 Marines. Official U.S. Marine Corps photo.)

Able Company 1st. Tank Battalion, 1st Provisional Marine Brigade, July 1950, loading for Korea. Pictured here are Robinson, Harlin, Gokee and DiNoto. (Courtesy of Paul DiNoto, A/1st Tank Bn, 1st Prov. Marine Bde)

including absorption of the helicopter contingent from Quantico, which did not arrive until July 9. Gottschalk discovered that there were not enough OY observation aircraft available at his base at El Toro. To solve the problem, he took eight planes to Korea, planning to use four for spare parts when needed.

Officers and enlisted men who otherwise would not have been part of the 1st Provisional Brigade volunteered to go with it. Among these were lieutenants Tom Johnston, (DSC, 1st Naktong); Francis W. "Metz" Muetzel (Silver Star, 1st Naktong and Bronze Star, Inchon); and Baldermo Lopez (MOH, Inchon).

Marines poured in from 105 posts and stations throughout the U.S. The men who came from a life of recruiting stations and guard units would be among those who suffered the most from the oppressive heat, humidity and almost-continuous hill-climbing and marching in Korea. But all of the new men had undergone weapons qualification and individual military training that the Corps required of everyone not serving in field units.

The Brigade was fortunate that 90 per cent of the officers and 65 per cent of the NCOs were combat veterans — percentages higher than most Army commands of comparable size. Even the 10 per cent of corporals and PFCs with combat experience may have been somewhat higher than in Army units first sent to Korea.

Many young Army and Marine enlisted men credited the combat-experienced NCOs and officers with saving their lives, while making efficient use of small arms, automatic weapons, mortars and artillery to inflict heavy casualties on the enemy. They were showing the young warriors the "tricks of the trade."

Companies A and B, 1st Battalion, had been together for some time, having been previously part of the 6th Marines. Co. B had been the division's elite demonstration troop for combat exercises and what military men call "dog and pony shows": Exercises or demonstrations for VIPs and others.

The 3d Battalion, 5th Marines also was well trained. Most of the men had been together one to two years, many with the battalion on Guam between 1947 and 1949. There, the only game was combat training. The men of 3-5 Marines, as well as the others from the 5th, had undergone live-firing exercises and had conducted assault exercises on Horno Ridge at Pendleton and/or been in amphibious Exercise Demon III.

Robert D. Bohn commanded G-3-5 Marines, a unit formed on Guam after WW II. Except for company officers and NCOs from first sergeant to platoon sergeant, all the other men came straight out of boot camp. There were no corporals or sergeants. "Although that may sound like a disadvantage, it worked out," he said. "We could pick the best people to promote to corporal and sergeant. As a result, they performed beautifully in Korea." Bohn said that this battalion "was probably the best peace-time battalion the Marine Corps ever had." During the two years on Guam company commanders were allowed the latitude to develop their own individual unit training programs, then implement them.

Enroute to Korea, the companies continued training aboard ship, including instruction on

131

preparing booby traps, which they blew up off the ship's fantail. The Marines also took the opportunity to fire weapons off the fantail, he recalled.

1LT Bohn recalled the first night ashore after landing in Korea. "The whole brigade went into positions and some of the companies...did a lot of shooting. But we were shooting at each other.... I think cooler heads prevailed and got them stopped."

LTC Robert D. Taplett, commanding 3-5 Marines, recalled that during this first jumpy night, one of the men of his battalion, out of his foxhole, was challenged by a sergeant. The man couldn't remember the password and tried to get by the sergeant. The NCO hit the man with a rifle butt-stroke, breaking his jaw. "That was our first casualty in Korea," he recalled.

LTC Taplett remembered that, on Saturday, July 8 the division had a review. Afterwards "We were informed that they were going to organize a brigade to be sent immediately to Korea..." he recalled. From that time on, "We spent the days...working 18, 20 and 24 hours a day, getting our equipment ready...and we had to strip the unit of all people who had short tours. As a result, we probably had about a 50 per cent turnover on our personnel." But, he added, "We had a highly-trained corps, a well-trained battalion as well as a well-trained regiment, which was the core of the brigade.... They all knew what they were doing, and that's why we were able to expeditiously get our gear together and embark aboard [the USS *Pickaway*] combat-loaded to go to Korea."

As the 1st Provisional Marine Brigade was preparing for immediate deployment, plans were set in motion to organize the 1st Marine Division for later deployment. Personnel for this division came from Marine barracks personnel on the West Coast, elements of the 2d Marine Division on the East Coast, and a major call-up of reservists. As COL Fenton so aptly put it, "If it hadn't been for these well trained reserves, many of them 'retreads' from World War II, the accomplishments of the Brigade would have been greatly diminished."

The original destination of the Brigade, like that of the 5 RCT and 2d Infantry Division, was Japan, but that was changed to Pusan while the ships were at sea. As Taplett recalled, when his ship docked in Pusan late on Aug. 2, "Everything was in turmoil, as it was rush, rush to get everybody off the ship...." Pusan was bulging with refugees and an air of desperation hung over the place. The attitude of the Army officers and some of the Navy officers at the briefing held for the newly-arrived Marine officers did not help matters. Information about the enemy was sketchy and the maps issued at the briefing were very poor. The maps used early in the war were based on Japanese surveys of 1937 and U.S. aerial photos from 1946 and 1947. Many had no grid lines. They were very inaccurate.

The 3d Battalion was first ordered to Changwon by rail. "We...rode all day, open windows, coal-burning engine; we got stalled in a tunnel a couple of times and damned near suffocated," Taplett remembered. The battalion set up for the night near Changwon, with 25 percent alert all night.

On Aug. 6, LTC Taplett received orders to report to the CP of LTC Michaelis, commanding the Army's 27th Infantry Regiment, near Chindong-ni. Michaelis commanded all troops in that sector at that time. When the 27th went into Eighth Army reserve a few days later, GEN Craig was given command of all troops in that area. Taking a runner, radio operator and a "shotgun" rider, Taplett set out for the CP late in the day.

Michaelis briefed Taplett, and told him to move his battalion onto Hill 255 and relieve 2/27 Inf. (LTC Gordon Murch) the next day. The 2/27 had their CP in the same schoolhouse which had been attacked by the enemy on Aug. 3. It was right after this fight that Michaelis moved his CP forward about a mile to a point on the road and at the foot of another finger ridge. An officer of 2/27 Inf offered Taplett the schoolhouse for his CP. He refused, saying that he would "go up the reverse slope of the mountain and set up there."

Taplett's battalion took over the 2/27 Infantry battle positions. Initially, he placed Co. G atop a hill 2,000 meters north of the 27th's CP and Co. H, less one platoon, on Hill 255, just north of his own CP. One platoon of H was sent to a smaller hill 600 or 700 yards south of the Chindong-ni-Masan road, which ran along the base of Hill 255.

Young James Sanders went to Guam just out of boot camp. He recalled that the NCOs were all veterans of the Pacific war. Training on Guam, he wrote "was constant field hikes, amphibious maneuvers, weapons proficiency, field tactics and coordination of close-air support," Returning to the States, he was assigned to Camp Pendleton and G-3-5 Mar.

"One major field maneuver took place," Sanders wrote. "Hot! Near 100 degrees in May 1950. After long marches through the hills and fire breaks — we finally assaulted the major objective, a great steep hill.... Marine Corsairs streaked in firing 20mm just yards in front of the rifle companies in the assault. Upon gaining the hill, the Corsairs then directed their attack on the far side with rockets and napalm."

Sanders remembered that "as a rifle company supply sergeant my life became hectic," when orders came forming the Brigade for Korea. He supervised crating and marking gear for an amphibious landing and prioritized weapons ammo, water, food etc., for tactical unloading.

When Sanders and his comrades learned they were headed for Korea, their reaction was, "Hey, we've prepared for this. Let's go and show them our stuff," Sanders wrote. "Many Marines...re-enlisted to go with the company. When we arrived in Pusan a pathetic [Korean] band was trying to play the *Marine Hymn*, Marines were shouting from the deck, 'Have no fear, the Marines are here!'" Others hurled insults at the soldiers and at the band, which they mistook for a U.S. Army band. Sanders wrote later: "This sounds like a gung-ho fanatic, but I'm not. This was our mental set."

Once the company jeep and trailer were unloaded, Sanders drove it in convoy with other Marine vehicles to the battalion assembly area near Changwon. "Drove most of the night," he wrote. After unloading the jeep and trailer, he parked it part-way up a hill, then dug in at the unit CP. That night, one of the company sergeants

received a grazing scalp wound and LT John D. Counselman had the stock of his carbine split by a rifle bullet. Sanders wrote that he realized that his survival and that of Co. G was "going to be an all-for- one and one-for-all deal."

DuWayne A. Philo was already a sergeant and career Marine at the outbreak of the Korean War, a combat veteran of the Pacific. He, too, had been on Guam for two years, and had just returned to Pendleton and married. Philo and his wife were looking forward to a three-year tour at the camp.

"I always seemed to end up as the NCO directly in charge of a hold," he wrote of his voyage to Korea, "and had the job of keeping the men (and the hold) clean."

Like the Army, the Marines reassigned men from all over to fill up the units going to Korea. Robert Roberts graduated from boot camp in 1948 and was sent to the Marine Corps supply depot, Barstow, CA, where from Nov. 1948 to July 1950, he served as a fireman. When the 5th Marines needed men to fill it up, Roberts and a number of other men from his fire station were sent to Co. G. He recalled that, in all, around 50 firemen from a number of points were tapped for the Brigade.

At 8 a.m. one day, he and a number of other men from his fire crew were ordered to pack up and travel to Pendleton by buses provided for the purpose. They arrived about 11 p.m., drew field equipment and got to bed some time after 1 a.m. Rolled out at 5:30 a.m., they had "chow, a lecture, cargo net training, shots, dental check and a day later boarded ship at San Diego and sailed," he wrote. Aboard ship, he and his comrades were briefed about the enemy and "what we as infantrymen should expect."

Jack E. "Archie" Wright said, "We graduated from boot camp June 24, 1950." About a week later "we were sent to Camp Pendleton to the 1st Provisional Marine Brigade.... [When] we got to Pendleton...it was mass confusion as far as we were concerned." He recalled that he and his buddies were bedded down, then rousted out to be issued equipment, sent to another place where they turned that equipment in, then to another barracks and repeated the whole business. Once, they were sent to a mess hall for some chow. "It seemed like this went on for two-thirds of the night," he recalled. The next morning his group was split up; half went to Co. G and half to Co. H.

He was with Co. G about a week before shipping out, during which they ran a few short field problems. Finally the unit boarded the personnel transport *Pickaway*. Three days out, the roll of the ship made "everybody...seasick. That's when I learned a little secret about being aboard ship," he said.

As the junior member of a fire team, Wright had the bottom bunk. "At first I thought was making out like a champ," he said. But his bunk was in the center of the ship. As the vessel rolled, everything not fastened down slid or fell near Wright's bunk. "Since I was centrally located, everything ended up underneath my rack [bunk]." Every morning, he returned "machine gun barrels, machine guns, rifles, and packs to guys whose bunks were on either side of me." He also found out the hard way the disadvantage of the bottom bunk when someone above him became seasick.

LT Jack Westerman, Wright's platoon leader, once told him that "he didn't care what the outside of a rifle looked like, as long as the inside was clean and ready to go and [to] keep that rifle clean and dry even if you have to lay on it," as Wright recalled.

A few days after their arrival in Korea Wright's unit was in an assembly area when it began to rain. He had dug a prone position, a hole big enough to lie down in, but not as deep as a foxhole, about 2 feet wide, 2 feet deep and as long as the occupant is tall — "two by two by you," as the saying went.

Although the veterans around him had removed their packs and made little tents over their prone shelters with ponchos or shelter halves, Wright had not. He figured that it would be a lot of trouble "redoing it" in the morning.

"Lt Westerman comes along...about midnight," Wright recounted. "I'm in my hole. It's full to the top. Water is running out of it. I'm miserable, wet, angry and cold. I'm hungry and I'm grumpy. He asked me where my rifle was. I told him, 'Sir, its right where you told me to put it to keep it dry and clean. I'm laying on it.' And I was - under all that water, in the mud, was my rifle and I was laying on it. How dumb can you get! LT Westerman went on down the line muttering...and shaking his head."

When the Korean War started, Jerry D. Rocky was a sergeant at Pendleton. He served with H-3-5 Marines in the Perimeter. Rocky said that "the cream of the crop" were selected to fill up the 5th Regiment for Korea.

One day after the word came that the 5th was headed for Korea, SGT Rocky was teaching machine gun headspace adjustment to some newly-assigned Marines. One of the youngsters said, "Gee, I hope the war won't be over before we get there. We can get a campaign ribbon if it isn't over." Some "old timer" Marine NCOs standing nearby rolled their eyes at this. One of them said, "Don't worry, the war will still be going on. You'll get your campaign ribbon, all right."

The experiences of the men of the 1st Battalion were similar to those of the other two battalions.

CPT Francis I. "Ike" Fenton Jr. was assigned to the 5th Marines. When the regiment was ordered to Korea, he volunteered to go as a rifle company XO, and was assigned as XO, B-1-5 Marines. Fenton credited the tough training at Pendleton preparing the men for Korea and Demon III for helping to mold the companies. In another exercise, helicopters were used to carry out "wounded" and to resupply ground troops in mountainous terrain, an excellent preparation, for some of the battles the Marines would face in Korea.

The 1-5 Marines shipped out on the *Henrico*; both generals Cates and Shepherd were on hand to say farewell and good luck to the Brigade as it departed. Their appearance and expressions of best wishes were a boost to all the men. A few days out, the *Henrico* developed turbine trouble and had to return to Oakland, after transferring the regimental commander and some of his staff to the *Pickaway* and *George Clymer*.

While the *Henrico* was being repaired, the Marine units aboard ship took turns on the docks, conducting limited tactical training, emphasizing fire team formations and arm and hand signals. Lectures on machine guns and 60mm mortars, calisthenics and body building also were conducted. Training continued enroute to Korea, including orientations on the T-34 tank. Just before shipping out, the Brigade was issued 3.5-inch rocket launchers. Although nobody had fired one, they studied the manual and became as familiar as possible with the weapon.

Upon arrival in Korea, like the remainder of the Brigade, 1-5 Mar. was ordered to Changwon. Fenton recalled they were there about three days.

* * *

"The sound of a radio drifted out of an upstairs window. 'We interrupt this broadcast to announce that North Korea has invaded South Korea.' The date was 25 June 1950."

Thus begins the remarkable 100-page personal account of PFC Herbert R. Luster, a BAR-man of Co. A, 1st Bn, 5th Marines. He had joined Co. A from boot camp just the day before, June 24. Luster named the BAR he took to Korea "Patty."

On July 2, a fellow Marine gave him a beautiful and expensive Bible, that became a prized possession, and which he turned to daily. Unfortunately, upon arrival in Korea he had to leave the Bible behind when the unit stripped down for combat.

When the unit was preparing for Korea, Luster was sent to help load the ship. Civilian dock workers were on strike. "When the Marines got off the trucks, tension was high," he wrote. But the striking dock workers didn't want to take on the Marines.

He was aboard the *Henrico* and recalled that it had to return to port for repairs, then proceed to Korea alone. One night, a radar contact was made and General Quarters was sounded. The contact proved to be a whale, and the ship soon secured from General Quarters. Speeding along as fast as possible, the *Henrico* caught up to the rest of the convoy carrying the Brigade just one day out of Pusan. The debarking Marines, Luster recalled, were full of bravado.

During the night of Aug. 3-4, in their first assembly area, Robert J. Cazzalio of LT Muetzel's platoon lit a cigarette. Another Marine mistook him for the enemy and fired at Cazzalio, fatally wounding him.

Roger C. Solheid and some friends, having enlisted in the Marine Corps in 1948, were discussing what they were going to do when their enlistments were up in 1951. Solheid was company clerk for Co. A, 1st Tank Battalion. The news of the Korean War ended all talk of what they would do in 1951. Solheid was astonished at the rapidity with which M-26 Pershing tanks were obtained, demothballed and shipped from Barstow to his unit at Pendleton. "At that time even requisitions for simple office supplies were back ordered," he recalled.

The tank company sailed aboard the *Fort Marion*. About noon July 13, the ship's well deck accidentally flooded to a depth of five feet, and it took the ship's pumps an hour to drain the compartment. By that time, the sea water had damaged 14 of the new M-26 tanks, 300 rounds of then critically-short 90mm ammunition and 5,000 rounds of .30-cal ammunition. All the ammunition had been combat-loaded on the tanks. Twelve of the tanks could be repaired at sea, but the other two would require parts, and it would take days to repair them upon arrival in Korea. The damaged ammunition was jettisoned at sea.

GEN Craig already had contacted Barstow and was promised that 14 replacement tanks would be ready and on the way to San Diego within 24 hours. The news that 12 of the tanks could be repaired halted shipment of the promised 14. Four M-26s were sent in the first resupply shipment to the Brigade. Spare parts and replacement ammunition were flown to the port of debarkation.

As August began, significant and decisive reinforcements arrived in Korea, reinforcements sufficient to stem the steady advance of the North Korean Army. The 9th and 5th RCTs and Marine Bde together brought in between 12,000 and 13,000 additional troops.

Chapter Notes:

P. 130 In all, 141 of the 670 members of the West Point Class of 1950 were sent to Korea in August 1950. Eventually about half of the class served there during the war. Casualties: 29 KIA, five DOW; two died as POWs; three MIA, presumed dead; and three killed in air accidents in Korea and Japan. Total: 42 dead, 84 WIA.

The first 141 members of the class to go to Korea were not permitted to undergo the branch school (Infantry, Armor, Artillery, Engineer, etc.), considered a requirement for basic qualification for every new officer. Although they had undergone the demanding academic, military and physical regiment of the U.S. Military Academy, they were not yet branch-qualified, a serious shortcoming. The few who had prior military service during WW II, some in combat, had few problems. However, those who did not have that experience were at a serious disadvantage. Quinn, for example, knew little about tanks, but was now a tank platoon leader.

P. 130 Army and Marine rifle and weapons companies were organized differently. For example, the Army rifle platoon had three rifle squads of nine men each. The squad had one BAR and eight M1 rifles. The Army platoon also had a weapons squad, consisting of a .30-cal light machine gun team and a rocket launcher team. The Marine rifle platoon had three 13-man rifle squads but no weapons squad. Each squad consisted of three BAR teams of four men each. The Marine platoon had nine automatic weapons vs. four in the Army platoon.

P. 130 Principal Leadership of the 1st Provisional Marine Brigade: Brigade Commander — BG Edward A. Craig; 5th Marines — LTC Raymond L. Murray; 1st Bn, 11th Marines (105mm how) — LTC Ransom M. Wood (12 105mm howitzers); Co. A, 1st Tank Bn (3 plt; 15 tanks) — CPT Gearl M. English; VMO-6 (4 HO35-1 helicopters; 8 observation planes) — MAJ Vincent J. Gottschalk; 1st Marine Air Wing — BG Thomas J. Cushman; Marine Air Group 33 (MAG 33) — COL Allen C. Koonce (to Aug. 5), COL Frank G. Dailey.

CHAPTER TWELVE - Task Force Kean

Character of Perimeter Battle

(Author's note — As more troops arrived in Korea and the fight became general along the Perimeter, it is difficult sometimes to sort out the complexities of battle actions occurring simultaneously along the line. A series of savage, brutal battles took place in a number of areas at the same time. They may have started or ended on different dates, but several major battles were in progress almost all the time during the Perimeter days. For logic and sequence, the major actions are covered in a series of chapters (e.g. Task Force Kean; The First Battle of the Naktong Bulge, etc.). Smaller but significant battles or other actions which occurred in the same geographic area near the time of the major engagement are covered within the appropriate chapter.)

Too many people, including the soldiers and marines who fought in Korea during July and Aug. 1950, never understood that the mission of Army troops in Korea all during July 1950 was to <u>delay</u> the enemy, fall back to another position and <u>delay</u> again. There was no line! There was never an "American forward wall," as Edwin P. Hoyt wrote in his *The Pusan Perimeter*. The battles were usually by an isolated company or battalion, a terrible way to fight a war. But the enemy <u>was</u> delayed. Because of this ignorance, the troops who fought this bloody, frustrating delaying battles often have been mistakenly called "ill-trained," "bug-outs," or labeled "yellow" or "cowards."

When the Naktong River was reached, the time for delay was at an end. The mission became defend; ground would not be given up without a fight. Every enemy penetration would be counterattacked and beaten back.

Walker exhorted his commanders to conduct an active defense by utilizing patrols, raids and other offensive actions to obtain information and keep the enemy off balance. The attack by 1/27 Infantry on Aug. 2 was an example of what he had in mind. Unfortunately, a similar foray by 1/29 Infantry on the same day along a nearby road met an enemy attack and was halted with heavy casualties

The Planning Section, G-3, Eighth Army, carrying out the offensive spirit exemplified by GEN Walker, developed plans for two offensives. The first would capitalize on the imminent arrival of the Army's 5 RCT and the 1st Marine Brigade — six infantry battalions with tanks and artillery, plus the Marine air element of the Brigade. The second was based on the arrival of the 2d Infantry division and three tank battalions in Korea by mid-August.

The first attack, to take place between Aug. 5 and 10, would mount out of the Masan area toward Chinju; the second would continue the advance west of Yosu, then north via Sunchon, Chonju and Nonsan toward the Kum River. The planning study stated that the first attack "should experience no difficulty in securing Chinju," which may have been true about July 31, but it was no longer so by Aug. 4.

Advance Parties

The Marine Brigade advance party, consisting of generals Craig and Cushman, plus selected staff members, arrived in Japan on July 19. The 2d Infantry Division advance party, under BG Joseph S. Bradley, arrived on July 25. That same date, GEN Craig was informed that the Brigade would be sent directly to Korea and not to Japan first, as originally planned. On July 27, GEN Bradley was informed that the 2d Division also would go directly to Korea, as would the 5 RCT. The North Korean Army was pressing the Americans and ROKs very hard; significant reinforcement was needed immediately.

Craig and his party flew into Korea on July 26 Bradley and his group on July 29. Two days later, elements of the 9 RCT arrived in Pusan.

Between July 26 and 30, GEN Craig and his staff were briefed thoroughly and began completing arrangements for the arrival of the Brigade. The general also took the opportunity to reconnoiter the battle area, utilizing Walker's plane and pilot. On July 30, Walker informed Craig that the Brigade would be committed to battle on the southern front. However, even as the ships bearing the Brigade steamed into Pusan late on Aug. 2, he still had not been informed exactly where on this front his command was to be deployed the following day.

Just before the Brigade arrived in Pusan, Craig's G-4, LTC Arthur A. Chidester, was able to obtain 50 trucks with Army drivers, several jeeps, radio vans and some other equipment. The official Marine history recorded that officers of the Pusan Base Command reacted to Chidester's requests with as much generosity as their meager stocks...would allow."

Aircraft of MAG-33, supporting the Brigade, MATCS-2 and VMO-6 were deployed in preparation for the Brigade's commitment. VMF-124 arrived July 4 on the carrier *Sicily*, VMF-323 aboard the *Badoeng Strait* on July 5. VMF(N)-513, the night fighter squadron, was based at Itazuke. VMO-6 and MATCS-2 went to Chinhae, Korea.

GEN Craig developed an operations plan for debarking and moving forward, to include provisions for one battalion to be the advance guard of the Brigade and sent it via Eighth Army headquarters to COL Edward W. Snedeker, his Chief of Staff, who was enroute aboard the *Clymer* with the ship convoy. He assumed that the Brigade staff, under Snedeker's direction, would prepare an operations order. He was amazed when he discovered that Snedeker never got his message, necessitating a hurried conference at 2100 hours (9 p.m.) on the day of arrival for the Brigade staff, COL Murray, battalion commanders and the commanders of supporting units.

After being briefed on the situation, they were told: "We move out tomorrow at 0600 hours, but we don't know where we are to go." It was an absolutely bizarre situation. The order came by phone at 2325 hours (11:25 p.m.), when COL Landrum, Walker's Chief of Staff, called GEN

Craig to say that the Brigade should assemble near Changwon, west of Pusan. There the Brigade would be in Eighth Army reserve — to be moved only on Walker's specific orders, but if an emergency arose and communication with Eighth Army failed, the Brigade would then be under the control of GEN Kean, of the 25th Division.

The Army's 9 RCT had arrived on July 31 and been sent north to Kyongsan, where it could back up the 24th Division. The advance CP of the 2d Division also was located there.

The 5 RCT, upon arrival, was attached to the 25th Division. Its 2d Battalion was deployed west of Masan near the village of Chindong-ni near 1/27 Inf. The other two battalions initially were located at Usan-ni.

The newly-arrived Army units and Marines fought with phantoms and shadows during their first nights ashore, but their leaders restored order. At dawn on August 4, GEN Craig not only restored order, he called in the leaders of the most obvious offending units and "severely reprimanded" them, as one officer who was present put it. While in the Changwon area, about August 3, 2-5 Mar was hit by 122mm mortar fire.

The *North Korean 6th Division and 83d Motorcycle Regiment*

In the south, facing elements of the 25th Division as July faded into August 1950 were the *NK 6th Division* and *83d Motorcycle Regiment*.

The 6th was composed of combat veterans of the Chinese civil war, and had suffered about 400-500 casualties before August 2-3. On Aug. 2, elements of the *6th* fought a pitched battle with a battalion of the 29th and another from the 19th. They also had a smaller engagement the same day with 1/27 Inf. at the Chinju Pass, about 10 road miles east of Chinju. On Aug. 3, two battalions of the *6th Division's 14th Regiment* suffered heavy casualties, close to 600 men, at the hands of the 1/27 Inf. and 8 FAB. Even so, the battle-wise *6th Division* with the attached *83d Motorcycle Regiment*, estimated at a combined strength of 7,500 men, proved to be a formidable opponent of TF Kean. (See Chapter Notes.)

Hill 342 — Fox Hill (August 2-7)

Hill 342 (Yaban-san), to be known forever to the 5 RCT as Fox Hill, was the site of the first pitched battles for both the it and the Marine Brigade. The hill was initially occupied on Aug. 2 by a platoon of G/5 RCT. On Aug. 3, the North Koreans attacked and seized the peak. During the night of Aug. 3-4, F/5 RCT took it back and remained there until relieved by a Marine company on Aug. 8.

PVT David E. Eckert was a member of Co. F when it attacked Fox Hill. "I crawled up Fox Hill on my belly," he wrote, "and pretty much stayed in that position the whole time. The only time I remember standing up was when I volunteered to go back down the hill to get some water. While I was down there I decided to take a bath in the stream, but no one told me there were Gooks down there. To make a long story short, I ran back up the hill carrying several canteens and my pants.... I can hardly believe I ran so fast, but I was 'pickin' 'em up and layin' 'em down!'"

Two more or less parallel ridges run northwest from the valley generally above Chindong-ni, eventually meeting on Hill 342 and forming a single ridge. This ridge line meanders northwest of that hill, climbing eventually to Sobuk-san (Hill 738). Across the valley to the west of Hill 342 about a mile are the peaks of another ridge which is slightly higher than 342. From this point, an enemy equipped with binoculars easily could overlook Hill 342. The slopes leading to Fox Hill are steep in every direction, but the top of the hill is relatively flat and in 1950 was devoid of concealing foliage except for some grass and scrub pine. Any daylight movement brought immediate and accurate enemy fire.

Further, all during the time that F/5 RCT, the platoon from G-3-5 Marines and D-2-5 Marines were on the hill, enemy soldiers were on the lower slopes, often within grenade range, almost surrounding the peak. The enemy also could observe the peak of 342 from Hill 297, about a mile north, and from another ridge about a mile across the valley to the east. In short, without friendly troops on nearby hills, troops on Hill 342 were isolated and subject to the most severe enemy mortar, machine gun, small-arms and grenade attack by day and enemy assaults every night.

Fox Co.'s XO was 1LT Frank B. Brooks Jr. He had been in Korea before, when his unit of the 5 RCT supplied platoons to demonstrate attack and defensive techniques to South Korean officers. As XO, he was not present with the rifle platoons of the unit when they went atop Hill 342, but followed them. "I met the weapons platoon in the saddle just to the rear of 342," he wrote. "Got a messenger, phone wire, a phone and went up to set up an OP." Because of the accuracy of enemy mortars, Brooks believed that the position had been pre-registered for their fire.

Every man, Army or Marine, who survived Fox Hill remembered the terrible heat and chronic, severe shortage of water. Fox Co. supply people and cooks came up at night with Korean "chiggy bearers," or "choggy bearers" with ammunition, food and water. They also carried off the dead and wounded from that day's action. The route up to 342 was steep and perilous, particularly areas under enemy observation and fire.

Brooks recalled that about 120 men from Co. F went onto the hill on Aug. 3-4, commanded by CPT Stanley Howarth. Other company officers included Brooks and lieutenants Kenneth S. Hino and Angway. In addition to being XO, Brooks also commanded the Weapons Platoon; Hino and Angway each commanded rifle platoons. CPT Howarth told the company that they would "hold the hill at all costs because it was the key to the whole area." The first night on 342 "all hell broke loose," Brooks wrote. "My OP was too close to the edge of the hill and we got grenades all around us. We were lucky to not get one in the hole."

The company had two sets of foxholes. One set was forward to oversee the slopes of the hill,

Fox Hill and locations of 2/5 RCT Units in defense. Fox Hill (Co. F) in the center. Co. G on hill to the left. Sobuk-san in the far distance center of picture. Co. E tied in with 24th Infantry there. Co. H(-) near clearing right center. CP, 2/5 RCT in a draw behind photographer.(Courtesy of Toshio Uyeda, HC/2/5 RCT)

which were occupied at night. Another set was 25 to 30 yards in rear of the first and was occupied during daylight hours. From these holes the men could see the enemy coming over the crest of the hill. The rear line of holes acted in a manner similar to a reverse slope defense and gave partial protection from enemy observation, since they were not on the forward slope. The enemy could still observe the Americans, but they were less of a target than forward slope positions would have been.

Communication with the battalion CP and the artillery was poor. Radio batteries of WW II vintage often failed, so supporting mortar and artillery fire often was impossible to obtain. The situation for Fox Co. on Hill 342 was confusing and deadly, out on this knob by itself. Every day, the company was whittled down more and more by dead and wounded.

Many of the wounded who still could fight stayed on the hill, like Gerald Pack. On Aug. 6, an enemy grenade flew into the hole occupied by Pack, Eckert and LT Hino, wounding Pack. He recalled that two of his friends in the unit were killed on Fox Hill. One he identified simply as PVT Wadsworth, "was too brave for his own good," he wrote. "He would stand up and go for the enemy." The other buddy was Dale B. Morse.

Ivan W. Russell, who died in 1992, was also with Fox Co. on 342. He wrote that the only shade on the hill "was that made by your steel helmet, which soon got too hot to touch. The only respite from the heat came at night, but that was when the North Koreans attacked. We somehow managed to hang on.... Since we had trained together as a unit in Hawaii, we all knew each other. So every time a man was hit, it hurt; even if you didn't especially like the guy."

One thing Russell was very definite about: "I want to emphasize," he wrote, "that the term 'bug out' was never used by our unit."

CPT Howarth, he wrote, was well liked and respected. The captain made Russell his company runner. One night Russell was sent forward with a message for a couple of machinegunners on the forward slope. As he moved forward, enemy mortar fire dropped in. He hit the ground until it let up, then went on to the gun position. He started talking, but was quickly told to keep his voice down; the enemy was very close. The two machinegunners were William F. Swearingen and John J. "Robie" Robichaud. "They used to wave to each other as soon as it was light before hosing down [firing into] the enemy positions," he wrote. "They both died on Fox Hill."

When he saw his friend, Robichaud, being carried down the hill, Russell cried. "A sergeant told me to go and see the medics. I told him to go to hell, picked up my M-1 and proceeded to fire at the enemy until [oil ran out of the upper hand guard] and burned my hands. I never cried again," Russell concluded.

The company was issued the 3.5-inch rocket launcher at Pusan, but never any ammunition, Brooks recalled. "I saw one of my rocket launcher crewmen on Fox Hill with the launcher lying on top of [his dead body]." He never had the opportunity to fire one round from the launcher. Some time during the fighting on Fox Hill, LT Brooks was wounded in the hands, but he stayed.

On Aug. 7, CPT Howarth received word that the Marines were going to relieve the company. He selected Russell to go down and lead them up. Russell had never been off of Fox Hill since his arrival the night of Aug. 3-4. It is apparent from subsequent events that other elements of 2/5 RCT were not informed that a party of Marines would be passing through the area to Fox Hill.

"CPT Howarth cautioned me to be careful and to remember that there were friendlies on the next hill [to the rear]," Russell recalled. "I took off at a good clip. When I had gone just a short way from the [company] perimeter, a stream of bullets hit the trail in front of me. I skidded to a halt and looked to where the fire was coming from." In the valley to his right he spotted a machine gun with two men. Since the gun was fairly close to the hill "where the friendlies were supposed to be," he thought it was a U.S. machine gun. "Then what were they doing firing at me?" he asked himself. Angered, he shook his fist and rifle at them "while calling them names I would be embarrassed to repeat," he wrote. Russell then went on his way back to the battalion CP.

There were, of course, other company runners at the time. One of these, CPL Jack R. Starkey (awarded the DSC) was killed at the base of Fox Hill.

Plans for Task Force Kean

While F/5 RCT fought to survive on Hill 342, Walker and his planners finally settled on a limited objective attack in the south. This division-sized attack would drive along two main axes toward Chinju. The missions of this attack were to relieve pressure on the Taegu front to the north by forcing the diversion of enemy troops to meet this U.S. thrust in the south; and throw the North Korean offensive off balance. This was a spoiling attack.

U.S. air attacks from late Aug. 5 through 6 were made to isolate the battlefield and to destroy North Korean forces behind the front between Masan and the Nam River.

The operational directive was issued on Aug. 6, and the attack was to begin at 6:30 a.m., Aug. 7. The attacking force, built around the bulk of the 25th Division, was to be known as TF Kean. Principal forces consisted of the 24th and 35th Regiments (the latter with but two battalions), the 5 RCT and the Marine Brigade. Artillery consisted of four battalions of 105mm howitzers (64th, 159th and 555 FABs and 1-11 Marines, the latter two battalions had only 12 howitzers each —short 6 guns in each battalion) and a battalion of 155mm howitzers (90 FAB). Armor included the 89th Medium Tk Bn (M4A3) and Co. A, 1st Tk Bn (Marine) (M-26). The 1/27 Inf and 8 FAB, from the 25th Division were in Eighth Army reserve. Task Force Kean numbered about 20,000 men.

The geography lent itself to this more or less isolated attack. The zone of advance was bordered on the north by the Nam River and on the south by the sea. The zone, averaging some 17 miles wide, did not permit mutual support by the three main attacking forces. The objectives of this limited objective attack were the high ground just south of Chinju (5 RCT) and Sachon (Marines), over eight air miles to the south. Chinju was 27 air miles west of Masan. By the shortest road it was 40 miles.

Most of the terrain consisted of relatively low hills, water-filled rice paddies and small streams. A major hill mass was located east of Chinju. The main route through it was via the Chinju Pass. In the center of the division's defensive sector was another major mountain mass —the formidable Sobuk-san (Hill 738), soon to earn the name "Bloody Sobuk."

Two roads lead to Chinju from the Chindong-ni-Kogan-ni area. The most direct route is via Kogan-ni, northwest through Pogam-ni to Muchon-ni, where it joins the road coming southwest from Chungam-ni and the infamous Notch, then heads west through the Chinju Pass to Chinju. The entrance to the Pass is about 9-10 miles road miles east of Chinju. The second road branches south from a point just east of Koganni, splitting after about 500 or 600 yards, with one branch, little more than a widened trail, snaking through mountainous terrain, terminating at Paedun-ni. The other branch turns due west for about three miles, then turns south through a narrow valley, meeting the mountain road at Paedun-ni. From there a road leads almost due south to Kosong, then westward about 9-10 miles to join another that leads northwest to Sachon, then turns almost due north toward Chinju. About 7 miles north of Sachon it joins the east-west road from the Chinju Pass. It is less than five miles from that junction to Chinju. The southern (Marine) route is longer and more circuitous than the road via Muchon-ni.

It is important to remember that elements of the 25th Division and the *NK 6th Division* had been in contact in the Chindong-ni - Sobuk-san - Notch areas for about five days before TF Kean jumped off. The 25th was deployed along a front about 20 miles wide, but there was no line. Elements of 1/29 Infantry were deployed north near the Nam River; 2/35 Infantry was positioned in the Notch area. The 27th Infantry was near Chindong-ni, and the 24th Infantry was in three blocking positions near Masan.

F/5 RCT, on Hill 342 had been engaging the enemy and North Koreans had been detected on the slopes of Sobuk-san and the rugged mountains nearby. In short, major portions of the *6th Division* would be in rear of TF Kean when its three assault forces began the attack. This should have been apparent to the attack planners. It led to the ambush of the 555 FAB, elements of the 90 FAB and part of the 5 RCT on August 11 and 12.

Task Force Kean's Scheme of Maneuver

The 35th Infantry was to attack from the Notch toward Muchon-ni, securing the Nam River line on the task force north flank, to meet the 5th RCT, then continue the attack with the 5th RCT toward Chinju. The 5 RCT would attack from vicinity of Chindong-ni to take the high ground overlooking the road junction near Kogan-ni, then attack generally northwest to Muchon-ni, meet the 35th and continue with that regiment toward Chinju. The 5 Marines would follow the 5 RCT to the Kosong turnoff, then attack south to Kosong, then west and north to seize Sachon. The 24th Inf. would attack enemy concentrations in the Sobuk-san area, and secure the north-south road between Koman-ni, via Haman to Chindong-ni.

A battalion of ROK Marines and a ROK Army battalion were attached to the 24th Infantry, but were sent elsewhere a few days later, before the conclusion of TF Kean. The Sobuk-san complex is a series of very high and rugged mountains running four miles northward from a hill mass over 540 meters high located about 2 1/2 Km northeast of Hill 342. This rugged complex embraces Sobuk-san (Hill 738), Pilbong (Hill 743) and Battle Mountain (Old Baldy) (Hill 665). The 1/24 Infantry was given the Battle Mountain area and 3/24 Infantry the Sobuk area. It should be noted here that this four mile complex of mountains is the most formidable and rugged terrain anywhere along the western face of what was the Pusan Perimeter. The slopes are steep, requiring extraordinary stamina and energy to negotiate under the best of circumstances. When these slopes become wet from rain they are very slippery, making it almost impossible to climb, and when an enemy is rolling grenades down slope and lashing the approaches with mortar machine gun and small-arms fire, uncommon valor is needed to continue an attack. This is what the 1st and 3d Battalions, 24th Infantry faced, while 2/24 Infantry was to secure the lateral road.

To facilitate the attack, the 5 RCT and 5 Marines were to relieve the 27th Infantry west of Chindong-ni on the night of Aug. 6-7.

On Aug. 6, the Brigade was attached to the 25th Infantry Division. Departing Changwon at 10:40 a.m. that day, 3-5 Marines arrived near Chindong-ni by 12:40 p.m. The 1st Bn, 11th Marines, a 75mm recoilless rifle platoon and an engineer platoon accompanied the 3d Battalion. Although LTC Taplett had wisely declined to occupy the old 2/27th Inf. CP in a schoolhouse there, the artillery emplaced in the positions formerly occupied by the 8 FAB. Both the schoolhouse and artillery positions had been registered in by enemy mortars during the earlier battles with the "Wolfhounds."

1LT Robert D. Bohn deployed his 2d and 3d Platoons on Hill 99, across the valley to the west of Hill 255, placing his 1st Platoon (2LT John H. "Blackie" Cahill), with an attached 75mm recoilless rifle, on a small knob at the base of Hill 255, overlooking the main road. CPT Joseph C. Fegan's Co. H (- 3d Plat.) was positioned about 500 yards south of the crest of Hill 255. His 3d Platoon was placed on high ground south of the Masan road to protect against infiltrators from the sea and mountains southeast of the Masan road.

Jim Sanders wrote that a patrol was sent out from Co. G on Aug. 6, under SGT Blackmon, to find an Army unit which was reported to be cut off. The patrol was attacked by the enemy and Blackmon was killed. Enemy artillery fire landed in the schoolhouse area where Sanders was located and he took shelter in a foxhole. A battery of 1-11 Mar. returned fire and the enemy artillery ceased.

Sanders was placed on the company perimeter that night to help fill in because the patrol had not yet returned. Hearing noises on the slope below him, he rolled two grenades down the hill. A few minutes later GySgt Beaver, a Bataan veteran, "slid next to me," wrote Sanders. "'See anything?' he whispered. 'No, it's too dark but it sounded like troops moving up here.'" Beaver slipped away and got Co. H to fire machine guns across the front of G below Sander's position, halting any enemy attempt on G that night. Co. H. was probed by the enemy. One of Sander's friends, Paul Dougherty, a machinegunner in How Co., was killed that night. The unit also had a number of men wounded. The G Company patrol returned after dark.

The same night a boot-camp comrade of Jack Wright's, named Richardson, saw a figure approaching in the darkness. Richardson "just sat there waiting for him to get closer," Wright said. "When he got close enough [that] he couldn't miss, Richardson fired once." The next morning a dead North Korean soldier lay in front of his foxhole.

Temporarily, all Marines in the Chindong-ni area were under Taplett's command, and 3-5 Marines, in turn were under the operational control (OPCON) of COL John H. Michaelis (CO, 27th Inf.)

As mentioned earlier, this whole area had been the scene of hard battle between 1/27 Infantry, regimental headquarters and the 8 FAB against two battalions of North Koreans. A few days later, when the Marines had arrived, most of the enemy dead had been removed at night by the enemy themselves. A large number of these dead had been in the valley west of Hill 255, where they were caught unloading from trucks by the 8 FAB.

Hill 342 — F/5 RCT and Cahill's Platoon, G-5 Marines, Aug. 7-8

Just before midnight on Aug. 7, LTC Taplett received a message from Michaelis to send a reinforced rifle platoon to relieve the defenders of Hill 342 (F/5 RCT). Taplett protested sending one of his six available platoons on this mission, but was told in response that GEN Kean wanted Hill 342 held at all costs. LTC Taplett cleared the mission with GEN Craig, then selected George Co. to supply the platoon. Then it was LT Bohn's turn to protest: It seemed that Army leadership was micromanaging front line commitment of troops. He, like Taplett, was very reluctant to commit a single platoon by itself at night in strange territory. Having voiced his objection, Bohn set about complying. 2LT "Blackie" Cahill's 1st Platoon, with a machine gun squad and an SCR-300 radio operator, were sent on the mission. He was told that his mission was to relieve the Army company on Hill 342 and hold it with his platoon. The reinforced platoon numbered 52 men.

Cahill led his platoon forward on the MSR to Michaelis' CP near some bridges near Hill 99. There, he was told that an army guide would meet him farther forward, at the CP of 2/5 RCT. A soldier escorted the platoon to that CP, located north of the MSR at the foot of the eastern ridge leading to Hill 342.

The guide from Co. F, Ivan W. Russell, met Cahill at the battalion CP and began leading the platoon toward Fox Hill. They skirted the western edge of the ridge. After a few hundred yards, Russell said he had started off wrong and the platoon had to retrace their steps. (Russell later declared that he did not recall having lost his way, as the Marine account in *The Pusan Perimeter* avers.) LT Cahill recalled later that he was "mad" because "the guide had taken the wrong route in the darkness."

It was well after midnight as the column moved slowly forward. Men slipped and stumbled on the narrow pathway. As the platoon reached a point near the end of the valley separating the two ridges leading to Fox Hill, rifle fire spat out into the darkness, wounding Marines Niemczyk and Wyman. Other units of the 5 RCT apparently had not been notified that the Marine platoon was coming through the area. (See Chapter Notes.)

About 5 a.m. on Aug. 7, Cahill's platoon neared the lower slope of Hill 342. Russell advised the platoon leader to wait for daylight to make the climb. Even in daylight, it was a steep, arduous climb to the summit. At some point, too, Russell told Cahill about the machine gun he had encountered on the way down the previous afternoon. He wrote, "I told the leader [LT Cahill] to pass the word that there was a machine gun up ahead and everyone should stay low." Acting on this advice, Cahill moved his platoon on the left (defiladed) finger leading to Hill 342.

Cahill tried to reach LT Bohn on the radio to inform him that the platoon was holding up until daylight.

At first light on Aug. 7, the lieutenant started his platoon off again. It soon became a fearsome test of physical stamina, with oppressive, terrible heat adding to the problem. The men struggled up, slipped back, but crept slowly upward, cursing all the while. The unmerciful sun and heat caused the men soon to empty their canteens.

About half-way up, enemy automatic weapons fire struck the platoon, wounding platoon guide SGT Tom Blackmon. PFC William Tome returned fire with his BAR, but the slope was so steep that he had to be held in position by PFC Melvin Brooks. With Blackmon down, the platoon had lost three men thus far.

Cahill, SGT Lee Buettner, a squad leader and Russell pushed on ahead, reaching the summit about 8 a.m. "We reached the military crest of the hill without incident," Ivan wrote. "When we reached the perimeter, mortars were coming in on top of the hill. PVT William G. Millan came crawling over the reverse slope of the hill with blood spouting from a throat wound. The Marine medic patched him up in a professional manner...."

Cahill found CPT Howarth in a foxhole in a slight depression amidst a cluster of burial mounds atop the hill, vainly trying to raise someone on his radio.

Cahill introduced himself and told Howarth that his platoon was relieving the Army unit. Some writers have stated that Cahill's platoon was to reinforce Co. F. Recently Cahill wrote this on the matter: "There was no doubt in my mind then, or today, that my mission was to relieved the Army company and hold the hill at all costs. I had...planned to put squads in where the Army company had platoons, if I could cover the area.... I believed the decision [of F/5 RCT] to remain temporarily was due to their inability to extract their men in the forward positions."

CPT Howarth said he had pulled his "men into a tight perimeter for the night and now they can't get back into their day positions."

At this point F/5 RCT could not have had many more men than Cahill now had in his platoon, about 40 men. In addition to battle casualties attaining Hill 342, the platoon had lost several more men to heat exhaustion, and a few others were helping seriously wounded to the rear. The combined Army-Marine force could not have been more than 100 men. It is doubtful if either unit by itself could have survived until relieved.

Frank B. Brooks Jr., F Co. XO, told the author on Aug. 6, 1994 that CPT Howarth sent the mortars back because there was no ammunition for them. Blackie Cahill wrote on Jan. 24, 1995: "I recall being told by the Army commander [Howarth] that their mortars had been sent back because they had received too much enemy fire to be effective." Cahill's observation "that their fire support could have been used," is all too true. When the Marines arrived, Brooks was surprised. CPT Howarth had not informed him that Marines were coming to the relief of the company.

The increased activity on Hill 342 precipitated increased enemy fire on the position. Hugging the ground, SGT Jack Macy led PFCs Tome and Brooks to a position on the left of the perimeter. Still prone, the three men began digging in, when a burst of machine gun fire hit Tome. Macy snatched up the BAR and returned fire, telling Brooks to look after Tome, but Tome was dead. The enemy quit firing and Macy put his hand on Brooks' shoulder, saying, "They're zeroed in on this spot— I'll move you." As he spoke, Macy saw the back of Brooks' dungarees give little jerks as bullets tore through his body. Brooks died instantly. PFC Lonzo Barnett, nearby, rose and hurled a grenade toward the enemy gun, silencing it. Macy crawled over to Barnett and said, "We'll hafta leave that hole open. Keep it covered."

PFC John Johnson was killed at his machine gun position, shot through the jugular. "The blood gushed out and he was dead in an instant," recalled Cahill. All of these men were Marines; three other Marines and five soldiers, including CPT Howarth, were wounded.

Kermit A. Wilhelm was a machinegunner attached to Cahill's platoon. He was attempting to clear a stoppage in the gun, he recalled. "My assistant gunner was shooting at the North Koreans with his and my .45 caliber pistols. (He killed two or more.) I heard the bullet hit him. He looked at me and fell dead at my feet." This had to be Johnson.

Three Marines were killed and eight wounded in going into position. A number of soldiers, thinking the Marines were relieving them, began to leave their foxholes. A Fox Co. officer got them back into position.

LT Brooks took over Fox Co., but command arrangements on the hill were confusing. Cahill apparently had the only working radio, so to him fell the responsibility for communication to the outside world. Cahill called for Army artillery fire, through a 3-5 Marine artillery net, in an attempt to silence enemy mortar fire falling on the perimeter, but the mortar fire went on unabated.

He asked for an air drop of water and ammunition. An air force transport responded, but everything except one packet of carbine ammunition fell into enemy territory. Brigade OY-2s took over the resupply mission. including water. VMO-6 donated every 5-gallon water can it had. Although the little planes came in as low and slow as possible, all the cans burst on impact. As a result, the defenders received little more than a mouthful or two of water. In one drop Brooks recalled that SGT William Straney, unit communications sergeant had a radio knocked off his back by a falling ammunition case.

The need for water on the hill became almost overwhelming. Marine SGT Jack Macy organized a party of volunteers to go to a stream near a village at the base of the hill. CPL Arnold Hutchinson and PFCs David Wilson, Lonzo Barnett and George Paz went with Macy. They carried three canvas waterbags. Almost immediately they came under long-range fire. Plunging on, the party made it safely to the stream. The men, ignoring the use of Halazone tablets to purify the water, drank from the stream, then filled the bags.

Lugging the heavy bags, Macy's party started up the hill. A half-mile from the hamlet, they met LT Arthur Oakley, a platoon leader in CPT John Finn's D-2-5 Marines. Oakley told Macy that D Company was on its way to relieve the Army-Marine force on Hill 342.

Later in the day, the enemy raked the entire peak with small-arms and machine gun fire, and used American grenades which had fallen into their positions from the air drops against the defenders. But the remnants of F/5 RCT, under LT Brooks and the rapidly dwindling Marine platoon, under LT Cahill "hung tough," refusing to be driven from Fox Hill.

PFC John D. Wagner, of How Co., wrote of a 12-man patrol he was on during one of the first nights in Korea. He recalled that the patrol traveled about 2 miles. "I was frightened because of the black darkness and the howling of the wind," he wrote. "I did not know what to expect and was pretty nervous as a rookie BAR-man." Wagner was a member of CPL William J. Chirkis' squad.

Wagner led a charmed life for a while in Korea. Once he took a bullet through his canteen. On another occasion he was in a foxhole when he developed a cramp in his leg. "I raised my leg out of the foxhole [to relieve the cramp]," he recounted, "and a sniper shot the heel off my boot." On Sept. 23, 1950, outside Seoul, he was hit by a bullet which went through his thigh without hitting a bone. He returned to duty the next day. "The Man Upstairs was with me," he concluded.

The Remainder of the Brigade Moves Up — August 7

At 2 a.m. Aug. 7, the remainder of the 5th Marines started forward from Changwon to the Chindong-ni area, led by LTC Roise's 2d Bn, reaching the schoolyard at the foot of Hill 255 about 6 a.m. and unloading from their trucks. The empty trucks then turned around to return to the rear. This great movement of trucks turned the schoolyard into a quagmire of mud. Then enemy artillery and mortar fire began falling on the area, halting all traffic on the road. Mortar fire killed one man in Co. E and wounded 11 others, including the company commander, CPT George E. Kittredge Jr. 1LT William E. Sweeney took command of the unit.

Men of both 2-5 Marines and 1-11 Marines remembered Aug. 7 at the schoolhouse.

"We were marshaling our men and equipment in a schoolyard.... A battery of 105 howitzers were...nearby...firing interdictory fire every now and then," wrote Chuck Hitchborn of Weapons Co., 2d Bn. "All of a sudden we started to receive incoming. We determined later that this was enemy 120mm mortar rounds.... I can remember tasting the cordite, hearing the tremen-

dously loud explosions, and most of all experiencing the intense fear of a...first time under fire.... Nothing is so fearsome as that 'first time' you're taken under fire. I'll never forget it."

The company gunnery sergeant got most of the men behind the schoolhouse, where they dug in. Hitchborn and Ed Grunder were told to stay with the motor carts, ammunition and equipment piled in front of the school building. Hitchborn dove under a water trailer for protection, but mortar fragments blew holes in the trailer, sending water in all directions. He spotted an Army tank retriever 60 or 70 yards away, and thought he would be safe behind it. "I took off running for it," he wrote. "The next thing I knew, I was sitting by the rock wall in front of the schoolhouse, very dazed...still 30 yards from the tank [retriever]. A shell . . . blew me up against this little rock wall.... As I regained my senses, I saw that I had blood on my left arm from a shrapnel wound; also had a small hole in the left side of my face and part of a tooth was gone"

His buddy Gunder was hugging the ground near a truck. Hitchborn discovered a TAC officer lying prone directing a flight of Corsairs onto the enemy by radio. He reasoned that if the officer could lay down in the open like that and be OK, "Why couldn't I?... So I laid down beside him.... He asked me to punch him when I heard an incoming round as he couldn't hear with the radio headset covering his ears. When I'd hear a round coming, I'd punch hell out of him and we'd flatten ourselves as flat as possible. This was the only time... that I punched the hell out of an officer at his direction." When the Corsairs began strafing and rocketing, the enemy fire ceased.

Then came the "screams and moans and shouts for 'Corpsman!' from others who had been wounded," Hitchborn continued. He and the other 12 men who had been wounded in the mortar attack were assembled in the schoolhouse for treatment and evacuation. Another Marine was killed by a tree burst. Hitchborn pictured enemy rounds coming through the roof and exploding in the schoolhouse. "I felt alone...," he wrote. Then he heard voices and his gunny directing the men to saddle up and move out. "I knew I wasn't hurt bad and felt the need to be with my unit and my buddies for safety..." he continued, so he climbed out through a window and joined his unit. The company corpsman, Chipman by name, bandaged his wounds and advised him to stay at the aid station. "But I said to hell with that. I wanted to be with our unit.... I was scared, confused, in...a daze and just had this incredible desire to be with guys I knew where I would feel safer...." Hitchborn concluded.

Richard C. Blevins and Raymond Johnson were PFCs in H&S, 2-5 Marines at the schoolhouse that day.

"Incoming mortar fire started hitting one of the line companies in the hills above us," Blevins recalled. "I remember seeing little puffs of smoke and it didn't look bad until we started getting hits in the yard were we were. One Marine was leaning against a tree.... He was killed from wounds to the head. Then I knew the little puffs of smoke were deadly."

Johnson wrote, "Shell bursts striking trees — 1 KIA and 11 WIA. I remember it as traumatic and brought tears to my eyes at the sight of our

first casualties. It...burned into my mind and made me toughen up emotionally for the many battles to follow."

PFC Malachy Lyons, also of H&S, 2-5 Marines, was at the schoolhouse that day, too. He recalled that they "were hit hard by enemy mortar fire.... The one thing I feared was mortar fire...." As luck would have it, it was a mortar round that wounded Lyons after the Inchon and Seoul operations.

Most of the enemy fire on Aug. 7 was directed at the artillery positions which were across the road from the schoolhouse and on the outskirts of Chindong-ni.

LTC Ransom M. Wood (ROTC, Auburn University) commanded the 1st Battalion, 11th Marines (105mm howitzer) on July 6, 1950. When his battalion moved into the Chindong-ni area, he found that likely positions for his command were scarce, so he moved his battalion into the position which had been occupied by the Army's 8 FAB. He registered his guns before the 8th pulled out.

"This position area was partly in the center of...Chindong-ni, while the remainder was on the outskirts of town," he wrote in the June 1951 issue of *Marine Corps Gazette*. "This was an undesirable position because the North Koreans had [it] plotted even before we moved in. That night...extremely accurate counterbattery fire...resulted in the loss of one howitzer and all of the gun crew." He would like to have displaced, but "there just were no alternate [positions] available.... So we had to dig in and stick it out as best we could." LTC Wood paid tribute to BG Bittman Barth, 25th Division Artillery commander. At the time, 1-11 Marines was under the operational control of the 25th Division. "He had learned much about the enemy and his tactics. He gladly passed the information on to us," Wood recounted, "and I knew that accepting his advice and applying his suggestions contributed to the efficiency of the battalion during its later encounters with the enemy."

The chaplain of 1-11 Mar. was Father Otto E. Sporrer (Lt Cdr). "He didn't spend much time with our unit," wrote LTC Wood. "Instead he was near the front lines, caring for the wounded." A number of Marines who responded to the author with their recollections and experiences of the Pusan Perimeter also mentioned Chaplain Sporrer. They remembered him as giving, caring and fearless, a fighting man's chaplain, successfully combining both toughness and compassion. "A familiar figure at the front," Wood recalled, "frequently exposed to enemy fire as he administered to fallen Marines was Lt. Cdr. Otto E. Sporrer, beloved chaplain of 1-11."

Steve Spanovich was a cook in 1-11 Marines. He pointed out, in the Marines he was trained "to be a rifleman first and a cook and baker second." He was about 75 feet from the artillery piece which took a direct hit from an enemy round. Two men were killed and four more were wounded. The BC "took the loss of the men very hard," he recalled. During the bombardment, the cooks took shelter next to a stone wall on the edge of the school yard.

Bill M. Murley belonged to Svc, 1-11 Marines. He was in the school yard at the foot of Hill 255 when the enemy mortar attack began and was "scared stiff," he recalled. His officer,

LT Skaggs, ordered the men to dig emplacements for the battalion howitzers. As they dug, Murley recalled, there was a fire-fight going on between the Marines and North Koreans. In the darkness, some Marine units fired at other Marine units, he wrote. In the midst of the firing and digging in, an enemy platoon approached his battery position from the rear. "Master Sergeant Altom ordered us to fight hand-to-hand," Murley wrote. "I remember using a bayonet on a Korean soldier against a tree and could not get my bayonet pulled out so left it there. [In all] we killed about 30." They also captured five more of the enemy. "The next day," Murley continued, "I found the soldier [I had] bayoneted to the tree [was] dead . . . . According to a Korean interpreter, he was only 15 years old. That haunts me to this day."

Charles C. Marquis, also a member of Svc, 1-11 Mar, recalled that the enemy hit on the howitzer killed a man named Porter and another named Petillo.

Henry G. Ammer, of C-1-11 Marines, was a World War II veteran. He recalled that the first enemy 120mm mortar round burst "about 5-6 feet from me," he wrote. "It caved in my foxhole, destroyed [my] radio, telephone [and] pack and gave me ringing of [my] ears. I gave the air controller the azimuth (compass direction) for search attack. He called in the mission and that was the last artillery fire I experienced."

Lieutenant Robert J. Harvey, USNR, was the surgeon for 3-5 Marines. He arrived at Pendleton one day in July and left for Korea two days later. His first battle was at Chindong-ni during the enemy's mortar attack. "I was appalled at the horrible carnage inflicted. 'This is sheer madness.' is what I thought. However, not for long — was too busy with [the] wounded."

When the remainder of the Brigade moved into the Chindong-ni area, its Co. A, 1st Engineer Battalion was put to work building a landing strip for the Brigade's OY (light observation) aircraft. CWO Willard C. Downs, who died Mar. 30, 1994, was chief warrant officer, Engineer Equipment Officer and HQ Plt Leader in the unit. He wrote that Co. A was constructing a landing strip at Chindong-ni "when North Korean artillery registered in on our site. Their attack was not very effective, but scary." The unit "came under heavier fire as we advanced toward Kosong."

LTC Murray tried to bring the remainder of his command forward. Riding behind Roise's battalion, he radioed ahead, ordering that unloading and movement of trucks should continue in spite of the shelling. Roise replied that the churned-up condition of the school yard was the real hold-up. But the battalion assembled, LTC Murray arrived, directed 2-5 Mar. to occupy and defend Hill 255 above How Co. Company's positions, and sent 1-5 Mar. to Hill 99, relieving G Co. (- Cahill's platoon) to return to Taplett.

1/5 RCT, Chindong-ni Area — Aug. 7

When Aug. 7 dawned, the area was enveloped in a dense fog, a common condition at that time of year in South Korea, preventing a scheduled air strike from being made before 1/5 RCT (LTC John P. Jones) began its attack as part of TF Kean. A planned twenty-minute artillery

preparation was fired. The mission of 1/5 RCT was to attack and seize a hill mass northeast of and dominating the road junction at Tosan, where the southern route split off the main road to Muchon-ni.

Elements of the command turned left and south short of Tosan and ended up 2 to 3 miles south of the MSR, some of them fighting on Hill 308, 2 miles south of the MSR. The battalion did not advance along the MSR, as it should have, to take the ridges northeast of Tosan, so the enemy still held that high ground and controlled that road junction. GEN Kean was furious about the mistake, blaming COL Ordway.

Chaos reigned in the Chindong-ni area as dawn broke on Aug. 7. The North Koreans were in strength and attacking too, besieging Hill 342 and on Hill 255 overlooking and blocking the MSR to the rear. Elsewhere in the 25th Division zone, other enemy forces were heavily engaging elements of the 24th and 35th Regiments. The MSR between Tosan and Chindong-ni was clogged with Army and Marine traffic. Troops trying to get forward for their attack, along with supply vehicles trying to bring up ammunition and other supplies vied with other troops and their vehicles which had been relieved trying to move to the rear. Enemy on the heights above Tosan blocked the attack, while the enemy roadblock in the rear on Hill 255 and nearby ridges blocked the MSR in both directions.

This was the situation when GEN Craig arrived in the Chindong-ni at about 7 a.m. Orders were received to provide a Marine battalion to relieve 2/5 RCT on Hill 342 and the ridges leading to it so that that command could begin their attack as part of TF Kean. Receiving this order, LTC Murray halted his 2d Battalion, which was then ascending Hill 255, sending it to relieve 2/5 RCT.

E/5 RCT - Aug. 7

While Fox Co., 5 RCT, held Hill 342, Easy Co. occupied a ridge to its south. On the night of Aug. 6-7, the enemy forced a platoon of Co. E out of position and seized a point from which they could overlook the MSR, the CPs of the 5 RCT and 5th Marines and the artillery positions near Chindong-ni.

The platoon in question was probably that of 1LT Gordon M. Strong, who was killed in the fight. CPL Frank Valvo, a squad leader and machinegunner with the unit, wrote that the "platoon suffered 10 KIA, including my platoon leader, LT Strong." He also recalled that a Japanese-American member of the platoon, BAR-man PFC James Kawamura, "personally killed 40 or more of the enemy" that day and..."helped us get out of the encirclement." Kawamura was awarded the DSC for this action.

Horace "Andy" Anderson of Co. E, wrote his recollection of being relieved by the Marines on Aug. 7. Co. E had been on this ridge for a few days and had fought the enemy a few times, including the night of Aug. 6-7. The men knew that the enemy could observe their positions from nearby high ground and routinely fired mortars on the Americans.

The Marine unit (possibly E-5 Mar.) came up on the position for a daylight relief, which was observed by the enemy. "We were ordered

to wait until after dark [to pull off the hill]," Anderson wrote, "so the North Koreans would believe we were being reinforced.... I had a recoilless rifle (57mm) squad on a saddle along the ridge."

A Marine platoon came up to an area near Anderson and apparently gathered for an orientation by the platoon leader. "I thought I should go over and tell the lieutenant about the mortar rounds," Anderson continued. The Marines had not started to dig in. "The lieutenant told me he had everything under control, so I went back to my foxhole."

He and his buddy, a man named McCoy, got in their foxhole and waited. "In a little while three mortar rounds came in.... One poor Marine had lost his leg and several more were wounded," Anderson wrote. "The rest were digging in."

This Marine unit had not yet experienced combat. The 5 RCT had been on the line only a few days, but had learned the importance of cover, concealment, dispersion and foxholes. Anderson was trying to share some of knowledge with the Marine lieutenant.

CPL Eugene R. Lakatos, a rocket launcher gunner with E/5 RCT, injured his ankle during these first few days, was returned to duty soon after and was slightly wounded by shell fragments.

GEN Craig Given Command at Chindong-ni - August 7

At 11:20 a.m. on Aug. 7, GEN Kean, determined to get things on track at Chindong-ni, directed GEN Craig to assume control of all troops in that area, giving him operational control of the 5 RCT and any other Army troops in the area, in addition to his own Marine Brigade. Craig immediately went forward and determined that elements of the 5 RCT were not moving very fast, although enemy resistance appeared light. The confused nature of the fighting may have contributed to the slow advance. He observed that enemy snipers and infiltrators had the MSR under fire and that American troops were searching the nearby hills for them.

At the conclusion of Aug. 7, the advance out of Chindong-ni had definitely not gone according to plan. GEN Craig ordered the 5 RCT to take the high ground at Tosan on July 8, directing 1-5 Mar. (LTC Newton) to move forward from Chindong-ni at 6 a.m. that day then attack southward from Tosan over the route which had been designated for the Marine Brigade in TF Kean.

2-5 Marines Take Over for 2/5 RCT

When 2-5 Mar. reached the point where Cahill had been met by the Army guide, LTC Roise sent Dog Co. along the eastern spur with orders to take that ridge and Hill 342. Easy Co. (1LT William E. Sweeney) was ordered to take and hold the western spur. This deployment ensured covering the two ridges and intervening valley.

MAJ Morgan J. McNeely, battalion S-3, and CPT John Finn, Jr. (Co. D), went ahead to the base of Hill 342. McNeely briefed Finn for his attack. Both McNeely and a guide from the 5

RCT said that the company would meet no organized resistance in their climb.

The men of Co. D already were pretty tired, having had little or no rest for over 24 hours. As they assembled to ascend to Fox Hill it was midafternoon and the fearful heat of the day began to fell a few of the men. At the same time, enemy rifle and machine gun fire slammed into the unit from the high ground above the road and a village on the right. The immediate reaction was that the Army was firing at them, but the distinctive sound of burp guns soon dispelled that notion.

David S. Van Dommelman of Co. D recalled that moment. "While moving to our jump-off point we came under long-range fire from our right and [I] hit the dirt like everyone. I felt some fear, but quickly followed orders and went into the attack to clear the first objective."

Ignoring the fire from the village, Finn briefed his platoon leaders. Then 2d Platoon (2LT Wallace J. Reid), moved forward up the hill at its juncture with the spur; 3d Platoon (2LT Edward T. Emmelman), headed directly for the top of the spur; 1st Platoon (2LT Arthur A. Oakley), moved forward on the right flank and then advanced up the southern slopes of Hill 342 itself. Oakley's platoon flushed out and chased off a small party of the enemy. The ridge grew steeper and many Marines were overcome by the relentless heat, humidity and constant struggle to climb the steep, treacherous slopes. Twelve men passed out and the remainder of the company was near exhaustion as it attained the crest of the spur. PFC George Mayo of Emmelman's platoon fell and broke his leg on the way up; five other men of the company had been wounded.

Frank Kerr, a member of Emmelman's platoon, wrote about the lieutenant that day: "Second Lieutenant Edward T. Emmelman was some-ticked at us. Or so it seemed, as he sauntered contemptuously above our heads, disdainful of the hellfire raging around him, suggesting that we take up some other line of work since we lacked the guts for his proud profession.... In minutes he shamed, prodded and inspired us toward our first objective, designated Hill 342...."

With night approaching and his unit beat out by their climb, Finn stopped the company short of 342 and radioed Roise to tell him the unit was exhausted. He had earlier directed his XO, 1LT Robert T. Hannifin, to establish a CP and set up the company 60mm mortars on the high ground just above the MSR.

When the unit stopped, LT Oakley was sent to contact the defenders of Hill 342. Enroute, he met Macy's water detail. David Van Dommelman accompanied Oakley, his platoon leader, to the Army-Marine perimeter, and wrote: "My platoon leader, LT Oakley, was told to contact LT Cahill and the CO of F Company [5 RCT] on Hill 342 to tell them we had orders to hold for the night and relieve the morning of [Aug.] 8. I went with the lieutenant and reached their command post with just spasmodic fire from the North Koreans. LT Cahill told LT Oakley to tell the skipper [CPT Finn] he would be wise to relieve at night as the __ was sure to hit the fan again in the a.m. We returned to our company and reported this to CPT Finn, but battalion said to hold 'till morning."

In 1990, LTC (then 1LT) Frank Brooks, who commanded the remnants of F/5RCT on Hill 342 at the time wrote this recollection: "We were relieved by a company of the 5th Marines...in a daylight pass through, which was against my wishes." Brooks had replaced CPT Howarth, who had been hit in the lungs by mortar fragments.

These two recollections are at variance with the account on page 114 of *The Pusan Perimeter*, which states that Oakley returned to Finn with Cahill and "the Army company commander. In the hurried conference that followed, the Army officer advised Finn against finishing the rugged climb and assured him that his soldiers and Cahill's platoon could defend the peak through the night. Informed of this by radio, Roise allowed Company D to hold its present position and relieve at dawn."

The Army officer who accompanied LT Cahill was not the Army company commander. He was 2LT Angway, a Fox Co. platoon leader. Cahill (and possibly Angway) did advise Finn to make the relief at once. "I told Finn that he would be better off coming up now," wrote Cahill. "(He wasn't that far down, maybe 600 - 1,000 yards as I recall.)"

LTC John Finn (Ret.), confirmed that Cahill advised making a night relief. Finn said he disapproved the idea because of three factors: (1) He and his men were unfamiliar with the terrain; (2) Finn had been with Co. D only a short time and did not know the men too well; (3) He felt trying to effect a night relief would cause heavy casualties. He said that he accepted responsibility for the decision to wait until daylight.

Co. D was suffering terribly from a lack of water. Marine helicopters made a low altitude free-drop of water cans. One hit PFC Leonard Mateo on the shoulder, knocking him out and breaking the stock of his BAR. Many of the cans broke, so each man got only a few sips of water.

While Co. D went up the eastern ridge toward Hill 342, LT Sweeney led Easy along the western ridge. Although the unit came under long range machine gun fire, it was ineffective. The real cause of casualties was the heat and hard climb. By dusk, the company was about half-way along the ridge, where it dug in for the night.

Situations of 3d and 1st Battalions, 5th Marines

The 3-5 Mar. (- Cahill's platoon) remained on Hills 255 and 99 on Aug. 7, calling periodically for artillery or mortar fire to disperse enemy troops sighted moving toward Chindong-ni. Shortly after 10 a.m., 2LT Lawrence W. Hetrick's 3 Platoon, Co. A, 1st Engineers finished laying mines across the Haman road a half mile above Chindong-ni.

That afternoon 1-5 Mar. relieved Bohn's G Co., which redeployed on the lower slopes of Hill 255, facing the Haman road. The company took some sniper fire during the night. At daylight on the 8th, the Marines discovered four North Korean soldiers dug in less than 100 yards away in the valley. They were quickly dispatched.

August 8 — Chindong-ni Area
Hill 342 — Aug. 8-9

The enemy tried one more time at dawn on Aug. 8 to wrest Hill 342 from the Army-Marine defenders. Having snaked their way forward in the darkness, enemy soldiers attacked at close range with rifles and machine guns. The defenders fired back and hurled grenades down on the North Koreans. But a small group of the enemy assaulted the northern face of the perimeter. The Marines and soldiers fought off the attackers in a short, sharp and bloody hand-to-hand battle. Marine PFC Michael Yercich was killed and three soldiers of Co. F were wounded. Cahill "pulled Yercich out of his hole and his wounds just sucked air," Cahill wrote. "He had multiple bayonet wounds and was dead. It was still not quite light."

Just after daybreak, Finn's company, deployed with all three platoons on line along the southern face of Hill 342, started out for the summit.

PFC Russell A. Albert was a PFC in Co. D, with his brother, John. "It was still dark, dawn was just breaking," he wrote. "Two green flares fired by the enemy, lit the sky and ground around us. Someone shouted 'They're attacking! We're moving to the top of the hill!' It seems at that moment a hand was on my left hand. In the green glow of light I knew immediately it was my brother, John's. He had crawled over from his position and somehow found me. His last words to me were, 'Keep your head down, Rusty, these bastards are playing for keeps.' Within a half hour he was killed." Russell was wounded in one arm above the wrist.

Albert recalled that MSG Harold Reeves, the company gunnery sergeant, told the unit aboard ship that they "would be facing a well trained army, and that there where a lot of one way tickets aboard [the ship]."

Van Dommelen wrote, "The morning of [Aug.] 8th we moved up and as predicted by Blackie the __ hit the fan as the North Koreans were launching an attack on the hill from three sides. We effected the relief, but it was costly. Lieutenants Oakley and Reid were killed while getting their platoons into position to repel the attack. The other platoon leader [LT Emmelman] was wounded. CPT Finn was wounded while checking out Oakley and Reid, leaving the XO [LT Hanifin] in command. He was evacuated with heat prostration [soon afterward]. Master GySgt Reeves assumed command of the company."

The ordeal on Hill 342 was finally over for the survivors of F/5 RCT and Cahill's platoon of G-3-5 Mar. Co. F had defended the hill from the night of Aug. 3-4 until joined on Aug. 7 by the Marine platoon. Cahill's reinforced platoon of 52 men lost 6 KIA and 12 WIA. LT Brooks said that only about eight men from Fox Co. came off the hill with him. He admitted that his recollection of that number may be faulty, but he said there were few of the original 120 men left on the hill when Finn's Marine company finally relieved them. Like Brooks, some of the survivors were wounded.

The two units had made a valiant, determined and successful stand, denying the enemy criti-

Brothers Three. A Navy chaplain (above) leads Russell (left) and William in prayers for the dead at the grave of their brother, John Stewart Albert. (Source: P. 133, Pictorial History of the War in Korea, *Veterans of Foreign Wars, 1951)*

cal ground that would have given them a hill mass dominating more than 2 miles of the MSR and lower hills, ridges and valleys for many more miles to the south and east of 342.

Co. D's appearance on Hill 342 precipitated renewed enemy efforts to make the summit untenable and wrest it from the Americans. Emmelman's platoon took position on the left, Reid's on the right and Oakley's moved straight ahead to the center. As the platoons moved forward, the enemy raked the area with grazing fire.

LT Emmelman received a serious head wound when a bullet penetrated his helmet, paralyzing the left side of his body. Reid was killed as he ran over a bare knob. Oakley was shot down as he went forward to locate enemy positions. SGT George Chapman and PFC Charley Heckman were cut down. Sergeants Douglas Bell and William Pascoe were wounded.

CPT Finn received his wounds trying to retrieve Reid's body. Returning with Reid, he was struck in the head and shoulder by enemy bullets. Blinded by blood and barely conscious, Finn crawled back into his lines on his hands and knees. After being treated by a corpsman, he was helped down the hill by the first sergeant. On the way, they met LT Hanifin leading the Company Headquarters and Mortar Section forward. Finn informed Hanifan that he now commanded the company. The lieutenant started for the summit at once, arriving barely in time to reorganize the emplaced 60 mm mortars before the enemy struck again. The Marines beat off the attack, inflicting heavy casualties on the enemy.

LTC Roise phoned Hanifin from his OP on the eastern spur at 11:30 a.m. No sooner had the conversation begun when Hanifin collapsed from heat prostration. It was then that Master GySgt Reeves assumed command of the company.

The only officer left on the peak was the FO from 1-11 Marines, 2LT Leroy K. Wirth. He recalled that the maps issued to FOs in the early days of the war "were of no use whatsoever. Nearly impossible to perform my mission as forward observer of artillery in support of [the] infantry company to which [I was] assigned." He remembered that the unit on the ridge had "no food/water and little ammunition." Wirth was "unable to bring in artillery support because of poor maps" He conducted "one air strike but [it was] of little assistance to the hard pressed troops."

Other Marines recalled that empty shell casings from the Corsairs fell into their positions on Hill 342 as the planes rocketed and strafed the attacking enemy troops. After that, the North Koreans never seriously threatened the position. CPT Andrew M. Zimmer, assistant regimental S-3, was sent forward to take command of Co. D.

The 2/24 Inf. was scheduled to relieve 2-5 Mar. during the afternoon of Aug. 8, but it was delayed fighting, along with elements of Taplett's 3-5 Marines, for Hill 255. By the time 2/24 Inf. did take over Hill 342, Dog Co.'s casualties had risen to 8 KIA and 28 WIA. Marines losses there between Aug. 7 and 9 totaled some 14 killed and 40 wounded. F/5 RCT, having been on the summit they called Fox Hill between Aug. 4 and 8 had even more casualties. American losses totaled between 120 and 160 men; that of the enemy approached 400. On Aug. 8, E-5th Marines moved forward a few hundred yards on its ridge and dug in.

Hill 255 — Aug. 8-9

In the 3d Battalion's area, some men from CPT Joseph C. Fegan's Co. H saw a column of troops climbing Hill 255 from the Haman road. The Marines at first thought they were ROK soldiers and watched them climb to the peak forward of the plateau occupied by Co. H. When the "ROKs" began setting up facing his unit, Fegan alerted his riflemen and machinegunners. No sooner had he spread the word than these soldiers opened fire; they were North Koreans.

The enemy's seizure of Hill 255 and nearby ground overlooked and blocked TF Kean's MSR. Supplies, ammunition and replacements could not go forward and casualties could not be evacuated. In this position, the enemy also stopped 2/24 Inf. from coming forward to relieve both the 2d and 3d Battalions, 5th Marines.

LTC Taplett ordered Fegan to drive the enemy from Hill 255. Co. H had only two rifle platoons available for the job; 2LT John O. Williams' 1st and LT Lucius DiLorenzo's 3d. LT Post's 2d Platoon was still positioned east of the MSR. CPT Fegan sent Williams' platoon in a skirmish line, echeloned to the right, across the plateau leading to Hill 255. The men employed marching fire, moving forward to within 30 yards of the hill's summit. There, they were stopped by a rain of enemy grenades and machine gun fire, pinning down the platoon. Fegan ordered Williams to try to get around to the enemy's left flank, but that failed.

The 3d Platoon (DiLorenzo) had also sustained a number of casualties. Some men who had tried to work around the steep slope leading to the enemy position were sent rolling down the hill when struck by enemy fire. Fegan felt that the 1st Platoon could not carry the hill. He ordered Williams to pull his men back and reorganize, and directed the 3d Platoon to pass through the 1st and continue the attack, but nothing happened.

The captain, realizing that the men were temporarily dismayed and confused by the first attacks failure, took charge of the 3d Platoon and led it forward. Energized by the company commander's leadership, the men of the 3d Platoon moved out. The platoon advanced in a wedge formation, with one squad at the apex and the other two echeloned to the left and right. Half way across the plateau, the formation passed through Williams' reorganizing platoon. Air strikes and artillery fire had not destroyed the enemy, but the position was taken in a deadly close-in small-arms and grenade fight.

SSG John I. Wheatley and several others were wounded. SGT Edward F. Barrett, made helpless by gunshot wounds to an elbow and a hip, was carried to safety by CPT Fegan.

The two trailing squads moved forward, flanking the enemy's position. CPL Melvin James and his squad worked through the North Korean position from the left, while TSGT Ray Morgan and PFC Donal Terrio collapsed the enemy's right by each knocking out a machine gun. James and another Marine made six trips through fire-swept terrain to rescue six wounded comrades. The platoon swept forward another 200 yards to a point where the ridge dropped off. Beyond this deep swale rose Hill 255 itself, dominating everything around it. Thus far Co. H had lost six dead and 32 wounded.

A platoon of North Koreans tried to reinforce Hill 25, but were spotted by troops from Co. G. The enemy began moving across the valley between the high ground on the ridge above Hill 99 and Hill 255, and the Marines of George Co. blasted the enemy platoon with every weapon available. Survivors ran back in panic.

While the Marines were attacking Hill 255 and the enemy roadblock from the south, 2/24 Infantry, supported by mortars, artillery, air strikes and tank fire, attacked the block from the other end. Hill 255 was but one promontory along a ridge two miles long which dominated the MSR. The highest point on this feature was Hill 395, a mile north of 255. The 2/24 went after Hill 395. Supporting the Marine-Army assaults were the 1-11 Marines, Batteries B and C, 159th (24 RCT) and, at the Marine's request, part of the 555 FAB. The two batteries of the 159th alone fired 1,600 rounds against the roadblock on August 7-8.

Taplett was ordered to halt the attack for the day and dig in. Enemy artillery and mortar fire harassed the Marines as they prepared for the night. Marine Corsairs of MAG-33 and artillery pounded the North Koreans. Marine artillery and the 3d Battalion's mortars laid a wall of fire across the battalion front during the night, discouraging enemy activity.

At 8:25 a.m. on Aug. 9, 1-11 Mar. plastered Hill 255, then Corsairs came in with air strikes featuring the first recorded use of napalm in the Korean War. Minutes before Co. H began its attack, the airborne TAC announced that the objective had been neutralized. Fegan's men climbed to the summit of Hill 255 virtually unopposed, finding two destroyed machine guns and a few dead North Koreans.

Grid line 1350 on the map more or less divided the Hill 255 - 395 complex in half, east and west. There, the 24th Regiment and H-5 Marines were to meet. At 11:25 a.m. the two commands met near line 1350, secured the ridge, freeing the MSR. The Marines lost 16 KIA and 36 WIA in taking Hill 255. Most were in Co. H, representing 25 per cent of its strength.

3/24 Infantry, Sobuk-san Area — Aug. 6

On Aug. 6, units of 3/24 Inf. experienced a series of misfortunes which temporarily disorganized companies L and I, as well as heavily engaging Co. M.

Love Co. advanced into the town of Sobuk and found it deserted. They were returning to friendly lines when ambushed by the enemy with a suddenness and fury that disorganized the unit and scattered the men.

Co. M was struck by the enemy on the night of Aug. 6. PFC William Thompson, a machinegunner, took on the enemy, allowing his platoon "to withdraw to more tenable positions," as the citation for his Medal of Honor read. Thompson, although wounded repeatedly by enemy grenades and small-arms fire, ignored pleas from his comrades to withdraw. He cut down numerous enemy soldiers and pinned the remainder down until finally killed by a grenade. His selfless action and sacrifice undoubtedly stemmed the enemy's attack and saved the lives of a number of his comrades.

BG Vennard Wilson, 25th Division ADC, assembled a task force consisting of Co. I, 24th Infantry, elements of the Regimental I & R Platoon and 3d Platoon, 77 ECC. CPT Daley, commanding Item Co., was task force commander. LT Chester Lenon commanded 3/77 ECC. The task force was to make contact with other U.S. units near Chindong-ni.

CPT Bussey, 77th commander, pieced together what happened to the task force from about a dozen survivors of Lenon's platoon.

The platoon had formed the task force rear guard.

The force moved into an upsloping valley, rimmed by crags where the enemy lay in wait. The first mile of so of the march was uneventful. When the whole force was well into the valley, the enemy sprung their ambush. CPT Daley and about half the task force escaped over the crest of a hill, but the other half, including Lenon's platoon, was pinned inside the valley. Most of this element of TF Daley were left dead or dying. Once over the crest, Daley and his party kept on going. As LTC Bussey wrote in his *Firefight at Yechon*, it was "a debacle." Later, part of Co. I linked up with elements of the 27th Infantry. Appleman, in *South to the Naktong*, states that the unit had 12 KIA. Whether this included the dead from the attached Engineer Platoon is unknown. Lenon and several other members of the platoon, all badly wounded, remained behind. They hid out together from the enemy.

After hearing what happened, Bussey sought out Daley. "I felt sorry for him," Bussey wrote. "His eyes were begrimed, and he was dirty from head to toe. Spatters of blood, shed by one of his wounded, covered his shoulder. His troops were sprawled out on the ground more like cattle than men."

Bussey tried to find out from Daley where this valley was. His men had told him that Lenon and a number of engineer soldiers with him remained in the valley. Daley could not recall much about how to find it and told Bussey that there was no chance that Lenon and the other engineers with him could have survived the devastating enemy fire. Saddened and discouraged, Bussey returned to his company.

COL Horton V. White was relieved of command of the 24th Infantry on Aug. 6 by COL Arthur Champeny, age 57. He was older than White by about eight years, and also older than GEN Kean. COL White realized that, at 49, he was not up to commanding the 24th, and neither was Champeny. A number of officers in the RCT were disappointed with the appointment of Champeny as commander. CPT Bussey considered him an incompetent. He commanded the "Deuce Four," as the men of the regiment sometimes called it, for only one month.

During the Aug. 6 battles, 3/24 Infantry lost its commander, LTC Samuel Pierce Jr., wounded in action. The battalion got an excellent new commander in LTC John T. Corley (West Point 1938). Corley was 36, and had been awarded a number of medals in WW II as commander of 3/26 Infantry.

The 35th Infantry Defends, then Attacks — Aug. 6 - 8

The North Koreans probed the "Cacti" (35th Infantry) defenses during Aug. 6, then an estimated enemy battalion assaulted Easy Co., driving it from its positions. Baker Co., supported by mortars and artillery, drove the enemy from the captured ground and restored the line. In spite of this pitched battle, 2/35 Inf. was ready the following morning to attack toward Muchon-ni as part of TF Kean.

From this point on, the day-to-day actions of each major component will be followed as closely as possible. The principal subordinate

commands, being separated geographically, operated pretty much independently of one another. The least complicated operation was that of the 35th Regiment; the most confusing and complex were those of the 5 and 24 RCTs. The Brigade advance over the southern and longest route more or less involved leapfrogging battalions.

It should be noted that 1/29 Infantry was dissolved on Aug. 6 and reconstituted the same day as 3/35 Infantry. The 3/29 Infantry became 3/27 Infantry on Aug. 7. At last, the 27th and 35th Regiments had their authorized complement of three battalions.

On Aug. 7, 2/35 Infantry began their attack as part of TF Kean after a 20 minute preparation. They battled the North Koreans for five hours before taking the initial objective. At one point, an estimated 500 enemy with self-propelled guns held up the advance. An air strike knocked out two T-34s and dispersed accompanying enemy infantry. The 35th drove on toward Muchon-ni, where it was to meet the 5 RCT coming from Chindong-ni. Near Wonbong-ni, the Cactus soldiers killed or wounded an estimated 350 North Koreans and captured truck loads of abandoned weapons, ammunition, several briefcases of documents, three POWs, and destroyed a 76mm SP gun and five antitanks guns. Near Pansong, about 2 miles northeast of Muchon-ni, they found several large Russian-built radios and other headquarters equipment, leading COL Fisher to believe that they had overrun the *6th Division* CP.

During this action, CPL Leroy Durst, a BAR-man, was providing covering fire for his unit's attack. The enemy tried to knock him out with grenades. Young Durst picked up the grenades and tossed them back over the hill's crest onto the enemy. As a witnessing war correspondent wrote, "he engaged in a calm game of catch in the midst of the assault...."

Then the enemy tried to get him by hurling several grenades at a time. Durst responded by kicking them back down the hill toward the enemy. "I was in a good position to cover the others and didn't feel like moving," Durst explained. The assistant platoon sergeant, SFC Donald Gray, saw the exchange and said Durst was "amazingly cool. Durst just picked up the grenades and threw them back like he was in a friendly game."

By evening of Aug. 7, the regiment stood on its initial objective. On Aug. 8, the 35th advanced on to the high ground just short of Muchon-ni, where GEN Kean ordered it to hold until the 5 RCT arrived. The cocky men of the 35th bragged that if they had not been ordered to stop at Muchon-ni, they would have been half way to Seoul before some of the other units had cleared their foxholes.

The regiment screened the task force right flank with men along the Nam River, the north (right) flank of the task force. The enemy took these troops under mortar and machine gun fire, then launched an attack on the new 3/35 Infantry. The battalion repelled the enemy assault after a three-hour battle.

On the night of Aug. 7-8, an enemy force also attacked Battery A, 64 FAB, but was repelled, leaving 15 dead. The high morale of the 64th matched that of the 35th, which it supported as the regiment's direct support artillery battalion.

1-5 Marines, Aug. 8

LTC Newton's battalion readied itself to move out on Aug. 8, as ordered; 1/5 RCT, however, was engaged with the enemy up ahead and his battalion was blocked from getting forward. LTC Newton went ahead to the Army battalion's CP on a hillside near the village of Singi. The situation was so confusing that LTC Jones, commanding 1/5 RCT, believed his forward units were cut off.

About 2 p.m., 1-5 Mar. reached Newton and was halted again, 1 1/2 miles from their Line of Departure. (LD - a point, or easily defined terrain feature such as a road, trail, stream, dike, etc., from which an attack is launched.) About this time, MAJ Merlin Olson (XO, 1-5 Mar.), recalled that a bedraggled, wet and muddy Army staff sergeant showed up. The sergeant reported that he had just come from Hill 308, south of the Tosan junction. His unit of 1/5 RCT was heavily engaged, he said. Enemy machine guns covered the paddy between the road and 308, and he had crawled almost the whole distance, he reported.

GEN Kean, meeting LTC Murray on the road near Chindong-ni, ordered him to arrange to relieve 1/5 RCT that night. Kean said that he would inform Brigade headquarters of these orders as soon as possible. Meantime, Newton radioed Murray for instructions and was told of the change in plans.

The 1-5 Mar. went into an assembly area near the western ridge which led to Hill 342. The battalion was ordered to make the relief at midnight on Aug. 8 and to secure the Tosan road junction.

5RCT — August 8 - 9

When Throckmorton's 2/5 RCT was relieved by 2-5 Marines on Aug. 8, he was ordered to seize the high ground northwest of the junction that 1/5 RCT should have been taken on Aug. 7. Throckmorton had only two effective rifles companies, G and E. Co. F, after Fox Hill, was all but destroyed. The attack, weakened by the lack of artillery support, failed.

GEN Kean was in no mood for failure. As COL Ordway stood nearby, Kean told Throckmorton, "I want that hill tonight."

"LTC Throckmorton gathered his Company Commanders and myself to issue his order for the night attack," wrote then-LT Keith W. Whitham, leader, 2d Platoon, 5 RCT Tank Co. "It was dusk...the most prominent feature...was a blown bridge over an almost dry streambed. Immediately after crossing the streambed the narrow road took a sharp right turn up a very steep hill.... The narrow road was bounded by a high bank on the left and a very deep gulch on the right.

"Shortly before midnight we jumped off in deep darkness," Whitham continued. His tank platoon moved with a rifle company. "Upon rounding a curve near the top of the pass an anti-tank gun (perhaps two) opened up, hitting my tank.... My gunner, SGT Carlton Kaiser... and my loader, a...Neisi named Kitaguchi, jumped out of the tank. On the embankment just above us were North Korean soldiers, firing and shouting 'Hey Joe, Hey Joe!'"

Whitham ran to the platoon sergeant's tank (MSG Archie Craig) "and told him to look for a place wide enough" to turn the tanks around. Keith tried to turn Craig's tank around, but the bank gave way. "The tank turned over completely into the deep ravine," he continued, "and landed on its tracks." Four crew members scrambled up the bank from the tank. Only the tank's loader CPL "Pourtgee" was hurt, suffering a gash on the head from a radio which broke loose. "Perhaps 50 soldiers and tank crewmen loaded up on the decks of the remaining [three] tanks and we didn't stop until we reached the bottom of the hill."

At the bottom of the hill, Whitham discovered that his tank driver, a man named Palermo, and his bow-gunner, a private known as Rocky, were missing. About an hour later, the two men came in: Palermo had saved himself and Rocky by dropping the escape hatch in Whitham's disabled tank and evading the enemy soldiers surrounding the stricken vehicle.

The night attack, supported by tanks, 81mm and 4.2-inch mortars, was successful, but the men were near exhaustion as they gained the objective.

Both the 2d and 3d Battalions of the 5 RCT were strongly opposed by the enemy on Aug. 8. In spite of this, the leading battalion was 2 miles west of the crossroads from which the attack had commenced.

MSG James W. "Hap" Easter, USA, Ret., was a member of 3d Platoon, Tank Co., 5th RCT. 2LT Vance McWorter commanded the platoon, which was in support of 3/5th RCT at the time. Easter's tank was in hull defilade on one of the first days of TF Kean, when it was struck by .51-cal AT fire. He determined that the fire came from what he described as "a mud shack." The tank returned fire from its .50-cal and one of its .30-cal machine guns. Then Easter eased the tank forward to fire the main gun. The first round blew up the shack and exposed a T-34 hidden there. The T-34 was destroyed either by a mine or tank fire, Easter couldn't remember which. He was wounded in the leg a few weeks later, but remained in combat.

LT McWorter was killed after TF Kean when struck by a tank track which had been blown off by a mine. The same track severely wounded 2LT Frank "Bull" Bullanto, who had gone to Korea as the unit supply sergeant, but his reputation as a fighter earned him assignment as tank commander, then platoon sergeant, and finally, a battlefield commission.

The 555 FAB (Triple Nickel) took a pounding that day. The battalion consisted of three four-gun firing batteries, a HQ Battery and a Svc Battery. Both flat-trajectory and 120mm mortar fire fell on the Battalion FDC, plus Service and B Batteries. One mortar round landing in Baker's CP killing and wounding a number of officers and NCOs, as noted in Chapter 11. CPL Gaffey, Battery Recorder, standing just outside the CP was unhurt.

General Barth wrote, "So many officers and key enlisted specialists were hit that the battalion commander, LTC John P. Daly, was forced to hastily reorganize his three four-gun batteries into two six-gun batteries." Battery A remained with six guns. Battery B and C were combined into a single battery. The rifle companies needed replacement FOs, so a number of NCOs, such as MSG Earl J. Law, SFC Ray Reddiford and

1SG Wyatt Logan, were sent to the units. LTC Daly even pressed LT William Motley Sr. of Service Battery into service as an FO on Aug. 11, although Motley had never been through the Field Artillery course and had never directed artillery before. Daly sent "a visibly disgruntled NCO" along with Motley, as Motley put it.

PFC Albert F. Semasko, (B/555 FAB, CPT Perry Graves commanding), recalled the bombardment which caused all the casualties. Six men of the battery were killed, he recalled, when a shell landed in the CP. The round landed "about 25 yards in front of me. It seemed like B Battery...was...jinxed," he wrote. In addition to the CP being hit, "the chow truck got hit," he wrote. "While this was going on my buddy spotted what he took to be an enemy forward observer about 150 yards away on top of a hill. We started shooting at him. I think we got him...." Friendly aircraft made a strike and the enemy bombardment stopped. "Those flyboys were like a band of angels to me," Semasko remembered. "I will forever be grateful to them."

Richard Lewis (HQ & B batteries, 555 FAB) recalled that on Aug. 8, the battalion was deployed along the MSR according to the order of march when taken under enemy fire. Battery B was forced to move because the fire was so heavy. Lewis and two other men were placed on a listening post for the night, he recalled, and SGT Matthew's howitzer was located on the opposite side of the road from the remainder of the battalion to act in an antitank role.

The Marine Brigade Launches its Attack, Aug. 9

Newton's battalion was at the 1/5 RCT CP by 10 p.m. on Aug. 8, an hour ahead of schedule. Guides were supposed to lead Newton's men to Hill 308. The Marines discovered that 5 RCT troops already were leaving Hill 308 and there were no guides. The 1-5 Marines halted on the MSR about a half mile east of Tosan, where a narrow dike designated as the Marine's route of approach went south from the road through a large paddy. Since soldiers from Hill 308 were using it to withdraw, Newton had to wait until the 5 RCT troops completed their crossing. Just after midnight the dike was cleared and two Korean civilian guides arrived. Led by South Korean guides of unknown loyalty, the Marine advance on Sachon began in the first hours of Aug. 9.

The Marines had been led to believe that the area was "crawling" with the enemy, but they reached the base of Hill 308 without encountering a single North Korean. There they were reformed into their squads, platoons and companies in preparation for continuing the advance. It was dawn before the last of the battalion crossed the dike.

With the dawn came orders from LTC Murray for 1-5 Mar. to attack southwest at once and seize Hill 308. Tobin's Co. B led out. It was a hard 1 1/4-mile climb to the summit, a thousand feet above the rice paddies below. These paddies were just above sea level. There only were a number of temporary heat casualties. Luckily, only a few snipers were encountered. By noon on Aug. 9, the 1st Battalion had attained the Brigade's first objective during TF Kean.

COL Murray did not allow Newton to stop on Hill 308, but ordered him to withdraw his battalion to the road northwest of the hill and continue the attack to Paedun-ni. Intelligence indicated no enemy ahead of the battalion and Murray wanted to take advantage of the situation.

Close to half of Companies A and B were down with heat sickness. Since he couldn't call upon those units for the mission, Newton formed up his Headquarters and Weapons Platoons, with an attached tank platoon. When he arrived in the valley northwest of Hill 308, he discovered that his Japanese map and the actual terrain did not match.

Six hundred yards south of Tosan on the MSR is a road junction at Oso-ri. One route headed south as an unimproved serpentine road through mountainous terrain; the other was good, by Korean standards, and went west, then south, through a long valley to Paedun-ni. Newton and Murray each had a different map of the area. Murray's map showed both roads, but the southern route was depicted as the better of the two. Newton's map, however, showed only the improved, "good" road. He formed up and moved out on this route.

The column had traveled barely 300 yards before it came upon what appeared to be a heavily-mined area. Marine engineers were sent forward to clear the mines and discovered that they were American, apparently fallen from an Army truck.

COL Murray arrived on the scene and told Newton he was on the wrong road, but Newton believed he was on the correct route. The two officers compared maps, then Murray directed that the column reverse itself and take the southern route through the mountains. He then left to fly over the area to confirm his decision.

While the column of trucks, tanks, infantrymen and engineers was trying to get sorted out, turned around and on the route designated by the regimental commander, GEN Craig arrived on the scene. Not knowing the situation, he let it be known that he was unhappy with the confused state of affairs.

During this time, the Marines were informed by Korean civilians that a badly-wounded soldier was in a nearby house. The Marines found the man and evacuated him.

LTC Newton radioed the two rifle companies and told their commanders to descend into the valley west of Hill 308 and meet the rest of the battalion. About a mile south of the Oso-ri junction, a lone enemy machinegunner fired from a hut on the 1st Battalion point. A Marine launcher team quickly silenced the gun. In late afternoon, the battalion reached a pass between Hill 308 and a hill about 240 meters to the west, where it dug in for the night.

Ike Fenton, XO of Co. B, remembered that hot, miserable day. He said that the battalion was ordered up Hill 308 at 4:30 a.m. on Aug. 9. "You expect hardship in war," he said, "but the men had been up since 0600 [6 a.m.] the previous morning and 50 per cent of them had been up half the night of August 7-8. The men were tired after crossing the rice paddy. Worst of all, our water was practically out. There was no water available on the hill, and it was quite a problem to get water up to us."

The battalion attacked at 6 a.m., he said, and were on Hill 308 by 9, having met no resistance.

Then Co. B was ordered to investigate a ridge line to the left front. It took three hours to gain the assigned ridge. Again, there was no opposition. The extreme heat and lack of water caused heavy heat prostration casualties, and two were so bad they had to be evacuated by helicopter.

At 5 p.m. on Aug. 9 GEN Craig's operational control of all troops in the area ended. COL Ordway finally had the 5 RCT headed out on the road to Muchon-ni.

When LTC Newton was ordered to descend to the road, Fenton recalled that the battalion commander ordered the two rifle companies to send all available men down. "But we [Co. B] only had 30 men and two officers that were in good enough shape," Fenton said. "The rest of the men just couldn't make it. They were out...lying on the ground...."

Company commander CPT Tobin "was in fairly bad shape," Fenton said. "He stayed with the men on the hill while I led the 30 men down to the road with one officer." When the group reached the road, CPT Fenton passed out, too. The troops coming off the hill were given water and an hour's rest, then moved out.

The temperature reached 114 degrees, Fenton recalled. The men of Co. B left on the hill were in such bad condition, Fenton believed they would have been unable to stop even a weak enemy attack.

The battalion advanced about a mile and a half by 5 p.m., slowed by heavy enemy sniper fire. The battalion then dug in, as noted previously. "The irony of this situation was that B Co. was given the mission of protecting the battalion's left flank, which would place it on the same high ground it had just come off. Fortunately, about 85 per cent of the company was

still on top of the hill," Fenton said. By this time civilian "chiggie bearers" had arrived with water for the men on the hill, but 15 men of the company still had to be sent for treatment at the battalion aid station.

LT Frank Muetzel brought up Co. A's rear coming off Hill 308, "with orders to leave no stragglers," he wrote. "Some men did overdose on salt tablets and convulsed," he added. He also stated that "Co. A was never in the kind of trouble [from lack of water and the extreme heat as has been reported]." When he finally reached the road, "there were approximately 10 men being revived or resting with corpsmen in attendance. The balance had already formed and moved out."

It was probably during the advance on Aug. 9 that 1LT George C. Fox, commanding Able Company's 3d Platoon, received his baptism of fire. "My platoon had the point on the road," he wrote. "We came under long-range small-arms fire and occasional mortar fire. The platoon sergeant, Stanley G. Miller knocked me into a paddy, then said, 'Well lieutenant, now you know what incoming mortars sound like.' I did."

"The pre-dawn hours [of Aug. 9] brought rain," wrote PFC Herbert Luster, of Co. A. It was the first time he had ever slept in the rain. To protect his BAR's action, he turned the bolt handle down. "The shower cooled things down temporarily, but after a couple of hours on the road, the parched earth was once again calling out for water and so were the Marines."

Co. A climbed Hill 308 with the battalion. "It was a hard climb, with intermittent stops," Luster recalled. "As the day came to a close, the men received their water, and then had to walk later than usual before deploying for the night."

He also wrote that his unit met "some soak-

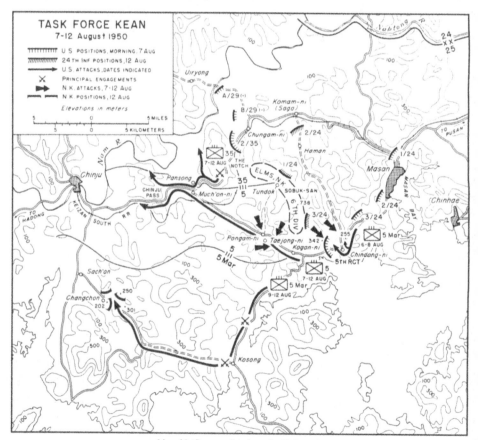

Map 19 (Source: South to the Naktong)

144

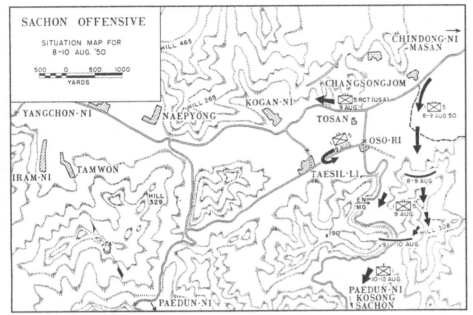

Map 20 (Source: p. 131, Pusan Perimeter)

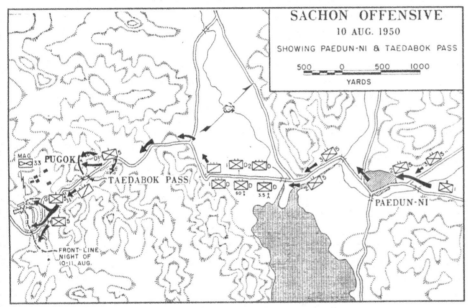

Map 21 (Source: p. 133, Pusan Perimeter)

ing wet black soldiers who looked scared to death." (LT Muetzel wrote that he believed these men were from a black 81mm mortar unit located near the CP of 1/5 RCT.)

The 2-5 Marines became available to the regiment at 4 p.m. that day, but the 3d Battalion was delayed until early on Aug. 10. Once relieved in the Hill 342 area, LTC Roise's 2-5 Mar. was trucked to an assembly area near Hill 308, arriving about 9 p.m. GEN Craig was determined to take advantage of the absence of significant enemy ahead (as reported by intelligence). He ordered a night attack by the 2d Battalion to seize Paedun-ni before daylight on Aug. 10.

Paedun-ni to Pugok, 2d and 3d Battalions, 5th Marines — Aug. 10

The 2d Battalion passed through the lines of the 1st at 1:15 a.m. on Aug. 10. Three M-26 tanks

from 1LT William D. Pomeroy's tank platoon were with the point. The column moved along without difficulty until 5 a.m. Less than a mile from the battalion's objective of Paedun-ni, a tank dropped through a concrete bridge. There it remained, impossible to move or retrieve. The next tank in line threw a track in midstream trying to go through a narrow bypass next to the bridge. The entire column's advance was delayed two hours by these incidents. South Korean laborers and an engineer dozer built a detour around the stranded tanks.

Paedun-ni was reached at 8 a.m. and found to be free of the enemy. By 9:30 a.m. the battalion was on the road to Kosong, the Brigade's next objective.

LTC Murray decided to shuttle the battalion on to Kosong, 8 miles south, an area believed to contain no enemy. A delay ensued while he tried to get trucks forward for the shuttle. At midmorning, GEN Craig arrived on the scene in a helicopter. Unsatisfied with the stalled situation, he directed colonels Murray and Roise to ad-

vance on Kosong with "all speed." A short distance out of Paedun-ni, five 2 1/2 ton trucks managed to get through to the lead elements of the battalion.

A column of 10 jeeps and five trucks was formed, with a detachment from the Recon Co. leading in the first four jeeps. The 1st and 2d Rifle Platoons, the 60mm mortars, an assault squad and a machine gun section from CPT Zimmer's Co. D followed on the remaining jeeps and trucks. The remainder of the 2d Battalion followed on foot until more vehicles could be brought forward.

The motorized column set off, lacking both artillery and air support. Zimmer's orders were to occupy Kosong and coordinate its defense with the mayor. Two and a half miles south of Paedun-ni the road makes a sharp turn to the right (west) then another to the left (south), then climbs through the 1,000-yard long Taedabok Pass. Northwest of the defile entrance about 500 yards is Hill 130, which overlooks the entire pass. The village of Pugok lay near the base of this hill.

At 3 p.m., the first jeep of the recon detachment approached the turn near Pugok. An enemy machine gun opened up from Hill 130. Other North Korean automatic weapons on the high ground adjacent to the pass swept the Marine-filled trucks and jeeps.

The Marines dove for cover in roadside ditches. An enemy AT gun, firing from Hill 130, hit one of the Recon jeeps. The Recon element worked their way back from the ambush site. Zimmer took stock of the situation, then sent the 1st Platoon to take the high ground to the left of the road about halfway through the Pass. Meeting no resistance, the men set up and returned the enemy fire. Meantime, the 2d Platoon cleared small parties of the enemy from high ground on both sides of the road and advanced up on the right.

The AT gun was spotted and knocked out by the company mortars, expending all the 60mm mortar ammunition in this action. Zimmer decided to await Brigade support. At 4:30 p.m., two tanks arrived and drove the enemy from concealment.

David Van Dommelman of Co. D wrote, "On the morning of [Aug.] 10th we mounted up again to continue our drive. We were rolling along pretty good when we ran into an ambush. The troops bailed out fast and began to return fire. It was then that we lost Gunny Reeves. I believe he was wounded in both legs, The fighting went on...until our tanks finally caught up and blasted away with their 90s, dispersing the North Koreans. We lost another 10 men in this action."

Marine air joined the tanks in smashing the roadblock. At the same time, the 3d Battalion, finally released from Chindong-ni, arrived in trucks at Paedun-ni. The command had driven over the more direct valley road, rather than the one Newton had been ordered to take. Murray ordered Taplett to prepare to pass through the 2d Battalion and continue the attack.

LTC Taplett sent Bohn's G Co. to attack and seize high ground to the right of the road and Fegan's H Co. to the high ground on the left of the road. The battalion passed through the 2d Battalion and attacked about 5 p.m. The objective was close to 300 meters high.

When G Co. was attacking their hill objective, the exact location of the enemy was in doubt, so MAJ McNeely (S-3, 2d Bn) volunteered to take a patrol out to find out. About 5:30 p.m., accompanied by a radio operator and a fire team in his jeep, he set out.

Taplett, in an OP to the left of the road, was now in a position to determine the situation for himself. He saw that McNeely was headed into danger but his radio call to Bohn to stop the jeep came too late. MecNeely's vehicle disappeared behind a hill around a bend in the road. A short, sharp barrage of machine gun and rifle fire rang out — followed by silence.

Meantime, G Co. had pressed their attack with 1LT Jack Westerman's 3d Platoon leading. When enemy fire held them up, LT Bohn sent 2LT Edward F. Duncan's 2d Platoon to envelop the enemy's left flank. The maneuver drove the North Koreans from the hill. From the crest of the newly-won hill, Westerman could see McNeely's bullet-riddled jeep. The major and his five men were sprawled motionless beneath and behind the vehicle.

Fred Davidson provided covering fire, as "Big Jack" Westerman dashed down the hill. He ran to the right of the jeep, picked McNeely up and carried him back on his shoulders. Westerman hurt his back retrieving the mortally wounded major and was evacuated. Miraculously, the jeep driver escaped unhurt, Davidson recalled. Three men were killed and two badly wounded, including McNeely.

Davidson was a PFC rifleman in Co. G, already a veteran of a year and a half each in the Army and the Marines.

When Co. G tried to continue the attack, it was held up by two machine guns located at the far end of the road bend. Co. H was sent to the high ground on the left of the road opposite G's position. Just before dark, the Marines knocked out two enemy machine guns. At 8:15 p.m., the regimental commander directed 3-5 to dig in for the night, forcing the company to dig in after dark. "That's bad," Bohn said. "Then I was ordered to kick off the next morning at 6 or 7.... G Co. was supposed to be leading the whole Brigade the next morning." No further attempt was made that night to go to the wrecked jeep, believing the enemy probably had the area set for an ambush.

3-5 Marines — Aug. 11

"The noise of bullets whizzing above my head brought me out of a light sleep," wrote Fred Davidson. It was daybreak, Aug. 11, and the enemy was attacking G Co. Keeping his head down, Davidson got his boots on, grabbed his carbine, ran up the hill, and jumped into a small depression with four other Marines. The enemy machine gun kept firing.

Off to the left, 1LT Bohn, George Co.'s skipper, directed the fire of a 3.5-inch rocket launcher, exposing himself to the enemy gun to get a fix on its location. He and the launcher crew spotted the gun; the loader put a rocket into the launcher. As the gunner was ready to fire, an enemy bullet hit the launcher, putting a 6-inch groove in the tube.

Enemy machine gun fire was joined by a barrage of hand grenades, but LT Bohn continued to expose himself to enemy fire so as to direct his men in responding to it. "I tell you," Davidson

wrote, "it was worth your life to lift your head above cover." He was firing his carbine at the enemy. Once, he saw Bohn "trying to do three things at the same time. He was directing fire from a BAR...yelling for [another rocket launcher] and trying to fire his carbine on full automatic at the enemy.... All this time he was standing out in the open as though he were bullet-proof."

Finally, another launcher was brought forward. As other men gave covering fire, the gunner fired one round, destroying the enemy machine gun. With that, the enemy broke and ran, with the Marines right on their heels. "None of them got away," Davidson wrote.

"At daybreak [Aug. 11] we were hit," Bohn recalled. "I was wounded by a grenade. My mortar section chief, standing next to me, was killed." SSG Charles F. Kurtz Jr. called in effective 60 mm mortar fire while ducking submachine gun bursts and throwing grenades.

The enemy apparently had homed in on the noise made by Bohn's radio. "They attacked my command group," he said. "I think we killed them all. I was hit in the neck and shoulders by fragments of a grenade." A corpsman dressed his wounds. Bohn suddenly realized that the enemy had been driven off, and quickly began organizing the unit to get down to the road, since Co. G was to lead out that day.

"I was late arriving at the Line of Departure," he recalled. COL Murray came up "to give me hell and Taplett was coming from the other direction." LTC Taplett interceded with Murray on Bohn's behalf. Even so, Bohn said, "I remember Murray telling me, 'You know, when I say cross the Line of Departure at 0800, I don't mean 0801.' He was right. But I couldn't disengage and get down there in time."

The advance started at 8:30 a.m. "It was probably one of the most successful, satisfying experiences a rifle company commander could have," Bohn recalled. "I felt that I was the most powerful man in the Marine Corps that day.... I had everything in support — tanks, artillery — air constantly overhead and I had a FAC...with me. We were doing it just like the book says. We had the main body on the road and had flank patrols and flank guards up on the high ground. People on the flanks were running to keep up, so I relieved them frequently...."

Bohn's march CP was directly behind his leading platoon, the 3d, under 2LT John D. Counselman. CPL Raymond Giaquinto was in charge of the leading element. During the march, a Marine aircraft mistook some of Bohn's flank people for the enemy and made a firing pass. Fortunately, no one was hit and the FAC got the attack called off.

Patrols also checked the roadsides and culverts for mines. About a mile beyond the LD, Giaquinto halted his unit as it approached terrain where the enemy might be set up. The flankers converged on an enemy machinegun position, killing all five North Koreans there before they could fire a shot.

SGT Lyle R. Engle, Co. A, 1st Engineer Battalion of the Brigade, vividly described being under enemy artillery fire on the road to Kosong. Engle and other men of his unit were further back in the column of Marines advancing on that town, but were busy keeping the road passable by fill-

ing shell holes and smoothing it out. Enemy artillery fire made their job very dangerous.

"It was very accurate and effective. They literally walked the shells up and down the road and then traversed and reversed cross-wise, killing and wounding many Marines," he wrote. Being on the road, of course, "all any of us could do was hug the ground and hope the round we could hear coming in was not *the one*. Shrapnel was flying and literally skipping across the surface of the ground, like when we were skipping flat rocks across a pond. One piece came to a stop inches from my left hand. Acting like any green Marine, I picked it up and dropped it immediately. It was hot like it came from a blacksmith forge."

In spite of the artillery, the engineers had to smooth the shell craters so that the wounded could be evacuated and ammunition and other supplies brought forward. "The screaming of the wounded as they were taken to the rear aid station was enough to make all hands turn to shoveling and the dozer operators do their best," Engle wrote. "The intense summer heat, the artillery and mortar shells coming in one behind the other, plus a burning...T-34 tank with the crew inside frying like bacon made the road work seem like condemned men working in Hell."

By 10 a.m., Bohn's company reached a bridge north of Kosong. Here Co. H passed through G and continued the advance on into the town. Fred Davidson recalled his first sight of Kosong. "I'll never forget it.... Painted in English on the roof of a two-story building on the right of the road was 'KOSONG.'"

Fegan easily cleared the northern end of town with a rifle platoon and two tanks, then wheeled right on the road to Sachon. The remainder of How Co. continued south to seize a high hill southeast of Sunam-dong. In moving through Kosong, some Marines decided to "blow" the locked safe of the town's bank. Korean won notes flew in all directions. Nearby Marines crammed the money in their pockets before moving on.

As Taplett began establishing his CP in a schoolyard north of town, GEN Craig arrived in a jeep. A small party of enemy snipers nearby opened fire, but battalion sniper teams quickly wiped them out.

Meantime, Co. G moved to the right of the town and began an attack on Hill 88 southwest of Kosong. While moving up to make the attack, the unit sustained a few casualties. One of these was CPL Donald Sowl, leader of the 1st Squad of LT Edward Duncan's 2d Platoon. Sowl had turned his men to return fire coming from the right rear of the company. As he did so, his right arm was broken by an enemy bullet. He stayed with his squad until it destroyed the enemy snipers. Marine aircraft and artillery blasted Hill 88 and the hundred North Koreans entrenched on it. The enemy fled and G Co. took the hill by 1:30 p.m.

GEN Craig, wanting to be on with the drive to Sachon, ordered Taplett to recall his men and move out toward that town.

While Co. H was assembling, Corpsman William H. Anderson, driving a jeep ambulance, dashed into the area to pick up some Co. G casualties. SGT Lamb rode "shotgun" on its hood. Anderson mistakenly sped out on the Sachon road. Two enemy AT guns positioned west of

Kosong destroyed the jeep as it rounded a bend. Anderson was killed and two passengers, including Lamb, were thrown from the vehicle. Lamb was injured.

Anderson was a friend of Herbert R. Pearce, Corpsman with the Marine Anti-tank Co. He found Anderson shortly after he had been killed; the shell had hit directly in the chest.

Later the same day Corpsman John Marquez was killed trying to bring a wounded Marine to safety across a fire-swept area.

CPT Fegan led two tanks forward. Three rounds from TSGT Johnnie C. Cottrell's 90mm gun destroyed the AT guns, ending all enemy opposition in the Kosong area.

Harvey G. Frye Sr. was also a tank commander in the company's 3d Platoon. He recalled that during the tactical road march to Kosong "we came under heavy small-arms and small mortar fire. My first experience being 'buttoned up' and trying to direct fire. After a few hectic moments we were able to see and engage targets of opportunity. The infantry also directed our fire over the tank-infantry phone."

Donald R. Gagnon, the loader in Platoon Sergeant John Cottrell's tank (A-25), wrote a description of the Marine tank company and their tank, the M-26. The company had three platoons of five tanks each, plus two in company headquarters, for a total of 17 tanks the same as in tank company of the Army's tank battalion. Gagnon wrote that the M-26 had live steel tracks. On dirt roads there was no problem. But on hard surfaces, such as cement, the tank had a tendency to slide rounding corners or short turns. Tank refueling was usually done by manhanding 55 gallon drums of gasoline into position, then hand-pumping the fuel into the tanks; generally about 100 gallons.

In their move to the southwest, Co. G passed through the western edge of Kosong. Davidson was walking along just behind the leading fire team. Suddenly, they were fired on by an enemy machine gun located in one of the top windows of a two-story building to the left. All five men dove for cover in a ditch. Each time the men tried to move, the gun opened up again, so they stayed put. The enemy gun quit firing. In a few minutes, the company XO, 1LT Edmund "Skeeter" Jaworski, walked up and asked, "What's the hold-up here?" Almost in chorus, the five men said, "Get down, Skeeter! There's an enemy machine gun in a window of that building! Get down before you get shot!"

Jaworski responded, "Let me have the BAR." As he took the weapon from the BAR-man, the enemy machine gun fired at him. With bullets kicking the dirt up all around him, the lieutenant stood there and calmly aimed the BAR at the window. He fired the entire 20-round magazine, then stood there for about half a minute. Then he handed the BAR back to the BAR-man and ordered, "Get your asses out of that hole and get on with it!"

The 1st Battalion entered Kosong well after the 3d Battalion had passed through. But the Marines in the 1st were alert, nevertheless. PFC Luster's unit was informed that three people were hiding in a cluster of houses, so he joined the search.

"Something soft was found in a haystack," he wrote. "Luster stood ready to open fire.... A pitiful grandmother and three year old emerged, trembling with fear — the old and young. The

Marines were glad they didn't shoot first." Then, "a healthy young man, trying to look innocent," according to Luster, was found and turned over to the South Korean police.

The Kosong Turkey Shoot, MAG-33 and 1/11 Marines — Aug. 11

As the 3d Battalion approached Kosong, the 11th Marines prepared to support them. LTC Wood recalled that the battalion was "adjusting fire on a crossroad between Kosong and Sachon, around which an enemy force, estimated as a regiment [83d Motorcycle Regiment], was camouflaged in...various native houses.... After we fired a few rounds the Reds, no doubt assuming that we knew of their position and were about to work it over, attempted to move westward over the road leading to Sachon. We fired on the column until it was out of range."

Bolting as they did was a great mistake by the enemy. Overhead were Corsairs of VMF-323 (from the carrier Badoeng Strait), already on a search and attack mission. MAJ Arnold A Lund's squadron was given a marvelous target — some 100 enemy vehicles, including jeeps, trucks and motorcycles.

The Corsairs swooped down the column, bringing it to a halt. The first flight began to play havoc on the enemy. Vehicles smashed into one another, enemy soldiers ran for cover. The first Corsairs set 40 vehicles afire, then were replaced by another flight from VMF-323. Air Force F-51s joined the attack.

Not all of the enemy turned and ran. Two of the first four-plane flight were so badly damaged by anti-aircraft fire that they had to try emergency landings. LT Doyle Cole had to ditch in the bay. Fortunately, GEN Craig in his helicopter, piloted by Gus Lueddeke, was nearby. The general operated the hoist that lifted the downed pilot to safety.

As he was pulled into the helicopter, Cole happily slapped the general on the shoulder, saying, "Thanks for the lift, buddy —." Then he

realized it was GEN Craig. His grin faded. "Thank you, sir!" he said. "Glad to be of service, lieutenant," Craig responded.

CPT Vivian Moses, in the other crippled plane, crash-landed in enemy territory and drowned in a rice paddy just minutes before a rescue helicopter arrived. Moses had been shot down behind enemy lines just the day before, but had been rescued by a helicopter. The captain was the first man from MAG-33 killed in action.

Several hours later, elements of the 3d Battalion arrived at the scene of destruction wrought by the artillery and air strikes. Most of the enemy vehicles were twisted, charred junk, but a number of motorcycles with sidecars and Soviet jeeps were found in working condition.

Donald R. Gagnon described what well may have been part of this scene. "The temperature had to be over 100 when our air support routed out enemy in their vehicles making a run down a dirt gravel road. [Marine] tank-infantry teams were in position on line. As we approached the crest of the hill we could see the enemy making a run down the road in their Russian jeeps. A few well placed 90mm HE rounds and a few thousand .30-cal rounds from each of the five tanks along with small-arms fire from the infantry, made short work of the battle." (It lasted less than five minutes.) Several jeeps were destroyed and "enemy dead [lay] along both sides of the road," Gagnon wrote. The Tank Co. Maintenance Section captured one of the jeeps, made necessary repairs and used it for a time.

Jack Wright with Co. G followed H out of Kosong. He recalled that some of the motorcycles had signs on them saying "Mine" or "Booby Trap." A biker riding with Wright in a truck looked "at these bikes and he said, 'The hell with them,' and jumped out [of the truck]...went over and ripped the sign off, grabbed the bike and gave it one hell of a good yank." The motorcycle didn't blow up, but was out of gas. The biker got some gas and filled the tank. "[T]he next thing I know," said Jack, "he and I are buzzin' up and down the road in a Russian motorcycle. I was riding in the sidecar and having a ball!"

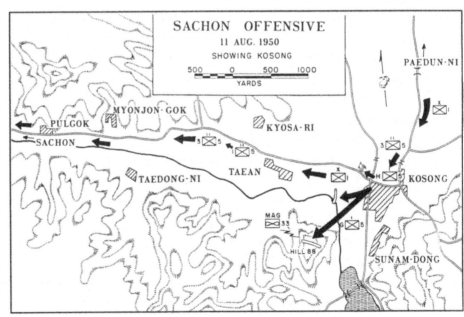

Map 22 (Source: p. 134, Pusan Perimeter)

Wright and his buddy were not the only ones zipping around in captured motorcycles and jeeps. Some Marines wondered why the Soviet jeeps had Ford dashboards. Fred Davidson wrote that he thought the Brigade "ended up with about 12 Russian jeeps and four motorcycles, with...sidecars." Jerry D. Rockey, of H & S, 2d Bn., said that for a couple of days the Marines were "mechanized" as the men confiscated and used the captured motorcycles and jeeps.

During the TF Kean operation, Rockey's unit approached a small village. Word was passed, "Snipers ahead!" The column halted on the edge of the village, and Rockey's men fell out on the edge of a rice paddy. He took off his helmet and, using it as a seat, squatted on the other side of the road and lit a cigarette. Soon an officer came by and ordered, "Rockey, get your ass off the road and on the other side there with your men!" "Aye, aye, sir!" Rockey replied. He scooted across the road, still in a squatting position. As he moved — CRACK! — the sound of a bullet passing overhead rang out. Had he stood up, or even paused before obeying the order, he would have "got it right between the headlights," as he put it.

Tactical Air Support and Marine Tactical Air Control Squadron 2 (MTACS-2)

During the first weeks after the Marines came to Korea, the Brigade had a huge edge on the Army in close-in, tactical air support — the aircraft of MAG-33. The pilots of these Corsairs were infantry-trained officers, which gave them a perspective in their missions never achieved by the USAF. Tactical air support for the Brigade was their primary mission, and this added perspective probably also gave then an edge in performing that mission. The Army never had their own "air force" in this respect; this is not to say that the USAF pilots did not perform thousands of very professional and successful tactical support missions. Air Force doctrine did not permit attachment to Army commands, or assignment of squadrons or other formations to the tactical support of particular Army regiments or divisions.

However, without TACs, having direct radio contact with aircraft performing these missions, the level of performance would have been much less effective. MATCS-2 provided this radio contact and control.

MAJ Christian C. Lee, commander of MATCS-2 , wrote, "My command was responsible for controlling air support for the 1st Marine Brigade and Army units when requested. We operated a mobile control facility designed to operate from positions close behind attacking units. From our control center we had communication with the aircraft carriers, the airplanes and all the infantry units down to battalion.... We had an intelligence section to provide up-to-date front line positions and enemy target information. The close air support missions near front line units were controlled in the attack phase by a forward air controller assigned to battalion level using portable radios. Airplanes on deep support missions were briefed and controlled from the control center."

MTACS-2 control center initially was set up at Chinhae. The squadron later moved to the Miryang area to support Brigade in the 1st and 2d Naktong Bulge operations. Between these operations, it returned to Chinhae.

CPT Earl H. Falk recalled that Chinhae was the site of the South Korean Naval Academy. There also was an airstrip which the USAF used in training South Korean pilots to fly F-51s. Falk was the security officer of the Squadron Air Support Section, "responsible," he wrote, "as the camp commander of the site, to select locations from which we [MTACS-2] could communicate with all engaged Marine outfits...aircraft carriers and the 27th Infantry." The area, he noted, had to be defensible by the unit's 65 officers and men. However, when friendly artillery batteries were emplaced nearby, enemy counter-battery fire sometimes became dangerous.

He recalled an incident in Korea (date unknown) when MTACS-2 was involved in freeing and retrieving an American soldier who had been captured by the enemy. A Marine air observer saw an American soldier being marched from the front lines by two North Koreans. "Our pilot reported this to out air control unit," he wrote. "We directed an F4U [Corsair] Marine pilot to contact the observation pilot for direction to the prisoner. The fighter pilot strafed and killed the Koreans, and a [Marine] helicopter" rescued the soldier," Falk wrote. "The prisoner was astonished, I'm sure."

MATCS-2 traced its lineage to HQ Squadron 43, activated at El Centro, CA, on Jan. 1, 1943. On July 1, 1947, the squadron was redesignated Marine Tactical Air Control Squadron-2 and assigned to the 1st Marine Air Wing, El Toro, in October. During 1949-50, MTACS-2 participated in joint operations with the 1st Marine Division and 1st Marine Air Wing. The squadron, in these exercises, controlled all close air-support operations.

When deployed to the Far East for Korea, the Air Defense Section went to Itami Air Base, Japan, and the Air Support Section went to Chinhae. Flights of Corsairs and helicopter observers were on station during daylight hours as the Marines advanced to Kosong, then on toward Sachon.

Sachon Ambush, The Changallon Valley, 1-5 Marines — Aug. 12-13

Co. H proceeded along the road from Kosong toward Sachon without difficulty. Tanks with the leading elements employed "reconnaissance by fire," that is, they fired into places the enemy was likely to occupy and attack the Marine column.

About 6 p.m. a lone enemy machinegun opened fire from a point 500 yards across a rice paddy to the left of the road. Three men of How Co.'s lead element were wounded. Tanks quickly destroyed the enemy gun.

SSG James W. Abrahamson, Co. H, was behind the leading squad with his machine gun squad when the enemy gun opened up. "I froze prone tight to the deck [ground]," he wrote. "The next thing I knew one of the rifle squad came back and said to move out.... I could still hear and feel the crack of bullets going around in my mind. From there on I was 'baptized' and became OK."

After the enemy machine gun incident, the advance was halted for the day.

By the end of Aug. 11, the North Koreans seemed disorganized and demoralized on the Sachon road.

At 6:30 a.m. on Aug. 12, the 1st Battalion passed through the 3d to continue the drive to Sachon. A 15-man detachment from the Recon Co., commanded by CPT Kenneth J. Houghton, led, followed by CPT Tobin's, B Co., with the 1st (1LT Hugh C. Schryver), 2d (1LT David S. Taylor) and 3d (2LT David R. Cowling) Platoons, in that order. Two tanks were behind the 1st Platoon and three others followed the rifle company.

The column had the good fortune of being accompanied by a water trailer from which the men could refill their canteens. A stream flowed near the road, and on breaks, many Marines plunged into the water to cool off

The advancing Marines knew that the Army's 5 RCT on a road to the north seemed to be fast approaching Chinju, and were determined to be in Sachon before the Army got to Chinju. The morning was ominously quiet as the battalion marched steadily along the road. By noon the head of the column was only about 3 miles short of Sachon. CPT Houghton's point was approaching the village of Changchon. Two enemy soldiers were sighted and several Marines opened fire.

In response, enemy machine guns opened up on the Recon detachment from the high ground to the front and both flanks. Tobin sent Schryver's platoon forward to reinforce Houghton, and three men were hit moving up. Taylor's 2d Platoon moved up behind three Marine tanks. The company HQ and 3d Platoon, further back on the road, also were pinned down in the valley by automatic weapons from Hill 250 on the right. LTC Newton called upon his air controller, 1LT James W. Smith for an air strike. Air was the only support Newton had at the moment, except for 60mm mortars, tank guns and machine guns. The heavy mortars and the artillery were not yet set to fire.

Tobin sent an ambulance and stretcher-bearers up to Houghton. In *The New Breed*, Andrew Geer made the point that Marine cooks, bakers and bandsmen formed the stretcher bearer teams. SGT Albert Keller, a battalion intelligence scout, also went forward under heavy enemy fire to aid the wounded. He utilized the tanks at the rear of the column for their evacuation.

After the Corsairs hit Hill 250, 2LT Cowling's 3d Platoon was sent to attack, as CPT Fenton had recommended to Tobin. At the same time, LT Tom Johnston's rifle platoon and machine gun section from Co. A were ordered to seize Hill 301 on the right of the road.

As Tobin moved forward with two runners, they were fired on by an enemy machine gun less than 100 yards away. The three dove for cover behind a dike. Then Tobin noticed one of the runners was jerking and shaking uncontrollably. "What's the matter?" Tobin asked. "I'm scared, Cap'n." Scowling, Tobin then said, "Don't you know, lad, Marines are never scared?" As he uttered these words, the enemy machine gun stitched the top of the dike. The captain said, "I see what you mean. Let's get the hell outa here."

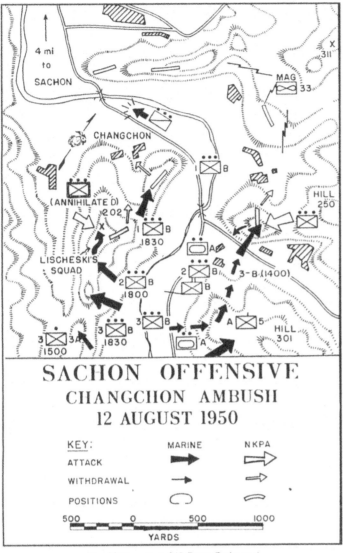

SACHON OFFENSIVE
CHANGCHON AMBUSH
12 AUGUST 1950

KEY: MARINE   NKPA

ATTACK

WITHDRAWAL

POSITIONS

500   0   500   1000
YARDS

Map 23 (Source: p. 145, Pusan Perimeter)

"I was with 2LT Dave Cowling's 3d Platoon," wrote CPL Manuel J. Brito. He recalled that "the trek [that day] was made tolerable because a water trailer...going up and down the road dispensing water to the troops." The enemy "had dug in at Changallon Valley, which commanded the approach of the Brigade..." he wrote. "I shall never forget the entrance to this valley. The high ground to the right and left was approximately 200 meters high. To the front was another ridge which formed a pocket with high ground to the right and left." On either side "of the narrow road were rice paddies covered with a foot of water that ran 800 yards to the base of the high ground that paralleled the road."

When Houghton's point fired at the two enemy soldiers "all hell broke loose," Brito recalled. "We began taking fire from both sides of the road."

The company quickly deployed into the paddies on both sides of the road and returned fire. Tanks moved up and added their 90mm guns and automatic weapons to the fire. "LT Cowling's platoon was ordered to...assault the high ground to the right. Because of water and mud in the paddies," Brito reported, "weapons jammed and the radio went out."

Tobin called artillery and air in on the 3d Platoon's objective. Under this fire, Cowling's

men reached the base of the hill. While waiting for the Corsairs to finish their runs, his men hastily cleaned their weapons. At the end of the air strike, the platoon swarmed up the hill, overcoming opposition. "But when the crest was reached," Brito wrote, "the North Koreans who were dug in on the reverse slope counterattacked. Being outnumbered more than two to one we were forced back half way down the slope before [staving off the counterattack]." CPT Fenton put the number of enemy counterattacking at between 75 and 100.

"Because of a water-logged radio, a runner was sent across the fire-swept paddies to advise Tobin of the 3d Platoon's predicament," Brito recalled. When the supporting artillery and mortar fire ceased, Co. A attacked through Co. B's 3d Platoon, seized and held the contested hill. The 3d Platoon lost 2 KIA and 7 wounded, including LT Cowling, who had been shot in the foot. SSG Cirinelli assumed command of the platoon.

After their strike in support of Newton's battalion, two of the Corsairs had a few minutes of fuel left and were sent to hunt along the road to Sachon. There they found and surprised a number of enemy vehicles and personnel. The North Korean motor column was left in flames. It was almost a repeat of the "Kosong turkey shoot."

Meantime, Baker Co.'s 3d Platoon fell back to Hill 301. CPT Stevens, with the rest of Co. A, was sent to secure high ground on the right of the road. The enemy still had a firm grip on Hill 250, but the Marines pounded it with 113 mortar rounds followed by an air strike. This combination silenced the enemy on that hill, securing Co. B's right flank.

PFC Luster's platoon was part of CPT Stevens' attack. The men ran across the paddy on its dike and into a heavily wooded hill on the right. "The Yellowlegs fanned out to search for the enemy," Luster wrote. (See Chapter Notes.)

Houghton's detachment and Baker's 1st and 2d Platoons all this time had been engaged in a spirited duel with the enemy. Then Marine artillery began asserting itself, blasting one enemy position after another. The guns were complemented by three more air strikes. The artillery and air strikes allowed the 1st and 2d Platoons

to attack up the slopes of Hill 202 on the left of the road.

SGT Walter Wolfe's machine gun section in Co. B delivered overhead fire from the road during the battle. "One of my squad leaders, CPL Jerry Schultz, was hit in the shoulder area," Wolfe recalled. "Unfortunately it hit his spine, rendering him chair-ridden to this day [1994]."

About 5:30 p.m., as Co. B was mopping up on Hill 202, LT Taylor saw an enemy platoon coming up the other side of the hill. He ordered TSGT F. J. Lischeski, with a squad, to ambush the approaching enemy. Lischeski waited until the North Koreans were within 75 feet before giving the command to fire. Thirty-eight of the thirty-nine enemy soldiers were killed. The lone survivor, an officer, died on the way to the regimental CP.

The battle had lasted all afternoon. The Marine history gives Marine losses of 3 KIA and 13 wounded. It was believed that an enemy company had opposed the Marines, as a rear guard for withdrawing elements of the *6th Division* and remnants of the *83d Motorcycle Regiment.*

In reacting to the ambush, the Marines had great difficulty in locating the enemy because, as Fenton observed, "their camouflage was outstanding." He also recalled that Marine wounded were evacuated by "putting them on the back of the tanks. The stretcher-bearers and the corpsmen and the men of the battalion motor transport section did a terrific job during this time. They showed almost complete disregard for their own personal safety."

At this time, each Marine rifle company had only two medical corpsmen, well short of the number of one per rifle platoon authorized.

Fenton also commented on the battalion's deficiency in communications and the failure of some weapons due to water and mud. "CPT Tobin's SCR 300 to the battalion went out, and our company SCR 536's went out of commission. Some of our weapons were out of action due to water and mud in the rice paddies.... Consequently, we only had one 300 radio operating on the battalion net, and we had borrowed that radio from the platoon leader of the tanks."

At the conclusion of the fighting on Aug. 12, Co. B was ordered to occupy Hill 202 and the adjacent ridgeline. Darkness fell before the company could be reunited, moved into position and establish a defense. Fenton recalled that, even with all three platoons on line, "we were still unable to defend the entire ridge line." The company occupied the Hill 202 complex with the 3d, 1st and 2d Platoons, from left to right, in that order. The company front was about 1,500 yards, almost a mile, with a large ravine running between the 1st and 2d platoons. Since it could not be physically occupied in its entirety, Fenton said, "quite a bit of the terrain had to be covered by fire."

Brito recalled that the 3d Platoon began digging in just before darkness fell. This "proved to be a costly mistake, for the Gooks had pinpointed every location on their maps... Two machine guns from the 3d Machinegun Section were set up at the extreme point of Cirinelli's left flank," Brito recounted. BAR-man Brito and his partner, PFC Chapman, were positioned "about 50 yards to the right rear of the nearest machine gun to cover their fire and the approach to the entrance to the ravine." The two men found that large rocks prevented their digging in where assigned. So after dark they moved some 10 yards to the left and dug in a clump of scrub pine. They had a better field of fire "and a good point of resistance against attack," Brito recalled.

The battalion disposition for the night did not permit a tight perimeter. While Co. B was on the Hill 202 complex on the left of the road, Co. A occupied Hill 301, 800 to 900 yards away. "Companies A and B were, in all respects, out by themselves," said Fenton. "We had to prepare very few foxholes on that ridge line," he remarked, "because this area had been well prepared for a defensive stand by the North Koreans."

The battalion expected an enemy attack the night of Aug. 12-13. Initially Co. B had a 25 per cent alert, with one-fourth of all men awake and ready. "We later changed that to 50 per cent," said Fenton. "We made a mistake in making that change." The men simply were nearing exhaustion. They had been on the move and keyed up for three days.

The enemy did not attack until near dawn. "It was close to midnight before we were completely set up," he recalled. It was near dark when the position was taken, and the unit had to reorganize, evacuate the dead and wounded, establish the best communication possible with battalion and supporting arms, and resupply ammunition, weapons, food and water. About midnight, the unit received orders from LTC Newton to pull off the hill at dawn and return to the battalion area. The battalion had received orders to move to another area and was to be assembled by 6:30 a.m. Company commanders were ordered to alert their men for the withdrawal at 4 a.m.

The enemy crept up on Co. B in the darkness. About 4:45 a.m., enemy machine gun fire began. Illuminating rounds from 60mm mortars revealed enemy infiltrators in the 2d Platoon area. Two red and one green flares arched into the night sky at 4:50 a.m., signaling the real enemy attack. The 3d Machinegun Section (11 men), attached to the 3d Platoon, was overwhelmed in a rush of enemy troops. Ten of the men were killed and one wounded, and two guns were turned on the marines. One wounded marine recalled that the enemy was "right on top of the 3d Platoon in a few seconds" with grenades and burp guns.

Manuel Brito described the action: "About three hours before dawn, Chapman and I heard movement to our right front. Within minutes enemy flares lit the skies above 202. The enemy then launched a furious counterattack." Manuel's BAR jammed, then Marine flares lit the ravine, revealing "great numbers" of enemy "moving forward" in that area. "Chapman and I spotted four enemy soldiers standing directly over the foxholes we had earlier attempted to dig. We each lobbed a grenade in that direction and began to fall back towards the 1st Platoon. I got up and ran a few yards, tripped and fell down. A grenade went off behind me. I got up again, tripped and fell down. A second grenade went off behind me." He crawled the rest of the way to the 1st Platoon. "Chapman was already there. I picked up a BAR from a wounded Marine and joined in with the 1st Platoon in repelling the attack."

The enemy, using the two captured machine guns, forced the 3d Platoon "down the hill some 75 yards," Brito recalled. Although artillery and mortar fire fell on the enemy they "kept coming out of nowhere," he wrote.

Fire from the 1st Platoon front increased in intensity and the enemy tried to drive a wedge between the 1st and 2d Platoons. But the three rifle platoons finally consolidated on the 1st Platoon's position. "Our consolidated fire," wrote Brito, "forced the enemy to pull back." Manuel lost many good friends that morning, including PFC Alfredo Carrizales and PFC Carlos Robles.

Warrant Officer Robert A. Clement, a veteran of Bataan and Corregidor in WW II and a pretty savvy Marine, led Baker Company's 60mm Mortar and 3.5-inch Rocket Launcher Sections.

When the North Koreans penetrated the company lines that early morning, "they were so near to us that at a normal elevation of 85 degrees my mortar rounds [exploded] behind the North Koreans," Clement wrote. He obtained Tobin's permission to increase the angle to 87.5 degrees. "This change put my mortar rounds right on target. Soon there in the darkness, we scored a direct hit on one of the two of our machine guns being used against us." Continued mortar fire forced the enemy to move the other gun. Dawn was just breaking and Robert saw where it had been moved to. He called on rocket launcher gunner PFC Rippy. Rippy's first round went just over the target; the next round was a direct hit. By this time Marine artillery fire started "walking" along the ridge from left to right through the abandoned positions of the 2d and 3d Platoons. It actually began to land in the 1st Platoon area before it could be halted.

One of the men of Co. B wounded on Aug. 13 was Delbert Bell, who recalled that the hill "was zeroed in [by the enemy] from all angles from the surrounding hills." Many of the Marines tried to use enemy foxholes already dug on the hill, but they were far too small. During the night, he recalled enemy soldiers tripping flares trying to approach the Marine position.

He wrote, "All hell broke loose — mortars from every angle and most of them direct hits." He thought they were pounded by enemy mortars for about two hours. Finally, the platoon sergeant came to his foxhole and told him "to go to the machine gun area to see if any of the members were alive.... I could find only a boondocker (boot) and a foot and one gold tooth. I knew [they] belonged to Sergeant McCoy, the machinegun sergeant.

"Another barrage commenced. This is when I got hit," Bell wrote. The unit had had their first mail call in Korea on Aug. 12 and Bell had all his letters stuffed in his helmet. The helmet and his entrenching tool, which, luckily was hanging down from his belt in front of his body, took most of the force of a mortar round's concussion. Bell was thrown to the ground and "grabbed my face and said 'God I can't die!' I had blood on my face, and as I wiped my hand across my face I staggered to my feet [then] fell over the crest of the hill [and into a clump of bushes]. How I ever got to the aid station...is a mystery.... I believe I rolled down most of the other side of the mountain.... I remember awakening and looking up to see General Craig." Bell was put on an LST and sent to a hospital in Japan.

The Marines had positioned an LST off the southern coast of Korea to which they could rapidly evacuate their wounded for treatment, much faster than taking the wounded overland to an Army medical facility.

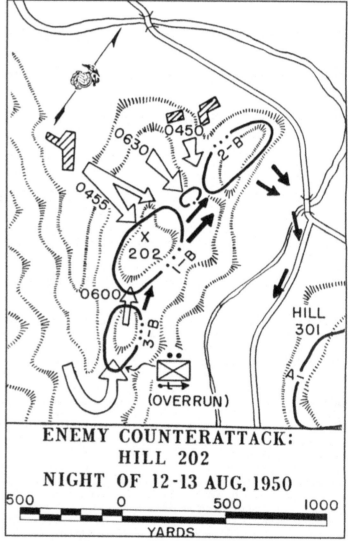

ENEMY COUNTERATTACK:
HILL 202
NIGHT OF 12-13 AUG. 1950

Map 24 (Source: p. 154, Pusan Perimeter)

When the enemy first attacked in the predawn darkness, artillery FO LT Kenneth Stewart was able to call in fire on his own radio, but a burst of machine gun bullets knocked it out. There was no wire communication with battalion, "because we never [got] resupplied that night," said Fenton. The day before, the company had lost two reels of wire in a rice paddy when one of the wiremen had been hit, and had only two more reels left, which were used to provide wire communication in the 3d and 1st Platoons and company CP. The 3d Platoon had only their 536 radio. "The SCR 300 we had been using was getting weaker and slowly going out of commission," Fenton recalled. Battalion could receive company transmissions, but the company could barely hear those from battalion.

Just as the FO's radio was destroyed, the enemy changed the direction of attack. Their main effort now was directed up the draw between the 1st and 2d Platoons. If successful, this attack would split the company position. The company, however, managed to get very effective artillery, 4.2-inch and 81mm mortar fire on the enemy. Fire commands were relayed via Co. A to the appropriate battery. The artillery landed within 50 - 75 yards of the Marine position, with an occasional round landing in the B Co. perimeter. The 81s, Fenton recalled, "Were putting them right in our lap; it was a terrific job of shooting," but the company 60s ran out of ammunition shortly after the battle started.

The enemy cut the telephone wires and two runners from Tobin to his left flank were killed. The third runner got through with orders for the remnants of the 3d Platoon to pull back into the position of the 1st.

Protected by concentrated close-in artillery and mortar fire, the company pulled tightly into the 1st Platoon area. With the coming of daylight, Tobin wanted to counterattack and retake the ridge. Permission was denied; he was ordered to withdraw his company. Tobin protested, notifying battalion that Marine dead lay in positions now occupied by the enemy. "We thought that we could go back up without too much difficulty," Fenton said, "and seize that ground and at least take out the dead." Permission was still denied; the battalion was urgently needed elsewhere and had to pull off at once. Eight men remained unaccounted for, and Fenton said that "this was very demoralizing to us."

After the 2d and 3d Platoons withdrew into the 1st Platoon area, Tobin sent his XO, CPT Fenton, with the 3d Platoon, Co. HQ personnel and the wounded down to the road. Tobin remained on the hill with the 1st and 2d Platoons.

Brito's reaction epitomized the Marines' feelings. "Walking down the hill supporting a wounded Marine, I turned around with a raised, clenched fist in the air with tears streaming down my dirty face, shouting 'We'll be back you S.O.B.s, we'll be back!'" (See Chapter Notes.)

Once CPT Fenton and his party were well underway, Tobin sent the 2d Platoon to the road. Then the 1st Platoon disengaged, one squad at a time. The company commander came off Hill 202 with the last squad at 8:15 a.m.

When the unit finally reached the battalion area, they were told that the enemy had broken

through an Army outfit and that the Brigade was being sent to plug the hole.

"The men were whipped, a lot of them were crying. The word was out now that we were pulling out of the area, that we would no longer continue our advance toward Sachon... just...3 miles [away]," Fenton recalled. The fact that the unit was denied the opportunity of bringing off their dead was a severe blow, against every Marine teaching and tradition. A Marine knew that if he were killed or wounded, his comrades would get him out, and, dead or wounded, he would be treated with dignity and reverence, as befitted a comrade.

The official Marine history states that there were 12 KIA, 18 WIA and 8 MIA on Hill 202. Neither it, nor the men of Co. A, 5th Marines who provided information for this book mentioned that unit's losses in the Changallon Valley on Aug., 12-13.

In their anger and sorrow, many Marines cursed the Army (and some still do to this day) for "bugging out" — running away, requiring the Marines retrieve the situation. They could not know that there had been a breakthrough, not a "bug-out," with several Army units being overrun as their own Co. B had been that day.

LT Hetrick's 3d Platoon, of the Engineer Company and Robert S. Winters 2d Platoon of the Tank Co. were the Brigade's rear guard, as it pulled back from Sachon.

The First Battalion, 11 Marines (105mm howitzer) in Task Force Kean

Marine Brigade direct support artillery was provided by field artillery from 1-11 Marines. Marine designation did not specify "Artillery" in referring to its field artillery.

In the Sachon operation, LTC Ransom M. Wood wrote, "the battalion more often than not had one battery laid on an azimuth generally south, one battery on an azimuth generally west and the third laid north." Each battery of the battalion at this stage had but four guns, so the battalion had only 12 of its authorized 16. Between Aug. 7 and 9, the battalion fired 81 missions, totaling 1,892 rounds.

The battalion received an attachment of forty-seven ROK policemen as security troops. LTC Wood recalled that these Korean policemen proved invaluable in providing security. LT Muetzel wrote that SSG Jack Carres, who spoke a little Japanese, "turned them into his private army.... They were devoted to him [presenting] him with a brand new Colt .45."

The battalion made its first displacement on Aug. 10, moving about 5 miles from Chindong-ni in order to support the Brigade during TF Kean. Between Aug. 11 and 14, the battalion had to displace a number of times to keep up with Marine infantry.

Normally, Wood wrote, artillery doctrine called for the guns to be displaced forward to within 2,000 - 3,000 yards of the front when the front line had advanced from 6,000 to 8,000 yards beyond a battery or artillery battalion position. At times, however, the 11th Marines moved to within 500 - 1,500 yards of the front. They did this "knowing the risks... of being

within easy enemy mortar range," he wrote. "But we did not want the distance to grow too great between us and the infantry [giving] the North Koreans an opportunity to pass wide around the infantry flank and surround our position area."

LTC Wood recounted a humorous incident which occurred in the early days of the Perimeter.

On one occasion, the artillery battalion CP was in a defiladed position when the enemy started shelling the area with 76mm howitzers. "During the shelling, one of my Marines jumped out of his foxhole," Wood recalled, "ran down the hill where there was a large shell fragment and calmly wrote his name on it and declared, 'I feel safe now, there is the shell with my name on it.'"

Background to the Redeployment of the Marine Brigade

The Brigade CP was set up in Kosong about 8 a.m. on Aug. 12. While the 1st Battalion headed toward Sachon, GEN Craig received telephone orders from GEN Kean to send one reinforced Marine battalion to "give assistance to 24th Infantry engaged [along the MSR in the rear] and to recapture artillery pieces." (Quotes here and below pertain to entries in GEN Craig's field notebook.)

At noon, Craig set out by helicopter for the CP of the 5th Marines to issue necessary orders. Enroute, he stopped twice to assemble trucks for the troop lift.

"1300 — The reinforced 3d Bn, 5th Marines, now on way to Chindong-ni area."

A half-hour later, GEN Craig sent his G-3, LTC Stewart and LTC Taplett (3d Bn CO) by helicopter to the bridge where GEN Kean had said they would be met by a liaison officer. Stewart and Taplett were to reconnoiter and develop a plan before the battalion arrived. The battalion would operate directly under 25th Division command.

GEN Craig wrote this in his notebook: "1400 — We are out on a limb with only two battalions left and Sach'on still to take. Went to leading elements to check." He found them heavily engaged in the enemy's attempted ambush. (This was the 1st Battalion.) He noted that the battalion took the enemy position and that both battalions were digging in.

At 5:30 p.m., Craig was again summoned to confer with Kean. He arrived at the Division CP at 6:30 p.m. Kean ordered him to begin a tactical withdrawal from the Sachon area. At 7:45 p.m., GEN Craig returned to his Kosong CP "and issued necessary orders."

The Marine history noted, "The...reason for the Brigade withdrawal was a decision by Eighth Army command and staff." The enemy had crossed the Naktong, pouring through a 2-mile gap in the defenses of 3/34 Infantry of the 24th Division. Without his helicopter GEN Craig could not have handled this fast moving situation on Aug. 12.

Muetzel recalled that "Co. B led the way and we [Co. A] were last out; picked up [by LST]."

Craig selected the 3d Battalion for the task of helping the 24th Infantry and going to the aid of elements of the 90th and 555th FABs. In order to better understand the reason for diverting a Marine battalion, it is necessary to trace the action and battles of the 5 RCT, including the 555 FAB (105mm), and elements of the 90 FAB (155mm). The latter command was the general support field artillery battalion of the 25th Infantry Division.

5 RCT — Aug. 10

On Aug. 10, the Combat Team began its drive toward Muchon-ni, via Pongam-ni. LTC John P. Jones led the 1st Battalion on the ridges north of the road, while LTC Throckmorton's 2d Battalion moved along those to the south. Aerial observers failed to sight enemy troops or installations. However, Naval aircraft attacked the enemy north of Pongam-ni and at Tundok, further north in the mining area of Sobuk-san.

The 1st Battalion engaged some enemy on the hills near Pongam-ni but took the town and established its CP there. At the time, Pongam-ni, Appleman wrote "was a nondescript collection of perhaps twenty mud-walled and thatch-roofed huts clustered around a road junction." A few hundred yards to the east lay the similar village of Taejong-ni. Both villages were east of what became known as the Pongam-ni Pass. The east-west road here was hardly more than a country lane.

The road leading from the south to Taejong-ni, and the village itself, lay in a valley about a half mile wide. For almost 3/4 of a mile along its length, the road lies at the western base of a gradually sloping ridge which runs more or less parallel to it. The ridge terminates in a knob over 330 meters high overlooking Taejong-ni at its foot. Just before entering the hamlet, the main road to Muchon -ni makes a sharp left turn, passes through the village and on to Pongam, 500 or so yards to the west. The road coming south from Tundok (not much more than a dirt trail) joined the Muchon-ni road at Taejong-ni. North, up the valley from the village, is the end of another east-west ridge ranging from 340 to 430 meters high. The North Koreans occupied this promontory.

Pongam-ni lies at the entrance to a long, narrow valley which climbs to the Pongam-ni Pass, some 1,500 meters to the west. The Pass itself was about 500 meters long and about 160 meters high. This narrow valley is dominated on the north by a ridge mass ranging from about 270 to about 320 meters in height. A series of north-south ridges come down to the valley on its southern flank. One of these ridges joins the northern ridge mass to form the Pass. Pongam-ni, Taejong-ni and all the roads in the area are completely dominated by surrounding high ground.

Except in the two towns and along a dry creek bed, the valley contained extensive rice paddies and a stream. At the western edge of Pongam-ni this stream and another join to form a single creek, crossed by a concrete bridge.

By the end of the day on Aug. 10, 2/5 RCT held the ridge just south of Pongam-ni. Companies B and C of the 1st Battalion were on the eastern end of the hill mass just north of the village. The enemy held the rest of this promontory and controlled the pass.

Thomas E. Will (Co. A), describes an action which may have taken place about this time. The

Pongam-ni and vicinity. Most houses were surrounded by stone walls about four feet high. The large building on the left is the village rice and grain storehouse. The enemy attacked from high ground to the rear of the village. Picture taken in 1969. (Courtesy of Toshio Uyeda, HC/2/5 RCT)

Pongam-ni Pass, northwest of the village. The pass was the site of an enemy ambush. Picture taken in 1969. (Courtesy of Toshio Uyeda, HC/2/5 RCT)

company moved up the side of a mountain, and as it reached the military crest, the enemy opened fire. In the ensuing fight, he recalled, two officers and 10 enlisted men were lost.

Ivan Russell, also of A, was wounded during TF Kean. He and two men were about half way up a hill, the two men were in a foxhole, and Russell sitting on the ground above them. "All of a sudden everything went black," he wrote. "I felt a sharp pain in the front of my left ankle." But his toes and foot still worked. When his vision returned a few minutes later Russell saw "the two men...were half buried in their foxhole." He hobbled up the hill and took shelter in a foxhole until the shelling stopped. Then he found an NCO and reported the two men half buried in

their foxhole and that he was wounded. "I showed him the hole in the top of my combat boot," Russell wrote. "He said we were moving out and if I wanted to go to the medics I would be left behind. The pain didn't seem so bad, so I stayed with the company."

Kenny Freedman D/5th RCT wrote of some of his experiences during TF Kean. "We took our basic load of 81mm ammo out of the trailer and sanded the rust off of the WW II rounds." The next day the unit assembled to move out on TF Kean. As they waited they heard the explosion of a tank hitting a mine. "We moved out walking along the side of the road next to our vehicles. After a mile or two [we] heard flat-trajectory incoming fire. Then I heard outgoing tank fire. The tanks had knocked out a Russian SU 76 [a full-tracked self-propelled 76mm artillery piece]. There were four or five NKA soldiers laying dead on the road.

"Soon after we passed the burned-out SU 76 we entered a valley shaped sort of like a rice bowl. We set up our mortars just off the road without digging them in. I was led to believe this was a temporary assembly area for 1st Bn, with elements from the 555 FA, Tank Company, 72 Engineers and Heavy Mortars. Our gun was...in front of a bombed out Korean house in a very small village." The jeep was parked behind the house. The mortar crew "unloaded a token amount of 81mm ammo," Freedman wrote.

"We were told to point the guns toward the west hills," he continued. "All of a sudden we heard a bunch of small-arms [fire] west of us. It looked like the area of Able Company.... More small-arms started up all around us. All of a sudden incoming flat trajectory (FT) started with much MG fire. We heard our first sound of "burp" guns in all directions. Bullets were zipping near and it occurred to us that we were being fired at.... The mortar crews got no fire orders either from their FOs or the FDC."

Freedman's squad leader was supposed to be an FO with Co. C, leaving Freedman as acting squad leader. They were "on their own" in what Freedman described as "a hell of a big messy ambush." The crew began to fill empty ammo boxes with dirt to form a parapet around the mortar. Then an enemy 57mm AT gun started to fire at them from a range of about 1,000 yards to the west, its rounds hitting a fence about 10 feet behind the mortar position. It was armor-piercing ammunition, so it went through the fence before exploding, keeping Freedman and his companions shielded from shell and rock fragments from the wall.

"I could hear the Triple Nickel starting to fire almost point-blank. They were only about 200 yards or so from us. I could see dust flying up all around the gun crews from bullets!! I directed our fire to the area where I saw the 105s hitting hoping they could see the NKA better than I could. By this time we had a double wall of dirt-filled boxes in a semi-circle around the gun about five feet high. Small arms kept hitting it but couldn't go through." They fired up the entire basic load of 81mm ammunition. Somehow, PFC Vickery, the jeep driver, managed to go back and bring up more, and the crew fired all of that, too. Then 1SG George LaFountain came up and told Freedman that the 1st Battalion was going to fight its way out.

Freedman wrote that he vaguely recalled "many attacks, explosions, and tracers flying around" that night, "but that's all. I can't...recall details of what I did or others did." (See Chapter Notes.)

Lieutenant James A. Johnson's 1st Platoon, 72d Engineer Combat Co., supported 1/5th RCT. Johnson was a 1947 graduate of West Point. The night before the battalion went into the valley, his platoon was sent up a hill to help secure the regimental CP. About 10 or 11 p.m., the platoon was ordered back down to provide close in CP security. When Johnson got back down the hill, he told his platoon sergeant, Emmitt D. Parish, "I'm going to sleep right on this trail because if

anybody comes across they are going to have to trip over me." About 5 the next morning (probably Aug. 11) a North Korean scout did trip over Johnson. (See Chapter Notes.)

COL Ordway began to worry about the hill overlooking his CP. He sent for LT Johnson. When Johnson reported to the colonel, "He said, 'Go up and take that hill.' [I said,] 'Yes, Sir.'" Taking about two squads, Johnson set out for the hill. They reached the hill about daybreak. Johnson and an assistant squad leader named Copeland were in the lead, "way up front when...a concussion grenade came flying in. I dropped down right along side a rock. Copeland had disappeared. Then the grass in front of me was being chopped by [enemy] machine gun fire.... I started to back up,...but it was being chopped up behind me too. The rock was saving me."

Johnson called out to Copeland. He called back, then threw two grenades. Johnson shouted for the platoon "to hose down the area.... They yelled back that they couldn't see anything. I yelled, 'Fire at everything!' Then they started to 'hose down' the sides of the hill and Copeland jumped up and ran back... [and] plopped down along side of me.... Well, we took the hill.... That morning...we moved into the valley."

Battery A, 555 FAB went into position under a concrete bridge that spanned a dry creek bed, and Battery B/C dug in along the stream bank north of Pongam-ni. Appleman states that all the artillery pieces were north of the east-west road. A sketch, drawn by Richard Lewis (Hq Btry, 555 FAB) for *The 5th RCT in Korea* shows B battery south of the road, near Taejong-ni.

HHB and Battery A, 90 FAB were emplaced west of the north-south stream and north of the Muchon-ni road.

3/5 RCT — Aug. 10 - 11

The 3d Battalion passed through the 1st and 2d Battalions on the afternoon of Aug. 10 and moved on to contact the 35th Infantry. It was the only element of the 5th RCT which attained its objective of the high ground near Chinju, after linking up with the 35th Infantry.

The battalion "raced on vehicles through the gauntlet of hills," wrote LT Daniel R. Beirne of King Co. "We received small arms fire. The trailer I was on turned over and I ended in a ditch." The jeep trailer was righted and Beirne continued on. "The battalion did not receive any casualties." But, according to Keith Whitham (5 RCT Tk Co.), the battalion did discover LT Kenneth Hino (Co. F), who had lain wounded all night long. Because he was Neisi, the enemy did not recognize him as an American and left him alone.

Once through the Pongam-ni Pass, the battalion bivouacked near the village of Kasan-ni for the night, unmolested by the enemy.

The next day the battalion set out again, moving west along railroad tracks which looped through the mountains. The battalion walked, Beirne wrote, while "the Battalion Commander, LTC Heckemeyer rode in his jeep [bouncing] along over the ties...."

The battalion made contact with the 35th that day at Muchon-ni. As 3/5 RCT moved along the railroad tracks, the 35th Infantry paralleled their advance on the road just to the north.

The battalion had little or no enemy contact until it came to a railroad tunnel about 6 miles west of their point of departure that morning. "Several North Korean guards in the tunnel were totally surprised to see us," Beirne wrote. The enemy soldiers were guarding the packs and other equipment of at least an enemy company "and maybe a battalion," Beirne recalled. "The...owners were out attacking the U.S. Army somewhere. They refused to surrender...and we shot."

On that date, Aug. 11, 3/5 RCT reached high ground near Sangong-ni, overlooking a 2-mile wide valley just 5 air miles from Chinju. "We dug in and spent the night there," Beirne wrote. Elements of the 35th Infantry were on their right. The battalion's left flank was unprotected, nor did it have any artillery support.

Situation of Task Force Kean at the Conclusion of Aug. 10

The situation of TF Kean at the conclusion of Aug. 10 was this:

24 RCT: 1st Bn north of Tundok; 2d Bn blocking the road south of Haman; 3d Bn in the hills above Chindong-ni. 35 RCT: Muchon-ni area, awaiting 5 RCT. 5 RCT: B and C Co. on eastern end of the ridge north of Pongam-ni; 2d Bn on the ridge just south of Pongam-ni; 3d Bn enroute to 35 Inf. at Muchon-ni and Chinju Pass; 555 FAB and 90 FAB (less batteries B and C) in firing positions in the valley vicinity of Pongam-ni and Taejong-ni. Mar. Bde: 3d Bn vicinity Pugok and west of Taedabok Pass; 1st and 2d Bns vicinity Paedun-ni.

5 RCT, Night of Aug. 10 -11

The enemy fell on the 1st Battalion and the artillery at Pongam-ni on the night of Aug. 10-11. LTC Daly lost communication with his A Battery, so he and LTC Jones (CO, 1/5 RCT), with some infantry, tried to reach the battery. Both officers were wounded, Jones seriously. 1LT Howard W. "Big Steve" Stephenson, 1st Battalion S-4, also was wounded in this action. Daly assumed temporary command of the infantry battalion, retaining command of his 555 FAB at the same time. Meantime, farther to the rear in the valley, the regimental CP and a nearby battery of the 159th beat off an enemy attack.

"The next morning [Aug. 11] I was awakened by several kicks on the sole of my boots by CPT Ecoff, S-3, 2d Battalion," wrote LT Whitham. "He told me to go back to Regimental Headquarters and bring up a convoy of 2 1/2-ton trucks loaded with ammunition." Whitham asked a Co. A sergeant named Silva and two or three other infantrymen who were helping with local security asked to ride along back to Regiment.

Two miles down the road, Whitham's three tanks and the infantrymen came upon the ammunition convoy, which had been ambushed. "Two trucks were burning, and everyone had dismounted and were firing at the North Koreans from the side of the road," Whitham continued. "SGT Silva was on the .50-caliber machine gun on my tank and we began firing the main guns at the...ambushers. At about that time I was hit in the forehead by small fragments of something which had apparently splintered after hitting a part of the tank turret." A few minutes later, Whitham got his left elbow tangled up with the 76mm breechblock during the firing. "It was pretty mangled, but not broken," he recalled.

The enemy was driven off and the lieutenant went on to his tank company CP, located near the regimental CP, where a medic treated his wounds. When he and his party arrived at the regimental CP area, he found it under enemy attack also. LTC Thomas Roelofs, Regimental S-2, was directing the fire of an 81mm mortar mounted on the Tank Company Vehicle (VTR). From a small hill, Roelofs "would watch the round hit, then run back within 'hollering distance' of the VTR crew to adjust fire," observed Whitham. Soon after, the enemy was driven off "and things quieted down," he wrote. "The Regimental Commander, COL Ordway, was sitting in a gully, shaking his head...."

The CP of the 2d Battalion also was attacked, and Throckmorton pulled Co. E out of its Pogam-ni position to help repel the enemy.

On the morning of Aug. 11, GEN Barth drove to the 5 RCT CP. "During the night," he noted, "the road had been...mined between Masan and Chindong-ni. Two supply vehicles were blown up, causing a number of casualties but the road was cleared and free of mines shortly before daylight.... Almost every night for the next month, one of the main roads was either mined or cut off by enemy fire. Often several hours were required to re-open the supply routes.... Just as I arrived, the 5th Command Post was attacked by enemy coming from the hills north of the road. One battery of the 555th...was close by. It swung its guns around and poured direct fire into the attackers. Three Marine planes, coming in low and only about three hundred yards to our right, pounded the enemy with rockets and .50 caliber machine guns. Nothing further was heard of the enemy force."

COL Ordway planned to continue the attack on Aug. 11, with the 1st Battalion first securing the north ridge and pass. The 2d Battalion would then withdraw from the south ridge and start the movement to the west, with regimental trains and the artillery following the 2d Battalion in that order. The 1st Battalion would then pull off the ridge and bring up the rear. Events on the night of Aug. 10-11 and during the day on Aug. 11 precluded executing this plan.

When the wounded LTC Jones was evacuated, Ordway sent LTC Thomas B. Roelofs to take command of the 1st Battalion, since he had commanded it before. He arrived in Pogam-ni and assumed command at 2 p.m. on Aug. 10. Roelofs consulted Daly and the 1st Battalion staff, made a personal reconnaissance then decided on a plan of action.

Co. B made the main attack. Roelofs brought the unit down to the valley from the north ridge. There the men rested for a short time and received a resupply of ammunition. Just before dusk, the company moved to attack the hill commanding the north side of the pass. Simultaneously, Co. C attacked west along the ridge to meet B. The 2d Battalion and artillery laid down heavy and accurate supporting fire, and Co. B seized its objective.

Meantime, a rifle platoon of Co. A, with a tank section, maintained a roadblock north of Pongam-ni on the Tundok road. Co. A(-) took

over some of the positions of 2/5 when it pulled off the south ridge about 9 p.m.

With the successful accomplishment of the battalion's mission, LTC Roelofs established his CP in a dry stream bed south of the road and about 300 yards west of Pogam-ni. He crawled under a trailer attached to his jeep and fell asleep.

COL Ordway decided it would be safer to move the regimental trains and artillery through the pass at night. He planned to do so after dark on Aug. 11.

GEN Kean, however, was being pressured by Eighth Army in a radio message, which ordered him to occupy and defend the Chinju Pass area; to send the regimental-sized ROK formation known as TF Min to Taegu for release to the ROK Army; and to be prepared to release both the 5 RCT and Marine Brigade on Army order. These orders soon were confirmed in writing. The loss of all these troops would end TF Kean and virtually assure that the 25th Division would have to return to the positions from whence it started the attack.

GEN Kean radioed COL Ordway the afternoon of Aug. 11 with instructions to move forward rapidly. A battalion of the 24th would come up to protect the 5 RCT's right flank, Ordway was told. A lengthy conversation between the two officers ensued. Kean, not believing the strength of the enemy as reported by Ordway, reluctantly approved the latter's proposed night movement.

GEN Lynch recalled that Walker was furious that TF Kean seemed to be going slowly, overall. He applied heavy pressure on Kean to get things in hand and unstuck. Kean "was trying to show [Walker] that he was a tactical commander," Lynch said. But the problems which the 5 RCT and 24th Regiment were encountering were wrecking Kean's efforts, so he put pressure on Ordway and others.

In the confusion and fighting on Aug. 11, LTC Daly was wounded again. One of the wounds was to a hip, where a mortar or artillery fragment had torn out a fist-sized chunk. Jim Richardson, 5 RCT Assistant S-2, talked to the colonel shortly after Daly received this wound. Daly apparently meant to stay with the 555th and continue to try to lead it. Richardson recalls advising Daly to "get on [an] ambulance and go to the rear and get a proper dressing put on that and come back in the morning." Daly was evacuated, never to return to the 555th.

About 9 p.m. on Aug. 11, the 2d Battalion and trains were forming on the road when COL Ordway received a written order from GEN Kean to move the 2d Battalion and a field artillery battery through the pass at once. The remainder of the troops were not to move until daylight. Ordway was dismayed, feeling that to do so would be disastrous. He tried to establish communication with division to protest the order, but could not get through. Finally, after further consideration, he decided that factors known only to the Eighth Army and division commander must have prompted the order, and issued orders implementing the division directive.

2/5 RCT — Aug. 11 - 13

The 2d Battalion, with C/555 FAB cleared the pass and went out of communication with

Ordway. Several times during the night of Aug. 11 he tried unsuccessfully to reach Throckmorton by radio. Throckmorton could not be supported by the rest of the combat team and was out of communication with Ordway.

In negotiating the pass that night, 2/5 RCT and C/555 FAB encountered heavy enemy fire from the high ground on their right. However, the force moved through it to Taechon-ni, 5 miles beyond, and stopped for the remainder of the night.

Buddy Ford and Gene McClure were with Co. H when they went over the pass; Ford was with the 81mm Mortar Platoon.

"That night we were riding in a jeep through a small village," Ford wrote, "and machine guns opened fire on us. I was riding in the front seat. A guy in the jeep in front of me jumped out of the back seat and...had a bullet go between his helmet liner and helmet [but wasn't hurt]." As Ford dove for a roadside ditch, a bullet went through his sleeve and he yelled, "I'm hit!" The bullet missed his arm, "but I felt the heat of it," he recalled.

McClure recorded that "withering small arms fire of rifle and machinegun weapons swept the convoy from the hills on both sides of the road. This was one of the heaviest walls of small-arms fire I was ever to pass through.... We would move the vehicles a few hundred feet, stop and pile out into the roadside ditches, then when the vehicles started to move again we would...jump back onto them and go a little farther and repeat the process. We laid down in the beds of our vehicles and stacked anything we could get our hands on around the sides of the truck beds to protect us.... Machine gun tracers coming from the hills bounced all over the place." McClure's vehicle was struck several times. "A bullet ripped through one man's leg," he wrote.

Toshio Uyeda of the 2d Battalion's HC wrote, "The North Koreans came down the mountainside firing burp guns and shouting 'GI, you die!' 'Don't shoot!' etc., with some profanity thrown in. The guys behind us got shot up pretty bad." All Uyeda and those around him could see were flashes of gunfire. He and the men nearby did not shoot "because we couldn't see anyone to shoot at." LTC Throckmorton came along and ordered the men to fix bayonets and start firing. Although Uyeda still could not actually see enemy soldiers, he obediently began firing. "By then," he wrote, "the North Koreans were withdrawing...going back up the hill."

Daly recalled William A. Motley from his FO duties and sent him with a 3/4-ton and a 2 1/2-ton to get some artillery ammunition from the 64 FAB. As luck would have it, Motley knew the 64 FAB commander, LTC Arthur H. Hogan, from a previous assignment, and got his ammunition.

Motley once more was sent out as an FO, this time with Co. E. Walking along with the company commander, about half-way across the bridge, headed for the pass west of Pongam-ni, when heavy enemy small-arms and machine gun fire struck the column from the right front and right rear. "I hit the bridge and could see guys getting hit trying to get on across and...the ones trying to get back." Motley wrote. He and a number of others jumped off the bridge into the dry creek bed 12 to 15 feet below. The creek bed was covered with rocks and stones "up to bowling-ball size."

Motley fell backward when he hit, "landing on my entrenching shovel handle, which didn't break. I had landed with my full weight on my tailbone. I thought I was paralyzed." As he struggled to get out of the creek bed, "a black lieutenant grabbed my shoulder and helped me to cover." This was 2LT Clarence Jackson, a platoon leader of E/5 RCT, then the only black lieutenant commanding white troops. Well-liked and highly-respected, he had been assigned to that position in 1949, a year and a half before official integration took place in January 1951.

Motley was evacuated to Masan, where he was treated. Looking around he saw many badly-wounded and dying men in the aid station, with more arriving. "I felt like an ass," he wrote, so he left the aid station and got a ride to the 555 Field's Service Battery. There a "Korean camp boy took me to...an old, old Korean man" who massaged his back. The massage, though very painful, resulted in Motley being able to "at least straighten up and walk." Over the next few days, he flew as an observer in an L5 observation plane.

When 2/5 RCT and C/555 FAB arrived near Taechon-ni, the 5 RCT then was broken into three separate elements: The 3d Battalion with the 35th Infantry on its way to the Chinju Pass; 1st Battalion in the Pongam-ni area with the 555 FAB(-), plus HHB and Btry A, 90 FAB. At the moment, both the 2d and 3d Battalions were relatively unmolested, probably because the bulk of the *North Korean 6th Division* then was engaging the 24th Regiment and about to pounce on the 1st Battalion and artillery at Pongam-ni.

Ordway could not reach the 2d Battalion by radio and his 3d Battalion was beyond radio range. There was no wire communication available.

At Taechon-ni, the 2d Battalion was on high ground adjacent to a valley which resembled the one at Pongam-ni. There was even a concrete bridge, and artillery in the valley C/555 FAB. This similarity and a rough sketch of the Pongam-ni area made by Bill Motley, appearing in *The First Fifty Days*, have caused several veterans of 2/5 RCT to place battles which actually took place near Taechon-ni back near the pass west of Pongam-ni. Another point of coincidence between the struggle at Pongam-ni and Taechon-ni was that the enemy attacked the artillery in the valley. At the same time, 2d Battalion infantrymen were under attack on nearby hills.

It may have been during this action that Buddy Ford and his comrade from the Co. H 81mm mortar section, who he identified as "Stott from Pontiac, Michigan" shared a foxhole. Stott, suffering from diarrhea, fell asleep during his two-hour tour of guard in the foxhole, and they awoke to discover small-arms fire passing over the hole. They quickly located their squad, which had moved during the night, and managed to rejoin it. Later in the day, when 81mm mortar ammunition was running low, Stott and Ford volunteered to get more at the ammunition trailer "because we had screwed up earlier that day" he wrote. They and some other men braved enemy rifle fire to successfully resupply the mortars.

Gene McClure (Co. H) recalled that it took about three hours to clear the pass west of Pongam-ni. "In the early morning hours of 12 August 1950 the section I was assigned to...was sitting around a small fire we had started [to heat some bullion and C-rations], down in a foxhole within a hundred yards of a concrete bridge which crossed a dry creek bed," McClure wrote. Fighting had gone on most of the night. The Machinegun Platoon was a few hundred yards farther up the hill and off the road. McClure's position covered the road with a crew-served weapon. Before they could finish their C-rations the enemy resumed their attack. "It became more intense by the hour," he wrote. "We had to break up our early breakfast and go to work...."

McClure could see the enemy firing small arms and mortars on the artillery in the valley and the machinegun platoon was in a hot firefight. He observed the artillery firing "point-blank into a hillside within a few hundred feet of their emplacements.... The hill was covered with enemy." The North Koreans attacked Co. H and other elements on one side of the road and the artillery on the other side "down a ways from the bridge," he wrote.

Aiding the enemy were hundreds of refugees on the road. South Korean police were dividing them into two groups, McClure recalled, the males up one trail into the hills and the women over another. Shortly, F-51 fighters came over and struck the area into which these refugees had been sent. The planes had been called to attack enemy soldiers, but the North Korean soldiers had so frequently tried to disguise themselves by dressing in civilian clothing that pilots sometimes attacked refugees, believing them to be enemy soldiers. The police also separated eight of the refugees, having identified them as enemy soldiers or sympathizers, and summarily executed them.

During the day Co. H destroyed an enemy personnel carrier which had made a dash towards the artillery position. "There were four North Korean soldiers in the truck and some were still alive," McClure wrote, when he and some other men "went down...to investigate the wreck." One of the enemy was an officer. The Americans found papers, maps and a satchel full of North Korean money. The documents were turned over to one of the regimental officers. McClure and some other men kept large amounts of the worthless money for a few days, then threw it away.

McClure had no idea the number of losses sustained by the 5 RCT, but he did recall that three members of his company were killed on Aug. 12. One, PVT Bobby G. Martain of the machinegun platoon, was a friend. Another was PVT Leland W. Robison. McClure and some of his comrades wrapped the three dead men in their ponchos and took them down to the road. Soon a medical front-line (jeep) ambulance came by. When the driver refused to take the three bodies, one of the men with McClure threatened to kill him. The driver quickly changed his mind and took the bodies.

MSG Earl J. Law, FO with Co. E at the time, recorded a tragic incident which could have taken place during TF Kean. As FO, it was his job to get timely and accurate fire on the enemy. "At the time," he wrote, "we were under heavy [enemy] infantry attack." Law desperately tried to call in supporting artillery fire. But "my phone lines had been cut by the North Koreans and my radio would not operate. The [infantry] lieutenant died begging for artillery, and I was unable to get it to him."

1SG Wyatt Logan was detailed as FO to Co. E, 5 RCT on Aug. 8. CPT Perry Graves (BC, B/555 FAB) "called me over and asked me if I ever fired a fire mission," Logan wrote. "I said I had so he gave me his binoculars and compass," and sent him to Easy Co. He was with Co. E only one day and was sent to be FO for G Co., but he considered himself lucky. In his absence, the battery had taken crippling losses in men and equipment. He wrote, "When I got back to the battery, I found out it had lost three guns, the...FDC Section, the Mess Section... and Supply Section and several trucks." The battery had one gun left.

Deployment off 1/5 RCT and Artillery in the Pongam-ni - Taejong-ni Area — Aug. 11 - 12

The 1st Battalion, 5 RCT was positioned on the hills north of the road leading west out of Pongamni. HHB and Btry A, 90 FAB, were in an area just north of the concrete bridge at that village, and A/555 FAB was under the bridge in a dry creek bed. Service and HHB were south of A, in that order, in the same creek bed. Battery B was in position south of the road between road Taejong-ni and Pongam-ni, but close to the former hamlet. Its guns were pointed generally pointed generally north along the toad to Tundok and Chungam-ni.

The terrain afforded the 90th some incidental protection from enemy direct fire, But the 555th was essentially in the open on the valley floor, vulnerable to enemy observation and very accurate fire. The 5 RCT CP, trains and elements of the 159 FAB were located somewhat over a mile farther south in the Pongam-ni valley.

1/5 RCT — Early Morning, Aug. 12

Engineer LT Johnson recalled the enemy attack. "They laid down a base of fire," he said, "and the muzzle flashes were like watching fire flies on the hill. I mean all the hills around us.... The only hill that I guess fire wasn't coming from was...the hill on the right side of the pass. That was a cut through the mountain. I remember the valley going around this S-curve and then through the pass. The First Battalion was on that part of the hill."

Companies A and B were on part of the hill; the enemy controlled the rest of it. In the fight, LT Stan Crosby, a platoon leader in Co. B, and one of Johnson's West Point classmates, was killed in action.

About 1 a.m., CPT Claude Baker, XO, 1/5 RCT, awakened LTC Roelofs to inform him that battalion had lost contact with Co. C, but could hear sounds of battle from that quarter. The unit was on a ridge north of Roelofs. He tried to re-establish contact by radio and phone, finally sending out runners and a wire crew to restore communication. He also notified Ordway of the situation and recommended that the regimental trains and artillery be sent through the pass to the west without delay. Ordway, however, stuck to division orders not to move until daylight.

Roelofs and two staff officers set off in his jeep to visit his A Co. roadblock on the Tundok road. Enroute, he saw the regimental trains assembling and apparently waiting orders to move out. He noticed several officers of the 555th on the bridge at Pongam-ni who also seemed to be waiting for movement orders.

Arriving at the roadblock, manned by an A Co. rifle platoon and a tank section, he heard firing and grenades bursting from the Co. C position on the hill mass to the west (left).

When he returned to his CP, Roelofs was informed that there was still no contact with Co. C. Runners had returned, having been unable to find the unit, and the wire team was missing. His staff reported hearing the sounds of fighting and of seeing flares from the company area, and they believed the flares meant that the enemy had taken the position.

Meantime, from his location with the regimental CP in the valley, Ordway could see that part of the 1st Battalion was being driven from its position, probably Co. C. Roelofs again strongly recommended that the trains be sent out of the gulch.

Although he still could not reach division, Ordway finally decided to move the trains and artillery westward under cover of the night. He believed that with the enemy taking control of the ridges overlooking Pongam-ni, waiting for daylight would result in heavy losses, if it were not entirely impossible. No help had arrived from the battalion of the 24th Infantry, which had been promised by GEN Kean.

5th Regimental Trains — Aug. 12

Ordway waited about as long as he could, finally giving the movement order at 4 a.m on Aug. 12. Order of march was to have been regimental trains, artillery and 1/5 RCT, with the infantry to hold open the pass for the trains and artillery.

Well before dawn, vehicles were assembling on the road, but things were not moving because the trains were not organized and ready to move. The intervention of staff officers, messengers and even Ordway himself failed to unsnarl a major traffic jam. What should have been a 20-minute march through the pass consumed several hours. Part of the problem developed when a Medical Co. ambulance tried to get into the column from its location near 1/5 RCT's CP. Appleman records that an ambulance, hung up in a ditch, held up the column until it could be pulled out.

About dawn, LT Johnson pulled his trucks onto the road. "When dawn broke, it was like a curtain goes up at a play.... In this instance all hell really broke loose," he said. "We received fire from all directions." His radio, an SCR 300, was on the operator's back, but with a long whip antenna, which drew enemy fire. Johnson had the operator get the radio out of sight, then began firing off to the left of the road where most of the enemy fire was coming from. The enemy shot off some flares, "then I really started shooting," he said. Johnson was using the jeep to steady his firing. Suddenly WO Bradley from his company "grabbed me and slammed me down on the ground," Johnson said. "He did so

just as a burp gun opened up on me. I told him, 'Godammit, mind your own business.' And he started laughing. That broke the tension, but he obviously saved me. In fact, all of the tires on the jeep were flattened." Johnson was hit in the leg, a wound that "just went through flesh, no bones."

LT Whitham, now being transported in a jeep since badly injuring his elbow, recalled being "stopped for what must have been hours." He finally walked forward along the column and found that a driver had fallen asleep during one of the halts. It was impossible to determine how long the sleeping driver had delayed the remainder of the convoy behind him. Whitham believed that "had this not happened many of the men and vehicles who were caught in the gulch would have been clear of the...pass when the North Koreans struck at dawn."

At first light, enemy fire began to fall on the column. At first, it was inaccurate and ineffective. Ordway, in his jeep, tried with little success to hasten the column on. He got over the Pass shortly after daybreak. Looking to the rear, he could see that the 1st Battalion was holding the pass and high ground north of it.

Once clear of the Pass, he wanted to get the trains off the road to clear it for the artillery. Finding no suitable area, he continued on to the CP of the 2d Battalion. The leading elements of the regimental trains already were there, and he ordered them to continue on westward to clear the road for the artillery. One of his staff officers located a schoolyard where the trains were able to assemble off the road.

"About dawn we arrived at 2d Battalion Hq," Whitham recalled, "which was under fierce attack.... One of the tank commanders, in the 2d Platoon was SGT John McMillin....He was standing atop his tank shooting North Koreans with the turret-mounted .50-caliber machine gun." LTC Throckmorton told LT Whitham to "get that idiot off the top of that tank before he gets shot." Soon afterward, the enemy withdrew. Then the men of the 2d Battalion and the regimental trains "could...clearly hear the furious firing taking place over the pass," Whitham recorded. Some vehicles and a few men came in from that direction, he wrote, and "it became clear that a catastrophe was in progress on the other side of the hill."

Most of Tank Co.'s maintenance section was in the gulch near the artillery, and most of the section got out alive, thanks to maintenance sergeant MSG Emrick. He "loaded as many [men] as possible in our M-39 utility vehicle," Whitham reported. They "made a run for it back to Chindong-ni and made it with all guns blazing." Corporals Schuman and "Friday" Van Hoosen, section mechanics, were killed before Emrick could get them out.

As the regimental trains were pulling into the schoolyard, an artillery officer from Pongam-ni arrived to inform Ordway that the artillery back in the valley had been savagely attacked. The colonel went back to the 2d Battalion area, then on eastward toward Pongam-ni. Enroute, he met the 1st Battalion on the road. They appeared nearly exhausted. In a short conference, Roelofs told Ordway that he thought the artillerymen had escaped into the hills, whereupon, COL Ordway ordered 1/5 RCT into an assembly area and di-

rected Throckmorton to take his battalion back to Pongam-ni to cover the area and rescue any troops found there.

Just after dawn, LTC Roelofs had been observing the column of troops passing by when, he discovered the A Co. platoon and tank section. The platoon leader insisted that he had been ordered to withdraw from his roadblock north of Pongam-ni. Angered, Roelofs ordered the platoon and tanks off the road near his CP, intending to find out later who issued such an order and when. He planned to send the force back to the roadblock until dissuaded by COL Ordway. The regimental commander feared that the platoon would block the artillery's movement through the pass. The untimely departure of this platoon and tank section from a blocking position north of Pongam-ni opened the way for enemy troops to approach the artillery in the valley without opposition. Their removal was a serious, and costly error.

When the 1st Battalion assembled on the road heading west out of Pongam-ni, the 555 FAB and HHB and Btry A, 90 FAB were left without any infantry support or protection. These commands were concentrated in the northern part of the valley, in an area to be known ever after by the survivors as "Bloody Gulch."

The enemy detected the infantry's pull-out and the *North Korean 13th Regiment* struck ferociously against the exposed and vulnerable artillery commands from three sides, a disaster for the artillerymen. The infantry, according to Ordway's plan and orders, was to hold the pass open until the artillery passed through. Why it was assembled for a pull-out before the artillery has never been explained.

LTC Roelofs, standing in the road, hurried his motor column along. He looked toward Pongam-ni and suddenly saw fire streaking across the valley, followed by heavy explosions. A truck on the bridge blew up in a brilliant ball of fire, stopping the trucks behind. Men jumped from these vehicles into nearby ditches. The colonel could make out enemy tanks and SP guns attacking from the north down the road where the A Co. roadblock had been located. The artillerymen later reported that the enemy force was two tanks and several AT guns.

As this attack began, the North Koreans on high ground north of the east-west road out of Pongam-ni increased their fire on 1/5 RCT and 4.2-inch mortar crews. This fire drove the 4.2-inch crewmen from their guns, but Co. D's Machinegun Platoon, well dug in, continued heavy return fire on the enemy above. When one enemy machine gun opened up from a position to the rear and south of the road, a .50-cal gunner on a truck destroyed it and the crew. Other enemy soldiers, trying to infiltrate the column, were killed or driven away.

An artillery lieutenant colonel, accompanied by three or four men, came up to Roelofs on the road and told him that the artillery pieces were knocked out, the trucks were destroyed and that the men were getting out any way they could. When the bulk of the truck column went by, LTC Roelofs sent the 4.2-inch Mortar Platoon through the pass, followed by the Heavy Machinegun Platoon. All the wounded of the battalion were taken along, but there was no room left on the few available trucks for the dead. They were left behind.

Tank Co., 5th RCT on the Masan front. Left to Right: SGT Singleton, Gunner; SFC Charles Shepherd, Tank Commander; PFC Freyer, Loader (or Friar). (Courtesy of Charles shepherd, TK/5 RCT)

As the last of 1/5 RCT headed for the top of the pass, three medium tanks came up from Pongam-ni. Roelofs was surprised; he didn't know they were there. He stopped one of the tanks and told the commander to hold up until a check could be made for dead and wounded. The tanker said that everyone he had seen at or near the bridge was dead. Roelofs and some men started back from the pass anyway, and soon met Chaplain Francis A. Kapica, whose jeep was loaded with wounded. Kapica reported this was all the wounded he could find. Roelofs then boarded the tank and headed west. At the pass were 23 men of Co. C — all that was left of 180. They reported that the unit had been over-run. The colonel organized his battalion for movement west of the pass with Co. A leading, followed by the remnants of C. Co. B disengaged by platoons from the enemy on the ridge north of the pass, and the three tanks acted as the rear guard. The column cleared the pass about 10:00 a.m.

LT Howard W. Stephenson (1st Bn S-4) was wounded near the pass. He recalled spending a night in a ditch with "constant 37mm anti-tank fire over our heads," he wrote. At daybreak the next morning the North Koreans on the hill above "opened fire and I moved behind a 2 1/2-ton loaded with ammunition, which soon caught fire," related Stephenson, "so I went across the road to a rice paddy.... Just then a bullet went through my right arm just above the elbow."

SGT Charles Shepherd's Tank With Task Force Kean

The 1st Platoon, Tank Company, 5 RCT normally supported the regiment's 1st Battalion. One of the tank commanders of that platoon was SGT Charles Shepherd. He recalled the platoon leader as a LT Lowry. LTC Keith Whitham, who commanded the 2d Platoon, wrote that 1LT Robert B. McGhee commanded the 1st Platoon at the outset in Korea, but that he left the unit shortly after Aug. 8 and was replaced by Lowry.

Shepherd, then 28, said his crew included Herman Singleton, 30, as gunner; a man named Ramer, 17, as driver; bow gunner Long, 18, and loader Friar, 17. He gave no first names. "They were all good men," he wrote. "They were cool in combat, did what they were told and became efficient at what they were doing."

Shepherd's tank was on the infantry perimeter. "I was near a little bridge with part of the tank sitting catty-cornered in a rice paddy," Shepherd said. "About 3 o'clock in the morning we saw a red and green flare going up and then a white one....We knew...that we were going to be attacked.... Artillery started coming in and a lot of small-arms fire. Machine guns hitting my tank.... Every once in a while this elephant gun was popping off and every time...[it] hit around a turret ring fire would fly inside.... One of the elephant gun rounds...went through the side of

the barrel recess on the turret shield and braided the side of the barrel bushing in the recess and shoved the barrel back...[so] that the gun wouldn't go forward and fire.... My coax machine gun was disabled."

All the while, an infantryman and an artillery observer were on the back of the tank firing the .50-cal machine gun. "The infantry boy had that machine gun barrel almost red hot," Shepherd said. The tankers were firing the bow gun (.30-cal machine gun) and the 76mm main gun. The enemy were "just a few yards in front of the tank behind an embankment near a creek," Shepherd recounted. "Then North Korean bullets hit the infantryman and he pitched off the tank." But the line held until daylight. After daybreak, the bow gunner spotted the elephant gun. One WP round from the tank's 76 knocked it out.

Later in the day, Shepherd's tank destroyed a cache of enemy weapons and ammunition with WP fire into a village.

The following morning "we ran into a lot of fire," he said. His tank and several others were under intense fire for a time. When this fire slacked off, Shepherd's tank and others of the platoon moved to a new position and "pulled our tanks in around some trees," he said. " I got out of the tank and was back-talking to some of the guys and small-arms and machine gun fire started picking up again.... I'm back of the tank and a round ricocheted through the tracks and grazes me on the right shoulder. It felt like somebody slugged me...."

His whole crew was out of the tank, but Shepherd managed to get them back in by having them move to the side of the tank away from the fire and jump into the turret hatch, one at a time.

Once he got the tank back on the road, he received a call on the external phone, "Sergeant, will you back up and cover us while we get the wounded back up the road?" Shepherd replied, "OK." He took an enemy machine gun on the left of the road under fire to aid the infantrymen evacuating the wounded, but the tank engine quit. The driver had failed to have both gas tanks on. Once the second gas tank was turned on, he restarted the engine. Shepherd was very upset about this — what he called a "stupid mistake." Because of this, the GI infantrymen, crawling along the ground near his tank, came under enemy fire again and "were getting shot up," he said.

"By that time we had to pull over into an area and [gas up]. We were still under fire," he recalled. In spite of that, Shepherd and his tank returned safely from TF Kean.

Bloody Gulch, the 555th and 90 Field Artillery Batteries at Pongam-ni — Aug. 11 - 12

In the northern area of a long, flat valley, dominated by surrounding hills, the two battalion were concentrated near the two villages of Pongam-ni and Taejon-ni, and now devoid of infantry protection. Battery B, 159 FAB (105mm), of the 25th Division, was near the southern end of the valley, over a mile away.

The 555th went into position at Pongam-ni on Aug. 10. Robert Lewis (Survey Section) recalled that the battalion received flat trajectory enemy fire early on Aug. 11. Most of this fire was directed at Battery A.

Eugene Mathews of Baker Battery recalled that "about breakfast time [on Aug. 11] we started taking small arms fire." His section already had eaten, so Mathews "went to the mess truck to get my favorite breakfast of S.O.S." (Hamburger in a milk gravy, served over toast.)

Mathews continued, "As I put my messkit up to the [serving] pan of S.O.S. a [bullet] went through the pan...." The bullet just missed hitting Eugene in the head. No one was injured by the bullet, but that ended Mathews' desire for breakfast that day.

On his way back to the section, CPT Perry Graves, his BC, stopped Mathews and asked him to accompany an infantry sergeant to guard the battery's right flank. Enemy soldiers could be seen to the front and the battery 105s were firing almost direct fire on them. Mathews took the section's BAR and the infantryman. As the two men jumped over a stone wall on their mission, enemy bullets hit the rocks, or ricocheted into the air, but both made it safely, and successfully protected the battery's flank. The enemy attack, he recalled, broke off at noon.

The enemy also cut the MSR behind the 5 RCT on Aug. 11., so wounded were taken out on trucks escorted by an M-39 armored vehicle. SFC Manner, S-2 sergeant of the 555th, although severely wounded in the elbow, manned a .50-cal machinegun on the M-39. LTC Daly was

wounded for the first time this day, but refused evacuation. Among the other wounded on Aug. 11 were Able's motor sergeant and SGT Joyner, the Battalion message center sergeant. Three tanks from the 89th Tank Battalion and an assault gun escorted supply vehicles into Pongam-ni. The enemy was in the Pongam-ni area in some strength beginning the night of Aug. 10 and built up from there on Aug. 11 and 12.

Arlen S. Russell was a member of the 555th's FDC. Early in the morning of Aug. 12, he walked over to visit a friend in Battery A, "When small arms fire broke out all around me," he wrote. "I jumped into a foxhole with another artilleryman and pointed to some figures scurrying around near the top of a ridge overlooking the village and river bed area. Since we had no troops on the ridge to our knowledge, we took them under fire. Oddly enough, I didn't notice any return fire. After...approximately 10 minutes, an officer came running down the river bed yelling for everyone to cease firing on friendly troops. The men ceased firing and the troops on the ridge did not shoot." The officer was wrong. North Korean soldiers were deploying on that ridge. Later, an enemy machine gun began firing into the stream bed from that hill.

Enemy armor struck the artillery in the valley very early on Aug. 12. Shortly afterward, their infantry began attacking with small arms and automatic weapons. In spite of this incoming fire, three of the Triple Nickel's 105 howitzers continued to fire until about 9 a.m. when the enemy overran their positions. Some of the other battalion guns were struck by enemy fire. Men of the 555th fought back from whatever shelter they could find under the bridge and behind he walls in the village. The enemy hit and destroyed almost every artillery vehicle in the valley during this fight; some were hit north of town and ammunition trucks blew up. Guns of the 555th engaged the enemy armor, without success. The 90th could not depress its 155mm howitzers low enough to take these enemy vehicles under fire.

WO Sal Bosco (HQ, 555 FAB) recalled when the command was overrun. "We were pinned down under a bridge, some wounded, including myself," he wrote. The supply sergeant, SSG Cook, was badly wounded. "He had been machinegunned across his chest," Bosco wrote. "He asked that we place sandbags across his chest to relieve the pain. This was done. There were about 25 of us pinned down." After dark this party of men headed south down the dry creek bed. Moving at night and hiding by day, five of them reached finally reached friendly troops. The remaining 20 had been lost or captured during the escape attempt. Richard Lewis wrote that there was an air drop of supplies in the gulch on Aug. 12 and that Bosco helped to retrieve the packages.

Kenneth J. Thornton was a medic with the Triple Nickel. He recalled that he was busy answering the call of "Medic!" Then, as he put it, "my skinny butt caught the eyes of a North Korean. Then I didn't move fast enough." Thornton was wounded.

"We were trapped in an ambush known as Bloody Gulch," wrote PFC Albert F. Semasko, of Baker Battery. He and a man he identifies only as PVT Zimmerman set trip flares around the battery perimeter. "None ever went off," he

wrote. "That battle was at close quarters and lasted all day and night," Semasko recalled. "My best friend, PFC Mike Gbur, was killed right beside me.... That really shook me up." He recalled that he and a number of other men were selected to try to get out of the ambush area. "We all made it out," he wrote.

LTC James V. Sanden (CO, 90 FAB), with his headquarters and Battery A, came under attack on Aug., 11 at the same time that the enemy struck the 555th. PVT Virgil Corless, Battery A, "jumped up onto a half-track and tried to return...fire with a .50-cal machine gun," Corless said. [O]ne of the officers hollered and told me to get the hell off " that he was firing on friendly troops. "The guys told him (the officer), 'Look at the rounds,' because [enemy] rounds were hitting the half track . . . I was standing on."

That night, amid what Corless described as "a madhouse" of explosions and fighting, he heard moaning. Crawling in the direction of the sound, Corless found a wounded soldier. He tried to pick up the wounded man but he "couldn't figure out why [he] kept slipping out of my hands," Corless said, "then I realized at a terrible moment...I'll never forget...he didn't have anything on [his] right side...." The man's one entire right hip and leg were gone. Corless managed to carry him to a jeep. "I put him into the passenger side.... I tried to start the jeep.... The thing was saturated with holes...from shrapnel flying all over the place.... About that moment, there was a terrible explosion...within arm's length on the left side of me — a big orange explosion.... I felt a burning sensation in my arm and was propelled out of the jeep...." Corless was knocked out by the explosion and the soldier he was trying to save was killed outright.

"The small arms fire [continued] to be poured in on us and shouting and hollering and crying for help and everything imaginable was taking place," Corless continued. Finally, orders were given to get out. Corless teamed up with a man he remembered as "McCullough." (Probably PFC James H. McCalla.) The two men headed back through the positions of the 555th, slipped into a rice paddy and encountered enemy infantry. Corless had no weapon; McCalla had his, but no ammunition. "There was a hell of a lot of them," Corless remembered, "and we slid deeper into the rice paddy and they moved past us...."

The two men eventually left the paddy and walked south along the road, soon running into the positions of B/159 FAB. "As we arrived," Corless said, "this...outfit was under heavy fire.... Trucks were up in flames and small-arms fire and shrapnel was going everywhere.... The place was lit up almost like daylight in an orange glow."

In this light, the two men saw a litter jeep with a wounded man strapped to one of the stretchers. Some men of the 159th nearby were discussing the plight of the man, but no one made a move to go to his rescue. Corless guessed the jeep was about 150 yards away, and he and McCalla decided to rescue the soldier.

Running across the open to the jeep, Corless said that he never was "as scared in my life as I was [then]...because there was so much shrapnel buzzing." They reached the jeep safely. "God, I've never been so glad to see anybody as I am you guys!" said the wounded soldier gratefully Corless' hands shook so badly that he had diffi-

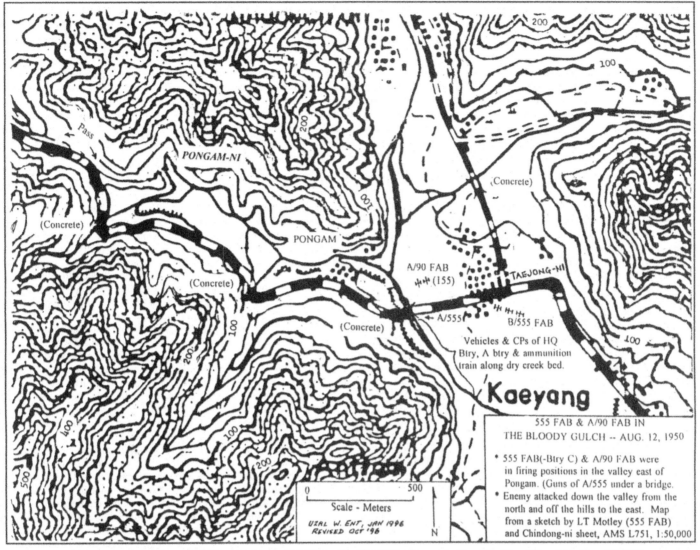

(Concrete)

Pass

PONGAM-NI

(Concrete)

(Concrete)

PONGAM

(Concrete)

A/90 FAB
(155)

(Concrete)

A/555

TAEJONG-NI

B/555 FAB

Vehicles & CPs of HQ
Btry, A btry & ammunition
train along dry creek bed.

Kaeyang

555 FAB & A/90 FAB IN
THE BLOODY GULCH -- AUG. 12, 1950

* 555 FAB(-Btry C) & A/90 FAB were
  in firing positions in the valley east of
  Pongam. (Guns of A/555 under a bridge.
* Enemy attacked down the valley from the
  north and off the hills to the east. Map
  from a sketch by LT Motley (555 FAB)
  and Chindong-ni sheet, AMS L751, 1:50,000

0 — 500
Scale - Meters

UZAL W. ENT, JAN 1996
REVISED OCT '96

N

Map 25 (Source: A sketch map by William Motley, Svc/555 FAB for The 5th RCT in Korea. The First Fifty Days, *Albert J. McAdoo, E/5 RCT.*

culty unstrapping the litter from the jeep. The wounded man tried to calm him down. "Okay, just take your time," he said. "I'm all right." Corless took the front of the litter and McCalla the other end, and the two men ran back toward the stone wall from whence they came. Suddenly, Corless felt the back of the litter fall. They stopped. "I said, 'Mac, Mac, are you all right?' He said, 'Yeah, I think I'm hit through the hand, though.'" By this time, daylight was coming.

Shortly thereafter, officers of B/159th asked who had rescued the man from the litter jeep. A number of soldiers who had seen Corless and McCalla make the rescue remained silent, and Corless and McCalla decided that they would not identify themselves. As Corless said, "There was a life saved...and I will go to my grave feeling good about that." At Masan, Corless was finally treated for his wound and returned to duty.

SGT Francis J. Behr (HHB, 90 FAB) recalled that enemy guerrillas dressed in GI fatigues got into the battery area on Aug. 9 and wounded PFC Donald Blaesing, 1SG Wilbur McCarthy and several other men. Behr and SGT Bobby G. Lowery loaded them into a jeep and set out for the aid station. Enroute, mortar shell fragments hit Blaesing and wounded Behr in his right index finger.

But Behr's real "baptism of fire" came on

Aug. 11 and 12, when the battery area was overrun. Few undamaged or destroyed vehicles remained, and many men had to get out on foot. Behr was lucky enough to get aboard the last vehicle out. The unit's kitchen truck was taken by the enemy. When recaptured in North Korea a few months later, all the original markings were still on it.

Alfred G. James, of A/90 FAB, was on a .50 cal machine gun in a battery outpost near a farm house, with a staff sergeant he remembered only as "Papa." He recalled the battery's 155s firing direct fire into the enemy to stave them off. In turn, he wrote, "we received mortar and artillery rounds. Some were going off in the trees above us, giving...air bursts."

In the general melee, Roger A. "Andy" Chapdelaine, of the 90th's HQ. Battery, was wounded in the back by grenade fragments. He described the battle that day as "pure hell... seeing buddies wounded and dead, made me wish I had never been born." Of the survivors, he wrote, the experience "made men from boys."

Very early in the attack, the enemy hit two of A battery's 155mm howitzers and a number of ammunition trucks. The artillerymen fought back with machine guns and small arms. PFC William L. Baumgartner of HQ. Battery, helped break up one enemy assault by manning a truck-

mounted machine gun. Comrades fell all around him. Then his gun was hit and he was knocked unconscious from the truck. When he came to, Baumgartner secured a rifle and kept fighting.

LTC Sanden turned the howitzers of A Battery to fire directly into the oncoming enemy. Meanwhile, men of both the 90th and 555th fired at the attacking North Koreans from pits, foxholes, from under the bridge, behind walls in the village — any shelter they could find. Like artillerymen throughout the ages, the men fought courageously to protect their guns.

Shortly after daylight, Corsairs flew in for a strike. Since there was no radio communication between the ground troops and pilots, the airmen guided in on tracers fired by the artillerymen at the enemy. In spite of this very welcome help, the artillery position was untenable by 9 a.m. Loading the wounded onto the few remaining trucks, the survivors withdrew under the protection of F-51s.

Amazing as it may seem, in the midst of the North Korean pre-dawn attack, plans were going forward to send elements of the Survey Section, wiremen, radiomen and FDC forward to select gun positions for the 555th so it could support the 5th Infantry in its move toward Chinju.

Richard Lewis and Arlen S. Russell were

members of this advance party, but enemy fire soon stopped them. Lewis got his men off the trucks and, he recalled, the Survey Section went "to the nearest ridge line, secured it and stayed until the convoy started moving out."

"I was driving the Wire Section 3/4 ton weapons carrier with a half dozen wiremen as passengers," Arlen wrote. "There were 8 - 10 vehicles in our little convoy.... (Lewis recalled a tank leading the convoy.) "As we rounded a curve in the road near the top of a hill we began receiving a lot of small-arms and heavy machinegun fire from a hill about 300 yards to our right. The firing brought the convoy to an abrupt halt. Bullets shattered the windshield of my truck," Russell wrote, "and shot out both rear tires. We piled out of the vehicles into a ditch on the left side of the road and started returning fire towards the opposite hillside."

The men of this convoy remained pinned down for the rest of the day and into the night. Then orders came to make a run for it. "We all piled back into the trucks," Russell continued. "A wireman by the name of 'Okie' took the wheel of the Wire truck and I rode alongside firing into the darkness towards...the North Koreans.... Since both rear tires were flat, 'Okie' put the truck in 4-wheel drive to better get it moving. In this manner we raced out of the ambush area and drove...until we came upon our infantry...."

B/159 FAB (CPT Curtis Walton) was also under a heavy enemy attack. Enemy gunfire set afire a number of trucks loaded with ammunition and gasoline. A number of men courageously drove other ammunition and gasoline trucks away from the burning vehicles By 8 a.m. the enemy was driven away from the 159th unit. The battery later displaced to a position 3 miles west of Chindong-ni. "This fine battery was destined to defend its guns three more times against strong attacks at close quarters," wrote GEN Barth.

Two 25th Division Recon Co. tanks arrived in Bloody Gulch shortly after the artillery positions had been overrun. They tried to drive the North Koreans away and clear the road. MSG Robert A. Tedford was killed while standing in the turret of his tank, firing the .50-cal machine gun and giving instructions to his crew. The tank counter-attack failed.

In accordance with COL Ordway's orders, LTC Throckmorton took his 2d Battalion back to the Pongam-ni Pass. By the time the battalion arrived there, the battle in the Gulch was over. A few survivors straggled into the battalion position before noon, then no more. Throckmorton, believing that the enemy was making its way through the hills to Taechon-ni, requested permission to return there, and was granted it at 3 p.m. by the regimental XO.

GEN Barth had tried to get to the Gulch earlier in the morning, but was halted by an enemy roadblock. He telephoned GEN Kean, who ordered him to take command of the two battalions of Marines which had been ordered to the area. He also placed Corley's 3/24 Infantry under Barth's command, which Barth wrote, "was to attack west from the vicinity of Chindong-ni, reopen the main supply road and recover the lost guns and ant remaining personnel... at Taejongni." Barth quickly utilized LTC Walter Preston's

159 FA headquarters as his CP and some of the 159th officers as his temporary staff.

The North Koreans also ambushed a platoon of the 72d Engineer Co. on Aug. 12. Gerald D. "Jake" Holler was in the ambushed platoon. "We were trying to knock out a roadblock and were ambushed...coming back," Holler wrote. "I was the last one back and [the] only one... wounded." He had taken shelter behind a rock, but one leg was unprotected, and was hit there. Holler didn't get medical treatment for three days, but he dismissed the injury as "just a flesh wound."

3-5 Marines — Aug. 12 -14

Pursuant to orders, LTC Stewart and LTC Taplett flew back to Chindong-ni early on the afternoon of Aug. 12 to perform a reconnaissance and plan for employment of Taplett's battalion. Army estimates gave the strength of the enemy in the area as between 2,000 and 2,500 men. The two officers were told to fly to a bridge over a dry creek bed, where they were to meet and be briefed by a 25th Division liaison officer in a jeep with a red air panel in its hood. Arriving at the bridge, they found no jeep nor liaison officer. Members of an Army tank crew nearby knew nothing about the arrangement. GEN Barth, stated in his monograph that LTC Raymond Murray (CO, 5th Marines) and the Marine Brigade S-3, LTC Stewart, landed by helicopter at his headquarters at 2 p.m. on the 12th.(See Chapter Notes.)

Discovering a number of telephone lines in a ditch, Taplett and Stewart began checking each one, trying to establish communication with someone who could give them some information on the situation and the action expected of the 3d Battalion, 5th Marines. At last, they reached the 25th Division G-3, who told them to "look the situation over" and settle on a course of action which would drive the enemy from the area and protect the only artillery battery remaining in the area, B/159 FAB. The Marine officers then were to report to GEN Barth when he arrived to assume overall command. Stewart and Taplett made a helicopter reconnaissance of the area then flew back to the MSR to locate 3/5. When they returned, they met LTC John Daly (CO, 555 FAB). He briefed them on what had happened — the onslaught of the enemy armor, mortars and infantry on his battalion (less Battery C) and elements of the 90th FAB, and told them where the enemy had been at the time of the attack. (See Chapter Notes.)

The two Marine officers decided to seize ridges commanding the MSR. Just as this plan was formulated, the 3d Battalion, 5th Marines arrived and unloaded from their trucks. LTC Taplett immediately sent Co. H on the attack, with Co. G following. LTC Daly provided a 15-minute artillery preparation on his own and Taplett's FAC somehow obtained a flight of Corsairs which still had unexpended ordnance and napalm aboard. CPT Fegan picked out some enemy targets after receiving some fire from the ridge. How Co. seized its first objective without a casualty. Only one wounded enemy was found, probably from a rear guard element.

GEN Barth finally got through at 7 p.m., and asked when the Marines would be ready to attack. LTC Taplett informed him that they had

already taken the first objective. Barth congratulated the Marines on their prompt action, then approved Taplett's's plans for continuing the attack.

The general provided several Army light tanks and three M-44 armored personnel carriers and an Army artillery battery to support the attack when it jumped off at 7 a.m. on Aug. 13. Battery C, 11th Marines also took part in the attack, and two rifle companies of 3-5 quickly took the remaining objectives against almost no resistance.

Fred Davidson (G-3-5) wrote, "The next day [Aug. 13], we started out on a climb up Hill 265 overlooking the abandoned Army artillery [555 FA]." His unit received a few ineffective bursts of machine gun fire, but attained the crest of the hill without enemy contact. That night it rained, slowly at first, "then it really started coming down," Fred recalled. "I spent the rainy night in my foxhole." He couldn't sleep "because it was too damned cold! This was a hell of a thing, all day it was hotter than hell and now, at night in the rain it was cold."

Although his men encountered virtually no opposition, LTC Murray had a very close call while attempting to deliver a message to survivors of the 555th reported to be under a bridge near Pongam-ni. He was thwarted by heavy enemy fire that drove his helicopter away.

The Marines continued their advance early the next morning. Men of Co. G observed How Co. climbing Hill 334 on their left. Neither unit made any contact with the enemy — they had faded away. Later that day 3-5 Marines were reassembled and headed for Miryang and the First Battle of the Naktong Bulge.

Plans had been under consideration for the 2d and 3d Battalions, 5th Marines, to attack west across the valley floor at Pongam-ni while 2/5 RCT attacked east to meet them. When the Marines were ordered away, the plan was abandoned and 2/5 RCT instead relieved 3-5 Marines at Kogan-ni on Aug. 14.

GEN Barth wrote, "We said goodbye to the Marine Brigade with real regret. During their short time with us they...certainly did their part to uphold the Marine tradition. Their artillery, the 11th Marine Artillery Battalion, under command of LTC Wood, was highly competent and cooperative."

3/24 Infantry — Aug. 12 - 13

On Aug. 9, LTC John T. Corley was given command of the 3d Battalion, 24th Infantry. Three days later the battalion was given the mission of attacking through the high rugged mountains just south of mighty Sobuk-san (Hill 738). These mountains consist of deep valleys and high, very steep ridges, often topped by very narrow promontories. A prolonged, bloody struggle for control of some of these ridges took place from mid-August until the breakout from the Perimeter more than a month later.

Corley's battalion failed to negotiate the terrain. On Aug. 12 the 3d Battalion's two assault companies were unable to make any headway. Battle casualties where reported as 10. By noon on Aug. 13, the battalion was stopped cold by the enemy and terrain some 2 1/2 miles from Bloody Gulch. "Corley reported to me at about four o'clock [P.M.]," Barth wrote, "that his battalion had been driven back and badly scattered."

3/5 RCT — Aug. 12 - 13

"Early the next morning [Aug. 12]," Bierne wrote "as the sun came up we noticed a woods moving slowly up the hill towards the position where I Co. was dug in. North Koreans had trees (actually tree branches) tied to their backs as they crept up on I Company.... We drove them away in our first real firefight of the war."

Later in the morning the 3d Battalion, 5 RCT was ordered to withdraw. In doing so, they came upon several men and vehicles of the battalion which had been ambushed the night before in the Chinju Pass. At Muchon- ni, trucks from the 35th Infantry met the 3/5 RCT and transported it to an assembly area near Chindong-ni.

Losses Suffered at Bloody Gulch

The 1/5 RCT probably suffered the most infantry losses in the vicinity of the pass near Bloody Gulch. The loss of 157 of 180 men in Co. C, coupled with the losses in other companies, substantially reduced the strength of the 1st Battalion. The 2d Battalion also had hard fighting at Taechon-ni and suffered losses. The 3d Battalion escaped TF Kean with small loss.

The great losses of the 90th and 555 FABs were the most cruel. The 90th lost all six guns, two by enemy fire. The others were rendered useless by the artillerymen when the position was overrun. The 90th managed to get out three tractors and about 15 other vehicles. Appleman gives the vehicular losses of the 90th as 28, including two M-5 tractors. This battalion had 10 killed, 60 wounded and 30 missing — 50 per cent of the men of the two batteries present. Twenty of the missing were dead, found five weeks later during the breakout.

The 555 FAB, according to GEN Barth, lost six guns in the Gulch; Appleman writes the loss was eight. The fact that 12 guns were issued to the 555th a few days after the Gulch substantiates Barth's figure. The 12 guns were given to the 555th in order to bring the battalion up to its full complement of 18 guns. The battalion brought out six guns. According to *The First Fifty Days*, the 555th lost 20 2 1/2-ton trucks, 9 3/4-ton trucks, 18 jeeps, one 4-ton wrecker and one ambulance, all destroyed. Between 75 and 100 men of the battalion were killed and another 80 wounded.

In all, the artillery lost a total of 12 guns (six 105mm howitzers and six 155mm howitzers about 100 vehicles and some 300 men. HHB and battery A, 90 FAB, were awarded a Presidential Unit Citation for their valiant efforts to defend their position on Aug. 11 and 12.

When the 25th Division regained the Gulch area in September, it found in a house the bodies of 55 men from the 555th and in another area close by the bodies of 20 men from the 90th. The latter group all had been shot in the head.

On Aug. 13, LTC Clarence E. Stuart arrived in Korea and was assigned command of the 555th on Aug. 16. In addition to 12 replacement 105mm howitzers for the 555th, GEN Barth arranged for the 90th to receive six replacement 155mm howitzers.

The Results of Task Force Kean

By Aug. 14, TF Kean was back where it had started. The entire battle, from Aug. 7 to 13, was a confused melange of fighting both at the "front" and in what should have been rear areas. Enemy mines and booby traps in the rear areas constantly cut supply roads. For 10 days tanks and armored cars were required to open a road to permit resupply of 1/24 Infantry in the Sobuk-san area. Enemy troops virtually swarmed in the Tundok region of that mountain, where they were easily sheltered from air attack by abandoned coal mines. Attempts by the 24th Infantry and ROKs to drive these North Koreans away failed.

TF Kean was officially dissolved by a 3:30 p.m. radio message on Aug. 16. The task force had been partially successful in accomplishing its mission, but the enemy's success against elements of the 24th Infantry and ROK troops in the area, and their destruction of the 555th as a viable artillery battalion and of Battery A, 90 FAB, in the deep center of the task force's zone of action, negated American successes. Had it not been for these disasters, the Marines most assuredly would have seized their objective of Sachon and the 5 RCT would have attained theirs, supported on their right flank by the 35th Infantry.

Large numbers of the *NK 6th Division* were in the 25th Division's rear areas before TF Kean was launched. Two battalions of the *14th Regiment* had engaged 1/27 Infantry at the Chindong-ni schoolhouse on Aug. 3 and the *15th Regiment* infiltrated the high ground southwest of Masan a day or two later. Both the Marines and the 5 RCT engaged the enemy in some heavy fighting in the Chindong-ni area on the eve of TF Kean's jump-off.

The clash of TF Kean with the *North Korean 6th Division* and attached *83d Motorcycle Regiment* was not a meeting engagement. The actual enemy line up went something like this: 35th Infantry — Opposed elements of the *6th Division*. The 5 RCT, 24th Infantry (and attached ROKs) — Elements of the *13th, 14th* and *15th Regiment* were identified through a captured copy of the enemy's order as the force which attacked the artillery in Bloody Gulch. Marine Bde — Opposed principally by the *83d Motorcycle Regiment*.

The thrust of TF Kean was not due west of Chindong-ni toward Chinju; rather, the Marines on the left made a wide looping envelopment, while the 5 RCT attacked northwest. Both of these advances followed the logical axes of principal roads. Only the 35th on the northern flank made a direct east to west advance.

The configuration of elements of the 5 RCT between Bloody Gulch and the Chinju Pass, with the bulk of the infantry near or beyond the pass just west of Pongam-ni, left the artillery vulnerable to attack from a large force of enemy infantry. North Koreans on the high ground north and east of the valley completely dominated the artillery positions, and when the infantry passed to the west, the enemy struck hard at the almost unprotected artillery. In its passage up the valley to Pongam-ni, the 5 RCT unwittingly bypassed a large number of enemy in the hills on their right flank. Many of these enemy soldiers took part in stalling the 1st and 3d Battalions of

the 24th Infantry, as they tried to attack in the Sobuk-san area and the high mountains south of it.

Most Marines were very frustrated, and some were angry that they were directed to the 5 RCT zone and later to what became known as the First Battle of the Naktong Bulge. However the bigger situation dictated their redeployment. Soldiers who had been on the receiving end of North Korean attacks were happy to be "dishing it out" for a change, particularly the 35th Infantry. Their morale went way up. Finally, the troops who participated in TF Kean gained valuable battle experience.

The offensive failed to attract any enemy troops from other sectors, but gained time to organize and prepare defensive positions between Sobuk-san and Chindong-ni.

The enemy's *83d Motorcycle Regiment* lost large numbers of vehicles and numerous casualties to Marine air and artillery. The *North Korean 6th Division* was reduced to about half its strength at the beginning of the battle, about 3,000 men. Enemy personnel losses can only be estimated; conservatively, perhaps 3,500 to 4,000 men.

Fred Davidson gave Marine casualties as 315 (66 dead; 240 wounded and 9 missing). Army artillery in Bloody Gulch lost some 300 men. The 35th had comparatively few casualties; the 5th and 24th Regiments both suffered moderately. Although no one has given a loss figure for TF Kean, it can be estimated at about 1,000 - 1,100 men.

As TF Kean prepared to begin its offensive, the *North Korean 4th Division* crossed the Naktong River and drove deep into the defensive positions of the 24th Infantry Division. In the midst of Kean's attack, the enemy threatened to break through on the east coast near Pohangdong. Along the Pusan Perimeter battle front, over 150 miles long, several major struggles were always in progress at the same time. Walker always had two or three simultaneous crises.

At the conclusion of TF Kean, Eighth Army gave up hard-won terrain because the area jutted forward many miles, lengthening the Perimeter defense line to an untenable degree.

The Colonel Eckert Briefing — Aug. 9

COL Eckert (no first name given) was sent by GEN Mark Clark's Army Field Forces headquarters to inspect Eighth Army in late July-early August, shortly after the entrance into combat of the 1st Cavalry and 25th Infantry Divisions and as Eighth Army was changing its mission from delay to defense.

Eckert briefed GEN Ridgway on his findings and conclusions Aug. 9, 1950, with only Eckert, Ridgway and his aide, LTC Frank W. Moorman, present. Moorman prepared a Memorandum For the Record of the briefing, classified SECRET until Nov. 18, 1982. (See Chapter Notes.)

Eckert verbally ripped the officers and enlisted men of Eighth Army apart. He had little positive to say. Almost without exception, the problems and ills which he pointed out were caused by the lack of training, poor equipment and leadership failure, beginning at the top in Washington, D.C.

The Moorman memo records the substance of COL Eckert's comments to GEN Ridgway, summarized below. (Material in quotation marks are verbatim extracts from the original, which is included in the Ridgway Papers, USAMHI, Carlisle Barracks, PA.)

The three "principal deficiencies" of Eighth Army were a) a lack of knowledge of infantry fundamentals; b) a lack of leadership in combat echelons; and c) the absence of an aggressive fighting spirit.

Eckert next listed the "unavoidable handicaps" under which U.S. forces were operating: a) units and individuals incompletely trained; b) units at reduced strength; c) operations being conducted on very wide frontages; d) a well-trained enemy "in superior numbers"; and e) U.S. troops "operating over very difficult terrain."

Mooreman's memorandum bearing on Eckert's elaboration and additional comments will be quoted below, with the author's comments in brackets following each point.

"a. Our troops are easily stampeded. When attacked they do not respond with the fundamental infantry reaction of fire and movement, but instead call for artillery and air support and then withdraw if this does not suffice to interrupt the attack. Our troops do not counter-attack an enemy penetration."

[No doubt some units may have reacted in the manner Eckert described, but he obviously did not understand that through the end of July and the first few days of August 1950 the mission was to delay the enemy, not to try to fight him to a standstill. In delaying actions, the defender does not usually counterattack a penetration, except to facilitate disengagement. If GEN Ridgway failed to understand the delay mission of Eighth Army, it is a reflection on him; it seems that Walker was the only one who knew what he was doing. Since he had to deal through Almond to communicate with MacArthur, it is doubtful that Almond could have accurately relayed this to that officer. The statement that "our troops are easily stampeded" is not supported by facts.]

"b. Our forces do not maintain outpost protection nor flank protection. Weapons are not properly emplaced to obtain a good field of fire. Troops take positions on tops of hills, apparently so they can be sure to see the enemy, and withdraw before he reaches them."

[It is no doubt true that some weapons were not emplaced to obtain a good field of fire, a criticism which could be leveled at any large military organization. In some instances, this was the fault of the junior leader selecting the position. The fact that high ground was key terrain in the Korean War dictated securing and fighting from ridges and hill crests, often forcing weapons to employ plunging, rather than grazing, fire.

His remark about troops taking position on hill tops in order to see the enemy and withdraw before he reaches them was unduly cruel, and demonstrates COL Eckert's ignorance of the character of fighting in Korea, where it was absolutely vital to success to seize and hold the high ground, except during delaying operations, as the troops had been executing all during July. High ground was sought in order to deny it to the enemy, just as the enemy did the same thing for the same reason.]

"c. With some individual exceptions, morale is good. (Note by COL Moorman: During my very limited observation I felt the morale was too good, i.e., the individual soldier is not sufficiently concerned or upset over the fact that he is being decisively defeated.)"

[Here, Eckert is correct. Few troops believed they were "being decisively defeated." Most of the front-line soldiers of Eighth Army felt at the time that they ultimately were going to beat the SOBs. I agree with COL Moorman on his admission of "very limited observation."]

"d. Junior officers are good except for a lack of knowledge."

[The junior officers who survived the first days on the front learned on the job. Most developed into good combat leaders.]

"e. Our troops do not dig in and make no pretense at camouflaging their positions. They do not seek cover and concealment while moving by day. They would be easily visible by enemy air were there such. They are visible to the enemy by terrestrial observation. The lack of camouflaging is concurred in by General Walker on the theory that he does not wish to harass his forces with a precaution which is not now necessary because of the lack of enemy air."

[Some units, might not have dug in, but even a prone shelter offers some protection. American troops are notoriously bad in utilizing camouflage, concealment and cover to hide from enemy observation and to protect themselves from his fire. COL Eckert was correct in his remarks about this failure.]

"4. Signal communication within front line regiments is poor. This is partly due to equipment which is in marginal operating condition. It is also due to the lack of knowledge on the part of the personnel involved and a lack of knowledge on the part of individual operators as to how to get the best out of marginal equipment."

[In addition to bad equipment, the lack of batteries or batteries which were no good also contributed to the problem. The lack of knowledge on the part of operators was due to the fact that radios were out of order or lacked batteries back in Japan before the war.]

"5. With minor exceptions, there has been no breakdown in the supply of front line units."

[The fact is that there were significant breakdowns in resupply to many front-line units, particularly to those in remote hills and ridges. Once South Korean civilians were recruited to carry supplies and ammunition forward and evacuate the dead and wounded, some of these shortages were reduced. Nevertheless, small-arms and machine gun ammunition issued at the front was sometimes corroded or often had to be reloaded into clips or metal-link machine gun belts on the front line.]

"6. The combat infantryman does not like the carbine. Some artillerymen dislike the carbine. In either case the preference over the carbine is for M-2s and light machine guns."

[This was very true, since the carbine was not accurate at any great range, did not have stopping power and was prone to jam too easily.]

"7. Tactical air support of front line units is not satisfactory. There are not enough Forward Air Control Parties. Those available do not have sufficient equipment nor enough knowhow."

[Except for the Marines, this is true. The jeep-mounted Air Force FAC radio at this stage of the war often failed by being jolted around as the jeep negotiated the roads and trails of Korea. The USAF already was striving hard to correct this deficiency.]

"8. All forces engaged in Korea regardless of arm or service, should have fundamental infantry training as the situation is sufficiently fluid to occasionally require those units in rear of the front lines to engage in close combat."

[COL Eckert was absolutely correct in this recommendation.]

"9. The quality of the soldier now engaged in Korea is not up to World War II standards."

[The soldier of World War II knew exactly what was at stake: That the enemy had to be defeated or the U.S. would not survive. The issues at stake in the Korean War were unclear to the average soldier. The soldiers who came from Japan and Okinawa falsely were led to believe that the North Korean soldier was poorly trained, poorly armed and poorly led, that the appearance of U.S. troops would cause the North Koreans to pull back and that the affair in Korea would be over in a few weeks or months. They were deluded on these points on a grand scale by the leadership, starting with MacArthur's headquarters, which should have known better.

Finally, Eckert forgot the defeat of untried U.S. troops in the Kasserine Pass of North Africa, or the less-than-stellar performances of other troops in their first battles. He was comparing the veterans at the end of WW II to the untested soldiers who first went to Korea, hardly a fair or accurate comparison.]

10. In this, COL Eckert points out that the ROK divisions "had small amounts of artillery" and "no 4.2 mortars."

[This was true. The ROK divisions also had no armor.]

"11. The Republic of Korea forces are doing better than U.S. forces. They are imbued with the only offensive spirit observed in Korea."

[The ROK troops did fight the advancing enemy with ferocity. Many of their soldiers sacrificed themselves to destroy enemy tanks. On a number of occasions, ROK formations ambushed large numbers of the enemy and annihilated them. Their "offensive spirit" perhaps did appear greater than of American units, but they were fighting to defend their country. The American soldier had no such motive. Pride in unit and self, however, soon overcame this and U.S. troops fought with as much bravery and determination as the enemy or the ROKs.]

12. This point centered on the names of key ROK commanders, Eckert's evaluation of Walker's Chief of Staff (COL Landrum) and of Eighth Army regimental commanders. COL Eckert was "not impressed" with COL Landrum, who was then almost 60. He felt that Walker should have a younger, stronger Chief of Staff. He believed that some of the regimental commanders were "poor" and "lacked experience and aggressiveness," and also said that "many senior staff officers appeared to be lacking in energy and ability."

[COL Levin C. "Lev" Allen, 56 (University of San Francisco 1916), was appointed as

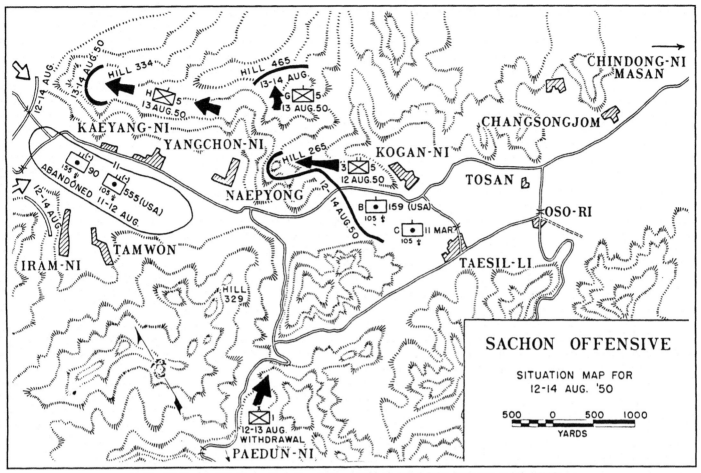

Map 26 (Source: U.S. Marine Operations in Korea 1950-53. Vol. 1, Pusan Perimeter, P. 149, USMC)

Walker's Chief of Staff soon after Ridgway returned to Washington, D.C., but Walker retained Landrum in Eighth Army headquarters.

Of the regimental commanders then in Korea, six were considered too old for regimental command, as mentioned previously. Of these, White was relieved of command Aug. 6, 1950, Rohsenberger on Aug. 7, Nist on Sept. 20, and Palmer Dec. 15, 1950. Stephens (21st Inf.) and Fisher (25th Inf.) were doing well.]

When Ridgway, Eckert and their associates visited Eighth Army, Walker had been in command less than three weeks. It would seem that a visit asking what could be done to help him would have been more in order than an inspection. Further, Almond already had succeeded in undercutting Walker with MacArthur, so the general had lost almost all faith in his commander. Ridgway, too, thought that Walker's leadership was so poor that he should be relieved of command, and seriously contemplated recommending Walker's relief to MacArthur, but thought that MacArthur would think Ridgway was hinting for the job. Ironically, MacArthur considered Ridgway the best man in the Army to replace Walker. Had Ridgway broached the subject, he undoubtedly would have succeeded to the command of Eighth Army in early August 1950 instead of upon the death of Walker four months later. In conclusion, GEN Walker brilliantly led the successful defense of the Pusan Perimeter, providing the time MacArthur needed to stage his "spectacular" — the Inchon landing.

Chapter Notes:

P. 134 Battleground Korea, a history of the 25th Infantry Division in Korea, gives the effective strength of the 6th Division as 9,335, not including the Motorcycle Regiment. Appleman gives about 6,000 men for the division and another 1,500 for the motorcycle regiment, for a total of 7,500 men. There is no way to reconcile the difference in estimates.

P. 137 Cahill's platoon traversed this route during the hours of darkness after midnight on Aug. 7 and arrived on the summit of the hill after pausing a short time for the coming of daylight, not August 6-7 as indicated in the official Marine history.

P. 149 "Yellowlegs" was a name the North Koreans had given to Marines for the lace leggings they wore, a name of respect for the ferocity and determination of Marine attacks. The leggings weren't really yellow, but a light dun color. The Army had discarded similar leggings early in WW II and adopted the combat boot, with a high-topped drill shoe (boondocker) with a leather collar about four inches wide sewn onto the shoe top.

P. 151 Bodies of seven of the missing men were recovered in September when the Army broke out of the Pusan Perimeter. The other man was carried as MIA until November 1953, when he was assumed to be dead. The names of the eight dead Marines who were left on Hill 202 were: SSG Eugene L. Lawson, CPL Richard D. Garcia, PFC Alfredo Carrizales, PFC Spencer C. Meldrum, PFC Bobby R. Poare, PFC

Gerald A. Schick, PFC Bernard V. Stavely and PFC Lawrence A. Wilcox.

P. 153 Kenny Freedman died Feb. 7, 1995, shortly after writing the articles for the 5th RCT Newsletter quoted in this narrative.

P. 153 Appleman misidentifies the unit as the 72d Engineer Combat Battalion.

P. 160 This does not agree with the account in the official Marine history, nor the recollection of COL Taplett, which agree the first personal contact with the Marines and GEN Barth was about 7 p.m. on Aug. 12. There is no dispute that Barth had been given temporary command of the Army's 5 RCT and 3-5th Marines.

P. 160 The Marine history erroneously states that the enemy attack was on C/555 FAB. It was on the entire 555th, less Battery C. That unit had gone forward with 2/5 RCT.

P. 161 Appleman was unaware of this document when he wrote South to the Naktong, North to the Yalu. A capsulized version of the document, without comments, is on page 186 of Clay Blair's The Forgotten War.

CHAPTER THIRTEEN - The First Battle of the Naktong Bulge

Introduction

Once the Naktong was reached, the North Koreans paused to regroup, while the Americans and ROKs began to establish defensive positions with some flank protection. The "line" thus established along the Naktong was so long that U.S. divisions were forced to defend on extended frontages, with huge gaps between defending units. The 24th Infantry Division, deployed northward from the confluence of the Naktong and Nam Rivers, on a 22 air mile front. The 1st Cavalry Division, north of the 24th, was deployed on a somewhat shorter frontage along the Naktong. To its north was the ROK 1st Division, also primarily along the Naktong. The 25th Division was located south of the 24th, from the Nam-Naktong confluence south to the sea.

Walker's Defense Plan and the North Korean Plan of Attack

GEN Walker's defensive plan required holding the road and rail lines running northward from Pusan via Miryang to Taegu, eastward from there through Ancien to Kyongju. At Kyongju, the road-railroad system turned back south to Pusan. These road and rail lines had to be held in order to successfully defend the Perimeter.

The North Koreans, on the other hand, determined to exploit four routes of attack in order to breach the Perimeter and gain Pusan. These were:

1. The route through Masan to Pusan in the south, the shortest, most direct route. The capture of Pusan virtually would ensure the destruction of U.S. and ROK forces far to the north.
2. Through what became known as the Naktong Bulge to Miryang, cutting the road and rail lines to Taegu as well as all U.S. and ROK troops north of Miryang along the Naktong and near Taegu.
3. Through Taegu, striking the center of the ROK-U.S. perimeter and cutting it in half, opening the way to roll up the line by driving east and south from Taegu.
4. Through Kyongju south toward Pusan. In addition to driving on Pusan, this avenue would destroy the eastern anchor and outflank the Perimeter.

A success along any one of these routes would virtually assure victory for the North Koreans. The North Korean high command decided to launch major drives along each of these avenues early in August.

The Naktong River and Vicinity

A discussion of the Naktong River and vicinity was touched on briefly in Chapter 10. It is essential for an understanding of the fighting which took place along that stream. The Naktong, second longest river in Korea, forms a wide, looping moat in its journey through South Korea to the sea. Behind this moat, a defender might make a stand.

Deployment of the 24th Infantry Division — August 3-5

The 24th Division went into Eighth Army reserve on July 22, but also had the responsibility of protecting the air strip near Pohang. Two days later, Walker ordered the 24th to the south to counteract a North Korean thrust via Chinju. Subsequently, the 24th, and the other U.S. divisions passed behind the Naktong. By Aug., 3, the entire 24th Division, except the 19th Infantry, had reached its new Naktong River sector. The 19th was enroute there. By Aug. 5, the entire division was deployed in the sector. On that date, the division, with attachments, numbered only 12,368 men. The number breakout was:

24th Division: 9,882. Estimated combat efficiency was 53 per cent. A partial breakdown of this strength figure shows the following:

19th Infantry: 1,910. No battalion figures available.
21st Infantry: 1,670. (1/21: 540. 3/21: 360.)
34th Infantry: 1,402. (1/34: 515. 3/34: 493.) Combat effectiveness 40 per cent.

Field Artillery: Consisted of the battalions shown, but two of the battalions had only two firing batteries and the other two had one firing battery each. The B/13 FAB had only five guns. Since all battalions were short firing batteries, artillery support for the division could not have amounted to more than 35 guns, the equivalent of less than two full battalions or half the complement of a division's artillery. The battalions were:

13, 52, 63 FABs (105mm howitzer) 11 FAB (155mm howitzer)

Armor: A/78 Medium Tank Bn. This company had only two M-24 light tanks, one of which was attached to the 24th Recon Co.
A/ 26 AAA/AW Bn (Automatic Weapons)
3 Engr Combat Bn
14 Engr Combat Bn: Strength of 472.
Division support troops, including Recon, MP, QM, Signal, Replacement and Ordnance companies, the Medical Battalion, a Division medical detachment and the Band.
Attachments: 486 men. Included ordnance and engineer units and the 8076th Surgical Hospital.
Operational Control: ROK 17th Infantry Regiment, strength of 2,000.

Disposition and Missions of the Principal Elements of the Division

34th Infantry (COL Charles E. Beauchamp, 1,402 men). The regiment, seriously short of vehicles, 4.2 inch mortars and BARs, was given the southern portion of the division sector to defend with a ground distance of 34,000 yards. (See Chapter Notes.)

The sector occupied by the 24th Infantry Di-

vision extended north of the confluence of the Naktong and Nam Rivers to the village of Hyonpung, an air line distance of 22 miles, but the loops and turns of the Naktong made the actual ground defensive line about 34 miles long.

In this area, the average width of the Naktong was 350 meters (about 438 feet). It was from three to nine feet deep. Before the war, the river could be crossed in the 24th Division sector by the Chogye-Changnyong bridge and a number of ferries. None of these were available at the time of the battle. The river was fairly low in the Summer of 1950. As a result, a number of areas were fordable by foot, but steep banks at or near the river's edge precluded crossing vehicles without engineer preparation of the approaches.

In the 24th Division's area, the hills flanking both sides of the Naktong averaged 200 meters high, with some rising to 300 meters. The hills facing one another across the river were about the same height, so neither the Americans nor North Koreans gained a military advantage from occupying any of these hills. Only Hill 408, on the eastern bank of the Naktong in the extreme north of the Division's sector, dominated the surrounding terrain. On the eastern side of the river, many gullies extended inland from the river, which the North Koreans took advantage of to conceal their crossing and penetration of the 24th Division line. There were no wooded areas. The hills contained clumps of grass and scrub pine.

The bulk of the 34th Regiment's sector was what became known as the Naktong Bulge, formed by a great loop in the Naktong River. In straight-line distance, the bulge was about 5,000 yards deep and some 6,000 yards wide at its base. The regiment also was responsible for the security of the bridge in the rear at Namji-ri, leading into the sector of the 25th Division. In all, the regimental front extended from the village of Masuwan in the north to the junction of the Nam and Naktong rivers.

3d Bn, 34th Inf (LTC Gines Perez, 493 men). Perez, 41, just arrived from the states, was given command of 3/34 Inf. effective Aug. 5, 1950, giving him no time to acquaint himself with his battalion, the terrain, or the situation.

All three rifle companies of the 3d Battalion were placed on the line. Co. I, in the north, reinforced by part of A/26 AA (AW), acting as infantrymen, was responsible for a 5,000-yard front. Co. L was positioned in the salient formed by a giant loop of the Naktong, with an 11,000-yard front. The I & R Platoon manned two OPs to the left (south) of L's main position. Co. K held the extreme left (south) flank of the regiment and division on a 7,500 yard front. These frontages made it completely impossible for the units assigned to defend. The best that they could do would be to alert higher headquarters of an attack, and try to slow down, or divert the enemy along certain avenues of approach. Accordingly, LTC Perez established a series of platoon-sized strong points overlooking the river, built around each of the company's four machine guns and generally covering ferry sites that provided avenues of approach into the regimental rear via roads or trails.

William Menninger, who was the 34th Regiment's operations sergeant, detected a general improvement in morale once the command went on line behind the Naktong. "For the first time in two months, we were fighting as a Division, with our supporting units actually supporting us," he wrote He related this story to illustrate the improved morale: "The colonel's driver had been in a state of constant depression since our entry into the war. He never smiled, talked to no one, and usually exhibited a 'Woe is me' attitude. One morning we were in the Operations Tent, working on an attack order, when the colonel remarked, 'Surely, that can't be Willis out there whistling.' It was Willis, whistling, smiling from ear to ear and polishing the jeep. The colonel asked him, why the abrupt change in demeanor. Willis replied, 'Sir, I looked around this morning, and for the first time since we got over here, ALL OF THE ARTILLERY IS POINTING IN ONE DIRECTION.'"

A/26 AAA (AW) Bn (- men committed as infantrymen with 3/34 Inf): This amounted to four half-tracks. Mobile reserve.

1st Bn, 34th Inf (LTC Harold B. Ayres, 515 men): Regimental reserve. Located on the Yongsan road, 4 miles behind the CP of 3/34 Inf.

Heavy Mortar Company (4.2 inch): Four mortars at the base of the salient near the 3d battalion CP in the village of Kogon-ni. Remaining three mortars in the same valley 2,000 yards to the north.

21st Infantry (COL Richard W. Stephens, 1,670 men): Positioned on the Naktong north of Masuwan on a 12,000 yard front. There were not 1,670 men present, since Co. C and a section of 81mm mortars were still near Yongdok, on South Korea's east coast.

3d Bn, 21st Inf (MAJ Charles B. McConnell, 360 men): Manned the regimental front line. In addition to the battalion headquarters element, the battalion had been consolidated into two line companies, Co. I attached to K and Co. L attached to M. The bulk of the regimental heavy mortar company was attached to the 3d Battalion, to act as its third rifle company. The severe shortage of 4.2 inch mortar ammunition made this weapon virtually useless to the regiment and made most of the men of that unit available as riflemen. The battalion deployed companies M, K and HM (Heavy Mortar) from north to south in its sector. Because McConnell's frontage was much smaller, he was able to deploy platoons with interlocking bands of fire.

14th Engr (C) Bn (472 men): Attached to 21st Inf. Seven .50 cal machine gun teams attached to 3/21 Inf.

D/14 Engr: Attached to 1/21 Inf to replace Co. C.

A & C/14 Engr: Vicinity of Changnyong. Contingency mission, mobile reserve.

Additional fire support for the front-line battalion was provided by five 60mm, two 81mm and six 4.2 inch mortars from just behind the infantry positions.

1st Bn, 21st Inf (LTC Charles B. Smith, 540 men): Regimental reserve. Positioned in separate reserve positions several thousand yards behind the 3d Battalion. From these, the 1st Battalion rapidly could aid any front-line unit.

ROK 17th Inf (2,000 men): Deployed on a 30,000-yard front north of the 21st.

3d Engr (C) Bn: Co. A and C. Primary mission of maintaining roads in division rear areas. Be prepared to serve as part of a division counterattack force if needed. Co. B: Construct barriers in ROK 17th Inf sector. Co. D: Prepare minefields for 34 Inf. Prepare to ac act as regimental reserve.

Division Artillery:

13 FAB (105mm): Btry A: DS ROK 17th Inf.

Btry B (5 guns): DS 34th Inf.

52 FAB (105mm): Btry B: Located 3,000 yards in rear of 1/21 Inf. DS 21st Inf.

63 FAB (105mm): Btry B: Located 3,000 yards in rear of 1/21 Inf. DS 21st Inf.

11 FAB (155mm): Btry A: Reinforce fires of 105mm batteries.

Btry B: Located near B/13 FAB. Reinforce fires of B/13 FAB.

Division Reserve:

19th Inf (COL Ned D. Moore, 1,910 men): 1st Bn, 19th Inf (LTC Robert L. Rhea): 2 miles northwest of Changnyong. 2d Bn, 19th Inf (LTC Thomas M. McGrail): 4 miles south of Changnyong.

A/78 Hvy Tk Bn: Pugong-ni, behind the Division left flank. The unit had only one M-24 tank present. The only other tank the company had was attached to the 24 Recon Co. As a result, members of the unit began classes in infantry tactics.

24 Recon Co.: Security for division headquarters. Be prepared to serve as part of the division counterattack force. The Recon Co. had only five of its seven M-24 light tanks in running condition; two had been lost to enemy action, and only three had operable main guns. The company also had lost 10 jeeps.

Because the division was so low in strength, the HHC, signal company and medical detachment formed composite defense platoons for either a "last stand defense" or to be used as part of the division's counterattack force.

Defensive Preparations — Aug. 3-5

GEN Church planned for the river line to be lightly held by platoon or smaller sized elements and the gaps to be covered by observation in daylight and by patrols at night. Both primary and alternate positions were to be well dug-in. Minefields were to be placed on all possible crossing sites. The civilians in the area encompassed by the river and the north - south road through Changnyong and Yongsan were evacuated. All boats and rafts were destroyed except for those needed for patrolling. Each regiment had its own local reserve, while selected division commands constituted a general reserve.

Most of the 24th Division was in position by the end of Aug. 4. Preparation time, the severe shortages of personnel and equipment all were against the division. Further stocks of almost every type of ammunition were low; particularly critical was 4.2 inch mortar ammunition. Illuminating rounds of every type were also in short supply, so it was impossible to keep the river lighted at night. The plan for preparing obstacles to the enemy also was severely hampered by the lack of tools, barbed wire and antipersonnel (AP) mines.

The situation of the 24th Division was well

recognized by GEN Walker and his staff, which had recommending replacing the 24th Division on Aug. 8-9 with two regiments of the arriving 2d Infantry Division. The Army G-3 disapproved this because he believed that the 24th was needed on the front. On Aug. 6, Walker told one of MacArthur's staff officers that the 24th Division would have little combat value until it had been rehabilitated.

The following figures reflect just how bad matters were for this command. There were only six artillery batteries instead of twelve and they had no more than 35 guns. Other divisional shortages included 13 4.2" mortars, 68 3.5 inch rocket launchers, 103 BARs, 57 57mm recoilless rifles, 7 75mm recoilless rifles, 16 M-24 tanks, 335 1/4-ton trucks, 85 3/4-ton trucks, 81 2 1/2-ton trucks, 17 dump trucks, six 4 ton trucks, three repair trucks, 158 1/4- ton trailers and 105 1-ton trailers. The 19th Infantry was so deficient in trucks that 20 2 1/2- ton trucks were assigned to it.

COL Beauchamp established his CP at Yongsan, and the 34th began its defensive preparations late on Aug. 2. The 3d Battalion prepared, then improved, defensive positions, set up OPs and ran patrols along the east bank of the Naktong. Since no boats were available to the battalion, no patrols were sent across the river. D/3 Engineers laid some AP mines in front of K Co. and improved roads in the regimental sector. The artillery established OPs, registered its guns and prepared the artillery defensive fire plan. Regimental units received a small amount of new equipment.

To the north of the 34th, the 21st Infantry likewise dug in and improved its position between the Aug. 3 and 5. Having more engineer assets available, the regiment was able to emplace more AP obstacles at possible crossing points. Improvised booby traps, made from TNT, tin cans, nails, gas drums and artillery shells were used to supplement the mines and flares. The 21st had no boats either. Late on Aug. 5, however, Stephens obtained several boats from the 14th Engineers and the 3d Battalion was directed to send night patrols across the Naktong in them.

The 19th did not reach its assigned area until 8:30 p.m. on Aug. 4, and spent most of the next day in making lists of equipment shortages and receiving small amounts of material from division depots. In addition, the regiment conducted road reconnaissances throughout the division sector for counterattack plans.

Church deployed his division with the preponderance of his combat power in the center and north of the command's defensive sector, believing that the southern area was the easiest to defend and also believed that the main enemy thrust would be in the center or north. As a result, he had the weakest regiment positioned in the Bulge area, right where the enemy chose to attack. From the standpoint of the North Koreans, his deployment could not have been much better, for it facilitated their river crossing into the Bulge.

When MAJ McConnell combined his rifle companies, he appointed LT Floyd Gibson to command the combined Co. L/M. Gibson found that the combat elements of Co. M consisted of a sergeant first class and 17 other men. They were not then on the hill position which they were to occupy on the Naktong. He obtained a good breakfast for the men and orders from McConnell to return the men to their Naktong River positions. LT Gibson found that the positions were about a mile forward and the men were reluctant to return to what they believed was certain death; they had been severely bombarded by an enemy SP gun. He finally said, "Who goes with me, follow me." Gibson had only a vague idea of where the position was located. As he began walking, PFC Ben Knight spoke up. "I'll show you the way, lieutenant," he said. After "a long walk in the dark and a back-breaking climb," Floyd wrote, they reached the center of the L/M position. All 18 men were with him. It was one a.m.

At daylight, he relieved the Co. M commander, who was ordered to the battalion CP. "The men were in sorry shape," Gibson recalled, "worn boots, torn and worn fatigues, no shaves, all hungry." The combined company numbered 68 men, including Gibson and a (non-combat arms) lieutenant who joined the unit the next day. It was to defend 4,000 yards. Armament consisted of one heavy .30-cal machine gun, two A-6 light .30-cal machine guns, a 60mm mortar with nine rounds, one 3.5 inch rocket launcher with three rockets, four BARs and an 81mm mortar tube, but no baseplate. The men carried M-1 rifles, carbines or .45-cal pistols, but there were no hand grenades.

Gibson organized five outposts, placing the heavy machine gun on the right flank where he was told the Naktong was fordable, and the 60mm mortar behind his CP in the center of the position. Gibson moved the A-6 machine guns several times a day. He had the guns fire a few bursts in each position to give the impression to the enemy that there were more machine guns than there actually were. The 81mm mortar tube was located so that it could be rolled down a path against the enemy if they came that way. Large boulders also were positioned at the top of the hill, to be rolled down in the event of an enemy attack. "I was desperate," Gibson wrote.

He went to each outpost and told the men that "we were not leaving this position unless ordered to..." that "we would hold or die...."

It took two days to organize the position, he recalled. Then he called the mess sergeant in the rear CP and ordered that beginning the next day, the Mess Section would bring hot coffee, scrambled eggs, bread, butter and jam "and anything else eatable he could steal, scrounge, etc. and have it on the hill at 0800 hours." When the sergeant replied that he didn't think they could do that, Gibson said, "Get your steel pots, cartridge belts and two bandoleers of ammo for your M-1 rifles and report to me at 0800 hours, I can use seven more riflemen." He then instructed the supply sergeant that at 0800 hours the next day, he would have on the hill all the fatigues (field uniforms), boots, socks, foot powder, insect repellent and hand grenades he could find. When the supply sergeant reacted like the mess sergeant, Gibson ordered him, his clerk and the armorer artificer (the man responsible for simple weapons repairs) to report to him on the hill at 0800 hours, equipped like the mess section personnel.

Not surprisingly, the Mess Section came through with all the food LT Gibson had asked for, plus freshly made doughnuts. Supply brought everything requested, plus underwear and four cases of hand grenades. "My men...were amazed

and from that day on, I could do no wrong," Gibson wrote. From then on, the Mess Section brought C-rations forward every other day, augmented by hot coffee, bread and butter. On alternate days, they brought a hot meal.

"I have wanted to tell this story for a long time," Gibson wrote. "MSG Ben Light (Ret.) will vouch for it."

LT Planter M. Wilson was the XO of the 21st Infantry's HM Co. He recalled that the unit lost one platoon with TF Smith and another with 3/21 at Chochiwon. The remnants of the unit were placed on the line as infantry, covering several thousand yards of front on the Naktong just north of 3/34 Infantry. All they could do was form a series of outposts, Wilson recalled, each of from four to six men, widely scattered across the front. B/21st Infantry, he wrote, was behind HM Co. on "the first dominant terrain feature."

A quad-.50-cal half track was located "On the river bank right at the boundary" between the 21st and 34th. "I talked to the crew," Wilson wrote, "and had them move to where they could fire all along our front."

Co. K was between Co. M in the north along the Naktong and HM Co. in the south. LT Elmer J. Gainok, leader of King's Weapons Platoon, wrote that a road ran along the opposite bank between the Naktong and high ground farther west. His men, observing enemy troops and vehicles on this road, tried to hit the vehicles with 3.5 inch rockets, but the range was too far. The next day, he tried unsuccessfully to find a unit which would loan him a 57mm recoilless rifle. He had to use two 81mm mortars against the enemy instead.

"Just prior to dusk, " he wrote, "they (the enemy) felt they could move a truck convoy along this exposed section of road." But it was a clear shot for the 81s. "We hit one of the lead transports with troops with a direct hit [blocking the road].... We inflicted more casualties until we couldn't see the target and [then] continued harassing fire."

"There were only 11 men in my platoon," said James Jones, a rifle squad leader in Co. I, 34th Infantry. "We were given an area of responsibility [along the Naktong] that should have been covered by at least a company or more. We maintained contact with other units periodically by running two-man patrols."

Co. I closely watched the far shore "for any kind of movement." but most of the enemy activity was at night. "Even so," Jones continued," some mornings...we could see a change.... On one occasion the village across from us looked different. A couple of the houses had been slightly moved." A tank had "come through the back of the house to get a field of fire and hide at the same time.... But by using field glasses we could see their gun sticking out, even though [it was] covered with straw, etc." Due to a shortage of artillery ammunition, Jones recalled, they could not get artillery fire on the tanks, but did call in air one day. Jones recalled that the pilot flew so low that the men on the hill could look down on the pilot in his cockpit.

The unit did not receive much enemy artillery fire until one of the men decided to take off his shirt, exposing his T-shirt "and all hell broke loose," Jones said. "That was the last time that ever happened regardless of how hot it got." The

man didn't "relish the idea of getting shot by his own buddies."

Jones was sent on a patrol across the Naktong into enemy territory. The patrol found the narrowest point they could and started out across a wide, sandy beach to the water. "The farther we went the softer it got," said Jones. "I was in front and just before I reached the water my right leg was sucked up [in the sand] all the way to the crotch.... One of the men took hold of my rifle and pulled me out and that ended the mission."

"Gun positions in Korea, in the south in the summer, are very hard to find, wrote then 2d LT Ellsworth "Dutch" Nelsen, XO B/13 FAB. "Every bit of ground that is usable is...used — mostly for rice paddies." Occasionally, artillerymen could find a cotton or soybean field or schoolyard in which to establish a battery firing position. "But many times," Nelsen pointed out, "we simply had to drop trails and fire from the road bed itself."

When the battery went into position near Tugok, "there was a hard, dry road with a wide ditch on each side," Nelsen wrote. "I put the guns in one ditch and the 2 1/2-ton prime movers just behind them in the other ditch. Battalion commander LTC Stratten came by and said this was totally unacceptable since 'counterbattery fire' would knock out my cannons and trucks at the same time. He ordered me to put the trucks in a bamboo thicket about a half mile away. I argued that if the 'S' hit the fan, we might not be able to get the trucks back to the guns. But second lieutenants always lose arguments with lieutenant colonels, and the trucks were moved away."

On Aug. 5, a jeep and a half-track mounting a 40mm gun with no sights drove into Baker Battery's position. The men, probably from the 26th AA/AW Bn, gave the 40mm half-track to the battery and left in the jeep. Fortunately, two members of the battery knew how to load and fire the gun.

Also on or about Aug. 5, "Colonel Beauchamp came roaring into the battery [position] in a polished jeep," wrote "Dutch" Nelsen. "He had on starched and ironed fatigues." He asked Nelsen what the battery was using as a "base point," turning to exchange smiles with his driver as he asked the question. Nelsen replied that the battery was using the [Ohang] ferry. Beauchamp then asked how far the guns could fire. Nelsen told him 12,000 yards. Seizing a map from his driver, "Beauchamp did the 'split finger' measuring off of distance," Nelsen wrote. "He turned to me," Nelsen continued, "and said, 'You can't reach the ferry crossing from here!' I wanted to tell him we had been firing on it for two days, but the man was obviously an ass so what was the use. He flung the map back to his driver and standing up holding onto the windshield,... roared out of the battery in a frenzy of spinning wheels and clouds of dust. Very impressive! Very impressive indeed!" Nelsen concluded.

"My company numbered about 50 men," wrote then-PFC Leonard Korgie, Co. L, 34th Infantry. "Captain Douglas W. Syverson (the company commander) deployed my platoon of about 10 men right across from the [Ohang] Ferry — at ground level with the river in an area about 300 yards wide. Left and right of this [position] was high ground...."

"The physical condition of our platoon was terrible — as a result of fighting the holding actions, the heat, bloody dysentery, fatigue, malnutrition and lack of heavy weapons... Everybody knew the North Koreans were coming through the 10 of us in that river valley. It didn't take long. About dark the 10 of us were moved up closer to the water...as a listening post.... We were the first position hit in the penetration of the Bulge."

North Korean 4th Division — Aug. 3-5

The *4th Division* included the *4th, 16th* and *18th Infantry Regiments*, plus the usual artillery regiment, antitank and SP gun battalions and combat service support elements. The artillery regiment had one 122mm howitzer and two 76mm gun battalions. Authorized division strength was 10,381 including three 2,590-man infantry regiments. MG Lee Kwon Mu, a veteran of the Chinese Communist forces and former chief of staff of the NKPA, commanded the division. As it poised to attack across the Naktong into the 24th Division, the *NK 4th Division* numbered about 8,000 men, its artillery reduced to only 12 guns.

On Aug. 3, aerial observation and reports from the South Korean police indicated that the enemy was moving slowly but surely toward the Naktong. The 24th Division G-2 (Intelligence) Section believed the enemy capable of five different courses of action, ranging from attacks in different sectors to a continuation of their buildup. The G-2 selected the last as the most likely course to be taken.

Over the night of Aug. 3-4, however, the enemy became more active. Two patrols crossed the river near the right flank of the 21st early on the morning of Aug. 4, but retreated, one after being fired upon by members of the ROK 17th Infantry. Later in the day, small parties of the enemy were observed on the west bank of the Naktong opposite the juncture of the ROK 17th and U.S. 21st Infantry Regiments and at the nose of the salient in the 34th Infantry's sector. Aerial reconnaissance and air strikes claimed hundreds of enemy casualties. The G-2 stayed with his original estimate: The enemy was continuing his build-up. On Aug.

4, the *NK 4th Division* actually was concentrated near Hyopchon, intending to make what is known as a "hasty river crossing" — quickly, with little advance preparation.

At daylight on Aug. 5, aerial observers, artillery FOs and infantry OPs all reported movement of large bodies of enemy troops just behind the hills along the west bank of the Naktong, with the largest concentration opposite the ROK 17th. The number and size of enemy sightings were fewer opposite the 21st and fewer still opposite the 34th. These enemy concentrations were hit by artillery, but with limited results; the results of air strikes were never reported back to the 24th. The G-2 did not change his estimate of continued buildup; in his estimate, the likelihood of an enemy attack across the Naktong into the 34th was third on the list of possible actions.

The enemy continued its activity into the night of Aug. 5 without letup. Just before nightfall, 34th Infantrymen observed a party of people across the river stacking boxes of ammunition in a grove of trees. Several hours later, flares shot into the air from hills to the west. At 8:10 p.m., outposts on the right of the 21st Infantry line heard vehicles moving eastward toward the river. Thirty-five minutes later, they reported seeing large numbers of men moving in the same direction. A patrol from the 21st crossed the Naktong near midnight, landing near the boundary between the 21st and 34th Infantry and detecting sounds of enemy personnel in a nearby village and trucks moving near the river. Upon returning, the patrol called artillery in on the village, but since no one could observe the fire, results were unknown.

In spite of all this reported activity, the 24th displayed no sense of concern. The division was content to rest and re-equip itself as long as the enemy stayed on its side of the river. The water barrier presented by the Naktong lulled many of the 24th Division men into a false sense of security.

24th Division Sector, August 6, 1950

The *North Korean 4th Division* Assault Crossing of the Naktong — Midnight Aug. 5-6

With soft "pops" red and yellow flares burst eerily in the warm August night. It was one minute after midnight on Aug. 6. Eight hundred men of the *3d Battalion, 16th Infantry, NK 4th Division*, began crossing the Naktong River near the Ohang Ferry. There is some evidence that the regiment's *1st Battalion* also crossed that night. They brought no heavy weapons nor mortars. Many of the enemy soldiers used rafts which they had built earlier. Others simply waded across. A few drowned.

An enemy POW gave the strength of the entire *16th Infantry* as 2,300 men: *1st Bn*- 500; *2d Bn* - 300; *3d Bn* - 800; *Arty Bn* - 300; all other units - 200.

After crossing, the enemy dressed, formed into a column of platoons and moved stealthily through a draw leading into American lines. Their objective was Yongsan, about 8 miles inland. The first contact was recorded at 1:15 a.m. on Aug. 6.

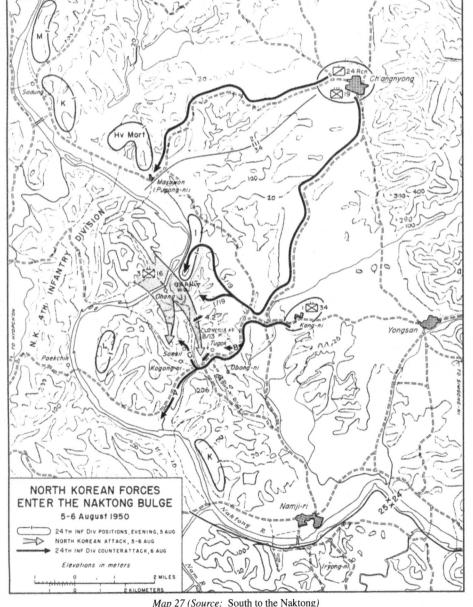

Map 27 (Source: South to the Naktong)

Right Flank, Co. L, 34th Infantry — 10:30 p.m. Aug. 5 to Approximately 2 a.m. Aug. 6

"CPL Ed Metkowski . . . and I heard small noises to our front about 10:30 p.m. [Aug. 6] but saw nothing," Korgie wrote. "We were right at the apex of the Bulge. Frank Pollock and Eugene Singleton on our left were also awake and mumbling. Alvin Ginn was readying his M-1 on our right. We opened fire. The shots set off what sounded like a rush of North Koreans from [our] rear and sides. They jumped all over us from the rear and sides and wrestled the weapons from us as we fired. They pushed Metkowski and me into our foxhole." Once the enemy soldiers had taken the Americans' weapons, they tried to take prisoners. "Nobody said anything. The North Koreans were obviously taking prisoners to get information. I was captured alive — something I dreaded worse than death itself. I knew I would never survive POW camp. I recalled the lieutenant at Ft. Riley told us, 'If you're going to escape, go at the earliest opportunity. The longer you wait, the tougher it'll be.'

"I threw my helmet right into them and yelled, 'Let's go, Ed!' We jumped from the hole right into them. I thought the North Koreans would burp gun me. I broke and ran through the weeds to the platoon CP. The North Koreans obviously followed me cautiously. They must have grabbed Ed.

"The platoon sergeant, MSG Brown, was on the phone calling for mortars. We heard a burst from Smitty's BAR followed by a blood-curdling scream." An enemy soldier had grappled Smitty for his BAR. The North Korean grabbed the barrel and Smitty the stock. "Smitty pulled the trigger and shot the gook in the crotch — hence the scream," Korgie wrote. "Now the North Koreans were coming across the Naktong noisily and shooting flares. The sergeant gave me his M-1 and pulled out his .45."

Figures were running up the hill toward the two men. As Korgie yelled "Halt!" about 15 enemy soldiers jumped up about 40 yards away, yelling "Manzai! Manzai!" and spraying the area with burp gun fire. Brown and Korgie fired into them. When his rifle was empty, Korgie began to withdraw while fumbling for another clip of ammunition. As he ran, he noted that he was running parallel to a group of enemy soldiers advancing in a skirmish line. He knew they were North Koreans, but they thought he was one of them. "It was comical — I think I was nervously laughing," he remembered. After running up and down three hills, Korgie collapsed at the top of the third succumbing to fatigue, bloody dysentery and heat, pitching head-first over the hill and rolling about 40 yards down the slope. About then, the enemy realized who he was and some sniped at him and began calling one another. He finally managed to reload his rifle, figuring he would kill as many of the enemy as he could before they killed him. "Strangely, they left," he recounted.

Of the 10 men in Korgie's platoon when the enemy attacked, four were lost: CPL Ed Metkowski was captured and died of malnutrition as a POW February 1951; corporals John A. Kerns and Robert D. Malkiewicz and PFC Alver H. Ginn were killed in action

"I was with a machine gun on the extreme right of L Company (1st Platoon)," wrote Robert Bayless. "There was still a gap of about a mile between us and the extreme left of 'Item' Company.... The [enemy] thrust across [the Naktong] at the Ohang Ferry caught the bulk of L Company cut off." Once across the river, the enemy had swung in behind Co. L. "Lieutenant Wheatly led us upriver to join forces with 'Item' Company," Bayless continued.

His group wandered into the sector of the 21st Infantry. As he and his comrades fell, exhausted, into a roadside ditch, Bayless dozed off. "I was awakened by a marching column coming up the road," he wrote. He identified them as the 24th Reconnaissance Co., enroute to counterattack along the southern flank of the 21st Infantry. Bayless joined the column and began calling the names of men from his company. When they discovered he was trying to find L/34 Infantry, recon men told him to follow the road back to the 34th CP in Yongsan. Tired, hungry "and totally disoriented," he recalled, Bayless started back. A field-grade officer in a jeep gave him a lift to the CP. There, he was told that he couldn't get back to Co. L "unless I knew how to parachute." What was left of Co. L was now in enemy territory. He was given some beef stew and a slice of bread — the first food he had in 48 hours. "Emotionally strapped," he wrote, " I allowed myself the luxury of a few tears...." He realized "that an entity with heart and soul and spirit...by the name of 'L' Co., 34th Inf. was out in those hills, and I could not find them." In short, Bayless had lost his "home," and all his close friends — his "brothers."

Bayless was given permission to go find his unit. Luckily, he came upon Ralph H. Owen, a friend from Co. I, who had been to the aid station for treatment and now also was trying to get back to his company. After getting a ride on a commo jeep as far as Co. A, the two men stayed there the night. Early the next morning, they arrived in Co. B's area, and asked company commander CPT Johnson to pick them up on his morning report. The captain, short of personnel, was happy to accommodate them. Both men were "quite relieved to be finally accounted for," as Bayless put it, and believed this was about Aug. 7. He served with Co. B as a rifleman and 60mm mortar crewman.

Once across the Naktong, the enemy brushed aside the right flank of L/34 Infantry, passed southeast down the valley to the rear of the company's position and headed for the road between the Naktong and Yongsan. In their path about 2 miles from the crossing site was the 3/34 Inf. CP and 4.2 inch mortar position at Kogon-ni, and B/13 FAB, near Tugok. *Counterattack on the Naktong* refers to Kogon-ni as "Kogono-ni."

At 2 a.m. on Aug. 6, the 34th reported to 24th Division that the enemy had penetrated between companies I and L. Artillery batteries in the regimental sector were warned to be alert for infiltrators. At 2:05 a.m., the Regimental S-3 notified division headquarters that increased firing had convinced him that an attack was in progress.

About 3 a.m., the enemy attacked the 4.2 inch mortar position, alerting the nearby infantry battalion CP. LTC Perez, with his command group and some mortarmen, made good their escape. Around 3:30 a.m., Perez arrived at the 1st Bat-

talion CP, 4 miles to the rear along the road at Kang-ni. He quickly informed LTC Ayres of the situation as he knew it. This was news to Ayres, but no one bothered to inform the regimental commander of what had happened. As a result, at 4:30 a.m. the 34th simply reported that from 30 to 80 enemy soldiers had crossed the river, engaged Co. I briefly in a firefight, then had withdrawn back across the river.

Battery B, 13 FAB — Dawn to 10:30 A.M, August 6

Once the enemy drove off the 4.2 inch mortar unit and Perez's CP, they continued on down the valley and slammed into Battery B, 13 FAB. "Right after first light," wrote Dutch Nelsen, "we were attacked by about 200 North Koreans. Their first fire...was machine gun which perfectly enfiladed the row of howitzers and drove off the cannoneers. Immediately thereafter 82mm mortars began to fall. The first one took out my aiming circle, and the second hit my fire direction center [killing] FDC Sergeant David O. White and [taking] the left arm off Gunnery Officer 2LT Sam Hoover."

At the same time, other enemy troops attacked the truck park in the bamboo thicket from three sides. "A few men tried to get back to the battery position," he wrote, "by running across a stretch of rice paddies. None made it."

The battery had five howitzers, but only four were in firing condition. The fifth was hitched to a prime mover, ready to be sent to the rear for repair.

The battery fought off the enemy for two hours, Nelsen wrote. The shooting at the motor park shifted to the main battery position, indicating that the men there were lost. "Any hope of getting the guns out was also lost," he continued. "The firing...was now coming from three sides." The only route open was the road behind the guns. Although he did not know where this road led, LT Nelsen knew it was the only way out.

"I sent any and all trucks that would still run down this road," he recalled, "and led the men on foot." Almost at once, they were under machine gun and rifle fire, forcing the men into the rice paddies and onto their stomachs to crawl out. Most of the men made it, either then or over the next few days. Appleman writes that the BC assembled about 50 men about 10:30 a.m. and withdrew over the road with one howitzer, four 2 1/2-ton trucks and three smaller trucks. Four howitzers and nine vehicles were left behind. He gives the casualties as 2 KIA, 6 WIA and 6 MIA. Nelsen believed that more howitzers could have been withdrawn had the prime movers been closer to the gun positions.

Ellsworth Nelsen concluded by writing: "We gave everything we had, and if they had been lesser men none of us would have made it at all. I am proud of my men and what they did that day."

34th Regiment Reacts — Morning, Aug. 6

Finally, regimental headquarters obtained more definitive information. At 5:20 a.m., Beauchamp reported to Church: "Enemy are across river in force in center of my sector. It's pretty dark and situation is obscure. I am committing my reserve [1st Bn] at daylight to clear up the situation. Get me a liaison plane in the air at dawn." The division G-3 duty officer notified the G-3, arranged for the liaison plane and requested Eighth Army's Air Operations Center to provide air strikes at dawn. The 19th, 21st and ROK 17th Regiments and division artillery were all notified of the situation and projected counter actions by 5:45 a.m. At 6 a.m., 2/19 Infantry was alerted, and at 8:35 was ordered to support the 34th Infantry. While these events were transpiring with elements of L/34 Inf., K and HM/21st Inf. and B/13 FAB, the 1/34 Inf., 2/19 Inf and the 24th Recon Co. were moving up to counterattack.

The 1st Bn, 34th Infantry Moves to Counterattack — Morning, Aug. 6

Arriving at the CP of 1/34 Inf, LTC Perez woke LTC Ayres and gave him the news. Perez was amazed when Ayres went ahead and had breakfast. It seemed fairly obvious that what he had reported was not entirely believed. Perez later said that he was regarded as "a newcomer [to combat], scared, and just bugging out." But Beauchamp had been informed. He later told Perez that they had been watching him "like a hawk"; if his report had proven to be false, Gines would have been summarily removed as battalion commander. Once Ayres received the counterattack order at his CP in Kang-ni, he had his battalion XO, CPT Leroy Osburn (former A Co. CO) mount Co. C (CPT Clyde Akridge) on the battalion's five trucks with orders to drive toward the Yongsan-Naktong until he, Ayres, stopped them. A, B and Weapons companies were to follow on foot, under CPT Osburn's command. The entire battalion contained only 20 officers and 471 EM when it moved out for this counterattack — a half-strength battalion.

SFC Robert Moser, Co. B, recalled that his unit was in reserve at the time in the village of Yu-ri, just south of Kang-ni, where the battalion CP was located. While there, the men were able to shower and clean clothing. The battalion also received 187 replacements. Robert remembered that two of them for his platoon were "black volunteers. This was the first we were integrated," he wrote. There were a number of instances where integration commenced, unheralded, in several Army units before the 24th Infantry was officially dissolved and integration began with some fanfare. Generally, black soldiers who were assigned to white units during this early "quiet" integration were accepted without problem. They were judged, as other men in the unit, in their ability as soldiers, not by skin color.

While at the aid station to receive dysentery medication, Moser met an old friend, SFC Slaick, who he had served with before in F/31 Infantry. The two men were talking when the orders came for Co. C to board trucks and head west.

Although the battalion had received replacements, unit rifleman Robert Witzig remembered that Co. C had only "about 100 men or less" when they were trucked forward that day moving by 7 a.m.

LTC Ayres, with his S-3 and Assistant S-3,

preceded Co. C in a jeep, to reconnoiter and determine the situation. They drove through the Battery B position and on to the deserted 3d Battalion CP without encountering any enemy. Here, Ayres stopped to reconnoiter. Just as the trucks carrying Co. C arrived, Ayres and his party were fired on from the hills above them.

The trucks stopped and the men hurriedly dismounted. This sudden attack temporarily caused some confusion. "We came into a valley with hills on all sides, both front and rear," wrote Robert Witzig, "and came under heavy attack.... The small arms fire was massive and as we had no cover except a creek bed and a small grist house, we were suffering enormous casualties as we were totally surrounded."

Ayres quickly went to CPT Akridge, who had commanded the company only a few days, and ordered him to attack and seize the high ground overlooking the former 3d Battalion CP. Ayres took position in a culvert, from where he could direct the fire of the company's 60mm mortars. LTC Ayres said that he was pinned down under a bridge and that they were able to "puff some rounds from" a 60mm mortar.

"We...set up a 60mm mortar in the creek bed," Witzig recounted, "but my assistant gunner stood up to see where the shells were landing and was killed almost instantly. I used [the] mortar ammunition we had then helped drag some wounded over to a small bridge where we were putting some wounded." His platoon leader, 1LT McDonald Martin, was shot in the stomach. Other men nearby were also hit.

CPT Akridge was wounded three times and the attack bogged down. (He was successfully evacuated.) Ayres realized that the remainder of his battalion was needed as quickly as possible. Having no radio communications, he had to return himself to bring the command forward. Accompanied by several staff members, he made a dash across the paddy. "I had never heard a bullet hit water," he said later. "It was a weird sound.... We ran about 100 yards across the paddy," coming to a deep little stream. They jumped in and made their way to the other side. MAJ Curtis Cooper, Battalion S-3, was shot in the hand and the S-2, 3/34 Infantry, struck in the arm in making the escape. But the party reached the foot of Obong-ni Ridge and around the now abandoned artillery position. The remainder of Ayres' battalion was two miles behind Co. C and it took Ayres several hours to return to it.

Right after Ayres left the culvert, 1LT Charles E. Payne (Asst Bn S-3) and the wounded LT Martin also made a dash from the under the bridge and into a grist mill near at hand. By that time, enemy fire had strewn the creek bed with the dead and dying men of Co. C. Over half the company were cut down in this hail of gunfire. The survivors ran into the grist mill, joining Payne and Martin. The grist mill and the artillery positions were in valley flat areas occupied by farmer's homes and by rice paddies and other cultivated areas.

Defending the Grist Mill, Co. C, 34th Infantry — August 6

Men, wounded and unwounded, made their way to the grist mill, where they determined to make a last stand. The defenders also used the

.50-cal machine gun on an abandoned personnel carrier to hold off the enemy. "At time they would get within grenade range but with the carrier we were doing OK," Witzig wrote, "even though we continued getting casualties. This horrible fight went on for several hours." LT Payne finally asked for volunteers to go for help. SGT Carmichael and Witzig volunteered, even though anyone who had tried to leave had been shot by the enemy as soon as they left the grist mill.

"SGT Carmichael started to go but all hell broke loose," Witzig continued, "and we came under intense small arms fire. I told Carmichael to get going, but he refused and went back into the grist mill." Witzig headed for a field about twenty or thirty yards away and started crawling in its furrows. "I probably got about 20 yards and was blown up into the air and landed on my back. I had been shot three times in various areas of my back." His web belt was blown apart and he was knocked unconscious. Coming to, "I looked up and there was a Korean trying to take my grenades." Witzig killed him with his .45 automatic pistol.

The enemy then opened fire again on the field and Witzig. "All at once my helmet flew and I felt pain on the left side of my head." Witzig recounted. "[I] thought my brains were coming out because I had blood and particles of flesh on my hands." Then he realized this the blood and flesh were on his hands were from the back wounds he had patched up with his aid packet. Retrieving his helmet, he discovered the whole right side of it was blown away. "It also dawned on me I couldn't be shot in the head or I'd be dead." Witzig remained lying in the field for some time, until he heard someone calling from the grist mill that someone had gotten through and the 3d Battalion was on the way. Hearing this, Witzig stood up and "yelled that I was a GI."

Two of his best friends, Corporals John Nearhood and Harold Tucker, braving intense enemy fire, came out and dragged Witzig back to the dubious shelter of the grist mill. By this time, the mill was filled with dead and wounded men. They were "all over the place," Witzig recalled. The dead were piled along the walls to protect the living. Every man who could handle a weapon helped to stop enemy attacks, which often came to within grenade range. The beleaguered men held out, crawling about on the floor to find ammunition for their guns. The .50-caliber machine gun on the carrier burned out from firing. Witzig guessed there were only about 15 men left alive in the grist mill, which was lashed by enemy small-arms and automatic weapons fire. After several more hours, LT Payne called for a volunteer to go up the creek bed to cover a breakout. CPL Nearhood went out, but was quickly killed trying to get over a fence.

Companies A and B, 34th Infantry Make their Attack — Aug. 6

While LTC Ayres and Co. C moved forward by vehicle, the remainder of the battalion started out on foot. It did not get very far before it, too, was engaged by the enemy.

"I deployed the battalion with B Company (CPT Raymond Johnson) on the right of the road and A Company on the left," Osburn wrote. "Enemy resistance was heavy but we managed to slowly advance forward. Two .50-cal AA half tracks led the advance. "Some time...I received word that COL Ayres and C Company had been cut off and was now in the trap with the 3d Bn."

Co. A attacked over low ground, while Co. B, some 200-300 yards to its left, moved over a series of low hills in its attack.

Robert Moser, of Co. B, recalled that the unit formed a skirmish line when the company deployed with his 3d Platoon was on the left of the line. There was no company reserve. "B Company moved up to the crest of the hill and engaged in a firefight," he wrote. The company suffered a few casualties but killed 10 of the enemy.

Meantime, COL Beauchamp had sent two M-24 tanks to help the battalion, and came forward himself. Moser met him on the hill and directed the colonel to the unit CP. About this time LTC Ayres made it back to the battalion. It was early afternoon. Soon after meeting Beauchamp, Moser was summoned to the CP and ordered to attack the ridge to his front with his 15-man platoon. The direction of attack separated the platoon from the rest of the company. Moser was ordered to support the two tanks. Osburn pointed out in his narrative that the addition of the two tanks speeded up the battalion's advance.

"I boarded the lead tank and manned the .50-cal machine gun on the turret," Moser wrote. "SSG Brennon followed behind the tanks with the remainder of the platoon." As the little column rounded a sharp curve, enemy small-arms and antitank fire crashed into it. At that point on the road, there was a small hill on the right and a steep drop off to a valley on the left, Moser recalled. Across the valley was Obong-ni Ridge. SSG Brennon and three other men of Moser's platoon were hit.

Co. A on the left of the road, and B on the right, engaged the enemy on Cloverleaf Hill, supported by two quad-.50 AA vehicles. One of the quad-.50s was knocked out. Co. B's attack stalled, but CPT Albert F. Alfonso's A Co., led by one of the tanks, continued its advance with only a few casualties. At the abandoned artillery position, Alfonso searched for survivors. "I had the [artillery] ammunition gathered up from the...site," Osburn wrote, "and removed the breech-blocks (actually breech-locks) from the guns." Osburn then climbed onto the rear of the lead tank and pointed out targets to the tank commander. "Upon jumping from the rear of the tank I was hit by automatic fire — twice through the right lung and twice in the right arm."

Relief of the Grist Mill — Late August 6

Upon reaching the grist mill area, the lead tank fired one round into the mill, decapitating SFC Carmichael, mortally wounded two and less severely injuring several members of Co. C inside and knocked LT Payne unconscious. The tank and men from Co. A then charged the mill. Then they discovered that the survivors of Co. C were inside — about 35 men. The dead and wounded were loaded on some abandoned but still operable 2 1/2-ton trucks. Robert Moser's friend, SFC Sliack, was among the dead. When

he was thrown on a truck, Payne regained consciousness long enough to hear a man say, "Payne is as dead as a mackerel." With a driver and two riflemen on each truck, the vehicles started back through enemy gunfire.

The wounded Robert Witzig was also put on one of the trucks. He remembered that enemy fire on the vehicles was heavy. "The driver got shot," he wrote, "and we turned over in a rice paddy. That was the last I remember 'till I came to in an aid station." Payne's truck also ended up in a ditch. He was able to crawl and walk out to safety.

The bulk of Co. B was unable to join Co. A in the advance. It was still fighting the enemy back at Cloverleaf Hill. There it would dig in for the night. Some men from B/13 FAB returned to the artillery position and recovered two more howitzers and some trucks before being driven away by enemy fire.

Once the dead and wounded from Co. C had been loaded on trucks and sent to the rear, CPT Alfonso's company, along with what was left of Moser's B Co. platoon and a few men from Co. C, continued the attack toward the river. (How Moser and his men came to be with Co. A is somewhat of a mystery. However, Moser's platoon had been ordered to accompany the tanks. One of the tanks stayed with Alfonso's company when it continued the attack after relieving the grist mill. Quite likely, Moser and some of his men were with that tank. However, Alfonso does not remember ever seeing or meeting SGT Moser and was unaware that this small Co. B contingent was with his company.) Co. A met heavy enemy resistance. Alfonso employed 60mm mortars against the enemy, and his troops moved forward. "As we moved we fired right and left alongside the road," Moser wrote. Just after sunset, the Co. A column entered the perimeter of Co. L, on a low hill surrounded by rice paddies and some 700 to 1,000 yards east of the Naktong but south of the Yongsan road. Alfonso sent the tank to the rear. He felt that providing security for it at night would be difficult and that it could safely "barrel down the Yongsan road without too much probability of meeting any anti-armor resistance...."

All the troops on the L Company position were attached to Co. A. This included Co. L, the few men of Co. B with SGT Moser, and one or two others, such as Stewart Sizemore, who had been attached from Co. D to Co. C. How he came to be with Alfonso's men is another mystery.

Moser recalled that L was on a small hill next to the road. He had been wounded. The bullet had entered his right cheekbone at eye level, also penetrating his right ear. There was no way to be evacuated, so he dug in with the combined force. This composite unit numbered only about 90 men, so they dug in a tight perimeter in the darkness. Fortunately, Alfonso could communicate with the 1st Battalion CP with his SCR 300 radio, relayed through Co. B ("when I could get through," he wrote). An artillery FO with Co. L provided much needed radio communication for artillery support. "This AM radio was a godsend," Alfonso wrote, "because it provided...reliable communications through artillery channels.... "That evening...I forwarded a request for an aerial resupply the following

morning for... ammunition, medical supplies, rations, water and radio batteries."

Company I and Other Elements Withdraw to the North — 10:30 a.m., Aug. 6.

As the 1st Battalion counterattacked, the 34 Regiment's right flank collapsed, but not from enemy pressure. Hearing the gunfire of fighting moving to the unit's left and rear, the lieutenant commanding Co. I, believing the unit was cut off, led the unit into the sector of the 21st Infantry about 10:30 a.m. He apparently did not attempt to reach higher headquarters for orders. Men from the 34th Regiment's HM Co., M Co. (Heavy Weapons) and A/26 AA/AW joined this exodus. The 21st HM Co., on the southern flank of that regiment, reported the incident to regimental headquarters. The 21st passed this information on to division at 10:55 a.m. Of course, division had been unaware of this unauthorized withdrawal. At 11:10 a.m., the 21st reported that the enemy was occupying I Company's old position. GEN Church was upset and concerned. The valley behind Co. I led to a road which went directly to the division command post at Changnyong. He immediately ordered COL Beauchamp to do whatever was necessary to restore the I Company position and to relieve the officers responsible for the withdrawal. Church authorized COL Stephens to direct artillery fire at the enemy troops on those positions. Beauchamp sent his XO, LTC Wadlington, to the scene. At 11:50 a.m., Church also sent the 24th Recon Co. down the road from the Division CP area to help Co. I restore their position. The composite security and defense platoons at division headquarters quickly manned a defensive perimeter. In the interim, Co. I had withdrawn some two miles and close to one of the 21st Regiment's reserve companies. There, some of the I Co. men reported having faced several thousand North Koreans.

2/19th Infantry Prepares to Attack — Late Morning, Aug. 6

Meantime, 2/19 Infantry departed from is location on the Changnyong-Yongsan road by truck at 10 a.m. It reached its Yu-ri assembly area, five miles away, about 11 a.m. Within ten minutes thereafter, Church ordered COL Moore (CO of the 19th) to "get up there and clean out the enemy. I'll send your other battalion to you." Concurrently, he directed 1/19 Infantry to move from its position northwest of Changnyong and proceed to Yu-ri . The battalion took two hours to make the eleven mile trip by truck. So, before noon on the 6th, the 1st battalion, 34th was actually counterattacking, 2/19 Inf. and the 24th Recon were enroute to counterattack, and 1/19 Infantry was poised to assist, as needed.

Counterattack of 24th Recon. Company and I/34th Infantry — 3 p.m. - Dusk, Aug. 6

The 24th Recon Company organized its cooks and mechanics into an extra platoon and set off from Changnyong just before noon. Encountering no enemy, the unit reached the Naktong about 1 p.m. The Recon CO contacted the I Co. commander and then developed a plan to retake Co. I's lost position. The unit, reinforced by the infantry elements from Recon. and supported by that unit's tanks, began an attack about 3 p.m. They attained the first hill without difficulty, but once over its slope, they were heavily engaged by automatic weapons and mortar fire from the next hill to the south. Artillery was called in on that promontory while Co. I withdrew back to the supporting tank position. Men of the company reported being "surrounded" by up to 4,000 of the enemy. But the commander of the 21st Infantry's HM Co., observing the action, estimated the enemy as about 150 men. With this failure, the commander of the Recon Co. pulled both units back to high ground near the road and dug in for the night.

Counterattack By 2/19th Infantry — 3 p.m. - Dusk, August 6

By 3 p.m., LTC Thomas McGrail's 2/19 Infantry had moved to a line of departure northeast of Sangnigok. The mission of the battalion was to restore the southern half of the old Co. I positions. About 4 p.m. the battalion set off slowly to the west toward Hill 146, about a mile west of Sangnigok. Once Hill 146 was taken, the battalion was to turn north and seize Hill 174 a mile from 146. Having taken Hill 174, the command was to turn west again and secure the hills overlooking the river. The rough terrain and terrible heat of August made McGrail's assignment pretty ambitious. Although the enemy offered little resistance, it did further delay the advance. COL Moore held LTC Rhea's 1st Battalion in reserve pending the outcome of McGrail's advance.

2/19 Infantry pressed forward late on the 6th and reached its first objective, Hill 146 by 5:15 p.m. Co. F was dropped off and the remainder of the battalion turned north toward the second objective, Hill 174. That hill was seized by Companies E and G by 7 p.m. LTC McGrail estimated that some 300 enemy soldiers were caught in the village of Chongdan, between the two hills. Believing his battalion too weak to attack the town, he called down heavy mortar and automatic weapons fire on it until darkness. The enemy withdrew, but their destruction was reported to division.

Counterattack By 1/19th Infantry — 6 p.m. - Dusk, August 6

The original plan was for 1/19th Infantry to follow 2/19th to Hill 146, then turn south to sweep through the Naktong Bulge. COL Moore had the 1st Battalion available to him since 1 p.m., but did not commit it to battle until 6 p.m. At that point, only three hours of daylight remained. As a result, too little time remained for the 1st Battalion to more than begin to execute what would have been an ambitious plan under the best of circumstances. This destroyed any

hope that Church had of restoring the front before dark.

The 1st Battalion moved out to the west with Co. C on the left and Co. B on the right. A was in reserve. Elements of Co. B attained Hill 146 without problem, then its 2d Platoon received enemy fire from Hill 165 to the south. Enemy fire from this hill, repulsed Co. C. With darkness approaching, LTC Rhea established a battalion perimeter near Hill 146 and established communications with 2/19th Infantry to the north and B/34th Infantry at Cloverleaf. This ended counterattacks that day in the 34th's sector.

Korgie from L/34 had joined about 40 other men from the 34th along the river bank. This group had not been attacked. The unit prepared to make what Korgie called a "Custer's Last Stand." "Damn that was exciting!" he recalled. Instead, the Battalion XO, MAJ David Rosen, pulled the unit off the hill.

Korgie wrote a vivid account of one of the counterattacks in the 34th Regimental sector that day. The men were ordered by MAJ Rosen to counterattack a village, which, in Korgie's words was "heavily wooded and infested with heavily camouflaged North Koreans." Korgie wrote that the lieutenant refused to lead the attack, saying, "These guys are in no physical condition to attack." The officer was replaced and the group seized the village.

"Then the North Koreans opened up from everywhere. Guys were being hit and dirt was kicking up all over," Korgie recounted. The enemy were hidden in the trees. "Then CPL Benedict Ales...saved our butts and got most of us out alive," he continued. "We called him 'Water-Cooled.' He took his water-cooled .30-cal machine gun crew to an exposed, open rice paddy and started working over the trees. The North Koreans rimmed him with fire. The camouflaged [enemy soldiers] started dropping out of the trees as he yelled at 'em, 'Water-Cool's gonna get you gooks!' He silenced them, then Major Rosen had us withdraw — we were so outnumbered.... But we knocked the North Korean attack off balance and caused them a lot of confusion." CPL Ales never received any recognition for his daring, brave action. As Korgie pointed out, "The situation was so fluid and chaotic the next few weeks nobody had time to write him up for an award."

PFC Edgar (Sinnett) Pawelski, of D/34th Infantry also related an incident that took place during one of the counterattacks on the Naktong. They had "set up [their] mortars in a small village," he wrote, "but the GI in charge of the air panels had left them behind when we jumped off that morning." As a result friendly "planes started to strafe us. Their napalm had been used up in another attack before us. One of my buddies who I had raised hell with in Japan, James Mason, caught a 20mm round [from one of the planes] in the stomach up with one of the rifle companies." After working over the U.S. infantry-held ridge, the planes turned on the mortar position in the village. "We tore up C-ration cartons and made a panel from them. As they [the airplanes] came in for another run they saw the panel, dipped their wings and went away."

The ROK 17th Infantry Sector — Aug. 6

About two squads of enemy soldiers crossed the Naktong in the ROK sector, but were quickly and decisively dealt with. However, Eighth Army had already determined that the ROK 17th Infantry would be withdrawn from the 24th Division sector. It had been scheduled to depart on Aug. 6. The enemy's major attack against the division delayed the move by one day. So, in the midst of trying to cope with a major penetration of his defenses in the 34th Infantry's sector, GEN Church was forced to create a composite force to replace the ROKs. He formed TF Hyzer, commanded by the LTC Peter C. Hyzer (West Point, 1937). Three companies of Hyzer's own 3d ECB, A/ 78th Hvy Tk Bn, and later, the 24th Recon Co. made up the force. In all, it numbered about 800 men, who were lost to the division's already critically low reserve.

The Enemy Attacks 21st Infantry — Aug. 6

The enemy also tried to cross the Naktong in the 21st Regiment's sector, but were driven back. In the HM Co. area, LT Wilson wrote that the unit's outposts were knocked out in about fifteen minutes by artillery fire, but that the enemy crossed the river "against the poor old worn-out 34th Infantry" to the south.

The village of Sadung lay on the east bank of the Naktong, squarely on the boundary between M Co. on high ground and Co. K on a ridge to the south. About 10 a.m. on Aug. 6, a party of South Korean police went to the village to evacuate any remaining civilians. They were met by a large body of enemy soldiers who were hiding there. They had crossed the river undetected during the night. The South Koreans were driven from Sadung. The enemy then fired on a nearby squad of Co. K. The battalion XO called for mortar and machine gun fire on the village. Unfortunately, his request was delayed due to communications problems. During the afternoon, more North Koreans attempted to cross the river and join the force already in Sadung. Floating their equipment across on rafts, most of them were successful. Others were killed by American fire from the nearby hill positions.

The artillery which finally was brought to bear on Sadung in midafternoon had little effect. About 4 p.m. about 50 North Koreans attacked King Co.'s right flank. At 4:30 p.m., COL Stephens, hoping to wipe out the enemy in and near Sadung before dark, ordered LTC Smith to do the job. Counterattack plans had been prepared, yet it took A/21st infantry several hours to get into position. In this time interval, the enemy began infiltrating to the east through a draw leading into the rear of Co. M. Artillery fire was called in to discourage the enemy. A South Korean policeman managed to escape during one of the artillery barrages and reported at least 150 enemy soldiers in Sadung.

At 7 p.m., Co. A launched its counterattack. The enemy put up a spirited defense and U.S. artillery was less effective because of continuing communications difficulties. In spite of these problems, the company drove the enemy back into Sadung. As night fell the unit even gained a foothold in the north end of the town and held on through the night.

LT Gainok gave an account of the enemy's action against his unit. When they crossed into K's area, "we took the enemy under fire on our platoon high ground and they slipped round us," he wrote. "I lost communication with my C.O. Later found out that my battalion pulled back to new positions. Out of contact, my platoon stayed in place." He sent two messengers to the company commander. Neither got through. At dawn, armed with his M-1 rifle, LT Gainok followed telephone wires back to the K Co. CP. He found it deserted. "I continued down the road," wrote Gainok, "and met the Battalion moving back into their original positions. I had a few unkindly words for the Battalion S-3 leading the column and returned to my platoon area, just a bit angry."

Summary of Action, Aug. 6

The enemy thrust just after midnight on Aug. 6 quickly drove deep into 3/34th Infantry's rear areas and drove the commander from his CP. In effect, at that point, he lost command of his battalion. His principal contribution to subsequent defensive actions was alerting LTC Ayres to the situation. His battalion passed the bad news on to division. The counterattacks made to drive the enemy back and restore the line were made piecemeal, and some were tardy in getting started.

GEN Church was very disappointed with the results of the counterattacks. The enemy had not been destroyed. With the commitment of the 3d Engr Bn and A/78th Hvy Tk Bn to TF Hyzer in the ROK 17th Infantry sector, Church had no more reserves of his own. TF Hyzer took over the ROK regiment's sector on Aug. 7.

The lack of timely, coordinated counterattacks was partly due to the very confusing situation. Little was known of the enemy's whereabouts or strength. Further, it was very hot, the terrain was rugged and the 24th Division was in poor condition after the battering it had taken over the previous month.

To help offset the loss of the engineer battalion and tank company as a division reserve, Eighth Army gave Church the newly-arrived 1/9th Infantry and a battery of the 15 FAB (both of the 2d Division). Both commands arrived in the division sector the evening of Aug. 6. The infantry assembled at Changnyong as division reserve and the artillery battery went into firing position west of Yongsan in support of the 19th Infantry.

24th Division Sector, August 7

The North Koreans reinforced their forces on the east bank of the Naktong overnight. The following morning, GEN Church had no option but to continue counterattacking with the units he had used the previous day.

The 34th Regiment — Aug. 7

The 34th Regiment, however, had little to contribute. What remained of companies A, C and L, under CPT Alfonso, held a small perimeter at the nose of the Bulge overlooking the Naktong. However, enemy troops in the area kept them in place. The combined force had to be resupplied by airdrop. The mission dropped badly needed food, water and ammunition, but about half of the bundles landed outside the perimeter. A number of men were wounded dashing out trying to retrieve some of these supplies. The perimeter was maintained, however, as was that of Co. K, about a thousand yards to the southwest.

B/34th Infantry was ordered to attack east from its position near Tugok along the road to Alfonso's position. The 19th was also to attack. The troops were near exhaustion, the heat and high humidity were enervating and the troops lacked both food and water. The attacks were largely failures. Co. B did rescue a few men from the HM Co., but then fell back in the face of heavy enemy resistance. Co. I did manage to regain the northern end of its former position about 1 p.m., supported by the tanks of the Recon. Co. At 2 p.m. Co. I made contact with a platoon of G/19th Infantry attacking from the south. The two units formed a perimeter for the night. At day's end, the 34th numbered 1,090 troops and was at 30 per cent effectiveness.

SSG James A. Jones, of Co. I, was in this counterattack. MSG Henderson was his platoon sergeant. He recalled that Co. I had not been driven from the hill; they had left it. The enemy moved in and seized the position. The attack went over the same route the unit had used in withdrawing. "We took the first part of our objective," Jones said, "and got pinned down with mostly artillery fire. They were really laying it down...." Jones, in his haste, dug into the side of a Korean grave on top of the hill. "I dug in pretty deep," he recounted, "and could smell him good (the Korean buried in the grave) [but] I thank him for possibly saving my life. We continued on and took the rest of our objective and tied in with a battalion of the 19th Regiment. My platoon was on the next hill from them [Ohang Hill] on the right facing north.... This was also about the time I was promoted to SFC."

19th Infantry's Counterattacks — Aug. 7

The 19th's 1st Battalion was to attack west and south in order to establish an anchor on the river and reduce the enemy's bulge space. Simultaneously, 2/19th was to attack west and north toward the river and link up with L/34th Infantry. Essentially, this was a continuation of the previous day's attacks. Company commanders received their orders at 7 a.m., with the attack to begin at 9.

The 1st Battalion attacked about 8:45 a.m. Co. C attacked northwest toward Ohang Hill while Co. A moved due south to seize Hill 165. Co. B remained on the hill overlooking the village of Sinam-ni as a base of fire for Co. C. Co. C, advancing in a skirmish line across the valley got half way up the hill on the far side when they were fired on by the enemy. Overcoming this resistance, the unit went on to seize the objective. In less than ten minutes about 50 North Koreans staged a counterattack, but were repulsed with heavy losses.

As Co. C moved against Ohang, Co. A headed south for Hill 165 and two villages nearby. The unit moved out with the 1st Platoon on the right, 2d on the left and the 3d in support. Although the 1st Platoon took a finger of the hill after a short, sharp fight, the 2d Platoon was driven off after one of its squads reached the crest of Hill 165, itself. A message to the company commander relating the 1st Platoon's success never reached him. The 2d Platoon withdrew from Hill 165 by 9:20 a.m. Co. C was in a bad situation.

Meantime, 2/19th had little trouble reaching the hills overlooking the Naktong. Co. F was in contact with Co. C on Ohang Hill by noon. E took the next hill to the north without meeting resistance, although it later was hit by both friendly and enemy fire. On the battalion's north flank Co. G also reached the river then sent one platoon north to contact Co. I, 34th Infantry. At last, the gap created by the precipitate withdrawal of Co. I was finally closed. The advances of the 19th on the morning of Aug. 7 reduced the northern shoulder of the enemy's penetration.

The terrible heat did what the enemy could not; it stalled the 19th Infantry's attack. Regiment radioed division at 2:45 p.m.: "Had to slow down our attack. Lots of heat exhaustion. Men are dropping out like flies. However it appears that we have them on the run." Meanwhile, Church had come to Moore's CP and ordered him to send his 2d Battalion north by truck to support TF Hyzer, but rescinded the order before it could be executed.

Heat continued to plague the 19th. A journal entry for 5 p.m. stated: "Troops suffering from heat exhaustion, lack of rations and water. Too tired to advance." Just before nightfall, as it became a little cooler, their advance resumed. Companies C and F formed a common perimeter on Ohang Hill. Co. A assaulted Hill 165 again, utilizing its 3d Platoon, reinforced by two squads from the 1st Platoon. By sunset (8:30 p.m.) the company dug in on the hill for the night.

About an hour later, North Korean counterattacks hit Companies A, C and F. At 9:50 p.m., Co. A reported being overrun on Hill 165 and that an enemy force of unknown strength was headed toward the 1st Battalion CP. While the battalion's 81mm mortars provided covering fire, Co. A quickly withdrew northeast toward the battalion CP. About 11:30 p.m. the unit was halted and reassembled near that point. The enemy also attacked Co. B on Hill 146, but the unit beat them off.

Sadung, 21st Infantry Sector — Aug. 7

Over in the 21st sector, the North Koreans clung to their hold on Sadung. Co. A tried, unsuccessfully, to push them out. The unit was thwarted by a combination of tough enemy resistance, coupled with an inability to get effective artillery support. The only support came from 155mm illuminating shells fired regularly over the area to prevent the enemy from reinforcing. (See Chapter Notes.)

Impatient with the situation, LTC Smith decided to withdraw Co. A if it could make no further progress by 4:30 a.m. on Aug. 7. Smith ordered C/14th ECB to move from reserve to the high ground overlooking Sadung in order to help Co. A disengage, but the company withdrew under cover of darkness before the engineers could arrive. Smith and Stephens planned to now destroy the enemy in Sadung by heavy artillery fire and air strikes. They were thwarted in both efforts. The lack of radios and forward observers throttled artillery, and the regiment's request for an air strike was denied at 8:30 a.m. Units farther south had a higher priority for air support.

About 10 a.m. a patrol from K/21st Infantry entered Sadung. They found no enemy, alive or dead, only bloodstains and some enemy equipment. After it was too late, just after 11 a.m., an air strike was made available to the 21st. Since the enemy had left the area, the strike was no longer required and the aircraft were released for other missions. About 15 minutes later, enemy troops returned to Sadung. Before 1 p.m., a number of them had moved between companies K and M and had surrounded an OP. A platoon from 3/21st got through to the OP just after 1 p.m. Then Smith sent in C/14 ECB. By 4:40 p.m. Sadung was taken. Fifteen enemy dead were found.

Engineers moved in to mine the town. First, an infantry lieutenant stopped them, saying that artillery would be firing into the village later. This was soon cleared up, but then enemy snipers hidden nearby fired on the engineers. This was followed by artillery. COL Stephens pushed the engineers on, however. They quickly completed the task and withdrew shortly after sunset. Soon after, chickens in Sadung began to set off the mines.

Shortly after nightfall, trucks could be heard on the far shore of the Naktong, opposite Sadung. At 10:30 p.m., 3/21st Infantry reported that about a company of North Koreans had again crossed to Sadung and were in the draw between companies K and M. Another crossing was reported about 2,000 yards downstream near the destroyed highway bridge. Detonating booby traps there disclosed this. Only Smith's A and B companies were now available to counterattack. Co. C, 14th ECB was then engaged in extending the 21st Infantry's line to the north in order to narrow TF Hyzer's sector. (Elements of the 1st Cavalry were extending that division's sector southward for the same purpose. As a result of these moves, Hyzer's front was reduced by 20,000 yards.) The remainder of the 14th Engineers, which had been part of the reserve, was providing security for the artillery. A and B/21st were alerted by midnight and 10 trucks were ready to take them forward at daybreak.

Loss of Cloverleaf Hill and Obong-ni Ridge — Aug. 7

In the south, North Korean troops took most of Cloverleaf Hill (Hill 165) and part of Obong-ni Ridge. From this critical terrain astride the main east-west road in the Bulge area, the enemy could see all the way to Yongsan, five miles to the east. Cloverleaf, as its name implies, is shaped like a four-leafed clover, with the stem pointing north. It is somewhat higher than Obong-ni Ridge, across the pass to the south. Obong-ni Ridge (or No-Name Ridge to some Marines) is a mile and a half long, curving somewhat southeast in a series of knobs known as Hills 102, 109, 117, 143, 147 and 153. The village of Tugok lies at the base of Cloverleaf Hill,

north of Obong-ni and north of the road through the pass between the two hill masses. Obong-ni village is at the eastern base of the ridge a half mile south of the road

Summary of Action, Aug. 7

Two things were in the 24th Division's favor as Aug. 7 came to a close. The 19th Infantry had scored gains on the northern flank of the enemy penetration, narrowing the enemy's area. And the North Koreans did not significantly reinforce their bridgehead during the night of Aug. 6-7 and were unable to cross significant numbers of troops during the day.

But the strength and combat effectiveness of the 24th Division continued to erode, 11,441 personnel and combat efficiency of 46 per cent. The sole reserve was the newly-arrived and untested 1/9th Infantry, which had been sent to the 24th Division sector late on Aug. 6. The battalion was assembled near Changnyong.

At 10:25 p.m., Eighth Army ordered the remainder of the 9th Infantry (- 3d Battalion) to Changnyong and under the operational control of the 24th Division. The 27th Infantry (25th Division) was also alerted for possible commitment with the 24th Division.

The Night of Aug. 7-8

The North Koreans made a series of attacks against the 19th and 21st Regiments over the night, all of which were reportedly repulsed. However, a squad of enemy got into the CP of K/21st infantry about 1 a.m. Company commander LT Childers, was there, alone. He quickly vacated and made his way to a 4.2 inch mortar position, where he organized a party of men from the 14th Engineers and mortarmen into a roadblock for the remainder of the night.

Eight miles south-east of Childers, five miles from the river and at least two miles behind infantry lines, A/15 FAB, at Yu-ri, was attacked. The artillerymen, drove the enemy away in a short fight, killing at least 13 of them. The significance of this incident was that the two-mile gap between Companies B and L of the 34th Infantry provided direct, unimpeded access to the 24th Division rear area villages of Kang-ni, Yu-ri, Yongsan and the Division's MSR back to Miryang. Had the enemy stayed south of the Naktong-Yongsan road, there was nothing to prevent their movement on to the east. However, neither the 24th Division commander nor his staff apparently recognized this at the time.

The North Koreans also sent at least two more battalions across the Naktong that night, using more than 70 boats. The crossing did not end until after daylight. CPT Alfonso's men spotted one of the crossings just after daylight, engaged the enemy with long-range .50- cal machine gun fire, and called in an air strike. The planes bombed and strafed. As soon as the aircraft left, the crossing resumed. Alfonso then called for artillery, but the number of rounds delivered were so few they caused hardly any casualties to the enemy, nor slowed up their crossing. By 8:15 a.m., aerial reconnaissance reported the Bulge to be full of North Koreans. At 8:52 a.m., Alfonso's perimeter reported that Co. A was under enemy fire. But the North Koreans did not

attack Alfonso; they were more intent on completing their reinforcement efforts.

24th Division Sector, August 8

The 34th Infantry — Aug. 8

It was now obvious that the enemy's main thrust was in the sector of the 34th Infantry. The enemy proved a nuisance at Sadung, but no threat. There was virtually no activity in TF Hyzer's sector. These factors demonstrated that the *NK 4th Division's* objective was to punch through the 24th Division's southern sector to Yongsan.

The men of Companies A, C and L, in their perimeter, and Co. K, far to the south along the Naktong remained in place all day, trading intermittent fire with the enemy. I/34th, to the north, was attached to the 19th Infantry, since it was within the sector of that regiment. B/34th Infantry, on the ridge east of Tugok, made the only attack of the day, by trying to break through to Alfonso that afternoon. Elements of the unit went through Tugok and on to the hill beyond. The enemy threw them back. After holding Tugok for four hours, they withdrew to their starting point. The only positive result of this action was the rescue of some men from the 34th's HM Co., who had been in hiding since Aug. 6.

Robert R. Bayless of Co. L temporarily joined Co. B after the enemy had plowed through his position on the first day's action, and was with the party who went to rescue these men. He identified them as being from Co. L, not the HM Co. This is his recollection of the incident: "A walking wounded man managed to reach our Perimeter and reported that there were about five others on the hill to our left front," he wrote. "A couple of them were seriously wounded and the others would not leave them. A volunteer patrol was asked for to try to bring them in. These men were L Company survivors, so it was my honor and privilege to be one of that patrol." The patrol went out with some litters, found the men, and brought them in. One of the wounded had been shot through the left knee joint. The wound was covered by a rubber compress. Carrying the litters, the party started back up the face of the steep, rocky hill, under persistent enemy sniper fire. The men slowly climbed, slipping, barking shins and elbows and ignoring sniper bullets "ricocheting off the rocks, which we could neither take shelter from nor do anything about." The young soldier with the wounded knee kept apologizing, Bayless wrote, saying, "I'm sorry fellows, I'm sorry."

A few days later, one of the volunteers, Clifton Lundy Jr., was killed when the enemy attacked Co. B's position, Bayless wrote.

The two surviving M-24 light tanks from A/ 78th Hvy Tk Co. supported Co. B's failed attack. As the two tanks moved forward, they were attacked by several 14.5mm AT rifles. The commander of the lead tank was wounded. The loader, PFC Louis Kappler, assumed command of the tank. In spite of being wounded in both arms, he continued the fight. When Keppler passed out from loss of blood, SGT Ervin Yates, whose own tank had been disabled by a round to its engine, dashed to Keppler's tank and took over. The tank moved forward, blasting one enemy heavy weapons position after the other. When nightfall forced him to withdraw, he attached a tow cable to the other tank and dragged it to safety.

Counterattack By 19th Infantry — Aug. 8

The 19th Infantry made the principal counterattack on Aug. 8. An air strike, scheduled for 7 a.m. failed to come off; the planes did not arrive. At 7:30 a.m., artillery rounds marked the target, Hill 165 and vicinity. Still, no planes. Not until 8 a.m., when 155mm WP rounds again marked the target did aircraft appear. To COL Moore's great disappointment, they carried neither rockets or bombs. He had specifically requested napalm and rockets. After strafing the target with bullets, the planes left at 8:30 a.m. Moore then resorted to an artillery barrage in preparation for the infantry assault.

Church had ordered Moore to discover the enemy's strength and dispositions while maintaining pressure through a limited attack. Moore planned short advances while consolidating the companies which were scattered across the hills. Co. E moved up on line with F and C on Ohang Hill. The enemy made a platoon-sized probe against Co. E but were driven off. Then the three companies jumped off in their attack, but were soon halted by heavy enemy fire from the ridge beyond the village of Ohang. They consolidated their position on a hill overlooking the village. From there they fired on North Koreans trying to remove U.S. vehicles which had been abandoned in the Aug. 6 fight.

The 9th Infantry Enters The Battle; Counterattack — Aug. 8

COL John G. Hill (West Point 1924) commanded the 9th Infantry Regiment. His 1st and 2d Battalions (commanded by LTC John E. Londahl and LTC Fred L. Harrison, respectively) were available to him, but the 3d had been held in Eighth Army reserve. Hill started his command forward toward the bulge area at 1:30 a.m. on Aug. 8. Enroute, he received word that GEN Church wanted to confer with him. Leaving the regiment to follow, Hill hurried forward. About 8:30 a.m. he arrived at the Division CP and found Church seated on a box, getting his hair cut. The general filled Hill in on the situation, saying, "This fellow had busted right through my center and is looking down my throat. I will give you planes for reconnaissance and my artillery to help. I want you to attack at once." Hill replied that his troops had been on the road since 1:30 a.m., were not yet concentrated at Yongsan, and needed time to be oriented on the situation and terrain before making an attack. Church then proposed 3 p.m., but after Hill passionately pressed for delay, set the attack for 4 p.m.

The two battalions of the 9th were to assault due west at the nose of the enemy penetration, Cloverleaf Hill. Artillery support would come from Batteries A and B, 15 FAB and the batteries of the 11 and 13 FABs, which were already supporting the 34th infantry

Hill concentrated his command at Yongsan. At noon he met with his battalion and company

commanders, during which he outlined this plan of attack: 1st Bn on the right, 2d on the left. Co. F and the I&R Platoon regimental reserve. Ultimate goal: East bank of the Naktong. The attack was to be continued until dark, but was not to be hurried. These oral orders were confirmed in an operations order issued at 1:15 p.m. The initial objective was Cloverleaf Hill, and Co. F was retained near there in reserve.

The two battalions of the 9th were up to strength in weapons and men, each numbering over 800 personnel. Morale was high, but neither command had yet experienced combat. The men, bored by the sea voyage and depressing camps near Pusan, were itching for battle. There even were salt tablets to help the men cope with the heat exhaustion and dehydration. The men had yet to experience the devastating heat and humidity and terrible toll these would take as they climbed and crawled up and down the hills, dragging their weapons and equipment with them. The only shortages were in 4.2 inch ammunition and 3.5 inch rockets.

The assault started at 4:45 p.m. Enemy resistance and many heat exhaustion casualties stopped the attack almost before it started. The 1st Battalion withdrew a short distance, then drifted northwest and out of the fight. The 2d Battalion went forward over high ground previously taken by B/34 Inf. The enemy offered little resistance. At nightfall, the 1st Battalion was in contact with the 19th Infantry's left flank and the 2d Battalion was on the high ground south and east of Tugok near B/34th Infantry.

The 9th Infantry's counterattack merely plowed into old ground without making any real contribution to the destruction of the enemy, or reduction of the bulge. But Church's orders were not definitive and Hill did not have time to make a thorough reconnaissance. Perhaps, too, the intelligence may not have provided him information upon which to base a different course of action. Church wanted to hurl troops at the enemy just where Hill's men attacked. Striking hard at the southern flank of the Bulge may have been a better option. It would have required the enemy to divert troops to meet this threat. Further, doctrine called for counterattacks against penetrations to be made against the flanks, preferably near the base of the penetration.

Summary of Action, Aug. 8

In spite of the commitment of the 9th Infantry and counterattacks by elements of the 24th Division, the situation had not improved. In some respects it was worse. The enemy had significantly reinforced its Bulge bridgehead and large numbers of enemy soldiers were into the 24th Division's rear areas. They had briefly set up a roadblock on the Changnyong-Naktong road, some two miles from the Division CP. Enemy artillery fire increased markedly during the night of August 8-9 in the vicinity of the 21st Regimental and Division CPs. The 24th Division estimated its combat efficiency at only 40 per cent. The 34th Infantry (1,100 men or less) was at about 24 per cent; the 19th (about 1,700), 42 per cent and the 21st Infantry (at 1,800 men) about 40 per cent. The Division numbered 9,883 personnel; with attachments, the strength rose to 13,476. Replacements were not keeping up with losses.

The division was still critically short of BARs, machine guns, 81mm and 4.2 inch mortars, M-24 tanks, jeeps and trucks. Ammunition resupply, particularly artillery, was going poorly. A critical shortage of 155mm artillery fuses was solved only by an emergency airlift from Eighth Army stocks at Taegu. But GEN Church had no choice but to continue to counterattack.

The Withdrawal of CPT Alfonso's Troops — Night of Aug. 8-9

Before addressing this withdrawal it is appropriate to summarize the experience of the men of Companies A, C and L who constituted the composite force CPT Alfonso commanded in a small perimeter on a hill overlooking the Naktong. The perimeter had been isolated in a hill above the river and two miles behind enemy lines since Aug. 6.

CPL Stewart Sizemore, Co. D, and SFC Robert Moser, Co. B, were both with Alfonso. Sizemore had been attached to Co. C and Moser's rifle platoon had gone forward in the attack on Aug. 6 with Alfonso's Co. A.

"At dawn [on Aug. 7] we received fire from all sides although [the enemy made no attempt] to take the hill," Moser wrote. "The hill provided no natural cover [but] it was a good vantage point, although we were surrounded." Alfonso wrote that the fire was not really from all sides, "except from the hill in extension of our position and at a higher elevation about 300-400 yards away. We countered with artillery fire which kept the enemy quiet for awhile. Knowing that we had an aerial resupply mission to take place in the morning, I did not report the small-arms fire received earlier that A.M. to battalion for fear that the air drop would be canceled. It arrived about mid-afternoon; half the drop reaching our position and the remainder outside...between our position and the enemy's."

Some supplies landed in the paddies, Moser noted. Stewart Sizemore said "that they weren't very successful in dropping the water to us but I can recall that they dropped cans of beer. You can imagine what cans of beer at 110 degrees in the shade [would be like]; in any case it was wet." (Alfonso wrote that he had no knowledge of beer being dropped; that if it was, he had *not* requested it.)

Of the drop and afterward, Alfonso wrote: "A pallet load of 5-gallon cans of water fell near my foxhole and burst all over the position. The troops started to get out of their foxholes to recover the supplies, forgetting that we were still under enemy observation. My 1st Sergeant and I yelled for them to return to their foxholes when the enemy opened fire and caused more casualties to our limited force. A recovery effort after dark was attempted but was not very successful. My 1st Sergeant, MSG Hammond, was killed trying to save our troops from further injury or death. He was a soldier's soldier.... Looking back, I wish I had requested more litters, but withdrawal from our position was never on my mind."

In addition to battle casualties, some of the men with Alfonso were debilitated by dysentery. One of these was Stewart Sizemore. "I had dysentery so bad," he said, "that I went down to 99 pounds and about all I could do was sit in a machine gun emplacement with a shelter half over me on two poles overlooking the river."

On Aug. 7, Alfonso had radio contact with his battalion CP and was able to call for an air drop of supplies, as noted above by SGT Moser. On Aug. 8, the enemy decided to eliminate this small band of Americans deep in their rear. Alfonso's men spotted six boats crossing the Naktong just below their position. Each boat held 10 to 12 enemy soldiers. Alfonso engaged them with a .50-cal machine gun at about a thousand yards range then called in an air strike. But the strike was never made according to Alfonso, who wrote this of the event: "When the enemy's recon/combat patrol crossed the Naktong, they were beyond our observation when they reached the near bank. There was a lot of noise emanating from the opposite bank where the road continued, had it still existed. Masked by the high ground on each side, I requested that heavy artillery fire be conducted in what I presumed to be a buildup area for a possible river crossing." He also asked that artillery fire intermittently into that area after the first barrage. "This request was executed," he continued. "The large enemy force walking toward the bridge site was also engaged by artillery fire. Air attacks against this force were not approved due to other higher priority missions." This is contrary to what Appleman wrote.

That afternoon, the enemy registered mortar and artillery on the perimeter, ceasing fire as soon as the registration was completed. The men also spotted a large party of enemy in the distance moving toward their position. The registration of fires and sighting of enemy moving toward his position convinced Alfonso that he would be attacked over the night. He requested permission to withdraw beginning at 11 p.m. that night. The request was approved.

Alfonso wrote: "For the movement to the rear, the platoon leaders were given the following instructions:

"1. One squad will be the point and will move about 500 yards forward of the main body The platoon (-) is the advance party.

"2. The main body will consist of the wounded carried by the non-wounded in litters made of shelter halfs [sic], as needed. The remainder of the non-wounded will follow the wounded being carried.

"3. One platoon was designated as rear guard.

"4. When change in carriers is ordered, carriers will leave the wounded in position on the road and move to the side. The non-wounded will move up to the front and pick up the first wounded and begin walking the litter, and so forth, with the following non-wounded until all wounded were picked up. The relieved carriers will take their places as the rear of the main body reached them.

"What I never realized in planning the withdrawal was the noise from the screams of pain made by the wounded," he wrote, "with each movement made to put [them] on a poncho and carry [them] down the hill. Fortunately, we started our preparations...early enough after dark to get all troops on the road to begin our movement on schedule." He decided to use the Yongsan road in order to expedite his withdrawal. In doing so, he ignored LTC Ayres' advice to take a circuitous route to avoid the enemy. But, as Alfonso observed, it was "fortunate... that we did not have to carry our wounded into the rice paddies [as they probably would have had to do by taking a circuitous route]. "We never would have made it to our lines before daylight."

The column was assembled on the road at 10:30 p.m. and set off on schedule. No sooner had the Americans started than the enemy attacked the vacated positions. Discovering the perimeter to be undefended, the North Koreans began firing automatic weapons down toward the road. This heavy volume of fire stopped Alfonso's plan to rotate litter bearers. "Fortunately," he remarked, "the firing was off in direction and no additional wounded were sustained during this phase."

By the time Alfonso's men reached the vicinity of Tugok, the column was beginning to break up. The captain halted his party at the entrance to a narrow pass at that point. "The advance guard did not hear or see the guide provided by battalion to get us into the perimeter in the safest manner," Alfonso wrote. "As a result, not knowing the latest enemy situation, I determined that a small recon party to find the safest route to friendly lines without detection was the solution. I placed the force in a covered assembly area and told my executive officer to wait for me and that I would return with help. After avoiding areas where the voice[s] of the enemy could be heard, we were able to find our battalion CP. It was still dark. After showing my battalion commander, LTC Harold B. Ayres, where the company was located, he got the staff to organize a convoy of trucks and ambulances to transport the troops back to safety. He ordered me to remain at the CP but permitted my sergeant to accompany the rescue party as a guide." Alfonso recalled that he and his party had walked about 1 1/2 miles to find the battalion CP.

But the party Alfonso left behind had broken up. Twenty-five men from Companies A and L had evidently followed Alfonso; they appeared at the battalion CP at 1:40 p.m. Other groups, on a longer detour, came out about a mile west of the CP on the Yongsan road. Unfortunately, a large group of 70 men were pinned down for a number of hours in the morning by heavy enemy machine gun fire. Some 40 men escaped, leaving the dead and wounded behind. The survivors of Alfonso's composite unit were fed a hot meal, then given a little time to rest and reorganize near the regimental CP.

"I was with the wounded in the rear of the column," SGT Moser wrote. "We moved out carrying the most serious[ly] wounded in shelter halves heading east on the same road we [had come] in on. It was slow going.... The last rest stop...was in a valley with a long ridge line in front of us." This was Obong-ni and the enemy was engaging American troops from its slopes. "They would fire down on us periodically. When under heavy fire they [the enemy] would move down the reverse slope for cover." About daybreak, Moser discovered that "all able bodied troops were gone except for SFC Lopez. He had a radio and contacted our forces, who identified themselves as the 9th Infantry."

Lopez and Moser thought they said 19th Infantry. "SFC Lopez asked me if I would get to Headquarters and inform them where we were." Moser climbed the hill to the rear, then decided to head south and cross Obong-ni where there were no enemy troops. He was fired on a few times, but was then picked up by some 9th Infantrymen in a jeep. He was taken to their headquarters, where he reported the location of the wounded he had left. Moser was then evacuated himself to a hospital in Japan. Moser obviously became separated from the main Alfonso party. As Alfonso has pointed out, the wounded were not at the rear of the column. But Moser may have gained this impression in the darkness and confusion of that night.

Robert L. Hysel, a combat medic with L/34th Infantry during the Naktong Bulge, recalled the first few days after the enemy crossed the Naktong and ripped deep into the 24th Division's rear area. He was apparently with that part of Co. L that CPT Alfonso joined, with his Co. A and part of Co. C (and a platoon of Co. B). "We were down to 19 men in this company [L/34th Inf.].... I had bandaged 23 men on a rock overhang. I was out of morphine [and] bandages; in fact, all medical supplies. God! The screams of my buddies still ring in my ears.... Some had arms or legs off; others had belly wounds. [Dead] North Koreans were all around us. We had them piled up in front of us like cords of wood. But we of Love Company were surrounded. King Company was on our left flank. Our captain asked them for help. But none came. We ran out of ammo. We had to leave all those wounded men to be taken prisoner. I brought a guy off the hill who had his leg blown off." (In 1958, Hysell met this man again and learned that they were both from Huntington, WV.)

Possibly Hysell was thinking of L Company's first position when he talks of wounded being left behind. CPT Alfonso wrote that he had taken special action to ensure that no wounded were left behind. "Not only that," he continued, "before vacating the position, I required that all the dead be buried [there] and a dog tag be left on his neck and the other to be given to the appropriate company commander. My 1st Sergeant was buried in the foxhole he and I shared. With the map of burial locations on my map, I'm almost sure that all the buried brave were recovered.... I turned this map over to my battalion commander."

24th Division Sector, August 9

Counterattack By the 9th Infantry — Morning, Aug. 9

The withdrawal of Alfonso's composite unit from the Naktong further opened the river for North Korean crossings. Now only K/34 Infantry on position along the river. Enemy pressure on the company forced it to relinquish about a mile of front along the river, then to contract into a small L-shaped perimeter along the Naktong. Enemy troops threatened to pin it there while they exploited the gap in the 24th division's sector.

The 34th Infantry had been fought to ruins and the 19th was not much better off. Less than 300 riflemen remained in each of its battalions. The only viable force left to Church in the Bulge area were the two battalions of the 9th Infantry.

Faulty staff work and the poor physical condition of its men had prevented the 9th from success the previous day. The men were still largely untried in battle. Church's plan was a continuation of the attack in the 9th Infantry's zone of action centering on Hill 165 and Tugok. A diversionary air attack was to be made against the enemy facing the 19th Infantry on the right of the 9th.

The air strike was diverted by the 1st Cavalry Division to the north, and never took place as planned. The 9th jumped off at 5:45 a.m. The 1st Battalion soon bogged down. Only B Company got a platoon on the first objective, but it was soon driven back. The 2d Battalion, a mile to the south near Tugok, initially made good progress with Companies E and G, supported by B/34 Infantry and the last remaining tank of A/78th Tk Bn. A platoon of Co. E reached the ridge beyond Tugok and Companies B and G seized part of the ridge across the road to the southeast. A fierce North Korean counterattack, however, hurled all three units back to their starting positions, with heavy casualties, including the 2d Battalion's commander, LTC Fred L. Harrison, who lost a leg. Battalion XO, Major Joseph A. Walker assumed command of the battalion. The Surgeon, 2/9th Infantry, was LT Gene N. Lam. He wrote that by the time LTC Harrison got to the aid station, gangrene had set in the ankle wound he had. As a result, the colonel's leg had to be amputated.

By noon, the 9th Infantry was back where it started and the men were exhausted, out of water. Fresh water, salt tablets and ammunition were quickly sent forward and plans were made for another attack, this time by both the 9th and 19th Infantries and B/34 Infantry. Plans were made during a conference attended by Moore, Hill, Beauchamp and BG Pearson Menoher, Assistant Division Commander. A 10 minute artillery barrage would start at 4:50 p.m. At 5 p.m., the 19th would attack against the high ground beyond Ohang and Sinam-ni while the 9th Infantry's 2d battalion, supported by B/34 Infantry and its attached tank assaulted Tugok. While the conference went on, observers reported small parties of the enemy were reinforcing Hill 165.

Hill 165 dominated ground to the east. B/19th Infantry was less than 500 yards away. It suffered 11 casualties from enemy sniping before a SGT Dudley organized a counter-sniping party, which neutralize the enemy. Dudley was awarded the DSC for his actions.

Meantime, enemy infiltrators and artillery fire became such a nuisance on the morning of the 9th that Church decided to move the Division CP to Kyungyo, eight miles east of Yongsan and about fifteen miles from Changnyong. The move consumed most of the afternoon. As a result, the division commander and staff were diverted from giving their full attention to the forthcoming counterattack and continued erosion of the division's left flank.

Counterattacks by 9th and 19th Regiments — Late Afternoon, Aug. 9

The 10-minute artillery preparation began on schedule, employing, for the first time in the battle 18 105mm howitzers (A and B/15 FAB and B/13 FAB, with new guns) as well as the 155s of B/11 FAB. An air strike also was made against enemy targets on both sides of the Naktong.

The attacks by both the 1/19th and 2/19th went nowhere. The 2/19th Infantry, already with less than 280 riflemen, suffered many casualties, including its commander, LTC Rhea and the S-3. Neither the 1/19th Infantry nor B/34 Infantry even moved forward.

The 1st Battalion, 9th Infantry, attacked Hill 165 from the north while Co. E assaulted from the southeast. The troops would be converging from different directions of terrain which limited observation. The timing of the attack broke down, or there might have been casualties from friendly fire. Co. E was moving up the slopes of its objective by 5:15 p.m. But the 1st Battalion had trouble coordinating supporting artillery and delayed their attack.

By that time, Co. E was in bad trouble, stalled on the southern slopes by a stubborn enemy. The three rifle companies of 1st Battalion battled southward onto the western slope. This neutralized the crest of Hill 165 to the east, but the hill was not taken. Meantime, Co. G, a mile to the south, moved through Tugok and the hill beyond. There, it was isolated. With nightfall fast approaching, the scattered elements of the regiment dug in where they were. COL Hill planned to continue the attack on the 10th, but did not depend too much on his 2d Battalion, since it had lost its commander (LTC Harrison) and operations officer and had suffered numerous other casualties.

First reports to GEN Church indicated success. But when Hill sent in his report about 11:30 p.m. a truer picture of very limited success was obtained. About an hour after sunset, reports from the 19th and 34th Regiments, plus another from an artillery spotter plane, indicated that the enemy had isolated K/34th on the river and were about to drive into the area between the southern flank of the 24th Division and the northern flank of the 25th, endangering Yongsan and the MSR to Miryang.

The Night of Aug. 9-10

Apprised of the situation, Moore, Hill and Beauchamp warned their men to increase their vigilance over the night. Beauchamp also ordered the reconstituted L/34 to move at once to a position behind Co. K. The depleted and worn company had only rested near Yongsan a few hours when this order reached it at 9 p.m. The unit dutifully responded, contacting Co. K at 1:15 a.m. on Aug. 10. Three hours later it dug in on Ks right flank. This again narrowed the river front available to the enemy, but did little more.

Even after dark, the division CP remained split between its old and new locations. This hampered both staff and command operations, and as Dr. Robertson points out in *Counterattack of the Naktong, 1950*, may have accounted "for the division's slow response to the North Korean flanking maneuver, already far advanced." When certain actions were taken in division headquarters is not known, but reports indicated that the North Koreans were moving in large numbers into the divisions rear areas.

24th Division Sector, August 10

Shortly after 12 noon, Aug. 10, GEN Church took action to close the gap. It is almost inconceivable that the report of "significant numbers" of enemy moving into the rear areas was not relayed to GEN Church by either the G2 or G3 Duty Officer as soon as possible, or personally by G2 or G3, especially since it was considered important enough to relay to division units and be included in the G2's intelligence summary for Eighth Army.

Counterattacks by 19th and 9th Regiments — Aug. 10

Counterattacks on Aug. 10 were continuations of those the previous day. A 15 minute artillery preparation and air strikes along the river preceded the attacks. The 9th and 19th Regiments, helped by part of the 34th were to drive over the hills to their front on to the Naktong. The artillery preparation began at 5:45 a.m. MSG Lester H. Thomas (HM Co., 9th Inf.) recalled that the regiment's 4.2 inch mortars fired their first rounds in Korea on this date. Both the 19th and 9th Regiments started their attacks at 7 a.m.

Part of 1/19 Infantry's front was masked by part of the 9th to its front and only the 2d Battalion of the 19th attacked. Co. E and F moved out, followed by G, far to the rear in reserve. Referring to these units as companies is not accurate, since each one numbered hardly more than a platoon. In short, the 1st Battalion's three rifle companies more closely resembled three rifle platoons. The enemy stopped Co. E within 15 minutes and the whole battalion attack stalled. By 7:25 a.m. the company was in deep trouble and two hours later was surrounded by the enemy. Co. G was committed along the river to break through to E. Just before 11 a.m., Co. C was also sent forward to Co. E's aid. G and C helped the beleaguered men of Easy to break out. The North Koreans pressed all three companies closely, retaking Ohang Hill in the process, and driving 2/19th back some 750 yards.

It was possibly during this battle that LT Ernest P. Terrell, FO from A/11 FAB was frustrated in his attempts to call in supporting fire for 2/19th Infantry. The 9th Infantry, on the 19th's left flank, had launched an attack early in the morning. "Shortly [there]after...the 19th was attacked by North Koreans," Terrell wrote. "I called in for fire support from the 13th F.A. (D.S. 19th Inf). They were firing in support of the 9th Inf Regt's attack and I could not get missions fired for the 19th. I asked the 2d Bn C.O. to notify the 19th Regt's C.O. of the situation and we received some F.A. support shortly thereafter. The attack on the 19th was repelled...but I do not believe that the 9th Inf. attack was coordinated with the 19th and I certainly had not been notified that our D.S.F.A. [direct support field artillery] was supporting the attack of another regt. The C.O. of the 13th F.A. was upset with me going through Inf. channels to get F.A. support, but my Bn C.O. [of the 11 FAB] said I did the right thing." Terrell should have been informed of the field artillery support plan.

The 1/9th Infantry was assailed by very heavy artillery and mortar fire almost from the start, but pressed forward. Its objective was to seize and hold Hill 165 then take the villages of Maekok and Sugae-ri further west. Co. A took Sugae-ri without much problem and Co. B cleared Hill 165 by noon. But Co. C failed to take Maekok. The 2d Battalion lost ground when Co. G was forced to pull back from Tugok, where it was out by itself. B/34 and the 34th's HM Company, on the lower slopes of Obong-ni, did well to hold in place.

The 2d Battalion, 9th Infantry, had also suffered heavy casualties in the past few days. Co. F was the only rifle company in the battalion with more than one officer. The battalion was commanded by MAJ Joseph A. Walker, who had taken command the day before when LTC Harrison was wounded. At 10 a.m., a strong enemy counterattack against the Tugok and Obong-ni areas sent the battalion and the two companies of the 34th rolling back. The fury and rapidity of this attack drove the shattered 2d Battalion back some 2,000 yards. During the attack, MAJ Walker dashed back to the regimental CP and reported to COL Hill that the battalion could not hold. Hill reprimanded the man for leaving his command, then returned with him. They found the Battalion XO in charge of the situation, aided by Co. F, which had remained relatively unshaken during the battle and retreat.

William R. Ellis, a WW II combat veteran of Europe, was a platoon leader in a Heavy Weapons Company of the 9th. In an April 15, 1985 letter to Clay Blair (*The Forgotten War*), he wrote that the "9th fought magnificently" in the Naktong Bulge. The regiment suffered terrible losses, especially among officers. In his letter, he praised the original officers as being "gallant (far beyond those who followed) and far underranked as well." He wrote that most rifle company commanders were just first lieutenants, "which was a disgrace in itself. They were forty-year-old, gray haired World War II combat veterans — and still lieutenants in combat in 1950. I knew all of them...they by-and-large died unknown and unrewarded for their bravery." (The letter is quoted more fully in *The Forgotten War*.)

2LT Lester H. Thomas (HM Co., 9th Inf.) wrote that on Aug. 10, the HM Co. fired its first actual combat fire mission and in support of 2/9th Infantry. He recalled that the enemy attacked about the same time that the 2d Battalion did. "Each [side was] stopped cold for several hours.... Then the North Koreans beat us to the punch [and] were so close in that we [the Heavy Mortars] could not help much. The period 10 Aug. to 14 Aug. was constant close in fire fights...." During these first few days, LT Harry Hall, the HM Company Commander, was wounded bringing forward observers to the front. LT Rolfe Hillman then assumed command of the unit.

Results of North Korean Counterattacks

North Korean counterattacks widened the Bulge area and provided them more opportunities to infiltrate to the rear and to go around the 24th Division's southern flank. On Aug. 9, enemy soldiers entered the town of Namji-ri, on the north bank of the Naktong River, and just inside the 24th Division's sector on the border with the 25th Division to the south. A good bridge remained standing across the Naktong at the town, which would facilitate North Korean egress into the 25th Division's northern flank. By noon on Aug. 10, enemy forces were moving toward Yongsan and had set up a roadblock south of that town. The troops were not told of this blocks. As a result, a number of men, including a party of five men from B/26 AA/AW Battalion, were stopped at the roadblock and captured about 2:30 p.m.

General Church Reacts to the North Korean Success

After division operations and intelligence officers visited each regimental headquarters on the morning of Aug. 10, and he had obtained information about the 34th Infantry from his G2 about 11 a.m., Church finally took positive action to deal with the situation.

Realizing that he needed fresh troops, and fast, he considered bringing 1/21st over to reinforce. Before actually taking the 1st Battalion from Stephens, Church went to the latter's CP, reaching it about 1 p.m. The 21st front was then fairly quiet, so the general directed COL Stephens to send Brad Smith's 1st Battalion for commitment south of Yongsan. The battalion had only two rifle companies (A and B) and the Heavy Weapons Company (Co. D). C Co. was enroute from the east coast. Stephens believed that the enemy would detect the movement of his 1st Battalion. Church assured him that Co. C and an artillery battery were enroute to replace the departing battalion. Church then went on to TF Hyzer. By 4:45 p.m. 1/21st Infantry (-Co. C) was headed south, followed by enemy artillery fire, as Stephens had predicted.

Enroute to Hyzer, Church and his assistant division commander, BG Menoher, passed through Yongsan about 4 p.m. Only then did he learn of the roadblock on the MSR south of town. The situation in this part of the division's area was far worse than he had thought. Church called his G3, LTC James Snee, at the Division CP and told him to find help anywhere he could. Snee was unable to telephone either Eighth Army or the 25th Division to the south; the lines were out. At 4:10 p.m. he wrote out a Flash message and sent it in the clear over the radio to Eighth Army. Fifteen minutes later, he sent a similar message to the 25th Division by liaison aircraft. Both messages requested the 27th Infantry (25th Division), which had just gone into Eighth Army reserve near Masan.

The 24th Division's Southern Flank — Late Aug. 10

GEN Menoher remained at Yongsan to coordinate the defense of the area. He had only the 34th Regiment's HM Company to start with. That unit had been forced back from Obong-ni earlier. At 4:40 p.m., the company was ordered to move south of Yongsan toward Namji-ri. Just after 5 p.m. Church ordered the 24th Recon. Co. from TF Hyzer, where he had sent it a few days previously, to proceed at once to Yongsan. At 5:30 p.m., Eighth Army ordered the 27th Infantry to send one battalion to secure the Namji-ri bridge.

By 8:50 p.m., North Korean troops were within two and a half miles of Yongsan and pressing forward. Just in time, the 24th Recon. Co. (CPT John A. Kearns) arrived in town. When he reported the situation to Church, the Division Commander ordered Menoher to remain at Yongsan to "get the place cleaned up," as Walker had put it.

2LT J. L. Bragg's 2d Platoon, 24th Recon Co., began its attack down the Yongsan - Namji-ri road at 8 p.m.. It met no resistance during the first three miles and did not stop until met by an enemy machine gun position, supported by infantry. The recon men had been told that a following 34th Infantry company was to secure any ground taken so they halted to wait for it to catch up. After dark, when no infantry appeared, the platoon leader prudently pulled back about 500 yards and established his own roadblock. It was 11 p.m.

Meantime, 2/27 Infantry (LTC Gordon Murch), with B/8 FAB, started out for Namji-ri at 7:30 p.m. Murch knew by one of his patrol reports to expect enemy action. Swarms of refugees slowed the battalion's march. A refugee cart overturned, revealing a load of guns and ammunition. With that, a number of enemy soldiers, disguised as refugees made a run for the hills. The Wolfhound soldiers cut them all down.

Reaching the bridge long after dark, Murch sent Co. F across to establish a bridgehead and deployed the rest of the battalion along the south bank of the river.

Glenn V. Ellison and Milton R. Olazagasti were members of CPT Martin L. V. Merchant's Fox Company. Ellison was in a rifle squad and Olazagasti was in the Weapons Platoon, commanded by 2LT Troy E. Moody Jr. "It was raining and hot," Ellison wrote. "We all had our ponchos on and our weapons slung under our ponchos to keep them dry." He recalled the "refugee" incident, when a cart tipped over, spilling weapons and ammunition onto the road. "Approximately twelve North Korean soldiers disguised as refugees fled across an open field," he wrote. "Infantrymen...killed eight of them."

As the battalion moved toward Namji-ri, some troops were deployed in the rice paddies to flush out any enemy soldiers hiding there. "We waded through the rice paddies and the rice was quite tall, near harvest time.... We stumbled into North Korean soldiers hiding" in the paddies. At first, some of the men thought the soldiers were American. "Some one hollered, 'They are Gooks, shoot 'em!' We engaged and dispersed [or] killed approximately 200 enemy soldiers. This was at Iryong-ni before crossing the bridge at Namji-ri."

When Fox Co. crossed the bridge at Namji-ri, it dug in on a horseshoe hill along the road for the night. The men expected the enemy to attack during the night. They did. "A quad-.50...down on the road started firing," Ellison recalled. From his foxhole all he could see were tracers from the quad-.50. "Then our water cooled machine gun lower down on the hill started firing." The enemy was coming up the draw. "I threw an illuminating grenade out," he continued. He didn't see anything.

"All of a sudden, slugs were whistling over head and then around my foxhole [in the center of the horseshoe] at the top of the hill. I was down in my foxhole watching red tracers fly and zing overhead." Hazardous as it was, Ellison had to find out where the fire was coming from. Finally, he took a quick look. "It was coming from our own machine gun." He was puzzled by this, so the next morning he went down to the machinegunner and "asked the gunner what the hell he was doing." The man replied that he figured if he raked the horseshoe with fire, the enemy would be unable to get up the draw. "He was probably right," Ellison admitted. There were seven dead enemy soldiers in the draw, probably victims of the machine gun.

Summary of Action, Aug. 10

The day's counterattacks were failures, except that 2/19th Infantry recaptured the locally important Ohang Hill. In doing so, the command was reduced to about 100 effectives in the rifle companies. (Co. E - about 25; Co. F - about 25; Co. G - about 40) The 1/9th Infantry pulled back near Hill 165 and tied in with the 19th Infantry on its right, but this left a big gap between it and 2/9th Infantry on the left.

The 24th Division numbered 9,755. Some 5,401 men in attached units brought the total force to 15,156. TF Hyzer the 21st Regiment (-) plus their supporting artillery and divisional ordnance, signal, medical and other service support units, not in the Bulge, were included in this total. The replacement flow was improving, but individual straggling partially offset these reinforcements. The division was also being slowly resupplied with weapons and equipment. Ammunition, except for mortar rounds, was adequate. The supply of salt tablets for the troops, however, was not. Emergency distribution of this item had to be made.

The enemy exploited a huge hole in the Division's southern sector to flank it on that front and to gain egress to the rear, cut the MSR, and threaten Yongsan deep in the rear on the MSR. Capture of this town would cut the division off from resupply and reinforcement.

As the day ended, feeble numbers of reinforcements were moving from the 24th Division's right and center to help defend Yongsan and a battalion of the 27th Infantry was poised to strike the enemy from the south. Events over the next few days would prove that these troops were not enough to defeat and eject the *NK 4th Division.*

By the morning of Aug. 11 the entire *4th Division* was across the Naktong and in the Bulge. Completely frustrated, GEN Church placed the division's counterattack efforts under one command, TF Hill, named for COL John G. Hill, the senior regimental commander. Hill would command his 9th Infantry, Moore's 19th, Beauchamp's 34th and 1/21st Infantry, which had assembled southwest of Yongsan.

The Division G2 believed the enemy would attack from the bridgehead area to link up with the force now nearing Yongsan. Division HC conducted patrols along the roads from the Naktong to the Yongsan-Miryang MSR. Supply convoys headed toward the front were especially alert for snipers and roadblocks. These were the only steps taken to secure the Division CP or the lines of communication with the front.

24th Division Sector, August 11

Colonel Hill's Counterattack Plan for Aug. 11

Once named task force commander, COL Hill assembled Moore, Beauchamp, their S3s and the commanders of the 13th and 15th FABs in a schoolhouse at Yongsan that night. Time of attack: Twelve noon. Scheme of maneuver:

9th and 19th Infantry Regiments: Continue the attack toward the Naktong.
1/21st Infantry (-): Attack the enemy's right flank and to the northwest behind Obong-ni Ridge.
34th Infantry: Protect left flank of 1/21 Inf. (-) as it advances.

The plan ignored the deteriorating situation at Yongsan and did not consider the fact that Smith's assembly area was dangerously close to the enemy's route of advance from Namji-ri. The plan had the grossly under strength 1/21st Infantry (-) attack through the terrain south of Obong-ni Ridge.

Attack by 2d Battalion, 27th Infantry — Aug. 11

At dawn, Murch moved the remainder of his battalion across the Naktong to join Co. F, then moved north along the road toward Yongsan. Co. F was on the road, with G on its left and E echeloned to the left rear of G. This protected the battalion's flank as it moved along the road. Co. F had advanced almost a mile, when it received machine gun fire from an enemy force concealed behind a dike crossing the road ahead. Fox Co. sought shelter and Murch called in artillery fire and an air strike. Covered by these actions, Co. G flanked the western end of the dike and drove the North Koreans off in confusion. Heavy concentrations of artillery fire hastened the enemy along. By noon Murch's men were cautiously moving forward again.

When the enemy were driven from the dike by an air strike and ground attack "We killed many...and captured a number of their weapons," wrote Fox Co.'s Glenn Ellison.

During the fight, Olazagasti was asked to take some machine gun ammunition forward to the 2d Platoon. He had to crawl along a ditch beside the road. "I could hear the rounds... you could hear 'zing, zing,' the funny sound the bullets make when they go past you," he wrote. "As I approached the machine gun there was a jeep turned over.... I started to seek cover under the jeep because the enemy fire was coming in rather heavy. As I crawled under the jeep, there was a dead GI under it." Olazagasti got away from there quickly, risking death rather than sharing the overturned jeep with a dead man.

He delivered the ammunition, then remained with the machine gun team for awhile, firing his carbine at the enemy. As they advanced, the men came upon an American halftrack which had been set ablaze by enemy fire. "The track was still smoking," he wrote, "and there were four charred, black bodies burned totally beyond recognition. And the smell that came out was some-

thing.... I still have dreams about the incident...."

The 2d Battalion lost nine KIA and 25 WIA that day. LT Moody was killed and 2LT Walter J. Zarnowski (Co. G) was wounded. Ellison recalled the stench from dead bodies "blown into pieces and the heat of the day."

The 2d Battalion briefly exchanged fire with elements of the 34th Regiment that day before establishing identity. Casualties, if any, on the 34th are unknown..

At 3:30 p.m., Murch's battalion continued the attack, moving into the high ground west of the Yongsan-Namji-ri road. In the face of this, the enemy moved back toward Yongsan, or dispersed into the hills on either side of the battalion. As night fell 2/27th Infantry was isolated between Namji-ri and Yongsan, in contact with no friendly troops. Murch prudently pulled back to the dike, where the command dug in about 11 p.m.

As they dug in, "sleep was a luxury we could not...afford," wrote Glenn Ellison. As was customary in the 27th, the men dug in two-man foxholes. This served two purposes; it provided a buddy system of defense and allowed for a two shift security system at night. Unless told otherwise, when on the line a 50 per cent alert at night was standard in the regiment. "We were hurting for sleep," he continued. Ellison's buddy committed a cardinal sin — he fell asleep while on watch. Two enemy soldiers stumbled into the hole in the dark, waking Ellison and his buddy.

"In a state of confusion," and "scared me half to death.... Being on the bottom of the heap and suddenly awakened, I made some comment like, 'What the hell is going on?'" Ellison continued. "The chatter in Korean told me it wasn't my foxhole buddy." There was a mad scramble by both the GIs and enemy soldiers to get out of the hole. "I managed to stand up and so did my partner," Ellison recounted. "I fired my .45 pistol at them, as they took off. I don't know if I hit either one,... I think they were as scared as we were.... Needless to say, there was no more sleeping.... At daylight, we moved out with grumbling bellies and no sleep. We were out of rations...."

Surprise Attack on the 1st Battalion, 21st Infantry — 9 a.m., Aug. 11

One and one half miles west of Tochon-ni, where the bulk of the 24th Recon Co. was located, 1/21st Infantry was in an assembly area along a road on the western shores of a lake named Sokki-ho. The command was preparing for an attack it was to make at noon. Just after 9 a.m., a large party of enemy soldiers swooped down and overran the area. They quickly disappeared, but caused at least eight casualties and destroyed several trucks.

The 24th Reconnaissance Company on the Approaches to Yongsan — Aug. 11

About the same time, heavy, well-directed enemy artillery began to fall on Yongsan. CPs and logistical installations were hit; the hardest being the CP of the 24th Recon Co., which lost two killed and five wounded. Continued shelling forced many of those with access to vehicles to evacuate the town.

CPT John A. Kearns' 24th Recon Co. left Yongsan at dawn on Aug. 11th. LT Bragg's 2d Platoon headed south on the east road, and the remainder of the company (two platoons) moved south on the main road toward Namji-ri. The 2d Platoon drove the enemy from the village of Non-ni, but was thwarted in moving farther by the North Koreans, who had moved to the hills above the town. The rest of the company was also stopped by enemy resistance just south of Tochon-ni, about a mile and a half south of Yongsan.

A very heavy barrage of artillery (possibly from Murch's supporting artillery) struck the force near Tochon-ni about 10:30 a.m. just as it made ready to continue the attack. This artillery fire was so violent that it caused the two recon platoons to withdraw hastily to a point almost a mile north of Yongsan.

Meantime, heavy artillery fire continued to fall into and around Yongsan, creating havoc. Command and logistical installations were forced northward out of town. The CP of the 13 FAB and B/11th FAB were also struck by this fire, but remained in position. B/13 FAB, a mile and a half closer to the front, was forced to move nearer Yongsan by enemy small-arms fire. A few days previously, Yongsan was pretty secure. Now it was virtually under siege by enemy fire.

The only element of the Recon Co. still opposing the enemy south of Yongsan was the 2d Platoon at Non-ni. At 2:30 p.m., North Korean 14.5mm antitank rifle rounds set one of the tanks on fire and destroyed LT Bragg's vehicle. Just as the enemy was about to outflank his platoon, Bragg pulled it back to the south edge of Yongsan. There CPT Kearns set it up as a roadblock, then went in search of the remainder of his company.

TF Hill Attacks and Fails — Aug. 11

TF Hill began its attack at noon, as planned. From left to right Hill's command was lined up with 1/21st Infantry (-) on the left. Companies A and B, 34th Infantry were next, northeast of the 21st. Then came the 9th Infantry, and finally the 19th Infantry, also echeloned to the northeast. The right flank of TF Hill and of the 19th Infantry was anchored by Co. E on the Naktong. Because 1/21st was off balance from the enemy's sudden, unexpected assault, Hill shifted the main attack to the 9th Infantry in the center.

The 1/9th Infantry laid down a base of fire from Hill 165 for the 2d Battalion. The 2d quickly gained 1,500 yards through the valley and hills on the right of the Yongsan-Naktong road. There was little enemy resistance. Most of the terrain lost the day before was regained. The two 34th Infantry companies advanced slightly. The 1/19th Infantry was to make an attack of its own, in coordination with that of the 9th. But, because of casualties, stragglers and heat exhaustion, the battalion never moved, in spite of calls for help from the 9th, which was exposed by the battalion's failure to attack.

Crisis at Yongsan — 5:55 p.m. - Midnight, Aug. 11

By 5:55 p.m. on Aug. 11, COL Beauchamp believed that Yongsan's fall was imminent. He so informed the G3, LTC Snee, stating that all available troops had been committed to its defense. At 6:45 p.m. increased enemy pressure from the south was reported. Then, B/13 FAB again came under enemy small arms fire in its new position. The battery returned fire with one of its howitzers and 40mm and machinegun fire, driving the North Koreans away.

American and North Korean troops experienced numerous encounters near Yongsan. As one regimental commander put it, "There are dozens of enemy and American forces all over the area. And they are surrounding each other." In one of these PFC Lawrence Y. Bater, a member of a patrol from HC, 9th Infantry posthumously earned the Distinguished Service Cross. To cover the escape of the other members of the patrol, Bater remained behind, and with his rifle held off the enemy until killed. When his body was recovered three days later, numerous enemy dead surrounded his position.

GEN Church needed to bring more troops to Yongsan's defense. At 7:05 p.m., he ordered COL Stephens to send another company to the town as quickly as possible. With phone lines dead, the message was dropped from an aircraft to Stephens at 7:40 p.m. Another message arrived at 7:50 p.m. By that time, Stephens already had taken action. He tapped the 14th Engineers to send every man available to Yongsan. An advance party reached Yongsan at 8:30 p.m. The main body, composed of part of A/14th Engineers plus cooks and staff personnel from the battalion HHC, reached Yongsan at 9:15 p.m. The force, however was pitifully small — less than 100 men.

It is believed that much of the pressure on Yongsan from the south was generated by the advance of 2/27th Infantry out of Namji-ri that day. The Wolfhounds compressed enemy forces northward against Yongsan.

Summary of Action, Aug. 11

The 24th Division's main counterattack by Task Force Hill failed. But now the main threat to the 24th Division was the enemy on the MSR and the imminent fall of Yongsan. Division service elements began to make arrangements accordingly.

The narrow and sometimes twisting road from Yongsan to Kyungyo, site of the Division CP, went south to Tochon-ni, then turned east through hills and valleys to Kyungyo. It traversed two passes, the first five miles west of that town, the other two miles west. Between the two passes, the road passes through the bottom of a narrow valley three miles long. From Kyungyo, the MSR went north for about five miles, then east for five more miles to the Rear CP at Miryang. In some places, this narrow, tortuous road through mountains and valleys was only one lane wide.

Yongsan and Miryang were about twenty miles apart. It was the only route capable of meeting the logistical requirements of the 24th Division. Any prolonged break in it would be disastrous. As a result, GEN Church had to turn his primary attention from trying to eject the enemy from the Bulge to securing his rear area and the critical MSR. Even a report that a sizable enemy force had crossed the Naktong north of TF Hyzer could not be responded to by any division troops; none were available. Hyzer's engineers were stretched very thinly as it was. For example, LT Maurice K. Kurtz Jr.'s two squad platoon of B/3d Engineers, he wrote, was responsible for eight miles along the river, backed by some artillery.

All the 3d Engineers could do was send a 17-man recon patrol across the Naktong to try to discover what the enemy intended. Church had stripped a battalion of infantry, an engineer company and a battery of 155mm howitzers from the center of the division's sector to meet the threat to the MSR. So there was no help for Hyzer from that quarter.

Preparations to Defend Yongsan and the MSR — Night of Aug. 11-12

As Aug. 11 came to a close, CPT Kearns had reunited his Recon Co. and had it deployed on the southern approaches to Yongsan. The composite company from the 14th Engineers moved out and established a series of four platoon-sized roadblocks at about 800 yard intervals over a one and one half mile span of the MSR eastward from a point just east of the village of Chukchon-ni. The positions were numbered Post Numbers 1 though 4, from west to east. Post #1 (LT Henderson) had 17 men; Post #2 (LT William Moore) (West Point, 1949) 15 men; Post #3 (LT McMillan) 24 troops; Post #4 (LT Martin) had 25 men. A five man jeep patrol, under CPL Hurst, ran periodically from block to block. The commander of this composite force, CPT Gass, established his CP in Yongsan. The CO of the 14th Engineers, MAJ Miller, also set up in Yongsan.

Just east of the last engineer position was the village of Simgong-ni, and a half mile farther east lay what was known as the Wonjon Pass. Both were likely points of enemy ambush on the MSR. East of this point, the MSR followed the lower slopes of high ground on the south side of a narrow valley for about a mile, slowly descending to the floor. At that point, the valley widened and the MSR crossed it, a distance of about another mile. The road climbed into the lower reaches of the hills north of it and meandered another half mile or so to another pass, and potential ambush point. This was the last pass before the MSR entered Kyungyo (Division CP) another one and a half or so to the east.

No combat troops were available to guard the MSR from the last engineer post to the Division CP. The CP of A/26th AA/AW Battalion, not a roadblock, was at the last pass before Kyungyo.

But a security force was necessary for this segment of the MSR. To this end, a task force was formed late on Aug. 11, under command of CPT George B. Hafeman, CO, 24th Division HC. The task force numbered 135 men, drawn from the HC, MP Co., Signal Co., Division Band,

724th Ordnance Battalion, South Korean police and possibly one or two other units. Many of the men, like PFC Francis Baker, 724th Ordnance Maintenance Battalion, were volunteers. Hafeman deployed his force in two strong points. The first was barely five hundred yards east of Engineer Post #4, at Simgong-ni. This was his Post #1. He established his second position in the Wonjon Pass (Post #2). From that point east, there were no more troops along the MSR except the A/26 AA/AW CP, some two and a half miles or more farther east.

24th Division Sector, August 12

Defending the MSR — Aug. 12

Vehicles passed over the MSR with relative ease before midnight on Aug. 11. Only a few sniper shots were encountered. One of these killed a man at Hafeman's Post #2. At 1:40 a.m. on Aug. 12, two ambulances of the 1st Ambulance Platoon, loaded with wounded, started out from Yongsan. They were preceded by CPL Hurst's jeep patrol. As Hurst's patrol neared Engineer Post 4, about 2:20 a.m., the two ambulances were between Posts 2 and 3. There they were suddenly hit by automatic weapons fire. The driver of the second ambulance was wounded and his vehicle lurched into the ditch. Two medics dashed back to warn Post 2. The first ambulance turned around, quickly loaded the men from the crippled vehicle and headed back to Yongsan. They alerted Moore's Engineer Post 2 and the Recon Co. roadblock. Moore sent a corporal in a 2 1/2-ton truck back to inform MAJ Miller's CP. The corporal could not locate the CP, but he alerted LT Henderson's Engineer Post 1.

Unaware of the ambulance ambush, CPL Hurst's patrol ran into the same enemy roadblock. Hurst's driver was hit, and the jeep came to a stop. The corporal pulled the wounded man under the vehicle and he and another man took shelter. One of his men ran to warn LT Moore's Engineer Post 2. But Moore already was aware that something was wrong. It was 3:30 a.m. When the jeep patrol did not return on schedule, two lieutenants from the 14th Engineer's CP drove to LT Henderson's Engineer Post 1 to investigate. Henderson, hearing firing up ahead, advised the two officers to hold up until daybreak. Back at Yongsan, the word was passed that the MSR had been cut around a mile and a half east of town.

At 5:20 a.m., in the pre-sunrise daylight, heavy enemy rifle and machinegun fire assailed LT Martin's Engineer Post 4. At 6 a.m. LT McMillan's Engineer Post 3 was also attacked. Here, the enemy had crawled to within grenade range during the night. Grenade fragments wounded McMillan and several other men.

For a number of hours the enemy kept up a steady heavy volume of small-arms and machine gun fire. Fearing his 25-man force would be cut off, Martin split his force to attempt an escape. Martin and two NCOs made for LT McMillan's Engineer Post 3. He sent SGT Churchill and most of the men east to join TF Hafeman's Post 1.

However, at McMillan's Post 3, after the officer was wounded, SGT Kavetsky, the senior NCO, decided to take men and make a run for Moore's Post 2. Devastating, accurate enemy fire cut down every man except Kavetsky. He dove into a roadside rice paddy, saving his life. From there, he watched LT Martin's group drive up to the deserted Post 3, be fired on, and then taken prisoner. The enemy had captured Engineer Posts 3 and 4.

TF Hafeman's Post 1 was attacked at 6:30 a.m. by an estimated company of North Koreans. Hafeman was able to maintain radio contact with Post 1 until 7 a.m., then the radios failed, but came back up a half hour later. In the meantime, the captain sent back for more ammunition, hand grenades and an 81mm mortar. When radio contact was reestablished, he learned that Post 1 had lost three men. At 8:30 a.m., Hafeman decided to try to break through to Post 1. At 9 a.m., he ordered three jeeps, armed with .50-cal machine guns and BARs, to make a run back from Post 1 to Post 2.

The tiny convoy dashed through enemy fire, arriving at Post 2 at 9:35 a.m. One jeep had been shot up, another had lost a tire and one machine gun was damaged, but the patrol leader believed they had also hit some of the enemy. Loaded up with ammunition and grenades, the three jeeps charged back to Post 1 at 10:05 a.m. They arrived safely. Now, reinforced by SGT Churchill and his men from Engineer Post 4 and resupplied with grenades and ammunition, Hafeman Post 1 was in pretty good shape for the moment.

Back at Yongsan, ambulances and supply vehicles gathered in anticipation of the MSR being reopened. North Korean soldiers threatened them from hills southeast of the town. The Recon Co. drove some of them back by mortar fire. About 8 a.m. a group of 41 men from B/21 Infantry withdrew from southwest of Yongsan into the Recon Co. position. Kearns sent them to take the hills where the enemy had been spotted. These *ad hoc* formations of men from different units muddled chains of command and reduced cohesive action just when a strong, united effort was most needed.

Church, knowing this, at 8:45 a.m., directed COL Hill to take command of all units around Yongsan. He told Hill that he could withdraw one rifle company from the battle line to help. COL Hill was already deeply involved with the battle along the Bulge front. He, therefore, ordered LTC Brad Smith to do the job, by creating TF Smith and sending F/9th Infantry to him. The 1/21st Infantry was also heavily engaged with the enemy southwest of Yongsan. As a result, Smith had to hang on at Yongsan with the Recon Co. and what was left of A/14th Engineers. At that moment, Engineer Post 2, about a half mile or so east of Chukchon-ni was the most advanced position on the MSR, and the enemy was closing in on it from three directions.

In the early morning hours of Aug. 12, LT Moore moved his little force onto a knoll overlooking the road and started them digging in. During the night, he had tried unsuccessfully to contact his battalion by radio. A patrol came in to inform him that Engineer Posts 3 and 4 had fallen and that the officers and men in each had been found with their hands tied behind their backs and murdered.

Shortly thereafter, LT Ralph Buffington, one of Moore's West Point classmates and now assistant commo officer of the 14th Engineers, arrived to try to get the radio working. Moore busied himself digging in while Buffington stood erect nearby. Suddenly, a burst of enemy machine gun fire hit Buffington and two others. Buffington had been struck by three bullets. Enemy fire pinned Moore's party down for a short time until an armored recon patrol took the enemy under fire. (This was probably a tank from A/78 Hvy Tk Bn. See below.) Under this covering fire, LT Moore and another man carried Buffington to a jeep for evacuation, but he was already dead.

Two attempts were made that day to reach the abandoned Engineer Posts 3 and 4. The first was made at 9 a.m. by 1LT William Coghill, XO of the Recon Co. and the communications chief, SGT James Keelan coming by jeep from Miryang to Yongsan. At the first enemy roadblock, the jeep was hit by a 14.5mm AT round which ricocheted into Coghill's leg. Coghill ordered Keelan to keep driving so that he could report personally to CPT Kearns. The next attempt was made by an M-24 tank of A/78 Hvy Tk Bn at 2 p.m., driving out of Yongsan in search of a wounded man, reported to be somewhere beyond Engineer Post 2. The tank searched in vain, taking 14.5mm rounds in the gas tank and an ammunition storage rack, before returning to Yongsan.

At 1:30 p.m., CPT Hafeman was given permission to evacuate Post 1, but he decided to wait until the 81mm mortar he had requested arrived. The mortar arrived at 3 p.m. and he had it cover the withdrawal of men from Post 1. The captain then had all automatic weapons on the available vehicles to provide covering fire for men who had to walk out.

Unknown to CPT Hafeman, TF Cody, consisting of two rifle squads from F/9th Infantry, with three 24th Recon Co. tanks and two M-39 personnel carriers, was on its way to the relief of his Post 1. CPT Cody, commanding F/9th Infantry, commanded the task force. The force rescued SGT Kavetsky, but another soldier farther along the road was killed by enemy fire as he rose from the rice paddies to jump aboard a task force vehicle. As Hafeman's men prepared to vacate Post 1, they saw TF Cody advancing to their aid. All the men at Post 1, plus TF Cody, moved together out of Post 1 for Post 2, virtually raked by heavy enemy gunfire. By 5:05 p.m., the task force, along with the survivors of Post 1 gained the dubious protection of Post 2 in the Wonjon Pass. One man had been killed in the withdrawal. BG Menoher reversed the instructions for TF Cody to return to Yongsan and ordered it to remain with Hafeman's last position.

At 6 p.m., Hafeman decided to reorganize his command and fall back to the next pass to the rear. His *ad hoc* command included men from the Division HC, signal men, MPs, bandsmen, ordnance soldiers, engineers, men from F/9th Infantry and the 24th Recon Co. He sent the MPs back to their unit, established five outposts on hills above the Wojon Pass, then pulled almost three miles to the next pass. This was less than two miles east of the Division CP at Kyungyo. In the day's fight, TF Hafeman lost one man killed, PFC Francis Baker, a volunteer from the 724th Ordnance Company, and 10 wounded. Hafeman, himself, was ordered to return to the Division CP to brief officers of 1/23d Infantry, which had been ordered to try to reopen the MSR the next day.

Back near Yongsan, Engineer Posts 1 and 2 were abandoned. What was left of A/14th Engineers was deployed to a hill northeast of Yongsan. The company had lost 23 KIA, 4 WIA and 3 Missing during their defense of the MSR. About sunset, a tank from A/78th Hvy Tk Co. and a tank and personnel carrier from the Recon Co. made one more attempt to run the enemy blockade on the MSR. Recon troops got through, but the other tank turned around and returned to Yongsan. The remainder of F/9th Infantry arrived about 9 p.m. and CPT Cody moved them in to position to fill gaps in the Recon Co.'s line southeast of town. Enemy artillery fell on their position as the men dug in, but created no casualties.

The enemy's success that day left almost 3 1/2 miles of the MSR in their hands. The loss of the MSR forced the wounded to remain in Yongsan, where medical supplies and medical personnel were limited. Far worse, was the loss of land line communication between the Division CP and subordinate commands at the front. Radio messages had to be encoded for transmission, then decoded upon receipt, increasing the time for a message to get through and be decoded to about 3 1/2 hours. Even messages dropped from aircraft took a long time to reach their destination. As a result, GEN Church had little concept of what was happening in the division area most of the day.

This communications problem caused COL Hill to be delayed two hours in getting to a meeting at division headquarters. When he finally arrived, GEN walker was there. Walker asked Hill if his troops could reopen the MSR. Hill said they could. Just to be sure, however, Walker gave Church another battalion; 1/23d Infantry, part of the now-arriving 2d Infantry Division. The plan was for 1/23d Infantry to advance west and south on the MSR, while the 27th Infantry advanced north from just above Namji-ri.

TF Hill remained on the defensive during Aug. 12, making only some slight adjustments to their lines. Closer to Yongsan, several artillery batteries and some CPs, including that of the 34th infantry, displaced northward a short distance to get away from threatened enemy approaches. The road to Changnyong became jammed up by traffic diverted from the MSR and medical personnel of the 21st Infantry tried manfully to keep up with the heavier volume of casualties brought to them from both the front and fighting on the MSR.

Potential Crisis In the North — Aug. 12-13

At 5 a.m. on Aug. 12, five survivors of the 17-man patrol returned to Hyzer. Only the sacrifice of his own life by patrol leader LT Ward Neville had saved these men from death or capture. They reported being attacked by a large number of enemy, indicating that the North Koreans were in force on Hyzer's right front. Two

and a half hours later, the 21st Infantry's I &R Platoon was ambushed by an enemy force near Hyonpung. The platoon escaped, however, with one man wounded and one jeep destroyed. The men placed the number of enemy at two companies, TF Hyzer's troops thought a battalion, and a patrol from the 1st Cavalry thought that an enemy regiment had crossed the Naktong. Alarmed, Stephens requested the return of his 1st Battalion several times. Church turned him down.

To meet the threat, Hyzer and Stephens were on their own. Hyzer put two of his companies into a roadblock and moved both his CP and Service Co. into more protected locations. Stephens had only one uncommitted unit, Co. C. This, he put into a mobile reserve near his CP. B/63d FAB, which was being reconstituted nearby, was ordered to be prepared to fire into the suspected enemy location. One 155mm howitzer of A/11 FAB was also positioned to fire toward Hyonpung. Both commanders also established OPs and the artillery placed unobserved fire on the suspected crossing point.

There were too few Americans troops and too great a front to defend. Hyzer had four companies, Stephens, a weak infantry battalion plus an additional rifle company and two engineer companies. Enemy forces in the Hyonpung area were estimated at 900. Adding to the problem, Eighth Army extended the 24th Division's sector northward to encompass the site of the enemy's crossing, which had been on the south flank of the 1st Cavalry Division. This enemy force never moved out of their shallow bridgehead.

From GEN Church's perspective, the division center seemed to be temporarily stabilized, and although the enemy appeared to be threatening his right, the most critical problem at the moment was to wrest the MSR from the enemy and restore his lines of communications and logistical support.

Preparing for the Counterattack on the MSR

Walker attached the entire 27th Infantry to the 24th Division at 2:40 p.m. on Aug. 12. COL Michaelis gave his 2d and 3d Battalions the mission "of attacking north to Yongsan, clearing enemy from area south of road extending from Yongsan east to Pugong-ni." Most of A/89th Tk Bn was attached to the regiment. One 4.2 inch mortar platoon was attached to each of the assault battalions and a platoon of tanks was attached to the 3d battalion.

The 27th Infantry's 3d Battalion had been the 3/29th Infantry, until reorganized and redesignated on Aug. 7. MAJ George H. DeChow (41), formerly XO of the 1/27 Inf., was given command of the 3d. He was a calm, assured, combat-experienced officer.

To facilitate the attack of Aug. 13, Murch's 2d Battalion, attacked at 7:30 p.m. on Aug. 12 and retook the high ground they had reached the day before. They met no enemy resistance. The 1st Battalion, with a tank platoon, remained in a blocking position near Namji-ri, prepared to assist the other two battalions. At the other end of the disputed MSR, LTC Hutchin's 1/23d Infantry relieved TF Hafeman during the night.

24th Division Sector, August 13

Attack of the 27th Infantry and 1/23d Infantry to Free the MSR — Aug. 13

The attack by the 2d and 3d Battalions, 27th Infantry is perhaps best summarized in the 27th RCT Historical Report — August:

"The 2d Battalion crossed LD at 0930 13 August and reached initial objective, high ground east of 2d Battalion by 1100. Final objective, the high ground north and east of Yongsan, was reached by 2d Battalion at 1500 and by 3d Battalion at 1630. Contact was established between battalions and 34th Infantry on arrival. 1st Battalion, 23d Infantry advancing from east toward Yongsan, contacted 3d Battalion patrol approximately 2,000 yards east of Yongsan. Enemy encountered in this operation consisted of small groups dispersed or destroyed. I & R Platoon maintained contact by patrols between 2d and 3d Battalions and RCT CP."

During the day, 1st Battalion patrols made contact with 3/34th Infantry. A patrol to the southwest made no contact with the enemy. At 2:30 p.m. on Aug. 13, the 2d and 3d Battalions of the 27th were ordered back to their former positions. On Aug. 14, a reinforced rifle company of the 35th Infantry arrived and took over defense of the Namji-ri bridge. The 27th was relieved from attachment the same day and reverted to Eighth Army reserve.

Glenn Ellison (F/27th Infantry) remembered Aug. 13. He wrote that his battalion "managed to make contact with Task Force Hill...without getting the hell shot out of us." When they took the final objective, many enemy soldiers were still there, but would not come out of their foxholes. Some holes, he recalled, held six soldiers. Some of the enemy blew themselves up. Others were killed when Ellison and his comrades threw hand grenades into the foxholes. He also wrote that the battalion captured four pieces of artillery, two of which were U.S. 105mm howitzers the enemy had captured earlier.

William Molton, who was a private in M/27th Infantry during this operation wrote an anecdote of one of his experiences. He wrote that he and "another 18 year old GI . . . were sent to guard a bridge...wired with explosives.... They believed the NK (North Koreans) would cross the bridge that night.... My orders were to let the NK get half way across the bridge and then blow it up. During the night there was a lot of water splashing in the river and I thought it was men swimming across." Molton called the unit CP and an officer came up. Investigating, "we found out it was large fish jumping out of the water," he concluded.

The 1st Battalion, 23d Infantry did not attack until 10 a.m. It was scheduled to start at 5 a.m., but a combination of unfamiliarity with the terrain, ruggedness of that terrain and the heat and humidity, and generally poor physical condition of the troops prevented all the troops from getting into position on time. When it did move out, Co. C was south of the MSR, B to the north and A on the MSR, itself. There was little en-

105mm Howitzer M2A1 and 4.2-inch M2 Chemical Mortar (left and right) returning enemy fire on 6 August. Note shelters built by the troops with heavy logs, rice straw and matting. (Source: P. 99, Korea, 1950, Chief of Military History, Washington, D.C., 1982)

Destroyed enemy self-propelled gun. (Source: P. 109, Korea, 1950, Chief of Military History, Washington, D.C., 1982)

emy contact. At 1:30 p.m., leading elements of the battalion met part of the 27th Infantry's I & R Platoon in Simgong-ni. The battalion halted there and LTC Hutchins went on into Yongsan, with some men and met COL Hill. Only one battle casualty and nine heat exhaustion casualties had been suffered by 1/23d Infantry. A/23d Infantry, with two tanks remained in the Wonjon Pass while the remainder of the battalion was withdrawn to Kyungyo. TF Hafeman was also dissolved. Afterward, although small groups of North Koreans sometimes harassed convoys and others on the MSR, for practical purposes the crisis there was over.

Some time during a conference on Aug. 13, Church told Walker that the entire enemy *4th Division* was across the Naktong in his division sector. Walker reportedly replied, "That is not my information." Church was right. Based on enemy POW interrogations, Appleman wrote that apparently, the "*5th Regiment* [was] on the north in front of the 19th Infantry, the *16th Regiment* on the Cloverleaf and Obong-ni, part of the *18th Regiment* back of the *16th*, and the rest of it . . . mostly in the south and east." Given the pattern of enemy attacks and counterattacks, this is certainly very plausible.

TF Hill — Aug. 13

Regiments of the task force spent the day in trying to fend off ferocious enemy attacks. The 1/19th infantry had some of the heaviest fighting. Some of the enemy got to within 30 yards

of Co. B's position and a point-blank firefight ensued. At another point, hand-to-hand fighting took place. Fire from 81mm mortars, called in almost on top of the defenders, finally drove the enemy away. Four hours after they started attacking, the North Koreans were finally driven back to their starting positions.

The 9th Infantry, left of the 19th, in the Cloverleaf-Obong-ni region, repelled three enemy attacks early in the day. The regiment lost 140 men to the enemy and 59 more to non-battle causes. Most of these were heat exhaustion cases. Co. E lost all officers on five occasions during the battle. Each time, MSG Warren H. Jordan took command. For this he was later awarded a battlefield commission. The 19th Infantry reported that 1/9th seemed too exhausted to remove its own dead.

The enemy also attacked 1/34th Infantry, driving Co. B 200 yards to the rear. During this time, COL Beauchamp ordered his K and L Companies to withdraw from their isolated positions near the Naktong. When COL Michaelis of the 27th objected, GEN Church canceled the withdrawal, over Beauchamp's objections. The two units were successfully withdrawn the next day to positions behind 1/34th Infantry.

Near Yongsan, TF Cody, which included most of F/9th Infantry and a platoon from B/21st Infantry, attacked a hill southeast of the town in midmorning. Fire support for the attack was provided by the 24th Recon Co. on the west and A/14th Engineers to the north. During the attack, a 60mm mortar round from F/9th Infantry landed short, killing two men and wounding four others. Otherwise, light enemy resistance was easily overcome and contact made with the 27th and 23d Infantries. A/78th Hvy Tk Co.'s two beat-up M-24s were finally allowed to go back for much needed repair and maintenance. What was left of A/14th Engineer Bn was returned to the battalion north of Changnyong. The company had been by itself during the operation — some-

times ill-used and improperly supervised. It was what soldiers call a "bastard outfit." No one claimed ownership, but anyone who outranked the unit commander seemed to be able to issue orders to the company.

Summary of Action — Aug. 13

At the end of the day, the MSR was again opened although telephone communication forward of the Division CP was still out. A second radio net, established by the 24th Signal Co., helped offset the problem. The enemy had been repulsed along the division's main battle front, and remained quiet in the north. But 4.2 inch and 81mm mortar ammunition and illuminating rounds in all calibers were all in critical short supply. Replacement weapons were reaching the division, but not personnel replacements. The number of replacements did not meet the number of losses. The division was at 52 per cent combat efficiency, but some units were at barely 20 per cent. The combined strength of the three rifle companies of 1/34th Infantry was equivalent to less than one full strength rifle company. The 1/9th Infantry reported 599 enlisted men, and the 2d Battalion 609. (A full strength battalion had 883.)

Then enemy tanks were reported in the bridgehead.

24th Division Sector, August 14

Plan for TF Hill's Counterattack — Aug. 14

COL Hill's plan to continue the counterattack started several days previously, was set out in OPORD #5. These are the main points of that order:

9th Infantry: Main attack astride the Tugok road with the Naktong as the objective.

1st Bn north of the road: Initial objective, Cloverleaf Hill.

2d Bn south of the 1st Bn: Initial objective the heights above Tugok. Then advance south of the road to seize the north end of Obong-ni Ridge.

19th Infantry: Secondary attack. 1st Bn: Seize Sinam-ni. 2d Bn: Retain positions along the Naktong.

1/34th Infantry: Attack and seize the southern end of Obong-ni Ridge.

1/21st Infantry: Attack around south end of Obong-ni and into enemy's south flank.

Air: An air strike of 100 planes to precede the attack.

Artillery: Four batteries of 105mm howitzers (24 guns); one battery of 155mm howitzers (6 guns). Fire a ten minute preparation. Then priority of fire to 9th Infantry.

If the infantry formations had all been close to full strength, this plan may have had some prospect of success. But the six infantry battalions of TF Hill were numerically closer to little more than two full battalions.

TF Hill's Counterattack — Aug. 14

Torrential, wind-driven sheets of rain began falling about 3 a.m. Dark, rain-soaked clouds descended low above the battlefield. Foxholes filled with water and the men were all thoroughly drenched. The planned air strike had to be canceled. Only the 10 minute artillery barrage was fired in preparation for the attack. The men struggled forward, their vision impaired by torrents of rain. Surprisingly, 2/9th Infantry gained Cloverleaf. But other commands were totally unsuccessful. The 1/34th Infantry was stopped cold at the foot of Obong-ni. Co. B almost reached the top, but was driven back by 8 a.m. The 1/21st Infantry, to the 34th's left rear was also

stopped by the stubborn enemy. The 2/19th did not advance. The 1/19th, on its left and on the right flank of 1/9th infantry, was supposed to attack in support of 1/9th. But the leadership of 1/19th was apparently reluctant to move until the 9th's Infantry battalion had taken more of Hill 165. As a result 1/19th did not attack until afternoon. By that time, it was too late. This failure to launch an attack as scheduled severely hampered the 9th Infantry. The regiment's 1st Battalion lost over 60 men in one hour of fighting.

It took COL Moore's personal intervention to get his 1st Battalion moving. At mid-afternoon, the 40-man Co. A began its attack, supported by fire from Co. B, on its right. The advance of the 9th Infantry on the left also aided the unit. With this help, Co. A gained the hills above the village of Maekok. Meantime, GEN Church had visited the 19th Infantry's CP. After determining that things were now moving, he left after a 10 minute visit.

The rain stopped during the afternoon and American aircraft came over the area, making strike after strike on the enemy. Artillery spotter planes

went up and directed numerous fire missions against enemy troops. It was too late. By late afternoon the counterattack was over. A/19th Infantry still moved forward north of Maekok, but by day's end, was down to 25 men.

That night, after digging in, Co. A could hear the enemy preparing to attack. After darkness North Korean troops infiltrated between A and B Companies, isolating Co. A. Just prior to 10 p.m., the enemy assaulted and drove the men of Co. A southward into the sector of the 9th Infantry. The 9th ended the day struggling up Clover-

Motor Carriage M19 mounting twin 40mm guns (top) and motor carriage, combination gun M15A1 (bottom) prepare to move forward near Yongsan. These are primarily designed as antiaircraft weapons. Note .30-caliber carbine on door of motor carriage in bottom picture. (Source: P. 119, Korea, 1950, Chief of Military History, Washington, D.C., 1982)

M-4 Sherman tanks and infantry attack along the road, August 14, 1950. (Source: P. 24, Korea, 1950, Chief of Military History, Washington, D.C., 1982)

82d AAA/AW Bn Quad .50 Half Track, M-16 "Liberated" and manned by Intelligence Section (S-2), 2d Bn, 23d Infantry. (Courtesy of John H. Ramsburg, HQ/2/23 Infantry)

leaf, which it never quite took. Elsewhere, units of TF Hill were digging into the muddy earth in preparation for a most certain North Korean counter stroke. On average, the task force gained only 500 yards.

The enemy had battled fiercely from reverse slope positions. They had suffered high losses, particularly after the rain stopped and U.S. air and artillery could get to them. But they had held. The enemy first used T-34s in the Bulge on Aug. 14. The 19th Infantry reported a tank in its sector at 10:45 a.m. Repeated attempts to destroy it by air and artillery during the day all failed. At 4:30 p.m., the pesky tank opened fire on B/34th Infantry, and again escaped retaliatory fire. At 6 p.m., it fired at Co. A. A mortar barrage and air strike were delivered, but the tank escaped again. The appearance of the tank confirmed that the North Koreans had been able to bring heavy equipment and weapons into the Bulge.

The remainder of the division's area was fairly quiet, and 289 replacements reached the 21st Infantry. Most of them were sent to the badly depleted 3d Battalion. GEN Church had made the decision to send this large contingent of replacements to the 21st rather than to the 19th. He felt that the 21st needed all the men they could get just in case the enemy at Hyonpung decided to attack.

One of the replacement officers was 2LT Harry J. Maihafer (West Point, 1949). On Aug. 14, he was assigned as S2, 3/21st. The next day he was moved to Co. I as leader of the 3d Platoon. 1LT Floyd "Gib" Gibson, a World War II veteran, commanded the unit. Company XO was 1LT Ruff Lynch. A Maihafer West Point classmate, 2LT Tom Hardaway, led the 1st Platoon. The 2d Platoon Leader was 2LT Jim Exley. Gibson and Exley were Citadel graduates. Maihafer was fortunate in having Mont Robinette as his platoon sergeant. LT Gibson considered Robinette "a fine platoon sergeant." Maihafer wrote that his first impression of SGT Robinette was that he "looked wise but weatherbeaten." (Quotations are from page 35, *From the Hudson to the Yalu*, by Harry J. Maihafer.)

After the replacements joined Item Company, Gibson led it back to positions along the Naktong on the northern flank of 3/21st Infantry. There, the company positioned itself on the left flank and south of the 3d Engineer Battalion. A detachment of the battalion, under 2LT Monk Kurtz, manned a strongpoint on a knob two miles north of Co. I. 2LT Earl Lochhead, an FO from A/52d FAB was also at this strongpoint. Kurtz and Lochhead had been West Point roommates in Maihafer's 1949 class.

COL Stephens sent daily 3d Engineer patrols into Hyonpung. But the 1st Cavalry Division also daily shelled the town. Church asked the Cavalry to stop bombarding it. Although the Cavalry agreed to stop, when an Engineer patrol went to the town the following day, they were driven out at 10 a.m. by friendly fire. The enemy was finally identified as the *10th Division*. A prisoner, wounded by his own squad leader because he couldn't keep up, reported that the division was very weak and lacked heavy weapons.

By the end of Aug. 14, telephone communication had been restored between the Division CP and forward commands. Companies K and

L/34th Infantry had been withdrawn and placed in reserve near a cluster of villages on the main road about two miles north of Yongsan. Two companies of 1/23d Infantry patrolled the MSR and the remainder of the battalion became division reserve. The 27th returned south of the river at Namji-ri, and a company of the 35th Infantry was stationed at the town to secure it and the bridge. The 24th Recon Co. ran contact patrols to the 35th unit. The enemy force which had attacked the MSR, estimated at battalion size, had disappeared and could not be found. Church, with a battalion of his own now to protect the MSR, if need be, turned his attention again to the enemy main body deployed along Obongni, Cloverleaf and the hills to the northwest.

MSG Lester H. Thomas, of the 9th Infantry's HM Co., wrote that officer casualties between Aug. 10 and 14 were heavy. This included his company CO. "LT Harry Hall was hit getting F.O.s forward [and] LT Rolfe Hillman became company commander." A few days later, he continued, "Delmar Cox, our supply sergeant, became a forward observer."

24th Division Sector, August 15

TF Hill's Counterattack — Aug. 15

24th Division Operations Instruction #23 was issued at midnight of Aug. 14-15. The plan of attack remained as it had been for Aug. 14, except for the 1/21st infantry. Instead of attacking the enemy's flank, the battalion was to remain in place to protect the task force's left flank.

Shortly after midnight, the enemy seized the initiative, launching an attack on Smith's battalion from three sides. By 2:30 a.m., at least 20 of the already low-strength battalion had been wounded (the number KIA is not reported). Calmly and quietly, Smith called Hill on the phone and requested permission to withdraw back along his communications wire. Hill obviously misread the calmness in Smith's voice. He recalled having responded, "You sound calm and perfectly all right to me. I hate to see you withdraw. On the other hand you are on the ground and should know best. I don't want to lose you. Think it over for half an hour and call me back." Smith reluctantly acquiesced, but warned COL Hill not to call him since the telephone's ringing might reveal Smith's location to the enemy. At 3 a.m., Smith again called for permission to withdraw. Hill granted the request, then ordered up 3/34th Infantry to cover the withdrawal and reorganization of Smith's command. The 34th Infantry battalion had fewer than 300 men — not much more than a reinforced company.

Meantime, enemy attacks spread all across the task force front. The annoying enemy tank fired at close range into the positions of 1/19th Infantry. Tank rounds also fell on Co. C, 9th Infantry. At 3 a.m., four T-34s clanked up the road from Tugok, headed toward Yongsan. Smashing through the lines of 2d Battalion, 9th Infantry, they went on a rampage in the rear. The tanks crushed one jeep and shot up several company rear CPs. This preoccupation with destroying small supply dumps, and their unfamiliarity with the terrain, prevented the tanks from continuing on to more vital installations nearer Yongsan. At

daybreak they were still deep in the American rear area, but not near that town.

CPL Robert C. Carroll of Co. H, 9th Infantry mounted a one-man attack on the four tanks. With a 3.5 inch rocket launcher, Carroll crawled to within fifty yards of the lead tank, knocking it out with one shot. But the crew of the disabled tank kept its guns blazing. As the other three tanks withdrew, Carroll charged the crippled one with a hand grenade. Removing an ax and sledge strapped to the outside of the vehicle, he used them to pry open the hatch cover. As the cover flew open, an enemy soldier appeared, firing a burp gun. Startled, Carroll fell off the tank. The tanker then closed the hatch. But the corporal wasn't finished. He took a five-gallon can of gasoline from a nearby abandoned vehicle, crawled back on the tank and poured gasoline around the turret and deck. Igniting the gasoline with a rag torch, he jumped free. The crew remained in the tank, firing all its guns until they burned to death. Carroll was awarded the Distinguished Service Cross for this action.

About 8:27 a.m., TF Hill tried to renew its counterattack. Far fewer aircraft were available to help, although the weather was clear. Other sectors of the front had a higher priority of air support. Neither the 9th or 19th made any progress. The survivors of Co. A, now led by a sergeant, remained in the 9th Infantry's zone. The 2/19th Infantry tried to find enough men to fill the gap created by Co. A's withdrawal.

After repelling an enemy attack, 1/34th Infantry launched its own attack, in a column of companies. Co. A, following an artillery preparation, gained a ridge. Dr. Robinson, in his *Counterattack on the Naktong, 1950*, writes, "Suddenly, it was flanked from both sides. Suffering heavy casualties, the company fell back with only forty men left." In his April 1995 comments to the author of this book, not Dr. Robinson, COL Alfonso, who commanded Co. A at the time wrote that this is not a true statement. He also commented that the attack was over a narrow ridgeline, allowing no room for maneuver. He also disputed Robertson's statement that Co. B then took up the attack, while Co. A reorganized. This is Alfonso's account of that day:

"With Co. A leading, the supporting artillery marked the enemy positions on the ridgeline with WP rounds to assist two fighter aircraft in locating the target area. They flew over the enemy-occupied ridgeline on a dry run before coming in for their strafing run. In the meantime, Co. A was moving forward up the ridgeline toward the enemy positions. However, in the interim, the smoke cloud had drifted over our advancing troops while the aircraft were coming in to strafe the enemy positions. Before I realized what had happened, the two aircraft began their strafing run with Company A as their target. Fortunately, their armament consisted of .50-cal MG and air-to-ground rockets. You can never experience the demoralizing effect of your own aircraft attacking you until you look directly into their weapons spitting fire and see the rockets' exhaust. Fortunately, the troops reacted swiftly by jumping off the ridgeline. My battalion commander, who was observing this disaster from his Bn OP called the air strike off while I had the task of reassembling a demoralized rifle company. Needless to say, the 1/34th attack was halted.

When the injury reports were finally tallied, only one soldier was reported wounded by rocket fragments and evacuated."

Co. B attacked, supported by fire from Co. A, on Hill 91. LT M. Dean Schiller's platoon of Co. A laid down some of this fire. Schiller, an expert rifle shot, personally took an enemy machine gun position under fire, causing the enemy gun to cease fire. In spite of fire support from Co. A, Co. B was repulsed. U.S. artillery broke up an enemy counterattack.

"We don't have the stuff," reported the 34th Regiment's S2 to division at 10:30 a.m. This was true of the entire task force.

Attack Along A Ridgeline — The Attack of A/34th Infantry, Aug. 15

On the morning of Aug. 15, A/34th Infantry numbered 4 officers and 158 EM. But 87 of these men had joined the unit just three and a half days before. The company had no 60mm mortars and no recoilless rifles, no radios for communication between the commander and platoon leaders and very few automatic weapons. LT Schiller recalled his own 35-man platoon had one BAR and no machine guns; that the company had possibly one light and one heavy .30-cal machine gun. The platoon leaders had no maps. Schiller had a wrist compass.

1LT Albert Alfonso, 25 (West Point 1948) commanded. He had already distinguished himself in Korea and had been awarded two Bronze Stars with "V" device for valor. The 1st Platoon was led by 1LT Melvin D. Schiller, 24; the 2d by 1LT Edward L. Shea (age unknown). His platoon sergeant was MSG Willie C. Gibson. 1LT George Back, 38, commanded the 3d Platoon. He, too, had also distinguished himself in battle, earning a Silver Star for his leadership of his platoon between Aug. 6 and 8 and had led men in battle in WW II.

SFC Regis Foley was his platoon sergeant. Schiller was a 2d Lieutenant at age 18 and was a machine gun platoon leader in Italy by the end of WW II. Foley was a veteran of combat in the Pacific. Less is known of MSG Gibson. SFC Roy E. Collins, a squad leader in Shea's platoon, and Foley had both been sent to the 34th Infantry from the 35th Infantry (25th Division) at the beginning of the Korean War.

The ridge which Co. A was to attack was the southern end of what became known as Obong-ni Ridge. Alfonso wrote about the terrain over which the attack took place. It is important to know something about this terrain in order to understand how the attack developed and how two of the platoon leaders became casualties. "What I feel is an important consideration but which has been overlooked is the terrain over which this operation took place. It was bare of any vegetation except for a few grassy areas. The ridge is from ten to twenty yards in width with a couple of burial mounds that provide limited protection. Because the ridgeline is generally flat, it provides excellent fields of fire to both forces. High points on the ridge are from 4-5 feet high except in the saddle area which has a rock outcropping along the ditch. Fields of fire, therefore, favors [sic] the force which has prepared positions; in this case, the enemy."

The company attacked in a column of platoons against the southern end of Obong-ni Ridge. The attack originated from the low ground south of the south end of Hill 91. Objective One was the most southern knob of Obong-ni Ridge. 1st Platoon (Schiller) led, followed by Shea's 2d. Alfonso and his command group were at the head of the 3d Platoon.

LT Schiller once wrote that he had "only sufficient time to take my squad leaders to the top of the hill and point out the general route to be followed and move down to the base of the hill and take up our attack formation prior to the 15 minute artillery preparation...." The company

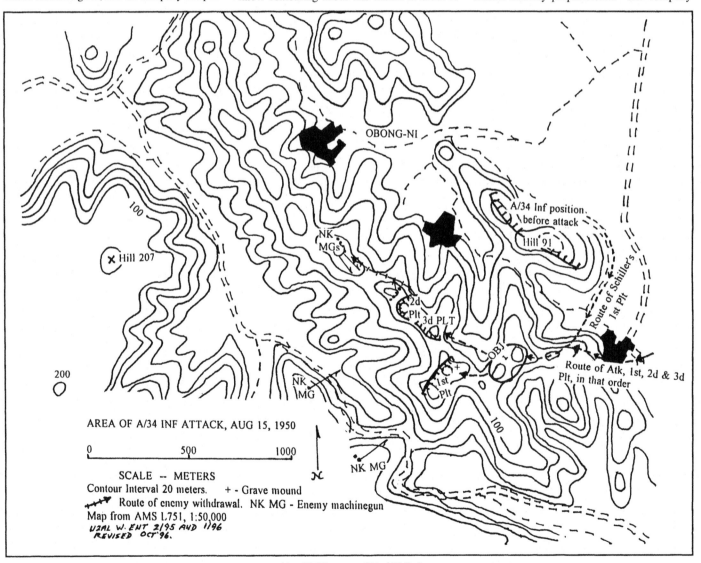

AREA OF A/34 INF ATTACK, AUG 15, 1950

SCALE -- METERS
Contour Interval 20 meters.   + - Grave mound
Route of enemy withdrawal. NK MG - Enemy machinegun
Map from AMS L751, 1:50,000
UZAL W. ENT 2/95 AND 11/96
REVISED OCT '96.

Map 28 (Courtesy of Uzal W. Ent)

moved to its jump off point and waited for a fifteen minute artillery preparation to be fired. Then the 1st Platoon moved out, with LT Schiller up with the leading squad. He positioned himself well forward behind the two point men and squad leader because he felt that he needed to be "responsive to the realities of the moment and to make the split-second decisions that had to be made," Schiller wrote. He had only been with Co. A since the night of Aug. 10; many of the men in his platoon had joined at the same time.

Placing himself well forward set an example for his men and placed him where he could observe the developing situation for himself. The attacking column gained the top of the first hill. As the point men of the 1st Platoon reached this part of the ridge, an enemy round believed to be about 76mm landed near them, wounding two or three of them. Another enemy artillery round came in, bursting among Schiller's men farther to the rear, creating more casualties. In spite of this, the platoon pushed on to the next peak. The enemy fired no more artillery after the two rounds. As they reached the second promontory, an enemy machine gun opened up, seemingly from the left front. Schiller directed his platoon to move to the right of the hill and continue the attack, using the hilltop to mask the enemy's gun until it could be dealt with.

However, when the men moved to the right, they were fired on by another machine gun off to the right. All avenues of advance were now under heavy and accurate short-range enemy machine gun fire. The lieutenant realized that the enemy guns would have to be destroyed or neutralized. He removed his combat pack to be less conspicuous and crawled up to the left of a burial mound — the only cover for him from the enemy fire.

"It was accurate small-arms (including machine gun) fire," Schiller wrote, "peppering the hilltop and spur running off to the right of this second hilltop.... The [enemy] gunners were well zeroed-in on these terrain features during previous actions repulsing elements of our battalion. By staying to the right of the ridgeline crest we could take cover from the machine guns firing from our left, but we had to locate the source of fire from the front and right front before we could get over the spur in front of us. The enemy was well camouflaged...."

Alfonso recalled "that the enemy machine gun and rifle fires came from both the front and left flank of our direction of attack. MGs on the high ground parallel to the ridge were about 500-700 yards away and difficult to locate." Heavy enemy fire from the front and flank created heavy casualties, stopping the attack. The ridge along which the unit had to advance was very narrow, dropping off steeply on each side. As a result, no more than one squad of men could be deployed on the company front as it advanced along the ridge.

When Schiller's platoon was stopped by the enemy, LT Alfonso called forward to LT Shea, "Shea, take your platoon through the First and continue the attack!" Shea and SFC Roy Collins, leader of the 1st Squad, exchanged glances, then the lieutenant began moving his 2d Platoon forward. This platoon, like the 1st, had about 35 men. They advanced about 60 or 70 yards. Shea moved up to Schiller's position and took shelter

on the opposite side of the mound. Then both officers tried to locate the source of enemy fire. Schiller called to his men to look for the muzzle flashes of the guns. He stood up momentarily to draw their fire, then dropped to the ground and tried to locate them with his binoculars.

As he did so, a burst of machine gun fire hit the mound. But neither he, nor his men could locate the enemy gun. Soon afterward, Schiller dropped his head and closed his eyes to clear the blur "from looking through binoculars dampened by the light rain [which was falling]." As he did so, an enemy bullet passed through his helmet, struck his head, on through his shoulder and lodged in LT Shea's leg just above the knee. Shea was still on the other side of the mound from Schiller. Schiller was evacuated after directing his platoon to neutralize the enemy guns.

Co. A had few automatic weapons with which to counter this fire. Therefore, Alfonso contacted LTC Ayres, reported the situation and requested artillery support. None was available; priority of fires were to an adjacent sector. LT Alfonso could not communicate by radio with his platoons because there were no platoon radios and he had no artillery forward observer, even if artillery support had been available. Further, enemy troops were observed digging in forward of the company to stop it.

When the two officers were hit, LT Alfonso moved up to the 1st Platoon position. Under his leadership, the two platoons gained the first objective about 8:30 a.m. They employed a technique of moving forward alternately, one providing fire support as the other advanced. The advancing platoon would then stop and fire to cover the other platoon's advance. There were freshly dug enemy positions on the objective, but no enemy soldiers. Beyond the objective, the main ridge extended northwestward some 500 yards to a hill formed by a rocky cliff. The intervening ridge was narrow, with three small knobs along its spine, before reaching a saddle leading to the foot of the rocky cliff. The men could see enemy soldiers moving around in the saddle.

Alfonso placed the 1st Platoon in position as a base of fire. He then directed MSG Willie C. Gibson, who had taken command of the 2d Platoon, to lead out in a continuation of the attack. The 2d Platoon was to take the saddle, then hold up as the 3d Platoon was to join it there. The 1st Platoon would provide covering fire for the attack. Once he had given these instructions, Alfonso moved from the 1st to the 3d Platoon. Alfonso took the radio himself and moved to within 150 yards of the 3d Platoon. Artillery support was still unavailable to his company.

MSG Gibson, meantime, moved out in a column of squads, 1st Squad (CPL Leo M. Brennen, a WW II veteran of the Pacific, who had joined the unit three days previously), leading and the 2d Squad behind the 1st. The 3d and 4th Squad followed in that order. Gibson ordered SFC Collins to follow the 4th Squad and not let anyone straggle. Gibson placed himself between the 1st and 2d Squads. CPL Brennen said, "I'll be the first to go, the rest of the squad follow me." With that, Brennen began running forward. Collins glanced at his watch. It was 8:45 a.m. Three men of Brennen's squad followed him at 15 yard intervals. They all kept to the right of the ridge, and just below the crest to avoid most

of the enemy fire. As the fourth man began running, an enemy machine gun on the cliff to the front began to fire short bursts, killing two men in the 1st Platoon. One was hit in the eye, the other in the neck.

"It was like jumping into cold water to jump over that ridge," recalled one of the survivors. The remainder of the platoon, one at a time, in 10-15 yard intervals, dashed forward. No one was hit. Finally, only Collins and CPL Joseph H. Simoneau were left. As Simoneau rose up, he was hit in the leg and stomach by a burst of machine gun fire. Calling out, "I'm hit!" he fell back. Collins caught him and called for a medic, but Simoneau died in a few minutes. Collins notified LT Back, coming up with his 3d Platoon, that he was the last man of the 2d Platoon, then jumped over the ridge and ran forward.

The 3d Platoon, which had trailed the 2d, had maneuvered to secure the company's right flank as it attacked. The platoon was passing up a gully, when it became apparent that it was vulnerable to enemy grenades being thrown down from above. Back tried to pull the platoon to the rear for another start, but it became split. The lieutenant moved to his left as the firing began. Platoon Sergeant Foley had done what he could with the new men, but there wasn't much time for any training or orientation. Foley had just crossed an open area and looked back, the rest of the platoon wasn't there. Not knowing what had happened, he took the few men of the 3d Platoon who were with him on to join the 2d out on the ridge. (Actually, the man behind Foley had mistakenly turned into another narrow area about two-thirds of the way across.) The 3d Platoon became pinned down, by itself, somewhere between the 1st platoon (base of fire) and the 2d Platoon several hundred yards forward at the saddle. There, it suffered heavy casualties. LT Back was with his 3d Platoon.

Brennen ran the entire distance, then hit the ground behind a small hump of ground. Not 20 yards away was an enemy machine gun position. Three North Koreans there seemed to be relaxing. Brennen had a grenade in his hand, with the pin loosened. He threw it. Just as he did, he detected movement in another machine gun position on his left, but only about 10 yards away. Brennen fired at the position just as the machine gun opened on him. He emptied an eight-round clip at the gun, hitting both enemy soldiers there, believing he killed them. But in the engagement Brennen was shot in the leg and slid down the hill into a protected area.

Following Brennen, the remainder of the 1st and 2d squads arrived and built up a firing line behind a low hummock of ground. From there, they rose up individually to fire at the enemy. The North Koreans responded. The machine gun on the cliff brought the line of GIs under fire, hitting several of them. It was a battle at very short range. The wounded slid down the hill, joining Brennen. There MSG Gibson and a medic treated them. Collins said that, "from two wars, this was the most confused and furious [fighting] I had ever seen." The noise of battle was continuous. With Gibson temporarily occupied with the wounded, Collins took over the fight.

Almost immediately a burst of burp gun fire

came from his left. Collins, too, had a grenade in his hand, with the pin loosened. Running to the left end of the American firing line, he took a quick glance over the ridge. Just as he did, an enemy soldier rose up to fire into the line of GIs. Collins tossed his grenade at the North Korean and instinctively dodged to one side as a burst from the burp gun plowed into the ground beside him. The grenade exploded, throwing the burp gun into the air. Stealing another glance over the ridge, Collins saw another enemy soldier pick up the gun and try to reload it. The sergeant shot him with his M1.

About this time, SFC Foley came up behind Collins. Collins told him to watch the left flank "and don't let them come up." Collins went back along the line. By this time, about half of the men were casualties. Some men had run out of ammunition, although each one had carried two bandoleers and a full belt of M1 ammunition — 176 rounds. He took ammunition from the dead and distributed it to the men still on the line. Collins, knowing that casualties were rapidly destroying the platoon, sent a runner to LT Alfonso asking for reinforcements, or at least, more grenades. Collins had no way of knowing that the 3d Platoon was also in trouble. The runner came back with a note from Alfonso ordering Collins to withdraw. It had taken the runner just eight minutes to make the round trip. But the sergeant went on with the fight.

The machine gun on the cliff was especially deadly. The 1st Platoon's covering fire kept it quiet part of the time, but every time there was a lull in the 1st Platoon's fire, the gun opened up again on the 2d Platoon. On the right of the line, CPL Joseph J. Sady called for a grenade. "They're pulling up a machine gun here!" he shouted. Collins ran over and tossed a grenade to him. Sady threw it down on the enemy. Collins asked if he needed another grenade. "No, that took care of them," Sady responded. Within two minutes, Sady was killed, shot in the temple by an enemy from a distance of 10 steps. The man next to Sady killed the North Korean.

On the other flank, SFC Foley fought at close range with several North Koreans. He killed two of them, but the third shot at him with a burp gun, knocking his weapon from his hand and wounding him in the forehead by a bullet fragment. Collins bandaged him and asked Foley to go back to Alfonso and ask for help. Foley soon returned with the same message — "Pull out." Collins stubbornly refused to accept this order. SFC Claude V. Hawthorne volunteered to go back to Alfonso, vowing to "get results."

Shortly after Hawthorne left, Collins had second thoughts. He decided to withdraw. Going down to Gibson, he told him to start getting the wounded men out. There were six of them, two seriously hurt. Gibson started them back along a gully to a road at the bottom of the ridge.

Near the center of the line was a black soldier, PFC Edward O. Cleaborn, who concentrated on picking off enemy soldiers who kept trying to re-man the machine gun Brennen had knocked out. Often, he would stand up on the ridge to get better shots. Collins recalled that Cleaborn burned up four rifles. One that he handed to Collins burned the sergeant's hands. Cleaborn ignored enemy fire, shooting at them

rapidly, and shouting, "Come on up, you sons of bitches, and fight!' Repeatedly Collins called to him to get down. Cleaborn replied, "Sergeant, I just can't see them when I get down."

While Hawthorne was gone, Collins was removing ammunition from one of the dead GIs when an enemy soldier leaped over the ridge and on top of Collins with hands up, in surrender. Then he grabbed Collins around the waist from behind and held on. Cleaborn, seeing this, wanted to shoot the man. "They were playing run around the mulberry bush," Collins recalled, "with me." The enemy soldier wanted to surrender. Collins pushed the prisoner down to Gibson. There, he was given a wounded man to carry out.

By this time Hawthorne came back with the same order — withdraw! With the men almost out of ammunition, and the wounded on the way to the rear, Collins told the men to fire up the ammunition they had, then pull out. The men let go with a heavy volley, then ran off the ridge — all but Cleaborn, who was reloading his rifle. Collins called to him to come on, but Cleaborn said, "Let me just fire this one clip." With that, he jumped up on the ridge to fire and was shot in the head. He fell dead just as the last man ran past him.

The five survivors, with Collins, ran back the way they had come out on the ridge. All of them, except the platoon runner, PFC Billy B. Vance, made it safely. Vance was hit in the leg. Collins' trousers were torn by several bullet holes.

Gibson evacuated nine wounded men. Of these, three died enroute to the rear. Platoon leader LT Shea had been wounded early in the fight and was not with the platoon during the battle far out on the ridge.

In all, the platoon had started with 36 personnel. At the end of the fight, only 10 remained unhurt. When Collins got back to Alfonso's location, he again looked at his watch. It was 9:32 a.m. The whole episode had taken only 47 minutes.

LT Alfonso, who took position with the 1st Platoon, could observe what was happening to his 2d and 3d Platoons. Both were being severely punished, and Alfonso could do little to help. He had no mortars or recoilless rifles of his own, and could not get artillery fire to support his company. Under the circumstances, the captain realized that all he could accomplish was to lose more men needlessly. The unit was not strong enough and did not have the supporting weapons or supporting fire to complete the mission. Raising the battalion commander, LTC Ayres, on the radio, he outlined the situation and requested permission to withdraw his company. Ayres approved.

After permission was given to withdraw, CPT Alfonso's radio operator and runner both were wounded. SGT Gibson was subsequently awarded a battlefield commission. CPL Cleaborn was awarded the Distinguished Service Cross, posthumously.

In all, Company A lost 7 KIA, 15 WIA and 17 MIA that day; almost 25 per cent. Two of the company's four officers were among the casualties. These two officers were the leaders of the lead platoons of the company. Most of the missing were subsequently declared dead.

When interviewed by CPT Alexander D. Kendris in 1987, retired COL Alfonso said

that he had recently reflected on the option of "Urging the 3d Platoon to get together with the 2d Platoon at that point to launch a coordinated attack." But, he noted, his "leadership did not extend to the Second platoon [at that time in the battle]. If it could have helped or whether it would have helped, we will never know. And it's easier to say that it would have after the smoke has cleared." (See Chapter Notes.)

As TF Hill's attacks ground to a halt, Walker was visiting Church at the 24th Division Rear CP in Miryang. Impatient with the failure to drive the enemy back across the Naktong, he decided to commit another of his reserve commands to the fight. "I am going to give you the Marine Brigade," Walker told Church. "I want this situation cleared up, and quick." He then returned to Eighth Army Headquarters, arriving just before noon. After hastily conferring with his staff Walker confirmed his decision just before 1 p.m. The Marines were already enroute to Miryang, where they were to become part of the Eighth Army reserve. COL William A. Collier was sent to Miryang to meet Marine BG Craig and brief him on the situation. The 24th Division would provide the Marines with logistical support and transportation once they arrived.

At 11:30 a.m., COL Hill sent this message to Church: "The situation is serious, particularly on south flank. It is under heavy attack. Strongly recommend we go on the defensive." Hill indicated that BG Menoher, the assistant division commander, was with him and concurred in his estimate of the situation. Since Walker had promised substantial reinforcements, Church agreed. Heavy North Korean attacks had already forced most of the task force onto the defensive. The enemy kept up pressure into the night, first at one point and then at another. Most of these attacks were halted by artillery fire. Division artillery fired 2,222 rounds in 91 missions on Aug. 14 and 3,540 rounds in 128 missions on Aug. 15. This very rapid expenditure of ammunition caused the division artillery commander to think that some infantry officers were calling in artillery support too freely. The artillery support given to the combat-weary and terribly depleted infantry units was vital to their survival on Aug. 15.

About the time he received Hill's request to revert to the defense, Church was given permission by Eighth Army to employ 1/23d Infantry in the north to block the enemy from moving out of their Hyonpung bridgehead. By this time, the town was in a no-man's land, visited only by occasional U.S. and enemy patrols. The bulk of the *10th Division* was concentrated on and around massive Hill 409. And there it stayed. Church issued orders to 1/23 Infantry at 10:45 p.m. to join the 3d Engineers near Hyonpung by 4:30 a.m. on Aug. 16. Only the 24th Recon Co. remained as security on the MSR.

Condition of the *NK 4th Infantry Division* at the Conclusion of Aug. 15

Signs that the *4th Division* was also suffering badly from the past 10 days of fighting were beginning to show. For one, the number of POWs increased. On Aug. 15, three were taken from the *4th* and one from the *10th*. There may have been more, except for an unfortunate incident in the 34th Infantry's sector. There, about 25 enemy soldiers threw down their weapons and attempted to surrender. Apparently, the Americans misunderstood their actions, and a squad fired on them. Angrily, the North Koreans picked up their weapons and resumed the fight, killing several Americans. One of these enemy soldiers survived and surrendered. He said ammunition, supplies and morale were all low in the *4th*. This was corroborated by statements from other POWs.

The *18th Infantry*, for example, reportedly received its last ammunition resupply on Aug. 14. Prisoners also said that desertions among replacements was about 40 per cent. Half these replacements did not have weapons, so they were employed digging positions, carrying ammunition and foraging for food. Enemy soldiers who were slightly wounded were returned to the front; the more seriously wounded usually died from lack of medical care. Only the hardened squad and platoon leaders who had come from the Chinese Communist Forces maintained high morale. Given all the problems confronting the *4th Division*, perhaps one heavy counteroffensive by the Americans was all that was needed to eject it from the Bulge and back across the Naktong.

General Walker's Command Problems

The crisis in the 24th division's sector was only one of several that Walker faced at the time. In TF Kean, the 5th RCT's artillery suffered terrible losses at Bloody Gulch on Aug. 12. At the same time, the enemy had crossed the Naktong farther north and were menacing Taegu. And on the east coast, the North Koreans were slowly and steadily pushing the ROKs back.

From mid-August to almost the end of September, the North Koreans were locked in almost continuous struggle with U.S. and ROK forces almost all across the 150-mile front of the Perimeter. While it was impossible for GEN Walker to concentrate his attention on one battle at a time, he conducted a superb defense, meeting each enemy thrust, or multiple thrusts, with the number and mix of troops and weapons to blunt or throw back each attack. The situation was always what military men call "fluid," constantly changing, sometimes very fast and very radically. Edwin P. Hoyt, in *The Pusan Perimeter*, called GEN Walker the unsung hero of the Pusan Perimeter.

In this author's opinion, few American generals of the time could have done as well. One of these was Lieutenant General Matthew B. Ridgway, the officer given command of Eighth Army when Walker was killed in a vehicle accident Dec. 23, 1950. Ridgway was a charismatic and forceful commander. Only a man with inordinate ability, tactical skill and iron will could have successfully defended the Perimeter against the strong, determined attacks by the North Koreans, who must be given credit for their zeal and determination in the face of absolute U.S. air supremacy. They continued to press resolutely on every front.

24th Division Sector, August 16

North Korean Attacks — Aug. 16

The 24th Division intended to spend the day on defense and plan for a massive counterattack for Aug. 17. But the North Koreans had no intention of letting up. They attacked all across the task force front. The center held firm, but the enemy made gains on either flank. Only 1/34th Infantry faced the North Koreans in the south. Companies B and C were dug in on Hill 91, about a thousand yards from the southern end of Obong-ni Ridge. (The same Hill 91 from which Co. A had launched its attack on Aug. 15.) The enemy assault came at 4:30 a.m., supported by automatic weapons and 76mm SP gun fire. The two units held for half an hour, then were forced off the hill. Co. A, on lower ground to the north, now outflanked, also fell back. Once the men left Hill 91 and vicinity, they had to traverse a mile-wide valley of marshes and rice paddies to attain the next high round. Covered by fire from the 13th FAB, the companies withdrew across the valley. Once they passed the position of the artillery FO, he destroyed his radio and joined the retreat. Gaining the high ground a mile northeast of Hill 91, the battalion reorganized and dug in after daylight.

The enemy also successfully struck the right flank on the Naktong. There, companies E and F held a ridge just north of Ohang Hill. Co. G was on a separate hill across a narrow valley to the southeast. The North Korean attack was preceded by a barrage of artillery and mortar fire, which the troops at first took for American. At 7 a.m., enemy infantrymen dashed forward and ferociously attacked the ridge held by companies E and F. Battalion commander LTC Tom McGrail reported the attack to regiment and requested permission to withdraw. He received no answer. Slowly, pressed hard by the North Koreans, the survivors of the two units gave ground, punishing the enemy heavily for every foot. Shortly after noon, McGrail informed regimental headquarters: "Situation critical. E-F...cannot observe river, want more troops." Moore responded: "Doughboy [19th Infantry] will send I and R Platoon. White [2d Battalion] must hold." With the addition of this small platoon, companies E and F finally stopped the enemy. They had lost 600 yards. The units reorganized. Aided by the element of surprise and flanking fire from George Co., E and F swept forward and re-took their old positions with relative ease. Appleman records that CPT Barszcz, CO of Co. G, distinguished himself by bravery and leadership in this battle.

SGT James H. Griffin, a squad leader in 2/19th Infantry's Pioneer and Ammunition Platoon was sharing a trench that day with his squad and the platoon leader, a young lieutenant. "A Russian mortar [probably 120mm mortar round] hit in the middle of us. I was the only survivor.... I was blown into a rice paddy, where I was found later." Griffin had multiple wounds over most of his body, but survived.

Both battalions of the 9th were heavily attacked. Those against the 2d Battalion began before dawn. The enemy employed artillery, mortars and automatic weapons preparatory fire.

Their infantry actually attacked in successive waves. During each attack, some enemy soldiers would just stand in position, screaming and shouting, while the others charged forward. Each wave was stopped in turn, until the attack stopped. Fire from the 15 FAB contributed materially to the repulse of the enemy in this sector. Farther north, where the 1st Battalion, defending the Cloverleaf and Maekok Hill, artillery also ripped through the attacking North Koreans. They attacked all morning, at one point breaking into the positions of Co. C on Cloverleaf and Co. B on Maekok. Enemy soldiers jumped into the holes of dead or wounded GIs. Hand-to-hand fighting ensued before the enemy was hurled back. As the North Koreans withdrew, the 9th Infantry called in air strikes.

The 1st Battalion, 21st Infantry arrived in the Hill 409 area at 4:30 a.m. Co. C prepared to make a probing attack. To provide cover, a heavy air strike was called in on Hill 409. As the planes struck, they set off numerous secondary explosions. Co. C moved out, but soon began suffering heat exhaustion casualties. Encountering North Koreans in a village at the foot of Hill 409, the unit withdrew to its starting point. Late that afternoon, the company moved out again, this time supported by several M-4 Sherman tanks. The enemy responded with heavy machine gun fire. Since it was late in the day, COL Stephens called off the operation. But he was unhappy with the 23d, especially with their apparent inability to coordinate artillery and mortar fires.

Operations Directive Number One — Counterattack of the 24th Division and Marine Brigade, Aug. 17

TF Hill was abolished at 2 p.m. Aug. 16 and all units reverted back to 24th Division control. On Aug. 15, the Marine Brigade was added to the Division for the Aug. 17 attack.

Operational Directive #1 envisioned this scheme of maneuver, from the division's right to left. Time of attack: 8 a.m., Aug. 17.

19th Inf: Objective 1, Ohang Hill. Objective 2, Hill 223. Objective 3, north end of a ridgeline about a thousand meters south of Hill 223. This ridge consisted of a series of long promontories trending south about two miles from the Naktong. Most of the ridge was about 200 meters high.

34th Inf: Assist 19th Infantry by fire in taking Ohang Hill. Objective 2, Hill 240. Objective 3, the center of the ridgeline which was the 19th Infantry's Objective 3. Objective 2 was an extension of the ridge which included Hill 223, the 19th's Objective 2.

9th Inf: Objective 1, the ridge west of Tugok. There, the 9th Infantry would be "pinched out" by the zones of advance of the 34th Infantry and the Marine Brigade. If the situation permitted, the regiment would then go into Eighth Army reserve.

Marine Bde: Make main attack on Aug. 17, in a column of battalions, with the 2d Battalion leading to seize Objective 1, Obong-ni Ridge. The 1st Battalion would pass through the 2d to seize Objective 2, Hill 207 and a peak about 900

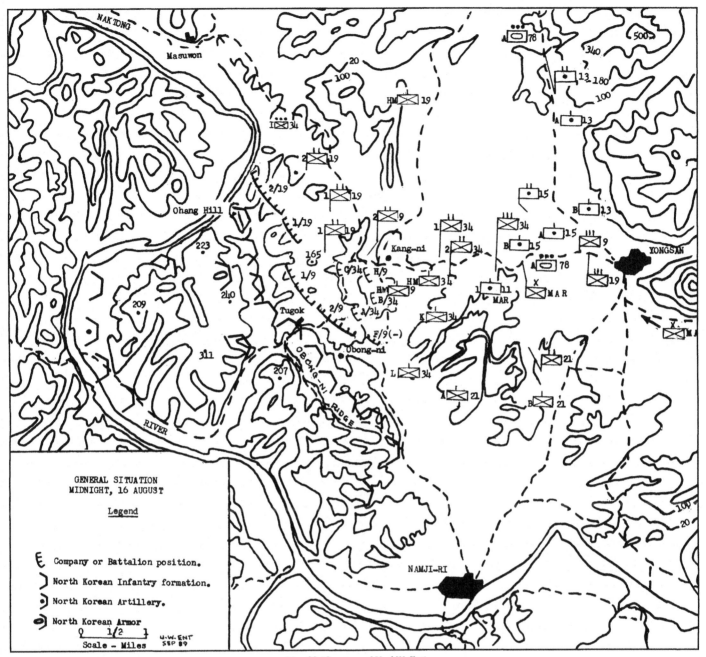

Map 29 (Courtesy of Uzal W. Ent)

meters south of that hill. Both were part of the same ridge. The 3d Battalion, following the others, would then pass through the 2d and take Objective 3, Hill 311. This hill was about a mile and a quarter slightly northwest of Hill 207 across a wide valley.

1(-)/21 Inf: Protect the left flank of the Marine Brigade.

Artillery: Fire a thirty minute preparation beginning at 7:30 a.m. Appleman gives the number of artillery pieces available to support the attack as 54 105mm howitzers and a battalion of 155mm howitzers. After the attack started, the fires of one Army 105mm howitzer battalion and the 155mm battalion would reinforce those of 1-11th Marines, supporting the Marine Brigade.

Air: Air strikes would also support the attack. Since the air assets available from the Marine Air Wing far outnumbered those provided by Eighth Army, MATCS-2 was designated to control all air support during the attack.

The seizure of the three objectives labeled Objective 3 would effectively wipe out the enemy in the Bulge and push him back across the Naktong. For this operation, the 34th Infantry was to be moved into line between the 19th Infantry on its right, and the 9th on its left. In so doing, it would relieve 1/19th Infantry, which moved over into the sector of 2/19th.

During the planning conference on Aug. 15, GEN Church outlined his concept of the operation. The 9th Infantry and Marine Brigade would attack side by side, in cooperation with one another. The Marines would attack from what they called Observation Hill to seize Obong-ni south of road leading to the Naktong. Simultaneously, the 9th Infantry would attack north of the road to take the high ground beyond Tugok, called Finger Ridge. This required close coordination and cooperation between the 9th Infantry and the Marines.

During the conference, GEN Church agreed to furnish 145 trucks to move the Brigade from their Miryang bivouac to an assembly area for the attack even though his own division was still woefully short of trucks.

Redeployment of the Marine Brigade — Aug. 14

While GEN Craig and other Brigade leaders were preparing for the Aug. 17 attack, the men were transported to a bivouac near Miryang.

Part of the Brigade traveled by LST from the southern coast of Korea to Masan because of an enemy roadblock on the Masan-Chindong-ni road. CPT Fenton's Co. B was one of the units utilizing the LST. His unit boarded the ship about 2:30 a.m. on Aug. 14 and arrived at Masan between 9:30 and 10 a.m. The company moved on to the railhead, where they were to get their first hot meal in over a week. In the midst of handing out the meal, the train came in. As a result, only about half the men were fed. The company arrived in Miryang, with the rest of 1-5th Marines, about 7:30 p.m.

Part of the Brigade traveled by motor convoy. Then-PFC Cleo P. Stapleton, of Service Battery, 1-11th Marines, wrote of the experience of riding in truck convoys in Korea during this time: "Those bone jarring night trips that left you caked with dust were for many of us adventures into the unknown, since we were leaving a place only a few of us knew by name and [were] going to another unknown place to find another unknown."

In the Perimeter that summer, two vehicles traveling together kicked up a small cloud of dust and dirt; convoys created huge clouds of dirt and dust impenetrable by the eye. Trucks stayed well away from those in front, just so the driver could see the road. Troops riding in the vehicles quickly became totally covered with a thick coating of road dust, and resembled creatures from another planet. Water was always in short supply, so the poor GI or Marine rarely had an opportunity to wash off the dirt or to wash his clothing. The terrible heat caused the men to sweat, turning the dust to mud. Traveling in the rain was almost as bad; then the roads turned to very shallow, muddy rivers. The troops, unprotected by canvas covers over the troop compartments, were soaked by rain, with no prospect of changing into dry clothing. They dried off with the passage of time, or when the sun came out. Showers and a change of clothing for the men came at infrequent intervals, measured in weeks.

When the Brigade assembled at Miryang there were many holes in the ranks, the result of casualties in its first week in combat. In that time, the Brigade lost 66 KIA or died of wounds; 240 WIA and 9 MIA, a total of 315 men. The first replacements for the infantry battalions of the 5th Marines were volunteers from Brigade service support units. The Brigade was "eating its own tail" to keep the infantry units up to strength. Even so, the rifle platoons could not be brought back up to full strength. "This practice," wrote LT Muetzel, "continued up to and including the 2d Naktong. [The] first Stateside replacements reached C Co. [5th Marines] for Inchon."

Miryang

At Miryang the tired Marines bivouacked in a grove of trees. There, they were able to bathe in the Miryang River, have their clothes washed by Korean women and get a hot meal. Geer, in *The New Breed* writes that the men could hear the guns firing in the west and that "the 25th Division had been badly mauled...." It actually was the 24th Division.

Herbert Pearce, a Corpsman with the Marine Anti-tank Company, like many other Marines, wrote a letter home. What he wrote epitomizes how most of the Marines felt there at Miryang. "I got a chance to wash all my clothes, shave and take a bath. I never thought it could feel so good just to get cleaned up, but boy I can tell you it is heaven. We even had hot chow this morning (eggs and bacon). That sure beats 'C' rations all to pieces."

A number of Marines recall that the swim in the Miryang in the buff apparently caused some embarrassment for correspondent Marguerite

(Maggie) Higgins, of the New York *Herald Tribune.*

Jack Wright (G-3-5 Mar.) described Maggie's visit as "a very historical moment for the 3d Battalion, 5th Marine Regiment." He recalled that the Corpsman had some "sick bay brandy" and "sick bay alcohol" cooling off in the Miryang. "We were getting ready for a nice evening.... We were all in the river bare ass, as you might say, and there's Maggie Higgins up on the bridge. We greeted her quite ceremoniously. She started screaming for our battalion commander, Colonel Taplett."

LT George L. Fox, a platoon leader in Co. A, was relaxing near the river, watching his men enjoying their swim. He was attired in trousers, but no shirt. Suddenly, he heard a woman's voice ask who was in charge. Fox replied that he was. "She started giving me hell," Fox wrote, "and said I should be ashamed of letting good American boys swim naked in a dirty Korean river! I was speechless for a second, and finally said, 'You and I are next,' and started taking off my trousers. She beat a retreat back up the path."

Higgins complained to Brigade headquarters. CPT Fenton recalled that he "got the word that all the men had to get their clothes on and get covered up because there was a woman present. I thought, here we are fighting a war...and these kids are tired, dirty and hungry. If a woman is in the area then she ought to take her lumps for the guys that are naked. It won't be the first time she's seen someone naked.... That sort of soured me on her."

However, COL Taplett wrote this of Maggie Higgins at Miryang: "She didn't bat an eyelash when she arrived at Craig's C.P. while the regimental commander, battalion commanders and staff were having a conference and all were naked except for Maggie."

Final Preparations for the Attack

GEN Craig reconnoitered the area for the Brigade's attack the next day. He visited COL Hill's 9th Infantry CP. Hill reportedly told Craig that his regiment was in good condition for the attack. Following Craig, LTC Murray arrived to conduct his own reconnaissance and complete plans to coordinate his attack with COL Hill. In spite of Hill's statement that the 9th was ready for the attack, the 24th Division rated the 9th RCT (-) at 47 per cent strength and 44 per cent estimated combat efficiency. Division morale was considered "fair."

The Marine attack would originate on what the Marines called Observation Hill. Some 300 yards of rice paddies separated this promontory from Obong-ni Ridge to the west. At the northern edge of the two hills ran the road from the Naktong to Yongsan. The road also marked the boundary between the Brigade and the 9th Infantry to the north. Co. F, 9th Infantry was then on Observation Hill. G/9 Infantry occupied the hill just to the north of this. George's hill was 125. The Marines would replace Co. F and jump off from Observation Hill. At the same time, the 9th Infantry would attack from Hill 125 to seize the hill mass just west of the village of Tugok. Tugok lay north of the road and almost due north of the northern end of Obong-ni ridge. Obong-

ni is a long spine ridge, trending southeast. There are a series of small knobs spaced out along the ridge top, each one somewhat higher than the last. They were numbered successively, from north to south, Hills 102, 109, 117, 143, 147 and 153. There were pronounced gullies between each of these hills. Marine accounts refer to the 9th Infantry's objective as Finger Ridge.

Many Marines remember Obong-ni as "Red Slash Hill," named because of a deep erosive gully of exposed red clay and shale extending down from the saddle between Hills 109 and 117. It was also called "No Name Ridge," apparently so named by correspondents.

Originally, the 9th and Marine Brigade were to attack at the same time. LTC Murray concluded from his reconnaissance that if the two commands attacked simultaneously, they would both be exposed in the low ground on their respective axes of advance at the same time. Obong-ni was closer than the Army objective and dominated both Tugok and Finger Ridge. Murray suggested to Hill that the 5th Marines attack alone at 8 a.m. on the 17th and the 9th Infantry support them by fire. When his men took Obong-ni, they would reciprocate by supporting the 9th Infantry as they advanced to seize Finger Ridge. Hill agreed. Murray made this recommendation based on tactical factors and because he realized that the 9th Infantry had already suffered great casualties and was battleworn. Although GEN Craig apparently was not informed of this change, General Church was. He deferred to the commanders making the actual attack, and approved the changed scheme of maneuver.

GEN Craig had settled on an attack in a column of battalions, first, because he could not have envisioned an attack on the enemy's left on Obong-ni through the zone of the 9th Infantry, and second, he believed that trying to attack the enemy's right flank on that ridge would unduly spread the Brigade's effort. The element(s) assaulting that flank would be separated from the remainder of the brigade by several thousand yards. The low marshy area on this approach would have impeded the employment of tanks and other supporting weapons. LTC Murray visualized fire support from the 9th Infantry to help him capture the north end of Obong-ni. If he had to employ troops simultaneously to attack the south end of Obong-ni, it would dissipate the potential force of both attacks and place the command making the flank attack at a disadvantage from the standpoint of supporting fire. Further, the hills on the south end of the ridge were higher than those in the north. An assault by a column of battalions ensured the strongest, most sustained attack possible. LT Muetzel wrote: "From the moment we first saw Obong-ni, we in the rifle companies screamed about a frontal attack and wanted to attack from the left [south] flank."

The 5th Marines were scheduled to depart by truck from Miryang at 4 p.m. on Aug. 16. First, the 539th Truck Co. arrived three hours late. Instead of 144 (or 145) trucks, it had but 43. The 24th division scraped up 29 more, but the total was still not enough. The Marines were forced to organize a shuttle. Even this succeeded in transporting only two of the 5th Marine's infantry battalions to Yongsan by midnight. The delay in moving the Brigade also delayed relief of the 34th by Marine units. This, in turn prevented the 34th from moving to relieve 1/19th Infantry as a prelude to its (the 34th) attack. The attack had not even begun and things were starting to come apart.

In the event, Taplett's 3-5th Marines left Miryang by truck about 7 p.m., Aug. 16, rode to the 5th Marine CP some 3,000 yards behind the lines, then marched forward to relieve the 34th infantry in position. However, COL Taplett wrote that the 34th had already vacated the position before his men arrived. Taplett assumed control of that area at 4:45 a.m., Aug. 17. (See Chapter Notes concerning "Cloverleaf" Hills.)

H-5th Marines relieved 1/34th Infantry on the hill the Marines called "Cloverleaf" and G-5th Marines relieved L/34th Infantry farther south, on a hill overlooking the long valley stretching westward to Hill 91. GEN Church had directed GEN Craig to occupy the 1/34th Infantry position in order to protect the Yongsan road. GEN Craig decided to also place some of his command to protect the Brigade's left flank, since 1/21st Infantry was so far out in that direction. The placement of Co. G took care of that.

LTC Harold Roise's 2d Battalion proceeded on foot to their assembly area near the (Marine) Cloverleaf at 1:30 a.m. on Aug. 17. Elements of the battalion relieved F/9th Infantry on Observation Hill. The Army unit then moved to the northern side of the road and prepared to lead the 9th's attack in the morning. The men of 2-5th Marines and F/9th Infantry got little sleep as they prepared to attack. Due to the truck shortage, LTC George Newton's 1st Battalion did not arrive in its assembly area until midmorning of Aug. 17.

Observation Hill(125), Obong-ni Ridge, and the area around them had been fought over by the North Koreans and 24th Division for a number of days before the Marines arrived. Dead GIs and enemy soldiers were to be found throughout the area. Only two factors come to mind to explain why Army units had not retrieved its dead. One is that the units were overrun and did not have the chance to get the dead out. The other is that, at the time, the Army had what was called "Graves Registration" units, specifically charged with collecting the dead. Most of the bodies had blackened and rotted in the sun, having been there for one or more days.

LTC Wood recalled that, on Aug. 14, when his artillery battalion began displacing to Miryang, "the weather was the worst it had been since our arrival. It was raining heavily and the wind blew hard and cold." At the rail head in Masan, the colonel stopped the motor convoy and placed all his men on the train, except drivers, gun crews, essential fire direction and communications personnel. He wanted as many men as possible to be as comfortable as possible. Colonel Wood wrote that the train took 17 hours to make the trip from Masan to Miryang and that the motor march was almost as long. As a result, the artillery battalion arrived at Miryang in the early hours of Aug. 15 "in no condition to appreciate, then, the rest area in a beautiful grove of trees along the river."

The Marine artillery battalion was under the operational control of the 24th Division Artil-

lery Commander, BG Henry J. D. Meyer (West Point 1919). Wood recalled that he was informed by Meyer's S-3 late on Aug. 16 that the attack was scheduled to begin the next morning, instead of on Aug. 18, as he had originally been told. Fortunately, the Army's artillery had occupied most of the suitable positions during the previous week or two. LTC Wood left his XO, MAJ Francis R. Schlesinger in the Yongsan area with orders to select a position and to make plans for communications with the 24th Division Artillery. Wood then returned to Miryang to bring his battalion forward. He returned just before sunset to find that Schlesinger had not only selected a position, he had telephone lines in to the 24th and to the Brigade's assault battalion. He also had obtained all available information from the 24th Division Artillery on check points, base points, concentrations and survey data. The 11th Marines were in position to fire and registration was completed by evening of Aug. 16. As a result, as COL Wood wrote, "when the attack began on the morning of Aug. 17, we were in a position to furnish almost any amount of artillery fire requested."

He also recalled that, in keeping with a recommendation made to him by BG Barth (CO, 25th DivArty), one gun in each battery near the road was sighted so that it could fire AT fire on any enemy tanks if they broke through.

The North Korean Defenders of Cloverleaf and Obong-ni Ridge

Information gained later indicates that the *18th Regiment*, plus a battalion from the *16th* , (a reported total of over 1,000 men) defended Obong-ni and that other elements of the *16th* were on Cloverleaf. COL Chang Ky Dok commanded the *18th*. He had attended military school in Russia and was a combat veteran of the Chinese Communist Army in North China. He reportedly had deployed all three of his battalions on Obong-ni to repel the Marines. There is no information as to where the battalion of the *16th* was located.

Also, he reportedly had assembled his battalion and company commanders on the night of Aug. 16 and exhorted them, saying that intelligence stated that they were to expect an attack by American Marines. He said the *NK 18th Regiment* would have the honor of being the first to defeat these U.S. Marines, and that the *18th* would win where others had failed. He said he considered the regiment's positions impregnable, and that the Marines would have to attack up a steep slope. In conclusion, he ordered his officers to tell their men that there would be no retreat, and that he would take instant action against anyone who showed weakness.

Attack of the 2d Battalion, 5th Marines — Aug. 17

Marine air and artillery were to blast the ridge from 7:25 to 8 a.m. Then at 8, as the Marine infantrymen began their attack, Corsairs were to work the ridge over one more time to cover the advance. The first air attack, scheduled for 7:25, did not take place. Brigade artillery, however, plastered the area for five minutes, begin-

ning at 7:30. At 7:40 a.m., 18 Corsairs zoomed in, strafing and dropping 1,000 lb. bombs and napalm on Obong-ni. From a distance, this attack seemed to be devastating. But the enemy was well dug in on the reverse slope of Obong-ni and were not badly hurt. From 7:50 to 8 a.m., the artillery fired again, joined by the mortars of 2-5th Marines, the 4.2s, and 90mm guns of the 3d Platoon, A/1st Tk Bn. Unfortunately, the artillery preparation also was not as effective as desired. Due to errors, either in registration or by forward observers, much of the artillery fell beyond Obong-ni. Because the air and artillery preparation had not materially hurt the enemy, were ready to meet Roise's men with deadly fire and hand grenades.

Companies D (CPT Andrew Zimmer) and E (1LT William Sweeney) began the infantry attack at 8 a.m. Co. D was on the right, next the road, heading for Hills 102, 109 and 117. SSGT Albert Crowson's 1st Platoon came up on the right and 2LT Michael Shinka's 3d Platoon was on the left. The 2d Platoon, under TSGT Sidney S. Dickerson. was in reserve on the south slope of Hill 125. Zimmer had his OP there, too. A rocket launcher section took up a position at the bend of the road. Shinka's platoon made contact with 2LT Charles Christiansen's 2d Platoon, which advanced on the right of Easy Company's line. 2LT Nickolas Arkadis's 1st Platoon was on the left. 2LT Rodger E. Eddy's 3d Platoon was in reserve. In all, the four assault platoons totaled about 130 men.

After the ferocious air strike and the artillery and mortar preparation had all stopped, an eerie silence fell over the battlefield as the assault platoons made their way across the paddies toward the base of Obong-ni. Ironically, the first casualties were to Dickerson's 2d Platoon of Dog Co. on Hill 125, caused by enemy long range machine gun fire.

"Finally...the infantry moved out," wrote Harold H. Martin, in a *Saturday Evening Post* article. "They went in long, thinly spaced files across the emerald rice paddies, walking upright despite the sniper fire,...these men were going into battle tired. They reached the terraced lower slopes where patches of peas and red peppers and scraggly cotton lay, and then they were moving upward into the scrubby pines."

As the troops advanced, Crowsen's platoon gradually turned its back on Tugok and began to move up the draw on the right of a spur leading to Hill 102. Shinka's platoon entered the draw on its left.

From the vantage point of an OP on Observation Hill, "it seemed that it might be a walkover, for the little figures were half way up now, and still moving." When the skirmish line was almost halfway up the slope, dozens of machine guns began raking the hill. PFC Douglas Koch, 3d Platoon, Dog Co., observed the advance of the other platoons from his location with the reserve platoon on Observation Hill. He was firing his BAR at the top of the ridge to keep the enemy down. He recalled that the two units were in good shape and that the formation was "textbook." However, once the formation got about two-thirds of the way across, he saw some of the men fall, hit by enemy sniper fire. At the same time, long range machine gun fire began to hit in the 3d Platoon's area.

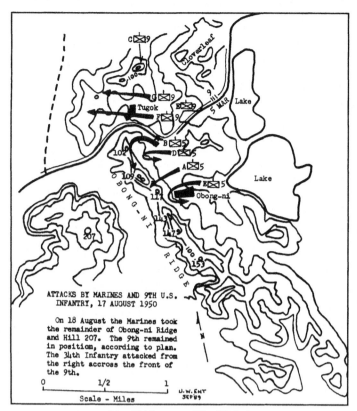

Map 30 (Courtesy of Uzal W. Ent)

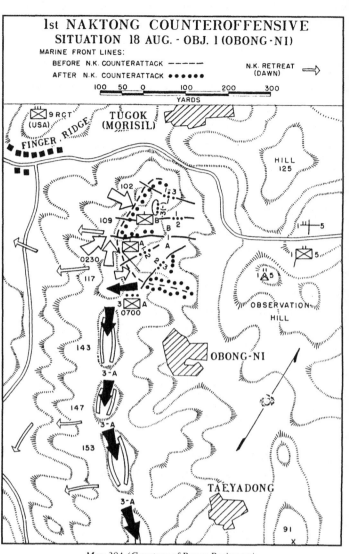

Map 30A (Courtesy of Pusan Perimeter)

In spite of being swept by enemy machine gun fire, Crowson and Shinka's men moved slowly forward. Enemy grenades flew down on the advancing Marines. "It was hellaciously hot," wrote SGT Lester M. Fulcher, 4.2 inch Mortar Co. He, too, watched the men inch up the hill. They would move - "always upward by fire and maneuver, roll under a bush or other ground cover...quickly catch a few breaths, then get up and charge upward a few more precious yards."

Finally, the fire from Hills 117 and 143, off to the left and forward of Co. E, became so heavy that Shinka's platoon was unable to emerge from its gully. At almost the same time, withering machine gun fire pinned the 1st Platoon down, creating heavy casualties. Crowson's men were being attacked by enemy fire from Tugok and the hills nearby it. Enemy mortars had joined the concentrated enemy fire.

About 10 a.m., Shinka, with 20 of his original 30 men, got to the top of Hill 109 and jumped into some abandoned enemy foxholes. Suddenly, machine gun fire ripped across the top of the hill, and enemy soldiers charged from their holes on the reverse slope. A bloody melee ensued. CPL Bill McCarver and a man named Lenz were killed. More men were wounded, among them, Mateo, Ceniceros, Mackison and Mayberry. The platoon could not long stand this. With 15 effectives, Shinka withdrew into a down-slope gully.

Seeing that his attack was faltering, Zimmer sent Dickerson's 2d Platoon to support the 1st Platoon, where he believed he had the best opportunity of success. Meantime, Crowson had eliminated two enemy machine guns with carbine fire. But his platoon could not move.

Dickerson called out to his men that they were going to support the 1st Platoon. Koch recalled that soon after they moved out, his platoon began taking casualties. He ran to the base of the hill, then began climbing. Ten feet beyond a wall he had crawled over, he dropped to the ground. Looking around, he discovered that, except for two dead Marines, he was alone. After firing several magazines at the ridge top, Koch went back behind the wall, where he met two other Marines, one his buddy Dick Fletcher. Much of the enemy fire was coming from the vicinity of Tugok. By agreement, the 9th had not attacked at the same time as the Marines, freeing the enemy in and near Tugok to attack the Marines by fire.

Zimmer spotted the enemy above Tugok. First, he tried to have supporting fires from the 2d Battalion take on the enemy. When he got no response, he had his FO, LT Leroy K. Wirth call in fire from the 11th Marines. "I commenced to adjust artillery fire," Wirth wrote, "but when the Bn FDC discovered it [the enemy machine gun] was outside my zone of action, fire was suspended." Three times, Wirth tried to get artillery fire on the enemy gun. Each time he was denied. Then he was wounded, and evacuated. CPT Zimmer tried to silence the enemy gun with his 60mm mortars, but the range was too great.

LT Donald D. Sisson, an FO from 1-11 Marines, was in LTC Roise's OP, watching the attack. He wrote that his "remembrance of the entire action was our seemingly inability to coordinate supporting arms.... Whether it was lack of maps, good communications or what...my experiences since have convinced me that we did a lousy job of utilizing supporting arms." One of the major problems for both artillery and mortar FOs were the poor maps. Sometimes poor communications contributed to the problem, and, of course, on occasion, the human element entered the equation. Sometimes, a commander may have failed to fully utilize the supporting weapons available to him.

2LT Granville G. Sweet's 3d Platoon, Co. A, Tk Bn concentrated its fire on enemy antitank weapons on Obong-ni. "My platoon accounted for many antitank guns and NKPA heavy weapons," wrote SGT Harvey G. Frye Sr. The four tanks of the platoon sustained 23 hits by antitank rifle fire, but none penetrated the armor. One tank was hit three times by enemy mortars. Officially, the platoon was credited with destroying at least 12 antitank guns and several automatic weapons. Unfortunately, because terrain features masked their guns, the tanks were unable to fire into the Tugok area.

As the battle progressed, the enemy attempted to drag a heavy machine gun into position on the saddle between Hills 102 and 109. Twice it was hauled up and twice hastily pulled back again under heavy Marine fire. Finally, Zimmer asked that a 75mm recoilless rifle be employed. When the enemy gun appeared for the third time, a 75mm round destroyed it.

After being driven from the hilltop, Shinka reported his status to CPT Zimmer. The captain asked for an air strike in support of the 3d Platoon. The strike came in at 11 a.m., then LT Shinka and his men stormed up and seized Hill 109. He now had only nine men. Enemy troops on the reverse slope and some in the saddle toward Hill 117 battled back. The best account of this last assault on Hill 109 is best told in LT Shinka's own words, as recorded in USMC's *The Pusan Perimeter*:

"Fire from Hill 143 was gaining in intensity, and they had observation over our position. Fire was also coming from the hill to our front [Hill 207]. I reported the situation to Captain Zimmer. A short time later phosphorus shells were exploding in Hill 143. This slowed the fire but it never did stop.

"My resupply of ammo did not arrive. Running short of ammo and taking casualties, with the shallow enemy slit trenches for cover, I decided to fall back until some of the fire on my left flank could be silenced. I gave the word to withdraw and take all wounded and weapons. About three-quarters of the way down, I had the men set up where cover was available. I had six men who were able to fight.

"I decided to go forward to find out if we left any of our wounded. As I crawled along our former position (on the crest of Hill 109), I came across a wounded Marine between two dead. (This was a man named Hric.) As I grabbed him under the arms and pulled him from the foxhole, a bullet shattered my chin. Blood ran into my throat and I couldn't breathe. I tossed a grenade at a gook crawling up the slope, didn't wait for it to explode, turned and reached under the Marine's arms and dragged him as far as the military crest.

"Another bullet hit my right arm, and the force spun me around. I rolled down the hill for a considerable distance before I could stop myself.

"I walked into my lines and had a battle dressing tied on my face and arm. I learned that the ammo was up and that relief was contemplated; and then I walked back to 2/5's aid station where they placed me on a jeep and took me to regimental aid."

In addition to Hric, who was hit in the stomach, the platoon lost a man named Reese, shot in the leg, breaking it. Two other men, CPL Walter Baker, leader of the 3d Squad, and another named Cedargren carried Hric to safety in a poncho. Reese crawled down the hill.

Eighteen year old Howard Varner, of Co. D, was also one of the casualties that day. "I was laying in my foxhole," he wrote. "Got shot in the hand from a shell. I was too scared to report it."

While Dog Co. battled for Hills 102 and 109, Easy Co. centered on the village of Obong-ni, below Hills 143 and 147. The assault platoons, like those of Co. E, encountered little opposition crossing the rice paddies. However, as they drew near the village, preparatory to ascending the ridge, heavy enemy fire tore through the platoons from Obong-ni village. Two of the company's earliest casualties were Richard Tryon, Jr. and his platoon sergeant, who he identified as Russ Borgomainerio — this was Russell J. Borgomainerio.

"My squad was forced to take cover behind a bank in a rice paddy," wrote Thomas Burke, of Co. E. "We remained in the rice paddy most of the late afternoon.... We were prone to take advantage of any cover we could get."

LT Arkadis took his platoon through the village amidst heavy enemy fire. But on the right LT Christiansen's platoon slowed and lost momentum. About this time, several enemy machine guns opened a storm of flanking fire from Hills 147 and 153. CPT Sweeney, seeing his forward platoons bogged down, had his FO try to get artillery fire on the enemy. But the FO couldn't get through. Sweeney next thought of the 4.2s, but could not locate their FO. With no other alternative, he sent his 3d Platoon forward, under 2LT Eddy. The platoon headed for the spur to the left of the village. The lieutenant worked his platoon up toward Hills 147 and 153 and was able to suppress some of the fire from these two positions. This relieved the pressure on the other two platoons.

"LT Eddy ordered me to take my fire team up the left flank to a knoll that could overlook a saddle where he thought machine gun fire was coming from," wrote Robert P. Burkhardt. He was a fire team leader in the 2d Platoon. He continued, "After climbing and running through four or five small rice paddies up the hill under fire, PFC Phillips, Barnett and Kelsey reached the knoll. The only cover was a small grave at the top. I ran to it and hugged the earth. I swear the whole ridge was firing at it, or me."

Enemy fire from apparently new positions on the lower slopes south of Obong-ni village increased. In response, Sweeney sent all of the mortar section and his headquarters personnel into the valley as a block on the south. He placed 1LT Paul R. Uffelman, his XO, in charge there then dashed to the base of the objective. Every man of Co. E was now committed to the battle.

The 2d Platoon was leaderless and disorganized, but the 1st had battled its way up the hill under excellent 81mm mortar fire. Unfortunately, just as the men neared the crest, a barrage of friendly white phosphorous artillery fire dropped on them.

By late morning part of Easy Co. was almost on the crest. But just before 11:30 a.m., they were ordered to pull back for an air strike. Some of Easy's men, within 25 yards of the summit, were strafed.

Burkhardt was in the shelter of a grave mound, when, he recalled, "someone yelled to pull back for more air strikes. It took all my nerve to get up and run back to my men.

"The air strike was a thing of beauty, with six F4U Corsairs diving right at us with guns and rockets firing away. Some shell casings hit us."

The 3d Platoon had moved back about 100 yards during the Corsair attack. When the planes left, almost smothering fire erupted from the enemy on Hills 147 and 153. The attack went to pieces.

As the battle raged along Obong-ni's slopes, enemy infiltrators sometimes harassed troops farther back. One incident involved 2d battalion's 81mm mortar platoon. A couple of the mortar positions were under fire by a sniper believed to be in a house on the right about 300 yards. No one had been hit, but the enemy's fire pinned the men down and created some confusion each time someone had to get out of the mortar pit for ammunition or supplies.

"Gunny Sergeant McVay finally had enough of it," wrote Chuck Hitchborn, a member of the platoon, "and directed me and a guy named Toomey and...I think Ed Grunder to go to that house and clean it out." Taking some fragmentation grenades with them, the three men crawled along the edge of rice paddies until within throwing distance of the house. "We heaved several grenades through the open doors and windows and then approached the house to clean it out," Hitchborn wrote. "As I stepped up on the front porch, a concussion grenade came rolling out and went off as I dived for cover. Toomey was hit in the gut; just a flesh wound but it [made him very angry]. We tossed a few more grenades inside and then heard men speaking in Korean."

Hitchborn called for them to come out. Two enemy soldiers, "who appeared to be 17 or 18 years old came out with their hands on top of their heads." The two were in uniform "and appeared to be scared," Hitchborn recalled. The prisoners were searched and the house was checked. No other North Koreans were found. They took the prisoners back to the 81 position. There, Kim, the Battalion interpreter questioned them. Grunder and Hitchborn then gave each prisoner a cigarette "and directed them to dig our hole deeper.... They started to dig and then one of them started to cry.... The prisoners thought they were digging their own graves. "They were bowing to us and chattering in Korean, apparently begging us." A jeep came from battalion about this time and took the prisoners away.

PFC Colin S. Jones Jr. was the instrument operator, responsible for assisting to lay the mortars in. He recalled in this battle that enemy fire shot the tripod of the instrument away while he was using it.

One group of men in combat can never just hug the ground or find shelter, they are the Corpsmen (Medics). When everyone else is down on the ground, trying to make themselves inconspicuous and smaller, the medical aidman must always respond to that terrible cry — "Corpsman!" At Obong-ni, many Corpsmen were among the killed and wounded. John Babbick was killed with Arkadis' platoon. Corpsmen Bill Leeke, Warren Albin, Alford Green and Herald Williams were all wounded in the battle. CPL Charles Scribner organized and led a brave little group of South Korean civilians. Six times this band went up the slopes of Obong-ni, carrying ammunition and water, and six times it brought badly wounded Marines back to the Battalion Aid Station. There, the over-worked surgeon of the 2d Battalion, Navy Lieutenant Bentley Nelson, did all he could for each one of them.

Someone once asked Conrad L. Pope, a Corpsman, how a man could go out into enemy fire like that, wrote SGT Lester M. Fulcher (4.2 inch Mortar Co.). "Con" quietly replied, 'You just know that it has to be done so you get up and do it.'"

Because of the heavy casualties among platoon leaders, LT Esten C. Carper, the 2d Battalion Naval Gunfire Officer, asked LTC Roise to assign him to a rifle company. Roise refused, saying, "One of these days the Navy will get in close enough to shoot and then I'll need you." Carper had a unique experience during this battle — he shared a foxhole with the ubiquitous Maggie Higgins!

By noon, after four hours of grueling battle, the 2d Battalion had lost 23 dead and 119 wounded — almost all the casualties in the two rifle companies. It was at this point that the shortage of a third rifle company in the battalion was hardest felt. That third company just might have added the punch needed to wrest the ridge from the enemy. As it was, the six rifle platoons had been shredded by enemy fire and grenades.

Earl J. Graves (HM Co.) described some of the enemy positions on Obong-ni thusly: "They were in the hills, [dug in] rooms just like a house. They used window sills cut in the [hill] to rest their machine guns and rifles on for support when they fired...."

The Marines did not know it at the time, but the defenders of Obong-ni had also taken a severe beating. Dead bodies, weapons and discarded equipment littered the entire north end of the ridge. In addition, Marine air and artillery attacked enemy rear areas, mortar and artillery positions, supply dumps and troop concentrations. There were definite signs of confusion in the enemy's rear area.

Only after the attack had started and he noted that the 9th was not moving, was GEN Craig informed of the Murray-Hill agreement. He then ordered Tugok be taken under fire.

When the 9th Infantry failed to attack, however, LTC Murray tried to contact COL Hill and request that he attack. He couldn't get through to Hill and had to let the matter drop in order to give his attention to the Marine attack on Obong-ni.

According to *South to the Naktong, North to the Yalu*, Murray then contacted GEN Church, who told him that the 9th would attack after a short artillery preparation. LTC Murray informed Church that 1-5th Marines would attack at 4 p.m. These statements are based on Appleman's interviews of Church and Hill on 9/25/52 and 10/1/52 respectively.

Attack of the 1st Battalion, 5th Marines — Aug. 17

At 12:45 p.m. LTC Murray ordered Newton's 1st Battalion to attack through the battered 2d and seize Obong-ni Ridge. Newton received this order at 1:30 p.m. As the 1st moved up, air, artillery and tank fire raked back and forth across the Ridge.

Just after 1:30 p.m., as he was reporting the situation to LTC Roise, CPT Zimmer was wounded by enemy machine gun fire which laced through the OP, causing several other casualties. Zimmer crawled to his CP on the reverse slope of the hill and turned command of the company over to LT Hanifin, who went forward.

On his way to the aid station, Zimmer met CPT Tobin leading his Co. B forward. He warned Tobin about the enemy guns in Tugok.

As Dog Co. prepared to withdraw to Observation Hill, Newton established his OP near that of Roise, on the same hill. His CP and aid station were co-located with those of the 2d Battalion just behind the road cut. Farther back, MAJ John W. Russell put the 1st Battalion's Weapons Company into position.

The 1st Battalion's plan of attack was similar to that employed by the 2d Battalion: Two rifle companies abreast, each with two assault rifle platoons. At 3 p.m. Co. B advanced on the right and A on the battalion left. CPT Tobin placed his 3d Platoon and machine guns on the forward slope of Observation Hill in order to support the attack. The 2d Platoon (LT David S. Taylor) advanced on the right and the 1st (LT Hugh C. Schryver Jr.) on the left. In Co. A, 1LT Robert C. Sebilian's 1st Platoon would advance on the right, and the 2d Platoon, led by diminutive 2LT Thomas H. Johnston, would be on the left. The 3d Platoon (1LT George C. Fox) was in both company and battalion reserve, which meant that Tobin could not commit the 3d Platoon without authorization from his battalion commander. Co. B would pass through Co. D and A would pass through E.

"John Tobin...called me [and the platoon leaders] forward up to a cut in the road in the little draw there," recalled Captain Fenton (then Co. XO), "to discuss the fire maneuver we were to undertake, and was pointing this out to me. John was on my right and a radio operator was on my left.... An automatic weapon opened up and caught John across the chest, somehow missed me, but hit the radio operator...on my left. But the only thing I could think of...as John went down...was 'My God, the map!' It was the only map we had.... We had one map for the company commander.... All I could think of was that, without the map, we were in trouble. John had been carrying it up in his dungaree pocket and...it was badly blood splattered. That was my first reaction. I got the map and then John was evacuated." CPT Tobin survived his wounds.

The two rifle companies began their attack at 3 p.m., as planned. Schryver's platoon headed for Hill 102, and Taylor's for Hill 109. In Co. A, Sebilian's platoon was to move up the draw between 109 and Hill 117, seizing 117. Johnston, on his left, moved up another draw between Hills 117 and 143, with the objective of taking 143. As with the attack platoons of the 2d Battalion, those of the 1st moved across the rice paddies to the slopes of Obong-ni without much opposition. Of course, Marine air, artillery, mortar and automatic weapons fire was blasting away at the objective during this move.

Since the enemy near Tugok seemed to provide the only effective fire on the Marines in the crossing, they were taken under artillery fire. While artillery and mortars shelled the Tugok area, recalled Manuel Brito, (Co. B) the men sought "cover in rain gulleys."

"When the shelling stopped we proceeded with our frontal assault," he wrote. The men got part way up Hill 102, but, he continued, "the frontal assault soon became impossible because of heavy machinegun fire from the top. The 1st [Platoon] worked its way back down the hill and around the base to the road, making a flanking attack on the hill. We captured and held the top with fewer casualties than would have been possible with a frontal assault."

LT Schryver called in 81mm mortars to suppress enemy fire from Tugok, which was severely impeding his platoon's advance. The 81s took care of Tugok. Schryver then worked his platoon around, taking the enemy position in flank, and seizing Hill 102 by 5:10 p.m.

After reporting Tobin's wounding and that he was assuming command of Co. B, Ike Fenton, with his gunnery sergeant, MSG Edward A. Wright, went forward to the 2d Platoon. Taylor's men had gotten about half way up the slope when accurate and heavy fire from Hills 109, 117 and 143 began cutting his men down. Taylor was mortally wounded.

When Fenton got to the 2d Platoon, both it and the 1st were stalled. He radioed back for the 3d.

In the meantime, the 1st Platoon took Hill 102 and began attacking Hill 109 by fire, while B Co. machine guns raked Hills 117 and 143. SGT Walter L. Wolfe Jr. wrote that his 2d Machinegun Section initially fired "overhead fire across the top of Red Slash in the 2d Platoon's zone of action. Occasionally a gook would pop up but was soon dispatched." Aided by the company machine guns, the 2d Platoon surged up and onto Hill 109 at 5:25 p.m.

"When the 1st and 2d Platoons overran the enemy's former positions," Wolfe recounted, "my section then diddy-bopped ASAP to the forward slope to further fire upon the retreating enemy. The gooks were not only stoppable, they were routable as well. Even though the action was fast and furious, we immediately consolidated our gains and our positions...."

On Co. B's left, Co. A moved through the survivors of E and reached a point almost half way up the slopes toward Hills 117 and 143.

As the 1st Battalion moved up the road toward the front earlier in the day, Billy Ogan, a rifleman in Co. A's 2d Platoon was daydreaming as he walked along. "Just three months ago," he wrote, "I had been sitting at a bar drinking all the beer I could consume and afford and contemplating selling my '49 Pontiac and returning to the Marine Corps so that I could get back into Officer's Training. Some poor planning on my part...."

Herbert Luster, a BAR-man in the same platoon, recalled the march forward that day. As his platoon walked up the road he saw that "a dead soldier lay face up on a slab of rock, "he wrote. As the platoon took a path to the left off the road, "they walked by a...hut with three dead American soldiers lying beside it...."

As both platoons of Co. A advanced beyond the half way point up the ridge, enemy fire began to exact a heavy toll. Dead and wounded Marines pitched forward here and there, and rolled limply down the hillside. 1LT Robert C. Sebilian led his 1st Platoon up the draw between Hills 109 and 117. He ignored the veritable hail of enemy bullets to stand up and urge his platoon forward. Soon he fell, one leg shattered by an explosive bullet. TSGT Orval F. McMullen immediately took command and pressed on. As a result, the 1st Platoon reached the saddle above the draw as Co. B took Hill 109. The sergeant tried to push the platoon on toward 117 to the south, but, what the Marine history describes as "a solid sheet of Communist fire" stopped it cold.

On the left, Johnson's platoon soon lost half its men, but the lieutenant pushed on. When enemy fire finally halted what was left of his platoon, he courageously went by himself up the draw between Hills 117 and 143. Observers could not believe that the enemy held on so stubbornly in the face of the pounding by Marine guns. Then, to their amazement, they saw one man dart forward of the stalled 2d Platoon and run up the hill. This was LT Johnson, in a single-handed, but suicidal, attack on the heart of the enemy defense. He reached the saddle between 117 and 143 and kept going. Finally, at the base of 143, he sagged to the ground, dead. TSGT Frank J. Lawson took over the platoon, and, with outstanding leadership, tried to move the platoon forward. But frightful enemy gunfire and showers of grenades were too much. The 2d Platoon now numbered no more than a squad.

CPT Stevens then radioed LTC Newton from his OP and asked to commit his 3d Platoon. The 3d Platoon, although in reserve, had come under 82mm mortar fire. One of its men was literally blown to pieces by a direct hit from one of these rounds.

1LT George Fox led his men forward from Observation Hill to a point on the company's left. While traversing the rice paddies, an enemy mortar barrage killed one of his men. Fox's platoon joined the remains of the 2d, and the combined force tried again to attack. But enemy machine guns lashed out and grenades rained down on the men. Fox twice tried to continue the attack, but was thwarted each time by what the Marine history describes as a "curtain of fire." The Marines could not move forward from the gully. Leaving TSGT Stanley G. Millar to reorganize the skirmish line, Fox and PFC Benjamin C. Simpson, of the 2d Platoon tried to reach Johnston. They crawled to a position just above the gully where Simpson could see the fallen platoon leader. He was dead. Thus assured, and prevented from getting to him by fire from several enemy machine guns, the two men slid back down into the draw. Simpson was killed in the Second Battle of the Naktong Bulge in early Sept.

About this time Stevens had arrived at the base of Obong-ni, but had lost radio contact with his rifle platoons. He could see the 2d and 3d Platoons above him, but had no contact with the 1st. As a result, he was unaware of that unit's success, which he could have exploited.

"I suppose we got to within 75 yards of the crest by 1700 (5 p.m.)," Fox wrote of the action. "Casualties were heavy. I was told to consolidate, hold and dig in for the night. The ground was terrible, but we did manage to scrape out shallow holes and pits for the MGs.... [W]e were receiving scattered fire while we did [this]. We...distributed ammo, evacuated the casualties, got resupplied with water, [placed and sighted in] weapons, etc." He thought that wire communication with the company CP was also established.

TSGT Joseph Fedin, with Co. A's machine guns, and Raymond E. Stephens, a Fire Team Leader in the 2d Platoon, recalled the fighting once the 2d and 3d Platoons gained the crest. "They were prepared on the reverse slope, fox-holes and all," Fedin wrote. "As we got near the top they would throw hand grenades and we would back down, then start up again."

"One grenade I threw didn't make it quite over the ridge," Stephens wrote, "and rolled back down directly toward me. I flattened out face down and it exploded harmlessly about 10 feet in front of me." Later a PFC Martinez of Stephens' squad tossed grenades up to him and Stephens would then throw them over the ridge

to clear the reverse slope before going over. Enemy grenades flew back toward Stephens, but he remained flat on the ground, and they exploded harmlessly.

Billy Ogan and Herbert Luster (2d Platoon, Co. A) wrote of their experiences in Co. A's attack. Both were wounded.

Ogan wrote, "I started up, with the rest of my fire team and the whole scene reminded me of several war movies I had seen, only this time I was a participant. We could not see the North Koreans but they sure as hell could see us.... It was a bloody mess. Explosions on both sides, bodies to jump over; I still couldn't see a damn thing to shoot at. I had Marines on both sides and in front — they were getting hit, dropping like flies." But Ogan couldn't stop to check on any of the fallen men; his fire team kept climbing up the hill. Then he spotted a BAR on the ground. Thinking it would increase his firepower, he stopped to pick it up. "By stopping, I made my first mistake," he wrote. "The enemy now had an immobile six foot two, one hundred and eighty-six pound Marine to zero in on. I felt like I had been hit by a truck; was picked up and thrown to the ground. What the hell hit me? No immediate pain...then confusion and a little shock. One minute I was standing and now I was on the ground. It was all so unreal. I was in a daze and still hadn't seen an enemy or even fired a shot. What kind of war was this? Nothing like what I used to see in movies."

His Fire Team Leader called down, "Ogan, are you hit?" Billy felt his right side, and his hand came away bloody, and the pain started. "Yeah, I'm hit!" he called back. The Fire Team Leader came down and was in the process of applying a compress to Ogan's wound, "when there was one hell of an explosion to my immediate rear." An enemy grenade landed behind the Fire Team Leader. One of his eyes popped out of its socket. Both men slid down the hill to a point where it was relatively safe to stand up. Ogan had two wounds, but his Fire Team Leader was in worse shape. Both men managed to make their way to the aid station, were treated and evacuated.

"Off they went, passing a .30-caliber air-cooled machinegun," Herbert wrote. "The gunner wished them well...."

At the base of the hill Luster's fire team was sent to one side to flank a saddle several hundred yards away. The men of the platoon spread out to present a poor target to the enemy. The hillside was covered with scrub pine bushes "and a whole platoon of enemy could be concealed there," Luster thought. He put the BAR sling over his head to free both hands for the up hill climb. "The BAR hung in front of him," wrote Luster, "so he could fire quickly, if needed." A 75mm recoilless rifle suddenly fired nearby, momentarily startling the entire team. As they climbed, Luster was virtually crawling, for he recalled that "he couldn't see ten feet ahead of himself, the young pines were so thick."

Emerging on the top of the ridge, he spotted what he believed to be enemy soldiers in the saddle crawl to their guns. Luster called to his Fire Team Leader, CPL Dale W. Ellis, "Do we have anyone in that direction?" "No!" he replied. Luster then called back for some machine gun fire. He could see an A Co. fire team heading for the enemy po-

sition he had spotted. It was evident to him that he was the only one who could see the enemy. Since his sergeant had told the men to save their grenades for night, Luster decided to engage the enemy with his BAR. Readying the weapon, Herbert "settled back on his right foot and opened fire," he recounted. "The flying dirt and tracers told him where his rounds were going. He emptied the rifle" At first, he couldn't get the magazine to fall out, so he pushed the release with his right thumb "and pulled the empty magazine out, stuck it in his jacket pocket, loaded and raised the BAR to his shoulder," he wrote. "Before he could get it all the way up, red dirt kicked up in his face. A big tug at his right arm told him he was hit. He looked down and saw blood squirting onto his broken BAR stock." Herbert laid back in the shallow ditch he was in and tried to relax, then called out that he was hit. When asked where, he responded, "In the arm."

About then a Corsair came over on a strafing run and Luster shielded his face from falling empty shell casings with his left arm. Ellis got to him briefly, then left. Someone called for a Corpsman. Luster got into position and began skidding down the hill on his bottom. His right arm flopped loosely, then got caught on a scrub pine. He couldn't get free. He was unable to get his fighting knife out because he had wired it to the sheath because the snap was broken. With the loss of blood, his mind wandered. "Suddenly, he saw his father's face," Herbert wrote. "He was back in Hearne, Texas, and he was seven years old."

His reverie was broken by CPL Koehler, who was applying a tourniquet made from a bayonet sheath and rifle ammunition bandoleer. Unable to stop the blood, Koehler disappeared. Luster prayed. Suddenly he heard the call, "Corpsman, Corpsman!" To his surprise it was his own voice. Homing in on his calls, two Corpsmen finally reached him, treated him and got him back to the aid station.

The enemy bullet had shattered PFC Herbert R. Luster's right arm and it had to be amputated. But Luster never lost his sense of humor. On Aug. 24, a doctor reminded him that there were many things he would no longer be able to do. "There was a sudden, heavy silence," he wrote. Then Luster said, "I can do something you can't do."

"What's that?" the doctor asked.

"I can stand in front of an officer and not salute!" said Luster. "The other patients roared with laughter," Luster wrote, "and [I] smiled, surprising even [myself] with that one."

"A runner came up [to the Brigade CP] with a report on the fighting strength of the two battalions on the hill," reported Harold H. Martin in his Oct. 14, 1950 *Saturday Evening Post* article, "The Epic of Bloody Hill." "Out of 200 men and 4 officers in each company, Able had 4 officers and 68 enlisted men alive.... Baker Company had 2 officers and 103 men left. Dog Company had 2 officers and 85 riflemen; and in Easy Company only 3 officers and 78 men were still in shape to fight."

North Korean Tank Attack

"About three nights ago just about dusk, we were coming up this road when 2 jeeps came running back shouting 'the tanks are coming.' I never saw our guns set up so fast. Three tanks came around the curve and never knew what hit them. They only fired 4 rounds at us before they turned into blazing infernos." These few lines from Herbert R. Pearce's Aug. 20, 1950 letter to his parents succinctly describe the disastrous enemy tank attack on the evening of Aug. 17. Pearce was a Corpsman with the Brigade's AT Co.

Both observation planes and ground observers spotted the approaching enemy tanks. One of those who saw the advancing T-34s was Manuel Brito of Co. B. "Towards dusk," he wrote, "I heard a faint, distant clanking sound coming from our front. Taking the scope from a dead Korean's sniper rifle, I scanned the rice paddies facing 102. About 700 yards [out] on the Naktong-Yongsan road...to the right of the paddies I spotted three enemy T-34 tanks headed towards us. Where the road curved to the left and about 1,000 yards behind the third tank was a fourth coming up the road and a company-sized enemy [force] moving through the rice paddies and behind the tank.

"I stood up and yelled, 'Enemy tanks with infantry moving towards 102!' The word was relayed back to CPT Ike Fenton's Command Post."

CPT Fenton recalled that he was alerted to the approaching tanks about 8 p.m. He sent a "Flash" message, reporting "enemy tanks in the area. About then some F-51s began engaging the tanks, but could not stop them. (The Marines finally called the planes off. The tanks, LT Muetzel recalled, "managed to shoot us up.") Fenton was ordered to let the tanks through, to be taken care of farther back. He recalled that there was firm ground on either side of the road, but the enemy tanks did not take advantage of it to maneuver. He wrote that it was "just like sitting on the 50 yard line of the Rose Bowl about 150 feet up. We had a good seat for the show that was about to take place."

"As we were rearming and refueling late the evening of the first day we received a 'Flash Purple' over the infantry radio, which was the code word for enemy tank attack," wrote SGT Harvey G. Frye Jr., A-1st Tk Bn. The crews had been refueling using 55-gallon drums which they had hoisted onto the tanks, and flexible nozzles. Quickly rolling the drums off their tanks, three of the M-26s, main guns loaded with armor piercing rounds, took off down the road toward the base of Obong-ni. Encountering some vehicles blocking the road, lead tank commander TSGT Cecil Fullerton yelled for them to get out of the way. As the American tanks entered one end of a narrow cut, the T-34s entered the other. Fullerton pulled the right track of his tank part way up the incline, allowing SGT Harvey G. Frye, Jr. to bring his up on the left. SGT Swinckie pulled the third tank up on the left of Frye's.

As the M-26s came forward into position, the 1st 75mm Recoilless Gun Platoon (2LT Paul R. Fields) on Observation Hill and the rocket section of the 1st Battalion on Hill 125, across the road, prepared to meet the oncoming T-34s.

As the enemy tank reached the bend in the road, it was hit in the right track by a 3.5 inch rocket fired by Casper A. Tartalone, H&S, 1-5th Marines. "I got one round off [and] hit the lead

tank in the treads." recounted Tartalone. "He spun, stopped, but opened fire with his machine guns, [killing] the other man [with me]." The T-34 then continued, firing wildly, until stopped by 75mm fire that blasted its left track and front armor. The tank lurched forward to face TSGT Fullerton's M-26.

"We commenced firing," wrote SGT Frye. "As my gunner started to depress the 90mm to fire down at the T-34s the gun stopped.... My elevating mechanism was somehow jammed, and I couldn't bear on the target! Sheer frustration! Fullerton and Swinckie were firing point blank at the T-34s.... In his haste to get the gasoline drums off his tank, Swinckie apparently spilled a lot of gas around the exterior turret ring of his tank. When Fullerton opened fire, Swinckie's tank caught fire. As Fullerton fired again, the back blast from the 90 put out the fire. Shortly there were three burning T-34s in front of us."

The lead tank exploded after taking two 90mm hits. An enemy soldier jumped from the burning wreck, was struck by small-arms fire, crawled under the tank and died. The second tank was first hit by one rocket in the right track, causing it to wobble forward aimlessly. A second hit the T-34's gas tank, then a 75mm round slammed into it. The vehicle slewed to a stop behind the first tank, and its main gun fired off into the air. Marine tanks next blasted it with six 90mm rounds. Amazingly, the enemy tank continued to fire, although wildly. Seven more rounds tore into the hulk. When an enemy tanker opened its turret to escape, a 2.36 inch WP round hit the open lid and ricocheted into the turret. The tanker fell back into the tank which had been turned into blazing furnace by the rocket round.

The third tank tore around the bend and stopped abruptly behind the first two. It was overwhelmed by rocket, recoilless rifle and M-26 90mm fire. The T-34 blew up and the wreckage began to burn. Corsairs had already destroyed the fourth tank before it reached Marine lines. The Army's Second Division history states that F/9th Infantry also knocked out an enemy tank by 3.5 inch rockets this day.

SGT Paul Santiago, H&S, 1-5th Marines, was with a litter team taking a badly wounded Marine back to the Aid Station when the enemy tanks came up the road. The men were in a shallow draw nearby, but were unaware of what was happening. The tank advance on the road cut Santiago and his party off from the Aid Station. "As we came out on the rice paddy," he wrote, "we heard all the commotion and stopped.... It seemed best to remain where they were; a 1,000 yard stretch of open rice paddy lay ahead. There was heavy firing in all directions, he recalled. "One of the litter bearers shielded our casualty when a couple of rounds came very close. I spun around to hit the deck. Unfortunately I was too close to the hillside. My helmet hit first and smashed down on the bridge of my nose. No harm was done but the other guys thought it worth a chuckle (it's always good to be able to laugh at a sergeant openly)." When the fire slackened, the team continued, arriving safely at the Aid Station with their casualty.

The Marine history makes a reference to "shattering the myth of the T-34" in this fight. The "myth," was dispelled at Taejon almost a

month previously, when infantrymen of the 24th Division destroyed 8 T-34 tanks there with 3.5 inch rocket launchers on July 20. The same day, artillery fire destroyed 2 more there, and the USAF knocked out 5 more. The latter number was confirmed by an enemy prisoner.

Attack of the 9th Infantry — Afternoon, August 17

The 9th Infantry finally made its attack about 1 p.m. with Co.s F and G abreast moving on Tugok and the hills beyond. Shortly before 4 p.m., Army artillery and mortar fire plastered the Tugok area. Some of the artillery fire was in the form of proximity fuze rounds, which scattered shell fragments in deadly profusion throughout the area. The 2/9th Infantry battled through the village and attacked the ridge beyond. This is the ridge the Marines dubbed "Finger Ridge." Although thrown back several times, the battalion persisted, winning the ridge line just before nightfall. The two companies dug in there, while Co. E was retained in reserve along the original line of departure. Only the 2d Battalion took part in the attack. The 1st Battalion remained in place, as planned. The seizure of Finger Ridge completed the 9th Infantry's part in the counteroffensive to drive the enemy's *4th Division* back across the Naktong.

Had the 9th attacked at the same time as the Brigade, as originally planned, it would have occupied the enemy in and near Tugok, north of the road in the Army's zone of attack and these enemy soldiers would have been unable to deliver such destructive fire on the Marine's right flank. Closer, more efficient communications between the 9th Infantry and Marines would have permitted better coordination of all types of fire. The attempt to fire Marine artillery into the Tugok area could have been cleared quickly and the mission could have been fired, or Army artillery supporting the 9th Infantry could have fired the mission. The Marine seizure of Hills 102 and 109 would have been made with more rapidly and with fewer casualties.

COL Fenton clarifies what caused the communications problems when he wrote: "The lack of communications was due to the lack of hardware, not the lack of desire or planning. Radios and wire were at a premium. Wire was hard to come by and the 9th [Infantry] had a shortage of communications personnel in their wire sections."

Attack of the 19th Infantry — Afternoon, Aug. 17

The attack of the 19th Infantry was held up because 3/34th Infantry was delayed in relieving 1/19th Infantry on the line due to the same shortage of trucks which had slowed the redeployment of the Marine Brigade. The same trucks had to be used for both lifts. The 3d Battalion, 34th began its relief of 1/19th about 9 a.m. The 1/34th infantry occupied an assembly area about 500 yards behind 3/34th. Both battalions would support by fire the attack on Ohang Hill. Once Ohang Hill was taken, the 34th would advance on its own Objectives 2 and 3. So, until the 19th actually attacked, the 34th took no overt action.

For some reason, 1/19th Infantry took a

roundabout route through the confusion of hills behind the lines. Of course, the projected attack time of 8 a.m. had long since passed. It was not until 1:30 p.m. that the 1st Battalion reached their assigned assembly area. The men were nearly spent from their protracted march to that point. In the meantime, the 2d Battalion conducted patrols toward enemy positions on Ohang Hill. These patrols revealed that the North Koreans were still there in force. The 1st Battalion's attack was then reset for 5 p.m. Repeated attempts to get air strikes on Ohang Hill were unsuccessful; no aircraft were available. Several artillery, the regimental HM Co. and the 1st Battalion's own Heavy Weapons Co. provided support for the attack.

Co. B, on the right, next to the Naktong, had 117 personnel. Co. C, on its left (south) had 144. B attacked with the 2d Platoon on the right and the 1st on the left. The 3d Platoon was company reserve, following the 2d. As the assault platoons climbed the hill far enough to mask supporting fires, the enemy opened a high volume of fire which raked the nearly exhausted infantrymen. Both assault platoons were stopped. But a sergeant from the 2d Platoon charged forward to the crest on his own and knocked out an enemy machine gun there. At his call, his squad joined him, but the remainder of the platoon was unable to, although it maneuvered to the right. The 3d Platoon was sent forward between the other two and also was pinned down. Again, one man took the initiative and charged. He destroyed the enemy holding up the attack. The company commander then pulled the 3d Platoon back and sent it up to reinforce the 1st. The two platoons then surged to the top of the hill. An enemy counterattack was beaten off, and the two platoons destroyed the enemy machine guns holding up the 2d Platoon. The entire company was then reunited on the top of Ohang Hill.

Co. C also experienced blasts of enemy fire and showers of grenades, once it advanced far enough to mask supporting fire. This pinned down the 1st Platoon advancing on the right, and part of the 3d Platoon on the left. The few men of the 3d not pinned down, moved to the right. Two men crawled to the crest and spotted a lone machine gun crew. This enemy was destroyed, allowing the rest of the company to reach the top. A weak counterattack by about 20 North Koreans was easily repulsed. Companies B and C, joined by 65 men from Co A, dug in for the night. The enemy plastered the area with an hour-long barrage of 120mm mortars and, after dark, tried another attack by about 100 men. This, too, was easily beaten off. The 19th was firmly in control of Ohang Hill.

On the division's northern flank, enemy infiltrators roamed the rear areas. One group attacked a medical detachment of the 21st, but were driven into the hills by the regimental I & R Platoon and South Korean police. The 1st Battalion, 23d Infantry, continued to probe enemy positions near Hill 409. Co. A, supported by artillery and air strikes, probed the eastern approaches to the hill mass. The enemy fought back spiritedly with small arms, machine guns and light mortars. An enemy prisoner said that the North Koreans were short of ammunition. This may explain why they did not employ heavier mortars or artillery against Co. A.

Evacuation of Marine Dead and Wounded — Aug. 17

Marine casualties were very heavy and extraordinary measures had to be taken to evacuate the dead, treat the wounded and get them to hospitals where they could be cared for. Surgeons Lieutenants (jg) Bentley G. Nelson (1-5) and Chester L Klein (2-5) did all they could. The shortage of hospital corpsman was so bad that the Brigade's Malaria and Epidemic Control Unit was pressed into service to reinforce the medical staff. In the rear, LT CDR Byron D. Casteel commandeered every ambulance he could, including 16 Army vehicles, to evacuate the wounded to and from his 5th Regimental aid station. More serious cases were flown by helicopter from the regiment to the 8076 MASH at Miryang, twenty miles away.

Chaplains LT CDR Orlando Ingvolstad Jr., LT CDR Otto E. Sporrer, LT William G. Tennant and LT (jg) Bernard L. Hickey toiled hard to meet the spiritual needs of casualties. Sporrer was especially conspicuous as he frequently exposed himself to enemy fire administering to wounded Marines. Muetzel wrote: "Sporrer was really Gung-ho and carried a .22 [caliber] pistol. When this was pointed out [to him] as illegal and somewhat inadequate, he later got a .357 Magnum. He was outspoken to a fault...." Colonels Fenton and Taplett also wrote about the chaplains. Fenton: "Hickey was the very ultimate in Chaplains. Sporrer was the Brigade Headquarters Chaplain. Hickey was up on the front lines with the Bns and Cos. He was tireless and a great comfort to the troops. Not enough good things can be said about this man!" Taplett: "One of the unsung heroes of the brigade was Father Bernard Hickey (now deceased).... He was always up front where the heaviest fighting was taking place night and day. He'd come to me and say, 'Tap, which company is going to have it worst today?' and that's where he'd head for."

1LT Wayne E. Richards 2d Platoon, Co A, 1st Engineers was engaged most of Aug. 17 in removing unexploded ordnance from forward assembly areas. The company's 1st Platoon, meantime had to demolish most of an unoccupied village for material with which to reinforce a section of road which was sinking from the incessant ambulance and truck traffic.

Disposition of the 1st Battalion, 5th Marines — Night of Aug. 17-18

At about 8:30 p.m., right after the enemy tank attack had been smashed, CPT Stevens (Co. A) contacted his 1st Platoon to learn that it occupied the saddle between Hills 109 and 117. The company had been unable to seize Hills 117 and 143, both of which were strongly defended by enemy troops. The platoon was in contact with B on the right, but a 100 yard gap existed between it and Stevens' other two platoons on the left.

Stevens conferred with Fox, Lawson and McMullen near the base of the ridge. These officers advised against continuing the attack. Darkness was coming and their men needed rest, food, water and ammunition. Furthermore, the

enemy's tank attack convinced the platoon leaders that the enemy was planning a heavy counterattack. Stevens reported to Newton, who ordered him to break off the attack and tie in with Fenton's Co. B for the night. Night had fallen before the 2d and 3d Platoon shifted to tie in with the 1st in a continuous company front.

Fenton's company went into position on Hills 102 and 109 with the 1st and 2d Platoons on line and the 3d in reserve on the reverse slope. To help ensure communication with his platoons, the captain had two telephone wires run to each.

On Fenton's left, on the southern part of Hill 109, Co. A was deployed southward to the saddle between 109 and 117. From there, the company line bent back and down the eastern slope of the ridge to the rice paddies. The Battalion HC was to have continued the line across the paddies between the base of Obong-ni and Observation Hill. Casualties and the workload of headquarters personnel prevented this from happening. As a result, the left flank of Co. A and its 3d Platoon was left dangling.

CPT Stevens placed Able's CP at the top of the draw leading to the saddle between Hills 109 and 117. The 60mm mortar section was behind the CP in the gully itself.

Paul Santiago (H&S, 1-5th Marines) was placed on the forward slope of Obong-ni, near the Battalion OP. He and another Marine manned a listening post. "I learned a lesson from my partner," he wrote. "He said we should lie on our backs with out feet towards the area we had to watch. Anyone moving through there would be visible against the skyglow. A device I used often in my work later on."

"I took position in a shallow foxhole," wrote PFC Carl T. Lawendowski, of Baker Co., "presumably occupied by the NKPA earlier, and was taking what I deemed to be a well deserved break...with my eyes shut. When suddenly I was jolted to reality by someone's boot, nudging me. It turned out to be the skipper's, Captain Ike Fenton, with accompanying words like, 'Wake up — 100% watch tonight.' Needless to say I got my second wind...right about then." Just before darkness, Lawendowski was paired up with BAR-man PFC Charles Beeson in a foxhole on the left side of Baker's hill. Carl felt confident with Beeson, who had been through actions with TF Kean.

On another part of the B Co. line was Manuel Brito. "We settled down for the night," he wrote, "in anticipation of the enemy counterattack which we were sure would come. Throughout the night, the burning enemy tanks below kept setting off ammo from within."

North Korean Counterattack — 2:30 a.m., Aug. 18

Just before 10 p.m. a heavy shower of mortar rounds fell on Co. A. This was followed by a concentration of white phosphorous fire which blanketed the company's center. The entire mortar section was knocked out, every man dead or wounded. Muetzel recalled that this barrage was from the Marine 4.2 inch mortars — short rounds. The barrage also struck part of the 3d Platoon, wounding Fox and a number of his men. Two men from the 3d had to be evacuated, but Fox and the others received first aid and remained in position. After this short, furious bombardment, an uneasy silence came over the area.

"About 0230 (2:30 a.m.) we heard movement and the entire company got hit hard by a counterattack shortly thereafter," wrote LT Fox (3/A Co.). "The gooks were all around us and occasionally one or two would get in the perimeter. I...got one with my .45. Commo went out. I don't know if we were surrounded, but it was pretty nip and tuck. I must have moved the same BAR man for the 2d or 3d time to plug a hole. As he passed me, he said in a stage whisper, 'G_ D_ it, Lieutenant, is this trip really necessary?' Everybody burst out laughing. That broke the tension. We held."

The enemy came off Hill 117, following heavy machine gun fire and a shower of hand grenades. An enemy platoon swarmed into the 2d Platoon. The platoon, under TSGT Lawson's courageous leadership battled the enemy for a half hour before being overrun. Lawson was wounded three times in the struggle. The North Koreans penetrated the line through the 2d Platoon's sector.

The enemy attacked with two platoons against Hill 109, ignoring 81mm illuminating rounds. They alternately attacked with grenadiers, then with burp gunners. The attack was covered by heavy, raking machine gun fire from Hill 117. One enemy squad came out of the gully between Hills 102 and 109, but was repelled. Thereafter it contented itself with sniping.

The enemy never exploited its breakthrough in Co. A, although Stevens and his CP group were forced slowly down the draw by what the Marine history describes as "methodical grenade and submachinegun fire from above." Steven's 1st Platoon, its left exposed, fell back into Baker Co.'s sector.

It was also about 2:30 a.m. when CPT Fenton's 2d Platoon, on the company left flank, where it tied in with Co. A, reported enemy activity to the front. "A few minutes later, a flare went off," Fenton recalled, "and the enemy hit us with great force right where the two companies were tied-in.... Their ferocious attack managed to break our lines where the two companies tied in." The North Koreans also pushed back Co. A's left flank

When he learned that the enemy had broken through between the two units, Fenton pulled his 2d Platoon back to form a tighter company perimeter That platoon was overrun and some of the enemy got into the Baker Co. CP and a furious hand-to-hand battle ensued.

"Darkness fell and we were told that the South Korean carriers would bring up rations," wrote SGT Bob Baughman, of Co. A. "We could hear the jabbering and assumed it was our chow. Instead, it was the *Inmun Gun* [sic] and right upon us. We were told to merge into Baker Company on top of the hill. In our movement, the *Inmun Gun* [sic] fired at us and then Baker Company also fired on us.

"My friend CPL Charles Avery [and I] were bringing up what we thought was the rear — on our bellies, he on my right. He said 'Let's move.' Then a grenade exploded at his right hip and he said, 'I'm hit; don't leave me.' I looked at his wound as a star shell went off and told him he had a broken leg. He was [actually] open[ed]

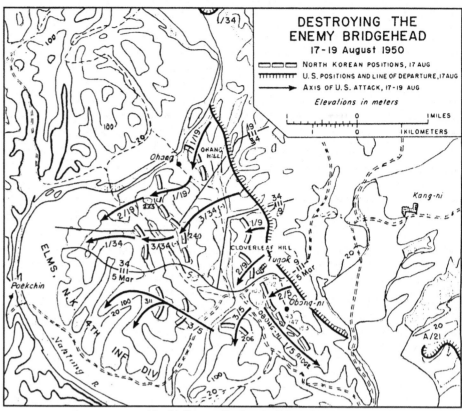

Map 31 (*Source:* South to the Naktong)

from the belt line half way to his knee. This was a U.S. grenade."

Enemy troops were now all around the two men. A couple of North Koreans came by and shook the men, but they successfully feigned death. The enemy soldiers passed on. Then Baughman helped Avery slide down the hill. By that time, it was getting light. Looking around, Baughman could see no one — friend or enemy. Recalling that an aid station had been about a quarter mile away, Baughman marked Avery's position with a C-ration carton, and ran for the station. Enroute he was struck in the lip by a bullet, then was held up by a mortar barrage. He discovered that the aid station had been moved back another 1/2 mile. When he got there, there were no stretcher bearers available, so he told the corpsmen where Avery was located. They loaded Baughman on a jeep and evacuated him. A few days later he rejoined his unit. Avery was alive when the corpsmen found him, but he died enroute to the aid station; he had lost too much blood.

LT Francis W. Muetzel commanded A Company's machine guns. When the unit dug in on Obong-ni for the night, his guns were all attached out to the rifle platoons. Muetzel had his platoon sergeant, TSGT Berlin Caldwell, on the right flank to tie in with Co. B. Caldwell was killed there. Muetzel remained with Steven's CP. "The attack began with a shower of grenades," he wrote. "followed by infantry armed with burp guns. They penetrated and overran one machine gun. I was hit by grenade fragments above my right eye and in my scalp, knocking me cold and shredding my steel helmet." Upon regaining consciousness, Muetzel realized he was behind the enemy "and could see them, hear them and smell them moving around me. The CP was abandoned and I had been left for dead. Oddly

enough, I wondered if it would be considered cowardly if I got the hell out of there. I threw my only grenade and between illuminating flares, I leaped to my feet and ran downhill in a crouch, diving headfirst into the Red Slash that ran up the hill. I rolled into the CP group before they could react and fire at me. We held what we had and at first light resumed the attack."

The Marine history states that "by 0400 [4 a.m.] Stevens had temporarily lost control of Company A, although the situation looked worse than it actually was." Fox, with his 3d Platoon and some men of the 2d, were "hanging tough" on the company left, while elements of the 1st had folded back into the left flank of Co. B. Stevens' XO, 1LT Fred F. Eubanks and LT Muetzel worked at keeping the enemy at bay in the gully between the two flanks of Co. A. Stevens, meantime, began getting things in hand.

Over in Co. B, PFC Lawendowski was still in the foxhole with BAR-man PFC Beeson. Once they settled in, "the next several hours the peace and quiet were disturbed occasionally by bursts of machine gun fire," Lawendowski wrote. "I half dozed off during the infrequent quiet intervals, due to exhaustion but also...due to the confidence I had in Beeson."

"Some time around 2 or 3 a.m....all hell broke loose to our front and on our right. I crouched at the ready every time illuminating flares went up and cursed them when they burned themselves out. I felt that I had a better than even chance if I could see what I was shooting at." Also, Lawendowski did not want to accidentally shoot any fellow Marine.

Brito wrote, "Upon signal, the enemy launched a furious counterattack...driving a wedge between Able Company and the 2d Platoon [of Co. B], turning that flank with a larger force than what hit the 1st Platoon. Our artillery and mortars, which were already registered... opened up with a deadly barrage. Illuminating rounds from our 81s lit up the entire area. What we saw was a squad-sized group of the enemy, lobbing grenades, [then] rise to their feet in a staggered formation, spray the front and both flanks with burp guns, and fall down. Another squad would rise and repeat the same moves. These tactics continued until dawn, but fire from our lines kept them in check." With the approach of dawn, the enemy withdrew to high ground on Obong-ni, south of the Marines.

LTC Newton responded to the news of Co A's withdrawal by calling down such a heavy volume of artillery fire on the enemy that 1-11 suggested he conserve some ammunition for the attack scheduled for 7 a.m. Newton replied that if he didn't get the artillery he needed, they would be trying to retake Objective 1 at 7 a.m. The battalion commander added the fire of his 81mm mortars.

Co. A, 5th Marines Secures the Remainder of Obong-ni Ridge — Morning, Aug. 18

As dawn broke, CPT Stevens prepared to continue the attack along Obong-ni Ridge. His wounded gunnery sergeant TSGT Paul A. Hodge had regained contact with Fox's men. At 7 a.m., Stevens moved out with Fox's 3d Platoon leading.

Fox shouted to his men to move out and they rose as one to the attack. An enemy machine gun cut loose from Hill 117. Spotting the gun, Stevens called in an air strike. Very quickly, a Corsair swooped in over the 3d Platoon and dropped a 500 lb. bomb directly on the enemy position. Fox's men were so close that they were all knocked to the ground by the concussion and the point man was killed. "But the rest of the attack was a cake walk," Fox wrote. "I think I had about 20 men left in my platoon that morning, from the 43 the day before."

McMullen's 1st Platoon swept in from Hill 109, and the enemy fled, panic-stricken, from the top and reverse slope of 117. What seemed to be an entire company of North Koreans ran down the western slope. Steven's riflemen, BAR men and machinegunners had a "turkey shoot." The 3d Platoon moved smoothly to Hill 143, taking it against little resistance, then on to Hill 147. From its crest, the Marines saw a formation of about 150 North Koreans, withdrawing down the western slope in a column of fours. Marine fire soon broke the formation into a gaggle of frightened men, fleeing for their lives.

Fox finally reached Hill 153. Believing that the enemy would make a stand for this, the highest point on the ridgeline, the Marines were pleasantly surprised to find the hill occupied by a few enemy dead, abandoned weapons and equipment and half-destroyed foxholes. They were startled however, when what seemed to be a stand of scrub pines arose from the reverse slope and rushed down the hill. It was a large party of enemy soldiers, camouflaged with scrub oak bushes. It happened so fast that few marines could get off a shot at the fleeing enemy.

During the morning's attack, LT Fox came upon a wounded enemy soldier. Fox motioned for him to get his hands up. "Instead, he raised his rifle and tried to get out of his hole," Fox wrote. "I pulled the trigger on my carbine and nothing happened. I threw the damned thing at him as I hit the deck and a bullet whizzed by my right ear. The radioman dropped him." The carbine failed because there was dirt in the bolt. "I threw it down," Fox continued, "[and] picked up an M1, and never carried a carbine the rest of my time in Korea."

The 2d Platoon's leader had been killed on the 17th, so LT Muetzel accompanied them on the attack the morning of the 18th. He was hit in the right foot by a rifle bullet. "I was prone at the time," he wrote, "and the slug entered my boot, burned my second toe, tore the meat off the third, burned the fourth and then exited my boot. Two holes." He immediately lost feeling in the foot, but found that he could limp along. "So I stayed with the Platoon 'till we overran the hill crest and secured the objective" Later in the day, he went to the aid station, where he was treated, "Had a cup of coffee, rounded up the A Co. stragglers (walking wounded) at the aid station and led them back up the hill to the company."

As Able Co. consolidated on Hill 153, and searched the slopes beyond, the 1st Platoon, Co A, 1st Engineers checked out the paddies and swamps to the east. This action secured Stevens' left flank.

As Co. A began their attack that morning, Fenton, sent a 15-man patrol to sweep the slopes in front of his unit. By midafternoon Obong-ni Ridge was the property of the U.S. Marines.

The North Koreans left behind 43 machine guns, 63 rifles and submachineguns, 8 AT rifles and 150 dead. Captain Fenton recalled that many of the machine guns were American. Also found, he said, was an SCR 300 radio, tuned to the 1st Battalion's command frequency, plus several of the smaller SCR 536 radios (which were used for internal company communication). The two rifle companies of the 1st Battalion aggregated 216 personnel. Co. A numbered somewhat over 100 personnel; Company B, about 90 or so. A number of these men had been wounded, but either remained with their units, or came back after getting first aid.

Fenton recalled LT Nick Schryver returning to the company that morning after having been wounded the day before. When he arrived at the company CP, the lieutenant's head was covered in bandages. "He looked like a mummy," said Fenton. "I was flabbergasted. I said, 'Nick, what are you doing here?' He said, 'While I was in the aid station I got to thinking that very seldom does a Second Lieutenant ever get a chance to command a company, and I thought your luck is running short; you haven't been hit yet. I figured I'd get back and I might get the company.'" It became a big joke between the two men, because Fenton was never wounded in Korea.

Completing the Mission: The Attack by the 3d Battalion, 5th Marines — Aug. 18

LTC Murray issued a warning order to Taplett at midnight on Aug. 17 to be prepared to continue the attack on Aug. 18. Just before dawn, Taplett and his two company commanders, Bohn of George Co. and Fegan of How Co., made a visual reconnaissance of Hill 207 (Objective 2) from points north and south of the MSR. As the battalion set up an OP on the northeast slope of Obong-ni, the two rifle companies moved to an assembly area at the base of the ridge.

Taplett arranged for smothering artillery, air and mortar preparations of the objectives. Occasionally, some fire was shifted to engage enemy troops fleeing to Hill 207 from Able Co.'s attack on Obong-ni.

Two fingers, or ridges, ran south from near the MSR, and Finger Ridge to converge at the summit of Hill 207. Co. H led out at 10 a.m. from the MSR between Obong-ni and Finger ridges, headed for the eastern spur. Bohn's G Company followed H, then slipped to the right to assault the western spur. As the two companies climbed toward Hill 207, the 3d Platoon, Co. A, of the Tank Battalion provided overhead and flanking cover fire.

Just before the two units moved out, Gunnery Sergeant Novobiliski, of Co. G, had a section of his heavy machine guns firing indirect fire on the enemy near Hill 207. The range, GEN Bohn recalls, was some 700 to 800 yards. At that distance, the enemy had no idea where the fire originated, but it was creating casualties.

How Co. was about half way to the top when Marine tankers spotted a platoon of enemy trying to flank the attackers. Tank 90mm and machine gun fire quickly disposed of this threat.

SGT Wayne Knott, of Co H, wrote, "As our 1st Platoon [LT Willams] came close to the summit some of the entrenched enemy stood up and threw grenades at us. When the explosions were over, we got up and charged the positions. Most of the enemy retreated along the ridge. The rest were killed.... During the last minutes of the fight for this hill, the entire North Korean unit broke and ran."

SSG James W. Abrahamson was with How's machine guns. His men were slowed by the steep climb, heat and humidity. "I finally took over carrying the machine gun . . . . When we attacked the top, I was there with a gun and no tripod and only one ammo carrier, with some riflemen. I wrapped the end of the [ammo] belt around the barrel and fired standing up as they [the enemy] ran down the other side [of the hill]." Once the hill was taken, one of Abrahamson's gunners lifted the corner of a poncho covering a dead Marine. He "became white as a ghost," James wrote. The body was that of the section leader, who had been with Abrahamson until they had reached 30 to 40 yards from the crest of the hill. He had been killed by an enemy grenadier hiding in a "spider hole."

SGT Duwayne A. Philo, a Section Leader in G Co.'s Machinegun Platoon, remembered that one gun from a 105mm howitzer battery was apparently set a little off from the rest of the battery. In every salvo, he wrote, one round would burst short. One of these short rounds killed his buddy in the company.

Robert Robert's squad of George Co. toiled up the hill with the unit. "[T]he hill was very steep," wrote Roberts, "and we ran out of breath and our legs were like lead." The tankers in the valley below sent round after round of 90mm gunfire ahead of the struggling infantrymen. The rounds, "were hitting the ground and exploding just above our heads.... "as the round passed over out heads we fell to out knees. At the top of the hill we killed a North Korean who carried a pack full of 1000 and 100 North Korean Won notes. We offered to pay any North Korean who would come in."

George Co.'s charge over the crest completed the seizure of Objective 2.

As the fighting on Hill 207 came to an end, the whole Naktong Bulge area seemed to swarm with North Korean soldiers, in panic-stricken flight. Some headed for Hill 311, the Brigade's next objective, while others made for the Naktong River.

Every heavy weapon which could be brought into play pounded the fleeing enemy —aircraft, artillery and mortars slammed into the North Koreans, many of whom were streaming into the banks of the Naktong. Marine aircraft blasted the suspected CP of the *18th Infantry* on a hill-

top south of 207, destroying weapons and communications equipment. Held up by the river, hundreds of enemy soldiers were killed trying to cross. LTC Taplett, meantime, attacked enemy soldiers sighted in the valley and on Hills 207 and 311 with mortars, machine guns and tanks. He was ordered to delay continuing his ground attack against Hill 301 until the North Koreans trying to flee across the Naktong could be dealt with.

Finally, he was allowed to continue. At 3:30 P.M., George and How Companies descended into the valley, meeting 1LT Pomeroy's 1st Tank Platoon. Accompanied by the tanks, and while Marine air, artillery, mortars and 75mm recoilless, bombarded and burned Hill 311, the two companies crossed the valley and began ascending the objective on two finger ridges which converged on the top of the objective. All went well until H Co. was within 200 yards of the crest. A volley of rifle fire from an enemy platoon sent

the Marines to the ground. Heavy scrub pine growth not only concealed the enemy, but prevented the effective use of unit machine guns. Fegan's men also were restricted from maneuvering by the steep sided ridge they were on, also well covered by enemy marksmen. Further, the late afternoon sun was in the Marine's eyes, severely restricting their vision. A few Marines did try to run forward, but were cut down by the enemy.

The enemy troops, without machine guns or grenades, kept up methodical and deadly rifle fire on the Marines below, eventually wounding Fegan, himself.

SGT Wayne K. Knott was with the company mortars. "I crawled through the brush as far as I could go," he wrote. "Every time I moved a volley of fire would go over my head.... The bushes moved and 2LT Jerry Fly, our artillery FO came back. He must have been within 50 yards of the enemy. LT Fly asked CPT Fegan to allow him to call in artillery but CPT Fegan refused because we were too close to the enemy and [he] was afraid some shells might fall on his own men.

"As the two officers stood to evaluate the situation, Captain Fegan was shot. He was hit in the leg," Knott wrote. Command of the company fell to 2LT Thomas P. Lennon. "After the Captain's evacuation our company dug in for the night. We fixed...our bayonets as we thought the enemy might try to attack us during the night," Knott concluded. But the night passed without incident for the company.

Co. G reached the southern portion of the long, narrow crest at 5:30 p.m., easily handling some light resistance. Bohn's lead men carried air panels on their backs, so that Marine pilots could see the location of the advancing troops. "Corsairs would come down shooting parallel to our front," he recalled.

"As we were getting to the top, I asked them to stay right over us and make the last run a dummy run so we wouldn't get any stray rounds." The company attained the hill's crest without much difficulty. "When we got to the top," Bohn said, 'there was a plateau about 300 yards long and you couldn't stick your head up. Whoever we were up against were tough people." As the route of Co. G developed, the

First Battle of the Naktong Bulge–A view from Marine Objective 1. On the left is the north edge of Objective 2. In the valley is the road between Objective 1 and 2. Objective 3 is on the horizon. From a 1981 photograph. (Courtesy of COL John H. Cahill, G-5 USMC, Ret.)

First Battle of the Naktong Bulge–View of Marine Objective 2 from Objective 3. From a 1981 photograph. (Courtesy of COL John H. Cahill, G-5 USMC, Ret.)

First Battle of the Naktong Bulge–Marine Objective 3, seen from Objective 2, at a lower level. From a 1981 photograph. (Courtesy of COL John H. Cahill, G-5 USMC, Ret.)

unit actually got behind the enemy confronting Fegan's company.

Near the crest, Co. G got into a fire fight with the enemy, "that had us pinned down," wrote Fred Davidson (of Co. G). "LT Bohn sent LT Cahill's 1st Platoon around to the left of the enemy that was holding the crest. The platoon overran the NKPA positions on the north half of the summit, but were stopped cold by the enemy on the forward slopes of the hill facing How Company. Because of darkness closing in, LT Bohn ordered Cahill to withdraw his platoon back to the lines of George Company. LT Cahill reported that his platoon had suffered 10 casualties, including two KIA. LT Cahill was one of the wounded." The wounded could not be evacuated. The company dug in for the night.

"I remember going up the spur to the Objective," Blackie Cahill wrote. "I established a base of fire to pin the enemy to our front down. Then I proceeded to send SGT Charles R. Richmond's squad around the left flank in an envelopment of the enemy position on top. The squad reported that they were receiving fire from across the Naktong. I told them that the distance was too great to be effective and [to] move out. It was then, as we received casualties that I realized the fire was coming from the objective. With the casualties and darkness setting in, I brought the squad back. While trying to locate the enemy over the crest, I was shot through the shoulder and Corpsman Wagner patched me up. Reporting the situation, I was ordered to pull back into the company perimeter. I remained in the CP overnight and in the morning was evacuated along with SGT Richmond, James C. Weikert and Wesley F. Jaska."

Some time earlier in the day, LT (jg) Robert J. Harvey, 3d battalion surgeon, had the grisly task of examining an Army aid station which had been overrun by the enemy a week previously. There, he found about 30 dead soldiers, brutally murdered by the North Koreans.

The 3d Battalion's 81mm mortars opened up at 6:10 a.m. on Aug. 19. 2LT Lennon, closely following this preparation, led Co. H up and over the objective. There was no opposition. Objective 3 was secured by 6:45 a.m.

LT Edward F. Duncan commanded a platoon of G Co. His platoon was on the Brigade's [and battalion's] right flank, clearing the area toward the Naktong River, when "seven gooks opened up from a gully on the left, hitting one [of my men] in the arm. My messenger and I killed six of the seven of them and captured a machine gun."

As previously noted, an SCR 300 radio had been found on Obong-ni, set on the Marine command frequency. GEN Bohn relates an anecdote illustrating how his battalion dealt with radio security. "I'd just say, 'Tap, this is Dewey.' Then he knew. [Dewey is GEN Bohn's middle name.] "I knew his voice and he knew mine, and we'd talk in cryptic language so they didn't know what we were saying or planning. Fegan was 'Joe.' I did the same thing with my platoon commanders. My platoon commanders were 'Blackie' [Cahill], 'Count' [Counselman], 'Big Jack' [Westerman] and 'Skeeter' [Jaworski]. It really worked well." Other commands resorted to similar devices to thwart an enemy who might be intercepting radio or telephone traffic.

During the First Naktong, Jack Wright (G, 5th Marines) had another adventure. Once, when he had gone forward with his supply train, Wright was ordered to take out five wounded men — three walking wounded, one walking but serious, and one on a stretcher. He had some 15 or 20 Korean laborers with him. It was dark by the time that his little column of wounded Marines and South Koreans got down to the base of the hill. Wright had organized the party, with four Koreans carrying the stretcher and two more helping the walking Marine who had been seriously wounded. To keep the group together in the darkness, he had the others hold hands, with the leading Korean holding onto the belt of one of the stretcher bearers.

"I didn't figure I was going to have a problem," he said. But when enemy bullets kicked up dirt on his side of the road, he went to cross to the ditch on the other side. Bullets were flying there, too. Since the road was not under fire, he led his charges to the rear on it. "It was pitch black," he recalled. "I came to one of our machine gun outposts. I was challenged. I told them 'PFC Wright.' They didn't know a PFC Wright, but when I told them 'Archie,' they all knew Archie, 'OK, come on in.' Wright counted his men. He had the five Marines and six of his Koreans. First, he looked to getting the wounded to the aid station. He was told "it was down the road and around the bend." Wright called the station on a field phone and was told that "they weren't going to send a jeep up to pick up the wounded," he recalled.

"Well, I raised all sorts of hell and bloody murder.... The next thing I knew here came a jeep with a couple of volunteer corpsmen to pick up my wounded." Once the wounded boarded the jeep, Wright went out to find his missing charges. The machine gun crew thought he "was nuts," but, as he said later, "they were my people, I was responsible for them, I had to get them." A little way down the road, he found them, "very scared, and when they saw me, very grateful." He brought the his wayward charges in, then discovered that the aid station. "Down the road and around the bend was less than 20 yards," he said. "I could have brought the whole works in without having to bother with battalion med, but I didn't know."

Wright went off into the night and fell asleep. The next morning, he awoke to find himself lying on a paddy dike. He noticed dark spots all over the area. He had slept through an enemy mortar barrage. When he appeared to his comrades, they were quite surprised. Seeing Wright's body on the dike earlier, they had concluded he had been killed by the mortar fire. "The bad penny always turns up," he concluded.

On Aug. 19, the Marines mopped up their zone of responsibility. SGT George Hawman, of the 1st Battalion's H&S Co. wrote, "We had a field day against the enemy when they retreated back across the river."

Casper A Tartalone, of the 1st Battalion's S-3 Section also related an incident which occurred during the First Naktong. He was a member of a patrol. They were on a road, studying a map, "when our chief scout [SSG "Red Dog" Keller] said he would move up the road" to get any enemy ahead to reveal themselves. He was quickly

"shot in the shoulder by a rifle bullet and I had to pull him off into a ditch and back under this cliff with the rest of us," Tartalone wrote. An older enemy soldier then appeared up on a cliff "about 20 feet high," continued Tartalone. "I spotted him and he dropped." He called to him in Korean to come here. The enemy soldier surrendered. He was armed with a large number of grenades. The prisoner and Keller were sent to the rear. The sergeant's wounds were not serious, wrote Tartalone.

The 1st Battalion occupied Obong-ni, the 2d Battalion Hill 207 and the 3d Hill 311. Marine patrols swept the intervening area to the Naktong. The First Battle of the Naktong Bulge cost the Brigade 66 dead, 1 MIA and 178 wounded. (USMC *The Pusan Perimeter.*)

Attack of the 34th Infantry — Aug. 18

As the Marines seized Obong-ni and went on to take Hill 207 from the enemy, elements of the 24th Division were progressing north of the Naktong-Yongsan road. Since the 9th Infantry had been "pinched out" by the zones assigned to the 34th on the north and the Marine Brigade to the south, its role consisted of providing supporting fire to flanking commands. The 34th and 19th Infantry Regiments were to make a coordinated attack, but the 19th was delayed because it was unable to resupply its 1st Battalion with ammunition in time for the attack The battalion was situated several thousand yards from the nearest roads and the ammunition, carried by supply bearers overland, was late in arriving. (Actual arrival was some time after daylight.)

At 6:30 a.m. 3/34 Infantry started its attack, with Co. L on the right and Co. K on the left. Co I was not available to the battalion, being employed to guard the Naktong River north of the 19th Infantry. The battalion objective (Objective 2) was Hill 240, the highest point on a 2,500 yard ridge running northwest to the Naktong. The 19th was to take Hill 223, and the rest of the ridge, on the 34th Infantry's right. Meeting little resistance, 3/34th reached their objective by 8 a.m. Then, without warning, Love Co.'s front and open right flank were assailed by a fierce enemy counterstroke. This flank should have been covered by the 19th. Co L was quickly driven several hundred yards back down the ridge. More than twenty of its men were lost in a few minutes. At 9:20 a.m. COL Beauchamp received the message: "L Company is cut up bad — do not think they will be able to do anything.... They are picking L Co. off like flies."

Leonard Korgie, one of the few survivors of the original L/34th Infantry, was now a squad leader. It was now that he saw hand grenades for the first time in Korea. He had never thrown one during his Army career to that date. It seemed to him that the whole battalion numbered only about 250 men. Korgie wrote that his squad had six or eight men. One of his men, a replacement, was PVT George Brown, a black soldier. The company also had another black replacement, PFC Newgames Hicks. Both "very good soldiers," Korgie wrote.

He continued, "As we approached the first ridge, guys started falling. The NKs were firing

A Marine patrol moves out from their Third Objective to mop up North Korean troops, August 19, 1950. The Naktong River is in the middle distance. USMC photo.

Tanks fire at North Koreans near Yongsan, Korea, August 18, 1950. The near tank is a Sherman M4A3 with a dozer blade on its front and mounting a 105mm Howitzer. The tank in the background is a Pershing medium M26, mounting a 90mm gun. The Pershing is from the Marine 1st Tank Battalion. (Courtesy of U.S. Army

those Russian water-cooled machine guns. The fire was whithering [sic]. We had a light .30- cal machine gun firing over our heads. There was so much collective noise from the Marine Area [to the south] that we couldn't pinpoint the enemy fire. I searched the bare ridge but couldn't see anything.

"A kid dropped on my left. As I opened his jacket, a fly lit on his lip. He didn't bother to brush it away. He was hit through the heart. Our radioman, PFC Newgames Hicks, fell on my right. He had a small hole in the back of his head and a large one to the front, obviously hit from the rear. Our BARman, PFC Leopold Soto, was [also] hit from the rear. He survived."

The enemy was too much for the company. CPT Syverson, unit CO, called in artillery, which landed about a hundred yards forward of the company. F-51 fighters dove in "and raked the ridge with their machine guns," Korgie recalled. "When the supporting fire lifted, we rushed the ridge, firing, and took it. We [also] cleaned out the two ridges to our front." After the battle, GIs pulled dead enemy soldiers from their foxholes. One of them had five American wrist watches on his arm.

PVT George Brown shared Korgie's foxhole. The next day, Brown left the hole for a few minutes. While he was gone, an enemy shell exploded in a tree to the rear of the hole. "Brown didn't come back," Korgie wrote, "so I went to

These 20 men are the survivors of a 58 man unit after the first Naktong battle. First row left to right: Cpl. Horton M. Jarrett, Rome Georgia; Pfc. Billy D. Lindley, Surgess, South Dakota; Pfc. Bobby R. Johnson, Dallas, Texas; Cpl. Richard E. Brown, Los Angeles, California; Pfc. Roy A. Grove, Litchfield, Minnesota; Cpl. Robert L. Judy, Baltimore, Maryland. Second row left to right: Cpl. Henry S. Adams, Alvin, texas; Pfc. Cleylon R. Camper, Beaumont, Texas; Pfc. Lynn D. Edds, Topeka, Kansas; Pfc. Benny B. Bagwell, Houston Texas; Pfc. Raymond Miller, Russell Kansas; Pfc. Raymond C. Risse, Davenport, Iowa. Third row left to right: 2d Lt. Francis W. Muetzel, Coronado, California; Cpl. Raymond E. Stephens, St. Louis, Missouri; Pfc. David J. Bohlke, Sioux City, Iowa; Pfc. Lawrence M. Esquivel, Tuscon, Arizona; Pfc. Jerry M. Freeman, Indio, California; Sgt. Clarence H. Vittitoe, Newport, Kentucky; T/Sgt. Jesse Johnson, Denham Springs, Louisiana. USMC photo.

check on him. I found him with a shrapnel wound through the side of his head — he was dead."

King Co. tried to help Love, but 1/19th, arriving tardily, made the difference. Covered by a base of fire from Co. B on Ohang Hill, Companies A and C started their struggle up the steep slopes of Hill 240. By 10 a.m., the assault companies were about a third of the way to the top and nearly abreast of Co L, which was being blasted by mortar fire. Moving forward resolutely the 61 men that were A Co. gained the crest with little resistance. However, Co C, far to A's right, was held up by a heavy volume of automatic weapons fire. Finally, a sergeant charged forward with a .30-cal machine gun, breaking the enemy's resistance. With that, Co. C quickly gained the hill. By 11:45 a.m., 1/19th had secured its objective. Fifteen minutes later K and L joined to secure Hill 240.

The 1/34th Infantry was brought forward to continue the attack toward Objective 3, and 2/19th Infantry also displaced to resume the attack in that zone. The 1/19th Infantry required an airdrop to supply it with rations, water and ammunition. The battalion needed only 300 individual rations.

Companies A and B, 34th Infantry passed through the 3d Battalion late in the day. Co. C, now numbering only 37 men, was left behind. A and B arrived on the objective by 6:40 p.m., but pockets of enemy resistance prevented them from securing it until after dark. To the north, the 19th was again late in making its attack, not starting until 1/34th Infantry was already on their part of the objective. The 2/19th Infantry did not secure their part of Objective 3 until an hour after dark.

On Aug. 19, the Marines patrolled to the river, then assembled behind the Bulge as division reserve. A Marine patrol contacted elements of the 34th, on their right, at 8:45 a.m. The 19th and 34th consolidated their positions, then moved on to dig in overlooking the Naktong. Farther south, the 9th Infantry and 1/21st Infantry conducted a sweep south of the Marines to clean out the 24th Divisions southern sector.

The *NK 4th Division* after the First Battle of the Naktong Bulge

The enemy division lost almost all its heavy equipment and weapons in this battle. Marine ordnance personnel, who gathered up most of the destroyed or abandoned enemy artillery and mortars collected 34 enemy artillery pieces, 18 of which were lined up along the Naktong-Yongsan road to fire along the main enemy axis of attack. The cache of artillery included 76mm guns, three U.S. 105mm howitzers in working order and Soviet 122mm howitzers. This was in addition to the machine guns and other weapons taken on Obong-ni Ridge. The 24th Division buried 1,200 enemy dead after the battle. Prisoners reported that the three regiments of the *4th Division* numbered no more than 300 to 400 men each after they re-crossed the Naktong. They also said that about half of the wounded died for lack of medical care. The *4th Division* was believed to contain no more than 3,500 men at the conclusion of the battle. The defeat of the *4th* was a major blow to the North Korean Army — the worst to that time. The division was not reconstituted until after the Chinese entered the war during the Winter of 1950-51. Ironically, on Aug. 19, the day it was defeated, the *4th Division* was designated "Guard Division" by the North Korean headquarters for its "outstanding accomplishments" in battle at Taejon.

Deployment of the 24th Division and Marine Brigade — Aug. 20

The Marine Brigade was returned to the Bean Patch and Eighth Army reserve. The 19th Infantry went into position on the southern half of the Bulge and the 34th took over the northern half. The 9th became division reserve near Yongsan. The 21st Infantry and 3d Engineers remained along the Naktong and at the foot of Hill 409 in the north.

On Aug. 24, the 24th Division was relieved on the Naktong by the newly-arrived 2d Infantry Division. The 24th had been in combat for 55 days. It assembled near Kyongsan on the 25th for a well-earned and much needed rest and refitting.

The First battle of the Naktong Bulge in Retrospect

This battle was one of epic proportions in the Korean War to that date. It was also an example of the employment of a type of mobile defense — not a classic example, but example nevertheless.

When the 24th Division took position along the Naktong it had certain advantages and disadvantages. Some of the advantages were theoretical, because other factors mitigated what seemed to be a plus. Some of these advantages and disadvantages are listed below:

Advantages

1. The Naktong River was an obstacle to the North Korean advance. It was both a moat and antitank ditch. The enemy would have to cross on boats or rafts, neither of which were readily available on the river; all had been removed or destroyed by the 24th Division.

2. The series of hills and ridges close to the river provided positions overlooking the Naktong. This high ground afforded long range observation and relatively long fields of fire.

Disadvantages

1. The convoluted course of the Naktong, particularly the great bend just north of its confluence with the Nam River almost tripled the front to be defended.

2. Behind the first hills and ridges, the terrain was considerably cut up by more hills and ridges. This system did not lend itself to long range observation or decent fields of fire. Long range observation could be attained only on the highest peaks.

3. Gullies and ravines provided egress into almost every battalion-sized sector that could be established.

4. The personnel strength and heavy weaponry available to the 24th division when it occupied the Naktong line was inadequate for the mission. Battle losses and other casualties had reduced many commands to 50 per cent or less. Artillery battalions came to Korea already short 1/3 of the number of guns authorized. Battle losses further reduced the number of artillery tubes, tanks, mortars, recoilless rifles and machine guns. These shortages led to the forward units having to spread themselves even more thinly than otherwise would have been the case. (Even at full strength, the three companies deployed in the Bulge would have been inadequate to provide the "tripwire" alert desired.) The severe shortage of personnel and heavy weapons also helped to doom most counterattacks to failure.

Deployment of the 24th Division

The 24th Division had, in fact, a frontage of 34 miles to defend. In addition to its own assets, the command had the 2,000-man ROK 17th Regiment. Church realized that his battle-weary and battered division, even with the ROKs, was inadequate to successfully defend along the river. He opted for a style of mobile defense. The ROK regiment, 21st and 34th Regiments were each assigned huge sectors of the river to outpost. The largest of these was given to the 34th. The 19th Regiment became division reserve. The 21st and 34th Regiments each placed one battalion on the line and kept the other as regimental reserve. The key to Church's defensive scheme was counterattack.

No less than 61 battalion- or company-sized counterattacks were planned for elements of the 24th Division, or attached units. Some of these were never executed and some were not executed with force and determination. Most of them failed to achieve the objectives desired.

The battalions which constituted the regimental reserve for the 21st and 34th Regiments were greatly reduced in strength and lacked many crew-served and heavy weapons due first, to the pre-Korean War military austerity program, and second, to battle losses prior to arriving at the Naktong.

Reducing a Penetration

Doctrinally, penetrations should be attacked at their base. In the 24th Division's counteraction to the enemy's penetration, this did not happen. In the north, the 19th Infantry did halt the enemy's expansion of their penetration. But in the south, 1/21st was too weak for this task. Then the battalion was attacked by the enemy in its assembly area before it could launch its own attack. And the area in the south was far too great for any battalion to handle.

The appearance of the powerful force Marine Brigade on their southern flank would have forced the enemy commander to shift major forces from the center to meet the threat. Another possibility, would have been to turn the two battalions of the 27th Infantry around after they had helped clear the 24th Division's rear area, and send them against the enemy's southern flank. The 27th reverted to Eighth Army reserve on Aug. 14, but would have been available to the 24th Division until Aug. 16. The decision to insert the Marine Brigade or the 27th Infantry into the battle on the southern flank was Church's to make. History does not reveal if this option was considered by the 24 Division's commander or staff.

The enemy was pushed out of the Bulge. The major attacks, delivered by the Marine Brigade and a battalion of the 9th Infantry on Aug. 17, were made directly into the strength of the *4th Division*. A bloody battle of attrition ensued.

Intelligence

The 24th Division's estimates of North Korean capabilities and intentions were very conservative. The obvious open area on the division's left flank was not pointed up, nor the sightings of enemy troops moving through that area to the rear given any significance. An attack by infiltrators on an artillery battery some distance to the rear was disregarded. Not until the MSR was cut were troops diverted in that direction. The division staff should have been concerned about the south flank early on.

Unified Command and Control

A single entity should command and control counterattacks. Not until Church formed TF Hill did this happen in the Bulge. But Hill had no previous experience fighting the North Koreans nor had his regiment. He had to command the task force and his regiment simultaneously. His span of command was too great. Although Hill was the ranking regimental commander available, Church should have given the job to his assistant division commander.

The Importance of Training
All Soldiers to Fight as Infantry

The sometimes desperate struggle by essentially "rear area" soldiers for the MSR points up the necessity for all soldiers to be trained in the basic infantry combat, to include small team and unit tactics and proficiency with infantry weapons— rifles, automatic weapons, mortars, grenades and the like. The battle included division headquarters personnel, MPs, ordnance personnel, bandsmen, and many others. Given the limited or nonexistent infantry training they may have had, these men fought gamely, if not completely successfully.

The soldiers and Marines who fought in the First Battle of the Naktong Bulge fought hard, took heavy casualties, but in the end, dealt the North Korean *4th Division* a death blow. The beating administered to that enemy division kept it out of the war for over two months.

Chapter Notes:

P. 164 U.S. doctrine specified a full-strength division front to be no more than 10,000 yards. At 1,402 men, the 34th was at a little over 1/3 strength. Counterattack on the Naktong, 1950 gives 10,000 yards as a regimental frontage.

P. 172 South to the Naktong, *states that the enemy was repulsed on the 21st front by running into a minefield, being shelled by artillery and machine gunned by infantry. Appleman does not mention the enemy in Sadung at all.*

P.___ Given the personnel and equipment of Co. A, company and platoon leadership was good and positive. The leaders of the two lead platoons led by example, and paid for it early in the fight by being seriously wounded. Collins and other NCOs with the 2d Platoon took command and continued the fight. LT Back's platoon was effectively taken out of the fight by being pinned down for most of the action. The 1st Platoon did what it could, with feeble weaponry to support by fire, as ordered. LT Alfonso placed himself with the 1st Platoon, where he could control the 1st Platoon's efforts and could observe his other platoons. Some may criticize him for not going forward to the 2d Platoon. From there he could have commanded that platoon, but nothing more. His presence there would not have influenced the outcome of the battle. If he had been killed or wounded there, it might have resulted in even more of a disaster.

P.___ The Marine history states that 3-5 Marines relieved the 34th on "Cloverleaf Hill." The map opening Part 3 of Donald Knox's The Korean War *copies the Marine location of Cloverleaf. The hill which 1/34th occupied resembled a three leaf clover, with its stem pointing generally north. This is not the same "Cloverleaf Hill" in the Army's official history. That hill mass was about 500-600 yards west of the three-leaf hill, was considerably larger, and roughly resembled a four-leaf clover, also with its stem pointing north. The dominant feature within this hill mass was Hill 165, situated more or less where the four "leaves" came together at the base of the stem. It also included Hill 125 (the southeastern "leaf") and Finger Ridge (the southwestern "leaf").*

P.___ This narrative does not seem to match the official account of this battle, but it graphically reflects what the action appeared to be from the perspective of a young soldier who was there. It may be, too, that Korgie's recollections are of the final surge of his unit to take Hill 240 a little later, with the help of 1/19th Infantry.

Infantrymen seem amused as they stand guard over a prisoner of war who nonchalantly has a smoke as he waits to be interrogated, 11 August. (Source: p. 109, Korea, 1950, *Chief of Military History, Wash., D.C., 1982)*

CHAPTER FOURTEEN - Meeting the Threat in the East

From early to late August 1950, GEN Walker faced four crises along the Perimeter simultaneously. Two were examined in previous chapters. Another was the enemy's threat to drive through Pohang and enter the Kyongju corridor to Pusan. This chapter addresses that crisis. The fourth, but not the least of the threats, was the enemy's concentrated drive to seize Taegu. That is the subject of Chapter 15.

East Coast Terrain — Corridor to Pusan

Among the avenues in to the Pusan Perimeter was the Kyongju corridor to Pusan. A key highway and railroad ran between Taegu and Pohang-dong on the east coast. In air miles the distance is 50 miles. This is the first valley route to South Korea's east coast south of the corridor running from Seoul through Chorwon and Pyongyang to Wonsan, 225 miles to the north. About half way between Taegu and Pohang on this route lies the town of Yongchon. At that point the only important north-south road between the east coast and Taegu runs down through the mountains from Andong, via Uisong, to the east-west valley road. East of this road for some 40 air miles to the coast, lies an almost trackless, rugged mountainous area. This region contained no improved roads.

The town of Angang-ni lies in the Taegu corridor twelve miles west of Pohang-dong. Six miles north of Angang-ni is the town of Kigye.

A number of trails and a poor road come out of the mountains near this town, entering a north south valley which intersects the Pohang-Taegu lateral valley, then continues south some 60 air miles to Pusan. Twelve miles south of Angang-ni lies the town of Kyongju. A rail line and road from Taegu (through Yongchon meet another road and rail line from Pohang, via Angang-ni. From there the railroad proceeded south through Ulsan to Pusan. This was one of only two north-south rail lines in the Perimeter. The other ran south from Taegu. Both terminated in Pusan. Two roads ran south from Kyongju, one via Ulsan to Pusan; the other almost due south to the city.

Pohang-dong had little military importance, except as a port to assist in supplying ROK and U.S. troops in the east. The Angang-ni-Kyongju-Pusan valley corridor was the critical feature in this region. If the enemy could seize and hold Kyongju, Taegu would be outflanked and have to be abandoned. It was not necessary for the enemy to reach Pusan to attain this result. By holding Kyongju, they would cut the main routes of supply to the entire eastern half of the Perimeter's northern flank. The road and railroad from Pusan to Taegu were inadequate to provide the logistical support cut off by an enemy in control of Kyongju.

As a result, the battles for Kigye, Pohang-dong and Angang-ni were important.

GEN Walker had too few troops to be strong throughout the Perimeter. In some places he was forced to take a calculated risk. One of these

places was the east coast. In making his decision to confront the enemy with fewer troops in this area, Walker took into consideration that the terrain over which the enemy would have to advance there in the region contained few roads; the only major highway ran along the coast for many miles. It could be interdicted by sea bombardment, as well as by air attack. He believed that the enemy would be unable to bring forward heavy weapons and equipment to exploit any success in the east. He could also rely on the road and railroad to rush reinforcements forward if the enemy should threaten that region. The Yonil airstrip, with its F-51 fighters, provided a uniquely responsive close air support capability in the east. Aircraft from this strip, known as K-3, could attack the enemy minutes after take off. (Later, when the enemy had seized Pohang-dong, the F-51s were barely airborne before they were over the target.)

Advance of the North Korean Army in the East

While the *8th Division* attacked down the Uisong road toward Yongchon in early August, the *12th* moved into the mountains southeast of Andong, heading toward Pohang-dong. About the same time the *766th Independent Unit* left the coastal road near Yongdok and headed southwest through the mountains toward Kigye and Angang-ni. and the *5th Division* continued the attack down the coastal road from Yongdok. El-

Pohang-dong two days after ROK units regained the town from the North Koreans. Note the rough, irregular mass of steep-sided mountains. (Source: P. 122-123, Korea, 1950, Chief of Military History, Washington, D.C., 1982)

ements of the *5th* swung inland then south to infiltrate the ROK 3d Division's rear area.

The ROK 8th Division caught part of the *NK 8th Division* in an ambush near Uisong on Aug. 9 and virtually annihilated a battalion of the *3d Regiment*, inflicting 700 casualties. The *8th Division's 2d Regiment* entered the battle, and although it also suffered heavy losses, the regiment won back the ground lost to the ROKs.

During the battle, five T-34s and a 76mm SP gun were destroyed. Two tanks were knocked out by mines. Then F-51s came in, attacking with rockets and napalm on these two tanks, plus the other three T-34s and the SP gun. All remaining tanks and the 76mm were destroyed by the air attack. The Air Force reported destruction of six enemy armored vehicles. The ROKs also reported the destruction of six enemy armored vehicles. This is a good example of multiple reporting.

The ROKs inflicted so many losses on the *8th Division* in this battle that it had to stop for a week. When it did start again the command could advance only a few miles south before being halted again by stiff ROK resistance. The division halted to await reinforcements.

Farther to the east, the *12th "Andong" Division* moved into the mountains, bound for Pohang-dong. The division's combat strength was very low. The *2d Battalion, Artillery Regiment*, sent its guns back to Tanyang on the upper Han River because ammunition could not be brought forward to supply them.

Elements of the ROK 3d Division defended on the east coast. The ROK Capital Division, to the west, was supposed to maintain contact with the 3d across the mountains. But the Capital Division was obviously unable to do this. Numerous reports came in of enemy groups in the mountains inland from the coast. One report estimated one enemy force to be 2,000 men. Eighth Army received a report on Aug. 9 that North Korean regulars were in what was known as the "guerrilla area" northwest of Pohang-dong, positioned to cut the coastal road and seize the Yonil Airfield.

To blunt the enemy's thrust from the mountains, the ROKs attacked north from Kigye on Aug. 9 with the 1st and 2d Battalions, 25th Regiment. The 25th was a newly activated regiment, with minimal training. Their mission was to make contact with the ROK 3d Division south of Yongdok. But an enemy counterattack swept the regiment back to a point two miles south of Kigye, confirming that no friendly units were in those mountains and that the 3d Division's left flank was open to enemy attack, and the rear areas to infiltration. The 3d held the coastal road from Yongdok south to a point twenty miles above Pohang-dong.

Formation of Task Force Pohang — Aug. 10

Walker had no U.S. troops to send to the coast at the time. The defense in this area would be conducted by the ROK Army. Accordingly, on Aug. 10, Eighth Army activated TF Pohang, consisting of the ROK 17th and 25th Regiments, the ROK 1st Anti-Guerrilla Battalion the ROK Pohang Marine Battalion and Battery C, U.S. 18th FAB (75mm). The ROK Army activated

the 26th Regiment the next day at Taegu, gave it a few days training, then rushed it to join TF Pohang at Angang-ni. Only the ROK 17th Regiment had battle experience. The task force mission was to attack north from Angang-ni to drive the enemy from the mountains near the coast.

The activation of the 26th Regiment was typical of how men were "drafted" and units of the ROK Army were formed in the early days of the war. The KMAG G-3 called CPT Frank W. Lukas in from the field and ordered him to activate a new regiment for the ROK 3d Division. Lukas first obtained two interpreters from ROK Army headquarters, then contacted the appropriate ROK Army staff officers in Taegu. These officers, with the assistance of police and other city officials, drafted young men off the streets of the city. Within a day or two they had almost 1,000 recruits. As the draftees were delivered to Lukas and his Korean staff, they were formed into squads, platoons and companies, then into two battalions. Lacking qualified personnel for the leadership of squads and platoons, the ROK trainers became company, battalion and regimental commanders and staffs. Once the two battal-

ions were organized, the KMAG G-4 found enough rifles to arm the men. Each man had the opportunity to fire nine rounds of ammunition. The force was still without proper uniforms. So, clad in various combinations of civilian clothing, school uniforms and parts of the U.S. Army uniforms, the regiment entered combat in less than a week after its activation. It received no formal training until April 1951.

The ROK 3d Division vs. the *NK 5th Division* — Aug. 5 -10

From late July into early August the *NK 5th Division* and ROK 3d Division were locked in bloody combat in and around Yongdok. On Aug. 5, the North Koreans finally drove the ROKs out of Yongdok and onto Hill 181, south of town. GEN Walker sent a personal message to COL Emmerich, KMAG advisor to the ROK 3d Division, saying that the lost ground must be regained. On Aug. 6, plans were made for a night attack.

At 7:30 p.m., an air strike hit the enemy on Hill 181 for 15 minutes. This was followed by a

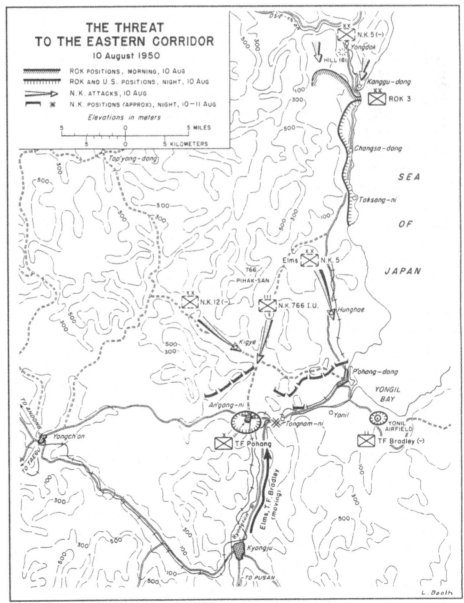

Map 32 (Source: South to the Naktong*)*

15 minute bombardment of naval gunfire and artillery. At 8 p.m., the ROK 22d and 23d Regiments began their attack, driving the enemy from Hill 181. Continuing the attack the next day, the ROKs, aided by naval and artillery fire, forced the enemy back to a point just south of Yongdok.

During the night attack, an enemy mortar barrage fell near the ROK 3d Division CP, killing several men. A short time later COL Emmerich sent a messenger to the CP for a situation report. The messenger returned, saying the CP was deserted. An interpreter was then sent to find the division commander. He, too, could not find the general or his staff. Finally, Emmerich and MAJ Slater searched the area with flashlights. Helped by some ROK soldiers, BG Chu Sik Lee, the Division Commander, and his aide, were found in a cave. Emmerich told the general to assemble his staff and return to the CP. The next morning, Emmerich requested that GEN Lee be relieved of command.

It was at this time that the 1st Separate Battalion and the Yongdungpo Battalion were inactivated and their men assigned as replacements in the ROK 22d and 23d Regiments.

On Aug. 7, Walker sent another message to Emmerich, telling him that the bridge south of Yongdok at Kanggu-dong must be held. An Engineer squad from the 24th Division had been manning the demolitions on the 520' bridge there over Osip-chon. The squad was called back to Taegu, and the ROKs took over the demolitions on the bridge. Their orders were to blow the bridge only on orders from MAJ Britton of KMAG.

At 5 a.m. on Aug. 9, a huge explosion jarred the bridge area. The commander of the ROK 22d Regiment had ordered the bridge destroyed without securing MAJ Britton's approval. About 350 soldiers from the regiment were still north of the Osip-chon when the bridge dropped. Many of these men were drowned trying to cross the deep water there. The ROK 3d Division chief of staff demanded that the regimental commander either be relieved or he would court martial that officer and have him shot by firing squad. The officer was immediately relieved.

The destruction of this bridge forced the ROK 3d Division to move its CP south to Changsa-dong the afternoon of Aug. 9. The next day, *NK 5th Division* soldiers infiltrated around the ROK 3d Division, and cut the road south of it at Hunghae, just five miles above Pohang-dong. This maneuver cut the ROK 3d Division off, isolating it.

As soon as GEN Walker learned that the ROK 3d Division was cut off, he notified COL Emmerich to meet him at the Yonil Airfield. There, the two officers met Air Force General Partridge and BG Francis W. Farrell, KMAG Chief.

Walker directed Emmerich to have the ROK 3d Division set up a defensive line around Changsa-dong and stop enemy tanks and artillery from going down the Pohang-dong road and possibly capturing Yonil Airfield. BG Kim Suk Won, the new ROK 3d Division commander, immediately placed his division in a perimeter extending along the coast from four miles north of Changsa-dong to a point seven miles south of the town.

On Aug. 10, strong enemy forces suddenly appeared near Pohang-dong, to the surprise of GEN Walker and many others. GEN Farrell had just assured Walker that ROK troops could defend Yonil without the help of American forces. He based this assessment on the belief that the enemy would be unable to move through the mountains in sufficient strength to pose a threat to the Pohang area.

TF Perry — 52d FAB and C/21st Infantry, Yongdok Area — Late July - Mid-Aug.

The official history doesn't mention Task Force Perry. This author learned of it through COL William E. Wyrick, USA, Ret., who commanded Co. C, 21st Infantry at the time. His unit provided security for the 52d FAB during this operation.

Toward the end of July 1950, the 52d FAB was sent to the vicinity of Yongdok, to provide artillery support to the ROK 3d Division. C/21st Infantry, under then-1LT Wyrick, was sent to provide security for the battalion. The company was attached to the artillery battalion for the operation. The whole force was designated Task Force Perry. LTC Miller O. Perry, commanding the 52d, commanded the task force.

"At Yongdok the artillery position was located just west of the coastal road," Wyrick wrote. "My headquarters and administrative area...were located just east of the road in an abandoned sardine cannery. The beach and ocean were immediately beyond the east edge of the building complex."

Wyrick remembered that the first replacements were received while on this duty. Most of them were NCOs, some very senior. He wrote that he used the "12-14 days...at Yongdok...to integrate this wealth of experience and expertise...into" his chain of command.

The rifle company mission soon evolved from static defense of the artillery to one of a reserve, with multiple missions. In addition to outposting the artillery's position, it provided security for FO parties and occasionally sent a rifle platoon forward to "show the flag," as Wyrick put it, "at one of the Korean infantry regiments during the daylight hours." At night, the outposts were reinforced. The remainder of the company was ready to deploy if needed.

Resupply came from the Air Force at Yonil. Wyrick sent one of his two 2 1/2-ton trucks back for supplies each day. His supply sergeant had a deal going at the airfield. Often, supply aircraft arriving from Japan would have one or more cases of weapons included in their load. The supply sergeant would take them "off their hands" and give them to the South Koreans. The ROKs gave the sergeant captured burp guns in exchange for the new weapons he had obtained from the Air Force. He traded the burp guns to Air Force supply personnel, "and they gave him almost anything," Wyrick wrote, and "everybody was happy!!!!"

Wyrick's greatest challenge was the health of his men. He had medical aidmen with his platoons, but the nearest medical unit (Air Force) was at Yonil. Diarrhea was epidemic; everyone was afflicted — true of almost every other unit in Korea at the time. Some cases were severe; the person had no control at all. The most severe cases were sent to the USAF medical unit at Yonil. Wyrick contracted a kidney infection. He was given sulfa tablets and told "to drink lots of water." The Air Force medics at Yonil gave Wyrick's aidmen "a great deal of medical supplies," which they used very effectively.

Because most of his men were deployed in hills and ridges, they had to be re-supplied and fed by choggie bearers. Normally, field mess gear was cleaned at a feeding site using three large galvanized cans; one of soapy water, one with rinse water, and one with clear hot water. After eating, the soldier dumped out food left uneaten into a garbage can, then cleaned his mess gear in the soapy water, using a brush. Next, he rinsed it in the second can, then dipped it into the third can of hot water. This system was not feasible in Korea at the time. Mess gear was collected after each "hot meal" served to the troops on position and sent back to be cleaned by mess personnel. The cleaned gear was brought forward with the next hot meal.

Wyrick's men were served two hot meals a day while with TF Perry. It was impossible to carry cans (each about 33 gal.) and water forward for each meal. Further, some of his men were so far away that the second meal was on the way to them before the carriers returned to the mess area after having delivered the first one. "Yankee ingenuity" solved the problem of having enough mess gear. Someone found crates of large new sardine cans, without lids. "The cans were oval and about seven inches long, four inches wide and about two inches high," Wyrick remembered. "Using heavy gauge wire as a handle for a can bottom, some very useable mess gear were fabricated."

There were few casualties, except to diarrhea. Wyrick remembered a Navy helicopter bringing in a load of ice cream from a cruiser standing off shore. The 52d FAB's FDC had been coordinating naval gunfire and the ice cream was a gift from the Navy for the artillery's help. "Everyone got some, even if it had almost melted. In early August 1950, it was certainly a treat!" he wrote. Everyone who was with TF Perry remembers this incident, even if everything else has faded with time.

TF Bradley — Aug. 10 - 11

GEN Walker returned to Taegu from the Yonil meeting. He sent a courier at 5:35 p.m. to MG Lawrence B. Keiser (commanding the 2d Division) at Kyongsan, ordering him to move the remaining elements of the 9th Infantry to the Yonil Airfield immediately.

A task force, formed to defend the airfield, was built around the 3d Battalion, 9th Infantry. The 3d Battalion was a black unit, similar to the 24th Infantry Regiment. Almost all the officers of these commands were white. LTC D. M. McMains commanded 3/9th Infantry. The task force was commanded by BG Joseph S. Bradley, Assistant Division Commander of the 2d Division. It was composed of 3/9th Infantry, B/ 15th FAB, TK/9th Infantry, A/2 ECB, A/82d AAA Bn, 3d Plat, HM Co., 9th Infantry, HQ, 9th Inf (Rear) and medical and signal detachments.

Moving out over the main road through Kyongju after dark on Aug. 10, the command group and 3/9th Infantry (- K Co.) reached Yonil Airfield shortly after midnight. But Co. K, riding tanks in the column's rear, was delayed three miles north of Kyongju by a destroyed bridge. As a result the company and tanks fell behind. Unable to catch up, they proceeded on alone. The 2d Division history states that infantry was riding on tank decks. Appleman's account implies that few, if any, tanks were with King Company at this time.

Ten miles north of Kyongju and about a mile east of Angang-ni, they turned sharply to the right, entering the Hyongsan River valley toward Pohang-dong five miles to the west. Appleman states seven miles. A map study indicates closer to five. As the road made this abrupt turn, it wound around the southern base of a steep hill, squeezed against the river near the village of Tongnam-ni. The lead truck of the convoy, consisting of Co. K and four vehicles from C/15 FAB was ambushed at this point at 1:20 a.m., Aug. 11. The driver of the leading vehicle was suddenly hit by enemy fire. His vehicle slewed around, blocking the road. The convoy came to a halt and was immediately assailed by automatic weapons, killing and wounding many men, and destroying some of the trucks. The men were thrown into confusion.

Upon learning of the ambush GEN Bradley at the airfield sent Co. I back to rescue Co. K. Before it could reach K, this unit was also ambushed. Bradley was informed of this by radio and sent two M-16 quad-.50 halftracks to the scene. The two M-16s were commanded by SFC Robert H. Stone and SGT E. Owens. The two vehicles "had to shoot their way through," wrote LTC Walter Killilea, who commanded the 82d AAA AW Battalion in Korea, "but their devastating fire relieved the pressure on the remnants of the two infantry companies and permitted them to withdraw." Each crew member of the two M-16s was awarded a Bronze Star Medal for this action. In addition to the two sergeants, this included corporals Paul D. Cumpton, Walter D. Emmons, PFCs Marshall W. Dunn, Hollis W. Neely, Elgenio Pedroza, Edgar L. Weems, Johnnie J. Whitmire, Jack Willis and PVT Herman L. Aycock. Aycock, Cumpton and Neely were wounded in the battle. The entire battery had numbered 7 officers and 151 EM when it landed in Korea on August 1.

Co. I lost 25 men and preliminary reports set the loss in Co. K as 7 dead and at least 40 WIA. C/15 FAB lost 25 men. The 2d Division history records that the survivors of King Company were forced to withdraw to Kyongju. There they were reassigned to other units of the 9th RCT.

It is believed that elements of the *766th Independent Unit* were the ambushers. This regiment had left the *5th Division* near Yongdok and had come through the mountains behind Pohang-dong.

In the early afternoon, Aug. 11, GEN Walker ordered the Tank Company north from Kyongju to Yonil. The unit had remained at Kyongju awaiting repair of the bridge. He also sent the ROK 17th Infantry from TF Pohang at Angang-ni to the airstrip.

Enemy troops still occupied the King Co. ambush site. Knowing this, CPT Darrigo, KMAG adviser to the ROK 17th Regiment, volunteered to lead an armored patrol through the area to Pohang. Darrigo rode in the lead tank of the five tank patrol. Four F-51s from Yonil made an attack on the enemy at the ambush site just as the tanks arrived there. The air strike forced a number of enemy troops from concealment. Tank machine gun fire cut many of them down. One group of 70 enemy soldiers was caught in the open.

The tanks arrived at the airfield about 8:30 p.m. on Aug. 11. Darrigo, then 30 years old, was said to have looked to be 50. This is the same CPT Darrigo who had escaped from Kaesong at dawn on June 25.

The USAF at Yonil Airfield

To the USAF, the Yonil Airfield was known as K-3, the Pohang Airfield. The Army called it the Yonil Airfield. Between Jul. 16 and Aug. 13, it was the busiest airfield in South Korea. Some airmen called it "The Cleveland Municipal Airport."

The U.S. Fifth Air Force organized the 6131st Base Unit there on Jul. 14. On Jul. 16, the 20 planes of the 40th Fighter-Interceptor Squadron set down at the base.

Almost from the outbreak of the Korean War, Air Force planners set out to rush aircraft and personnel to Korea. Runways on the air strips remaining in U.S. or ROK hands were too short for jet fighters to land and take off. The only fighter capable of being deployed to Korea was the F-51 (known as the P-51 during World War II and nicknamed "Mustang"). To secure the necessary planes and pilots, entire squadrons were re-equipped with F-51s. Since this propeller-driven aircraft was considered obsolete, trading in jets for F-51s was like being retro-fitted.

BG Edward J. Timberlake (West Point, 1932), Vice Commander, U.S. Fifth Air Force in Japan, recognized the value of having F-51s based in Korea. He said, "One F-51 adequately supported and fought from Taegu Airfield is equivalent to four F-80s based on Kyushu." What he meant by this was that the F-51, if stationed in Korea could be over a target in minutes, and stay on station making bombing and strafing runs far longer than an F-80 jet which had to fly from and back to Japan. What GEN Timberlake said about Mustangs flying out of Taegu, applied equally to those based at Pohang.

Other elements stationed at the Pohang Airfield, included an air weather detachment, a few B-26 bombers and several C-47 transport planes. William I. McKinney and Edward Vermillion were enlisted members of the Pohang Air Weather Detachment, which consisted of one officer and five EM. All volunteered for duty in Korea from Japan. Detachment Commander was LT Albert T. Watson, from Haneda Air Base, Tokyo. All the EM came from the 20-15 Air Weather Service Detachment, Tachikawa Air Base, about 30 miles west of Tokyo. LT Watson and MSG Peter Kobilsek were the Pohang Air Weather Detachment's forecasters. The Observers were corporals William Blommel and William I. McKinney, PFC Edward Vermillion and PVT Wendell Gene Priddy.

Within days after the Korean War started, Vermillion, "being young, adventurous and stupid...volunteered myself and Gene [Priddy]," he wrote. "Major Walker (his CO) let me know, in no uncertain terms, that I could not volunteer someone else and that, in any event, I wasn't going because I had not been in the weather service long enough to know anything about weather. He was wrong on both counts," Vermillion continued. "I immediately jumped on the old yellow weather station bike and headed for our barracks." There he awakened Gene Priddy from a sound sleep, and excitedly told him about the war in Korea. Finally, Priddy agreed to volunteer if Vermillion would promise him they would be back in time to play football on the Tachikawa football team. Vermillion assured him they would be back in time. "Seems to me a fellow will agree to almost anything when he comes out of a dead sleep...[and] all he wants is to get back to sleep," Vermillion observed. Both young men wanted to play on this team, coached by Arnold Tucker, who was quarterback on the Army teams during the Doc Blanchard and Glenn Davis era (1944-46). They got back in time; Priddy to play end and Vermillion to become an avid fan, "realizing that I couldn't possibly play football for anybody," Vermillion wrote.

Shortly, the detachment assembled at Ashiya, where they learned how to put up a tent, tested aneroid barometers and learned how to eat K- and C-rations, "or something," as Vermillion puts it.

The Air Weather detachment arrived in Pohang aboard a C-54 on Jul. 13. At that time the battle lines were well over a hundred miles north. The last thing the airmen expected was to be endangered by enemy ground forces.

Vermillion describes the area at the time: "Pohang was located in...a beautiful and idyllic setting. The city was...at the northern edge of the harbor...surrounded by the Sea of Japan on the east and mountains and rice paddies on the north and south. The air strip was located about [three road] miles south of the city on a piece of land that was perhaps 1/4-mile from the ocean. Between the airstrip and the ocean there was a beach, some land with a little grass...and a gravel and sand road. The air strip lay probably 20-25 feet above the road and 200 feet west of it. When we got there in the middle of July, it really was a lovely spot — the ocean in front of us, mountains all around and the war 126 miles north — made it feel like we were on vacation. We were laying rock-lined paths...and in general, sort of acting as if we would be there for awhile. About three weeks later, that whole area turned into some kind of hell but the first three weeks offered us lots of opportunities for laughs."

One incident of note was a typhoon which struck the field a few days after their arrival. Vermillion and his buddies had never been instructed on how to pitch a tent (except at Ashiya) but theirs was the only one which was not "collapsed or...blown asunder," Vermillion proudly recalled.

Somewhat later, the men dug a few trenches for shelter, just in case. Someone made contact with a Korean civilian, who provided Korean wine in exchange for articles of clothing. "At least we called it wine," Vermillion wrote. The men threw their empty bottles into the trenches. One afternoon, during an air raid warning a couple of the men jumped into a trench partly filled with bottles. "No one was hurt," Vermillion recalled, "but it was a lot more dangerous than the air raid [which was made by] one old single-engine Piper."

William I. McKinney recalled two other adventures at Pohang before things got nasty.

"Most of the pilots had gained their experience in World War II," he wrote. "One day after the F-51s had a successful mission...they decided to do an old World War II Victory Roll. This consisted of the lead planes doing a large loop, then landing, with the planes behind doing the same thing. This was very impressive to watch, except the pilots must have been a bit rusty on their victory roll maneuver.... Two of the rear planes landed too fast behind the lead planes and chopped up their tails. This proved very embarrassing.... Orders came out the next day: No more Victory Rolls after missions!"

On another occasion, one of the pilots spotted "a large group of North Korean forces just a few miles northeast" of the Pohang airfield. "The base was almost taken by surprise," McKinney wrote. "The Air Force personnel and mainly our small weather detachment...were mainly technicians and not trained for combat. In our poorly dug foxholes one night we heard some noises in our section...." The men of the detachment "poured out a murderous fire from our carbines; then all was quiet. The next morning we discovered...one dead cow and several dead pigs. One of our group said that they were probably Communist animals! A few days later the Air Force personnel were ordered back to Japan. I think the Army troops [at the airfield] were glad to see us leave because they only had to worry about enemy troops in front shooting at them and not the jumpy Airmen behind them"

Not all the suspected enemy incursions onto the Pohang airstrip were false alarms. The following narrative could be titled "How Vermillion Saved the Pohang Airfield":

One night in August, Vermillion was pulling the midnight guard shift and had been on duty about thirty minutes. He was sitting in the weather station tent, which had all flaps down and secured to prevent light shining outside. His feet were propped up on a small, wobbly table and he was reading a comic book by the light of a kerosene lantern hanging on the center pole. "I heard a noise outside the weather station," he wrote. "I immediately put down the comic book and grabbed my carbine, which was resting against the tent pole. In the next instant, I heard whispering in what was obviously not English. At the same time, someone stumbled over a stack of wooden ammunition boxes," stacked at the corner of the tent.

"In a state of youthful, frightened and foolish panic I turned back the tent flap and rushed out into a very dark night to do I don't know what with the enemy. It turned out I was chasing two North Koreans and they were running toward the gasoline dump (great numbers of 55 gallon drums) which was situated perhaps 100 yards from the tent and alongside the runway. I ran after them shouting for them to halt. After I got outside and started running after them I wasn't scared at all.... When I got close enough to one of them to shoot him, I said, 'All right, Joe, hold it right there.' He suddenly dropped into a squatting position and placed his hands

on top of his head. The other one kept running and by now was...among the [gasoline] barrels.... I decided not to fire [at him]."

Vermillion marched his prisoner back to the weather tent. "While we were standing there listening to the Air Police interrogate the prisoner," he wrote, Gene Priddy said, 'Look at your rifle.' I looked down to see that a live round of ammunition had taken a diagonal position in the breech of the carbine. When I was running after the guys [enemy], I pulled the bolt back as though I was going to shoot a .22 caliber rifle. In so doing, a live round was ejected and the next round wedged itself in the breech. I didn't know anything about the carbine." (When Vermillion was to undergo carbine familiarization firing at Lackland Air Base some time previously, he didn't go to the range. "I never did have much use for shooting anything anyway and, at the time, it never occurred to me that I would actually be in a position of killing somebody, so I didn't go.")

When he got off duty about 7 a.m., Vermillion went looking for "his" prisoner. An Air Policeman told him that the man had been turned over to the South Koreans for interrogation and subsequently shot. Upon hearing this, Vermillion wrote, "All kinds of things happened to me. I got angry, then sick at my stomach and head at the same time and then a kind of dazed feeling. I don't know to this day if he was lying just to be macho or if he was telling the truth. I didn't have the presence of mind to ask to see the base commander or his [the Air Policeman's] C.O.... I've been sick about this ever since. The kid couldn't have been over 15 or 16 years old...."

Another outfit sent to Pohang Airfield was Co. A, 802d Engineer Aviation Battalion. The mission of this unit was to improve the runways of the field, then cover them with pierced steel planking (PSP). These engineers were so pressed for time in trying to rehabilitate the field that they were unable to give much attention to sound engineering procedures.

The 40th Squadron averaged 34 sorties daily with just 20 aircraft (weather permitting). For one week the missions were flown in less than 150 foot ceilings. North Korean prisoners said that air attacks had knocked out almost all their transportation, and that the enemy commander reported to his superiors that he needed more men to accomplish his mission.

On July 30, five more planes were added to the 40th Squadron at Pohang, bringing it up to its authorized complement of 25 F-51s.

As July ended and August began, it became obvious that the enemy was getting closer. Air strike missions got shorter and shorter with each passing day. Finally, just before the Air Force abandoned the field, planes were taking off, making their strike and returning to Pohang without leaving the landing pattern.

On Aug. 7, the 39th Fighter-Interceptor Squadron received their allocation of F-51s. The next day, the squadron, plus the 35th Fighter-Interceptor Group headquarters moved to Pohang. Both the 39th and 40th Squadrons were part of the 35th. This brought the number of Mustangs operating out of Pohang to 50. Concurrently with this move, the provisional support unit at Pohang was expanded into the 6131st Fighter Wing, Single Engine. The 6002d Fighter

Interceptor Wing, Single Engine was simultaneously activated at Taegu. COL Robert W. Witty commanded the 6131st at Pohang.

On Aug. 8, COL Witty decided that half of each unit on the base would be evacuated immediately and that the remaining airmen would stay to defend the base until Army units could be brought up to take over. On that date, LT Watson chose Priddy and Vermillion to stay with him at Pohang. Priddy drove the jeep taking MSG Kobilsek, McKinney and Blommel 12 miles south to the port of Kuryongpo-ri, where they were taken off in an LST. The trailer was loaded with weather equipment. Priddy was to leave the men and equipment and return to Pohang. When he got to the port, he was ordered aboard the LST with the jeep and trailer. Although he told the officer that he had been ordered to return to the base, he was informed that Pohang was cut off by the enemy and no one could get through. Priddy waited until no one was looking and left the ship, caught a ride in an ambulance, and went back to the air strip.

LT Watson and Vermillion were enjoying a bottle of Ballantine scotch when Edward spotted Priddy coming toward them, "without [his] helmet and with his carbine over his head." Vermillion wrote. "Here comes John Wayne, Lieutenant," Vermillion said. "Think we ought to save him a drink?" Watson asked. "We were so glad to see him that we gave him the rest of the bottle," Vermillion recalled.

That evening Priddy and Vermillion were sharing a foxhole on the perimeter. The hole was a few feet forward of the holes to either flank. Just before dark the men on either side got out of their holes and ran to the rear. Vermillion recounts what happened:

"Gene said, 'What the hell...those bastards are running away! What do you think we ought to do?' 'They can't run to Japan,' I said. 'We're about to get killed, Gene, you know that?' 'Yeah, I'm afraid so,' he said. We talked for a little bit about how we might be able to avoid that but finally decided there was no escape and that we would rather have our folks see that we had been shot in the face and not in the back."

Shortly after dark a gentle rain began to fall. Vermillion held a blanket over the hole to keep the men and their ammunition dry, "while we talked and waited to be killed," Vermillion continued. "I said, 'Gene, did you ever go to church when you were a kid?' 'Naw,' he said. 'We lived next door to a Baptist church one time but I never did go. Momma would send us over there but I always went in the front door and out the side away from our house.' After a brief pause, he said, 'You know, those people sure could sing pretty, though.' I said, 'That's close enough. Why don't you kneel down and say a prayer for us?' I don't recall that he said anything...in response. He simply knelt or crouched down in the trench and said in a very firm voice, 'Lord, you get us out of this one and we'll get out of the next one by ourselves.' With that, he stood up, looked me in the eye and quite seriously said, 'Well, what d'ya' think?' 'I believe that will get it,' I said. And there was no more talk about running, getting killed, being taken prisoner or anything else about our predicament."

A few weeks later, back in Japan, LT Watson, Priddy and Vermillion were each awarded a

Bronze Star Medal. Vermillion had been credited with saving the base by capturing the enemy soldier and chasing off the other. "Somebody figured that those two kids I was chasing were attempting to blow up the gasoline dump," Vermillion wrote, "and my quick and heroic action saved the day. The medal has been little solace. I still have the kid's hat brass, a little tin star, and I have always wished I could have told his Mom and Dad how sorry I was about what happened to him."

Of his Korean experience, Vermillion wrote, "I found that I had more courage than I thought I had." He also paid tribute to "the strength and courage of my great friend..., Gene Priddy," and to Albert Watson, "a man of integrity and cool as a cucumber under fire." He concludes with this observation: "Still, there have been many, many times when I wished that I had let Gene Priddy sleep that June morning at Tachikawa."

Battle Actions — Aug. 11

In addition to the fight which the tanks had in joining TF Bradley at the Pohang Airfield there were several other battle actions in the area on Aug. 11.

That morning, TF Pohang attacked north from Angang-ni and ran into a buzz-saw. Two companies of the 25th Regiment were annihilated. It was a blazing hot day. Both the task force and the Capital Division lost ground to the enemy in spite of almost constant air attacks from the Yonil (Pohang) Airfield. One pilot recalled in *South to the Naktong*, "I barely had my wheels up before I started my strafing runs." North Korean ground fire could sometimes be deadly, for, on Aug. 10, they shot down four F-51s.

The enemy troops were from the *12th Division*, which had come south through Kigye. In the battles on Aug. 11, prisoners reported that the division lost about 800 men. Even so, by the end of the day, utilizing small-arms and automatic weapons almost exclusively, the enemy forced the ROKs back and had patrols operating three miles south of Pohang. Some 300 members of the *766th Independent Unit* and the *5th Division* entered Pohang and reportedly seized the railroad station. Within hours, however, they were driven out by Naval gunfire and air strikes. From then on, Pohang-dong lay between the lines, visited by night patrols from both sides.

Some time during the day Eighth Army headquarters ordered the ROK forces in the east to fall back to new positions during the nights of Aug. 12 and 13. That night, the planes at Yonil flew to another strip for safety, then flew back the next morning.

On Aug. 12, long range, but ineffective, enemy fire fell on the airfield. The same day, as ordered by GEN Walker, COL Kim Hi Chun (age 28) led his ROK 17th Infantry in an attack from Angang-ni to Yonil.

The Air Force Abandons Pohang Airfield — Aug. 15

As early as late July, COL Witty, the Air Force commander at the Pohang Airfield, had warned his superiors that enemy forces nearby endangered his installation, men and equipment. When the enemy was so close that his aircraft were

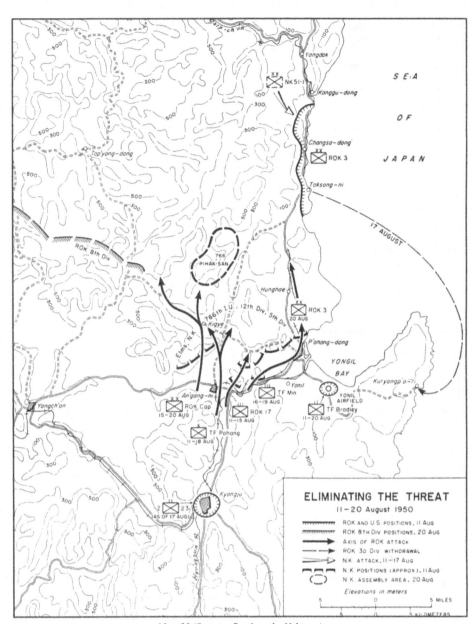

Map 33 (Source: South to the Naktong)

barely airborne before making their attack runs, he became much more concerned. Airmen serviced planes by day and helped man defenses at night. The arrival of TF Bradley and even the ROK 17th Regiment did little to allay his concern. On Aug. 8, some Air Force personnel, already were sent back to Japan. MG Earl E. Partridge (West Point 1924), commanding the Fifth Air Force, authorized abandonment of the airfield. Evacuation began on Aug. 14 and was completed the next day, when Witty's headquarters departed. At that time his command included 45 Mustangs.

But Fifth Air Force headquarters apparently failed to notify MacArthur's headquarters of the move. The information came at 4 p.m. on Aug. 13, in the form of a United Press report filed at 1:20 p.m. *South to the Naktong* quoted this report: "Air Force spokesman announced that the Air Force was evacuating Pohang air strip." The report said that the evacuation was being carried out because the strip was under North Korean machine gun and mortar fire. Eighth Army was immediately called on the telephone. This call confirmed that Fifth Air Force Advance

Headquarters in Korea had ordered the abandonment of the field, but disclosed that no mortar fire had landed on it.

Generals MacArthur and Almond were very upset at the news. MacArthur ordered one of his staff to notify the Far East Air Force Headquarters that he intended to hold the airfield and that he did not want the planes to return to Japan. In spite of this, the entire 6131st Fighter Wing redeployed to Tsuika Air Base on Kyushu. The enemy never brought the Pohang Airfield under effective fire. A large stock of aviation gasoline remained at the strip. After it was abandoned, damaged planes made emergency landings there, and many fighters used it for refueling as long as the gasoline lasted. The Air Force did not re-occupy the field later, claiming that the area was too infested with guerrillas.

Evacuation By Sea of the ROK 3d Division — Aug. 16 - 17

As North and South Korean forces battled in the Pohang-Angang-ni region to the south, the ROK 3d Division found itself pinned to the coast in a long, narrow beachhead by the *NK 5th Division*. The *5th Division* now renewed its efforts to destroy the ROK command. Under this pressure, the 3d Division reduced its perimeter and moved its CP four miles south to Toksong-ni on the coast. LSTs could land at this point to evacuate the ROKs. Only fire from the U.S. cruiser *Helena*, three destroyers and air attacks by the Fifth Air Force kept the enemy at bay. This support was guided by air control parties and artillery observers. Two of *Helena's* helicopters transported medical supplies in for the Korean wounded.

A supply LST evacuated 313 ROK wounded from Changsa-dong on Aug. 13. At Toksong-ni later in the day, this LST struck rocks which opened a hole in its hull. The wounded had to be moved to another LST over a walkway in a heavy sea. Amphibious trucks (DUKW), known as "Ducks," were used to transport 86 of the more seriously wounded ROKs to a Korean hospital ship. This vessel, just arrived, was anchored just 500 yards off-shore. The LST, once loaded, headed for Pusan. The DUKW was an amphibious 2 1/2-ton truck, capable of traveling on land as a truck, and on water as a self-propelled boat.

By Aug. 15, the situation of the ROK 3d Division became so critical that Eighth Army ordered its evacuation by sea. The division would be transported to the port of Kuryongpo-ri, 20 air miles to the south on the cape on the southern side of Yongil Bay. From there, it would relieve elements of the Capital Division on line below Pohang-dong then join in a planned coordinated attack to the north.

The evacuation by LST began at Toksong-ni on the night of Aug. 16. The entire command, including 125 wounded, was loaded and the last LST left the beach at 7 a.m. The entire 3d Division, consisting of the 22d and 23d Regiments (over 9,000 men), plus 1,200 attached South Korean policemen and 1,000 laborers, together with all their weapons, equipment and ammunition, were successfully brought away under the cover of night and heavy concentrations of naval gunfire. At dawn, aircraft joined the Navy in providing a curtain of fire along the beach. Escorted by the *Helena* and several destroyers, the 3d Division, in LSTs made its way to Kuryongpo-ri, arriving at 10:30 a.m. Unloading at once, the command was ordered to move into the battle line south of Pohang the next day.

The North Korean Advance in the East Thwarted — Aug. 13-19

Although some North Koreans entered Pohang-dong on Aug. 10 and 11, it was not until Aug. 13 that the enemy formally claimed its "liberation." A large body of troops from the *12th Division* entered the town that day. But they did not stay long. A captured officer of the *12th* said that the *1st Regiment* withdrew after only three hours because of heavy air strikes and a severe naval bombardment. The *12th Division* then positioned itself on high ground south and west of the town. The *2d Regiment's* 2d and 3d Battalions were on hills six miles southwest of Pohang and in position to threaten the Pohang Airfield. At the same time, elements of the *5th Division* had reached the hills just north of the town.

The Capital Division had been ordered to move from near Andong to the Angang-ni-Kigye area (about 25 miles). There, it was to go into line east of the ROK 8th Division. This move was completed by Aug. 14.

The savage battle near Pohang resulted in heavy casualties on both sides. On Aug. 13, the ROKs renewed their attack, when the 17th Regiment, back under Capital Division control drove forward. U.S. artillery and tanks from TF Bradley supported the attack.

About the same time, TF Pohang attacked from Angang-ni toward Kigye. Between Aug. 15 and 17, the Capital Division and TF Pohang, augmented by TF Min (commanded by ROK COL Min Ki Sik) from Eighth Army reserve, combined to force the enemy back north of the lateral Taegu-Pohang road and away from the Kyongju corridor near Angang-ni. (See Chapter Notes.)

The 2/23d Infantry arrived at Kyongju about dawn of Aug. 17 to stiffen its defense.

In the midst of all this fighting across the Perimeter, North Korea's Premier Kim Il Sung broadcast from Pyongyang an order for the army to drive the U.S. and ROK forces from Korea by the end of August. He correctly predicted that the longer they remained the stronger they would become. He called on his troops to "destroy the South Korean and United States [troops] to the last man." (Quoted from *South to the Naktong*.)

By nightfall of Aug. 17, the *766th Independent Unit* was all but surrounded by the advancing ROKs, and it withdrew into the mountains north of Kigye. The *NK 12th Division*, having suffered very heavily from air strikes and naval gunfire, began to withdraw that night. At 8 p.m., the commander ordered it to pull back through Kigye to the Topyong-dong area. In making this move, the division lost heavily. On Aug. 18, it ordered all units to assemble on Pihak-san (a mountain about six miles or so north of Kigye). There, the *12th Division* would try to reorganize.

By Aug. 19 the ROK Capital Division had pushed north of Kigye about two miles, the 3d Division had entered Pohang-dong and TF Min was a mile and a half north of the town. On Aug. 20, the 3d Division relieved TF Min and continued the attack to positions five and a half miles north of Pohang-dong. The Capital Division also made further advances north of Kigye. Also on Aug. 20, Eighth Army dissolved TF Pohang and TF Bradley and moved TF Min west between the ROK 1st and 6th Divisions. The American force at the airfield was redesignated the 3d Battalion, 9th Infantry, Reinforced.

North Korean Forces in the East After Aug. 20

In the rugged fastness of the 2,400 foot Pihak-san six miles north of Kigye, the *12th Division* and *766th Independent Unit* reorganized. As a result, the *766th* was deactivated and its approximately 1,500 men incorporated into the *12th Division*. The division also received about 2,000 replacements. With these additions, the *12th Division* reportedly totaled about 5,000 men. This figure attests to the terrible casualties which it had suffered in the Pohang battles. Originally the *12th Division* had been composed primarily of veterans of the Chinese Communist Army.

Then it was a highly trained command. The severe losses it had suffered, compelling the infusion of poorly trained replacements, reduced its fighting ability. Morale was low, but there was little desertion.

From about the end of July, the *12th Division* had been equipped primarily with captured U.S. M1 rifles and carbines. The men of the division originally had Japanese 99 rifles and ammunition. Once the U.S. weapons and ammunition became available, they turned in the Japanese rifles to the division supply dump.

By the time that the men of the *12th Division* arrived in the Pohang area, they were near exhaustion. Further, the command had left its artillery behind, and lacked an adequate food supply. The North Korean logistical system could not adequately support the *12th* nor any of the other forces in the East.

In a footnote, Appleman states that a survey of 825 enemy prisoners revealed that the shortage of food was the most important of all factors causing low morale.

The ROK Army reported that, between Aug. 17 and 20 its forces in the Pohang area had killed 3,800 North Koreans and captured another 181. It also stated that it had captured 20 artillery pieces, 11 light mortars, 21 82mm mortars 160 machine guns, 557 U.S. M1 rifles and 381 Japanese rifles.

On August 27 it started all over again in this area.

Chapter Notes:

P. 212 TF Min was rated as a separate regimental-sized force. It is the same TF Min which fought the North Koreans on the west coast of South Korea earlier in the war. Shortly after the battles near Pohang, this force was reconstituted as the ROK 5th Infantry Regiment.

CHAPTER FIFTEEN - On The Taegu Front

Walker's Command Style

GEN Walker believed that the success of his defense lay in the attack. He strongly urged his principal subordinate commanders to launch attacks as often as possible. He knew he could not win simply by constantly countering enemy blows. He said, substantially, "I wanted all commanders to attack, to raid, to capture prisoners and thus keep the enemy off balance. If that is done, more and more opportunities to hurt the enemy will arise and our troops will be better prepared to pass to a general offensive when things are ripe." (Quoted in *South to the Naktong*, p. 334.) But to meet all the threats he faced simultaneously throughout the Perimeter, Walker had to adroitly move his always meager reserves from place to place along the Perimeter to preserve the little real estate left to his command.

Few people can disagree that Walker managed his assets in a deft and timely manner. His defense of the Perimeter was masterful. There were few American generals at the time who could have successfully engineered such a defense. GEN Walker was anything but a "Headquarters" general. He left this routine to his staff. One of Walker's daily problems was to find reserves with which to meet enemy thrusts. For this, he depended upon COL Eugene M. Landrum, his Chief of Staff during August. Both ROK Army and U.S. troops were employed in reserve roles throughout the Perimeter. One of Walker's daily greetings to his chief of staff was, "Landrum, how many reserves have you dug up for me today?"

COL Landrum was charged with keeping GEN Walker completely informed on the situation around the entire Perimeter. Landrum did this by briefing Walker each day when he returned to the CP. To keep abreast of the latest situation, Landrum obtained information from the Army G-2, G-3 and G-3, Air, and contacted each major headquarters by telephone between 10 p.m. and midnight and talked either with the commander or his chief of staff. This provided the latest thinking of the commander concerned and the most up-to-date situational data. These nightly calls often formed the basis for Walker's trips the next day.

Walker went out each day, sometimes by jeep, but often by aircraft. He could cover a great deal of territory by air, and the light plane he used could land on dirt roads or open ground. The plane did not need very much space to land or to take off, so it was usually the most practical way for Walker to go from place to place around the Perimeter.

BG Eugene M. Lynch, then Walker's pilot, explained how Walker traveled around, gathered information, then took action: Walker had "an Assistant 3 by the name of [COL] Allen MacLean, who was later killed up at the Chosen Reservoir. MacLean was selected by Walker to be his Tactical 'Gofer.' His Administrative 'Gofer' was...[COL] Bill Collier. Collier would handle activities with a division staff, division

commanders and Mac was supposed to handle regimental commanders and staff."

When Walker came into a division CP, Lynch said, he would say, "Let me see your battalion disposition." Walker believed that division commanders fight by battalion and regimental commanders fight by company. This is Army doctrine.

Often, Walker discovered that the division commander "didn't understand how to fight," Lynch said. In these instances, he would take the division commander aside and have a private conference with him. The conference was not always cordial, if Walker thought the commander needed "jacked up," Lynch recalled.

On one occasion, Lynch related, Walker flew in to the 2d Division CP. He "walked in and said, 'Dutch, where's your division?' And Keiser said, 'Well I'm waiting for the liaison officers to come back. I understand they are having difficulty getting back.' Well, of course, the roads were jammed.

"Walker said to Keiser, 'You get this division under control right now or I'll take control over this division along with the Army.'

"So the two of us were walking over to the plane." There was a little embankment near the plane. "Walker walked over and sat down," Lynch continued, "so I sat down alongside of him.... I looked over and he was crying. He said, 'I can't let this Army be destroyed, yet I don't know what to do to stop it from being destroyed.' Here he was — you couldn't do anymore than we had tried to do that morning.... He said. 'Well, we've got to look at the rest of the area.... Except for that area [2d Division] things looked OK." (See Chapter Notes.)

When Walker visited division CPs, he sent his aide, LTC Layton C. "Joe" Tyner and Mike Lynch to visit the staff sections, talk to the officers and enlisted men and find out what was really going on. Lynch also queried division pilots who happened to be present. When they returned to the Army CP in Taegu, Lynch recalled, Walker would say, "OK, gentlemen, ...what's happening down at the platoon and company?' Joe would say, "I think Colonel Collier's gonna work with that G2.'... Then Collier would be on an airplane down to that division staff. Or, if it was a weakness in the regimental or battalion level, Walker would go by jeep someplace else [while] Mac and I would go down and he'd talk to the regimental or battalion commander. That's the way it worked."

Walker was constantly moving about the Perimeter, to be present at critical sites at the right time, mentor and tough teacher to his division commanders, intervening, when necessary, to call in reinforcements. Many times, he knew more about what was really happening in a division sector than the division commander. He was what is now called a "hands-on" commander. By that, it is meant that there was no doubt that he was in charge, because he took personal and direct charge of the situation if the division commander had not. He made all the major critical decisions and personally followed up to see that

his orders were being carried out. He saw that his job was to command; to lead.

The crises in the 24th Division sector, on the Pohang front and then on the Taegu front, all taking place in the same general time period in August, fully tested Walker's abilities. In meeting them, he proved a consummate tactician.

Disposition of the North Korean, ROK and U.S. Troops on the Taegu Front — August

The North Korean Army deployed five divisions and elements of the *105th Armored Division* in an arc along the Taegu front. Opposite these five divisions, from south to north, were the U.S. 1st Cavalry Division and the ROK 1st and 6th Infantry Divisions. The 1st Cavalry Division front extended from a point just north of Hyonpung to a point about two miles north of Waegwan, where it met the south flank of the ROK 1st Division. The frontage of this division extended northward to Naktong-ni, on the Naktong River, then eastward about six miles to the left flank of the ROK 6th Division. At Naktong-ni, the road from Sangju runs south to join another north-south road through Kunwi near the village of Chonpyong. This village lay near the mouth of a long, narrow valley (later called the "Bowling Alley"). The poplar-lined road went south through this valley toward Taegu by way of Tabu-dong. The 6th Division carried the line eastward another eight miles, covering the Kunwi road. BG Paik Sun Yup commanded the ROK 1st Division. He had been promoted to Brigadier General on July 27. COL Kim Chong O commanded the ROK 6th Division.

The *NK 10th Division* and part of the *3d* faced the 1st Cavalry. The *15th* and *13th Divisions* were opposite the ROK 1st Division, and the *NK 1st Division* opposed the ROK 6th. The *NK 1st Division* (about 5,000 men) was commanded by MG Hong Rim. The *NK 3d Division* (about 6,000 men) was commanded by MG Lee Yong Ho; the *13th* (about 9,500 men) by MG Choi Yong Chin; the *15th* (some 6,500 men) by MG Park Song Chol, and the *105th Armored Division* by MG Yu Kyong Su. The *10th Division* experienced no combat until it crossed the Naktong near Hyonpung on Aug. 12. (See Chapter 13.)

The 1st Cavalry Division had a frontage of about 35 miles along the Naktong. (This figure is from Appleman's *South to the Naktong*, p. 254.) The 1/7th Cavalry, occupying the extreme southern sector, was responsible for over 30,000 yards of front (9 miles). North of the 7th Cavalry was the 8th Cavalry, whose two battalions each guarded 10,000 yards along the Naktong. The 8th sat squarely on the shortest and most direct avenue to Taegu from the west. The 8th Cavalry made contact with the 5th Cavalry Regiment along the river forward of Hill 268, Triangulation Hill. The hill was within the 5th Cavalry's sector. The 5th also deployed both battalions on the front, with the 1st on the south and the 2d on the north. The extreme northern area of the Cavalry Division's sector was occupied by G/5th Cav, reinforced by elements of the Heavy Weapons Co. (Co H) on Hill 303.

The ROK 1st and 6th Divisions — Aug. 4 - 17

The ROK 1st Division's sector started just north of Hill 303. GEN Paik wrote that he was worried about the hill because that was where his division tied into the 1st Cavalry Division. He discussed the situation with the Americans. "We decided to cover the vulnerable approach to Hill 303 by swapping the positions of a U.S. platoon with those of a platoon from my 13th Regiment, including telephone lines and the artillery fire grids that went with each," he wrote in *From Pusan to Panmunjom*. He remarked that this was the first time such an exchange had been attempted. There was confusion, he wrote. "We watched with interest as the men of the two different cultures used hand gestures — and even foot gestures — to make the swap, but they accomplished the task in short order, and we were able to relax."

GEN Paik established his CP at the Osang school, on the road to Taegu. His division was responsible for 25 miles of front along the Naktong, plus another seven or eight from Naktong-ni to the east. The 13th Regiment, along the southern portion of the division line, guarded about ten miles along the river. To the north, disposed principally on an eight-mile front, was Paik's ROK 11th Infantry. His 12th Regiment was in the north, on the Naktong-ni approach. As the ROK 1st Division took up these positions, it numbered a mere 7,000 personnel

Paik wrote that Walker called the Naktong defense line "Line X" and that he had designated a second defense line as "Line Y." Line Y still embraced the Naktong River defenses as far north as Waegwan. From there, Paik wrote, Line Y curved east to the east coast, but still included Taegu. Planning ahead, GEN Paik, reconnoitered the area which would be within the sector of Line Y probably assigned to his division. He located excellent defensive terrain on the high ridges north of Tabu-dong, including massive Hill 902 — Kasan. The Kasan ridge line served as a defense line twice in the sixth century Japanese invasions led by Hideyoshi. The ruins of an ancient fort stood on the highest part of Kasan.

Paik's chief of staff, COL Suk Ju Am and his G3, Mun Hyong Tae, made a further examination of the ground. The high ridges of Uhak-san, north of Tabu-dong, west of the Bowling Alley road, and a similar high ridge line east of the road were selected for the ROK 1st Division's final defensive line. Uhak-san included a series of peaks, each over 800 meters high, stretching for over two miles. The comparable ridge east of the road included a summit well over a mile long that was at a height ranging from 670 to 770 meters.

The *NK 13th* and *15th Divisions* Attack the ROK 1st Division — Aug. 4-16

Paik wrote that his 7,000-man division was stretched "paper thin" along the Naktong. It could hold during the daytime, aided by U.S. air strikes. But it was vulnerable at night.

The enemy found relatively shallow places along the Naktong where they constructed "underwater bridges" at night. These "bridges" were constructed of sandbags and oil drums to make a ford just a few feet below the surface of the river. By this means, a number of troops from the *13th Division* crossed into the ROK 1st Division's sector. On the 5th, the bulk of the *13th's 21st Regiment* crossed the Naktong at Naktong-ni. When the crossing was discovered, the enemy was engaged by air strikes (some while still in the water) and ROK mortars and artillery. That night the enemy's *19th Regiment* also crossed into the ROK sector, leaving their heavy weapons and vehicles behind. On the night of Aug. 6-7, the *13th Division's* third regiment, the *23d*, made its crossing, along with two artillery battalions on rafts below Naktong-ni. On Aug. 8, the T-34s with the *13th Division* crossed the river.

The ROK 1st Division attacked the *13th* as soon as it crossed the Naktong, forcing it into the hills. About this time, the ROKs began receiving the 3.5 inch rocket launchers. Each regiment received two or three launchers. The ROKs formed tank hunter teams with these weapons. Some teams even ventured across the Naktong in search of enemy tanks. Over the next few days, the ROK 12th Regiment destroyed three T-34s and captured another. This tank was later put on display in Taegu.

In the early days of August, the logistical situation for the ROKs improved and they also began to receive replacements for their sorely depleted units. Unfortunately, these recruits were virtually untrained. None of them had fired more than ten rounds of ammunition from their individual weapons.

South of the *NK 13th*, the *15th Division's 45th Regiment* crossed the Naktong south of Sonsan on August 7. Although UN aircraft attacked during part of the crossing, the regiment was successful, and headed into the mountains, unopposed. The *15th Divisions* other two regiments, the *48th* and *50th,* accompanied by tanks, crossed at two ferry sites four and six miles above Waegwan. By 8:10 a.m., at least two tanks, along with at least two battalions of infantry had crossed at the upper site. Air observers reported that at least seven enemy tanks supported the crossing with direct fire. These tanks apparently also crossed the river later in the day. (This is the tank crossing mentioned above.) After seizing Hills 201 and 346, the *15th Division* headed east toward Tabu-dong, seven air miles away.

After the *15th Division* had crossed the river, the Air Force attacked the underwater bridge six miles above Waegwan with 1,000 lb. bombs, with unknown results.

On Aug. 9, the ROK 1st Division regained the high ground near the crossing sites, but by that time, the enemy *15th Division* had already moved deep into the mountains northwest of Tabu-dong. Between Aug. 12 and 16, the *15th Division* assembled near the towering Yuhak-san, where the *13th Division* was already grappling with the ROK 1st Division for possession of that key terrain feature.

The ROK 12th Regiment withdrew from its positions at In-dong and moved over the road to Tabu-dong, intending to occupy the high ridges north of the town. To their dismay, they found elements of the *13th Division* already on Yuhak-san, squarely in the center of the ROK 1st Division's sector of Line Y. A fierce and bloody struggle ensued. Meantime, enemy forces attacked the ROK 1st Division's 13th Regiment on Hill 328, near the Naktong, quickly taking it. GEN Paik was thoroughly alarmed by this loss. He rushed to the scene. As he watched his troops withdrawing on the road, a projectile suddenly burst in front of them. Their regimental commander, COL Choi Young Hi had fired a 57mm recoilless rifle ahead of them, bringing the men to a sudden halt. With that, the colonel ran to the road and angrily ordered his men to turn around and counterattack. The men immediately turned around and launched a counterattack on Hill 328.

As the regiment attacked, it was joined by a battalion-sized unit, adding significant impetus to the assault. Paik, amazed and puzzled by the sudden appearance of this force, demanded of COL Choi "where the hell these new troops had come from." The embarrassed colonel confessed that he had engaged in some unauthorized recruiting in Taegu. Paik had detailed his 3d Battalion to the 11th Regiment's sector, leaving Choi with only two battalions with which to defend his sector. The colonel simply dispatched a detail of "recruiters" to Taegu, where they rounded up enough men to equal a third battalion. He apologized to GEN Paik, who neither praised nor condemned the colonel. He realized that, without these additional men, the 13th Regiment would have been unable to retake the hill. Even so, it took the regiment two days to regain 328.

The ROK 11th Regiment, in the division's northern sector, meantime, was driven back two miles toward Tabu-dong. In the 11th's withdrawal, the ROKs ended up on the northern side of the road and the enemy on the south side. A close-in, swirling battle followed with, as Paik wrote, "the offense and defense each facing in the wrong direction."

While his 11th and 13th Regiments were thus engaged, Paik's 12th Regiment was locked in a hand-to-hand struggle for Yuhak-san. Both sides used hand grenades liberally. Bodies piled up almost everywhere. The living used the dead as protection. But neither the North Koreans nor the ROKs would back off.

By Aug. 15, with his division fully committed to desperate battle all along its front, GEN Paik asked Eighth Army for reinforcements. In response, the U.S. 27th Infantry (25th Division) and ROK 10th Infantry (8th Division) were ordered to Paik's assistance. In the meantime, he was ordered to hold fast.

The *NK 1st Division* Attacks the ROK 6th Division — Aug. 6-17

The *1st Division* received about 2,500 replacements, but many had no weapons and were employed in rear areas. On Aug. 6, U.S. aircraft spotted ten troop-laden barges crossing the river. Between then and Aug., 8, the *1st* crossed the Naktong between Hamchang and Sangju and attacked the ROK 6th Division. The ROK 6th Division stubbornly resisted the *1st* in a slow, fighting withdrawal, keeping this enemy division from reaching Kunwi until about Aug. 17.

Then the 6th punished it further before the *1st* could reach the Tabu-dong region farther south.

Timely Arrival of U.S. Armored Battalions in the Perimeter — Aug. 7 and 16

In Chapter 11, mention was made of the deployment of three battalions of armor to Korea on a crash basis. These battalions were more or less thrown together in a matter of days and shipped to Korea without having had the opportunity to assimilate personnel or equipment. Many officer and enlisted filler personnel had little or no armor training or experience. But all three battalions (6th, 70th and 73d) were built around cadres of experienced tankers.

With the arrival of these three tank battalions on Aug. 7 and the 2d Division's organic 72d Tk Bn on Aug. 16, plus the divisions' tank battalions, Walker had a powerful 400 tanks which could fight enemy tanks and give support to infantry counterattacks and the defense.

LTC John S. Growdon's 6th Tk Bn (M-46 Patton tanks) became Eighth Army reserve on Aug. 8. On Aug. 12, LTC William M. Rodgers' 70th Tk Bn (22 M-26s and 44 M4A3 Shermans) joined the 1st Cavalry Division. The companies of LTC Calvin S. Hannum's 73d (M-26 Pershings) were sent to support various fronts on the Perimeter. Co A went to Ulsan to help protect the eastern MSR; Company B to TF Bradley at Kyongju and Kigye, and Co. C was attached to the 27th Infantry in the Bowling Alley. Later, the 6th was attached to the 24th Division and the 73d was withdrawn from the Perimeter and attached to the 7th Infantry Division for the Inchon operation.

1st Cavalry Division — End July - Aug. 18

The 1st Cavalry Division executed a fighting withdrawal to the Naktong River. In one action, C/8th Cavalry was hit by the enemy in the predawn hours of a day late in July. Donald Summers, of Co. C, wrote: "We were digging in again. Our position was at the corner of two roads which formed a ninety degree angle. It was raining and the mud stuck to your shovels and hands. There were no flies or bugs during the rain, but they would come when it stopped. We dug our machine gun at the point so it could cover an attack down either road. We then dug our rifle squads in a semi-circle about one hundred yards up the hill. Another hundred yards and at the top of the ridge line was our command post, our anti-tank weapons and mortars. We watched as hundreds of Koreans who we believed to be civilians came past our position. It was getting dark now and the rain had stopped. We tried to get comfortable [but with] wet and muddy holes...most [men] laid outside [them], thinking they could take cover if something happened.

"A lot of the civilians had left the road and seemed [to be] settling down for the night. We were on fifty percent alert, but most of us were so exhausted [that] sometimes both [men in the two-man foxholes] would fall asleep for awhile.

"Just before dawn, yelling and shooting started and our mortar sent up flares. I could see them [the enemy] all over and mixed up with our machine gun and rifle squad down at the road. Most of them had white clothing on and made easy targets. But were we hitting our own men? It was hard to tell. Now the flash of an automatic weapon. They had turned our machine gun around on us. Each time I raised my head a spray of dirt erupted in my face. I [went] way down in my hole now and fumbled for my bayonet, fixing it on my M1. I thought any minute one [North Korean] would appear above my hole and I was going to take him with me. Suddenly, there were a couple of loud explosions and the machine gun fell silent. Our 57mm recoilless rifle had scored a direct hit on the nest. It was daylight now and the North Koreans faded, except for the ones who lay dead. We were now able to advance to our overrun positions." There, the men found a number of dead GIs, bayonetted in their foxholes. Three were still alive. These were evacuated.

On the afternoon of Aug. 2, the 7th Cavalry was given the mission of covering the withdrawal of the 1st Cavalry Division to positions behind the Naktong River. H/7th Cavalry was assigned a position on the main rail line between Kumchon and Taegu. Refugees became a major problem. In his *The Legacy of Custer's 7th U.S. Cavalry in Korea*, Ed Daily describes what happened: "Orders were issued that no refugees would be permitted to come near or pass through our sector. Enemy sniper fire...was increasing. Suddenly from the rear of our position, five enemy soldiers dressed in native refugee clothing, [having] infiltrated our line...immediately fired into us with rifles and burp guns. An enemy hand grenade ricocheted off the rail edge of the railroad and landed at my feet. Immediately, I kicked the grenade with my boot, which went forward and it detonated simultaneously. Luckily, it was only a concussion grenade and when the dust cleared all I sustained was a minor concussion and a small metal fragment in my right hand." There were no other friendly wounded. "Within a matter of minutes, four enemy soldiers were killed and one seriously wounded," Daily continued. He went to the aid station, had his wounds treated and returned to his unit. (See Chapter Notes.)

Joe Christopher was an ammunition bearer in the 60mm mortar section of F/8th Cav. On August 3, his unit was just west of the Naktong. The company's rifle platoons took up positions on a low hill. "The mortar section," he wrote, "set up on the sand wash [of a dry stream bed] in the open. We could see some of the company on the hill and CPL Donald Hewins [platoon leader and FO] was with them. The fire direction commands were very simple. Hewins gave hand signals which we had trained to do, the first aiming stake was the figure of CPL Donald Hewins. This was my first time to operate the gun. I had never done so even in training.... Someone suggested to me to put some willow sticks under the baseplate to prevent it from sinking into the sand.

"PFC Wayne Houchin's platoon...took position along a ridge on bare ground. Wayne and Claude Rutter were the crew for [a] light machine gun. They set up and waited," Christopher continued. "LT Matta, the C.O., was standing nearby cautioning everyone to be quiet and not fire until a mortar round landed on the North Koreans. LT Matta was Puerto Rican, with quite an accent. He was also very popular with the men, always ready to exchange friendly banter.... The enemy had not detected the presence of F Co. and five North Koreans raised up about twenty-five yards away. One was carrying an American SCR 300 radio. Wayne had his sight on them and wanted to fire but LT Matta said, 'Don't shoot.' Just then a mortar round hit in front of the machine gun, showering Wayne and Claude with dirt. Wayne could not see, but he started firing; everybody was firing. LT Matta was saying, 'look at those SOBs run' and firing his pistol. Wayne fired one box of ammo and reloaded the second. Hot brass was in his shirt making brands. A burst of machine gun fire from the N.K. hit under the tripod, kicking dirt into Wayne's and Claude's faces so hard it brought specks of blood. Both men thought the other was hit. They dragged the gun back from the crest. It was so hot it had to be handled by the tripod legs. The firing stopped."

Christopher fired the first mortar round. When the round was fired, "the baseplate skidded rearward a bit rather than dig in a little," Christopher wrote. "I called out that I was resetting the gun, and another one took up firing. I quickly cleaned away the sticks and picked up the new range and commenced firing.... The three guns (60mm mortars) fired non-stop for a few minutes, then increasing range as the Koreans were running off. CPL Hewins on the hill [gave] all [range and deflection] changes by hand signals." During all this, Christopher's mortar had a misfire. He removed it from the mortar tube "as we had been instructed to do. This got my attention more than the N.K. The firing was halted and word came back that the hill was ours.

"LT Matta was dead," he wrote. The officer had been cut down by a machine gun burst as he stood on the ridge firing at the retreating enemy. "Lloyd Poland 'Polock' had also been killed.

"The men now elated with the taste of victory examined the enemy dead and weapons. Wayne looked over a Russian water cooled machine gun. There was a dead N.K. half blown away..." Christopher continued. One enemy soldier was found alive in the bottom of a hole. "LT Matta and Polock were brought down and loaded on the ammo trailer. Fox Co. filed down from the hill and we marched back...and on to the Naktong River and the Pusan Perimeter," Christopher concluded.

A/8th Cavalry was the last of the 1st Cavalry Division to cross the Naktong on a bridge at Waegwan. Once all the troops had crossed, the bridge was to be blown, but the civilian refugees kept flooding across, ignoring the commands of the 545th MP Company and 2/7th Cavalry. Finally, knowing that the enemy was fast approaching and that many enemy soldiers were probably among the refugees, the order was given to blow the bridge. Hundreds of civilian refugees died in the explosion or drowned in the river.

LTC Clainos' 1/7th Cav was designated Division reserve, leaving the 2d Battalion to man the regimental front. As a result, Co. H, the battalion Heavy Weapons Co., was given a sector to defend. (See Chapter Notes.)

The 2/7th Cavalry employed Co F on Hill 360 in the southern part of its sector. Co. H, next in line, occupied Hill 209, from which the

Naktong could be observed for a number of miles to the north and south. The hill also dominated the ruins of a steel and concrete bridge, which had spanned the river below that point. The tiny village of Toksan lay just across the river. A bend in the Naktong in the sectors of these two units resulted in Co. F being generally east of Co H, facing south, while H, a mile and a half away, faced west. Co. G occupied a low hill mass near the village of Samni-dong north of Co. H. Farther north, one platoon of Co. E manned a similar low hill. The remainder of Co. E was on low hills near Kyohang-dong. E and G Companies faced rice paddies, which stretched for distances of from one half to about one mile to the banks of the Naktong. (See Chapter Notes.)

The huge front required the division to employ OPs, listening posts (LPs), patrols and trip flares in order to try to detect enemy attempts to infiltrate the lines. Ed Daily, of the 7th, wrote that it became "difficult to replace the flares that were tripped [by the enemy] because of short supply. Even our 60mm mortar illuminating shells had deteriorated [in depot storage] to such a degree that only 20 percent issued to the battalion were effective. Also the 155mm howitzer illuminating shells were in short supply from the 82d Field Artillery."

2LT John O. Potts, a rifle platoon leader in Co. F, wrote that "one of our platoons used jeeps to make contact with elements of the 21st Inf. some six miles south along the river."

Once back across the Naktong, the Cavalry was not content to just allow the enemy to move up to the river and prepare to cross. On the contrary, a number of patrols were sent back in order to gather information and to capture prisoners. These patrols were a vital part of the division's active defense.

The experiences related by CPL Alfred B. Clair (F/7 Cav) and Platoon Sergeant Walter Raisner provide some concept of the scope and variety of these patrols.

CPL Clair wrote, "The first patrol was led by SGT Leroy Arsenaux. We crossed in assault boats and very cautiously moved inland. In the first village we found some buildings very shot up by the Air Force. In one house we found a young boy." The boy had been hit in the shoulder by a machine gun bullet. "Our medic, Galagher, worked on the wound, cleaned it and gave the boy antibiotics," Clair went on. "We also left K rations, candy bars and water.

"We moved about five miles away from the river, up a very beautiful valley planted with beans and melons. At the head of the valley we found a village untouched by the war. There were several hundred people in this village. As we ate our ration, we talked about all the able bodied men we saw. It was suggested that they should be in the Army, fighting, as we were. So we lined all the young men up and marched more than a hundred of them back to the river. When we got close enough to use our radio, we reported that we were bringing more than 100 South Koreans back for the South Korean Army.... That ended my first patrol."

SGT Arsenaux was injured a few days later, and Clair took over as Platoon Sergeant, 3d Platoon.

"During August," Clair wrote, "I crossed the river 10 times in the daylight and 6 times at night.

Each time, we brought food medication and water to our little friend. Until he was strong enough to evacuate, this boy kept us up on any [enemy] troop movements near him."

On Aug. 7, Al Clair's good friend, SGT Coleman C. Hundley, led a patrol across the Naktong that was hit by the enemy. Hundley and a man named Arthur Williams were left behind when the rest of the patrol made it out. That night, Al swam across the river alone and went to the house where Hundley and Williams had last been seen. "I never did find them anywhere in the area," he wrote.

The day after his unit had dug in on the east bank of the Naktong, SGT Walter Raisner and his men spotted enemy soldiers digging in on the opposite shore. They found that the North Koreans were out of effective rifle and .30 cal machine gun range. Raisner had a .50-cal machine gun brought forward and emplaced to engage the enemy. The commander of a tank located nearby told the Sergeant he would have better luck with a telescopic sight for the gun. Raisner did not know that such a sight was available for the .50.

A few hours later, the tanker returned and presented the Sergeant with a telescopic sight for the .50-cal machine gun. Soon, Raisner had the gun zeroed in and ready. He spotted some enemy digging in at an estimated range of 2,800 yards. "I fixed my sights, and left a volley go," he said. "I hit two." He then shifted the gun back and forth, firing at enemy soldiers across the river..... "The closest enemy I shot was directly across the river from our position," Raisner said. "I estimated maybe 2,300 yards."

That night, Platoon Sergeant Walter Raisner was ordered by his battalion commander, LTC Gilman A. Huff, to select someone from his platoon to lead a small reconnaissance patrol across the river. "I told him that I was the most qualified and would take the patrol myself," Raisner said. Huff finally agreed to this, then gave his orders: "Go across the river. I want you to penetrate about two to three miles...then turn left and cover about five miles, returning to the river and back to safety." The colonel thought seven or eight hours should suffice for the patrol to complete its mission. Raisner disagreed, but said that he would do it as quickly as possible.

Under the cover of darkness the next morning, Raisner and eight other men crossed the Naktong at the point where the first enemy soldier lay that had been hit by the .50-cal machine gun. Moving back from the river about two miles, the patrol spotted some enemy tanks. Raisner had each man observe, but write nothing down. They all agreed that there were six T-34s in that area. The patrol then went on, but then saw an artillery spotter plane fly overhead. Shortly thereafter, American artillery rounds passed overhead, "and I thought nothing of it," Raisner recounted. "Soon there was another volley that came in.... This time a little closer. Now comes the odd part of this experience; we started...toward the Naktong River. All the time, the artillery was firing behind us. We finally passed through the whole North Korean Army that was dug in on the opposite side of the Naktong River.... Not one shot was fired from the North Korean[s].... The artillery followed us...to the river and the last rounds...hit into the

sand and lifted us completely off the ground." No one from the patrol was wounded, however. Raisner called across the river to get the artillery stopped. One more volley came in "and the sand went flying," he said. GIs worked a boat across the Naktong, fighting a swift current, and brought Raisner and his patrol back to safety. They were landed in George Co.'s sector. Their own unit, Co. E, was two miles north, on G's right flank.

When he reported to the battalion commander, LTC Huff, "seemed entirely indifferent to the report...and only was concerned that I did not finish the patrol," said Walter. "My explanation...continuously fell on deaf ears.

"The next morning, about half an hour after daybreak, I shot two North Koreans who were trying to make their way to the Naktong River. Each morning for the next several days, we were required to form a skirmish line and work our way through the pea patches killing North Koreans who were hiding there."

Other patrols by the 7th included those by LT Thomas H. Stone (Platoon Leader, 1st Platoon, Co. F) and SGT Lyle Gibbs (4th Platoon, Co. E). (See Chapter Notes.)

On Aug. 10, LT Stone was to take his platoon, reinforced, on a patrol. It was to cross the Naktong near Toksan, then move along the road northward toward Waegwan. To Stone, "the mission seemed that it should be a battalion operation," he wrote, "but who was I to question the command."

At the crossing site, he was met by LTs John B. Wadsworth Jr. and Herschel Fuson (Bn S2 and S3, respectively; Wadsworth, West Point 1948; Fuson in 1947.) These officers told Stone that his original mission was scrubbed and that he was to take one squad on a patrol across the river and recon to the west. The smaller patrol set out. "We had moved forward several thousand yards...and suddenly we found ourselves in [an enemy] bivouac area," Stone wrote. "Enemy troops were hunkered down, feeding was going on. They were completely relaxed with no security in our direction." The patrol observed from a number of vantage points for about an hour to determine the size and armament of this enemy force. "We remained undiscovered," Stone continued, "until a woman walked through our position.... We thought she was a friendly native until she neared the encampment. Then she yelled... turned and pointed in our direction." Stone immediately "signalled move out smartly, and we did," he wrote.

The patrol took off running, until the lieutenant decided it should turn and defend itself. To their surprise, no enemy pursued. The patrol continued peacefully toward the river. When within a few hundred yards of the Naktong, and crossing an open area, one of the men had to relieve himself. The rest of the patrol took up firing positions facing the enemy. "Suddenly we were bracketed by incoming 105mm fire. It was our own and it was intense for a time. I thought 'what a way to go.' Suddenly it was quiet." Then the man who had to relieve himself "came running up pulling up his trousers and said 'let's get out of here.' The patrol made it safely back across the river. "Later, we all laughed about it," Stone concluded. He reported the location of the enemy troops to the battalion CP.

SGT Gibbs wrote of a twelve man patrol, led by SGT Charles Barton of Co. E. The patrol crossed the river, never to return. "Two days later I woke up about 3 a.m. to hear three officers discussing the situation. They had decided to send 'SGT Lyle Gibbs' and four other soldiers across the river...to be back by 1 p.m.," Gibbs wrote.

Gibbs wrote that he was "scared to death [and] felt very insecure because they weren't sending men with any experience, just ones they felt they could spare." In briefing the patrol, Gibbs ordered the men not to fire unless fired upon first.

Luckily, Gibbs' small patrol was able to cross the Naktong at 6 a.m. the next day in company with a combat patrol, led by LT W. H. Travis, 1st Platoon Leader. Once across the river, Gibbs' patrol turned left and Travis led his group off to the right. Shortly thereafter, Gibbs heard firing from the Travis patrol. On the other hand, the Sergeant's patrol failed to see any enemy troops and returned to friendly lines without incident. The Barton patrol was found later. All the members had been killed by what appeared to be artillery fire, Gibbs wrote.

Shortly after the 1st Cavalry Division dug in along the Naktong, GEN Gay relieved COL Carl Rohsenberger of command of the 5th Cavalry, replacing him with COL Marcel Gustav Crombez (West Point 1925). As ADC, BG Charles Palmer put it in an interview by Clay Blair, "Carl was willing and brave, but just too old and too deaf." Crombez, at 49, was also "old" for regimental command, but Palmer told Blair he was a "hell of a good field soldier." COL Peter D. Clainos characterized him as "an aggressive commander and he was respected." Many officers and enlisted men of the 5th Cavalry, however, felt he was inept, insensitive to his losses and the welfare of his men, egotistical and a self-promoter; that his primary goal in Korea was to, in military parlance, "get his ticket punched" in regimental command to pave the way for promotion to general. (See Chapter Notes.)

Other command changes within the 1st Cavalry included LTC Morgan B. Heasley to 1/5th Cavalry, LTC Peter D. Clainos (West Point, 1933) to 1/7th Cavalry and LTC Gilman Huff to 2/7th Cavalry. Morgan Heasley had a serious drinking problem, wrote Clay Blair in *The Forgotten War,* but was kept on the job. Many officers of the battalion believed that the real tactical leader was the Battalion "3", James Gibson.

Under Clainos, 1/7th Cavalry became known to the press as "Clainos's Clouters," or "Clainos's Cavaliers." This was because the battalion, greatly reinforced, became the Cavalry Division's principal reserve. At one time, this reinforced battalion numbered some 1,500 men. On Aug. 8, the 16th Recon Co. was attached to the 7th Cavalry and positioned on the regiment's left flank to make and maintain contact with the 3d Engineers, 24th Division, to the south. Reports indicated that about 280 enemy troops had infiltrated through the 24th Division in that area, poising a threat to the 7th Cavalry's left rear.

The *NK 3d Division* Attacks the 5th Cavalry Regiment — Aug. 9

About 3 a.m. on Aug. 9, the *7th Regiment, 3d Division* began crossing the Naktong at a ferry

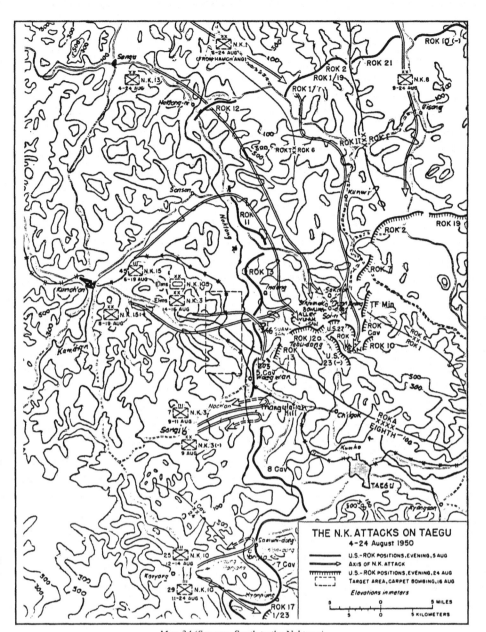

Map 34 (*Source:* South to the Naktong)

site near the village of Nochon, two miles south of Waegwan. Here, the river was only about five feet deep, with a firm sandy bottom. As a result, the enemy was able to wade across, holding their weapons overhead. The 5th Cavalry, discovering the crossing, engaged the enemy with preregistered artillery and mortar fire and automatic weapons.

In spite of this, the bulk of the enemy force reached the east bank and moved on into the hills. This is the Aug. 9 diary entry of Choe Sang Hwan, one of the enemy soldiers who made the crossing:

"Gradually advanced toward the river. Enemy shelling is fierce. Arrived at the shores of the river. The terrible enemy sent up flares. The Naktong River is flowing quietly and evenly. Entered the river. After advancing 200 meters, shooting began with the firing of an enemy flare. The noise is ringing in my ears. Have already crossed the river. Occupied a hill. A new day is already breaking." This diary, covering July 21 - Aug. 10, 1950, was captured on Aug. 12, 1950.

At 3:30 a.m., the *8th* and *9th Regiments* be-

gan crossing the river south of the *7th.*. The 5th Cavalry, fully alerted, lit the area with flares and star shells, then poured mortar and artillery fire on the enemy, catching them in midstream. A great slaughter ensued and the two regiments were driven back across the river. Only a few made it to the American side, where they were either captured or hid until the next night, when they recrossed the Naktong.

Some of the troops from the *7th Regiment,* which had crossed earlier apparently got into the rear of elements of 1/5th Cavalry. PFC Dallas Freeburg of Co. D recalled that a large body of enemy soldiers came marching down the road to the right rear of his company's position. The marching troops were challenged by a tanker. When he received no answer, "he cut loose with his machine gun on the tank and they fired up that damned tank and took off down the road in the opposite direction," Freeburg said. Then his company opened fire on the enemy, who took shelter behind a hill on the other side of the road. All was quiet for about 20 to 30 minutes, "Then we heard...'Manzai! Manzai!' screaming, yelling.... Then they came down over the hill right at us. I fired every round I had...a full belt and two bandoliers ...and they were coming right through us, jumping over the holes." Both Freeburg and his foxhole mate, being out of ammunition, beat a retreat to the platoon sergeant's hole. "We ran at a crouch, and I remember the air was just hot. It felt just hot with tracers and bullets.... My God, I never went through such flying lead."

"Get on that machine gun!" ordered the Platoon Sergeant, Freeburg recalled. Freeburg and his buddy "got on the machine gun and started firing that mother," Freeburg said. "At one point while we were firing the machine gun," Freeburg continued, "we heard one of the guys in another hole...just a few feet away shout 'There's a Gook right in front of us!' In fact [he would have] been right behind us...because they were coming from the opposite direction, the way we were set up. He fired a burst from his BAR and the gook fell.... He said, 'Everybody duck, I'm going to put a grenade on him!' The men kept firing until the last of the enemy ran through the position.

"When daylight came, my God!" Freeburg recalled. "There were dead gooks and a few wounded from the top of the hill all the way down and across the roadway, strung out all through our holes and out over the sandbar beach, into the water." The man killed by the BAR-man was a North Korean lieutenant. A grenade was clutched in his dead hand. He had not had time to arm it before being killed. Freeburg said that 152 dead enemy soldiers were counted and buried. The few wounded survivors were taken away in ambulances.

Triangulation Hill (Hill 268), 1/7th Cavalry — Aug. 9

At daylight GEN Gay learned of the enemy crossing south of Waegwan. 1LT Harry A. Buckley, Acting S-2, 5th Cavalry, had observed the North Korean crossing. Gay sent for him, then alerted 1/7th Cavalry for a counterattack on a one hour notice. Appleman quoted this statement of LT Buckley from a letter and comments from GEN Gay, dated Aug. 24, 1953:

"Just prior to daylight this morning, I with a small group of men from the I&R Platoon, was on reconnaissance. Approximately 45 minutes prior to daylight, I observed enemy forces moving up the ridge line just northwest of Hill 268. The enemy were moving at a dog trot in groups of four. Every fourth man carried an automatic weapon, either a light machine gun or a burp gun. I watched them until they had all disappeared into the brush on Hill 268. In my opinion, and I counted them carefully, the enemy was in strength of a reinforced battalion, approximately 750 men. General, I am not a very excitable person and I know what I saw, when I saw it, where I saw it, and where the enemy was going."

A few minutes after LT Buckley gave this report, GEN Walker arrived at the 1st Cavalry Division CP and asked GEN Gay what he planned to do. Gay responded that he knew that at least one enemy battalion had crossed the river and was now on Hill 268, while another North Korean regiment was attempting to cross under heavy fire from the 5th Cavalry. As soon as the situation cleared a bit, Gay said he planned to attack, drive the enemy from Hill 268 and back across the Naktong. Appleman quoted Walker as saying, "Fine, be sure you are right before you move because this enemy battalion might be a feint and the real attack could be coming farther to your left." Later events indicated Walker was probably right.

At 8:40 a.m., 1/7th Cavalry, with A/71st Tk Co. (five tanks) attached, moved out of its assembly area two miles west of Taegu. The force was supported by the 61st FAB. Clainos's men proceeded forward in a motorized column with the tanks to a position about 2000 yards short of Hill 268, known as "Triangulation Hill," or "Triangle Hill." This promontory, three miles southeast of Waegwan and 10 air miles northwest of Taegu, lay just south of the main north-south highway and the main double-tracked Pusan-Seoul-Harbin, Manchuria rail line. The hill was thickly covered with scrub brush about four feet high and some trees eight to 10 feet high.

While the infantry rode forward, the 61st began to heavily shell the hill. Once dismounted, 1/7th Cavalry deployed for the attack. Co. C was on the left; Co. B in the center, and Hq Co., elements of Dog Co. and a platoon of A on the right. Co. A (-) was in reserve. Heat exhaustion caused many casualties in the battalion as it advanced. Heavy enemy machine gun, small arms and mortar fire from a mountain known as "Observation Hill," however, is what stalled the attack. Co. B, fighting savagely, reached this hill, only to be thrown back by an enemy counterattack. The whole attack stalled and the battalion dug in for the night. Severe enemy artillery and mortar fire fell on the battalion CP during the afternoon, causing six casualties. Among the seriously wounded was MAJ F. A. Daubin, Battalion XO. His driver, PFC Edward Curry, was killed by the same round which had wounded the XO. (Edward Daily, in *Skirmish, Red, White and Blue*, writes this occurred on Aug. 9; Appleman states it was Aug. 10.)

Richard Dowell was a machinegunner in Co. B at the time. He wrote an account of the battle on Aug. 9. Although, since he writes that the hill was secured by nightfall, some, or all, of what he describes may have occurred on Aug. 10, when 1/7th Cavalry did take Hill 268. The unit moved out in a skirmish line "to the left of the main hill," he wrote. "We had to cross a rice paddy. I told SGT Taylor I didn't like the wind hitting the back of my neck. This means the reds could hear us, but we couldn't hear them. He just laughed and said he couldn't change the wind. We got about half way across the rice paddy and the water was splashing everywhere. Men were dropping. We couldn't hear the report of the rifles, but the battle had begun. We ran as fast as we could to the base of the hill; working our way to the top was very hard."

The enemy sniped away at the advancing men, some of whom used their helmets to lure an enemy to shoot and expose his position. Dowell, carrying his .30-cal machine gun, ignored the snipers and made it to a stone wall about 30 yards long and 2 1/2 feet high. As he paused there for breath, other men joined him. Enemy bullets struck the wall. "My face was burning from the bullets hitting in front of me, splattering dirt and small stones," he wrote. Taylor "laughed and said I looked like a raccoon." Shortly, eight or ten men were behind the wall. Almost as one, they rose up and charged forward. "It must have looked like a banzai attack to the Red snipers," Dowell continued. "When I got to the top I saw the Reds immediately."

Ignoring the shouting and shooting around him, Dowell recalled that all he cared about was what he had to do. "Once I got my belt [of ammunition] started in my light .30 it seemed as though the great fear left me. I had landed in a spot that was perfect for what I had to do.... It was directly across from a deep saddle which would be used by the Reds for their escape route later. I kept yelling for more boxes of ammo, a rifle and bandoliers of M1 ammo. About that time PFC Gerald G. Gerome...dropped off two boxes of machine gun ammo. I told him what I needed and away he went. Minutes later he was back with everything.... I used the M1 when I saw one to five reds and the light .30 for more Reds." The enemy was only about 100 yards away and skylined themselves, making them easy targets for Dowell. "They had to either come towards me or run the saddle," he recalled. "At one point, my second gunner took his hands and feet to push the empty cartridge [casings] away. I was losing my footing."

The remainder of their battalion, although stopped, kept a steady fire on the enemy. Co. B took the southern slope, and the enemy withdrew. From the new position, Co. B poured fire at the enemy. Dowell's machine gun got so hot that he switched to his M1. Then the men began pitching grenades over the hill onto enemy soldiers concealed there. "Boy, oh, Boy! Did that do the trick!" Dowell wrote. "They came pouring out of the bottom and up the north slope. They were everywhere.... You couldn't shoot fast enough to get them all.... I was knocking them off as fast as I could pull the trigger" He shot three enemy soldiers manhandling a wheel mounted heavy machine gun. "As I nailed them and saw the gun roll down the hill, I couldn't help but think that's one machine gun I won't have to worry about," he recalled.

Dowell fired from five to seven belts of ammo through his machine gun. The gun got so hot that it kept shooting by itself and he had to twist the ammunition belt to stop it. Then two enemy machine guns got his range and both opened on him, cutting down small trees around him and hitting his machine gun four times. The enemy bullets, however, failed to knock out his gun, or to injure Dowell. Richard swung the gun to the right and took out one of the enemy machine guns, then to the left and knocked out the other with a few well-placed burst. Dowell had loaded his machine gun belts with combinations of one tracer, three ball and two armor piercing rounds. He credited the armor piercing rounds with knocking out the enemy machine guns.

When the machine gun got too hot to fire, SGT Taylor took up the slack by firing his M1 as rapidly as possible to keep the enemy down while the machine gun cooled enough to be used. Finally, he ordered his assistant gunner to pour water from his canteen over the gun. This cooled the weapon off enough so that he could put it back in action.

Covered by air strikes and artillery preparations, the attack on Hill 268 began at 6 a.m. on Aug. 10. Co. A's 3d Platoon met fierce machine gun fire, which killed its Platoon Leader, LT Charles F. McGee (West Point 1948). The battalion made no progress, so drew back to allow their artillery and air strikes to pound the objective.

Following this, a platoon from the battalion HC and the Pioneer and Ammunition Platoon (P&A Platoon), also from the battalion HC, went forward with artillery FOs and occupied two hills about 1,000 yards in front of the CP. A number of enemy troops still occupied Triangulation Hill and a smaller hill to the left. Three M-24 tanks moved up the Waegwan road until they could fire from the northwest into the rear of the enemy-held hill. (Appleman states five tanks.) Co. D, added the fire of its 81mm mortars, from positions along the north side of a railroad embankment. With this support, Companies A and B moved to the attack. Supporting fire drove the enemy from their positions and into the rice paddies, where they were slaughtered by Co. A sweeping in from the right of the hill and Co. B from the left. The battle was over by 4 p.m.

When the enemy was driven from Hill 268, American artillery and mortar fire shifted to cut off the retreating enemy. A large body of enemy troops ran into a village. A time-on-target mission of WP fired by the 61st FAB struck the village. Later, GIs found 200 enemy dead there. Meantime, some 300 to 400 enemy dead on Hill 268 confirmed that at least one enemy battalion had occupied the position. A number of North Koreans, after firing off their ammunition, surrendered with UN safe conduct passes that had been dropped by aircraft earlier in the war. Enemy prisoners generally agreed that about 1,000 men from the *7th Regiment* had crossed the Naktong to Hill 268, and that around 700 of them had been killed or wounded in the battle for the hill. The force had received no reinforcement, food or ammunition once it crossed. The prisoners also confirmed that most of their casualties were from artillery and mortars. Some 300 survivors are believed to have withdrawn across the Naktong on the night of Aug. 10-11.

GEN Gay complimented LTC Clainos on the 1st Battalion's victory, which cost 15 dead, 48 wounded and one missing. The 1/7th Cavalry reverted to division reserve on the evening of Aug. 10.

The *NK 3d Division's* river crossing south of Waegwan was a disaster. Only its *7th Regiment* got across in some strength; the other two regiments were driven back with heavy losses. On Hill 268, the *7th* was decimated. As a result by Aug. 12 the *3d Division* was reduced to what Appleman called "a disorganized unit of some 2,500 men." The command had to be withdrawn into reserve to rebuild.

The *NK 10th Division* Attacks the 2d Battalion, 7th Cavalry — Aug. 11-14

The *NK 3d* and *10th Divisions* were supposed to make a coordinated attack across the Naktong. The *10th* had not been in combat previously. On July 25, it had started for the front, arriving op-

posite Waegwan about Aug. 8. On Aug. 10, the division was given its mission: Cross the Naktong River near Tuksong-dong, advance east and cut the Taegu-Pusan main highway. The *10th* assembled near Koryong on Aug. .11, astride the road east to the river and a partially destroyed bridge at Toksan. The bridge was passable to foot troops, but not to vehicles. It could be a trap to soldiers crossing it, because the crossing would be channeled at that point, making them easy targets for concentrated fire of all types.

Between Aug. 10 and 12, the Naktong River dropped three feet, facilitating enemy large-scale crossings.

The *10th Division's 29th Regiment* began its crossing at three ferry sites just north and northwest of the sprawling mountain known as Hill 409 during the night of Aug. 11-12. They were unopposed. To the north, the division's *25th Regiment* began crossing the Naktong at 3 a.m. near the partially destroyed bridge. The regiment's objective was to "destroy the enemy in Taegu City in coordination with the *3d Infantry Division*." (Quote from *25th Regimental* order, cited by Appleman.) The division's third regiment, the *27th*, was in reserve. The *2/29th Infantry* occupied Hill 265, a northern arm of Hill 409, and set up machine gun positions. Under this protection, the other two battalions of the regiment crossed and went on to occupy 409

itself. Reportedly, about 20 or 30 men of the *1st Battalion* drowned in the crossing. While *2/29th infantry* had no opposition, the *25th Infantry* ran into outposts of 2/7th Cavalry about 5:30 a.m.

Ed Daily of H/7th Cavalry, now a brand-new Second Lieutenant by way of a battlefield promotion, had a listening post near the partially destroyed bridge across the Naktong. LT Cillary, FO from the 77th FAB, with an SCR 300 radio, SGT Millard G. Gray, 81 mm mortar FO, and PFC Harry Shappell were all with him at his platoon CP.

At 30 minutes after midnight on Aug. 12, Daily talked to his company commander, CPT Chandler, on the radio. He reported that flares had revealed enemy movement to the front and that company listening posts had been driven back be enemy small-arms fire. Daily called Chandler again about 3 a.m. to report more enemy activity to his direct front and right flank. On Daily's right were two rifle squads from Co G. Chandler cautioned against firing on the enemy, in the belief that it might be just a small party of them. But Ed knew the enemy was very close; he could smell them. (See Chapter Notes.)

By 5:30 a.m., all the listening posts had been driven in. Daily left his observation post to converse with PFCs Norman Tinkler, J. P. "Smitty" Smith and Ray Scarberry, gunners on his heavy machine gun positions. He intended to give them

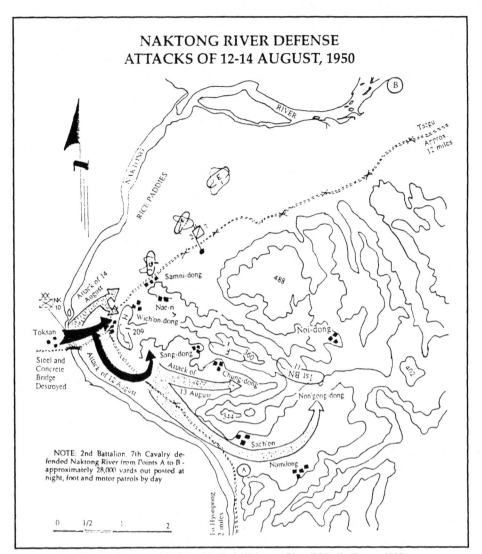

NAKTONG RIVER DEFENSE
ATTACKS OF 12-14 AUGUST, 1950

NOTE: 2nd Battalion, 7th Cavalry defended Naktong River from Points A to B - approximately 28,000 yards out posted at night, foot and motor patrols by day

Map 35 (Source: p. 36 Skirmish, Red, White and Blue, Ed Daily, Turner, 1992)

Beating off an attack on the Pusan Perimeter. (Source: The First Cavalry Division in Korea, 18 July 1950 - 18 January 1952*)*

instructions on the imminent enemy attack. Everyone firmly believed that a heavy enemy attack could come at any moment. All the small-arms fire had ceased, and an eerie silence suddenly set in.

Upon leaving Scarberry's position, Daily glanced at his watch. It was 6 a.m. As he made his way back to the OP, an explosion came from that quarter. He broke into a run back to it. He discovered that an enemy grenade had landed between SGT Gray and PFC Harry Shappell, badly wounding both men. Millard had been on the field telephone with CPT Chandler, reporting the approach of enemy soldiers. Daily called for a medic and began administering first aid. Soon, the aidman appeared with two litter bearers and the two wounded men were on their way to the rear.

"All hell was breaking loose now," Daily wrote, "as I attempted to use the radio which I soon discovered was inoperative due to the enemy hand grenade explosion." Then he realized that the FO, LT Cillary was missing.

Daily could see the enemy advancing in waves. The first wave consisted of white-clad civilians equipped with crude spears or captured weapons. They had been impressed into service by the enemy. Following this wave were the enemy regulars, well-armed. As many as six waves were included in each attack formation, with every other wave consisting of enemy soldiers.

"Everywhere I looked," Daily wrote, "the enemy had outflanked our company positions. Our machine gun positions were annihilating the [civilians] and enemy soldiers, but we were being overpowered by sheer numbers alone. I quickly threw the six hand grenades I was carrying. Then I put my trusty M-1 rifle to good use." He estimated some 1,000 enemy troops and civilians made this attack.

His men repelled the first four or five waves. On his left, Daily saw that PFC Norman Tinkler's gun position was in trouble. Running there, he found Tinkler badly wounded. An ammunition bearer lay dead nearby, shot in the head just be-low the eye. Sending the wounded Tinkler to the rear, Daily, loaded the machine gun and fired at the enemy to his front and left flank until out of ammunition. He then disabled the gun. Dead and wounded enemy soldiers lay all around.

"I looked to my rear toward Hill 209," he wrote, "and I could see the enemy moving upward to secure the high ground behind us. I knew our company command post was located near the rear of the hill; and I realized that all company positions had been overrun." He had lost his M-1 in the confusion. Pulling out his .45 automatic pistol, Daily continued to fire at enemy soldiers until out of ammunition for that weapon. He then ran down into a gully looking for another weapon. "As I approached the lower part of the gully, I came face to face with a North Korean soldier who jammed his rifle into the left side of my chest. He immediately made me put both hands on top of my helmet." Enemy soldiers quickly took all his personal items, then pushed and shoved him southwest along the Naktong to a collection point where other captured Americans were being assembled. At first, Daily thought he was in a dream. This gave way to guilt and shame, he recalled. "I had been stripped of my dignity," he wrote, "and I wondered how the hell it all came about." Ed Daily remained a POW until he escaped in the midst of a U.S. 155mm artillery barrage on his captors in Waegwan on Sept. 12.

As the situation in Daily's area had deteriorated, SGT Millard Gray called for 81mm mortar fire on the outpost position. "This was denied," he said.

"Suddenly, an enemy hand grenade landed next to PFC Harry Shappell and I shouted. 'Grenade, throw it!' As Shappell tried to toss the grenade out of the hole, it exploded, blowing off his right hand and wounding Millard with eleven shards, from his ankle to his shoulder. A few moments later, Daily arrived, then the aidmen, to evacuate Millard and Shappell.

CPL Barton M. Smith was assigned from the 1st Cavalry Division Band to Daily's 1st Platoon, Co. H on Aug. 10. He had the feeling that he wasn't wanted in the company. When the enemy attacked across the Naktong on Aug. 12, Smith's machine gun position was directly behind the village of Yong-po. "Our company command post was located up the ravine about 50-75 yards behind us," he said. "To our right flank just across the dirt road was an apple orchard and Company G was located there." (See Chapter Notes.)

Barton was given a few lessons on the .30-cal machine gun in the next day or so. Across the river, he could see enemy soldiers from time to time. When Barton had been assigned to the platoon, LT Daily, his platoon leader had called him a "horn blower." That stuck in his craw. "I started to wonder what in hell I was doing in a machine gun platoon to begin with," he recalled.

He recalled that the battle started at 6 a.m. "with a lot of shouting and shooting." His gun position was beside a Korean burial mound. "As I looked out across the open...all I could see was swarms of refugees and North Korean soldiers running towards us shouting and shooting wildly...."

"We continued to fire the machine gun.... This was my first experience in actual combat and I could feel my body going into knots.... Then a mortar round or a hand grenade exploded on the one side of the mound," momentarily stunning him.

"I looked down toward the village and saw five North Korean soldiers coming up a ravine toward us. I started firing at them and hit four, but the fifth one ran back into the village." Then a sergeant crawled over to Smith's position and told him and another man to go down to the village and shoot any refugees or enemy soldiers they found. Smith and the other man crawled down to the village and remained there until about noon. The man with Smith then decided to go back up the hill. Smith "told him he had better remain in the village with me. As he stood up to leave, a bullet tore through his head and he fell dead." Smith remained in the village another hour before crawling back to his position.

Enemy troops reached the high ground in rear

Tank killer team. (Source: The First Cavalry Division in Korea, 18 July 1950 - 18 January 1952*)*

of Co H. From there, they attacked the unit from the rear as other North Koreans assaulted from the front. Co H suffered heavy casualties, as the enemy overran the entire position.

CPT Chandler was able to rally about 25 slightly wounded men and the cooks, company clerk and supply men of his headquarters, and with them made an attack on the enemy force to the rear, estimated at about 125. They reached a point about 3/4 of the way up the mountain to their rear when they ran out of ammunition. There, they were pinned down by concentrated automatic weapons fire and hand grenades. Some enemy positions were only 10 feet away. Lt Robert M. Carroll, who had been wounded earlier in the battle, had been left at the foot of the hill to send up any reinforcements which might arrive. Instead, he rounded up three stragglers and led them in a charge on the enemy until badly wounded by grenade fragments.

CPT Chandler sent CPL Harry Straitman back to the company CP for more ammunition. Then he and PVT Thomas L. Palmer returned to the overrun 81mm mortar position. There they turned one of the 81s around to bear on the enemy in the rear. Removing all the powder charges from the mortar rounds and elevating the mortars to the maximum, they were able to bring effective 81mm mortar fire on the enemy barely 100 yards away. This fire enabled the pinned down How Co. troopers to disengage and return to the bottom of the hill for more ammunition. But their bold action had stopped the enemy in rear of Co. H.

Help was on the way. This included a force of 242 South Korean policemen, temporarily attached to the 7th Cavalry, under MAJ Charles G. King, the I&R Platoon, under LT Crawford Buchanan and 15 drivers, cooks and supply men from the Regimental Service Co. This polyglot formation, along with troops from Co G on the right and Co F on the left, drove the enemy back across the Naktong. Heavy artillery fire and air strikes cut down hundreds of the enemy, as they strove to get back across the river.

When Co. H was hit, Co. F was deployed on Hill 360 to the east. The company front was about 1 1/2 miles long. The 1st Platoon, with about 16 men, was on the right and the 2d Platoon on its left. 2LT Thomas H. Stone, commanding the 1st Platoon, had two listening posts forward of his position near the river. He communicated with them by small SCR 536 radios.

"On 12 August at BMNT (Beginning Morning Nautical Twilight — dawn) we saw troops coming from the direction of G Co. [to the right of Co F]. It wasn't light enough to distinguish who they were," Stone wrote. "At less than 50 yards we challenged them, still thinking they were GIs from George [Co.]." No word had come from his listening posts, nor had he received any information that Co G was withdrawing. When challenged, the unknown body of men cut loose with a heavy volume of small-arms and automatic fire on Stone's men. Stone responded with his .30-cal machine gun. Facing return fire, the enemy resorted to fire and maneuver to advance. (See Chapter Notes.)

The machinegunner was hit, and the assistant gunner took over. "All of us were firing," Stone wrote, "and they kept coming. As they closed in I started hurling fragmentation grenades

instead of firing my carbine. That was effective...our frags were superior to their concussion, which they were hurling at us. One enemy rose up and charged at us and I put at least four carbine rounds in him before he fell mortally wounded." With that experience, Stone resolved to get rid of his carbine and replace it with an M1 as soon as possible. The platoon beat off the attack. Ten dead enemy soldiers lay at the edge of the position and several more were sprawled farther out. Stone's platoon lost one KIA and three wounded.

LT John C. Lippincott's platoon was sent to help Stone's. He witnessed Stone exchanging grenades with the enemy. He said that grenades filled the air "as thick as blackbirds, and that he had to hesitate a moment to determine where to fire. LT John O. Potts' 2d Platoon also swung to the right in support of the 1st, while Lippincott's 3d Platoon counterattacked south. This maneuver brought Lippincott in on the enemy's left flank.

Meantime, LT Stone had picked up an M1, ammunition and a number of grenades. Observing the enemy moving to his left, he went that way too, so as to determine the situation. He had proceeded about 100 yards above the road which ran in front of his platoon position when he heard the sound of automatic weapons fire and a jeep motor. "The jeep was hit by the fire and I heard someone cry out in pain. I rushed down to the road. Two troopers were lying beside the jeep, which was being raked by small-arms fire coming from the direction I had just come," he wrote. "I crawled out to the two men. One was wounded and the other was not." Stone helped the injured man into a ditch and left the other man to look after him while he went for help. Crawling along the ditch on the hill side of the road, Stone came up behind two of the enemy, also crawling in the ditch. The enemy took no notice of him. "I fired a full clip into the two so they never knew what hit them," he recalled.

Then he heard voices on the other side of the road. Glancing over the road, he saw an enemy soldier duck down on the other side. Stone threw a grenade in the soldier's direction, just as he did the same. Stone's grenade landed in the ditch across the road; the enemy's hit on the road. "I heard jabbering and WHAMO! mine went off," he wrote. There was silence, "but I heaved another [grenade]. No response." The lieutenant crawled across the road to discover three dead North Koreans in their ditch. After making his way to the company CP to report the platoon's losses to the commander, he returned to his platoon. His experiences that day, sold Stone on the value of fragmentation hand grenades in a close fight.

CPL Donald A. Down, BAR-man, 3d Squad, 3d Platoon of Co. F, was on the extreme left flank of the unit with a 57mm recoilless rifle crew and a .30-cal light machine gun team. They were the company left flank outpost. He recalled that some ROK soldiers were supposed to be on the hill farther down to the left. The unit was so short of personnel that company cooks were being used as riflemen. During the fighting on Aug. 12, two of Down's friends, CPL Ralph Rathburn, a cook and PVT Vanhorn, a rifleman, were killed. CPL Paul J. Szezepanski, another cook and PVT John Harcula, a rifleman, were among Fox Company's wounded.

At day's end, 237 enemy dead were counted in the rear of Co. H. There were many other enemy dead in or near the 2d Battalion's position, but they were never tabulated. Another 35 enemy were captured. The 7th Cavalry lost 15 KIA and 60 WIA, mostly in Co. H. CPT Chandler was badly wounded by an enemy grenade. Several men, along with LT Daily, became POWs. LT William Kaluf was the sole remaining officer, and over 70 per cent of Co. H were casualties that day.

The 1/7th Cavalry was released to the regiment from Division reserve at 2 a.m. on Aug. 12, but did not reach the area until about 6 p.m. Elements of the battalion then occupied Hill 344, which overlooked the Naktong south of Hill 360.

2LT James W. Mann, an FO and LTC William A. Harris, commanding the 77th FAB accompanied a patrol from Co. A to Hill 344. When the patrol returned to friendly lines, Mann and Harris remained behind to direct fire on the enemy until nightfall.

The *10th Division* was not finished with the 7th Cavalry. Enemy troops infiltrated onto the high ground on 1/7th Cavalry's right flank along Hill 344. At 5:55 a.m., an enemy machine gun began firing from close in on Co. C. This was followed by a general enemy attack supported by automatic weapons that lasted four hours. The enemy failed to drive out the 3d Platoon of Co. C, ably supported by the unit's 60mm mortar section. As C stood its ground, Co. B was called in to assist. Baker moved forward to the vicinity of Hadong, where it was pinned down by machine gun fire from the eastern slopes of Hill 344.

The recollections and experiences of men from Companies B, C, D and F help to clarify how this battle developed.

CPL Stanley Dahl (81mm gunner, 81mm Mortar Platoon, D/7th Cavalry) recalled that about 1:00 a.m. on Aug. 13, the Mortar and 75mm Recoilless Rifle Platoons, both of which now included company cooks as replacements, were ordered out of reserve and sent forward. The two platoons "loaded up in about ten jeeps with trailers," Dahl wrote. "We moved out driving down a dark, dusty dirt road with blackout lights on.... It was pitch black out. No moon or stars." The convoy moved by starts and stops. Finally, after one stop, LT Frank Earle, the Mortar Platoon leader, had the convoy pull off the main road and down a small trail. Local security was established and the men bedded down for the night. Dahl wrote that guides were supposed to meet them to take the platoons into their new positions, but no guides ever arrived. Dahl felt the platoons were lost.

CPL Dahl spent the rest of the night trying to get a little sleep without rolling down the side of the hill. "As dawn approached, I could see a dry creek bed right below me. I would have slept a lot more comfortable in the creek bed than on the side of the hill," he wrote. Jeeps and trailers were parked along the creek bed. Beyond the creek bed was an open field several hundred yards wide, ending at the base of a large hill. The men of Dahl's unit were on a hill to his left and behind him. The D Co. platoons had bivouacked near Fox Co. defensive positions.

About 7 a.m., while the men were relaxing, drinking coffee and eating a C-ration breakfast,

"I heard several rifle shots to our front," Dahl recounted. "It seemed to be coming off the hill, beyond the open field. Somebody shouted 'GOOKS!' At that same instant I heard a loud 'HURRAH!'.... It seemed as though the whole hill to my front was moving. Camouflaged North Koreans were attacking.... It was like something you would see in the old war movies. Everybody ducked...behind the creek bank...to return fire."

MSG Nauweiler brought his 75mm recoilless rifle into action at point blank range against the enemy. "For a couple of minutes," Dahl wrote, "it created havoc in [the enemy] ranks. Then a machine gun opened up...and knocked [the 75] out of action."

PFC Alexander Stuart, ran to Nauweiler's position and gave covering fire so the badly wounded sergeant could be evacuated.

"Incoming machine gun and rifle fire was so heavy you couldn't raise your head to return fire," Dahl recalled. "Rocks and dirt were flying all about our heads. I would raise my rifle over the bank and pull the trigger as fast as I could. LT Earle yelled, 'Get your head up and see what you're shooting at!'.... The man kneeling beside me thought LT Earle was yelling at him and raised up to fire. A burst of machinegun fire caught him in the head and he fell back dead.... The soldier was the one I had been talking to earlier, one of the young cooks from Fox Company."

Then CPL Dahl saw one of the men sitting in the midst of the fighting, reading a Bible. "I asked him what the hell he was doing," Stanley wrote. "I told him to pick up his rifle and get rid of that Bible." The man crawled away. Another trooper, a medic from Hawaii, was mistaken for an enemy soldier. "Someone shot him dead." Enemy soldiers were known to dress in American uniforms to get through the lines.

Four men, Graves, Morrisey, Gebhart and Killian, were all near Dahl. Graves was on his left, Morrisey his right, Gebhart to his right rear and Killian to his left rear. Graves and Morrisey were two of the cooks which had been sent to the 81mm mortars. Dahl was reloading his rifle and trying to talk to the two men beside him. "All of a sudden a mortar shell hit on the bank to our rear," he wrote. "I turned to Graves and said, 'God Damn! Look at that!' Graves just looked at me with a blank stare.... He leaned forward on the creek bank and I heard a rush of air.... There was a hole in his back you could put your hand in." Dahl went to apply a compress to the wound, but was stopped by a sergeant called Pappy, a WW II vet. "'Forget him, he's dead,' Pappy said, 'Take care of the other wounded.'"

Gebhart, wounded in the stomach, was screaming. Morrisey, hit in the neck, lay moaning next to Gebhart. Killian, hit in the back by mortar fragments, had involuntarily stood up and was then struck by machine gun fire. Dahl and some others rendered aid to the stricken men.

About noon, an enemy machine gun moved in closer and raked the area where Dahl and some others were located. Its fire was getting too close, so Dahl and several others fixed bayonets, got some grenades and crawled up the toward the enemy gun. Fixing the gun's location by its fire, the men hurled several grenades in that direction, silencing the weapon.

At one point, the 81s which also were firing on the enemy were elevated for minimum range firing, the rounds landing within 200 yards of the mortar position.

The men began running out of ammunition and water. "It was hot!" Dahl recalled. CPL Swing took matters into his own hands. jumped up, ran to the wreckage of the shot-up jeeps and trailers and began throwing ammunition to the men in the ditches. Enemy fire hit two mortar rounds in one trailer, setting their powder increments afire. Swing was hit by enemy mortar or artillery fragments, but kept to his task.

Since enemy fire threatened to blow up ammunition remaining in the trailers, orders came to move down the creek. As Dahl began to crawl away, he heard a moan and someone say feebly, "Help me." It was Morrisey. "I grabbed him by his fatigue jacket and dragged him with me," Dahl wrote. On the way, they passed Gebhart, who was dead. "I felt bad, he was a friend.... While he was laying there wounded, he kept begging, 'God, let me die.' He was at peace."

About 3 p.m., Fox Co. "came to our rescue, just like in the movies," Dahl recalled. 'Here comes the Cavalry!' They came off the hill behind us in a classic bayonet charge through us and over the creek bank through the open field, routing what North Koreans [who] were still on the battlefield," Dahl joyfully remembered. As they were caring for the wounded after the battle, "I saw a sergeant from Fox Company. standing in the creek bed, looking down at the dead trooper [cook from Fox Co.]. The sergeant was crying. The dead trooper was his brother."

Of the battle, Dahl wrote that he had "seen the elephant." This is an ancient saying which means one has experienced the danger and fright of intense and bloody battle.

LT John Potts (Co F) wrote that the thrust of the enemy pre-dawn attack on the 13th was across the front of Fox Co. in an attempt to outflank the 7th Cavalry. "The enemy overran our Weapons Platoon...causing a great deal of confusion. Telephone lines were cut, so information regarding enemy locations was stopped. The enemy captured one 60mm mortar. They tried to fire one of our 57mm recoilless rifles (which we had received only about a week earlier) but only succeeded in killing several of their own men who happened to stand to the rear of the weapon."

CPL Down recalled that "there was sporadic fire coming from our left flank [about 7 a.m.] which we thought [were] the Republic of Korea soldiers...playing around testing their weapons. Shortly thereafter, I was crouched down when a bullet suddenly hit next to my foot. Then all hell broke loose...." The enemy was attacking F Co. from the rear. They were now above Down and the men near him. "We immediately had to reverse our weapon positions and fire on them as they came down on us. Needless to say, we were fighting like hell...while working our way to the bottom of the hill. CPL Robert Conlan, our machinegunner, got hit in his upper leg and his assistant, CPL Eugene Cossich got hit in his right forearm," breaking his arm at that point.

"The 57mm recoilless rifle crew was 'cut down like trees' while trying to change positions," Down recalled. At the bottom of the hill, SGT Hillary Logue took charge of the men, sending them "crawling along the ditches, rice paddies and road" toward the Fox Co. positions, about a hundred yards away across an open rice paddy. Patching up their wounded, the party slowly made their way, sometimes crawling, sometimes running, until they reached the unit's main position. SGT Logue was hit by a bullet in the right foot. Among the dead from Fox Co. on Aug. 13 were PFC Leonard Finley, CPL Clarence Deal and SGT Glen W. Taturn. Down also witnessed the enemy's attempt to use the captured 57. He recalled that the enemy turned a captured .30-cal machine gun on the Americans.

Some time during the battle, LT Gamble, SGT Steward and 18 men from 2/C, 7th Cavalry, with an artillery FO, were covering part of Hill 360. Gamble was ordered to take his men forward to Hill 344 to join the remainder of Co. C. As the platoon on Hill 344, it met some 25 to 35 enemy soldiers face to face. The platoon drove the enemy off the hill and through Co. D's position. Gamble was wounded in the action and SGT Steward took over. The platoon remained on the newly-won position for about an hour and a half, when concentrated enemy artillery fire forced them to move.

Co. B took part in counterattacking the enemy that day. Richard Dowell, with his .30-cal machine gun was there. He recalled that their attack was from the south to the north, with the 1st and 2d Platoons on the right and the 3d and 4th on the left. He could see the effects of the enemy attack on the 81mm Mortar and 75mm Recoilless Rifle Platoons of Co. D. Enemy fire drove Co. B to ground, but some of the men worked their way along the company flanks toward the enemy-held hill. As Dowell neared the Dog Co. position, an enemy machine gun opened up "from the hill on the right," he recalled. "In just a few minutes our boys got them." Dowell and a buddy paused in their advance. As they did so, a sniper's bullet cracked between them. My buddy dove behind a big rock to our left," he wrote, and I dove down a ditch."

He thought the ditch to be about three feet deep, but it turned out to be nearer eight feet. Then off to his left front he heard an enemy machine gun cut loose "and he didn't let up," Dowell recalled. "This was perfect. I ran as hard as I could along the ditch, not thinking about snipers or meeting a Red face to face." His machine gun was empty, but he had his .45 automatic pistol and a number of grenades. When he arrived at a point near the enemy gun, he found SGT Taylor and two riflemen. The riflemen made an improvised platform for Dowell with their rifles. Taylor told him how the enemy gunner out there had caught his buddy, Baker, in the open, and just emptied his machine gun into him. Standing on the two rifles, Dowell loaded and fired a full belt through his machinegun at the enemy position. He wanted to continue firing, but SGT Taylor stopped him. Dowell climbed down from his improvised perch. In the meantime, he recalled, the remainder of the company moved to the road and secured the area.

In the aftermath of the battle, while driving the enemy toward the river, CPT Eugene E. Fels, commanding Co. B, was struck in the left leg by enemy machine gun fire. The three rifle companies of the battalion, "A on one side and C on another, and my Company B, in the middle," he said, made the sweep towards the Naktong. The companies "went down a valley slowly, carefully, under sniper fire,...got almost to the river," he continued, "when machine guns had us pinned down and a couple of men killed...and I was wounded in the left leg, but ...it wasn't serious.... I made sure that the machine guns were neutralized and then permitted myself to be evacuated." The citation for Fels' Silver Star states that he was wounded while personally trying to locate the enemy machine guns, and that when he had done so, he remained to direct fire on and destroy the enemy guns. And that "he stayed with his men until assured they could move forward unmolested."

On Aug. 14, the enemy tested the 7th Cavalry again. The two battalions of the regiment were deployed with the 1st Battalion in the south and the 2d in the north. The HM Co. and 77th FAB were in support. A platoon of the 71st Tk Bn, A/8th ECB and a squad from B/8th ECB also were in support.

The enemy began their attack about 5:31 am., detected by listening posts of Co G. Pressing the attack, the North Koreans drove the defenders back. It was estimated that some 700 troops took part in this attack, which concentrated on G and H Companies. Their objective was to secure high ground to protect the crossing of other elements of the enemy division later on. By 6:20 a.m. about 400-500 enemy troops had reached Yonpo. Ten minutes later the 16th Recon Co. was committed to try to flank the enemy. Part of the 8th Engineers were also committed in counterattack. By 6:35 a.m., enemy troops had reached the village of Wichon-dong and fighting in the H and G Co. areas was now hand-to-hand.

SFC James Elkins wrote of the heroism of PFC Arthur H. Hunter, part of a G Co. machine gun team. The team was dug-in an apple orchard when the enemy struck. The company was under strength and stretched thinly. Hunter and PVT Theodore Hickman manned the gun and engaged the enemy. Suddenly the gun jammed. Hickman left to get a part for it. Hunter stayed behind and held the enemy off with his M1 rifle. He was also able to fix the machine gun before Hickman returned. "Hunter...was able to hold off the enemy until our tanks arrived," Elkins wrote. The enemy then started to retreat. Hunter never left his position all day...until the battle was over. In front of his position, we estimated close to one hundred (100) killed. I would say Hunter...saved us from being overrun before the tanks arrived." Another account states that PFC Hunter could be heard, over the sound of firing, calling out "GARRY OWEN! Yahoo! Look at em! I got one!"

PFC Robert D. Roberts, also of George Co., was manning a machine gun on the southwestern slope of the hill next to the company CP. At 7 a.m., he was struck in the helmet by a bullet, which entered through the front just above his head, passed through the helmet liner and out the back of the helmet without touching his head. A half hour later, another bullet pierced his helmet at almost the same spot as the first, grazed his scalp, and passed out through the back of the helmet. At the same time, he suffered a shell fragment wound to his back. After receiving medical treatment, Roberts returned to duty four hours later.

Russell McKinley wrote that he and gunner David Fetter "fired our 60mm [mortars] until they wouldn't fire anymore. Many times we were firing on our own [friendly] positions to kill North Koreans that surrounded and overran us." Running out of mortar ammunition, Fetter, McKinley and the rest of the mortar section used their M1 rifles against the enemy. At one point, McKinley wrote, a man named Thompson "fired just over my head, killing a North Korean who had his rifle trained on my head. Somehow, we held our position...."

Enemy troops overran the company CP while the CO, CPT Herman L. West was reporting the situation to his battalion commander, LTC Gilman A. Huff. Suddenly, West stopped talking. A moment later, he came back on the phone and calmly said, "Excuse me, Sir, I had to shoot a couple of Gooks that stuck their heads in my CP."

A smaller enemy attack began against 1/7th Cavalry about 5 or 6 a.m. Patrols from the battalion were ordered south along the road at 6:37 a.m. to contact the 24th Division near Hyonpung and a tank platoon was sent to the Samni-dong area to destroy a pocket of some 400 enemy soldiers. A report at 7:50 a.m. indicated that the enemy was on Hill 360 and that Co. B was attacking the position. Even as companies F and G closed in on the enemy in the rear, more North Koreans were trying to cross the Naktong. Co. H began to receive enemy tank fire from across the river. Air strikes were called in to destroy the enemy on the road and in the rice paddies from Yongpo back to the destroyed bridge.

By 9:18 a.m., all the enemy troops who had reached the Yongpo and Samni-dong areas had been killed or captured, but many more remained hidden in the rice paddies nearer the river. Units of the regiment spent the rest of the 14th and all day on the 15th rooting out these soldiers. Often some of them would feign death, then throw grenades at passing GIs.

Co. B took Hill 360, then sent a platoon to help Co. C sweep the terrain north to the road. Charlie Co. ambushed and killed seven of the enemy near Hill 360. Baker Co. went on a sweep of paddies to the northwest and made contact with Fox Co. Meantime, one of the patrols to Hyonpung ran into a minefield and one man was killed. The patrol went on and contacted elements of the 24th Division in the town at 4:28 p.m.

About 9:30 a.m., or so, the Air-Ground Liaison Officer reported that aircraft had spotted three barges loaded with enemy personnel near the partially destroyed bridge. An air strike hit the barges and pilots reported that the "river ran red" in its aftermath. About noon, pilots reported that they could see nothing but enemy dead on the west side of the Naktong.

The 1st Battalion reverted to Division reserve at 11 p.m.

Early in the day, while checking his platoon, LT Lippincott (3d Plt, Co. F) was hit in the leg by two bullets from a burp gun. As he crawled to cover, the enemy gunner sprayed more fire at him, but failed to score any more hits. Lippincott was evacuated, treated at division and returned to duty four or five days later.

The crossings had been made by elements of the *10th Division's 25th* and *27th Regiments*. The 7th Cavalry estimated that about 1,700 enemy

soldiers succeeded in crossing the river, but that 1,500 had been killed. Co. H buried 267 enemy dead and Co. G counted the bodies of 150 North Koreans in its position. The dead in the rice paddies to the front were never counted. Twenty enemy soldiers were captured. In all, the *10th Division* suffered 2,500 casualties. Some units lost up to 50 per cent of their men. In spite of the ferocity of the fighting, Co. G lost only 2 KIA and 3 wounded. The 1st Battalion lost 2 KIA and 2 WIA.

The bodies of two colonels were among the enemy dead. Also found were numerous enemy documents. One of these, dated Aug. 13, is quoted by Appleman as follows:

"Kim Il Sung has directed that the war be carried out so that its final victory can be realized by 15 August, fifth anniversary of the liberation of Korea....

"Our victory lies before your eyes. Young soldiers! You are fortunate in that you are able to participate in the battle for our final victory. Young soldiers, the capture of Taegu lies in the crossing of the Naktong River.... The eyes of 30,000,000 people are fixed on the Naktong River crossing operation....

"Pledge of all fighting men: We pledge with our life, no matter what hardships and sacrifices lie before us, to bear it and put forth our full effort to conclude the crossing of the Naktong River. Young Men! Let us protect our glorious pride by completely annihilating the enemy!"

Hill 303 at Waegwan — Atrocity Hill, 2d Battalion, 5th Cavalry — Aug. 14-18

On the very northern flank of the 1st Cavalry Division was G/5th Cavalry, on Hill 303. It was also the northern flank anchor of the U.S. Eighth Army. Just to the north was the left flank of the ROK 1st Division.

Hill 303 is a hill mass which extends to the northeast for almost two miles from the north edge of Waegwan. Its top, about 950 feet high, overlooks the Naktong for several miles; its northern slopes actually come down to the river's bank. The hill top also dominates the road and rail net from the town. One road ran north and south along the east bank of the Naktong. Another ran northeast through the mountains to Tabu-dong, then on to Taegu. The main north-south rail line came in from the south to Waegwan, crossed the river there, then went on north from that point. Hill 303 also dominated the rail line for some distance. The hill was key terrain in the area; he who had Hill 303 had the area surrounding it in control, militarily.

Early on Aug. 14, part of the *NK 3d Division*, supported by elements of the *105th Armored Division* crossed the Naktong six miles north of Waegwan on an underwater bridge into the sector of the ROK 13th Infantry. From there, a sizable force of the enemy turned south toward Hill 303. Co G, 5th Cavalry, with a mortar platoon of Co. H, held Hill 303. In the first light of dawn, G Co. outposts could see about 50 enemy soldiers and two tanks come marching down the river road. Another enemy column moved to their rear and attacked Co. F. In order to escape being surrounded, Fox Co. withdrew southward. By 8:30 a.m., Co. G and the H Co mortar platoon were isolated by the enemy on Hill 303.

That day, 2LT Adrian Beecher Brian (West Point, 1949) wrote home. He had been assigned as leader, 3d Platoon, B/5th Cavalry on Aug. 9. The platoon numbered 24 men. "B Co. is in support," he wrote. "We are spread thin over 3 hills, 5 miles apart. We have been busier than I can imagine for a reserve company. In the last three days I have been on three patrols trying to clear out the Gooks from the rear.... The river 'front' is very quiet — but the rear is (or was) crawling with Gooks." He describes how they took their first prisoner, who "just walked in on us in a sort of daze. We didn't see him until he was about five feet from our flank foxhole. When the guard yelled, 'Halt!' he jumped into a ditch." Brian threw a grenade near the man and he quickly surrendered.

Aug. 15 was Dennis Robinson's first day of combat with F/5th Cavalry. He had recently joined the unit as a replacement. He recalled that Fox Co. was on a small hill below Hill 303. The enemy spread their attack against Co. F. "We heard a vicious fire fight above us," he wrote, "and were told to fire on the right side of 303 where the North Korean positions were. I took it seriously and fired all but about 8 rounds of the 150 rounds I carried." He asked his squad leader, SGT Edward Hendricks, a WW II veteran, for more ammunition. "He gave me several more clips along with a lecture about what would I do if the North Koreans now attacked us," Robinson wrote. "He was right."

The 15th of August was also the first — and the last — day of combat for 2LT Cecil Newman, a West Point classmate of LT Brian. Newman was an infantry combat veteran of WW II, but he was in Korea less than a week before being killed in action with Co. F, 5th Cavalry.

The enemy also got into the rear areas on Aug. 15. At one point, they forced a platoon of the HM Co. to displace by their heavy fire. In the withdrawal, one of the platoon's vehicles was left behind. PFCs Lindsey C. Nelms and Richard Portwood volunteered to return and retrieve the vehicle. In spite of enemy heavy mortar and automatic weapons fire, the two men succeeded in extricating the vehicle.

Gerald D. Gingery of Co. H, 5th Cavalry, recalled that it was in the early days on the Naktong that they first heard enemy broadcasts by a woman the men called "Seoul City Sue." Most men laughed at most of her propaganda, but enjoyed the music she played. She often correctly identified units on the line and included the names of some POWs in her broadcasts.

Gingery's recollections of service on the Naktong as an Infantryman are typical of other soldiers who were in Korea. Korea had no base camps, no "China Beach" recreation areas, nor any of the amenities of Viet Nam. During the first weeks in Korea there was little respite from front line foxholes, dirt, dust, rain and at night, hordes of mosquitoes. It was not uncommon to wear the same clothing for one, two or three weeks, with no opportunity to wash properly, let alone have a shower. He wrote, "When it rained and we were in our foxholes, our clothes took on the color of the earth and we all looked like hell and smelled like it too." Obtaining untainted

water was also a major problem. Water treated with halazone tablets or other purifiers tasted terrible, and was always warm.

Gerald Gingery had been selected to be a radio operator with the mortar platoon that was to join G Co. on Hill 303. But his sergeant asked that Gingery be allowed to remain and help him. PFC Brook T. Powell volunteered to go in his place. Powell was captured and murdered on the hill a few days later.

In a January 18, 1987 interview for *The Sunday Independent* of Ashland, Kentucky, CPL James M. Rudd, a member of the Mortar Platoon, H/5th Cavalry, and survivor of Hill 303, gave his account of the events of Aug. 15-17, 1950.

The platoon asked for infantry help at the mortar positions early on Aug. 15, and were told that 60 South Koreans, under a LT Pak would be sent to them.

"A little later we saw some Koreans. We called out 'LT Pak!' and an officer answered us," he recalled. "Some of them had South Korean markings on them." Rudd said there were between 45 and 60 of them. At first, some of the Americans, including Rudd, and Truman E. Purser, fired on the Koreans. They were soon stopped by their officer, who said the approaching troops were the South Koreans he had asked for. But as the troops got closer, the GIs realized that the soldiers were North Koreans because of their uniforms and that some of them were carrying burp guns. At that point, Rudd said, "We disobeyed and fired again." Rudd told one of his ammunition bearers to slip down a ditch and shoot LT Pak in the stomach. Rudd's lieutenant "ordered me directly to not let it happen," he said.

By this time, the enemy soldiers were on top of the mortarmen. Rudd and Purser re-opened fire, but it was too late. Purser took an enemy bullet which entered the top of his shoulder and "came out of his body," said Rudd. As Rudd grabbed his aid packet to help Purser, enemy soldiers appeared, pointing their guns into his foxhole. At first, Purser held fast to his rifle, until Rudd was able to pry it from his hands.

Rudd recalled that 37 men from his platoon were captured then and another five from Co. G later on. The men's hands were tied with communications wire, then they were tied together into a line. Their shoes, and in some cases, trousers were taken from the men and they were marched off. Some of the men muttered death threats at the lieutenant for not letting them engage the enemy when they had the chance. As they stumbled along, SGT Ray A. Briley fell over a bluff and had to be pulled back by the others tied to him.

The lieutenant (identified by Gerald Gingery as a LT Hudspeth) succeeded in loosening the wire bands and escaped. But, according to Gingery, the lieutenant disappeared. Rudd said that the officer's bullet-ridden body was found tied to the front of a jeep in a nearby town. Rudd said that the enemy found the bindings slack on three other men, who they beat with shovels and rifles, then led away and shot.

"I got crazy mad and told them in English, 'If you S.O.B.s will untie me, I'll bite your throats out!'" Rudd thought they would kill him for this outburst, but nothing happened.

The enemy marched the prisoners around on the hill. "My feet were cut to pieces, marching barefoot," Rudd said. "I still had my pants, but my arms were cut from the wire. I was a long time getting feeling back in them.

"They gave us no water, and the only food was two apples. They started at one end [of the line of prisoners] and held them out for us to take a bite apiece. I was near the end and got a bite of core. They tormented us, ate in front of us and poured water out on the ground." Men who had to relieve themselves had to so in their trousers.

On Aug. 16, CPL Roy L. Day Jr., one of the prisoners who spoke Japanese, conversed with one of the guards. He overheard a North Korean lieutenant that afternoon say that if the Americans got too close they would kill the prisoners. That night enemy soldiers took five of the prisoners away and the others did not know what happened to them.

During a rest stop, the guards rifled the prisoner's pockets, throwing away what they didn't want. PFC Benjamin Bristow knew Rudd could speak some Japanese. He asked Rudd to get his fiance's picture back from the guards. Rudd asked a guard, who picked up the picture and put it in Bristow's shirt pocket.

Several other prisoners asked Rudd to talk to the guard about allowing them to have a cigarette. To Rudd's amazement, the guard responded in English. He had learned English from missionaries, who had raised him in North Korea. The guard said he was a Christian, who had been forced into the North Korean Army when the lives of his family were threatened. He also said that he purposely missed U.S. soldiers in fire fights.

Rudd remembered that two other guards came up as they talked, knocked the cigarettes from the prisoners' mouths, and berated the man for his kindness to the Americans. When the two men left, the guard relit the cigarettes. The two guards returned, knocked the cigarettes from the prisoners' mouths again, took the friendly guard aside and shot him dead.

The friendly guard told Rudd his name, but neither Rudd or any of the other survivors of the massacre on Hill 303 remembered it.

Platoon Sergeant Clifford Phillips of George Co. recalled that his platoon, along with the Weapons Platoon, were positioned along the left (south) base of Hill 303, near Waegwan. The Weapons Platoon was to the right of Phillips' platoon. He also recalled some South Koreans nearby. His platoon leader was LT Willis Honeycutt. He, Honeycutt, the platoon medic and a runner were located at the Platoon CP.

This is his recollection of the events of Aug. 15 on Hill 303. "I was asleep," he said. "Somebody shook me and said 'They are here.' When I woke up, a machine gun was firing. They [the enemy] had tanks. We were right on the road. It was shooting everywhere; firing along the road, in the bushes, and hollering 'Hajo! Hajo!' They killed or took prisoner all of our men, except myself and LT Honeycutt, the medic and the runner." He had no idea at the time what happened to the men. He had no communication with the Weapons Platoon, nor the squads of his platoon. There was a phone to the company CP, which was around on the other side of the hill. The company commander called LT Honeycutt on the phone and said, "Hold." "I told him that there was only four of us left. He told me he couldn't give me orders to withdraw so we stayed and gave him information on what was going on up in the front. They [the enemy] were in back of us on top of the hill." The four men stayed put all day on Aug. 15. The next day, they climbed the hill and joined the remnants of Co. G. He recalled that they numbered 32 men. By this time, the enemy was in Waegwan and on the slopes of Hill 303. What was left of Co. G was isolated on Hill 303.

Phillips went on to say that no help came, as promised on the radio to the rear, no tanks, no aircraft. What Phillips did not know was that on both Aug. 15 and 16, B/5th Cavalry, with tanks, did try to break through, but was driven back by the enemy, estimated to be a battalion of about 700 men. The 61st FAB and three 155mm howitzers from B/82d FAB fired on the enemy-held hill all day on the 16th

CPL Arthur P. Bartol, also of Co. G, wrote, "They [the enemy] came up at us both mornings [Aug. 15 and 16] screaming, yelling, blowing whistles. We had artillery support.... We held them off. During the day of Aug. 15, the North Korean Army spread all around the base of Hill 303 and through Waegwan. Our supporting units and part of Co. G to the rear and base of Hill 303 had to fall back, leaving about 30 Co. G men on top...completely cut off from the rest of the regiment."

Phillips recalled that the enemy brought the GI prisoners on Hill 303 up to the lines of Co G. Phillips was sent over to talk to the enemy, who called on the rest of Co. G to surrender. (This was probably on Aug. 16.) "I said I didn't come to Korea to surrender," Phillips recalled. "I talked to the men [prisoners]. They had them tied, hands behind, a rope around their necks. I said, 'If we surrender, they will only kill us and y'all. And they're gonna kill y'all anyway. They'll just add us to it." So we want to fight as long as we can." (See Chapter Note.)

American troops and the guards exchanged fire on the morning of Aug. 17. About noon the GI prisoners were herded into a gully with a few guards. Then a very heavy American artillery preparation and air strike fell on the hill. The approaching American infantry and the intense artillery bombardment and air strike convinced the enemy officer that the time had come to kill the prisoners. Accounts differ as to what happened next, one survivor (not identified by Appleman) said the entire 50 man guard force opened fire on the kneeling men resting in the gully. Other accounts state that about 14 to 20 soldiers ran up when two of the guards called out a signal and fired into the men with burp guns. Shortly thereafter, some of them came back and shot those who were groaning.

When the burp guns began firing, Day dove to the ground. Bodies fell all around him, most of them already dead. CPL Rudd escaped death when a man was shot dead at his side and fell on top of him. (The bodies of two soldiers shielded Rudd and he was not wounded.) PFC Roy Manring burrowed under the bodies of comrades, but was still hit in each leg and one arm. CPL Day was unwounded. In addition to Day, Rudd and Manring, Charles Ryan and Truman E.

Purser survived this massacre. Another survivor died in the hospital next day, according to Rudd. Ryan had been hit five times. Purser also was wounded.

Meantime, what was left of Co G, held on until almost out of ammunition. In the early hours of Aug. 17, the men broke through the encircling enemy. "We...walked straight through them," said Phillips. "They were cooking and eating and smoking[.]... When we reached the road where the [enemy] tanks were, they challenged us.... We opened up on them with what ammo we had." At this point, the group split up into small parties of two or three men. Soon, they met counterattacking troops of the 5th Cavalry.

COL Crombez was very much upset by the enemy's success in seizing Hill 303. He mustered everything he had to retake the hill.

In the pre-dawn darkness of Aug. 17, men of 1st and 2d Battalions, 5th Cavalry, supported by A/70th Tk Bn, attacked Hill 303. But concentrated heavy mortar fire from Waegwan stopped them. The infantry called on the artillery, which pounded the hill with heavy concentrations of fire. The 61st FAB alone pumped 1,159 rounds into 303. At 11:30 a.m., the 5th Cavalry asked for more help and learned that an air strike was scheduled for 2 p.m. The combination of the delivery of napalm, bombs, rockets and strafing from the air, and heavy concentrations of artillery broke the enemy's grip on Hill 303. At 3:30 p.m., the infantry assaulted and secured the promontory by 4:30 p.m. On the crest, Co. E and F found their combined strength was down to only about 60 men.

Dennis Robinson wrote that his first real battle came on Aug. 17, in the attack on Hill 303. "We started walking up the hill," he wrote, "on a road carved on the left side, then climbed up through brush, trees, etc. The front men spotted a North Korean sniper and started firing [at him]. I heard one [GI] yell that 'We got him!'

Robinson recalled seeing MAJ Claude E. Allen during this attack. Allen was XO of 2/5th Cavalry. It appeared to Robinson that Allen was in command of the attack. Because he often saw Allen at the front later, Dennis wrote that he "would develop a lot of respect for him." Allen was killed by a Chinese mortar round on March 2, 1951.

In the assault up Hill 303, Fox Co., Robinson recalled, was led by "a slim, young sergeant," whose name he could not recall. "He was a brave soldier, waving us forward, while he was ahead of everyone. It was a disaster.... The North Koreans sprayed machine guns and rifle [fire] into our ranks and Fox Co. was literally destroyed." Upon reaching the hill's crest, the men were exposed on the skyline. The sergeant ordered them to the reverse slope at once. "I yelled at three men near me," Robinson wrote, "to follow me as I dived to the right side of the hill.... As we dropped to the ground a very young soldier fell beside me. He looked about 17. I thought he was in shock, as he was crying for his mother."

Robinson turned the man over. "His side was open and I looked right inside his chest. I could see blood spurting from what I guess was a main artery. I felt like a fool, telling him it would be OK, I would get him to a doctor. We had no

chance of getting him anywhere...." He dragged the dying boy to the shelter of some fallen trees, where an enemy sniper began taking pot shots at them with an automatic rifle. Robinson made two or three snap shots in return. Finally, his basic weapons training kicked in, he recalled. "I thought of the big ex-paratrooper first sergeant, when I missed a target on the range. He kicked me in the legs and yelled, 'Robinson, you dumb S.O.B., hold your breath and squeeze the trigger!'"

Robinson sighted in on where the enemy soldier had kept popping up, took a deep breath, held it, and when the North Korean's head appeared, he squeezed off one round. "The bullet hit the enemy soldier in the head.... His head snapped back like he was hit by a big baseball bat when the .30-caliber bullet hit." Robinson then fired at other enemy soldiers. When it was over, he recalled, his unit had only about "15 or so men left who were not hit."

Co. F came upon some of Co. G in the advance. "G Company was a very happy bunch," he recalled.

While all this was happening, back at the scene of the massacre, Roy Manring managed to crawl away and down Hill 303, where he was found and treated. He told of the massacre. Orders were given for LT Paul Kelly to take his I&R Platoon and investigate. The platoon set out in nine jeeps, with Chaplain A. M. Kiner, who had insisted on coming along. The little column went through the deserted and burning Waegwan. At the edge of town, the jeeps were stopped, the men spread out and began their ascent of Hill 303. As they advanced, they first smelled the sweetish odor of the dead. The bodies of two dead GIs were found, killed by the attacking enemy. Then the platoon found the gully of death.

Charles and Eugene Jones, on pages 49 and 50 of their *The Faces of War*, write a graphic depiction of the scene:

"The boys lay packed tightly, shoulder to shoulder, lying on their sides, curled like babies sleeping in the sun. Their feet, bloodied and bare, from walking on the rocks, stuck out stiffly....

"Features were gray-green and waxen....

"All had hands tied behind their backs, some with cord, others with regular government issue Army communication wire. Only a few hands were clenched. Bullet holes as if put on with black paint, dotted and evenly spaced, crisscrossed the backs."

Chaplain Kiner knelt and performed the last rites for the dead soldiers. LT Kelly and his men looked on grimly, sadly. Some swore at the enemy, and wept. One soldier found the body of the lieutenant he had once driven for. The fondness he had for the dead officer was in his face and his actions, as he sat and mourned. Another soldier came to the grieving man and caressed the back of his neck with his hand. The BAR on his shoulder slipped to the ground. "Ah, Christ, Harry, he ain't alone," he murmured, consolingly, "they're with him." (See Chapter Notes for the names of the men murdered on Hill 303.)

Three enemy soldiers who had knowledge of the massacre were captured. They were Chong Myong Tok, Kim Kown Taek and Heo Chang Keun. Day and Rudd were able to identify the North Korean officer who ordered the killing.

He had been captured by U.S. troops. Rudd had to be restrained from attacking and killing the officer.

Interrogation of enemy prisoners revealed that the *4th Co., 2d Bn, 206th Mechanized Infantry Regiment (105th Armored Div.)* were the captors, although some men from *Hq Co,* of the *Anti-tank Bn, 105th Armored Division.* also were there. There is some evidence that the captives were then turned over to the custody of a company from the *3d Division*. It was this unit which perpetrated the massacre.

Appleman has the following incident occurring on Aug. 17; whether it was Aug. 17 or 16 is immaterial.

Co. A, 70th Tk Bn, fresh from the U.S., was attached to the 5th Cavalry just as the battle for 303 began. Aug. 16 was the first real day of combat for the 3d Platoon, commanded by LT Rodger Thrall. SGT Ashley C. Anderson was the Platoon Sergeant. Late that day, Thrall's platoon was moving down the road to the east, near Hill 303. The tanks did not have communication with one another. They often used arm and hand signals as a crude form of communication. Thrall's tank was leading. Some infantrymen were on the second tank. Anderson was in the third tank. "I noticed the tank ahead of me, with infantry on the deck," Anderson wrote, "had stopped and was pointing down the road where it turned north and up a grade. I had my tank pull around the one in front of me.... I saw the lead tank drawing all kinds of fire.... It was in trouble and I felt we should help. At that moment, we too came under heavy fire from both sides of the road." An infantryman on Anderson's tank manned the .50-cal machine gun. "He showed a lot of guts," Anderson wrote. "But it got too hot for him and he dove head first into the tank. He was wounded when he dove in."

Anderson moved his tank forward to the rear of Thrall's, which was off the road. It was now dark. Anderson tried to turn his tank around, "and we ran off the road, almost on the back deck of the Lieutenant's tank," Anderson continued. Both tanks were stuck. Anderson could get no one on his radio. Leaving his tank, he moved to a small bridge nearby. There, he found PVT Barner, from Thrall's tank crew and Levenduski, from his own, and two infantrymen, both wounded — one badly wounded, the other slightly. Anderson wondered where Thrall might be and he worried about PVT Eaton, his driver, who was only 16 years old. As the enemy approached the slightly wounded infantryman ran from the bridge and tried to surrender; the enemy killed him. Sending Barner and Levenduski back along the stream bed, Anderson set out for the tanks to try and find Eaton. Enroute he was wounded and dove into a rice paddy. "It had about 4" of water in it," he wrote, "and was as slick as glass. I must have slid 10-15 feet.... I tried to pull myself to a dry paddy. The rice paddies were very small; the North Koreans knew I was in there. They called, 'American come on out, its OK!' Like hell I am," he thought to himself. Then U.S. artillery began to fall nearby. This helped Anderson, who suffered from smoker's cough. He wrote that he "would almost choke to keep from coughing." When he heard the artillery rounds come in, "I would get set, and when the round would land...I would cough."

But he knew that the artillery was close; he was in danger of being killed by that, or by the enemy. But he couldn't get his legs to move. He was wet from the paddy, so he didn't know if some of the wetness was from that or his own blood. He didn't know where friendly troops might be, nor the other tanks of his platoon. He prayed. Anderson wrote that he actually heard a voice say, "Don't worry, you will be alright." Reassured, Anderson fell asleep, to be awakened the next morning by an air strike on Hill 303. He was thirsty, hungry, and hurt all over, but he began making his way slowly and cautiously toward Waegwan. "After some hours, I made it back to the road leading to Waegwan," he wrote. "I covered myself with shell casings and crates, and went to sleep."

Occasionally, through the sleep, he heard vehicles crossing the bridge. Eventually, he raised up as a jeep approached, and was almost shot by the startled driver. As he climbed into the jeep, the driver handed him an M1 rifle. They no more than started when the jeep ran out of gas — out in the open. They got some fuel from a passing vehicle and Anderson finally got to an aid station and on to a hospital. LT Thrall, SGT Arthur E. Reasor and CPL William Williams, all of Thrall's tank, had been killed, as well as CPL Robert L. Simons, SSG Roy Stam and PVT William Eaton of Anderson's crew. All had been murdered by their captors. PVTs F. McCarron and Barner of Thrall's crew had been wounded.

The enemy paid dearly for Hill 303. Of the 500 troops estimated to be on the hill, the bodies of 200 of them littered the area. The survivors fled in disorder after the air strike.

The execution of American prisoners by the enemy prompted GEN MacArthur to broadcast an announcement to the North Korean Army and have leaflets prepared, addressed to the Commander-in-chief of the Armed Forces of North Korea. The leaflet was dropped over North Korea in large numbers. MacArthur ended his message thusly:

Inertia on your part and on the part of your senior field commanders in the discharge of this grave and universally recognized command responsibility may only be construed as a condonation and encouragement of such outrage, for which if not promptly corrected I shall hold you and your commanders criminally accountable under the rules and precedents of war.

No evidence exists that the North Korean High command condoned the murder of prisoners of war. The killing of prisoners was done by individuals or small units, without orders or encouragement by the higher leadership.

GEN Kim Chaek, Commander in Chief and GEN Kang Kon, Commanding General Staff, *Advanced General Headquarters* of the North Korean Army, issued the following order:

1. The unnecessary killing of enemy personnel when they could be taken as PsW shall be strictly prohibited as of now. Those who surrender will be taken as PsW, and all efforts will be made to destroy the enemy in thought and politically.

2. Treatment of PsW shall be according to the regulations issued by the Supreme Hq, as attached herein, pertaining to the regulation and order of PW camps.

3. This directive will be explained to and understood by all military personnel immediately, and staff members of the Cultural Section will be responsible for seeing that this is carried out.

The Cultural Section of the *NK 2d Division* issued an order on Aug. 16, which read in part: "Some of us are still slaughtering enemy troops that come to surrender. Therefore, the responsibility of teaching soldiers to take prisoners of war and to treat them kindly rests on the Political Section of each unit."

But the damage had already been done. Hundreds, if not thousands, of U.S. and South Korean soldiers vowed not to take North Korean prisoners, but to kill them in vengeance for the men murdered earlier in the war.

The Carpet Bombing Opposite Wagewan — Aug. 16

The ROK 1st Division fought valiantly against the enemy, with its 13th Regiment still near the Naktong, and the 11th and 12th Regiments battled for Suam-san and Yuhak-san, west and northwest of Tabu-dong, 4 to 6 miles from the Naktong. Six miles north of Waegwan, in front of Hills 201 and 346, the enemy kept their underwater bridge in operation. Even hits by 155mm howitzer rounds seemed to do little damage.

As the enemy pressed in on the ROK 1st Division and the Hill 303 sector of the 5th Cavalry, the safety of Taegu became critical. To meet the threat, an additional 750 South Korean police were positioned on the outskirts of the city. Over 400,000 refugees had swollen Taegu's population from 300,000 to 700,000 souls. Early on Aug. 18, seven rounds of enemy artillery struck near the railroad station, damaging the roundhouse, destroying one yard engine, killing one Korean civilian and wounding eight more. The South Korean Provisional Government moved the capital and President Syngman Rhee to Pusan.

Once the people heard of this, they swarmed out on the road, heading almost panic-stricken to the south. The jam of people almost stopped military traffic and undermined the morale of defending troops. Extraordinary measures taken by the Co-ordinator for Protection of Lines of Communication stopped the exodus. The enemy gun shelled Taegu twice more, the last time on Aug. 20. Six battalions of South Korean police were then moved into reinforce the security of important rail and highway tunnels throughout the Perimeter.

GEN MacArthur decided to carpet bomb enemy troop concentrations west of the Naktong on Aug. 14. As a result, GEN Stratemeyer consulted MG Emmett "Rosie" O'Donnell Jr., commanding Far East Bomber Command. He said a fairly good job of bombing could be done on a 3 by 5 mile area. MacArthur's headquarters chose a 27 square-mile area 3.5 miles wide and 7.5 miles long west of the Naktong opposite the ROK 1st Division.

Knowing of the projected bombing, GEN Gay, commanding the 1st Cavalry Division, repeatedly recommended that the bombing include an area on the east side of the Naktong northeast of Waegwan, between the river and the Waegwan-Tabu-dong road. Fearing that bombing in that area would cause casualties in the 1st Cavalry and ROK 1st Divisions, his request was denied. Gay pointed out that terrain features clearly marked the area and offered Cavalry Division aircraft to lead the bombers to the target area, but was still overruled.

The strike was set for Aug. 16, employing the 19th, 22d, 92d, 98th and 307th Bomber Groups (ninety-eight bombers) from Japan and Okinawa. No enemy concentrations could be detected in the target area, so it was divided into twelve equal squares, with an aiming point in the center of each square. A B-29 squadron was assigned to attack each square.

The bombing attack lasted from 11:58 a.m. to 12:24 p.m. on Aug. 16. The attack was made from 10,000 feet. About 960 tons of 500 and 1,000 general purpose bombs were dropped. The area was so badly obscured in dust and smoke that the results could not be determined either from the air or from the ground. But ground patrols sent to investigate the bombed area were turned back by heavy enemy fire. There is little evidence that this "carpet bombing" had any significant effect on the enemy. Most of the enemy's divisions facing the 1st ROK Division had already crossed the Naktong. A marked reduction of artillery fire against the 1st Cavalry and 1st ROK Divisions seemed to be the only result of this massive aerial attack. However, GEN Paik Sun Yup, on page 40 of his *From Pusan to Panmunjom*, wrote, "Subsequent interrogation of enemy prisoners of war revealed...that the raid dealt a crushing blow to NKPA morale."

MacArthur wanted to stage a similar raid east of the Naktong on Aug. 19. Generals Walker, Partridge and O'Donnell reportedly all opposed any more carpet bombings unless there were clear enemy troop concentrations in the area and the tactical situation extremely critical. GEN Stratemeyer had to personally intercede with MacArthur to get the projected Aug. 19 raid called off.

The Bowling Alley Area — Aug. 14-26

(The ROK 1st Division and 10th Regt. and the U.S. 23d and 27th Regiments.)

27th Infantry — Aug. 14-17

On Aug. 14, the 27th Infantry was relieved from attachment to the 24th Division and sent northward to Kyongsan and Army reserve. The regiment arrived there on Aug. 16 and COL Michaelis was ordered to reconnoiter routes east, north, northwest and west of the town in preparation for Army orders to meet enemy thrusts in those directions.

That day, two T-34 tanks came through the ROK 1st Division lines near Rabu-dong but were destroyed by ROK 3.5 inch rocket launcher teams

At noon on Aug. 17, the 27th Infantry was ordered to move its headquarters and a reinforced battalion "without delay" to a point across the Kumho River three miles north of Taegu on the

Tabu-dong-Sangju road in order "to secure Taegu from enemy penetration" from that direction. The ROKs had reported that an enemy regiment, with six tanks, had entered the village of Kumhwa, two miles north of Tabu-dong.

Michaelis sent his 1st Battalion (LTC Gilbert J. Check), a 4.2 inch mortar platoon, and the 8th FAB (LTC Augustus T. "Gus" Terry, Jr.) less Battery B. This force moved north of Taegu at noon. Later, it moved two miles to Chilgok, where GEN Paik had his headquarters. By dark, the whole regiment, reinforced by C/73d Tk Bn, was north of Taegu.

Eighth Army then ordered the 37th FAB (LTC John B. Hector) less Battery A, to displace from the Kyongju-Pohang-dong area, where a great battle was in progress, for attachment to the 27th Infantry Regiment to reinforce the fires of the 8th FAB. It arrived on Aug. 18th. As the 27th Infantry, with elements of the two artillery battalions deployed in what became known as the Bowling Alley area, the struggle for Obong-ni and Cloverleaf Hill back south in the 24th Division sector was still going on.

The deafening noises and flashes of tank fire, exploding mortar and artillery rounds, punctuated by the staccato of automatic weapons and small-arms fire, echoing up and down this valley in the forthcoming series of battles led to the area being called "The Bowling Alley."

The *NK 13th Division* had fought its way into the Tabu-dong corridor against the ROK 1st Division's 11th and 12th Regiments. On Aug. 17 it was poised to drive through the deep valley there to finally assault Taegu. LTC Chong Pong Uk, commanding the *13th Division's Artillery Regiment*, surrendered on Aug. 22. He said that the division had suffered 1,500 casualties in breaking into the Tabu-dong corridor.

On Aug. 15, GEN Paik, commanding the ROK 1st Division, had urgently requested immediate reinforcement. To his delight, both the ROK 10th Infantry and the U.S. 27th Infantry were dispatched by Eighth Army and attached to his division. Thus, for the forthcoming Bowling Alley action, the Wolfhounds were attached to the ROK 1st Division.

"After sundown on August 17, 1950, a handsome U.S. colonel with piercing eyes arrived at my headquarters," wrote GEN Paik. The general was overjoyed to discover that the entire 27th Infantry, plus an artillery battalion and a battery of 155mm howitzers had been attached to his division. He was eager to use this added strength to counterattack at once, he recalled, but COL Michaelis replied that his orders were only to defend a thousand yard line in the deep valley on the Tabu-dong road. This valley was in the middle of the ROK 1st Division's sector almost in the center of the ROK 11th Infantry.

Enemy Situation in the Bowling Alley Area

Both the *NK 13th* and *15th Divisions* were just north of Tabu-dong. The *13th Division* was deployed primarily west of the Tabu-dong road. West of the *13th* on Yuhak-san, was the *15th Division*. On Aug. 15, the *105th Armored Division* received 21 new T-34 tanks and 200 replacements, which were distributed to the divisions on the Taegu front. The *13th Division* was re-

ported to have 14 tanks. At this point, the North Korean High Command made a decisive move. It ordered the *15th Division* from the Taegu area and sent it to bolster the *8th Division*, which was failing in its mission to cut the east-west road from Taegu to the Pohang area. The *15th* left the Yuhak-san area on Aug. 20. It ordered the *1st Division*, which had just arrived in the Kunwi area, twenty-five miles north of Taegu, to move forward and take position on the left (east) of the *13th*. When the 27th Regiment and two regiments of the ROK 1st Division were ordered to attack north on Aug. 18, elements of the *13th* and *15th Divisions* were in the zone of advance. Two days later, the *13th* and *1st Divisions* opposed the ROK-U.S. force in the area. For a week and a half, the ROK 1st Division, reinforced by the ROK 10th Infantry and the U.S. 23d and 27th Regiments, battled it out with two North Korean divisions which were determined to break through to Taegu.

Attack of the 27th Infantry — Aug. 18

At 8 p.m. on Aug. 17, the 27th was ordered to restore a salient in the sector of the ROK 1st Division the next day. ROK forces would attack on each flank of the regiment. The attack was planned to start at 1 p.m., with the 1st and 2d Battalions abreast and the 3d Battalion in reserve. One platoon of tanks from C/73d Tk Bn was attached to the 1st Battalion. The remainder of the company traveled with the 3d Battalion. The objective was to restore the original ROK line.

Crowded road conditions prevented the regiment from getting into position on time. As a result, the attack did not start until 3:30 p.m. In the attack, the 1st Battalion was responsible for the road and terrain to its left. The 2d Battalion advanced on the 1st Battalion's right. LTC Check deployed Co. C on the left of the road, gave the road to Co. B with the tanks leading. Co. A followed Co. C. C Co.'s path was along the paddies and lower slopes of Yuhak-san. The 2d Battalion, right of the road proceeded along the lower slopes of high ridges on that flank of the valley. The battalion advanced with Co. E on the left and Co. G on the right. Co. E was on B Co.'s right flank. Co. F followed 300 yards behind Co E. Batteries B and C, 37th FAB had been attached to the 8th FAB. The two batteries were placed in direct support of the regiment. The 8th FAB had its A and B Batteries present.

Wireman Harold W. Brixius, of B/37th FAB recalled that this was his unit's first combat, and "a lot of us were nervous," he wrote. "Mortars fell around our position almost from the beginning. However, the position was on terraces and the...rounds were hitting on a higher terrace and nobody in my outfit was hit. The outing went just like a training exercise."

Glenn V. Ellison with Co. F recalled seeing the ROKs and North Koreans fighting in the high mountains flanking the company as it rolled forward to the LD on trucks. The troops dismounted, and the attack began. The tanks fired at targets of opportunity as they rumbled forward. The infantry swept the lower hills, struggling to keep up with the tanks. Co. G experienced difficulty negotiating the slopes, delaying its advance. As a result, at 5:30 p.m., Co. F was brought forward and Co. E extended itself to the left. This placed G to the left rear of the battalion, along the road and following Co. F

The regiment moved forward without opposition for an hour, as enemy outposts withdrew. The enemy's main line was located about two and a half miles farther on. The 27th advanced about 3,000 yards when COL Michaelis received a message that the ROKs on either flank had been held up by the enemy. Of the fighting that day, GEN Paik wrote that it was one of attack and counterattack for his men, with bayonets and grenades doing most of the killing. Some of his men developed sore shoulders from throwing so many grenades. He also noted that enemy troops had infiltrated his lines and were poised to attack rear areas.

Michaelis was ordered to stop and establish a defensive position in the valley astride the road. In peacetime, this would have been a very pretty area. The road, almost straight, was lined with Lombardy poplar trees. Paddies and fields covered the flat areas of the valley, most of them to the west of the road, which was closer to the base of the mountain to the east. The mountains which rose steeply on both flanks of the valley, were covered with trees. The lower slopes contained some scrub brush. A small stream ran along the west side of the road. About a mile or so north of where the 27th halted, near the village of Chonpyong, the road forked. The left fork went northwest to Sangju and the right one northeast to Kunwi.

Dusk was approaching when the order to halt and set up a defense reached the forward companies. It was about 8 p.m. Some of the officers of 1st Battalion assembled on the road to receive orders for the defense. While they were standing there, an enemy column, led by two tanks and an SP gun came down the road. The second tank and the SP gun fired in the general direction of Fox Co. on the right of the road, but it was obvious that this fire was indiscriminate. The enemy did not know exactly where U.S. troops were located. Then enemy artillery and mortar fire began falling throughout the area. The officers scrambled back to their respective commands. (See Chapter Notes.)

The approach of enemy armor was promptly reported by radio to the 1st Battalion CP. When first sighted, the enemy armor, flanked by infantrymen, was near the village of Chonpyong, 800 yards forward of the leading elements of the 27th. The commander of the attached C/73d Tk Bn, overheard the report. To meet the threat, two M-26 tanks of the 1st Platoon were moved out in a column onto a stretch of road just north of a blown bridge. The remaining tanks of the platoon stayed deployed in a stream bed which was more or less at right angles to the road. The 3d Platoon was in a column on the road further to the rear. The tanks were each about 75 yards apart.

It was now a little after 8 p.m. The men in the 1st Platoon's lead tank could hear the approach of enemy armor about 550 yards away, and around a bend in the road. The lead enemy tank stopped and fired. The round was 25 yards short. The second round hit a U.S. vehicle, setting it on fire. In its light the American tankers spotted a T-34 about 300 yards away, accompanied by infantrymen in the ditches. Two T-34s,

following the first, opened fire on the M-26s to the rear with their main guns and machine guns. They apparently did not see the leading U.S. tanks. But the lead M-26 returned fire with an HE round, striking the front plate of the first enemy tank. Five HVAP (high velocity armor piercing) rounds were then sent into this tank, destroying it. The remaining tanks of the 1st Platoon then engaged the four remaining enemy tanks.

Before the enemy attacked, it had been decided that Co. F would be responsible for the road. It was Co F which met the enemy attack with effective 3.5 inch bazooka fire. It was only after this attack was beaten off that the two battalions were able to form the defensive position assigned to them.

As the enemy column approached, CPT Jung deployed half of his Co B into the paddies to the left of the road. Darkness was coming on fast. The enemy was taken under artillery fire and rocket launcher teams from Co. F engaged two tanks. The second tank was destroyed by a rocket hit. The first tank was struck by two rounds rocket rounds, which failed to explode, but the enemy abandoned this tank. Artillery fire accounted for the SP gun and two trucks. Co. B held its fire until the enemy infantry closed to within 50 yards then sent a blast of small-arms and automatic fire into them. Co. B's 1st Platoon attempted to get its 3.5 inch rocket launcher into play, but Fox Co. had already engaged the lead tanks.

LT Dixie Parker was an FO for the 8th FAB and was with Co F when the enemy attacked. He and his three men were in an observation post. One tank stopped about 15 to 20 feet from them. Parker and his companions could hear the enemy talking inside the tank. Then the tank's 85mm main gun fired. The concussion was unnerving. "About 2400 (midnight) I decided to do something about them stinking tanks," Dixie recalled. He ran to the rear, picked up a 3.5 inch rocket launcher and some ammunition and returned to the OP.

"We sneaked a quick peek and let fly," he said. "The instant it (the rocket) was out of the tube, we scuttled like mad about 10 feet to our right. We missed.... That rocket whizzing by from nowhere must have scared the pants off those Reds. They recovered rapidly and... (turning) their machine guns around, poured a hail of lead into the place we had been. They kept traversing, probing for us and the tracers were terrible, yet fascinating." Then Parker's men spotted a second tank. They got it with one rocket. "With a helluva roar and a big flash the tank was dead," Parker said.

Glenn V. Ellison of Co. F, with two others, was in a foxhole on a dike next to the road that night. Ellison had his carbine and a portable flamethrower. One of his companions was armed with a BAR and the other with an M1 rifle. To their right a crew manned a heavy, water-cooled .30-cal machine gun. Behind Ellison, partially shielded by the dike, was an American tank. As Ellison put it, "It was going to get real interesting."

When the enemy tanks and SP guns attacked that evening, a 76mm SP round hit next to Ellison's foxhole, showering the occupants with rocks and dirt. (This was probably the enemy

round, mentioned above, and was probably 85mm, not 76.) He was slightly wounded. But worse, the exploding round had blown their weapons out of reach down the front face of the hole. Machine gun fire from the tank behind them and answering enemy machine gun fire crisscrossed overhead. "Bullets and tracers were flying in all directions," Ellison recalled.

Lacking their weapons and afraid of being killed by the machine gun duel trying to retrieve them, Ellison and his buddies periodically rolled hand grenades out of their hole.

To add to the confusion, one of the men in the hole had been hit hard by a flying rock, which had dented his helmet. For awhile, the poor man thought he had been fatally wounded.

1LT Lewis Millett, who was awarded the Medal of Honor later in the war, was an artillery observer for the 8th FAB with the Wolfhounds in the Bowling Alley. He called in artillery fire on the enemy when their tanks got within 50 feet of his foxhole. By 30 minutes past midnight, the enemy had had enough. Three of the surviving tanks turned on their running lights and fled north. In addition to two tanks, the enemy lost an SP gun and at least two trucks to artillery fire, and about 100 men.

LT Posie L. Starkey, commanding the Machine Gun Platoon, Co. D, had his guns attached to B and C Companies. He was with B. He recalled that night as "a turkey shoot when the tanks and SPs tried to come into the battalion position. I can still see the silhouettes of the burning vehicles and the thunderous artillery fire concentrated on the attackers."

Another, weaker attack against companies E and F came about 2:30 a.m. on next day, but was broken up by artillery and mortar fire.

As 27th Infantry finally organized near the tiny hamlet of Soi-ri, the 1st Battalion was on the left of the road and the 2d Battalion on the right, with responsibility for the road. Co. B was just to the left of the road and Co. F, 2d Battalion. CPT Merchant of Co. F and CPT Jung, of B, wanted to ensure they were "tied in" where the two units met. "I remember getting together with Captain Merchant," Jung wrote, "and we exchanged squads at the road to make sure we were tied in." Co. B's 2d Platoon, under Platoon Sergeant James R. Wilson, occupied the company's right next to Fox Co. 1LT John B. Hammond's platoon of Co. F tied in with Wilson. Co. B carried the line west over the rice paddies and into the lower slopes of Yuhak-san. Co. C was to Baker's left front, occupying a finger ridge about 400 yards forward of Co. B, which afforded observation of the enemy's approach. Co. A was located on a ridge just behind Company B's left flank. On that flank, from front to rear, were Co. C, the left flank platoon (the 1st Platoon) of Co. B and Co. A.

The 2d Battalion's Co F guarded the road. Company E was to its right and up the slopes. George Co. held a ridge behind Co. E. (See Chapter Notes.)

The regiment presented a four company front with both flanks refused. Two tanks were placed on the front line, two more in the stream bed, and four more were farther back in reserve. The 8th and 37th FABs, each less one battery, were in position behind the infantry. The new 3d Battalion (recently 3/29th Infantry), commanded by

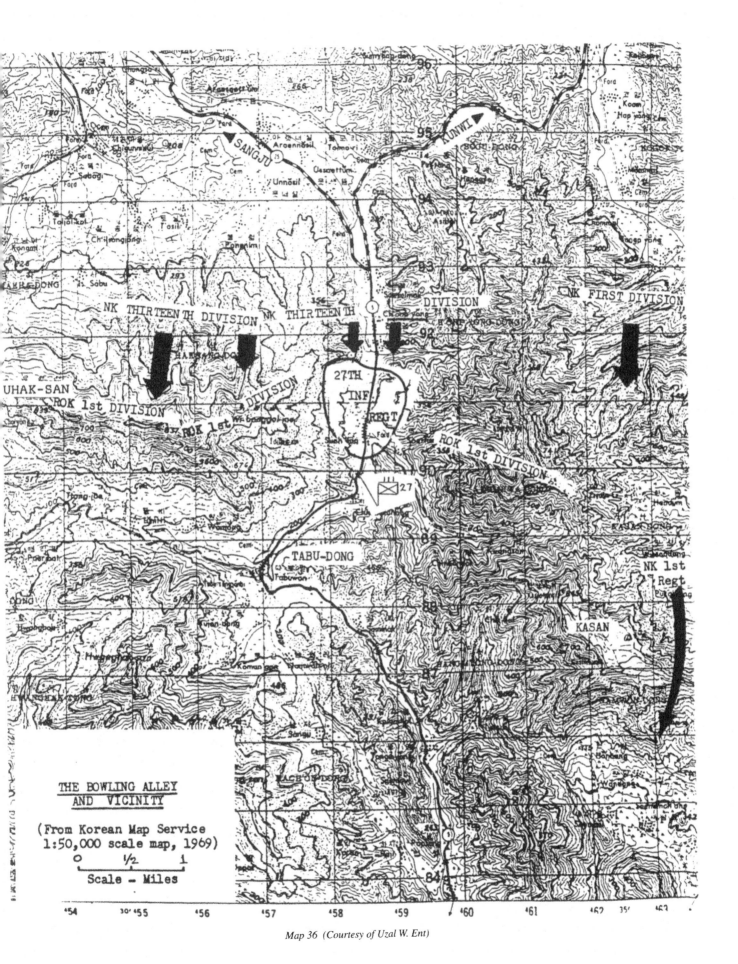

Map 36 (Courtesy of Uzal W. Ent)

MAJ George H. DeChow, was assigned the mission of securing the high ground on either side of the MSR near the village of Soya. In effect, this also was the rear of the regimental area. Companies I and K occupied the right of the road, overlooking the positions of the 1st and 2d Battalions, and Co L the left. "By darkness, positions were secured," reads the Battalion Operations Report for August. "Immediately thereafter enemy artillery and tank fire began falling in the Battalion sector. During the nights [of] 18 and 19 August, 1950, 300 rounds of enemy artillery landed in the Battalion area." Only two casualties, both wiremen, were killed by all this fire.

Bowling Alley Area — Aug. 19

On the morning of Aug. 19, the ROK 11th and 13th Regiments attacked along the ridges, making small gains. The ROK 10th Infantry was brought into the ROK 1st Division sector to close a gap in their lines. The 2d and 3d Battalions of the 23d Infantry were also brought to the rear of the Bowling Alley area that day. The 3d Battalion established a perimeter to protect the 8th and 37th FABs. The 2d Battalion went into position astride the MSR behind the 27th Infantry. CPT Frank U. Roquemore, Assistant S-3 of the 27th, made contact with COL Paul Freeman, commanding the 23d and relayed these orders to him.

Heavy enemy mortar fire forced the relocation of 3/27th Infantry's CP. The new location was in a deep, narrow cut, about 500 yards from the regimental CP, which was under a road bridge. At 5:22 p.m., enemy heavy mortars landed in the Battalion motor pool area, near the M Co. CP and the Battalion Aid Station. One man was killed and four wounded by this fire. The Battalion XO, CPT Robert M. Flynn, supervised the displacement of all the units in the area struck by the enemy mortars. Co. C, 65th ECB and C/73d Tk Bn (-one platoon) were attached to the 3d Battalion. The battalion perimeter was adjusted to include the engineer company.

A/8th FAB was subjected to heavy enemy artillery, mortar and small arms fire beginning about 3:45 p.m., resulting in 2 KIA and 12 WIA. The men stayed with their guns and continued to fire missions in spite of heavy counter-battery fire. During the worst part of the attack, some of the howitzers were turned to fire point blank at enemy infantrymen.

A number of air strikes were called in on known or suspected enemy artillery and mortar positions during the day, coupled with fire from the 8th FAB.

That night, a company-sized force of enemy troops attacked GEN Paik's CP. Luckily, a battalion of the ROK 10th Infantry was close by. The battalion quickly repelled the enemy. GEN Paik wrote that subsequent information revealed that the raid had been made to find and kill him.

Bowling Alley Area — Aug. 20

Aug. 20 was fairly quiet during the day. Aircraft strafed enemy positions, beginning their runs so close to friendly lines that their machine gun fire hit the air panels and expended .50-cal

cartridge casings fell into U.S. foxholes. In general, however, the Wolfhounds were able to improve their positions, lay mines, etc. The 1st Platoon of Co. B had the unusual experience of being deployed over an area which had been swept clear of earth by erosion. As a result, most of the men were able to construct foxholes by removing stones and boulders and piling them up to form parapets. However, in some places, they struck water about five feet down. The foxhole shared by the platoon leader and platoon sergeant was one of these. The platoon was on a 50 per cent alert every night. The platoon leader and platoon sergeant took their turns on alert. The person resting, or trying to sleep in the bottom of the hole <u>always</u> ended up with a wet behind. Even using empty C-ration cases to try to absorb the water did not work. Otherwise, the stay in the Bowling Alley was fairly easy for the platoon. Being above the valley, the men had a ringside seat for the nightly fireworks, as the enemy strove to break through. The company's 2d Platoon and neighboring platoon or two of Co. F turned back every attack, with very few casualties. GEN Walker, visiting the Taegu front during the day, later stated that Taegu "certainly is saved."

During the previous night, an enemy repair crew came out to work on one of the knocked-out T-34s. In the morning, 17 year old BAR-man Daniel Cooper and three other riflemen from G/27th Infantry were sent out on a patrol to disable the tank's main gun. "It was several hundred yards in front and within their [the enemy's] range most of the way," said Cooper. "We took off down the road, using whatever cover we could find and made our way to the tank." Cooper didn't remember being fired on, but he admitted, they were so intent on getting to the tank, disabling the gun and getting back to their lines, that the men ignored everything else.

When the patrol arrived at the tank, they decided not to open the hatch; it was probably booby trapped. They had nothing with which to disable the gun. As they puzzled over the problem, one of the men suggested stuffing mud down the barrel. And that is what they did, then returned to friendly lines. That night, Cooper, recalled, "They [the enemy] were back out there and fired one shot and that was the end of that barrel and anyone else that was standing around. The picture of that tank with the flared barrel made the Associated Press, *Life* Magazine and all. And that was my little part of the Bowling Alley."

At 5 p.m., enemy 120mm mortar fire struck the Heavy Weapons Co. area. Then, silhouetted by a bright moon, enemy tanks, with supporting infantry, ground forward down the valley. They were first taken under mortar and artillery fire. When the enemy infantry came within 150-200 yards of the foxhole line, American machine guns, BARs, rifles and company 60mm mortars opened a devastating fire, repulsing the attack. Milton R. Olazagasti with the 60mm Mortar Section of Co. F wrote: "We had set up our mortars in a gully...." He and another man from the section were dug in near the road. He recalled that, at first he was happy about this, because he didn't have to climb a hill to dig in. "Later on," he said, "I was to regret that be-

cause we were right in the middle of the action." When the enemy attacked, the 60mm mortars joined in to repel every attack. Olazagasti thought maybe they set a record for rounds fired. "Anyway," he said, "we fired a hell of a lot of rounds in those three or four nights...."

The leader of 3d Platoon, C/73d Tk Bn could not see the enemy tanks because the night was pitch black. His tank got off the first round, but missed. A T-34's answering shot also missed. After firing that one round, the enemy tank turned around and retreated, hastened by several more rounds from the M-26. Unknown to the ROKs and Americans, the *15th Division* left the Bowling Alley sector this day, to move east in support of the *NK 8th Division*, which was trying to cut the Taegu-Pohang-dong road.

Bowling Alley Area — Aug. 21

On the morning of Aug. 21 white flags were observed in front of the American lines. Korean civilians reported that enemy soldiers wanted to surrender. At 9:45 a.m., therefore, the 3d Platoon of Co. B a platoon from Co. G and the 1st and 3d Platoons, C/73d Tk Bn were sent out to investigate and to obtain an estimate of enemy losses. The patrol progressed about 1,500 yards, receiving some artillery fire and skirmishing with small groups of North Koreans. When enemy SP guns opened up on the patrol, it was ordered back. The patrol saw one destroyed enemy 37mm AT gun with its crew, dead; one disabled tank with crew; one 120mm mortar and two SP guns (already destroyed) and five disabled tanks, which were destroyed by thermite grenades. The patrol also saw the bodies of about 20 other enemy soldiers. The patrol returned to friendly lines without loss, except in Co D, supporting the patrol, where two men were killed and two more were wounded.

The 73d Tk Bn report records that the tanks accompanying this patrol knocked out one SU-76 SP gun in the pass to the right of the road and two T-34s parked in a schoolyard south of Chonpyong.

At dusk, the 2d Battalion placed an antitank mine field with antipersonnel mines and trip flares 150 yards in front of Co. F. A hasty mine field was placed about 100 yards forward of the buried mines to deceive the enemy. The mines were booby trapped and machine guns were sited to cover both fields. The enemy shelled the general area heavily from 8:35 p.m. to 10:35 p.m.

Meantime, GEN Paik had decided to launch an attack the next day. But the enemy beat him to the punch. He wrote that the enemy loosed barrages of hand grenades and mortar fire on his men, then followed up with massive infantry assaults. It was hand-to-hand fighting all over again. (See Chapter Notes.)

Bowling Alley — Aug. 22

C/73d Tk Bn carefully planned for the next enemy attack. The crews of the 2d and 4th Platoons took over the tanks of the 1st and 3d Platoons, respectively. The five tanks of 2d Platoon remained deployed in the creek bed on the left of the road. The five tanks of the 4th Platoon moved up in a staggered column along both sides of the road. The lead tank stopped just beyond and to the right of the T-34 which had been destroyed on the night of Aug. 18-19. The tank positions were selected to afford the best camouflage and fields of fire. All tank guns and rocket launchers were zeroed in on the road.

Enemy flat trajectory fire began about 10 p.m. from several thousand yards out. In all, about 250 rounds came in over the next several hours, most of it directed at the MLR. Responding U.S. artillery fire concentrated on the road junction. The 73d Tk Bn account gives the enemy as eight tanks, four 76mm SP guns, an unknown number of trucks and a regiment of infantry, advancing from a position about 2000 yards forward of the 27th Infantry's defense line. The artillery fire seemed to halt this advance.

A transmission came in from Co. C up forward. "Able Charlie to Amazing Able, over," it began. This was Charlie's commander, CPT Alfred S. Burnett, calling from his advanced position to report the sound of tanks to his front. The artillery fired illuminating rounds. It was 1:37 a.m. In their light, he counted 19 enemy vehicles in a column on the road. They were part of a major assault by the *13th Division* against the ROKs and 27th Infantry. Nine tanks, a number of SP guns and North Korean infantrymen moved rapidly on the road and flanking ground toward the Americans. The tanks and SP guns fired as they lumbered along. Most of the fire landed in rear areas.

American artillery and mortar fire poured down on the approaching enemy. They were joined by machine gun, BAR and rifle fire as the enemy neared the front-line foxholes. U.S. tanks held their fire until the lead North Korean tank stopped about 50 yards from the first M-26. The U.S. tank fired, hitting the leading T-34 abreast of the driver. About the same time, a rocket launcher round also struck the tank. The second vehicle, a tank, was disabled by a rocket fired by F Company's Frank Schivone. The crew was killed trying to escape. The M-26 then shifted its fire to the second enemy tank. The first round of HVAP missed. But the second struck the T-34 in the side, bogie and into the ground. Someone later painted "27TH INFANTRY COURTESY FOX CO." on the side of this tank. (See Chapter Notes.)

The third enemy vehicle in line was a 76mm SP gun. It had been firing up the draw east of the road. This SP gun fired the only enemy shot at U.S. tanks that night. The round hit the ground. Records of the 27th Infantry claim that a Fox Co. rocket launcher team disabled this gun; the 73d Tk Bn claims that the leading M-26 set the vehicle on fire with its fourth shot. Both accounts can be correct. The M-26 then pumped five more rounds into the leading enemy tank, joined by the fire from three other American tanks. The fourth vehicle in the enemy column, a T-34, quickly turned and fled.

About a platoon of enemy infantry were with the tanks; 10 of them riding on the first T-34. Ten of 15 of these infantrymen were killed, and the others withdrew. Most of the enemy infantry and vehicles never got close enough to be engaged by U.S. tanks. More SP guns, several

trucks and personnel carriers were destroyed by artillery fire.

Phil File, with Co A, described the action from his vantage point. "The NK tanks started shooting blindly down the center of the road," he wrote. From our vantage point, the red hot shells going straight down the road in the black of night suggested bowling balls rolling down a darkened alley." The enemy tanks were firing armor piercing ammunition. Each round flashed through the darkness as a flaming ball. Some rounds ricocheted off the road, and caromed off erratically into the night sky.

Tankers LT Jesse F. Vansant of the tank named "Alma" and SGT Howard Ezell of "Ida" got three T34s at point blank range. The battle raged on for five hours. The 8th FAB fired 1,661 rounds, the 4.2 inch heavy mortars 902. The 81mm mortars pumped out another 1,200 rounds and Fox Co.'s 60mm mortars fired 385. The 37th FAB must have fired almost 1,400 rounds. In a letter home, CPT Joseph W. Terman, who was working in the FDC, wrote, "We fired over 3,000 rounds during the night...."

Almost at first light, LTC Check went forward to get a first-hand report of the battle. CPT Merchant asked him to compliment Company B on their machine gun support. "Their machine-gunning was beautiful, just beautiful," he said, happily.

The enemy suffered terrible losses. Based on patrol reports after daylight, it was estimated that the North Koreans lost 1,300 men in the battle. Eleven prisoners taken by the patrol confirmed that only about one-quarter of the attackers survived. The 27th Regimental Historical report for Aug. 1950 put the number of enemy tanks destroyed that night at 9, along with 6 SP guns and two trucks. It was learned later that the North Korean division commander blamed MAJ Kim Song Jun, commanding the *19th Regiment* for incompetence and failure to coordinate the action of his regiment with the rest of the division in this battle.

While the Americans and ROKs battled the North Koreans in the valley and on the flanking ridges, the *NK 1st Regiment, 1st Division*, slipped around the eastern flank and appeared at noon of Aug. 22 six miles in rear of the 27th. They covered the MSR with fire over a five mile span northward from a point just nine miles above Taegu.

At 4:05 p.m., "the enemy began the most intense shelling of our position encountered during the campaign," recorded the 8th FAB War Diary for Aug. 1950. At 4:30 p.m., "the FDC received two direct hits instantly killing four officers and two non-commissioned officers," the War Diary continued. Killed were MAJ Byron D. Magee, Bn XO; CPT Sten E. Westin, Asst S-3; CPT Joseph W. Terman, Liaison Officer; 1LT Teddy B. Akins, Asst S-2; MSG Kenneth S. Richards, Intelligence SGT and SFC James O. Relogle, Communications SGT. Eight other men were wounded. Millard Fletcher remembered that he had just relieved MAJ Magee and had walked about a hundred feet from the FDC when the mortar fire came in. "I was knocked to the ground and rolled into a ditch, was not hit. One round made a direct dead center hit on the command post," Fletcher wrote. Just that morning Terman had written to his wife

about how he had been slightly wounded a few days previously. He ended the letter by writing, "Other than for scratches I am embarassingly [*sic*] healthy."

The individual batteries almost immediately took over control and continued to fire. The 8th FAB CP, however, had to displace under fire. "Some of the men had to move out on foot and make their way through the hills to one of the battery positions," the Battalion War Diary recorded. Lew Millett had been at the Battalion CP when it came under long range machine gun fire. He jumped on a truck and returned fire with its ring-mounted .50-cal machine gun until ordered to let the infantry get the enemy gun. Angrily, Millet jumped into his jeep and tore back to Co. F.

The 27th Regimental CP also came under heavy enemy attack. Machine gun fire laced the position. CPT Frank U. "Rocky" Roquemore, Assistant S-3, described the situation. "The regimental command post was receiving machine gun fire direct from [a nearby hill]. My driver and three others were wounded. The tanks, [in a little draw] placed direct 90mm fire and eliminated that particular position."

But the enemy attack continued so heavily that Michaelis called artillery down on his own position. He later described it as "awesome." Air support was then requested. B-25 bombers, looking for a target, were contacted. Michaelis' air controller asked them to drop their bombs. The flight leader responded that if they did it would hit the CP. The air controller said that it "didn't make a bit of difference because [they] would be dead anyway." The bombers dropped 4,400 pounds of bombs and, as Michaelis put it, "that blocked it."

In the midst of this crisis, COL Michaelis got a report that the ROKs of the 1st Division were being driven from the mountains on his left. Alarmed, he reported to higher headquarters that the ROKs had given way. Some American troops received word to force the ROKs back up the mountain, if they had to shoot some of them in the effort.

A platoon leader of Co. B, into whose unit ROKs had come for food, water, ammunition, or medical treatment over the previous few days, thought the order to be ridiculous. He could not accept the "shoot if necessary" order without personal investigation. He discovered, as Michaelis and other leaders did later, that large numbers of ROKs were out of ammunition, food and water. (See Chapter Notes.)

GEN Paik had received a report that a battalion of his 11th Regiment had been thrown off the ridge by the enemy. Soon after, he got an angry telephone call from Eighth Army. The voice at the other end wanted to know "what the hell's wrong with the ROK Army?" Michaelis threatened to withdraw, Paik recalled.

The general was highly offended that Michaelis had so little faith in his soldiers. He went to investigate himself and found the battalion, "retreating in a state of utter exhaustion." He learned that the command had been cut off for two days and had been without water all that time. He reorganized the troops. "Look at those American troops over there," he told them. "They're fighting because they trust the ROK Army, and if we retreat, we bring shame down on the entire ROK Army.... We're going to...kick the enemy off our ridge,..." And that's what they did. Some American observers said that the ROKs charged right into their own supporting artillery to get at the enemy.

Michaelis later apologized to GEN Paik. His men were having as tough a time defending the rugged mountain as the 27th did the lower slopes. The Wolfhounds greatly admired and respected the soldiers of the ROK 1st Division after this campaign.

Every night before an attack North Korean red or green flares eerily lit the sky at various points along the front. A red flare meant that they had located a strong American or ROK position. The green indicated a gap, or weak point in the lines. The 27th got some red and green flares and fired them to confuse the enemy or lure the North Koreans into killing zones. There is little evidence these flares deceived the enemy.

In the Bowling Alley, Michaelis was beset by correspondents, such as Joseph Alsop, Jim Lucas, David Duncan, Harold Martin and, of course, Maggie Higgins. The Regimental S-3 and his men hated to see them come. The culvert CP was very crowded and not a stand-up place. As a result, when these newspeople seated themselves to interview "Mike" Michaelis, their bodies usually inadvertently wiped out all grease pencil marks on the battle map.

Baker Company's CP was near a persimmon tree. One morning, at daybreak, the men discovered a lone enemy soldier sitting next to the tree eating a persimmon. He was starved. CPT Jung remembered that the man's belt "could have gone around his waist twice."

Baker's First Sergeant, George S. Hearn, described by New York *Herald Tribune* correspondent as "a massive man with a fresh shrapnel dimple in his cheek who learned ground fighting as a lieutenant in Merrill's Marauders," was the quintessential rifle company first sergeant. Alsop also described him as "fatherly." But Hearn was the top soldier in the unit in title and as a soldier. His fatherliness sometimes came out when dealing with very young soldiers, as when he gave a man named Prokov his orders for the night. "Now you, Prokov," he said, "you're a messenger tonight. Regardless of what's afallin' you've got to get out to the platoons on order. But you'll be all right if you learn where all the platoons are at." Hearn could also be very tough.

Jim Trumble rejoined Co. E in the Bowling Alley, after recovering from wounds. "All I had to do was dig a foxhole and relate how nice it was back in the hospital with all those beds, clean sheets, ice cream, cold drinks [and] showers...." But then he relented and passed out new socks he had brought back. What impressed Jim the most about the Bowling Alley was that "we were able to stand our ground and stop those Russian tanks."

The surrender of LTC Chong Pong Uk, commander of the *13th Division* artillery, on Aug. 22 was of great importance to the defenders of the Bowling Alley area. Smarting from a rebuke by his commanding general for failure to shell Tabu-dong, he deserted by walking up to a ROK 1st Division position about 10 a.m. and surrendering. He believed that terrain obstacles prevented his artillery from reaching the town. Chong reported that seven operable 122mm howitzers and thirteen 76mm guns were dug in and

camouflaged in an orchard four and a half miles north of Tabu-dong near a village on the north side of Yuhak-san, and that 700 rounds of ammunition remained on hand. Fighter bombers and U.S. artillery pummeled the orchard. He also said that the *13th Division* was down to about 3,000 men, only 1,000 of which were infantry and that the division had only three tanks and seven of its original sixteen 76mm AP guns.

Aug. 22 also was a day of triumph for the ROK 1st Division. Over the previous several days, its 12th Regiment had unsuccessfully assaulted the peak of Yuhak-san. But in an attack that night the regiment destroyed the enemy there, and drove the survivors away.

CPT Merchant's F Co. had borne the brunt of the nightly enemy attacks in the Bowling Alley. A *Time* Magazine article of Sept. 4, 1950 provides a vignette of Merchant and one of his platoon leaders, 2LT Doyle D. Lummus. Lummus had been awarded a battlefield commission on Aug. 14. The article described the two men thusly: "They looked like Bill Mauldin's Willie and Joe. Both wore filthy fatigues and week's growth of beard. Their shoulders slumped and their buttons were unbuttoned.

They were perfect examples of what ...officers should never, never look like." The dead bodies and parts of bodies of the enemy were strewn around the area. "The flies were terrible and the stench worse," the article continues. A dog wandered up and began gnawing at one of the bodies. A GI hurled a rock at the dog, hitting it in the ribs, sending it away howling.

As they sat there, Merchant held a cup of C-ration coffee. Three flies flew into the cup. Merchant just looked at them. "You're not going to drink that stuff now?" asked a correspondent. "Those flies just came off those dead over there in the ditch."

Without emotion, Merchant looked at the flies and said, "What the hell, I've been drinking coffee with flies in it for a month and it ain't hurt me yet." With that, he took a big swallow.

The *NK 1st Regiment* Attacks the 2d Battalion, 23d Infantry — Aug. 22. (See Chapter Notes.)

On Aug. 20, the 2d Battalion, 23d Infantry (LTC James W. Edwards) was ordered to the

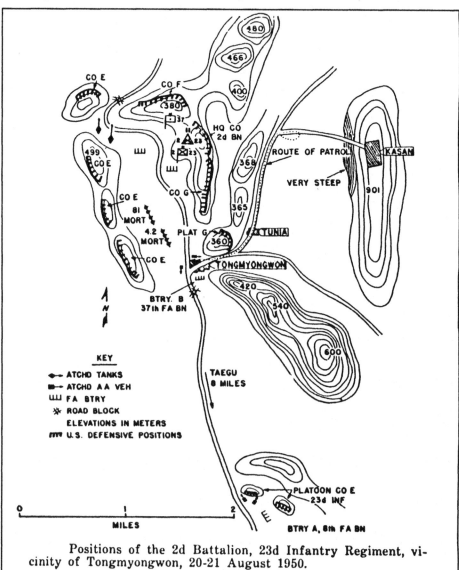

Positions of the 2d Battalion, 23d Infantry Regiment, vicinity of Tongmyongwon, 20-21 August 1950.

Map 37 - Positions of 2/23d Infantry, vicinity of Tongmyongwon, 20-21 August 1950. (Source: "Action at Tongmyongwon," LTC James W. Edwards, Infantry School Quarterly, Jan. 1951)

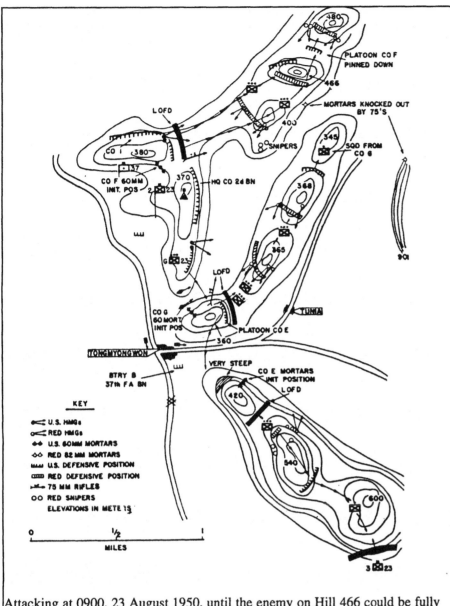

Attacking at 0900, 23 August 1950, until the enemy on Hill 466 could be fully occupied by Company F's attack.

Map 38 - Action on 23 August 1950, attacking at 0900 until the enemy on Hill 466 could be fully occupied by Company F's attack.

Tongmyongwon area to provide security for the 8th and 37th FABs in that area. The battalion was at about 75 per cent of full strength, with 60 per cent of the officers and 30 per cent of the enlisted men combat veterans of WW II. The bulk of the artillery was positioned in a long, narrow valley running north-northwest from the village, with Battery A, 8th FAB, about two miles south of the town. Edwards formed a perimeter on the nearby hills, with Co. E on the north and along the western flank. Co. F also started in the north, with its line running generally south along a ridge across the valley to the east of Easy Co. Elements of the 2d Battalion HC was south of Fox Co., with Co. G completing the line on that flank and on a small knob on the southern flank. One platoon of Co E was sent to provide security for A/8th FAB farther south. One section of two 75mm recoilless rifles and a 3.5 inch rocket launcher, part of each section, was emplaced on either flank of the battalion perimeter. The 75's

on each flank were placed so that they could be mutually supporting.

About a mile and half to the east was mighty Hill 902 — Kasan. On its summit were the ruins of an ancient fort. Whoever occupied Kasan had the dominant terrain feature for many miles around.

Although 75 rounds of 82mm and 120mm mortar and some artillery fire hit the area the night of Aug. 21-22, only two artillerymen were slightly wounded. Richard Shand of Co. E wrote, "We dug in. That night all Hell broke loose. Mortar fire was very heavy. We held." Leslie C. Sholar, H Co., remembered that the unit's 81mm mortar platoon was set up near the artillery positions. From there they supported the battalion's infantrymen, including firing illuminating rounds during the night.

During the night, the .50-cal machine gun from the 75mm Recoilless Rifle Platoon was integrated into the defensive fires of the battal-

ion. The "50" helped silence the enemy for the rest of the night.

At 8 a.m., five mortar rounds landed in Tongmyongwon. Then How Co.'s 81s began firing on suspected enemy positions on Hill 902. At 11 a.m., a 4.2 inch mortar platoon arrived and was attached to 2/23d Infantry. It soon also began firing on suspected enemy OPs on Kasan. Since enemy mortar and artillery fire became more accurate, it was obvious that the enemy observers were adjusting it. The battalion then placed a 75mm recoilless rifle in G Co.'s area so that it could also take enemy OPs under fire. LT Phil R. Garn commanded the 75mm Recoilless Rifle Platoon. "Our first targets at Tongmyongwon were bunched personnel and crew-served weapons," he wrote. "One gunner spotted a machine gun firing. Range — about 1500 yards. Score — direct hit with the second round." No other targets being in sight, the gun was left aimed where it was. "In about ten minutes another enemy machine gun was observed going into the same position," he continued. "That gun was destroyed by the first round."

Replacements arrived at 8 a.m., bringing companies of the battalion up to 98 per cent of full strength.

About 1 p.m. on Aug. 22, the 2d Battalion OP reported an estimated 50 enemy soldiers approaching Hill 360. A platoon of Co. G occupied the reverse slope of this hill. Coincidentally, a group of 150 engineer recruits for the ROK 1st Division appeared near Hill 360. Battalion sent a Japanese-American soldier to contact the leader of this contingent and request their help in securing the crest of Hill 360. By this time, the enemy force had increased to some 200 men. G Co.'s platoon charged to the crest. The green Korean troops added what help they could. On top of the hill the North Koreans and Americans met head-on. The G Co. platoon kept attacking, although their platoon leader and platoon sergeant had been felled by enemy fire. To help meet this threat, a platoon of Co E was ordered to the G platoon's assistance and the remainder of Co. E was brought down from their hill positions to assemble behind Co. G's right flank as battalion reserve.

The E Co. platoon came up on the G platoon's right flank, and the two units pressed the attack, supported by artillery and 4.2 inch mortar fire. The E platoon advanced in the face of heavy machine gun fire, forcing 50 enemy soldiers off Hill 360, killing most of them. At the same time, the G Company platoon with the 150 South Koreans, attacking abreast of E's platoon cleared another 150 North Koreans from the rest of Hill 360. All units had used marching fire in the attack. By 3 p.m., Hill 360 belonged to the 23d Infantry. Almost immediately, enemy machine gun and mortar fire came from the nearby village of Tunia. Artillery and heavy mortar fire set the village aflame, ending the enemy fire. The South Korean recruits were released from Hill 360, but the platoons of Companies E and G remained.

At 11 a.m., a squad of Co. F was sent about 500 yards or so forward of the unit to outpost Hill 400. The squad was on position within the hour. The 4.2 inch mortar platoon leader, seeking a better OP, also went to Hill 400. At 1 p.m., an enemy force estimated at 500 men, or an enemy battalion, suddenly dashed at Hill 400 from a nearby hill. The rifle squad successfully retreated, firing at the enemy as they did so. But the officer was cut off by enemy soldiers, run down and bayonetted to death. U.S. machine guns, in turn, cut down several of the enemy soldiers who had killed the lieutenant and kept the others from his body.

Then the enemy made a concerted attack on F Co. Pre-registered artillery and 81mm mortar fire decimated the oncoming North Koreans. Automatic weapons, small-arms and the company 60mm mortars dropped many more, driving the enemy off before they could get within 200 yards of the company position.

During the attack, MSG Jesse L. Bishop, commanding Co. F's Weapons Platoon, obtained permission to move one mortar squad "to high ground in rear of First Platoon in order to give riflemen better close in support." The squad, with men from the other mortar squads acting as ammo bearers, "immediately moved forward to high ground and took up fire on enemy positions," Bishop wrote. One of his men, PFC Joe Cannon, was wounded in the hand, but refused medical attention.

At 3:30 p.m., Co. E (less two of its platoons), was ordered to take Hill 420, at the southern end of the perimeter, just above the location of B/8th FAB's firing positions. The enemy was firing on Hill 360 from that 420. Hill 420 was very steep and high. A 10-minute artillery preparation was fired on it, then Easy Co. moved out, supported by 81mm mortar fire. Enemy troops not driven away by the mortar and artillery fire were shot down or bayonetted by the steadily advancing infantrymen. By 5:30 p.m., the hill was in Easy's hands. The company chased about 50 North Koreans. Only about 15 of them reached the village of Tunia, a few hundred yards away.

About 2 p.m., LTC Edwards, who had been directing the battle from his OP, asked the regimental commander, COL Paul Freeman, for the loan of a rifle company to replace Co. E on the hills to the battalion's left flank. Freeman immediately sent Co I, which arrived at 4 p.m. The 2d Battalion XO placed the unit on the positions vacated by Co. E.

A patrol from Co. E was sent south on the ridge from Hill 420 to Hill 540, arriving there about 6:30 p.m. No enemy was encountered, and the patrol returned to Hill 420.

Just about the time that Item Co. arrived to cover the battalions left flank, an estimated enemy battalion launched a heavy attack on Hill 360. The U.S. battalion met them with barrages of artillery and 4.2 inch mortar fire. This fire, coupled with automatic and small-arms fire from the Co E and G platoons killed large numbers of the enemy and by 4:45 p.m. sent the rest of them running back to their original positions.

About this time, more enemy troops began assembling forward of Co. F and the center of the battalion right flank hills. At 4:50 p.m., four F-51s came in, dropped three 500 pound bombs and strafed and rocketed this concentration of troops. The air strike ended at 5:45 p.m. Five minutes later, another enemy force, estimated at battalion size, started down Hill 400 toward Co. F. These troops, unlike the others this day, wore Russian type steel helmets instead of cloth caps, and were well equipped. Each man had small tree or shrub branches tied onto him. When the man squatted down, he was almost impossible to see. However, there were so many enemy troops, some were moving all the time. It created the impression of a forest of small trees approaching.

At the same time, another large force of North Koreans on high ground north of Hill 360 started toward the battalion's center on the hills that formed the right flank of the perimeter. But a flight of six A-20A attack bombers, led by a South Korean spotter plane came overhead at 5:55 p.m. The spotter located both enemy forces, and the bombers went to work. They dropped eighteen 500 pound bombs then strafed the enemy. One North Korean force was driven off in panic, but the steel-helmeted troops continued their attack as soon as the planes departed. Co F was soon under heavy mortar and machine gun fire.

At 7 p.m., the four F-51s returned to attack these enemy troops. When they left at 7:30 p.m., a flight of F-80 jets continued to pound the North Koreans. Some planes strafed just 200 yards in front of the infantry foxhole line. This unremitting bombardment finally broke up the steel-helmeted force, and they fled in disorganized confusion.

The platoon of Co. E protecting A/8th FAB was attacked at 7 p.m. by about 125 North Koreans. But the platoon, which was supported by one quad-.50 and one dual-40mm anti-aircraft vehicle from the 82d AAA Battalion and seven .50 caliber machinegun teams and BARs from Battery A, soon repulsed the attack, killing 60 enemy soldiers. Battery guns were sighted down the ravines, prepared to fire over open sights if the enemy had broken through.

Although the battalion experienced some small arms and occasional mortar fire, the night of Aug. 22-23 was fairly quiet.

Attacks of the 2d and 3d Battalions, 23d Infantry — Aug. 23-24

At 6:50 a.m. on Aug. 23, a ten minute artillery and mortar preparation was fired on the enemy occupying Hill 400 and the ridge beyond. At 7 a.m., Co. F jumped off in an attack, with two platoons abreast. Each platoon had a 57mm recoilless rifle attached. As the company advanced, 81mm mortar fire "walked" up the hill about a hundred yards forward of them. Some enemy riflemen and a machine gun opened fire, but were put out of action almost at once by American heavy machine guns, 60mm mortars and a 75mm recoilless rifle. The 75 hit the enemy gun with its second round. The enemy left 53 dead on Hill 400. A 75mm recoilless rifle located on Hill 360 destroyed an enemy 82mm mortar on the reverse slope of Hill 400 with one shot. Supporting fire from Co G and battalion headquarters personnel protected F Co.'s flank. Two tanks between Hills 360 and 370 also knocked out several enemy machine guns.

It is worthy of note that command and coordination was almost flawless because, unlike in the earlier days in the units coming from Japan, 2/23d Infantry had excellent radio and wire communication throughout the command and with supporting artillery.

Fox Co. had Hill 400 by 8 a.m. and the body of the 4.2 inch mortar platoon officer was recovered. A platoon of Co. I occupied the original positions of Co. F, and Fox continued on to the next objective. Once Fox had the enemy fully engaged there, LTC Edwards sent Co. G on their attack along a more or less parallel ridge from Hill 360 at 9:25 a.m., leaving one platoon to support the attack by fire. G's commander leapfrogged his two assault platoons from objective to objective, each with a 57mm recoilless rifle attached to it. The E Company platoon remained on Hill 360 for the time being. Co. F had all the artillery support, but 4.2 inch, 81mm and the unit 60's provided support to Co. G. The unit employed marching fire as it advanced. Every time the enemy rose to face them, the mortars and machine guns killed them. A 75mm recoilless rifle destroyed an enemy mortar setting up on Hill 902, with its second round at a range of some 2,000 yards. Co. G took its first objective at 10:50 a.m. The enemy left 38 dead behind. The trailing platoon assumed the lead, and George Co. made for its second objective, taking it by 11:45 a.m. The company was ordered to hold up there and reconnoiter the next hill forward. A patrol went forward, found the hill unoccupied, and stayed there the rest of the day.

Since Co. G had received so much flanking fire from Hill 902, an air strike was called in on it at 11 a.m. The planes started a fire on the hilltop, effectively silencing enemy guns from that quarter.

Meantime, Co. F, lacking the heavy mortar support it had in taking its first objective, became bogged down by heavy enemy fire, including that from 82mm and 120mm mortars. But at 11:30 a.m., the 4.2s and 81s were again shifted to help the unit. With this help, Co F moved out again and assaulted their objective from both the left and right flanks. Fearing encirclement, the enemy ran off the back side in flight. But when the company started for its final objective, enemy machine guns opened up on them and a number of supposedly dead North Koreans rose up and shot several men at point-blank range. Very quickly, the platoon leader and 10 enlisted men were seriously wounded and the platoon sergeant and three others killed. The survivors managed to extricate themselves, bringing out all the wounded and two of the four dead. The other two dead could not be retrieved without further casualties.

During Fox's advance, Bishop's platoon lost two killed in action and at least one wounded. One of his dead men and a KIA from another platoon were on the forward slope of a hill being swept by enemy machinegun fire. Bishop and PFCs Xavier Benziger and Holbert went to retrieve their bodies. Benziger was wounded in the right shoulder and chest, but the dead were brought back.

Co. E attacked along the ridgeline extending southeast from Hill 420. Meeting little resistance, the company seized its last objective, Hill 600, at 1:35 p.m. Five minutes later the lead elements of 3/23d Infantry made contact there with a squad from Easy Co.

While 2/23d Infantry attacked the enemy near the artillery positions on Aug. 23, the regiment's 3d Battalion swept a three mile stretch of the MSR. The actions by these two battalions pretty well cleaned up the enemy force in that area.

Although enemy artillery and mortar fire had been a nuisance in the rear areas of 2/23d Infantry, and had caused B/8th FAB to displace, it caused few casualties. At dawn on Aug. 24, the enemy had disappeared. Two ROK battalions assaulted and took Hill 902 that day. The 2d Battalion, 23d Infantry sent out a number of patrols to check the area, gather enemy weapons and count the dead. The counted dead numbered 523, in addition to pieces of bodies. Six POWs were taken, including one officer. The flag of the *NK 1st Regiment* was also found. It was riddled by machine gun bullets. This flag was to have been flown over Taegu when the North Koreans captured it. The 2/23d Infantry lost 6 KIA and 31 WIA in this, their first battle in Korea.

Bowling Alley — Aug. 23-26

On Aug. 23, Michaelis reported to Eighth Army that the *NK 13th Division* had blown craters in the road to his front, had mined it and was pulling back.

Just prior to noon that day, however, about 100 enemy soldiers hit K/27th Infantry and the 1st Platoon, C/65th ECB. The enemy penetrated the position, but were quickly driven off, leaving 50 dead behind.

The enemy made their final attack on the 27th just after midnight of the 24th. The estimated two companies and a few tanks were easily repelled, causing the loss of two more tanks.

During the day, technical teams from Ordnance tried to evacuate a damaged T-34. The effort attracted several onlookers. As the retriever pulled the tank, a U.S. mine, caught under the tank, blew up, badly damaging the tank and injuring 12 men standing nearby.

That night, GEN Walker ordered the 27th to return to the Masan area. The ROK 1st Division would take over 27th's positions, but the 23d regiment would remain north of Taegu in support.

At 2:30 p.m. on the 25th, a small force, composed of one platoon from Co. B and one from Co F, supported by a platoon from C/73d Tk Bn launched a limited objective attack to secure a line of departure for ROK troops. The attackers progressed 2,000 yards without opposition. While waiting the arrival of the ROKs, the force, and ROKs, was taken under enemy mortar fire. As a result, the ROK force lost all its officers, and the Americans suffered a number of casualties. When the Americans withdrew, the leaderless ROKs did too. They were reorganized, with new officers, and returned to their attack. MAJ Arthur B. Butler, S3, 2/27th Infantry, was killed as the regiment withdrew.

The North Koreans lost heavily in men and equipment in the Bowling Alley area. In the valley, itself, between Aug. 18 and 25, 13 T-34 tanks, 5 SP guns and 23 other vehicles were destroyed. The enemy's *1st Regiment, 1st Division* was reported to be down to just 400 men and had lost

Photos above and below are two views of the tank destroyed by a rocket launcher team from F/27th Inf. The arrow in picture below points to the location of a mine which detonated when a technical team tried to move the tank. (Note the lettering on the turret, barrel and side of tank.) (U.S. Army photos, courtesy of David Bradley, E/27 Infantry)

all its 120mm mortars, 76mm howitzers and antitank guns in opposing the 23d regiment.

In addition to the 37 casualties suffered by 2/23d Infantry, the 27th Infantry lost some 17 KIA, 88 WIA and 4 MIA. The 8th FAB 4 KIA, 32 WIA and 2 MIA. GEN Paik wrote that the ROK 1st Division lost 56 officers and 2,244 enlisted men. He estimated the North Korean dead at 5,690.

Glenn Ellison (F/27th Infantry) proudly attributed the 27th Infantry's success in the Bowling Alley "to the outstanding leadership we were fortunate to have."

The relief of the 27th started at 6 p.m. on Aug. 25 and was completed at 3:45 a.m. on Aug. 26. The regiment completed its move to the Masan area by 8:30 p.m. on Aug. 31, just in time to meet another crisis on the Perimeter.

The Miryang Cemetery — Aug. 24-Sept. 7, 1950

Thousands of U.S. war dead were buried in South Korea. One of the first cemeteries was at Miryang, known as "The United Nations Cemetery Number Two, Miryang, Korea." Interments started on Aug. 24, 1950. Donald W. Hoffman, F/23d Infantry, was detailed on Aug. 23 to duty gathering and helping to process and bury dead in this cemetery. He did not volunteer and knew nothing about how bodies were gathered or "processed." He recalled that there were about 20 soldiers in his contingent, commanded by a master sergeant. Hoffman was assigned to one of several 2-man teams who picked up bodies. This was a particularly horrible task, since many of them had been killed several days or weeks before. Hoffman was there Aug. 24 to Sept. 7, 1950, during which 1,026 U.S. and ROK soldiers were interred.

Chapter Notes:

P. 212 This is from Lynch's Clay Blair interview. A copy of the interview's transcript is in *The Clay and Joan Blair Collection, U.S. Army Military History Institute, Carlisle Barracks, PA.* The author extracted the Walker-Keiser quotations and the Walker-Lynch conversation from this transcript.

P. 215 This was totally unorthodox; a heavy weapons company provided machine gun, 81mm mortar and 75mm recoilless support to the rifle companies of an infantry battalion.

P. 216 This description is based on a map, page 30, *The Legacy of Custer's 7th Cavalry in Korea,* and a study of a 1:50,000 map of the area, prepared from Japanese surveys of 1939 and U.S. aerial photos taken in 1947.

P. 216 Other regiments of the 1st Cavalry Division also conducted patrols across the Naktong at this time, but the author received no accounts of them.

P. 217 In his chapter notes to *The Forgotten War,* Clay Blair listed those favorable to Crombez as Palmer, COL Peter D. Clainos and GEN Harold K. Johnson. He wrote that detractors included CPT Harry A. Buckley (CO, L/5 Cav), LT John C. Barrett Jr. (A/5 Cav) and PFC Victor Fox (I/5 Cav).

P. 219 When North Korean soldiers approached near one's position, they could actually be smelled; they had a distinct odor which experienced soldiers could detect although the enemy might not be seen. (Personal experience.)

P. 220 The story of CPL Barton Smith, to include all material quoted from him, is contained on pp. 32-33 of Daily's *The Legacy of Custer's 7th U.S. Cavalry In Korea.*

P. 221 Fire and maneuver involves some men firing from concealed positions to cover the advance of others. When one group has moved forward, or to the flanks, and taken up the fire, then the group which had been providing covering fire moves, covered by those who had moved. Thus, in small parties, the entire force works its way forward in an attack.

P. 225 Neither this, nor a similar account of the enemy using prisoners to induce the remainder of Co. G on the hill to surrender is included in any other account of Hill 303 which the author has found.

P. 225 Lindsey C. Nelms, then a PFC in HM Co., 5th Cavalry provided the author with the names of the men who were murdered on Hill 303.

Their names are listed below in honor and memory. State where enlisted, where known, is included:

PVT Leroy Abbott, KY; PVT Leo W. Jacques, NY; PFC Leroy Bone; PFC Richard Jahnke; PVT Arthur Borst, NY; PFC Ramond J. Karelsky, NY; SGT Ray A. Briley, MI; PVT Herbert R. McKenzie, OK; PFC Benjamin Bristow, KY; PVT Milton Mlaskac, IL; PVT Billie J. Causey, AL; PVT Houston Montfort; PVT John W. Collins, OH; PVT Melvin W. Morden, MI; PVT Johnny K. Dooley, AL; 2LT Cecil Neuman, Jr., GA; PVT Cecil C. Edwards, AR; PVT Robert J. O'Brien, NJ; PFC Harlon C. Feltner, MI; PFC Brook T. Powell, KY; PVT Richard Finnigan, PA; PVT Bruce A. Reams, PA; PVT Kenneth G. Fletke, MI; CPL Ernest Regney, PA; PVT Arthur S. Garcia, CA; PFC Walter Schuman, MI; PVT Charles Hastings; PVT George Semosky, Jr., PA; PFC Antonio Hernandez, TX; PFC John W. Simmons, UT; PVT Joseph M. Herndon; CPL Glen L. Tangman; PVT John J. Hilgerson Jr., FL; PFC Tony Tavares, CA; PVT Billy R. Hogan, AR; PVT William D. Trammel, SC; PVT Glenn E. Huffman, OH; CPL William W. Williams; SGT Robert A. Humes, OH; CPL Siegfried S. Zimnluch

P. 228 This account differs from that of Appleman, but is from the personal experiences of the author, who was one of the officers on the road.

P. 228 Appleman's deployment, on page 355 of *South to the Naktong* is incorrect. The disposition described above is from the 1st and 2d Bn, 27th RCT Operation Reports for Aug. 1950 and the author's recollections as a platoon leader, 1st Platoon, Co. B.

P. 230 Not enough credit has been given to the staunch fighting of the 1st ROK Division in the Bowling Alley. They were not down in the valley, but they successfully held the high mountains on each of its flanks. Had the ROKs been unable to hold, the 27th Infantry could have been subjected to the greatest slaughter by the enemy from those peaks. Also, the role of the 2d and 3d Battalions, 23d Infantry, has never been told, nor the vital importance of their battles along the MSR in the rear of the Bowling Alley. The entire battle was one of the finest examples of international cooperation in battle to come out of the Korean War. Each command, ROK or American, performed in a superb fashion, where the failure of even one battalion anywhere could have doomed the entire effort to failure.

P. 231 A bogie is one of a series of weight-carrying wheels on a tank which serve to keep the tread, or track, in line

P. 231 ROK soldiers had come down off the mountain in ones and twos during these days. Some were wounded; others were looking for a little water, food or ammunition. The wounded were treated and evacuated. The others, once they received the supplies they sought, always climbed back and resumed the fight. The relationship between the Wolfhounds in the valley and the ROKs in the mountains was always excellent.

P. 232 The account of 2/23d Infantry for Aug. 22-26 is based primarily on "Action at Tongmyong," by LTC James W. Edwards, *Infantry School Quarterly,* Ft. Benning, GA, Jan. 1951. The personal experiences of participants are also included.

Two platoons of F/27th Inf., with three Pershing tanks, move out on patrol toward Ch'onp'yong-dong. A machinegun team and riflemen in the foreground move along the flank.

CHAPTER SIXTEEN - The Southern Front Again

Deployment of the 25th infantry Division

While the 27th Infantry was in the Bowling Alley, with the bulk of the 8th FAB in support, the remainder of the 25th Division, with the 5th RCT attached, was deployed south of the confluence of the Nam and Naktong Rivers, carrying the Pusan Perimeter to the sea in the vicinity of Chindong-ni.

The northern sector was manned by COL Fisher's 35th Infantry, with the 64th FAB (LTC Arthur H. Logan) in support. The regimental front was about 26,000 yards long, beginning on the south bank of The Nam River opposite Namji-ri southward to a point about one mile north of Haman. The 2d Battalion (LTC John L. Wilkins, Jr.) manned the northern half of the regimental front from Namji-ri southward along the Nam River. The 1st Battalion (LTC Bernard G. Teeter) extended the line almost due south to the boundary with the 24th Infantry. Battery C, 90th FAB (155mm) was attached to the 64th FAB. A/89th Tk Bn was attached to the 35th Infantry. BG Barth, commanding the 25th DivArty, wrote that five batteries of 105mm howitzers from the 64th and 159th FABs (LTC Walter J. Preston commanded the 159th) plus C/90th FAB (155mm) supported the Division's "northern front." Barth implied that this included the 24th and 35th Infantry's sectors when he wrote that the thirty-six guns in these six batteries represented a little over two guns per mile of front, very thin coverage. The combined frontage of the two regiments was over thirteen and a half air-line miles. The configuration of the Nam River and ridge system made the actual front to be defended much longer.

COL Champeny's 24th Infantry carried the division front southward starting on a range of relatively low hills west of Haman, thence through the most rugged terrain on the entire Naktong front. This included Battle Mountain (Hill 665), Pil-bong (Hill 743) and the peak called Sobuk-san (Hill 652). The 2d Battalion (LTC George R. Cole to Aug. 18, then LTC Paul F. Roberts) occupied a lower ridge line west of Haman. This was the second ridge line west of town. The southern half of the sector, the rugged Battle Mountain-Pilbong area, was occupied by LTC Gerald Miller's 1st Battalion. The 3d Battalion (LTC John T. Corley) was in reserve. The 159th FAB supported the regiment. There was a gap of 4,000 yards between the 24th Infantry and the 5th RCT to the south. On Aug. 16, GEN Kean sent 432 ROK policemen to Champeny, who placed them in this gap near the critical Sobuk-san peak.

Initially, the 5th RCT (now commanded by LTC John L. Throckmorton) was deployed along the ridges south of Sobuk-san and onto the relatively flat area to the coastal road to Chindong-ni. LTC T. B. Roelofs' 1st Battalion was on the higher ridges south of the 24th Infantry. The 2d Battalion (LTC Albert W. Ward) defended the regiment's center. LTC Benjamin Heckemeyer's

3d Battalion carried the line south to the coastal road. ROKs defended from there to the sea. The Triple Nickel FAB, under their new commander, LTC Clarence E. Stuart, supported the 5th Infantry.

Over 1,200 miles of barbed wire, 30,000 pickets and 350,000 sandbags were employed to help strengthen the division defenses, in addition to trip flares and antipersonnel mines. But the division's rear areas were not secure. On Aug. 14 it was estimated that about five battalions of enemy troops were in this area. As a result, all service support troops had to be ready to fight as infantrymen.

The *NK 6th* and *7th Divisions*

Following the terrible fighting in opposition to TF Kean, the *6th Division* was ordered to take up defensive positions until replacements could be sent to it. The division deployed its *13th, 15th* and *14th Regiments* from north to south in that order. About 2,000 replacements had arrived in the division about Aug. 12. Another 2,500 replacements conscripted in Seoul arrived about Aug. 21. This brought the *6th Division* up to about 8,500 men. At the end of August and during the first week of September another 3,000 recruits joined the division. These men were first used in labor details, then later in combat.

The *7th Division* began arriving on the southern front about Aug. 15. It numbered about 10,000 men. Its *1st* and *3d Regiments* reached Tongyong at the south end of the Korean peninsula about Aug. 17. Its *2d Regiment* went to garrison the port of Yosu on Aug. 15. In effect, the *7th Division*, deployed near the southern coast, protected the *6th Division* from envelopment from the sea.

But the enemy reinforced battalion which was left to garrison Tongyong was soon driven from the town. American naval vessels supported an attack by three companies of ROK Marines, drove the enemy away. The North Koreans lost about 350 men, about half of the command. The ousted troops pulled back to Chinju.

The *6th* and *7th Divisions* moved on the 25th Division line and by Aug. 17, began a series of probes that eventually became full-scale attacks. The struggle in this area continued into mid-September.

The North Koreans Attack the 35th Infantry — Aug. 17 - 25

When the North Koreans renewed their attacks in the 25th Division sector, they started against one of the ablest regimental commanders then in Korea, COL Fisher of the 35th. He did not have the dash and news copy character of COL Michaelis. Rather, he was unassuming, calm, but a true professional. He had what Appleman described as "an exact knowledge of the capabilities of the weapons" of an infantry regiment "and was skilled in their use." Fisher was also a master tactician. Shortly, these two

officers would be joined by another excellent regimental commander, John T. Corley, a highly decorated combat veteran of WW II. He was a no-nonsense leader, brave and determined. The 24th Infantry Regiment improved immeasurably under his leadership.

The 35th placed trip flares all across its front. But, when the enemy tripped them, they soon became impossible to replace. They were in short supply. Even worse, 80 per cent of the illuminating rounds for the 60mm mortar were defective. Illuminating rounds for the 155mm howitzer were also in short supply. Further, even when 155mm illumination was requested, it took so long for the mission to be fired that the enemy was often gone from the area. (See Chapter Notes.)

Nine of the M4A3 tanks from the attached tank company were used as artillery. Three of them placed interdicting fire on Chungam-ni and six others similar interdictory fire on Uiryong west of the Nam River.

At 3 a.m. on Aug. 17, enemy artillery fire hit the CP of 1/35th Infantry at Komam-ni. At 4 a.m. enemy infantry attacked Co. A. "Just before dawn we could hear the sound of oxen at the bottom of the hill," wrote PFC Robert Liberty, a BAR-man in Co. A. His platoon leader, 2LT Kinney, on Liberty's right, also heard the noise. Kinney had Liberty lay out some BAR magazines so he could keep Liberty supplied with ammo when the enemy attacked. About a half hour later, the attack came, accompanied by bugles and whistles. They opened fire when enemy soldiers could be seen from the waist up as they climbed the hill.

"It was terrible," Liberty recalled. "We were overrun by them." He first saw a line of about 15 or 20. "I opened fire.... I could only get two magazines of 20 rounds each off. I believe I got about 10 of them before they got me with a grenade. It blew me right out of the slit trench. My platoon leader...dragged me to a foxhole...."

At daylight, the men with Liberty discovered they were surrounded by the enemy. A tank on a nearby hill began to engage the enemy with its guns. Then aircraft came in on the North Koreans. About an hour later, tanks escorted some trucks forward. Liberty and the other wounded were evacuated.

The enemy attack pushed two of Co. A's platoons out of position and overran the mortar position. After daylight, Co. B counterattacked and retook the lost ground. Thus began a five day fight between elements of the *6th Division* and 1/35th Infantry. Co. A was thrown off its position again on Aug. 18, but took it back in a counterattack. Two companies of ROK police arrived to reinforce the battalion's right flank.

Two additional companies of ROKs were sent in to bolster the 1st Battalion's right flank. Elements of A/29th Infantry counterattacked the enemy on 1/35's left flank.

During the night of Aug. 18-19, the artillery fired an average of 200 rounds an hour in support of the battalion. The battle raged for three days and nights. On Aug. 19, artillery fire destroyed fifteen enemy trucks which were moving forward to resupply their forces. Then, on Aug. 20, C/35th Infantry and A/29th Infantry were brought up astride the Komam-ni road to backstop A and B of the 35th on Sibidang, an east-west ridge about 1,500 yards long about a mile west of the road. As the two companies came into position, COL Fisher, from his OP, detected a large force of North Koreans approaching for another attack. He called in artillery and an air strike, breaking up the enemy force and killing about half of them — 350 men.

The enemy tried one last time before dawn on Aug. 22 against 1/35 Infantry. This time, the North Koreans did not fire any artillery or mortar preparation. Rather, they quietly approached in the darkness, cut the barbed wire and attacked with small-arms and grenades. This battle engulfed three U.S. rifle companies, again driving Co. A from its position. However, the unit counterattacked and threw the enemy out again.

Rifleman James F. Waters of Co. C recounts an incident which could have been part of this battle. CPL Bartolome S. Ribac and PVT Roy N. Fomby "manned a .30-caliber machine gun...covering a pretty good sized draw," Waters recalled. He was dug in with another rifleman on a small finger of the hill on the machine gun's left. "Early one morning a group of North Korean soldiers, estimated to be company sized, [came] up the draw using a heavy blanket of fog as cover to mask their movements.... Unfortunately for them and fortunately for us, the...fog suddenly lifted.... They were out there like sitting ducks." Ribac called in 4.2 inch mortar fire. One of the rounds hit among an enemy squad, killing all of them. Ribac and Fomby stayed on their gun, continuing to fire it, "though...under very heavy, intense small arms fire from the approaching enemy," Waters wrote. After the battle, between 75 and 100 enemy dead were counted in the draw, most the victims of Ribac and Fomby and their machine gun.

Although there was little action in the 35th's sector on Aug. 24 and 25, the enemy did try to slip a force through on the left of Co. C. During the action, the North Koreans pretended to surrender by waving a white flag. But when Co. C ceased firing, the enemy force attacked. They were repulsed with a loss of 20 counted dead. A patrol from Co. E had a similar experience when it crossed a river to accept a surrender. It was hit by a heavy volume of enemy fire.

Battle Mountain - Sobuk-san — Aug. 15-31

The Terrain

Sobuk-san was the name given to an entire five-mile long, high, rugged mountain range, as well as one of its peaks, Hill 665. In the north, the range springs from a series of relatively low ridges east of the Nam River. Hills 225 and Sibidang were the highest hills in the 35th Infantry sector, in its south-central area. Farther south, entering the 24th Infantry's sector, the ridges and hills are lower for a little over a mile, until coming to Hill 212. South across a valley from Hill 212 the terrain starts to climb into Battle Mountain. Battle Mountain was also

known as Old Baldy, Napalm Hill and Bloody Knob. South of this promontory, the ridge narrows into a rocky ledge, known to the troops as the Rocky Crags. This ridge trends southeast to Pilbong, a very narrow ridge over 700 meters high, running south for over 1,000 yards. The ridge meanders farther south then, still over 600 meters high and very steep, to Hill 644, a thousand yards due south of the end of Pilbong. It then climbs slowly for just over another thousand yards to a promontory 700 meters high. From there it runs southeast about 1,000 yards

to Sobuk-san, which embraced Hills 652 and 734. Originally, the 24th Infantry's sector included Sobuk-san. However, the regiment was about 4,000 yards short of that peak. First, 432 ROKs were placed in this gap. Sobuk-san was eventually assigned to the 5th RCT.

From Sobuk, the ridge line continues to meander southward, first through points 600 and 500 meters high, then into lower elevations as it approaches the Chindong-ni area. Hill 342, Fox Hill, is on one of the lower arms of the range.

A road ran south from Chungam-ni gener-

Photos above and below depict the rugged terrain typical of the Battle Mountain, P'ilbong and Sobuk-san areas defended by the 24th, 35th and 5th RCTs in August and September 1950. (Source: P. 95 and 138, Pictorial History of the War in Korea, *Veterans of Foreign Wars, 1951)*

ally along the western base of the Sobuk range. On the western side of Battle Mountain, this road climbed a pass 1,100 feet up the slope of Battle Mountain — about half way to the top. This was a decided advantage to the North Koreans in reinforcing and resupplying their troops on this hill. A trail system led up to the top of both Battle Mountain and Pilbong from the villages of Ogok and Tundok. The two towns were only one and a quarter miles from the crests of these two hills. Numerous mine shafts just west of Battle Mountain provided the enemy with bomb-proof shelters for reserves and supply stores. From the summit of Battle Mountain, U.S. troops could dominate any enemy in the valley to the west. The enemy, on this mountain, could look down into the Haman valley, where the CP of the 24th Infantry, MSR, artillery positions and other rear area installations were located. Battle Mountain and neighboring Pilbong were key to holding the Perimeter in the center of the 25th Division sector.

The eastern (U.S.) side of Battle Mountain and Pilbong had no trails or roads to aid climbing. Climbers in condition required 2 to 3 hours to reach the top of Pilbong, 3 to 4 hours to climb Battle Mountain. It took supply bearers 6 hours to make a Battle Mountain round trip and messengers often required 8 hours for the journey. At the steepest places, rope "hand rails" were stretched along the trail. Maintaining wire communication was a nightmare. Enemy patrols constantly cut the wires. Night and day, wiremen then had to try to find and repair the line. This was also true of Pilbong.

Even worse was the long, tortuous task of evacuating the wounded from these two mountains. It took a team of six stretcher bearers, often with an accompanying aidman, to carry one man down the mountain. Often, too, the litter had to be escorted by riflemen to protect the party from enemy snipers. The trip took many hours and, as a result, many of the critically wounded died on the way down. When it was raining, trails were almost impossible to negotiate in either direction. If wounded, many men were afraid they would die before reaching an aid station. This had an adverse affect on the morale of some 24th Infantrymen fighting on Battle Mountain and Pilbong. At this stage of the Korean War, the Army had no helicopters to evacuate wounded from the front. Further, air evacuation of the critically wounded, when finally instituted, was from a forward aid station or clearing station to a MASH. (See Appendix C — Medical Support.)

A Daring Rescue

On Aug. 6, as recounted in Chapter 12, LT Chester Lenon and a number of members of his platoon were missing in action. His company commander, CPT Charles M. Bussey was distraught by this loss.

Lenon wasn't dead, but was badly wounded. In the battle on Aug. 6, he and his men had been at the tail end of L/24th Infantry, when the force was ambushed by the enemy. Many men of Co. L made their escape. Lenon's group, in the rear, fought up a hill. He and about half a dozen men moved to flank the enemy. As Lenon and his platoon sergeant, SFC Collins A. Whitaker, threw two grenades at an enemy machine gun position, an enemy bullet plowed through Lenon's upper left thigh, knocked off a corner of his femur, and exited through his buttock. He was rendered unconscious, not recovering until late that afternoon. He must have passed out again, or fallen asleep, because he remembered only awakening the next morning with the sun in his face. He was on his back. Looking around, he could not see or hear anything. He called out. "Finally, I raised six voices," he said. All were wounded, but he managed to get them together. It was early afternoon of Aug. 7. No one had any water and Lenon's canteen had a hole in it, but he remembered a tiny stream, not more than a hundred yards away. The group slowly inched their way toward it, pausing often to allow the more seriously wounded to rest. They crawled until about dark.

CPL Jerome Barnwell, one of the more seriously injured men, gave out, so the entire party stayed with him. "He told me, 'I'm just in too much pain. I can't move at all.' So I crawled over to him," Lenon said. "I put his head up on my side.... I just kind of nursed him a little bit, and after a few minutes, he said, 'I'll see you Lieutenant.' and that was it."

The men finally reached the stream at 9 a.m. on Aug. 8. There, five of the men stayed from Aug. 8 until Aug. 12, when Bussey came with a rescue party and found them. The men built a little dam in the stream, so they had water but no food. About Wednesday, Lenon recalled, one of the men (PFC Edwards) volunteered to go for help. Edwards had one ankle smashed by an enemy bullet, but believed himself to be the most mobile of the group. Reluctantly, Lenon permitted him to go. Somewhere along the way he was discovered by enemy soldiers, who severely beat him, took his clothes and left him for dead.

At 3 a.m., Aug. 13, Bussey received a phone call in his CP that PFC Edwards was at the medics and insisted in talking to him. Bussey found Edwards in deplorable condition; the bullet had plowed through the bones of his left foot. Strong muscles on the sole pulled the foot under and backward. What clothing he had was in shreds and the skin on his hands, knees, elbows and thighs was worn off from his painful crawling. A snake had bitten his right cheek and his entire face and head was swollen. Edwards filled Bussey in on Lenon and the others and where he thought they were located.

CPT Bussey assembled about 150 men of his company, with some extra automatic weapons, some litters and a large bag of candy bars (for the wounded, who hadn't eaten for almost a week). He had no authority to take the men of his unit on this mission into what was considered enemy territory. He placed his unit at risk by this action. Bussey could have been court martialed, even if his unit did not encounter the enemy. With some men on nearby hills as flank protection, the rescue column headed out. Bussey could see enemy soldiers on the ridgeline ahead. After a march of seven or eight miles, he and his men arrived at the ambush site. They came across a large number of dead GIs, apparently cut down while attempting to flee.

When Bussey neared the place that Edwards had indicated Lenon and the other wounded were located, he started to call, "Chet Lenon! Chet Lenon!" Lenon heard the approaching troops, but thought they might be enemy, until he recognized Bussey's voice. Then he called out, "Over here! Over Here!" Homing in on the voice, Bussey and his men located Lenon's party and immediately rendered first aid. PFC Semedo, one of the wounded with Lenon, said, "I knew you'd come for us sooner or later, and when I woke up this morning, I knew that today was the day." Bussey's men collected both the wounded and the dead and returned, without incident, to the company CP. Chester Lenon, for his leadership and heroism was awarded the Distinguished Service Cross.

The 24th Infantry and Battle Mountain — Aug. 15-21

As TF Kean ended, 2/24th Infantry was still trying to seize Obang-san (Hill 525). This hill is somewhat less than two miles west of Battle Mountain. The North Koreans were on Obangsan in strength and parties of enemy soldiers infested the area near Ogok and Tundok. U.S. patrols approaching this area were always ambushed or driven back.

Originally, the 159th FAB was located in the valley south of Haman, along with the regimental 4.2 inch mortars. On Aug. 19, the 159th, except for Battery C, was relocated. COL Champeny insisted that one battery of the battalion remain.

The North Koreans attacked Battle Mountain for the first time on Aug. 18. They overran part of Co. E on the northern section of the hill, killing the company commander. The troops renewed the attack the next day, driving Co C from its position. Officers assembled 40 survivors. Likewise, the enemy drove most of the ROKs from their position; only about 56 stayed on the ridge. U.S. officers collected the scattered ROKs and got most of them back on the hill.

The perspective from part of Co. A's position was considerably different from what is portrayed above.

2LT Lyle Rishell's 2d Platoon, A/24th Infantry, had about nine men at the time, he recalled. The North Koreans attacked at dawn. To his left "one of our machine guns commenced its staccato chatter," he wrote in *With a Black Platoon in Korea.* "Soon other weapons began a chant...." Through his binoculars, Rishell could see enemy troops moving forward in the attack, "evidently determined to break through our lines. We were just as determined to stop them." Enemy heavy mortar and artillery fire started dropping onto his platoon. But because of the very steep terrain to its front, the enemy drove around the platoon's right flank. Heavy barrages roared in on the defenders, slacked off, then started up again.

On Rishell's right flank, Co. C, called in an air strike of F-80 jets and F-51 fighters. A slow-moving, light spotter plane his men called "Cheezie" directed the air strike. The attacking aircraft rocketed and napalmed the enemy. "Burning globs of jellied gasoline flushed the attackers out of the rocks before us," Rishell recalled. "Someone named it the Devil's Brew. The men were ecstatic, shouting encouragement to the planes" as the enemy soldiers ran for cover. The air attack drove off the enemy. "Along our immediate front all activity ceased."

In succeeding days, Rishell's platoon received replacements, swelling to 27 men. Lyle was proud of his platoon, his platoon sergeant (SGT Nollie) and the four squad leaders (SGTs Mims, Hicks, McRoberts and Rochelle). He wrote that they "were all I could have hoped for. They handled their squads deftly and efficiently." Nowhere, he continued, "could squad leaders have been more dedicated than these men." Of the four, Mims was later KIA. Rishell wrote, "Sergeant Nollie was Regular Army and it showed in everything he did.... He was good natured.... A serious soldier.... He was the consummate non-com; I couldn't have asked for any better. He was indispensable, and I loved the man."

Appleman wrote that by the end of the day on Aug. 18, "a gap of nearly a mile in the line north of Pilbong existed in the 24th Infantry lines...and an unknown number of North Koreans were moving into it."

Appleman's version of events in the 24th Infantry sector on Aug. 20 and that of the 25th Division historian are somewhat different. Appleman wrote that "all of C company except the company commander, CPT Lawrence M. Corcoran, and about twenty-five men abandoned their positions on Battle Mountain." They reported that Corcoran had been killed, the position surrounded, then overrun by the enemy. As a result of this report, heavy concentrations of U.S. artillery and mortar fire were directed at Battle Mountain and the Air Force flew 38 sorties against it. The end result was that CPT Corcoran and the men remaining with him had to abandon the unit position. He also wrote that a platoon of Co. E, "except for eight or ten men, also left their position on the mountain under similar circumstances." He made no mention of a counterattack to regain the lost ground.

The 25th Division history states that the enemy first struck the 1st Battalion at 6:45 a.m., then spread the attack to include part of the 2d Battalion.

"C Company positions were overrun at the first onslaught," the Division history states. "The men rallied and counterattacked, but were driven back into D Company positions." It was then that artillery, mortars and air strikes were directed at the enemy. "Following this preparation," the history continues, "elements of the 24th's 3d Battalion counterattacked the former positions and moved close in without strenuous resistance from the Reds"

Appleman mentions that a ROK patrol from the Co. K position on Sobuk-san captured the commander of the *NK 15th Infantry*, but that he was killed a few minutes later trying to escape. The patrol found important documents on his body. During their attack the enemy drove the ROKs from the 24th Infantry's left flank on Sobuk, opening the area to infiltration.

"Move out, Lieutenant," ordered LT R. P. Stevens, 2LT Ted Swett's CO, pointing to the top of Battle Mountain. That was the entire attack order for Swett's 3d Platoon, Co. L, 24th Infantry on Aug. 20, 1950. LT Swett (West Point, 1949) was the ninth platoon leader that the 3d Platoon had so far in the war. He led his platoon up the narrow path, soon passing members of Co. C, in groups of two or three, some wounded, making their way down the mountain. Then up

ahead, he saw a party of troops he thought were remnants of Co. C which had been sent back up the hill. Investigation revealed that the group was his battalion commander, LTC Corley, and his communications officer. Corley took Swett's platoon to protect his Battalion CP, located in a saddle about 150 yards from the top of Battle Mountain. The night passed peacefully for the lieutenant and his men

The struggle in the 24th Infantry sector continued on Aug. 21. During one enemy barrage, an enemy round burst behind a battalion switchboard, badly damaging the equipment and seriously wounding the operator. After calling for medics and seeing to the evacuation of the injured man, PFC James T. Patterson, a standby operator, repaired the switchboard and had it back in operation so quickly, "that most of the companies never knew the switchboard was hit," said SFC Harden Walker.

Aug. 21 dawned hot and sultry. Love Co. would attack in a column of platoons to take the crest of Battle Mountain. Swett's platoon struggled up the rocky incline. A few scattered trees and bushes provided some concealment, but when the platoon emerged from the trees, it was met by small-arms fire. The platoon, deployed with two squads up in a skirmish line, fired back, employing marching fire. The third rifle squad and a 60mm mortar, set up in a draw, provided covering fire for the advancing men. The attack went "just like he'd been taught at Ft. Benning," Swett recalled. The platoon lost only two wounded and the crest was secured within an hour. The view from the crest was spectacular; it was a beautiful sunny day, and for a few minutes, at least, Swett thought there was no war.

Swett called for his squad leaders to assemble for orders. Suddenly, enemy mortar rounds began exploding in the position. He was crouched at the edge of the shallow hole he had made his CP. The squad leaders were approaching for their orders. At that instant, a mortar round burst near his left hip. His radio operator and two squad leaders were killed.

Swett tried to move his legs, but couldn't. Mortar rounds burst all around. He saw no live GIs; he was alone. Then he saw the fingers of an enemy soldier reaching for a grip on a ledge about 20 yards away. He realized that he had no weapon; his carbine had apparently been destroyed in the explosion. With no other alternative, Swett dragged himself from the hole, rolled down the hill away from the approaching enemy and into a clump of bushes. The platoon medic, who was hidden in the same clump, began to dress the lieutenant's wound. Some enemy soldiers about 50 yards away, detecting movement in the bushes, began to fire. The medic ran away, with Swett's first aid compress just as he was struck above the knee by another bullet.

Enemy soldiers now began walking around the position, kicking at bodies which lay near the CP. Swett remained motionless, hoping the North Koreans would think he was dead. At that point, he lost consciousness. When he awoke, a fire fight was in progress, diverting the enemy's attention. Swett began to crawl painfully down toward where the Battalion CP had been. He was terribly thirsty, but his canteen had been blown

open by the mortar round which had wounded him. Soldiers on the hill began shooting at him as he got closer to the tree line. A bullet narrowly missed his head. Swett reached up to adjust his helmet, only to discover, he had none. Then he spotted a helmet nearby and clamped it on his head. Between periods of unconsciousness, he continued to crawl toward the CP. Suddenly, he heard the ominous click of an M1 being taken off safety, and a voice whispering, "Here comes one now!" Swett rose unsteadily and called, "Don't shoot, its Lieutenant Swett!" Just as he was about to pass out again, he saw the faces of some men from another platoon looking down on him curiously. Swett was wearing an ill-fitting North Korean helmet.

It took five hours to get LT Swett down off Battle Mountain. Enroute, he was dropped by the litter bearers, when a short round of friendly artillery landed close by.

Apparently, both Companies I and L made this attack, for Appleman wrote that officers "tried to assemble L and I Companies on the eastern slope." He stated that part "of E Company left their position during the day."

The Division history states that the 3d Battalion "performed well [on Aug. 21, 1950], placing I and L Companies in the strategic positions after seven hours.... But at 2 p.m., one hour later, an enemy force estimated at two battalions counter-attacked and drove the two companies back off the heights." Following this, however, the 24th Infantry made plans to attack again to regain the crest of Battle Mountain

The battles along the sectors of the 24th and 5th RCTs continued in varying degrees of intensity for over a month — so long that the men who were there are often unable to remember the day or dates of any given encounter. The experiences of a number of these men are included the following narrative as being part of the whole, but are impossible to place exactly as to date. One of these is the recollection of Isaac S. Smith.

"First Lieutenant Philip King and I were ordered to set up a forward aid station in the Third Battalion's perimeter on top of 'Ol' Baldy,' a portion of Battle Mountain," wrote Smith, a member of Medical Company, 24th Infantry. "The most convenient site appeared to be located in K Company. Digging a foxhole is difficult in that area. Preparing a place to receive and treat patients is much more difficult."

Smith recalled some of the fighting for Old Baldy. "The front was quiet until about 11:30 p.m., then the enemy started blowing horns, shooting flares, firing small arms and throwing mortar [rounds on the defenders]. The attack had begun. We collected a few patients; walking wounded. We were fortunate that we had only one or two litter patients." At daylight, orders were given to abandon the positions; the enemy had infiltrated into the unit's rear. Moving back with litter patients and walking wounded in broad daylight could have been fatal, except for what Smith called "Divine intervention." "A heavy fog so thick that one could only see a few yards away rolled in," he wrote. The enemy was all around the evacuation route, but Smith and those with him reached the rear aid station safely. "[T]he next the day mountain was retaken," he concluded.

The 5th RCT on Sobuk-san — Mid -Aug.-Aug. 23

On Aug. 15, GEN Kean relieved COL Godwin L. Ordway as commander of the 5th RCT. LTC John L. Throckmorton succeeded him. James C. Richardson, Regimental Assistant Adjutant, recalled Ordway's relief. Richardson drove the jeep carrying Ordway and Throckmorton back to the Division CP. "I asked COL Ordway were he wanted to go and he said he wanted to go to 25th Division Headquarters." Ordway was angry because he felt division was responsible for the foul-up which led to the heavy losses the 5th had just suffered in the vicinity of Pongam-ni. (See Chapter 12.)

"I knew where it was so I took him [there].... He went in there mad as a wet hen and he was going to find out about the terrible mess they'd made out of something or other, the reason we'd [been] cut up and lost those 350 dead men.... He was in there for a relatively short time and he came back out and walked to the jeep and said to no one in particular, 'I'm no longer your CO.' Colonel Ordway was a man that thought first of his men and he was inclined to take very good care of them. Anything that they had coming to them, he got them. Anytime they were in trouble, other than a major felony, he did everything to get them out. He looked like a soldier. He was a former enlisted man who had made it through West Point [but] he just didn't have the heart for combat." Richardson remarked that under battle pressure Ordway became disorganized, and that he was also night blind. "We all felt very sad for him," he concluded. (See Chapter 20 for a different version of Ordway's relief from command.)

LTC John L. Throckmorton became commander of the 5th RCT on August 15, as it went into defensive positions from Sobuk-san south to the coastal road to Chindong-ni.

The 1/5th RCT manned the regimental right, on the southern slopes of Sobuk-san. the 2d Battalion held the center and the 3d Battalion carried the line south to the coastal road to Chindong-ni. ROK troops anchored the line from there to the sea (the Korea Strait).

Sobuk-san was a vital part of the 25th Division defense. The 24th Infantry had its hands full on Battle Mountain and elsewhere in their sector. Sobuk lay on its extreme southern flank and the regiment was hard pressed to spare enough men to defend it. Efforts by elements of the regiment, along with some ROK troops, had been roughly handled. As a result, GEN Kean ordered COL Throckmorton to attack Sobuk from his regimental sector south of the 24th. On the morning of Aug. 21, 1/5 RCT (-Co A) seized Sobuk against light resistance. That night, an attack by about two enemy battalions drove the battalion off the mountain. At noon the next day, the 1st Battalion went after the peak again, with Co. B taking it five hours later. GEN Kean now changed the boundary and gave Sobuk-san to the 5th RCT. On the night of Aug. 22-23, the enemy attacked again, preventing 1/5th RCT from consolidating its position.

The following morning, Co. A attacked to secure some high ground about a thousand yards southwest of Sobuk and make contact with Co. B. The enemy stubbornly halted the attack, while keeping Baker Company under almost constant small arms and automatic weapons fire. Thereafter too, for a number of days, the North Koreans kept Able Co. under almost daily attack. LTG Henry E. Emerson (West Point, 1947), first a platoon leader in A/5th RCT, then its commander, recalled that Co. A beat off 27 major enemy attacks during the 19 days his unit was on the slopes of Sobuk-san.

GEN Emerson also recalled one of the first offensive actions which Co. A made once it took position on the approaches to Sobuk-san. (This may be the engagement mentioned above, but that is not certain.)

Emerson recalled the action as a reconnaissance in force by Co. A. CPT Robert Timmins, commanding the company, protested the recon order to the battalion CO, LTC Roeloffs, as being "suicidal," in his opinion. The order stood. There were three objectives: OBJ A-1, a knob somewhat lower than the other two; and Objectives A-2 and A-3 which were farther forward. Objective A-2, on the right, was the highest of the three.

Co A moved out with 1LT Henry E. Emerson's platoon on the right and 1LT Charles Worley's (North Georgia College 1947) platoon on the left. The third rifle platoon, under 1LT "Cactus Jack" Zerbe, followed as reserve. Zerbe was also the company XO. The company seized OBJ A-1 without opposition. "The North Koreans just let us come out there and as soon as we got on the intermediate objective [A-1] they fired at us from all directions.... It was a nightmare that...put a lot of men down almost immediately. Strangely, for that part of the country, there were some trees there...."

As a result of this, the enemy 120mm mortar rounds falling on the Americans caused a number of tree bursts. Timmins went forward and called Emerson and Worley to him. The three men lay on the ground between the two platoons. Suddenly a machine gun bullet struck Worley near the clavicle, plowing downward through his heart and body, killing him instantly. Timmins then quickly decided to send Emerson and his platoon to attack the knob to the right. Emerson assented.

With that, the lieutenant jumped up and ran, zig-zag. He had gone about 40 yards toward his platoon, some 150 yards from where the three officers had met, when a barrage of mortar rounds landed. The blast of one of them knocked Emerson forward into a small depression in the ground. In the depression was a dying GI. Emerson could do nothing for him. He called to his platoon sergeant, Robert Lyons, to get the platoon ready to attack the right knob. He was about to jump up and make another run to join the platoon, when someone yelled, "Lieutenant Emerson, come back! Captain Timmins has been hit!"

"I raced back," he said. "[Timmins] had a gaping hole in his side; obviously a mortal wound," Emerson said. "He was very gallantly trying to hang onto the radio and direct fire.... The lieutenant gave the dying Timmins a shot of morphine. LT Zerbe came forward, but refused to take command. Emerson took over at that point. Picking up the radio handset, he discovered that the regimental commander, COL Throckmorton was on the other end. Emerson filled him in and told the colonel he was assuming command. "What are your intentions?" asked Throckmorton. Emerson responded that he intended to attack the high ground on the right, but that if the company didn't get ammunition soon they would have "big problems." He also told the colonel that if litter bearers didn't come very soon, he was going to have "bigger problems" — the company already had 50 or 60 men down. Throckmorton promised to send ammo and litter bearers to him at once.

2LT William A. Motley Sr. was the artillery FO with Co. A. He wrote a narrative of this action from his perspective. He recalled that the initial firing from the enemy lasted "no more than 10 or 15 seconds and then stopped." Infantrymen had been carrying his artillery radio. In the confusion, it disappeared, never got to him. "Most of the wounded crawled or were helped to cover," he wrote. "I was near the CO [CPT Timmins], who immediately had battalion notified that we had been hit; that it was too early to report casualties. All platoon leaders had not reported in. 2LT Charles L. Worley had been hit in the butt and slid in next to us to report on the platoon and tell the CO he was OK. He had hardly finished and was still propped up on his elbows when the small-arms started for another few seconds and stopped. LT Worley was hit and never moved.

The CO was hit in the back and couldn't move his legs, but continued to give orders to assemble the wounded near his area, which was behind a small rise and provided some cover." Timmons updated battalion on the situation on the radio, including his own wounding and Worley's death. "By now," Motley wrote, there was only one platoon leader left [LT Emerson].

The recollections of Emerson and Motley do not completely agree, but are close on the essentials. Motley recalled that Timmins requested battalion's permission to hold up, but he was ordered to continue the attack. "Units on both flanks were progressing as scheduled," wrote Motley, "and failure to take this objective would leave their flanks exposed." Motley recalled that Timmins wanted Emerson "to take all the men who could walk and go into the ravine on our right then proceed up the other side, bearing to the left toward the final objective and hit them from their rear."

Motley also recalled that Emerson recommended that the entire company should "stay together until we could find out what we were facing and we'd stand a better chance of making it. Although I didn't...have a voice in the matter, I agreed." But Timmins repeated that battalion orders were to continue the attack. He had all the wounded moved to the little shelter afforded by the rise of ground near him and all the small arms of the wounded brought there, too.

Motley accompanied the attacking force, now led by LT Emerson. "Everything was going as planned until we neared the ridge on the other side of the ravine. The firing broke out again in the area we had just left...." By this time, due to enemy fire, Motley wrote that he didn't think they "had over 20 or 25 men left. We discussed our alternatives. We still didn't know the strength of the [enemy] group who had hit us.... The Lieutenant reported this to battalion," but the orders to continue the attack stood. Two men were sent to investigate the ridge line; only one came back.

Tired and covered with grime after 43 days at the front, SGT David K. Brood of Laie, Hawaii, rests before rejoining his squad of the 5th Regimental Combat Team. (Source: P. 151, Pictorial History of the War in Korea, *Veterans of Foreign Wars, 1951)*

Emerson had another conversation on the radio. It must have been obvious to the officers on the scene, if not at battalion, that the unit could not continue the attack. Emerson ordered a withdrawal. This ends Motley's recollections.

Lyons and about sixteen or seventeen men finally gained the crest of A-2. Emerson was just below. The unit was "completely out of ammunition," Emerson said. "I mean completely out. About then, we heard this heavy firing in the valley maybe a mile below us. It went on...for about 20 minutes and...we surmised what had happened.... The North Koreans had cut behind us and completely chopped up the chiggies [South Koreans] bringing the resupply of ammunition and the litters." Emerson was notified on the radio "to withdraw as best I could and to ensure there were no wounded left," he recalled. "We did that." Emerson said that he and SGT Lyons covered the company withdrawal.

The company started out with "around 180 men," Emerson recalled, and suffered over 70 casualties. The next day Co. A attacked "the left ridge line going up to the highest ground on Sobuk-san.... We successfully got up on what was a major approach to friendly lines from the highest ground.

Co. B was on Sobuk-san, then, with Co. A on its left (south). Emerson recalled that there was a gap of about 800 yards between the two companies. Co. C, he said, was on a ridge to the rear of A and B.

Emerson had Co. A dig in an oblong perimeter about 125 yards long and 25 to 30 yards wide. He obtained additional machine guns. "I wound up with eight machine guns — two heavies and six light.... Four of the guns were positioned facing the avenue the enemy always took to attack." The company also had four 60mm mortars. The ground on the company right flank was too steep for an enemy attack, dropping almost straight down. The enemy could have come up on the left, but never did. Barbed wire was strung about 40 yards beyond the perimeter, and repaired or replaced every day. Antipersonnel mines were also placed between Emerson's company and Co. B on Sobuk-san by 1LT James H. Johnson's platoon of the 72d ECC. Johnson and Emerson were West Point classmates.

Since artillery fire would completely destroy the wire, Co. A employed their 60mm mortars against the enemy as they approached or got into the wire. Since barbed wire was so close to the mortars, less than 100 yards, they had to be fired at below recommended minimum range. The tubes were pointed almost vertically. So much mortar ammunition was used that the company had to be resupplied at least once a day, sometimes twice. Trains of a hundred or more chiggie bearers was common. In addition to water, these bearers brought water, food and litters to take out the wounded.

Every enemy attack, Emerson said, was begun by the enemy firing a red flare into his company position and then the enemy would come in blowing bugles and sounding sirens. To counteract the enemy's use of noise, Emerson's supply sergeant got a hand-cranked fire siren from a village and sent it up to the company. From then on, when the enemy attacked, Emerson had his radio operator crank the fire siren "It sounded like the London air raid.... "It really was an eerie sounding thing [but] it served two purposes. One, if...radio communication was out, it indicated to the people down below that we were under attack [and] to put down the protective artillery fires. Two, it blanked out the bugles, sirens, whistles and all the yelling [of] the North Koreans. So it helped psychologically."

Emerson said that the enemy attacks at night "were really mass attacks. They would come in waves.... From a captured enemy soldier, they learned that often the men in the second or third wave were not armed. They were expected to pick up weapons from the dead and wounded who had preceded them.

GEN Emerson also spoke highly of the soldiers he fought with. "You just can't say enough for the American infantry soldier that fought there," he said. "They were fighters, and fought in the best traditions of the U.S. Army.... I'm awfully proud that I was associated with them."

Emerson recalled that 2/5th RCT was on his left, but seven or eight hundred yards away. He thought Co. F was over there. Both Co. F and Co. A called artillery fire into that gap from time to time to discourage the enemy from exploiting it. Finally the Americans strung a piece of engineer tape across between the two companies, then hung signs on the tape stating that there was a minefield there. The enemy never attacked through that gap.

Over the span of 19 days on line there, Emerson's company took casualties almost every day. About mid-way through this period, the company went down to Emerson and 42 enlisted men.

Battle Mountain — Aug. 22 -31

Just before dawn on Aug. 22, Companies I and L, 24th Infantry launched an attack. LT R. P. Stevens led Co. L in the attack while Item laid down covering fire. 2LT Gerald N. Alexander's testimony in the Inspector General's Report, 24th Infantry Regiment, 1950 condemns the men of his platoon (cited on pp. 372-373, *South to the Naktong*). He testified that it took him an hour to get his men to move 200 yards, even though they were receiving no enemy fire; that when they reached the objective three enemy grenades wounded six of his men and the others withdrew without orders. He halted them about 100 yards down the slope and ordered them to go back up. No one would go, so he and a BAR-man climbed back and found no enemy. After that, his men rejoined him. (See Chapter Notes.)

Communications equipment was very scarce early in the war. One day 2LT Carroll N. LeTellier (Citadel, 1949) and his 1st Platoon, 77th ECC were returned from laying mines and stringing barbed wire, when they met the battalion commander, LTC Gerald Miller and his staff coming up the trail. LTC Miller spotted LeTellier's SCR 300 radio, and asked him for it. LeTellier obliged him.

On another part of the mountain, the enemy

attacked CPT Laurence M. Corcoran's C Co. Many of the enemy were killed or wounded in the band of antipersonnel mines and barbed wire entanglements which the 77th Engineers had emplaced. But an enemy 120mm mortar round came in, striking LT Mathis and four EM of the unit. With the loss of Mathis, Corcoran was the sole officer in Co. C until the end of August. The Division History records that Co. C employed flame throwers to help fend off the enemy attack.

Bussey recalled that most of the replacements coming to the 24th RCT at the time were not infantrymen; they came from the technical services such as signal, ordnance, medical, etc. This was true with other infantry commands. Replacements were being scraped up from service units in both Korea and Japan. Still, except possibly for the 24th RCT, the number of replacements did not meet the losses of the infantry companies.

Reserves were scarce in the 25th Division at the time. GEN Kean found it necessary, therefore, to order the 65th Engineer Battalion to be prepared to assemble three of its companies on two-hour notice to counter-attack in case of a breakthrough in the Haman area. About the same time, GEN Walker alerted the Marine Brigade for possible commitment to the 25th Division sector.

The struggle for Old Baldy continued on Aug. 23. ROK police units reinforced companies I and L. Supported by accurate, deadly 81mm and 4.2 inch mortar fire, the combined force wrested the crest from the enemy.

CPT Bussey's 77th ECC was pressed into service as a front line rifle company about this time, he recalled. Given a quick and very incomplete briefing by the 25th Division Engineer, a lieutenant colonel (his immediate commander), Bussey led his 200-man force up the a 400 meter high ridge to defend a 4,100 yard front, he wrote. They put out mines and barbed wire and awaited the enemy.

Bussey wrote that the Division Engineer ordered that all artillery fire missions had to have his personal approval, an unworkable arrangement since he would be nowhere near the front line during any fight; one that perhaps should have been reported to the Division Artillery Commander GEN Barth.

Charles Bussey detected some smoke from trees to his front, then observed the area through binoculars. He estimated the enemy force there at about 350 men. He called the Division Engineer, he wrote, and asked for artillery fire. The colonel refused authorization; he felt the enemy too close for artillery. Bussey stirred the enemy up a bit with long range .50-cal machine gun fire. This revealed that the enemy force was closer to 600.

Just before nightfall, a young replacement reported in, PVT Crosley. He was a chaplain's assistant, and had no knowledge of infantry or engineer work. He did not even know how to fire the M1 rifle, Bussey recalled. Bussey gave him a quick orientation, then sent him on to SGT Joseph Knight. Knight gave Crosley a very quick orientation on the M1 rifle and use of the bayonet, then put him into the line.

LaVaughn E. Fields, of the 3d Platoon, wrote, "From my position we looked out [and] could see cows with six and eight legs. Needless to say that the enemy was hiding behind the cows as they walked across our line of fire. Bussey called down and told us to hang tight. We knew we were going to get hit that night."

That night, there was a full moon, what Bussey called "The Chinese Moon." In the eerie light of that moon, the North Koreans came. The Engineers fought back with rifles and automatic weapons. When the enemy got into the foxhole line, the fighting became hand-to-hand, very personal and very deadly. In one encounter, Bussey wrote of bayoneting one enemy soldier who charged forward firing a machine pistol. The enemy attacked in waves.

Then it became quiet. The Engineers were exhausted.; many were dead, including, Bussey wrote, a PVT Hargrove and SGT Walker. He found the sergeant slumped on the parapet of his foxhole, dying. "Thanks, Cap'n," he croaked through his blood choked throat, lifted his hand up an inch or two and died.

A heavy enemy mortar bombardment heralded another attack. Again it became a hand-to-hand struggle. Bussey was struck from behind and fell down. He instinctively scuttled sideways and groped for his rifle. His hand found an entrenching tool, which he swung at his attacker, striking him in the head. Blood and brains spewed onto Bussey, he wrote.

By about 2 a.m., CPT Bussey contacted his platoons and found that he had only about half his men. Some of those who took wounded to the rear had not returned and a number of others were dead. The men repelled one more attack, then Bussey gave the order to withdraw. In all, he recalled, the enemy attacked six times that night before the Engineers pulled out. Bussey and his men made their way to the artillery and there reinforced their perimeter. At the time, hundreds of enemy soldiers were in the rear areas. They were attacking the artillery position and the gunners were firing back over open sights. Bussey called the Division Engineer to report the action and his withdrawal, but that officer was asleep, he wrote, with orders not to be disturbed. The enemy troops around the artil-

lery were too numerous, he recalled, forcing the battery to relocate. In addition to the wounded, Bussey's 77th Engineer Combat Company lost 20 KIA The Night of the Chinese Moon.

The enemy fiercely attacked 3/24th Infantry on Battle Mountain on the morning of Aug. 24, but were repulsed. Other enemy attacks of lesser force later in the day were also turned back. ROK National Police units then relieved 3d Battalion units on the hill.

Appleman wrote that, before its relief on Old Baldy Love Co. reported a foxhole strength of 17 men "yet, halfway down the slope its strength had jumped to 48 men, and by the next morning it was more than 100." The implication is that the bulk of the men had left the mountain without authority, possibly even had "bugged out." (See Chapter Notes.)

The enemy almost always attacked Battle Mountain by way of a long ridge from the northwest, starting near the village of Tundok. On Aug. 25 and 26, they launched several more attacks along this avenue, now against C/24th Infantry. Co. C was part of TF Baker, under command of LTC George R. Cole (West Point 1937). He commanded 2/24th Infantry Aug. 12-25, then was Regimental XO.) In addition to Co. C, the task force included a platoon of Co. E, 24th RCT and a company of ROK police. The task force was charged with the defense of a portion of Battle Mountain, according to Appleman. During the battle, he relates, U.S. aircraft caught about 100 enemy soldiers in the open and attacked them with rockets, napalm and machine guns. Few escaped.

LTC William J. Nelson, USA, Ret. was a First Lieutenant in the Operations section of 2/24th Infantry at the time. He recalled that TF Baker was formed to go to the aid of one of the battalion's companies which was cut off on Battle Mountain. As the force got close to their objective, the commander called for an air strike. The TF had no air panels of its own; they were all atop Battle Mountain. The aircraft came in and attacked TF Baker creating many casualties, before they could be redirected.

A 24th Infantry 75mm recoilless rifle crew in action on the Haman front. (Source: P. 127, Pictorial History of the War in Korea, Veterans of Foreign Wars, 1951)

Rishell's platoon of Co. A changed places with the left flank platoon of the unit on Aug. 26. That platoon had suffered a number of casualties from repeated enemy attacks. Rishell didn't get much information from the platoon leader; he was too eager "to get the hell off the mountain," Rishell wrote. His 1st Platoon passed a quiet night, but early next morning, Sunday, Aug. 27, the chatter of a BAR announced that the enemy was attacking. Rishell saw the point men of the enemy force less than a hundred yards away. The platoon opened fire, dispersing the enemy. Although the North Koreans made no more advances against the platoon that day, Rishell was ordered to take out a recon patrol. The three previous patrols which had been sent out in this sector had been caught in interlocking bands of enemy machine gun fire forward of the defensive position.

Rishell was unable to obtain artillery fire into the area from which other patrols had been fired on, and no air strikes were available. Finally, he arranged for the company 60mm mortars to fire smoke rounds to screen the patrol's departure and return, and for company machine guns and the rest of his own platoon to provide supporting fire, if necessary. With seven volunteers, he set out. As the men started to climb a hill the enemy opened fire on them. Since his orders were to make contact and withdraw, Rishell quickly pulled his men back without loss.

Rishell recalled that his unit was in this mountain position his men called "The Rock" for 20 days before being relieved and going into reserve.

On Aug. 27, 3/24th Infantry relieved 1/24th Infantry in the Battle Mountain-Pilbong area. Before dawn the next day a company-sized enemy force attacked between C and L Companies. After dark, enemy mortar fire hit Co. C, most of it directed at the CP. Some time after midnight, an enemy infiltrating force captured the CP. When the enemy attack began at 2:45 a.m. on Aug. 29, some of the men of the unit left their positions. The North Koreans then swung their attack against Co. E, overrunning part of the position. What was left of C Co. on Battle Mountain was resupplied by air while artillery fire sealed off the enemy from receiving reinforcements. The enemy occupying the part of Easy Co.'s position was pounded by artillery and air strikes. That night Co. E took the area back.

At 11 that night, an enemy attack sent some of the men in the left flank of Co C running to the rear in panic. Yells of, "They have broken through!" made matters worse as other men got up and ran, too. CPT Corcoran was left with 17, including several wounded, in and around his CP. With the coming of daylight, the enemy was again plastered with artillery, mortar and tank fire and air strikes. A wounded man who had hidden out, then had made his way down the mountain, reported that the most of the North Koreans had withdrawn to a wooded area west of the peak. Only a token force occupied the summit. Co. B, supported by 3/24th Infantry attacked and retook the crest at 11 a.m. on Aug. 30.

Battle Mountain changed hands repeatedly between Aug. 15 and 31. Often it fell to one side or the other several times in a day. The Intelligence Sergeant of 1/24th Infantry calculated that

A 105mm howitzer of the 159th FAB firing. (Source: Chapter 3, Battleground Korea - 25th Division in the Korean War*)*

it had fallen to the enemy and regained by the 24th Infantry 19 times.

Appleman described how Battle Mountain was retaken each time. "Artillery, mortar, and tank fire raked the crest and air strikes employing napalm blanketed the scorched top." The infantry then attacked from beneath a hill on the east slope of Old Baldy, "where supporting mortars set up a base of fire and kept the heights under a hail of steel until the infantry had arrived at a point just short of the crest. The mortar fire then lifted and the infantry moved rapidly up the last stretch to the top, usually to find it deserted by the enemy." The enemy did not attempt to occupy the crest during daylight hours, knowing that the Americans would blast the area. They attacked under the cloak of night for the same reason. The reduced visibility was a great equalizer for the North Koreans. They took advantage of it to mass overwhelming numbers of troops at the point of attack. If the defenders did not withdraw, the enemy kept attacking in waves, eventually overwhelming the position by weight of numbers.

Battle Mountain and Pilbong also resulted in heavy casualties. Battle Mountain alone accounted for the loss of seven FOs and eight other men in the FO parties, all from the 159th FAB. Aug. casualties in the 24th Infantry were 75 KIA and 425 WIA.

The 5th RCT on Sobuk-san — Aug. 24-31

The 5th RCT, from Sobuk-san to Chindong-ni, was also often heavily engaged. This was particularly true of 1/5th RCT, up on Sobuk itself. Early in the series of battles around Sobuk-san, Francis (Frank) Colbert, then a PFC in a .30-cal machine gun crew of Co. D, recalled that his squad was supporting a rifle company. "The infantry company had gotten on top of the mountain," he wrote. "We were on a knoll below them...." The enemy drove the rifle unit off the hill, and they "came running down off the top.... I was so damned mad, I couldn't talk." The company was quickly turned around and retook the summit.

At 8:30 p.m. on Aug. 25, enemy flat trajectory fire began to strike the positions of 1/5th RCT. Within 15 minutes, the entire area was under heavy enemy artillery, mortar and machine gun fire. Under this fire, the enemy launched a vicious and determined attack. The battle lasted all night, but the North Koreans were repulsed. Fighting continued the next day. During this protracted and savage engagement, MSG Melvin O. Handrich, Co. C, 5th RCT, distinguished himself as an outstanding and heroic leader. Near midnight on Aug. 25, Handrich discovered about a hundred enemy soldiers trying to infiltrate the position. He moved forward to direct fire on this force and stayed there for eight hours.

Often, the enemy approached within 50 feet of his position. The next morning, when a large enemy force tried to overrun the company position, Handrich first rose up and engaged them with his rifle, then personally kept part of the company from abandoning its position. He directed fire on the North Koreans. Although severely wounded, he remained in a forward and exposed position, directing fire. Finally, an enemy assault overran his position and MSG Handrich was fatally wounded. When the ground was retaken over 70 enemy dead were counted in the area he had defended. The Division History credits Handrich with being largely responsible for the success of the 1st Battalion's defense on Aug. 25 and early the next day. During the latter day, the North Koreans were able to penetrate the positions of companies B and C. Under close-in artillery fire, counterattacking troops restored the line.

1LT Gordon J. Duqueman, then platoon leader of the 81mm mortar platoon of Co. D, recalled his "first real battle" while on the slopes of Sobuk-san. Co. A was on the left of the line and Co. B on the right. Co. C was on a ridge in the center and slightly behind the other two rifle companies. The mortars and CP of Co. D were behind C. "The North Koreans attacked in the morning," he wrote, "overrunning part of Co. C and killing CPT Carter Hillgard." Co. B stood firm. This was the day Co. A made their "reconnaissance in force," losing CPT Timmons and LT Worley. "CPT Baker [Claude Baker, C.O., Co. D] and I gathered what was left of Co. C and counterattacked and restored the position," he continued. "Co A [also] held."

"In this engagement the North Koreans broke through C Company's perimeter, but never made it over the top of the hill. D Co. CP and my mortar platoon CP were on the reverse slope of the hill, so we received mortar fire and later rifle fire from the top of the hill and flank," Duquemin wrote. His mortarmen joined the counterattack. The attack was made "by going around each flank. Baker on the left and me on the right...." he related. The 555th FA Bn gave us great support."

Once a patrol from King Co. boldly attacked a fortified position containing four antitank weapons. The attack was successful and all four guns were destroyed.

Co. K was on the extreme southern end of the 5th RCT and the whole Perimeter, in a valley next to the sea. The unit's position was near the road fork at Tosan, where the Marines turned south during TF Kean. Co. L occupied the first high ground north of Co. K. Co I was in reserve on a ridge behind L.

The night of Aug. 27 was brightly lit by a full moon. 1LT Daniel R. Beirne (West Point, 1948), wrote this to his family about the events of that night: "About midnight we observed a fairly large group [of enemy troops] sneaking in across the rice paddies. I waited until they got in and were stretched along a road in front of our position and then gave the order to open fire. The entire position cut loose with every weapon we had. We really burned up that road. We must have surprised them because they never fired a single return shot. We could see them running

back into the rice paddies...." Farther on in the letter, he wrote that a person dressed as a Korean woman opened fire with a burp gun on several of his men.

On the morning of Aug. 28, the enemy again attacked 1/5th RCT, but made no headway. The following day, Co. A was attacked by about 40 enemy soldiers, supported by a mortar barrage. The North Koreans closed to close quarters, but were thrown back.

The Navy was of great assistance to the 5th RCT. Since the regiment was emplaced on the southern flank and coast, the smaller naval vessels could come in close. Taking advantage of this, the destroyer *Wiltsie*, and later the *Endicott,* stood in close to shore and added their guns (about 5" or 6") to the artillery support for the 5th RCT, and later the 27th RCT when it relieved the 5th. It was the equivalent of an additional battery of heavy artillery. At the time, the heaviest Army artillery available in Korea was the 155mm howitzer, which fired a round about equal that fired by the ship's gun.

2LT William A. Motley, an FO with the Triple Nickel wrote about how he adjusted fire with the help of illuminating parachute flares fired by naval ships lying off the southern shore. "This, to me, was a real accomplishment of the FDC.... They were timing the firing of the batteries so that my rounds were landing just seconds after the flare exploded. I could give the correction and the batteries could fire again while the flares were still up," he wrote. This required skillful timing and good gunnery on the part of both the ship and the field artillery personnel. Motley cited it as an example "of what could be done with instant communication and coordination between the Services."

Duquemin recalled that the 5th RCT traded North Korean weapons to the destroyers in exchange for ice cream and vegetables.

A number of other veterans of the 5th RCT recalled some of their experiences during this time on the Perimeter. Gerald Pack, Co. F, wrote that he and a major were walking along beside a tank one day. The tank hit a mine and the track was blown off. "We both thought we were KIA. The major raised up and a Gook hiding in the weeds shot at him." The officer shot him. "We walked up to him [the enemy soldier]. He was going to shoot again, but we finished him off."

MSG Robert W. Potter, USA, Ret., came to the 5th RCT as a staff sergeant replacement while the regiment was defending the southern flank. He was assigned to Co. G. William G. Price was also a member of George. Both men recalled the one time that Co. G was driven from its position on Sobuk. It was Potter's first battle in Korea. "It happened early...Sunday morning before dawn," Potter said. "They broke through our machine gun nest and we were pushed off the hill.... "We regrouped and...retook the hill."

"We had great foxholes, dug deeply and as comfortable as possible considering the situation," Price wrote in the May 1994 *Newsletter of the 5th RCT Association.* "We were usually under attack, both day and night, but we lost the mountain one time. We lost it one night and regained it...the following day."

The company got one hot meal a day, he recalled, brought up the mountain in large, insulated marmite cans. The men went back a few at

a time to get their meal, then returned to their foxholes. The "one hot meal a day" routine was fairly typical of many rifle companies on the Perimeter. Unit commanders and mess personnel tried very hard to provide front-line soldiers with this amenity. Often, mess personnel risked their lives to deliver this meal.

He also recalled the short time during that first summer in Korea when every man in Eighth Army received an issue of one can of beer per day. This was what was called "three point two beer." That is, it contained 3.2 per cent alcohol. Back in the U.S., the Women's Christian Temperance Union and other anti-alcohol groups succeeded in stopping this issue on the grounds that many of the soldiers were under the legal drinking age. (See Chapter Notes.) "Some time in late August...or early September 1950 we were kicked off Sobuk-san during an NK night assault," Price wrote. The foxhole which Price shared with Ray Warner "was on the extreme forward slope of the mountain, so we had to retreat by going toward N.K. lines. The two men somehow got into a ditch "that was loaded with anti-tank and anti-personnel mines," some trip wire activated and some pressure activated. But they returned to their unit in time to take part in the counterattack which retook the position. There, he wrote, "we discovered some positions where the men had been killed while sleeping in their foxholes."

"My foxhole...was dug in just below the crest of a hill and we were under artillery fire," wrote Buddy Ford, 81mm Mortar Platoon, Co. H, 5th RCT in a 1990 issue of the 5th RCT Association *Newsletter.* "One shell came screaming in and suddenly went quiet, which meant it was falling close." It was a dud, and he watched it skid on down the hill. He also recalled for a time in August when ammunition was rationed.

CPL Robert B. Hardin of Item Co. wrote this: "Battle Mountain had a saddle running to our positions. We put 2 outposts...there — one BAR and one rifle. The N.K would come up that way and hit us.... We had two [sets of foxholes], one for day and one for night." The enemy could see into the night foxholes, so the day positions were dug on the reverse slope of the hill. He recalled that a BAR-man and one rifleman were killed in the saddle on the flank while the unit occupied these positions.

"One day, I volunteered to go on a roadblock," wrote then-PFC Albert F. Semasko, of Battery B, 555th FAB. "There were 15 of us. We were at a bridge with a mine field on one side of it. One night, my buddy, PFC Betencourt, whispered, 'Here come some Gooks.' When they came to the bridge, he hollered some Korean word for surrender. Those five Gooks threw their hands straight up in the air. If they would have done anything else, I would have cut them down.... We stripped them naked. They had enough arms and ammo to start their own war."

The 72d Engineer Combat Company

The 72d ECC served the 5th RCT in much the same way that the 77d ECC did the 24th RCT. Two members of the 72d, MG James A. Johnson, then a platoon leader, and SFC Raul DeLuna, then a young enlisted man, recorded their experiences with the unit during the early days of the Korean War.

DeLuna was a member of a detail of engineers, under 1LT Albert A. Van Patten (West Point, 1947) which had been working in a rear area for about three days, building a culvert. At night, they returned to a bivouac area and returned to the work site in dump trucks the next day. On the fourth morning, the three trucks carrying the engineers to work passed a walled village — one they had passed each of the previous three days. The wall, made of mud, stone and rock, was about 6 feet high and about 2 feet thick in places. There were a number of gates through the wall. DeLuna was riding in the back of the first truck. The first hint of danger was a loud explosion in front of the lead truck. The truck "shook like the front wheels had fallen in a ditch," he said. The explosion was from an enemy hand grenade. It was followed by machine gun fire directed at the truck and its occupants. The other two trucks hastily backed out of the fire zone. The sudden stop by the lead truck threw one of the sergeants standing on its bed against the back of the truck. "In the process," DeLuna said, "the ammunition clip fell out of his .45 [automatic pistol]."

"Somebody yells, 'AMBUSH!' The first thought was to get out of there.... We started jumping off the back. One of the first people to jump out...got hit on the way..." This was a man named Lipscomb, hit in the back, but not killed. "The rest of us fell on him, jumping on top of him in a mad scramble to get out of the truck. One of the squad leaders...jumped off the truck and landed on his rifle, breaking its stock." He ran through a gate into a compound. Everyone from the truck followed him. "One of the guys ahead of me...got shot through the helmet into the back of his head. He fell face down. We jumped over him. The squad leader picked up the fallen man's "rifle and cartridge belt, thinking he was dead."

DeLuna and several others ran into what he described as "pig pens that had roofs and a back wall and low wall at the front about 3 feet high. There were several of these cubicles along one side of the patio and the same thing across the patio from us."

The man who had been shot in the helmet "laid there for 15 or 20 minutes," said DeLuna. "We knew that he was dead.... We could see the hole where the bullet went in his steel pot and it had a hole on the back where it had been shot through."

Then "he...started moving. A couple of guys...near me ran out...and dragged him in.... He continued to be in a daze." The helmet saved his life. The bullet apparently entered the front of the helmet at his forehead, passed between the helmet liner and the steel helmet itself, then exited in the rear, blowing a hole in the helmet at that point. (See Chapter Notes.)

Enemy troops across the patio kept the engineers under fire in the pig pens. The sergeant who had lost the clip from his .45 had just one round in the pistol's chamber. He later jokingly remarked, "I didn't know whether to use that round to kill one of those guys or to just use it on myself."

"We spent most of the day there," DeLuna said. An American tank was brought up to attack the enemy, but DeLuna remarked, it couldn't lower its barrel far enough to fire into the wall, so was ineffective.

A squad leader from one of the other trucks jumped over the fence into the patio, "coming to see what he could do about getting us out. He got three slugs across the stomach.... His stomach was all muscle. The doctor said that if he had not been so muscular in the stomach he would have died," DeLuna said.

Another soldier, named Sparks, was shot in the left cheek by a burp gun. "I could hear him gurgling as blood poured into his mouth. The guy who was with him was frantic (and scared)," DeLuna continued. He called for help and asked "What should I do?" Someone called back, "Hey, calm down and get his first aid kit! Get the bandage out...and put it on. Its an open wound so tie it up good and strong...so he stops bleeding."

At some point in the day's action, LT Van Patten was wounded in the cheek and had the tip of a finger shot off.

The enemy kept the GIs down in their pig pens, firing burp guns at every voice, every noise. "They had small slugs and...were not very effective at any great distance," DeLuna observed.

An air strike came in hitting another part of the village. The metal links from the strafing aircraft fell on the roofs of the pens and into the patio where DeLuna and his companions were located.

Under cover of the air strike and other diversions, the men slipped out of the compound by ones and twos, unknown to DeLuna. Suddenly, he found he was all alone. He called out, but got no answer. Even the enemy seemed to have gone. DeLuna decided it was time he left, too. "I made a mad dash out the gate...ran across the road into the rice paddy and started to run away from the village." A burp gun opened fire. DeLuna "heard . . . slugs hitting around the water fairly close." He dove into the water-covered paddy and started crawling. After crawling about 40-50 yards, he became angry. "I was so tired and exhausted from the events of the day and now from crawling through the mud, that I stood up and said, 'What the heck, if I get shot, I get shot.'" Luckily, there was no more firing.

Some GIs, a great distance away, saw him. Two of them ran to DeLuna. "They grabbed me by one arm each and literally dragged me out to...the others...."

DeLuna was fortunate to have gotten out of the village when he did. Just after he made his escape, the village was leveled by direct artillery fire. He remembered the date very well — Aug. 21, 1950 — it was his 19th birthday.

During one mine-laying operation between Companies A and B on Sobuk, LT Johnson's platoon began receiving heavy fire. Johnson thought it came from Emerson's company and stormed up to protest. He found out that the fire was not from Co. A. Emerson promised to get it straightened out. When Johnson got back to his platoon, which had continued to work laying mines and trip flares, the men were brought under .50-cal machine gun fire from the 2d Battalion. Johnson, disgusted, pulled his men off the project and Sobuk-san. He told Emerson, "When you get this straightened out, I'll be back."

With all three battalions committed on line, the 5th RCT was slim on reserves. More than, once, Johnson recalled, his engineer platoon was all or part of the regimental reserve, ready to be committed at a moment's notice. When in this role, Johnson stayed at the regimental CP so that he could be contacted without loss of time.

The 77th Engineers also sometimes were sent in to man part of the front line. In one case, Johnson recalled, they took the headlights from a destroyed truck up on the front with them. The lights were fastened to a rod, and ropes were attached so as to be able to move the lights. The lights were attached to a battery in a foxhole. "When we'd hear something, we'd turn the lights on." When the lights were turned on, it looked to the enemy as though there was a vehicle up on the mountain.

DeLuna recalled one time when his platoon dug in on the front. His position, with a .30-cal machine gun, faced to the rear overlooking the route which the platoon had taken up the hill. He was about eight feet behind the crest. About five of six feet to his right was a huge rock about seven or eight feet high and about the same width. His squad leader sat with his back against the boulder, talking to Raul. Suddenly, they heard an explosion about half way down the rear slope of the mountain. They turned and saw three tanks down in the valley. Both men thought the tankers were zeroing their guns. "I turned back to...digging.... All of a sudden, we heard the tank fire again. This time, we heard the shell zooming towards us.... I dropped down into the hole...and [my squad leader] dropped almost on top of me. . . . Luckily, the shell hit the upper third of the boulder.... The shrapnel flew upward.

But the force of the concussion threw DeLuna out of his hole. "The next thing I knew," he said, "I was rolling down the mountain.... I was stunned." His squad leader jumped forward, grabbed DeLuna, and stopped his rolling. "He grabbed a branch," DeLuna said. "I was lying face down." Certain that he probably had lost arms or legs, he asked, "Take a look and see if I'm all here." The squad leader made a quick inspection, then responded, "Well, it looks like you're all here. I don't see any blood anywhere." DeLuna then sat up and checked himself out, "flexing my hands and moving my feet." Although he and his squad leader had escaped unhurt, some infantrymen farther up the mountain were hit. One or two were killed. DeLuna and his squad leader rejoined the platoon.

Later that night, DeLuna was again dug in with his machine gun, guarding the back trail. About 2:30 or 3 a.m., fighting sleep, he went over to the next foxhole, "about 15-20 feet away," he said. "I sat down...with one of my buddies and we started whispering.... About this time...both of us...heard noise coming up the trail.... No one was supposed to be there." It turned out to be his platoon leader, LT Van Patten and a Salvador Parmona, returning with 5-gallon cans of water for the platoon. DeLuna didn't know they had gone on this mission, and was not expecting anyone on the trail. The only thing that saved the two men was the fact that DeLuna was not at his machine gun. He would have most certainly killed his platoon leader and Parmona, his good friend.

Ambushing the Enemy

The 25th Recon Co. ranged throughout the division sector, principally in rear areas to ferret out infiltrated enemy troops. At one point, a message from one North Korean commander was intercepted in which he complained that this unit was seriously interfering with the operations of his command.

One day a patrol discovered a shallow draw where enemy troops would assemble at night to infiltrate American lines. The draw lay between the sectors of the 24th and 35th Regiments. A platoon of the 35th was positioned on the rim of the draw to intercept the infiltrators. Each day thereafter, the Recon Co. made a sweep to drive along the hills and nearby terrain to drive small parties of the enemy into the open end of the draw. When the enemy attempted to infiltrate through the other end of the draw that night, the 35th platoon sprang their ambush. The enemy dead were removed and the trap set again. This scenario repeated itself for a number of nights. Then the enemy sent a patrol in to investigate. The Recon Co. attacked the patrol, forcing its withdrawal. That brought the nightly ambushes to an end; the enemy never used the draw again.

The Recon Co. encountered about 30 of the enemy in the rear on Aug. 27 in a village just north of Masan. A number of North Koreans were killed and the rest scattered. Documents on some of the bodies revealed that they were from the *6th Reconnaissance Company.*

The 25th MP Company

CPL Milton Melhorn, 1st Platoon, 25th MP Company recalled some of the Military Police Co. activities. The company performed the normal traffic control duties, but it also provided convoy escort and patrol duty. "We...ran night jeep patrols back and forth between... Masan and the three 25th Division regimental command posts along the MSR. The purpose was to make sure the MSR remained open to the ambulances, supply trucks and other vehicles.... We reported back by radio to our Headquarters in Masan of any disruption and Division would decide what to do.... There was frequent guerrilla activity along the MSR and our job was to report this.... At least two of our patrols were ambushed by guerrillas. One MP named Kitchen was killed in one ambush and another MP was captured." This MP was rescued during the breakout, after being shot and left for dead by his guards.

Melhorn wrote that MPs enjoyed being "dropped off to stay with other units for periods of time to direct traffic at bombed out bridges, defiles, detours, etc. "We were on our own and had to fend for ourselves.... We preferred this type duty. We worked (out) our own schedule.... We enjoyed eating and bivouacking with non-MP units. This brought us together, causing us to have pride in being an MP; camaraderie and cohesion...."

The Southern Front Holds

The *NK 6th* and *7th Divisions* strove mightily to breach 25th Division defenses in August, but the division stood fast, inflicting huge losses on the enemy. One member of a 25th Division rifle company recalled that the ground was littered with North Korean dead, which rotted in the hot sun, creating an almost nauseating stench. Lime was brought up to cover the bodies. This

was typical of the condition in many front-line units of the division at the time.

It is possible that the 159th FAB fired the largest number of rounds of the three 105mm field artillery battalions of the 25th Division in August. Their count was 26,527 rounds. The 64th fired another 15,174 rounds. Figures for the 8th (105mm) or the 90th FAB (155mm) could not be found.

What appears to be a destroyed U.S. tank. (Courtesy of SFC Edward N. Arendell, HQ, 34th Infantry)

The coordination of mortar, artillery, naval gunfire and air support was fine tuned during August. Supporting fire and air strikes came on target more quickly, the fire more concentrated and more deadly.

On the other hand, attrition, and the lack of sufficient replacements, brought rifle company strength way down. The losses among platoon leaders and company commanders was very high. By Aug. 24, four front line rifle companies each had but one officer. Critical shortages of ammunition, vehicles and signal equipment added to the command's problems.

Refugees entering the lines and wandering around rear areas created major problems. First were the infiltrators who concealed themselves with the refugees. Sometimes, firefights with them also caused tragic, severe casualties among the real refugees. Another problem was that these poor displaced people often clogged roads, including the MSR, impeding supply and reinforcement efforts. Finally, all these people had to be rounded up and evacuated. In August alone, 120,335 refugees were evacuated from the 25th Division sector and resettled.

Choggie Bearers (Chiggie Bearers)

Every front-line soldier and Marine veteran of Korea remembers what he called choggie or chiggie bearers. These bearers were a mixture of old men and young boys. The poundage of ammo, food and equipment which each could carry on back packs called "A-frames" was astounding — often far more than the bearer's weight. Their pay was a pittance, often little more than food and a place to sleep when not engaged in a resupply mission. Untold hundreds, if not thousands, of them were killed or wounded. Unheralded, unsung, their story never told, these bearers contributed immeasurably to the success of the Americans and ROKs in the Perimeter and later.

Later, the bearer situation was formalized into what was known as the Korean Service Corps. The bearers were more organized into teams, and received pay for their work (still a pittance by U.S. standards).

Chapter Notes:
P. 237 Similar conditions prevail in the U.S. Armed Forces today. Even for Desert Storm, it required five months to muster the force required for the operation. In the early days of the build-up, troops and

equipment were sent to Saudi Arabia, with not enough ammunition for even a token defense by the forces available in the country. Had the Iraqis chosen to attack early on there could have been a far different outcome to that adventure.

P. 242 The actions of this platoon may seem shameful, but Appleman's narrative is sketchy and incomplete. There is no information in the South to the Naktong *account as to the nature of the terrain the platoon had to traverse in the 200 yards; nor is there any indication as to the number of men in the platoon. Battle Mountain is notoriously steep. The rapid wounding of six men by three grenades could have temporarily unnerved a few men, who might have precipitated the retreat of the others.*

P. 243 Throughout South to the Naktong, *Appleman cites various officers and Eighth Army Inspector General reports to support many negative conclusions. This author has written statements and narratives from other officers and NCOs, which indicate more positive conduct of individuals and units of the 24th Regiment.*

LTC Corley, then commanding 3/24th Infantry, wrote: "My chain of command stops at company level." Obviously, he found company, platoon and squad leadership less than satisfactory. However, the turn-over rate of the 3d Platoon, Co. L, (nine platoon leaders in about a month of combat) could be one reason that leadership suffered. While some units may not have behaved as well as expected, Appleman seems to condemn the whole regiment.

Another factor possibly contributing to the poor showing of some units was the Army's segregation policy. As LTC Charles Bussey wrote in Firefight at Yechon, *"assignment and utilization policy specified only that replacements to the 24th Infantry Regiment be Negroes. It didn't matter if they were properly trained or qualified in the proper skills. It only mattered that they were black. That policy guaranteed the weakening of the 24th Regimental Combat Team."*

P. 245 Many were. But the loss of the beer issue created a short lived, minor morale problem. It is doubtful if anti-alcohol groups attracted any members from the veterans of the Perimeter.

P. 245 This happened to a number of soldiers with this style helmet. The helmet consisted of two main parts, a thin, laminated plastic liner, molded to fit the inside of the steel helmet itself, the other part of the helmet.

Far East Air Force (FEAF), Tactical and Strategic Missions — August 1950

The number of tactical air control parties (TACP) available to ground forces steadily increased between July and August, 1950. One TACP was assigned to each U.S. regiment and division, and one to each ROK division and corps. During July FEAF flew 4,635 close support sorties. In August, this jumped to 7,397 sorties. This equates to 238 close-support sorties per day. That month, an average of 40 sorties daily were flown in support of each American division in the Perimeter. This does not include the considerable number of sorties flown by Marine air. Between Aug. 3 and Sept. 14, 1950, the three squadrons of MAG 33 flew 995 close support missions; 244 of them for the Army. MAG 33 had two squadrons of Corsairs for daylight operations and one all-weather squadron for operations at night or periods of bad weather. By the end of August, FEAF had eight fighter squadrons available for close support missions.

FEAF close support aircraft normally left their bases at Itazuke and Ashiya two planes at a time every fifteen minutes. Tactical aircraft were brought on target by Forward Air Controllers and AT-6 Mosquito aircraft. By Aug. 23, twenty-nine AT-6 planes were operating in Korea. They operated, dawn-to-dusk over six stations. Each plane stayed on station for two hours, being relieved by another at the end of that time.

Appleman credits this close support "in determining the outcome of battles [in August] than in any other month of the war." Robert F. Futrell, in his *The United States Air Force in Korea 1950-1953*, writes, "No American army...had ever received so much close support as the FEAF supplied to the Eighth Army [in August 1950]."

Often, during enemy breakthroughs, Walker was able to obtain tactical air attacks on enemy concentrations before he was able to commit his reserves. These air assaults usually inflicted heavy casualties on the enemy, destroyed supplies and equipment, delayed his advance and caused him to disperse his forces to avoid annihilation. As a result, the force of the penetration was usually somewhat diminished. The attacks bought valuable time for reserves to assemble and launch counterattacks.

One Air Force pilot who most of the men in Korea in the early days remember, was MAJ Dean Hess. Hess, a combat fighter pilot of WW II, had the mission of training ROK pilots. In WW II, he flew 63 combat mission in Europe. In Korea, in only two months, he flew 95 more, earning him the sobriquet of "The One-man Air Force." The Air Force, fearful that this valuable officer would be lost, grounded him.

Ground support, or fighter, aircraft soon made daylight activities by the North Koreans near suicide. They destroyed or damaged railroad rolling stock, trucks, artillery pieces and tanks. This forced the enemy to move most of their supplies and reinforcements at night or during periods of very bad weather. Air power contrib-

uted in large measure, to the destruction of the enemy's tank force. Troops encountered numerous burned out enemy trucks and tanks during the breakout and pursuit late that September.

The Army, Air Force, Marines and Navy cooperated in a ground-air-sea operation in the early days of Korea long before such a term was officially used.

A shortage of aviation engineer units (another "casualty" of post-World War II cuts) slowed the construction of six planned bases in Korea. The loss of ground by U.S and ROK forces during July and early August also prevented work on some of these sites.

Amply complementing tactical air power was the strategic operation of bombers. The 22d and 92d Bombardment Groups were sent to the Far East. These two groups, equipped with B-29 medium bombers, joined the 19th Bombardment Group, already in FEAF. These three groups, along with the 31st Strategic Reconnaissance Squadron and other support formations, were organized into the Far East Air Forces Bomber Command (Provisional), under the command of MG Emmett "Rosie" O'Donnell, Jr. (West Point, 1928). After a distinguished record in WW II, O'Donnell had commanded the Fifteenth Air Force since 1948. There were also at least three B-26 light bomber wings — 3d, 98th and 307th, which flew both tactical and strategic missions.

North Korea had five major industrial centers: Wonsan, Pyongyang, Hungnam, Chongjin and Rashin. All but Pyongyang were located along the northeast coast of North Korea. Wonsan was a major port city, railway center and the site of the Chosun Oil Refinery — the largest oil refinery in Korea and one of the largest in Asia. Five miles south of the city was a large petroleum tank farm. The rail yards were one of the three most important in all Korea and its locomotive repair shops were the second largest in Korea.

Pyongyang was a major road and rail hub. It also was the site of the North Korean Army's arsenal (the second largest arsenal in Asia), and a vast array of war manufacturing enterprises, producing weapons, ammunition of all types and military vehicles. It also had extensive rail yards and a large railway repair installation. The Hungnam area contained the most extensive ba-

sic-chemical and light-metal production complex in the Far East. Chongjin had two harbors, important rail yards and workshops and two iron works. Far to the north was Rashin, a significant port and naval base, including naval oil-storage facilities and railroad yards of importance to both the North Koreans and the Soviet Union.

All of these complexes were targeted for destruction early in the war, along with all key bridges north of the 37th parallel. This interdiction campaign was waged in August by both B-29 medium bombers and B-26 light bombers. A total of 32 rail and highway bridges were targeted. These bridges lay on the three main transportation routes in Korea at the time: Sinanju south to Pyongyang, then northeast to Wonsan on the east coast; the Munsan-Seoul-Chunchon-Chumunjin-up on the east coast; Seoul south to Chochi-won, then east to Wonju, thence to Samchok on the east coast.

B-29s attacked the five principal complexes in August and September. On Aug. 7, most of the Pyongyang arsenal and rail yards were destroyed. Concentrated bombing on Aug. 7, 9 and 10 completely destroyed the Chosen petroleum refinery at Wonsan. Between July 30 and Sept. 19, the Air Force heavily bombed the chemical complex near Hungnam. It also attacked the docks at Najin, a bare 17 miles south of the Siberian border. In the last few days of August, it bombed the Songjin metal-working facilities and heavily damaged the aluminum and magnesium plants at Chinnampo.

On Aug. 6, nightly aerial reconnaissance was implemented. Late in August nightly aerial interdiction began over North Korea. This involved B-29 bombers dropping parachute flares at 10,000 feet. The flares deployed at 6,000 feet and B-26 bombers attacked enemy targets in their light. Many of the flares were WW II leftovers, and failed to work, sometimes hampering the success of these missions.

As the war continued the enemy took extraordinary measures to counteract attacks against rail lines and truck convoys. They established numerous supply points, stocking ties, spare rails and tools along the rail lines. Work parties were also scattered along these lines. Damaged or destroyed rolling stock was quickly moved away and the lines repaired, often overnight. Also, listening for approaching Ameri-

T-6 Mosquito (Source: PP.83, U.S. Air Force in Korea, Futrell, USAF, Wash., D.C., 1983)

can aircraft, they were able to establish anti-aircraft ambushes, destroying or damaging the attacking planes.

Shelters were built along roads to protect trucks from attack. Large convoys were split up into several smaller ones. And large amounts of supplies were hand-carried by soldiers and civilians, in long-range relay systems.

From July through September 1950 FEAF increased to 16 groups and 44 squadrons with 657 aircraft. At war's end, this had expanded into 19 groups, 69 squadrons and 1,536 aircraft. By WW II standards, this was still a very small force of aircraft.

Army Logistics and Personnel

Very early in the Korean War the Far East Command instituted "Operation Rebuild" in Japan to repair and rebuild vehicles, weapons and equipment and rehabilitate ammunition. In August alone, 950 2 1/2-ton trucks were repaired. In the first three months of the war, almost all the ammunition used by the UN and ROKs came from rebuild stocks in Japan. This did not totally prevent the issue of faulty ammunition to the troops on the front. By the end of 1950, "Rebuild" employed 19,908 people (almost all Japanese) in eight shops. The Korean War provided a valuable impetus to restarting many Japanese commercial endeavors, giving a significant boost to its post-WW II economy.

The daily Yokohama-Sasebo-Pusan Red Ball Express, started on July 23, operated with increased efficiency, delivering supplies to Korea consistently within 60-70 hours. Air delivery varied from 12 hours to five days. In four deliveries (Aug. 5, 9, 22 and 25) Red Ball delivered a total of 2,234 tons of supplies to Pusan. It was more efficient and cheaper than airlift. But GEN Partridge, commanding FEAF, complained on Aug. 10 that the Army was not utilizing the Air Force's 200-ton daily airlift capability. As a result, Eighth Army curtailed Red Ball express deliveries, effective Aug. 15, except on Tuesdays and Fridays. Ostensibly, this was done because it was feared that Pusan would be unable to handle the flow of seaborne supplies. Airlift tonnage then dramatically increased. In four deliveries (Aug. 16, 19, 28 and 29) the Air force transported 1,666 personnel and 1,198 tons of supplies.

Battle losses in July and August were so great that extraordinary measures had to be taken to try to replace them. By Aug. 5 losses totaled 7,859, but only 7,711 replacements had reached the Far East and only part of these had actually been sent to Korea. MG William A. Beiderlinden, MacArthur's personnel chief, was optimistic. He believed that, once the defense line stabilized along what became known as the Pusan Perimeter, casualties would decrease and the flow of replacements would increase; that the return to combat duty of soldiers wounded and recovering in FEC hospitals would also ease the situation. For example, the number of men returned to combat duty from hospitals on Aug. 4 equaled 30 per cent of the casualties suffered on the same day.

But his beliefs were shattered within two days; every division in Korea was dangerously short of officers and men. On Aug. 7, the Far East Command sent an urgent message to Washington for 8,000 men to reach FEC within 15 days. James F. Schnabel, in *Policy and Direction: The First Year,* correctly writes: "All infantry regiments in Korea were so weakened that unless these men reached them in two weeks, they would deteriorate so badly that

B-26 Invader (Source: PP. 327, U.S. Air Force in Korea, Futrell, USAF, Wash., D.C., 1983)

major steps would be necessary to rebuild them. Most urgently needed were infantry and artillery soldiers and company-grade officers." Most rifle companies numbered fewer than 100 EM on the line and had but one or two officers. B/27th Infantry had two officers and not more than 60 or 70 EM in the rifle and weapons platoons — typical of the time among units which had gone to Korea from Japan.

The replacement situation became so critical in Korea that MacArthur cut the short orientation period replacements underwent at Camp Drake to only the time required to issue them individual weapons and equipment. As a result, in addition to sending men untrained, or poorly trained in infantry subjects, these replacements were shipped to Korea without having the opportunity to become familiar with the characteristics and proper sight setting of their individual weapons.

Part of the problem of replacements for Korea rested in the units stationed in Japan. Less than half of the 16,000 replacements arriving in Japan between Jul. 1 and Aug. 15 went straight to Korea. Some went to the badly depleted 7th Division, but many more went to non-divisional units in Japan. Some 25,000 men and officers of Eighth Army remained in Japan. This was later remedied, when all of Eighth Army was moved to Korea.

As in every war, higher headquarters suddenly found that authorized staffing did not seem to meet staff work requirements. As a result, staff agencies in Japan took experienced officers and enlisted men from among the replacements to fill their own perceived needs. These same staff section chiefs also kept many officers and enlisted men who should have been sent to Korea as replacements. At lower headquarters, the scenario was repeated: keep the people you have, and add more. These section chiefs appeared to be trying to enhance the staff section's importance and expand the number of personnel assigned — "empire building" in military parlance.

Beiderlinden asked GEN Almond to inter-

B-29 of the 19th Bomb Wing provided a strategic punch during the war. (Source: PP. 409, U.S. Air Force in Korea, Futrell, USAF, Wash., D.C., 1983)

vene to stop the practice. Almond talked to the section chiefs, stressing the importance of keeping GHQ manpower requirements as low as possible.

On Aug. 19, Eighth Army Rear in Japan implemented "Operation Flushout." Under this plan, all Eighth Army units in Japan were required to reassign part of their troops as replacements. As a result, 229 officers and 2,201 EM had been assigned to Korea by Sept. 6. A total of 11,115 replacements arrived in Korea during Aug. 1950.

On Aug. 19, looking to the future, MacArthur requested troops to activate I and IX Corps. Walker was controlling four U.S. and five ROK divisions, too large a span for a commander. In the U.S. Army five major subordinate commands is considered the maximum number that most commanders can effectively control. Most of I Corps arrived in Japan Sept. 3; IX Corps was due about Oct. 10.

In August, the Department of the Army decided to deploy the 3d Infantry Division to Korea, to activate four Army National Guard divisions and to recall individual reservists. The 28th (Pennsylvania), 40th (California), 43d (Rhode Island, Connecticut and Vermont) and 45th (Oklahoma) National Guard divisions were all activated between Sept. 1 and 5. The 196th RCT (South Dakota) and 278th RCT (Tennessee) were also called at the same time. The 31st (Mississippi and Alabama) and 37th (Ohio), 44th (Illinois) and 47th (Minnesota) National Guard divisions were also called to active duty, but not until early in 1951. In addition to these major commands, another RCT and 714 company-sized Army Guard units were called to active duty during the Korean War totaling 138,000 Army Guardsmen, or 34 per cent of the total Army National Guard strength.

Twenty-two Air National Guard wings, numbering about 45,000 men (84 percent of Air Guard strength) were activated in the first weeks of the Korean War.

The Army claimed later that it took a year to get National Guard divisions up to a proper level of training for deployment, but did not reveal that the activated Guard divisions were used as a pool of individual replacements. For example, the 28th Infantry Division was activated Sept. 5, 1950. On Feb. 2, 1951, well into its training program, the division was ordered to provide several thousand individual replacements. Of course, this took a large number of trained men and severely undermined the training status of divisional commands from the platoon on up to regiment. Then in March, several thousand more men were taken from the division. That the 28th trained and processed over 6,000 replacements for overseas shipment in record time and in peak condition won commendations from the Commanding Officer, Ft. Lawton, Washington and the Commanding Generals of Fifth and Sixth Armies and Camp Atterbury, but did not alter the fact that the sudden loss of one-third of the division's strength crippled the progress in training company, battalion and regimental level training which had been achieved. Consequently, it took the 28th Division almost a year to ready for deployment to Germany after distinguishing itself in August 1951 Army maneuvers.

The Korean War quickly became a UN operation, with GEN MacArthur as commander of all UN troops committed to the fray. Great Britain soon contributed a significant ground force in the 27th Infantry Brigade (Brigadier Basil A. Coad). The brigade included two fine, old commands. They were the 1st Battalion, The Middlesex Regiment, and the 1st Battalion, The Argyl and Sutherland Highlanders. These troops sailed from Hong Kong, arriving in Pusan on Aug. 29 to the tune of bagpipes playing "Auld Lang Syne" and "The Campbells Are Coming." The Brigade was moved that night by train to an assembly area near Kyong-san, 10 miles south of Taegu. (See Chapter 18.)

The Refugee Problem

Between Aug. 12 and 19, the 25th helped ROK police screen and remove more than 50,000 refugees from the battlefront area between the Nam River and Chindong-ni. In mid-August, the 24th Division estimated that 100,000 refugees were in its southern sector awaiting the opportunity to cross the Naktong. On Aug. 24 some 300,000 refugees began moving from collecting points near Yongsan and Changnyong, under ROK police escort, to assembly points well away from the battle area.

The 1st Cavalry and ROK 1st Divisions had similar refugee problems. Refugees being escorted to the rear were cautioned to stay on the assigned route, lest they be mistaken for guerrillas and shot. ROK police always worked in conjunction with local army commanders in screening and relocating these people.

Guerrilla activities in rear areas was generally a nuisance, causing few casualties and only occasionally disrupting travel and communication. At times, however, an attack was militarily significant. One of these was a guerrilla attack against a VHF radio relay station on Hill 915 eight miles south of Taegu on Aug. 11. About 100 guerrillas attacked the station at 5:15 a.m., driving off the American operators and 70-man ROK security force. Two U.S soldiers were killed, 2 wounded and 3 missing. A ROK police unit, counterattacking later in the day, found that the enemy had disappeared.

In early September, a similar attack was carried out by guerrillas against another VHF radio relay station on a hill top about five miles from the 25th Division CP. In this case, due to very bad, rainy weather, the party of 5 American soldiers and 3 or 4 ROK security guards simply holed up in their squad tent and posted no guards. At 10 p.m., a party of guerrillas attacked and killed them all with small arms and grenades. The next morning, Sept. 4, a CID agent and a reporter began climbing to the site, were both wounded by grenades, but were able to get back and report in to the 8063d MASH, located in the village of Chang.

Later in the day, LTC Barton O. Baker, 25th Division Ordnance officer was visiting the MASH. Learned of the disaster on the hill, Baker called GEN Kean and apprised him of the situation. Kean approved using the 725th Ordnance Co., located in the area to provide a security force for the MASH, and appointed Baker to take charge of the area and all troops there until the 25th Recon Co. (CPT Torman) arrived the next

day. The force was dubbed Task Force Baker. LTC Baker built his force around 3 officers and 150 EM from CPT Ira Snyder's 725th Ord Co., augmented by an engineer platoon located nearby and troops from an ammunition company which was operating an ASP. With these troops he established a perimeter around the MASH, the ASP and on the MSR and rail line running nearby.

During the night a tank platoon then a battalion of ROK marines came into the perimeter. Baker integrated both into his defenses. During the night a jeep, coming along the road, failed to stop when challenged. The vehicle was stopped by gunfire, killing the local police chief, a passenger.

The following morning, Torman's Recon Co. arrived. The tank platoon encircled the enemy while the Recon Co. and ROK marines assaulted the VHF radio station on foot. The enemy fought back with machine guns and mortars, but were overwhelmed with a loss of 17 guerrillas were killed or captured, including three women. An unknown number escaped. Two Americans were killed. The number of ROK casualties is unknown.

Barton wrote that "[The 725th Ordnance] company showed that well-trained technical troops can be of decisive importance during critical periods."

The ROK Army

As the Pusan Perimeter began forming, the ROK Army was reduced to only five divisions. These divisions required a constant flow of replacements. But it was also necessary to increase the size of the ROK Army. A three part program was adopted: (1) Fill the five existing divisions to full strength; (2) Activate new ROK divisions; (3) Attach large numbers of South Korean recruits to the U.S. Army.

To implement these plans, the ROK Army opened a series of training centers and schools. The first two of these centers each turned out 150 trainees a day for the five ROK divisions. At first KMAG plans envisioned a ten-day training cycle, emphasizing rifle marksmanship. Unfortunately, even this short period had to be reduced because of the critical need for replacements at the front. Recruit training was hampered further by the lack of weapons and equipment. Small arms and machine guns were in acute short supply. None could be spared from combat units. As a result, trainees were given old Japanese rifles, unserviceable weapons and even captured enemy guns to handle and fire. At least, with these, the recruits were given the opportunity to handle and fire some sort of weapon before actually entering combat.

Three more training centers were opened; two in August and one in September. All the centers were supervised by KMAG officers. By this time the 1st Replacement Training Center at Taegu was graduating 1,000 recruits a day; Kumhae and Kupo-ri 500 each. Samnangjin produced 200 graduates per day and the center on Cheju-do 750 daily.

The ROK Army suffered terrible losses among officers and NCOs very early in the war. As a result, it needed large numbers of lieutenants and NCOs, in addition to massive numbers of recruit replacements. To meet the need for junior leaders the ROK Army's Ground General School was activated at Tongnae, near Pusan, on Aug. 15, under the supervision of MAJ John B. Clark, who had organized the ROK Infantry School in 1948. Its first class arrived on Aug. 23. Officer candidates received training in infantry, artillery, ordnance and signal subjects. OCS was six weeks long; four weeks of general training and two weeks of specialized branch training. The first class began on Aug. 28 with 200 students. As the officer candidate program started, the school also began two-week courses for 200 ROK NCOs and a special two-week course for lieutenants of the ROK National Defense Corps. The Corps was roughly the equivalent of America's Army National Guard.

GEN MacArthur asked the Department of the Army for authority to increase the size of the ROK Army. Permission was granted on Aug. 10. On Aug. 18, Walker recommended to MacArthur that five new ROK divisions (each with 10,500 personnel) be activated and equipped on the basis of one per month, beginning in September. MacArthur disagreed with this because of the pressing need for weapons and equipment in the units already in being. He authorized activation and equipping of new divisions, but not on Walker's proposed timetable. MacArthur reported his decision to Department of the Army.

The ROKs had their own agenda and began reactivating the 7th Division at the end of August. They started the process by activating at least one battalion each of the 3d, 5th and 8th Infantry Regiments. TF Min was dissolved and became the 1st and 2d Battalions, 5th Regiment, ROK 7th Division. They also planned to next activate the 11th Division. ROK divisions were still woefully short of field artillery. To help remedy this situation one U.S. 105mm howitzer battalion was attached to each ROK division. These attachments were completed by Sept. 10. Even with this augmentation, ROK divisions still had only about one-fourth the artillery support of a U.S. division in Eighth Army. Appleman observed: "It should not have been surprising that sometimes the ROK divisions did not perform as satisfactorily as the U.S. divisions." This shortage of organic artillery still prevailed into 1951 and the Chinese intervention. It, therefore, should not be surprising that the North Korean and Chinese Armies usually concentrated their offensives against ROK troops later in the war.

Korean Augmentation to the U.S. Army (KATUSA)

Since American replacements failed to keep pace with losses in combat units, extraordinary measures were required. The extraordinary, and to many, controversial, measure which was taken was to attached large numbers of Korean recruits to U.S. Army divisions in Korea and Japan. The Far East Command planned to integrate between 30,000 and 40,000 ROK recruits into the four American divisions in Korea and the 7th Division in Japan. On Aug. 9, MacArthur directed Walker to fill up each U.S. rifle company and artillery battery with 100 ROK soldiers. These soldiers would still be members of the ROK Army, but would be attached to units of the U.S. Army. Pay and administration came from the South Korean government.

KATUSAs could not be promoted beyond Private First Class. Command and control while attached to American forces came from the units to which attached. The Americans also provided rations and special service items. The Far East Command envisioned that each Korean would be paired with a GI. The program was known as the Korean Augmentation to the United States Army (KATUSA). ROK replacement centers produced some 2,950 recruits daily. Of these, 500 per day were siphoned off to fulfill the KATUSA plan. This set back efforts to increase the size of the ROK Army, but the shortages in U.S. Army front-line units was so critical that little else could be done.

LTC Clainos, commanding 1/7th Cavalry, seems to have pioneered the KATUSA program about Aug. 1, when he accepted four ROK officers and 133 enlisted volunteers into his battalion on the unofficial basis that 1/7th Cavalry would provide them with food and weapons to the best of its ability. A LT Chung, a Korean trained in Tokyo, wearing a Japanese samurai sword, marched the Korean units to Clainos' CP. The colonel attached Chung to his headquarters and the three other officers to Companies A, B and C. He then attached two South Korean policemen to each rifle squad in the companies. Nine days later, these South Korean soldiers took part in the battle of Triangulation Hill. Two were KIA and seven WIA. All of the wounded refused evacuation except one who was unable to walk.

Since the 7th Division in Japan had been badly depleted due to levies on it for replacements in Korea, it received some of the first KATUSAs. Between Aug. 16 and 24, 8,625 Korean officers and EM had been attached to the division (almost 50 per cent of its authorized strength.) Korean recruiting methods would have been illegal in some other countries. Men and boys were simply rounded up and marched to centers, then on to training posts. Groups sent to Japan included boys still carrying their schoolbooks. One young man, who had gone to get medicine for his sick wife still had the medicine with him when he arrived in Japan.

The American divisions in Korea began receiving their augmentations on Aug. 20. That day the 24th and 25th Divisions each got 250 men; the 2d and 1st Cavalry Divisions 249 men each. Each division averaged 250 more men per day for the next week. On Aug. 29 and 30 the 1st Cavalry received an average of 740 each day, while the 24th Division averaged 950 recruits on each of these days. The plan changed near the end of August so that each division received 500 recruits every fourth day until each had 8,300 Korean recruits.

KATUSAs were not always paired with GIs, as envisioned. Some units formed all-Korean platoons — a fifth platoon — in the company, usually led by an American lieutenant, with assistance from a few GIs from the company. Other units formed all-Korean squads, with one or two GIs as leaders. Still other, relegated them to ammo handlers, laborers and choggie bearers. B/27th Infantry received their first KATUSAs on the line in the Sobuk-san area in early Sept. Since there were still a number of men who had been in the unit in Japan, the KATUSAs could be integrated into the existing squads on a buddy system with a GI. (See Chapter Notes.)

Soon 50 per cent or more men in rifle companies were KATUSAs. Some became very fine soldiers. One of these was rifleman Kahn Suk Koo, 1st Platoon, B/27th Infantry. In January 1951, Kahn single-handedly covered the withdrawal of the company when it was attacked by a superior Chinese force. For this, Kahn was awarded the Bronze Star Medal, with "V" device for valor, the highest U.S. medal he could be given. Had he been a GI, he would have been recommended for the Distinguished Service Cross.

Appleman writes that the buddy system "gradually broke down and was abandoned." Many of these recruits, like Kahn, matured into good soldiers, if they survived. About late October, before the Chinese intervention, most KATUSAs were returned to the ROK Army, leaving six or less in rifle platoons. The ones who remained were selected by the unit concerned to be kept with the company or platoon. Only the 7th Division retained large numbers of KATUSAs into 1951. The infusion of over 32,000 young Koreans into the ranks of U.S. divisions provided the added numbers needed to fight on to victory in the Perimeter.

The United States Eighth Army

From the very beginning of the war, with TF Smith, American troops were hurried into battle. More thought was given to placing troops to slow or stop the enemy than to command integrity. The 24th Division did not fight as a division until the First Battle of the Naktong Bulge, in Aug. 1950, a month after the division arrived in Korea. The two battalions of the 29th, from Okinawa, were each thrown into separate battles as soon as they arrived in Korea. Both were badly mauled. The 5th RCT was first attached to the 25th Division, then later to the 24th Division. When it arrived in Korea, the 9th Infantry from the 2d Division was immediately attached to the 24th Division during the First Battle of the Naktong Bulge. The order of battle was very confusing. Even after the Perimeter was formed, some commands, such as the 27th Infantry, remained detached from their parent command. The 27th was detached from the 25th Division during most of August.

The last regiment of the 2d Division to arrive in Korea was the 38th Infantry (Rock of the Marne), which landed in Pusan on Aug. 19. The 2d Division, now compete, relieved the 24th Division on the Naktong effective at 6 p.m. on Aug. 24. The 24th Division on Aug. 25 numbered about 10,600 men, short of full strength by some 8,000 personnel. It also needed considerable amounts of arms, equipment and vehicles. The 24th was temporarily split up, with the 19th Infantry and 11th FAB being attached to the 2d Division as a reserve, the 21st Infantry becoming Eighth Army reserve, and the rest of the 24th Division assembling near Kyongsan, 12 miles southeast of Taegu.

Two days later, after discussing the matter with GEN Church, GEN Walker reduced the 34th Infantry to paper status and transferred its personnel and equipment to the 19th and 21st Infantry Regiments. The 1/34th Infantry became 3/19th Infantry and 3/34th became 2/21st Infantry. The 34th Infantry had entered Korea with 1,898 men. Of these, only 184 were still with the regiment when it was broken up. Between Jul. 5 and Aug. 23, the regiment lost 98 KIA, 569 WIA and 773 MIA, plus 274 non-battle casualties. Most of the MIAs were eventually declared dead. COL Beauchamp was transferred back to command his old regiment, the 32d Infantry of the 7th Division. At the same time, Eighth Army disbanded the 63d FAB, which had been the 34th Infantry's direct support battalion. The three firing batteries became Batteries C/11th, 13th and 52d FABs. The artillery reorganization became effective on August 26; that of the infantry on Aug. 31.

Most of the veterans of the 34th Infantry remained bitter ever after that their regiment was disbanded and lost its identity. There is little doubt that Walker was influenced in his decision to break up the 34th Infantry by remarks by Generals Dean, Church and others. Appleman noted that "given his choice, General Church chose to have the 5th RCT as his third regiment rather than rebuild the 34th Infantry with replacements."

The men of the 34th fought as well as any other command, but suffered far more losses of commanders and key staff officers in a very short span of time than any regiment in Korea then, or later. Disbanding the 34th was an expedient which solved the problem for Walker and Church of providing the additional battalion needed in the other two regiments of the 24th Division. By taking the 5th RCT Church avoided the task of rebuilding the 34th Infantry. It certainly was the easier course of action for him.

Walker attached the 5th RCT to the 24th Division at the same time he disbanded the 34th Infantry and 63d FAB. The 6th Tk Bn was also attached to the division at this time. The 5th RCT brought 3,550 men to the 24th and the tank battalion 650 more. This still left the 24th division short by about 4,000 men.

1st Cavalry Division regiments received their third battalions on Aug. 26. These battalions had been formed in the United States specifically for this purpose. The 3/7th Inf, 3d Division, Ft. Devens, MA, became 3/8th Cav.; 2/30th Inf, 3d Division, Ft. Benning, GA, became 3/7th Cav.; a battalion was formed at Camp Carson, CO, and designated 3/5th Cav.

At the end of August, too, Eighth Army took action to reunite commands with their parent divisions. On Aug. 28 it sent the 23d Infantry from the Taegu area back to the 2d Division at Miryang. On Aug. 30 it ordered the 27th Infantry to rejoin the 25th Division near Masan and ordered the 5th RCT north to join the 24th Division.

GEN Walker, realizing that the old boundary between the ROK 1st Division and the 1st Cavalry Division near the Sangju-Taegu road was militarily unsatisfactory, moved it. Effective Aug. 26, the new boundary ran from a point two miles north of the Walled City of Kasan to a point east of and below Taegu. The Sangju-Taegu road was now in the 1st Cavalry Division sector. To cover this extension of front, the 1st Cavalry Division's right boundary was placed on the Army boundary.

On Aug. 28, GEN Gay ordered the 7th Cavalry to occupy what had been the left (western) portion of the old 1st ROK Division sector and the 8th Cavalry to take over the right (eastern) portion. This placed both regiments in very mountainous terrain, increasing the task of resupply, reinforcement and evacuation of casualties. The 3d Battalion, 23d Infantry, relieved the 7th Cavalry in the southern part of the 1st Cavalry sector on Aug. 29. The 7th then relieved the ROK 13th Infantry and part of the 12th. On Aug. 30, the brand-new 3/5th Cavalry took over the 14,000 yard front of the 8th Cavalry. This gave the 5th Cavalry a 32,000 yard front. The 8th Cavalry then took over the sectors formerly occupied by the ROK 11th Infantry and part of the 12th. The ROK 1st Division moved to the east, still on the 1st Cavalry Division's right flank.

Walker had planned to move the 2d Division boundary northward, but the area could be supplied only by the road net from Taegu. Accordingly, on Aug. 30, he re-established the old boundary and attached 3/23d Infantry to the 1st Cavalry Division.

On Aug. 30, a little-known and unsung battalion became responsible for operating the approximately 500 miles of rail lines in the Pusan Perimeter. This was the 714th Transportation Railway Operating Battalion.

American and ROK Casualties

For U.S. troops, July 1950 was the bloodiest month of the entire war; August ranked fourth and September number two, in terms of the number of men killed in action. October, 1950 ranked third; February fifth and September 1951 sixth. During these six months in 1950-51, the Army suffered 48 per cent of all the KIAs and 37 per cent of all the WIAs in the entire war. November, 1950, when the Chinese intervened ranked seven, with 946 KIA and 4,595 WIA.

During July, August and September, 1950 the Army lost 5,672 KIA and 17,019 WIA. These figures represent 29.3 per cent of all KIAs and 18.4 per cent of all WIAs in the 37 month long Korean War. Based on division War Diaries, Appleman gives these battle losses for August: 24th Division, 1,941; 25th Division, 1,800; 1st Cavalry, 1,503; 9th Infantry, 2d Division, 827.

Considering the number of U.S. Army troops in Korea in the first three months of the war, the casualty rate is very high. The mean strength of the Army in Korea during July, 1950 was 29,610; in August, 59,139; in September, 93,321.

Non-battle casualties (15,9150) were also high in these first three months of the war compared with the number of troops in Korea at the time, but very low, when compared to the amazing 460,685 non-battle casualties during the entire war.

Some of these were from disease, such as respiratory infections, digestive system problems, infective and parasitic diseases, a high number of psychiatric disorders and a great number from fevers of unknown origin. Others were non-battle injuries such as sprains, broken bones, etc. The vast majority of these casualties were returned to duty in a very short time — usually a matter of days. Some of the men suffering what were called "psychiatric disorders" were kept in an aid station or clearing station overnight, and

returned to duty. The sick were often given some medication to take, such as pills or liquid medicine and returned to duty. The fact that they were evacuated and were absent from the unit long enough for one Morning Report to be rendered resulted in them being carried as a casualty, even if for just one day, so, the 460,685 figure is not as alarming as it seems.

Although battle and non-battle casualties were high within U.S. forces, the battle casualties in the ROK Army were higher; the non-battle losses lower. At times the number of ROK battle casualties was much greater then American. For example, on Aug. 6, U.S. battles losses were 74, the ROK 1,328. On Aug. 21, the Americans lost 49; the ROKs 2,229.

Relative Strengths, US/ROK Forces and North Korean Army

The U.S. and ROK figures below are as reported by major organizations as of Sept. 1 and include Eighth Army and ROK headquarters troops and the ROK corps. Those for the North Koreans were derived from enemy material and interrogation of enemy POWs as of Sept. 1. The figures for the North Korean Army are estimates only, but do not include figures for their headquarters nor their corps. Therefore, the total for the North Korean Army is higher than shown. There is no way to determine how much higher, perhaps 2,000 or more. (See chart top of next page.)

GEN Walker's Contingency Plan of Defense

One contingency plan for defending Pusan was for the establishment of a defensive position generally south of the Perimeter. MacArthur outlined such a position to Walker. On Aug. 11, Walker orally directed BG Garrison H. Davidson (West Point, 1927), an engineer officer, to lay out this secondary line. After examining the terrain, Davidson recommended to Walker that better defensive terrain lay a little closer to Pusan than what MacArthur had envisioned. GEN Walker told Davidson to construct the line where MacArthur had indicated.

BG Crump Garvin's 2d Logistical Command and the 2d and 25th Divisions helped to construct the line, although there were few resources available. The line, soon known as the "Davidson Line," ran from the high ground northeast of Masan north to Muan-ni, thence to a point northeast of Miryang, then east along high ground to Sodong-ni on the east coast about eight miles north of Ulsan. The line was about 70 miles long, encompassing an area about 35-37 miles from north to south and about the same from east to west.

Davidson recommended removing all houses from in front of the line in order to clear fields of fire. Walker disapproved. Davidson laid out the line, removing all obstacles to fields of fire, except houses. He ordered necessary materials for field fortifications and had some of the positions dug before he was assigned as assistant division commander of the 24th Division. The line was never used.

In spite of the preparation of a second line of defense, it was always Walker's plan to ulti-

US/ROK Forces and North Korean Army

U.S. Eighth Army	78,762**		North Korean Army			97,850**
2d Inf. Division	17,498	1st Division	5,000	9th Division	9,350	
24th Inf. Division	14,739	2d Division	6,000	10th Division	7,500	
25th Inf. Division	15,007	3d Division	7,000	12th Division	5,000	
1st Cav. Division	14,703	4th Division	5,500	13th Division	9,000	
ROK Army	91,696	5th Division	7,000	15th Division	7,000	
1st Prov. Marine Bde	4,290	6th Division	10,000	104th Security Bde	2,000	
British 27th Inf Bde	1,578	7th Division	9,000	105th Armd Div	1,000	
U.S Fifth Air Force	3,603	8th Division	6,500	16th Armd Bde	500	
17th Armd Bde	500					
FEAF	33,651					
Royal Australian AF	330					

* These numbers are deceiving because they do not show relative combat strength. By adding the numbers for each of the four U.S. divisions, we learn that the combat strength of Eighth Army was 61,957. The Marine Brigade and British 27th Infantry add 5,868 to this, for a total of 67,815 men. The ROK Army had five divisions on the front with the new 7th being activated. ROK divisions at this time probably numbered no more than 9,000 to 10,000 men, and could easily have been smaller. Therefore, the front line strength of the ROK Army could not have been more than about 50,000 men. Comparing battle strength to battle strength, the U.S. and ROK forces numbered, at most, 117,815 and the North Korean Army, an estimated 97,850.

mately go on the offensive and break out of the Pusan Perimeter and chase the North Korean Army completely out of the South.

The North Korean Plan for September 1950

The North Korean Army High Command and the North Korean soldiers kept up the pressure in the Perimeter. They displayed an uncommon will and determination to win through, although suffering horrendous casualties. All through August and into September, they pounded away over multiple avenues. Although they gained temporary local numerical superiority, they were unable to sustain it in the face of aerial superiority and Walker's ability to rush reinforcing infantry and artillery to critical fronts on a "just in time" basis. Enemy tactics never altered: frontal attack, coupled with an attempt to flank the position and gain the rear area. This worked in the early days, forcing the defenders out of position. But, once the Perimeter was formed, most commands stayed in position and allowed counterattacking troops to push the enemy back out. The Perimeter's flanks on the sea were secured by overwhelming naval gunfire and aircraft.

Walker exploited his interior line of communication to shift forces from one front to another, ejecting the enemy, or blunting his thrust and frustrating every enemy attack.

The enemy did a remarkable job of resupplying its troops with ammunition, but fell short in providing replacement small arms. The first wave(s) of attackers had weapons but succeeding waves often did not. Men in these waves were expected to pick up their weapons from the dead and wounded of the first wave(s). The North also failed to resupply men with clothing and, more importantly, food. The lack of food was so acute that many enemy soldiers lost stamina and combat effectiveness. UN air power had destroyed or damaged almost all of North Korea's trucks, particularly in South Korea.

North Korean Order of Battle

Marshal Choe Yong Gun, Minister of Defense and Deputy Commander, *North Korean Armed Forces,* had served in the Chinese Communist *8th Route Army.*

Front Headquarters, Kumchon. CG, Aug. and Sept. was GEN Kim Chaek.

Chief of Staff, LTG Kang Kon (KIA Sept. 8)

I Corps, Chunchon. LTG Kim Ung. (Graduate, Whampoa Military Academy; *8th Route Army.*)

2d Division	7th Division	16th Armd Bde (43 T-34 tanks)
4th Division	9th Division	104th Security Bde
6th Division	10th Division	105th Armd Division (elements)

II Corps, Mungyong. LTG Kim Mu Chong. (Graduate Whampoa Military Academy. Accompanied Mao Tse Dong on the "Long March." Reportedly one of only 30 Koreans to survive that march.)

1st Division	8th Division	15th Division
3d Division	12th Division	105th Armd Division (elements)
5th Division	13th Division	17th Armd Bde (40 T-34 tanks)

I Corps front extended from the Chindong-ni area in the south northward to opposite Taegu. Form south to north, its divisions were deployed as follows: *6th, 7th, 9th, 4th, 2d,* and *10th.* Elements of the *105th Armd Division* and *16th Armd Bde** supported the divisions and the *104th Security Bde* was deployed behind the *6th Division.*

II Corps front extended from northwest of Taegu east to the coast. From west to east were the *3d, 13th, 1st, 8th, 15th, 12th,* and *5th Divisions.* Elements of the *105th Armd Division* and *17th Armd Bde** supported the corps. (* The two brigades were actually regiments.)

The estimated total strength of the North Korean Army around the Perimeter was about 98,000 men. There were several new commands at the front. These included the two armored brigades and the *9th Division.* Elements of the *7th Division,* but apparently not all of it, had seen battle.

The North Korean planned to attack over the same five avenues as before. Two of these were in the *I Corps* zone of action and three were in that of the *II Corps.*

These were the groupings and orders to each:

> *I Corps:* The following division groups attack 11:30 p.m., Aug. 31:
>> *6th* and *7th Divisions* (Est. 19,000): Break through U.S. 25th Division. Seize Masan.
>> *9th, 4th, 2d* and *10th Divisions* (Est. 28,000 [+]): Break through U.S. 2d Division.
>> Seize Miryang, Changnyong and Yongsan and the Pusan-Taegu railroad and highway in that area.
>
> *II Corps:* The following division groups attack 6 p.m., Sept. 1:
>> *3, 13th* and *1st Divisions* (Est. 21,000): Break through U.S. 1st Cavalry and ROK 1st Divisions. Seize Taegu.
>> *8th* and *15th Divisions* (Est. 13,500): Break through ROK 8th and 6th Divisions.
>> Seize Hayang and Yongchon on the highway east of Taegu.
>> *12th* and *5th Divisions* (Est. 12,000 troops): Break through ROK Capital and 3d Divisions. Seize Pohang-dong, the Yonil airfield and Kyongju corridor to Pusan.

Chapter Notes:

P. 251 These early KATUSAs had almost no training and no concept of fighting and battle. Some had barely fired more than eight rounds from an M1 and had no individual or combat training, nor even an orientation as to what to expect. Most were less than a week from a peasant civilian life. They could not understand English and were totally ignorant of any part of western culture. They were little more than cannon fodder, doomed to early death or injury in their first battle.

All the Koreans could speak and understand Japanese from the 40 years of Japanese occupation. But, except for the surviving soldiers from the pre-Korean War Army garrison of Japan, the Americans neither understood nor were interested in learning any Korean or Japanese. This led to many needless combat deaths and injuries among KATUSAs and GIs, alike. Writers, to date, have not touched on another significant barrier to the effective use of KATUSAs. That barrier was racial prejudice on the part of many American soldiers. To them a Korean was an inferior being and nothing a KATUSA did, or did not do, changed this bias. The cultural, language and racial barriers inherent in the KATUSA program made it almost impossible to implement with the efficiency that otherwise would have been possible.

From Pohang-dong to Yongchon, August 27 - September 15

TF Jackson- Aug. 27-Sept. 7

Just as American and ROK leaders were congratulating themselves on having thrown back the enemy in the Pohang area, the *NK 12th Division*, 5,000 strong, attacked elements of the ROK Capital Division at 4 a.m., Sunday, Aug. 27. The attack overran a company of the ROK 17th Regiment north of Kigye. Soon, the entire regiment fell back. The ROK 18th Regiment, on the right of the 17th, also fell back to protect its flank. The 17th lost Kigye and the whole Capital Division then fell back three miles to the south side of the Kigye valley.

Later that morning, GEN Walker was briefed about this setback in the east. MG John B. Coulter, who had arrived in Korea about a month previously, was present at the briefing. Thirty minutes afterward, Walker called Coulter in and said, "I can't get reliable reports. I want you to go to the eastern front and represent me. I am sending a regiment from the 24th Division to help."

Walker appointed Coulter Deputy Commander, Eighth Army, giving him command of the ROK I Corps, plus the U.S. 21st Infantry, 3/ 9th Infantry and the 73d Tk Bn (-Co. C). GEN Coulter flew into Kyongju at noon and formed the American commands into TF Jackson. He assumed command at 12 noon, Aug. 27 and established his CP in Kyongju with the ROK I Corps and KMAG contingent CPs.

Coulter's missions: (1) Eliminate the enemy penetration in the Kigye area, and; (2) Seize and organize the high ground from north of Yongchon northeast to the coast at Wolpori, about 12 miles north of Pohang-dong. The "high ground" of this objective started about 10 miles north of Kigye, ending near Wolpori.

ROK I Corps morale was very low, and that entire command was on the point of crumbling. Assembling the ROK commanders and staffs, Coulter reminded them that a failure to hold would jeopardize the entire Perimeter. Walker had told him to issue orders to the ROK I Corps commander and his chief of staff in the form of advice, and he did. He planned to attack immediately with TF Jackson to seize the high ground just north of Kigye.

The 21st Infantry was moving to a position north of Taegu the morning of Aug. 27. Walker changed the orders and sent it to Kyongju instead. The regiment arrived at Kyongju that afternoon and Coulter sent the 3d Battalion into position behind the ROK Capital Division.

LT Maihafer of I/21st Infantry recalled that the trip took three hours. His truck driver told Maihafer that he had been shuttling units constantly to plug holes in the Perimeter. Maihafer wrote that when the unit unloaded, he hated "to see the trucks pull out, since they represented a link to the safe rear area, if...there was such a haven." (Quotes in this and the next two paragraphs are from COL Maihafer's book, *From the Hudson to the Yalu.*)

The 3d Battalion was deployed along the base of a mountain on the edge of a wide valley. Behind the battalion was a ROK 75mm howitzer battery. The entire battalion was on line — K, I and L, in that order, from left to right. Shortly after the Americans went into position, the ROK artillery began firing. Soon, enemy counterbattery fire started coming in. Maihafer's company was between the two. He wrote that the ROK artillery was "ruining the neighborhood."

Shortly, enemy artillery began falling into the 21st Infantry, causing casualties. Maihafer moved his men farther up the hill to get out of the impact area. The artillery duel continued through the night. To make matters worse, too, the ROKs occasionally fired too low, and some of their rounds also landed among the Americans. A SGT Sullivan, of Item Company quipped, "If someone will give me a whistle, I'll stand up and direct traffic."

The next morning, 1LT Floyd Gibson, Item's Commander, and the platoon leaders went on reconnaissance, using a ROK Capital Division OP. A Korean captain and an interpreter pointed out the objective to the company officers. As they studied it with binoculars, a bullet snapped overhead. The shot seemed to have been fired from the hill they were on. Maihafer raised his head to continue studying the objective. 2LT Thomas Hardaway, commanding Co. I's 1st Platoon stood next to Maihafer. Another shot was fired. This time, the bullet seemed to pass between the two officers. They quickly ducked down. Through the interpreter, the ROK captain asked that they keep their heads down. He had told his men to shoot anyone who exposed themselves. It was a harsh, but very effective way to enforce camouflage discipline.

On the way back to their position, the jeep which the officers were riding in came under observed enemy artillery fire. Hardaway, the driver, jammed his foot on the accelerator, and the jeep careened forward and around a sheltering bend in the road.

The attack was canceled and 3/21st taken on trucks to the Pohang area.

There were "too many enemy, too many casualties, troops tired," said the ROK I Corps commander to GEN Coulter, in defending his decision not to attack on Aug. 28, as planned. In addition to this, the *NK 5th Division*, north of Pohang was beginning to attack the ROK 3d Division, which was showing signs of imminent collapse. COL Emmerich, advisor to this division, recommended to its commander, BG Kim Suk Won, that the 3d should counterattack. GEN Kim refused. The following day, Kim told Emmerich that he was going to move his CP out of Pohang-dong. Emmerich replied that the KMAG advisors were going to stay. Appleman wrote that Kim became hysterical, but, in the end, decided to stay in Pohang-dong to save face.

On the same day, Aug. 28, GEN Walker issued this special statement to the ROK Army and the ROK Minister of Defense, calling on the ROKs to hold fast on the Perimeter:

"It is my belief, that the over-extended enemy is making his last gasp, while United

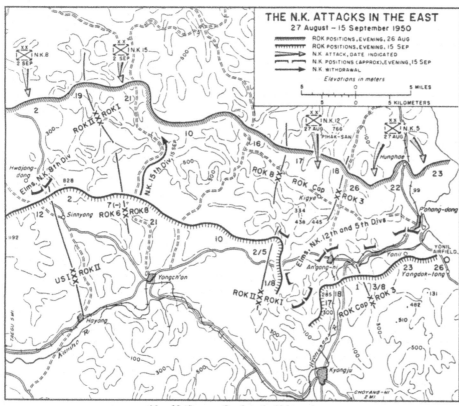

Map 39 (Source: South to the Naktong)

Nations forces are daily becoming stronger and stronger. The time has now come for everyone to stand in place and fight, or advance to a position which will give us greater tactical advantage from which the counter-offensive can be launched. If our present positions are pierced, we must counter-attack at once, destroy the enemy and restore the positions.

"To you officers and soldiers of the Army of the Republic of Korea, I ask that you rise as one and stop the enemy on your front in his tracks."

The ROK 17th Infantry's loss of a high ridge to the north at a bend in the Kigye valley and the general ROK disorganization caused TF Jackson's counterattack on the 28th to be canceled. The 21st Infantry was in an assembly area two miles north of Angang-ni. The ROKs regained, then lost their position during that afternoon and night.

Meantime, the *NK 5th Division* penetrated the lines of the ROK 3d Division southwest of Pohang-dong. GEN Coulter ordered COL Stephens to eject the enemy. On Aug. 29, B/21st Infantry, supported by a platoon of tanks from B/73d Medium Tk Bn, attacked northwest from the edge of Pohang-dong and took 1 1/2 miles of ground from the enemy. Following ROK troops occupied the new forward position. U.S. troops withdrew to Pohang-dong. That night, the ROKs also withdrew. The next day another U.S. tank-infantry team retook the lost ground.

The ROK 3d Division needed help to hold its front. As a result, on Aug. 29, COL Stephens was ordered to take over a portion of its line with the 21st infantry. The regimental sector extended 1,000 yards north and 3,000 yards northwest of Pohang-dong.

On the same day, the ROK Capital Division, supported by American tanks and artillery, recaptured Kigye, held it during the night against enemy counterattacks, then lost it finally at daybreak.

The U.S. Navy continued to support the ROKs with gunfire and air attacks. On Aug. 29 and 30, a cruiser and two destroyers fired almost 1,500 5-inch shells into an enemy troop and supply site in the Hunghae area five miles north of Pohang-dong, in support of the ROK 3d Division. On Aug. 31, the aircraft carrier *USS Sicily* launched 38 sorties against enemy ground targets. The ROKs reported finding the bodies of many enemy soldiers, apparently killed by air attack. They also found many articles of white clothing, dropped there by enemy soldiers changing into uniforms. In spite of all this naval and aerial support, the ROKs were losing the battles at Kigye and Pohang-dong.

Kigye Area, Sept. 1-3

On Sept. 1, aerial observers reported enemy troops moving south in the mountains above both Kigye and P'ohang-dong. The next day, the North Koreans attacked north and northwest of Kigye. By that afternoon an estimated 2,500 enemy soldiers had penetrated a gap between the ROK Capital Division's 17th and 18th Regiments. At 1:30 a.m. on Aug. 3, the *NK 12th Division*, as part of the *NK II Corps* offensive, attacked the ROK 17th and 18th Regiments on the

high hills south of the Kigye valley. The 18th, on the left, lost Hills 334 and 438, while the 17th, on the right, relinquished ground near Hill 445. By daybreak, enemy troops had reached the vital east-west road three miles east of Angang-ni. In one night, the enemy gained five miles, bringing the Capital Division to the brink of total collapse.

The situation was so critical that GEN Coulter immediately withdrew the 21st Infantry from the line northwest of Pohang and concentrated it near Kyongju. There it was joined by its new 2d Battalion, LTC Gines Perez, commanding (formed from 3/34th Infantry on Aug. 31). The 2d Battalion had been in TF reserve at Angang-ni. While the remainder of the regiment went into an assembly area north of Kyongju, the 2d Battalion formed a horseshoe-shaped defensive position around Angang-ni, with elements on high ground two miles to the east where they dominated the Kyongju-Pohang-dong highway. Concurrently, Walker began moving the newly activated ROK 7th Division toward the enemy penetration. The division's 5th Regiment closed at Yongchon that afternoon, the 3d Regiment (-1st Bn) at Kyongju that evening.

The two AA batteries (D/865th AAA/AW Bn and A/933d AAA/AW Bn) were ordered to remain at Yonil, except in an emergency, but Walker authorized Coulter to employ all other U.S. Army commands located there as he deemed appropriate. This included 3/9th Infantry, Tank Co., 9th Infantry, and the 15th FAB.

Attack By 3/21st Infantry — Sept. 2

The enemy's *5th Division* held fast to Hill 99 in the Pohang-dong area. No amount of air attacks, artillery and naval gunfire could help the ROK 3d Division to capture it. On Sept. 2, the 21st Infantry launched an attack, supported by a tank platoon of the 6th Tk Bn, mortars, artillery and naval gunfire, including the 16 inch guns of the battleship *USS Missouri*. The attack followed the valley road between Pohang-dong and Hunghae. The 3/21st Infantry attacked with all three rifle companies on line, I, L and K, from left to right. Co. K was assigned to take Hill 99 itself. The Line of Departure (LD) for Co. I was the top of a ridge. Item Co.'s 3d Platoon, under LT Maihafer, was on the company left, and also the battalion's extreme left.

Artillery fire started to soften up the objective. The Air Force took over, firing rockets and machine guns into likely enemy locations. Then enemy artillery and mortar fire started falling on the waiting Americans; mostly on L and K Companies. One three-round cluster of enemy artillery rounds landed squarely into a group of bunched-up King Co. men.

Soon after daylight, the infantrymen crossed the LD. In the valley before them, burning houses, hit by air strikes, sent columns of smoke into the air. F-51s still attacked forward of the advancing infantrymen. One plane swooped down over Co. I and sent a salvo of rockets into a burning village to the front. The rockets sounded like the whole world was being ripped apart as they sped from the plane.

Item's 3d Platoon went down the forward slope in single file, with two scouts in the lead.

LT Maihafer, the platoon leader, followed them. As the men started across a dry rice paddy, a salvo of enemy artillery rounds burst all around the platoon. In his book, *From the Hudson to the Yalu*, Maihafer wrote: "I dropped to one knee, wanting to hug the ground, but when caught in the open, it was best to run through the concentration, even though every instinct screamed for you to stay down. But what if I started running and no one followed? I was scared, my mind was racing, and those thoughts flashed through my consciousness faster than it takes to tell about it."

Overcoming his fear, Maihafer stood up and ordered, "On your feet, let's go." One by one, his men stood up and followed, as he started walking forward. Maihafer began jogging, and his platoon stayed with him. By this time, most of the enemy artillery fire was behind them. The platoon ran to the base of the objective hill, spread out and moved to its top. A quick check revealed 3 wounded by the enemy artillery barrage. One of them, a BAR-man named Archie, had been badly hit. A member of the platoon had remained behind with him until a medic could provide treatment. Archie died before a medic arrived. Meantime, the platoon dug in and awaited orders to proceed to the next objective. Off to the right could be heard the "pop" of M1 rifles the chatter of American machine guns and the "burrrp, brrrrp" of enemy burp guns.

Then Co. I moved out again for Objective Two, taking it without much problem. Once on its crest the artillery FO spotted a large body of enemy soldiers at the foot of Objective Three, heading north. He called a fire mission in on them.

Meantime, King Co. was taking a beating in trying to take Hill 99. Enemy artillery, mortars and automatic weapons rained down on the company. The noise of battle was incessant. Companies I and L held up and dug in, hoping that K would be able to seize Hill 99. It was hot; the sun beat down. Canteens were slowly emptied by thirsty soldiers.

F-51s were called in to work over Hill 99. The F-51s came in perpendicular to the American lines. The first plane passed almost directly over Co. I's 3d Platoon. The second plane mistook the company's position for that of the enemy and swooped to the attack, firing rockets. The first one made "a rushing sound like a freight train," Maihafer recalled, "followed by an explosion." The round struck between him and the Company XO, 1LT Ruff Lynch. He sensed a roaring sound right on top of him. It was a moment of pure terror. The concussion slammed him down like a punch from a huge giant. Clumps of earth and stone struck his helmet. Stunned, he lay there shaking, not wishing to look up; fearful of what he might see. It might have hit Lynch. Then he heard Ruff call, "You all right, Harry?" Maihafer, ears ringing, staggered to his feet. He felt groggy; he felt lucky. Meantime, the FO was screaming profanely into his radio to lift the air strike.

By 3:25 p.m., Co. K was down to 35 men. The company was never able to take Hill 99. The 3d Platoon, Co. I moved out and took a hill to the unit's left without opposition and occupied it for the night.

Co. L, between I and K, was commanded by

1LT Planter Wilson. Planter had been the XO of the 34th Infantry's HM Co., but was given command of L/21st Infantry in August. The unit had but 17 men at the time. A few days later, it "received something over 100 American replacements and a small platoon of KATUSAs," Wilson wrote. The company's artillery FO was LT Olin M. Hardy, 52d FAB. Hardy recalled Pohang-dong. "The movement never stopped. We were shelled at night by direct high velocity fire," he wrote, "and by mortar and sniper fire during the day. The mortar and self propelled fire was much more effective than the sniper fire. The 'whap' of the sniper fire was annoying and the dropping of leaves from the camouflage as the rounds knocked them from the limbs caused the sweat to itch all around the collar of my dirty fatigues. No one was hit from the sniper fire, but a self propelled round landed two feet in front of my foxhole, blowing me in the air and turning me over and deafening me for over an hour. My wireman, CPL James T. Dossett, repaired the line to the artillery.

"We held the position for two days then another crisis developed and we were called out to reinforce another unit.... I was left to guard our departure with artillery fire." U.S. artillery fired in support of the ROK Capital Division. Hardy and his FO party were cut off "at one point...and had to go north to escape," but without casualties to his party.

While the 3d Battalion attacked, the 1st Battalion, nearer the coast also jumped off in its own assault. The FO with Co. C was LT Earl Lochhead (West Point 1949). The company commander was still CPT Jack Doody (West Point 1948). As the unit approached the LD, Navy 16 inch shells "so large they could almost be seen with the naked eye, and sounding like freight cars" passed overhead.

The company took its objective on three north-south finger ridges. Lochhead's artillery FO party was with one platoon and the 4.2 inch mortar FO was with another. The platoons were spread out, with a gap of 50 to 100 yards between them. That afternoon, Lochhead saw his first enemy, a Maxim heavy machine gun with a square metal gunshield. It opened fire from a ridge crest about 75 yards from him. It was a difficult artillery target and the FDC told Lochhead it didn't want to waste too much ammunition on it. Later, he called a fire mission in on a T-34, backed into a house and camouflaged by vines. He could not determine if the artillery had knocked out the tank.

Later in the day, Lochhead lost communications with his FDC. The telephone lines had been cut, possibly by enemy artillery or mortars, and the batteries went out in his radio. Two more sets of left-over WW II batteries were defective. Like many another soldier in Korea, Lochead cursed the practice of trying to use equipment salvaged from the fighting in the Pacific. He decided to repair the telephone line. However, an enemy sniper zeroed in on him almost as soon as he started out. Unable to locate the sniper, and in imminent danger of being shot by him, Lochhead went back up the hill and tried another battery.

Shortly after dark, he was given a case of hand grenades. The infantrymen around him didn't seem to want any, until later that night,

when the enemy attacked. Lochhead suddenly became grenade resupply officer for the GIs.

During the night, Lochhead thought that an enemy soldier was in their position. He told a sergeant about it. The sergeant suggested that Lochhead go and capture him. With drawn .45-cal pistol, Lochhead approached the "North Korean" — it turned out to be a bush, gently moving in the wind.

As the enemy attacked the side of his hill, Lochhead called in artillery, but they kept advancing. He brought the artillery in closer and closer, keeping pace with the oncoming North Koreans. At one point, he used himself as the base point for the fire. Fragments from bursting artillery rounds fell on his own position, before the enemy attack was repelled. Dawn on Sept. 3, revealed the bodies of many enemy dead outside the unit perimeter.

As night fell on Sept. 2, the enemy penetrated on the boundary between the ROK Capital and 3d Divisions three miles east of Kigye. The next day, the commander of the ROK 3d Division at Pohang-dong began preparing to withdraw. COL Emmerich promptly reported this to GEN Coulter. Coulter immediately went to the commander of the ROK I Corps and had him order the ROK 3d Division to remain in place. GEN Coulter checked every half hour afterward to ensure that the 3d Division stayed in place.

G/21st Infantry, Sept. 3-4

The ROK I Corps front gave way on the night Sept. 3-4. Three T-34s overran a ROK artillery battery then chased off two battalions of the newly-arrived ROK 5th Regiment. Covered by mortar fire, enemy troops entered Angang-ni at 2:20 a.m. About an hour later the Capital

Division's CP left the town and fighting became even more confused.

Enemy troops began attacking the horseshoe-shaped defensive position of 2/21st Infantry about 2:30 a.m. They first hit an outpost on the west end of town. LTC Perez pulled the outpost back into town along with three Patton tanks guarding the western approaches. The embattled battalion then repelled three enemy attacks. By 4 a.m. U.S. tanks quit firing because troops of the Capital Division were hopelessly intermingled with those of the enemy. "We couldn't tell friend from foe," said LTC Perez. He ordered a withdrawal. But Co. G (LT Douglas W. Syverson) didn't get the word. At dawn, he discovered G was alone in Angang-ni, almost surrounded by the enemy. Neither U.S. nor ROK troops were in sight. A patrol confirmed that the enemy had the unit completely cut off.

Homer Bigart's Sept. 5 dispatch to the New York *Herald Tribune* told the story of the fight and escape by Co. G, quoting LT Syverson, the CO, and Battalion Commander, LTC Perez.

"The road was cut all along the way," LT Syverson said. "So we pushed our tanks in column, with infantry moving beside them right and left of the road. We just had to put everything on that road because the rice paddies on either side were interlaced with deep ditches. As we withdrew, the lead tank fired straight down the road. Other tanks kept up rapid fire on the steep slopes on our right and left."

Co. G had received two replacement officers on Sept. 1 and 3, both brand-new Second Lieutenants, from the West Point Class of 1950. They were Dwight L. Adams (Sept. 1) and Frederick Dickerson on Sept. 3. The battle at Angang-ni on Sept. 4 was their baptism of fire. Adams was assigned as platoon leader of the 1st Platoon; Dickerson got the 4th (Weapons) Platoon. The

60mm mortar crew in action. (Source: 24th Forward *A Pictorial History of the Victory Division in Korea, Tokyo, 1953)*

This 57mm recoilless rifle has just fired. (Source: 24th Forward A Pictorial History of the Victory Division in Korea, Tokyo, 1953)

1st Platoon had 18 men, recalled Robert Bayless, one of its members. He wrote, "We were moved to the P'ohang sector to shore up the ROKs, taking up positions above the town of An'gang-ni, still hardly numerically superior to our strength of the previous few weeks, but with one distinct advantage: The First Platoon...had just acquired a recent West Point graduate, 2LT Dwight L. Adams, who was in action with us the following day. His presence was a morale boost, as we had been desperate for enough line officers up to this point." Jose Leyba, a newly promoted staff sergeant, and acting leader of the Weapons Platoon, recalled that Dickerson was from his home town of Trinidad, Colorado.

"My platoon was not touched during the night," wrote COL Dwight L Adams, "but the other two were. Just before dawn the company commander said that the company was to withdraw and my platoon...was to be last out. When it was time for us to go we were brought under fire by heavy machine guns; we returned the fire and after awhile it stopped. I believe that, on hindsight, it may have come from our own tanks (two M-26s) who apparently had been engaged and were jumpy.... We joined the rear of the company and entered An'-gang-ni. The entire column came under fire at very close quarters. Men were being hit up and down the line and returning fire to both sides. The wounded were placed on a tank. The column was apparently stopped at a railroad overpass held by enemy infantry."

Adams went to the front of the column to discover for himself what was holding it up. He was told about the enemy at the railroad overpass and that the move was also delayed because the tankers did not want to run over wounded GIs lying on the road. "In order to do something," Adams continued, "I took a couple of men and went off the main road to the right to try to flank the overpass. There were rice paddies between my small party, separating us from the overpass

by about 10-15 yards. We came face to face with a North Korean and I dispatched him, emptying my carbine magazine in my excitement (and inexperience). Another North Korean ducked behind the overpass and we got rid of him by tossing a couple of grenades. (These grenades were handed to me by Fred Dickerson.... He [had] killed his captors and showed up at our little fracas.) The column began to move again and we escaped from An'gang-ni."

The official history states that G Company withdrew from Angang-ni at 6:10 p.m. "and dug in along the road eastward near the rest of the 2d Battalion at the bridge over the Hyongsan-gang. North Koreans held the town and extended southward along the railroad."

Dickerson wrote: "Our forces started moving to the rear mostly by crawling through fire from three sides. Our company was badly separated and attempted to regroup on the east side of the village. I saw part of my mortar section and attempted to gather them together. I told them to wait while I searched for the rest. I saw two men standing on a railroad overpass and I yelled at them and they waved their arms. One man came down the bank and put out his hand. At that time, I saw that he had a red star on his hat. Several other people came over and escorted me to the other side of the overpass, took my weapon and gave me some pamphlets welcoming me as a POW. I stayed with them for approximately 45 minutes until my company came through on the road under the overpass."

Jose Leyba wrote that when they learned that LT Dickerson had been captured, "we went looking for him. It wasn't long before we spotted him being guarded by two North Korean soldiers. We worked ourselves as close as possible and opened fire on his guards, and good Lieutenant Dickerson broke loose and joined us."

When men of his company approached, Dickerson decided to make a break. "I decided

to depart and dispatched my guard by stealing back my carbine and bashing him in the head. I then rejoined my company. My reaction was a bit traumatic as I didn't realize that I had a gunshot wound in the arm and was totally grateful not to be left behind." Leyba recalled that Dickerson was unaware that he was wounded until SFC Leyba pointed it out to him. With Dickerson a casualty, Leyba was platoon leader once again. "It seemed that I was always taking the Platoon back," he wrote.

In the meantime, the bulk of the 2d Battalion withdrew under orders from COL Stephens, to join the rest of the regiment above Kyongju. The battalion fought its way through a roadblock on the east side of Hyongsan-gang three miles south of Angang-ni. Then Perez discovered that Co. G was not with the battalion. COL Stephens ordered him to go back and get the company. He found George Co. back at the bridge, holding against dwindling enemy pressure. The reunited battalion then turned around again to fight its way out. Tanks fired down the road to the front of the column and into the hills on both flanks. Three tanks were crippled when enemy fire knocked off their tracks. American artillery destroyed them. The 2d Battalion arrived back in the Kyongju area just before noon. LTC Perez praised his three rifle company commanders when he said that the action of CPT Norm E. Brown (CO, Co. E), 1LT Robert E. Thompson (CO Co. F) and Syverson, of G was "one of the most magnificent pieces of leadership I've ever seen."

The Deteriorating ROK Situation — Sept. 4 - 6

The tactical situations in the ROK 3d and Capital Divisions got worse during Sept. 4. By noon, the enemy had roadblocks on the Kyongju-Angang-ni road within three miles of Kyongju. There was a two mile wide gap between the 3d and Capital Divisions near Pohang-dong. But a really huge gap of eight miles existed in the high mountains west of the Hyongsan valley and southwest of Angang-ni between the ROK 8th Division's right flank and the left of the Capital. An enemy thrust from this direction posed a threat to the railroad and road net going south in the Kyongju-Pusan corridor. More concerned about this threat than that in the Pohang-dong area, GEN Coulter deployed the 21st Infantry in the large valley and bordering hills northwest of Kyongju to block the enemy in that quarter.

The evening of Sept. 4, the ROK corps commander again suggested evacuating Kyongju. He contended that the enemy was on the hills only three miles to the north, poised to attack and take the town that night. Coulter would have none of it. He told the ROK general that they were all staying in Kyongju. To reinforce his resolve, Coulter stationed four tanks around the CP building and sent KMAG advisors out on the road to stop any ROKs trying to pull out. COL John F. Greco, Coulter's G2 and Majors William C. Hungate Jr. and George W. Flagler, of Coulter's staff were there that night. One of the majors stopped a party of fleeing ROKs at gunpoint. The staff found Coulter grouchy and difficult to please that sleepless night, but he was determined that Kyongju would not fall to the enemy.

Tankers on the road just above Kyongju, talking among themselves on the radio, revealed that enemy soldiers had tried to knock them out by climbing aboard. The tankers knocked the enemy soldiers off. But an enemy attack on Kyongju never came. Instead, the North Koreans turned east, crossing the highway a few miles north of that town, headed toward the Yonil Airfield. On Sept. 5, Air Force planes attacked enemy gun positions four miles north of Kyongju and found other targets in the Kigye-Kyongju-Pohang-dong triangle.

At 2 a.m. on Sept. 5, COL Emmerich, still advisor to the ROK 3d Division, hastened to Yonil to advise LTC McMains (CO, 3/9th Infantry) of the situation in the Pohang-dong area and to confer with him about it. Obtaining a tank platoon from McMains, Emmerich hurried back to Pohang-dong. Placing the tanks into position, he awaited the expected enemy armored attack. By 5:30 a.m., the ROK 22d Regiment had given way and the enemy was entering the gap. By 11 a.m., the U.S. tanks in Pohang-dong were under heavy machine gun fire. Five enemy SP guns entered town and began firing. At a range of one city block, tankers destroyed the lead SP gun, killing three crewmen. The others were driven away by more tank fire. Emmerich called in air strikes and artillery, which destroyed the remaining guns. But at 2:35 p.m., orders came to evacuate all material and supplies from the Yonil Airfield.

The end in Pohang-dong came during the night of Sept. 5-6. At midnight, 10 rounds of enemy artillery landed near the ROK 3d Division CP. The CP moved, but enemy artillery, obviously observed fire, followed it to the new location. Then the ROK commanding general, his G-2 and G-3, all "got sick," as Appleman put it. The command withdrew from Pohang-dong. The enemy occupied it on Sept. 6. Both the ROK I Corps and 3d Division commanders were relieved of command by ROK Army Headquarters.

The eight mile gap between the ROK 8th and Capital Divisions was too large for the ROK I Corps to control actions of the 8th Division. As a result, the ROK Army shifted control of the 8th from the ROK I to the II Corps, effective at 10:30 a.m. Sept. 5. At the same time, it attached the 5th Regiment (ROK 7th Division) to the 8th. As this shift was being made, the *NK 15th Division* penetrated the ROK 8th Division positions and took Yongchon on the Taegu-Pohang-dong road. From its location west of Angang-ni, the ROK 3d Regiment attacked toward Yong-chon, still attempting to close the gap.

The rapidly deteriorating situation in the east caused GEN Walker to shift the 24th Infantry Division to the Kyongju area. The 24th had been slated to relieve the Marine Brigade on the Naktong, and had moved from its reserve position near Taegu to the vicinity of the town of Susan-ni on the banks of the Naktong. There it bivouacked for the night in a downpour of rain. The new order came to GEN Church on the morning of Sept. 4, before relief of the Marines could be started. GEN "Gar" Davidson, the assistant division commander, was sent on ahead to Kyongju by jeep. He arrived that evening. The 19th Infantry and Division troops set out on muddy roads at 1 p.m. on Sept. 5, with most of

them arriving at Kyongju before midnight. GEN Church arrived there earlier in the day. By 7 a.m. on Sept. 6, the rest of the division was also there.

On Sept. 5, the 21st Infantry received a number of new officers from the West Point Class of 1950, including Charles W. Newcomb, Co. A; Clifton A. Pritchett Jr., Co. I; Volney F. Warner and Thomas F. Dreisonstok, both Co. L., William B. DeGraf (Co. M), Francois X. Therrien Jr. and John Ufner. Newcomb, Pritchett and Warner wrote of their arrival. Newcomb wrote: "I was...sent up to A Company, commanded by Captain Earl F. Babb and...taken to the side of a ridge up on a mountain top where I assumed my first my first military duty and my first command — Platoon Leader of the 2d Platoon.... I told the platoon sergeant MSG Anthony Treadwell, to continue to lead the platoon until I got my feet on the ground." Treadwell had been reassigned from the 1st Cavalry Division as a replacement in the 24th Division's 21st Infantry. He was not then happy about it. "We got along reasonably well," Newcomb continued, and managed to keep the platoon going. I had the great good fortune to join the platoon in a quiet sector...and had a chance to at least meet the members...before having to take them into combat."

Pritchett became leader of Item Co.'s Weapons Platoon. His platoon sergeant was a man named SGT Sumpsky, who reminded Pritchett of movie actor Guy Kibbee. Sumpsky briefed him on the forthcoming attack and what the role of the Weapons Platoon would be. Pritchett had never commanded troops before, so he too, took the platoon sergeant aside. "I told him I would appreciate it if he would, as discrete as he could, tell me what to do and I would issue the orders and hopefully get through it that way and I assured him that I was a fast learner and in a short time I could assume my full duties and would not have to work this kind of arrangement out.... He was a solid understanding type and did just what I asked him to do and it wasn't long before I could take over and do what needed to be done on my own."

Volney Warner was assigned to command the 3d Platoon of Co. L. At the Co. CP, the platoon's position was pointed out to him — on top of "an enormously steep hill," as he described it. "I simply had no idea of what was to follow.

"As I reached what I later learned was the platoon sergeant's position, I squared away my steel pot, and reported as 'replacement Warner.' Platoon Sergeant Michael Thiel promptly pointed down the ridge line at a spot of ground where I was to...dig in.... I dutifully went down the hill and began to dig. Shortly thereafter, Sergeant Anderson, the squad leader...came over to check my progress and remarked on how young the replacements seemed to be getting these days. After a brief interrogation, it dawned on Anderson that I was a 2LT and he came to attention and saluted. After checking over my shoulder and discovering I was the only one there, it dawned on me that this was my new platoon and I was at the wrong end of it. With great glee Sergeant Anderson took me back to SGT Thiel and introduced me as their new platoon leader.... In the following 32 years in the military, there were times when I thought Theil's initial assessment of my military ability was right on target!"

Volney Warner retired from the Army as a four-star general.

Planter Wilson, commanding L/21st Infantry wrote this of his platoon leaders and platoon sergeants: "I was fortunate in having some of the most outstanding officers I have ever known as platoon leaders. Volney Warner, 'Toady' Dreisonstok, Carl Bernard and Joe Epton. The platoon sergeants were experienced, highly skilled, competent and courageous: Hugh Brown, Mike Thiel, Anderson. All successes of L Co. were due to the leadership, courage and ability of the above men. They took care of their platoons, led them wisely and bravely and never lost control of the situation."

During WW II, Bill DeGraf had been awarded a battlefield commission and was a 1st Lieutenant at war's end. But he opted to resign his Reserve commission and graduate from West Point (top of class and a cadet regimental commander), securing a Regular Army commission. He went to Co. M.

The 3d Transportation Military Railroad Service

It is a little-known fact that American military personnel eventually took over the operation of most railroad service in the Perimeter. Personnel of the Service did not replace train crews, but worked with them. This was the 3d Transportation Military Railroad Service. Within this command were 714th and 724th Transportation Railway Operating Battalions (TROB). CPL Francis M. Carpenter was a member of the 3d Transportation Railway Military Railroad Service. His detachment operated out of Kyongju. Carpenter, himself, was stationed at Kyongju for 10 of the 14 months he was in Korea. He wrote of that they evacuated the town only twice in that time. The Railroad Service men from Kyongju also were responsible for controlling the railhead at Pohang-dong, where the rail line dead-ended.

"The fighting units usually kept us informed and we...would notify our company of what was happening," Carpenter wrote, but he was never in "a true or large battle," Occasionally he experienced sniper fire when riding in a jeep, but most of his "official travel [was] by railroad locomotive...." This was much safer because, even though getting shot up the trains usually got through.

TF Church — Sept. 7-9

Knowing that the *NK 15th Division* was heading toward Kyongju from the Yongchon area, GEN Coulter ordered the 21st infantry to attack northwest from the vicinity of that town toward the advancing enemy. The 21st attacked on Sept. 7, but encountered little resistance. Later in the day, an enemy patrol attacked the CP of Co. I. In the ensuing gun battle, LT Tom Hardaway, the 1st Platoon leader, was killed.

Eighth Army redesignated Task Force Jackson as Task Force Church at 12:30 p.m. on Sept. 7. About 1 p.m., GEN Coulter left for Taegu to continued his planning duties. Church, believing that the attack by the 21st Infantry into the mountains was a useless dispersion of troops, canceled its orders and instead, concentrated it near Kyongju. On Sept. 8, he displaced his CP to the vicinity of Choyang-ni, four miles south of Kyongju. He felt that the CP could be more easily defended in the more open terrain around Choyang-ni than in the town of Kyongju and that traffic would be less congested there, too.

Sept. 9 and part of the 10 were marked by heavy downpouring, typhoon-driven rains and low hanging clouds. In spite of this, battles in the hills adjacent to the valley between Angang-ni and Kyongju continued almost unabated. The newly-arrived 3/19th Infantry became engaged there on the night of Sept. 8-9, when King Co. was driven from Hill 300 by the enemy. The position was midway between Angang-ni and Kyongju. Counterattacks on Sept. 9 failed to dislodge the enemy.

PFC William W. Garry was serving in the U.S. Army in a Topographic Engineer unit in Japan shortly after the Korean War started. "The food was so bad there," he wrote, "that I volunteered to go [to Korea] in 7/50." In Korea, he was assigned to the 4th Platoon, K/19th Infantry. He reported to the company, with a number of other replacements after dark on Sept. 8. They were at the base of Hill 300 when the enemy attacked. The NCO in charge of the replacements left them and did not return. This left Garry, a PFC, the senior man present. "Firing was going on all around us," he wrote. "Another soldier wanted us to go up the hill to help out. I talked him out of it."

Garry and the other replacements remained at the base of the hill that night. "Most of the battalion came down through our position," Garry recalled. The replacements joined the company and he was assigned to the 4th Platoon. "We tried to retake the hill but were pinned down and could not advance any further. After several attempts I passed out [from exhaustion] and was tagged by a medic. Went to the Regimental Aid Station via a narrow gauge railroad. The railroad was under constant enemy mortar fire." At the aid station Garry was given a short rest and salt tablets then released to return to his unit. When he got back to Co. K, the company had been reorganized and was about half way up Hill 300. From this vantage point, the men watched a South Korean unit take the hill.

To the north, on the left side of the valley, the ROK 17th Regiment, supported by the U.S. 13th FAB (105mm), captured Hill 285 and held off several enemy counterattacks. On the right (east) side of the valley the ROK 18th Regiment made some modest gains.

PFC Carpenter, of the railway service, described Kyongju during the fighting around it in early to mid-Sept. 1950. "Everything in the world was dug in around the town.... Mortars within sight of the railroad station. Tanks dug in to be used as artillery on the outskirts of town. The 105s [howitzers] in the railroad yard. We simply spotted a box car loaded with ammo for each gun. The 155s [howitzers] were about a half mile away out of town to the South. They broke most of the glass in the railroad station when firing." His railway detachment at the time "was never larger than 2 officers and 4 enlisted men. We simply worked 12 hours a day, every day and assisted in the railroad yard when we were off. We evacuated the rail station of everything except ammo and our personnel. We kept several

locomotives available. If the town fell, we planned to take all freight cars and locomotives with us in one train." Kyongju was the end of the line in the east (there was a single track spur to Pohang-dong). The line to Kyongju was also single track.

There were usually over 200 cars in the Kyongju station, he recalled. "There is no way to describe the confusion and congestion," he wrote. But, "it worked remarkably well despite mass confusion at all times — management by crisis, I guess."

TF Davidson — Sept. 9-13

At this time, the *NK 5th Division* had troops on the hills west, southwest and south of Pohang-dong. An estimated force of 1,600 men were on Hills 482 (Unje-san) and 510, some four to five miles southwest of Yonil Airfield. Two regiments of the ROK 3d Division, in defensive positions on the hills along the west side of the valley, faced this enemy force. The North Koreans threatened to drive a wedge between the two ROK regiments.

To eliminate the threat to the Yonil Airfield GEN Church formed TF Davidson the evening of Sept. 9. BG Davidson commanded the force, which consisted of the 19th Infantry (-3d Bn); 3/9th Infantry; 13th FAB; C/15th FAB; A/3d ECB; Tk Co., 9th Infantry; two AAA/AW batteries; and other miscellaneous combat service support units.

Since the enemy controlled all other approaches to the Yonil area, the task force had to spend all day Sept. 10 taking a roundabout southern route to the objective. Early that morning Davidson had flown ahead from Kyongju to the task force assembly area at Yongdok-tong. As his plane came to a stop after landing on a road, COL Emmerich stepped forward to meet him. Davidson noted that there seemed no evidence of the enemy in sight. Emmerich advised him that the enemy had taken Hill 131 from the ROKs. The hill was between the two regiments of the ROK 3d Division. Davidson and Emmerich agreed that the ROKs would have to retake Hill 131 so that the task force could attack through the ROK 3d Division to seize the main enemy position on Hill 482. They reasoned that if the ROKs could be placed on that hill they would be able to handle the situation afterward. Emmerich and Davidson then went to meet the ROK 3d Division commander. Davidson informed Emmerich that he now commanded in the area and told him of the attack plan. The ROKs took Hill 482 that night. In the attack, the ROK 3d Engineer Battalion, led by KMAG advisor Major Walter J. Hutchins, fighting as infantry, materially assisted in capturing the height.

Meantime, the task force arrived in its assembly area at Yongdok-tong, a mile south of Yonil Airfield. There it prepared for its attack on Sept. 11.

The attack started on the morning of Sept. 11, passing through the ROKs on Hill 131. The 1/9th Infantry led. It captured the first objective two miles beyond the LD by 9:30 a.m. The 2d Battalion passed through the 1st to continue the attack toward Hill 482, a mile to the west beyond a steep gorge. There, deeply entrenched North Koreans stopped the battalion by machine gun fire.

The following morning, four Australian pilots hit the enemy position with napalm. This was followed by an artillery preparation. The 2d Battalion attacked and seized the promontory by about noon. That afternoon ROK troops relieved TF Davidson on Hill 482. The force went into an assembly area in the valley southwest of Yongdok-tong. The official history notes that Walker visited the task force CP two or three times that day. The task force returned to Kyongju on Sept. 13.

The ROKs took Hill 300 on Sept. 11. That afternoon, 3/19th Infantry (which was attached to the 21st Infantry at the time) relieved the ROKs there. The Americans counted 257 enemy dead on the hill and found large quantities of abandoned weapons and equipment. Fighting continued there. The U.S. 3/19th Infantry lost eight lieutenants and 29 EM killed.

By Tuesday, Sept. 12, the *NK 12th Division* was all but destroyed and the *5th Division* was trying to assemble its survivors near Pohang-dong. Aerial observation confirmed that many groups of enemy soldiers were heading north.

ROK troops followed up the enemy; the ROK 3d in pursuit of the *5th Division* and the Capital Division after the *NK 12th*. Elements of the Capital Division reached the southern edge of Angang-ni on Sept. 15. It seemed evident that the enemy was withdrawing toward Kigye. The enemy threat in the East was over; TF Church was dissolved at noon that day. The ROK Army resumed control of its I Corps and the 24th Division (-19th Infantry, retained at Kyongju in Eighth Army reserve) was ordered to reassemble near Kyongsan, southeast of Taegu. The 21st had moved there on Sept. 14.

The rapid deployment of U.S. and ROK reinforcements to the eastern front, plus the massive naval gunfire and aerial support tipped the scales against the enemy. Their lack of the ability to adequately communicate with, reinforce or resupply their forces doomed the attack in the east to ultimate failure.

On the Yonchon Front — ROK 6th and 8th Divisions — Sept. 1-12

On Sept. 1, the *NK 8th* and *15th Divisions* readied themselves to attack the ROK 6th and 8th Divisions, respectively. The *NK 8th Division* attacked from a point on the main road 20 air miles northwest of Yongchon to seize Hayang, 12 miles east of Taegu on the lateral Taegu-Pohang-dong road. The *15th Division*, just below Andong, attacked to take Yongchon, 20 air miles east of Taegu on the same lateral road as Hayang.

Between Sept. 2 and 12, the *8th Division* made little progress, having advanced only as far as the town of Hwajong-dong, 14 air miles northwest of Yongchon. Losses to that point had been very bad. Particularly telling was the loss of almost all of the 21 new T-34s in the supporting *17th Armored Brigade*. Just below the town, the road enters a pass between the massive Hill 928 (Hwa-san, 3,000 feet high) on the east and peaks about 2,000 feet high on the west. In this pass, the ROK 6th Division all but destroyed the *NK 8th Division*. The diary entries of Pak Han Pin, of the *NK 83d Regiment, 8th Division*, tell the story: Sept. 2, "Today we opened a general attack." After Sept. 6: "We underwent extremely desperate battles. With no place to hide or escape from the fierce enemy artillery bombardment our main force was wiped out." Sept. 8: "We suffer miserably heavy casualties from fierce enemy air, artillery, and heavy machine gun attacks. Only 20 remain alive out of our entire battalion."

The *15th Division*, however, attacking on Sept. 2 against the ROK 8th Division, reached Yongchon in four days. This was quite an achievement, since the three regiments of this division totaled only about 3,600 men. One regiment of the ROK 8th Division was panicked by a single enemy tank behind its lines. By midafternoon of Sept. 6, elements of the *15th Division* were in the southern part of Yongchon. They moved on out of town to occupy the hills south and southeast of it, dominating the main east-west road. The next day elements of the *15th* established a roadblock 3 1/2 miles southeast of the town, while other elements attacked a ROK regiment a mile south of it. Later in the day, the 5th Regiment of the new ROK 7th Division, attacking from the east along the road, recaptured Yongchon then took up defensive positions north of town. On Sept. 8, reinforcing elements of the *15th Division* took Yongchon back again. But that afternoon, the 11th Regiment of the ROK 1st Division arrived from the Taegu area and drove the enemy out of most of the town and adjacent area. The enemy clung to the railroad station to the southeast.

This is where the artillery regiment of the *15th Division* got ahead of its infantry. After expending all of its ammunition, the regiment was all but destroyed by ROK counter-battery fire, which also killed the artillery commander. Once the ROK 5th and 11th Regiments arrived to reinforce the shaken 8th Division, "ROK battle action was so severe against the enemy units," states the official history, "that they had no chance to regroup for coordinated action." On Sept. 9 and 10, ROK troops surrounded and almost wiped out the *15th Division* southeast of Kyongju on the hills overlooking the Kyongju road. The division chief of staff, COL Kim Yon and a number of other high ranking officers were among the dead. The official history notes that KMAG officers played an important part in collecting stragglers from the demoralized ROK 8th Division and in reorganizing its units into effective commands. The fact that the 8th was brought back to effectiveness so quickly "was an important factor in the successful outcome of these battles," it asserts. For example, on Sept. 10 the ROK 8th Division cleared the enemy from the Yongchon-Kyongju road and captured 2 T-34 tanks, 6 howitzers, 1 76mm SP gun, a number of AT guns and many small arms.

An interesting story surrounds the capture of the SP gun. An enemy soldier drove the gun, followed by a truck full of soldiers, from the southeast through the ROKs to Yongchon. There he stopped and was "quietly eating dinner with ROK troops when he came under suspicion," the official history records. He made a dash for it, closely pursued by the ROKs. He finally surrendered to a lone ROK soldier 4 miles to the north, explaining that he could not drive the gun and shoot at the same time.

The ROK 8th Division and 5th Regiment (ROK 7th Division) pursued the fleeing remnants of the *15th* without meeting significant resistance. On Sept. 12, ROK units, now eight miles north of Yongchon, captured 4 120mm mortars, 4 AT guns, 4 artillery pieces, 9 trucks, 2 machine guns and a large number of small arms.

The *15th Division's* breakthrough of the ROK 8th Division and seizure of Yongchon placed the enemy in a position to either turn west toward Taegu and take Eighth Army and the 1st Cavalry Division in reverse, or to turn east and attack the left and rear of TF Jackson. The enemy was beginning to execute the latter maneuver when the ROK 5th and 11th Regiments, quickly dispatched to the scene by GEN Walker, thwarted the enemy. The official history credits Walker with accurately determining what reinforcements were needed in the Kyongju-Pohang-dong and Yongchon areas and promptly shifting reinforcements to those areas to meet the threats. Appleman wrote that this was "a notable command achievement in the battles of the Pusan Perimeter."

The Taegu Area, September 2 - 16

The New Third Battalions for the 1st Cavalry Division

The 3/5th, 3/7th and 3/8th Cavalry, which had joined the Cavalry Division Aug. 26, would face their first battles at the beginning of Sept. All three battalions were commanded by West Pointers. The 3/5th Cavalry was led by LTC Edgar J. Treacy, age 36, Class of 1935. A veteran of WW II, where he was an intelligence expert, Treacy had never led troops in battle. The battalion was at full strength (900 personnel) and had been trained in cross-country skiing and mountain climbing. As a result, the men were in excellent physical shape. The 3/7th Cavalry was commanded by 36-year-old James H. Lynch (West Point, 1938). He had only about two weeks to train his battalion before embarking for Korea. Lynch had been in WW II, but never commanded troops in combat. When the battalion joined the 7th Cavalry on Aug. 26, it numbered 33 officers, 5 warrants and 685 EM; about 170 men short of full strength. LTC Harold K. "Johnny" Johnson, 38 (West Point, 1933) commanded 3/8th Cavalry. Numbering 704 personnel, the battalion had not even trained at platoon level before embarking for Korea. The battalion had been literally thrown together and Johnson rated its combat effectiveness as "zero." But, he recalled, the Battalion XO was a "very good technician" and a tough disciplinarian who "loved soldiering." He also recalled that the battalion had excellent lieutenants and some long time, good, professional NCOs.

The North Korean Plan of Attack in the Taegu Area

Three enemy divisions, the *1st, 13th* and *3d,* in that order from east to west, were in position north of Taegu. These divisions, along with *5th, 8th, 12th* and *15th* (estimated to total 21,000 troops), were part of the *NK II Corps.* (Maj Kim

Song Jun, S-3, *19th Regiment,* surrendered on Sept. 2. He stated that the *13th* had just been reinforced by 4,000 replacements, 2,000 of them without weapons, and now contained about 9,000 men.) The *1st Division* was to attack south through the high ridges east of the Sangju-Taegu road. The *13th Division* was to advance south along the ridges west of that road, while the *3d Division* was to attack more or less eastward from the Waegwan area. Taegu was the ultimate objective for all three divisions.

To oppose these three enemy divisions were the U.S. 1st Cavalry on the left near the Naktong, and the ROK 1st Infantry on the Cavalry's right flank in the mountains north of Taegu.

Deployment of the 1st Cavalry Division, Sept. 2-5

The 1st Cavalry Division had a front 35 miles long. Again, all GEN Gay could do was outpost likely avenues of approach and hope to eject the enemy by counterattacks. Initially, he also had 1/23d Infantry (U.S. 2d Division) attached to the Cavalry, manning the division's southern flank. On Sept. 5, this battalion was returned to its parent division, and the newly-arrived British 27th Brigade took its place in line. The 5th Cavalry was deployed north of the 27th Bde, defending a sector which included the Naktong around Waegwan and the main Seoul road southeast from there to Taegu. The 7th Cavalry, next in line, guarded the mountainous region between that road and the hills near the Sangju road. The 8th Cavalry, on the Division right flank, was positioned on the mountains on either side of the Sangju road. (The initial positions of elements of the 8th were in the old Bowling Alley area, formerly occupied by elements of the ROK 1st Infantry Division and the U.S. 27th Infantry.)

Units of the British 27th Brigade

The British 27th Bde entered Korea from Hong Kong on Aug. 28, 1950, with the 1st Battalion, The Middlesex Regiment and the 1st Battalion, The Argyll and Sutherland Highlanders. The Americans supplied the brigade with tanks, artillery and trucks. Later, as more British troops arrived, they included artillery, mortar, tank, transportation, medical and other support troops. (See Chapter Notes.) Both battalions left Korea Apr. 26, 1951, replaced by other battalions.

American troops who worked with, or who came into contact with British troops in Korea had nothing but the highest praise for them; they were good, solid, brave and determined men, and fine allies.

Hill 518, 7th Cavalry — Sept. 2

On Sept. 1, in an attempt to relieve enemy pressure on the 2d and 25th Divisions on the southern flank of the Perimeter, GEN Walker directed GEN Gay to attack to the north and northwest. Initially, Gay wanted to attack up the Sangju road, but allowed his staff and regimental commanders to talk him out of it. They recommended that the attack should be made against Hill 518, in the 7th Cavalry's sector. Two days previously, this hill had been in the ROK 1st

Division's sector. It was considered an enemy assembly point.

On Aug. 30, B/7th Cavalry sent a patrol to Hill 518. Battalion reinforced the patrol with the rest of Co. B and all of Co. A. Just 200 yards from the summit, very heavy enemy mortar, small arms and automatic weapons fire stopped the attackers in their tracks. The two units pulled back and dug in on the slopes for the night. They had lost 10 KIA and 36 WIA.

All day on Aug. 31 both Hills 518 and nearby 346 were hit by harassing artillery and mortar fire. An air strike also hit the north side of Hill 518. About midmorning Co. C made contact with the 8th Cavalry and preparations were made to close the gap between the 7th and 8th Cavalry Regiments.

Heretofore, the 7th believed only about one enemy "reinforced company" was on Hill 518. The enemy increased their artillery and mortar fire and more aggressively engaged Cavalry patrols. There was increased activity and noise across the Naktong. On Sept. 2, while walking along near Hill 518, LT Otis Lane and SGT John Jano, of Co. E, were both felled by an incoming shell. When the dust and smoked cleared, PFC Marvin C. Daniel saw that the officer had multiple wounds from the neck on down and one leg had been blown almost off. "He looked at me eye to eye," Daniel recalled, "and...said, 'Don't bother with me, I'm dead!' With that, he fell over and died in a few minutes. SGT Jano was very badly wounded, but survived.

The plan of attack against Hill 518 called for 1/7th Cavalry to make the main attack, while the 2d Battalion blocked on the left (west) and the new 3d Battalion was to be behind the 2d Battalion and in a gap between the 2d and Hill 518. Air strikes and artillery were to soften up the objective. Once Hill 518 was taken, the regiment was to continue west along the ridge to seize Hill 346. Two companies of the new 3/8th Cavalry were to make a diversionary attack toward Hill 490 on the right flank of the 7th Cavalry. This would leave the 8th with only one company in reserve. The Cavalry Division had its three 105mm howitzer battalions and one 155mm howitzer battalion, plus the 9th FAB (155mm howitzer). These battalions totaled 90 howitzers: 54 105mm and 36 155mm. The 77th FAB (105mm), A/61st FAB (105mm), B and C/9th FAB (155mm) and a platoon of B/82d FAB (155mm), a total of 24 105mm howitzers and 14 155mm howitzers were designated to support the 7th Cavalry's attack on Hill 518.

The attack began at 9 a.m., with a 37-minute long air strike, during which 24 napalm pods were dropped on the enemy. Then the artillery pounded them, followed again by more air strikes. Tanks added their support with direct fire. Just after 10 a.m., the 1st Battalion started its attack. F/7th Cavalry opened supporting machine gun fire on the objective at 10:22 a.m. Seven minutes later, the 1st Battalion reported that it and the supporting artillery fire were being held up by an unscheduled air strike on Hill 518 by four F-80 jets. The jets were diverted to Hill 346 and other enemy targets and the 1st Battalion resumed its attack. (See Chapter Notes.)

What was supposed to be a battalion attack by 1/7th Cavalry, in fact became an attack by a column of rifle squads against a well dug-in en-

emy. The approach to Hill 518 for the battalion was along a very narrow, almost razor-backed ridge. There was barely room to deploy a single squad in an attack formation. But the battalion struggled on in the face of telling mortar and machine gun fire. By 1:20 p.m., this intense enemy resistance had halted 1st Battalion's attack. At 4:10 p.m., the battalion reported enemy fire from Hill 490, on its left. The battalion commander requested permission to shift Co. A so as to attack from the north and northwest, while two other companies were moved to make the main attack. Permission was granted, but the commander was told that 3/7th Cavalry would attack from Co. I's position in a northwesterly direction from Hill 490 later that afternoon. The 1st Battalion withdrew to regroup at 4:15 p.m., then resumed its attack at 5 p.m.

2LT William H. Marslender (West Point 1949) joined A/7th Cavalry at the end of August and was assigned as a rifle platoon leader. On Sept. 2, therefore, he barely knew his men when the company made its attack on Hill 518. The company CP was in a Korean hut "in an open field...approximately a mile and a half to two miles from the mountains [one of which was Hill 518]," he said. The company CO pointed to a hill on the map and told LT Marslender to take his platoon and occupy it. Platoon leaders did not then have maps, as they did later in the war. The unit CO stayed at his CP. The lieutenant shot an azimuth to what he believed to be the assigned hill. He took the platoon, numbering 38 men, to what he and the platoon sergeant agreed was the right position. The following morning (Sept. 3), the company commander ordered Marslender's platoon "to attack along the ridge line to the front of my position," Marslender said, "towards a hill called 518." At about 8 a.m., he recalled, the platoon set out toward the objective in a column of squads. The company commander had told him nothing about fire support and "I did not know where any of the other platoons of the company were," he remarked.

Marslender's platoon moved forward for about an hour. Then he discovered another rifle platoon from Co. A on his left. The two platoon leaders met and introduced one another. Neither of them had much information, nor were sure that they were attacking along the correct ridgeline. They decided to continue the attack with the platoons abreast; the other platoon on the left and Marslender's on the right. The two platoons presented a two-squad front. The two platoons moved forward, over a knob which they thought might be the objective. Beyond the knob, "the ridge opened up into a broad plateau on the left, and on the right a sharp ravine," he recalled. This put his platoon on a ledge. His men had to climb up on the ledge to fire at the enemy, which Marslender could see on the hill to his front. "They appeared to be in foxholes three deep," he said. The position...was heavily fortified and we were receiving intense small-arms and 82mm mortar fire. They were also rolling hand grenades down the hill into our positions.... A potato masher type grenade landed close enough to me that I could reach it to throw it back, but in my nervousness I only flipped it a few feet.... The grenade was a dud."

A short time later, Marslender discovered that some of his men had drifted away. The enemy

mortar fire was dropping mostly in the ravine behind his platoon, where some of his men had moved to. The platoon on the left, being in the open, was taking heavy casualties. Neither platoon could call upon mortar or artillery support. After discussing the situation with his platoon sergeant, Marslender decided to pull back to the knoll, about 150-200 yards to the rear. An enemy mortar round hit the platoon machine gun position, killing all three men there. He called the company commander on the radio to request permission. That officer called the battalion CP for permission; Marslender was to wait.

While he was waiting, the other platoon leader came over and asked, "Sir, what are we to do? What ARE we to do?" He was bleeding from a head wound, probably caused by a mortar fragment, and was probably in some shock. Marslender grabbed him by the lapels and shook him, then told him to withdraw his platoon, one squad at a time, to the knoll to the rear. Marslender would send his men out in the same fashion and come out with his last squad. The other officer was to put men into a defensive position on the knoll as they withdrew. In the midst of the withdrawal, the company commander called to tell him to hold. Marslender told his radio operator not to acknowledge the transmission and to turn off the radio. He, with the last four men, started to pull out, but came upon two wounded from the other platoon. They took the injured men with them in improvised litters.

Upon gaining the knoll, Marslender discovered that there was no one there. He set the men with him to digging in and sent the platoon sergeant to round up what men he could find. Darkness was coming on. The sergeant returned in about an hour with 16 men. The platoon remained on the hill undisturbed all during the night.

They were attacked the next morning, but beat it off with no problem, then were subjected to a 45-minute 82mm mortar barrage, again with no losses. About 10 a.m.. Marslender received a radio message to return to the jump off point. He sent a detail of men back to the Company CP with the two wounded with instructions to bring back water and ammunition. The detail returned to the platoon about dark, with the rumor that the Company Commander was going to court-martial Marslender for disobeying a direct order (to stay on Hill 518). The next rumor was that he would not be court-martialled. His platoon sergeant allegedly told the unit commander that if Marslender was court-martialled, he, the sergeant, would report that the company commander never left his CP during the attack. That ended the threatened court martial.

Co. C was also part of the attack on Hill 518. CPL Peter J. Mariotti came into the unit in late August as a replacement. He recalled that. in spite of artillery and fighter (air attacks), they were unable to take Hill 518. Although Peter is not specific, this is where he was probably wounded while trying to withdraw. He injured his back about 2 p.m. and was dragged to safety by one of his buddies.

Richard Dowell and James W. Dodgen were in Co. B. Dodgen wrote this of his first impressions of Korea: "I came. I saw. I was ready to leave." Of Hill 518, he recalled that the com-

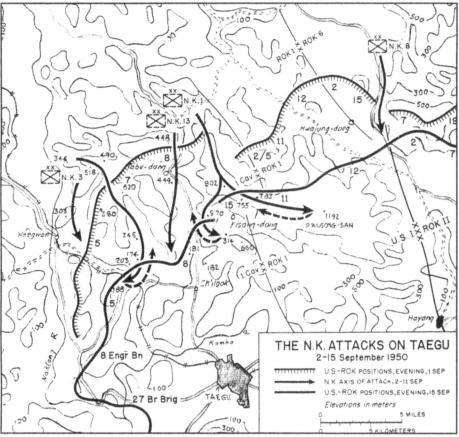

Map 40 (Source: South to the Naktong*)*

pany "lost most of our men. Support fire was called in...called walking fire. We moved up as the support[ing fire] was moved." He remembered that the hill was dotted with enemy dead. "You couldn't walk any place on or down that hill for dead Koreans."

"C Co. made an attack on Hill 518," Richard Dowell wrote. "I couldn't see them, but did hear the terrible screaming. The Reds really did a number on our boys. That evening I ran a belt through my light .30 at the top of Hill 518 so our men could get out. I had only a foot left of my machine gun belt when a heavy round [of enemy mortar or artillery] came in and landed in front of my foxhole. The concussion went by me and hit this huge boulder that was to my back, and then pushed me forward into the front of my foxhole. It stunned me...." His squad leader told him to finish the belt and quit. "The Reds knew I was there," Dowell continued. "While sitting in the bottom of my foxhole, I pulled down on my .30 and pulled the trigger. My second gunner wondered why I did it that way. I told him I wanted the Reds to think they got me. This way we wouldn't get any more big stuff on us. It seemed to work."

The 81mm mortars of D/7th Cavalry added their fire in support of the 1st Battalion's attack on Sept. 2. The mortars were positioned "on a small plateau near a trail, approximately 2,500 yards east of the...summit of Hill 518," wrote then-Corporal Stanley Dahl. Dahl was a gunner in this platoon. "Our only problem was we were rationed on 81mm mortar ammo; we were only allowed to fire so many rounds per day. We had the forward observers with the rifle companies screaming at us over the radio, calling for fire

missions. We didn't have the ammo. A supply SNAFU that led directly back to the States. We even had a problem getting C-rations. It was a nightmare. Who suffered? The Infantry, Queen of Battle!"

Returning wounded said that the enemy was deeply entrenched on Hill 518. That was evident to the mortarmen by the large number of dead and wounded passing to the rear through their position.

Other elements of the 7th Cavalry also had contact of varying degrees with the enemy on the morning and early afternoon of Sept. 2. For example, at 11:01 a.m., harassing enemy artillery fire fell on Co. I while about 35 enemy soldiers moved across its front. The enemy infantry was taken under fire. Another group of about 40 enemy, with three field pieces were sighted on Hill 346 by a 3d Battalion outpost. Jets were called in and hit the enemy position at 11:32 a.m. "Good results" were reported from the strike.

A tank from C/70th Tk Bn, supporting 2/7th Cavalry was hit by a 120mm mortar round at 12:10 p.m., killing three crewmen and wounding two others.

Thirty minutes later the I&R Platoon reported that an air strike had caused explosions and black smoke in a village forward of the 2d Battalion. Enemy tanks were reported to be burning furiously later on, as a result of attacks by F-51s and F-80s.

Platoon Leader, LT Richard L "Rigger" Morton (West Point 1949), F/7th Cavalry, wrote that his battalion had relieved a ROK battalion on Hill 324 "just north of Waegwan and the notorious Hill 303" in the last week of August. He

recalled that there was a gap of 800 yards between his battalion and the 5th Cavalry on the left, but that they were tied in with the 7th Cavalry's 1st battalion on the right.

Almost at once, it was obvious that the enemy could observe any activity on Hill 324 from their vantage point of Hill 464 to the east. "Mortar and artillery fire descended on us whenever three or more men exposed themselves together," he wrote. Enemy observed mortar fire soon prevented the men of Co. F from dropping back on the reverse slope of the hill for their one hot meal a day. The company commander, 1LT Marvin Golding, was killed and a number of unit CP personnel wounded by a direct hit from a 120mm mortar round.

From Hill 324, Morton was able to watch the efforts to take Hill 518 from the enemy. All were thwarted by the stubborn enemy. In 1966, he had the opportunity to re-visit the area and climbed Hill 518. Then he discovered why the 7th Cavalry could not take the hill back in Sept. 1950. "The final altitude on 518 was almost vertical and I could not have climbed it unopposed without climbing gear," he wrote. In somewhat of an exaggeration, he concluded that "one NKPA soldier at the top with a bag of grenades could have held off a division of Eighth Army."

3/7th Cavalry and Hill 490, Sept. 2

At 5:15 p.m., 3/7th Cavalry fired WP and smoke shells at the hills to its left front, then launched an attack through Co. I, northwest toward Hill 490, as planned. The 3d Battalion's attack permitted the 1st Battalion to try for Hill 518 from the west about 5:30 p.m. The 1st Battalion started for Hill 518 as the 3d moved to the base of 490.

As 3/7th Cavalry neared the top of Hill 490 at 6:30 p.m., it was held up by heavy machine gun fire. However, the battalion reported that it would continue the attack on 490 while the 1st Battalion attacked Hill 518 at 6:50 p.m. The 3d was stopped again at 7:20 p.m. by two enemy machine guns on 490. Cavalry machine guns responded, suppressing the enemy fire, allowing the 3d Battalion to continue its advance. Ten minutes later, the battalion was on Hill 490 and within 200 yards of Hill 518. There, very heavy small-arms, automatic weapons and mortar fire forced the Americans to pull back and regroup.

The 1st and 3d Battalions were instructed to establish contact on Hill 518 once it was taken. The boundary between the two was to be the large draw going northwest from Hill 518. The 2d and 3d Battalions were to contact one another and the 1st was to establish contact with the 8th Cavalry on the 7th Cavalry's right flank.

The enemy heavily shelled the entire 7th Cavalry's sector that night with artillery and 120mm mortars. The I&R Platoon was forced from the regimental outpost and the forward medical collection station had to withdraw because of this fire. Heavy fire between 8 p.m. and 9:15 p.m. knocked out all telephone lines. Companies F and G observed and reported small groups of the enemy crossing the Naktong during the night.

8th Cavalry Regiment — Sept. 2

The 8th Cavalry Regiment manned the Cavalry Division's right, next to the ROK 1st Division's left. The regiment's line was astride the Sangju-Taegu road in the area which had been occupied by the ROK 1st Division and U.S. 27th Infantry just a few weeks previously. The 8th Cavalry's 2d Battalion held the right sector of the regimental front on Hill 740. At the end of August, the 8th Cavalry took over the former positions of the ROK 11th and 12th Regiments (ROK 1st Division). BAR-man CPL Richard I. Benedict later wrote an account, "The Battle on Hill #740 - September 2 & 3, 1950." (Apr. 1986 issue of *Military* magazine.)

He wrote that the 8th Cavalry had but 25-30 men to put into position where the ROKs had 50. Benedict was a member of 3d Platoon, E/8th Cavalry. His platoon "was placed on a knoll approximately 150-200 yards in front of the rest of the company connected by a narrow spine [ridge] with steep sides." Benedict, and his assistant BAR-man, Lionel Lavoie (one of the company cooks), were placed between the 3d Platoon and Co. F as a listening post. About "90 yards out in front and approximately 100 yards further north were two men from F Company who were also manning a listening post approximately 200 yards from the rest of their company." Co. G, he wrote, was about 200-250 yards forward of Co. F. George's position started at the Sangju-Taegu road and ran east along two ridges to high ground "that ended with steep drop-offs at the top. A long narrow spine, which varied in width, connected us [elements of Co. E] to F and G companies along the top of the ridge."

From their post, Benedict and Lavoie could see a small village about three miles to the northeast. They also observed small groups of enemy soldiers, of from two to six men, on the road from time to time, sometimes pulling carts. At times, when larger groups of from 10 to 30 men were spotted, the artillery FO tried to get artillery fire on them. Each time the mission was denied, Benedict wrote, because the artillery was short of ammunition. The enemy had to be in parties of 50 or more to get an artillery fire mission.

The *NK 13th Division* faced elements of the 8th Cavalry Regiment. The division was scheduled to begin their major attack at dusk on Sept. 2.

"At approximately 1700 hours [5 p.m.], 2 September 1950, G and F Companies came under attack with the most fierce artillery and mortar barrage I had ever seen," Benedict wrote. "As soon as the barrage ended, the NKs started to blow bugles, whistles and different colored flares were shot off. Then they attacked in force all along G Company's positions." The enemy came running, yelling and throwing grenades. Their numbers and firepower overwhelmed Co. G. The enemy then surged on to overrun Co. F, using the same tactics. "A deathly silence settled over the battle field in front of us as all firing ceased."

An officer of Co. E called up to the Fox Co. position repeatedly, trying to determine if any U.S. soldiers remained there. Finally, just as he was about to call artillery fire in on the Co. F position, a group of men called back. When they did, "the NKs screamed and went after them," Benedict recalled. Artillery fire was called in at that point. "We heard no more from the F Company men after that."

Joe M. Christopher was a member of Fox Co. at the time. When the enemy overran the company position, Christopher and four others were captured by the enemy. He escaped a few minutes later, but it was four days before he could get back to friendly lines.

When Benedict and Lavoie saw that Co. F was being overrun, they pulled back to their platoon, since they had the discretion to do so. Once back in the platoon position, Benedict shared a foxhole with a new replacement sergeant. After he got into the hole, Benedict began to tremble uncontrollably. He couldn't stop. He wrote that it didn't affect his fighting ability, "but it sure was aggravating. All night long, enemy soldiers followed a path which led right up to his BAR. "We took a terrible toll of NKs," he recalled, stopping every thrust.

While at the LP, Benedict had rigged noise devices using empty C-ration cans into which he had put a few stones and metal fragments. He suspended them with commo wire from bushes, making several rows of the devices. Anyone trying to crawl or walk through the area who disturbed a bush having one of the cans fastened to it could be detected by the noise of the stones or shell fragments rattling in the can. When the enemy started toward Benedict's and Robert Mueller's foxholes, they disturbed the stone/shell fragment cans. The cans revealed a number of enemy attacks early enough so that the Americans could direct fire on them before they got to U.S. positions.

There were about 25 men on the knoll. To Benedict's left was a light machine gun manned by William Taylor and another man. The sergeant replacement, with an M-1 rifle was in the foxhole with Benedict. On their right was another light machine gun manned by Herbert Mueller and another man. On the right of this gun was Boyce M. Walker, armed with an M-1 rifle. These 7 men were the company front because the ridge was so narrow, with steep sides. Their lieutenant, who had taken all the grenades into his hole, was about 10 yards behind Benedict. Further up the slope was Terry Campbell, also with an M-1 rifle. With him was the FO radio to the 99th FAB. Because of the ground's slope behind the men in front, no one could fire down on the enemy from above without the danger of shooting their own men in the back. As a result, Benedict wrote, "almost all of the firing... that night was by the 2 light machine guns, 2 M-1 Garands and my BAR."

An enemy attack came at about 8 p.m., with the enemy blowing bugles and firing different colored flares. The first men in the enemy attack, Benedict recalled, were South Koreans, dressed in white, being driven forward to attract American fire. Benedict wasn't biting. The night was partly cloudy and the moon occasionally broke through the clouds to bathe the landscape in a faint, eerie light. He was able to detect the darker shapes of enemy soldiers behind the people in white, and fired on them. His BAR opened the American defense, cutting down several North Korean soldiers. The others opened fire, and the enemy charged forward, yelling, and shouting "Manzai! Manzai!"

While the front 7 engaged the enemy with small arms and automatic weapons, the officer, yelled and threw grenades at them. He shouted out something about the knoll being held by 120 men. Some time during the battle, the lieutenant was killed by a burp gun burst. Three bullets from the same burst stung Benedict on the upper lip, right earlobe and the right side of his neck. The platoon sergeant, SGT Campbell, took command.

Again and again the enemy attacked. The first attacks were accompanied by screams, yelling and noise. But American weapons fire homed in on the noise, dropping many of the enemy. Then they shifted tactics and crawled up to within grenade distance of the defenders before revealing their presence by throwing showers of grenades. They would then jump up and charge forward firing their weapons and throwing grenades. At times, North Koreans got to within 6 feet of Benedict before jumping up. Each time, he cut them down.

Just before the attack that night, the platoon was resupplied with ammo. Benedict was given a burlap bag with about 500 loose rounds of .30-cal ammunition. During lulls in the battle he refilled his empty magazines. Knowing that ammunition was scarce, he fired only short bursts, and only at targets he could see. Even the wounded enemy soldiers were dangerous. Many of the wounded would get up and continue their attack. Benedict and his comrades believed that the enemy may have been drugged, they acted so irrationally.

At one point, the platoon fired some 3.5 inch rockets into the enemy, but nothing seemed to stop the enemy attacks; they kept coming, one after the other. Believing that they were in imminent danger of being overrun, SGT Campbell called the 99th FAB to walk the artillery fire in to the foxhole line. The fire started about 50 yards out, then crept nearer. "It was really terrifying," Benedict remembered. "They fired salvo after salvo of high explosive...and white phosphorous shells. The ground literally shook and moved from the force and power of all the shells exploding. Dirt, stones, dust, rocks and shrapnel flew all over the place and all over us. It scared the living daylights out of us.... We all thought we would probably be killed by our own artillery, but...our lives were spared.... The 99th Field Artillery fired with such precision, its still hard to believe to this day." The artillery stopped the last enemy attack about 3:45 a.m. When the artillery lifted, CPT Fred R. White, commanding Co. E, ordered Campbell to withdraw the platoon. Except for the lieutenant, no one had been killed and only a few wounded in the terrible, hard fight during the night.

Benedict and his BAR were left to cover the withdrawal. When he started to get out of his foxhole, his legs wouldn't function, so he began to crawl. Soon, feeling came back into them and he was able to catch up to the platoon. The artillery had so badly mauled the enemy that the withdrawal was made without interference. One man from the 3d Platoon, deafened by the noise of battle, had not heard the order to withdraw. He came into the company line the next day, also without interference from the enemy.

2LT David E. Bolté' (West Point, 1949) joined H/8th Cavalry near the end of August, and was understudying 1LT Roy Duggan as platoon leader of the machine gun platoon. The two officers had visited the rifle companies to which machine guns from the platoon were attached. Duggan stayed with the guns and company on the left of the Sangju-Taegu road, and Bolté' was given the responsibility of the guns with the rifle elements on the right.

About dusk on Sept. 2, while checking on platoon machine guns, LT Bolté' "found a rifle platoon strong point...which had been abandoned; many weapons, including an M-1917-A6 machine gun, abandoned, and much blood. about," he wrote. "A rifleman some 30 to 50 yards farther on told me some men had been wounded and the others evacuated them." Bolté' went back and manned the machine gun in the abandoned strongpoint. He fired "on attacking enemy infantry moving up the slopes and fingers of the ridge to the front until I was wounded in the forearm and shoulder, my shoulder being 'smashed,'" he wrote. "I then contacted the infantryman to my left, who helped me, explained to him what I knew of the situation, and then embarked on the trip to get myself helped, as my left arm was useless."

Appleman's account of events in the 8th Cavalry sector on Sept. 2 is somewhat different than Benedict's. He wrote that the enemy overran Hill 448 the night of Sept. 2-3. This hill is two miles north of Tabu-dong and west of the Sangju-Taegu highway. He stated that Co. E, on the battalion right, was not attacked, but was cut off and had to withdraw.

7th Cavalry — Sept. 3

Battle action started in the 7th Cavalry zone shortly after midnight on Sept. 3. By 1 a.m., 3/7th Cavalry was again within 200 yards of the top of Hill 518, the 1st Battalion was stopped short of the crest of Hill 490 and the 2d Battalion reported all quiet on its front. The 2d Battalion's respite was cut short at 3:56 a.m. by heavy artillery and tank fire. Co. E repulsed a probing attack. From an observation post the I&R Platoon reported sighting one large and one small artillery piece across the Naktong, which were firing on the slopes and crest of Hill 464, directly in rear of the 2d Battalion's positions. The battalion itself received occasional tank and artillery fire.

At 5:15 a.m., Fox Co. was attacked by the enemy, heavily supported by artillery fire. First, the company was forced from their forward positions. By 6:40 a.m., it had been driven from Hill 300, exposing the battalion's right flank. Artillery fire was directed onto the hill to prevent the enemy from reinforcing. A report from 1/7th Cavalry at 7:25 a.m. stated that an unknown number of North Koreans had gone through F Co. and to the bridge on the MSR. It requested that the I&R Platoon attack this enemy force. Meantime, Co. F counterattacked and took back Hill 300.

LT Richard Morton (Co. F) wrote that the unit was hit hard by the fighting for Hill 300, with the loss of 1LT Marvin Golding, the CO and 2LT Jay Rash, a platoon leader and some 37 EM. "The company was so weakened," he wrote, "that we were put into reserve near the bottom of Hill 324 but on the dangling left flank be-

tween us and the 5th Cav.... The entire 7th Cav was now in danger of being circled. In...fact, the 2/7th was already behind enemy lines...."

Meantime, at 6:33 a.m., LT John C. Lippincott was ordered to take elements of the Regimental HQ Security Platoon to find and destroy the enemy which had infiltrated the rear near Hills 464 and 380. LT Homer C. McNamara, I&R Platoon leader spotted Lippincott's group under heavy fire from about 25 North Koreans on Hill 464. Lippincott later confirmed that his men were under mortar and automatic weapons fire from Hill 464 and that the North Koreans had a radio and one 82mm mortar on the hill. He prepared to move against the hill from the south and requested that a force from 3/7th Cavalry attack from the west. At 11:35 a.m., the 2d Battalion was directed to send a combat patrol to Hill 464. At 1:06 p.m., Lippincott's men drove the enemy from their positions and they were in pursuit. Less than a half hour later, the enemy force was heading southwest on the trail from Hill 464 to the village of Changja-dong. The 8th Cavalry was notified and requested to dispatch a combat patrol to intercept it. Lippincott lost 5 men seriously wounded.

At 8:44 a.m., 1st Battalion again tried to take Hill 518. At 9:26 a.m. the 3d Battalion joined this attack. The 3d Battalion reported slow, but steady progress. At 10:40 a.m., 8th Cavalry observers reported an enemy penetration between the 7th Cavalry's 1st and 3d Battalions on Hill 518. About that time, LT Talbert reported an enemy force had penetrated to the village of Songok-tong between the 1st and 2d Battalions. Just before noon, he had to withdraw to Hill 400 and reported the draw northwest of that hill was alive with enemy troops. Shortly before 1 p.m., two squads of infantry with a tank platoon in the 3d Battalion area attacked to clear the MSR toward the 8th Cavalry. Enemy troops now were on Hill 326, while Talbert's force remained on Hill 400. The 1st Battalion had Co. A about 500 yards short of the crest of Hill 518 at 2:50 p.m. But at 8:28 p.m., elements of the battalion were locked in hand-to-hand fighting with the enemy.

8th Cavalry — Sept. 3

In the early morning hours of Sept. 3, 2/8th Cavalry had to give up Hill 740. The 3d Battalion was sent to stop the enemy's advance near Tabu-dong. Just north of the town two T-34s and a force of enemy infantry attacked Co. I at about 2 a.m. on Sept. 3. The unit suffered many casualties, but repelled the enemy.

2LT Bill Wilbur (West Point, 1949) had been a platoon leader in Co. I, 8th Cavalry for only a few days. The enemy had already captured Tabu-dong and actually was then in rear of Item Co. The North Koreans had to be kicked out of the town for the company mission to be successful. LT Wilbur volunteered to lead a 30-man detachment into town. Against enemy small-arms fire, Wilbur's men succeeded in clearing a section of Tabu-dong. Then he took his men across town in the face of heavy small-arms and machine gun fire and rescued a badly wounded soldier. The enemy then made a concerted attack on the detachment. Six of the attackers were felled. About 75 enemy troops launched a second attack almost overwhelming Wilbur's small force. The

lieutenant called artillery fire down on his position, allowing his men to withdraw. LT Wilbur was awarded the DSC.

Nearby, 2LT John V. "Jack" McDonald, also West Point, 1949 was an artillery FO from the 99th FAB with another 8th Cavalry rifle company. There, too, the battle situation became critical. LT McDonald, recognizing that only concentrated artillery fire would stop the enemy attack in the area, moved to an exposed position where he could better observe and direct fire. Heavy enemy automatic weapons and small-arms fire whipped about near him, but he stayed in his position until the next day, directing artillery fire which prevented the enemy from overrunning the company.

The 2d Battalion managed to pull back through the 3d. At day's end, the 3d was in a defensive position south of Tabu-dong. The 2d was behind the 3d.

The efforts of the 8th Cavalry on Sept. 3 were futile. The enemy continued to advance, seizing the dominant Hill 902, Kasan, from the 8th Cavalry's I&R Platoon and a detachment of South Korean police.

Enemy artillery moved into position just north of Hill 902 and began light, sporadic fire on American positions, causing minor damage in the 99th FAB. To meet the threat of the enemy, now pressing hard on the 8th Cavalry, Eighth Army ordered a ROK battalion from the Taegu Replacement Training Center placed in rear of that regiment. The 1st Cavalry also took extraordinary steps by organizing a task force of two provisional battalions from personnel out of the division headquarters, service support units, the division band, replacement company and other troops. Known as TF Allen, and commanded by the Assistant Division Commander, BG Frank A. Allen Jr., it was to be committed as infantry if the enemy broke through to Taegu. Walker ordered the 1st Cavalry to retake Hill 902.

7th Cavalry — Sept. 4

The 2/7th Cavalry began receiving tank fire on their right and small arms fire in the center at 1:30 a.m. Some 20 to 40 North Koreans and two T-34s were in a draw between the battalion and the 5th Cavalry on its left flank. Enemy troops in unknown strength were reported within 100 yards of the 3/7th Cavalry CP at 5:20 a.m.

About 6 a.m. the enemy attacked LT McNamara's I&R Platoon on Hill 464. Contact with the platoon was lost. By about 7:20 a.m. the enemy had taken the hill. The platoon had to destroy its radio and one machine gun to prevent them from being captured.

The fight for Hill 518 continued on Sept. 4. Both the 1st and 3d Battalions attacked it, but were unsuccessful, little ground being taken due to the strong enemy positions and heavy automatic weapons fire. An enemy POW reported that Hill 518 was held by 1,200 troops, with 82mm and 120 mm mortars.

Meantime, Co. L was sent to regain Hill 464. The attack started that afternoon. About dark, the 3d Battalion reported that the enemy was well dug in on the hill but that their troops were about 500 yards from the top.

That afternoon the enemy established a strong roadblock on the MSR behind the 8th Cavalry.

The fight for Hill 303, infamous "Atrocity Hill." (Source: The First Cavalry Division in Korea, 18 July 1950 - 18 January 1952*)*

The regiment had committed tanks and engineers to replace its 2d Battalion on the right flank of 3/7th Cavalry Shortly after 8 p.m., 1/7th Cavalry established contact with 1/8th Cavalry on its right flank. Thus, all avenues of approach between the two battalions was now covered. Elements of 1/7th Cavalry attacked Hill 400 again. An outpost on this hill was withdrawn at 8:42 p.m. after receiving enemy mortar and automatic weapons fire. About this time the 2d Battalion reported that a large number of enemy vehicles and troops were assembling to their front and that it was taking the enemy under fire.

"After sundown on 4 Sep our new Co. C.O. found me and explained that my weapons platoon was now too small and ineffective to be called a platoon and that I was needed as Plt Ldr, 1st Plt. which, of course, was a rifle platoon," wrote Co. F's LT Richard L. Morton. In a hard monsoon that night, he had trouble finding the platoon. He finally found them about 8 p.m. Platoon Sergeant Almacy introduced the lieutenant to the squad leaders during a firefight. It rained all night.

2/5th Cavalry, Hill 303 — Sept. 4

The infamous Hill 303, upon which the enemy had butchered men of the 1st Cavalry so short a time ago, was attacked and captured by the 2d Battalion, 5th Cavalry on Sept. 4. CPL Arthur P. Bartol of Co. G, was wounded in the attack. In a letter which he sent to his parents on Sept. 6, he wrote of his experience. The company started the day on hills near 303. The enemy attacked the unit there early in the morning. "It was foggy," he wrote. "They came up the hill at us screaming and yelling. We drove them back down twice, but some of them stayed on the side of the hill. All this time we were shooting like mad at them. We stayed in our foxholes and all morning we fired back at each other. Then about noon the shooting stopped, and everything was quiet until 3 p.m. Then we got orders to attack the 3 small hills next to Hill 303. We had to chase the Gooks off the hill. We knew it would be a suicide attack, being in the open like that.

"I was in charge of the 1st Fire Team, and I was in the first bunch to go. At 3:15 [p.m.] we started the attack. We made the first hill O.K., but as I was going over the second hill I got hit in the left foot by a bullet. I couldn't stand the weight on it and fell to the ground and started rolling downhill. I rolled into a shallow foxhole and was laying there thinking what to do next, as I was between our men and the enemy.... One of our men jumped in the same hole...on top of me. I told him to keep his head down.... [A] minute later he got a bullet in his ribs and it came out thru his shoulder. He started to bleed all over me. I kept telling him it wasn't bad." About 10 minutes later, the two wounded men made a run for it and got to the rear and medical attention. After recovering from his wound, Bartol was sent back to Korea Dec. 26, 1950 and was assigned to Co. F, 5th Cavalry.

That night, a large enemy force infiltrated through the gap between the 3d Battalion on the southern slopes of Hill 518 and the 2d Battalion to the west. The attackers then turned and climbed Hill 464, occupying it in force. By daylight on Sept. 5 there were probably more enemy soldiers on it than on Hill 518.

Company D, 8th ECB, Hill 902 (Kasan) — Sept. 3-5

When the 1st Cavalry Division took over lines of the ROK 1st Division on Aug. 29, it was not clear if Hill 902 was included in the Cavalry's sector. A patrol from the 8th Cavalry's I&R Platoon found 156 South Korean policemen manning the summit. This indicated that the hill "belonged" to the ROKs. The responsibility for this promontory was not settled. GEN Gay felt that his division, already stretched over a 35-mile front should not have the responsibility for Hill 902. On the afternoon of Sept. 3, the enemy seized Kasan. The Eighth Army G-3, called COL Ernest V. Holmes, 1st Cavalry Division Chief of Staff (West Point, 1925) and told him that the 1st Cavalry had responsibility for the hill. Holmes responded that GEN Gay, who was then absent from the CP, would not like that decision, but said he would send a company of engineers

to Kasan, pending his return. When Gay got back to the CP, he was unhappy, but, since the order came from Army headquarters it had to be obeyed. He approved Holmes' decision to send an engineer company to the summit.

When he finished talking on the phone to the Eighth Army G-3, Holmes directed LTC William C. Holley, commanding the 8th ECC, to report to COL Raymond D. Palmer (CO, 8th Cavalry Regiment) That afternoon, Palmer briefed 1LT John T. Kennedy, commanding D/8th ECC and the commander of E/8th Cavalry on his plan to take Hill 902. Kennedy's unit would lead and Co. E would follow. Once the crest of Hill 902 had been secured and Easy Co. established in defensive positions, the engineer company would withdraw. Fortunately, D/8th ECC had a number of combat infantrymen from WW II.

Co. D set out that evening in trucks, in a driving rain, bound for the foot of Hill 902. Enroute, they met two truckloads of ROK policemen heading south, some of them wounded. These men, with a detachment of the 8th Cavalry's I&R Platoon, had been forced from the hill that afternoon. The Engineer Company awaited orders in a rain-drenched assembly area. When none came, it returned to camp.

While at breakfast the following morning, Co. D was ordered to move as infantry against Hill 902. One platoon had no time to eat, and the company carried no rations. The following E/8th Cavalry was to bring food and water with them. The assembly area was in the little village of Kisong-dong, about 3,000 meters (somewhat less than 2 miles) from the summit of Hill 902. LTC Holley had a communications CP there. The company set off in a column of platoons. About a half mile from the village, it received some sniper fire. Information was that about 75 disorganized North Koreans occupied the hill. (In fact, the *NK 2d Bn, 2d Regt, 1st Division* held Kasan.)

Co. D started its ascent of the hill about noon on Sept. 4, over a trail up a southern spur. The platoons were in single file, 1st, 2d and 3d, in that order. COL Palmer and his S-2, CPT Rene J. Guiraud accompanied the engineers. COL Palmer felt that the mission was important enough for him to be there. James N. Vandygriff,

Platoon Sergeant of the 2d Platoon, recalled passing LTC Holley as the column moved out. "Who got us into this mess?' he asked the colonel. Holly responded, "The Chief of Staff of the Division did."

"It looks like a suicide mission, but we'll make it," said Vandygriff to Holley. Holley replied, "Sergeant, take care of yourself."

"Yes, Sir," Vandygriff responded.

With LT Robert Peterson, of the I&R Platoon as guide, D Co. moved up the road about 1,500 yards, then onto a little trail and started up the hill. About this time it came under enemy machinegun fire, which wounded two of Vandygriff's men. He asked CPT Kennedy for permission to take a squad and silence the gun. Kennedy ordered the men to keep moving and pass the weapon's position as best as they could. A BAR from the 3d Platoon silenced the enemy gun.

"We moved about 12 to 14 hundred yards up the hill into a small village which had a stone wall about 2 ft. thick and 4 ft. high running around it," Vandygriff wrote. "The 1st and 3d Plt. had got disorganized and I moved the 2d Plt. up and took point." Farther along, another enemy machine gun took the column under fire from the right. Artillery fire was called in by radio and the enemy gun was silenced.

The wide trail dead-ended, so the single-file column of men moved into a ravine on the left and continued to climb. While they toiled through the ravine, enemy mortar fire killed two men and wounded eight or 10 more. Vandygriff's platoon leader collapsed from a kidney ailment, and the sergeant took command of the platoon, which was leading the company.

The unit reached the summit of Hill 755 about 5 P.M., after passing through a tunnel under a small ridge and a stone wall. The hilltop was bowl-shaped, with a stone wall around part of the summit. Vandygriff describes the wall: "It was made of rocks, about 4 to 6 ft. thick. It didn't run around Hill 755. It was to our left. It started at the top of the hill and came back to where we were dug in. At this point it was about 15 ft. high." Appleman's account states that the wall was more extensive than Vandygriff's description. He wrote: "The D Company position was entirely within the area enclosed by the stone wall, which was nearly intact except on the northeast near the 3d Platoon where it had crumbled and was covered with brush and trees." Vandygriff also mentions that there was a temple on the right of the hill. Hill 755 was on a southern ridge extension of Hill 902.

COL Palmer was within 50 feet of the summit, when he was ordered off the hill by GEN Gay, who had discovered that the colonel had accompanied the expedition.

The remainder of the company quickly followed the 2d Platoon to the crest. The unit numbered about ninety men. It had already lost about a dozen to enemy machine gun and mortar fire on the way up. LT Kennedy placed the company in an arc, with the 2d Platoon on the left near the stone wall, 1st Platoon in the center on a wooded knoll, and the 3d Platoon on the right at the edge of a woods. The company line faced west to northeast.

2LT Thomas T. Jones, leader of the 3d Platoon, spotted and heard three enemy mortars fire, about 1,000 yards away on a grassy ridge to the east (right). He suggested to Kennedy that artillery fire be brought in on them. Kennedy did not act on the suggestion. The company CP was established in the tunnel behind the 2d Platoon.

Vandygriff dug his platoon in about 10 ft. inside the wall in an L angle position. LT Jones oriented his platoon sergeant and squad leaders on where he wanted the platoon to go into position. They would be in the edge of woods facing the grassy ridge where Jones had seen the enemy mortars. After talking briefly to LT Kennedy, Jones went to his 3d Squad at the edge of the woods. There he learned that the platoon sergeant, with rest of the platoon, had continued toward the narrow grassy ridge. At this point, one of the squad called him to the edge of the woods and pointed out 10 or 12 enemy soldiers, in camouflage, coming down the ridge toward them. One had a machine gun. About a third of the way down the ridge, the enemy group disappeared from view.

Jones decided to go after his two squads and bring them back to form a cohesive line. Thinking he would be gone only a short time, he did not take his SCR-300 radio with him. He found one squad, but the other one was farther out. He sent a messenger to find and bring it back. Jones studied the terrain while awaiting the messenger's return. Suddenly, the enemy attacked the company position to his rear. The firing and yelling convinced him that the enemy were in the woods between him and the company position. When the firing ceased, all he could hear were enemy voices. This convinced him that the company had been overrun, and that he and the few men with him were on their own. The lieutenant, and two of his squads were isolated in enemy territory, although the two squads were not together.

Jones, and the eight men with him, spent the night in the heavily wooded ravine. "When morning came...and our planes began strafing the ridge about 25 feet above us...our belief...was confirmed," Jones wrote, "that the left two platoons had been wiped out and we were now on our own in enemy territory."

LT Kennedy was unaware that his right flank was exposed because two squads of the 3d Platoon had continued to move and did not go into position. Later, when he could get no response on the radio, he sent a patrol to the 3d Platoon area. It returned to report that the 3d Platoon was not there; only rocket launchers and two machine guns could be found.

Within 30 minutes after Co. D arrived on Hill 755, it was hit by an estimated enemy battalion attacking from Hill 902. The attack was directed mainly at Vandygriff's platoon. He had two machine guns. With these guns, and the protection of the stone wall, his platoon was able to turn back the enemy attack. He lost one killed and three wounded. Sending the wounded back, Vandygriff then checked with his squad leaders. SFC John J. Phillips, leader of the 3d Squad, which was at the point of the main enemy attack, told him that his men could hold if "the ammo held out." Vandygriff, thinking that E/8th Cavalry would arrive soon with ammunition, water and food, was not worried about ammunition. As darkness set in, the enemy began to hit the company with small-arms and mortar fire and

small probing attacks. It began to rain. The enemy fire, probes, and the rain continued all night. Vandygriff ordered his men to dig in deep and stay awake.

In the foggy drizzling-wet dawn on Sept. 5, the enemy attacked again. The engineers drove the enemy back, but Vandygriff lost a BAR-man and his radio was destroyed by enemy fire, forcing him to use runners to communicate with the Co. CP. One of them returned to tell him that an air strike was scheduled for the morning. Before the strike, three C-47 planes came over for a drop. Kennedy put out orange air panels, and saw the enemy do the same thing. The drop went to the enemy. As the C-47s left, two F-51s came over and attacked Co. D. They dropped two napalm pods. One failed to ignite, and the other did not hit anyone. The planes followed this with a strafing run right through the company. Miraculously, again, no one was hit. Soon after the air attack, CPT Kennedy was wounded in the leg and ankle by burp gun fire. (Vandygriff wrote that the air drop occurred between 1 and 2 p.m.) By this time, his platoon had no rations and very little ammunition.

E/8th Cavalry was to follow Co. D, 8th Engineers up Hill 755, but was delayed. CPL Richard J. Benedict (E/8th Cav.) wrote that the unit "started up the mountain at approximately 1330 [1:30 p.m.], 4 September." Enemy mortar fire was falling on the trail as the company began to climb. Several men were killed and wounded. The company commander radioed to COL Palmer that, because of this the unit could advance no farther. Palmer relieved the officer, and designated LT Gill to take charge of the company and continue the advance. Benedict records that Gill was soon shot in the foot and could not go on. Appleman wrote that "the second officer broke his glasses," but was ordered to go on. Shortly afterward, he was shot in the foot.

Palmer then appointed LT William A. McCain to take over and hurry on to join the engineer company. Under McCain, Co. E started out again about 8 P.M. Enemy fire stopped the company about "500 yards short of the crest before dawn on 5 September," Benedict wrote. Appleman stated that the morale of Co. E was not good at this time. The company had been cut off by an enemy attack a few days previously, and had traveled a roundabout way to rejoin the battalion. When the company overcame this enemy fire and started again, some members of Co. D fired on them. Fortunately, no one was hit, and the firing was stopped. Benedict states that the infantry unit joined the engineer company "shortly after dawn." Vandygriff puts the time at "about 1000 (10 a.m.)."

The infantry company's 3d Platoon was positioned to the right of Vandygriff's Engineer platoon. Whatever the actual time of arrival may have been, shortly thereafter, the enemy attacked. Neither company had any mortars to help in the defense. At one point, Vandygriff fired into the enemy with a 3.5 inch rocket launcher. This broke up the attack. He then had his men collect all the weapons and ammunition they could from the enemy dead. "We picked up 30 or 40...rifles, 5 burp guns and a few hand grenades," he recalled.

While so engaged, Vandygriff noticed the foxhole of BAR-man PFC Melvin L. Brown of the 3d Squad. He was on the platoon's extreme left flank. "The wall was about 6 or 7 feet high at this point," Vandygriff wrote. "There were 15 or 20 dead enemy at the bottom. I asked Brown, 'What happened?' He said, 'Every time they came up I knocked them off the wall.' He was wounded in the shoulder...[but] he had taken care of it." CPT Kennedy had seen Brown about 8 a.m. At that time, there were about five enemy dead that Brown had killed with his BAR. Later, when he ran out of ammunition, he killed the enemy with the few grenades he had, and finally, used his entrenching tool to hit the enemy soldiers in the head when they tried to climb over the wall.

As the battle on Hill 755 continued, rain and fog came in again. Vandygriff recalled that one could see barely "over three or four yards." Taking advantage of rain and fog, the enemy attacked again. An assistant squad leader was wounded in the neck. Vandygriff sent him back to the CP. Shortly afterward, the man returned to say that the CP was deserted. All that was there were some enemy dead.

What had happened can be partly reconstructed. When the infantry company arrived on Hill 755, LT Kennedy turned over command of the area to LT McClain, commanding E/8th Cavalry. Kennedy then assembled twelve wounded men and descended the mountain for medical attention. The party was under small arms fire most of the journey. It is unclear where McClain established his CP.

A South Korean carrying party, led by an American officer had started up the mountain early in the morning, but turned back after enemy fire had killed a number of them. When he discovered the engineer CP was gone, Vandygriff conferred with the infantry platoon sergeant on his right. The two NCOs decided that it was best to withdraw their men. Actually, GEN Gay had decided to abandon the mountain. He felt that his division was too extended already, without putting men on this mountain. He also felt that the enemy did not have enough ammunition to exploit having the high mountain as an artillery observation point. Benedict wrote that he was with LT McCain in the infantry CP when the order came to withdraw.

Once the two platoon sergeants had conferred, Vandygriff assembled his squad leaders and told them that the platoon was going out the way it had come in. He gave the wounded a thirty minute head start. He would pick them up on the way. "By that time we were getting hit from all sides again," he wrote, "and I didn't think any of us would be getting out."

As SFC Phillips started breaking up the weapons which the platoon could not take out, Vandygriff noticed that Brown was not with the assembled men. Phillips didn't know where he was, but went to look for him. He found Brown, dead. Phillips asked Vandygriff if he should take the dog tags off the dead, Vandygriff. "I told him, 'No,' that their dog tags were the only way" to identify the dead. Putting the platoon into a V formation, he led them down the mountain the same way they had come up. Enroute, he picked up four wounded.

Several groups of men, some from D/8th Engineers and some from E/8th Cavalry, came off Hill 577. Each party thought it was the last

survivors, and each told conflicting and confusing stories. When LTC Holley assembled Co. D, he found that losses amounted to about 50 per cent — 18 wounded and 30 missing, and the dead PFC Melvin L. Brown.

An officer of Co. D was among the wounded carried off Hill 755. He had been hit in the leg just before jumping off a high ledge. Two soldiers carried him down the mountain and, at his request, left him in a Korean house. The men were to come back in a jeep for him. Men from a later escaping group heard his screams. Two weeks later, when the Cavalry Division recaptured the area, his body was found in the house. His hands and feet were tied, his eyes gouged, a thumb pulled off, and his body had been partly burned. He had been bound, tortured and a fire had been built under his body. Co. E, 8th Cavalry also suffered a number of casualties, but not as many as the Engineer unit.

PFC Melvin L. Brown was awarded the Medal of Honor, posthumously, for his heroic action on Hill 755.

On Sept. 4, members of the ROK 1st Division captured an enemy soldier near Kasan. He said that about 800 North Koreans occupied the Kasan area and that three more battalions were coming in from the north. By Sept. 5, the Kasan area was well in enemy hands, with five battalions totaling 1,500 men. An enemy ox train carrying 82mm mortar ammunition and rice apparently reached the summit of Hill 902 that day. Troops of the ROK 1st Division captured this train a few days later south of the mountain.

Among the missing were LT Jones and two squads of his platoon — about 16 or 18 men. When the infantry and engineers left Hill 755, Jones and these men, two of them wounded by mortar fire, were left behind in a ravine. Enemy troops were all around, but none searched this ravine, filled with heavy underbrush. The Americans stayed there four days, surrounded by North Koreans. Every day, U.S. planes bombed and strafed the area, but never hit the ravine. Finally, Jones decided to make a break. "Moving out on the fourth night, we made a slow and tortuous descent during the next few days," he wrote in "Two Hundred Miles to Freedom," in *The Military Engineer*, Sept.-Oct. 1951, "taking advantage of a heavy fog for cover. Movement by night was difficult because of the steep cliffs, and by day because of the sudden lifting of the fog. We had to hide constantly from nearby bands of North Koreans.

"It rained steadily and we were soaked to the skin. This, plus the fact that we had no rations, did a lot to discourage our inclination to move out rapidly, as we knew we should have."

When the sun did come out, clothing dried and morale vastly improved. Although the men felt stronger, they were weak from the lack of food and water. The men laid down and fell asleep. Jones suddenly awoke to find the ravine swarming with enemy soldiers. Resistance was useless. An enemy NCO had been leading a party of about 50 enemy soldiers up the mountain and had stumbled on the slumbering GIs. The North Koreans and Americans were both equally frightened by the experience. The enemy took the men's weapons, rings, watches and wallets, then started the prisoners up the mountain. (See Appendix A — Prisoners of War and Missing in Action.)

7th Cavalry — Sept. 5

The 7th continued to battle for Hill 518. Appleman stated that the regiment never took the hill. But Stanley Dahl, 81mm Mortar Platoon, D/7th Cavalry, writes that they did take it. (This account is included in actions of September 5, but the actual date is uncertain.)

About the third day of the attack against this enemy stronghold, a TOT (Time on Target) was ordered to be fired for 30 minutes by all the 105mm and 155mm howitzers and the 4.2 inch and 81mm mortars at 12 noon. In firing a TOT all the guns and mortars are fired so that their first rounds all land on the target at the same time. Then, for the duration of the TOT, each weapon is fired as fast as it can be re-laid on its correct azimuth and elevation and reloaded. A TOT devastates the target area. After the TOT was fired this day, 10 jets made an air strike. Dahl describes the scene as the TOT began. "The sky over Hill 518 turned black, the first shell of all guns of the division were set on time fuze to create air bursts over the hill. The noise was thunderous, roaring and deafening; there just is no way to describe the sound. The barrage went on for 30 minutes. Nothing could live through that. How wrong we were!

"Next came the air strike. Ten Sabre jets came streaking over our heads firing their guns as they went by; empty shell casings falling all around us. We thought one of the cases would hit us on the head." The men donned their steel helmets. The jets worked the enemy hill over for half an hour with bombs, napalm and strafing.

"The battalion attacked...in a blinding rain storm. The rifle companies assaulting the hill ran into murderous heavy machine gun fire, rifle fire, burp guns, hand grenades and mortar fire. After the heavy pounding the hill had received, we were shocked that anyone could have survived on that hill. The well disciplined, hard core enemy was still there, fighting as savagely as ever." The assault companies took heavy casualties, Dahl wrote, but took Hill 518 before dark. He stated that the battalion was now down to about half strength.

The next day, he went up Hill 518 as an assistant FO. Near the hill's crest, he noted "enemy dead in groups spread out in grotesque positions of death.... What surprised me were the wounds. They were all killed by small-arms fire; the bombardment hadn't touched them. It didn't make sense. On the ridge you could see what the napalm and bombing had done. It was appalling. The summit of the hill extended for several hundred yards...north and south. Everything had been burned off by the napalm or blown to hell by the bombing. I had never seen such destruction."

About 3 a.m., enemy harassing fire fell on the Security Platoon's post on Hill 400. Three enemy tanks were spotted in the valley between 2/7th Cavalry and the 5th Cavalry on their left at about 4:05 a.m. A 3.5 inch rocket launcher team was sent after them. But the enemy continued to infiltrate between the two commands, building pressure on the 5th Cavalry on Hill 303. The 2d Battalion was directed to send a reinforced platoon to take and hold the hill.

On Hill 490, the 3d Battalion, 7th Cavalry was attacked at 9:15 a.m. By 1:50 p.m., the enemy had penetrated the battalion's position. At about 1:45 p.m., the 1st Battalion was sharply attacked from the northwest of Hill 518. Lippincott's Security Platoon was sent after an enemy patrol of about 20 men who had infiltrated to a point near the regimental CP.

5th Cavalry — Sept. 5

MAJ John W. Callaway (West Point, 1942) came to 2/5th Cavalry as its XO while the battalion occupied Hill 303. "When I arrived all was quiet," he wrote. "We sent patrols at night and our artillery fired on enemy positions using our FO on Hill 303 to spot the targets.... One day two news reporters came to the CP and requested permission to accompany one of our patrols. They were told that this was against division policy and they could not go." One of these correspondents was Randolph Churchill, son of Winston Churchill, the WW II Prime Minister of Great Britain. Gerald Gingery, 81mm Mortar Platoon, 2/5th Cavalry gives a more detailed account of this incident.

"He came in a British jeep along with a driver and a Korean interpreter and all his equipment." The men in the company thought the patrol was staged for Randolph Churchill. This was not the case. Churchill accompanied the patrol against orders. Gingery wrote that the patrol was discovered by the enemy while crossing the Naktong in a boat. One man was killed, a couple wounded, and Churchill was nicked in the arm, Gingery recalled. When the patrol returned, Churchill "was cussing and giving his interpreter hell because the man was having trouble trying to figure out what Churchill was saying," wrote Gingery. "One of the men hollered to Randolph and said, 'If you're so damn smart talk to him in Korean!' And that was the last we heard anything out of him."

"I was told that the reporters had been drinking," Callaway wrote, "and were noisy and careless while accompanying the patrol." When GEN Gay heard about the incident, "he was furious," Callaway continued, "and chewed out the Bn CO." The general was especially concerned because it involved the son of Winston Churchill.

Early on Sept. 5 the enemy hit Hill 303. Callaway wrote, "The Bn CO ordered the S-3 to go up and take charge of the company. I was disappointed in not being selected but said nothing." During the battle, wire communication went out and a wireman was dispatched to find the break. "He followed the wire to the company on the mountain," Callaway recalled. "The wire appeared to be OK.... On the return trip, the wireman discovered that the enemy had cut only one of the two wires to make it more difficult to detect.

"The company held its position," Callaway continued, "but suffered heavy casualties. That afternoon the Bn CO sent a second company to reinforce our position. The enemy continued the attack. We suffered heavy casualties but held the position. The S-3 was wounded and evacuated. The enemy has suffered severe casualties, but had not been able to seize Hill 303. I volunteered to take charge of the remaining troops on 303 but was ordered to remain at the CP."

By midnight, the enemy had surrounded G/5th Cavalry on Hill 303. Second Lieutenants James A. Scholtz and Alan G. Brown (both West Point, 1949) were platoon leaders in this unit. In the early morning hours of the 6th, LT Scholtz decided to fire a 3.5 inch rocket launcher at some enemy behind a knoll about 200 yards away. As he rose to get a better shot and placed his eye to the launcher's sight, an enemy bullet struck him in the left shoulder, passed through his body and exited through his right shoulder. He managed to get down the hill with some help and into a litter jeep. The vehicle was fired on enroute to the aid station and the wounded man next to Scholtz was hit again.

Order to Withdraw — Sept. 5

The situation was worsening in the Cavalry Division's sector. The division was on an over-extended line and under attack by the *NK 3d, 13th* and part of the *1st Divisions*. The enemy had heavily infiltrated rear areas and had blocks on part of the MSR. By the end of the day on Sept. 5, Tabu-dong had been captured by the enemy, in the center the enemy had heavily infiltrated south of Hill 518 and on the left, Waegwan was in a no-man's land. The lines needed to be shortened and the regiments re-organized and consolidated. GEN Gay discussed this critical situation with GEN Walker and COL Collier. Walker cautioned Gay not to withdraw beyond terrain from which the 1st Cavalry Division could defend Taegu. Appleman wrote that "on one occasion early in September he told one of his division commanders in effect, 'If the enemy gets into Taegu, you will find me resisting him in the streets, and I'll have some of my trusted people with me and you had better be prepared to do the same. Now get back to your division and fight it.'" Clay Blair in *The Forgotten War*, surmised the general was Hobart Gay. At this critical moment during the Perimeter battles, Walker told one division commander that "he didn't want to see him back from the front again unless it was in a coffin." (Quoted from *South to the Naktong*.)

Contemplating Withdrawal of All forces to the Davidson Line — Sept. 5

Not only was the situation near Taegu becoming critical, but also to the south in the old Bulge area, now in the sector of the U.S. 2d Infantry Division (Chapter 19), the Pohang-Kyongju area (discussed above), and in the sectors of the 24th and 35th Regiments of the 25th Division on the southern flank (Chapter 20). Walker discussed the situation and the possibility of withdrawing to the Davidson Line with most of his division commanders, his staff and his deputy, GEN Coulter. His G-3, COL Dabney, confessed that for once, he did not have a recommendation. Remarking that the decision was a hard one to make, he said that he hoped the Army would stay in place. He made a good point when he reminded Walker that past enemy attacks had lost most of their steam within a few days and that this might be the case again. However, just to be prepared, COL Landrum ordered Dabney's G-3 Section to begin drafting withdrawal orders immediately. The staff worked on this plan all night

and it was ready to be issued at 5 a.m. on Sept. 6. Walker stopped its issuance; he had decided that the Army was sitting tight and fighting where it was.

However, the Eighth Army Main CP displaced south to the former Fisheries College, between Pusan and Tongnae, north of Pusan. About the same time the Main ROK Army CP relocated to Pusan. Their new CP opened at 8 a.m. on Sept. 6 and that of Eighth Army at 4 p.m. Walker, with key staff personnel, remained in Taegu in a forward, or tactical, CP.

The principal reason Walker chose to send the main CP south was to protect the irreplaceable communications equipment of his headquarters. The principal components were a MARC-2, four van teletype system and a 1,200 line switchboard. No replacement equipment was available in the Far East. The teletype and 1,200 line telephone system were the principal means of communications with Japan. Army operations would have been severely handicapped if the equipment were captured or destroyed. Other equipment was utilized for communication to the ROKs, divisions, and other commands subordinate to Eighth Army.

BG Crump Garvin (West Point, 1920), commanding the 2d Logistics Command in Korea, issued verbal instructions that service support personnel should be prepared to take up defensive positions in and around Pusan, if the tactical situation required it.

Many South Korean civilians, who could afford to pay to be smuggled aboard small vessels, sought safety in sailing to Tsushima Island. Similarly well-to-do Chinese living in the Pusan area planned to sail for Taiwan, also smuggled out in small vessels. The first group of Chinese planned to leave on Sept. 8.

Not generally known is the fact that Walker's intelligence experts had broken one of the North Korean's codes. Walker used the information gleaned from intercepts of this code in helping him determine enemy plans and operations. Perhaps this led to some of his more memorable shifts of his reserves at the right time, in the right numbers and at the right place. Since GEN Walker did not survive the war, and there is little information about this subject from staff officers and commanders who served with him, there is not much to go on in determining how much information he received, when he received it and how he used it in decision making.

Withdrawal of the 7th Cavalry — Sept. 6

The 1st Battalion withdrew without any problems. The 3d Battalion withdrew by passing behind Hill 303, formerly occupied by 2/5th Cavalry. The 2d Battalion, already involved with enemy to its front, was ordered to take Hill 464 in its rear. "We all questioned this...order because of the clear evidence that 464 was well-populated by the NKPA," remarked LT Richard L. Morton (F/7th Cavalry). Co. G, with elements of Companies F and H headed toward that hill, while the 2d Battalion HHC, Co. E and elements of Companies F and H made for Hill 380. The battalion began its withdrawal at 3 a.m. Two tanks had to be abandoned. One had a mechanical failure and the other was stuck in the mud.

LT Morton recalled that withdrawing under cover of darkness was good, "because the T-34s were now in position to deliver cannon and MG fire directly on our route of march."

If a daylight withdrawal had been attempted, it could have led to a great slaughter. The enemy soon discovered that the battalion was withdrawing. Co. E, with part of Co. H, turned west toward the 5th Cavalry area, skirmishing with small groups of the enemy along the way. In one of these little battles, CPT James T. Milan, former C.O. of Co. E, but now Battalion S-3, was killed while covering the withdrawal of the last element of Co. E. Meantime, the main battalion group began its attack on Hill 380. MAJ Omar Hitchner, battalion commander, sent LT Pennel J. H. Hickey and a body of men forward as point. The enemy allowed the attackers to approach to within 50 yards of the top of the hill before firing. Then they sent a heavy volume of automatic fire into Hickey's party, stopping them cold. The men could not detect the enemy's positions and were pinned to the ground by the deadly fire. A few minutes later, MAJ Hitchner sent a machine gun up to take the enemy under fire.

Morton's platoon of Co. F was the battalion's rear guard. "By 1000 hours [10 a.m.] the head of the column was completely stopped by heavy automatic weapons fire," he wrote. "I was ordered to report to our acting Bn C.O. (MAJ Hitchner). He explained that my platoon was...ordered to move to the far right and, as soon as the weapons from HHQ and G Co. began to lay down suppressing fire, to 'storm' the dug-in enemy. That was the last time I saw the major alive. Ten minutes later he stood up to direct the fire and was immediately killed.

"Meanwhile, my platoon had arrived and was ready to clear a small crest and move out smartly. Our horribly inaccurate maps showed a fairly modest rise ahead of us. What the maps did not show was a large ravine which ran perpendicular to our route of advance. The ravine had steep sides. It was about 50 feet deep and about 150 feet wide. The north side of this ravine had been heavily fortified and occupied by the NKPA. Only sustained heavy artillery fire or an air strike could have softened up this brilliantly prepared fortification.... I waited for our own fires to begin and then called, 'Follow me!' This was a mistake. Only one man followed. And this was just as well. Had the entire platoon gone...as a body we would all have fallen into the ravine and been sitting ducks. As it was, a bullet creased my helmet and a round penetrated my canteen. Before I jumped back I had a clear view of an enemy dug in and ready...and our understrength battalion was no match for them. Fortunately, the NKPA was also precluded from storming us by the same ravine. But they could have flanked us. They did not...."

When Hitchner went forward to locate the enemy, an enemy antitank rifle round killed him. CPT Melbourne C. Chandler (former H Co., CO), but now Battalion XO, quickly assumed command of the battalion. CPT Albert B. Cassidy, 77th FAB Liaison Officer, had the only operational radio with this element of the battalion. About 11:30 a.m., using this radio, contact was established with Co. G on Hill 464. At the time the enemy had Chandler and the part of the battalion with him, firmly pinned down. A number of men had already been hit by enemy fire trying to pull back. After losing three more men in this attempt, the remainder stayed put. Finally, Chandler was able to reach regiment on the radio, informed them of the situation and told them that he was going to go around Hill 380 that night and attack it from the opposite side the next morning. Because the radio battery was becoming weak, it was turned off for the remainder of the night.

When darkness fell, the battalion marched west for about 1,500 yards then east another 1,200 yards to get to the other side of Hill 380. The march was over almost vertical rocky hills, covered with thick underbrush. CPT Chandler and LT John B. Wadsworth led the way. As the column crested the ridge, an enemy patrol was detected to the immediate front. The men waited until it passed. From the top of this ridge, Ed Dailey (Co. H) wrote, "looking northward, the entire valley across the Naktong River appeared to be filled with green flashes from the enemy artillery firing toward Taegu."

Traveling without food or water and low on ammunition, the column reached a point about 900 yards south of Hill 380 (1,500 yards south of their previous day's position). About 4 a.m. Chandler called regiment on the radio, informed them of the situation and repeated his intent to attack Hill 380. He was informed that CPT Fred DePalma was on the way with a group of replacements and that a train of 100 Korean carriers was being sent with water and ammunition. DePalma arrived at 7:10 a.m. and LT Wadsworth with two EM were sent to guide the carriers in. The entire 2/7th Cavalry in the vicinity of Hills 380 and 464 was surrounded by enemy troops. COL Nist thought the battalion would be destroyed. But Chandler, nevertheless, had the battalion element with him attack Hill 380. The attack was a success. The hill was taken. About 50 enemy troops were killed and a large amount of enemy equipment was captured. This included radios and telescopes which had been used to direct artillery and mortar fire on the 7th Cavalry during the previous few days.

When radio contact was again made with regiment, at 1 p.m., it was learned that the carriers could not get through. The battalion was surrounded and ordered to get out on any route it could. The only friendly lines then known to CPT Chandler were those of the 5th Cavalry, about 3,000 yards to the southwest. The battalion, however, had no map to help guide it to those lines.

Chandler assembled the men with him, distributed the last available ammunition and set off toward what he believed was the 5th Cavalry. The ammunition distribution amounted to about two clips per M-1, two magazines per carbine, one box (250 rounds) for each of the three light machine guns and seven rounds for each of the two 60 mm mortars. The column by-passed several enemy groups and halted for a rest about 4 p.m. During the rest, scouts reported seeing troops near the former 5th Cavalry CP. Through the Artillery Liaison Officer's field glasses, Chandler saw a figure emerge from a bunker. The man signaled for the troops to come on, calling, "Hey, GI, this way!"

Then the captain realized he was an enemy officer. Further study of the terrain through the binoculars revealed many enemy soldiers scurrying along the ridge north and parallel to his troops. Chandler immediately got the column moving south through water-filled rice paddies. Before the enemy could get much fire on them, most of the men were across. Even so, CPT Chandler was hit in the heel by a bullet, and discarded his boots. About 40 enemy soldiers hotly pursued the rapidly moving men. A spotter plane suddenly appeared and directed artillery fire on the pursuers, permitting Chandler's group to reach 2/5th Cavalry positions about a thousands yards farther south.

The men were exhausted, hungry and thirsty, having had no sleep, no food and little water for thirty or more hours. They reached 5th Cavalry lines late in the afternoon of Sept. 7. An officer and three EM had been killed in the withdrawal and nine EM wounded. Chandler, barefooted, wet and covered with mud, had difficulty convincing officers at the 2/5th Cavalry CP that he was the battalion commander of 2/7th Cavalry. He and his men were transported to the rear to join other survivors of the battalion and reorganize.

LT Morton and the 2/7th Cavalry's Rear Guard — Sept. 6-7

When the 2d Battalion began the move to go around Hill 380, LT Morton's platoon, "now not more than a large squad," he wrote, "had the honor of being the rear guard."

"I posted SGT Almacy at the head of the platoon...and took up the position as the last man out. At darkness the HQ personnel moved out smartly. It was drizzling again and the visibility was almost zero." He recalled that the march started about 8 p.m. By 10 p.m., his platoon had not moved and they could hear enemy soldiers talking behind them. "My people, although bushed and nervous, maintained discipline.... Shortly after 2200 hours [10 p.m.] SGT Almacy worked his way down our platoon column with a soldier from G Co., found me, and announced: 'Lieutenant, there is nobody ahead of me. I don't know where the column went!'" What had happened was that the troops, worn out by the events of the past few days, dozed off whenever the column slowed or halted. Often a man fell asleep at this time and failed to get up and move with the column. As a result, the column was broken several times, and small groups of men became separated from the main body. Thus, Morton found his platoon alone. Morton decided to head for 77th FAB. He had previously shot a compass azimuth to their location. The route traversed what he described as "some of the roughest terrain in the Pusan Perimeter." The "area was...devoid of any civilian population. There were no roads, trails or works of man of any kind. We seemed to be climbing either straight up or straight down.... And my platoon...had two wounded aboard."

It began to rain about 1 a.m. on Sept. 7. Men having raincoats put them on, but the raincoats made so much noise as the men walked through the underbrush that Morton soon ordered them removed and abandoned. The rain was heavy. At 1:30 a.m., he called a halt and counted the men with him: 21 GIs and 4 KATUSAs. Almost immediately, most of them were asleep. Very soon afterward, he and the platoon sergeant detected the unmistakable smell of *kimchee*. "This was ominous," he wrote.... One of our...KATUSAs grabbed my knee and whispered the only American slang word he had mastered: 'GOOKS!'

"And there they came...at a range of no more than 10 yards. All of us were lying or sitting. Not one man moved. The sleeping troopers never snored." Fifty North Koreans walked by Morton and his men. The lieutenant did not choose to engage the enemy because his men had only about one clip per rifle and the wounded BAR-man had less than one 20-round magazine. Further, the group did not include a medic. After waiting 15 minutes, Morton's party moved on as fast as the terrain (still very rugged) would permit. During the next break someone accidentally stepped on the wounded hand of the BAR-man. He screamed in pain. Everyone thought this would bring on the enemy, but their luck held.

A little farther, they began to pick up other stragglers from the battalion. One still carried his 57mm recoilless rifle, but no ammunition. The soldier wanted to abandoned it, but Morton said no. "A few minutes later," Morton recounted, "the oaf got rid of his weapon by pretending to stumble and drop it into a crevasse. The crevasse turned out to be more of a canyon...and we all listened in horror as the 57 tumbled and bounced...to the bottom. Again we felt the enemy had certainly heard this noise and would soon be on top of us."

By daylight, Morton's party numbered over 100. He put them into a perimeter in a wooded area and allowed the men to rest. No one had any food nor water. "Many were sucking on leaves and pine needles to assuage their thirst," he recalled.

At noon he "made a recon to our southeast and came to the edge of a plateau. Across a wide rock and shrub-filled valley and the ridge beyond, he heard the booming guns of the 77th FAB. The valley appeared uninhabited. As he inspected the terrain, the monsoon clouds parted and the sun came out," he recalled. "I regarded it as an omen."

While looking for a way down to the valley, one of his men spotted a small stand of pines. A wisp of smoke drifted up from it. Cautious investigation revealed that 2LT Pennel J. Hickey and another party of men from the battalion were there. Hickey's group of about 40 men was also headed for the artillery position. The two parties joined, and led by the two young lieutenants, moved down into and across the valley. Enroute, they came upon F Co.'s 1SG Early and some wounded with him. The march across the rocky, scrub brush-filled valley was slow and painful. The sun was unmercifully hot. A small, dirty stream of water along the way provided some relief to the men, most of whom had been without water for over a day.

The combined group reached the ridge above the artillery toward evening and one of the 77th's outposts. The outpost had the party under observation for some time, but were directed not to fire by LTC Harris (77 FAB CO) until positive identification could be made. Harris, in the belief that the party of soldiers in the valley were

Americans, ordered his battalion mess to prepare food. "When we finally arrived...he surprised us with all the scrambled eggs (powdered) and bacon we could eat. It was a Godsend. I still remember it as one of the greatest meals I ever consumed." Hickey and Morton brought in 150 EM, including a man from the 5th Cavalry. After debriefing at regiment, Morton was taken to the battalion bivouac. He had a case of fifty cartons of cigarettes to distribute to the men. He found them all asleep in a cotton field. He dropped to the ground, but instead of lying parallel to the furrows, he laid down perpendicular to them. "When they awakened me an hour later my spine was bent in all the wrong directions and the pain persisted for over a week. But hey," he concluded, "we were alive and back inside friendly lines!"

Co. G, 7th Cavalry and Hill 464 — Sept. 6-7

Co. G, with elements of F and H, was to attack Hill 464. Hills 380 and 464 were both in the rear of the 2d Battalion. In effect, the attack was to the rear. To do this, the battalion had to first disengage from a battle with the enemy in front, withdraw, then attack an enemy to the rear. This is a very tricky maneuver. Units of the 7th Cavalry had attacked Hill 464 unsuccessfully on three previous days.

Co. G disengaged from the enemy about 3 a.m. on Sept. 6. During its withdrawal the unit was subjected to sporadic enemy tank and artillery fire. Rain and mud slowed the movement. The company numbered about 80 men. CPT Herman L. West commanded. Bill Williams was the First Sergeant. Four young Second Lieutenants from the West Point Class of 1949 commanded the four platoons: Richard E. Tobin, the 1st; Arthur H. "Curly" Lindeman Jr., the 2d; Lawrence J. Ogden, the 3d and Harold R. Anderegg, the 4th. The unit suddenly found itself isolated from the remainder of the battalion. But it attacked Hill 464, as planned, with Tobin's 1st Platoon in the lead. At 8 a.m., near the crest, it came upon three enemy soldiers eating breakfast and killed them.

West ordered Tobin's platoon to lay down a base of fire while Ogden took his men around to the left. Ogden's men were stopped by heavy enemy fire just 50 yards from the crest. Every avenue to the top was blocked by the enemy. All three rifle platoons were heavily engaged but the unit could make no progress. In midafternoon, the company was ordered to withdraw that night, move to the east and attack the hill from a new direction the next morning. Seven dead had to be left behind, but five wounded were taken along on litters improvised from ponchos and tree branches. The men groped and slid down the shale slopes in the darkness and rain. About half way down the hill, a round of friendly artillery exploded near the column, killing an NCO. A rock hurled by the exploding round inflicted a painful back injury to CPT West. The bursting artillery round startled and scattered the unit, but West reassembled them. He cautioned his men to move quietly and not to fire under any circumstances, so that the enemy might think them one of their own units. He led the company to the eastern base of Hill 464 and went into a de-

fensive perimeter for the night. Only the company Weapons Platoon was missing.

The 2d and 3d Platoons were ahead of Anderegg's Weapons Platoon when the company came off the hill. Tobin's 1st followed Anderegg. Near the base of the mountain, Anderegg's platoon came to a trail intersection, his men turned right instead of left, and got lost. Soon Anderegg realized that he was out of contact with the column, but decided to continue on, since the path seemed to lead toward the hilltop. He had to call a number of rest stops. The platoon was short-handed, had a mortar and machine gun to carry, as well as three wounded men. The men had been bone-weary when they started. The march in the rain-soaked night took a further toll. Appleman wrote that several times during the night, the little column passed groups of enemy soldiers along the way, but they passed with neither side firing a shot. Once, Anderegg discovered that five of his men were missing. Backtracking, he found that they had dozed off at the last rest stop. An hour before dawn, they reached a small flat area, where they took another rest halt.

As daylight came, Anderegg's platoon set out for the summit. To the east they could see Hill 464. Upon reaching the top of their own hill, the men found a number of unoccupied enemy foxholes. Two men quickly occupied each of four of the holes. CPL Louis T. Tebodo (who graduated from West Point in 1955) and PFC Harper, with a light machine gun, spotted another hole, covered with pine branches, about five yards away. As they watched, something moved in the hole. COL Harry J. Maihafer, in *From the Hudson to the Yalu*, describes what happened next: "Tebodo yelled at Sergeant Link, 'I think there's somebody in this hole.'

"'Hey,' Link shouted, 'GIs in this hole?' The only answer was a cough. Sergeant Link left Tebodo to cover the hole and moved up to Sergeant Reed's hole.

"'I think there are gooks over there.'"

Anderegg, arriving on the scene, said, "'Well, clean them off.'"

While Tebodo, with his rifle, and Harper with the machine gun covered the hole, Reed walked up and pulled the pine branches from it. In the hole sat four enemy soldiers, their rifles between their legs. Reed motioned for them to come out, but no one moved. He reached down and pulled a man wearing officer's insignia out of the hole. The man twisted loose and began to run. Harper shot him down with the machine gun. Other members of the platoon killed the other three men in the hole and fired into another nearby foxhole covered with brush. Two more enemy were killed there.

Suddenly, a party of enemy soldiers appeared about 25 to 75 yards away. A gun battle ensued. When it was over, seven more North Koreans had been killed and three taken prisoner. A briefcase found at the scene revealed that this had been a regimental CP and the man who had fled was the regimental commander. They also showed that Hill 464 had been an assembly point for elements of the *NK 3d Division* during its advance from Hill 518 toward Taegu.

Meantime, the bulk of Co. G was about to be attacked by U.S. aircraft. The men scrambled to make a hasty signal out of paper, branches and rocks, reading "SOS-GI." Seeing this, the planes veered off and left the area. A bombing mission had been planned for the hill, which was believed to be in enemy hands.

Just after the close call with friendly aircraft, the company made contact with a patrol from 1/7th Cavalry. Two platoons of G were sent to the 1st Battalion area, while CPT West waited for the party carrying litters to catch up. A runner reported to the captain that the litter bearers where exhausted and could proceed no further. West, making his way through an artillery barrage, took charge and led the group to safety. Anderegg's men, in getting "lost," had discovered an enemy CP, killed at least 13 of the enemy and captured three more. Of more importance was their capture of documents and maps of great intelligence value.

CPT Chandler, with the remainder of 2/7th Cavalry learned of G Co.'s location from an aerial observer. He then sent a patrol which guided the company to the rest of the battalion at the foot of Hill 464.

Withdrawal of 2/5th Cavalry — Sept. 6

The 5th and 7th Cavalry Regiments began withdrawing to new positions on Sept. 6. MAJ Callaway, of 2/5th Cavalry was the only officer in the battalion CP who knew the way up Hill 303, where elements of the battalion were deployed. He set out for the hill. The battalion was to pull back about a thousand meters to another ridge across the valley to the east. "I moved with great haste," he recounted. "I contacted the company CO and told him of my plan for evacuation." The men would come off the hill in single file. "I would lead the column and he would bring up the rear. There were about 75 men left on the hill. There was to be no firing and men were to stay closed up. The night was clear and the moon was out. There were trees on the side of the mountain but no thick underbrush.

"All went well until we reached the bottom of the hill. I was carrying my .45 pistol in my hand. As I opened two evergreen limbs to walk through, I was challenged by a person with a foreign voice. I was tempted to shoot, but I knew that my column would disperse, so I pushed the branches back and did a right turn and walked away. The column followed. I could almost feel the bullet in my back. About fifty yards away I turned to the left and came into the open valley. As we crossed this open area we spotted a tank about fifty yards away with a squad of infantry around it. The tank and soldiers began firing in all directions, mostly in the air. I increased my pace to a trot and the column followed. No one in the column fired a shot."

Upon arrival in the new position, it was discovered that about 20 men in the rear of the column were missing. They joined the unit safely early next morning. Two days later, MAJ Callaway was sent to take command of 2/7th Cavalry.

1st Battalion, 7th Cavalry — Sept. 7

The 1st Battalion took up new positions extending from the base of Hill 464 to Hill 620 to the east. Co. A was on the left of the line. At 4:15 a.m. on Sept. 7, battalion reported hearing the enemy on the flank near that unit. Shortly afterward a lively firefight developed in that quarter. A call from HM Co. revealed that Able Co. and 1st Battalion personnel were no longer on that flank. An enemy force, estimated as 150 personnel, made five attacks on the 1st Battalion in the first hours of the day. Two platoons of the HM Co. had to withdraw under enemy machine gun fire. They took the mortars with them. From their new positions, they took the enemy under very effective mortar fire. SGT Eddie L. Fletcher distinguished himself in directing platoon fire and in evacuating eight wounded men.

LT Marslender's platoon of A/7th Cavalry numbered 37 men on Sept. 4. By Sept. 6, it was down to six. That day he was ordered to take his men forward as an outpost in the valley to the front. He was not told how far out to go, however, nor when he was to return. With a borrowed SCR-300 radio, Marslender and his tiny platoon set off after nightfall in a heavy rain. About a mile out, he called a halt, and arranged the men in a little perimeter. The men covered themselves with ponchos against the rain.

To their rear, during the night, the battalion was heavily attacked. The following morning, Marslender was unable to get any response to his radio calls. He believed that the battalion may have been overrun. Even after he tried again to call on the radio from a nearby hill, he got no response. The lieutenant and his radio operator climbed to a higher ridge nearby. Marslender was standing behind the operator, holding the radio's handset, when he spotted four North Koreans coming down the ridge. With no time to say anything, he handed the handset to the operator and went for the carbine under his poncho. One of the enemy, possibly an officer, judging from his cap insignia, fired at them with a burp gun. Then the four enemy soldiers began to run away. Marslender raised his carbine, squeezed the trigger, but the weapon failed to fire. The burp gun fire brought the rest of his platoon up the hill. As they arrived, the radio operator said he had been shot; there was blood on his shirt and pantleg. A quick check revealed no wounds. The blood was from LT Marslender. Bullets had struck across the fingers of his left hand, shattering the carbine. This explained the carbine's malfunction and the blood.

Soon after, to their horror, they saw a force of men coming toward them in a deployed combat formation. With no place to go, Marslender had his men spread out and hid. As the force got closer, he detected a voice calling out instructions. Suddenly it dawned on Marslender that it was the voice of his West Point classmate, Larry Ogden, calling out to Curley Lindeman, another classmate. It was a most happy reunion. Ogden and Lindeman led the two platoons of Co. G which CPT West had sent to contact the 1st Battalion. The wounded Marslender was evacuated.

That night 1/7th Cavalry was attached to the 5th Cavalry. The rest of the 7th went into division reserve near Taegu. On division orders, the 5th Cavalry, on the night of Sept. 7-8, moved still farther south of Waegwan. On Sept. 8, an enemy broadcast claimed the capture of Waegwan. The enemy *3d Division*, meantime, continued to reinforce its troops on the east bank of the Naktong, to include the movement of artillery to that shore.

Richard Dowell, now an assistant platoon sergeant in B/7th Cavalry, wrote of the withdrawal of his company in those days of September. The unit withdrew at night, he wrote, and left booby traps on positions when they abandoned them. When the booby traps went off, "it was a real morale booster," he wrote. The rain "was a real blessing from God," for without it, "we surely would have been caught."

Finally, they made radio contact with an element of the 5th Cavalry, and were asked to throw a WP grenade for identification. The 5th Cavalry said that they could not see the WP grenade's smoke, so Dowell's unit went closer to the 5th Cavalry's lines. Then the company received fire from a small walled village. "Our C.O. said, 'Go get them!'" The men couldn't believe the order, until it was given again. "I started screaming our battle cry, Garry Owen! running as fast as I could towards the village...and shooting my M1 from the hip. SGT Taylor said, 'Cover that man,' and the battle was on. It seemed that gunfire relieved the pressure that had built up in each of us from night after night of sneaking past the [enemy] and not being able to do anything about it."

Enemy snipers hit a number of men. SGT Taylor stood up several times to draw their fire so his men could spot them. "We finally did," Dowell wrote. "They were firing out of slots in the straw roofs. We used tracers to start them [the buildings] on fire. It was just a matter of picking them off as they ran out.... Each house had a stone wall around it, which made it more difficult. We had to check out each house. Just as we thought we had the village taken, the Reds would make another attack from all sides." Enemy troops jumped over the wall into the village. Their supporting mortar fire killed and wounded men from both sides. "The men [Americans] on the west wall ran out of ammo so used their rifles to knock the Reds off the wall," Dowell related. "If they thought there were enough of them they would throw grenades over it." One man reportedly broke his carbine hitting enemy soldiers, then began using his fists or throwing grenades.

Dowell was on the eastern side of the village. "Everyone around me was hit," he recalled. "I was firing out a doorway of a house. Three other men covered the windows. They finally quit coming. I stood up just as a mortar landed about 2 ft. from the door. I saw the flash, then my hands and feet were together and then I saw the house move. But that was really me flying across the room. I don't remember hitting the floor. It knocked me out." When he came to, the other three men in the house were tending their wounds. Dowell couldn't find his rifle. He was hit by mortar fragments in the right knee, breaking the joint in five places. "I got to my feet, but went down. The pain drove me to the floor." The wave of pain soon left. Dowell was about to try to get up again, when a wounded soldier, holding his rifle in his right hand and his wounded stomach with the other, came by and told the men they were pulling out. "I thought, by Jove, if he can make it, I know I can," Dowell wrote. A medic was about three houses away.

During the battle, about a dozen men from the 8th Cavalry pitched in to help Dowell's unit in the village. "It was just the relief we needed," he wrote. "Other troopers rallied around them, beating off the last attack. Many of us were down to our sidearms and knives. We didn't need another attack, but what could we do for one last punch at them. I thought of SGT York, World War I. Why not. I told the interpreter to yell at the Reds, telling them they were surrounded, throw down their weapons and surrender. They didn't believe it. OK, so I lied." SGT Taylor told Dowell that he had fought all through Europe against the Germans, was wounded in the left elbow at the Battle of the Bulge, but never saw fighting like he experienced in Korea.

5th Cavalry and 1/7th Cavalry, Hills 174 and 203 — Sept. 10-14

The 5th Cavalry and 1/7th Cavalry battled in see-saw fights for Hills 203 and 174. Before it left the sector to join its parent regiment, 1/7th Cavalry captured Hill 174. It took four assaults. In one of these battles, SGT H. P. Flerchinger, a platoon sergeant with Co. B, distinguished himself in hand-to-hand combat with the enemy. His platoon leader was wounded. The company commander ordered Flerchinger to take over the platoon, reorganize it and take the objective. The mission was successful against some sniper fire. When two of his men were wounded, Flerchinger decided to go after the snipers himself. Setting up a machine gun to cover him, the sergeant set out. After advancing a few yards around a rocky ledge, he suddenly confronted six of the enemy. They scattered when he tossed a grenade at them. Continuing, he encountered a group of four more North Koreans. But this time he didn't have time to use his pistol or hurl a grenade. Instead, he threw his steel helmet at them. Three of the enemy tried to get their rifles up to fire, but Flerchinger jumped into their midst and the three ran off. He and the remaining enemy soldier locked in a bitter hand-to-hand fight. At one point, Flerchinger lifted the enemy soldier up on his feet. Flerchinger was lying on his back on the ground, with the enemy soldier balanced on his upturned legs and feet.) He hoped his men would shoot the enemy soldier while he held him up. Eventually he tossed the man over the ledge where machine gun fire killed him. This ended enemy sniper fire that night.

The 5th Cavalry barely held their positions on Hill 203 on Sept. 12. A major enemy attack, however, between midnight and 4 a.m. dislodged Co. E from Hill 203, Co. L from Hill 174, B and F from Hill 188. The regiment regained Hill 188 on the south side of the road, but made no headway against Hill 203. In the attack on Hill 188, Co. C feinted a frontal attack, while Co. B, reinforced by platoons from A and C, flanked the hill from the north. The feint by Co. C was successful and Co. B (reinforced) swept up and over Hill 188 at 3:55 p.m. The hill was secured at 5:20 p.m. Co. L, reinforced by a platoon from Co. I, attacked Hill 174, seizing it by 5:30 p.m. Because of rocky ground, the force did not dig in very well. As a result, Co. L lost the hill about 8:10 that night. Co. I attacked Hill 174 again on Sept. 14 and seized one side of it at a cost of 82 casualties. The 2d Platoon started with 27 GIs and 15 ROKs. At the end, it had only 11 Americans and five ROKs. With the enemy on one side

of the hill and U.S. and ROK troops on the other, grenade battles continued for a week. Co. I and its experiences attacking and holding Hill 174 are narrated below. Appleman wrote that the strengths of the battalions of the 5th Cavalry were so low that they were barely combat effective.

"Sept. 13-'50 fifteen of us left the Bn HQs to go to our company," wrote Eric C. Bogard, then a young replacement. just assigned to G/5th Cavalry. Five of the replacements were hit by sniper fire before they could join their units on the front. He recalled that when he and the other replacements arrived on the line, Co. G "had only 26 men left out of 60 until we showed up." On Sept. 12, he wrote, the company commander and three or four men were killed in the unit. Bogard capsulized his experiences over the next several days thusly:

"That night [Sept. 13] we went into attack with bayonets fixed. Another GI and I got out front of the attack, hit a wash in the ground that saved our lives....

"The next morning we attacked again. Received little fire from the enemy soldiers. That evening we attacked again and got surrounded by the North Koreans. The Co. Commander found [an] opening and led us out through it. The North Koreans [thinking we were still there] fought each other there for awhile."

When the 5th Cavalry had to withdraw, Jim Keppel and the 81mm mortars of Co. D were displaced too. "Our position was exposed in several places," he remembered, "so the second night we heard a tank moving and then 3 quick rounds into our area. This continued every night for three nights." The enemy flanked the main position. The company pulled back again. This time the 81s dug in near a church, where they stayed, until the breakout.

3d Battalion, 8th Cavalry and Hill 570 — Sept. 8; 11 and 14-15

The first effort to capture Hill 570 from the enemy was made on the morning of Sept. 8 by LTC Harold K. Johnson's 3/8th Cavalry. The battalion had to withdraw from one position in order to make this attack. Dawn revealed the triple peaks of Hill 570 to be hidden in a shroud of clouds, preventing air strikes and effective artillery and mortar support. The battalion attacked with all three rifle companies — one to each peak. Two companies took their objectives with no problem, one with no opposition. The other caught the enemy asleep on the ground. But an enemy counterattack re-took this peak.

The highest peak was firmly held by the bulk of the enemy force. Eighth Army estimated that about 1,000 North Koreans manned Hill 570. Co. I and L lost heavily in attacking it on Sept. 8. Item's commander and Love's XO were both killed in the attempt.

Eighth Army was very much concerned about the hill, since it was a major peak only eight air miles from Taegu.

The 3d Battalion, 8th Cavalry continued to struggle for possession of Hill 570 on Sept. 11. Companies I and K made the assault. But, by now the sizes of the rifle platoons in each company were so small (15 -20 men each) that the attack was more like one by two platoons rather than two companies. 2LT Kenneth W. Miller's

platoon of K/8th Cavalry was one of those 15-man platoons. Miller was another West Point '49er. In the beginning of the climb, the terrain provided protection from enemy detection and fire. When his platoon gained the military crest, LT Miller looked back to the knob from which the attack had began, and saw his company commander motion for him to continue the advance.

"Let's go!" Miller ordered. After taking a few steps, he looked back to see that no one was following. He repeated the command, this time with a few rather profane words for emphasis. The men got up to follow and were quickly met by mortar and automatic weapons fire and grenades rolling downhill at them. Moments later a bullet struck LT Miller in the stomach. The force spun him around and to the ground. It felt like he had been hit by a sledgehammer. A soldier ran over and applied a first aid dressing to the wound. Miller told him to go on up the hill. As the man rose to obey, a bullet struck him in the head. He fell beside Miller, holding his face, murmured "Mama" and died.

Fortunately, the platoon sergeant, MSG Ray Caplette, was still with the platoon. He took charge, and the platoon went on to capture the hill. Two men lifted LT Miller up and literally dragged him off to safety. In the ensuing enemy counterattack, the platoon lost the knob. At day's end there were just seven men left, including Caplette. Miller survived.

On Sept. 14, it was 2/8th Cavalry's turn. The battalion, along with the attached 16th Recon Co. and supporting 2d Platoon, HM Co., 8th Cavalry were awarded a U.S. Presidential Unit Citation and a Korean Presidential Citation for their actions on Hill 570 between Sept. 14 and 19.

The hill was subjected to intense concentrations of artillery and mortar fire in support of the attack. In a fierce three hour battle the battalion wrested the promontory from stubborn enemy defenders.

SGT Richard Benedict, Co. E, 8th Cavalry recalled some of his experiences in this attack. On Sept., 14, his company attacked some hills on the way to Hill 570. "Our squad was following the side of the hill when we were fired upon by a burp gun. Boyce M. Walker was leading the way and when [we were] fired upon he did a perfect flip in the air and hit the ground. I was right behind him and approximately 5 or 6 men were behind me. We all hit the ground and some grenades came down the hill towards us, exploding harmlessly.... I jumped up to see where the firing and grenades were coming from and saw two NKs looking at me from a foxhole approximately 75 yards away." Walker had not been hit by the burp gun. "I told him I saw the two NKs and...he said he was going to put me in for a bronze star medal. . . . I said, 'What for, I just wanted to see where they were.' The NKs kept throwing grenades down on us. I was the only one who knew where their foxhole was located." Benedict went around the rest of the squad, asking for grenades. "Nobody had any grenades." The squad was pulled back, and other men from the company, farther up the slope killed the enemy grenadiers. The attack continued and the three knobs were taken.

Benedict was wounded the following day on Hill 570. He remembered that the company commander, CPT William McLain, had promised the men cold beer if they took the hill. McLain couldn't deliver on the cold beer, but he did provide 5-in-1 rations instead, "which was perfectly alright with me," Benedict recalled. The 5-in-1 ration had been developed to provide a compact ration for five-man tank crews. On some occasions other troops also were issued, or otherwise came into possession, of some 5-in-1 rations.

"We had just about finished our early supper at approximately 1600 hours [4 p.m.] when the North Koreans started to 'walk' mortars in on us," Benedict wrote. In the ensuing mortar barrage, Richard was badly wounded by fragments in the neck, left shoulder, below the left breast and right ankle.

As the 2d Battalion gained Hill 570, 3/8th Cavalry fought a tough battle for possession of Hill 401. At the end of the day, the outcome was still in doubt; both sides had troops on the hill. SFC Earl R. Baxter (2d Platoon, L/8th Cavalry) was posthumously awarded the DSC for covering the forced withdrawal of his platoon. In this action he killed at least 10 North Koreans before he was killed.

3d Battalion, 7th Cavalry and Hill 314 — Sept. 11-12

The attack by 3/7th Cavalry on Hill 314 was the subject of an exhaustive study by the Operations Research Office, Johns Hopkins University, completed in Jan. 1954. That study is the principal reference for this section.

On Sept. 11, the enemy seized the crest of Hill 314, driving the 16th Recon Co. from it. The timely arrival of the ROK 5th Training Battalion from Taegu prevented the enemy from taking the entire hill mass. Three times this ROK battalion tried to take the crest, and the 3/8th Cavalry, attacking through it, also failed. The ROKs then clung to the reverse slope.

On Sept. 11, the 3d Battalion was occupying a blocking position on the Taegu-Tabu-dong road seven miles north of Taegu, preparing to attack Hill 570. Its attack on Hill 314 on Sept. 12 was part of a major counterattack against the *NK 13th* and *1st Divisions* by the 1st Cavalry and ROK 1st Divisions. The 2/7th Cavalry was to attack that day to secure Hill 660, while the ROK 1st Division drove Hill 902.

The Plan of Attack: Co. L on the left, Co. I on the right, with Co. K in reserve initially in vicinity of LD. Assault companies to attack in a column of platoons. Order of march for Co. L was 2d Platoon (MSG J. H. Mitchell), 1st (LT Holder) and 3d (1LT R. B. Sheridan); for Co. I it was 3d (1LT Marvin H. Haynes), 2d (2LT Marshall G. Engle) and 1st (2LT Marion Weston). MSG Roy E. McCullom commanded the 4th Platoon. Mitchell and Sheridan in Co. L were WIA. In Co. I, Fields, CO; Engle, Weston and 2LT J. Perez-Chiasa (possibly Company XO) were wounded, and Haynes and McCullom were killed.

Companies I and L each had one section (two guns) of heavy machine guns attached from Co. M. These guns initially supported the attack from positions on the LD. Each company also had three flame-thrower teams attached from the P&A Platoon. These teams moved with the attacking force. The 3d Platoon, C/70th Tk Bn was attached to the battalion. Kept under battalion

control it was not used to deliver preparatory fire. One squad of C/ 8th Engineers, attached to the battalion, was further attached to Co. I.

Preparatory Fires Scheduled: Air strike 9:30-10:30 a.m. Artillery (77th FAB) 10:30-11 a.m. 81mm mortars and four heavy machine guns 11-11:10 a.m. A platoon of HM/8th Cavalry was to have provided general support, but this did not materialize, due apparently to an FO problem. L/8th Cavalry was to support the attack by fire. This unit was on a lower knob of Hill 314. Its front became the LD for the attack.

The Objective — Hill 314: Hill 314 is, to an extent, the southern extension of a hill which rises to some 500 meters. From its summit, the hill slopes steeply to the valley in all directions except in the south. There it drops into a gully about 350 meters deep. From this gully, the ridge climbs further south to a knob 380 meters high, then begins to drop off again toward Hill 314. The approaches to Hill 314 are steep on both flanks and from the south. The hill itself, is composed of three knobs, which were known, from south to north as Knobs 0, 2 and 3. L/8th Cavalry was on Knob 0. For control and reporting purposes during the attack, a series of phase lines was designated. In the plan's final form, Phase Line 1 was the map grid line passing through Knob 2.

Phase Line 2 was the line of the edge of the map sheet crossing Hill 314 just north of Knob 2. Phase Line 3 was the map grid line passing through the north end of Knob 3. The ground distance between Knob 0 and Knob 3 was between 1,150 and 1,200 yards. The ridge line from the 314 meter point to the 500 meter point is one mile. The enemy could observe the left flank and crest of Hill 314 from Hill 570, to the northwest. The North Koreans also had some observation of parts of Hill 314 from the ridge's summit, about 500 meters high, to the north.

The Enemy: Information gathered after the battle indicates that Hill 314 and vicinity were occupied by about 645 men, many of them recent replacements and ill-trained. This force probably included *3/19th Regt. (13th Div.),* two companies *1/14th Regt.* and three companies *2/2d Regt.* (both from *NK 1st Div.*) Hill 314, itself, held about 400 enemy troops. Enemy fire support included at least four 82mm mortars, six 120mm mortars, four 76mm howitzers and four 45mm AT guns.

3/7th Cavalry: The battalion (LTC James H. Lynch) totaled 785 personnel at the start of the battle on Sept. 12. Of this number, the two assault companies, I (1LT Joseph A. Fields) and L (CPT Robert W. Walker), numbered 351 personnel. To this must be added the flame thrower teams and the engineer squad. Even so, the grand total of men in these two assault units could not have exceeded 400. Co. K, the reserve company, numbered 181 at the beginning of the battle. Co. M, the heavy weapons company, totaled 125 and the Battalion HHC, 128. The flame thrower teams came from this unit. Co. K was eventually committed to the fight. The Johns Hopkins study states that 610 men from 3/7th Cavalry actually made the assaults. This figure includes 145 attached KATUSAs.

The First Assault: Companies I and L reached the LD at 10:30 a.m. The supporting tanks, which were to be at the base of the hill by 6:30 a.m.,

did not arrive until 10:18 a.m. Knobs 1, 2 and 3, in that order, were the battalion objectives. Although the slopes of the approach to Hill 314 were steep all around, the purpose of the two companies deploying one platoon each in the assault was to bring a greater number of men and heavier firepower to the leading elements of each company.

The air strike part of the preparation was actually carried out from 9:50 a.m. to 10:45 a.m., with three missions by 11 F-51s. The artillery preparation was canceled due to a restriction on ammunition expenditure! To partially make up for this, four more F-51s were brought in on another strike. In all, the aircraft delivered five bombs (possibly 500 lb.), 16 napalm pods and 51 rockets, plus several thousand rounds of .50-cal machine gun rounds on the target. 81mm mortars and heavy machine guns then fired from 11 a.m. to 11:10 a.m. In the meantime, the assault companies crossed the LD at 11:10 a.m.

The jeep-mounted 75mm recoilless rifles from the Heavy Weapons Co. were not employed to fire preparatory fires, nor in support, until later in the battle. Why these weapons were not used at the outset is unknown. The Johns Hopkins study surmises that, "in the absence of exposed enemy bunkers," the 75s were not appropriate for preparatory fire. Enemy 120mm mortar fire was falling on and behind the LD as the two assault companies moved out.

Knob 1 was occupied by about 12 to 15 enemy soldiers, equipped with two machine guns and two automatic rifles. Few, if any Americans were hit in this phase. Fighting had occurred there previously, as evidenced by several enemy and American bodies. The knob was seized by 11:30 a.m. and all defenders killed, except one, who escaped to the rear. The enemy bodies were thrown out of their foxholes. The two companies reorganized. In L Co., LT Holder's 1st Platoon took the lead; LT Sheridan's 3d moved to cover the left flank. In Co. I, LT Engle's 2d Platoon became the lead; LT Weston's 1st covered the left flank. MSG Mitchell's 2/L Co. and LT Hayes 3/I Co. remained temporarily on Knob 1.

The enemy, reacting to the attack, delivered 120mm mortar fire on the LD, causing some casualties in L/8th Cavalry. K/7th Cavalry had stayed further to the rear just to avoid such an eventuality.

At 11:35 a.m, the attack continued toward Knob 2, covered by overhead light machine gun fire and 81mm and 60mm fire on the objective. Two platoons were abreast in the lead and two others echeloned to protect the flank as they started down into the saddle between the two hills. The two forward platoons each had two squads deployed in a skirmish line, followed by the third in a wedge formation. A squad from each of the flank platoons went down slope to sweep wooded areas. The ridge contained areas of woods and dense underbrush. The two company's weapons platoons deployed forward to Knob 1. The Co. I sweep squad killed the crew in an enemy automatic weapon position.

Soon, inaccurate enemy rifle fire was directed toward Co. L from a group of rocks on the left side of the saddle. A squad quickly silenced this annoyance. There were no American casualties in this episode. Four enemy soldiers were flushed out. Three ran to the rear; one went across the saddle to the right. He was killed; the other three apparently escaped.

Moving rapidly, the two units reached the bottom of the saddle about 11:43 a.m. At this point they were struck by very heavy fire from 120mm, 82mm and 50mm mortars, machine guns and American BARs. Enemy fire quickly destroyed Co. I's radio communication to the rear. Radio communication within the two companies was also knocked out at the same time. The companies plowed on for 200 yards, escaping the mortar fire, but were finally stopped by casualties from enemy small-arms and automatic weapons fire from the crest of Knob 2. LT Weston, 2/I Co., was among the casualties.

The companies were about 200 yards short of Knob 2 when pinned down. Off to the left, they detected an estimated 400 enemy soldiers preparing to counterattack. An air strike was requested, but was delayed; the aircraft were refueling. The counterattack was broken up by a heavy (about 120 round) 81mm mortar barrage.

The advance got underway again about 11:50 a.m. Once the internal radio communication system had been destroyed in each company, the initiative for continuing rested mostly with the platoon leaders. Enemy mortar fire fell over the entire saddle and on troops moving forward from Knob 1. Enemy 76mm SP fire hit the west side of Knob 1. About this time the four heavy machine guns of Co. M moved up to Knob 1 and began to fire overhead onto Knob 2. Some infantrymen at first thought this was enemy fire.

It is believed that part of 3/L Co. gained Knob 2 first. About this time, SGT D. C. Jones was killed by an automatic weapon. Seeing a gunner cut down, he had run forward, and kneeling, was in the act of unjamming the dead gunner's weapon. He caught a concentrated burst of enemy machine gun fire about waist high.

"121200 [12 noon]. Now on Phase Line 2," read the message. "Reorganizing and pushing on to Phase Line 3."

The two units were ready to continue the attack, but heavy fire from dense underbrush on a transverse ridge overlooking the shallow draw on the left side of Knob 2 was partly responsible. Co. L moved over the crest to avoid this fire. Co. I, advancing on the right of the saddle, saw enemy troops withdraw to the northeast reverse slope. When L moved to avoid the fire from the left, it ran into these enemy troops. It is unclear if the enemy actually made a counterattack at this time. The two units were repulsed in trying to advance. Friendly artillery and mortar fire prevented the enemy from following up.

The 3d Platoon, Co. L became disorganized from the devastating fire from the left. A runner came to LT Fields in Co. I to inform him that Co. L was in deep trouble. Fields moved to make contact with CPT Walker of Co. L. "They're killing all my men," Walker said. LT Hayes, on his own, moved his 3d Platoon over to back LT Sheridan's L Co. 3d Platoon. The Weapons Platoon, Co. I, was sent to back up the Love Co.'s 1st. Both company commanders left Knob 1 to go to the critical point of the attacking echelon of their units.

In the draw to the left of Knob 2, the two officers found the troops "stunned." Enemy mortar fire fell behind them while enemy small arms and automatic weapons fire came from the heavy underbrush along the transverse ridge ahead and to the left. No enemy was in sight, but the firing and showers of grenades from the bushes confirmed that the enemy was there. Fortunately, the grenades were concussion, rather than fragmentation. Only R. H. Joyce, Co. L, was wounded by these grenades. About 12:15 a.m., resolved to get the men moving again, both Fields and Walker stood up and began hurling fragmentation grenades at the hidden enemy. After each officer had thrown five or six grenades, their men also began to toss grenades at the enemy. This stopped the enemy grenades. Surviving enemy soldiers probably withdrew on up the main ridge to more defensible positions in the woods there.

As this transpired, men from LT Engle's, 2/Co. I detected about a dozen of the enemy, in groups of three or four, pulling back toward the northeast side of Knob 2. About the time Co. L was being stopped on the left, Weston's 1/Co. I was stopped by fire from underbrush from the right. Engle was wounded at about 11:55 a.m. He refused evacuation until more seriously wounded were evacuated. As a result, he laid on the hill for twelve hours, receiving another mortar wound during that time. When Engle was wounded, his platoon sergeant, SFC N. B. Lancaster took over, and was wounded in turn. Ignoring his wounds, Lancaster took charge and deployed the platoon to meet two enemy attacks. He then led the platoon forward to capture its objective.

Co. I's 1st and 2d Platoons were deployed along a ditch which ran down from the right side of Knob 2 along the top of the finger. At the top, this ditch was about six feet deep and eight feet wide. Farther down, it was about 15 feet deep and 15 feet wide. There was no concealment on the friendly side, but dense scrub pine growth on the enemy side. Enemy fire caused the men to fall back and they had to be urged forward again. Although LT Fields did not recall if they were receiving general small arms fire, he saw dust puff from the back of the jacket of one man who was hit "like a stone wall" and killed.

Hayes' platoon was attached to Co. L about 12:15 p.m. LT Sheridan stood up. As he did so, a mortar round burst, killing him. Hayes, his friend, ran over, saw that he was dead, turned away, dropping his hands. At that moment, another mortar round burst, killing him. This precipitated a short withdrawal of the men of these two platoons.

The Second Assault: About 12:30 p.m., the 2d Platoon, Co. I (MSG Mitchell) moved up across the finger to the left. Enemy SP gun fire hit the northern slope of the finger which the platoon had to cross, and some enemy troops in the woods higher up the finger to the left made some movement toward Knob 2. Enemy small-arms fire and grenades caused heavy losses, stopping Mitchell's platoon short of the left side of the nose of Knob 2. Both 81mm and 105mm howitzer fire were called in. The 81's fired beyond Phase Line 1 while the artillery worked over the objective. This chased the enemy down the draw to the left beyond Phase Line 2 and out of the battle. LT Holder then moved his 1st Platoon, Co. L onto Knob 2 without opposition. The two company commanders, the Co. L radio operator, an artillery liaison officer, one artillery forward observer, the two 81mm mortar FOs and some messengers moved up to a depression just short of the crest of Knob 2 called "the shallow." This was a semi-circular depression about 20 feet across, enclosed by a four foot high wall. From "the shallow" the ridge beyond the crest could finally be seen, but the reverse slope of the ridge, the flanks of the hill and much of the sides of the ridge were still out of sight.

Mitchell continuously exposed himself to enemy fire as his platoon moved up the steep slope of Knob 2. The Johns Hopkins study quotes an affidavit from one soldier who was there at the time: "As we neared the top of the hill...I saw him [Mitchell] and he was wounded in the chest and was bleeding very much, but kept the platoon and himself going up to the top of the hill. He was one of the first to reach the top of the hill despite his condition.... When the enemy had been driven from the hill (much later), SGT Mitchell asked the medic to get treatment.... I saw him start down the trail." Mitchell was killed by a mortar round while going to the aid station.

Mitchell's platoon had taken a commanding portion of Knob 2. It was at about this time that two squads of LT Holder's 1/L Co. moved up the draw and seized the left side of the nose and this 3d Squad moved onto the right side. Position was everything in attaining observation. For example, a sergeant of 2d Squad, 1st Platoon, Co. L, located just to the left in the shallow noticed one of his men firing over Knob 2. He asked the man if he was sure he was firing at enemy soldiers. The man invited the sergeant to see for himself. There, on the northeast reverse side of Knob 2 were 15 or 20 North Koreans.

More artillery fire was directed at the enemy, this time with about 36 rounds of VT-fuzed 105mm rounds, set to detonate just above the ground, producing a larger, more lethal spread of shell fragments. This fire was designed to prompt the enemy to evacuate the objective. The 81s also fired two more concentrations at this time.

The advance stopped again. It was near 1:10 p.m. Twenty minutes later, an air strike was requested. All this time, fighting continued, with small-arms, automatic weapons and mortars. Enemy 120mm and 82mm mortars created about one casualty every two minutes among friendly troops.

During this interval, an enemy soldier kept popping his head up from behind a huge boulder about 150 or so yards from friendly troops. He did this periodically for about 15 minutes, escaping GI fire all the time, but was finally hit in the leg and felled as he tried to run away.

Around 2:10 p.m., enemy small-arms fire from thick underbrush down the right slope of Knob 2 created some casualties in Co. I's 2d Platoon. Enemy 120mm mortars hit some men already wounded, as well as some others walking back down the evacuation trail.

At 2:10 p.m., the long-awaited air strike came in. Three F-51s worked over the enemy with napalm, bombs, rockets and machine guns until 2:45 p.m. The planes made their runs over the heads of friendly troops and through the enemy mortar fire. They flew very low, hitting the enemy only 75 to 100 yards forward of the friendly troops. Metal links from their machine gun belts rained down on the men. CPT Walker's helmet was blown off by the airwash. One napalm pod went over the northeast end of Knob 2. Another landed just beyond a little knoll about two-thirds of the way to Knob 3.

At about 2:15 p.m., COL Nist (CO, 7th Cavalry) talked to LTC Lynch. At that time the issue was in doubt on Hill 314. A half hour later, Nist reported this to Division: "[Lynch] was getting ready to jump off for his third phase line. He doesn't know whether or not he can make it. I am going to stop him at 1630 [4:30 p.m.] because he must get dug in for the night. He is having quite a few casualties...."

A ROK police battalion was then getting into position to the rear to back up 3/7th Cavalry. The situation in other areas of the 1st Cavalry sector was also grim. The CO, 8th Cavalry issued orders about 2 p.m. that the command must hold its objective. "If unit stops, men must dig in," the text of a message from 8th Cavalry read. "They must hold their present position even though they are going to get casualties. If you lose any ground, you have to take it in the morning. Plan all prearranged fire of organic attack or supporting weapons...."

As soon as the planes left, the assault companies were ordered to renew the attack. The losses among platoon leadership left them somewhat confused, but CPT Walker took charge himself and lead the charge. LT Fields and a dozen men from Co. I, joined in. Walker was among the first men on the crest of Knob 3. "Come on up here where you can see them," he called to his men, "There are lots of the bastards and you can kill them!" The troops responded in a rush, yelling and shouting, as they swarmed up a 60 degree slope for the last 150 yards. Wounded enemy soldiers were killed in the mad rush. Fields moved to the right, hunting for the enemy, but found only five enemy bodies instead. The enemy scattered in disorganized retreat. One enemy soldier was captured hiding in the rocks. But some enemy soldiers did fight back. At least two members of Co. I's 2d Platoon, some 150 yards down the ridgeline, were hit by small-arms fire. SGT J. Manuel, Co. I, charged a fanatical enemy soldier who was holding up two squads of the 1st Platoon. He killed the North Korean with a grenade, allowing the squads to advance. In the action, the sergeant was wounded in the right leg and right hip.

About 3 p.m., enemy mortar fire created a few casualties in Co. K, which was moving to close on the leading units. The company suffered heavier losses a little later.

By 3:30 p.m., Knob 3 was captured. Walker reorganized both companies on the objective. During the last phase of the attack, LT Fields, I Company's commander was wounded. With his wounding, every officer of Company I had become a casualty in the attack. The first head-count on Hill 314 showed a total of 80 men, about evenly divided between the two companies. A little later, as the companies assembled and reorganized on the objective, more men arrived. GEN Gay had a special study made of the battle. This study indicated total losses in 3/7th Cavalry of 229 men in the first two hours of the battle. This figure included 38 Americans KIA, 167 WIA and the remainder KATUSAs.

These figures do not agree with those derived by the Johns Hopkins study, published in Jan.

1954. That study gives these figures: American: 32 KIA, 97 WIA. KATUSA: 6 KIA; 15 WIA. TOTALS: 38 KIA; 112 WIA. The total loss, then was 150 men, including 8 officers. Of this number, 141 were from the three rifle companies. One-third of the men in the two assault companies I and L became casualties, with I losing all its officers. The Johns Hopkins figures are probably more accurate, since its author had access to more data and had more time to study and analyze records and reports. The battalion had already experienced one tough and bloody fight for Hill 518 just nine days previously. It now had experienced another bloody and traumatic struggle.

Although the 3d Battalion's losses were heavy, the enemy suffered more. An unknown number had been wounded, no doubt 200 or more, but there were 250 dead bodies scattered from Knob 1 up to and including Knob 3.

3d Battalion, 5th Cavalry and Hill 174 — Sept. 14

(Conversations quoted in this section are from *The Korean War, Pusan to Chosin*, by Donald Knox, unless otherwise cited.)

The 5th Cavalry had been engaged for a number of days, contesting for such terrain features as Hills 188, 203 and 260. Its 3d Battalion relieved 1/7th Cavalry about 6 p.m. on Sept. 11. Co. K occupied Hill 203 on the left, L the nose of 174 in the center and I another hill mass on the battalion right. Co. I had to go forward and occupy its position at night. No one from the company had an opportunity to scout and there were no guides. The company crossed rice paddies and began to climb. The men were wearing full field packs. Finally, CPT Norman F. J. Allen called a rest halt. At its conclusion, he ordered the column to move out. To his dismay, when he got to the top of the hill, only 10 or 11 men were with him. He discovered that a man had stopped to tie his shoe, breaking the column. Allen set up a little perimeter with the men he had, to include two listening posts and waited out the night. The next day he was able to assemble the entire unit. That night, he heard and could see a battle going on Hill 174. He alerted his men for possible action.

On the night of Sept. 12-13, Co. L lost its toehold on Hill 174: Co. E lost 203.

PVT Carroll G. Everist recalled that among the casualties in the loss of Hill 174 were five KIA. The first man killed, he wrote, was CPL Carl W. Cook, shot in the head. During the battle, Everist and another man took over a machine gun when the original crew was knocked out by shell fragments. He wrote that the man with him declared that, if he got out of the fight alive, he would go to church every Sunday. Everist, who became a Baptist, often wondered if the man stuck to his vow.

Co. L was ordered to counterattack and regain Hill 174. This it did. The leading elements of the unit were on the hill by 4:50 p.m.

The 3d Platoon, Co. I helped Co. L in this attack, due to the losses Love had suffered. SGT Dale M. Larsen commanded the 2d Squad, 3d Platoon, Co. I. He wrote that when the attackers topped the first of three hills, the enemy ran away and that the Americans "eliminated the entire

company." Roy F. Richards was a Corporal in Larsen's squad. Richards always attacked just to the left of Larsen. He confirms Larsen's claim to eliminating an enemy company when he said: "He finally pointed his carbine in another direction, then I saw going around the hill. They [the enemy] were down in the valley going.... We did have a field day there. They say we killed more than 200...."

At 5:20 p.m., 3/5th was notified that all ammunition restrictions were lifted; all possible targets could be engaged. Twenty-five minutes later, CPT Gerald Perry, Love's commander, reported the company was taking casualties from 120mm mortars. He didn't know how long the unit could hold. Shortly after 7 p.m., about 60-70 enemy were discovered assembling on the north edge of Hill 174. They were engaged by 81mm mortars. At 8:05 p.m., Co. L was authorized to withdraw and tie in with Co. K's right flank. At 10 minutes after midnight (0010 hours) Sept. 14, Co. L was under a severe enemy ground attack, what was known as a "banzai attack."

The boom of mortar and artillery explosions mixed with the much lighter, but irregularly spaced "tat, tat, tat" of small-arms fire, the more sustained "tat-tat-tat-tat" of automatic weapons fire, pyrotechnic tracer streams in the dark and their arcs into the sky as they ricocheted told the story too well: Co. L was under a furious attack. CPT Allen alerted his men, in case the enemy came their way.

With the help of artillery, Love repulsed two enemy attacks, but the third one swept up and forced the unit off the hill. The 3d Battalion S2/3 Journal entry for 1:45 a.m., Sept. 14 records the loss of Hill 174.

At 6:05 a.m., the journal records that at least 300 enemy are atop Hill 203 and that Co. K. is directing 4.2 inch mortar fire on them. Less than a half hour later, it records that Co. K reports the enemy digging in on that hill and an adjoining ridge. Meantime, the regimental commander, COL Marcel G. Crombez, resolved to retake both hills. The journal entry for 8:43 a.m. states that White (2d Bn) will attack Hill 203 at 11 a.m. and Blue (3d Bn) "will attack and hold hill 174 by night fall." At 8:45 a.m., the journal shows that CPT Allen has been notified to assemble Co. I "and prepare for attack. Item 6 to CP immediately." ("Item 6" was the communications code for CPT Allen.)

The 3d Battalion S2/3 journal records as of 1:40 a.m., Co. L had only 88 men left out of a strength of 193 which it had when it attacked Hill 174 the day before.

LTC Treacy and COL Crombez got into a heated argument about sending Co. I to take Hill 174. Treacy pointed out to Crombez that the hill had been attacked several times before. CPT Allen recounted the encounter: "The enemy knows that we'll be coming, and no matter how Allen attacks it, it went that way at least once before and the gooks will be ready for them," Treacy told Crombez. He also reminded Crombez that Co. I was the only of any numeric strength left in the regiment; that if it attacked Hill 174, it would "be the last strong company, gone to hell." Crombez, livid with rage, accused Treacy of being a coward. The order that Co. I attack Hill 174 stood.

CPT Allen conferred with the Battalion "3,"

CPT Robert Humphries about the impending attack of Co. I on Hill 174, returning to the unit just before 10 a.m. He ordered his XO to prepare the company to move in a couple of hours and to be sure that everyone had plenty of ammunition and grenades. He also ordered a hot, cooked meal, not the usual fare of C-rations. He then took a radio operator and headed for the Battalion OP.

I/5th Cavalry Attack on Hill 174 — Sept. 15

The company would attack with all three platoons abreast; 1st (2LT Joseph D. Toomey Jr.), 3d Platoon, which had been released from attachment to Co. L, (MSG Wally Nelson) and 2d (2LT Adrian Beecher Brian), in that order from left to right. Toomey and Brian were 1949 West Point classmates. Toomey was captured later in the war and died in a POW camp on Feb. 28, 1951.

The company was ordered to an assembly area in an a grove of peach and persimmon trees, behind a stone wall near the foot of Hill 203. PFC Victor Fox of the 3d Squad, Nelson's 3d Platoon, recalled that enemy shellfire was falling in the rear area up to the point where his unit had detrucked two days previously. LT Geer briefed the platoon leaders on the attack; they, in turn, briefed their squad leaders. Fox remembered SGT Steve "Blackie" Furlan, his squad leader orienting the squad on the attack and supporting fires to expect.

LT Toomey posted PFC Jerry Emer near a ditch in the vicinity of the assembly area, with instructions to watch for the platoon, then point them in the right direction. While he, the lieutenant and the officer's runner stood there, they heard a loud <u>whoosh</u>. Instinctively they all hit the ground. As they did so the incoming round exploded — *BLAAM!* Clods of dirt and branches rained down on the prone men. Almost immediately, two more rounds landed farther down the ditch. "Damn, they're close," Toomey muttered. His runner just nodded in agreement. Emer felt shaky and weak. Toomey and his runner went on, leaving Emer alone. The enemy shelling continued.

Then he saw members of the platoon running bent over, toward him. He called to them, pointing the way. Just as one of the KATUSAs ran by, a round landed, throwing the man's body into a ditch near Emer. Emer crawled over to the man and discovered that the Korean was terribly wounded. One arm had a large, ugly gash near his elbow, one side was ripped open from the rib cage to the hip and there were numerous lesser wounds all over his body. His cartridge belt was smoking (probably from rifle ammunition set off when the man was hit.) Emer tore off the cartridge belt and tossed it away. Then, using his own first aid packet, dressed the arm wound to stop the bleeding. Emer recalled that he was shaking badly and didn't do a good job. As the Korean mumbled something, Emer reached for the man's canteen. By the heft, it was full. It was, all right —full of sugar. (Emer's canteen was already dry.) "Oh, God help me," he muttered.

As Emer tended the fatally wounded KATUSA, the platoon ran by. One of the last men was Doyle Smith, the medic. He took one look at the dying KATUSA, then gave him a shot of morphine to ease his pain. The Korean became quiet and still in a few minutes, then Emer and Smitty went to join the platoon. Enroute, they passed the blood spattered bodies of several Korean farmers. Enemy mortar fire was already causing casualties in the assembly area; two machine gunners were killed on the edge of the grove of trees. Five or six other men had been wounded. Emer filled his canteen and washed the Korean's blood from his face and hands as best he could. "I thought of Pontius Pilate," he wrote.

CPT Allen was forward by the stone wall and orchard, watching the artillery preparation on Hill 174. SGT Nelson came up, very agitated about the plastering the company was taking from enemy 120mm mortars. Allen was "scared as hell" himself. He knew that the longer the unit stayed in the assembly area, the more casualties it would suffer. But he also wanted badly for the scheduled air strike to come in on the objective before the men attacked. He moved the tanks up to bring direct fire on Hill 174, perhaps hoping that one of them would knock out the enemy observer responsible for the deadly mortar fire. The tanks then drew some of the mortar fire and wanted to pull out. Angry, Allen ran over to their commander and yelled at him that the tankers had "all that goddamn armor around him when all we had was our field jackets, and that he damn well better stay...."

About this time, the battalion CO, LTC Edgar J. Treacy, came up to Allen and asked him why he hadn't started the attack, scheduled to have taken place at 2 p.m. It was now after 2 p.m. Allen explained that he was awaiting the air strike. But Treacy insisted that the attack commence at once. He told Allen that he (Treacy) had been up on the near knob of Hill 174 and no enemy were there.

Almost as the men conversed, four F-80 jets came in and began the strike. Allen then called battalion and asked for a signal when the air strike was ended. Battalion told him that a WP round fired on the hill would be that signal. When the fighters left, the WP round burst on the objective and Allen called out "OK, let's go!" With that, Item Co. rose up and moved forward quickly to get out of the enemy mortar fire in the orchard area.

Each platoon was deployed in a skirmish line to cross the rice paddies. which had a waist-high growth of rice in them. Weighted down with extra ammo, the growth- and mud-filled rice paddies were very hard to walk in.

Brian's platoon headed for the left flank of Hill 174, in the valley between it and Hill 203. The platoon was to attack the western flank of the objective, while Nelson's 3d went up the front and Toomey's 1st attacked the eastern slope. The three platoons were to meet on the top. Fox recalled that his 3d Platoon ran out of the orchard and across the rocky, dry streambed. CPT Allen recalled that good progress was made in about the first 150 yards, with only some mortar fire. But, as the 1st and 2d Platoon's cleared the shield of a forward knob of Hill 174, enemy small-arms, mortar and artillery fire swept through the entire company. Allen could see men from the 2d Platoon as they fell to enemy fire, taking its toll in dead and wounded. Cries of "Medic!" "I'm hit!" and the like soon were heard. Skirmish lines all but disappeared and the men of the unit went forward in, as one man put it, "a column of bunches," or a "herd of turtles." U.S. tanks fired their main guns and machine guns, while outgoing artillery rounds sighed and moaned overhead to slam into Hill 174.

"As we moved toward the objective we got caught in a dry creek bed," wrote Gordon L. Davis, of Co. I. "The North Koreans already had us under heavy 120 mortar fire as well. We had to move forward from the creek bed in order to survive because the mortars, plus the flying rocks, were taking too heavy a toll on us. Once out of the creek bed, we had to cross a sparsely treed apple orchard to get to the base of the hill. We lost many good men crossing that piece of ground."

LT Brian was folded over at the waist from the blast of one of the first mortars. A KATUSA nearby was badly wounded and Smitty the medic had a shrapnel hole the size of a silver dollar in his lower abdomen. Brian sent his runner (a man named Covington, he recalled) back to guide litter bearers forward. He then attempted to help Smitty. When he tried to raise the medic in order to apply a bandage, Smitty screamed in pain. He told Brian that he felt sick in the stomach and stuck a finger down his own throat. As he gagged on the finger, Brian remembered, about a foot of intestines came out of the hole in the man's stomach. The lieutenant was torn between his duty to his platoon and caring for Smitty. Knowing he had to rejoin and lead the platoon, Brian draped a bandage over the wound to keep the flies off, then strung a linen strip from Smitty to the nearest paddy dike, where he tied it to the medic's carbine and laid it on the dike where the litter bearers were certain to find it. He then rejoined what was left of the platoon at the base of the hill. Only five minutes had passed since Smitty was wounded. Finding the platoon at the base of the hill, he got them moving on up.

"When we finally reached the base of Hill 174, we were quite disorganized and everyone was thoroughly bushed," wrote Jerry Emer (for Donald Knox. Knox did not use this material in his book.) "There was an erosion gully which also served as a natural pathway to the top of the hill. About 10 of us were laboring up this 'gulch' when we heard that familiar ghastly rushing of incoming rounds. We flattened ourselves out.... Four or five shells tracked right across the ditch; they exploded in rapid succession, like a stick of bombs." One round struck on the left of the ditch and the others burst down slope and to the right of it. "The air was gray and acrid with smoke and dust," Emer wrote. If just one of the rounds had landed in the gully, most, if not all the GIs in it, would have become casualties. While lying there after the last round had exploded, Emer looked up to see SGT Woods hurry by, his left arm and shoulder covered with blood. "But he looked quite calm and self-possessed," Emer remarked.

As the attack continued, battalion began pressing Allen for status reports. The captain, trying hard to get fire support on the enemy, told them to clear the (radio) net so that he could get through. Battalion insisted that regiment wanted to know his progress. Allen profanely responded that if regiment wanted to know what was going on, they could come up and see for themselves. Again, profanely, he told battalion to clear the net so he could manage his fire support. With that, he quit talking to the battalion CP.

About 20 yards from the crest of Hill 174, Allen, to his horror, saw a squad of his men cut down by a volley of artillery rounds. The squad immediately following the first was also swept away by another flurry of artillery rounds.

"The sun had come out and it was dry," wrote SGT Larsen. We started up the hill right at noon. I had gone only about 10 yards when a mortar [round] landed about 10 feet from me, on my right. It lifted me 2 feet into the air and pushed me 5 feet to my left. I felt my right arm and leg get hit. It dazed me for several minutes. It was as if someone had slapped me with a baseball bat on the side of the head."

He found a small wound in his arm and another in his leg. He didn't think that he was badly hit, so decided to keep going, and ordered the squad to move out. "There were enemy troops everywhere. The squad kept moving until it reached a plateau about two thirds of the way up. There it "ran into a solid hail of bullets. We were stopped dead. About this time, our machine gun crew, located to my right, and about 100 yards behind me, started firing — long bursts...."

When the machine gun fired again, Larsen jumped up and called to his squad to charge. He started running toward the top of the hill, and what he thought was an empty foxhole, firing his rifle. Suddenly, an enemy soldier popped up from the hole and fired a burst from his burp gun at Larsen. "He hit me with the first burst," Larsen recalled. "I remember stiffening up real hard with my legs, I threw up my hands so hard, I threw my rifle about 10 feet away. I fell on my right side. I could not move my legs." The enemy soldier aimed the burp gun at Larsen's head. "I turned my head to the right and his bullet hit the ground by my left cheek. I called to John Duff that I had been hit." The enemy soldier fired another burst, which passed over Larsen's body. Larsen began pushing himself away, "rolling as fast as I could," he wrote. "Suddenly, John Duff appeared, running toward me as fast as he could, firing as he ran." Duff killed the enemy soldier. He laid down for a moment, then jumped up, grabbed Larsen by the wrist and dragged him about 100 yards. Duff sprinkled sulfa powder on his wounds and Larsen was carried to the rear in a litter improvised from a poncho and two rifles. Roy Richards recalled that Larsen had killed two of three North Koreans in the charge before being wounded.

Victor Fox and his friend William (Bill) Haltom were the point of the 3d Platoon. SGT Furlan was nearby. The remainder of the platoon advanced in a skirmish line, covered by machine gun and BAR fire. Fox was oblivious to what was happening to either side or behind him. He did hear the noise of a major firefight off to his left. The enemy and Fox's platoon exchanged heavy fire. Near the hilltop, the platoon charged to the summit with bayonets fixed, firing all the way. The enemy had withdrawn. Fox looked around quickly and saw a narrow-spined ridge leading out 300-400 yards to another knob designated Hill 174.1 on the map. The tops of Hills 174 and 174.1 were totally bare. The slopes of the connecting ridge were cut up by deep erosion ditches which reached to the valley on either side. Dusty shrubs and brush dotted the ridge. Fox described the landscape as "moonlike."

Fox and Haltom moved to the right side of the narrow ridge and crawled from gully to gully toward Hill 174.1 The two men found themselves literally under the gunsights of enemy defenders. But the North Koreans were concentrating on the bulk of Co. I further up the ridge and on the other side of it. Fox and Haltom stopped and looked around, seeing only LT Toomey, crouched in another gully. A terrible battle was taking place all around them, but, oddly to Fox, no friendly fire fell on the enemy positions.

When Allen gained the summit, he knew that Nelson's platoon had been all but destroyed. LT Brian joined him there and reported no more than 15 men left in his platoon. Allen ordered Nelson and Brian to hold on Hill 174.

Toomey, from his advanced position on the right, near the summit of Hill 174.1 radioed Allen and recommended sending the remainder of the company to join him. Allen refused. Toomey argued that he was almost at the crest of 174.1, that all that was needed was the balance of the company to take it, thus securing the entire hill mass. Allen wanted to say yes, but he knew better than Toomey how bad-off the company was. Heavy casualties had reduced two platoons to a strength of less than a single platoon; the men were exhausted and low on ammunition. Further, the enemy was raking the company front with fire. An attempt to advance would be suicide. It would be hard enough to hold what they had, without taking many more casualties in trying for more. CPT Allen also wrote that battalion, unaware that Hill 174, was in reality two knobs — 174 and 174.1 — did not expect Co. I to go beyond where he had stopped on Hill 174. He ordered Toomey to withdraw and rejoin the company.

Toomey crawled over and convinced Fox and Haltom that they could not take Hill 174.1 themselves; they had no grenades left, for one thing. It was then that the enemy spotted the three men and opened fire on them. It was touch-and-go for a time. Toomey, Fox and Haltom, timing their runs, made short dashes from one gully to the next, followed by enemy fire.

SFC Donald Pate, leader of the 4th (Weapons) Squad, 3d Platoon, was a premier machine gunner and combat veteran of WW II. Spotting the three men trying to get back to the company, he opened up with the platoon's light .30-cal machine gun to give them covering fire. The stream of bullets just cleared the heads of the crouching, running men. Pate had taken over the gun when the gunner, CPL William (Bill) Taylor was wounded in the head by mortar fragments. He left the tripod with Taylor, firing the gun during the rest of the attack by bracing the pintle against the nearest rocks.

The ground on Hill 174 was very rocky, making digging in nearly impossible. LT Brian recalled that about all they could do was build little walls out of loose shale. "You couldn't get a tool [entrenching tool] into the ground if your life depended on it, which it did," he wrote to Donald Knox.

Pate wrote that to dig a foxhole, the rocks [shale] had to be broken up and taken out in layers. He also recalled that the company found quite a bit of ammo, left behind when Co. L was driven from the hill the previous night. He collected a number of parachute flares, which could be fired from a rifle, using a grenade launcher, as well as quite a few fragmentation grenades. He and others also gathered enemy concussion grenades for possible use. This grenade resembled "a can of beans, with a detonator" on the top. Pate showed some of the men how to rig the grenades with a trip wire so anyone disturbing the wire would set off the grenade. (See Chapter Notes.)

"When we reached the crest of the hill, no enemy in sight," Emer wrote, "only a few corpses lying about. The hill had numerous shallow slit trenches left over from L Co.'s. 'occupation' (We piled into these for cover, expecting more mortar fire or a possible enemy counterattack.) Instead a brief lull ensued." CPT Allen and the officers and senior NCOs used the time to reorganize the company and prepare a defense. LT Brian selected a slit trench about 15 to 20 yards behind the foxhole line as his platoon CP. CPT Allen established his CP in a bushy gully to the left of Brian's. Telephone wire was strung from the Co. CP to each Platoon CP and to crew-served weapons positions. Except for a very short lull, Co. I was under a continuous bombardment by enemy mortars and enemy small-arms and automatic weapons fire for many hours. Fox thought that the concussion from continuous mortar bombardment had made some of the men punch-drunk.

When Item took Hill 174 that day, it was the tenth time that U.S. forces had taken it. The 8th Cavalry had taken and lost it six times, L/5th Cavalry twice.

Most of the enemy fire came from Hill 174.1 and Hill 203 on the left of Hill 174. The enemy machine gun and small-arms fire was so heavy that CPT Allen finally moved his men onto the reverse slope. This stopped the effectiveness of this fire, but enemy mortars kept up their pounding. Occasionally, a mortar round landed in an occupied foxhole, usually tearing the men in the hole to pieces, or shattering their bodies with multiple, fatal wounds. The men never knew what hit them. At one point, Victor Fox, not thinking, stuck his head above the hill crest for a peek. SGT Furlan yelled at him to keep his head down. Fox quickly ducked. Just as he did so, a burst of machine gun fire kicked up stones and dirt where his head had been.

Fox recalled that I Company's perimeter was not large. He remembered, however, that the 57mm recoilless rifle, a shoulder-fired weapon, always drew a flurry of enemy retaliatory fire every time it fired. This type of weapon depended upon the gases generated by its firing to keep the gun stable on the gunner's shoulder. Fox called it a "one-man walking artillery piece." The back end of the weapon had a series of openings to allow gases to escape to the rear. When the gun fired, the gases escaped through the perforated shell casing and through the openings in the base. The escaping gases known as "backblast" created a killing force behind the gun by hurling dust, dirt and rocks some distance to the rear of the gun each time it fired. As it fired, the gun also sent out a cloud of fire and smoke

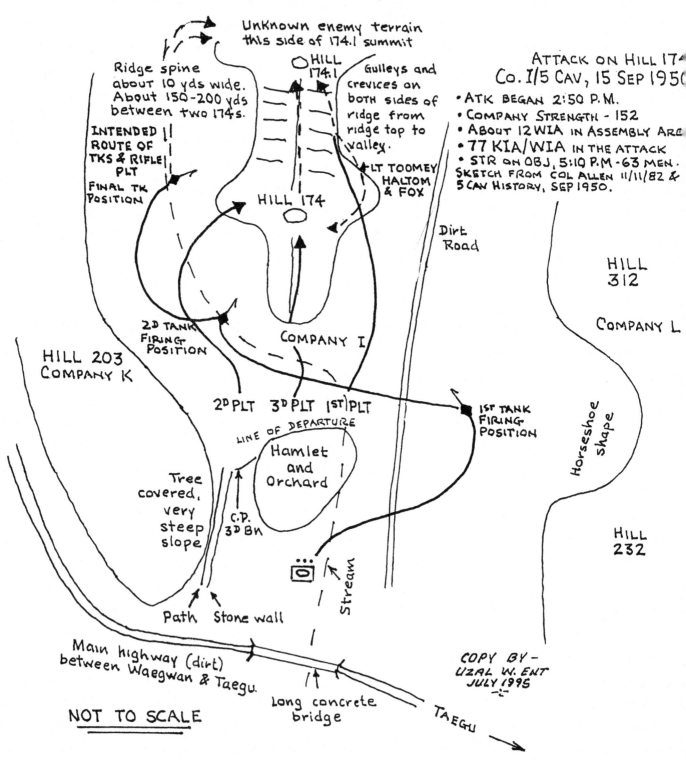

FROM 5TH CAVALRY REGIMENTAL HISTORY, SEPT. 1950
SEPTEMBER 14, 1950

Unknown enemy terrain this side of 174.1 summit

Ridge spine about 10 yds wide. About 150-200 yds between two 174s.

HILL 174.1

Gulleys and crevices on both sides of ridge from ridge top to valley.

ATTACK ON HILL 174
Co. I/5 CAV, 15 SEP 1950

- ATK BEGAN 2:50 P.M.
- COMPANY STRENGTH - 152
- ABOUT 12 WIA IN ASSEMBLY AREA
- 77 KIA/WIA IN THE ATTACK
- STR ON OBJ, 5:10 P.M - 63 MEN.
SKETCH FROM COL ALLEN 11/11/82 & 5 CAV HISTORY, SEP 1950.

INTENDED ROUTE OF TKS & RIFLE PLT

FINAL TK POSITION

LT TOOMEY HALTOM & FOX

HILL 174

Dirt Road

HILL 312

COMPANY L

2D TANK FIRING POSITION

COMPANY I

HILL 203
COMPANY K

2D PLT 3D PLT 1ST PLT

1ST TANK FIRING POSITION

LINE OF DEPARTURE

Horseshoe shape

Tree covered, very steep slope

Hamlet and Orchard

C.P. 3D BN

HILL 232

Path Stone wall

Stream

Main highway (dirt) between Waegwan & Taegu.

Long concrete bridge

TAEGU

COPY BY - UZAL W. ENT JULY 1995

NOT TO SCALE

Map 41 (Courtesy of Uzal W. Ent)

to the front, as well. As a result of all this, as soon as the weapon fired, it was usually necessary for the gunner and crew to move *at once*. Enemy responding fire was almost certain and deadly. So it was on Hill 174. The RR gun crew would scurry into a firing position, shoot a round and depart in haste. The infantrymen left in the foxholes near where the rifle was fired were left to take the enemy's return fire.

Looking back over the route which his company had taken to attack the hill, CPT Allen was appalled, sick and frightened when he saw the landscape dotted with the bodies of his dead and wounded men. He reported to the Battalion XO, MAJ Edward Mayer, that he had between 80 and 90 wounded. It was obvious that Allen did not have men available to care for and evacuate all these wounded. Mayer asked him why he had not reported during the attack. Allen said that he was so busy dodging from one point to the other, firing, throwing grenades and shifting fire support, that he hadn't had time for progress reports.

The 3d Battalion S2/3 journal records that at 4:20 p.m., the Battalion S-1 was ordered to "get as many litters here as quickly as possible." Five minutes later CPT Allen called to report that friendly artillery fire had fallen on his men and asked that it be "moved forward." Resupply of ammunition was of paramount importance if Item expected to hold the hill. At 4:38 p.m., the journal states that the company had requested that "all available MG ammo be sent forward immediately." At 5:15 p.m., the Battalion S-3 called the Regimental Medical Co. to "send plasma, litters and morphine with doctors." The battalion had heavy casualties in Co. I, as well as more from other units which were involved with the enemy elsewhere, although not attacking.

Darkness overtook the litter parties as they tried to get to all the wounded. Allen believed that there was one man who the parties never found. In all, he wrote, Co. I lost 89 men taking Hill 174. Allen found that the CP which his XO, LT. Robert Geer, had selected was nothing more than another erosion ditch. Allen was too tired to do anything about it. He laid down in the ditch to get what little sleep he could.

When Co. I retook the hill, it was dotted with enemy dead, some starting to decompose. About 20 of them were grotesquely sprawled in front of the foxhole of Haltom and Fox. That number would increase in the days ahead. Like most soldiers who have been in heavy battle for some time, the two men were accustomed to the sight of dead bodies; they were able to eat their C-rations, indifferent to lifeless stares of dead enemy soldiers.

Just before dark, LT Brian had the 57mm recoilless rifle fire into a Korean house in the valley. The building burned far into the night. An attacking enemy would be silhouetted against the light of the fire.

Darkness fell. It was totally black. Fox and Holtam laid out a supply of grenades, the pins partially pulled. U.S. artillery fired harassing fire through the night, including WP and parachute flares. WP rounds gave off a comparatively low-intensity illumination; parachute flares destroyed one's night vision (the ability to see in darkness). The enemy probed stealthily, crawling slowly up erosion ditches and gullies, trying the get the

GIs to fire and reveal their positions. Once detected, enemy grenades would kill or wound anyone so revealed. Throughout the night, Fox recalled, company machine gunners periodically worked the machine-gun bolts. Both enemy and friendly soldiers recognized that someone was apparently jacking a round into a gun, preparing to fire. For a time, this froze enemy activity. A high state of tension gripped everyone — friend and foe alike. Fox swore that he could hear North Koreans whispering and could detect the tell-tale smell of garlic which always emanated from enemy soldiers.

On Hill 174, Co. I was 700 yards from the nearest friendly troops, with the enemy on all sides. CPT Allen remembered the night of Sept. 14-15 as one of pure hell. He was determined that Item would not retreat; that dead or alive, they would be on that hill in the morning. CPL Howard Bowhall, of the CP group, positioned himself as a self-appointed guard over CPT Allen. After probing the position for several hours, the enemy launched a heavy attack about 11:40 p.m. It was beaten off. In the second attack, some of the enemy got into Allen's CP area.

"A few minutes before midnight...," Allen wrote, "Bowhall nudged me and said, 'Captain, wake up, they are right out there, I can smell them.'" Another man in the CP group gave the challenge. He was answered by a flurry of grenades, "Dozens and dozens within seconds," Allen recalled. Fortunately, most were concussion type, with little fragmentation. As quickly as the grenade attack started, it stopped. Suddenly a dark figure loomed up on Allen's right, just a few feet away. Moving rapidly, he stepped on Allen, then halted and crouched about six feet away. "I guess he knew he had stepped on something besides hard ground."

The captain could dimly make out the man against the night sky. Still lying down, Allen eased his .45 from its shoulder holster, slowly pulled the slide to the rear, chambering a round, then cautiously guided it forward. "Then in the most godawful firing position . . . pistol in my right hand, I crossed the hand across my prone body until the hammer was at my right left ear; couldn't aim, just leveled it and fired. He rose up to a kneeling position and toppled over, his outreached arm falling against my body." Allen holstered his pistol and took up his carbine. No one else fired, or uttered a sound. About 10 minutes later, he recalled, another figure loomed up, coming fast. This one impaled himself on Allen's carbine bayonet. As he did so, the figure cried out, "Oh, Mother of God!" Allen was convinced he had bayoneted one of his own men, Hackney by name.

He had little time to check this out, for the enemy now tried to get a fix on the company CP by softly calling "I Companee CP. CP I Companee." They were very close. Then the man who had been bayoneted (in the right abdomen, as it turned out), who was in the ditch with Allen, began talking. The captain told the man to shut up, or he would kill him. Allen got the company aidman, McKenna, who was very close, to check the wounded man out. McKenna reported that he would probably live through the night. Allen asked the injured man who he was. "'Merican soldier," came the reply. By this reply, Allen knew the man was an enemy soldier. Enemy soldiers were still

crawling around softly calling "I Companee CP." McKenna inspected the man closely and told Allen that he was not Hackney.

About 20 yards away lay a mortally wounded man of the company. The medic could do nothing for him. All he or Allen could do was make him comfortable. Just before dawn, the young soldier died, crying for his mother and asking for God.

Allen decided that it would be best to kill the wounded enemy soldier in his hole. As he fumbled with the bolt of his carbine, the enemy soldier made a lunge for it. In the ensuing struggle, Allen got possession of the weapon and aimed it at the man's throat. The enemy soldier raised his hands defensively in front of his throat and said "No. No!' It was too late, Allen had pulled the trigger. The carbine was on automatic and a stream of bullets ripped into the man. He gasped and slumped into Allen who expected a shower of grenades. But nothing happened. A short time later, mentally and physically drained, CPT Allen fell asleep. The next morning he was jolted awake. A trickle of dirt was falling onto the crook of his right arm. He was prone in the hole. One dead enemy soldier was slumped over him and another lay with his arm dangling over the side. Someone was standing above him. Allen assumed it to be the enemy. He resolved to jump up, shoot everyone around him, then run away as fast as possible. "Jesus look at that," he heard, "the captain has killed two right in his own hole!" Weakly, Allen rose up to see two of his men. Relief swept over him.

Jerry Emer heard the grenades and firing near the CP, but apparently he, and those near him, had little contact with the enemy that night. Victor Fox and Bill Haltom however, exchanged grenades with enemy soldiers all night long. Fox described the explosion of the enemy concussion grenade as resembling a heavy WHOOMP and that of the GI fragmentation grenade sounding like an explosive ZINNG. Occasionally, they could hear the sound of an enemy soldier being hit by the full blast of a fragmentation grenade, then the muffled sound of a body being dragged away. Fox and Haltom teamed up to combat enemy grenades. Fox was the lookout and Haltom, with longer arms, batted or swept incoming grenades away from their foxhole. Other men teamed the same way in their own foxholes.

With daylight, the machine gunning started again. The dead bodies on the hill absorbed more bullets. Mortar fire also started, joined by an enemy SP gun. By 8:35 a.m. plans were being made to withdraw Item from Hill 174. Less than an hour later, the company was expecting an enemy attack. CPT Allen saw large groups of North Korean between his position and Co. K, on the left and other groups moving down the valley to his right and a ridge which ran parallel to Hill 174. Companies I and K opened fire on these groups and soon Allen had more targets than he could get fire missions for. He reported to LTC Treacy that if Companies I and K were not soon withdrawn, they would be cut off by the enemy. Treacy asked the captain to hold until 11 a.m. Allen spread the word to his company that they would soon be in "one hell of a fight in just a few minutes and would have to hold until noon, no matter what." (In Knox's book, Allen says that they had to hold until 11 a.m.)

1st Platoon, Co. I, 5th Calvalry after Hill 174. Standing in back left to right: MSG Ed Rueter (Plt. Sgt.), Jefferson Davis Brown, Smith, Blanchard, Hopkins, Wyatt, Whiteside, Lee Carpenter, Boullon, Purner, Unknown, Mike Havilla. Kneeling left to right: Unknown, Unknown, Dark, Tapehouse, Unknown, Possibly Joe Blunt. Sitting left to right: Robert Grant, Unknown, Purdy, Percy, Heiman, Unknown. (Courtesy of Victor Fox, I/5 Cavalry)

The captain's plan for withdrawal was to send the 1st Platoon, which was by itself on the right side of the hill, down first. Then the other two rifle platoons would leapfrog one another back down the ridge.

When the order came to withdraw, no one ran. Fox remembered that, in addition to Co. I, K and L were also under heavy attack nearby. The noise of battle increased to a crescendo. Heavy enemy small-arms and automatic weapons fire followed the men until the ground provided a mask. But nothing could stop the incessant mortars. By 11:15 a.m. an estimated 200 enemy were east of Co. I and another 150 to the west.

Fox heard someone shout "Every man for himself!" His ears rang from the noise of the firefight. At the bottom of the hill he discovered a wounded GI who needed help to walk. Fox helped the man to his feet, then put the wounded GI's arm around his shoulders and together they stumbled toward the streambed in the rear. Suddenly he heard a man's voice telling him not to worry; that everything would be all right.

There was no one route down the hill. Each man found his way down. In the valley, a terrible battle was in progress, as the enemy attacked in mass down the dry streambed. The 3d Battalion sent cooks, clerks, drivers and commo men forward to help fend off this attack. The enemy almost made it to a nearby bridge. Fox got his wounded man back, then joined some other Item Company men behind a low mud wall with some other Item Company men. Then he found one of his friends, Joe Blunt, in shock. A few steps farther on was John Irons, lying on the ground, gasping for air. Standing near a group of soldiers, Fox heard a rush of air and saw a flash of light, then silence. A section of the wall blew up. Fox and a number of other men were

hit, some killed. Fox refused evacuation. Later that afternoon John Irons and several other men ran into a salvo of three exploding mortar rounds.

About 4:30 p.m., Treacy told Allen that Co. I would have to go back and take Hill 174 before dark. Allen angrily refused, telling the colonel that he would have to come up and beat him up before he would carry out such an order because he (Allen) would have to whip each of his men to get them to go back to the hill that day. The entire company was mentally and physically exhausted, hungry and thirsty. Treacy heard Allen out, said he would intercede at regiment, but warned that the unit better be ready to attack in the morning.

In all this grimness, death and destruction, a note of humor came through. Some time during the day, a squad leader came to CPT Allen and told him that he was probably in a lot of trouble. During the attack the previous day, he noticed a man who couldn't seem to keep up. The squad leader, angered, went over and kicked the man hard in the butt. The unknown soldier then turned toward the squad leader. He had kicked the battalion commander! Allen found out later that Treacy, who had never been in an infantry attack, and stung by COL Crombez calling him a coward, had accompanied Co. I in its attack on Hill 174.

The next afternoon, Sept. 16, Co. I set out again with three platoons abreast. Allen ordered fixed bayonets and an all-out rush for possession of the hill. There would be no stopping because of casualties, enemy fire or anything else. They met no resistance! Allen had the men occupy the same foxholes they had before, and he employed artillery to keep the enemy nearby at bay.

On Sept. 17, Victor Fox broke his glasses. This misfortune, plus the wounds he had suf-

fered on Sept. 15 caused him to be medically evacuated.

Co. I stayed on Hill 174 until about Sept. 21, fighting off a number of enemy attacks and engaging in numerous grenade fights during the period. During this time, Sergeants Donald Pate, William Taylor, CPL Roy F. Richards and "French" Marquillas shared a large hole. Taylor was playing what Richards described as "hide-and-seek" with an enemy soldier. They were sniping at one another. Once, as Taylor raised his rifle to fire, the enemy soldier fired first, knocking the rear sight off Taylor's rifle. The sight struck Taylor beside his right eye and flew back to cut his ear. Taylor was temporarily blinded by blood and shock.

The battles in the 1st Cavalry Division during the first two weeks of September caused heavy casualties. LTC Johnson said that any company of his 3/8th Cavalry which could assemble half strength (about 100 men) was his assault "company" that day. The three battalions of the 5th Cavalry were so low in strength that they were virtually not combat effective. A typical company of the 2d Battalion numbered about 69 or 70 men. The 3d Battalion had lost 600 of its 900 men. Most of these were from battle casualties and the remainder due to transfers to the other two battalions. One company in 1/7th Cavalry had but 50 men.

Anecdotes of the 13th Signal Company — Mid-September

"The situation in the Perimeter could not have been worse," wrote Robert Thompson, 13th Signal Co. "The line was stretched to the breaking point. The rain had kept our air support grounded. Division had ordered service units to move farther back. The 77th Field Artillery [1st Cavalry

Division] was firing from the schoolyard of the Taegu Medical School, the [site of] the 1st Cavalry Division CP, when the Signal Company left the Division CP for the rear." (The 13th Signal Company was then attached to the 1st Cavalry Division.)

"We bivouacked that night on a riverbank. It poured all night and we were drenched. The river was about to flood. Our company commander was CPT James Olaf Johnson, a burley Swede with sandy red hair and a big walrus mustache.... He was one of the finest, most decent men I have ever met."

That morning, in the rain, CPT Johnson climbed onto the back of a 2 1/2-ton truck and addressed his assembled company: "Men, I have just come back from Division. The situation does not look good. The division commander [MG Hobart R. Gay] told the COs of the service units that they may return to Taegu or they may continue to move back to Miryang. The decision is up to the service unit commanders. Now, if we return to Taegu and the line does not hold, there will be no possibility of escape. If we move back to Miryang, the chances may be a little better. I am ordering LT. S____ to pick some men and set up a rear CP at Miryang. As for myself, I'm going back to Taegu. I'll take my chances with Division. Those of you who want to go with LT. S____ to Miryang are free to go over with the lieutenant."

"No one spoke," Thompson wrote. "I guess the same thought went through the mind of every man there. If die we must, I guess Taegu was as good a place as any. Not one man moved. The 13th Signal Company returned to Taegu."

Among other things, the 13th Signal conducted psychological operations, broadcasting surrender messages to the enemy in Korean. Along with the messages, it broadcast music familiar to North Korean soldiers. Quite often, the broadcast trucks were subjected to enemy artillery or mortar fire during the broadcast. Francis A. Venuto Sr., a member of the 13th was in one of these broadcast teams. "Our team," he wrote, "consisted of a GI jeep, with driver, towing a 75KVA engine generator. A powerful amplifier and floating speakers. A 3/4- ton . . . with four to six Korean interpreters a ROK 1LT and various musical instruments. They [would play in broadcasting Korean tunes]. Our biggest problems were when we had a commitment or assignment on the lines we always had a tendency to attract...enemy fire. Many of the...outfits resented seeing us come on to their position because of what was to come when we started to broadcast. There were times that the enemy fire was so severe we would have to make a fast exit."

The British 27th Infantry Brigade Committed to the Line

On Sept. 4, the British 27th Infantry Brigade (Brigadier Basil A. Coad, commanding) relieved 3/23d Infantry on the Perimeter and was placed under command of the U.S. 1st Cavalry Division. The Brigade's sector was on the division's southern flank. The three companies of the 1st Bn, The Argyll and Sutherland Highlanders (1st Bn, A&SH), commanded by LTC Leslie Nielson, were scattered across a number of hills. The battalion occupied the extreme left flank of the di-

vision. LTC G. I. Malcom of Poltalloch, in his book, *The Argylls in Korea*, wrote that a gap of 6,000 yards existed between the battalion and the 2d Infantry Division to the south.

The battalion sent frequent patrols into this area in order to locate enemy troops or infiltrators. A patrol, on the afternoon of Sept. 6, led by CPT Neil Buchanan, ran into enemy fire and Buchanan split his patrol into two parties. LTC Malcom wrote what happened from then on: "The fire increased, thus disclosing the strength and disposition of the enemy. And as the fire was returned by the patrol, and the small-scale but uneven battle developed, it became clear to Buchanan that his little party had accomplished their task and ought to get back with their information. His sergeant (Walker) was wounded, as well as three men (volunteers from the Leicesters), and he himself rendered incapable of being moved except with great danger to his comrades. In these circumstances he properly ordered his men to withdraw and leave him behind." Buchanan had to repeat the order before it was obeyed. His batman, PVT T. Taylor, also wounded, also stayed behind. The rest of the patrol escaped. The captain and PVT Taylor were killed and five other men wounded in this action. (See Chapter Notes.)

A few days later, CPT J. A. Penman led a patrol to the Naktong, intending to cross in a small assault boat. The current proved too strong for the men to control the boat. Penman, taking his batman, Lance CPL A. Mitchell along, swam the river. Enroute, Mitchell's weapon, a Sten gun, which was slung around his neck threatened to pull him under. Penman grabbed the man in time. The two completed the reconnaissance and swam safely back.

At 3 a.m. one morning, an enemy patrol assaulted an Argyll machine gun section, but was driven off. But the section suffered several casualties. The next evening, just after dark, the section moved to another position, this time within Co. A's perimeter. Once this was done a Sergeant Morrison took out a patrol. He returned to report an enemy patrol on the way. The enemy patrol came upon the old machine gun position to find it vacant. The old position was within the Argyll's lines. The enemy would have to get out again before light. Co. A's 1st Platoon, under SGT J. Robertson, was along the route the enemy would have to take in withdrawing. Forty-five minutes after the enemy had attacked the abandoned machine gun position, the North Koreans cut the platoon telephone line and attacked. Normally, this would have drawn heavy responding fire and flares. Instead, no one in the platoon responded with grenades or fire. As a result, the actual platoon position remained undisclosed to the enemy. Robertson's company commander called him on the radio and asked him what the situation was. Robertson told the officer that there was a large enemy patrol around his position, but he was waiting for daylight to shoot and "let him have it." A few minutes later, in the early dawn, the platoon opened a heavy and sustained volume of fire all around its position. The enemy, terrified, broke and ran, leaving 10 of their number dead on the ground.

The 27th Brigade defended their sector until it crossed the Naktong on Sept. 21.

Chapter Notes:

P. 260 The Middlesex Regiment was formed in 1755. It was known as "Diehards," "The Mids," or "Steelbacks." It served in America in 1776 at Cape Fear, New York and Yorktown. The Argyll and Sutherland Highlanders were known as the "Thin Red Line" from the battle of Balaclava in the Crimean War. They distinguished themselves in America in the defense of Penobscot in 1778. Many other distinguished, old British battalions later fought in Korea, but these were the first. Both battalions left Korea Apr. 26, 1951, replaced by other British battalions.

P. 261 Most times given in describing actions by the 7th Cavalry between Sept. 2 and 13 in this chapter are from the 7th Cavalry battle reports.

P. 277 To rig the grenade for this, it is fastened to a stake in the ground, or a small bush. The cotter pin which holds the striker from hitting the detonator is loosened just enough so that it remains in place but will be pulled out by a little tug. A wire, in this case commo wire, is tied to the ring on the cotter pin and stretched to another stake or bush perhaps five to 10 yards away. The wire should be about a foot from the ground to "trip" an enemy trying to sneak up.

P. 281 British units were under strength at the outset of the Korean War. Volunteers from other formations were needed to fill out the Middlesex and Argyll battalions sent to Korea. As a result, men from the Royal Leicestershire Regiment, the King's Own Scottish Borderers, the Kings Shropshire Light Infantry and the South Staffordshire Regiment were used to fill out the ranks of these two battalions. As to the term "batman," he/she is a personal servant to an officer. The U.S. Army specifically forbids personal servants of this nature. The closest U.S. equivalent are the enlisted and officer aides assigned to generals and admirals.

CHAPTER NINETEEN - The Second Battle of the Naktong Bulge

Deployment of the U.S. 2d Infantry Division

The 2d Infantry Division relieved the 24th Infantry Division along the Naktong effective at 6 P.M., Aug. 24. On Aug. 29, 3/23d Infantry relieved the 7th Cavalry Regiment in the southern part of the 1st Cavalry Division sector. Since the 3/23d Infantry could only be supplied over the road net from Taegu, Eighth Army attached the battalion to the 1st Cavalry Division. In its final form, then, the sector of the 2d Division stretched along the Naktong from the town of Hyonpung in the north to the village of Agok in the south. This village lay at the confluence of the Naktong and Nam Rivers.

Because of the serpentine Naktong and the locations of hill masses, the division front was about 35 miles long according to the 2d Division history. Appleman gave a frontage of 20,000 yards for the 9th Infantry and 16,000 yards for the 23d. A map inspection by the author indicates that the frontage of the 38th Infantry was about eleven or twelve miles. Using the figures of 16,000 and 20, 000 yards, plus eleven miles, would give the division a front over 32 miles long.

Whether it was 32 or 35 miles, makes little difference. With the troops and weaponry available, it was an area impossible to defend. GEN Walker miscalculated when he placed the 2d Division where the 24th had been. He believed, with the defeat of the *NK 4th Division* earlier in August, that front would be relatively quiet, allowing the 2d Division time to get some experience without becoming immediately engaged in heavy fighting.

The 2d Division had a total of seven infantry battalions available. The division had to employ the same tactics as the 24th Division did; outpost the front and depend upon counterattacks by reserves to meet and eject enemy penetrations. The 3/9th Infantry was on detached service at the Yonil airfield and the 3/23d was attached to the 1st Cavalry Division. Some other supporting elements of the division were with these two battalions.

The division deployed the 38th Infantry from Hyonpung in the north on a front of almost twelve miles to the south. The 23d Infantry (-3d Bn) held the center on a front somewhat less than ten miles wide. The 9th Infantry (-3d Bn) held the southern sector, including the Bulge area on front of eleven and a third miles.

The 9th Infantry placed a total of five of its six available rifle companies on the front. This was in the same area where the 24th division had deployed three rifle companies when it occupied this line. The 1/9th Infantry occupied the southern half of the regimental sector and 2/9th Infantry the northern half. The 1st Battalion placed all three rifle companies on the front, with Co. A in the south, C in the center and B in the north. Co. A's left flank overlooked Agok and the Kihang ferry site. Companies C and B were within the Bulge area. Co. F was to the north of

Co. B, and was also within the Bulge. Co. G held the north of the regimental sector. Co. E was in reserve about four miles in the rear in an assembly area along the road between Tugok and Yongsan. This placed it in a central location from which it could be deployed in any direction.

The 23d Infantry's sector commenced north of G/9th Infantry at a point just to the south of the village of Pugong-ni (Masuwon). The 23d deployed its 1st Battalion along the Naktong; Companies C, B and A in that order from south to north. The 2d Battalion (- Co. E, which was moved into the 9th Regiment's sector on Aug. 29 as an additional reserve unit for the 9th) was in reserve about eight miles in rear, from which it could guard the regimental road net. Of the eight rifle companies deployed facing the Naktong in the 9th and 23d Regiments, A/9th Infantry, in the south, probably had the shortest front; it was "only" about 1 1/2 miles long. A/23d, on the northern flank of that regiment, probably had the longest; almost 4 1/2 miles. Here, the unit was in three enclaves of about a mile each, separated by gaps of almost a mile each. The gaps were "covered" by patrols and outposts.

The 38th Regiment, in the north, adopted an unusual defensive scheme. Co. G outposted a front over four miles wide, generally facing the Naktong, with its right flank refused. A gap of over a mile existed to its north, where Co. E took over. Part of E faced a mile of river front, but the bulk of the unit faced north spanning about three miles of low hills facing massive Hill 409. Co. F was spread over a series of hills to the rear, running north for about 2 1/2 miles from a point just north of Lake Yong-ho. Both flanks were refused. In the far north of both the regimental and division sectors, Co. C occupied a horseshoe-shaped position of about a mile and a half at Hyonpung. The nose of the position thrust westward toward Hill 409. It had no physical contact with any other part of the regiment.

None of the regiment's units seem to have had much physical contact with one another. Co. B occupied defensive positions a little over a mile south of Hyonpung, astride the main road south from Hyonpung. The company also blocked a road which branched off to the southwest just within their line. The company's left flank was refused to face Hill 409. Co. A was deployed about a mile south of Co. B, also astride the north-south road and facing north. Its line was about a mile long, with almost half of it bent back to on the left flank so as to face Hill 409. The deployments of Companies B and A protected the north south road in some depth. But the flanks, being oriented toward Hill 409, invited an enemy envelopment of each unit's left. Such an envelopment would force the company out of position. The regiment's 3d Battalion was in reserve.

Clay Blair, in *The Forgotten War*, wrote that GEN Keiser "did not encourage the customary (and prudent) use of sandbags, barbed wire, and other measures to strengthen defensive positions on the dubious ground that it would rob the

troops of their offensive spirit." The lack of barbed wire, sandbags and mines with which to strengthen the positions materially assisted enemy attacks against them.

The North Korean Plan for Attacking the U.S. 2d Infantry Division

The contemplated North Korean attack against the 2d Division was part of the enemy's overall plan to break through somewhere and destroy the Perimeter. The prize was Pusan. The sector of the 25th Division in the south was the most direct route. (See Chapter 20.) But a penetration and exploitation in the southern half of the 2d Division, just north of the 25th would have the same effect, if the North Korean Army could smash through, then swing south behind the 25th Division, while pinning that command on its front by heavy attacks from other enemy divisions.

To breach the 2d Division's sector, the North Korean *I Corps* planned to employ the *9th, 4th, 2d* and *10th Divisions*, a total of at least 28,000 men. At the same time, the *6th* and *7th Divisions*, some 21,000 men, were to assault the 25th Division. In the north, the enemy *3d, 13th* and *1st Divisions,* (19,000 troops of the *II Corps*) tried mightily to smash through the 1st Cavalry Division to Taegu.

In these attacks, the enemy had the initiative because he could assemble enough troops to gain overwhelming superiority at the point of attack. The Americans, being in the defense, had to spread thousands of men in small groups across many miles of terrain just to maintain some surveillance of possible routes of enemy attack. This left too few troops and weapons for powerful and doctrinally sound counterattacks. Readers, and even students of Korean War history fail to understand this and have repeatedly and unfairly condemned soldiers for failing to stop the enemy until he had achieved major breakthrough(s). (See Chapter Notes.)

In the last few days of August, men of the 2d Division noted some enemy activity across the Naktong, and the 9th Infantry was experiencing enemy infiltration and patrol activity. One man wrote of his experience during this time:

"I had been back to Hq for something and on my way back the Mess Sgt (SGT Garnet L. Igo) asked if I needed a ride back," wrote Willis Fredericks (H/9th Infantry). "So I got in the jeep with Igo and driver. We got about half way and ran headlong into a North Korean tank. Igo jumped from the jeep and hollered, 'Get out of the way!' They [the enemy] started firing machine guns. We all jumped...into ditches. When the others [GIs] heard the firing they came running and firing on the tank. About this time LT Edward Schmitt ordered us to quit firing. As did he jumped on the tank and tried to pull open the hatch. As it came open the enemy [soldier] was firing pistols.... One of the rounds hit LT

Schmitt through the neck. But before he jumped [off the tank] one of the men handed up [a] 5 gal. [can] of gas and LT Schmitt doused the tank with gas and set fire to [it]. The troops that were in the tank were captured. It took hours to get that tank moved. There were 3 more in back of this one. They were knocked out."

The enemy did not know that the 24th Division had been replaced by the 2d. Directly facing the 2d Division was the enemy *10th Division* (7,500 men) on the Hill 409 complex against the 38th Regiment. The *NK 2d Division* (6,000 men) was opposite the 23d Regiment and the *NK 9th Division* (9,350 men) was opposite the 9th Infantry. The *2d* and *9th Divisions* were augmented by what was left of the *4th Division* (5,500 men). In the 9th Infantry sector, this meant that seven rifle companies, including two reserve companies would oppose more than one enemy division. The situation was even worse for the 23d Infantry. There COL Freeman had but five rifle companies against another enemy division, plus. It is fortunate that the enemy *10th Division* was not more aggressive against the 38th Infantry in the north, for COL Peploe had only two of his battalions available to him, and fighting in parts of his sector became fierce. But GEN Keiser had to send Peploe's reserve, 3/38th Infantry to the aid of the 23d Regiment.

GEN Pak Kyo Sam, commanding the *9th Division*, defined the division's mission in his operations order, issued Aug. 28: "To outflank and destroy the enemy by capturing the Miryang and Samnangjin areas, thereby cutting off his [Eighth Army] route of withdrawal between Taegu and Pusan...."

The main axis of advance for the *9th Division* was astride the road from the Naktong via Tugok, to Yongsan. The *NK 2d Division* attacked in two major columns. The southern column followed the road east from Pugong-ni through Poncho-ri to Changnyong. Its northern column advanced along the road which ran for several miles generally north near the eastern shore of the Naktong, then turned east, passing through Mosan-ni joining the southern road just east of Changnyong. The *10th Division* was to attack to the east from Hill 409.

To facilitate their river crossings, the enemy utilized rafts and barges as well as so-called "underwater bridges." These were constructed of rocks and sandbags, providing a manmade ford about three feet deep. These "bridges" were almost impossible to detect from the ground and difficult to locate from the air. On Aug. 27, the 38th Infantry observed the enemy building bridges and assembling rafts and barges. Artillery and mortar fire was directed on them, with little effect. But the Americans were determined to destroy as many rafts and barges as possible.

1LT Clifford Philipsen and three enlisted men of K/38th Infantry volunteered to cross the river and do the job. The operation was carefully planned and was carried out in daylight. The four men pushed four drums, partially filled with gasoline, across the Naktong, covered by a very heavy volume of automatic weapons and recoilless rifle fire. With this protection, the men were able to saturate the rafts with gasoline and set them afire, then make good their escape back across the Naktong.

Their comrades of King Co. helped provide the covering fire. Lieutenants René' Ramos and Harry S. Morrison, Jr. crewed a 57mm recoilless rifle. Ramos was the gunner and Morrison, his assistant. "We destroyed two enemy machine-gun positions [with the 57]," Ramos wrote. "We started receiving either mortar or artillery air bursts and as soon as we noticed that they had bracketed our position we withdrew."

On the Northern Flank of the 9th Infantry — Aug. 31 - Sept. 1

Enemy attacks struck most heavily in the 9th Regiment's center and into the 23d Infantry's left flank and center. In the division's northern sector, lighter attacks were made simultaneously from Hill 409 against the 38th Infantry.

Between about 9:30 p.m. and midnight on Aug. 31, elements of the *9th Division* crossed the Naktong at several places and stealthily climbed the hills toward and into the 9th Infantry lines along the river. North Korean mortars and artillery began pounding 9th Infantry positions from about 10 p.m. to 1 a.m. on September 1. The beginning and ending of this bombardment varied from one position to another along the line. When the artillery/mortar preparation ended, North Korean infantrymen were in position to assault American positions. The assaults began in the northern part of the regimental sector and spread to the south. (See Chapter Notes.) The three front-line companies of 1/9th Infantry were pretty much overwhelmed by large enemy forces early in the battle, which tore the regimental front to pieces.

The enemy attack struck Co. G in the far north of the regiment. John L. Mason, a black soldier (probably the only one in the company), wrote that the enemy "hit Co. G's lines around 10 P.M. They were repulsed." Again, "Air cover caught enemy moving up behind us (Bn size unit.) All hell broke loose with M-1s, 50 cal., etc.; yelling, bugles, grenades flying everywhere. No time to think, just fire away. Wave after wave trying to get up the hill. [I] became nervous after it was over!! (Can you believe that?)"

2LT Edward B. Quinn (West Point, 1950) led a tank platoon of A/72d Tank Bn which supported the right flank of the 9th Infantry from positions within the lines of Co. G (commanded by LT Frank Muñoz). He had no opportunity to undergo any armor training before being sent to Korea.

For the two weeks before the North Korean attack, main gun ammunition was rationed to a maximum of seventeen rounds per gun per day. "We didn't do any firing;... So we accumulated a reserve of ammunition," he wrote. Knowing of the projected Operation Manchu, LT Quinn moved his tanks into position in the north where he could see the proposed crossing site. "I thought I would offer support on the flank of the crossing if they flushed anything out across the river." Quinn's platoon included a tank dozer, which he used to prepare positions for his tanks in a saddle on a ridge overlooking the Naktong. While the dozer worked one enemy artillery round came over and hit one of the hilltops on the ridge. At sundown on Aug. 31, the platoon moved into these positions overlooking the Naktong. Quinn's tank platoon was with G Co.'s 1st Platoon, commanded by LT Green (or Greene), a black officer. "An unusual circum-

stance then because the Ninth Infantry was segregated [at the time]," Quinn wrote.

He recalled that the enemy attacked Co. G's 2d and 3d Platoons but left Green's platoon pretty much alone. The 2d Platoon withdrew into the 1st Platoon's position, but contact was lost with the 3d. Enemy troops got into the rear of the 1st Platoon, so Quinn took a tank and "a couple of squads and...cleared [them out] and continued on back to the company CP," he wrote. "Captain Munoz was concerned about his 3d Platoon and so I volunteered to...counterattack up behind the 2d and 3d Platoon positions and see if I could reach them."

Quinn employed his entire tank platoon in the attack. "We engaged the North Koreans in a fierce firefight and then someone started yelling that we were firing at our own people, so we stopped." He tried to establish voice communication with the supposedly friendly troops. This was particularly difficult, since it was still dark. He noted that twin-40 and quad-.50 vehicles from the antiaircraft artillery battalion were in the 3d Platoon position, but he could see no firing from them.

These vehicles were from LT Higgins' platoon, D/82d AAA/AW Bn. He had three vehicles south of the town of Masuwon, on the boundary between the 9th and 23d Regiments and one north of it. These weapons were well forward on dikes overlooking the river. The 1st Section, 2d Platoon, B/82d AAA/AW Bn was also on a dike just to the north of Higgins, supporting C/23d Infantry. The enemy attack in this sector overran C/23d Infantry. The quad-.50 with this company got mired in mud and had to be abandoned. The crew walked four miles to reach friendly lines. The twin-40 withdrew with the remnants of C/23d toward Changnyong.

LT Higgins tried to withdraw his vehicles. He led them in a jeep toward the only exit road. Enroute, his jeep was ambushed in an enemy roadblock and Higgins was wounded in the face. Three of his vehicles then tried a different route, but found it impassable. They returned to the block and fought as infantrymen. The other vehicle made it through the block. Higgins, his platoon sergeant, Louis Goings, and a number of their men were captured. The enemy stripped the dead of their boots and left the bodies where they lay.

Meantime, Quinn wrote, "We decided to wait it out until morning and then see what we would do." Stragglers came into the perimeter all night and into the next day, Sept. 1. By midafternoon 350 men had gathered there, many of them wounded. Radio transmissions revealed that the 9th was in trouble all along the line and was withdrawing. Enemy roadblocks in rear of Co. G ambushed a jeep load of wounded which the unit had sent to the rear. Orders came for Co. G to hold; the 38th Infantry was to counterattack from the north.

Just north of the company perimeter was a dry creek bed running east and west. To its north was another ridgeline. The men expected the 38th Infantry to attack from that direction. When they saw troops on that ridgeline, they thought them to be from the 38th. A patrol, however, discovered the troops to be North Korean.

During the day, the enemy "put some pressure on us," Quinn recalled. "[W]ith the tanks we were able to keep them at bay, although we were heavily outnumbered.... As it started to get dark, I told Captain Muñoz that we would not be too effective at night if we were attacked, and that I was running low on ammunition for the tanks...so we decided that we would withdraw and try to get back to the MSR."

The wounded were loaded on two 2 1/2-ton trucks the company had. One section of tanks led the little column and the other section followed. Thus organized, the group started out along the dry creek bed. The bed was about five feet deep, providing cover for the infantrymen, and the tanks kept the enemy's heads down. In this manner, they succeeded in safely reaching the MSR. A South Korean outpost was located there. A phone call revealed that the 9th Infantry had left Yongsan. Quinn sent a tank section down the road to locate the 9th and have trucks and ambulances sent back for the 350 men. "Back came the trucks and ambulances and picked us up and we were then taken back to Yongsan," Quinn wrote. They reached Yongsan about nine or ten that night. The 72d Tk Bn was deployed on a ridge south and east of Yongsan, overlooking the town.

The Battle at Agok — Aug. 31 - Sept. 1

A/9th Infantry occupied a long finger near the river, north from Hill 95, opposite the Kihang Ferry. The road from Namji-ri crossed the Naktong at this point. The tiny village of Agok lay at the base of Hill 94. Near Agok, the Americans established a roadblock, with two rifle squads from Co. A, two medium tanks from A/72d Tk Bn and two AA vehicles from D/82d AA/AW Bn. One of these, an M-19, mounted twin-40mm guns and the other, an M-16, quad-.50. SFC Marian A. Ceylon commanded the two AA vehicles.

On the evening of Aug. 31 Co. A, in compliance with orders, moved off the finger into positions along the river below the ridge. One of the tanks from A/72d Tk Bn developed gun trouble. SGT Ernest R. Kouma brought another Pershing tank to Agok to replace it. He placed his tank to the west of Agok and about 40 yards from the Kihang ferry. A heavy fog rolled in from the river about 8 p.m. At 9 p.m., dogs were heard barking on the far shore of the Naktong and continued until enemy mortars began firing on American positions at 10 p.m. At 10:15 p.m., this fire extended into the positions of Co. A. U.S. artillery and mortars began counterbattery fire. Splashes could be heard from across the river.

The fog suddenly lifted about 10:30 p.m., to reveal a bridge under construction from the enemy's side of the river. It was almost two-thirds completed. SGT Kouma had the tank's main gun open fire on it, while he engaged the target with the .50-cal machine gun. The other tank (commanded by SFC Oscar V. Berry) and both AA vehicles joined the attack. Within a minute, the bridge collapsed and two minutes later the pontoon boats used to hold the bridge in place broke loose. Most of them were then sunk by machine gun fire. Then, except for the barking dogs and an occasional enemy mortar round, the area fell silent.

This quiet ended at 11 p.m. when a small-arms fight began suddenly on the left of Co. A north of the tanks. About two or three minutes after this gunfight started, the two rifle squads with the tanks and AA vehicles were ordered on their field phone to return to the main position. One of the infantrymen called out, "We are moving out, tankers." In his letter to Appleman, Kouma told what followed:

"The infantry outpost had hardly left when I spotted seven men running towards me from the direction of where Able Company's CP formerly was located. I halted them and noticed that they were wearing the division patch. One of them spoke excellent English. All seven came next to my tank...three of them crawled on the deck of the tank and informed me that a large force had crossed the river farther down approaching my position and that most of Able Company were killed or captured. At the time I had the idea that they were part of the 9th Infantry. During this time I was on top of the turret checking my .50-cal. machine-gun. At a given signal they leaped from the tank and began throwing grenades on the tank and about the same time a steady spray of machine gun and rifle fire began hitting the tanks and AA guns from the crest of the high bluff about 150 yards to my right. My gunner at once took them under fire as well as SFC Berry's and the AA guns. I got back in the turret and threw about 7 or 8 grenades over the house as well as inside the house through the door which faced us."

During one of many enemy attempts to destroy his tank, SGT Kouma opened the hatch of his tank so that he could man the .50-cal machine gun mounted on it. Exposed to heavy enemy fire, he manned the gun, killing and wounding a number of the enemy at point blank range. When the machine gun was empty, the Sergeant continued to fire on the enemy with his pistol and grenades. The tank remained in position for over nine hours, subjected to one enemy attack after another. Kouma was wounded twice.

The enemy attacked both tanks and the two AA vehicles. Using the correct password, the enemy was able to approach and capture the quad-.50. One crew member managed to escape. The dual-40 also escaped, although several crew members were wounded. Berry and Kouma were left alone with their two tanks. They moved the tanks to open ground which provided clear fields of fire for 200 yards in every direction. There the enemy made repeated attacks. Some enemy soldiers got within 20 yards of the tankers before being driven off, leaving their dead and wounded behind. Berry's tank engine began overheating about 1:30 a.m., and he informed Kouma that he was withdrawing. Berry's tank caught fire about a mile to the rear and it was abandoned. Kouma stayed in position all night.

By daylight, the enemy attack stopped. At 7:30 a.m., Kouma started back through enemy lines, firing into them in passing. His tank destroyed three enemy machine guns in this phase. SGT Kouma brought his tank and crew safely through eight miles of enemy-held territory into friendly lines. It was estimated that the tank had killed 250 enemy soldiers during its stand and withdrawal.

SFC Ceylon had to finally withdraw his AA vehicle due to running short of ammunition and a defective traversing mechanism. About a mile back, they met a tank crew, who gave them some ammunition. With this, SGT Ceylon and his crew were able to fight the enemy with their individual weapons until forced to withdraw to avoid capture. SGT Kouma was awarded the Medal of Honor and SGT Ceylon was awarded the Silver Star.

The enemy attack on Co. A hit the 1st Platoon near Agok and seemingly ignored 2LT Albert J. Fern, Jr.'s 2d Platoon to the north. (Fern was West Point Class of 1950). The North Koreans also heavily attacked Co. C, on his right. Two men came into Fern's position and reported that C Co. had been overrun. 1LT Adam B. Rodriguez, commanding Co. A, had to displace his CP back up the hill soon after the battle started. He ordered his company to pull back, too. Fern's platoon skirmished with a small group of the enemy enroute. Atop the hill, Co. A assembled and formed a perimeter. The rest of the night passed quietly for them.

At daylight, Co. A could see enemy soldiers on the surrounding hills. Most of the North Koreans were heading east. Several hours later, LT Fern sent a patrol down to Agok to retrieve some supplies left behind the night before. The patrol ran into some of the enemy, killing three of them and sustaining two casualties themselves. But the patrol returned with much needed ammunition, rations and water.

Still later in the morning enemy barges crossed the river, out of range, below Co. A's position. LT Rodriguez then sent a rifle squad and a light machine gun team to the southern tip of the ridge overlooking Agok to take these enemy troops under fire. About half way to this position, the squad found a critically wounded black soldier in the midst of 10 enemy dead. Taken back to the company CP, the man died that afternoon.

The squad detected enemy soldiers in Agok and reported this to LT Fern. He called for artillery fire, through the FO. A few minutes later, the artillery concentration came in on target, sending the enemy scurrying for the river. The light machine gun took them under fire, as did another machine gun from the 35th Infantry (25th Division) to the south. Then proximity fuse artillery fire felled great numbers of the fleeing enemy. It was later estimated that the combination of machine gun and artillery fire caused 300 enemy casualties.

That afternoon, light planes dropped food and ammunition to Company A. Only a part of it was recovered. The unit was ordered to withdraw that night.

Fern's platoon led out that night, heading east down the hill. As the column neared the bottom, men in the lead saw a column of some 400 enemy marching along the road about 200 yards below them. Several of them were pulling wheel-mounted machine guns. Rodriguez had the company circle back up the ridge, away from the road. Fern's platoon, with the company wounded (two on litters) was to bring up the rear. Carrying the litter cases in the rough terrain at night slowed the platoon so that it gradually fell behind. By the time Fern reached the bottom of the ridge, he had lost contact with the rest of the company.

At this point, a ferocious gunfight broke out ahead of Fern's platoon. Enemy machine gun fire

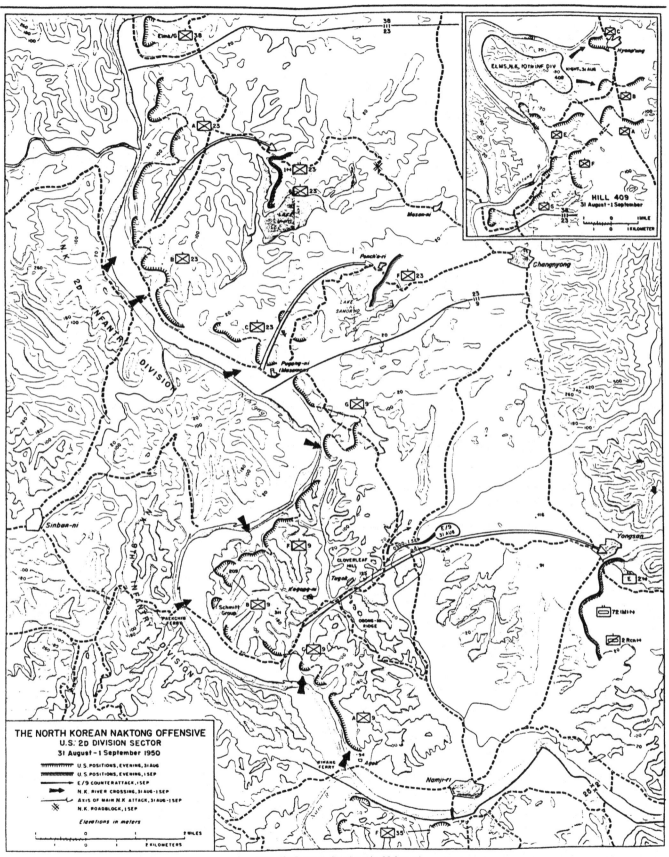

Map 42 (Source: South to the Naktong)

from this battle pinned his platoon down. He decided the safest thing to do with the wounded was to send them back into the ravine the platoon had just left. He put Platoon Sergeant Herbert H. Freeman in charge of them. He gave Freeman 10 men to help.

Rodriguez and the rest of the company had run into a large enemy force. He and most of the men with him were killed at close range. The survivors scattered. Some of these ran back and informed LT Fern. PFC Luther H. Story, a weapons squad leader, was posthumously awarded the Medal of Honor for his deeds that night. Although badly wounded, he refused to be carried along with the others. He stayed, fought and died, overwhelmed by enemy soldiers. Only about 10 of the men who had been with Rodriguez escaped.

Just before dawn, Fern decided that the platoon must try to escape before daylight. He sent a runner to notify Freemen, who should have been about 500 yards to the rear, to rejoin the platoon. The runner returned to report he could not find the platoon sergeant. Since there had been no firing to the rear, Fern deduced that Freeman had not encountered any enemy. He sent two other men back to search, but they returned without finding a trace of the sergeant, or the men with him.

Fern decided to waste no more time and try to get out with the men he had. Under the cloak of a heavy fog, so thick that one could barely see 25 yards, Fern and his men set out early Sept. 2. Using a compass, he headed toward Yongsan. The fog burned off by midmorning. At noon, the platoon crested a hill and saw the battle underway at Yongsan. Fern brought the 19 men with him into the lines of the 72d Tk Bn, near Yongsan that afternoon.

When he reported to his battalion commander, LTC John E. Londahl, Fern asked for permission to take a patrol back to search for SGT Freeman's party. Londahl denied the request because he needed every man possible for the defense of Yongsan.

SGT Freeman had taken his party back up to the top of the ridge during the battle in which LT Rodriguez was killed. There they stayed all day on Sept. 2, watching enemy activity all around the valley below. Freeman believed that most of Co. A had been killed or captured. He, the squad with him and the four wounded remained behind enemy lines for five days. Freeman then led them to safety. He was awarded the Distinguished Service Cross.

Co. C, just north of Co. A, also fared badly, being overrun early in the battle. The enemy employed green flares and whistles in a violent assault. There, another AA section, consisting of a quad-.50 and twin-40 from D/82d AA Battalion, under SGT Robert L. Wood, covered the withdrawal of Co. C. Many Charlie Co. men escaped into the Co. A perimeter, while many others made their way all the way south to the lines of the 35th Infantry (25th Division). On Sept. 2, the 25th reported that 110 men from C/9th Infantry had come into its lines.

SGT Wood wrote this: "About 11 P.M. the North Koreans came after us with everything they had. They just overran us. Took my M-19. I lost 3 men out of six.... My M-16 made it out OK with the loss of a few men, I found out later.

"We laid along the road that night [after the loss of the M-19]. We watched [the enemy] march by us for about 4 hours on the road. Then there was a break [and] we got across the road into a corn field."

The group that Wood was with included infantrymen, engineers, anti-aircraft crewmen and others. "About daybreak a machine gun opened up on us. We only lost 3 men.... We got into the mountains. Every time we tried to get water [the enemy] would machine gun us. It took us about 3 days to work our way out."

In his book, *82d AAA AW Battalion in Korea*, LTC Walter Killilea wrote that SGT Klosky was with this group. SGT Woods wrote that it was he, not Klosky. It is possible that Klosky and Wood were both in this group.

TF Manchu — Aug. 31 - Sept. 1

The Paekchin ferry crossing was located at the very nose of the Naktong Bulge. B/9th Infantry occupied Hill 209, about a mile east of the ferry site. On revised maps, this hill is numbered 210. In this narrative, it will be referred to as 210 in order to avoid confusion with another Hill 209, which was located north of Lake U-po. This Hill 209 was also the site of other fighting. The Paekchin ferry was about five miles north of Agok.

Near the end of August, two patrols from the 9th Infantry crossed the Naktong and from a hilltop observed enemy tank and troop movements about two miles west of the river. They correctly suspected the site was an enemy division CP, that of the *9th Division*. Based on these reports, and impelled by Walker's order to conduct aggressive patrolling, the 2d Division planned a reinforced company combat patrol across the river. Its mission was to attack the enemy division CP, destroy it, capture prisoners and seek information about enemy plans. On Aug. 25, COL John G. Hill, 9th Infantry CO, announced the plan for what was called "Operation Manchu," named for the regiment's nickname, the Manchu Regiment. COL Hill had proposed three crossing sites. GEN Keiser selected the one at the Paekchin ferry.

TF Manchu was built around the 9th Infantry reserve, Co. E. It included a section of light machine guns (two .30-cal light machine guns) attached from Co. H. The unit was further reinforced by 57mm recoilless rifles, 60mm mortars and demolition teams. In support were 15th FAB (-) (105mm); one battery, 38th FAB (155mm); Companies A and B, 72d Tk Bn; two quad-.50 and two twin 40mm vehicles (commanded by LT McCabe) from D/82d AAA/AW. Companies D and H, 9th Infantry, were each to provide one section of heavy machine guns (.30-cal water cooled guns), a section of 81mm mortars (two guns per section), and a section of 75mm recoilless rifles (two rifles). A platoon (four mortar tubes) of 4.2 inch mortars was also in direct support. The 1st Platoon, D/2d Engineers was to transport the assault elements of the Task Force across the Naktong in assault boats the night of Aug. 31. The entire force, including the engineer platoon, numbered nearly 700 men. The redeployment of tanks, AAA/AW vehicles, allocation of artillery support, machine guns, mortars and recoilless rifles further thinned out the already over-extended 9th Infantry, making it even more vulnerable to enemy attack.

Of course, Keiser, Hill and others realized this; taking weapons and troops for TF Manchu was a calculated risk. In their minds, the potential dividends of a successful raid obviously offset the risks. Unfortunately, concentrating many of these weapons and men well forward played into the enemy's hands.

First Lieutenants Charles I. Caldwell (Co. D) and Edward Schmitt (Co. H) brought their men and weapons to the base of Hill 210. within Baker Co.'s perimeter just after dark on Aug. 31. Co. E was still in its reserve position some two miles west of Yongsan, preparing to move up with the engineer platoon. The two officers oriented their section leaders on where they wanted the weapons emplaced. Carrying parties, with weapons and ammo, soon followed. Meantime COL Hill, his S3 and Thomas A. Lombardo (West Point, 1945), Keiser's aide-de-camp, had come forward with the 4.2 inch mortar platoon to its position at the base of Hill 210. The mortarmen began setting up their weapons. It was a little after 9 p.m., and full dark.

CPT Lewis B. Sheen, the regimental chaplain, and his assistant had gone forward that afternoon (Thursday, Aug. 31) to conduct services in B/9th Infantry. Services were conducted at 3:30 p.m. Afterward, the Chaplain "visited around," as he put it. He continues: "Just before supper, LT. Cary [C.O., Co. B] returned with the information that we [Co. B] were to make certain preparations to cover the patrol of the following morning. [This was TF Manchu.] All the company, or most of it, was to move from its positions on the hill, and go down to the edge of the river and dig in.... When it became dark enough, the men started to move out. I went up to the top of the hill where the company OP was located.... LT Cary soon came up, and I moved over into the foxhole with him and a sergeant, and we started to settle down for the evening.

"Before long, however, we thought we could hear the sound of swishing water, and after looking closely at the river through field glasses, we could make out lines of North Koreans wading across the river. I don't recall that at the time we heard any firing.... It later developed that the men who had gone down to dig in were caught red handed just across the road that ran along the base of our hill." When these men reached the bottom of the hill, they had no time to dig in before the enemy attacked. The North Koreans were upon them before they realized what was happening.

"Most of them [Co. B men] hid in rice paddies and under bridges. This occurred at about 2100 hours [9 p.m.]. We watched and waited, hearing an occasional shot fired, but outside of that, only deadly silence broken occasionally by the sound of more troops wading across the Naktong. On the hill to the left of us, our artillery observer was firing a mission, and in the distance to the west, we could see the flash of an enemy artillery piece firing over us," Sheen continued.

"At 2300 hours [11 p.m.], our calm was shattered by an enemy artillery and mortar barrage which continued until 0100 hours [1 a.m.]. The air above us was solid with singing lead for those two hours. Some of it landed near us, and we could hear the whine of shrapnel flying through the air. But most of the barrage seemed to be aimed at Hill 311, just behind us, and farther to the rear. During the barrage, SGT Segars and the remnants of his platoon came back up on our hill, and the sergeant dispersed his men among foxholes in a pretty good perimeter defense"

This initial enemy crossing at the Paekchin ferry also caught the 4.2 inch mortar platoon setting up their weapons and most of the men from D and H Companies at the base of Hill 210, about a half mile from the crossing site. Many of these men were quickly captured. COL Hill escaped, but his S3 and Lombardo were killed. The first carrying party for the heavy weapons was about half way up the hill when the enemy overpowered the men at its foot. The party quickly made its way to the top, joining the advance group. There the two groups dug in a small perimeter. The enemy left them alone for the remainder of the night.

SGT Richard L. Feaser, a member of the 4.2 inch Mortar Company FDC, wrote that "this is where we lost LT Bruce Bromley and much of one of our platoons."

"At 9:30 on August 31, LT Bromley, myself and our Third Platoon moved to Agok to support the 1 September crossing [of Co. E] of the 9th several hundred yards upstream," wrote MSG Lester H. Thomas, of the Heavy Mortar Company.

"LT [Rolfe L.] Hillman [Jr., West Point 1945] helicoptered across the Naktong as observer.... He reported no enemy sighted. I spent 4 hours observing with field glasses, sighting none — no movement. One platoon of D Company was 300 yds to our right on a small hill.

"About 9 p.m. I heard some sound like a mess kit dropping on a rock and some water sounds. I looked through the glasses. (I was told later that they [the enemy] had at least 2 companies across and were already on the road to our left.) We left a few [mortar rounds] go and went out of action; secured our equipment."

Just after the platoon left this area, what Thomas described as "a respectable artillery barrage" hit where they had been. Mortar Company headquarters informed the platoon that it was displacing to Yongsan and that it could not send trucks to carry out the mortars ammunition and equipment. The platoon was ordered to try to carry out the baseplates, but to throw the tubes and ammunition into a lake they would be passing on the way to the rear. Thomas, a combat veteran of Pacific fighting in WW II, wrote that this was the first time he had ever had to abandon equipment.

"There were three firefights [going on] behind us now, plus Companies B and D to our right. The enemy ignored us, so we were able to hide our base plates and tubes in the lake." Thomas, and the men with him made good their withdrawal. However, eleven members of the platoon split off and joined the machine guns of Co. D, which were in Co. B's position. These men became part of the group who were cut off with LT Edward Schmitt, H/9th Infantry.

Thomas wrote that LT Raymond McDaniel was also with the Schmitt group. He was wounded in the head and thrown into the Naktong by enemy soldiers. Some men from the 35th Infantry fished him, still alive, out of the river several miles downstream.

Thomas's party of about a dozen men got to the old HM Co. CP about 3 a.m. It was occupied by the enemy, so the men went on, headed for Tugok. They, and a group of enemy soldiers, arrived at Tugok at the same time. Friendly tanks began firing; the enemy went one way, and the mortarmen joined the tanks. These tanks were protecting a battery of the 15th FAB, which was preparing to displace. Thomas recalled that CPT James Beaver and SGT Kouma were with these tanks. It was Sept. 1. CPT Beaver pressed Thomas and his mortarmen into service as infantry for a counterattack, with tanks, to keep the enemy at bay while the artillery displaced. "We advanced 3/4 of the way on tanks," Thomas recalled. "Then got off beside them. We did fair, as the only assault training we had was in basic."

Here LT Bromley, CPT Beaver, SGT Cox and a number of others, were killed, Thomas recalled, but the scratch tank-infantry team held the ridge for two hours, allowing the artillery to get safely away. MSG Thomas's platoon had numbered 33 men on the morning of Aug. 31. At noon, it numbered just nine men, "and that was just the start," he concluded.

From his position in Co. B's perimeter, Chaplain Sheen could hear the noise of battle. "When the barrage lifted at 0100 hours [1 a.m.], 1 Sept., the enemy began attacking the hills on which our troops were so thinly spread. They started way up to the right in the second Battalion area, and worked their way down. We could hear their cries of 'Manzai!' and the air was lighted up with all sorts of flares. At the same time, we could hear men working up to our right on what must have been their underwater bridge, and soon the sound of tanks and trucks and shouting men. Once in a while the two-beat of a Korean drum could be heard above the rest of the commotion. Every so often, after a fierce firefight, we could hear a massed shout, which I took to be the Koreans gloating over the capture of our hills."

At 3 a.m., a truck stopped at the foot of B Company's hill, and a whistle was blown. A North Korean leader shouted "Manzai!" and enemy troops started up the slope to Co. B. "We let them have it," Sheen wrote. "The [enemy] attempt was rather half-hearted, and before long they passed on to the hill on our left. We prayed for daylight, and once in a while, we would shoot at a Korean trying to get up the hill." While Co. B defended itself, there were firefights all around them, to include on Hill 314, to the rear.

With dawn came a renewed enemy effort to subdue Co. B. Eight enemy soldiers had crept within grenade range of an American machine gun on the unit right flank. They tried to knock out the gun with grenades, fatally wounding one of the crew. In the end, all eight enemy soldiers were killed, and the gun remained in operation. As the day progressed, ammunition became critical, and there was little carbine or M-1 ammunition in reserve. The machine gun had three boxes (750 rounds, total) and there were a few rounds left for the 60 and 81 mm mortars.

Then they spotted a group of North Koreans with a horse-drawn artillery piece down to the right. The enemy was taken under rifle fire and scattered; some went back across the Naktong. Other soldiers took their places, trying to get the gun into position. To Sheen, these enemy troops

seemed different from others he had seen. They were taller and were wearing packs. Some men thought, at first, that they were Americans. "But their persistent efforts to get the field piece into position soon convinced us that they were enemy," Sheen wrote. Then some men on the left flank spotted an enemy ammunition truck. This was set on fire by mortar fire. "The sound of the thing blowing up was music to our ears," Sheen recalled.

The enemy's attack was a complete surprise. Catching, as it did, the regimental CO and a number of men from several companies not dug in and not expecting an enemy attack, it created chaos in the center of the 9th Infantry's line. Reports from other sectors, and the very heavy enemy mortar and artillery barrages caused the 2d Division to cancel Operation Manchu at 11:55 p.m.

Most of the men of the 9th Infantry were unaware that the operation had been called off. Besides, they were too busy with their own little units and groups of individual situations. This applied to Co. B, which had expended a considerable amount of their rapidly dwindling supply of ammunition on the enemy field piece and ammo truck. "It began to dawn on us," Sheen wrote, "That we were ill-prepared to fight off any determined attack that night.... We guessed that from the trouble we had caused that morning, there was little doubt but that they would try to eradicate us during the night. LT Cary, after taking due notice of...[the] shortage of food, ammunition and water, decided that we had better get out with whole hides, if possible.... We determined to try to make it up to Hill 311.... As preparation, we sent two scouts on about an hour ahead of us, to try to get to 311 and determine the nature of the troops there.

Co. B and the troops with it, were divided into two groups for the trip to Hill 311. They were joined by about 15 men from the hill on the left, which included AAA men and an artillery FO party. As the groups climbed a hill just west of Hill 311, they noticed troops coming down the forward slope toward them and taking position behind a slight rise. Some of the GIs thought these to be friendly troops and began to wave and shout. There was no response. It suddenly became apparent that the troops were enemy. Trading shots with them, the Americans scrambled over a ridge away from them. After creeping along this ridge, which was parallel to Hill 311, the men dug in. One soldier skylined himself, Sheen recalled, and was shot in the back and right eye by enemy snipers. The ridge was very steep and a poor position. The wounded man had to be propped against a few trees to keep him from rolling down the hill. Finally, LT Cary decided that they could not stay there.

As darkness fell, they moved out again, with MSG Beard and SGT Fairfield, both from the FO party, in the lead. Fairfield was limping along on a wounded heel. The strain of battle, being on the move to evade the enemy, lack of food and water, and the tension of being behind enemy lines began taking its toll on the men. Many involuntarily dozed off during rest stops. Finally, LT Cary counted his men, discovering that only thirty of them were present. He went back for the stragglers. It was about 2 a.m., Sept. 2. They had reached the old site of the 4.2 inch mortars on the east side of Hill 311. As the party crossed the road at that point, they were discovered by some enemy, who took them under fire. The whole party "slammed head first into a rice paddy," Sheen wrote. "Then crawled on our bellies like reptiles through several more of them." Making good their escape, they next came upon a north-south road, from which they could see Obong-ni Ridge and Hill 165.

SGT Heard asked if it would be best to continue toward Hill 165, or head north toward the 23d Infantry. It was decided to hide out for the remainder of the night and make a decision in the morning. At 6 a.m., Sheen and others were awakened by the sounds of men digging in and the voices speaking Korean. They were in the midst of an enemy unit! The Americans decided to break out. SGT Fairfield found a weak spot in the enemy line. The party set out stealthily, evading one party of four enemy soldiers, but were soon discovered by others. An enemy burp gun cut loose. The Americans returned fire and ran out of the enemy perimeter, then headed north. Some enemy soldiers followed and the GIs traded occasional shots with them.

After traveling north for some distance, the men found a mountain stream to fill their canteens, then headed east toward the MSR. At one point they were able to see the former site of 2/9th Infantry's CP. But, seeing tanks there, and unsure whose they were, the party did not approach the CP. Finally, about 3 p.m. on Sept. 2, they reached the MSR near Yongsan. The sounds of battle came from the direction of the town. An eight man patrol was sent to investigate, but quickly returned, having been chased by a large group of the enemy. The party then turned toward Changnyong. In the village of Changnak, they came upon a stalled tank dozer. In it they found several large cans of beets, a five gallon can of water and two cartons of cigarettes. The beets, water and cigarettes were rationed out and then prepared to continue the march. The beets were the first food the men had since Aug. 31.

Before they could start out again, four tanks from the 72d Tk Bn arrived to establish a roadblock. Chaplain Sheen's group stayed with the tankers that night. The next morning the tanks went to assist in a counterattack by the 9th Infantry and Marine Brigade and Sheen's party went on to the 23d Infantry CP. Finally, Sheen got a ride to the 9th Infantry CP, borrowed a 3/4-ton truck from the HM Co., and transported his men back to the 9th's CP. Their odyssey ended at 4:30 p.m., Sept. 4. "We all arrived back at the 9th CP, very happy souls, not to mention thankful," Chaplain Sheen wrote.

On Aug. 1, near Taegu, LT Gene N. Lam was assigned to 2/9th Infantry as its Battalion Surgeon. "I met my medics on a tranquil hillside," he wrote. "I assumed command of the 2d Battalion Aid Station on Aug. 3 and for the first time met the rest of my Aidmen, as well as the Battalion Staff. Not so incidentally, all medics were issued arms and any indication that we were medics was not present. Never before had medics been armed or unidentified." Lam was the 2d Battalion Surgeon when the 9th Infantry was attached to the 24th Division during the First Battle of the Naktong Bulge.

Lam wrote about medical evacuation and treatment during the Naktong Bulge battles.

"Evacuation was a medical nightmare," he wrote. "The battalion was extended probably 15-20 miles along the river. If a man were seriously wounded, he usually was dead by the time he reached the Aid Station. Those who survived the initial trip were transported to the Regimental Collecting Station 15 miles away. The lucky one reached a MASH at Miryang, 35 miles away." What Lam wrote applied to the medical evacuation and treatment of casualties in any battalion defending along the Naktong in August and September 1950.

"I moved an Aid Station near the river to support [the Operation Manchu] attack," he wrote, "but by morning was in full retreat with what wounded we could carry. We were pushed back toward Yongsan, not knowing where to go."

The Schmitt Group — Aug. 31 - Sept. 4

The men from Companies D and H who had made it up the hill before the enemy overran the valley on the night of August 31 - September 1, were on a southern knob of Hill 210. The knob was about 150 meters high and a half mile across a saddle from Co. B's higher position. During the night a few more men wandered into their perimeter. In all, the group probably numbered between 60 and 70 EM and five officers. A count was never made. The officers included LT Schmitt (H/9th Inf.); LT Caldwell (D/9th Inf.); LT Raymond J. McDoniel (Plt Ldr, D/9th Inf.); LT Paul E. Kremser (Plt Ldr, H/9th Inf.) and LT Edmund J. Lilly III (Plt Ldr, B/9th Inf., West Point 1950). They had one SCR-300 radio; 2 heavy machine guns (1 operable); 2 light machine guns; 1 BAR; about 20 M-1 rifles and about 40 carbines and pistols.

During the night, LT Schmitt made radio contact with 1/9th Infantry and was told that he would get help the following day. In the morning (September 1) he found that the enemy occupied Co. B's old position atop Hill 210 and that the enemy was continuing to move supplies and equipment across the Naktong.

About 2 P.M., the enemy made his first attack on the Schmitt perimeter, but were repulsed. An estimated enemy company attacked three times that night, but were driven off without penetrating the perimeter. Daylight on September 2 revealed many enemy dead scattered on the steep slopes.

That day CPL Clovis Taylor, a machine gunner from Co. H with the Schmitt group, was wounded during one of the enemy attacks. He refused medical aid, saying that, they should be used on men injured more seriously than himself.

CPL William R. Swafford was a member of a 75mm recoilless rifle crew who found himself with the Schmitt group. He recalled running up the hill to escape advancing enemy troops, of digging in a Korean cemetery, and of a tank or SP gun firing at their position. He wrote that a bazooka team went down into the valley and destroyed the enemy weapon. Of the enemy crossings, he recalled: "I could hear vehicles and N. Koreans coming across the Naktong River all night and the nights following my stay on the hill." He also wrote that the enemy night attack was accompanied by the blowing of whistles.

After the night battle of September 1, the shortage of hand grenades became acute. Swafford wrote: "[A] man stood up in his hole [the morning of September 1] and began shooting his M1 rifle at N. Koreans. He killed 3 of them; one he hit blew up. He was carrying ammo or something." The man Swafford refers to was probably MSG Travis E. Watkins (Co. H). About 9 a.m., Watkins shot and killed two enemy soldiers about 50 yards outside the northeast side of the perimeter. He then jumped from his hole to get the weapons and grenades from the dead men. About 20 yards from them three enemy soldiers jumped from hiding and fired on him. Watkins killed the three, took the weapons, ammunition and insignia from all five enemy dead, and returned to the perimeter.

Around 10 a.m. six enemy soldiers made their way to a protected spot 25 yards from a perimeter machine gun position and began grenading it. Watkins, although already wounded in the head, rose from his foxhole and began firing at them. As he did so, enemy machine-gun fire struck him in the left side, breaking his back. In spite of this, Watkins managed to kill all six of the enemy before sliding down in his hole, paralyzed from the waist down. Valiantly, Watkins shouted encouragement to his comrades. He would not accept any rations, saying he did not deserve them, since he could not fight.

CPL Taylor observed a long column of enemy climbing Hill 210 carrying large mortars which, if set up on that promontory, could be used against the Schmitt perimeter. Anticipating that the enemy column would stop for a rest, he had his machine gunners hold fire. When the enemy troops did stop, he ordered his guns to fire, cutting down 67 of them and destroying the mortars.

That afternoon (Sept. 2), Schmitt radioed a request for an airdrop of supplies. A division liaison plane made the drop, but the perimeter was so small and the hill slopes so steep that almost everything fell to the enemy. "Spotter planes came in . . . and dropped duffel bags [filled with C-rations], ammo and 5 gal cans of water; also cans of beer," Swafford wrote. "The duffel bags of food bounced off the hill. The water cans burst on impact with the ground. We recovered some of the ammo and cans of beer. During the airdrop I was afraid some of the items would fall into our foxhole."

Limited supplies were salvaged from a drop made at 7 p.m. These included a case of carbine ammunition, 2 boxes of machine gun ammunition, 11 hand grenades, part of a package of medical supplies, 2 1/2 cases of rations and 21 cans of beer.

PFC Joseph R. Ouellette, Co. H, went out of the perimeter to get some of the airdropped water cans, but found them all broken and empty. He also left the perimeter a number of times to gather weapons, grenades and ammunition from enemy dead. On one such trip, he killed an attacking enemy soldier in hand-to-hand combat.

"That afternoon a twin engine plane (DC-3) came flying through the valley, the side door...was open," Swafford wrote. "I thought troops would be dropped, but instead, it circled back into the valley and strafed the N. Koreans with a .50-cal M.G. from the plane's open door.

"The same day two jet fighter planes came

and strafed and rocketed vehicles that were by the knocked out tank. I saw two N. Koreans leave the road running and leaping down the hill, with the planes strafing them. They both made it to a ditch and the planes left."

That afternoon, the enemy sent an American POW to Schmitt with the threat: "You have one hour to surrender or be blown to pieces." It was fairly obvious that the enemy planned to stop infantry assaults and shift to pounding the perimeter into submission by observed mortar and other heavy weapons fire. The enemy didn't wait an hour; forty-five minutes after delivering the ultimatum, they opened up with antitank fire and with two machine guns from the north and higher up the ridge. These weapons were soon joined by enemy mortars positioned on a finger ridge to the east. The mortars registered in on the perimeter, then pounded it until dark. After dark, enemy infantry attacked again and again. All were repulsed, but each had created more American casualties. Food, water and ammunition were all badly needed. The medical supplies remaining were just those carried by an aidman.

LT Schmitt was wounded that evening while helping to retrieve airdropped supplies, but retained command. Appleman wrote that he "encouraged the diminishing group by his example."

Sunday, Sept. 3 was the worst day to date. It was stiflingly hot and the men were completely out of water. Food for the day consisted of one can of C-rations per man. For close to twelve hours, now enemy mortar and concentrated machine gun fire had alternated with infantry attacks. Survivors later estimated that there were about 20 separate infantry attacks — all of them repulsed. Dead or dying GIs were in almost every foxhole. Mortar fire destroyed the radio. Requested artillery and air strikes never materialized. Enemy machine gun and mortar fire continued throughout the day.

The CP was hit and LT Schmitt was killed. LT McDoniel, D/9th Infantry took command. Under this enemy fire North Korean soldiers crept within grenade range then rained grenades into the perimeter. Six times Ouellette jumped from his foxhole to escape exploding grenades. Each time he did, enemy soldiers fired at him from close range. At last, he was killed. So many mortar rounds landed within the perimeter that, eventually, most foxholes had taken one or more direct hits.

Swafford wrote graphically of this: "[T]he N. Koreans mortared the hill for several hours then attacked us with small arms. The CP was knocked out by a mortar; all the men were killed and radio destroyed. I looked just below me about 8 feet and saw Saylors and Simmons, sitting in their hole, dead. A mortar [round] fell in their foxhole.... The N. Koreans tried to take the hill two or three times that night. One man behind me got out of his hole and was shot in the stomach.... He was crying for a medic to help him. He died in about three minutes."

CPL Taylor distinguished himself again on September 3. Standing in the open, he killed 25 enemy soldiers that day with his rifle.

Relief, in the form of rain, came to the beleaguered Americans. LT McDoniel spread out two blankets, which had been included in an airdrop. When wrung out, the blankets produced 5 gallons of water. The men took off their cloth-

ing to soak up enough rainwater to fill their canteens.

Apparently some of the men broke under the strain of the past several days, jumped from their holes and tried to escape. They were all killed. Swafford recalled: "Three men and the man in the hole with me left the hill. I did not go because I thought it would be safe[r] to go alone. They made a lot of noise going down the hill. I think they reached the road below when I heard small arms fire that lasted about three minutes. Then it was silent."

CPL Swafford was scared and very thirsty. He decided to go in search of water. "So I went quietly down the hill," he recounted. "I came to a rice paddy and drank all the water I could hold." He then went on down to the road. "I was walking on the road when I heard North Koreans coming up...behind me. I jumped in the ditch beside the road, face down. The N. Koreans stepped within 15 feet of me. One Korean said something and shined a flashlight up the ditch over me. I thought I was going to be shot. but instead, they crossed the ditch onto a path and left. They thought I was dead."

Swafford got up and again walked along the road until he heard the sound of approaching vehicles. He moved about a hundred feet off the road and sat down. As the vehicles approached, a propeller-driven plane came over and dropped a flare. The enemy trucks stopped and North Korean soldiers jumped from them and headed toward Swafford. He moved away from them. When the plane did not come back, the enemy soldiers returned to their vehicles and drove off.

Swafford found a small stand of pines and decided to hide there. He cut down two of the small trees (each about four feet tall) with his pocket knife. "I backed up against one tree and put the other two in front of me," he wrote. "To my surprise, I had not gone very far that night. I could see the hill I just left that night. I saw the N. Koreans go up the hill, firing their weapons and into the foxholes. There was another N. Korean patrol about 125 feet from me. [They were] watching also." (See Chapter Notes.)

At daylight on Sept. 4, only Lieutenants McDoniel and Caldwell and about half of the men who had taken refuge on the hill were still alive. By the end of the day, ammunition was down to about one clip per M-1 rifle, a few grenades, and no help in sight. McDoniel decided to make a break after dark. He told Caldwell that the men would split up into small groups and try to return to friendly lines. Shortly after dark, enemy leaders tried to get their men to launch another infantry assault. Shouted orders and cries of "Manzai!" failed to get the enemy soldiers to move. The "attack" consisted of a few hand grenades. The North Korean infantrymen had enough.

At 10 p.m., McDoniel and Caldwell and 27 EM slipped out of the perimeter in groups of four. Only SGT Watkins remained behind. He refused to go along. "I'm helpless and I'd only be a burden," he said.

"The last time we saw him," said SGT Grover Bozarth, "he was wearing a big smile and wishing the survivors the best of luck on the way out."

The two officers started off together, planning to go down to the river and follow it south toward the 25th Division sector. But there was

so much enemy activity on the road that they had to wait about an hour for the tanks, artillery and carrying parties to get by before they could cross. There, they found themselves in an enemy artillery battery position. Escaping unobserved, the two officers hid in a field near the river at daybreak. They became separated that night when running away from an enemy outpost. Two North Koreans captured Caldwell the next morning, took his boots and identification, hit him on the head with a rock and threw him over a cliff into the Naktong. Not badly hurt, Caldwell pretended to be dead and escaped that night. On Sept. 10 he entered positions of the 72d Tk Bn.

CPL Taylor again rose to the occasion on Sept. 4. He led six men out of the little perimeter that night. He brought four of the six through enemy territory and several firefights.

Twenty-nine men escaped from their hill position the night of Sept. 4. Twenty-two reached friendly lines. Many of them followed the Naktong downstream, hiding by day and traveling at night toward the 25th Division.

CPL William Swafford was not one of them. After hiding in the pines all day, he set out on the road that night. Nearing a bridge, he heard someone under it. He made a wide detour into a field along the Naktong. "I walked about 3 hundred feet and came upon a foxhole. I got in the foxhole. Lying next to the hole was a blanket rolled up with dried rice on it. Two small bowls and chop sticks were [also] lying next to the hole. I heard two N. Koreans talking. They were coming from the direction that I just came. I crawled out of the hole into some weeds, about six feet away. One N. Korean got into the hole beside me and the other Korean got into another hole several feet past this one."

Swafford waited until the two enemy soldiers began to snore, then crawled away about 100 to 150 feet to a stream about 10 feet wide. He almost drowned when he went in over his head in stepping into it. Some way, he got to the other side and up onto the creek bank. He then walked to a nearby hut about six feet square, built on pilings about five feet off the ground. He crawled into the hut and fell asleep. The next morning he was awakened by two Koreans talking. They were under the hut eating. "They stopped talking and one of them reached up and got my carbine, that was lying next to the hut entrance," Swafford wrote.

"Then they pulled me down. They slapped me three or four times.... [They] took me back to a village. In the village were more soldiers, men and women. One of the women gave me a boiled sweet potato." The enemy soldiers then made Swafford strip to his shorts, including his boots and took him back across the Naktong over knocked out steel bridge which had been put back in service with heavy wooden timbers. Swafford remained a POW until freed at Namwon by advancing U.S. troops.

The survivors reported valuable information about enemy activity at and near the Paekchin ferry site. At the ferry itself, the enemy had constructed an underwater bridge. A little way downstream they placed a metal floating bridge across the river every night and took it up before dawn the next day. Appleman wrote that "carrying parties of 50 civilians guarded by four soldiers crossed the river continuously at night at a dog-trot, an estimated total of 800-1,000 carriers being used at this crossing site."

Privates James F. Brisco and Vincent A. Krepps were each responsible for single-handedly saving, then driving to safety, an anti-aircraft vehicle of D/82d AAA/AW Bn. At about 11 p.m. on Aug. 31, the crew of the AA vehicle which Brisco was in had to abandon it because of "superior enemy forces," in the words of his Silver Star citation. Heavy enemy fire prevented Brisco from exiting the vehicle. He waited while most of the enemy went on. However, when two enemy soldiers prepared to destroy the vehicle with hand grenades, he shot both of them. At dawn on Sept. 1, Brisco discovered that there were no enemy nearby. Brisco knew that AA half tracks were valuable to the defense. Therefore, although he had no experience driving half tracks, he started it and drove several miles to friendly lines. He was under intense enemy mortar and small-arms fire most of the distance and smashed through at least one enemy roadblock.

PVT Krepps' battery was preparing to defend itself against an enemy attack. He saw that a disabled AA firing vehicle was blocking the road preventing a tank from passing. Krepps dashed out, crossed several hundred yards of ground swept by heavy enemy fire to the vehicle and was able to move the weapon enough to allow the tank to pass. Krepps then made emergency repairs to the vehicle and drove it back to the battery perimeter. All this time he and the vehicle were the targets of enemy AT and mortar fire. Once inside the perimeter, he organized a crew for the recovered weapon and commanded it until the enemy was repulsed.

About 3 a.m., on Sept. 1, COL Hill ordered Co. E, his only reserve company (which was to have been the main element of TF Manchu) to move west on the Yongsan-Naktong River road and establish a block at the pass between Obong-ni Ridge and Cloverleaf Hill. This point was three miles east of the river and about six miles west of Yongsan. This is the same area fought over so fiercely during the First Battle of the Naktong Bulge about two weeks previously. Tankers from A/72d Tk Bn had begun fighting at this pass at 2:30 a.m. At that time MSG Jack A. Mac Sloarrow's tank knocked out a T-34 at Tugok.

Most of Cloverleaf Hill and Obong-ni Ridge were in enemy hands before dawn on Sept. 1. Appleman stated that these two terrain features were "the best defensive terrain between Yongsan and the river." Now, in the southern portion of its sector, the 2d Division had to try to defend on the low hodgepodge of hills west of the town: poor defensive terrain.

Calamity in the Center — Aug. 31 - Sept. 1

The 23d Regiment relieved 3/38th Infantry along the Naktong just north of the 9th Infantry on Aug. 29. The regiment had but two battalions available for a 16,000 yard front. LTC Claire E. Hutchin Jr.'s 1/23d manned the river front, outposting the "line" with all three rifle companies. The 2d Battalion (LTC James W. Edwards) was in reserve about eight miles to the rear, commanding the regimental road net. Co. C, 72d Tk Bn supported the 23d Infantry, along with B/82d AAA/AW Bn.

On Aug. 31, the 2d Division took E/23d Infantry from this reserve battalion and moved it south into the 9th Infantry sector.

Two roads ran east through the regimental sector from the river to Changnyong. The southern road was the main route to that town. It went from Pugong-ni (Masuwon) near the Naktong, skirted the northern shore of Lake Samor-ho to Poncho-ri, then on to Changnyong. The northern road led east from a junction with a north-south route that more or less paralleled the Naktong. It then curved around marshland and Lakes Mok-po, U-po and Saji-po, through the town of Masan-ni. It then trended southeast to join the southern road about a half mile west of Changnyong. The 2d Battalion was deployed to cover these two routes.

Along the river, Co. A in the north outposted over five miles of hills near the river. A section of heavy machine guns and a section of 81mm mortars were attached to Co. A from Co. D. Twenty thousand rounds of machine gun ammunition and 300 rounds of 81mm mortar ammunition were stockpiled on site. To the south, across a gap of about a half mile, Co. B was scattered across another three and a quarter miles or so of hills. Co. D attached a section of 75mm recoilless rifles to the unit. A gap over a half mile wide existed between Co. B and Co. C. Co. C had the 2d Platoon on the right, nearest Co. B, the 1st Platoon on the left to the boundary with the 9th Infantry to the south. The two platoons covered about two miles near the river. The 3d Platoon was in rear of the front along a series of hills about a mile long. The company CP was with the 3d Platoon. A section each of heavy machine guns, 81mm mortars and 75mm recoilless rifles were attached to the company. The 81s had almost 300 rounds available at the tubes when the fighting began.

"We had good vision to the front," wrote Richard L. Ballenger, an assistant BAR-man in the 2d Squad, 2d Platoon of Co. C, "but at night the gap to our right [between B and C companies] concerned us. Our 1st Platoon overlooked a road junction which was important to the approach to Changnyong."

At 10:50 a.m. on Aug. 31, a PFC Nuzzo brought an enemy map into the D/23d Infantry CP. It showed the left part of the battalion sector. The enemy had circled the location of the D company observation post in red. Nuzzo had found the map the previous night near a town in the sector. At 7 p.m. that day, CPT Tassey, commanding D/23d Infantry moved his CP closer to the right of the battalion sector. He had good communication to the elements attached out in this part of the sector, but none to the others some 17 miles away in the other part of the sector.

As if extended frontages which could only be outposted was not enough, the 2d Division also had to contend with ammunition shortages (as did other forces on the Perimeter). The 2d Division history records critical shortages of ammunition for 57mm recoilless rifles, 105mm howitzers, 60mm, 81mm and 4.2 inch mortars and 3. inch rocket launchers. As noted above, certain tank main gun ammunition was also in short supply. The problem of shortages of ammunition plagued Walker's Eighth Army from early September into October, 1950. At the time, soldiers on the Perimeter did not know what caused these shortages.

In retrospect, however, it is fairly obvious that the shortages in September were caused because MacArthur's headquarters was diverting large quantities for the Inchon landing. The problem continued into October because MacArthur decided to redeploy the U.S. X Corps out of Inchon harbor and onto the east coast of North Korea. This so tied up Inchon that it was almost impossible to get any supplies in through that harbor. This left Pusan, in October, far to the rear. All supplies had then to be transported by road and rail to division supply points hundreds of miles away.

The two main enemy thrusts in the 23d Infantry sector were through the right flank of Co. B and then veered north behind Co. A before turning east along the northern road to Changnyong. The second thrust was through the positions of the 1st and 3d Platoons, C/23d Infantry and along the southern road to Changnyong.

The story was the same in the 23d's sector as in the 9th's; some enemy forces attacked forward positions while other forces bypassed through gaps to strike CPs, supply points, artillery and mortar positions and to ambush reinforcements in roadblocks. By daylight strong enemy forces were across the Naktong in both regimental sectors.

"It came on the evening of August 31," wrote Richard L. Ballenger, of C/23d Infantry. "Sergeant Graham, our acting platoon leader, sent the First Squad down to an outpost position for the night.... I was uneasy because during the day we lost contact with [the] company CP and I had to string communication wire to the command post." Ballenger found that the old wire had been cut. His report of this at the CP was ignored. Ballenger took a different route back to the platoon and made the same report to SGT Graham, who posted additional LPs.

At about 10:30 p.m., Ballenger's foxhole mate, CPL Wallace, woke him to say "there was a lot of extra activity going on all along the front." Within a half hour, the platoon outpost opened fire. A heavy volume of fire broke out from that direction. "Wallace said to me, 'I think we have lost our First Squad, get prepared.' About this time...mortar rounds and small-arms fire came in on us. SGT Graham came over and said to Wallace, 'Get your BAR over on the right and cover our flank.'" Wallace jumped from the hole, with Ballenger right behind him. As they ran to the flank, a friendly 57mm recoilless rifle fired. Wallace had cleared the backblast area before the gun fired, but Ballenger had not. The backblast knocked Ballenger down, but he was all right.

Arriving on the flank, as ordered, Wallace put the BAR into action. The enemy, however, ignored the two men and the BAR. "They only wanted to get by us," Ballenger remarked. About 3 a.m., Sept. 1, SGT Graham, on company orders, directed his men to pull out. "It was very dark," Ballenger recalled, "so we stayed close and moved slow. On the way, we encountered a North Korean patrol and destroyed them." This was the only encounter the platoon had on its way back to the Co. CP. The company commander ordered SGT Graham to deploy the platoon as a roadblock. The commander said that, to his knowledge, this one platoon was all that was left of the unit. There was one tank to reinforce Co. C. The commander posted it near his CP, facing north. Ballenger gave the time as 5 a.m. when the platoon arrived at the CP, "because we had little time to set up and dig in." The 1st Squad was placed on the road; the 2d on adjacent high ground and the 3d somewhat to the rear and opposite side of the road.

Shortly after daylight the Americans saw a column of enemy approaching on the road. "There was an American made truck in front and on each side a column of soldiers as far as the eye could see," Ballenger wrote. The tank pulled onto the road and lowered its main gun to aim at the truck. The truck driver blew his horn to get the tank to move. Instead, the gun fired and the truck blew up in a burst of flame. "The battle was on!" Ballenger continued. "Everyone opened up and it was like a turkey shoot. There were so many targets that you didn't know where to shoot first. We had stopped them cold. Now came the wait. From his vantage point on high ground, Ballenger could look down on the 1st Squad and the foxhole of his friend, John Trail. The two men waved to one another. "We didn't have to wait long. Mortars and artillery came in on us...so heavy that you didn't dare get up and look around. After 30 minutes or so, it lifted and the small-arms fire came in, machine gun fire from two different angles. The company commander decided that it was best to withdraw. He gave the order. "It was disorderly confusion," Ballenger recalled. He first went to John's foxhole and found that it had taken a direct mortar hit. "There wasn't much left and I knew it was over for him," Ballenger observed.

In the time it took for him to check on his friend, the rest of the unit had withdrawn. Ballenger began to run to catch up. He made it to the top of the first ridge. "When I started down [the other side] a hail of machine gun fire cut loose. If I had not fallen and rolled to the bottom, I don't think I would have made it. A lot of guys didn't." At the bottom of the hill, he decided to hide out until dark. He crawled into a field of sweet potatoes. After about an hour, he heard a noise to his rear. He checked his rifle. It contained just four rounds — all the ammunition he had. "It turned out to be another G.I.," he wrote.

"I told him to lay still and not to move, but he looked on a ridge that faced us, and said, 'There are G.I.'s on that ridge.' and he got up and started waving. Fire came in from different directions." The man fell, killed instantly. Ballenger crawled off, alone again. He had been hit in the left arm and side by the fusillade of bullets which had cut down the other soldier. But he all but ignored the wounds, they were "only flesh wounds and it wasn't hard to stop the bleeding," he remembered.

A short time later, still crawling, he came upon about 15 other men from Co. C. The group included CPT Carl S. Bartholdi (his CO), Sergeants Kirkpatrick, Eurich and Graham, and CPL Wallace. The little band was surrounded by the enemy, who were moving in. The ditch where the GIs had taken shelter was being swept by enemy automatic weapons, firing from several

directions. The group had to surrender. After stripping the men of valuables and their boots, the enemy placed them into a large drainage pipe which ran under the road. This was the enemy's POW collecting point. On Sept. 3, the men were lined up on the road, their hands tied and marched off. About 70 per cent of them were wounded in one way or another. But they helped one another as best they could. The march lasted three weeks, always at night. One night PFC Ed Gregory (B/23d) slipped away, but was recaptured. The North Koreans then said that if another man escaped 10 POWs would be shot.

"Everyone was losing weight and strength because...our diet...consisted of one handful of rice or barley a day," Ballenger wrote. "Our feet were [a] bloody mess from walking barefoot. The roads were all gravel and dirt. On about the 21st day of September we got to a town called Namwon." There, he met MSG Louis Goings. Ballenger wrote that Goings "kept us close together as a group and we worked as a team instead of individuals" at Namwon until they were all rescued by SGT Raymond Reifers' tank of the 25th Recon Co. on Sept. 28.

PFC Jack Carter, also of Co. C, recalled fighting and running, fighting and running. At dawn, he and two other men were joined in a valley by two more GIs. One of the men saw figures on the crest of a nearby hill and began to shout "We're GIs, we're GIs!" The figures were enemy soldiers. Carter and his companions took off running, with the North Koreans, firing, in hot pursuit. They ran into a Korean cemetery. There, they made a brief stand. Two of their number were killed by enemy fire. Carter and two other men went into a gully. When an enemy soldier popped his head up to Carter's right, Carter fired at him three times. But the enemy was closing in. They surrendered. Enemy soldiers took their dog tags and boots. Taken down to the Naktong, Carter was ordered to carry an enemy officer across on his back. The rocky bottomed river cut the young GI's feet.

On the third day of captivity, Carter and two other American soldiers were ordered to lie out on the forward slope of a hill to bait five U.S. tanks into an ambush. The rest of the POWs and about 125 enemy soldiers waited on the reverse slope. When the tanks got close, the enemy attacked them. The tanks buttoned up and engaged the enemy. Then three planes came in and strafed the hill where Carter and the other two men lay. One man was hit in the ankle by a bullet and the other had his stomach sliced open by another.

Between the tanks and air strike, most of the enemy soldiers were killed. The survivors took the prisoners, except the two who had been wounded, to a hut at the foot of the hill and near a road. They were left there, guarded by a wounded enemy soldier. The rest of the enemy party went on to nearby high ground and dug in. The two wounded men who had been left behind began to call for help. Using sign language, Carter and some others, indicated to the guard that they were going out to bring in the injured men. Amazing as it seems, the guard made no move to stop them.

The others cared for the two wounded men the best they could that night. Carter dozed off, to be awakened early in the morning by voices shouting, "We're GIs, don't shoot!" A U.S. tank-

infantry patrol had found and rescued them. Carter prevented the rescue party from harming their guard, who was badly wounded, himself. The uninjured ex-POWs were loaded on a tank and a jeep was sent for to take the wounded back to an aid station. Carter and the men with him were dropped off at the regimental CP, where they got new boots and weapons. Later in the day, Carter rejoined what was left of Co. C — 12 men. By Sept. 4, there were still only 20 men accounted for in Co. C.

Co. B, in the center of the regimental sector. was also badly mauled by enemy attacks. Many of its men were captured. One of these was PFC Edward Gregory, Jr. His 18th birthday was Aug. 30. The enemy attacked on Aug. 31. He recalled that his unit fought hard, hoping to hold out until reinforcements could arrive. Casualties mounted and the perimeter shrank. He wrote that they did what they could with the weapons and ammunition they had. He remembered that the order to pull out came about sunset on Sept. 1. The enemy was all around them that night.

At daylight, they saw a tank with a white star on it — an American tank. Someone on the tank called out, "Hey, Joe, over here!" The men stayed down and the tank opened fire on them. The enemy had captured this tank. Gregory's party got out of the area, regrouped and tried to organize a new position. But enemy fire came from all directions. Gregory jumped into a water-filled rice paddy trench. The water was up to his hips. Twenty men from Co. B were in this trench. The men fired back at the enemy in an all-around defense. Gregory recalled CPL Crumpus firing toward the front while he, Gregory, fired to the rear. Enemy bullets "thunked" into the mud around them. Then Gregory heard a loud clang and a yell. Turning around he saw that Crumpus had been hit in the head, dying instantly.

A few GIs remained. Then an enemy bugle sounded a call for a charge. Enemy fire came from high ground to the rear. From the opposite direction, other enemy soldiers charged, holding branches in front as camouflage. Gregory fired at them with his BAR. Enemy soldiers fell, some screaming. As the enemy closed in, he threw his last two grenades, then turned to fire on another group of North Koreans coming from a different direction. His BAR was now empty, as was his .45 pistol. Young Gregory didn't know if any other GIs were still alive in the trench.

He dropped the BAR and his pistol into the mud, pushing them down into the muck with his feet. He hoped, in this way to bury them. Scared, he then climbed from the trench and made a run for it. Enemy bullets followed him, cracking all around. One of them hit his right arm, knocking him to the ground. Very frightened, he tried to play dead, but his heavy breathing gave him away. Enemy soldiers yelled and kicked him. One tried to slip a wire noose around his neck. Gregory jerked his head away.

He and SGT Jose Fernandez were captured about the same time. The enemy took their boots, watches and wallets. One North Korean took Gregory's first aid packet away from him to prevent him from using it on his wounded arm, which was bleeding profusely. Fernandez tied an old hankie around the wound and the bleeding soon stopped.

More enemy soldiers appeared, along with

SGT Hanson and tank crew from 4th Platoon, Tank Co., 23d Infantry, near Obong-ni, August 1950. (Courtesy of Charles N. Prince, Tank Co., 23d Infantry)

three more American POWs. The GIs were herded along, prodded and struck by enemy rifle butts, and the words, "Hubba, hubba, pallye, pallye!" (Meaning hurry up.)

About two hours later, Gregory and his companions were joined by a larger group of POWs. He recalled that the combined party numbered 128 Americans. The group set off, with some men carrying the badly wounded and others helping those less badly hurt.

William H. Jones, of D/23d Infantry may have been among the 128 American POWs who Gregory recalled. Young Jones was also captured early in the North Korean attack across the Naktong on Aug. 31-Sept. 1, 1950.

CPL Roy H. King, B/23d Infantry, wrote this account of the enemy attack: "They came across [the Naktong] under [cover of] darkness...set up...mortars and artillery [and] knocked out our machine guns. We only had one heavy and one light [machine gun] at the point of the hill.... Our [artillery and mortar] support stopped. Then they rounded up all the civilians they could find in the surrounding villages and forced them [carrying torches] to go in front of them up the hill.... We began to fire. We were so spread out and so short of ammo that we were overrun very quickly." Two days later the unit "pulled a counterattack and regained the lost ground," he wrote. On Sept. 2, King, hit by grenade fragments, was treated at the Battalion Aid Station and returned to duty.

2LT William M. Glasgow's 2d Platoon, B/23d Infantry numbered 42 men on Aug. 31, 1950, (LT Glasgow's birthday.) With that many men, he had a full platoon, plus one or two additional men. But the platoon had the responsibility for a 2,600 yard frontage. Glasgow had the men deployed in outposts on a series of seven hills north of Pugong-ni. During the afternoon of Aug. 31, his men could see two large bodies of enemy soldiers in rice paddies across the Naktong. Artillery fire was called in from time to time to disperse them.

Just as dusk began to settle on the landscape

that evening, Glasgow and the men of his 2d Squad saw a truly amazing sight. "Just before dark," he wrote in the Feb. 1952 issue of *Combat Forces Journal*, "a big torchlight parade began to wind out of the hills across the Naktong.... Why would the enemy do such a crazy thing here at the front, make themselves so conspicuous?" Only Glasgow and the men of his 2d Squad could see this enemy parade. He immediately reported this bizarre spectacle to CPT Martin Coker at Battalion headquarters. Glasgow's FO thought that the enemy had forced refugees to parade by torchlight to attract U.S. artillery fire. As a result, he refused to call in a fire mission. This changed when COL Freeman called over the artillery phone line, and asked the FO, "Do you see that torchlight parade?" "Yes, sir," the FO replied. "Well, then get some damn artillery fire on them!" Freeman ordered. Glasgow estimated the torch-lit column to number some 2,000 people. The fire soon came in and each bursting round knocked out some of the torchbearers. But others took their places and the march continued without pause toward the river bank. One small group broke off and marched down another slope.

At 9 p.m. enemy artillery and mortar fire began falling on Glasgow's platoon. The barrage continued without letup for two hours. Under this fire, enemy soldiers crossed the Naktong and climbed the hills. At 11 p.m., an enemy green flare signaled their attack. Within minutes, enemy grenades rained onto the 2d Platoon positions. This was followed by a short, sharp hand-to-hand struggle.

"I jumped from my hole and ran through grenade fragments and small arms fire to... my platoon sergeant. Benjamin Rubio," Glasgow wrote. "I told him to take the platoon command post group to the first squad's area and form a perimeter defense. I would cover their move with the second squad. Then I ran to find Corporal Buswell, leader of my second squad. He was hugging the ground but trying at the same time to stop some of his men from flight. 'We're go-

ing to fall back on the first squad,' I told him. Then you and I will cover the withdrawal of your squad.'"

He and Buswell fell back, firing as they withdrew. Glasgow was concerned; he had been ordered to hold the position at all costs and had visions of having to counterattack to get it back the next morning. But he was more concerned at the moment of living to fight another day.

When he and Buswell got to where the first squad should have been, it wasn't there. He sent his runner, PFC Louis Burch, down to the road. Two of Buswell's squad showed up. The enemy was on three sides of his position. Glasgow vowed to stay put and fight until driven from the hill.

A green flare went up and a wave of enemy soldiers, silhouetted against the skyline, swept forward. "I opened up with my carbine and so did the others," he wrote. "The enemy stopped...and returned the fire. The night was full of carbines on full automatic with the Russian-type burp guns replying." The enemy was in overwhelming strength. Glasgow and the men with him ran back over the ridge toward the position occupied by the 3d Platoon. Enroute, he could "see the tiny golden sparks of the first platoon's machine guns" pouring fire into the enemy. But the enemy was between Glasgow and the 1st Platoon. Upon reaching the 3d Platoon position, it was deserted. Buswell, Glasgow and the two men from Buswell's squad paused for breath. Glasgow was relieved that he wasn't the only one pulling out.

Then the enemy made for Glasgow's position. "At less than 100 yards we opened fire and once again began to run," keeping to the high ground. They suddenly came upon a sleeping soldier, who they mistook for a GI; he was a North Korean. Figuring that one meant more, the four Americans got away without firing on him.

A short time later, Glasgow's left forearm began to hurt; he had been shot, but had not noticed it at the time. Buswell acted as scout, checking the bushes and shrubs as the little band walked on. They were thirsty, hot and plagued by mosquitoes. Once, Buswell spotted an enemy soldier in a rice paddy below and fired at him. The man let out a piercing wail.

With the coming of dawn, they hid out in a thick clump of bushes. In the mists of early light, they saw the figures of 20 men coming down a hill into the saddle where they lay concealed. Upon closer inspection, the party proved to be men from Co. B, including Sergeants Wajnoraski and Mackrell. Wajnoraski told Glasgow that there were more GIs on the hill he had just left. It was agreed that they would go back to the hill from a different direction and try to get the group to join them. Enroute, they came to a small stream, where Glasgow had the men with canteens stop to fill them. He and 10 men were in this group.

Firing broke out from the hill. Two men from Glasgow's party ran to join Wajnoraski. Glasgow and his men were pinned down by the fire, which proved to be from enemy soldiers. Several of his men were hit. He prayed, asking that God show him a way out. Finally, he had the small party begin crawling down a gully, heading for some trees on another hill. Enemy fire followed them, including the fire of a .51-cal enemy machine gun. Glasgow's men stopped periodically and fired back, hoping to hit some of the hidden enemy gunners. An enemy bullet carried away a nail from the lieutenant's boot.

Reaching the end of the gully, Glasgow had the men make a dash for the trees, one at a time, covered by the fire of the others. He was last out, followed closely by a group of enemy soldiers. He jumped behind a tree, cast aside his empty carbine, and drew a .45-cal WW I 1917 Colt revolver, which had belonged to his father. He rapidly fired all six shots from the pistol and ran to the shelter of the trees and brush up the hill.

Rejoining his eight men, he sat trying to figure a way out. A man named Cummings looked at him and said, "Lieutenant, if you get us out of this, I'll do anything for you."

"Cummings," Glasgow replied, "I'll get you out, and some day when we get back to 'Frisco you can buy me a drink." He then administered first aid to two of the men, who were both badly wounded. Glasgow knew only two of the eight men, but "had the strongest feeling that it was my job to protect them though I knew only two of their names," he wrote. For the rest of the day, they played cat-and-mouse with enemy patrols.

Checking his map, Glasgow decided to go through the same rice paddy they had traversed that morning, then work their way through enemy lines to Lake U-po. He reasoned that the enemy would not have troops in the middle of the lake surrounded by hills. The group would travel at night, hid by day.

The lieutenant took his Bible out, turned to the 23d Psalm, and read the words, "Yea, though I walk through the valley of the shadow of death." He recalled that, with these words, "a great sense of calmness came over me. We were going to be O.K."

At 9 p.m., they set off and, three nerve-wracking hours later, reached the paddies leading to the lake. They removed their shoes to prevent the sucking noise they made in the mud. But they had gone less than 50 yards before a water party of enemy soldiers heard them. Glasgow and his companions dropped flat on their backs in the water with only their noses above it. The enemy stumbled and thrashed around calling to one another, looking for the source of the noise. Glasgow whispered to the men that if discovered, they would jump up firing their weapons.

Reaching the lake, they cautiously waded through it, keeping their faces down to avoid the moonlight from shining on their white faces. They were able to wade most of the way, and swam over the few places which were deeper. Once they reached the far shore, they still had a thousand yards of enemy territory to traverse. Firing broke out to the front; the enemy was attacking friendly positions. Glasgow and his men prepared to hide in the rushes along the lake's shore. Some of the wounded feared that they could not last through another day with its searing, hot sun. Then, miraculously, a heavy fog rolled in. Taking advantage of the fog, the men moved rapidly toward American lines. All around them they heard yelling from small groups of enemy soldiers. As they neared friendly lines, the fog lifted and Glasgow saw some C-47 cargo planes in the air. He waved, but the pilots seemed to take no notice.

Soon they arrived outside the lines. Glasgow called out, "What outfit is up there?" "Headquarters Company, 1st Battalion," came the reply.

Glasgow asked, "What's your company commander's name?"

"If you want to know our company commander's name, then get the hell in here and we'll tell you," came the answer.

After seeing to the care of the wounded, Glasgow went to the company commander, CPT George White, of Co. G. He found out that the 1st Battalion, along with Co. G, were cut off and manning an isolated perimeter. The C-47s had been on a supply drop mission to them. This was the Hill 209 position.

Glasgow discovered that, in addition to the eight men who had been with him, his platoon sergeant, his runner, the men of his 1st Squad, and several others from the 2d, had all made their way safely into the 1st Battalion perimeter.

The D/23d Infantry OP took very heavy artillery and flat trajectory fire, along with long range enemy machine gun fire all night, but there were no casualties. The enemy penetrated up the draw between Companies A and B, then were able to overrun both units. In the subsequent withdrawal of these units, a 3/4-ton truck, containing a 75mm recoilless rifle and equipment was destroyed by a direct hit. One Heavy Machine-gun Section, with 1LT Carl J. Johnson with a platoon of Co. A, were cut off by the advancing enemy. CPT Tassey ordered the section to withdraw with the A Co. Platoon, upon their own initiative.

PFC James Coulas was a member of the 23d's HM Co. He recalled seeing the enemy's green flares the night of Aug. 31-Sept. 1. The rifle companies to the front were overrun, he recalled. "We abandoned our position and mortars," he wrote. "Enemy controlled the road on our left and we had to retreat through a swamp and up a hill, under fire. I did not think I would make it. The first gunner in our squad, CPL Leo Englehart, was not seen again. Someone I never saw before or after helped me through the swamp. I'll never forget his kindness. Half way up the hill I collapsed from exhaustion. Only the thought of my family got me started again. Enemy fired a small cannon at the hill but there was only one minor wound.... We ended up next morning in the company kitchen area (Changnyong). This was the hardest day of the war for me. I was mad at myself for panicking in the swamp — I thought it was quicksand — and took a lesson from it: 'If you think you can do it, you can do it.'"

SSG Harley E. Wilburn was a 4.2 inch mortar FO with HM, 23d Infantry at the time. He, too, recalled that the mortar position was overrun that night by the enemy, forcing the abandonment of the mortars.

During the night, LTC Hutchin pulled the bulk of the battalion, less Co. C, back to near his CP just north of Lake U-po and the high ground there covering the northern road to Changnyong, three miles east of the Naktong and five miles west of the town.

Meantime, COL Freeman, aware of the disaster which had befallen Co. C and his 1st Battalion, secured Companies G and F from the division reserve. He sent Co. G to help LTC Hutchin. He sent Co. F along the Pugong-ni road

toward Co. C. MAJ Lloyd K. Jensen, 2d Battalion XO, accompanied Co. F. They were unable to reach Charlie Co. However, the major gathered in stragglers. With Co. F and this pick-up group, he seized the hills on the main road to Changnyong near the shore of Lake Samor-ho and just east of Poncho-ri. On Sept. 2, E/23d Infantry was also released to the regiment and joined Co. F at Poncho-ri. This position became the main defense area for the 23d. LTC James W. Edwards assumed command of the position.

Andrew E. Reyna was a tank section leader in the 3d Platoon, 23d Tk Co. Charles N. Prince was also in this platoon. Both recalled some of the fighting in the last days of August and the first days of September 1950. Prince wrote that the tank section he was with engaged a large force of North Koreans in a fire fight along the crest of a hill. "Our tank section was attacked by a group of N. Koreans, platoon size or larger," he wrote, "supported by a self-propelled gun.

"Within a few minutes the second tank of our section was knocked out, the driver killed and the bow gunner injured. The other three tanks of our platoon came up and fired on the self-propelled gun and set it on fire. We succeeded in driving them back towards the...river when we were attacked on our left by a company sized group from the North Korean Second Division. We fired and maneuvered constantly until daylight. At that time our Division Artillery came into action along with some P-51 Mustang and Corsair fighter plane support. The enemy broke off contact and withdrew towards the river."

Reyna's section was attached to 2/23d Infantry for a time. At one point, they were in support of Co. F, along the Naktong. An F Co. LP was down the road. Late in the afternoon of the day after joining Co. F, Reyna's gunner was cleaning the gun tube when he (Reyna) saw a large number of troops skylined on a ridge about 600 yards away. He instructed his men to wave to them "so that the enemy would think that we thought they were friendly, Reyna wrote.

"I knew that it was an enemy force.... I told my gunner to put away the gun cleaning equipment, and we alerted the line company platoon leader who was nearby." But there was no attack, even by artillery or mortars. He and the other tank commander, SFC Melvin Surface, selected alternate positions for their tanks. From these positions the tanks could still cover the same fields of fire. Just after dark the two tanks moved into these positions for the night. "Soon after," Reyna recalled, "the Sergeant in charge of the outpost reported to me that his detail was back in our perimeter, and that trip flares and booby traps had been set forward of the outpost position. That any activity to the front of our position was going to be North Koreans."

Reyna instructed his men not to fire until he gave the command, and then only with machine guns. He wanted the enemy to make the first move. He repeatedly scanned the front with his field glasses, but could detect no movement.

"Sooner than I expected, a trip flare was set off out on the road where our outpost had been," he recorded. "I saw a group of the enemy on the road moving in our direction. Our tanks opened fire simultaneously with our four caliber .30 machine guns (2 on each tank). The enemy returned fire with small arms and anti-tank weapons. I was shoulder high, directing fire in my 'Tank Commander's hatch,' when suddenly a tremendous explosion occurred right in front of my face, rocking our tank and knocking me down into the tank and blinding me momentarily. I had felt the heat on my face from the explosion. I recovered and then I kicked the back rest of my gunner's seat and said, 'Dammit Smitty, I told you not to fire the main gun unless I told you to!' Sergeant Smith said that he had not fired. We had gotten a direct hit on the front slope of our tank, apparently from an anti-tank weapon. At that point our artillery forward observer directed fire from the artillery battalion upon the enemy troops with devastating effect, causing then to withdraw and ending the battle."

During the night of Aug. 31- Sept. 1, enemy troops passed by Hutchin's right flank and attained the road three miles to his rear near the division's artillery. The HQ Co., Svc Co., with parts of other 23d Infantry units stopped this enemy drive near the 23d's CP five mile north of Changnyong.

Before noon of Sept. 1, it was evident that the enemy had succeeded in cutting the 2d Division in two. To the north were the 23d and 38th Regiments and the bulk of the division artillery. To the south was the 9th Infantry, division headquarters and miscellaneous service units. Losses had been heavy. The 1st and 2d Battalions of the 9th Infantry and 2/23d Infantry were only 50 per cent effective. The 1/23d Infantry, having suffered severe losses was isolated from other friendly troops near Hill 209, north of Lake U-po. By 5 p.m. that day, the 82d AAA/AW Bn had lost three M-16s (quad-.50s), four M-19s (dual-40mm), two M-39s, two jeeps, 14 one ton trailers and two 1/4-ton trailers. Personnel losses were 2 officers and 44 EM MIA. This included 2 platoon sergeants and 5 section leaders.

The 2d Division CP was at Muan-ni, seven air miles east of Yongsan and on the Miryang road. From his CP, GEN Keiser decided that the only way now to fight the division was with someone in charge of each of the two sections. He placed the DivArty commander, BG Loyal M. Haynes, in command of the northern force. Haynes established his CP seven miles north of Changnyong, about two miles from that of COL Freeman. The force, known as TF Haynes, became operational at 10:20 a.m., Sept. 1. In addition to the 23d and 38th Infantry Regiments, this force included the 37th FAB (105mm), C/503d FAB (155mm), Btrys A,B, and C, 82d AAA/AW Bn and C/72d Tk Bn. Troops in the southern sector (9th Infantry, 2d Engineer Combat Bn, 72d Tank Bn [-Co. C] plus other miscellaneous divisional units) were designated part of TF Bradley, named for its commander, BG Joseph S. Bradley, Assistant Division Commander.

Clay Blair wrote that Haynes and Freeman clashed. According to Freeman this was over Haynes repeatedly calling Freeman to his (Haynes') CP at critical times in the battle. Haynes, angered by Freeman's balking, finally came to the 23d Infantry CP, summarily relieved him of command and ordered him back to the division CP. (See Chapter Notes.)

The Division G-3, COL Maurice G. Holden recalled that Freeman came into the Division CP "totally exhausted." Freeman fell asleep almost immediately. Keiser liked Freeman and did not want to relieve him. Accordingly, he sent COL Holden up to the 23d to find out what was really going on. Holden discovered that "the 23d staff thought Haynes was terrible; he'd never been near the front" and "had no idea what was going on," Holden told Blair in a July 25, 1985 interview. Keiser, happy with the report, woke up Freeman and sent him back to the command of the 23d. From then on, Blair wrote, Freeman ignored Haynes and ran the regiment his way.

Some time during the Bulge fighting, COL Freeman visited the 37th FAB's FDC. Young CPL Earl Dube was a computer there at the time. "They [the battalion] always adjusted with Baker battery," he wrote.... I spoke low over the phone and I told the people on Charlie's guns that I want to see a good show, because the Colonel [Freeman] was in the Fire Direction Center.... We were ready in nine seconds, and... I yelled, 'Charlie's ready!'... The Colonel stood up and said, 'Maybe we should adjust with Charlie battery.'... From that time on, we ran a little bit of a game between the three computers to see who could get...these batteries adjusted the fastest and it was like a little contest between the three batteries." CPL Dube also wrote that the battalion fired WP rounds against tanks. If a round hit near or on the tank's rear deck, the tank's air intake would pull the phosphorous smoke into the vehicle's interior, killing or incapacitating the crew. (See Chapter Notes.)

The 38th Infantry and the *NK 10th Division* — Aug. 29 - Sept. 1

1/38th Infantry:

Charlie Co. of LTC William P. Keleher's 1/38th Infantry was deployed in the far north of the regimental and division sector, covering the town of Hyonpung. The company's main line faced west toward the massive, towering Hill 409. The hill was occupied by major elements of the *NK 10th Division*. To the south of Co. C a mile and a half or so, Co. A was deployed on a series of hills astride the MSR and facing north. Co. B was another mile and a half south of A, also positioned astride the MSR, facing north.

In the closing days of August, the enemy sent a number of patrols and groups of infiltrators into and through the 1st Battalion's sector. Many of these patrols and infiltrators were intercepted and destroyed. Bruce M. Ritter (A/38th Infantry) and BAR-man Jerome Baker (B/38th Infantry) wrote accounts of actions against enemy patrols.

Ritter's account was very short. "An enemy patrol had been scouting in force. They carried heavy weapons including several water cooled machine guns through the rice paddies. They evidently ran into us by mistake on their return path. I believe we killed or captured the majority of them with very few casualties on our part." Ritter was an "old Korean hand," having served there for two years before the Korean War.

Jerome Baker recalled that his company was dug in along a rice paddy when his platoon sergeant, MSG Chester Mathis ordered his BAR team to join a skirmish line being formed by platoon leader 1LT Serohum. The line moved forward "to clear out the area to our front," he wrote. "As we started forward the N.K. patrol jumped up to engage us. Our platoon fired in unison with rifles [and] rifle grenades. The N.K.s did not stand a chance and we killed all thirteen of them with no injuries to any of our men. This was our first combat action. During the fight I had mild panic. Not because of the action, because my BAR jammed. I thought, 'Boy, I am going to catch Hell from the platoon.' In the fight I squirted oil on the working parts as quickly as possible. It (BAR) started working. We collected the N.K. weapons and returned to our positions."

Roy Hill, assistant squad leader, of the 1st Squad of what he believes was the 2d Platoon of B/38th, about an American attack on the base of Hill 409 which he stated took place on Aug. 30. "About 11 a.m. (on our left) some company, with tank support, went west about a mile to the base of Hill 409. The tank had to stop at the base of the hill and we sat there and watched this company of Americans try to go up the hill. They didn't get very far and suffered very high casualties. Hill 409 was just too heavily fortified and defended."

What Roy Hill may have seen was a platoon-sized patrol from A/38th Infantry which went out toward Hill 409 to develop enemy positions on the north side of Hill 409 on August 29. The platoon passed through the lines of Co. C. CPT Leonard Lowry, CO, Co. C, wrote: "The platoon was ambushed and was forced back through C Co. position. Many were wounded and at daylight there were five MIAs. I ordered the 2d Platoon Leader, SFC Martin Vandy, to send a rifle squad with an M4 tank, to attempt to locate the missing. SFC Vandy, who had fought every campaign with the 1st Inf. Div...in World War II, was a complete rifle platoon leader. He elected to personally lead this small rescue force and boldly moved it to the base of Hill 409. This action limited the artillery and mortar fire of the enemy as the rescue force closed within 100 yards of their forward positions (although [enemy] artillery and mortar fire was attempted).

"Enemy small-arms fire was intense, but Vandy skillfully used the tank as a shield for his men and would have them dart out in pairs and return quickly to the protection of the tank and return fire as they searched for the missing. Meanwhile, the tank was firing its 76mm and machine guns steadily throughout this action. PFC Witt manned the tank's .50-caliber AA machine gun, and thus was completely exposed to enemy fire. Three bodies were recovered and carried out on the deck of the tank. This action took about 30 minutes and was broken off when ammunition ran low. Upon its return, the tank had been hit 12 times by the NKPA's 14 mm antitank rifles, with penetrations of an inch at each hit. This would indicate that thousands of rounds of...rifle and machine gun rounds had been directed at the rescue force. Yet, neither PFC Witt, or others were hit and miraculously returned intact."

On the night of Aug. 31, C/38th Infantry was heavily attacked by troops from the *NK 10th Division*. CPT Lowry related the course of the battle: "As darkness descended on August 31 my company...was the right flank of the 2d Infantry Division. I was informed that the left flank of the 1st Cavalry Division was two miles to our right. My foot patrols were unable to make contact. Approximately at midnight the heaviest enemy artillery and mortar preparatory fires that

I had ever experienced began. Far more than [the] Japanese placed on our unit (32d Inf. Div.) in WW II. Initially, I and my artillery FO, a 2LT Van (?), were lying on the parapet of our foxhole. When the fires became so intense, I said, 'Let's get in the hole,' and I slid back into it. The FO said, 'I will in a little while. Maybe I can pick up some targets.' At that moment, he was killed by a direct hit. The two KIAs and other WIAs that night were generally from direct hits on their foxholes. With my FO dead, by radio I got some support from the A Co. FO. The enemy preparatory fires lasted about 30 minutes, then lifted and their infantry attacked. I always feared a flank attack on my open flank. This did not transpire and the enemy...hit us 'head on' and against our strong points.

"Penetrations did occur, but all of these were eliminated the next day.... Some [enemy soldiers] were killed by their own...fires. Many tried to straggle back to Hill 409, which necessitated crossing a large rice paddy, and this offered good marksmanship firing to many men of my company.

"During the night I ordered my Executive Officer, 1LT Paul A. Stough (West Point 1945), to move the AAA quad fifties and twin forties, with a rifle squad, out in the open right flank and place flanking fire on Hill 409. This apparently paid off as at daybreak a NKPA 76mm self propelled gun was [discovered] disabled at the base of Hill 409."

During the defense of Hyonpung, the AAA vehicles knocked out a number of enemy machine gun positions. One M-19 was hit by enemy AT fire, wounding two men. While evacuating wounded for C/38th Infantry the AAA platoon lost a jeep and three ammunition trailers to enemy fire. The AAA platoon was attached to B/38th Infantry when Hyonpung was abandoned. The jeep was then recovered, but not the trailers.

"In the afternoon, a worried motorized patrol from the 1st Cavalry contacted us here in Hyonpung, and were most happy to know that we were still holding that town," Lowry wrote. "They also notified us that the British Commonwealth Brigade would be filling the gap between their division and the 2d Infantry Division."

CPT Lowry wrote that "it was the leadership of veteran NCOs who established mutual trust and confidence in their men that resulted in the company holding their positions like 'The Rock of the Marne,' our 38th Infantry regimental motto."

Some time after the visit by the 1st Cavalry patrol, LTC Keleher ordered Co. C to withdraw from Hyonpung. Enemy forces were between the company and the rest of the battalion. 1LT Stough described the withdrawal as "highly successful.... With very, very close support of our Air Force jets, we loaded tanks and other vehicles and blasted our way out of the trap. The jets zoomed down the road on each side and pinned the N.K.s down. What a show they put on!"

Once back from Hyonpung, Co. C was trucked into a rear area and given the mission of cleaning out an enemy force threatening support units. "Our unit...was trucked about 4-5,000 yds to the rear," Stough wrote. "We detrucked and prepared for combat." CPT Lowry led his unit

into a valley with rice paddies and small hills. "To the right was high ground with spurs extending out into the valley," Stough continued. "Off to the left side of the valley was a gravel road. The enemy was dug in on one of the spurs." CPT Lowry used one platoon, with machine guns and mortars as a base of fire. He sent one platoon to the right to attack across one spur and into the enemy position on the 2nd spur. "Heavy enemy small-arms fire stopped the platoon before it reached the enemy position."

A number of its men had been killed or wounded. "They were evacuated," Stough wrote. "Lowry called on Hogan's platoon (in reserve) to attack across higher ground still farther to the right and come in on the enemy from above. Hogan moved to high ground and started his assault using 'Marching Fire.' The whole platoon moved forward firing rapidly from the shoulder or hip, pinning the enemy down in their holes and then tossing grenades in ...to finish them off. Those still alive were finished off with rifle fire. A few tried to escape in the rice paddy were hunted down and killed. We counted 55 enemy dead, armed with rifles, MGs and mortars. All the enemy weapons were piled up and Hogan used hand grenades to destroy them." (See Chapter Notes.)

2/38th Infantry:

Enemy troops also attacked the 2d Battalion, overrunning elements of both E and F Co.s. Cecil Sherrod, an ammo bearer in a 57mm recoilless rifle squad of Co. E, recorded that his squad leader, a SGT Wolk, was killed early on by a sniper. He also recalled that they found few good targets for the 57 and did not fire it very often. "We just got run over on the mountain during the night," he wrote. "We just did not have the manpower." By Sept. 1, only Sherrod and a man named Shaw were the only ones left from the squad. Sherrod was hit in the helmet with a hand grenade, denting it, but leaving him unhurt. But Shaw was lost, but was found "near the hill, OK," the next day when the company retook the hill, Sherrod recorded.

In Co. F, LT Frederick Henry sacrificed himself to hold off the enemy when they overran his platoon position. On the night of Aug. 31-Sept. 1, his platoon occupied a hill in the vicinity of the village of Am-dong near the base of Hill 409. That night an estimated reinforced enemy company attacked, and Henry's platoon was cut off.

Although wounded in the side and shoulder, LT Henry moved around the position directing the fire of his men and encouraging them. As dawn broke, the platoon ran out of ammunition. LT Henry ordered his men to bring their now useless weapons to his foxhole and then make their way back to friendly lines any way possible. When last seen, he was standing in his foxhole, throwing empty weapons at the enemy as they made their last assault and overran the position.

Nine men survived. Among them was Henry's runner, Roger Hallenback. He remained with LT Henry, until wounded and ordered evacuated. On his way back through medical channels, Hallenback saw both COL Peploe (C.O., 38th Infantry) and the 2d Battalion commander, LTC Skeldon. He filled both officers in on what had happened to the platoon. LT Henry

was posthumously awarded the Medal of Honor for his courageous and unselfish sacrifice.

A/72d Tk Bn was attached to the 38th infantry at the time. Tank ammunition was stacked outside the tanks. The tanks were firing indirect fire during the enemy's attack. A man was outside each of them passing main gun ammunition up a round at a time for the firing. Richard A. Schultz was one of the men passing up 90mm ammunition, when enemy mortar fire began to fall among the tanks. The tankers "buttoned up" and the men on the outside dove under them. Schultz was caught with a 90mm round in his hands. He laid it on the tank and dove under the vehicle. He recalled that he was under that tank for about four hours.

Walker Faces Another Crisis — Sept. 1

By daybreak, Sept. 1, the 2d Division was in deep trouble. Split asunder, it was threatened with defeat. At 8:10 a.m., GEN Keiser called Eighth Army and briefed them on the situation as he then knew it. The deepest penetrations seemed to be in the 9th Infantry's sector. Walker was puzzled by the report, since a major battle had taken place in that sector a couple of weeks previously and the enemy had been ejected and soundly beaten.

At 9 a.m., GEN Walker asked Fifth Air Force commander, MG Earle Partridge to make a maximum effort to support the 2d Division. He wanted the Air Force to isolate the battlefield to prevent resupply and reinforcement of the troops on the east side of the Naktong confronting the 2d Division. The Far East Command called on the Navy to assist. The Navy responded by sending the Seventh Fleet back from its interdiction of the Inchon-Seoul area so that its aircraft could participate in attacks on the advancing enemy.

But the 2d Division's situation worsened during the morning. Lacking information from the front, liaison planes were used on an hourly basis, from 9:30 a.m. on, to fly throughout the division sector to assess the situation. These light planes also made 14 drops of food ammunition, water and medical supplies to cut-off units.

Gradually, the scope of the disaster became more clear. The enemy had made a major penetration some six miles wide and eight miles deep in the center of the division's sector, effectively cutting the command in two. In addition, there were several lesser penetrations at other places. The front line battalions of the 9th and 23d Regiments were disorganized and some of their companies seemed to have been wiped out.

Walker closely followed reports from the 2d Division and the 25th Division during the morning hours. In addition to breakthroughs in the 2d, elements of the *NK 6th* and *7th Divisions* had penetrated the lines of the 25th. But in the 2d Division sector, the enemy was at the edge of Yongsan, deep into that command's rear area. Unless they could be dealt with decisively, the entire Perimeter was in danger. Down in the Tropic Lightning (25th) Division sector, elements of the 27th were available to counterattack. That regiment had just arrived at Masan at 8:30 p.m. the previous evening. The original plan was for this regiment to relieve the 5th RCT. The 5th was then to join the 24th Division as its third regiment, replacing the 34th Infantry, which was to be disbanded.

Walker had the largest reserve to date: The 27th Infantry, the Marine Brigade, the 19th Infantry (24th Division), plus the newly-arrived and incompletely equipped two-battalion British 27th Brigade. He rejected employing the British Brigade because it was not yet fully equipped for battle and the 27th Infantry because it was already in an excellent position to counterattack in the 25th Division sector. He alerted 24th Division and 19th Infantry to prepare for the regiment's commitment to the line at a moments notice. He issued the same warning order to GEN Craig, commanding the Marine Brigade.

The enemy's rapid advance to Yongsan threatened Miryang and the principal road and rail line of supply and reinforcement to the center and northwest corner of the Perimeter. At the moment, this was the critical area of the Perimeter. About 11 a.m., Sept. 1, Walker ordered the Marine Brigade to move at once. Shortly after noon, the order arrived at Brigade headquarters and the Marines were ready to move by 1:30 p.m. It was back to the Bulge.

BG Mike Lynch, who was Walker's pilot at the time, was interviewed by Clay Blair for *The Forgotten War*. Lynch recalled that the 2d Division seemed to be disintegrating. "Everything coming out of the 2d Division made absolutely no sense," he said.

Just before noon, Lynch flew GEN Walker to the 2d Division sector. They were fired on. "We started flying back to our landing," he continued. "When we saw this column of the 2d Division soldiers pulling back." One group appeared to be about a company. Walker became very upset because the unit was withdrawing, although no enemy seemed to be near and it was ignoring defensible terrain on which to make a stand. Further this unit and others appeared to be moving into areas which were not defensible.

Lynch would shut the throttle and glide down to about 50 feet above the withdrawing troops and Walker yelled out of the plane's window at them.

"You're not under attack! Stop where you are! You've got a good defensive position," he shouted at them.

"I don't know...whether they actually heard him," Lynch remarked, "but he was yelling like the devil. Then he said, 'Let's go back to the 2d Division CP.'"

They landed at the 2d Division airstrip and Walker went into the CP. "Dutch," he asked GEN Keiser, "Where's your division?" Keiser replied that he was waiting for the return of liaison officers to bring the latest information. Lynch recalled that the roads were jammed.

Lynch recalled that Walker was very unhappy, and told Keiser: "You get this division under control right now or I'll take control over this division along with the Army." Blair also quotes Walker as telling Keiser, "We shall not surrender another inch and we shall hold regardless of cost." Keiser quickly relayed this edict to his division. With that, Lynch and Walker walked back to the aircraft. There was a little embankment near the plane; Walker sat down on this and Lynch sat beside him. Glancing toward the general, he noted that Walker was crying. Walker said, "I can't let this Army be destroyed, yet I

don't know what to do to stop it from being destroyed." Lynch recalled, however, that Walker had done all that anyone could have done that morning to save his army. With this remark, Walker rose and climbed into the plane, saying, "Well, we've got to look at the rest of the area." In the interview, Lynch said, "Except for that area, things looked OK."

Meantime, elements of the 2d Division fought on as best they could. Rear area troops, who rarely, if ever were called upon for real battle, were pressed into service. One such *ad hoc* force was TF Strom, commanded by MAJ V. E. Strom, Division Special Service Officer, composed of the Division Band and clerks from Division Headquarters. TF Strom dug in on two mountain passes on the MSR and stayed there for a week. COL Maury Holden, USA, Ret., (2d Division G-3 at the time) wrote about how the Band came to be committed to a defensive position.

"Around Sept. 2 or 3, GEN Keiser and I were examining our lines on an Operations Map," Holden wrote. "He pointed to one hill mass that was not on the front, but would have been a key position if we failed to hold our present front line positions against the NKA.... 'Maury, we have got to put some troops on that hill in case the North Koreans break through the 9th Infantry. What do we have in reserve that we can use?' I explained to him that we had committed everything we had — all our infantry, including all of the 2d Engineer Bn. I racked my brain for a solution, and then I thought of a solution — the 2d Division Band, which had 40 members, as I recall. That would constitute one infantry platoon, which, if dug in properly should be able to hang on to the hill. GEN Keiser said that was a great idea and to get them on the hill as quickly as possible."

LTC Holden sent one of his assistant G-3 officers to lead the Band to the hill and be sure that they knew which direction the enemy might attack from. The Band had only pistols and carbines and no automatic weapons, but the situation was critical; they would have to defend with what they had. Division headquarters "rejoiced" that troops were "on that key terrain feature," as Holden put it.

Holden's announcement at the Operations briefing the next morning that the Band occupied a key hill brought a laugh from the assembled staff. "GEN Keiser turned to the G-1, LTC Jim Tanner," Holden wrote, "and said, 'Jim, the Band belongs to you. Why don't you go down and visit the Band today and see how they are doing?'" Tanner visited the Band. When he returned, he happily reported that the their morale was great. The Warrant Officer commanding was ready to fight. He had scrounged some extra weapons and had even issued grenades to his men. "Jim asked the Band Leader to see his Operations Map so he could show him where the North Koreans were, but the only map the Band had was clipped out of the *San Francisco Chronicle*, Holden recalled. The Bandmaster said that all he had received were verbal orders, but no map, but he thought the *Chronicle* map was all he needed to fight a battle. The Band was never called upon to fight in the Perimeter, but Holden wrote that "it was comforting to the Division Commander to know that the Band as-

sumed its secondary role as infantrymen without a sour note."

The 2d Engineer Bn had its three line companies out supporting the division's three regiments. Co. A was in support of the 9th, B the 23d and C the 38th. When the tactical situation became critical, the engineers were tapped to fight as infantrymen. Combat engineer companies had a number of automatic weapons and some rocket launchers, but no mortars. When the 2d Engineers were called upon to help defend Yongsan, the battalion had to regain control of one or more of the companies out with the infantry. Retrieving Co. C with the 38th was out of the question; Co. B with the 23d was a remote possibility and Co. A was a better bet. Radio contact with the two units was almost nil.

Accordingly, SGT Harry L. Lohmeyer and a captain were sent from the engineer battalion in a jeep to contact the two units and direct them to move to the engineer area. Shortly after they set out, the captain became so distraught at the sight of so many wounded men being evacuated by jeep and truck, that he ordered the jeep back to the engineer CP. There, he reportedly said that they couldn't get through because the action was too intense. Lohmeyer wrote that he told the authorities at the CP that they hadn't gone far enough to make such assessment. As a result, he, the Battalion S3 (MAJ Price) and a buddy, SGT Shirley, set out again by jeep. They met Co. A on the road. The company had received the order by radio and was coming in.

The Battle of Yongsan — Sept. 1-2

BG Sladen Bradley and COL Hill desperately tried to gather the badly shattered 9th Infantry in order to stop the rapidly advancing enemy. Bradley recalled that Hill suffered a mental shock at having his regiment so badly manhandled by the enemy and was physically exhausted by his efforts to piece the remnants together for a stand. Bradley recommended to Keiser that Hill be temporarily relieved for a rest at the Division CP. Keiser, who had already decided to relieve Hill and place COL Chin Sloane back in command of the 9th, refused the request. But Hill made a rapid recovery and displayed uncommon leadership in bringing what was left of the 9th together again. The reconstituted 9th fell back on Yongsan.

The *1st* and *2d Regiments* of the *NK 9th Division* were putting severe pressure on the 9th Infantry. As Appleman observed, the situation for the *9th Division* must have appeared favorable to its commander, Pak Kyo Sam. The *1st Regiment* approached Yongsan on the north and the *2d Regiment* on the south. The *9th Division* was supported by a battalion of 76mm artillery from the *I Corps*, an artillery battalion from the *4th Division*, an AA artillery battalion and two tank battalions from the *16th Armored Brigade*. The far under strength *4th Division*, short of weapons and with untrained replacements, crossed the Naktong behind the *9th Division*. The enemy considered these two divisions as the *I Corps* "main force." Part of the *9th Division* reached the hills just west of Yongsan on the afternoon of Sept. 1.

That morning, with only what was left of Co.

E, the 9th Infantry had few troops with which to defend the town. GEN Keiser attached the 2d Engineer Bn to the regiment and the 72d Tk Bn (- elements with the 23d and 38th Regiments to the north) and the 2d Recon Co. were also incorporated into the defensive force. The tank battalion and Recon Co. were placed into positions close to Yongsan and COL Hill planned to position the engineers along a chain of low hills northwest of the town.

Later on Sept. 1, the Engineer Bn deployed along the road about two miles west of Yongsan, with CPT Frank M. Reed's Co. A on the south and 1LT Lee E. Beahler's Co. D on the north. About 300 enemy engaged Reed's company in a battle. Two quad-.50's and a twin- 40, of D/82d AAA/AW, under LT William R. Webster, supported Co. A. The 82d history records that the enemy had pinned down two squads of engineers and that fire from the AAA vehicles relieved the squads and inflicted heavy casualties on the enemy in the fight.

Meantime, Beahler protested his company's position; the frontage was long and the flanks were unprotected. GEN Bradley authorized him to move the unit to a hill immediately south and overlooking Yongsan. An infantry platoon took up positions behind him.

Reed's Co. A was ordered to withdraw to the southeast edge of Yongsan. There it took up positions along the road. C/2d Engineer Bn was on its left. To C's left was the Recon Co. D/2d Engineers was on the western tip of a large mountain that lay southeast of Yongsan. The D Company position overlooked the town, itself, as well as the road to Miryang, which came south out of the town, rounded the western tip of the mountain, then turned eastward along its base.

LTC Clark Webber's 72d Tk Bn (-Co. C) and CPT Wallace A. Kydland's 2d Recon Co., on the southern approach to Yongsan, opposed a determined enemy drive on the town from that direction. In this fight, MSG Jack A. Mac Sloarrow's tank (of A/72d Tk Bn) knocked out the first T-34 for the battalion.

The 2d Recon Co. was on the extreme left flank of the 2d Division's line defending Yongsan. The enemy attacked elements of the 2d Recon Co. at 5:30 a.m. on Sept. 3, driving the 3d Platoon from its position. CPT Kydland organized and led a counterattack with the 2d Platoon and survivors of the 3d. The enemy resisted with a heavy volume of machine gun and small arms fire. In the final assault against the enemy main position, Kydland led six men in a bayonet assault which drove the enemy out. The enemy lost some 114 men to the counterattack. Kydland's citation for the Silver Star states that the lost ground was regained and the enemy threat to the division's left flank was eliminated.

Roy Mogged, a tank crew member in the Recon Co., wrote that "Captain Kydland was a very gallant man — just a super CO."

SFC Charles W. Turner, of the Recon Co., mounted a tank and manned the .50-cal machine gun on the tank's turret. There, he was exposed to return enemy fire. In spite of this, he kept up his fire and directed the fire of the tank's main gun. Seven enemy machine guns were destroyed in the ensuing battle. The enemy directed heavy fire on the tank, trying to kill Turner and knock out the vehicle. The tank absorbed over 50 enemy hits, the periscope was destroyed and its antennae was shot away. Although wounded, Turner remained at his position until killed. He was later awarded the Medal of Honor posthumously.

The Fight for Yongsan, Sept. 2

From its positions overlooking the approaches, D/2d Engineer Bn detected a long line of white-clad people moving quietly through Yongsan toward Co. A. The word was passed to Able Company about 3 a.m. on Sept. 2. Intelligence estimated an enemy battalion, with four tanks in the town at the time.

Enemy struck the Engineer Bn about 4 a.m., trying for a breakthrough. However, once daylight came, the North Koreans could no longer reinforce the effort because D/2d Engineers commanded the town and its approaches. A savage, bloody fight continued until 11 a.m., with heavy casualties on both sides. Companies A and B, 72d Tk Bn joined the engineers in stopping this enemy thrust. The engineers, lacking artillery and mortar support, partially made up for the deficit with nine 3.5 inch rocket launchers and nine of the older 2.36 inch rocket launchers, four heavy and four light machine guns. 1LT Lee E. Beahler Jr., commanding D/2d Engineers, was the only company officer not killed or wounded. He was awarded the Distinguished Service Cross for his valorous leadership.

The company had beaten off two enemy attacks, losing 12 KIA and 18 WIA in the effort. LT Beahler directed the unit's small arms, automatic weapons and rocket fire to regain fire superiority. The enemy's third attack penetrated into Yongsan. Beahler then moved some of his men to counter this thrust. The attack was blunted when the engineers knocked out a T-34. "The town was saved and the threat to the whole position was eliminated," by his "superb leadership and aggressive actions," read his citation. Enemy dead and wounded and destroyed and abandoned enemy equipment dotted the edge of Yongsan and the hill slopes south of town at the battle's conclusion.

SGT Robert P. Gifford (D/2d Engineers) wrote: "About midnight the bugles started and we could hear the tanks.... The tanks had to come down the road, because the hills were on one side; the rice paddies on the other. We were on the hill just above a small village. Down the hill to my left the C.O. had put a machine-gun. The mortar company let go with flares. We could see the enemy and their tanks. The bazooka people were called and my bazooka operator got a tank that night. We had a firefight that night. Just after sunrise the enemy pulled back, but not before we got three more tanks."

While these battles raged, COL Hill reorganized about 800 men of the 9th Infantry who had arrived near Yongsan from their overrun river positions. Only Companies F and G had escaped relatively unscathed, but with no heavy equipment or crew-served weapons.

That afternoon, the reorganized 2/9th Infantry and tanks from B/72d Tk Bn attacked through A/2d Engineers and retook Yongsan from the enemy at 3 p.m. "GI's of the Second Division, gagging on acrid smoke of burning thatch roofs, slugged their way through fiery Yongsan and took high ground to the west Saturday," is the way AP correspondent Bem Price described the action. He went on: "[A]n American tank, apparently immobilized, was pumping shells and machine gun fire into a defilade"

"The retreating North Koreans — broken up into small units — were suffering heavy casualties under rifle and machine-gun fire from American infantry from high ground directly to their front and rear.

"In the western outskirts of town a sniper, wearing white trousers and a mustard-colored jacket, leaped out at me from a bush 20 yards away. A GI, whose name I do not know, but to whom I am grateful, put two bullets through the sniper's chest."

A couple of "bazooka men" passed the U.S. tank in a jeep and stopped about 200 yards away. They then pumped three rocket rounds into a T-34. The third round burst inside the enemy tank. Among the American officers was a LT F. Reid, leading a six man patrol. Edward Parker, a very tired medic, told Price his unit had lost heavily in the attack.

"This is the second time I've had my company shot out from under me," he told Price. "We can locate only 45 guys. That is five better than the last time." (See Chapter Notes.)

Leonard T. Ferrell, of Co. G, 9th Infantry, also took part in the attack through Yongsan. Companies F and G, 9th Infantry, made the attack. He was a rifle squad scout, he wrote. Co. G went down through the main part of town. "One hundred forty [men from Co. G] went in and 50 came out in about four hours," he wrote.

The official history notes that two rocket launcher teams from A/2d Engineers knocked out three enemy tanks west of Yongsan later in the day and that U.S. ground and air attacks destroyed other T-34s during the day southwest of town.

One tank of A/72d Tk Bn was knocked out. Four crew members, including Corporals Richard L. Dailey, Robert T. Elmer and PFCs James Hurst and Lonnie Thronton, were killed. All elements of the 72d were committed to battle on Sept. 1 and 2, including the clerks, mechanics and cooks from Headquarters and Service Co. (H&S Co.)

A section of D/82d AAA/AW Bn supported A/2d Engineers in their attack on Sept. 2. The attack was to have begun at 6 a.m., but the clog of refugees on the road delayed it until 8 a.m. The Antiaircraft Battalion history records that "fighting all day against stiff opposition resulted in an advance of only 200 yards."

By 3 p.m. an M-16 supporting E/9th Infantry had been knocked out and the infantry trying to advance on the right flank had been stopped by enemy AT fire. Another AAA section, with close fire support from A/72d Tk Bn aided A/2d Engineers in the center. Both the M-16 and M-19 of the section were knocked out by enemy fire. The M-16 was withdrawn but the M-19 was left to be retrieved on Sept. 3. The M-16 covered the engineers with overhead fire. The battery lost one KIA and 3 WIA during the day. By 5 p.m., Battery D had only two quad .50s and two twin 40s left operational.

The attack of A/2d Engineers continued into the night, but it still was unable to reach its objective, the high ground which had been designated as part of the Marine's LD.

By that evening, however, the enemy had been ejected from Yongsan and into the hills to the west. The 2/9th Infantry and A/2d Engineers occupied the chain of low hills northwest and west of the town. G/9th Infantry was north of the road running west from Yongsan to Koganni; A/2d Engineers south of this road and F/9th infantry on the Engineer's south (left) flank. The remnants of 1/9th Infantry were even further to the south. It is important to note these dispositions. There were no significant elements of the 9th Infantry or other 2d Division commands on the right (north) flank of G/9th Infantry.

Planning a Counterattack — Sept. 2

At 9:35 a.m. Sept. 2, GEN Walker called MG Doyle O. Hickey, MacArthur's Deputy Chief of Staff, on the telephone. He outlined the friendly and enemy situations as he knew them. He said that he had started the Marines toward Yongsan but had not yet committed them. He wanted to be sure that MacArthur approved the employment of the Marines, since he knew that this would interfere with the plans for Inchon. Walker then said that he did not think that he could restore the 2d Division lines without the Brigade. Hickey responded that MacArthur had approved Walker's use of the Marines on Sept. 1, at the latter's discretion. At 1:35 p.m., Walker officially attached the Marine Brigade to the 2d Infantry Division. Simultaneously, he ordered that all available elements of the division and the Brigade attack to destroy the enemy east of the Naktong in the 2d Division sector and restore the river line. The Brigade was to be released from 2d Division control as soon as the mission was accomplished.

In the meantime, GEN Craig had established his Brigade CP in Miryang at 6 p.m. on Sept. 1. The 1-11th Marines was returned to the Brigade from Chindong-ni, where it had been firing in support of elements of the 25th Infantry Division. At 10:30 p.m., he received orders from Walker's headquarters to move the Brigade at first light to a reserve position south of Yongsan and to the rear of the 9th Infantry.

At 6:30 a.m. on Sept. 2, 2-5th Marines arrived at their assigned covering position on the Yongsan road. The balance of the Brigade arrived in the assembly area later in the day. At 8:30 a.m., GEN Craig, accompanied by his assistant G-3, MAJ Frank R. Stewart, Jr., helicoptered to the 2d Division CP for a conference to plan the move of the Brigade into 2d Division lines. After the conference, Craig spent the rest of the morning on a helicopter terrain reconnaissance. Enroute, he stopped at LTC Murray's CP and learned that the 5th Marines were well established along the road to the front.

The counterattack planning conference began at 2:30 p.m. BG Craig and MAJ Stewart attended the meeting for the Marines. GEN Keiser, his Chief of Staff, COL John M. Tulley and Colonels Collier and McClain, from MacArthur's staff, were also present. GEN Keiser and his staff emphasized the criticality of the division situation. They wanted the brigade to counterattack that very afternoon on a wide front.

GEN Craig objected to both proposals. First, it was already late in the day. Second, some Bri-

gade units had not yet arrived at their assembly areas, while others were still detraining or were in trucks. Third, smoke and haze over the battle area impaired the effective use of air support. Fourth, Craig did not then have contact with the carriers which would provide the tactical aircraft. In regard to the brigade attacking on a wide front, Craig suggested that the 2d Division assign objectives to the Brigade and let him decide what formation to employ. He also proposed that the attack commence the following morning. Faced with these logical objections, and his equally logical proposals, Keiser agreed with Craig.

The plan of attack, to begin at 8 a.m., Sept. 3:

9th Infantry (-1st Bn), on the right, supported by B/72d Tk Bn and D/82d AAA/AW Bn: Attack in zone to the northwest. Establish contact with 23d Infantry.

Marine Bde, in the center: Attack in zone, astride the Yongsan-Naktong River road.

2d Engineer Bn; remnants 1/9th Infantry; elements 72d Tk Bn, on the left: Attack in zone southward. Establish contact with the 25th Infantry Division.

The 2d Infantry Division Operations Directive of Sept. 2, 1950 stated that the attack mission was "to restore former 9th Infantry positions."

The Marine Brigade's plan had the 1st and 2d Battalions advancing westward abreast along the Yongsan road, with the 2d to the right of the road. The 3d Battalion was initially in reserve, blocking the southern approaches to Yongsan.

Meantime, Eighth Army ordered the 24th Division headquarters and its 19th Infantry to move into the Susan-ni area, eight air miles south Miryang and about 15 miles east of the junction of the Naktong and Nam Rivers. From there, it could be committed into either the 2d or 25th Division sectors.

COL Hill returned to his CP at 7 p.m. on Sept. 2 and conferred there with Marine Colonel Murray. He told Murray that the Marine's LD for the next morning was secured. (Hill was wrong.) This "line" was along a north-south ridgeline about a thousand yards east of Yongsan. This ridge started just south of the village of Myong-ni. The Yongsan-Naktong road ran east and west, cutting through the ridge. On Sept. 2, G/9th Infantry was deployed to the north of the road along the ridge and A/2d Engineers was south of the road on the same ridge. F/9th Infantry extended the ridge position farther south.

At dawn on Sept. 3, CPT Reed led his A/2d Engineers on another attack to seize the LD. The unit fought its way to within a hundred yards of crest. At that moment Reed was wounded by an enemy grenade which he had caught and was in the act of throwing back. The engineers withdrew, covered by the fire from an M-16. Then, aided by tank fire from Marine 2LT Robert M. Winter's M-26 tanks, the engineers advanced again to take the hill. This battle for the LD delayed the Marine attack until 8:55 a.m.

The Marine history and Geer's *The New Breed* create the impression that the 9th Infantry and other elements of the 2d Division were in the act of pulling back from the enemy. This is not entirely true. As related previously, F and G Companies of the regiment had just driven enemy troops from Yongsan late on Sept. 2. Both

companies lost heavily in that fight. There was a fight in progress between enemy troops and 2d Division Engineers for part of the LD. Just to their north was G/9th Infantry, the only significant force north of the road. No 2d Division troops were then available to cover, much less screen, the mountainous, and dominant terrain which lay just north of Yongsan and east of Myong-ni.

This mountain reached a peak over 600 meters high about 1,500 meters north of Yongsan and about 2000 meters east of Myong-ni. From this area, enemy troops could observe Army and Marine troops in the Yongsan and nearby valley and infiltrated Yongsan and adjacent areas after the town fell to the Americans on Sept. 2. This partially explains the confused situation which the Marines found in and around Yongsan early on Sept. 3. There was, undoubtedly, delay and confusion. The 9th Infantry (-), supported by A/72d Tk Bn and D/82d AAA/AW Bn began their attack at 8:30 a.m. The 2d Division history records that, after taking certain assigned objectives, this force was passed through by the Marines.

The 2-5th Marines detrucked at 4:50 a.m. on Sept. 3 about 800 yards east of Yongsan and marched through the town. Enroute, its column was fired on by a few snipers, who were quickly dealt with. By 6:30 a.m. the battalion reached the road junction at the western edge of town. At this point, a road branched off to the north to Myong-ni.

The battalion, although a thousand yards from its LD, began receiving fire from its front. There appeared to be confusion up ahead. LTC Roise moved forward about 500 yards to a low hill on the MSR. He saw what appeared to be 9th Infantrymen in retreat. "At this point," wrote COL Theodore F. Spiker, USMC, Ret., then a Major commanding Weapons Company, 2-5th Marines, "an Army colonel came up from the rear in a jeep and told us that they had to move back one ridge during the night. (No harm done.)"

There seemed to be no friendly activity to the right, but tanks (probably from the 72d Tk Bn) were parked to the south of the MSR and to the front were four U.S. and two T-34 tanks — all destroyed or abandoned.

Later in the day, PFC Paul F. DiNoto, a loader on Marine tank A-24, was sent forward to destroy two of these tanks with thermite grenades. In carrying out this task, he was wounded by enemy artillery fire.

On high ground three hundred yards to the west and south of the MSR, he saw American troops in retreat from the Marine battalion's LD.

GEN Craig and MAJ Stewart observed the confused situation from the general's helicopter. They landed near Yongsan, and proceeding on foot, located the 1-5th CP south of Yongsan and discovered that the battalion was slightly out of position. While waiting for the 2d Battalion to move through the town, COL Murray had ordered Newton's 1st Battalion to move to the west and align his battalion for the attack as best as he could. Darkness and the confused tactical situation near and on the LD caused the 1st Battalion to move south of Chukchon-ni instead of Yongsan. (Chukchon-ni was about 700 yards south of Yongsan, on the road to Namji-ri in the

25th Division sector.) The general ordered LTC Newton to make a 500 yard correction to the north during the forthcoming attack.

At 6:45 a.m., Roise called Winter's tank platoon forward to help the struggling soldiers on the hills ahead. It was this tank fire which turned the tide for A/2d Engineers. The tankers fired from hull defilade next to the 2-5th OP.

Counterattack, Sept. 3

The 2d Battalion, 5th Marines launched its attack at 7:15 a.m. to clear the Yongsan-Myong-ni road and secure the regimental right flank. Co. E was given the initial mission of clearing some low hills below Myong-ni. These hills had originally been part of the Marine LD. Meantime, 2d Division troops had cleared the 1-5th Marine's LD and LTC Roise immediately called in devastating tank, artillery, air, mortar and machine gun fire on it. In spite of this, as Co. E cleared its series of hills, it received fire from the enemy located on the high ground being pounded by Roise's fire.

"We spread out as skirmishers going up a ridgeline," wrote PFC Robert Q. Dickson, of the 2d Platoon, E-5th Marines. "We drew scattered small arms and some mortar fire. LT Eddy went down with an upper body wound. We all took turns carrying the boss off the hill."

However, Jaskilka's company completed its mission by 8 a.m. and LTC Roise ordered 1LT H. J. Smith's D Company to move through Myong-ni and seize the hill just northwest of the town.

Winter's tank platoon, on a small hill straddling the MSR west of Myong-ni, was joined by 1st Platoon, Co. A, 1st Engineers (Marine). About this time, an Army tank unit, unexpected by the Marines, went into hull defilade behind the southern portion of the hill and added its firepower to that of the Marines. This tank unit was part of the 72d Tk Bn. GEN Craig, his Chief of Staff, COL Snedeker and MAJ Stewart crawled to the crest of the hill to the right of the MSR to study the front from positions between the Marine tanks and Roise's CP.

Enemy fire concentrated on the hill where Craig had set up his OP. LT Winter was shot through the neck and one of his men was wounded giving him aid. Meantime, Chaplains Sporrer and Hickey began making their way up along the MSR toward the hill when the enemy took them under fire. "It's lucky they're poor shots," Sporrer observed. The two Chaplains arrived safely and just in time to administer to the wounded being carried to the rear.

"Our Company D was making advances... going through a village," wrote Howard Varner. "We came under heavy artillery fire; pinned us down for awhile. I was laying by a tank which was drawing fire. An anti-tank shell came in on us and wounded a lieutenant, another guy and myself." The wounded officer could have been LT Winter.

Emerging from Myong-ni, Dog Co. crossed the road leading north from the town and turned to attack south on an enemy-held ridge. It was apparently during this action that at least one Army tank mistakenly fired a number of its main gun rounds and a number of bullets from one or more of its machine guns on members of D-5th Marines as the latter assaulted the enemy-held ridge. (See Chapter Notes.)

"This is the incident as I recall it," wrote CPL Frank Raponi. "We jumped off in the attack early in the morning. We were supported by the 90mm guns of our [Marine] tanks. We were on the right hand side [the Myong-ni side] of the road. Our mission was to cross the road and follow a small stream that ran through a rice paddy to the base of a small hill that we were going to occupy. We were receiving a fair amount of casualties. About half way up the hill we were bogged down. Directly in back of us was the road we had crossed beyond the rice paddy. Our attention was called to a tank coming down the road from the direction of where we thought the enemy was. There was no mistaking it for anything but friendly because of the bright colored [air] panel on it."

The only road into the Co. D zone at that point came from the north out of the 9th Infantry on the Marine right flank. This leads to the conjecture that the tank was from Tank Co., 9th Infantry, or that it was an American tank which had been captured by the enemy. Unfortunately, no mention is made of this incident in either the Army or Marine histories, the 2d Division history, or the history of the 2d Division's 72d Tk Bn. There is also nothing from the 9th Infantry or its organic tank company on the subject.

"It stopped in the road just about where we crossed to follow the small stream," Raponi continued. "We saw the turret turn in our direction and were getting ready to cheer the Army's supporting fire. (We thought it was going to be directed to a higher hill beyond us.) Just then our cheers turned to horror when the coaxial machine gun started to drop rounds like rain all around us. To my amazement, I saw no one hit by the machine gun fire. That doesn't mean that it did not happen.... He was sighting in the big gun. Some of us got up and ran to our left — away from where the machine gun rounds fell. We ran maybe 5 to 10 yards and hit the ground just as the 1st round hit. Some of us got up again and ran another few yards farther to the left and hit the deck [ground] once again when the second round came. I don't recall any more than 2 rounds being fired."

SGT John Headrick was also up on the hill at the time. He wrote: "We disembarked [from trucks in Yongsan], started on foot.... We began receiving heavy artillery fire which was hitting on the hills on the right flank. The 1st Bn peeled off and began attacking...." His company moved on to Myong-ni, then his squad entered a plum orchard. There, a sniper in a tree shot the BAR-man of his first fire team. His platoon leader and platoon sergeant, standing under the tree at the time, killed the sniper. He observed enemy machine gun fire hitting near a Marine who dove behind a Korean grave mound. An Army tank was parked on the road with its main gun pointed at the ridge which was to be Co. D's next objective, Hill 117. "I could see a lone P-51 Mustang making a couple of strafing runs on the ridge [Hill 117]. SSG Crowson [platoon sergeant] got on the tank phone and requested a few rounds be placed on the ridge to aid our assault. The only cover we had was knee high rice paddy all the way to the ridge. After about 4 rounds from the Army tank we jumped off."

Headrick's 1st Platoon was on the right of the company and his squad was on the right of the platoon. The enemy took the advancing Marines under small-arms, machine gun and mortar fire. "I could see bullets clipping rice paddy stalks around my legs," he wrote. "I hit the deck and rolled over. SSG Crowson...casually walked up and kicked me in the butt and said, 'Get up and lead those men.' I stood up and yelled, 'Some SOB is trying to kill me!'" But Headrick moved his men forward on the double out of the paddy. They reached the ridge base, climbed a vertical 15-foot embankment and moved toward the hill's crest. They reached the top without casualties. Hearing enemy voices over the crest, they threw three grenades toward the sound. Once the grenades exploded, there was silence.

"About this time we began to catch hell. We had snipers in our rear — MG on our flanks, sweeping us with grazing fire, mortars and light artillery. The machine gun section attached to his squad took several casualties. His platoon leader yelled for the men to get down. Headrick dove into an erosion ditch about 5 inches deep. Three or four more Army tanks joined the first one down on the road, he recalled. They fired their main guns and coaxial machine guns into Headrick's squad, he wrote. One of his men was almost blown out of his clothing.

"He bounced three times," Headrick wrote. "On the third bounce, his belly split open and his intestines rolled out in my face." Headrick himself was propelled on his stomach, his face to the rear, down the hill toward the embankment. Unable to stop himself, his body hurtled over the embankment. He was without helmet or weapon as he sailed through the air. That's all he remembered until he regained his senses and found himself "squatting in the rice paddy at the base [of the hill] with helmet on and my carbine in my hand," he wrote.   Very soon, he found what was left of the machine-gun section, and started back with them to the CP. Within 25 yards, a sniper shot at Headrick. The bullet smacked the side of the ditch about an inch from his head, sending stinging dirt into his face. He and three other men crouched in the ditch with him. Then, one by one each of them was killed, shot in the head, as they tried to run on down the ditch. Finally, only Headrick was left. He lunged for the top of the ditch, wanting to get up and over and into the paddy beyond. Instead, he landed half in and half out of the ditch. Expecting to be shot momentarily, he pulled himself out of the ditch and, grabbing rice stalks, pulled himself along for a few yards, then went back into the ditch.

There he found five or six wounded Marines. One of them was the machine-gun section sergeant, with a bullet hole through his foot. Headrick bandaged the men he could and "got them back to the road and the same Army tank that blew us off the ridge and caused the sniper to catch us in the ditch," Headrick wrote. "One tanker opened the hatch to throw out empty shell casings. He said to me, 'We are sorry we shot you guys up.' I said, 'You b_____s go tell that to the ones we left up there.' He got down into the tank and closed the hatch and the tanks covered us to our CP." Headrick wrote that he later learned that his 2d Fire Team Leader, PFC Ferguson was killed by .50-cal machine gun fire from the tanks while waving an air panel, attempting to identify the Marines as friendly troops.

Valente U. Yruegas, who was on the hill with Dog Co. at the time, thought that the Army tank fire "decimated our ranks, to the tune of 40-plus casualties," he wrote. During this action Yruegas was hurled 8-10 feet. "Although I got concussion," he recalled, "I did not receive a scratch. But my ears kept ringing all the way to the Inch'on landing." His best friend was not so lucky; he was killed by the blast. One shell fragment tore a gaping hole in his chest.

William Albert, of D Company, was still down near the road in a ditch. Other men from his unit were already in the paddies and some on the slopes of Hill 117. "The Army tank stopped parallel to us [on the road], turned its turret towards the hill we were on and opened fire with its cannon on the Marines," he wrote. "LT Dunbar took off his helmet and started beating on the tank. The turret hatch opened [and] one of the tank crew manned a .50-cal. machine gun and started firing on the Marines in the paddy. LT Dunbar got up on the tank and yelled at the soldier that he was killing Marines.."

Lloyd W. Pasley, also a Company D man, wrote this: "On September 3, 1950, in the early morning darkness, the sky was ablaze with outgoing and incoming tracers and small arms fire. Dog Company was on the outskirts of Yongsan on the right side of the road. It was daylight when one of our rifle platoons was to my right and forward of me moving to our objective. They were in single column walking on a path just above a rice paddy by the side of the hill.

"There were several houses along our left side. The Army tank rolled up on the road just in front of me and to my left. Within a few minutes they opened fire with machine guns on the Marines walking on the path above the rice paddy. We managed to inform the tank crew that they were firing on Marines and the firing ceased. I don't believe there were any WIAs or KIAs from this incident.

"We moved on toward our objective. The hill that was our objective was on the left side of the road and across an open rice paddy. I was with machine guns and we set up a battery fire from the right side of the road while our rifle platoons moved out to assault the hill. The Company Commander, H. J. Smith (later KIA) was directly behind me about five feet and our 60mm mortars to my left.

"As the Marines were going up the hill we had to lift our machine gun and mortar fire. The Army tank came up the road and stopped just to my left front and fired the 90mm cannon into the Marines assaulting the hill. On this occasion there were casualties — dead and wounded. One of the dead was a Marine named Cavender. Gordon Jones, who was in my gun section, ran to the rear of the tank, grabbed the tank phone, and managed to inform the tank crew that they were firing into assaulting Marines. For a few seconds there was utter chaos trying to alert the tank crew."

Pasley's account indicates that there were two tank incidents that morning involving men from D-5th Marines.

PFC Alfred R. Jordan was a BAR-man in the 2d Platoon of Co. D. As his platoon assaulted Hill 117 the morning of Sept. 3, he was hit in the foot and lower legs by fragments from a mortar or artillery round. A Corpsman treated him then Jordan began crawling down the hill. "I inched downward," he wrote, "on my two hands and one foot. Enemy fire continued heavy and I kept hoping I wouldn't get hit again." At the bottom of the hill, he was carried in a poncho and placed into an Army tank for evacuation. "Blood had come through my foot dressing and was dripping inside the tank. I placed my foot in my helmet. I can remember an Army gunner firing a machine gun in the direction of the hill that I had come from. After a while I noticed that a pool of blood had formed in my helmet. I shouted to the gunner, 'Let's get this GD heap moving before I bleed to death!' His reply was that he had to expend his ammo before we could move. I wonder now if this could have been one of the Army tanks...firing in error on Dog Co. I do not know!"

Lloyd W. Pasley (D Co.) wrote a possible explanation of how a tank crew could have made such a mistake. "There is a logical reason for the tank crew's actions," he wrote. "They may have observed the machine guns battery fire in support of the rifle platoons. When we lifted the machine gun and mortar fire, the tankers may have figured they were assisting us with heavy supporting fire."

Co. D cleared Myong-ni of the enemy and took the hill across the road to the northwest. However, once on this lower hill, the unit began receiving galling machine-gun and mortar fire from Hill 117. This ridge ran northward about 500 yards from the MSR in the 2d Battalion's zone of action.

Smith's company, on the lower slopes of the Hill 117 was isolated about 500 yards from the remainder of the 2d Battalion and was being chewed up by enemy artillery, mortars and automatic weapons. The mounting casualties made it difficult to retain the position.

Meantime, LT Winter's 2d Platoon of tanks, now commanded by 2LT John S. Carson, moved westward along the MSR and became heavily engaged with enemy AT weapons. Tank commanders exposed themselves from unbuttoned vehicles to better detect enemy emplacements. LT Carson, so exposed, was killed instantly by enemy machine gun fire. This platoon had five M-26 tanks, numbered A-21 through A-25. PFC Paul DiNoto was a loader on A-24 in this battle. SSG William Robinson was the tank commander; SGT Hobson the driver; CPL Henry the gunner and PFC Desimone, bow gunner. "We were receiving heavy enemy fire," DiNoto wrote, "but managed to knock out one T-34 tank. I was in the turret of our tank and doing my job of loading the turret gun and the machine gun on top. I remember seeing the enemy swing their tank guns toward us. I was really scared.... When they fired at us they must have hit the ground because it threw dirt all over our tank. I was loading the gun again after they fired and that's when I got hit. I had blood in my mouth and my face and arms stung from pieces of shrapnel."

SSG Robinson wrote: "We were receiving heavy enemy fire. We knocked out one T34 tank and there was a flash in the turret and PFC Paul F. DiNoto had a bloodied face so I had him change positions with PFC Desimone, the assistant driver [and bow gunner]. PFC Desimone

loaded the 90mm tank gun and we started to move the turret to engage another T34. Sergeant Hobson, my tank driver, saw that PFC Paul F. DiNoto was not in the assistant driver's seat and via the intercom was telling us not to traverse the turret, as we were going to pin him [DiNoto] in the turret."

"I started crawling down head first from the turret to the assistant driver's seat," wrote DiNoto, "and realized the turret was being turned to aim at another tank. I thought that I would be pinned inside the tunnel and be cut in half." Hobson was able to move DiNoto and the turret could then be traversed. DiNoto and Robinson both needed medical treatment after the battle. DiNoto lost some teeth, had taken some fragments in the face and arms and hurt his back. The unit was so short-handed that both men were immediately returned to duty.

SGT Donald R. Gagnon commanded tank A-23 at the time. His crew included driver SGT Hopkins; assistant driver CPL Carolan; loader PFC. J. R. Davis and gunner PFC File. SGT Gagnon wrote of actions which could have taken place at this time, but certainly during the Second Naktong. "We moved into position on a ridge line that was long enough to accommodate six tanks, one of which was an M4A3 with 105mm howitzer. This M4 was able to lob some 105 HE over the ridge to our front on the reverse slope, as with our own artillery. The enemy swarmed over the hill towards our position like ants. All of them in American uniforms.

"They were about 5 to 8 hundred yards to our front. My crew and I thought we were shooting at our own troops. For once we had good radio contact with our leaders and the word was passed about the enemy being in our uniforms. (One tell-tale thing to identify Marines was their leggings. They always had on leggings and were easy to see.) When the battle was over and we traversed the area, it was hard to believe the number of enemy we had killed. We also engaged enemy T34 tanks in this same actions, which we destroyed. When this battle ended our confidence in our 90mm guns' ability to knock out the T34 tank was at its highest."

The platoon went into hull defilade and there surprised and knocked out three enemy tanks. Then the tankers turned their attention to all kinds of targets — from AT and machine gun positions to troop concentrations and parties either trying to withdraw or reinforce.

Around noontime, 2LT Sweet's 3d Platoon joined the 2d. Sweet's men fired into a stand of brush suspected of concealing an AT gun; they knocked out a T34 hidden there. The enemy abandoned another tank on the left side of the road. In all, four T34s had been knocked out by Marine tanks, and a fifth abandoned by its crew.

SGT George M. Wiles, of the 2d Battalion Weapons Company witnessed some of this action. "We...moved onto the roadway and forward toward the enemy. About 50 or so yards to our front were 5-6 Marine tanks on a ridge, all firing toward a fleeing enemy. The concussion from the tank fire was so intense that an 81mm mortar forward observer directing their fire was knocked to the ground each time a tank 'cranked one off.' [Fired its main gun.] Each round seemed to drive me deeper into the ground and I was convinced that my eardrums would 'implode.' As friendly fire intensified, the enemy began withdrawing at a more rapid pace, but not before firing a lot of automatic weapons and other types in our direction. Some of it made a neat 'tattoo' around me as I attempted to melt into the muddy rice paddy."

Still later, Wiles saw the bodies of a number of dead U.S. soldiers scattered here and there on the battlefield. He wondered why Graves Registration, or someone had not attended to them. No friendly troops, Army or Marine, had been in these areas to be able to retrieve these dead.

Meantime, 1-5th Marines had attacked at 8:55 a.m. from below Chukchon-ni with Fenton's B Company on the right and Steven's A Company on the left. In order to get into the correct alignment with the 2d Battalion to the north, the 1st Battalion had to move slightly northwest, then turn west as they gained the MSR. From that point, the battalion advance would be to the west with its right flank along the MSR. The objective, an enemy held ridge, lay a thousand yards to the front as the battalion moved out.

Ike Fenton recalled that this was the first time that the brigade could employ two battalions abreast, in accordance with doctrine. Shortly after the attack began, the 2d Battalion was stopped by heavy fire from Hill 117, north of the MSR. "But the 1st Battalion was able to move and seize the ridge line without encountering heavy opposition," Fenton said. "I don't believe the enemy realized that we had a battalion to the left of the road, because he was preparing to take that high ground himself. We beat him there by a good 10 to 20 minutes and caught him across another rice paddy. We really had a 'turkey shoot.'

"From our position we were able to support by fire the movement of the 2d Battalion. But the enemy defense was strong, and by nightfall the 2d Battalion had moved but a short distance."

2LT Edward C. Morris, a platoon leader in Co. B, recalled that the attack on the first enemy hill was fairly easy. "The first hill, after jumping off in the attack, was taken with very light resistance," he wrote. "As I expected the enemy shot and ran.... My unit suffered only one WIA, which pleased me."

PFC Carl T. Lawendowski, also of Co. B, remembered an easy attack. He wrote: "Baker Company started our assault for the hill objective...in the form of a wide skirmish line in a rice paddy. I recall the hill being peppered with preparatory mortar and artillery fire before we received the order to attack. As we trotted thru the paddy toward the base of the hill, I noticed some of the Marines in the line were firing their weapons at the hill from the standing position.... I proceeded to do likewise [fire at the hill] even though I saw no targets.... I just felt more at ease firing my rifle during the assault; gave me more confidence and felt the additional firepower couldn't hurt. In my thought, the hill fell rather easily but I learned later that two of my good friends were casualties."

Another casualty that day was SGT Walter L. "Waldo" Wolfe, Jr., a combat veteran from WW II. He was a B Company machine gun section leader. This was his third wound. "We're in position for the final assault," he wrote. "Only this time, I did not make it to the position. Just

short of where we would assault, at a point where I, along with a few other predicted an enemy mortar barrage would fire for effect, just as we were busting a__ through the bracketing point. We had 2 KIAs from the 2d Platoon and 5 WIAs, but it did not slow anything down."

Wolfe was one of the wounded, but he was happy! "To successfully attain a 3d PH [Purple Heart] without lights out [being killed], is cause for great joy and jubilation," he wrote, "and in my case, I added a few jumps with joy. Naturally, my Co. Cmdr was sure the shrapnel to my gourd [head] finally proved I was Whacky Waldo." Waldo was medically evacuated, but went AWOL from the medical facility to rejoin his unit on Sept. 6 or 7.

The Marine official history records that the 1st Battalion was subjected to enemy long range small-arms fire as its men waded through the knee-deep muck of a rice paddy. LTC Newton quickly acted to suppress this fire by "plastering the ridge with artillery and mortar fire." The battalion reached a drainage ditch about half way across the paddy. A short stop was made there to check the long skirmish line of the two assault companies and to place the wounded on dikes where they could be seen by corpsmen. In addition to artillery and mortars, the battalion called in air strikes to knock out enemy emplacements. Co. A even added an "Army tank destroyer" to provide overhead fire from a hill south of Chukchon-ni. Marine 75s joined the Army weapon on one occasion to knock out enemy guns in a little village at the foot of the ridge.

Co. B took their part of the battalion objective in somewhat over an hour. This placed the unit on a peak south, across the road from Hill 117, from whence Co. D was taking such a pounding. During the advance, Fenton had seen and reported large bodies of enemy troops running into the 2d Battalion's zone. The information was quickly relayed to LTC Roise.

Frank Muetzel recalled, "B Co. was on the right flank and A on the left.... The recon platoon was off to our left flank, out of sight, but watching the flank. The company commander briefed us alongside an M-4 Sherman (Army) that was atop a rise just south of the road from Yongsan to the river. We were facing a long ridge line extending from in front of Yongsan toward the west. A rice paddy of 500-600 yards was between us and the ridge. We had support from tanks, artillery and air and all three fired alternately as we crossed the paddy.... We were to guide on B Co., who in turn, was guiding on the 2d Bn. The 2d Bn ran into resistance in the village [of Myong-ni] itself and was delayed. As a result the Bn left flank soon was ahead of the 2d Bn. We slowed but didn't stop. If one kept moving, it reduced the chance of getting hit." Muetzel came across three soldiers in the paddy. One was wounded and the other two were helping him. They seemed to be doing all right, so he did not permit his corpsman to give treatment. Instead, he sent the three GIs back to an Army tank which could be seen to the rear.

The Marine history states that the attacking Marines encountered a number of wounded soldiers in this advance. Some of the men had been isolated for two or more days, according to that account.

At 11 a.m., Fenton and Stevens were ready

to make the final assault. When they notified LTC Newton, he blanketed the objective with 81mm mortar fire.

"On reaching dry ground at the edge of the paddy and at the base of the ridge," he continued, "I hesitated long enough for both A and B Co. to get aligned, called for supporting arms fire to be lifted and the entire line charged up the hill, firing as we went. There were bodies and body parts scattered throughout the small pines. There had not been enough time for them to dig in."

TSGT McMullen's 1st Platoon was on the right, Muetzel's 2d in the center and LT Fox's 3d on the left for the assault.

"We swept to the top of the ridge, set up a hasty defense and waited for the Company OP to catch up with us.... We were positioned with the 1st Platoon on the right, 2d on the left and 3d in reserve. As the machine guns came up they went into position along the line. While he was waiting for the CO, CPT Stevens, to come up, Muetzel learned that three men — Frank Weller and Charles Reynolds, both of the 1st Platoon, and his Corpsman, Ben Simpson had all been killed. Weller and Reynolds had gotten ahead of the others, and were hit. Simpson went to their aid and was killed. "I had TSGT Dan Carroll set up all 7 of the machine guns to cover the hill to our front and to put suppressive fire on it while we pulled all three [men] back. That guy [the enemy soldier] must have been some shot. All three had been pinwheeled through the chest and all three were dead. I almost lost it at that point. The whole exercise [attack] had been textbook perfect...until this moment."

The Marine assault was so fast and fearful that almost an entire enemy company jumped from their foxholes and scrambled up and over the hill in flight. Right after them the Marines paused at the crest to carefully aim and kill most of the fleeing enemy.

The 1st Battalion took its first objective about noon on Sept. 3. The next objective for Co. B were four peaks at the end of a thousand yard ridge south of and parallel to the MSR. Co. A's was a hill to the front beyond a 200-yard valley. There was a connecting ridge on the right, but it was a poor avenue of approach.

The two units paused on the newly-won ground to reorganize, evacuate casualties and resupply ammunition. While this was in progress, fire from the enemy's side of the objective and high ground to the west caused more casualties until LTC Newton got a Corsair strike. The strike caused large groups of North Koreans to break and run. Most ran north onto Hill 117, in the 2d Battalion's zone. Newton called in artillery, which created heavy casualties among the fleeing enemy. The hillsides and road were soon strewn with bodies and equipment.

Co. D, meantime, was clinging to a toehold on the northern end of Hill 117 and Co. E had been prevented from advancing by North Koreans in Co. B's zone south of the MSR.

LT Muetzel recalled Co. A's plan to continue the attack: "We must have waited the better part of an hour before Stevens called the platoon leaders together with the plan of attack for the next ridge.... A steep draw lay to our immediate front with another ridge line behind it, gradually sloping off to the left. The 1st Platoon was to lay down a base of fire on the ridge, with all machine guns in company control. The 2d Platoon was to go down to the ravine and make a feint at the ridge while the 3d Platoon was to circle to the left and out of sight and then make the attack from the left flank. Co. B, on A's right, started its attack at 3:15 p.m.

"Under cover of the machine guns my platoon did go down into the ravine and about 2/3 of the way up the slope on the other side." The platoon halted because they were about to go into the area being hit by the covering machine gun fire. They immediately were hit by enemy small-arms fire.

CPL Raymond Stephens and his squad of Muetzel's platoon had become split from the rest. The bulk of the platoon was on the left of the draw and Stephens and his men on the right. Fox had led his platoon around the enemy right flank behind the concealment of a rice paddy bank. He misjudged when the artillery preparation would cease and did not assault as soon as it lifted. This gave the enemy time to recover and meet his attack with small arms fire. Fox was wounded and TSGT George W. Bolkow took command. He worked the platoon up into the enemy positions.

CPL Virgil W. Henderson worked his 3d Squad, 3d Platoon around to the rear of an irritating enemy machine gun position and destroyed it. In this action, Henderson was shot in the jaw.

Muetzel heard on the radio that the 3d Platoon leader had been hit. He thought that the attack was stalling. "The choice was stay where I was and get shot, attack and get shot, or try to pull back without getting shot," he wrote. "I got John Stevens [the Company Commander] on the radio and told him that if he could give me 4 rounds of 60mm on the crest, that I thought I could take the hill. [Hill 91.] He told me I was too close for the 60s but [that] he would see if he could get something for me. Muetzel told his platoon to attack as soon as the last round hit. What he got was four rounds of 4.2 inch mortars. Three hit the enemy position and one fell on his platoon, killing two men.

Acting on his own, CPL Stephens, across the draw worked his squad up the razorback ridge and around the North Korean left flank. The enemy was then hit by a "triple envelopment," as the Marine history put it, when Stephens hit from the north, Muetzel from the east and Bolkow from the south.

"We took the crest standing up and found bodies and machine guns well chewed up by small-arms fire and also the mortars. These guys were dug in. As it was getting dark, we dug in using the enemy holes, got a carrying party to remove the dead and resupplies of rations, water and small arms ammo. The South Korean police we had with the company went forward to a cluster of houses to our immediate front and cleared them. We were in good shape for the night as we not only held the high ground, but received about a half dozen replacements dragooned from our supporting elements. Around midnight it began to rain and no enemy counterattack came."

PFC David J. Bohlke, from Co. A, was wounded early in the attack that day. "We were to take a hill — I forget the number, but it had a number, you can bet on that," he wrote. "On our approach the enemy sprayed us with automatic fire as we came across an open rice paddy. I got hit in the head, left hand and right arm. I was able to crawl back by myself as we were pinned down and no one could help me. Under cover of the growing rice I got to the road." He found the aid station in an old building with a bad roof. "It really rained that night," he continued, "and while the medics worked on the badly injured those of us who could, held ponchos up over the table they were working on...to keep the rain off of them." The next day Bohlke was transported to Japan on an LST.

Co. A reported it had seized its objective at 4:30 p.m. Both companies were then ordered to dig in for the night.

"There was a little ridge line that ran off the high ground we were occupying which formed an upside down 'T,'" Fenton said. "B Company was ordered to move down this ridge line and defend it for the night. A Company would defend the high ground to our immediate rear and another ridge about 800 yards on our left flank. Once again we were faced with the situation of having nothing on our right flank. The 2d Battalion was about 900 yards to my right rear. This gave us an exposed right flank and we felt like the point of an arrow ready to be shot from the bow. That night we had a few small counterattacks that were easily repulsed. Other than that it was very quiet, and we had the suspicion that the enemy was withdrawing."

The two Marine battalions were now confronted with extended frontages and huge gaps. The 2d Battalion front was 2,000 yards long and formed a right angle. There was a 500 yard gap between Co. D on the northern edge of Hill 117 and Co. E outside Myong-ni. This left the two units isolated from one another, with no flank protection.

South of the MSR, the 1st Battalion was 900 to 1,000 yards forward of the 2d Battalion, exposing its right flank along the whole distance. The 1st had a mile-long front, with a 200 yard gap between B and A Companies. The Recon Co. was deployed far out on the battalion's left flank, but not near enough to protect that flank from an enemy attack.

To help in defending the area, LTC Newton had the 1st Platoon, Co. A, 1st Engineer Battalion place dozens of antipersonnel mines, hand grenades and blocks of TNT wrapped with 60-penny spikes to the front and flanks of Baker Co.

TSGT David N. Duncan and SGT Bryan K. White and other engineers of the platoon set up similar devices for Co. A. Duncan put a nice touch to his handiwork with a 40-pound shaped charge hooked up in a gully with a trip wire.

At midnight, SSG Saweren J. Dennis led his 2d Squad of engineers forward 1,000 yards along the MSR and placed an antitank minefield across the road near the southern tip of Hill 117. Enroute, he discovered an enemy antitank minefield in the road. Although the men were not familiar with the Russian wooden box mine, they were able to detect, disarm and remove the mines. While they were so engaged, Dennis heard a clanking noise. He discovered it was being made by an enemy soldier, desperately trying to insert a loaded magazine into his weapon.

Dennis killed him. Before the engineers could finish their job, a rainstorm swept in with a heavy downpour.

Earlier in the day, SSG George M. Wiles and two sections of the AT assault platoon were walking toward the combat area. "A lot of small arms firing was taking place between Army and North Korean troops," he wrote. "Marines were on either side of a truck convoy carrying ammunition and other supplies. What appeared to be mortar shells began exploding all around the convoy. We dispersed and ran for the ditches on either side of the roadway. About this time, our CO, Major Theodore Spiker, approached from near the rear of the convoy, took a quick glance in our direction and stated: 'What are you guys doing down THERE? The war is up HERE!' He spotted me and half-grinned, being aware that I was the 'new kid on the block' and probably as 'green' as anyone in the company (in spite of the fact that I was an NCO, but had no combat experience)."

Total Marine casualties for the day were 34 dead and 157 wounded. Casualties in the 2d Battalion totaled 18 dead and 77 wounded. Co. D suffered most of these casualties.

During the night, although he made no serious attacks, the enemy harassed some Marines with mortar fire, which created a number of casualties. One of these was PFC Richard C. Blevins, H&S, 2d Battalion. "We started getting 120mm mortar rounds...during the late morning hours," he wrote. "We sustained 6 or 7 wounded. One died and I was the only one returned to duty... in time for the Inchon landing."

PFC Raymond Johnson and SGT James I. Higgins, also of H&S, 2d Battalion, recalled the 2d Naktong. Johnson remembered the hordes of mosquitoes. He recalled being in "rice paddies, wet and using citronella to keep the mosquitoes away.... The worst for me was the 2d Naktong Bulge and the heavy casualties we endured, especially our D Company to which I was attached."

Higgins recorded his experiences this way: "4 September 1950: Two squads to rice paddy - Not much room - Dug in men at dark four men to foxhole.... About 0400 [4 a.m.] false dawn crawled to 1st foxhole told men to get some sleep that I was up and about and would let them know if something was up. I was sitting between Dixon and Burke - mortars incoming.... 2d round hit foxhole between Dixon's legs - killed Burke - Blew me out of foxhole - I had given Burke my watch so he could trade off watch [guard duty] - Dixon didn't have leg was putting on tourniquet when CPL [Norman L.] Beal from Bn said, 'Sarge, let me do it.' Was using jacket sleeve — I didn't know I was wounded felt O.K. - Carried dead and wounded to high ground.... I think PFC Simmons from Bn drove a jeep to the edge of rice paddy - With the help of Beal and Simmons we loaded the jeep with dead and wounded - Beal drove it to the rear aid station. In ten minutes we had all the dead and wounded back to the aid station - I was sure glad to see those two fine Marines shag down a couple hundred yards to give me a hand - I again checked the paddy for dead or wounded - We had gotten them all - I found hand grip from my carbine; it had been between my legs - I wrote up a recommendation for a Silver Star for Beal and Simmons on a ra-

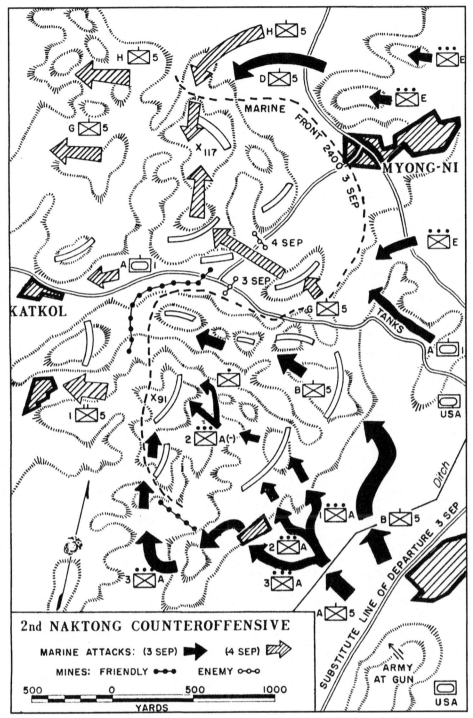

MARINE FRONT 2400 3 SEP

X 117

MYONG-NI

4 SEP

3 SEP

TANKS

KATKOL

X 91

A(-)

Ditch

SUBSTITUTE LINE OF DEPARTURE 3 SEP

USA

ARMY
AT GUN

USA

2nd NAKTONG COUNTEROFFENSIVE

MARINE ATTACKS: (3 SEP) ➡ (4 SEP) ⇨

MINES: FRIENDLY ●━●━● ENEMY ○━○━○

500   0   500   1000

YARDS

Map 43 (Source: U.S. Marine Operations in Korea 1950-53. Vol. 1, The Pusan Perimeter)

tion box and gave it to LT Gates he said he would see that it would get to Bn." Higgins had been wounded himself, with shrapnel wounds to the left side of his face and over the right eye. He refused evacuation.

The Brigade artillery was under the operational control of the 2d Division Artillery commander during this counterattack and its continuation the next two days. That officer, BG Loyal M. Haynes, was isolated in the division's northern sector, where he had been placed in command of troops with him. Two Army artillery battalions reinforced those of 1-11th Marines. Having been in the area previously, COL Wood's artillerymen were able to use the same fire chart as before. This expedited firing time and again during the three days' counterattack. In all, dur-

ing the period, the battalion fired some 5,000 rounds, destroying 6 AT guns, a light and a medium tank, 21 field pieces and numerous mortars and machine guns. During the operation, COL Wood noted, heavy smoke from burning villages and clouds made aerial observation very difficult, often impossible.

Kenneth D. Clothier, HQ, 1-11th Marines recalled that the Marine artillery battalion was able to go from three 4-gun batteries to three 6-gun batteries by utilizing Army 105mm howitzers captured by the enemy, then recaptured by the Marines.

The 9th Infantry, to the north, was to coordinate its attack with that of the Brigade. In fact, the 9th Infantry's attack was scheduled to started at 8:30 a.m. But the 9th's attack was never re-

ally coordinated with that of the Marine Brigade.

That night, LTC Murray ordered the 3d Battalion to pass through the 2d at 8 a.m. on the 4th and continue the attack. The 1st Battalion would attack south of the MSR at the same time. The Recon Co., out on the left flank, would coincidentally move forward to a new blocking position.

The Army's TF Bradley, in the southern half of the 2d Division sector, was split into two subordinate task forces for the counterattack scheduled for the next day. COL Hill, with what was left of two of his battalions, supported by tanks and AA vehicles, deployed north of the Marine Brigade was given the mission of driving west to clear the MSR in its zone, then push on to the Naktong. One section of D/82d AAA/AW, under MSG Ralph Klosky supported this force. COL Charles C. Sloane Jr., with companies of the 2d ECB, tanks and AA vehicles, south of the Marine Brigade, was ordered to attack southwest to the junction of the Naktong and Nam Rivers. Two sections of D/82d AAA/AW under LT Webster supported this force.

Counterattack, Sept. 4

Just before dawn, Marine engineers went forward and removed the mines ahead of the 1st Battalion. The artillery preparation began at 7:50 a.m., routing a party of enemy from a hilltop forward of Co. B. Marine rifle fire hurried them on their way, and the enemy soldiers threw away their weapons in flight.

The 1st Battalion attacked at 8 a.m. and moved rapidly south of the MSR against almost no resistance. Scattered groups of the enemy were frequently observed fleeing in all directions, and were usually wiped out by Marine air, artillery or mortar fire. The battalion captured 12 enemy in traversing the 3,000 yards to its part of Objective One, which it reached at 3:05 p.m. This objective was the high ground around and south of Kang-ni.

"We moved out rapidly," Fenton said, "and in about 20 minutes overran the enemy's old division command post. [The *9th Division* CP.] Tents were still up and equipment all about.... We captured two T34 tanks that were unmanned and in excellent condition. In the vicinity of the tank was a big ammunition dump which we blew up accidentally with a stray mortar round. Our advance continued very rapidly.... We had them on the run.... We had 12 [prisoners] by noon.

"By 1500 [3 p.m.] we had seized Objective 1."

Co. A had a similar easy time attaining their objective for the day; the enemy scattered before them, offering little resistance and a few prisoners.

Just after 8 a.m., the 3d Battalion started its attack against Hill 117. Co. G was on the left and H on the right. Co. G passed through E and moved through the rice paddies toward the objective. After crossing the paddy, the unit charged over a small knoll, to find it occupied by enemy dead and empty foxholes. From there, Co. G quickly moved on to Hill 117. That, too, was quiet. In taking the southern half of the hill, Co. G killed only 15 enemy soldiers.

Marine Bivouac Area in the Perimeter. (Courtesy of Eldon D. Heller, Wpns-2-5 Mar.)

Tank Numbers A-23 (SGT Gagnon); A-24 (SSG Robinson) and A-25 (TSGT Cottrell) of LT Winter's 2d Plt., A-1st TK Bn, 1st Provisional Marine Bde engage the enemy with indirect fire. PFC Dinoto was the gunner of Tank A-25, far left of photo. (Courtesy of Paul DiNoto, A/1st TK Bn)

Co. H, swinging wide, passed through Co. D, and attacked south on Hill 117 as Bohn's G came up from the south. Hill 117 was Marine territory by 8:40 a.m.

As LTC Taplett's CP was moving forward that morning over the road south from Myong-ni, the lead vehicle, loaded with communications personnel, hit a mine. Ten casualties resulted. Marine engineers, meantime, had been busy detecting and removing enemy mines on and near the road. The Marine history notes that the two anti-vehicular minefields which they found were the first encountered by UN forces in the Korean War.

After taking Hill 117, Companies G and H continued the attack abreast along the high ground north of the MSR toward Kang-ni. Contact was maintained with the 1st Battalion to the south, but could never be made with the slower moving 9th Infantry.

Enemy machine gun fire from a hill north of Kang-ni cut into Co. G about 10:45 a.m. Taplett responded with Marine air and artillery, quickly dispersing the enemy from that site. The aircraft and artillery continued to pound the hill and to chase fleeing enemy soldiers. Co. G took the objective at 3:15 p.m.

About 1 p.m., in the process of this attack, Fred Davidson was fired on by an automatic weapon while taking a drink from his canteen during a short break. He quickly looked for cover or concealment; there wasn't any. There were about four or five ROKs above him on the hill. The firing came from below and to his right. He called on the ROKs to fire in that direction. Two of them did, but the other two threw down their

weapons and ran. Davidson picked up one of the M1s and fired himself into the area where he thought the enemy to be. There was no more enemy fire after he emptied the rifle at them.

Later, after the objective had been taken, Davidson recalled, several Marines in his company began to fire at a lone North Korean running through a paddy toward the village of Hwyong-ni, almost 1,000 yards to the front. MSG Ryder soon got the fire stopped, although one of the Marines fired some 10 or 12 carbine rounds after his order. The order was to stop wasting M-1 ammo, but not carbine ammo.

The firing, however, brought a storm of return fire. "Suddenly the air was full of incoming automatic fire. It was just above our heads. Leroy [Goulette] and I jumped behind a burial mound on the top of the hill and laid on our backs, safe from the incoming fire." Soon, this fire stopped, and Davidson and Leroy left their place of shelter.

Across the stream bed north of their new positions, some men of Co. G discovered enemy infantry, with a T34, withdrawing into the zone of the 9th Infantry. They quickly dispersed this enemy with machine gun fire.

The enemy in front of the Marine Brigade had been routed. Its zone of advance was littered with enemy dead and abandoned weapons and equipment. At one point on the MSR a whole column of enemy dead lay, victims of Marine air and artillery. In the lead was the headless body of a lieutenant colonel. There was enough abandoned small arms, ammunition and equipment to outfit several hundred men. One of the dead was a paymaster. A number of Marines "paid" themselves with the worthless North Korean money found with his body. The Marines also recaptured a considerable amount of U.S. tanks, artillery pieces, mortars, vehicles, small arms and ammunition which had fallen to the enemy attack. Most of this materiel was returned to the 2d Division.

Taplett wrote of this incident: "Late in the afternoon of the 4th (before 1-5 was ordered forward) we observed an enemy force of about 150-200 NKs approaching along the MSR on our left flank and in front of the 1-5. I had my forward air controller (LT Danny Green), who had a flight of Marine Corsairs supporting 3-5 on station. [He] took them under immediate attack, along with arty and Bn mortar fire. The Corsairs did a perfect job and wiped out the entire force. Those still alive were finished off with rifle fire by 3-5.... After this action, which took place about 1600 (4 p.m.), the 1-5 moved ahead about 500 plus yards to the left front of 3-5's perimeter, which was the situation as night fell." He recalled that there was still no evidence of the 9th Infantry on his right flank.

The abandoned enemy division CP provided a "gold mine" of enemy information from documents, unit rolls, maps, orders, ledgers, textbooks and propaganda material.

Late that afternoon, the Marine history records, "the 9th Infantry moved into positions on the high ground northeast of" 3-5th Marines. This completed Phase One of the 2d Division's attack order. Phase Line Two was Hill 125 and Observation Hill, another 3,000 yards to the front. John Toland identified the Army regiment as the 5th RCT, but the 5th RCT was deployed on the southern portion of the 25th Division front line northward from the sea. Toland wrote that before dawn on Sept. 4, Taplett sent his XO to locate the 5th [9th]. The 9th was scheduled to begin its attack at 8:30 a.m., two hours or more after dawn.

Colonel Taplett wrote that Toland was wrong about when he sent the Battalion XO in search of the 9th. In fact, Taplett made repeated attempts during the day to try to establish contact with the 9th, all without success. "The 9th failed to jump off as ordered to attack abreast of 3-5," he wrote. "My battalion made fast progress that morning against moderate resistance after passing through the 2-5. By late morning it was becoming obvious that there was nobody on our right flank as our patrols to establish contact produced naught. So around 10-11 o'clock I sent my executive officer, Major John Canney [KIA Nov. 27-28 at Yudam-ni, Chosin Reservoir] back to the morning's line of departure. He found that the 9th hadn't even reached the line of departure. Later in the day after we had seized our final objective for the day, we found ourselves out on a limb so to speak. The 1-5 was on our left about 3-400 meters echeloned to our left rear and nobody on our right flank. I requested permission from COL Murray to send a reinforced patrol to our right again to try and contact elements of the 9th. This patrol was led by LT "Blackie" Cahill.... After reaching about 3,000 meters to our right was again unsuccessful. I ordered the patrol to return as it was after sundown, so we could establish a tight perimeter. Later in the day 1-5 moved about 500-1000 yards ahead on our left flank."

Once he was informed that the Brigade had attained its objective, GEN Keiser authorized GEN Craig to move on to Phase Line Two.

The Brigade right boundary narrowed down to the MSR just beyond Kang-ni, therefore, 3-5th Marines could advance no further. The Marine history states that LTC Newton was then ordered to continue the attack south of and parallel to the MSR to seize the Marine Cloverleaf Hill, about a thousand yards to the front.

A rice paddy about 1600 yards wide leading to this objective confronted the 1st Battalion. A dike ran through the paddy at a right angle to the line of advance. The only way to move vehicles forward was along the MSR. Co. B moved forward along the MSR, in a column of twos, one file on each side of the road. Its point was 400 yards to the front. "When we were about three-fourths of the way across the paddy," Fenton said, "we received very heavy enfilade machine gun, small-arms and mortar fire from our right flank and were pinned down without a bit of cover. I then decided to move forward under cover of close air support and kept the tanks moving between the small-arms fire and the troops. The amazing part is that we didn't have a single casualty. Not one man wounded or killed and the fire we received was just as intense as any fire we had received in any daylight attack."

The battalion commander had been notified of Co., B's hold-up, but Fenton, in the meantime had moved his unit onto the objective. Co. A came up on Fenton's left. The Marine Cloverleaf Hill was secure by 6 p.m.

The brigade front very much resembled the one of the previous night. South of the MSR the

1st Battalion was again about a thousand yards forward of the 3d Battalion, north of that road. Companies A and B were stretched along a mile of front, with the left flank open. Recon was off on the left, but not close enough to protect the battalion's flank in that direction. The 3d Battalion, isolated from the 9th Infantry to the north and the 1st Battalion to the south, established its own perimeter.

Again that night, the engineers laid mines to the front and flanks of the 1st Battalion. Enemy artillery and mortar fire harassed both battalions during the night. Fred Davidson recalled the fire lasted about three hours in the 3d battalion area, ending about 3 a.m. on Sept. 5. The 1st Battalion CP was hit, one blacked out tent was struck by a 120 mm mortar round. One Marine was killed and two wounded. Among the wounded was the Battalion Assistant S3, 2LT James R. Young. 1LT Joris J. Snyder, the artillery liaison officer, was knocked unconscious for several hours but suffered not a scratch from the explosion.

MAJ Joseph H. Reinburg's night fighters bombed the enemy mortar position at 2:30 a.m., then dumped general purpose and fragmentation bombs on other enemy targets. Enemy mortar fire slackened appreciably after this attack.

Both G and H Companies reported movement forward of their positions. Battalion 81s quickly fired illuminating rounds revealing several small parties of enemy. This precipitated a short flurry of firing, but there was no general attack. One enemy party stumbled into the 3d Battalion CP area and was taken under fire by a listening post from the Weapons Co. An enemy officer was killed and the others fled.

"We spent the night of 4-5 September under heavy artillery fire and frequent enemy probes of our perimeter," Taplett wrote of that night and early the following morning. "During the early morning hours G Company repulsed two enemy attacks. The next morning [Sept. 5] just after sunrise we discovered an enemy company marching up a draw about 3-500 yards to our right front in the zone of the 9th Regt. They had reached a point opposite the Battalion CP and the part of the perimeter manned by H&S Company." The 9th Infantry was still some distance behind, so the Marines took the enemy unit under fire, virtually wiping it out. "B Company, my mortars and command post personnel, especially the clerks, had what they called their first 'turkey shoot.' I am sure this facilitated the advance later that morning of the 9th [Infantry]."

Counterattack, Sept. 5

Just before dawn on Sept. 5, the enemy launched a heavy counterattack against the 9th Infantry north of the Marines. The main attack struck Co. G. The assault came in the midst of a downpouring of rain. 2LT Jack Murphy (West Point, 1950), who had just joined G/9th Infantry on Sept. 2, had his platoon, along with three tanks on a ridge 3,000 yards to G Co.'s right. Murphy recalled that the company had only two rifle platoons, and, with him, two officers. A master sergeant commanded the other platoon. Murphy's platoon sergeant was SFC Loren R. Kaufman, described as a "soft-spoken man with a large mustache."

When the enemy attacked Co. G, Murphy's

platoon was ordered back to help; the company had been knocked off its position. This is Murphy's recollection of events afterward, as reported in *Look* magazine, June 3, 1952. "We made our way back along high ground. Suddenly, in the darkness, we heard men in a ravine below. Kaufman...whispered he'd find out who they were. He walked ahead; I was about 10 feet behind him. Kaufman grabbed the first man by the helmet, looked into his face and yelled, 'Them's gooks!'

Ten enemy soldiers rushed Murphy. He bayoneted two. Men of his platoon scattered. The lieutenant then picked up a machine gun and fired it from the hip. Twenty-two enemy dead were found in that ravine the following morning.

The platoon pressed on to the G Company hill. There, Murphy, Kaufman and the two squad leaders (the platoon had only two squads) rushed the position. They ran into a machine gun nest manned by five of the enemy. Kaufman fired two rounds, then bayoneted the other three. The Army history records that Kaufman bayoneted four of the enemy and also killed an enemy mortar crew that morning. Murphy is credited with killing six or seven more of the enemy in this attack. American artillery, and Marine machine gun fire at a range of from 600 to 1000 yards helped to finally repel the enemy. By 11 a.m., 120 enemy dead littered Co. G's position, and the company had it back. Some of the enemy fled into a village at the base of the hill. SFC Kaufman took a patrol to the village and destroyed it. For their actions that morning, Murphy was awarded the DSC and Kaufman, who was killed by U.S. mortars six months later, posthumously received the Medal of Honor.

For the attack that day, 3-5th Marines would pass behind the 1st Battalion and come up on its left flank. This made 1-5th Marines the right battalion and the 3d the left in the attack. Co. B would become the right flank company of the Brigade. Elements of the 9th Infantry were to swing south to make contact with Fenton's right with its left.

The 1-5th Marines was preparing to continue the attack at 8 a.m. that morning to take Hill 125 and Observation Hill. Beyond these was a very special objective for the Marines — Obong-ni ridge. In the midst of these preparations, two F-51s suddenly dove to the attack on the Marine-held Cloverleaf. They strafed the hill from north to south. Fortunately, only one Marine was wounded in this attack.

About a half mile beyond Hwayong-ni the MSR makes a right turn southward for 1,000 yards, then turns west again through a cut between Hill 125 and Observation Hill.

It was raining heavily. Co. B received hot coffee, but the order to attack prevented its distribution — a bit of a blow to morale. The battalion began its attack at 8:20 a.m. with Co. B on the right and Co. A on the left. "We moved... against scattered resistance — mortar fire, sniper fire, and an occasional burst of machine gun fire," Fenton related. "It was enough to cause us to try an envelopment. In each case, the resistance fell back. We moved rapidly and... A and B Companies were working in close harmony. One company would take a piece of high ground on one side, and the other company would provide a base of fire.

"B Company advanced about 3,000 yards to a ridge line that ran parallel to Obong-ni Ridge, about 400 yards this side of it." (This was Hill 125.)

"The rain became so hard," wrote Edward Morris, then a platoon leader in Co. B, "it was difficult to see any distance. We met the enemy early afternoon and took him under fire. The rifle platoon led by LT Hugh Schryver clawed their way up the hill and soon entered a grenade-throwing contest with the NKPA.... We were receiving small-arms fire and being shelled by NK T-34 tanks."

Cornelius E. Fineran, also of Baker, recalled: "There was a tense time when we assaulted," he wrote. Of the action during the enemy counter-attack later, "Our battered company had only a few rounds in their belts remaining so we were told to fix bayonets and be ready because the enemy was getting ready to launch one more movement [attack]. Just as we were thinking the worst, somebody tapped me on the shoulder and said, 'Let's go.' I didn't question the order; found out that the Army was coming to replace us later."

The MSR turned south across B's front at the point mentioned above. Co. B continued on across the MSR there and on to Hill 125. Co. A, to the left, moved against Observation Hill at the same time.

"A Co. remained on the south side of the road," wrote LT Muetzel, "and also started up the slopes. It was so rainy and muddy that it was impossible to register the 60mm mortars with HE. They just got lost in the paddies. We had to use WP, which we did not like to do because it [WP ammunition] was in short supply. On gaining the high ground we found what we took to be an army outpost that had been overrun and [the soldiers] killed while trying to get out of their sleeping bags. They had been there long enough to begin to decompose. We moved to the crest and took Obong-ni under fire, although we could not really identify targets because of the rain and reduced visibility." Co. A received some machine gun fire from in front of Co. B, but there wasn't much A could do about it. (See Chapter Notes.)

When the 1st Battalion attained this objective at 11 a.m., it was ordered to hold up. Fenton and others believed that the enemy had withdrawn to Obong-ni and was fortifying it. Shortly after Co. B began digging in, "everything broke loose," Fenton said. By 2:20 p.m. the company was pinned down. Obong-ni was situated in such a position in relation to Hill 125 that the enemy was able to place fire on the forward slopes and much of the reverse slope of Hill 125. "The entire ridge line was being swept by fire," he wrote.

Because of the rain, the Marines could not call on air power. To make matters worse, the rain had also knocked out all of Fenton's platoon radios, the battalion tactical radio net, artillery and 81mm mortar nets all went down. Fenton had no communication with battalion. About this time, he received word via runner that the 9th Infantry was approaching from the right rear and was about 1,500 to 2,000 yards back. Co. B held Hill 125 and Fenton had the attached 1st Tank Platoon remain in the road cut, just to the rear of Hill 125.

Then the enemy attacked Ike's company. He recalled the force numbered between 300 and 400 men, supported by what proved to be two tanks, and a half-track personnel carrier. "It was a well prepared counterattack, preceded by a heavy mortar barrage and anti-tank...fire from Obong-ni Ridge," he said. "Intense enemy heavy machine gun fire made it practically impossible for us to move." He sent a runner to seek artillery help from the 9th Infantry, two more runners to the battalion commander with the current situation and another to the attached tanks to warn them of approaching enemy armor.

"Shortly after noon, CPT Stevens called me back to the OP and told me to collect my platoon, establish a dump and to leave all grenades and excess ammunition," Muetzel wrote. "He told me we were pulling out for Pusan to make an amphibious landing. We were extremely happy to hear this as it meant we would be rejoining the rest of the 1st Marine Division. Then I was told that B Company was in trouble.... Stevens told me to load up the 1st and 2d Platoons, 2 machine-gun sections and the mortar section and to get over to B Company post haste, along with my SCR 300 radio."

Muetzel got his men into Fenton's area and Ike fed them into the line to reinforce his badly pressed troops. Fenton had already committed every man of Co. B to defend the position. Muetzel's force arrived just in time; Co. B was running out of ammunition and grenades. The enemy was so close that the men took the grenades from the boxes, tossed them to others in forward foxholes, and they hurled the missiles into the advancing enemy.

During the fight, Fenton sent 22-year-old PFC William A. Wilson to contact the 9th Infantry for artillery support. When Wilson got to the Army unit, he found that the company commander had to be his own FO. Shortly after his arrival, that officer was wounded and evacuated. PFC Wilson took over the FO task, calling in several successful artillery missions. Fenton said that Wilson then assembled the Army platoon leaders, "brought them up to date on the situation, advised them as to the best location of their platoons, told them where to tie-in, and where best to place their machine guns. He then returned to me and reported that he had made contact with the Army and that the artillery fire had been fired as requested.... I found out later from one of the Army officers what a fine job my 'Lieutenant' Wilson had done.... I replied that Wilson wasn't an officer, just a good Marine PFC!"

During the battle, LT Pomeroy moved his tanks forward and around the bend so that his guns could bear on Obong-ni Ridge. As a result, when the first Marine tank rounded the bend, its main gun was aimed at that ridge, a quarter turn away from approaching T34s. The lead enemy tank fired and hit the M-26. Several more enemy rounds followed. The second M-26 tried to squeeze around the first and was also hit and knocked out. The crews managed to escape, although a few were wounded. The two knocked out tanks, however, prevented the other tanks of the platoon from engaging the enemy. But Fenton's 3.5 inch rocket launcher teams did the job, knocking out both T34s and the personnel carrier.

The dispatch of Muetzel and platoons from Co. A to the aid of Co. B came as 3-5th Marines were relieving Co. A, preparatory to continuing the attack.

Unlike Co. B, George Co., 3d Battalion got their hot coffee that morning, as well as mail call. The 3d Battalion then began moving behind the 1st Battalion in preparation for its attack on Hill 91. This is the same hill which figured in the attack of A/34th Infantry on Aug. 15. (See Chapter 13.) By mid-morning the 3d was ready to attack.

Co. H provided the base of fire while LT Bohn's G Company enveloped the objective. Bohn's command group led the unit. Looking back across the rice paddy his company had to traverse, the lieutenant was worried at first because he couldn't see his men crossing. Actually, they were moving so low in the newly-growing rice that it was almost impossible to detect them. The entire company got across the paddy without loss.

"It was like you read in books," he said. "It worked beautifully. We had very few casualties and secured the high ground.... We were smarter I think [than during the 1st Naktong]."

2LT David Duncan was wounded in the leg, and Bohn was ordered to send his XO, LT Charles Mize, back to battalion. There was no explanation.

During this battle, Jack "Archie" Wright was a runner for LT Bohn. In the midst of the attack, Wright recalled, LT Bohn noticed one of his platoons on the flank was getting too far from the rest of the company. He sent Wright to the platoon leader, with the message that the platoon leader was to pull his first squad back to his present position and hold. Archie took off on the run down the road. Enemy bullets soon convinced him to seek cover in a ditch. He jumped into the roadside ditch and "right into the middle of a dead dog," he said, "that had been dead for about a week or so." Wright jumped back on the road and reached the platoon. He gave the platoon leader to "pull back and hold." With that, he ran back to LT Bohn. Upon arrival, Bohn asked him what message he had given the platoon leader. Archie told him. "Archie, you get your G. D. a__ moving. You get up there and tell that man exactly what I told you word for word!" Bohn ordered. Wright again took off, running. "I was carrying a can of C-ration crackers and while I was going down this road, a bullet took that can out of my hand," Jack recalled. "I figured that road was no place for me, so I went back in the ditch, right back into the middle of that dog again. It was enough to gag a maggot." Wright made it back to the platoon leader and delivered the correct message.

This was the first battle for G Co. replacement Lloyd P. Summers. "To me it appeared just like a scene you see in the movies. We moved up in trucks so far and got out...at the debarkation spot and moved up [on foot]. It was early in the morning," he said. While waiting in the final assembly area, an enemy soldier came out of a camouflaged foxhole and surrendered. "We moved off...out over the rice paddies and the hills, sometimes in water and mud up to our knees." They met no opposition. The enemy seemed to have vanished.

After taking one hill, the unit paused to eat their C-ration. "The enemy from the ridge way out ahead of us opened up a small-arms fire and the bullets were stinging up all around our feet. Only about three feet from us." The startled Marines scuttled back to the hill's reverse slope and began looking for the source of enemy fire. Later, the company moved to another objective and began digging in. While so engaged, Marine artillery fired beyond the line. Then Summers heard one round coming in. "I thought, 'That sounds like its whistling awful low; its gonna hit. Sure enough, about 50 or 60 yards down from me, one of our own artillery shells...came in and landed right amongst a bunch of Marines that were digging in. I think it killed about five or six."

"Around 1000 hours [10 a.m.] on 5 September," Fred Davidson, Co. G, wrote, "we left the road and walked on a rice paddy levee to our left toward Hill 91, some 900 yards ahead." The point reached a spot where a dike six or seven feet high ran across the path of the levee. The company spread out in the shelter of this dike. Suddenly, the point was fired on from Hill 91. Davidson was still 800 yards or so back from them, but enemy bullets began hitting the ground around him. Since there was nowhere to find shelter, he just sat down and tried to ignore the incoming fire. "As I sat there," he wrote, "I'd say to myself, 'That one would have hit me if it were just six feet to the left — or to the right!'"

Finally, he decided to write some letters home. Pulling a poncho over himself to keep out the rain, he began to write, with a cigarette in his mouth. As he wrote, the ashes on the cigarette became longer. "Suddenly a big zoom comes ripping into my poncho, knocks off the ashes and exits out the right side! So help me! A bullet!.... The alignment of the entry and exit holes of the bullet indicated that it damned sure came close to knocking off the ashes."

George Co. led the move through the rice paddy south of Marine Cloverleaf Hill. Artillery and 75mm recoilless rifle fire fell on the objective, Hill 91. Upon reaching the slopes of the hill, LT Bohn requested these fires be lifted. They were then shifted onto Obong-ni. The company began ascending the hill and an attached 75 recoilless blasted an enemy wheel-mounted machine gun which was being placed on the crest. In the midst of this attack, Bohn got the order to withdraw.

In the attack to this time however, 1LT Edmund W. "Skeeter" Jaworski distinguished himself when he went to the aid of a wounded man lying in a paddy being swept by intense enemy fire. In the same fight, 2LT Edward F. Duncan, leader of G Co.'s 3d Platoon was wounded in the leg.

"We were to take a hill," recalled Paul Stanley Cobane, of H Co. "Lloyd Green and myself on point. About half way up grenades were coming at us like crazy. Green stood behind a tree and I laid down. Green's rifle quit working." About that time, an enemy soldier rushed Green. He killed the North Korean with a knife. Green went back down the hill, got another rifle and rejoined Cobane. The two men continued up the hill to a bunker containing several enemy burp-gunners. "Green got the bunker with a grenade," Cobane wrote. When Cobane passed the bunker, an enemy soldier emerged from it. "I shot BAR — one less gook," he wrote. "There were about 4-5 dead gooks in bunker when I went by. Green and I went up and over the hill. Gooks were running away up the next hill about 150 yards away." The two men shot at the retreating enemy until almost out of ammunition. Then they waited for the rest of Co. H. "To the best of my knowledge," Cobane wrote, "Green and I were the only two to get to the top. We waited and no one else showed up. It started to get dark, so we returned down hill. Everyone else was just standing around at the bottom of the hill!!"

In Co. G after dark, Charlie Mize came back and reported to LT Bohn that the unit was ordered to move out. "I'm not moving out!" Bohn insisted. "We just got up here!"

"I can't tell you anymore," Mize responded, "but Tap [LTC Taplett, battalion commander] got me down there so we wouldn't have to put this on the radio." Bohn complied, but "I still did not know why," he said.

Taplett had been called back to the 5th Marine CP late that morning and informed that the Brigade was to be relieved on position and that the 3d Battalion "was to make the initial amphibious landing of the Wolmi-do/Inchon Operation on Sept. 15."

CPT Fenton heard that the Brigade was being pulled back to Pusan from David Duncan, a *Life* correspondent. At 7 p.m., he was ordered to have his men dig in but not set up an elaborate defense; an Army unit was to relieve him. About two hours later, he heard a voice in the darkness called out repeatedly, "B Company! B Company!" It was an Army lieutenant, who asked why Fenton had not returned the call. Ike told him in a few well-chosen words. He recalled the Army force numbered about 40 men. Muetzel remembered about 60 — a ridiculously small force for the task. It was to relieve a Marine force of "5 rifle platoons, 8 machine-gun sections and 2 mortar sections and to hold against a group [of enemy] that had staged a fairly impressive attack the preceding day," Muetzel wrote. He also recalled that the group relieving him did not even have a machine gun with them; it was at the Co. CP. Muetzel took the Army unit to the top of the hill, where it set up a perimeter. He left several cases of grenades and a quantity of .30-caliber ammunition.

The small Army force sent to relieve Co. B upset CPT Fenton. "It was the same old story, the Army was going to relieve with a platoon where they should be relieving me with a company, and the first time the enemy started to feel out the line, this outfit would probably pull out. The so-called relief was made about 2230 [11:30 p.m.]"

The small Army force sent to relieve Fenton's unit was probably what was left of a rifle company. It is doubtful if any rifle platoon of the 2d Division had as many as 40 men in it at this stage of the battle. In short, the 2d Division had no rifle companies available on Sept. 5 which were not shadows of companies. Nor did Eighth Army have reserves with greater strength units to commit in the Brigade sector. It was not a case of the Army consciously relieving a company with a platoon, but rather of the Army relieving with what it had available.

So bad was the replacement situation in Army units of Eighth Army that ROK soldiers began to be sent in large numbers to fill out the rifle companies. Rifle platoons, at this stage, rarely had more than 10 to 20 American soldiers.

COL Taplett also recalled being relieved by a pitifully small Army contingent. "I returned to my CP," he wrote, "to learn that 3-5 positions were to be relieved by a Bn I believe was the 23d Regt. and 3-5 was to cover the withdrawal of 1-5. Our relief by the Army unit was delayed several hours. Then instead of a Bn, a LT brought up a decimated rifle company. He stated he was the Executive Officer of the unit, as the C.O., while defending in the area of Taegu had gone to the rear to get ammo and they never saw him again. He told me that they pulled out of Taegu less one platoon which was pinned down, so he had 2 platoons. We gave him radios, mortars, ammo, etc., as his troops only had their rifles. We were not relieved on position as ordered, as the LT decided to set up positions some distance to the rear of 3-5's C.P. (My staff and I really felt sorry for the LT and his men for the situation they were being placed in. It wasn't until after midnight that we withdrew from our forward positions on the reverse slope of Obong-ni ridge and commenced the long march back to the truck embarkation point for the long ride to Pusan, arriving there about 0630 [6:30 a.m.] on the morning of the 6th.)"

During the Second Battle of the Naktong Bulge, Fenton's company lost 2 KIA and 23 wounded. Taplett lost another 24 men. Total Marine casualties for Sept. 5, as recorded in *South to the Naktong*, came to 35 KIA and 91 WIA. During its time in the Pusan Perimeter the Brigade sustained 148 KIA, 15 DOW, 9 MIA (the bodies of seven of these were recovered reclassified KIA) and 730 WIA, for a total battle loss of 902 men. The Brigade was credited with inflicting some 9,900 casualties on the North Koreans, a ratio of over 10 to 1. On three occasions — TF Kean, and both the First and Second Battles of the Naktong Bulge — the Marine Brigade played a key role in the operation. The Marine history ranked the First Naktong among "the hardest fights in Marine Corps history." During the two Naktong Bulge battles, its contribution was swift and decisive.

While the Marines drove toward Obong-ni, the 2d Division mounted counterattacks with several forces. In the far north of the 2d Division sector, TF Haynes mustered the 23d Infantry (-3d Bn), 38th Infantry and C/72d Tk Bn. Just north of the Brigade, a force, consisting of the 9th Inf (-3d Bn), 3/23d Infantry, A/72d Tk Bn and D/82d AAA/AW Bn was to attack. South of the Marines was the 2d Engineer Bn force. The 2d Recon Co. screened the left flank near the 25th Infantry Division. Fire support came from the 15th, 37th, 38th and 503d FABs, the 82d AAA/AW Bn (-) and 72d Tk Bn (-). The 503d was a 155mm howitzer battalion. The 15th, 37th and 38th had 105mm howitzers.

While the Marines were attacking south of the 9th, that regiment also moved out against the Army's Cloverleaf Hill, which lay north of the MSR and the northern end of Obong-ni. At midmorning, they could see the enemy digging in on the hill. Again, elements of the 82d AAA/AW Battalion supported. Two sections of Co. D, under LT Owens and MSG Klosky supported 2/9th Infantry's attack. The 9th seized Hill 201 that day.

Meantime, TF Fry, under MAJ Fry and consisting of Companies A and D, 2d Engineers plus an AA section and two tanks. made a probing patrol to the village of Agok on the Naktong at Kihang Ferry. On its return trip, TF Fry came upon Companies B and C, 2d Engineers, which were pinned down by the enemy. TF Fry's AW vehicles and tanks came to their rescue. That night and into the next dawn, enemy snipers and patrols harassed TF Fry. At dawn, the force attacked and dispersed the enemy, many of whom abandoned their weapons and ammunition.

South to the Naktong states that Sept. 5 was a day of heavy American casualties. Army: 102 KIA; 430 WIA; 587 MIA. Marine: 35 KIA; 91 WIA; no MIA. Total casualties: 137 KIA; 521 WIA; 587 MIA. The huge MIA figure on that date reflects heavy enemy attacks all along the Perimeter line, including several penetrations, which he was still exploiting. Some of these MIAs were subsequently discovered to be men who were cut off during the action. Others were found dead as lost ground was regained in counterattacks.

Early in the battle, GEN Keiser had decided to replace COL Hill with the 9th Infantry's former commander, COL Charles C. "Chin" Sloane. On Sept. 5, he relieved Hill and put Sloane back in command of the 9th.

GEN Walker fought hard to keep the Marine brigade with Eighth Army as long as possible. He knew that the Brigade had to be released soon to prepare for the Inchon landing, but he wanted to retain this powerful force as long as possible because of the critical combat situation which he now faced in the Perimeter. His stubborn insistence brought a compromise, permitting him the employment of the Marines until Sept. 5. The timing proved to be just right, for the Brigade had soundly defeated and routed the enemy in their zone of action by noon of that date.

The 23d Infantry, Sept. 2 - 9

By daylight on Sept. 1, the two battalions of the 23d Infantry were, essentially, fighting as two independent commands, separated one from the other. The bulk of the 1st Battalion found itself generally north of Lake U-Po in the center of the regimental sector and the bulk of the 2d Battalion was assembling to make a stand on a series of hills east of the town of Poncho-ri, situated just north of Lake Samor-ho. Then, about 400 of the enemy overran the 23d Regiment's CP, causing COL Freeman to move it about 600 yards. It was then located about five miles northeast of Changnyong. There, the Regimental HHC, miscellaneous regimental units and the regiments staff officers beat back the enemy in a three hour battle. The Army history mentions that CPT Niles J. McIntyre, of the HC, "played a leading role," but does not explain.

The confusion attending the enemy's breakthrough and heavy infiltration of the 2d Division in the first days of September broke up some units. Individuals and small groups of men became separated from their companies. Others became separated due to the type of work they were about at the time. SGT Fred M. Liddel's wire team is a case in point. "My wire crew [of the 2d Signal Co.] went to our forward switch area to test some lines back to Division HQ," he

wrote. "I couldn't raise anyone except some foreign language speakers. After a couple [of] attempts...[with] the same results we decided to join the 23d Inf. Regt. HQ. Their CP was a short distance away. There we learned a breakthrough had occurred between the 9th and 23d. We also learned regt. had no communication with their Bns.... We were pressed into use as part of a perimeter."

An enemy SP gun delivered very accurate fire, he recalled. Enemy infiltrators, hiding in the surging crowds of refugees streaming to the rear, presented a different problem. One time, he recalled, "a 'pregnant' woman came through & the shelling started. Someone spotted the antenna of her radio & hollered out a description. We shot her. My foxhole was next to a tank. One day, as the refugees were coming thru, a woman with a 3' basket on her head, full of fruit, lobbed a grenade into the tank next to me. She also was shot."

A lieutenant in the tank was cut open from his shoulder to his buttocks. The man was pulled from the tank and "a medic sewed him up with no pain killer," Liddell recalled. He also recalled that they were cut off for five days, with no food, "except Life Savers." Almost all the medicine was used up in the first day. And there was no way to evacuate the wounded, he recounted. While in this position, Liddell shared a slit trench with two other men. One day an enemy artillery or mortar round came in and exploded next to the hole. The force of the explosion moved all the men to one side, tossing one of them out of the hole and down a five foot embankment.

The civilian population of Changnyong began to flee the town. When two large parties approached from the northwest and southwest, a local security force of 300 men, commanded by MAJ Jack T. Young and CPT Harry H. White, withdrew into the hills to the east.

During the day, GEN Hayes, discovered that communications to the 2d Division CP and the 9th Infantry to the south had been broken. He sent CPT Manes E. Dew, CO, C/72d Tk Bn, with three tanks, on a patrol to try to re-establish communication. The tanks had to fight through a series of enemy roadblocks. Only Dew's tank got through, but he was able to deliver an overlay of TF Haynes' positions to GEN Bradley.

Farther north, on Sept. 1, GEN Keiser had ordered 2/38th Infantry to move south to aid the 23d Regiment to establish a defense line west of Changnyong. Also that morning, GEN Keiser ordered 3/38th Infantry to launch an attack westward from the vicinity of the 23d Infantry's C.P. near Mosan-ni to open the MSR to 1/23d Infantry.

1/23d Infantry:

The 1st Battalion occupied positions on the shore of Lake U-po and astride the northern road to Changnyong. The nearest friendly troops were some three miles away. On Sept. 1, LTC Claire Hutchin (West Point 1938), commanding 1/23d Infantry, was ordered to withdraw his battalion to the Changnyong area. At 2 p.m., he sent a tank-infantry patrol back to determine if the road was open. The patrol found an estimated enemy battalion in the mountain pass about two miles to the rear of the 1st Battalion's position. Hutchin asked COL Freeman for permission to remain

in place and try to stop enemy reinforcements and re-supply from there. Freeman agreed. It was into this battalion enclave that LT Glasgow led the remnants of his platoon. The 2d Platoon, 82d AAA/AW Battalion supported the infantry battalion there.

In the midst of all this chaos, 2LT William R. Lamdin, another brand-new officer from the West Point Class of 1950, reported to COL Freeman for duty on Sept. 2. He was sent to Co. A as a platoon leader. There were two other officers; the CO and another rifle platoon leader. Lamdin recalled that the company at the time had only two rifle platoons. The Weapons Platoon, commanded by an NCO, had one 57mm recoilless rifle with no sight, two 60mm mortars (but only one sight) and "a couple of heavy machine guns."

"A and B Companies, with attachments, were ordered to withdraw to their rear positions," recorded CPT Tassey, commanding D/23d Infantry, in a daily journal he kept. In the withdrawal, a 3/4-ton truck from his company was destroyed by enemy fire. The unit also lost a 75mm recoilless rifle to the enemy. CPT Tassey wrote that the withdrawal was to the vicinity of his CP at a crossroad. A heavy machine-gun section, under LT Johnson, was cut off, but Tassey ordered it to come out with a platoon from Co. A. At 3 a.m. on Sept. 2, a 4.2 inch Mortar Platoon withdrew into Tassey's area and was attached to his command. The 4.2s provided supporting fires for the battalion as it withdrew. Unfortunately, his 81mm mortar section and a heavy machine-gun section had to withdraw, leaving a store of ammunition behind. The ammunition was booby trapped. At 2:30 p.m., the entire battalion withdrew to better positions and reorganized.

PVT Raymond C. Wisniewski, a medic with Co. A, recalled being in a litter jeep that was taken under enemy mortar fire as it made its way forward in the rain one night. One round knocked out the jeep, wounding the driver. Wisniewski and others crawled from the wrecked vehicle and went to the aid of the driver. His boot had been blown open and the side of his foot had been opened by shrapnel. "I took off his boot and patched the wound as best as I could," Wisniewski wrote. The wounded man was helped to a building about 50 yards away and another jeep came to evacuate him. Wisniewski was wounded on Sept. 2. "I had just given first aid to a South Korean soldier assigned to our unit as an interpreter," Wisniewski recalled. "I started to move down the mountain and a machine gun opened up and I got shot in the back and arm."

George Co., 23d Infantry arrived to reinforce the 1st Battalion (-). "One section of 81mm mortars was given a mission to support B Company in their attack to seize a hill leading to the Regimental area," Tassey's journal continues. "B Company was counter-attacked and withdrew to the main line of resistance. The enemy attacked our main line of resistance at 0350 hours (3 Sept.) [3:50 a.m.]."

Enemy mortar fire wounded six men in the 4.2 inch mortar platoon. LT Johnson's heavy machine-gun section repelled the enemy attack in its area by point blank fire. One of the guns knocked out an A Co. jeep which had been captured by the enemy. The jeep was loaded with ammunition. The machine gun fire detonated the ammunition, blowing the jeep to pieces. The enemy attack was beaten off by 8 a.m., but not before they had penetrated the perimeter. "The attack this morning was repelled by our tanks firing point blank from the vicinity of D Company command post to a hill overhead where the enemy had penetrated," Tassey recorded. "A successful counterattack (by Co. A and elements of Co. B) was made, and the main line of resistance was restored with 20 enemy known dead. A wounded enemy lieutenant was captured. Tassey wrote that the enemy was "feeling around in the dark for weak points and yelling 'banzai' during the attack. Tassey noted that, because his heavy machine guns were so effective, the enemy avoided them. (See Chapter Notes.)

The battalion (-) was isolated from the rest of the regiment and its supply lines had been cut. An air drop of food and ammunition came into the perimeter at 9 a.m., including halazone tablets to be used to purify water which the men had to take from a village well.

The enemy made one attack on the morning that Glasgow came into the perimeter, taking some commanding ground. MAJ George H. Russell, battalion "3," took Co. A and ejected the enemy from the position. The enemy withdrew, covered by an early morning fog. That evening the 81mm and 4.2 inch mortars registered mortar concentrations forward of the battalion MLR. An enemy artillery round landed in one of the heavy machine-gun squads, killing two men and wounding five others.

Early on Sept. 4, CPT Steele, of Tassey's Company D, was reassigned to command Co. B. The men got a hot meal on Sept. 3 and another the next day. An 81mm mortar section, which had been attached to Co. F, and which Tassey thought was lost, had gotten out with that unit. But a heavy machine-gun section and a 75mm recoilless rifle section were still missing. At 3 a.m. on Sept. 4, the enemy again attacked, crawling up the steep-sloped hills; 81mm and 4.2 inch mortar fire and artillery fire drove them away. But the enemy took the D Co. OP under direct fire, followed by mortars. Tassey wrote that the 4.2s knocked out an enemy OP, four mortar positions, a roadblock and several enemy troop concentrations.

Two enemy tanks were spotted about 4,000 yards from the battalion. Neither mortar or artillery fire was effective against them, but an air strike took care of the matter.

At 4:30 p.m., he wrote, the 38th Infantry relieved 1/23d Infantry and the battalion moved by truck to an area near Yongsan.

On Sept. 5, LT Raney, with the missing mortar section rejoined Co. D, as did a heavy machine-gun section commanded by Platoon Sergeant Roopes. From them, Tassey was able to piece together what had happened. The mortar OP and mortar position were overrun on the night of Aug. 31-Sept. 1. The FO, SGT Newton stayed at the OP, directing fire and was MIA. Raney fired all the ammunition on position, then sent back for more. As the enemy overwhelmed the position, Raney fired his pistol point blank at them. In spite of the onrushing enemy, he managed to organize his men and move his vehicles out of the enemy encirclement. CPL Jorgenson coolly drove the vehicles out of the area. Under cover of darkness, Raney guided his men to

friendly lines early on Sept. 5. Part of his men came out on the road and the remainder cross-country.

Meantime, Platoon Sergeant Roope's heavy machine-gun section fired until it ran out of ammunition. The jackets of the water cooled guns of PFCs Lynn P. Mathena Jr. and Genung burst due to excessive heat. SFC Clyde O. Munger was the section leader. The enemy was all around as the men made their way out. Roope dropped his weapon while moving through a paddy. He came upon two enemy soldiers. One of them was laying wire; the other was armed with a rifle. Roope attacked the armed soldier and disarmed him. The machine gun crews scattered as they pulled back.

PFC Nealy, a light machinegunner, dismantled his gun and threw the ammo belt into the Naktong before withdrawing. He stayed in a riverside village that night and made his way to safety on Sept. 5.

Tassey recorded that, on Sept. 5, the 4.2s knocked out some enemy artillery pieces and mortars. He noted that the 1st Battalion also sent out a patrol of two tanks and a rifle squad, looking for elements of Co. C, which had been overrun on the night of Aug. 31-Sept. 1. He took stock of Co. D's losses. They amounted to two 3/4-ton 75mm recoilless rifle trucks; one 1-ton trailer; two heavy machine gun 1/4-ton trucks, with two 1/4-ton trailers; two light machine guns and two heavy machine guns (destroyed on position) and two 75mm recoilless rifles. Personnel losses for D/23d Infantry between Aug. 31 and Sept. 4 were 7 KIA, 11 WIA, 10 MIA. Of the MIA, five were captured by the enemy and one was a non-battle casualty. Four men remained MIA. Over all, the 1st Battalion lost about 500 of its 1,100 men by Sept. 4.

A section of AA guns from B/82d AAA/AW Battalion, under LT George Keller and SGT Richard Rognrud, along with three tanks from the 72d Tk Bn, supported a 1st Battalion attack on Sept. 6. The attackers were hit hard by heavy mortar fire and two of the tanks were disabled, blocking the road. The automatic weapons section remained in position and became a radio link between the infantry battalion and regimental CPs.

On Sept. 7, the enemy attacked Co. A at about 4 a.m., but was driven off by concentrated artillery and mortar fire, leaving 50 dead in front of the company position. After an air strike and a ten minute artillery preparation, Co. A jumped off on its own attack at 11 a.m., supported by 81mm mortars, overhead fire from heavy machine guns and the fires from the left by Co. B.

"In a line of skirmishers, both rifle platoons abreast (about 50-60 men, total), the company advanced about 20 yards," wrote William R. Lamdin (West Point 1950), a rifle platoon leader of A/23d Infantry, "at which time it suffered about 50% casualties from a 120mm mortar barrage. My platoon of about 27 men ended up after it all with 9 effectives. The other platoon fared somewhat better. Needless to say...we advanced no further!!.... Shortly after this, as I remember, my platoon received a dozen or so KATUSAs; the Co. perhaps about 30."

Co. D lost one heavy machine gun to enemy fire and had 2 KIA and 2 WIA, all from the heavy

machine-gun section. In addition to the heavy casualties suffered by Co. A, Co. C was reduced to only about 28 men.

From that day on to Sept. 16, the enemy continued pressure on 1/23d Infantry. On the 11th, they got into barbed wire in front of Co. A and shifted their attack so that it struck between Companies A and F, where some of them surrendered.

Also on the 11th, a section of 2d Platoon, B/82d supported a reconnaissance in force by B/23d Infantry. The section fired about 400 rounds of ammunition on this mission, killing 17 enemy soldiers. About the same time, two M-19s supporting C/23d Infantry knocked out an enemy machine gun position, killing the three-man crew. Later, SGT James L. Dorrance's M-16 from the 2d Platoon fired about 600 rounds in supporting a C/23d Infantry attack.

An enemy attack was made on Sept. 15-16 against the part of Hill 125 held by Co. C. C suffered heavy casualties, but held. The D Co. heavy machine-gun section supporting Co. C was also hit hard. LT Johnson, the platoon leader and 2 EM were killed and 4 other men, also from the machine-guns, were wounded. The battalion counterattacked on Sept. 16 and took its objectives. The following day the 2d Battalion relieved the 1st.

2/23d Infantry:

The 2d Battalion (- Co. E, attached to the 9th Infantry) was returned to regimental control from division reserve. Co. G, reinforced, was sent to assist the 1st Battalion. MAJ Lloyd K. Jenson (Bn XO) with Companies F and H, reinforced, meantime, moved out on the Changnyong-Poncho-ri road to set up a block. The force traveled in darkness. The road ran south from Poncho-ri for a little over 500 yards, then curved east over a low ridge running northeast from the shore of Lake Samor-ho between Poncho-ri and the village of Haktong. The battalion named this "Hog Back Ridge." Jenson decided to set up the block astride the road just east of Haktong.

1LT Charles Klipstine, commanding Co. F, placed one platoon on high ground east of Haktong, named "Kuhn Hill." Another platoon was positioned on a hill south of the road, named "Duea Hill." Each platoon was reinforced by a heavy machine gun section. The 75mm rifle section manned a roadblock on the road itself. The hill immediately east of Kuhn Hill was dubbed "Battalion Headquarters Hill." The 81mm mortar platoon dug in behind this hill. The task force CP was located in a road culvert on the left rear of the hill. During the night, two M-19s (quad-.50s) and three tanks from the 23d Tk Co. reinforced the position, along with 15 men from Co. C. The tanks had been supporting Co. C. These men and vehicles had been cut off by the enemy, but fought their way out.

September 1

At dawn a squad from Co. F's support platoon, and an LMG were sent to a hill east of Duea Hill, which they named "Currie Hill." This provided additional security on that flank. A rifle squad and one tank were sent to a hill to the rear, which was named "Hill 2." An Intelligence squad from the task force, with an LMG went to outpost "Hill 1," also to the rear. A tank and M-19

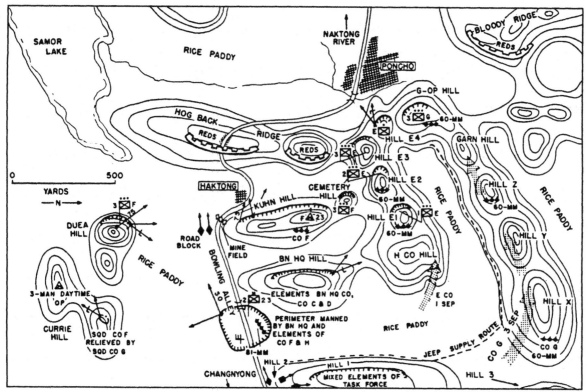

Map 44 (Source: "Naktong Defense," LTC James W. Edwards, Infantry School Quarterly, *Apr. 1951, Ft. Benning, GA)*

replaced the 75's on the roadblock and these guns were attached to the platoon on Duea Hill. The other tank and quad-.50 vehicle were located near Hill 1 to provide flank protection to the Intelligence Squad. The remainder of the Co. F support platoon, the 15 men from Co. C and 3 from Co. D were all placed on Battalion Headquarters Hill.

About 7:30 a.m., a column of 30 enemy soldiers came double-timing down the road from the Hog Back toward Kuhn Hill. The F Co. platoon waited until the North Koreans reached a point 50 yards from their foxholes. Then they let loose with rifles and machine guns, killing all of the enemy. At 1:30 p.m., two more tanks from the C Co. position entered the perimeter and were immediately incorporated into the defense. One joined the tank on Hill 2 and the other replaced the quad-.50 at the Kuhn Hill roadblock. That M-19 was sent back near Hill 1.

In the early afternoon, small groups of the enemy were observed moving around both flanks. One party of about 15 men, led by an officer came onto Hill 3, north of Hill 2. The Intelligence Squad on Hill 1 drove them away. Meantime, Co. F reported enemy build-ups on the Hog back and what the battalion called Hills E-3 and E-2. E-3 and E-2 were two of a series of knobs running from west to east, labeled by the battalion, from west to east as Hills E-3, E-2, E-1 and Co. H Hill.

Concerned for his flanks, MAJ Jenson sent an urgent message to the CO, 2d Battalion and the 23d Infantry CP for reinforcement. Fortunately, E/23d Infantry (CPT Perry Sager) became available, and was sent at once. LTC Edwards, the Battalion CO came with it and assumed command of the blocking position. The unit was immediately sent to seize Co. H Hill and the E-series of hills. The company took all but E-3 without much trouble, but was stopped cold by

heavy enemy fire from nearby high ground from taking E-3. The company was ordered to dig in on the terrain it had taken,

At 8:55 p.m. two enemy green flares sailed out from E-3 toward E-2. Five minutes later about 150 to 200 enemy assaulted the 2d Platoon, Co. E, on Hill E-2. Enemy troops crawled forward to within grenade throwing distance, then sprang up, screaming "Manzai!" The defending platoon cut down one wave after the other, but was finally reduced to grenades, bayonets, knives and fists. The number of enemy was too great, and the platoon was pushed to the reverse slope. But about 10:30 p.m., the attack slowed then stopped.

Meantime, Co. F, the Intelligence squad and the Fox Co. party on Hill 2 repulsed a number of small probing patrols. This activity kept the battalion on alert all night.

September 2

Enemy 82mm and 120mm mortar fire began landing on the Battalion CP area about 9 a.m., causing many casualties among Co. H and F personnel in that area. One of the wounded was Morris V. Evans, of the 81mm mortars. He observed an enemy mortar and took it under fire. "We both fired at the same time," he wrote. "I had a direct hit on him he likewise hit me. His shell hit close behind me. My LT said he thought it got my spinal column, so I tried to move my legs. Thanks to God I could [move them]. The medic...was going to give me a shot of morphine. I told him, 'No way!' He kept hollering 'Stretcher!'" Evans got to his feet, told the medic to forget the stretcher and walked back down the mountain and was evacuated. He rejoined his unit on October 2.

LTC Edwards, upon arrival in the area, decided to leave most of the staff and vehicles about

2,000 yards to the rear of the front line. He took the Communication Platoon and only headquarters personnel necessary to operate a forward CP. The CP remained in the culvert. The F Co. squad on Hill 2, replaced by an HC element, rejoined Co. F.

SGT Leslie C. Sholar, 81mm Mortar Platoon, H/23d, recalled the CP in the culvert. He was dug in nearby. "[CPT Payne's] Co. H was dug in [the] rice paddy. Same foxhole for 20 days or more," he wrote. "Not much ammo. Air Force dropped ammo, gas and water. Cut off. Could not retreat. No where to go but fight. We suffered heavy casualties." At one point, the 81s were given the mission of knocking out an enemy CP in a schoolhouse "across a small hill from my mortars," he recounted. "We used white phosphorous, HE heavy, HE light, [we] used everything. [The] schoolhouse was hard to take out."

Sholar related another unusual story: "F Co. retreated from a hill; left [its] guidon on the hill. Five soldiers tried to get [that] guidon. Enemy machine guns firing point blank killed three [of them]." Apparently the guidon was never recovered in that battle. (See Chapter Notes.)

John P. Parsley, also of Co. H, recalled that the schoolhouse actually hid one or more enemy 120mm mortars. These mortars fired out through openings in the schoolhouse roof, thus helping to conceal both the weapons and the flash from the tubes when they fired. "One evening they fired at dusk," he wrote. "They were in a schoolhouse about 300 yards away.... Aircraft or artillery [observers] — someone — saw the sparks from [their] tubes. Called on an M-4 tank. which took care of the problem." Later in his writing, Parsley recalled, "I remember the bugles and flares; the music they played over a loudspeaker before they hit us at night. They got in among us but never broke through."

Enemy SP guns on high ground west of Poncho-ri could fire down the valley road in and beyond the perimeter. Their gunners could see all the way to Changnyong. "Vehicles on the road were wide open as ten pins," wrote LTC Edwards in his "Naktong Defense," published in the April 1951 issue of *Infantry School Quarterly.* "The valley became known as the Bowling Alley...."

1LT John H. Ramsburg had one experience in connection with enemy infiltrators interdicting the MSR during the Naktong Bulge battle. The Battalion S-2 was fired on by infiltrators enroute back to the CP from regimental headquarters. "I took 4 members of the Bn Intell. Section and one M4 tank back to that area, along with the S-2 and a young 2d LT assigned to the

Bn HQ (LT Cam Hurst)," Ramsburg wrote. "When we reached the area where the S-2 had been fired on, we came under small-arms fire. I mounted the tank and manned the .50-cal MG, spraying the low, brush-covered hill with fire. The tank was buttoned up and would move forward 5 or ten yards and then back up again.

"I kept trying to get the tank commander to hold the tank in one spot where I had a good field of fire. I was having problems with the MG jamming and would eject several rounds, recharge the gun [by pulling the bolt to the rear a couple of times to clear the gun and seat a live round into the chamber], fire a few rounds and go through the process again." He noticed sparks near the ground and thought it was due to the tank treads running over and detonating the ejected .50-caliber rounds. Suddenly LT Hurst, who was standing near the tank, fell wounded. Hurst was evacuated and Ramsburg continued firing the tanks .50-caliber machine gun at the hill. Eventually, there was no enemy return fire.

Back at the CP, Ramsburg confronted the tank commander about continuously moving the tank, spoiling his aim. The tank commander pointed out several spots where the tank had been hit by an enemy anti-tank rifle ("Buffalo gun"). The sparks Ramsburg saw were strikes from the weapon. The tank commander kept moving the tank to spoil the AT gunner's aim. Ramsburg served in 2/23d as Assistant S-3 and as an interim commander of Co. F, then as Battalion S-2.

Edwards called for an air strike against enemy positions on Hog Back, Hill E-3, Hill G-OP and Bloody Ridge. Hill G-OP was a knob just north of Hill E-3. Bloody Ridge was located about 500 yards northwest of Hill G-OP. An air strike by four F-51s came in at 12:20 p.m., bombing and strafing the four hills. Taking advantage of the strike, Edwards ordered Co. E to attack the crest of Hill E-2 again. Co. F provided supporting fire. E Co. found a few snipers and a number of enemy dead on the hill. E's 3d Platoon, however discovered that the North Koreans had dug in on the reverse slope. Once the air strike was over, enemy troops on Hill G-OP, Hog Back and Garn Hill, opened fire with mortars and automatic weapons, pinning down the 3d Platoon. Thus covered, the enemy on the reverse slope of Hill E-3, crawled up and threw grenades over the crest into the platoon, causing many casualties. CPT Sager pulled the decimated platoon back to Hill E-2. The 2d and 3d Platoons had each lost 60 per cent of their men. He left the remnants of the two platoons to defend E-2, placed his 1st Platoon on E-1 and put the 60mm mortar section on its reverse slope.

Ralph H. Krueger was an "old" man by Infantry standards in 1950. He was 26, having been in the Army since 1938. In WW II, he fought in the Pacific, mostly as a platoon sergeant or platoon leader. He was awarded a reserve commission in 1946 as a result of a study program called "Series Ten," but was serving then as an NCO. Krueger reported to CPT Sager as a replacement during the first days of the Second Naktong battle. Sager "handed me a warm can of beer," he said, then "[He] said, 'I understand you have a commission. You can take it or not, that's up to you, but you are gonna lead the Third Platoon. Your platoon is up there.' He pointed up a

hill, 'and your objective is up there,' pointing to another hill. 'Jump off in ten minutes, good luck.'

"I went up and met Master Sergeant 'Toppie' [Robert J. Topping]; I'll never forget him. I said, 'I guess I'm taking over for you.' He said, 'Thank God. I'm from Ordnance. I don't know a damned thing about this Infantry stuff.' It seemed like they grabbed people from everywhere to fill up [infantry units], but that's the normal thing."

One time COL Freeman came into Krueger's platoon attack assembly area. "He saw one of my guys laying on the ground and he said, 'Son, are you gonna take that hill today?' The kid looked at him and said, 'Hi, Colonel.' Pointed at me, and said, 'If Pop goes (that was me) 'I go. If he doesn't go, _____.' The Colonel said, 'Well you got your job cut out for you.' I said, 'Yes, Sir.' But that's the kind of people we had."

Krueger described a remarkable display of marching fire, employed on one occasion by G/23d Infantry. "The most awesome sight that I saw [in marching fire] was George Company... any of the 23d.... 150 men walking up the hill and marching fire, everybody shooting tracers. It scared the enemy off the hill...and the hill on the other aside of him.... Scared us, too, because those tracers were bouncing all over hell."

SSG Richard H. Shand, a member of Co. E. wrote that the battle near Poncho-ri "was to be one of the biggest battles I was in during the Korean War. I was about to lose many buddies [who] I got pretty attached to.... I learned to never get attached to someone any more. ..." He recalled that the company was reduced by casualties to two rifle platoons.

Meantime, the enemy heavily attacked Co. F's left flank on Kuhn Hill with about a company. Artillery and mortar final protective fires caused heavy enemy casualties. In spite of these losses, the enemy kept coming, only to be cut down by F Co. small-arms fire from Kuhn and Duea Hill. At 2:40 p.m., the enemy fled, leaving 95 dead behind. Shortly thereafter, eight enemy soldiers approached the right flank of Kuhn Hill waving white flags. When an American squad approached them, the enemy dropped the flags and started throwing grenades. All eight were quickly killed by the patrol and a covering machine-gun.

Another air strike was scheduled against Hill G-OP, Hog Back and Bloody Ridge for 4:40 p.m. In preparation, the 81 mortars fired WP rounds at the target hills. This brought enemy soldiers out of their holes, where they became targets for 2d Battalion rifles and automatic weapons. Later that afternoon, the same thing happened when Co. F called for artillery fire on Hog Back. As LTC Edwards wrote, "The frightened Reds [enemy] gave the riflemen a full afternoon of target practice."

The battalion was heavily infiltrated that night. By midnight almost every telephone wire to the companies and artillery and mortar FOs had been cut, although two lines had been laid to each locale.

September 3

Between midnight and dawn three enemy companies attacked Co. E and F positions. All were repulsed. At 4 a.m., another enemy rifle company, reinforced by three SP guns, attacked

down the road from Haktong. A Russian 2 1/2-ton truck, leading the column, hit a minefield forward of Kuhn Hill. The 1st Platoon, Co. F opened fire with small-arms and a 3.5 inch rocket launcher. One SP gun was destroyed, another damaged and the third withdrew with the retreating infantry. The dark night started with a light rain, which soon became a heavy downpour.

The Battalion CP was protected by members of the HC, drivers of Companies F and H, the battalion staff and the 81mm Mortar Platoon. Infiltrators searched for the mortars. Since the enemy could use the flash of their firing to give away their position the 81s were ordered not to fire during the night. During the night, machine gun fire from the roadblock tanks interlocked with that from the tank near Hill 1. The fire crossed the paddy and met in the valley forward of Currie Hill. The next morning a patrol went into the paddy to count enemy dead and captured three prisoners. Then another 73 enemy soldiers, who had been pinned down by the tank's guns, got up from the paddy and surrendered.

North of the E-1 through E-3 series of hills was another line of knobs, dubbed, from east to west Hill X, Hill Y and Hill Z, terminating at its western end with Garn Hill. Co. G rejoined the battalion on the 3d and was immediately sent to attack these hills, beginning with Hill X. By 11:40 a.m., Hills Y and Z were taken without opposition. Then small parties of the enemy began firing on the lead platoon from Garn Hill. The men of Co. E on Hill E-2 could see about 100 of the enemy digging in on G-OP Hill.

LTC Edwards now planned a coordinated battalion attack, supported by air strikes and the fire of Co. E, Co. G was to seize Garn and G-OP Hills. Once these two hills fell, Co. E would attack and take Hills E-3 and E-4, assisted by fires from Companies F and G. At 2 p.m., four F-51s attacked G-OP Hill, Hog Back and Bloody Ridge with rockets and napalm. Because Hills E-3 and E-4 were too close to battalion lines to be bombed, they were strafed with the airplanes' .50-caliber machine guns.

Co. G, supported by 81mm mortar fire which was "walked" up the hill about 100 yards in front of the advancing infantrymen, and assisted by the fires of Co. E's 60mm mortars and machine guns on G-OP and Hill E-4, seized Garn by 3 p.m.

A second air strike of napalm and 500 lb. bombs was made on Hog Back; Bloody Ridge and Hills E-3 and E-4 were strafed with .50-caliber machine guns. Preceded by "walking" 81 mortar fire and supported by supporting fire from Co. E, George Co. attacked G-OP employing marching fire. The knob was taken by 4:30 p.m. Fifteen minutes later, Co. E seized E-3, supported by fire from Co. G. The enemy abandoned Hill E-4, so Co. E sent a reinforced squad to occupy it and establish contact with Co. G.

When E was seen on Hill E-3, about 5:35 p.m., Fox Co. attacked Cemetery Hill, a knob lying between the northern end of Kuhn Hill and Hill E-2 to its north. Co. E supported the attack by fire. The hill fell before 6:10 p.m. Co. F's 3d Platoon dug in on Cemetery Hill as the 2d Platoon dug in on the saddle between it and Kuhn Hill.

By Sept. 3, 2/23d was all by itself. The enemy was to its front, both flanks and to the rear along various parts of the MSR. About noon that day, COL Freeman ordered the 1st Battalion to move up on the 2d Battalion's left flank. The 1st was augmented by troops from the regimental headquarters.

The enemy never attacked the 2d Battalion's open flanks in those first few days of September. Later, a captured enemy operations order provides some explanation, at least for one flank. The boundary between the *NK 2d* and *9th Divisions* ran just south of 2/23d Infantry's left (south) flank. The boundary was too close to the battalion position for the *2d Division* to go around the left (south) flank without entering the *9th Division's* zone. This explains why that flank was not attacked, but does not explain why the enemy did not attack the right.

Captured enemy orders gave Changnyong and the mountains east of that town as objectives. It is possible that the enemy simply decided to fix the battalion in position by some troops and bypassing it to attain the primary objectives. If these objectives could be attained, the battalion would be hopelessly isolated and could be decisively dealt with at that time.

September 4 - 11

During this period, the enemy pounded battalion positions with SP and Mortar fire by day and fierce infantry attacks by night.

On Sept. 4th, GEN Haynes changed the boundary between 38th and 23d Infantry Regiments, giving the northern part of the 23d's sector to the 38th, permitting COL Freeman to send Hutchin's 1/23d south to aid the 2/23d and make a cohesive regimental defense.

That day Co. G seized a number of hills and knobs which protected the battalion and regimental right flank, including Emerson Ridge, north of G-OP and Garn Hills, and a hill southeast of Emerson overlooking the village of Chirdong.

On Sept. 5, the 1st Battalion took position on the 2d Battalion's left, including part of Kuhn Hill. Elements of A/23d took over that part of Kuhn Hill, while B/23d occupied Duea and Currie Hills. The 1st Battalion established its CP in the culvert which had been the site of the 2d Battalion's forward headquarters. Co. F now occupied the right half of Kuhn Hill and Cemetery Hill. It also had a squad on Hill E-4. Co. E was dug in on Hills E-3 and E-2. The 2d Battalion CP was moved behind Company H Hill. Co. H mortars and 75mm rifles moved into the same area, giving the hill its name.

Just after midnight on Sept. 5, the enemy launched an all-out attack across the entire battalion front. Artillery and mortar fire cut down large numbers of the enemy and battalion infantrymen took care of the rest with automatic weapons, rifles grenades and bayonets.

The 37th FAB supported the 23d Regiment. It fired large amounts of ammunition in this endeavor. On one night, it pumped out 2,300 rounds in support of the 2d battalion alone. On another occasion, in firing in support of Co. E's defense, it dropped concentrations within 50 yards of their foxholes on Cemetery Hill.

The 2d Battalion seized Manzai Hill and Bloody Ridge on Sept. 6 and 7. Manzai Hill was the northern extension of the Hog Back. On the afternoon of Sept. 6, a section of the machine-gun platoon, Co. H, came under very heavy machine gun and mortar fire and the section leader was wounded. Ignoring the enemy fire, PFC Richard L. Fleishmann, a medical aidman with Co. H, dashed forward to the help the section leader. He got the injured man to safety and gave him medical treatment. A few minutes later, the gunner of this machine gun was also wounded. Again, Fleishmann selflessly ran forward and rescued this man. Then, although wounded himself by now, he took over the machine gun and manned it until killed.

MSG Jesse C. Bishop (Weapons Platoon, E-23d Infantry) recorded in his journal for Sept. 5: "The final objective was taken with high morale for the number of casualties [in Co. F], which numbered about thirty-five[.] But was still not as bad as the enemy losses, which was abandoned equipment and dead."

The fire support for Co. F's attack on the 6th included machine guns from LT Charles Multop's Machine-gun Platoon (Co. H). He recommended that the section supporting Co. F fire into the objective over the heads of the advancing infantrymen. His recommendation was adopted. "Before the attack, no enemy was visible on the hill being attacked," he wrote in his article "A Heavy Weapons Company in Korea." (*Infantry School Quarterly*, 1951.) "But as soon as Co. F jumped off, several of the enemy popped their heads up over the ridge line. The machine gunners immediately went to work and delivered heavy fire against the top of the hill, each gun traversing half the width of the hilltop.

"In 10 minutes of firing, the section put 3,000 rounds [12 boxes] on the Company F objective. Just before the riflemen masked the machine-gun fire, it was lifted.... When the attack was successfully driven home, the company commander of Company F and his platoon leaders were unanimous in declaring that their attack would have failed if it had not been for the overhead fire from the machine guns."

On the night of Sept. 8, the enemy fired unusually heavy volumes of fire, then came in another fierce and bloody attack. The battalion responded with artillery, mortars automatic and small-arms fire, but the North Koreans came on. Even showers of hand grenades failed to stop the enemy before he gained the crests of several hills, forcing the defenders to the reverse slope. The battalion line was very nearly breached.

F Co.'s line was penetrated by the enemy. If the line could not be restored, the entire battalion position would be threatened. All company officers were casualties. 1LT Ralph R. Robinson, 2d Battalion adjutant, took command of the unit.

Infantrymen of F/23 Infantry near Manzai (Banzai) Hill, September 1950. (Courtesy of Donald Hoffman, F/23d Infantry)

While enemy soldiers were infiltrating the company position, Robinson made his way in the darkness and rain some 500 yards to Co. A. There, he borrowed that unit's reserve platoon, brought it back and placed it into the gap in Fox's line. The enemy attack finally receded, then resumed again on the night of Sept. 9. Air power was brought to bear on the enemy, but casualties mounted. Every available man in the HC was put into the fight. At one point, the entire regimental reserve was six men. Just after noon on that day, the enemy attack ended. By that time, the 23d was down to an estimated combat efficiency of 38 percent.

But the attack also decimated the enemy's *2d Division*. A few days later, the medical officer of that division's *17th Regiment*. was captured. He said that the division had evacuated about 300 men each night to a hospital in Pugong-ni; that in the first two weeks in September the *2d Division* had lost 1,300 KIA and 2,500 WIA in the battles west of Changnyong. In spite of these losses, the enemy division heavily infiltrated the rear areas near Changnyong, sometimes in company strength. Daily patrols had to be run to keep the MSR open.

Co. G withdrew from Bloody Ridge on the night of Sept. 8-9. At dawn, enemy artillery fire blasted the ridge, then an enemy company charged up the hill, screaming "Manzai!" At the top, they realized that the hill was unoccupied. But the Americans used it as a killing ground. From Emerson Ridge and G-OP Hill concentrated small arms, automatic weapons and 60mm WP rounds hit the enemy, skylined on the crest of Bloody Ridge. Enemy soldiers "were picked off like ducks in a shooting gallery," Colonel Edwards wrote in his April 1951 article in *Infantry School Quarterly.*

"On September 10th at about 1900 hours (7 P.M.) Fox Company got involved in one hell of a fire fight that lasted 'till about 2200 hours (10 P.M.)," wrote SGT Donald W. Hoffman, of Co.

F. "The North Koreans hit the hill with, what I believe, everything they had. After the initial onslaught things settled down to a grenade battle. Stan [CPL Stanley Ledbetter] and I had two cases of grenades in our hole, and when the fight was over I think we had six or so. I remember one man by the name of Elmer Ratliff was bayoneted through the stomach. During the thick of the fire fight he was running around trying to find a medic. I understand he survived. When the fight was over everyone was on alert till daybreak. Once daylight came we noted that our position was a mess; littered with dead and wounded from both sides. The day was spent cleaning up the mess."

MSG Bishop wrote that the Weapons Platoon suffered no casualties in this night battle. However, he wrote: "It was too close for the mortar observer to direct fire on the enemy so he gave assistance to the riflemen in throwing grenades, because of their [the riflemen's] casualties. The mortar sec. did fire when permission was granted. Sometimes bringing rounds in as close as twenty-five yds."

September 11 - 16

The enemy became increasingly weaker. On Sept. 12, an enemy loudspeaker broadcast called upon the Americans to surrender and urged the South Koreans to desert and join the "Glorious Peoples' Army." The GIs thought the broadcast was hilarious. Patrols were sent through Poncho-ri and other areas forward of the battalion on Sept. 12 and 14.

On Sept. 16 the 23d launched an attack to clear the enemy from its front. The 2d Battalion was to take Bloody Ridge and Jackson Hill, farther west. The 1st Battalion would attack at the same time on the left. Once the 2d Battalion took its objectives, 3/23d, which had been less engaged and almost up to strength, would pass through the 2d and continue the attack.

At 5:55 a.m., a 15 minute preparation of artillery and mortar fire churned over Bloody Ridge. At 6:05 a.m., George Co.'s 60mm mortars joined the barrage. Five minutes later, Co. G attacked, secured the ridge 20 minutes later. The 2d Platoon forged on to Jackson Hill, taking it by 6:50 a.m.

3/23d Infantry:

The 3/23d Infantry relieved the 7th Cavalry, 1st Cavalry Division on Aug. 29 and was attached to the 38th infantry (2d Division). But because of resupply problems, had to be reattached to the 1st Cavalry. On Sept. 2, enemy troops opposed elements of 3/23d near the Yongpo bridge across the Naktong. Robert N. Fogle, then a member of K/23d Infantry, wrote that "fighting here was light if at all. The enemy failed to mount a major attack in this area...." On Sept. 5, the British 27th Infantry Brigade relieved 3/23d Infantry. The 2d Platoon, K/23d Infantry was delayed in completing the relief because it was involved in a firefight with the enemy. Then the platoon was diverted to establish a roadblock near the old "Bowling Alley" area. It stayed on this position about two days.

Elements of 3/23d Infantry relieved part of the Marine Brigade on Sept. 5. Co. I was part of the relieving force. Harold L. Jennings, a pla-

toon sergeant of Co. I, wrote: "We moved to the hill top, started to dig in, but before we got settled in they pulled us back to the rear to guard an artillery battery." The company was relieved by another unit the next day.

About Sept. 10, he recalled, the company was sent to set up a block at the river to stop withdrawing enemy soldiers. When the company arrived it found the dead bodies of five GIs in two shallow trenches. Jennings deployed his platoon. "I had one machine gun squad at the river crossing," he wrote, "one squad at the back side of the hill behind us, plus, they gave me a 57 recoilless rifle squad and one rifle squad. Next day [Sept. 11] they gave me a .50-cal machine gun with scope. Never got to fire it." A day or so later, a platoon of tanks were brought up and dug in. Jennings recalled that the 57 squad destroyed four houses across the river suspected of being enemy gun positions.

Around midnight on Sept. 12, a South Korean unit which was also along the river with Co. I, waded across the Naktong, which Jennings wrote, was about 70 yards wide at that point. "The first troops had just started up the opposite bank when the North Koreans started firing.... The ones [South Koreans] in the water were bunched up," he wrote. "They had no idea of what to do. I started firing support fire. They all retreated back across the river. Not one man [of them had] fired a shot." Later in the morning, Jennings heard track vehicles across the river and asked the tank commander to fire on targets over there. "Tank plt com [platoon commander] refused — said they would give away their position if they did."

A few days later, he wrote, his company was relieved by a British unit.

As of Sept. 12, K/23d was dug in on Hill 189. "The men are in foxholes cut deep to protect them from the frequent shelling by enemy artillery and mortars," Fogle recalled. "Their positions are attacked, mostly at night, as the enemy 'feels them out' in preparation, no doubt, for a full scale attack. Snipers abound and have to be eliminated by individual platoons of rifle squads."

While in this position, Co. K received its first beer ration. "Ironically," Fogle wrote, "this is the same day that back home the U.S. Congress votes to discontinue giving free beer to its troops. Some of the non-drinkers around gave SGT Donovan, of the 3d Platoon, their beer because he's a good soldier and a likable guy."

Late in the evening of Sept. 15 a battle started in which Fogle's cousin, Robert Bennington, was killed.

1/38th Infantry:

"Day before yesterday [Sept. 1] the 'Gooks' came across the river — we couldn't stop them," wrote Roy Hill B/38th Infantry, to his family on Sept. 3, 1950. "We withdrew from our positions to the rear for over a mile, where we are now and will stay.... The 'Gooks' brought up tanks last night. Been lots of fighting today and last night.... Our supply route is cut off. I'll love the Air Corps as long as I live. Day before yesterday, they were wonderful the way they held back all those Gooks. They must have slaughtered them with jelly bombs (fire) and rockets and machine gun fire.... I'm still filthy dirty and have

a nice start for a beard. My hair is really shaggy, and the fleas are still crawling....

"We're supposed to be in a last ditch stand here and are trying to get ready for tonight. We don't know what's to be here tonight.

"We know the Gooks are preparing for tonight or tomorrow. Probably for early tomorrow a.m. about 4:30 or 5 a.m. Gooks have overrun the positions we left night before last. They were shelled today. I'm sick of all this. Most of the GIs are too. I can't even eat good what ration we get. I've forgotten when I last took off my shoes and my underwear has been on me about 8 or 9 days now. Going up and down these hills is getting me down. I'm sorry if it seems that each letter is full of complaining, but Hell, there's nothing nice to write about."

Hill's letter home aptly outlines the situation and the condition of many of the men along the Naktong at the time. Water was a problem; there was little enough to drink, let alone to wash or shave. Bathing, showers and changes of clothing at this stage of the war were almost unheard of. Typically, men did not have changes of underclothing, and very few had spare socks. No one had spare shirts or trousers. There was so much activity, too, that it was dangerous to take off one's boots.

On Sept. 4 Hill's platoon moved up on Hill 198. Hill 198 was about 2 1/2 miles south of Hyonpung and east of the MSR. The platoon CP was near the crest, with Hill's squad (he was Assistant Squad leader) dug in on a lower spur on the east side of the hill which extended northward. That night, a three man outpost from Hill's platoon, which was placed on a higher hill to the rear of 198, were all killed by an enemy burp gunner. The next morning this hill was retaken by another platoon of Co. B.

Jerome R. Baker, with a BAR team of Company B's 2d Platoon (Platoon Sergeant, MSG Chester Mathis) also wrote about this incident. Baker blamed the enemy's successful infiltration to the hill in the rear on a man on the right flank of the company position who fell asleep. The man was holding a grenade, with the pin pulled, in his lap. In his sleep, his hand relaxed and the grenade exploded, killing him.

"We assaulted the NKs behind us on the hill," Baker wrote. "We used a frontal assault and flanking fire. Once again we were blessed, because none of our men were hurt. It was during this battle that the NKs had also occupied a hill to the platoon's right front. The First Platoon, under SGT Welch, was ordered to attack this hill. My BAR team and our M. Gun [machine-gun] squad was to lay down a base of fire and supporting fire. SGT Welch's plt [platoon], using marching fire, went up the hill and, we thought, killed 65 NKs.

"About 20 min. later, after SGT Welch and his men withdrew, I and CPL Bearden's sqd [squad] was ordered into action as a clean-up team, to see if any NKs were still alive. As we reached the crest of the hill, several NKs jumped up! I wanted to take them prisoner, but Bearden fired on the enemy, killing them instantly. The reason I wanted to take them as POWs was [because] they had surrender leaflets (UN) with them, that they waved.... CPL Bearden had fought in the Pacific during World War II. He yelled at me not to take any prisoners."

On Sept. 4, A/38th Infantry reduced an enemy roadblock on the MSR, well supported by SGT McMahon's squad, 2d Section, 2d Platoon, C/82d AAA/AW Battalion. In this action an enemy tank and SP gun were destroyed. A Co.'s commander recommended the entire AA gun crew for Bronze Star awards.

The 1st Battalion relieved the 2d Battalion on September 6, LT John E. Fox (Co. F) recalled. CPT Gambos, his company commander sent him to meet his relief. "It was a platoon from C Company of the first battalion," he wrote. "I met them just as they were approaching our perimeter, brought them through the perimeter and took the lieutenant to the CP where he was briefed on the local situation. His men took over our positions and we began our withdrawal to an assembly area."

LTC Killilea wrote in *82d AAA AW Battalion in Korea* that C/38th was subjected to "a 'banzai' type attack" during the night of Sept. 6-7. "SGT Lawrence Mauritz' M19 [from the 2d Platoon, C/82d AAA/AW Bn] succeeded in breaking up the charge and killing 9 of the enemy," he recounted.

LT Paul A. Stough (West Point 1945), C/38th's XO, wrote of a patrol part of his company made from this new position. "Our unit [C/38th] occupied about 3,500 yd of front, with a big gap to the left and the enemy penetration to the right of us. The former 2d Bn CP was in front of us about 500 yds (hidden from our view). I was ordered to take a rifle platoon (reinforced with a tank platoon) & move forward to explore the area between us and the Naktong 2-3,000 yds to the west. We moved out and reached the CP. So far, no enemy fire. There were piles of supplies undamaged. Evidently the enemy hadn't moved into the CP area.

"As we moved farther on (with the tanks forward) we received small arms fire from across a small valley. It was evidently an outpost — not a strong defense. I was calling the tank commander to tell him where to fire. The phone was on the back of the tank. Unfortunately for me he let loose with his cannon right over my head. It knocked me down, my helmet flew off & my glasses were broken. The mission continued with the riflemen following the tanks. Our rifle LMG [light machine gun] and tank fire silenced the outpost. I was following the tank as we climbed a hill to get a better view of the enemy disposition and possibly, the Naktong. Right there we re-learned an old battlefield truth — 'Tanks Draw Fire.' None of us was hit. But the battalion commander on the radio ordered us to come back." The only casualty was Stough's glasses.

On the night of Sept. 15-16, the enemy attacked Hill 198 and B/38th Infantry. The attack seemed to concentrate on the 1st Squad of LT David Alcar's 2d Platoon. SGT Roy Hill, Assistant Squad Leader, 1st Squad and SSG "Pop" Kiniski, leader of the 2d Squad, shared a foxhole. The attack did not strike them, but Manuel Berain, the platoon medic and SGT Warren, the leader of the 1st Squad were among those right in its path.

Hill and "Pop" were on the alert and could hear the sounds of the battle. "All of a sudden here comes a figure in the very dim light leaping over the hill toward us," Hill wrote. "I already had my rifle pointed in his direction and

Hill 115 as seen in 1981. In 1950 the hill had no trees and was almost devoid of vegetation. (Courtesy of John E. Fox, F&G/38 Infantry)

almost shot him. Just in time, I recognized an American outline.... It was Manuel Berain.... He got into the foxhole with us (he was really scared) and told us that 1st Squad had been overrun out on its lone finger jutting out north of the hill. A few more minutes passed while we waited (seemed like an hour) and I saw someone crawling on his stomach toward our hole from the northeast side of the hill. Just as I raised my rifle to shoot, I heard him say, 'Hill, Hill, its me, SGT Warren. I'm hurt.'"

Warren crawled to the hole and laid along its north edge. A few minutes later, the order to pull out came. Kiniski left the hole. "Berain & I sat Warren on my rifle with his arms around our shoulders and we carried him west toward our CP. We were the last to leave our Hill 198." Resting every ten or fifteen yards, and taking frequent sips from Hill's canteen, the three men slowly made their way to the Bn CP and Aid Station. "Later, I found out that the safety was off on my rifle," Hill wrote, "and it's a wonder, that in stumbling around in the dark, that we hadn't fired it."

SGT Warren had fallen on an enemy grenade in his foxhole, trying to save his ROK foxhole buddy. The grenade went off, severely wounding Warren's stomach. Hill rode "shotgun" on the litter jeep back to a MASH unit. Returning to his unit, Hill laid down in a prone shelter and fell asleep. While he slept, the platoon attacked and regained Hill 198. In the attack, LT Alcar was hit in the face by enemy grenade fragments, losing an eye. Enemy dead littered the area. Two enemy dead were in one foxhole, but Hill detected five knees. "Pop" Kiniski, who was standing with Hill, fired into the hole.

Cisler, a member of Hill's squad, tossed a grenade into another hole which had been filled with enemy equipment, weapons and ammunition. As the grenade went off, it seemed that everything in the hole exploded at the same time. A huge blast erupted 20 ft into the air," Hill recalled, "picking up Cisler with it and tossing him aside. I just knew he'd been blown to bits. But he got up...laughing and started to dust himself off." The squad had lost a number of men in the attack, including several KATUSAs and Ben

Ehle, the assistant BAR-man. His body, riddled with burp gun bullets, was found two days later on a ledge half way down a cliff.

The night of Sept. 17, the enemy attacked again, but was repelled. In this fight, the 1st Squad BAR malfunctioned and Hill used a carbine, on full automatic, to take up its fire.

2/38th Infantry:

On Sept. 2, Co. G, supported by LT Antone Raposa's 1st Platoon, C/82d AAA/AW Battalion, destroyed an enemy roadblock on the MSR between Hills 208 and 285. This was in the 38th Infantry's rear area. Co. F attacked and seized Hill 115 on Sept. 4, also supported by Raposa's platoon.

On Sept. 4, three more lieutenants reported to the 38th Infantry. They were 2LTs John E. Fox, Louis V. Genuario (both West Point 1950) and a man named Lawson. They were all sent to the 2d Battalion and reported to Battalion Commander LTC James H. Skeldon, in his CP near the village of Yusan-dong. Fox and Lawson were sent to Co. F and Genuario to Co. G. Co. F was dug in on Hill 115 about a mile northeast of the CP. CPT Nicholas Gambos commanded. He had just been assigned to that position the previous day, along with 1LT Raymond Orth, from Co. E. (F Co. had lost all its officers.) Orth was from the 1946 West Point class. Gambos formed the 89 enlisted men left in the unit into two platoons and a headquarters section. The more experienced Orth and Lawson were made platoon leaders and the junior officer, John E. Fox, became XO. A 1LT Flack was the FO. Co. E was on Fox Co.'s left.

Over the next several days, the battalion remained in position, subject from time to time to enemy mortar fire. On Sept. 7, the battalion moved to positions near Mosan-ni. As LT Orth's platoon moved into position, one of the sergeants suddenly "threw off the bandoleers he was carrying and began firing his M-1 into the bushes," Fox wrote. "The sergeant hadn't seen the enemy, he had smelled them. Sure enough, a search of the bushes turned up two dead North Korean soldiers — and they had a strong odor."

2LT Louis Genuario's G Co. made an attack

Looking west from Hill 115 toward the Naktong River, which can be seen in the middle distance. This was enemy territory in Sep. 1950. Photo taken in 1981. (Courtesy of John E. Fox, F&G/38 Infantry)

Hill 409 as seen from Hill 115. Photo taken in 1981. (Courtesy of John E. Fox, F&G/38 Infantry)

on Sept. 12. His platoon numbered only 16 men. An enemy machinegunner pinned them down. Genuario, armed with his carbine and some grenades, crawled out and knocked out the gun and crew. For this deed he was awarded the Silver Star. But he did not believe he had done anything remarkable. When interviewed by J. Robert Moskin, author of "The Tragedy of West Point Class of 1950," *Look* magazine, June 3, 1952, Genuario said, "There are occasions when leadership means the lieutenant goes first. This was one of them."

Fox Co. received its KATUSAs on Sept. 15. CPT Gambos took this opportunity to reorganize the company. He took six men from each of the existing two rifle platoons in the company to form the 3d Platoon. He added twelve KATUSAs to fill out the platoon and placed 2LT John E. Fox in command of it. SGT Colvin, the ranking

NCO among the 12 GIs, became platoon sergeant. The next three ranking NCOs were appointed squad leaders.

The same day, the 2d Battalion received orders to attack and seize Hill 209. Fox described it as a north-south ridgeline about a mile and a half long. "Except for a few spurs, the sides and each end tapered steeply down to the surrounding paddies," he wrote, "most of which had elevations of less than twenty feet above sea level. The highest part of the hill was in the middle of the crest, but there were other high points along the crest. The northern-most of these lesser high points was F company's initial objective."

The 1st and 2d Platoons made the assault on Sept. 16. Fox's 3d Platoon followed in reserve. Having no radio, he kept his platoon close behind those in the lead. The company took its first objective by 9 a.m. Fox was fairly close to the

captain. "The attack along the crest of the ridge had barely gotten started when it bogged down," Fox wrote. "I left my platoon in a sheltered area and moved forward to get instructions." Enroute, enemy fire was directed at him, and Fox jumped into one of a number of foxholes in the area. He found it to be occupied by a badly wounded North Korean. He considered killing the man, but believing he posed no threat to anyone, settled for throwing the enemy soldier's weapon out of the hole. "Then I moved on to...Captain Gambos [who] was surveying the situation."

"From his position there was a clear view all the way to the top of Hill 209...about a thousand yards away. A short distance to his front, spread out in some disarray and hugging the ground were the men of the two lead platoons. There was very little firing [now] coming from the enemy, but somehow these men had allowed themselves to be 'pinned down' and Captain Gambos was beside himself to get them unpinned." He decided to commit Fox's platoon out to an intermediate high point about 200 yards farther up the ridge.

Fox went back to get his platoon and discovered two of his KATUSAs violently ill. He left another ROK soldier with them and took the remainder of the platoon to the attack. He formed them into a two squad skirmish line and moved along the ridge, flanking the enemy foxhole line. The platoon moved forward, knocking out one foxhole after the other. "Only five or six of us were directly involved in most of the fighting and I was right in the middle of it," Fox recalled. His skirmishers walked slowly forward, delivering a constant rate of marching fire as they advanced. This kept the enemy pinned in their holes.

"As we came near a hole," he recounted, "we would fire at its lip until we were looking down into it and then simply shoot the enemy who was usually huddled in the bottom." Once, Fox was changing carbine magazines when an enemy poked his head above the edge of a foxhole. Fox pointed the North Korean out to one of his ROKs, who killed the man. "It was like shooting fish in a barrel," Fox recalled. He had killed three or four enemy himself, and now vowed to capture the next one. Approaching another enemy foxhole, he found a young enemy soldier "cringing in the bottom. His rifle leaned against the side of the hole," Fox wrote.

Fox grabbed it up and threw it away. Then he grabbed the enemy soldier by the collar and pulled him bodily out of the hole. He was surprised at his own strength. He then reached to take a grenade from the soldier's belt. "One of my men yelled, 'Look out, Lieutenant!'" An enemy grenade had landed about a yard from his left foot. "Just as I saw it, it exploded, jarring me up and spraying me with pieces of metal," he recalled. "I was hit all over. My legs got the larger pieces, but my left hand was hit by a mass of smaller pieces and immediately welled up in blood." Another grenade was thrown at him, but sailed on by and exploded harmlessly a few yards away.

But his platoon had taken its objective. Fox, leaning on the enemy prisoner, hobbled around, and with SGT Cowen's help, organized a perimeter. The other two platoons then moved through Fox's and one of their medics bandaged his hand

and gave him a shot of morphine, then moved on. CPT Gambos came up and congratulated him on taking the objective, then also moved on. Next someone brought a litter up. Fox was placed on it and covered with a blanket. He laid there until midafternoon, then was carried off the hill. While waiting, he pulled the blanket over his head. Two walking wounded men came by and assumed Fox was dead.

Co. E attacked at the same time as Co. F. Cecil L. Sherrod, a member of Easy Co., wrote: "Sept.. 16. Still much rain. We took Hill 208 overlooking Naktong. Sniper took shot at me. It sounded as if bullet burst in my ear. Next shot hit top sling swivel of rifle, knocking it out of my hands. Only two shots fired. We were all on hill. Why me?"

HQ, 38th Infantry:

The 38th Infantry's CP was at the village of Sibi-ri, which was at the foot of Hill 284. This hill and Hill 209, several miles south in the 23d Infantry's sector, dominated rear areas. At 6 a.m. on Sept. 3, an estimated 300 enemy soldiers launched an attack on COL Peploe's CP from Hill 284. He scraped together a defensive force from his headquarters, the headquarters company, mortarmen, tankers and an AA unit. The AA unit was an element of C/82d AAA/AW Battalion.

The colonel requested a bombing strike. It was denied on the basis that the enemy was too close to his defensive perimeter. The air force did conduct an air strike, however, employing rockets and strafing.

The battle for Hill 284 went on until Sept. 5, when CPT Ernest J. Schauer's G/38th Infantry finally captured the promontory. Appleman wrote that Schauer employed two platoons from Co. F. However, John E. Fox, a platoon leader in F Co. at the time, wrote that his company had only two rifle platoons. On both Sept. 5 and 6 no one from Co. F was engaged at or near Hill 284. Schauer's men attacked four times before securing the crest. There, they found the bodies of 150 enemy soldiers. The other 150 or so had run away. Many of them were cut down by George Co.'s only machine gun as they tried to escape to Hill 409 to the north.

CWO Fred W. Merten, writing in the Dec. 19, 1952, issue of The Ranger, described some of the action. When the enemy was first observed on Hill 289, "our security platoon immediately took after them and brought in a few prisoners. From them we learned that an entire enemy battalion had gained the rear of our 2d Battalion in the course of the recent offensive, climbed Hill 289 and established a strongpoint on it crest. All that and the next day, fighter planes strafed and napalmed every inch of the mountain top, yet failed to dislodge the enemy from the deep bunkers which he had dug under the large boulders on it."

Finally, COL Peploe sent Co. G to root out the enemy on the hill. "I can still see the company commander shaking hands all around as we wished him good luck, before setting out on his mission at high noon. Supported by the direct fire of several of our tanks and heavy mortars, the men of George Company slowly yet steadily climbed the steep slope in broad daylight. The nearer they reached the top, the more

intense grew the defensive fire of the opponents, who had expertly displaced his heavy weapons so as to cover all approaches. Our tank and mortar fire support was marvelous. As soon as an enemy gun opened up and revealed its position by the flash of its fire, the gunner of the tank nearest me, a heavily bespectacled young corporal, would zero in within a matter of seconds and silence the gun, repeatedly, with the first round."

In three hours of crawling, firing and short rushes, the men of Co. G worked their way to within a hundred yards of the crest. The enemy emerged from their holes and bunkers to hurl grenades down on the Americans hugging the ground below. At first the attackers wavered, then got to their feet throwing grenades back at the enemy, and delivered a bayonet assault which swept up and over the hill. A few defenders engaged in a short, sharp hand-to-hand battle before being downed or fleeing from the crest.

Abandoned enemy equipment and weapons on Hill 284 included 25 U.S. BARs and submachineguns, 30 boxes of unopened American fragmentation grenades, some American rations and a "large" American radio. Appleman gave this tabulation, but he did not identify what he meant by a "large" radio.

It was obvious as early as the morning of Sept. 2 that the enemy had significant forces deep in the 2d Division's rear area. The experience of MAJ Thomas K. Voorhis, then the Assistant Regimental Motor Officer illustrates this quite well. He wrote a short narrative about enemy activity in the rear area on Sept. 2. He was told about a 38th FAB convoy being ambushed in mountain defiles in the rear. "Went back to see what could be done about clearing the road over mountain," he wrote. "Found convoy of 37th FA ammo trucks waiting to get thru. Took Sgt and some men on wrecker and went up. Found one truck burned completely and two others damaged. Also found MP jeep and dead MP. Located wounded truck driver down side of mountain where he had been thrown by attackers. Started to clear road of disabled trucks when Major from 38th FA took over, so I left. Returned to Svc Co. at about 1000 hrs [10 a.m.].... Received word that ration train had been ambushed at about 1200 [noon]. One man known dead (Lambert) one wounded (McDermott) and 8 missing.... Missing drivers turned up later, three wounded; had mixed in with 9th RCT trps who had been overrun in area where our trucks were [located]. [The trucks] were caught in middle of firefight, not an ambush as originally thought."

Infantry regiments of that time were authorized three chaplains. When the 38th Infantry deployed, it had but two, Chaplains (Majors) John Garron and Samuel Simpson. On Aug. 19, Chaplain James C. Carroll was assigned to the regiment. He was the single Catholic chaplain. These chaplains made their rounds among the units of the regiment, providing services and spiritual help to the men. Even at the height of the Second Naktong, they endeavored to help. Carroll wrote that he tried to visit a different battalion and company each day and offer Mass. "At night," he wrote, "I would stay at a Bn Aid Station, under fire, or return to the Regimental Collecting Station, to where all wounded were evacuated. During the Perimeter days, I admin-

istered to many wounded, with the rites of the Church."

3/38th Infantry:

As mentioned above, 3/38th Infantry, was ordered south into the 23d Infantry sector. There, it was to attack westward from the 23d Regiment's CP near Mosan-ni to relieve 1/23d Infantry fighting near the village of Poncho-ri

The advance elements of 3/38th Infantry broke through the enemy roadblock in rear of 1/ 23d and joined them at 5 p.m. on Sept. 2. William Temple, an ammunition bearer in the 60mm mortar section of I/38th Infantry, recalled, "it was a scorching hot day, terribly hot day, and we had no water since early morning.... And for the first time in my life I found out what it was to be thirsty...."

On Sept. 4, the 3d Battalion attacked Hill 209. An M19 (twin-40mm) from C/82d AAA/AW Battalion delivered fire from a range of 3,000 yards. The battalion commander, then-Major Everett S. Stewart directed this fire, using a captured Russian BC scope. The attack on Hill 209 continued the next day. A section of 2d Platoon, C/82d AAA/AW Battalion, under LT Richard Rein, consisting of an M16 (quad-.50s) and an M19 (twin-40 mm) fired preparatory fires for L/ 38th Infantry. During the assault, these guns provide rolling fire just forward of the advancing infantry from the flanks. With this very effective help Love Co. took the objective.

SGT Nordin's M19 was then placed in defilade behind the highest point of the hill just yards from the enemy who occupied the reverse slope. Only the crest separated them. Three tanks were sent to reinforce the position. However, one tank was hit in the tracks and rolled back down the hill. The other two then withdrew. Later, the M19 was employed to carry forward ammunition, food and water to the infantry, who had no other means of being resupplied. The enemy tried to knock out the M19 with mortar fire, but the rounds landed on their own men instead.

That night, the gun crew placed fire on the enemy over the slope. LTC Stewart told LT Rein that the M19 was the deterrent factor in preventing the enemy from making an attack that night and that its presence gave a great boost to Co. L, which had suffered heavy casualties to date. He considered Hill 209 the key terrain feature in the entire battalion sector. A day or so after the hill had been taken, another M19, commanded by SGT Arthur G. Smith replaced Nordin's. His vehicle brought out the bodies of several L Company men who had been killed, but who could not be evacuated earlier due to enemy actions.

On Sept. 6, mortar fire struck near the M19, wounding SGT Smith and four crew members. A scratch replacement crew, consisting of the injured members of the original crew and four infantrymen, manned the gun until a regular antiaircraft crew could be sent forward.

Meantime, I/38th Infantry occupied an L-shaped position in the roadblock area which 3/ 38th Infantry had taken over from the 1/23d Infantry. Third Platoon, Co. I occupied the short end of the L, which was on high ground south of the road. The remainder of the company was deployed along the long side of the L, facing west. Temple, and the 4th Platoon were dug in next to the road.

He recalled that the enemy probed the main company position for four days and nights. Then they made a concerted night attack, but against the 3d Platoon, on the left. "They just absolutely won the day," he said. He recalled that the 3d Platoon "caved in" under the weight of the enemy attack. The attacking enemy closely followed the men of the platoon down into the 4th Platoon positions. "And there was an effort, I believe, for the gunners on the 60mm mortars to grab the sights and to thermite the tubes. [Drop thermite grenades down the mortar tubes to destroy them.]... It got to the point where we were actually bumping shoulder to shoulder with the North Koreans who were mixed in among us. It was a melee and I think they were as confused and bewildered...as we were." Temple, and those with him, made their way toward the Battalion CP area, where two U.S. tanks fired on them, hitting several men.

Strangely, several men had remained on position until morning. They allegedly exchanged hand waves with enemy soldiers, then were allowed to pull back to the CP area. Temple said that in the four days at the roadblock, over half the company became casualties.

Temple said that he believed that the 3d Platoon hill, now occupied by the enemy, was only about 100 to 150 yards from the Battalion Aid Station, in the CP area. A new line had been established on the reverse slope of a hill in that area. The crest was under direct enemy small-arms and automatic weapons fire. Some men tried to place a machine gun on the crest, only to have it destroyed by enemy fire.

Temple said that the company displaced a few hundred yards to the rear and dug in again. It stayed on this position for another three days. It was during this period that Temple also experienced the U.S. artillery shortage. One afternoon, he spotted what he described as "a large body of enemy" move from one wooded area, across an open space and enter another woods. When this information was relayed in an attempt to get artillery fire on this enemy concentration, the company was told that "the only way that the artillery could fire was if we were under direct attack," Temple said.

On Sept. 11, during an enemy attack on K/38th Infantry, CPL John Gamez performed a series of actions which earned him a Silver Star. As the enemy closed to within about 20 yards of his platoon position, CPL Gamez was wounded. Ignoring his wound and orders to go to the rear for treatment, he stayed on to fight. A short time later, he was again wounded, this time by grenade fragments. Again, his platoon leader ordered him to seek treatment. Gamez, realizing that the platoon needed every man to fend off the attack, again refused. Instead, he moved to the right of the platoon position to protect that flank with his rifle. Gamez engaged the enemy until they were finally repelled, with over a hundred casualties. Only then did he permit himself to receive medical treatment.

HM Co., 38th Infantry:

Bradley Sutter was a member of the crew of Number 4 gun, 1st Platoon. On the night of Sept. 1, enemy infantry attacked Sutter's platoon for the second time in two days. The enemy was driven away in the first attack. When they tried

on the on Sept. 1, one of the North Koreans tripped a trip wire hooked to a grenade, warning the Americans of the attack. The GIs had recently reloaded their M1 clips. It turned out that the ammunition they used was armor piercing and tracer. "It was a real surprise when this group of North Koreans hit us," Sutter said. "The fire fight itself didn't last but maybe an hour or hour and a half due to the fact that all they saw coming at them was tracer rounds.... I guess they thought they ran into a nest of machine guns because it was real startling.... There was a lot of hollering and screaming going on their side.... We had learned the night before [when the enemy attacked] to keep our mouths shut unless we were hit.... The area was lit up, the machine guns worked fine." The next day, the mortar-men counted 27 enemy dead and took three wounded prisoners — an officer and two EM.

"We were never bothered after the 1st of September by any other attacks from the North Koreans," Sutter recounted.

On Sept. 2, a tank from the 72d Tk Bn came into the mortar position. The crew drove the tank into hull defilade on a small ridge on the right (north) side of the mortars facing a village located out to the front.

"The following day...in the afternoon, lo and behold, out of this village...comes this self-propelled Russian track howitzer," Sutter said. "I think the designation for it is SU76.... This little bugger come chugging up the road toward our position about zero MPH — barely moving.... Just as it reached the area of where a drainage culvert ran under the road, it stopped. We couldn't fire at it. We knew that if we fired...our small arms would attract unwanted attention [to us from the SP gun]. But this tank...from the 72d Tank Battalion just sat there with this 76mm pea shooter they had on the front.... They had buttoned up when this self-propelled came up the road. We kept yelling at it to open fire, open fire; do something! They had the opportunity of their lives at that time to chalk up one enemy self-propelled artillery piece. But they just sat there and did not fire.

"Then this enemy SP gun...slowly turns around and starts back into the village. And lo and behold, on the sloping back end of that thing a door opens. And some Gook sticks his head

Bradley Sutter and his revolver. A number of soldiers carried a personal weapon in addition to the one issued to them. (Courtesy of Bradley Sutter, HM/38 Infantry)

out and is looking over the area as they [progressed] back into town. This was the opportunity for that damned 72 tank...but he didn't fire.... Needless to say, everyone in the platoon was...highly ticked at these guys in the tank.... This 76 that they had could have blown that damned SP all to blazes.... This sergeant tank commander said that he was given radio orders from his leader somewhere (who was lord knows where) not to fire. Anyway, this SP went back into [the village] and we never saw it again."

Sutter's platoon leader, LT Jack D. Brown, told the tank commander "to get him, his crew and his broken-down tank out of the area," Sutter said, "that his presence was no longer appreciated or required.... It was rather comical in a way, but Brown told him to pack up his tank and get the hell out of there and if he didn't (Brown) was personally going to do something to that tank. I don't recall the exact words, but something on the order of a shaped charge in the bogey wheels, or something to that effect." (See Chapter Notes.)

Results of the Second Battle of the Naktong Bulge

The Marine Brigade's counterattack, Sept. 3-5 largely took care of the enemy *9th Division*. The U.S. 9th Infantry, 2d Division engineers and other elements of the 2d Division had inflicted casualties on the enemy during the first few days of September, but the three day counterattack, with the Marine Brigade attacking the heart of the enemy *9th Division* created huge North Korean casualties. The bulk of these enemy losses were inflicted by the Brigade and its supporting artillery and air. The result of this Army-Marine counterattack was the virtual destruction of the *9th Division.*

On the northern flank of the 9th Infantry's sector, the 23d Infantry, aided later by 3/38th Infantry, took on the enemy *2d Division* and trounced it. COL Freeman claimed that the 23d had created "more than 5,000 casualties" on the *NK 2d Division*

Several elements of the *NK 4th Division* also took part in this enemy offensive, but to what extent is unclear. The *4th* had been badly mauled in the First Naktong, but it is known that elements of the *4th* reinforced the *9th* for the Second Naktong. The *NK 10th Division* largely remained on or near the massive and extensive Hill 409. Parts of this division worked their way southward to engage battalions of the 38th Infantry, but did not completely press their attacks with the division's full force. Had it done so the enemy may just have broken through. As it was, both the *NK 2d* and *9th Division*s lost a combined estimated total of over 10,000 men and were pretty much destroyed as divisions. Records do not indicate the losses in the *NK 4th Division.* Until the 2d Division made its breakout from the Perimeter, enemy forces of varying strengths remained in its sector and a number of bloody battles were fought.

Chapter Notes:

P. 282 Anyone who says that his unit "saved" the Perimeter is deluded; it was the resolute and bloody, often heroic fighting by many units and thousands of men, both South Korean and American, which "saved" the Perimeter.

P. 283 John Toland's sketchy treatment of actions in the 2d and 25th Division sectors contains several errors, including location of the Marine Brigade, misidentification of the 23d Regiment as the 35th, the 9th RCT as the 5th RCT and conjecture that "the 9th must have panicked...." The 9th did not panic. Some men from A/9th Infantry and perhaps a few from Co. B made their way into the lines of the 35th infantry (25th Division) to the south, but there was no mass movement of 9th Infantry troops in that direction, ordered or otherwise.

P. 289 Swafford states that this occurred on the third night on the hill — Sept. 2-3 — which meshes with Appleman's account that a number of men left the hill that night, intent on escaping. But Swafford's recollection of seeing enemy soldiers attacking up the hill and entering foxholes of the perimeter does not match. The perimeter was abandoned by its defenders the evening of Sept. 4. If that is so, Swafford could have seen enemy soldiers attacking the perimeter, but not entering the foxholes. The author believes that he left the hill on the night of Sept. 2-3 and saw an enemy attack on the perimeter on Sept. 3. The author does not otherwise dispute Swafford's account.

P. 294 In a letter to Clay Blair, dated March 6, 1986, Freeman wrote his side of the affair:

"I scarcely knew Haynes. He was fifty-five

at the time, not robust.... Finding himself nearly in the front lines of desperate hand-to-hand combat did not appeal to him — to say the least. My first problem with Haynes was his calling me to report to him at his CP some miles to the rear. Twice this happened when we were at the critical stage of repulsing strong enemy attacks. Not only did I have to leave my CP but literally had to fight my way through rear area infiltrators to his CP. I finally told him in a respectful way that I believed it improper to summon a commander to the rear during a firefight and suggested he send one of his staff forward to my CP if he didn't want to come himself. Moreover, he diverted a tank company, sent to reinforce my sector, to reinforce the protection of his own CP."*

Farther on, Freeman wrote: "The only time Haynes came to my position was when he came mincingly through the mud to tell me I was relieved and to report to the division CP. I was so shocked and furious that I got in my jeep and drove right through the enemy positions to get there.... I had no respect for him from then on." (COL Freeman's letter quoted from page 249, The Forgotten War.)

P. 294 A "computer" in an FDC of the time was a human being, not the electronic device we now call a computer. The human computer performed mathematical computations in connection with laying artillery pieces on the right azimuth and elevation to hit the desired target.

P. 295 The "marching fire" technique was taught during basic training in 1951, if not before. CPT Lowry introduced this to his unit just before leaving Ft. Lewis, WA. In executing marching fire, the platoon, or company, advances in a skirmish line, each man firing his rifle or automatic weapon at known or suspected enemy positions to his front as he walks forward. The objective is to seize fire superiority from the start and maintain it as the unit advances into and over the objective.

P. 297 A copy of the Price article was given to the author by Willis Fredericks (H/9th Inf.)

P. 299 Where this tank came from and to which Army unit it belonged is still a mystery. Based on information supplied to the author by six veterans of D-5th Marines, this tank's fire killed at least two men and wounded another. But is doubtful that the number of casualties caused by the tank fire approached 40, as one survivor recollected. William Albert, John Headrick, Lloyd W. Pasley, Frank Raponi and Valente U. Yruegas, all of Co. D, witnessed or were on the receiving end of this fire. In piecing together their recollections of the incident, it is possible that two tanks were involved. Alfred R. Jordan, also of Co. D, having been wounded and placed in an Army tank, may have been in one that did this accidental, but deadly, firing.

P. 306 Unless the 2d Division was different from the 25th and other divisions, infantrymen did not have sleeping bags that summer along the Naktong, first, because they did not need them and, second, because it was much too hot. An infantryman carried his weapon, ammo, grenades, a poncho or raincoat, bayonet, entrenching tool, canteen and some toilet articles. Few had a change of socks, let alone a sleeping bag. The dead soldiers who Muetzel wrote about were not front-line troops. In a letter to the author dated September 14, 1995, LT Muetzel wrote that

"the bodies were wearing something over their fatigues but it could have easily been ponchos. I did not inspect them closely because of the conditions of their bodies. They were in their foxholes...and they were reclining when killed. Decomposition was advanced and I really didn't want to get any closer to them than I had to." Some enemy attackers had penetrated to the Hill 125 - Observation Hill area during the night of Aug. 31- Sept. 1. There can be little doubt that the enemy were on these sleeping men without warning.

P. 309 The enemy was actually shouting "Manzai!" the Korean equivalent of "Banzai!"

P. 310 The guidon is a small swallow-tailed company flag, in the color of the branch of service, with the branch insignia in the center and the company letter below the symbol and the regimental number above it. F/23d's guidon would have been blue, and in white, crossed muskets in the center, the letter "F" below the muskets and the number "23" above them.

P. 317 Eleven former members of Heavy Mortar Company, 38th Infantry were contacted in 1993 for their recollections/experiences. Only Bradley Sutter provided any input.

CHAPTER TWENTY - Breakthrough at Haman

Disposition of the 25th Division — August 31, 1950

The 25th Infantry Division anchored the Eighth Army's left (southern) flank, from the confluence of the Nam and Naktong Rivers southward to the sea. The 2d Division's southern boundary and the northern boundary of the 25th Division ran eastward from where the two rivers joined, following the Naktong. The division front stretched along almost thirty miles of front. Part of it ran along the east side of the Nam to where the northern slopes of Sobuk-san came down to its banks. The line then went south along ever higher ridges to Sibidang-san (Hill 276), across a saddle southward to Hill 665 (Battle Mountain) and Pil-bong (Hill 743), then along a lowering series of ridges to the sea west of Chindong-ni. The Chinju-Masan highway and railroad passed through the saddle. The south coast road ran through the line to Chindong-ni to Masan.

The front was held by the 35th Infantry in the north, the 24th infantry in the center and the 5th RCT as the division's southern anchor. According to Appleman, the 35th had a 26,000 yard front from the Namji-ri bridge south to, and including the Chinju-Masan highway. The 1st Platoon, F/35th Infantry, under LT Grady M. Vickery, guarded the Namji-ri bridge. There were no friendly troops to Vickery's right and a 3-mile gap between his left and the remainder of Co. F. COL Fisher, commanding the 35th, was very much concerned about this gap. The 35th employed all six companies of its two battalions on the front, plus a 300-man force of ROKs in its center. The 2d Battalion was deployed with F, G and E from north to south. The ROKs held a hill about 1,000 meters long in the center. The 1st Battalion was deployed with C Company in the north, Co. B in a perimeter atop Sibidang-san (Hill 276), and Co. A in the south. None of the rifle companies was able to present a cohesive company front. All of them were deployed in a number of platoon (and in at least two instances) reinforced squad perimeters. In short, the 35th Infantry's "front" was not a front, but rather a series of small defensive enclaves, most of which were unable to support, or be supported by, any of the others. These small perimeters, however, were sited to lie astride of, or overlook likely avenues of enemy approach.

The regiment's 3d Battalion newly-formed from the remnants of 1/29th Infantry and replacements, was in reserve in a perimeter around A and B Batteries, 159th FAB on the Saga-Chung-ni road. The regimental CP was located on the east side of the Chirwon-Chung-ni road about midway between the two towns.

COL Champeny's 24th Infantry held the high ground south of the road (and west of Haman) south to and including Battle Mountain and Pil-bong. The regimental front was about 12,000 yards wide. The bulk of the regiment's front contained the highest and most rugged terrain in the entire Division sector. All three rifle companies of the 2d Battalion were deployed across a front of about 6,000 yards. There was a large gap, partly in the 35th Regiment's sector to the north and the 24th Regiment's right flank. F/24th was deployed just south of that gap. The bulk of the Co. E was on the lower slopes of a spur trending north from the lower slopes of Battle Mountain with one of its platoons dug in on the northern end of Battle Mountain itself, more than 1,000 yards from the rest of the company. Co. B held the bulk of Battle Mountain. A force of ROKs occupied the left-center of the regimental sector, on the northern half of Pil-bong (Hill 743). On the night of Aug. 31-Sept. 1, I/24th Infantry occupied the southern half of this hill. Company L held Hill 644, across a saddle at the southern end of Pilbong and K held the southern end of the regimental line on a hill about 700 meters high, part of the massive Sobuk-san mountain complex. The 24th's CP was in Haman.

The 5th RCT, under COL Throckmorton, held part of Sobuk-san southward to the coastal road near Chindong-ni. The 1st Battalion held the Sobuk-san position. To its south was the 2d Battalion. The 3d Battalion carried the regimental sector to the Chindong-ni road. ROK Marines were dug in from there to the coast. Throckmorton's CP was in Chindong-ni.

NK I Corps Plan of Attack Against the 25th Division

LTG Kim Ung, commanding the NK I Corps issued Operational Directive No. 81 on Aug. 20, ordering the corps offensive to start all along the line at 10 p.m. Aug. 31. This order set in motion the attacks of the 2d, 4th, 9th and 10th Divisions, supported by the 16th Tank Brigade against the 2d Division and the 6th and 7th Divisions against the 25th Division.

The 7th Division was to attack on the left, north of the Masan-Chinju highway against the 25th Division, then turn left to the Naktong and wait for the 9th Division to the north and the 6th Division on the right (south) to join it. The 6th Division was to attack through Haman, Masan and Chinhae to capture Kumhae on the west side of the Naktong River delta and just 15 miles from Pusan by Sept. 3. Part of the 7th Division was assembled near Uiryong west of the Nam River. The 6th Division would be attacking the 24th Infantry and the 7th Division would assault the 35th Infantry.

On Aug. 24, MG Pang Ho San, the highly decorated commander of the 6th Division, issued a morale-building order. The division mission, he said, was "to liberate Masan and Pusan within a few days." He also admonished the command to adhere to stricter discipline and to persevere better than ever before. He said that tactics must be altered to adjust to the changes "this epoch-making conflict had introduced into the art of warfare." He summarized the battle lessons:

"Our experience in night combat up to now shows that we can operate only four or five hours in the dark since we start night attacks between 2300 and 2400 hours [11 p.m. and midnight], and therefore, if the battle continues until dawn, we are likely to suffer losses. From now on, use daylight for combat preparation, and commence attacks soon after sunset. Concentrate your battle actions mostly at night and capture enemy base operations. From midnight on, engage enemy in close combat by approaching within 100 to 150 meters of him. Then, even with the break of dawn, the enemy planes will not be able to distinguish friend from foe, which will enable you to prevent great losses. This is the most valuable battle experience we have gained from the Chinju operation." (From South to the Naktong.)

24th Infantry Regiment — Aug. 31 -Sept. 1

The 2/24th Infantry held the regimental right on hills west and southwest of Haman. The battalion front was about 6,000 meters long. The bulk of Co. F was deployed in the second ridgeline west of Haman. One of its platoons was on a ridge to the rear of the main force. Company 60mm mortars were at the eastern base of this ridge. The F Co. sector was about 1,300 yards wide. A dirt road to the south of these ridges formed the boundary between Fox Co. and George Co. to the south. G Co. also had a sector of about 1,300 yards. Co. E's sector measured almost twice as wide as either of the other two units. But the bulk of the company was deployed in the northern part of the sector, with one platoon 1,300 to 1,400 yards away on the top of Battle Mountain to the south.

"Just before midnight [on Aug. 31], the artillery and mortar barrage opened up all along our line and lasted for about two hours," wrote BG Barth of the 25th Division. "The enemy attacks started at midnight. On the left, the 5th Infantry held firm. In the center, Lt. Colonel John T. Corley's 3d Battalion of the 24th held, but the other two battalions were driven back, retreating east of the Haman road. Through this gap, poured hordes of Red infantry. By daylight, Gustav Franke's Battery C of the 159th Field Artillery was cut off near Haman and fighting at close quarters to hold its guns." GEN Barth is mistaken; only 2/24th Inf. was driven back. The 1/24th Inf., less Co. B., was in reserve.

The gun position, about a mile north of Haman, was attacked about 4 a.m. on Sept. 1. Two tanks from the 89th Tk Bn helped defend the battery and the artillery gunners fired direct fire at enemy soldiers. Finally, under the protection of small-arms, machine guns and grenades from some artillerymen, others were able to couple up his guns and make a dash over the newly completed Engineer Road. The battery lost only 1 KIA and 8 WIA. Within two hours the battery was again firing in support of the 24th Infantry.

This road had been constructed by the 77th ECC, utilizing an oxcart trail as its basis up to a shale hogback, impassable to vehicles. The engineers blew a hole through the shale and then completed the road and named it "Engineer Road." It was about three miles long. The road provided an auxiliary MSR which the 27th Infantry subsequently used when it was committed to counterattacks in the 24th and 35th sectors. CPT Charles M. Bussey wrote that the 77th had undertaken construction of the road so the 24th would have an MSR if the enemy penetrated the regimental lines.

G/24th Infantry observers noticed a lot of enemy activity about a mile to the front. They called in two air strikes which hit the enemy just before dark. The first enemy attack struck F Co. just before midnight. Appleman stated that there were ROK troops guarding the road and pass on Fox's left flank. This would have been in G Co.'s sector. The ROKs, he wrote, "left their positions and fell back on G Company south of the pass." The enemy captured a 75mm recoilless rifle in the pass and used it to knock out two U.S. tanks. The retreating ROKs left a hole in the 24th Infantry's line along this road early in the fight. Exploiting this success, the enemy continued on, overrunning the battalion 81mm mortar position at the east end of the pass. At dawn, 1LT Houston M. McMurray, commanding 1st Platoon of Co. G found that he had only 15 out of 69 men still with him. This included eight from his platoon and seven ROKs. This implies a strength of 69 men for Co. G, although that may not be true. The enemy attacked McMurray's position through an opening in the barbed wire which was supposed to have been covered by a BAR. Appleman wrote that the BAR-man had fled. The enemy attackers quickly overran the position.

Joel T. Ward was a squad leader in Easy Co. The squad, he wrote, was on outpost when the enemy struck just before dawn on Sept. 1. "The enemy used automatic [weapons], small-arms [fire] and grenades. We [the squad] were...covering a hill about 200 yards from the company MLR. We were spread very thin, but could talk to the person on either side of you. We were on a hill...covering a road to our left. We fought for about an hour, repelling two frontal attacks. Our ammo was running out. I told the men to move back as I called their last name." There were seven men. By calling out each name and seeing the man, Ward could account for his squad. "I moved back last, after emptying my M-1 clip. As I moved across the ridge, some enemy soldiers were coming up behind our OP position. One said something in Korean. While he repeated what he had said, I pulled the pin on a white phosphorous grenade. As they made their way up the draw, I threw the WP grenade and my last two fragmentation [grenades] followed."

Ward and his men got back to the Co. CP, where he met MSG Norwood, his platoon sergeant from basic. Noticing the men in the area huddled behind a burial mound, he asked Norwood why. Norwood responded that a tank was firing at them from a position in the rear and down the hill. It was a U.S. tank. Casualties from the tank fire lay nearby. "Some where crying out in pain," Ward recalled. One wounded asked to be shot and killed to stop his pain. "I asked Norwood if he wanted me to go and stop the tank." Norwood said yes.

Ward, armed with a BAR he took from a man, and accompanied by his squad and a replacement named Pete, crawled down to the road. Norwood ordered "Pete" to accompany Ward. By this time it was getting daylight. "We came upon LT Charles Ellis [CO, Co. E] and two men

standing on the road. He had a .45-cal pistol in each hand. Before I could say anything, he fired one shot between my feet and said, 'Get back up on the hill!' I pointed my BAR at him and told him not to fire toward me again. He said he was the CO of E Company and he was going to have me court martialed. I told him my mission and [that] I had orders from MSG Norwood to go and [that] we were not running. He told me to go on." Ward came upon the tank just as the gunner on the .50-cal was reloading his machine gun. "Seeing us, he asked, 'What's wrong?'" Ward wrote. "We told him he was firing on our company. The tanker became frightened and said, 'I'm sorry, but I couldn't tell the difference,' and pointed up the hill at the silhouettes of my company as they moved around. (I assumed they were taking care of the wounded.) I assured him we understood."

Shortly thereafter, Ward recalled, he saw LT Ellis in the middle of a rice paddy, firing his pistols in the air and calling out. Ward took his men back to the tank and provided close-in infantry support for it. Soon after they arrived there, an enemy machine gun opened fire from a small hill across a rice paddy. Ward's men returned fire from behind the tank and the machine gun ceased firing. He then informed the tanker that his squad could provide better protection from ridge on the other side of the paddy. Ward led still carrying the BAR. He recalled a ditch on the right side of the paddy. "I kept my eyes on the ridge for any movement," he wrote.

"As I reached the tree [which he had headed for] one of my men, Henry James...asked me if that was one of our MGs to our left rear. It was an American cal .30 water cooled MG. As I turned, the MG opened up on us. The men dropped into the ditch. I got behind the tree. I felt little stings on my legs and one arm." The BAR jammed and Ward was unable to get it to fire. He decided to jump into the ditch. His men gave covering fire. "As I leaped...in the ditch, there was an explosion and MG fire on the ground all around me. By the time I landed in the ditch, I was hit on my left side. Pete told me my BAR was empty. He took it and knocked out the MG."

Interestingly, this narrative meshes with a similar episode described by Appleman involving LT Ellis and a "platoon leader." Appleman recorded that Ellis fired a round from his .45 at the ground between a platoon leader's feet. Ward's recollection puts a different spin on the incident from what Appleman implied.

Appleman also wrote that Ellis and a number of men with him "stood their ground." The group stayed in their holes, he wrote for two days, repelling several attacks. Early in that time, three or four men tried to make a break, but were killed by enemy fire. At the conclusion of the second day, the lieutenant was able to withdraw his party to the south into the 3d Battalion's position. During the withdrawal, they came upon a man who had been wounded by a mine. Ellis went into the minefield and rescued this soldier.

Appleman's account of the North Korean attack on 2/24th Infantry on the night of Aug. 31-Sept. 1 is generally a condemnation of that battalion, plus the 1st Battalion, which was sent forward in a counterattack early in the battle. There is evidence that some men did not stay in

position. Subsequent statements and affidavits by reputable officers of other commands, relating their observations and experiences attest to this. Enemy forces penetrated both the 35th and 24th Infantry lines at a number of places. Map VII in *South to the Naktong* shows that North Korean thrusts penetrated the 35th in Co. G's sector, displacing that unit, and the ROK sector, sending the ROKs to the rear and along the boundary between A/35th in the north and F/24th in the south. Penetrations in the 2/24th sector are shown on the map to have taken place behind the northern flank of Co. F and between Companies F and G. North Korean attacks also hit elements of F, B and L/35th.

Clay Blair wrote in *The Forgotten War* that the enemy's *6th Division* attacked the 24th with two regiments. An equally large force from the *7th Division* struck the 35th. He points out that the 24th had suffered some 500 battle casualties in August on Battle Mountain alone (75 dead and 425 wounded). Battle Mountain changed hands frequently — some 19 times by one veteran's reckoning. In that month, 2/24th had three different commanders — Horace Donaho, George R. Cole and finally, Paul Roberts, the regimental XO.

Many veterans of the 24th vehemently dispute Appleman's condemnation of the regiment, particularly the 1st and 2d Battalions. One of these is LTC Roger S. Walden, USA, Ret., who commanded F/24. He was a WW II paratrooper, but had not experienced combat. LTC Walden provided his recollections of events on Aug. 31 - Sept. 1 in a July 18, 1993 letter to the author, quoted in the following narrative:

"The unimproved road through the center of the battalion sector was assigned exclusively to Company G. They had been given at least one or two tanks to use in defense of this avenue.... I don't recall any specific effort being made to coordinate our defensive effort at the coordinating points. (See Chapter Notes)

"Some artillery and mortar fires were planned in defense of this position, but to the best of my knowledge, not highly developed. We set up barbed wire forward of our lines to the extent that it was available. Our main effort was to dig emplacements, clear fields of fire, lay communication lines and set out bouncing betty AP mines along the avenues of approach. We received probing attacks prior to the main one on Aug. 31 and Sept.1. (See Chapter Notes)

"On our right was the 35th and there was quite a gap between my company and their left flank unit. When the attack started it began late at night with artillery and mortars all along the line. They kept us heavily engaged while the main effort was made down the unimproved road through the battalion center sector. Once they broke through they were shortly thereafter upon the battalion CP area. At the time I was still at the [company] observation post in my right platoon sector. We continued fighting all night, until daybreak, but contact with my platoons by radio and wire was out and it was out with battalion."

After daylight, Walden discovered that the battalion CP had displaced to the rear, leaving a number of knocked out vehicles and equipment behind. F Co.'s vehicles had also been destroyed. The unit's left platoon, nearest the road and Co. G to the south, were badly mauled in the fight.

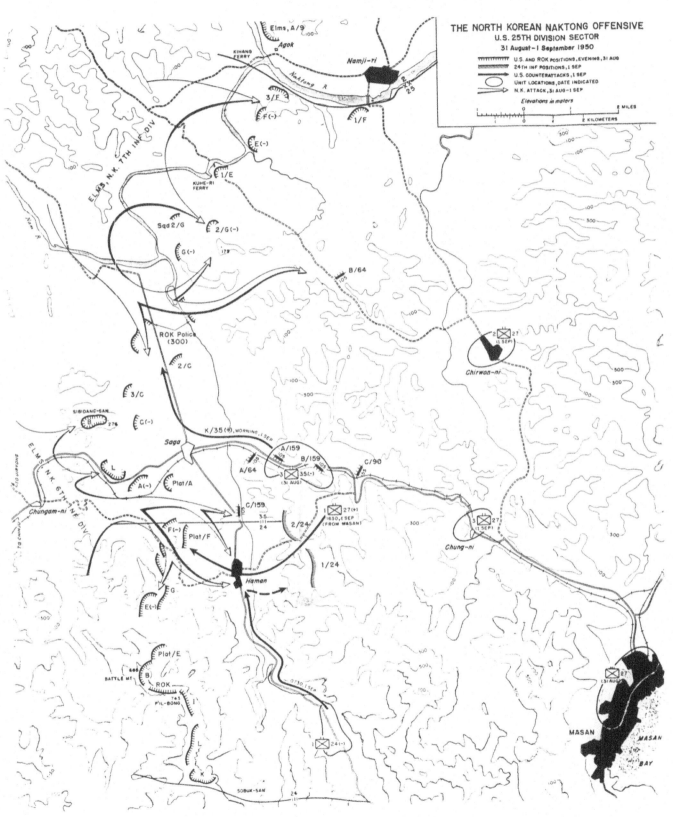

Map 45 (Source: South to the Naktong*)*

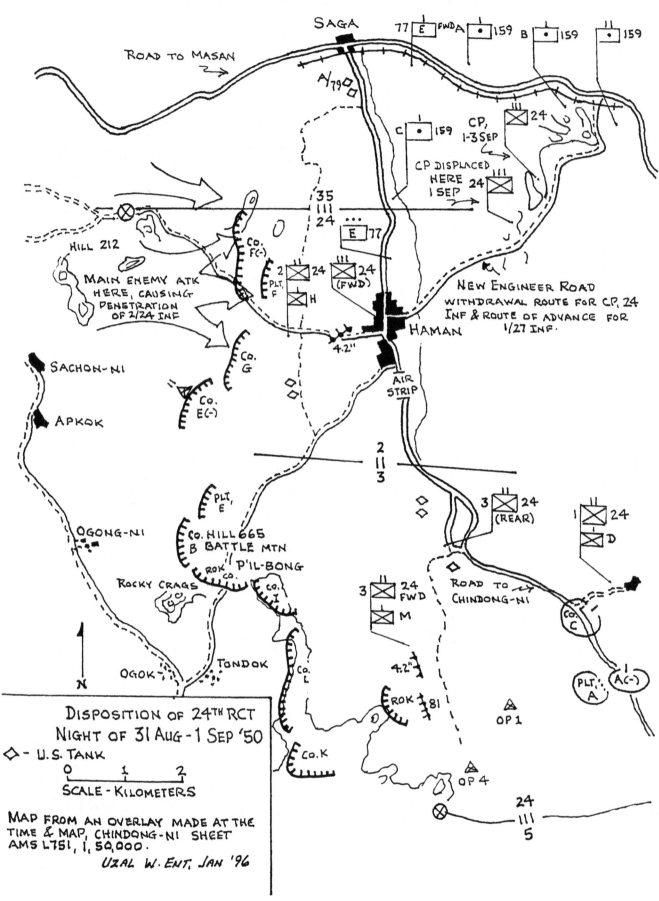

Map 46 (Courtesy of Uzal W. Ent)

The platoon on the ridge to the rear had few casualties, having been subjected to little mortar fire. At daylight, Walden stated that he had between 50 and 70 men left in his company

"I decided that our best option was to move to the terrain mass [to the rear] previously designated in plans for a penetration of this sort. Here I thought I would regain contact with battalion or other friendly elements. As we neared the crest of this hill, I saw many enemy troops moving along it to the north. I realized it would be sheer disaster to continue on and engage these forces under existing conditions, so I moved the remains of my force down from the hill and along the route shown on the overlay, northward to contact the left flank unit of the 35th RCT and explained the then existing situation of their exposed flank." Walden then took his men back south toward Haman. Once contact was made with friendly troops near there, "we were guided into an area...where we were assigned CP security until reorganization could be effected."

LTC Walden commented on Appleman's depiction of the 2d Battalion and what Walden called a public "lynching" of the 24th.

"I feel that the Army heaped exceptional abuse on the 24th in order to justify and make more palatable the break-up of segregated units and integrate the forces! Comparison of descriptive terms of other Korean (U.S. Army) forces with terms applied to the 24th are much softer and more acceptable to the general public than similar actions described for the 24th."

As to the charge by Appleman that "Most of the 2nd Battalion...fled its positions," Walden emphatically responds: "My company did not flee its position! The remnants were moved by my orders. I don't think that G or E Companies fled their positions either. I think that the attack came with such intensity and concentration of effort that they overwhelmed the defenders and smashed through to the rear areas and the Battalion CP. This happened to many other units throughout this 'Police Action.'"

He goes on, commenting about Appleman's statement: "The 2d Battalion was no longer an effective fighting force." Walden wrote, "Any unit losing communication and control ceases to be an effective force. Battles become isolated skirmishes."

Walden's unit was not called upon to participate in a counterattack.

When the enemy penetrated to the outskirts of Haman, LTC Roberts ordered an officer to gather remnants of the 2d Battalion and establish a roadblock. Appleman recounted that, although this officer ordered "a large group of men to accompany him, only eight did so."

At 4 a.m. on Sept. 1, COL Champeny displaced his CP from Haman to a point two miles northeast in a defile along the Engineer Road. It was about this time that C/159th FAB had to defend their guns and were helped by two tanks, recounted above.

Once it was apparent that the enemy had broken through the 2d battalion, Champeny ordered his 1st Battalion (- Co. B on Battle Mountain) to counterattack. This battalion (- Co. B) was assembled astride the road about three miles south of Haman. The battalion moved out at 7:30 a.m. It was supposed to make its counterattack along with elements of the 2d Battalion. LTC Roberts

succeeded in assembling about 40 men from his 2d battalion for the effort. Appleman wrote that "upon contact with the enemy, the 1st Battalion broke and fled to the rear." Not according to Waymon R. Ransom, 24th Regimental I & R Platoon and C. De Witt Dunn, A/24th. Both men were in this counterattack.

The squad of the I & R Platoon to which Ransom belonged led the 1st Battalion when it moved out toward Haman on the morning of Sept. 1. "1/24th was moved on trucks," he wrote, "from a bivouac area to the south edge of Haman. There were not enough trucks, so 3 or 4 round trips were made. Drew some fire on all trips. Last trip was after daylight. At this time a position of regt'l Security Plt...S. of Haman had apparently been overrun. Observed a dead American in the road." Ransom dismounted from his jeep to investigate. He found an enemy soldier, shot through the body, in a roadside ditch. The man tried to get a grenade from an American pack harness he was wearing when Ransom shot him above the left eye.

"As the 1st Bn troops entered Haman a CPL with shipping marks still chalked on his helmet noticed I was dechambering the round in my .45. He jumped on my case about not having been ordered to load. I corrected him and informed him that the noise he heard was NK fire within 100 yards and he had best look to his troops, if any, and look out for himself. It was plain that the NKA was in Haman in force." It was also obvious to Ransom that the 24th CP was also not in Haman. In the absence of orders, he had his men take position an a dike at the south edge of Haman "and sent two men to scout around the southeast edge of town to the 'Engineer Road.'"

While he waited there, a column of 200 to 300 ROKs, led by U.S. NCOs came up the road. A master sergeant asked the way to the 35th Infantry, and Ransom told him. He also advised the sergeant that there was a major enemy force in the way. "I got my orders," the NCO responded, and the column marched into Haman. It turned out that these were South Korean conscripts, on the way to their first battle.

His scouts returned with information as to the location of the regimental CP and Ransom led his squad to that site. The next morning, the CP area was hit by 120mm mortar fire then that of an AT (buffalo gun) rifle. "Numbers of troops were observed on the low ridge just above the CP position," he wrote. His men were ordered to take them under fire, but a company commander soon complained that they were firing on friendly troops. But Ransom could see the muzzle flash of the AT rifle, each time it fired, although the gun was some 900 to 1,000 yards away

"SGT J. Richardson, an assistant squad leader in the I & R," Ransom recalled, "climbed on a 2 1/2 [ton] with a ring mounted .50 [cal machine-gun] and eventually took it [the AT gun] out. The gent who claimed we were firing on friendlies ordered some of his people to 'shoot that SOB off that .50.'" But some of the men from the I & R Platoon held these soldiers at bay with their weapons until Richards had destroyed the AT rifle. But before it was knocked out, a round struck Ransom's rifle, destroying it and throwing him to the ground. Enemy 120mm mortar

fire began to fall in the area and the enemy cut Engineer Road between the new regimental CP and Haman. The enemy "had a very large force east of Haman and south of the Masan-Chinju road," Ransom wrote.

Ransom's platoon set up a roadblock along Engineer Road near the enemy and remained there until Aug. 4. During this period Platoon Sergeant J.H. Carter was wounded and Ransom was appointed to replace him. The platoon was then moved into a battalion CP (Ransom thought that of 1st Battalion) in Haman, where his Platoon Leader, LT P. Teague allowed the men to try to get some sleep. Some time after midnight, an enemy force attacked the CP. SGT R. Brown, of the platoon was killed at the outset. The I & R platoon was located in the angle formed by a stone wall and house ruins forming the eastern edge of the schoolyard and a road running on a stone embankment, forming the southern edge. Several enemy soldiers "jumped onto the road and emptied their weapons into the I & R jeeps and the school building next to the road," Ransom wrote.

CPL William Herndon was hit in the left temple by an enemy bullet almost immediately. "It began to rain grenades from the house ruins and walls. SGT Rivers called for cover and made it to the base of the wall with an armed grenade in each hand. He popped them and put them over. Immediate explosion and confusion. No more stuff from that direction." SGT Richardson was firing a .50-cal machine gun from a jeep when he was taken under fire by another .50-caliber. An enemy soldier had engaged him with the machine gun mounted on a nearby 2 1/2-ton truck. "Richardson put a burst into the truck and set it afire, and ended that," Ransom wrote. After daylight, the enemy dispersed and order was restored. CPL Herndon was found, alive. He survived 27 days in a coma, Ransom recalled.

"The 1st Platoon was on a truck, heading for Haman, as I recall," wrote Lawrence Dunn, of A/24th. He was writing about his experiences Sept. 1 and 2, 1950. "We ran smack into an enemy roadblock, but thanks to that truck driver, he shifted gears and ran right through it.... LT Collins, PFC Sam Mayo, and some other men were wounded, and evacuated that night. The rest of us went north to Haman but there was a lot of confusion. SGT Clarence Paul and I were in a foxhole overlooking a slight cliff. Enemy infiltrators, using GI slang, came down the road and started up the cliff, asking where was Heavy Mortar Company. We could tell they were North Korean by the smell of garlic."

U.S. flares were popping in the sky in an attempt to locate and engage the enemy. "Before the next flare went off so we could see them clearly, we were engaged in hand to hand combat right there in our foxhole. One of them was trying to get the pin out of his 'potato masher' but I managed to grab his hand as he switched hands and smacked me right across the nose with the [grenade]. Then SGT Paul had 'dispatched' the other one to 'Kingdom Come' and swung around with his M2 carbine on full automatic. And in his best Creole command, shouted, 'Hold him still mon, so I can shoot him!' That was funny later, but not then.... He got the NK infiltrator. But at the same time, CPL Freddie 'Firebug' Cage, thinking we were being overrun, opened fire on our position with his A6 [light machine gun]. By staying down in the hole with the bodies propped up on the edge, we survived.... Of course, a direct order from SGT Paul to cease fire helped."

There was considerable confusion and fire support was largely ineffective. In daylight, it became obvious that the enemy was trying to flank both sides of the position. Dunn shot an enemy soldier carrying a base-plate over a rise in the distance. He and CPL Gay, located just behind him, both ran out of ammunition. At that moment, SGT Melvin Schools ordered the men to withdraw. Then they realized that the position was almost surrounded. The platoon medic was shot in the thigh. Schools and three other men placed him on a door to carry him to the rear. With Dunn leading, and the medic's carbine slung over his shoulder, the party set out for the rear. Starting through a village, they came upon an enemy soldier trying to change into civilian white clothing. SGT Schools pointed him out to Dunn. Dunn aimed his rifle at the man, pulled the trigger and heard the tell-tale "click" of an empty rifle. Then, in what seemed slow-motion to him, Dunn got the medic's carbine off his shoulder and shot the North Korean.

LT Lyle Rishell (1st Platoon, A/24th Infantry) was ordered to go to the CP of 2/24th Infantry and investigate the situation. Communications had apparently been cut with it during the night of Aug. 31-Sept. 1. Rishell was given a tank for the mission. Appointing himself patrol leader, he selected a squad to go with him. "The morning was cool and crisp," he recalled. Rishell recounted the events of that patrol in *With a Black Platoon in Combat*.

"The Headquarters was utterly devastated, the charred remains of both men and equipment scattered around.... I did not see much indication of a fight. Most of the casualties had been killed in their sleeping bags, and if they awakened at all, it was too late for them to unwrap themselves before they died. The horror of that first sight was sobering beyond words." (See Chapter Notes)

He saw blood everywhere. Some bodies still oozed blood, which dropped into the blood darkened ground beneath their cots. Rishell and his men were shocked into silence by this scene of violent death and destruction. He wondered to himself how men could set aside war's danger and lull them into seeking shelter in their sleeping bags. The men with him never again had to be told to stay alert.

About a half mile away, Rishell found the battalion commander, "wandering along the edge of a field, emotionally and physically beaten by the enormity of the happening," Lyle wrote. He felt great compassion for the man, who had not yet grasped the magnitude of the massacre. COL John S. Komp, USA, Ret., 24th Infantry Assistant S-3, wrote that after the 24th CP relocated, they "were able to accomplish a makeshift set-up, but during the late morning we were again taken under fire with what we thought were recoilless rifles. Mass confusion reigned when we saw North Koreans on the near ridge line to the west." A number of casualties were sustained, including the S3, MAJ Owen H. Carter, wounded in both arms. Komp recalled that LT Erman Aynes organized the CP defense, but was soon

wounded. The chief of the POW interrogation team, LT Harry Iida, "then assumed command and rallied the defense." It was fortunate, he continued, that the Tactical Air Observer, in a small airplane was able to obtain a very effective air strike. A few days later, after the enemy had been cleared from the 35th and 24th Infantry's rear areas, the 24th's CP returned to Haman.

Appleman's narrative stated that, "shortly after daylight the scattered and disorganized men of the 1st and 2d Battalions of the 24th Infantry had fled to the high ground two miles east of Haman. The better part of two regiments of the *NK 6th Division* poured into and through the 3-mile-wide Haman gap." What Appleman does not say is that these two enemy regiments had made the attack through the 2d Battalion.

Neither the 3d Battalion, manning the southern part of the regimental sector, nor the 5th RCT, further south, was seriously attacked at this time, receiving only some artillery and mortar fire and a few light probes. About 2 a.m. on Sept. 1, an outpost on the 3d Battalion's right flank reported watching about 600 enemy soldiers file past about 100 yards away. They were headed for Haman. From the 3d Battalion's mountain position Haman seemed to be engulfed in flames. At dawn, the men saw about 800 enemy troops enter the town.

35th Infantry Regiment — Aug. 31 - Sept. 1

At 11:30 p.m. on Aug. 31 an enemy SP gun across the Nam River began firing into positions of G/35th Infantry. PFC Earl R. Green and three or four other men were on a G Co. outpost at the time. "Several hours after dark," he wrote, "a tank or SP gun rattled up in front of our position and fired. The round hit behind my hole on the slope above my head. It was within 20 feet of me and was a dud. A platoon sized force of North Koreans double timed in close formation past our position. Our NCO notified our CP by EE-8 and was told to withdraw. (Hell of a deal, since the company was under attack from at least two directions. To make matters worse it was in darkness and we had no password. We were at risk from friendly fire and from the NK. What followed was story book stuff)," Green continued.

"We decided to march up the road and sing the Marine Hymn! The shooting stopped and we went up the hill without incident. We found an officer at the base of the hill who had been shot in the ankle and carried him to the top. We grabbed a foxhole and spent the rest of the night under mortar attacks and several ground attacks. Our 60 mm Mortar Section was overrun, but the crew piled up 25 or so NKs," Green concluded.

A few minutes after the SP gun began firing, enemy artillery and mortar fire rained down on all the front-line companies of the 1st and 2d Battalions of the 35th. Thus covered, a reinforced regiment of the *NK 7th Division* crossed the Nam River and assaulted F and G Companies. Other North Korean forces crossed the river on an underwater bridge into the paddies near the boundary between LTC John L. Wilkins Jr.'s 2d Battalion in the north and LTC Bernard G. Teeter's 1st Battalion in the south. The contingent of ROK police manned some low hills in this sector, right in the path of this enemy force. COL Fisher had

placed this ROK force in this position to act as a warning unit. He expected them to hold long enough for him to counterattack with his 3d Battalion.

Unfortunately, the ROKs gave way very early on, creating a huge hole in the center of the 35th Regiment's line and between the 1st and 2d Battalions. Very soon, enemy troops were attacking the southern flank of Co. G and the northern flank of Co. C. Co. C and D, with the regimental I & R Platoon, formed a hasty defensive position along dikes at the north edge of Komam-ni. This village was located about a mile east of Saga.

Instead of turning south, as COL Fisher expected, the bulk of the enemy force which had broken through now turned east and north behind his 2d Battalion.

James F. Waters, C/35th, recalled defending his position. CPL Bartolome S. Ribac and PFC Roy N. Fomby manned a .30-caliber light machine gun covering what Waters described as "a pretty good sized draw.... I was over to the left on the small finger of the hill," he wrote. "I was dug in with another rifleman.... Early one morning a group of North Korean soldiers, estimated to be company sized, were coming up the draw using a heavy blanket of fog as cover to mask their movements.... Unfortunately for them, and fortunately for us, the blanket of fog suddenly lifted. There they were...like sitting ducks.... Corporal Ribac and Roy Fomby spotted them and Roy called in some 4.2 mortar and, as they were trying to pinpoint where the rounds should go, one of the rounds landed in our position. But the succeeding round — or one of the succeeding rounds — made a direct hit on one of the North Korean squads and literally blew them away. Corporal Ribac was firing his machine gun and continued firing even though he was under very heavy, intense small-arms fire from the approaching enemy. When the battle was over, some of us went down into the draw...to check out things.... There was an estimated...75 and 100 or so North Korean dead, and Ribac got credit for killing most of them." Waters does not recall Ribac receiving any award for this, but Ribac later was posthumously awarded the DSC for another action.

Sibidang-san (Hill 276), occupied by B/35th Infantry was the dominant terrain feature in the southern part of the regimental sector. Under the cover of a half hour artillery bombardment (11:30 p.m. to midnight Aug. 31) two battalions of the *NK 13th Regiment, 6th Division* made their way to within 150 yards of the defenders. Simultaneously, enemy tanks, SP and AT guns made their way along the road south of Sibidang toward Saga. An American M4 tank there knocked out a T-34 before midnight while a 3.5 inch rocket launcher team destroyed an SP gun and a number of 45mm AT guns.

The first wave of enemy attackers on Sibidang were stopped by an antipersonnel mine field. But the North Koreans continued to launch one assault after the other. All were turned back. By 2:30 a.m., the riflemen of Co. B were stripping ammunition from machine gun belts to use in their rifles. The emergency was met by the 1st Platoon, Co. C, located at the base of the hill behind Co. B. The platoon scrambled up Sibidang in forty-five minutes, bringing a resupply of ammunition. As daylight came, enemy attacks ceased and the defenders saw slopes littered with enemy dead and abandoned enemy equipment, including thirty light and three heavy machine guns. The commander, *NK 13th Regiment,* was among the dead.

At daybreak Sept. 1, Co. C headquarters personnel, with a tank, cleared the road to Sibidang and, just in time, resupplied Co. B's 2d Platoon with ammunition. The enemy launched another attack, which was repelled, leaving 75 enemy dead and 21 prisoners.

Division engineers counterattacked up the secondary road toward Chirwon on Sept. 1. They advanced slowly in the morning against stiff opposition; that afternoon, the enemy brought them to a halt. Co. B, 29th Infantry (soon to be redesignated K/35th Infantry), being in the 1/35th sector and subject to that battalion commander's orders, counterattacked to restore the position formerly held by the ROKs in the regimental center. The company attacked at 11 a.m. and regained the objective by 12:30 p.m.

About this date Combat Medic Harold L. Gamble, working with B/29th Infantry was called upon to go forward to the B Co. CO, 1LT John C. Hughes' CP. He and another medic set out with four litters and additional medical supplies. "At the base of the hill a jeep with 3 men hit a mine just in front of us," he wrote. "I went to them. They were seriously wounded by the mine." After the wounded had been treated, Gamble sent the other medic to the rear with them. Gamble, carrying two litters, his carbine and aid kit, started up the hill. About a third of the way up, "about 8 - 10 NKPA came around the hill from my right started firing at me, hitting my left hand," Gamble recalled. "I dropped the stretchers, rolled down the hill toward them and brought my carbine into firing position and caught them across the chest. My weapon was on automatic with a 30 round magazine in it. Two were left standing. I reloaded and opened fire again. One limped away very slowly; I doubt if he made it. I then retrieved my stretchers and proceeded up the hill to the Company CP. LT Hughes asked me which way I came up...[and] I told him and he said, 'My God, that hasn't been cleared yet!' I told him, 'Yes it has, I just cleared it.'"

When the battalion commander, LTC Wilson heard of this, he remarked, "That crazy medic went up the wrong side of the hill."

LT Hughes had 28 wounded men, "and a few prisoners during that time," Gamble remembered, "and over 800 NKPA were killed...." Gamble and another medic there treated and evacuated 31 wounded GIs "on the hill," he wrote. Hughes said that he was going to recommend Gamble for the Silver Star for his work.

Gamble, as well as Jesus Rodriguez and Edward F. Balbi, both of A/29th Inf. (I/35th Inf.), recalled one ridge they called "Tank Hill." The hill was part of the line along the Nam River then defended by 3/35th Infantry. Rodriguez recalled that the enemy sent "different platoons and different companies...to take this mountain. They would approach us from different fingers." One night an enemy soldier got into the unit perimeter and sprayed the area with his burp gun and walked out again, Rodriguez recalled. One of the bullets hit his foxhole buddy in the forehead, killing him.

"Tank Hill" was so-named because a dozer was used to cut a trail up the mountain so that a tank could be brought up. Gamble wrote that this occurred some time between Sept. 5 and 10. "I saw it," he wrote. "I Co. position was just west of K Co....fronting the Nam River. They used a dozer to cut a road up the side of the hill, then the dozer was used to help push the tank up the hill and into position.... When they [the enemy] hit I Co. they would become disorganized and filter back toward K Co., whose interlocking fields of fire wreaked havoc on them."

Rodriguez places Tank Hill as the site where half his squad was killed. The squad was known, unofficially, as the "Mexican Squad." The squad included Jesus Rodriguez; Manuel and George Gonzalez; Oscar Gillegos (BAR-man); Henry McCormick (Assistant BAR-man. McCormick was Mexican, Rodriguez said); and a man named Goodman, who was not Mexican. The squad was part of an attack to knock out some enemy machine guns near Tank Hill. "We tried to make a frontal attack on this high ground to knock out these machine guns on wheels," Rodriguez continued. "The only way we could do it was to just go over the top, down into a gully and come back and try to take that ridge. This machine gun caught us, and to my immediate right, Goodman dropped, George Gonzales dropped and Manuel Gonzalez dropped — three of them right with that first burst.... I lost half my squad... in an instant." Rodriguez did not say if they got the enemy guns.

G/35th Infantry — Aug. 31 - Sept. 2

"In the faint light of morning I observed movement about 50 yards east of my hole.... [A] small horse and an enormous iron wheeled machinegun and 2 or 3 NKs were skylined on top of a ridge. I brought down the horse and two of the enemy with a couple of clips rapid fire with my M1. When daylight came we had piled up a lot of the enemy. I have no idea how many. The bad news was that we had only one man left in many of our two-man foxholes." This is how Earl R. Green (G/35th Infantry) described the company's opening battle with the enemy, Aug. 31-Sept. 1.

Appleman wrote that Co. G received the hardest enemy blows in his attack against the 35th. Just after 3 a.m., the enemy overran 3d Platoon, HM Co. and drove it from its position. The mortarmen went up Hill 179 and joined the 2d Platoon, Co. G on its crest.

At the same time that the mortar position was being attacked, G Co.'s 3d Platoon, on a low hill along the Nam four miles south of its junction with the Naktong, came under heavy attack. With the coming of daylight, Co. G's CO, CPT LeRoy Majeske (West Point 1947), called in artillery fire and air strikes. The strikes were slow in coming and, by 11:45 a.m., enemy troops were nearing the crest of the hill. Only the narrow space covered by the American air panel separated the two forces. A few minutes after calling the strikes Majeske was killed and the 3d Platoon's leader, 2LT George Roach, once more reported the critical situation and asked for an air strike. Finally, the strike came in, hitting the enemy side of the hill, stopping the assaults for the moment.

But it came too late. Some enemy troops had already seized platoon foxholes, from which they hurled hand grenades into holes occupied by defenders. LT Roach was killed by one of these grenades early in the afternoon. Squad leader SFC Junius Poovey then assumed command. In the fight that day CPL Hideo Hashimoto, a Japanese-American, fought back with grenades by crawling within 10 to 15 feet of an enemy-occupied hole before tossing in a grenade. By 6 p.m., the platoon had only 12 unwounded men, out of a strength of 29. Ammunition was almost gone, so Poovey obtained permission to withdraw. After dark, some friendly tanks moved up and engaged the enemy. Under this diversion, the 29 men escaped, three of them being carried on litters. The party reached the G Co. position on Hill 179 at 11:30 p.m. on Sept. 1. (See Chapter Notes)

Benjamin F. Martin was B/64th FAB FO with G/35th Infantry at the time. The company was cut off for three days, he recalled, "but we remained on the hill," he wrote. He also recalled the Air Force coming in to "break enemy thrusts."

"The forty or so of us who survived did pull in to the only tenable position on the western side of our perimeter," wrote Earl Green. "It was from this position that we made the final stand. From this hill we could look down and see the dead lined up under ponchos."

Except for the forward platoon of Co. G, all of the companies of the 35th remained in their original positions as dawn broke Sept. 1. Only the ROK force in the regimental center had collapsed. Some enemy troops had penetrated to the high ground just south of Chirwon, more than seven miles in the rear of the 1st Battalion's front lines. K/35th Infantry, supported by tanks, counterattacked and regained part of it.

On Sept. 1, aircraft were employed for the first time against enemy troop concentrations in the 25th Division rear areas. Many more strikes would be made by aircraft in these areas during the next several days. Later, enemy POWs revealed that five enemy battalions, totaling about 3,500 men, were then operating in the Division's rear. Most of them were behind the 35th Infantry.

GEN Barth, in writing of the employment of air strikes, called the aircraft "flying artillery." In his monograph, "Tropic Lightning and Taro Leaf in Korea," he wrote: "Without the planes of the 5th Air Force on these crucial days, we would have had little chance of survival. Their performance was proof conclusive of the efficiency and power of Tactical Air properly employed."

Even after daylight, defying American efforts to stop them, the enemy continued to push troops across the Nam River into the gap between 1st and 2d Battalions, 35th Infantry. Aerial observers spotted one force of about four companies trying to cross. They called in proximity (VT) fuze fire from the 64th FA Battalion, which destroyed about 3/4 of the crossing force. (See Chapter Notes)

After the artillery finished firing, fighter planes came in and finished off the survivors. Later in the day, other aerial observers detected another enemy force near the river. This time VT fuze artillery produced an estimated 200 enemy casualties.

A/89th Tank Battalion was then in support of the 35th Infantry. One of its platoons was sent to break up a roadblock. CPT James Harvey, the company commander, rode along on the rear deck of one of the tanks. At the roadblock, he manned its .50-caliber machine gun. An enemy sniper wounded him with burp gun fire, but he killed the enemy soldier. Looking down at his wound, he exclaimed "God damn it, that's my second Purple Heart in two days!" He had been hit the previous day by grenade fragments.

It appeared that the *NK 7th Division* was to swing behind the 35th Regiment and cut the Namji-ri-Chirwon road while the *NK 6th Division* thrust east along the main Chinju-Saga-Masan road through the 1/35th Infantry. The road south from Namji-ri ran through Chirwon to join the main highway eight miles east of Komam-ni near the hamlet of Chung-ni, just four miles northwest of Masan. These two roads formed principal avenues into the 25th Division and Eighth Army rear areas.

The breakthroughs in the 24th and 35th Regiments threatened the collapse of the 25th Division's northern sector. GEN Kean had few troops with which to counterattack. He pressed the 65th Engineer Battalion into service as infantry.

By daylight on Sept. 1, GEN Kean realized that his division was in deep trouble. He called GEN Walker, at Eighth Army, and asked for the entire 27th infantry Regiment from Army reserve to counterattack behind the 24th and 35th Regiments to restore the front. His request was denied. Instead, he was given only LTC Gilbert Check's 1/27th. The battalion was reinforced by 1st Platoon, HM Co., a tank platoon from B/89th Tk Bn and A/8th FA Bn in direct support. The battalion, thus reinforced, was attached to the 24th Infantry Regiment. Its mission was to attack Sept. 1 to restore the former positions of 2/24th Infantry. The battalion moved to a position east of Haman at 7 a.m.

By mid-morning of Sept. 1, GEN Kean became alarmed at the large number of enemy troops in rear of the 35th. By this time, Walker had flown to Kean's CP. He asked Walker to release 2/27th Infantry to counter these enemy troops. Walker refused. But by 3 p.m. the situation in the 35th area was desperate.

Front line units were cut off and could not hold out indefinitely without resupplies of ammunition and food. The 25th Division history records the exploit of a 2 1/2-ton truck driver in getting ammunition to one cut off unit. CPL Ervin H. Edwardson was in the battalion CP when he learned of the unit's critical need for ammunition. He volunteered to drive a truckload of ammunition to it. On his first try, he ran into fire from several enemy machine guns, and withdrew. But he could find no alternate route. Determined to get through, he turned the truck around and drove it in reverse. As he approached the enemy guns, he hit the pedal and drove it to the floor. The enemy machine guns all fired on the speeding truck, but he got through unhurt.

Once through the block, Edwardson had to continue driving in reverse because the road was too narrow to turn around. He drove it three miles in reverse, but delivered the ammunition. The truck, however, was a total loss. Three tires had been shot away, the windshield had been de-

stroyed and the truck body was so badly chewed up by bullets that it couldn't be repaired. The ammunition boxes had also taken many hits, but fortunately none exploded.

Four artillery batteries were exposed to attacks by forces large enough to overwhelm them without infantry support. Walker could not be reached. Therefore, Kean, on his own initiative, now ordered LTC Gordon E. Murch's 2/27th from its assembly area at Chirwon to counterattack to clear the area behind the 35th Infantry and relieve enemy pressure on G/35. The 1/29th Infantry (soon to become 3/27th Infantry) still in Eighth Army reserve at this time, was placed in blocking positions on the MSR.

1/27th Infantry Counterattacks — Sept. 1-5

Alerted for movement at 2 a.m., Sept. 1, the 1st Battalion, 27th Infantry arrived at Champeny's new CP two miles east of Haman at 10 a.m. The battalion advance party, composed of Check and his command group, were met by a barrage of enemy mortar fire upon arrival there. COL Champeny oriented Check and his staff on the situation.

The 24th Infantry's rear area in this sector was chaotic. There were individuals and small groups of men, apparently from the 24th RCT, as well as numerous vehicles traveling about. An occasional enemy artillery or mortar round dropped into the paddies, without hurting anyone, or damaging equipment. There appeared to be no one in charge. Champeny's CP did not seem to have a grasp of the situation. Appleman wrote that SGT Jack Riley, 25th MP Company tried to clear the road, but men just went around him. During an Inspector General's investigation afterward, Riley testified to this and also said that some men were unarmed, had no helmets and some were even barefooted. He called for all officers and NCOs to stop, but none did. He chambered a round in his carbine and pointed at one man, who turned out to be a first sergeant.

The first sergeant told him to get out of the way. Some of the retreating soldiers jeered Riley when he asked why they didn't stay and fight. "We didn't see any MPs on the hill!" they retorted. At 4 p.m., 2/24th Infantry mustered between 150 and 200 men in an assembly area near the regimental CP. Not all the men of 2/24th were milling around the rear areas. CPT Walden (F/24) had kept his unit in hand. Although it had left its front line position, after having fought through the night and having one platoon decimated, Walden kept the company together as an organization. Later that day and the next, counterattacking 1/27th units found individuals and small groups of 24th Infantrymen still out on the front. After they had recaptured a portion of the former 2/24th front line, B/27 discovered a 24th Infantry rifle platoon in position, by itself, several hundred yards to its right (north) flank.

The situation in 2/24th Infantry was chaotic and men of the rifle companies which had been overrun or flanked were in the rear. But there were probably also men from the regimental Service Co., HM Co. and others who contributed to the indescribable confusion which seemed to have overtaken 2/24th and the 24th Infantry's CP. As 1/27th moved up to Haman,

the author recalls seeing an officer in a jeep, who was identified to him as COL Champeny. This officer, as his jeep moved slowly by the advancing 27th soldiers shook his head sadly and muttered, "I'm sorry, I'm sorry." The men felt sorry for him.

At 2:45 p.m., Check received his attack order. "A 30 minute air bombardment, followed by a quarter hour of destructive artillery barrages preceded the attack and all but leveled the town of Haman," stated 1/27's Report of Operations. The town was in flames from these attacks. At 4:30 p.m., 1/27 attacked astride Engineer Road, with Co. A to its north and B on the south. Another tank platoon, this one from A/79th Tk Bn, further reinforced the infantry. Infantrymen rode on the eight tanks of the two tank platoons. Co. C followed in reserve.

In spite of some resistance by enemy forces, the battalion moved into and recaptured Haman. The Operations Report states that the town "was a sea of flames, with everything demolished and burning." The attackers found abandoned weapons, equipment and vehicles; the units helped themselves to all these "goodies."

West of Haman is a low ridge, which the enemy occupied. "MG fire swept every approach," read the 1/27 Report of Operations, "and the green tracers seemed as thick as the rice in the paddies." One tank was destroyed and the infantry suffered heavy casualties. But by 6:25 p.m. the battalion had seized the first line of hills west of Haman.

Planes from the carriers *Valley Forge* and *Philippine Sea* attacked the enemy preventing him from reorganizing and consolidating. Darkness was approaching when Check called a halt to the attacks. The two sides exchanged small-arms and automatic weapons fire during the night. The enemy made no attacks but strangely, kept flares up over their own rear areas.

"A Company moved down the left side of the road," SGT Phil File, then leading its 2d Platoon, wrote of this attack, "2d and 3d Platoons abreast. We cornered a large contingent [of enemy] under a bridge. With the 3d Platoon pouring fire from one side and the 2d Platoon from the other we convinced about 20 of the NKs to surrender. They were made to lie prone along the road [with their] heads all toward the road. A couple of men guarded them. A tank attached to B Company came spinning around the curve and, before the guards could stop it... had run right over the prisoners."

He described the battle on the first hill mass west of Haman. "It got dark as we worked our way up the hill and our illumination was the streams of tracers going overhead. I explained to my men, everybody shoots high at night. All you have to do is hug the ground and move closer to the enemy. We got on top of the ridgeline and drove the enemy from their positions. During the battle I could hear the song *China Night* playing over and over. When daylight came I found a battery powered record player and a dead black soldier in a deep foxhole."

Lyle Rishell's 1st Platoon, A/24th Infantry was attached to the 27th Infantry during this counterattack. His platoon was apparently the only element of the 24th Regiment to take part in this counterattack. Rishell wrote of this and it has been confirmed by recent research by historians at the U.S. Army Center for Military History, Washington, D.C. Shortly thereafter, he was ordered to bring his platoon and rejoin A/24th on the line.

LT Bernard's B/89th Tk Bn supported the 27th Regiment. Under cover of a long dike that ran through American positions, the enemy infiltrated to within fifty yards of the tanks. The tankers fired on the enemy at point blank range. Other enemy soldiers got behind the position and cut the only road out of the area. Near the tankers were 40 wounded men, who needed to be evacuated for further treatment. These men were put into a number of M-39 armored personnel carriers. A platoon of tanks escorted the carriers, attacked the roadblock, freed the road, then convoyed the wounded back to an aid station.

On Sept. 2, 1/27 continued its attack to regain former 2/24th positions. This led to the bloodiest single day's combat for B/27. The company reached a ridge just short of its final objective. On the left, a ridge ran forward, connecting it with a much longer one. The longer one had been the forward position of F/24th on Aug., 31. Now it was in enemy hands. The ridge where Co. B was located and the one occupied by the enemy were covered with scrub brush — mostly scrub oaks. The connecting ridge had no such concealment. A stand of well-spaced trees were on it and ran on up to a small knob on the objective.

The objective was taken under fire by company and attached machine guns and mortars. When this concluded, the 1st Platoon started out on the connecting ridge, while the other platoons started down the face of B Co.'s ridge. The 1st Platoon got about half way to the objective and the other platoons had started up its slope, when enemy machine gun fire ripped into the two formations. The first burst into the 1st Platoon passed the platoon leader and tore into the stomach of the platoon medic to his rear. The soldier fell to his knees, his right hand clutching his abdomen, and rolled over, dead. Several other men were also felled by this fire. The adjacent platoon was also caught in the open by machine gun fire. Both platoons recoiled.

After reorganizing, B Co. machine guns and mortars again hit the enemy-held ridge. The company then sent the 1st Platoon down into the valley toward the objective while the 2d Platoon tried to flank it. Again, enemy machine gun fire, from totally concealed positions, drove the men to ground well short of the hilltop. The 2d Platoon's flank attack was a disaster. Its men were cut down, one after the other, just like in a movie. The attack stalled and receded.

CPT Gordon Jung, B Co.'s commander then placed all the surviving riflemen under command of the only other officer of the unit and ordered him to attack again. The entire force started out again in a long skirmish line, down into the valley between the ridges. As soon as the men cleared the B Co. position, its machine guns and mortars began firing on the enemy, this time continuing until the advancing infantrymen masked their fire on the objective. Topping the ridge, one of the men gleefully shouted, "Here they are!" and began firing his M1 rifle down the opposite slope as fast as he could pull the trigger. Other men quickly joined him and the firing became general. At least three enemy heavy, wheeled machine guns were found along the top of the hill.

The enemy had avoided casualties, during the first two Co. B assaults by simply going a little way down the reverse slope of the hill during the preparatory fires then returning to man their guns in time to catch the American infantry in the open. During the last assault, however, when the covering fire continued during the advance of the infantry, the enemy did not have an opportunity to return to its defensive positions.

Very shortly after the enemy was driven from their ridge, accurate, deadly automatic weapons fire came in on Co. B. The 2d Platoon was assigned to defend the connecting ridge, thus refusing the company's left flank. The 1st Platoon held the center. The 3d Platoon was on the right, following the contour of the ridge. This placed part of that platoon on a position generally facing across the rest of the company front. Shortly after the unit started digging in on the reverse slope of the hill, a young sergeant of the 1st Platoon had to have one more peek over the hill. He paid for it with his life. A burst of machine gun fire ripped his body from his head to his stomach. Co. B lost 15 KIA and 45 WIA, wrote 1SG George S. Hearn. "I know because I made out the reports," he wrote. Hearn was one of the finest "Old Army" First Sergeants one could have. He "ran" the company without infringing on the command prerogatives of the company commander. He and CPT Jung worked as a superb team, both in Japan and in Korea.

Co. A was to B's left. File had no communication with his company CP, so that day his platoon stayed in position. "I was in position to see the backside of the gap where the road climbed up and passed through the hills," File wrote. This road was between A and B Companies, with B on the north and A to the south. "Beyond effective rifle range I could make out a NK crew setting up a gun to cover the gap. With glasses I could make out that it was a 75mm recoilless rifle the NK had captured from the 24th. B Co. had a tank leading their push up the center. The NKs got their gun set up and ready. Then all the crew except the gunner laid down behind the gun. The tank poked its nose around the corner. The gunner fired a round that disabled the tank. The backblast [from the recoilless rifle] rolled the prone NKs like so many dry leaves. The gunner stood up, looked back at his comrades and took off running. B Co. eventually secured the position."

During the 2d, American air flew 135 sorties for the 25th Division. Many enemy soldiers were reported killed, several tanks and artillery pieces destroyed and three enemy ammunition dumps blown up.

That day, too the enemy counterattacked elements of 1/27, but was repelled.

Before dawn on Sept. 3, the enemy attacked again. Artillery, mortar and tank fire, and after daybreak, an air strike stopped this attack. In the battle, elements of 1/27 had to turn around and fight to the rear.

Part of this attack was an attempt by a platoon of enemy soldiers to infiltrate the lines of 1st Platoon, B/27th Infantry. The 2d Platoon was to the left rear of the 1st, on the connecting ridge. The boundary between the two platoons was on the crest of the knob where the two ridges joined.

1st Platoon had an attached D/27 machine gun, manned by SGT Gallup and PFC Nelson, on this knob. The platoon was deployed on the reverse slope from that point to where the ridge curved slightly forward. The boundary between the 1st and 3d Platoons was near this point. The 1st Platoon machine gun was sighted to fire in front of or on the top and rear of the knob. Another machine gun from D/27 was placed on the platoon's right flank to fire lengthwise along the crest of the ridge. It could also fire down the crest of the 3d Platoon ridge. The 1st Platoon CP was below and to the right of the knob.

During the day, a young replacement "medic" came up to the 1st Platoon. Late in the day, one of the platoon's men was wounded. Then it was discovered that the "medic" was actually a Medical Co. cook. That unit had run out of medical aidmen and sent forward anyone it could. But this soldier had no medical training. The platoon leader sent the injured man to the rear with another man from the platoon and the "medic" to help him.

That night the 1st Platoon leader, believing that the man had returned from the aid station, decided to crawl up to his hole to keep him company. He announced this to the Platoon Sergeant, who was sharing the foxhole, then began crawling up the hill. Suddenly, silhouetted against the skyline, he say the figure of a crouched man. As he watched, the man's left arm swung in a signal to others to move forward. The figure was an easy target, but the lieutenant believed that there were more men and his shot would bring on a firefight with an enemy force of unknown size. He decided, instead to place 60mm mortar fire on the enemy.

Quickly crawling back to his hole, he informed the sergeant, then crawled up to the platoon machine gun position. There he told the men not to fire unless enemy soldiers were actually coming into their foxholes. Returning to the platoon CP, he called the 60mm mortar section on his sound powered phone and began adjusting their fire. The enemy force was close in, so the mortars were firing almost straight up. Their fire was adjusted onto where the enemy soldier had been seen. Then the officer had the mortars change to hit the bottom of the enemy's side of the hill. He then worked it back up the hill and toward his own position. As the 60 mortar rounds landed closer and closer to the CP hole, the platoon sergeant became concerned. The lieutenant then shifted fire back to the base of the enemy's side of the hill, worked it up to his foxhole again, then repeated the process.

As he worked the fire closer to his hole, the mortar gunners had to adjust by quarter turns of their elevating and traversing wheels. This moved the strike of the round about 7 or 8 yards on the ground. This routine was repeated over and over again. SGT Laub and PFC Cressie Johnson, both of D/27, were located near the B Co. CP. Johnson recalled that, during the fight, a gleeful GI came up pulling a captured enemy wheeled machine gun. The soldier said he was going to fire it against the enemy. 1SG Hearn said to him, "Son, you're not going to fire that thing. If you do every GI around is going to open up on you." The man was disappointed, but obeyed.

Meantime, the officer had the 60s fire a mix

of HE and WP rounds. The WP set the clothing of two or three of the enemy on fire. The enemy fired small-arms and burp guns all around. At one point, a North Korean was silhouetted by the flash from bursting mortar rounds as he fired his burp gun in the direction of the mortar position. Soon afterward, he was felled by one of the mortar rounds. Johnson wrote that he and SGT Laub called in 81mm mortar fire on the enemy concentration. Some GIs saw one or more of the enemy fleeing with their clothing afire. Finally, there was no more fire from the enemy. The 60s were stopped and the night became silent again.

The next morning, the bodies of 16 dead North Koreans dotted the knoll and nearby slopes. The 1st Platoon CP hole contained hundreds of tiny shards of 60 mortar fragments. The platoon leader and sergeant were unhurt. However, two mortarmen had been wounded and

SGT Gallup and PFC Nelson had been killed by the enemy. That ended enemy attacks. The dead enemy bodies lay on the ground and slowly rotted in the hot sun. The troops spread lime on them, but nothing could dispel the horrible odor.

A day or two later, someone with field glasses detected enemy troops withdrawing up a hill far to the front. B Company machine gunners took them under indirect fire. Through binoculars, one could see that some of the rounds were dropping among them. A recent resupply of machine gun ammunition in the company consisted of rounds in cloth belts left over from WW II. The bullets were corroded fast to the cloth. Men were put to work taking this ammunition from the old belt and making new metal link belts for the unit guns. They couldn't make the new belts fast enough. CPT Jung allowed no one to come up to the unit position in those days, unless he brought ammunition or hand grenades with him.

PVT Donald Cable was among a group of replacements who joined Co. B on Sept. 2. There was a respectable number of replacements in this party. As they approached the hill, they passed through a deep. narrow valley between two ridges. While in that narrow pass an enemy mortar concentration blasted in on them. Half or more of the replacements became casualties. Cable recalled that, when he joined the 1st Platoon's 1st Squad, it numbered three men — Joe Zelinas, squad leader, Roy Ward and him.

2/27th Infantry and G/35th Infantry — Sept. 1-5

Pursuant to orders to move to the 35th Infantry sector, 2/27th Infantry left Masan at 10:20 a.m. on Sept. 1, arriving in an assembly area near Chirwon by 2 p.m. At about 5 p.m. the battalion received orders to clear the MSR behind the 35th Infantry and relieve the pressure on isolated G/35th Infantry. The battalion moved to the attack position by truck. From there on only the jeeps of the battalion commander, his artillery liaison officer, one from each rifle company and the Heavy Weapons Co. vehicles were permitted to accompany the attack. Two M-26 tanks from the 89th Tk Bn were attached.

The battalion attacked at 5 p.m. on Sept. 2. Stubborn enemy resistance slowed progress. James Trumble was a member of Co. E. He wrote of his experiences in this attack. "My squad was the left flank guard and we had our hand full keeping contact with the people on the road, as we went through the brush, hills rice paddies, etc. About 0200 (2 a.m.)... we did exactly what a flank guard is supposed to do — draw fire from the enemy. At first I thought it was only a small enemy group and that we could flush them out. PVT Lopez was point and I was right behind him with the rest of the squad behind us. I turned to call to them up...and discovered they weren't there." A new man had failed to pass the word for the squad to move out earlier. As a result, the men were not with Trumble.

View of Battle Mountain (Courtesy of John w. Akeson, A/89 Tk Bn)

Infantrymen of 1st Platoon, B-27th Infantry: Reclining, Salvatore Fiacco; kneeling in front, Tagliaferro. Third man not identified. (Courtesy of Donald Cable, 1st Plt. B/27 Infantry)

Earl Miller, Machinegunner, G/27th Infantry. (Courtesy of Earl Miller, G/27th Infantry)

As he discovered this, PVT Lopez was hit in the lower right side. Trumble discovered that the bullet had struck his bayonet and driven part of it into his side. Deciding that it would be unwise to move Lopez with the bayonet wound, Trumble dug a slit trench and put Lopez into it. He then returned to the platoon and reported the situation to his leader, LT Davis. Davis sent him and Bud Wood to bring Lopez in. On the way back with Lopez, Trumble was shot in the knee. "I rolled down an embankment," he wrote, "sat up and saw the lower half of my leg at right angles to the other and decided I was in 'sheep dip.' I made a tourniquet and went about getting myself into a better defensive position in case some NKs stumbled on me."

Then two new men from the platoon came by and Trumble asked them to have Bud Wood come for him. "Gradually the fire let up (we got help from some tanks to finish off the roadblock) and it looked like the NKs were pulling out. Just as it was getting daylight, old Bud Wood showed up with some morphine he had mooched off Tom, our medic." Wood gave Trumble a shot of morphine and saw to it that he was safely evacuated.

The battalion fought all that very dark night. By 3 p.m. on Sept. 3 it reached a point 1,000 yards south of G/35 Infantry's original positions. G/35th was still defending Hill 179.

On Sept. 3, PFC Anthony Fernandes was a replacement for G/35th. That day, Fernandes and five other men who were at 2/35th Infantry CP, were chosen to ride "shotgun" on a convoy of three supply trucks and two tanks destined for G/35th (and possibly other units). The convoy, led by a LT Nichols had a tank at each end of the column. Fernandes was seated on a box of rations in the third truck. "After a few miles," he wrote, "we hit this saddle in the road and we were fired on. The trucks stopped and I jumped off.... LT Nichols took charge. We were told to rush the machine gun position, which on signal, we did. We climbed the embankment and again there was [enemy machine gun fire]. We hit the ground and one man got hit. I never saw the machine gun nest, when, while laying there, bullets started to hit the ground...by my face and around my body. I was scared stiff! I laid there, motionless, making believe I was dead. (By the way, there were two machine guns firing — one to my front and another on my left flank. The tankers knocked out one, but I don't know about the 2nd."

The other men ran back to the protection of the road embankment. After what seemed like an eternity Fernandez jumped up and over the embankment onto the road. At this point, LT Nichols conferred with the tankers and decided to leave the riflemen behind and go on with the trucks and tanks. "It must have been essential that the companies got their supplies," Fernandes observed. He noted a wrecked jeep at the site, indicating that other ambushes had earlier taken place there. Fernandez and his companions made their way back to the 2d Battalion CP.

On Sept. 4, an enemy force attacked this CP. This force was "sizable," Fernandez wrote. "They fired a red flare and a green flare.... They came down the roads and fields with small arms machine guns and mortars. It didn't last long but the rice paddies were turned red from their blood

Two more members of 1st Platoon, B/27th Infantry: Donald Cable and ROK Yong Da Ri. Yong Da Ri, along with Kim Ha Ok and Kahn Suk Koo, were among the first Koreans to join the platoon in early September 1950. (Courtesy of Donald Cable, B/27th Infantry)

and mangled bodies. There must have been a couple hundred dead. Some GIs were captured [by the enemy] when they rode into the North Koreans with a 3/4-ton truck."

Other units of 2/35th Infantry were also heavily engaged during these first days of September PFC Donald Cholka recalled that his Co. E "was almost wiped out."

A coordinated infantry-armor-artillery attack was launched by 2/27th Infantry shortly after 3 p.m. on Sept. 3. By 6 p.m. the battalion had re-established the battle line. In this battle 2/27th Infantry killed 275 enemy soldiers and recovered most of the equipment which G/35th had lost earlier. The 2d Battalion remained on this position during the night Sept. 3. The following morning, Murch was ordered to attack to the rear to clear the route on the western edge of the battalion zone. G/35 relieved E/27 on the regained positions at 8 a.m. The 2/27 then began its attack back up the supply road, with Co. E in the lead, followed by F. Co. G occupied high ground from which it established a base of fire for the other two units.

An estimated enemy battalion was on high ground overlooking the road. Co. F passed through E to take the first finger leading to the ridge line. Heavy enemy automatic weapons fire rained down from three directions on the two companies and CP group. This fire stopped Co. F. At 5 P.M. it began to rain heavily, making observation almost impossible. The enemy took advantage of this to launch a counterattack. Companies E and F were ordered to withdraw. F fought a rear guard action supported by a tank. Rain turned the road into a quagmire. Wheeled vehicles had to be pushed by troops. The battalion lost three 60mm mortars and two 1/4-ton trailers to enemy fire. An enemy roadblock prevented wounded from being evacuated from the battle area. The battalion was now short of 81mm, 60mm and 75mm ammunition and the tanks were low on fuel.

At 3:10 a.m. on Sept. 4, Murch radioed for an air drop. He had no direct radio communication with higher headquarters, so battalion transmissions were relayed through the SCR 300 radio with the Battalion XO. The drop was scheduled for 12:30 p.m. that day, but did not come in until 1:30 p.m. But it was on target. The battalion received about 65 rounds of 81mm mortar and 43 rounds of 75mm recoilless rifle ammunition. Most of the 81mm ammunition was faulty. The drop included 90mm tank ammunition, but 76mm ammunition was needed. Another successful air drop came at 6:30 p.m. This time, the enemy fired at the planes. All three rifle companies of 2/27 responded by delivering heavy fire on the enemy-held ridge.

About 5:45 a.m. on Sept. 5, a strong enemy attack drove G/35 from its position. Murch sent his E and F companies to restore it. They were supported by fire from the 90th FAB. This fire killed an estimated 175 to 200 enemy and drove the remainder into a valley to the south. There, they were engaged by a 75mm recoilless rifle and a machine gun section. Under this fire, the enemy dispersed, moved southwest and were attacked by fire by other friendly forces there. The fighting had again exhausted 75mm ammunition and reduced the number of 81mm mortar rounds to 10. One tank had only eight rounds of HE left.

In spite of this, the battalion attacked again along the road at 12 noon that day, with Co. F and a tank. The objective was taken at 6 p.m. The battalion was then ordered to halt and prepare to attack northeast to link up with 1/27th Infantry.

3/27th Infantry — Sept. 2-5

After 2/27th Infantry left the Chung-ni area in its counterattack, the enemy attacked the 24th Regiment's CP and a number of artillery positions. To meet this new threat, GEN Kean, again on his own initiative ordered the 3d Battalion, 29th Infantry (soon to be redesignated 3d Battalion 27th Infantry), commanded by LTC George H. De Chow, to attack and destroy this enemy force. Kean notified Eighth Army of his action at 12:50 p.m. Sept. 2.

In the early morning hours of Sept. 3, the battalion fought several hundred enemy who were near artillery positions. DeChow's battalion began its attack at 3 p.m. over the high and rugged terrain west of a stretch of the MSR named the "Horseshoe," so named because of a deep, long curve resembling a horseshoe four miles east of Komam-ni. The mission was to clear and secure the high ground dominating the Horseshoe, then to relieve pressure in the 24th Infantry's rear area. Only one howitzer was in position to support the battalion's attack.

The battalion had advanced some distance, when an enemy force, estimated at over 1,000 men, suddenly counterattacked. The 3/27th suffered heavy casualties, including 13 officers. 1LT Elwood F. James, commanding K Co. was killed while leading an assault. More tanks were brought up to aid in securing the battalion right flank and rear, and air strikes were employed to contain the enemy. Finally, the battalion took its objective.

During the night, the 3d Battalion's orders were changed. Instead of continuing the attack toward the 24th Infantry CP, it was directed to attack straight ahead into the Komam-ni area, where the enemy was fighting in artillery positions. The attack began at 9 A.M. in the face of heavy North Korean small-arms fire. That afternoon, torrential rains slowed the attack. But I and K, fighting all day, aided by a number of air strikes, seized the high ground dominating the Komam-ni crossroads. Casualties in the battalion had been so great that GEN Kean attached C/65th Engineer Battalion to it

On Sept. 5, 3/27th turned and attacked southward through rugged terrain toward Haman, succeeding in reaching the 24th Infantry CP. The battalion counted over 300 enemy dead in the area it crossed that day.

Defending the Field Artillery Batteries — Sept. 2-6

On Sept. 2, all batteries of the 159th were under enemy small arms and mortar fire, forcing them to displace into the Horseshoe. Even there, they were subjected to almost nightly harassing fire for the next week. The 77th ECC, part of the 24th RCT, and a platoon of tanks were sent to provide them close in defensive support.

A/64th FAB (CPT Leroy Anderson) was positioned two and a half miles north of Haman, on the edge of the village of Saga. The battery was located south of the road. Anderson kept his battery position as compact as possible. About three or four hundred yards south of the road was a horseshoe shaped ridge. He placed five of the six howitzers in this area. Because the area would not accommodate the sixth gun, it was located to the north of a railroad track which ran through the area, paralleling the road. The FDC was in a tent over a four foot deep dugout behind the guns and near the inner base of the ridge. The guns were within shouting distance of the FDC. The battery switchboard was in a dugout north of the tracks and some 15 to 20 yards south

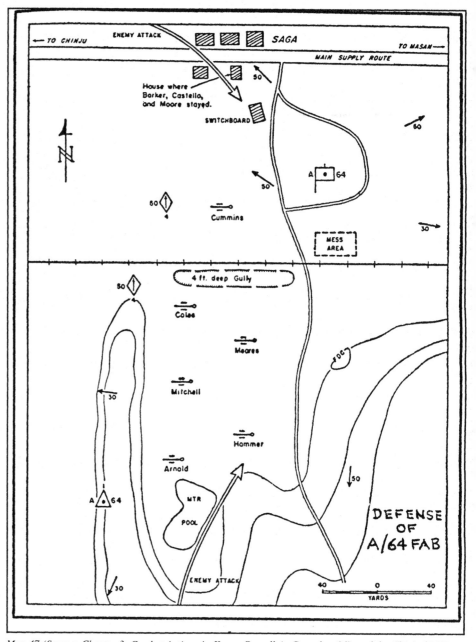

Map 47 (Source: Chapter 3, Combat Actions in Korea, Russell A. Guggeler, Office of the Chief of Military History, Wash., D.C., 1970 edition)

of a cluster of houses. The wire section used some of the buildings as living quarters. There was a long gully about four feet deep on the southern edge of the tracks, in the center of the battery position.

Ten defensive posts ringed the area, including four .50-caliber and three .30-caliber machine guns, an observation/listening post and two M16 (quad-.50) halftracks. Four of the posts were on the ridge next to the gun position and were connected by telephone. The others were within shouting distance.

The battery first sergeant, MSG William Parker, was standing near the switchboard dugout about 2:30 a.m. on Sept. 3, when he saw several men moving along the road through the fog-shrouded darkness. He called out "Who's there?" then shouted "Halt!"

The men he saw were three North Koreans pulling a heavy machine gun down the road. They moved on a few steps, dropped into a ditch,

turned the weapon toward the gun position and opened fire. They were quickly joined by other enemy, firing from several directions, but principally from the ridge. Three enemy machine guns were on this ridge, and soon, the gun on the road was joined by another. The ensuing battle was in two parts — one north of the railroad and one to the south of it.

Wire Team Chief SGT Herbert L. Rawls Jr. saw the enemy soldiers when Parker challenged them. He ran to one of the houses along the road to alert several men from the wire section who were sleeping there, then to the switchboard dugout to warn those men. As Rawls arrived there an enemy fired a burst of burp gun fire, killing him and SGT Joseph R. Pursley, who had been kneeling at the edge of the hole splicing wire. The North Korean then hurled a grenade into the dugout killing two of the three men there. CPL John M. Pitcher, the third man, was not seriously hurt. He stayed in the hole with his two dead companions for the rest of the night, manning the switchboard.

This all happened within a few minutes. Meantime, CPL Bobbie H. McQuitty reacted to the enemy attack by running to man a machine gun on his 3/4-ton truck, parked near the road. By the time he reached it, the enemy had rolled their second machine gun up just in front of it. The two guns faced each other less than 30 yards apart. McQuitty's gun failed to fire. He quickly jumped from the truck and ran across the paddies toward where he had seen a tank the previous afternoon. He hoped to get its help, but the tank was gone. By this time it was impossible for the other two American machine guns on that side of the tracks, nor the quad-.50 to fire against the enemy in that area without danger to the wiremen.

Meantime, the four men in the house whom SGT Rawls had awakened before he was killed, tried to get away from the it and join the rest of the battery. One man, in a room by himself, stepped from the building and was shot in the mouth by one of a group of North Koreans just outside the door. PFCs Harold W. Barker, Thomas A. Castello and Santford B. Moore were together in another room. Barker ran out of the house, but stopped short when he saw one of the enemy machine guns just ahead. He turned and made a dash for the house, but at the doorway he was struck in the knee by a bullet. The other two men dragged him into the room. Costello and Moore decided to stay in the room, so they put Barker on the floor then each stood in a corner of the room as close to the wall as possible. Two puppies which Barker and Costello had picked up a few days previously made an alarming amount of noise, but the enemy never came to investigate. From this time on, the two enemy machine guns fired toward the howitzers from the road, but the North Koreans did not move against them, nor search for the hidden Americans.

Two of the enemy machine guns firing from the ridge were on the left front of the howitzers and the third was at their left rear. About a half dozen enemy riflemen were also firing. The three howitzers nearest the ridge caught the heaviest fire. Gun crews ceased firing the howitzers and took shelter in the gun pits.

MSG Frederick J. Hammer's section gun pit took an enemy hand grenade, which killed one man and wounded several others. Another enemy grenade set off over a hundred 105mm rounds in a nearby ammunition pit. The artillery machine gunners on the ridge opened fire when the battle started, but soon discovered that the enemy had already gained the battery position. They withdrew northward toward the other quad .50. This weapon fired only a few rounds before its power-driven traversing mechanism failed. The crew was unable to traverse by hand, so they backed it a short distance to the gully beside the railroad.

About this time, the Battalion CP called Battery A to find out why it had quit firing.

"As I sat half asleep in the sandbag revetted... FDC tent just in rear of the guns," wrote then-Lieutenant Kincheon H. Bailey Jr. (West Point 1945), Battery XO, "the fire direction chief SGT Carl Francis...handed me the phone. 'Why have you stopped firing?' battalion wanted to know. Since I had sensed the gooks were planning some devilment, I had chosen to sit in the FDC to keep on top of matters. SGT Francis and his assistant, CPL McDonald, were very capable men but I sometimes assisted them in their duties." The Army's Table of Organization for a 105mm artillery battery did not provide enough men for a 24-hour FDC operation, Bailey remarked.

"Heavy fog surrounded the area this night and we could hear the infantry machine guns on the MLR firing occasionally; they sounded much closer than they really were. Comatose from grabbing some shuteye, I asked SGT Francis why we were not firing. He did not know so I told battalion to wait and I would find out. Leaving the FDC and heading for the guns, I saw much commotion in the gun pits. Five or so gooks were cavorting about Gun #1 [MSG Hammer] amidst flaming powder charges. Looked eerie. Then I saw Gun #2 [PFC Ernest R. Arnold] was overrun. The firing by the enemy while I was in the FDC I had taken to be our own infantry because of the fog's distorting sound. Jumping into Gun #3's pit [SGT Cecil W. Meares' section], I started firing my rifle at the gooks around the guns to the left. I urged SGT Meares, the crew chief, and his men to start firing their carbines."

Bailey was worried; the quad-.50 to the right front, was not firing. He thought the crew had been killed and that the enemy would turn the weapon on the battery. He sent some men to check on it. At that moment, he saw some enemy soldiers charge Meares' gun. The gun crew could not fire HE because if a round did not strike the enemy it would travel on and hit the rear of friendly infantry on the MLR. "Had to fire Fuze Time," he wrote. "Cutting fuzes to Time 4.0, 2.0 and then 1.0, our gun crew worked feverishly to stop the onslaught. But the rounds were bursting beyond the targets. So, I gave the command, 'Time 0.0!' I do not know how many of the crew thought as I did — these rounds will blow up the guns — but I was determined to stop the attack, even if some of us were KIA in the attempt. The battery would be saved. No heroics, just topnotch training and dedication of good soldiers.... The rounds burst 20 yards in front of the guns and the gooks panicked."

While Bailey was in Meares' gun pit, SGT Hammer, seeing his ammunition afire ordered his men to make a run to the gully by the tracks. His section, plus the men of two others made it to this point. At the same time, MSG Germanus P. Kotzer, a platoon sergeant, dashed to the gun located north of the tracks and ordered it to fire on the enemy-held ridge.

The two howitzers fired a total of eighteen rounds at a range of from 150 to 200 yards. Meares crew fired their howitzer for a number of minutes and threw grenades into Hammer's abandon gun pit. Then Bailey and Kotzer decided it would be best to get the men into the protection of the gully. To give covering fire for the move, SGT Henry E. Baker ran to a nearby 2 1/2-ton truck and climbed up to man the ring-mounted .50-cal machine gun. He was joined by PFC Richard G. Haussler, who fed the gun while Baker fired it. The two men, easy targets in the light provided by the burning ammunition, fired five boxes of .50-caliber ammunition (1,250 rounds) in about 10 minutes. CPT Anderson checked the battery area to make certain that none of his men were still in foxholes or gun pits.

All the cannoneers reached the gully about 3:15 a.m., just a half hour after the battle started. Chaplain (CPT) John T. Schag had been visiting the battery the previous day and had decided to stay overnight. When the fight began, he assembled the men sleeping near him and took them to the gully. Once there, he gathered the wounded in one place then helped care for them. CPT Anderson and SGT Kotzer organized the gully's defense. All battery survivors were now in there except three men in the FDC; CPL Pitcher, still on the switchboard and Barker, Castello and Moore, still hiding in the house in Saga.

Although what has been described as "a brisk exchange of rifle fire" continued, enemy actions dropped off after the gully position was organized. Battalion commander, LTC Arthur H. Hogan, had called a number of times on the phone, offering help from another battery. SGT Carl Francis, in the FDC, called to LT Bailey and asked if he wanted some 155mm fire in the area. Bailey said yes, on the hill in front of the guns. Hogan, familiar with the terrain at A battery, got the first rounds on the hill. Bailey called back to the FDC, "'Right 50 — drop 100. Fire for effect!' The wounded, not cottoning to my heroics and wishing selfishly to live even if some gook did, too, groaned at my wanton command. Feeling compassion for those unlucky souls, I changed the command to 'Drop 50. Fire for effect!' Whistle, whistle, CERACK! Those beautiful 155s dropped right on target and killed all gooks, no GIs."

The 155 battery fired two rounds from each gun, a total of twelve rounds. All fell just in front of the guns of Able Battery. Soon thereafter, a tank came down the Masan road from the north and started firing into the enemy. This was the tank CPL McQuitty had gone for. This considerably quieted the enemy, although there was scattered rifle fire until dawn. Then the enemy disappeared, leaving 21 dead in the battery position. The battery lost seven dead and 12 wounded. Among the wounded were gunner CPL Schuyler J. Berdan, hit by shell fragments in the left hand and left forehead, and CPL Chauncy E. Schick, gunner for Meares. He was struck in the shoulder.

Four trucks had been destroyed and the enemy let the air out of the tires of a fifth. They had written the numbers of their company, platoon and squad in chalk on three howitzer tubes. The battery quickly reorganized and resumed firing missions.

"I wasted my time worrying about Anderson's battery," wrote GEN Barth of his concern for the unit at the time. "I found them still in action and busy stringing more barbed wire and digging in. They had no thought of doing anything but staying right where they were."

The following day, Barth and LTC Hogan were in the B/64th FAB battery position when the North Koreans attacked it. "It [the attack] wasn't serious but might have been, if Hogan hadn't acted promptly," Barth wrote. "He called C battery that was about 2,000 yards behind us and brought its fire on the infantry that were coming up the hill in front of our position. In a matter of minutes, the shells came whistling over our heads and burst along about 500 yards in front of the battery position. Two of our guns joined in with direct fire along the hill top and the enemy retired. Hogan had demonstrated how artillery can use its fire power to help itself in an emergency."

Battle Actions in the Rear Areas

A group of 35th Infantry company mess parties in jeeps, pulling trailers with hot breakfasts were following tanks toward the front one day. About 1 1/2 miles from G/35 the column was fired on in a defile. The tanks went on through, but most of the jeeps, under 2/35 S-2, CPT Robert E. Hammerquist, turned back. However, at least one mess crew went after the tanks. Some of this group were taken prisoner. One of its members succeeded in hiding in a haystack and witnessed what transpired. One captive was tortured, mutilated and murdered. He recognized the man's voice between agonizing screams and sobs. At one point the man said, "You might as well kill me now." Later, the man's body was found. He had been castrated and his fingers cut off. The bodies of other soldiers were found in the 35th sector, their hands tied and their feet cut off. Still others were found with their tongues cut out. Members of the *NK 7th Division* were believed to have been responsible. This mindless cruelty led most GIs to kill enemy soldiers rather than take them prisoner.

On Sept. 3, two tanks from 3d Platoon, A/89th Tk Bn, named respectively "Antique" and "Honey Bucket," plus a rifle platoon of the 27th, were sent to reduce a road block. "We ran the road block; broke through," wrote SGT John W. Akeson. "In doing so, we lost (KIA) one crew member (Frenchy DeLaFance). [We] expended all our .30- and .50-cal ammunition. We even fired HVAP (High Velocity Armor Piercing) at [enemy] infantry targets.

"That night the infantry collected all spare .30-cal ammo from riflemen and gave it to us (2 tanks). We took ammo from the M1 clips and made up belts for our .30-cal machine guns. We [Akeson's tank] only had one left. We lost the bow .30-cal gun when Frenchy was lost. Morning came. We received an air drop. Water, food, small arms ammunition. Some one screwed up. The tank ammo dropped was for 90mm guns — useless to us. We left it behind. Half of the air drop landed with the Gooks.

"That afternoon, as many of the badly wounded as we could carry were loaded in and on [the two] tanks. We ran another road block to get medical attention. Many of the wounded we had tied onto the outside of the tanks were hit again, but we got them through."

In Masan, Han Gum Jo, manager of the Masan branch of the Korean Press Association, confessed to being the chief of the South Korean Labor Party and that he sent information to the enemy through a Pusan headquarters. The head of the guards of the Masan prison was the chief of a Communist cell and seven of his guards were members. GEN Kean believed the situation so dangerous that he ordered the evacuation of all civilians from Masan except public officials, the police, railroad and utility workers, and required laborers and their families. He

ordered the evacuation to be completed in five days. On Sept. 10 and 11 alone, the 25th Division removed 12,000 people by LST from Masan.

Behind the 35th Infantry — Sept. 6-9

The situation behind the 35th remained so serious on Sept. 5 that 1/27th was relieved on the front by elements of the 24th Infantry and sent to join Murch's 2d battalion. By evening 1/27 was in an assembly area behind the CP of 2/35th Infantry.

Early in the morning of Sept. 6, the enemy made what GEN Barth wrote as "their last large-scale attack behind the 35th." Their objective was the area occupied by the 2/35th CP and the 1/27th Infantry assembly area. Three artillery batteries were also there; B and C/64th FAB and B/8th FAB (all 105mm). "Machine gun and anti-tank fire poured into the positions from the hills overlooking the batteries," wrote GEN Barth. The enemy "advanced in the dark right up to the gun positions," he recalled, "but our murderous fire of all types, including direct fire by the guns of Battery C, 64th finally repulsed the attack with heavy losses. Battery C, newly arrived from the United States only two days before, stopped a 'Banzai' charge that reached within twenty-five yards of the guns." After the battle, North Korean dead were hauled away by the truckload. "Over sixty bodies had been taken from the rice paddies just in front of the guns," Barth recorded. "Many were killed in the hills above the position."

Enemy troops were now caught between the 35th Infantry, in position near the Nam River and the two advancing battalions of the 27th. In this action large numbers of enemy troops were killed. Reports indicate that sixteen different groups of North Koreans were dispersed with heavy casualties during Sept. 6. By the morning of Sept. 7 it was clearly evident that what was left of the *NK 7th Division* were trying to get back across the Nam. In the first seven days in September,, the 25th buried over 2,000 dead North Koreans behind its lines. This does not include the dead in front of its positions.

COL Fisher, traveling through the rear area about Sept. 9 was amazed at the large number of enemy dead littering the countryside. "The area of Trun in the Falaise Gap in Europe couldn't match it," he said. "Flies were so thick in some areas it limited vision."

Speaking later of this battle, Fisher said, "I never intended to withdraw. There was no place to go. I planned to go into a regimental perimeter and hold." In recognition of the 35th Infantry's stand, it was awarded a Distinguished Unit Citation.

The Defense of "Vickery's Bridge" — Sept. 5-9

On Sept. 8 and 9, heavy rains caused the Nam River to rise over two feet, reducing the danger of new enemy crossings. On Sept. 9 an F-82 jet mistakenly bombed the Namji-ri bridge, destroying one 80 foot section with a 500 lb. bomb. This bridge had been defended by the considerably reinforced 1st Platoon, F/35th Infantry, under the

command of LT Grady M. Vickery. In 1993 Vickery wrote a narrative of this defense. The platoon was reinforced by a 75mm recoilless rifle, a 105mm howitzer from the 64th FAB, a tank platoon, a master sergeant with an engineer squad and 25 or 30 ROKs. The artillery dubbed the 105 "Lancer Forward," Lancer being the radio call sign for the 64th FAB. The platoon had over a week to prepare, he recalled. The mission was to secure and defend the bridge, and blow it up only on order from 35th Infantry or 25th Division. Vickery defended the far end of the bridge with one rifle squad behind barbed wire, mines, booby traps and trip flares.

The first attack came about 9 or 10 p.m. on Sept. 5. "They got into our wire, minefield and a flare went off," he wrote. "We opened up with all pre-arranged fire from both sides [of the river]; 75, tanks plus rifle squads and other weapons. Shortly after the 'Mad Minute' of fire we had three explosions (boxes of American dynamite). You could hear it all over the valley. Everyone from regiment and division thought we had *lost* the bridge. We let them know we were being attacked across the river, where a rifle squad was dug in. The rest of the platoon, and attachments were dug in on this side of the bridge. We fought most of the night. At daylight I and my squad leaders checked the area. All types of bodies blown up. About 75 bodies laying on the barbed wire — legs, etc., scattered all over the area. Three other men and I had been on the far side of the bridge dropping hand grenades under it and killed 7-10 enemy. Other bodies were floating down the river." Then Vickery and the tank commander, with all the tanks, crossed the river in pursuit of the enemy. While he was gone, COL Fisher visited the platoon and discovered Vickery was pursuing the enemy with the tanks. "He gave orders," Vickery wrote, "that I and the tanks were to stay in position, not to cross the bridge." Vickery took him on a tour, showing the colonel the enemy dead and part of the dynamite boxes "Made in USA," which the enemy had tried to use. "Good night for us," he recorded, "so we got ready for the 2nd night."

September 6: "Rotated squads across the bridge about 2-3 o'clock each day. [That way] had plenty of time for them to check positions, etc.

"Ordered squad leader to put extra fire and security and expect attack from the east. Sure enough, force hit us there and later on in the morning, [their] main force hit again on the north. And he had the 'Mad Minute' again. Not that many [enemy] killed that night and few killed under the bridge." Vickery was there with four other men that night.

In preparation for the night of Sept. 7, Vickery ordered the squad leader "to put more security, weapons and trip flares to the South. [A] couple of hours after[ward] trip flares and 2 tanks did an exceptional job. Then [we] were hit again from the North [but we] were ready. [They] never got through barbed wire. Killed only a few that night; only one under the bridge."

September 8: "Ordered everyone to focus North. I felt [their] main force would hit us again. That afternoon at 3:30, one BAR-man wanted to know if he could place a trip flare in front of his BAR. Naturally, I said yes and helped him place it. Then he said, 'LT Vickery, I believe they

Corporal Carroll Vogles (pointing) and 1st Lieutenant Grady Vickery, Co. F, 35th Infantry. (Courtesy of Grady Vickery, F/35th Infantry)

The bridge at Namji-ri-"Vickery's Bridge." (Courtesy of Grady Vickery, F/35th Infantry)

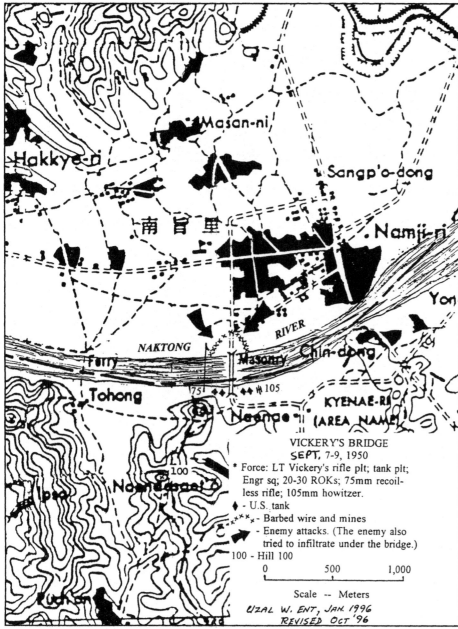

Map 48 (Courtesy of Uzal W. Ent)

Inside the map:

'Masan-ni
Hakkye-ri
Sangp'o-dong
南旨里
Namji-ni
Yon
RIVER
NAKTONG
Ferry
Masonry Chin-dong
Tohong
◆ 75
◆◆ 卅 105
KYENAE-RI
(AREA NAME)
Naangae-ni

VICKERY'S BRIDGE
SEPT. 7-9, 1950
* Force: LT Vickery's rifle plt; tank plt;
Engr sq; 20-30 ROKs; 75mm recoil-
less rifle; 105mm howitzer.
◆ - U.S. tank
×ˣˣˣ× - Barbed wire and mines
➤ - Enemy attacks. (The enemy also
tried to infiltrate under the bridge.)
100 - Hill 100

0   500   1,000

Scale -- Meters

UZAL W. ENT, JAN. 1996
REVISED OCT '96

100
Nam-dong

command of LT Melyar Oxendine. The gun was positioned to fire on the pass. It was ringed by barbed wire and protected by infantrymen. Fisher called the gun "The Little Professor." For 10 days it pounded the enemy supply line through the pass with its fire. Several times the gun position was attacked. But the gun and crew stayed in place, never losing a man to the enemy.

24th Infantry — Sept. 2-10

LT Carroll B. LeTellier's platoon of the 77th ECC was positioned around the town of Saga, with some elements of the 35th Regiment on Sept. 1. The next day CPT Bussey assembled the entire company, to include all the cooks and others. Only the First Sergeant, Motor Sergeant and Company Clerk were left at his CP. Everyone else came forward to fight. The company had two very new lieutenants, both form the West Point Class of 1950; 2LT David Carlisle and 2LT Robert Green had joined the 77th just days before.

On Sept. 2 the 77th was given the mission of providing security along the routes of withdrawal as the 159th displaced to the Horseshoe area. But first, he sent LeTellier back to the company CP to round up everybody except 1SG Roscoe Dudley, the Motor Sergeant and the Company Clerk. LeTellier wrote that he had a problem keeping 1SG Dudley from getting on the truck and joining the company for the mission.

LeTellier's platoon was sent to hold a defile overlooking the Haman-Saga valley until the 159th had passed through. "It was a good thing, for Haman was lost during the night and the artillery's sole route of withdrawal was over Engineer Road," he wrote. "The 159th had engaged the enemy practically all night and was still engaged in the valley. I must say it was a classic withdrawal. We stayed on the high ground until the last tube was withdrawn. The Battery Commander's jeep was pulling the last tube and there were wounded on his jeep and on the [artillery] piece."

His platoon was then sent on a patrol along the high ground to his north. This was the high ground just south of the Chung-ni-Saga road. They went out about a mile without contacting any enemy. He was ordered to stay there until enemy contact was made. LeTellier placed a strong point on high ground north of the main platoon position to provide warning of approaching enemy soldiers.

"The next morning the ground was covered with haze and about daylight our strong point...was attacked and overrun and we began to take fire from the hill to the North," wrote LeTellier. "Our position would have been completely exposed when the fog burned off, so we fell back, under fire, along the trail up the mountain to our East. We then established defensive positions along the high ground of the Horseshoe. The 159th...had taken up positions in the Horseshoe after displacing.... All of those [men] who had been on the strong point sustained some sort of wound. Most were rather minor with the exception of Sergeant Shaw, who had an ugly wound on his ankle, which later had to be amputated. How he got down that hill with that wound I shall never know."

The reorganized 1/24th and F/24th relieved

will get through the barbed wire tonight and this flare will save us.' Sure enough, that night the North Koreans got through everything (flares tied with grenades, mines and barbed wire). Then one flare went off — in front of the BAR. Needless to say, [the BAR-man] had a field day and a double, triple 'Mad Minute' went into effect. Lots of ammunition was fired. North Koreans, looked like about 30 - 40 in line right behind each other. Then this one 'Gook' got careless [and] tripped this one flare. We won and what a night! I was never so proud of all the troops, *especially* the BAR-man. Fought to about daylight then everything stopped."

September 9, about 6 or 7 a.m.: "I was on the other side [of the bridge] when we heard this plane. Looked up and the squad leader said 'LT Vickery, you better get to the other side.' I said 'I'm on the way — me and the radio operator.' The first time the plane passed I was 2/3 of the way across the bridge. Don't know if he dropped a bomb on that pass.... But he circled and dropped one the next time and missed. All the time the

troops are hollering and waving and showing our [air]panels on both sides [of the bridge]. Then he made another pass, [and] the bomb dropped the center span [of the bridge], which the master sergeant of the engineers had set to blow, [so that the whole bridge would not be destroyed]. So COL Fisher came again to see what [had] caused the explosion. [He] told me later he [wanted to] prefer charges against the pilot. We were all hurt. We [had] fought for the bridge and our Air Force bombed it."

But Vickery's men used the two engineer boats they had to search the bodies for information. The got a lot of information, Vickery wrote, and got a letter from the 25th Division G2 for their help.

It is unusual for field pieces to be used individually, but the one at Vickery's Bridge was one of two so employed with the 35th at the time. During the battle, the enemy was using a pass on the north road which was out of artillery range. Fisher asked Barth for a gun. Barth, sent a 155mm howitzer from the 90th FAB, under

1/27 on Sept. 4 and 1/27 moved to a secondary position a mile and a half east of Haman. COL Champeny moved his CP to Haman at the base of a hill 300 yards west of the center of town. Before daylight on Sept. 5, Appleman recounted, "two enemy companies, only half-armed, moved against Haman. A part of this force approached the hill at the western edge of Haman where H Company was posted as security for the 24th Regimental command post situated at its base." Appleman stated that the men of H Co. left their posts without firing a shot, abandoning two new machine guns. The men in the CP first discovered the enemy when they were fired on by the captured guns. A small enemy party got within 100 yards of the CP before being driven off in a grenade battle with the I & R Platoon. An enemy grenade blew up an ammunition truck. The exploding shells and fire created the impression from a distance that a heavy battle was in progress.

Some 20 of the enemy got close enough, undetected, to throw hand grenades and fire burp guns into the 1/24th Infantry CP west of Haman. There were about 45 men of the CP group and 20 Korean recruits present in the CP at the time. The enemy was driven off at dawn. MAJ Eugene J. Carson, battalion XO, stated that he then had only 30 men in the CP with him, seven of them wounded. Looking back down the hill, he said that he saw about 40 men get out of a rice paddy and go over to a tank at a roadblock. These men reported to regiment that they had been driven from the hill.

At the time this action took place, a white officer and from 35 to 40 black soldiers left their roadblock and withdrew to COL Check's 1/27th Infantry CP, a mile and half away. At 5 a.m. there, this officer reported that 2,000 North Koreans had overrun his position and several others near Haman, including the 24th Regimental CP. Check reported this to Kean, then sent a platoon of tanks and a platoon of infantry back toward Haman to investigate. Meantime, some of Check's staff had stopped about 220 men moving to the rear. Check ordered them to follow the tanks. Some did, reportedly at gunpoint. The tank-infantry team arrived at the 24th Regiment's CP without incident to find everything peaceful there.

Appleman stated in a footnote that these incidents were substantiated by an interview of COL Champeny on July 22, 1951; Eighth Army War Diary entry for Sept. 14, 1950; Interrogation Report of Yun Che Gun and Eighth Army IG Report; testimony of Champeny, Roberts, Carson, Check, and Captains Hickman and Hunsaker (1/27th Inf.)

Hundreds of 24th Infantrymen were found wandering the rear areas, leaderless, at this point, yet the entire 3/24th was still on line, as was the reorganized 1/24th and at least part of the 2d Battalion.

After Rishell's platoon of A/24th was relieved from attachment to the 27th, it rejoined the company on line. Co. A and C were in position, with A on the right and C on the left. Rishell's platoon was given the saddle to defend, on A's left. To his right was another platoon of Co. A, but there was a gap in between and its platoon leader was beyond "shouting distance" from Rishell. He recalled that his position was almost indefensible. The barbed wire in front of the foxhole line was haphazardly strung. There were trip flares on the enemy side of the wire, but Lyle couldn't imagine that the wire posed any obstacle to an attacker. The enemy occupied a parallel ridge about 500 yards to the front. There were a large number of dead, bloated bodies scattered between the two lines, some inside the barbed wire. To the rear was a small village, which Co. B was then clearing of enemy infiltrators. Rishell felt isolated in this saddle of ground, so deployed his platoon for all around defense.

About dusk that first night, an enemy tank began a methodical shelling of American lines. The tank fire was aimed to pass over Rishell's platoon and strike somewhere in the rear. But the rounds were not clearing the hill by much and he was concerned that one would hit a tree and produce casualties in the platoon from an air burst. He called the company CP for artillery fire on the tank, but does not recall that any was fired.

A second tank moved up and joined the first. Rishell was now very upset. When his platoon sergeant couldn't seem to convince someone in the rear that the tanks should be engaged, Lyle grabbed the phone from him and yelled, "I need some support! The rounds are passing right over the position! I don't give a damn what it is, lay in some mortars!"

Then to his right, enemy rounds began falling into the position. To his surprise, some of them were WP; he didn't know the enemy had this type ammunition. He suspected that the enemy was firing a captured 4.2 inch mortar. The firing stopped as darkness fell.

As was customary in the unit, his men manned the forward foxholes at night, then pulled to the reverse slope during daylight. This, Rishell said, prevented the enemy from discovering the strength of the position.

The 24th Regiment was fairly well sorted out by Sept. 6, back on line and defending their share of the division front. On that date, COL Champeny visited Rishell's platoon. (Clay Blair writes that Champeny was visiting F/24th, but Rishell states that the U.S. Army Center for Military History substantiates his claim. The two accounts are remarkably similar.)

In his book, Rishell writes that when the colonel approached and they had exchanged salutes (they were on the reverse of the hill, out of enemy observation) Champeny asked what was happening. He responded that there was an enemy sniper active and that one of his men was trying to locate and eliminate him. The colonel went toward the marksman, who was trading shots with the enemy, making a derogatory comment that he didn't believe the lieutenant. "I want to take a look for myself, Lieutenant," he said. Champeny raised his binoculars to his eyes. A shot rang out and he fell back into Rishell's arms, hit in the shoulder. Rishell applied a bandage to the wound and the colonel was evacuated.

GEN Kean selected LTC Corley, commanding the 3d Battalion as the new commander of the 24th. Kean was so delighted that Corley accepted the command that he promoted him to Colonel. This made Corley, at 36, the youngest regimental commander in Korea. Corley was a highly decorated battalion commander in North Africa, Sicily and Europe during WW II, being awarded a DSC and five Silver Stars.

Horton V. White took the 24th Regiment to Korea, and was relieved within a month of arrival because of his age and health. Arthur S. Champeny took over Aug. 8 and was wounded in action on Sept. 6. Corley assumed command the next day.

One of his favorite sayings was "Cash pays the rent." He was highly respected by the officers and men of the 3/24th Infantry and became equally highly regarded by the entire 24th Infantry. Corley made "Remember Yechon!" the battlecry of the regiment. He was determined to improved the regiment and went about it in a very logical and methodical manner. First, he issued this statement to the men:

"In sixty days of continuous combat you have witnessed a roughness of battle which I have not seen in five campaigns in Africa, Sicily, Europe with the 1st Infantry Division. You have held ground against superior odds. You have lived up to the regimental motto, *Semper Paratus* [Always Ready]. The first United States victory in Korea was your action at Yechon. It has been noted in Congress. The people back home cover in detail your efforts.... Other units have been unable to accomplish what depleted companies of the fighting 24th have done. I am proud of you." (Quoted from Blair's *The Forgotten War*.)

Next, he tackled the task of selecting battalion commanders. He kept LTC Gerald Miller as commander of the 1st Battalion. The 2d Battalion was originally commanded by LTC Horace E. Donaho, who was WIA Aug. 11. MAJ George R. Cole (West Point 1937), the battalion XO, then commanded until relieved by LTC Paul F. Roberts, who came from his job as regimental XO. Corley brought Roberts back to regimental headquarters on Sept. 11 and Joseph Baxter was named to the command. This, then, was the fourth commander for the 2d Battalion in two months. Baxter was succeeded near the end of September by the battalion XO, MAJ George A. Clayton, who went on to command the battalion for many months.

The command situation in the 3d Battalion was even more chaotic. LTC Samuel Pierce Jr. commanded when the 3d Battalion arrived in Korea. He was wounded Aug. 6 and temporarily replaced by MAJ Theodore J. Cooke, the battalion XO. On Aug. 12, LTC Corley was given the command and he then went to command of the regiment Sept. 7. Between Aug. 7 and 21, William Walton and battalion XO Graydon A. Tunstall each commanded a part of that time. On Sept. 21, LTC Melvin R. Blair was made 3d Battalion commander. Blair had been awarded a DSC and Purple Heart while a member of Merrill's Marauders in WW II. That's six commanders in about 2 1/2 months.

Neither the regimental commanders nor the battalion commanders of the 2d and 3d battalions of the 24th had the time in command to do much with it in the first two months or so of the Korean War. Under Corley and his battalion commanders, the 24th RCT improved considerably, in reputation and in deed.

This anecdote, provided by MG Carroll N. LeTellier (then a newly-arrived 2LT of Engineers) illustrates how Corley operated:

LeTellier had arrived in the 24th Regiment's CP just after it had sustained a severe mortar attack resulting in many casualties. Shortly afterward a tall Second Lieutenant, another officer from the West Point Class of 1950, reported to the Colonel that his company had just been run off the hill to the northwest. "Corley pointed to the damage in his forward CP and told the young officer that this was quite evident," LeTellier wrote, "for the mortar fire which just played havoc with his CP came from that direction. The lieutenant had just joined his unit a day or two before and hardly knew anyone's name in [it]. Corley asked where the Company Commander and the rest of the officers were."

The frightened young officer thought that he was the only officer left; the others were casualties. "Corley said. 'Then you must be the Company Commander, so where are your men?'" He responded that they were scattered along the valley road and were all very tired from the experience and needed rest. "Corley rejected this outright," LeTellier recalled, "and told him that he would gather up his men and retake the hill by nightfall.... The lieutenant tried to make Corley change his mind to no avail." Corley told him that he wanted a message from the young officer's battalion commander that his company had retaken this critical ground. "I understand that the officer was successful, but what a way to earn your stripes!" LeTellier observed.

On Sept. 8, a monsoon rain came down in torrents, rain which no infantrymen could escape unsoaked. Foxholes filled with water. It even seeped into bunkers. Blankets or ponchos, spread above holes to give shelter, soon collapsed under the weight of water. Eating was another frustration. Water got into open C-ration cans and mixed with the food while one tried to eat. If a hot meal was being served with mess kits, rainwater turned everything into a most un-appetizing, watery mess. Good infantrymen just looked at one another, laughed and made the best of it. Everyone was so thoroughly wet, so thoroughly miserable, that even this lousy, rain-soaked food was a treat.

All across the 24th Regimental front in the mountains, the bodies of hundreds of North Koreans rotted in the heat and the sickly sweet smell got into one's nostrils and seemed even to invade the taste. Even liberal amounts of lime on the bodies did little to help the situation.

The morning of Sept. 10 dawned with a brilliant sunrise, raising the men's spirits dramatically. Foxholes, clothing equipment, and the men themselves finally had an opportunity to dry out.

While heavy, bloody battles were taking place in the 35th Infantry and the northern segment of the 24th Infantry, enemy artillery and mortar fire, plus strong local attacks, kept the troops on Battle Mountain and Sobuk-san well engaged. The 1/5th RCT never succeeded in securing the southern, and highest peak of Sobuk-san. This would have provided observation into the enemy's rear areas. Kean ordered Throckmorton to send troops into the sector of the 24th in order to protect the right flank of the 5th RCT. E/5th RCT (CPT William Conger Jr., West Point 1937), 5th's reserve company, got the mission. Appleman wrote that every night Co. E collected 24th Infantry stragglers and sent them back to their companies the next morning.

Although things quieted down along the 24th Regiment's front west of Haman, the bloody fighting for the mountain tops in the center and

southern sectors continued until Sept. 20, when the 24th began their battles leading to the breakout. The fight for Battle Mountain ended Sept. 9.

3/27th Infantry and Battle Mountain — Sept. 7-9

On Sept. 7 the enemy drove the 24th from the top of Battle Mountain once more. Kean ordered LTC DeChow's 3/27 to retake the peak. Companies K and B, 24th Infantry were to follow 3/27 to take over and secure the mountain once it had been taken.

The 3/27th Infantry, with C/65th Engineer Bn attached, began its attack at 3 p.m. on Sept. 7. The battalion fought against a stubborn enemy until dark and then dug in on a lower part of the objective. It resumed the attack the next day, was unsuccessful and dug in for the night.

That night, about 9:30 p.m., an estimated 600 North Koreans counterattacked the battalion, but were repulsed by small-arms and automatic weapons fire and the fire of mortars and close in artillery.

At 7 a.m. on Sept. 9, the battalion continued the attack. CPT William Mitchell's I/27 gained the top of Battle Mountain. It was joined there by Co. K. Shortly, however, both units were ejected from the crest by the enemy. Then the enemy counterattacked several times, but failed to dislodge the 3d Battalion from its position on lower ground.

"I can remember going up this mountain very clearly," wrote PVT John L. Kirby, of L/27. "The First Platoon of Co. L went to our right and took some of the top. The Third Platoon (actually we were about a squad in size at the time) were told to dig in, which we did before dark." Kirby, with two other men, Harkins and James Ward, went forward of the position. Kirby rigged trip wires tied to grenades on the only approach to the platoon position. He recalled that it was next to a large standing rock which resembled a man. The three men then returned to their foxholes.

"About 1 or 2 in the morning we started taking hits from big rounds of some kind," he wrote. "A little later we were hit with a frontal attack. The grenades we placed helped us a lot, but some got through to us anyway. James Ward, with a light machine gun and Harkins were to my left. James' gun jammed and he was trying to clear it. A North Korean ran at him and got close enough to stick a rifle bayonet right in front of his hole." Kirby and Harkins both fired at the enemy soldier, killing him.

"The enemy withdrew, but poor Ward was so frightened [that] he turned himself in to the CO as being only 16 years old. [H]e was taken off the mountain at once.... We took a very bad beating on top of Sobuk-san, but we held."

Tank Hill. Then-Private Edward F. Balbi and Jesus Rodriguez, an assistant squad leader in LT Frank L. Griffin's platoon of A/29th Infantry (later redesignated L/35th Infantry), recorded their recollections of action on what they called "Tank Hill":

"They told us that there was one over strength Co. on the hill," Edward Balbi wrote. "When we began moving up the hill they opened up on us with interlocking fields of MG fire. We lost several men immediately and were pinned down

in a shallow draw where a deep breath brought enemy fire. It took us all day and into the night to work our way out of it. The next morning they sent us back in without any reinforcements. Part way up the hill they ripped us up again. We made a daylight withdrawal back into the valley." The battalion commander asked for artillery and tank support and the battalion attacked again. "They ordered us back up the hill again that afternoon and we got our butts kicked again." Although repulsed once more, the battalion was ordered to attack again. It was a repeat of the other times. Balbi recalled that his unit made it almost to the top, but was thrown back. "There were dead and wounded laying all over the place. That night, Balbi wrote, the 1/29th Infantry became 3/35th infantry. Their new regimental commander, COL Henry Fisher (CO, 35th Infantry) asked if the battalion could take the hill with some help. The battalion commander responded that he thought it could.

The 3/27 was released from attachment to the 24th Infantry and directed to assemble at Masan beginning at 10 a.m. K/24th Infantry and C/65th ECB took over the defensive positions which 3/27 had occupied.

GEN Kean decided to quit fighting for the top of Battle Mountain. He had K/24th and C/65th Engineers dig in on a lower hill to the east of the Mountain. There, the two units were surrounded by barbed wire and mines. Artillery and mortars were registered on all likely enemy approaches, and a number points along them were plotted so that all the infantry had to do was call in a concentration number. The artillery and mortar gunners knew exactly what elevation and deflection to set the tube on to fire the concentration requested. The enemy tried a number of times in succeeding days to dislodge the Infantry/Engineer strongpoint but were never successful.

27th Infantry Relieves the 5th RCT — Sept. 9

The 5th RCT was attached to the 25th Division, giving it four regiments instead of the usual three. While the 2d Division, reinforced by the Marine Brigade and other forces, battled to eject the enemy from its sector and the 25th fought to clear the enemy from behind the 35th, the 1st Cavalry Division, farther north and near Taegu, was in dire straits. By Sept. 7, Kean had regained control of most of the area that the enemy had penetrated, destroying most of the North Korean force there in the process. On that date, Walker ordered the 5th RCT be released from 25th Division control within 24 hours. He planned to send the 5th north and attach it to the 1st Cavalry Division.

The 1/27th relieved 2/5th at 2:30 p.m. on Sept. 9; 2/27th relieved 3/5 at 3 p.m. COL Michaelis formally assumed command of the regimental sector at the same time. The 3/27th was still engaged in the 24th Regimental area and was unable to arrive in the 27th sector until Sept. 10. Their relief of 1/5th was not completed until 11 a.m. on Sept. 11. The 27th, for the first time since early August, was back with its parent division and on the MLR. Up to this time, the regiment had been employed as a "Fire Brigade," first in the sector of the 24th Division, then in the Bowling Alley, and finally, from Eighth Army reserve to counterattack to restore lines of the 24th Infantry and to clear enemy from the rear of the 35th. It would remain in this position until the 25th Division's breakout on Sept. 18.

Once relieved, the 5th RCT began moving to Samnangjin on Sept. 10. The last train bearing its units left Masan at 4 p.m. the next day. When assembled at Samnangjin, it went into Eighth Army reserve.

End of the Beer Ration — Sept. 12

To many of the young soldiers in Korea at the time, Sept. 12, 1950 was a day of infamy; that is the day that the "Beer Ration" was stopped. This beer was purchased with appropriated funds and issued free to the men in Korea. All units received the issue. At least some units received up to one can of beer per man per day. This beer was what was known as "three point two" beer. That is, it contained 3.2 percent alcohol, instead of the usual 5 or 6 percent. The Women's Christian Temperance Union, other social groups and individuals brought pressure on the Army and Congress to stop the practice. The legal drinking age in many parts of the United States was (and remains) 21. Many of the soldiers in Korea were still in their late teens. One member of Congress, who favored the issue, declared that "Water in Korea is deadlier than bullets."

Many of the soldiers were angered when the Army bowed to this pressure and ordered that the free beer issue be discontinued effective Sept. 12. The prevailing rationale among these young soldiers was that, if they were old enough to be sent to fight and die in a war, they were old enough to have a can of beer which had almost no alcohol. Appleman quoted one soldier, typifying the thought: "Those organizations or whatever they are have nothing to do with us. We are doing the fighting over here and it gets pretty bad. One can of beer never hurt nobody." But, as of Sept. 12, Eighth Army units had to buy beer with nonappropriated funds through post exchanges. It was a very sad, sad day!

3/24th Infantry on Pil-bong — Sept. 14

Companies I and L, 24th Infantry occupied Pil-bong, located about an air mile southeast of the enemy-held Battle Mountain. Pil-bong (Hill 743) was 250 feet higher than Battle Mountain. A long, narrow ridge connected the two mountain tops. Appleman wrote that Co. L had 100 men in position. No figure was given for Co. I.

Before dawn on Sept. 14 an enemy force, estimated at 400 to 500 men, attacked I and L/24th Infantry. The men repulsed several attacks, but then control broke down. Shortly, only about 40 men of Co. L remained on position; some of the men had become casualties while others had left their foxholes without orders. MAJ Melvin R. Blair, the new 3/24th Infantry commander, took personal control of the unit. With them, he pulled back into Item Co.'s position. There, he discovered that the company had withdrawn without his knowledge. An enemy sniper, hiding near the trail, shot Blair in the leg. Refusing evacuation, he tried in vain to hold Pil-bong. The small remaining force was too weak; Pilbong was lost.

5th RCT — Sept. 2-10

At midnight on Sept. 2 the enemy began attacking Companies A and F/5th RCT. The attacks diminished as the enemy shifted their focus to G/5th RCT. Part of G was driven from its positions. But American firepower continued to whittle down the enemy force and it finally fled, leaving its dead and wounded behind. Thereupon, G reoccupied its position and mopped up any enemy troops who had stayed behind.

But the enemy was not finished with G Co. Shortly after 7 a.m. on Sept. 4, the enemy attacked the company heavily, driving into its position. Calling in an air strike, George Co. counterattacked, ejected the enemy and reoccupied the ground.

At 2:30 a.m. on Sept. 6, it was Companies A and F that were attacked, first by a mortar barrage, then by infantrymen. The attacks were turned back, but the enemy kept both units under sporadic fire all day.

Aerial observers and ground reconnaissance revealed that the enemy continued to bring supplies forward to the Uiryong area, indicating that he intended to continue attacking. Trucks brought supplies up at night, cramming the villages with boxes and bales. By morning each day, these supplies had been moved to areas giving protection from air or artillery attack.

By Sept. 6, the enemy's attack against the 25th Division was largely a failure. It is true that somewhere between 3,000 and 3,500 of them had penetrated deep behind the 35th, but 2,000 of them, by actual count, were killed and buried there. On Sept. 7, the enemy made a general attack, which lacked punch and gradually receded.

The 27th Infantry was to relieve the 5th RCT on Sept. 9. But 1/5th on the slopes of Sobuk-san and 3/5, further south, were both heavily engaged in battle. The U.S. destroyer *Wiltsie*, lying offshore near Chindong-ni, helped to defend the southern flank, providing support with its guns and searchlights. A number of times, the ship's searchlights were trained onto low-hanging clouds, which reflected the light from the searchlights downward toward the ground, providing "artificial moonlight." At one point, this provided light which G/5th RCT used to help stave off a 30 minute enemy attack. The relief was finally completed on Sept. 11.

A number of veterans of the defending 5th RCT have provided some of their experiences and recollections of the period of Sept. 2-10.

Platoon Leader Henry E. Emerson quickly found himself the only officer left unhurt in A/5th RCT. Part of his personnel shortage was made up when he received his first batch of 25 KATUSAs. These young Koreans had no more than three days' orientation and were still really civilians because they had not yet been properly trained and indoctrinated to understand what was expected of them. They arrived that day with about 100 chiggie bearers. "Just then," he said, "they [the enemy] threw in, I guess...20 or 30 mortar rounds right in amongst them," Emerson recalled. Six or seven bearers were killed and a number of others wounded. Three or four KATUSAs were also killed and several others wounded.

"Of course they were scared to death," Emerson said. Eighteen of the KATUSAs were unhurt. They were scattered around in the platoons, but some of them were placed together in two-man foxholes," he wrote. During the next night attack, Emerson found two of them huddled in the bottom of the foxhole, firing their rifles into the air. Emerson recalled that the unit had to train their KATUSAs "on the job." This is exactly how other American units which received KATUSA replacements had to train them. Most

Masaon Front - Left to right, PFC Raymor and PFC Freyer (or Friar), both 17 years old. Had the Army discovered they were under age, both young men would have been immediately discharged. (Courtesy of Charles Shepherd, Tk Co./5 RCT)

of these young Koreans turned into creditable soldiers, if given the opportunity. Because they had virtually no training, the losses in killed and wounded among KATUSAs were very high.

Another time, during an attack at night, two KATUSAs came running toward Emerson's foxhole. He and 1SG Earl Davis jumped up and tackled the two men. Shortly thereafter, two GIs appeared from the line. They had abandoned their position, leaving a machine gun behind. Emerson asked, "Where the hell are you going?" They stopped. One of them said, "They said withdraw." Emerson sent them back to their hole. Speaking of these two incidents, he said, "Just an example of how easy it is to start a panic at night in a defensive position when you are under heavy pressure."

In regard to the enemy's attacks on the 5th RCT at the time, he said, "When these attacks came in at night, they were really mass attacks. They would come...in waves and there were several occasions, we...found out that...the second and third wave wouldn't even have rifles, wouldn't even have weapons. They were told that they would pick up weapons off of the dead and the wounded from the first attempt. It was that fanatical.... " He said this of the American soldiers he led: "You just can't say enough for the American infantry soldier who fought there.... They were fighters, and fought in the best traditions of the U.S. Army. And I'm awfully proud that I was associated with them." Emerson also paid tribute to a number of superior NCOs of his company, including 1SG Earl Davis, Bob Lyons, Santiago Bunda and a man named Silva, who was a Nisei NCO WW II veteran of the 442d RCT, which fought in Europe

It was during the enemy's attack on Sept. 2 that Bill Motley, FO from the Triple Nickel was wounded. That day started with Motley back with the battery. Word came that one of the rifle companies needed an FO; theirs apparently had been isolated from them and they could not reach him on the ground or by radio. Motley was sent to the company with its chiggie train. "I was to rush them along since they were hauling badly needed recoilless rifle ammo to the unit.

"I pushed them as fast as I thought they could stand it and we made pretty good time. I dropped them off at the rear of the company area, and headed on up to find the CO. There was occasional small arms fire and I dropped into the first shell hole 'till I could find out where he was. I watched one of the lieutenants and a couple of NCOs run across in front of me to what I decided was his hole. He was still too far away to holler at, so while I was trying to make up my mind whether I should be brave and make a dash for it, or be smart and stay put until things died down more. I asked some of the men in holes around me if they knew where the FO was. They didn't."

Then Motley made a dash for another hole. He didn't draw fire. "I was now close enough to talk to one of the platoon leaders, who pointed out where the FO was. Again, I watched men running around without drawing fire and decided to make a run for it. I hadn't taken but a couple of steps when my left leg went out from under me. The [North] Korean wasn't fifty yards down the hill from me. When I hit [the ground], I rolled until my head was behind a stump about 10

inches high and 6 inches across. There was enough of a rise in front of me so that I wasn't worried from that direction. But as I lay there like an ostrich with its head in the sand, I could see weeds and blades of grass fall from stray (I hoped) rounds."

Motley believed that the enemy had seen him come into the area with binoculars and a radio and figured him to be someone of importance. He rolled back into the hole he had run from, to be joined very shortly by a medic. The medic cut his trouser leg to discover a wound above Motley's knee that resembled a knife slash. "He said, "Hell, Lieutenant, you just got a nick." Motley told the medic he would bandage himself, and the man rolled out of the hole to go to someone else's aid. He placed his own first aid bandage on the wound "and started to leave the hole too," he wrote, "but I had no use of my leg at all. I tore my fatigues further and saw about an inch of dried blood on the inside of the knee and realized it [the bullet] had gone through and blew open the flesh on the way out."

This left the slashed look. He and the medic had seen the exit wound but not the wound where the bullet had entered. Motley crawled to the medic, who applied another bandage. Then he crawled on to the rear of the company area and was evacuated on a litter by the same chiggie bearers he had come up the hill with just a short time ago.

The 77th ECC was the engineer unit in the 5th RCT. It had the same mission with the 5th that the 72d ECC had with the 24th RCT. 1LT James A. Johnson (West Point 1947) was a platoon leader in the 77th at the time. He recalled that his unit was kept busy laying mines, stringing barbed wire and installing other obstacles. On occasion during this period, he company also performed as infantry.

1LT Henry Emerson, A/5th RCT was one of Johnson's West Point classmates. Johnson recalled the aftermath of one enemy attack on Co. A. "They found 40 North Korean bodies in front of one platoon," he said.

The 1/5th RCT CP was located "right down in a draw between and below A Company on the left and B Company on top of the mountain in front of C Company," he recalled.

"Hank Emerson...asked that we place antipersonnel mines on the ridge line covering his front. He occupied the top of a steep hill above the battalion headquarters. Between his position and B Company was a saddle over which the North Koreans could infiltrate. We... started putting the mines in. I thought our action had been coordinated with everyone. Since we were in front of A Company the troops across the valley could see us."

As Johnson's men worked to put in mines, they started to receive artillery fire. Johnson got mad. "And so I went to Hank and I said, 'God dammit, you guys are shooting at me!' And he said, 'No, that's not us. I said, 'Like hell! It's coming from back here, it's not coming from out there. [Enemy territory.] All right, you get that squared away, and I'll go down here and put mines in behind your flank.' He [Emerson] had been attacked there, too, between his position and the 2nd Battalion.

"So we get down there, and we're putting in mines and trip flares.... Apparently people from

the 2nd Battalion saw us, and they started opening up...with their .50-calibers. So I went back to Hank and I said, 'To hell with you! When you get this straightened out, I'll be back.'" Johnson's platoon received no casualties from the artillery fire or from the machine guns.

Johnson recalled a different version of the relief of COL Ordway from what James A. Richardson related earlier in this book. He was ordered to dig the regimental CP in a position only about one hill mass behind the front. The platoon started to build an access road and Johnson took a squad with him to look for roof timbers. When he returned to the site, his platoon was gone. He found them about 5 miles to the rear. His platoon sergeant told him that COL Ordway had come up and told the sergeant he wanted the CP at this other site to the rear.

"We started working again," Johnson said, "when Major [Elmer] Owens [Regimental S3] happened by and sent us back to the original spot. So we loaded up and went back. Again, we started digging and then all of a sudden this jeep comes up the access road we had cut. It was the Assistant Division Commander, Brigadier General Vennard Wilson.... He comes up.... I saluted and said, 'General, how are you, sir?'

'Well, Johnson, what are you doing here?' I said, 'Sir, I don't know.'

'What do you mean you don't know?' I told him what had happened about the CP location." Wilson loaded Johnson in his jeep, and they head back to the regimental CP.

Upon arrival, GEN Wilson asked for COL Ordway, who was then shaving. The colonel ran from his tent to report to the general. Wilson ordered Johnson to repeat what he had told him. "So I said, 'Sir, I don't know where you want that command post built. I keep getting conflicting orders.' He [Ordway] pointed to a map and said he wanted it built in the back location. Wilson looked at him and said, 'I'll be God damned, Johnson, you build it where I saw you building it!' Then he said, 'You know, since I've been in the Army there are two ways to do things. The right way and the wrong way. Now there's the Ordway, and that's no damn good. You're relieved.'"

Whether this version or Richardson's is the correct account of Ordway's relief makes little difference. He was relieved by GEN Kean on Aug. 15, purportedly because Kean blamed him for the losses near Pongam-ni during the TF Kean counterattack.

SGT Gerald Pack and CPL Paul D. Comi were members of F/5th RCT. Pack recalled Sept. 1, 1950: "My squad, including Junior Mullins, was assigned LP [Listening Post] about 200 yds below [the] Co. Shortly after dark I looked up and there were Gooks almost in the hole with us. One shot me in [the] arm and leg. I pulled the pin and just rolled the grenade." The exploding grenade gave Pack a minor wound, but Mullins lost a leg. The enemy drove the company from the hill. Then overcome by hunger, the North Koreans stopped at the Co. CP and sat in the holes there and began to eat.

CPL Comi joined Fox Co. as a replacement and was assigned as a 60mm mortar ammunition carrier. His first task was to take mortar ammunition up the hill from the rear to the 60mm mortar position. The hill was steep and the weather hot. He could hear the sounds of battle on top of the hill. Then he saw two men carrying a wounded man back on a litter. "I have a vivid memory of looking at the position of the legs and feet of this man and the chilling recognition that this was reality and real blood and that you could get killed up there. And a wave of fear gripped me at the pit of my stomach. I numbly continued to climb up the hill...."

Comi arrived at the top of the hill at dark and was assigned to LP duty in a foxhole by himself on the forward slope facing toward Co. G. Other holes were about 20 feet away from him, he recalled. About 3 a.m, the enemy began a heavy mortaring of G Co., then followed with an infantry assault. In the noise of battle and mortar rounds exploding, he mistook sounds he heard to be of enemy soldiers crawling up on his hole. Desperately, he tried to pull the pin on a grenade, but he had bent the pin back so far that it was impossible to pull. He lacerated his finger in a vain attempt to pull that pin.

"As it was," he wrote, I probably would have tossed it into my buddy's foxhole and killed him in my panic.... Dawn arrived with the realization that the Gooks had taken the hill from George Company and now we were positioned between our company and the enemy and they began to exchange fire. Very soon after, G Company began an assault to recapture the summit." When this happened, the enemy on the G Co. hill shifted their fire to meet this threat. But the fire from Fox Co.'s main position to support Co. G continued to pass dangerously low over Comi's foxhole.

Eventually this fire also ceased and Comi and another man, named Morris, who was also out as a listening post began to zero their rifles "in on places in the rice paddy at the base of the opposite hill, Comi wrote. "When the Gooks began to reach that area, which they had to go through in their retreat, Morris and I had a real 'Turkey Shoot' popping off fleeing figures in the paddy below."

William G. Price and Robert W. Potter were members of G/5th RCT. Price had come to Korea with the regiment and Potter joined it later as a replacement. Price recalled a night when Co. G was driven from its position by the enemy. "Our foxhole (Ray Warner and me) was on an extreme forward slope of the mountain, so we had to retreat by going toward N.K. lines. We ended in a ditch that was loaded with anti-tank and anti-personnel; some were trip wire and others were pressure type. We finally worked our way to friendly lines and were returned via Bn Hqs to our company just in time for the attack to retake Sobuk-san."

Potter recalled the first attack he experienced as a replacement with Co. G. "It happened early Sunday morning before dawn.... They broke through our front and destroyed our machine gun nest and we were pushed off the hill. Then we regrouped...early that same morning and retook the hill."

The 3/5th RCT, on the southern flank of the regiment (and 25th Division) had Co. K in the low ground next to the coastal road, Co. L on the first high ground to the right of K. LT Daniel R. Beirne of Co. K, recalled that the enemy attacked the battalion. The night of Sept. 1, the enemy heavily shelled the rear areas. "It was our

first real artillery barrage," he wrote to his family. "Shells dropped around all night long but not a man was hit.

"That night I relieved another platoon on the front line. When I got up to the front there were a lot of dead [North] Koreans lying about. K Company didn't get a single casualty that night. L Company held a high hill and that was what they were after. K Company held low ground on the left of L Company but my platoon controlled the approaches. The 2nd night the N. Koreans didn't come in across the rice paddies yelling, etc., like they did the first [time], but came in quietly to attack L Company. My platoon heard them and we opened [fire]. I called mortar fire on them also. They very carefully went around my position (we were well dug in) and hit L from the other side. Before they attacked, however, they really gave L a pounding with direct fire weapons...yet L had only one casualty from that.

"Then they blew whistles, yelled 'Manzai' and charged. Well, one platoon in L Company got scared and broke and before long, the entire company was just about off the mountain. When the sun rose, only seven men remained on the top peaks and 'gooks' were all around the bottom. There was I in my position and high on my right rear, looking down on me, was a mountain just about completely taken by the 'gooks.' Fortunately, at this moment jets hit the hill with rockets and drove the [North] Koreans down a ways. My company re-equipped L Company and they regained the mountain," Beirne wrote.

The enemy infiltrated 5th RCT lines almost every night. On Sept. 4, I/5th RCT caught 75 of them in a trap and killed most of them. Any North Koreans caught in the open each morning were usually spotted and killed.

In the same letter home, Beirne described the days and nights on the front. "It's funny here. The days seem like normal days. You sometimes don't even know a war is going on. We walk around our positions in the open. We watch the 'Gooks' walking around. We sleep, bathe and so do they. Then at night all hell breaks loose. The difference is the air [support]. The enemy can only move at night. The air has saved us many times by smashing up [troop] concentrations right before an attack. They are a wonderful arm [of service]."

Homestead Hill: C/29th Infantry/L 35th Infantry — Mid-Aug.-Mid-Sept.

SGT David M. Williams, C/29th (L/35th) recalled a hill his unit occupied shortly after the end of TF Kean until about the time of the breakout. He called it "Homestead Hill," because the unit was on it for so long. The unit was assigned a hill position, he recalled. "There we prepared positions, including barbed wire, clearing fields of fire and other actions needed to hold at all costs.... We were tired of withdrawing and all hands were determined to hold

"The enemy attack was not long in coming. We knocked out their tanks first, then their infantry opened fire. There is nothing like the sound of a burp gun as the bullets crack over your head. We knocked out their lead tanks and many of their men. In spite of this they overran

one hill in our defense line and captured a heavy machine gun. We counterattacked and re-took the hill. A soldier named Profitt, although wounded in the stomach, re-captured the machine gun after killing the three North Koreans who had been firing it. I never knew what happened to PVT Profitt, but in my mind he was a true hero.... I lost my best friend that night, and was saddened by the fact that he was so young, like most in Company C at that time." (Quoted from a 29th Infantry reunion letter, by permission of David M. Williams.)

Battery C, 8th FAB — Tale of a New Battery

The two firing battery Field Artillery battalions received their third batteries late in August 1950. One of these new batteries was C/8th FAB. In late June 1950 the 537th FAB was engaged, along with 2/14th Infantry, in training ROTC cadets. The battalion also loaned equipment to individuals and units so that they could train properly. In addition, about 20 men daily, from a complement of 82 men in one battery, performed Post duties (KP, etc.).

The deployment of the battalion to Korea to make up the third firing batteries of battalions over there was kept secret. When the men were finally told, it was too late for many of them to take care of personal affairs (allotments, wills, etc.). Then the mode by which B and C Batteries were to return to Camp Carson, CO, became fouled up. On a Friday they were ordered to return by organic vehicles. Last minute maintenance to make "deadlined" vehicles operational. packing an loading were all done with all possible speed. Men called their families back at Carson to inform them. Then, on Saturday morning, the order was changed: Travel by rail. Box all equipment and place in boxcars. Vehicles on flatcars, troops in coaches. "Of course, no one had loaded flat cars before and no wooden boxes were available," wrote COL Robert E. Dingeman (West Point 1945), then a lieutenant in B/537th FAB. "By all night effort by the Post Carpenter Shop, boxes were packed and hastily loaded in the box cars and as the last engine pulled in, the last vehicle rolled on the flat cars."

Dingeman was a member of the Advance Party, so he had to race back to Carson with his family. Three days after he arrived at Carson, the troop train pulled in. "Then the real rat race began," he wrote. The troops had not yet been informed, but the civilians on the Post seemed to know. The batteries were stripped of unserviceable equipment and brought up to allowances on everything.

The batteries were short personnel. To bring them up to a reasonable strength, men were pulled in from everywhere; fire truck drivers, bakers, mule skinners, "everything but trained 105mm artillerymen," Dingeman wrote. Additional officers came from the 4th FAB, the last and only pack-mule artillery outfit in the Army.

Batteries B and C, 537th FAB became the 10th and 11th Provisional Batteries, respectively. Finally, on Aug. 10, 1950, they set sail for Korea and arrived there on Aug. 25. The 10th Provisional Battery became Battery C, 8th FAB and the 11th Provisional Battery became Battery C,

64th FAB. The 8th was the 27th Infantry's direct support battalion and the 64th was the direct support battalion for the 35th Infantry. LT Hart, an FO for the 11th, was killed the second day that the battery was in action. Initially, Dingeman's battery was emplaced in the south to work with the Triple Nickel, supporting the 5th Infantry. CPT Joel M. Genung commanded the 10th (C/8th FAB). His officers included Lieutenants Dingeman, XO; Roland B. Shriver; Rolly G. Miller; Henry J. Shaefer and Phillip Egert and Warrant Officer Willard D. Clark. MSG Hugh W. Philpott was the initial First Sergeant in Korea. Miller, Scheaffer and Egert were the battery FOs. CPT Charles Waddell commanded the 11th (C/64th FAB). His officers included FOs LT Hart and LT Seely.

"We shipped as a four gun battery," wrote SGT Allen M. Smith, "6 officers, 1 WO and 95 EM. They made us a 6 gun battery [in Korea]. We then should have had 7 officers, 1 WO and 131 EM."

Dingeman selected the forward slope of a hill for the battery's first firing position in Korea. It was dotted with little mounds, which he soon found out were Korean graves. "This made for interesting digging for the perimeter positions and gun emplacements," he wrote. But the battery was in position, ready to fire, in ten minutes. This first position was occupied Sept. 2, 1950. The battery occupied this position for 21 days.

Lew Millett, 8th FAB was the liaison officer to the new battery. It was called on to fire in support of 1/5th RCT. As a result, Dingeman came to know, admire and respect Henry Emerson, commanding Co. A.

In writing about firing from this position, SGT Smith said: "You could stand behind the howitzer and watch the projectile leave and hit the target (Sobuk-san) as it was a huge hill in front of us."

Also writing about the battery's first position near Chindong-ni, SGT Robert R. Minger said: "We went into Chindong-ni at night. Our battery had never fired at night or together. I had never laid a gun battery (which was my job). However, I learned fast from a 2d Lt and a World War II Artillery Sgt. They were a great help." Minger wrote this of LT Dingeman: "I was proud to be one of his men. When LT Robert Dingeman was in a battery, you were always best in his way of thinking. Everyone respected him...." And: "I will give 1st Lt Robert Dingeman, Exec. Officer, all the credit for leadership."

General Kean and the 24th Infantry

Appleman stated that "ever since its entrance into combat...in July [the 24th] Regiment had given a poor performance, although there were some exceptions and many individual acts of heroism and capable performance of duty." He also wrote: "Eighth Army and the 25th Division assigned officers of an unusually high caliber to the 24th Infantry to give it strong leadership, but this did not solve the problem." (See Chapter Notes.)

Appleman and other writers have failed to recognize high regimental and battalion leadership turnover as a problem. Certainly, it greatly inhibited the performance of at least two battalions of the 24th.

Nevertheless, GEN Kean tired of coping with the problem. The enemy breakthrough in the 24th's sector caused him to write a letter to GEN Walker on Sept. 9, recommending the removal of the 24th from combat and distributing its personnel to other commands in Korea as replacements. Kean harshly condemned the entire 24th with these words: "It is my considered opinion that the 24th Infantry has demonstrated in combat that it is untrustworthy and incapable of carrying out missions expected of an infantry regiment." Appleman asserted that "nearly all officers serving in the regiment agreed with General Kean, and so did many of the Negro non-commissioned officers and enlisted men themselves." (Letter, Kean to Walker, Sept. 9, 1950, quoted by Appleman.) Appleman, who had detailed references for almost everything he writes in *South to the Naktong,* has no notations or other references about these opinions of the officers NCOs and other ranks of the 24th.

Walker did not act on Kean's recommendation. Full integration did not occur until Oct. 1, 1951. On that date, the 24th RCT was dissolved and the 14th Infantry took its place in the 25th Infantry Division. The men of the 24th RCT were scattered into a number of regiments and separate battalions in Korea.

The Specter of Chinese Intervention

Coincident with the heavy fighting along the Perimeter intelligence came to U.S military leaders in Tokyo and Washington that Chinese troops were moving north through China and assembling along the Yalu River boundary between North Korea and China. On Sept. 4, a twin-engine bomber bearing a red star flew over a screening ship of the UN naval task force cruising in the Yellow Sea. The task force was then off the west coast of Korea about at the 38th Parallel. The plane flew on toward the center of the formation of ships and began firing on an American fighter plane patrol. The patrol shot the intruder down. The body of one of the bomber crew was retrieved from the sea. He was dressed in the uniform of the armed forces of the Soviet Union.

Results of the Enemy Attack on the 25th Division

The enemy had attacked the 25th Division with its *6th* and *7th Divisions.* Both of these divisions suffered terrible casualties. Prisoners of war disclosed that the *7th Division* was down to a strength of about 4,000 men. The *6th Division* had also suffered heavy losses. When they started their offensive Aug. 31-Sept. 1, intelligence sources credited the *6th Division* with 10,000 men and the *7th Division* with 9,000. We know that over 2,000 enemy dead were buried within 25th Division lines. The heavy losses of these two divisions closely approximated similar crippling losses by the other North Korean divisions along the Perimeter at the time.

The 35th Infantry was awarded a Presidential Unit Citation for its stand along the Nam River and its commander, COL Fisher was awarded a DSC. Michaelis's Wolfhounds also received a considerable amount of praise from the news media.

American Battle Losses to Sept. 15, 1950

From the start of the war to Sept. 15, American battle losses totaled 19,165 men. Of these, 4,280 KIA; 12,377 WIA (of whom 319 died of wounds); 401 reported POWs, and 2,107 MIA. There were more battle casualties in the first 15 days of September than any other two week period of the war, before or afterward, indicating the ferocity of the fighting.

Chapter Notes:

P. 320 A coordinating point is a location on the terrain marking the boundary between two units. Normally, adjacent unit commanders would meet to tie in and coordinate their defenses at or near this point.

P. 320 Barbed wire was often in short supply in the Perimeter.

P. 324 The author queried COL Rishell in a 1996 telephone call about his writing that some of the men were still in sleeping bags. He confirmed that it was sleeping bags, not blankets, and stated that this was a headquarters, not a line company, area which had been attacked. His men, as well as those of the author at that time, had no sleeping bags; they were lucky to have a blanket. This was also true of other rifle units in the Perimeter.

P. 325 Appleman wrote that during the grenade fighting on Hill 179 the practice of "cooking the grenade" developed. To do this, the grenadier pulled the pin on the grenade and held it for a few seconds before throwing it. This was done so that the enemy would not have time to pick up and throw the grenade back. The practice of "cooking" grenades started long before the Korean War, when some unnamed soldier discovered that the few seconds it took a grenade to detonate allowed his enemy to toss it back. So this soldier learned to pull the pin, count to about three and throw the grenade. The "cooked" grenade usually exploded just about the time it landed on the target.

P. 325 Proximity fuze (VT) rounds are set to detonate above the ground, gaining the maximum killing power from their explosion. The shell explodes when it comes into "proximity" of the ground. A sensor in the round detects this "proximity," exploding the shell. At times, when a battery was firing a number of these rounds, the shells would set one another off as they passed close to one another in flight. When a round was set off in this fashion it was called "sympathetic detonation."

P. 340 Horton White and Arthur Champeny were not, in the author's opinion "unusually high caliber" officers. Nor were some of the battalion commanders. Many veterans of the 24th Infantry also dispute Appleman's assertion about the high caliber of officers assigned to the 24th. In reality, there should never have been segregated units of commands this late in American history. That there were reflects at least indifference on the part of national military and civilian leadership. The 24th was not as bad as some writers have made it to be, nor as good, perhaps, as its advocates claim.

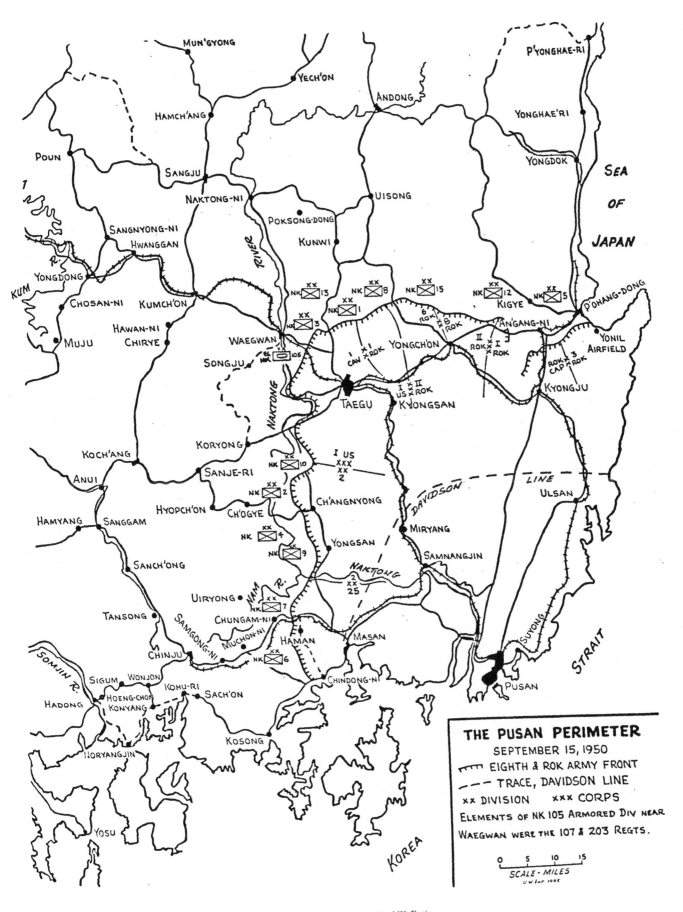

MUN'GYONG

YECH'ON

ANDONG

P'YONGHAE-RI

HAMCH'ANG

YONGHAE'RI

POUN

SANGJU

YONGDOK

SEA

NAKTONG-NI

POKSONG-DONG

UISONG

OF

SANGNYONG-NI

KUNWI

JAPAN

HWANGGAN

RIVER

KUM

YONGDONG

NK XX 13   NK XX 8   NK XX 15   NK XX 12   NK XX 5

P'OHANG-DONG

CHOSAN-NI

KUMCH'ON

NK XX 1   KIGYE

HAWAN-NI

NK XX 3

6   AN'GANG-NI   YONIL

MUJU   CHIRYE

WAEGWAN

NK 105

1 X ROK   ROK X 8 ROK   II X I   AIRFIELD
CAV ROK   YONGCH'ON   ROK ROK

SONGJU

ROK X 3   KYONGJU
CAP ROK

NAKTONG

TAEGU   KYONGSAN   I X II   YONIL
US ROK

KORYONG

I US   DAVIDSON   LINE
XXX
XX   ULSAN
2

KOCH'ANG

NK XX 10

SANJE-RI

ANUI   NK XX 2

HYOPCH'ON   CH'OGYE   CH'ANGNYONG

HAMYANG   SANGGAM   NK XX 4

MIRYANG

SANCH'ONG   NK XX 9   YONGSAN

NAKTONG

SAMNANGJIN

NAM R.

2
XX
25

UIRYONG   NK XX 7

TANSONG   CHUNGAM-NI

SUYONG

SAMGONG-NI   MUCHON-NI   MASAN

CHINJU   HAMAN   STRAIT

NK XX 6

SOMJIN R.   CHINDONG-NI   PUSAN

SIGUM   WONJON

HADONG   KOHU-RI   SACH'ON

HOENG-CHON   KONYANG

KOSONG

NORYANGJIN

YOSU

KOREA

THE PUSAN PERIMETER
SEPTEMBER 15, 1950

⌒⌒⌒ EIGHTH & ROK ARMY FRONT

– – – TRACE, DAVIDSON LINE

XX DIVISION   XXX CORPS

ELEMENTS OF NK 105 ARMORED DIV NEAR

WAEGWAN WERE THE 107 & 203 REGTS.

0   5   10   15
SCALE - MILES
UW ENR 1955

Map 49 (Courtesy of Uzal W. Ent)

1st SG George S. Hearn, First Sergeant Co. B, 27th Infantry, Japan and Korea, 1949-51.

Dependent Housing Project, Gifu, Japan, May 1947. Two families to a house - three and four bedrooms. (Courtesy of William E. Gott, Former Captain, 24th REGT)

Left to right: Clothier, Conz, Cavallero, Crivello, Radio School, San Diego, June 1950. (Courtesy of Kenneth D. Clothier, HQ, 1st BN, 11 Marines)

PART FOUR

BREAKOUT AND PURSUIT

We fought along the Naktong
And from outposts sea-to-sea.
In heat and mud we battled
To keep South Korea free.

* * * * * * *

We held along the river
Where the world saw us to be.
The ones who saved Korea
Though our backs were to the sea.

(From "The Pusan Perimeter," by MAJ Arthur F. Dorie.
Used with his permission.)

CHAPTER TWENTY-ONE – Breakout

The Inchon Landing

An event which changed the course of the Korean War was the U.S. landing at Inchon, September 15, 1950. The 1st Marine Division stormed ashore and seized a beachhead, which it and the Army's 7th Infantry Division expanded, then exploited. Then MacArthur decreed that the South Korean capitol, Seoul, be freed as quickly as possible. This was a political decision. As a result, the Marine Division and elements of the 7th Division and the ROK 17th Infantry Regiment were tied up in that city until September 28.

Meantime, elements of the 7th Division's 32d Infantry, 73d Tk Bn and 48th FAB had been ordered to turn southward along the road to seize Suwon and its airstrip. This was accomplished by the end of the day on Sept. 22. The next day, the 31st Infantry took over the area from the 32d. Elements of the 31st and 7th Cavalry linked up a few miles north of Osan late on Sept. 26.

The Eighth Army Breakout Plan

There were three natural axes of advance out of the Perimeter. The main effort would be along the highway from Waegwan to Kumchon, then over the mountains to Taejon. The second axis of advance would be northward over the Sangju road. Possible river crossing sites along this route were at Sonsan and Naktong-ni. The best routes for the ROK Army were via Andong and Wonju and the coastal road toward Yongdok and Wonsan.

Any plan to cross the Naktong and break out of the Pusan Perimeter was made more difficult for three reasons. These were: (1) The North Koreans still held the initiative; (2) There were only two pontoon treadway bridges available to Eighth Army to cross the Naktong, and; (3) There was an acute shortage of artillery ammunition. The shortage of bridging equipment and artillery ammunition was due to the necessity to divert personnel, equipment and ammunition assets to support the Inchon landing.

When the Marine Brigade was pulled from the Perimeter, the supporting Marine Air squadrons went with it. To compensate, GEN Stratemeyer had the 51st Fighter-Interceptor Wing and the 16th and 25th Fighter-Interceptor Squadrons transferred from the 20th Air Force on Okinawa.

Although Walker was unable to assemble a large force for the main breakout effort, he was able to move the 24th Division, almost unit by unit, to the center behind the 1st Cavalry Division. Initially, Eighth Army would stage a series of holding attacks just after the Inchon invasion took place. These attacks were designed to keep enemy troops in place on the Perimeter so they could not be sent to help defend in the north.

To boost Eighth Army morale, word of the Inchon invasion was quickly disseminated to the troops. The enemy kept the news from their men because of its adverse morale effect.

Walker's plan to break out of the Perimeter was published Sept. 6 and sent to MacArthur's headquarters for approval the next day. On Sept. 11, Eighth Army revised the plan and, on Sept. 16, made it EUSAK OPLAN 10, dated Sept. 6, with Revision, dated Sept. 11. Hour and date of attack: 9 A.M., Sept. 16. The order directed the U. S. Eighth and the ROK Armies to attack "from present bridgehead with main effort directed along the Taegu-Kumchon-Taejon-Suwon axis," to destroy enemy forces "on line of advance," and to make a "junction with X Corps" coming south from the Inchon area. The newly formed U.S. I Corps would make the main breakthrough. Four factors influenced this decision:

1. X Corps troops were the closest to the link-up area.
2. The best roads and easiest grades could be found in its zone of advance.
3. The road net provided the best opportunity to exploit a breakthrough.
4. The road net provided the best supply route for advancing troops.

Concept of the Operation: In the south, the 25th Division would attack west across the southern area of Korea, then turn north toward Kunsan. Following roads farther north, the 2d Division would also attack to the west, then swing northward. Meantime the 1st Cavalry Division and 5th RCT would cross the Naktong near Waegwan. The 24th Division would follow these commands, then pass through once the Naktong had been crossed, continuing the attack northwest to Taejon and beyond. Elements of the 24th Division were to meet elements of the 7th Division coming south from the Inchon-Seoul area. The ROK divisions on the northern flank of the Perimeter would attack at the same time as Eighth Army into the Taebaek Mountains and up the east coast highway.

Outline of Plan of Attack:

5th RCT and 1st Cavalry Division: Seize a bridgehead over the Naktong near Waegwan.

24th Division: Cross the Naktong through the 5th RCT and 1st Cavalry and attack toward the Kumchon-Taejon area.

ROK 1st Division: Attack in zone to seize Kasan. Be prepared to cross the Naktong River in conjunction with the 1st Cavalry Division. Attack and seize Sangju,

1st Cavalry Division: Follow 24th Division. Patrol its rear areas and lines of communication.

2d and 25th Divisions: Attack and fix the enemy in their zones. Exploit any local breakthrough. Strive to attain crossings of the Naktong below Waegwan.

ROK I and II Corps: Attack and fix the enemy in their zones. Exploit any local breakthrough.

ROK 17th Infantry Regiment: Move to Pusan for sea movement to Inchon to join X Corps.

For the first time in the Korean War, Walker would have Corps commands within the Eighth Army. The I Corps headquarters was formed back in the United States by changing the V Corps to I Corps on July 20, 1950. This headquarters arrived in Korea during the first few days of September. MG John B. Coulter commanded the corps when it was activated. Following World War II, Coulter served as deputy commander of U.S. Forces in Korea and XXV Corps, succeeding to the command on Aug. 26, 1948. Before the breakout started, Walker gave IX Corps to Coulter and I Corps to MG Frank W. "Shrimp" Milburn, who at the time commanded IX Corps. I corps became operational in Korea at noon Sept. 13. Milburn (West Point 1914), commanded XXI Corps in GEN Alexander Patch's Seventh Army in Europe during World War II. When tapped to command a corps in Korea, Milburn was deputy commander of U.S. Army Forces in Europe.

Clay Blair, in *Forgotten War*, states that Walker made the switch because he felt that Milburn was more aggressive than Coulter. He wanted an aggressive corps commander to lead the troops making the main breakout attempt. Blair also wrote that, if GEN Dean had been available, Walker would have appointed him to lead the main attack.

The IX Corps, now commanded by MG John B. Coulter, was activated in Korea on Sept. 23, 1950.

IX Corps controlled the U.S. 2d and 25th Divisions for the attack. I Corps consisted of the U.S. 1st Cavalry and 24th Infantry Divisions, the ROK 1st Division and the 5th RCT.

GEN Paik Sun Yup, who commanded the 1st ROK Division at the time, recalled that Milburn "proved to be a bold and aggressive soldier, in spite of his appearance." Paik described him as being short and mild mannered.

When the two officers first met, Milburn promised to give Paik more supporting firepower. True to his word, he attached the U.S. 10th Antiaircraft Artillery Group to the ROK 1st Division. The 10th included the 78th FAB (eighteen 90mm guns), 9th FAB (eighteen 155s) and the 2d HM Battalion (eighteen 4.2" mortars). Paik was overjoyed.

Milburn's breakout orders to Paik were: "You will attack from Palgong-san to Kasan and destroy the NKPA 1st Division there. You will prepare to cross the Naktong River and attack in concert with the U.S. 1st Cavalry Division toward Sangju." (Quotes describing GEN Milburn and the order to 1st ROK Division from Paik's *From Pusan to Panmunjom*.)

The Enemy

The Intelligence Annex to the battle plan credited the enemy with 13 infantry divisions on line supported by an armored division and two armored brigades. Six of these divisions and supporting armor, of the *NK I Corps*, were in the southern half of the front. The corps strength was put at 47,417 men. The *NK II Corps* consisted of seven infantry divisions, plus armor, and was estimated to be 54,000 men strong. The estimate put enemy organizations at 75% strength. This intelligence estimate stated that up to three enemy divisions could be diverted from the Pusan Perimeter to help defend the Seoul area without impairing his ability to defend around the Perimeter.

Appleman disputed this estimate. The *13th Division,* COL Lee Hak Ku, its chief of staff, claimed it had 2,300 men plus another 2,000 untrained and unarmed replacements. Eighth Army estimated the *13th* had 8,000 men. The *NK 15th Division* "numbered no more than a few hundred scattered and disorganized men instead of the 7,000 men in the Eighth Army estimate," Appleman wrote. The *NK 5th Division* "was down to about 5,000 men," he wrote, instead of 6,500, and the *NK 7th Division* was down to about 4,000 men instead of the 7,600 accorded it by the Eighth Army estimate. He also wrote that the *NK 1st, 2d* and *3d Divisions* "almost certainly did not begin to approach the strength of 7,000-8,000 men each in mid-September accorded to them in the estimate." In summary, Appleman gives the North Korean Army on the Perimeter an estimated strength of "about 70,000 men" with "probably no more than 50 percent of the original equipment."

North Korean Army morale was very low. The few veterans still alive ruled recruits by instilling fear of being shot for not obeying orders or showing reluctance to advance when ordered. Food was scarce. Lack of food was the most common reason given for low morale. But desertions were rare because the men feared being killed by their captors or being shot by their own officers if they made the attempt. (By Sept. 15, Eighth and ROK Armies had captured 3,380 North Koreans.)

U.N. Strength in the Perimeter

Far East Command Situation Report for Sept. 16, 1950 gave these strength figures for major U.N. commands in the Perimeter:

U.S. Eighth Army	84,478
U.S. I Corps (plus 1,110 KATUSAs)	7,475
U.S. 1st Cavalry Division (plus 2,338 KATUSAs)	13,904
U.S. 24th Infantry Division (plus 2,786 KATUSAs)	16,356
U.S. 2d Infantry Division (plus 1,821 KATUSAs)	15,191
U.S. 25th Infantry Division (plus 2,447 KATUSAs)	15,334
British 27th Infantry Brigade	1,693
ROK Army	72,730

Appleman pointed out that the assigned strength of the U.S. divisions did not accurately show the number of men in the rifle companies, "the men who actually did the fighting," as he put it. Some rifle companies had no more then 50 effectives — about 25% strength. Others, although of somewhat greater strength, were in bad shape. A 100-man company cannot perform a combat mission as effectively as one of 150 or more men. Many of the rifle companies fell into this 100-man category. It was about this time that young Korean recruits began being attached to U.S. forces. In the 25th Division, the basis was 90 KATUSAs per rifle company and 40 per firing battery of artillery. Since a full strength rifle company numbered 205 officers and enlisted men, the fact that KATUSAs were attached at the rate of 90 per rifle company gives one an idea how low in strength these units were at the time.

Both the North and South Korean divisions were low in combat effectiveness due to losses of personnel and equipment.

In summary, the records show an estimated North Korean Army strength along the Perimeter of about 70,000 and the U.N. divisional strength of about 130,000. But, since the logistical and service support portion of U.S. divisions was greater than that of the enemy, the actual front line strength was much lower. One must also remember that the North Koreans had retained the initiative. That is, they were "calling the shots" and the Perimeter defenders were still in the position of counterpunching — reacting to the enemy's action. While the U.N. had superior numbers of infantry, its margin of superiority in armor, artillery and air support was huge — particularly in air power. The enemy had none. And, of course, the North Koreans had no sea presence at all. The U.N. completely ruled the sea around Korea.

One must give the North Korean leadership high marks for their dogged determination to break through the Perimeter. They came again and again, absorbing horrible casualties. Their troops fought very hard, giving their all. They were tough battle opponents.

25th Infantry Division — Sept. 11-26

Fighting in rear of the 35th continued long after the bulk of the enemy had been ejected from the 25th Division's rear areas. At times, units outside of the regiment were called upon to help wipe out these pesky enemy pockets. On Sept.

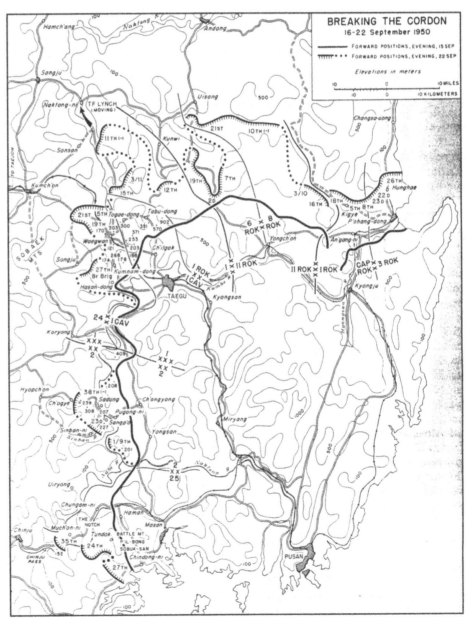

Map 49 (Source: South to the Naktong*)*

14, for example, B/65th ECC was called upon by COL Fisher, commanding the 35th, to attack and take a hill near Chungam-ni. E/35th had attacked the hill three times without success. The engineers had but two hours to prepare for their attack. Fire support was given by nearby infantry plus two heavy .30-cal machine guns from the engineer battalion. It was all over in a half hour, with Co. B on the hill. The cost had been high, with the loss of 14 KIA and 21 WIA. This included one officer killed and one wounded. The 3d Platoon was particularly hard hit, losing the platoon sergeant wounded, two squad leaders killed and another wounded and three assistant squad leaders wounded. The platoon numbered only 13 men at the end of the fight. As a result, it could not be given platoon missions until receiving replacements some five or six weeks later.

GEN Barth wrote of the severe artillery ammunition shortage which prevailed on the eve of and during the time of the ordered breakout. The artillery was "limited to 25 rounds of 105mm and 40 rounds of 155mm ammunition per gun per day. There was also a serious shortage of mortar ammunition," he wrote, "particularly for the big 4.2 inch mortars. It was, therefore, decided to make strong attacks on narrow frontages each day in order to give maximum fire support to each attack while remaining within the ammunition ration for the day. (See Chapter Notes.)

The first attacks were to be on the front of the 35th Infantry to the north, with succeeding days' attacks progressing southward along the line.

Elements of the 25th began their attack at 6:30 a.m. on Sept. 16. But tactical air support had to be canceled due to bad weather. However, C/27th Infantry did advance some 1,000 yards against stubborn resistance. F and G/27th also took the objectives against heavy resistance, then had to be withdrawn for another mission.

At 7:15 a.m. that day, 3/24th Infantry attacked to restore their former positions in the mountains. By 3 p.m., one company reported capturing its initial objective, but was halted by enemy automatic weapons fire from the front and flank. Another company was stalled after having moved forward a hard-fought 300 yards. A patrol got to the summit of the battalion objective but was forced back.

L/27th, meantime, was on the defensive, beating off several enemy attacks that day.

The 25th Division was still fighting major battles in its rear areas, as well as seemingly stronger enemy forces on Battle Mountain, Pilbong and Sobuk-san. GEN Kean and his staff realized that the division could not launch a full scale counterattack until the enemy was brought under control on the high ground in the 24th Infantry's sector. Kean did not want a repeat of his TF Kean experience, when large forces of the enemy in his rear caused severe problems. The failure of 3/24th infantry proved that the 24th needed help to eject the enemy from Battle Mountain and Pil-bong. On Sept. 16, therefore, Kean organized Task Force Woolfolk, named for MAJ Robert L. Woolfolk, C.O., 3/35th Infantry. OPORD #4, Sept. 17, 1950 was issued to organize the task force and give it the mission. The force consisted of A/27th Infantry, I/35th Infantry, B/65th ECC, 1st Plat., C/65th ECC, and a

tank platoon. The 25th Recon Co. and 3/24th's Heavy Weapons Co. gave support.

PFC Harold R. Brannon, I/35th, was wounded on Sept. 16. "When the bullet hit," he wrote, "it was like 20,000 volts had just entered my body. I remember rolling, crashing and tumbling down the hill 'till a small tree or plant stopped me. It was then I felt this intense burning pain. I thought my entire arm and shoulder had been blown off because I had no feeling in that area of my body." A medic quickly arrived and treated Brannon, who confessed to "screaming in pain at the top of my lungs." His heart "was pounding in such a manner that I feared that I was going into shock."

TF Woolfolk attacked at 1:35 P.M. on Sept. 17, with the mission of restoring the 3/24th Infantry positions. The 8th and 90th FABs provided heavy artillery support and numerous air strikes supported the task force. Enemy resistance was stubborn, stopping the task force. In the first 24 hours, A/27th Infantry lost 57 men. I/35th Infantry could not gain its objective and consolidate. On Sept. 19 TF Woolfolk was dissolved.

SGT Philip File, 2d Platoon and Frank Sandell, 4th Platoon, both of A/27th Infantry took part in this attack. These are their recollections:

File's 2d Platoon led Co. A. I/35th Infantry would attack up a ridge on A Company's left. When File's platoon secured the crest of its hill, known as the "Crow's Nest," 1st Platoon of Co. A was to pass through, cross a saddle into some woods and make contact with I/35th Infantry. Simultaneously with this, 3/A Company was to move up on File's right flank and the 4th (Weapons) Platoon was to come up in the rear. The 2d Platoon with its new replacements numbered 36 men, File recalled. "We suffered two wounded going up the hill and succeeded in killing and driving off all the enemy in our zone of operation."

"Pop" Aracid, "a forty-two year old Filipino who had been busted from MSG for decking a major who had a disagreement with him," File wrote, "led the assault as coolly as if he was at Ft. Benning." On the final approach to the objective, Aracid had to scale a 12 foot cliff to reach the top. He paused just before going over the top and tossed two grenades underhanded over his head onto the Crow's Nest. As they exploded, he finished his climb. File, noticing enemy bullets striking the rocks near Aracid, discovered their source and silenced the enemy gun. The platoon quickly followed and spread out over the objective. Digging in the rocky soil was impossible, so the men hastily piled up rocks to form small revetments.

Sandell's 57mm recoilless rifle squad was in the attack. "Going up the mountain it was kind of a mess," he said. "There were a few bodies here and there. There was a lot of debris; blankets, weapons, ammunition laying all over the place." Once they got to the top, he recalled, "It was nothing but rocks and cliffs," he said. "There was almost just a one-line path going through there. We couldn't flank out, it was just a movement one [man] after one [man] getting into position.... We took up our position with our 57 to his [the platoon leader's] right flank slightly to the rear."

It was getting dark when the 1st Platoon arrived on the hill. Contact with units of the 35th and 24th Infantry on the flanks had been lost.

"We could see movement in the thick woods on the hill across the saddle [where the 1st Platoon was to contact I/35th]. "CPT [John L.] Buckley [CO, Co. A] surmised that must be [the 35th]," File said. "I expressed my doubts but was overruled." The 1st Platoon headed for the woods. As soon as they got there "a brisk fire fight broke out," said File, "and men of the 1st Platoon, accompanied by NK troops, began coming back across the saddle. Confusion reigned."

The platoon aidman was kept busy that night with the wounded. A light rain began to fall and kept up all night. At daylight, though, File, what was left of his platoon, part of the 1st Platoon, some FOs and communications personnel still held on. Small-arms fire came from the enemy-held woods across the saddle and grenades were being exchanged at close quarters. A grenade exploded next to File. He was unhurt, but the wire section chief was killed by a fragment which cut his jugular vein. The next grenade killed a replacement, a reservist who had been recalled to active duty in July. Upon being hit, he looked up toward the sky, muttered, "Oh dear God!" and died.

File could not figure out where these grenades were coming from. He eased around a rock to look. "There was nothing but rocky, precipitous hillside seventy-five feet below me," he recounted. "Then about a hundred feet away a North Korean stepped out from behind a rock swinging a home-made sling around his head. I dropped him just before he made his throw." That stopped the grenades, but the small-arms fire from the woods was nearly overwhelming. File decided to withdraw. He went to the mortar section, where he discovered that only nine rounds were left for the unit's 60mm mortar. The Weapons Platoon leader left at this time, so File and a mortar gunner stayed to fire off these rounds.

The enemy was so close that the rounds went almost straight up. File could see them rise up into the air, start to fall tail first, then turn as the fins bit the air. "We fired all nine rounds," File said, "then a SSG named Sandlin [probably Sandell] fixed bayonets and charged back into the Crow's Nest.

"The line started pulling back just a little bit close to Buckley's headquarters," Sandell said, "and I yelled out, 'Hell we can't lose this hill! Five guys and we can hold it! Let's go — five guys!' I ended up with little more than that. We did advance. We took back what little position we had lost.... Looking around after we took it back, there were two from my squad and there were two from either the 1st or 2d Platoon, and of course myself and the four black fellows from the night before. Regardless of what I heard from the rumors prior to and what we thought about the 24th Regiment, those four were fighters.... They were good...and I respected them one hell of a lot. We held all that day. The fog cleared a little bit."

The men found a .30-caliber water-cooled machine gun which had been jammed. One of them got the gun unjammed and began using it on the enemy. "He used insect repellent to lubricate the damned thing," Sandell recalled, "and he got it going. About that time, the fog had lifted and we could see the other mountain top. It couldn't have been but 100 yards to our front and he had a field day playing with that thing until he got hit." Sandell thought the man was awarded a medal for this action. "The kid did a hell of a job," Sandell remembered. "He did expose himself and...laid down a lot of fire."

The machine gun fire broke up groups of enemy forming to come forward, but not those who were exchanging grenades with Sandell and his comrades. The enemy and Americans were too close for rifle fire, but grenades flew back and forth. Sandell had to send back for more grenades. Toward evening, orders came to withdraw. On the way back, enemy mortar fire caught them withdrawing and SFC Banks and CPL Needham coming forward. CPL Needham was badly hit, losing an arm and a leg. There were two men named Needham in Co. A at the time — H.L. and R. Sandell did not indicate which one it was. At the bottom of the hill, he discovered that CPL Lookingbill had been accidentally shot by another GI. The corporal died before he could be evacuated.

B/27th Infantry had, all in all, an easier time from Sept. 10 to the 19. But there were some significant losses. MSG Sam Bass, an outstanding NCO, was killed by an anti-personnel mine. Periodically, the enemy fired mortar concentrations on the company's position. One of these came in as the unit, a few men at a time was going through a chow line well on the reverse side of the hill. Once a man went through the line, he moved away. Some of them went back to their foxholes; others just some distance away and also some distance from other soldiers who were eating their meal. A mortar round landed near the line, killing one man. His body was moved aside; the chow line moved a little faster.

Another time, after dark, another mortar concentration came in while one of the platoon leaders was checking his platoon. He and another man dove into a small bunker, already occupied by two other men. The four men crouched in the cramped space — two enlisted men, then the officer and finally, the man who had jumped into the hole with him. This man was closest to the bunker entrance. The four were more or less lying against or on one another. Several mortar rounds landed close by, but the barrage soon quit. The lieutenant nudged the man next to him who was closest to the entrance. He got no response. The man was dead, but no wound could be found. On closer examination, a tiny drop of blood was discovered just forward of his left ear. A needle-sized piece of mortar fragment had entered there and on into his brain. He died instantly. If the man had tilted his helmet to cover the left ear instead of the right, he would not have been hurt at all.

It was in this position that Co. B received its first contingent of KATUSAs. These poor men were bewildered and most seemed lost. They were paired off with GIs in each squad. Their numbers almost doubled the strength of each of the rifle platoons. The 1st Platoon leader wanted to add one of the KATUSAs to the platoon command group. He and the platoon sergeant conferred. Both had noted one KATUSA who, almost immediately upon being assigned, began cleaning his carbine. Noting this, both men thought he might make a pretty good soldier. Questioning soon revealed that he could speak and understand English. Of course, he also was familiar with Japanese and Korean. From that moment on Kim Ha Ok became the platoon interpreter. Later in the war, it was discovered that he also able to interpret Chinese. Kim was still with the platoon when the platoon leader rotated home in late May 1951. (See Chapter Notes.)

During the time that the 5th RCT and later, the 27th Infantry, occupied the southern part of the 25th Division's sector on the Perimeter, the U.S. Navy stationed a small ship just off the coast but close enough to fire into or forward of the regimental lines. The ship was armed with either 5 inch or 6 inch guns. Every night, it would periodically fire parachute flares. The ship also was available to fire conventional ammunition in support of the defense. CPL David W. Bradley, who served in HHC, 2/27 and E/27, recalled the ship "firing its guns. Some of the rounds really seemed close going overhead and landing on the other side of the hill.... They made a heavy whooshing sound [as they passed overhead]." The flares were very large, providing bright light over a larger area than similar type rounds from the Division's field artillery.

"At noon on Sept. 16th, the 2nd Plt G Co. was called and told to get ready to move out," wrote Daniel Cooper, a BAR-man in the unit. "They took our Plt and added some extra BARs and a 57 recoilless rifle. We also had a 300 radio set." On the day of the patrol which the platoon was to make, a young, new lieutenant arrived. He announced to the platoon that he was to be in charge of the patrol, but that the sergeant should take complete charge since he (the lieutenant) wasn't even an Infantry officer and he would go along as an infantryman. The platoon was in a diamond formation as it moved out. It was misting rain, then began to rain in earnest. The men tried to shield their weapons. The 57 gunner stuffed a sock into the barrel of the gun. Along the way, the patrol found a group of dead American soldiers, their hands tied behind their backs. The patrol was to advance over seven ridges, then dig in on the seventh and wait for the rest of the battalion to catch up.

As the patrol traversed the sixth ridge "our part of the world blew up in our face," Cooper wrote. "The North Koreans were on the seventh ridge and opened up on us at point blank range with at least three machine guns, rifles and 120 mortars. All the automatic weapons survived the first shots and made it back to the top. I was on the left and all the other BARs were on the right. The 57 rifle was the first to fire...only [the gunner] forgot to take the sock out of the barrel. The 57 blew up, killing the gunner and loader. PFC Woolf set up his .30-cal machine gun and I don't think he even fired a shot, when he was hit...." This was the fifth time in two and a half months that Woolf was wounded.

The other BAR-men were quickly hit by enemy machine gun fire or 120mm mortars. "I was firing my BAR a whole clip at a time and while firing the third clip a 120 mortar fell right at my feet," wrote Cooper. "From the time the first shot was fired until now, it had been less than a minute. All the automatic weapons were out of action and [the men] either killed or badly wounded. I was lying in a prone position when the mortar round went off and numbed my whole body. I couldn't move. At first, I was afraid to look because I thought my legs were gone. My right pant leg and right boot were gone, but my leg was still there. I didn't have any feeling, but it was a bloody mess and broken in two places. I was also shot through the stomach and neck. I took my belt off and tied it as high and tight as I could, but I still couldn't move much. None of the patrol had made it back to the top of the ridge and all the firing had stopped."

As Cooper lay there, a man ran by him, then stopped and came back. It was his foxhole buddy, PFC Barnett. "I don't remember either of us saying anything," Cooper wrote, "he just took off everything that he was carrying except his rifle, managed to get me on his shoulder and took off down the hill as fast as he could. Barnett weighed about 160 lbs. and I was 6'3" and 220 lbs. I didn't know what was in store for us, but I did know that we were going to do it together. We had been together since we landed in Pusan."

Some way, Barnett carried, pushed and pulled Cooper all the way back. Barnett was exhausted early on, and Cooper helped as best he could, but kept passing out. The two men made it back to the reverse slope of the fourth hill. There, in the valley Cooper saw "the most beautiful tanks that I had ever seen." When the following enemy came over the hill, the two tanks, joined by two machine gun jeeps "blew the whole top off that hill," Cooper wrote. A litter team came up the hill and carried him down to a jeep. "While I was laying on the jeep," he recalled, I felt someone grab my hand. I looked up and it was our new 2LT. He was standing there, holding my hand and crying. He didn't say anything, but he didn't have to, because I knew exactly what he was thinking and how he felt. I bet that he made a fine officer, but he will never forget his first day on the job."

Milton R. Olazagasti was forward observer for F/27's 60mm mortars. Peering through his binoculars about the Sept. 16 or 17, directing fire, "I suddenly heard a crack," he said, "and my eyes were full of dust. I suddenly realized that someone had fired at me...directly at me, and didn't take long for me to realize that it came from the nearby hill or it may have come from someone attacking my position. So I threw two hand grenades...." That evening, he looked around and realized that the camouflage behind his foxhole was gone. That was the reason the enemy soldier had spotted him. He moved to his alternate position for the next day's operation.

From there he was able to just as effectively direct the fire from the company's 60s. "As I was directing fire to support [Easy and George Companies], it was like a movie," he said. "You could see the guys crawling up the hills and the North Koreans would pop out and throw hand grenades down on them. And our guys were supposed to crawl up towards them. You could see a couple of hand-to-hand actions going on and at that time it was exciting." Later Olazagasti thought more about the fight. "Now I think, not only of the GIs, our guys that got killed, but then I think of the ones [enemy soldiers] that I was responsible for.... That they had mothers and fathers and brothers and sisters, wives and children. And it makes war a very, very, very sad thing. Anyone who glorifies war, I think they are probably a little bit sick."

During G/27th's advance on Sept. 18, CPL Earl Miller had a close call when he was creased on the head by an enemy bullet.

On Sept. 19, things began to move in the 25th Division zone. That morning it was discovered that the enemy had abandoned the crest of Battle Mountain. The 35th moved forward against light resistance until it reached hills in front of Chungam-ni where enemy troops hidden in spider holes shot at soldiers of the 1st Battalion from the rear. The battalion captured the town the next day and 2/35 seized the long ridge running from it north east to the Nam River. Elements of the 24th Infantry in the center advanced some 1,500 to 2,000 yards on Sept. 19 against light resistance. A prisoner from *3/14th Infantry, 6th Division*, captured on Sept. 20, said that only about 30 men remained behind on Pil-bong. On Sept. 21, the 35th captured the old Notch area three miles southwest of Chungam-ni then advanced another eight air miles to the west without resistance on to the high ground of the Chinju Pass.

In the south, however, the 27th found hard going on Sept. 19 and 20. Between 17 and 19 September, the regiment lost 13 KIA, 102 WIA, 16 NBC and 34 MIA. As a result, regimental strength fell to 2,596 personnel. The 27th continued its attack in the mountains on Sept. 20. After pausing that night, patrols the next day discovered that the enemy had withdrawn all across the regimental front. The attack now became a pursuit.

The enemy *7th Division* completed its withdrawal north across the Nam River by the morning of Sept. 19. Then the *6th* withdrew from Sobuk-san. This general withdrawal was not immediately discovered by units of the 25th Division. In fact, stubborn resistance on Sept. 19 and 20, as well as forays by parties of enemy soldiers, created the opposite impression. In one instance, on the morning of Sept. 22, a party of enemy soldiers slipped into the bivouac area of A/24th Infantry.

1LT Robert J. Tews, a platoon leader awoke to discover a North Korean standing over him. He grabbed the soldier's bayonet and grappled with him until someone else shot the man. Nearby an enemy grenade killed one man and wounded two others sleeping in a foxhole. Shortly thereafter mortar fire came in on a company commanders' meeting in the 1st Battalion CP. The commander of the HC was killed and the Battalion XO, S-1 and S-2, plus three other men were wounded.

That day, too, troops of the *6th Division* blocked the 35th Infantry's advance at the Chinju Pass. Assault companies of 1/35th advanced to within 200 yards of Hill 152 in the pass but were stopped there by enemy action.

The 1st Battalion, 27th Infantry began an attack on Sept. 19, with Co. C headed for Hill 368 and B the "Camelback." The attack continued all day. 1LT Donald F. Darnell, then commanding Co. C, was wounded in both arms, but continued to lead his unit. By 5 P.M., both units had advanced some 2,500 yards, supported by air strikes, artillery and tank fire.

The 1st Battalion, 24th Infantry made its attack on Sept. 19 at 6 A.M. LT Rishell's platoon led out Co. .A. "At daybreak we started the descent from our position and moved forward," he wrote in *With a Black Platoon in Combat*. "There was only sporadic firing as the squad moved in a coordinated skirmish line. A few isolated pockets of resistance were found, but it was not until

we reached to the top of the ridge that we discovered the enemy had withdrawn during the night...." The company moved on to the next objective, unopposed. 2/24th also attacked that day advancing to a point two miles west of Haman.

Two members of the 25th Division earned the award of the Medal of Honor on Sept. 19. One was SGT William R. Jecelin, C/35th Infantry, near Saga. First, SGT Jecelin led his platoon across rice fields and rocky terrain which was being swept by enemy mortar fire in a direct advance on enemy held high ground. Once the unit gained a cliff where intense enemy fire stopped the advance, the Sergeant stood up and moved out firing his rifle and throwing grenades and calling on his men to follow. The troops surged forward, gained the crest of the objective, but were then forced to seek cover from enemy fire.

Again, Jecelin rallied the men and, with fixed bayonets, they charged the enemy in the face of strong antitank fire. The battle became hand-to-hand. Ejecting the enemy, the unit was then forced to take cover from an enemy SP gun. Once more, Jecelin led the men in a further attack. Just then, a well-camouflaged enemy soldier threw a grenade at the platoon. Jecelin immediately jumped on the grenade and absorbed the force of its explosion with his own body. By his action, he saved the lives of a number of men nearby.

In Co. C, 27th Infantry, it was CPL John W. Collier near Chindong-ni. He, too, sacrificed himself to save the lives of his comrades. CPT Burnett, commanding Co. C at the time, recalled CPL Collier as "a quiet, likable boy of 19 or 20 whom I classified as an average soldier." As he recalled the incident, Collier worked his way up this cliff, and although wounded, knocked out the enemy machine gun, killing at least four of the enemy. "Thinking the position had been cleared of the enemy, [he] waved the rest of the squad forward," Burnett wrote. "As the men came up...an unseen North Korean threw a large fragmentation grenade into their midst. Without hesitation, Collier threw his body over the grenade which exploded, killing him. This utterly selfless act of his cost him his life, but undoubtedly saved the lives of several comrades." (See Chapter Notes.)

The 27th Infantry continued the attack on Sept. 20. Both B and C Companies received some heavy enemy fire prior to the jump off time of 7 A.M. SP fire, striking the forward elements of Co. B, which were in and on a large outcropping of large rocks. wounded the company commander, CPT Jung in three places, including a head wound. This fire also killed or wounded a number of other men, including 2LT James R. Wilson, a rifle platoon leader, who received a gash to his cheek. Rock fragments destroyed the FO's radio.

Just at this time 2LT John S. York, another officer of the company, came up the hill from the rear. The leader of the reserve platoon, who was the senior officer, placed York in command of the reserve platoon. Then, moving forward, he assumed command of the company. He obtained a 30 minute delay in starting the attack, utilizing the time to assess losses and reorganize. The FO radio had been the only radio contact

with higher headquarters. Now, the only means of communication, except runners, was a single telephone line to battalion.

As it turned out, CPT Jung was not seriously wounded and returned to the company within two weeks. In recalling the incident, Jung wrote, "[The] N.K.s made a mistake; the SP shrapnel hit me in the head, so I was only out one week."

The company began its attack about 7:30 A.M., making good progress, with little opposition until it came to a ridge on the left which connected with a parallel ridge to the west. The connecting ridge was devoid of any vegetation and went up and down in a series of small knobs and small swales between each. There was no concealment and the only protection from enemy fire could be found in these little swales. The lead squad started out onto the connecting ridge. Almost immediately, it came under fire from two to three enemy machine guns from the ridge across the way and an SP gun way down in the valley to the left (north). The squad leader alertly threw out a WP grenade, which created just enough smoke to conceal the squad as they withdrew.

As it turned out, three enemy machine guns, concealed in rock bunkers, covered the top and both flanks of the connecting ridge. The northern flank of this ridge was also covered by an SP gun. Company 60 mortars were ineffective and no 81 or 4.2 inch mortars, nor artillery were available. Finally, the acting company commander was able to get an air strike, but this was a big disappointment. The "strike" was by a light bomber, which dropped a load of parachute fragmentation bombs. They exploded harmlessly on the enemy-held hill. The stone-built bunkers protected the enemy soldiers.

Don Cable of the 1st Platoon, Co. B, recalled the day. "After an air strike by F-51s we assaulted along the ridge. Despite the air strike some enemy were still dug in. Individual enemy [soldiers] would pop up, toss several grenades at us at once and pop down again. Someone had a flamethrower. I can still see Curtis Cook with his BAR aimed at the spot where a gook had stood up to throw grenades. Sure enough, in a moment the gook popped up again and Curtis shot him. We secured that hill. We moved then to a hill where we were pinned down for a time. We called in an air strike by light bombers (similar to a B-25 but with a single vertical stabilizer) that strafed and then dropped parachute bombs. I recalled thinking that the parachutes were leaflets and asking myself and all within hearing what could they be thinking of to drop leaflets at a time like that."

At one point after the enemy stopped Co. B with their machine guns and SP fire, the Battalion XO called and asked the acting company commander, "If they can see to shoot at you why can't you see to shoot at them?" The range was several hundred yards; the enemy used smokeless powder and the enemy guns were concealed within bunkers built of stone.

Co. B dug in for the night, but the acting CO got permission to make a pre-dawn attack across the ridge. About 4 or 5 A.M., Baker Company moved out and took the enemy ridge without opposition. The enemy had no doubt departed some time after darkness fell. The Battalion XO came up to Co. B at this time and the acting CO showed him the enemy bunkers and said, "This is why we couldn't see them."

From Sept. 20 on for the next several days, it was a pursuit.

Meantime, that day, Co. C advanced to the base of its objective, but was halted there by enemy fire. At 9:15 A.M., E and G Companies began their attack, making good progress until stopped by strong enemy fire about 11 A.M. At about 2 P.M., Co. E made a bayonet and grenade assault, routing the enemy from the objective. King Co., attacking southwest about 11:30 A.M., to help the 1st Battalion, was stopped after advancing a few hundred yards. Heavy enemy fire forced it back to its start point. However, by the end of the day all regimental objectives had been taken. But Co. C having suffered heavy casualties, was ordered to withdraw and form a defensive position with Co. A.

On Sept. 21 the regiment advanced some 6,000 yards to the southwest. The 27th was swinging southwest, following roughly the same route toward Paedun-ni and Sachon that the Marines had used in TF Kean. Paedun-ni fell to the regiment by 11:30 A.M. on Sept. 23. On the 24th, the regiment, less its 1st Battalion, moved to an assembly area near Chungam-ni to prepare to cross the Nam River. The 1st Battalion remained at Paedun-ni, joining the rest of the regiment on Sept. 25.

At 4 A.M. on Sept. 26 1/27th Infantry crossed the Nam River. Companies A and C went across in boats. Co. B attacked by wading across. Artillery fire supported the battalion attack. Co. B was to have crossed on an underwater footbridge. No one knew exactly where this footbridge was located. As a result, the acting company commander sent men up and down the river looking for it in the dark. Moments before 4 A.M., the attack time, it was found. But so many sandbags were missing from it that the "bridge" was actually a hazard.

The acting commander, close to the front of the company column in the crossing, stepped off the bridge to discover that the river was not much deeper, anyway. The whole company followed suit. The taller men rescued the shorter ones, including the KATUSAs, when they stepped into a hole over their heads. The far shore was deadly quiet as the unit waded slowly forward. Finally, the first man made it to shore, then another and another. There was no enemy. The plan of attack called for the 1st Platoon to split off at this point and head for a small hill some distance to the right of the line of march. The remainder of the company headed for a village farther inland.

The CO stood at the river bank until all of the 1st Platoon had passed on its way, then made his way to the head of the remainder of the company. The unit arrived above the village, its objective just before dawn. Suddenly a high volume of automatic and small-arms fire broke out on the 1st Platoon's objective. The platoon leader soon reported the hill secure. The platoon, it seemed, silently arrived on the objective and waited for the enemy to come out of his bunkers and holes at daylight. When they did, the platoon cut them all down in one brisk, short burst of fire.

Don Cable, with the 1st Platoon, wrote: "The squad walked onto a small knoll and found several foxholes around a mound. It turned out that these were the entrances to a bunker. Pee Wee

[Thompson] and I walked away from the mound. Shots from the area of the bunker. Roy Ward yelled, 'Hey, Cable, I got a wounded gook up here.' I went to him. He pointed to a man lying on the ground. I fired several rounds at the man's head. Pee Wee and I [then] moved away from the mound again. I saw what I thought was a hut against a tree. I whispered to Pee Wee to cover me. I fired a couple of rounds into the hut. Heard a scurrying sound. I fired more shots. More scurrying. Pee Wee and I both fired into the hut. Still the scurrying sound. The "hut" was a stack of rice sacks leaning against the tree. The scurrying sound was rice running out of holes in the sack [made by our bullets].

"Come daylight I took a Tokarev pistol, compass, some wallets and pens, taken from Americans, from the body of the gook on the ground — the one I had shot in the head. He was a [North] Korean Arty FO."

Meantime, with the coming of daylight, the men above the village noted the large number of Korean men wandering around its streets in civilian clothing. A platoon was sent down and rounded them all up — perhaps fifty or more. 1SG Hearn shouted out something which sounded like a command in Japanese. As he did so, the entire group of Korean men, to the amazement of the GIs, lined up in military formation. This gave them away. They were all North Korean soldiers, trying to disguise themselves in civilian clothing. They were all searched, then sent back to work on a bridge across the Nam River.

Also, while on the hill above the village, the CO saw what he believed to be a small enemy artillery piece or AT gun sitting in the middle of a road going over a hill off in the distance. It appeared that the "gun" was aimed at the company. Several other men examined the "gun" with field glasses and agreed that's what it was. Accordingly, one of the company recoilless rifles fired. The "gun" turned out to be a Korean cart, which was blown to pieces by the first round.

The 2d Battalion followed the 1st across the Nam at 5:15 a.m., then went on to expand the bridgehead. At 7 a.m. B/65th ECB began constructing a sandbag bridge of the river. Civilian laborers, enemy prisoners and ingenuity went into its construction. Some 38,000 sandbags were used to span the 600 foot stream.

Sept. 26 marked the date that the breakout started for the 27th infantry.

Meantime, the 24th in the center and the 35th also moved to the attack. The 24th attacked on Sept. 20. A/24th was part of this attack. The company objective was a road junction. Co. A was to take and hold this point until the rest of the regiment could pass through. As LT Rishell's platoon started down the slope toward its objective, small sized enemy mortar rounds began to fall on his advancing men. At first Rishell was not concerned about this fire; it was doing little damage. But then the fire increased in intensity and accuracy.

The platoon now had to cross a wide area of open, but muddy, ground to attain the junction. Once there, the platoon had to climb a nearby hill in order to control the objective. There was no other approach except across that open ground. The platoon began advancing across this area and the mortar fire began more intense. The

men began to bunch up. Rishell, Platoon Sergeant Nollie and the squad leaders yelled at the men to spread out and keep moving. One unlucky round could take out a number of men if they bunched up. The mud was deep and the men's boots became giant suction cups that held one's legs in place. It was exhausting work just to try to walk across this quagmire.

Suddenly, three mortar rounds landed directly to his front. Although the lead squad, which he was following, was spread out, the three rounds landed just far enough apart to knock out all eight or nine men. Although the rounds, landing in mud, drilled into the ground somewhat before exploding, this time, it did not save these unlucky soldiers. Other rounds now began to hit other men of the platoon. Some of them tried to take shelter in a river bed, but the mortaring followed them there. The medics had more casualties than they could treat. Some soldiers stopped to help comrades out of the mud. "How we managed to survive I don't know," he wrote, "but when we reached the top of the hill, the enemy had cut and run, and we collapsed on the ground...."

On Sept. 22 Rishell's men attacked again. The objective lay at the top of a very steep hill, covered with woods of bamboo-like trees. The men were soon near exhaustion. Those ahead often reached a hand back to help the man following. They had to pull themselves up laboriously by pulling themselves along from one bamboo trunk to the next. Suddenly, an enemy whistle blew and grenades began to rain down from above. Some of the men responded by firing wildly up the slope. Holding onto a tree with one hand, they fired their rifles with the other.

Rishell recalled that the din of small-arms fire and exploding grenades became deafening. Fortunately, most grenades exploded behind and below the men. It took three hours to inch up this steep hill. The men's legs were like leaden weights. Rishell was now too exhausted even to call encouragement to his men. Near the top, he lobbed a grenade over the crest, then another. Enemy fire stopped for a moment, and he stumbled to his feet. Then he saw a large shell hole. In it were an enemy officer and two enlisted men, all mortally wounded by grenade fragments. Rishell shot all three to put them out of their misery. Meantime, his men were shooting down other enemy soldiers who were running to escape. The few who tried to fight back were instantly cut down.

On Sept. 24, Rishell wrote, an armored task force passed through the regimental position and attacked south and west. The breakout had commenced for the 24th.

The A and B/35th took Hill 152 in the Chinju Pass area on Sept. 23. At dawn on Sept. 24 it became obvious that the enemy had withdrawn. The next day, infantrymen of the 2d and 3d Battalions of the 35th crossed the Nam River meeting on the far side beyond Chinju.

The advance of the 35th to the Nam River on the 25th was not without some casualties. One of these was CPL Jack J. Gates Sr., F/35th, who was shot in the right arm. Apparently, a number of suspected enemy soldiers were spotted in the open. Gates and his comrades were ordered not to fire at them. But the enemy soldiers opened fire, hitting Gates and several other men.

The bridge over the Nam River had been destroyed and the 35th was held up there on Sept. 25. The Nam River at Chinju was 300 feet wide and about 6 feet deep. The current was swift. CPT Richard F. McAdoo's A/65th ECB, supporting the 35th, was called upon to bridge the river there. McAdoo was West Point, 1947. Downstream from the bridge site was a ford suitable for tracked vehicles. There, TF Torman crossed the Nam. The wheeled vehicles of the force were towed across by tanks and a D7 dozer. (Note: TFs Torman, Dolvin, Blair and other commands formed for the breakout will be discussed in the next chapter.)

At 4 p.m. on Sept. 25, McAdoo recalled being faced with the responsibility of bridging the Nam in a hurry. First, he had only two platoons available; his 3d Platoon was with TF Torman. Second, he was short of material with which to build a bridge, some timbers and two truckloads of 3x12 inch wooden decking. Luckily, a unit recon party found 15 steel sections of what was known as sheet piling each 50 feet long, in the stream close to the bridge site. Another recon party located a large stock of timbers suitable for bridging just two miles from the site. Unfortunately, the road was clogged with traffic. Even with GEN Barth's help near the bridge site, it was a six hour round trip to and from the timber location. Although the engineer trucks had priority, five of these hours were consumed because of the road congestion.

The engineers used the steel pilings. As darkness set in, they worked with the aid of truck headlights. The river bottom was sand, making it very difficult to anchor any bridge to the bottom. To solve the problem 12x12 inch timbers 14 feet long were drift-pinned together on top of one another to form intermediate supports. This rig would not last long, but then it didn't have to. Since the bridge was just above water level, it was easy to float the supports out to position, set them vertically and attach the stringers. The company used the steel pilings as stringers, on 40-foot centers for the first three bridge spans. The remaining stringers were of either 6x12 inch or 12x12 inch timbers, varying from 15 to 20 feet long.

With only 140 pieces of decking material available (20% of what was needed), McAdoo decided to lay just two treads, one 2 feet wide and another 3 feet wide. The treads were spaced to accommodate a jeep, but with just 2 inches of leeway on the inside of each tread. The 2 1/2-ton trucks had no difficulty in crossing, but the wider ammunition trailers could just make it with their tires on the outside edge of each tread. To help prevent accidents, the engineers put in small curbings. The bridge capacity was estimated at 20 tons.

While the engineer company worked on the bridge, itself, 500 Korean civilians helped prepare approaches. Everything available was used as fill, even rubble. And 15 mines had to be removed from the approach on the far side of the river. But within 20 hours of starting, vehicles were moving across the bridge. Trucks were spaced out 50 feet apart and closely watched as each one drove slowly over the bridge. "It was both fearful and wonderful to watch the give in those steel-pile stringers," McAdoo wrote in his "Improvised Bridge," article in *Combat Support*

in Korea by John G. Westover, Combat Forces Press, 1955.

A/65th Engineers had to go with the 35th. C/65th took over the bridge, reinforcing it with additional sandbags at the base of the intermediate supports and adding more intermediate bracings — while traffic was crossing. The bridge remained in operation about 10 days, long enough to allow major elements of the 25th Division to cross the Nam River at Chinju.

2d Infantry Division — Sept. 14 - 20

The enemy still confronted the 2d Division, north of the 25th Division in mid-September. Although many of the enemy had withdrawn back across the Naktong, fighting continued east of the river. In one of these battles on Sept. 14, Ronald Peters, of B/9th Infantry was wounded. He returned to his unit on Oct. 12, to be wounded again Nov. 8.

On Sept. 15 strong enemy probing attacks on the flanks of the 2d Division were repulsed. An enemy battalion, supported by tanks, struck at 1/38th Infantry and an enemy company attack part of the 9th Infantry. North Korean artillery and mortar fire fell throughout the division sector.

Three days previous to this, the 2d Division received the Eighth Army order to attack to achieve a breakthrough. The plan called for the command to attack to the west. The 38th RCT in the north was to attack across the Naktong and hold a bridgehead. Meantime the 23d Infantry was to attack in the center. In the south, the 9th Infantry was to seize Hill 201, then support the attack of the 23d Infantry. The 2d ECB was division reserve, while the Ivanhoe Security Force, under MAJ Jack T. Young, secured Changnyong and cleared the enemy from the area east of the town.

The 72d Tk Bn was attached out to the infantry for the forthcoming offensive. Battalion HQ and Co. A were attached to the 38th Infantry, Co. B to the 9th RCT and Co. C (CPT James R Dew) to the 23d.

LTC McMains' 3/9th Infantry and the regimental Tank Co. returned to the regiment about this time. The battalion was close to full strength. On Sept. 15, 3/23d Infantry also rejoined its parent regiment. These were welcome and powerful additions to the two regiments. Both had been badly reduced in strength fighting in the Second Bulge.

The attack was set to begin at 7 A.M. on Sept. 16, preceded by air strikes. Because of bad weather, the strikes were never made and a saturation bombing of enemy positions in the Waegwan area was also canceled. Due to the shortage of artillery ammunition, the division was making its attack with less artillery support than it would have had. Since the air strikes were also canceled, the 2d Division sent an urgent message to Eighth Army to increase the allocation of artillery ammunition to help offset the lack of air support.

The 9th, supported by LTC John Keith's 15th FAB, began its attack on Hill 201. It fought hard, suffering numerous casualties, but was unable to dislodge the enemy. The 3/9th lost its XO, MAJ William Frazier, KIA. Platoon Leader Julius W. Becton Jr. was wounded in three places.

A savage enemy attack on C/23d Infantry in the pre-dawn hours of Sept. 16 left 25 men down, including all the company officers and 1LT Carl J. Johnson, leader of a machine gun platoon. A section of this platoon was attached to C/23d. The section lost 2 KIA and 4 WIA in the action.

COL Freeman had assigned the main attack of the regiment to his 3d Battalion. In spite of the enemy's predawn assault on Co. C, LTC Robert G. Sherrard Jr.'s 3/23d led the regimental attack on time, as planned. At first, the attack was unsuccessful. Then Sherrard ordered his battalion to attack at 10 A.M., supported by C/72d Tk Bn. The enemy fought stubbornly and successfully until mid-afternoon, when he began to pull out. To capitalize on this success, a task force, consisting of the 23d Tk Co. and B/82d AA Battalion was formed to cut off the enemy. From 4 P.M. until darkness cut off visibility, the tank and tremendous volume of machine gun and 40mm fire from the automatic weapons company cut down large numbers of the enemy along the Naktong. Baker Battery fired 10,000 rounds of .50-caliber and 640 rounds of 40mm ammunition that day.

The enemy on Hill 201 had been the hold-up for both the 9th and 23d. 1LT Stephen E. Gray, commanding 3d Platoon, L/23d Infantry distinguished himself that day. He led his platoon, first to take the initial objective under intense enemy fire and resistance. In this action he destroyed one enemy machine gun and helped to eliminate a group of 60 enemy soldiers. Reorganizing his platoon, he led it on to the next objective, more heavily defended than the first. Shell fragments hit the binoculars hanging around his neck, but Gray pressed on with his platoon. The assault routed the enemy. For the attack on a third objective, Gray was given some tanks. With them and his infantrymen, he took this final objective for the day, resulting in the rupture of the enemy's defense line in that area. In all, his actions accounted for some 100 enemy dead and wounded, the destruction of three enemy mortars, two fortified machine gun positions and one field piece. He was awarded the DSC.

BAR-man Charles A. McCave was in the L Company attack that day. About a half hour after the attack started, he was on the left flank of the unit with his BAR "and there was quite a gap between me and the ones on my left," he wrote. There should have been a rifleman closer on his left, to support him, but there wasn't. "We had gone over our first ridge," he continued, "and I had by-passed a [North Korean] foxhole too far on my left [for me to notice] and was down in the ravine below when they [the enemy] opened fire on me with a burp gun. I got hit in the finger and through [my] shoe. The [bullets] hit all around me like I was shot at with a load of buckshot." McCave's wounds were apparently not serious enough for him to be evacuated, but he was struck by shell fragments in the spring of 1951.

The 1/23d also attacked that morning. Bill Glasgow's Co. B, he wrote, made a "Near Perfect Attack" that day. (Article, *Infantry School Quarterly*, 1952.) Support for Co. B included a 30 minute artillery preparation, an air strike (which actually came the dusk of the day before), AA fire and mortars, plus an attached tank platoon. The objective was an enemy-held hill about 1,500 yards across rice paddies and a lower intervening hill. A dry stream bed off to the left of the route of attack passed within about 300-400 yards to the left flank of the objective, as one viewed it from Co. B's position. The plan was for the 3d and 2d Platoons to move out, in that order in platoon columns across the paddies to strike the left flank of the objective. The tanks were to move along the dry stream bed as the infantry moved through the paddies. A rifle platoon from A/23d was to move with the tanks to give them close-in protection from enemy infantry. The B's 1st Platoon was in reserve.

The air strike came in about 5 P.M. on Sept. 15. Three F-51s worked over the enemy hill with napalm and machine gun fire. Grass and underbrush on the hill were set afire. At 6:30 A.M. the following morning artillery fire, joined by that of the .50-caliber machine guns and twin-40s of the supporting AA unit began pounding the enemy. Then the 81mm and 60mm mortars and 75mm and 57mm recoilless rifles joined in. At 7 A.M., the tank platoon and the 2d and 3d Platoons of Co. B all attacked. The platoons moved as planned. To everyone's surprise, there was no enemy mortar or artillery fire on the advancing infantrymen. The tanks, now in position on the flank of the enemy hill, began firing on it. When the lead elements of Co. B reached a point about 100 yards from the objective, the artillery fire was lifted and the mortar fire was shifted to the right half of the objective.

For the assault, the two platoons came abreast and formed a long skirmish line. In the 2d Platoon, the leader employed only his 1st and 2d Squads on the line, followed by the Weapons Squad. He had the 3d Squad follow as a reserve. The left half of the objective was taken without trouble.

The 3d Platoon halted and the 1st and 2d Squads of the 2d Platoon began firing on the right half of the objective. The Weapons Squad moved up to add its firepower, but the 3d Rifle Squad was not yet committed. The 2d Platoon leader then signaled the 3d Platoon leader and the 3d Platoon moved out over the saddle between the two halves of the objective, firing assault fire. Mortar and AA fire was lifted, but machine gun and rifle fire from the 2d Platoon fired over the heads of the advancing skirmish line. Just before the 3d Platoon reached the hill crest, this fire ceased, but several "friendly" mortar rounds landed in their midst. The men pulled back a short distance.

The mortar rounds stopped and a grenade duel started between the men of the 3d Platoon and enemy soldiers just over the other side of the hill. The enemy began to turn the right flank of the platoon. The 3d Squad of the 2d Platoon was sent out to deal with that threat. The 2d Platoon leader then called the company commander on the radio and recommended that the 1st Platoon be committed to envelop the enemy position. The 1st Platoon attacked over a route to the right of that which the other two platoons had used. The 3d and 1st Platoon leaders were wounded. The leader of the 2d Platoon turned command of his platoon over to his sergeant and ran over to coordinate the actions of the now leaderless 1st and 3d Platoons. Both of these units were engaged in a hand grenade and small-arms battle with the enemy. Now enemy mortars en-

tered the fray, but some of them landed on their own men, ending the grenade battle. The Baker Co. men, on a hill without cover took shelter behind mounds of dirt, which turned out to be dead enemy soldiers with dirt heaped over them.

The enemy artillery and mortar fire was coming from the zone through which 3/23d was attacking, and soon quit. The remainder of the company displaced to the newly-won position and the men dug out a few enemy soldiers still on the hill. A prisoner said he was from the *4th Division* while most of the enemy on the hill were from the *2d Division*. They had been placed on the hill after the air strike of the previous evening. Over 60 enemy dead littered the objective. Co. B lost one killed and six wounded.

In the north, the 38th Infantry attained the southern part of the commanding ground in its sector, including Hill 209 and captured a small village just 2,000 yards short of the Naktong. That night, the *NK 2d Division* CP and its *4th, 6th* and *17th Rifle Regiments* and division artillery regiment began re-crossing the river. Their crossings continued into the following day.

The 2d Battalion, 38th Infantry assaulted Hill 209 on Sept. 16. (Described in Chapter 19.) Two M19s and an M16 of 2d Platoon, C/82d AAA/AW Battalion supported that battalion's attack. Later one of the M19s supported a tank-infantry recon patrol into enemy held territory. The 3d Battalion also attacked. Co. L, supported by an AW section of 1st Platoon, C/82d AAA/AW Battalion, led the battalion attack on Hill 208 that morning. The section's M-19, with the help of an M4 tank knocked out six enemy 76mm SP guns.

The action about to be described probably took place on the Sept. 16 or 17. Machine gunner George E. Hartley, of K Co. wrote that he had a "ringside seat" in his machine gun nest. "I was firing cover over the infantry's heads so they could advance," he wrote. "Five of our tanks were leading the way, with the infantry on both sides. Picture perfect. The lead tank got hit. [Enemy] self propelled; one shot, one tank. Set the tank on fire and the crew came pouring out. The 3d tank back got hit [by] something. Then at the crest of the mountain across the Naktong I saw the flash of the muzzle, so I directed my machinegun fire on the gun position. The 4th tank in line got hit next. Three tanks knocked out in probably 5 minutes. The 5th tank in line picked up the [enemy] gun's position. I kept firing [my] machine gun into the [enemy] position. It took 3 shots from the [tank gun]...to knock out the [enemy] gun.... But on the 3d [shot] the gunner on our tank got a direct hit. I could see the [enemy] gun and the men fly up in the air." Then an air strike came in and put the enemy to flight.

On Sept. 17, the 9th Infantry still was stalled by Hill 201. This hill, plus the enemy bridgehead nearby posed a threat to the division's flank. It had to be taken so that the 2d could get on with its offensive. Keiser gave LTC James Edwards' 2/23d to the 9th to help. But the enemy was pulling out in haste in the 23d Infantry's sector. They left behind large stocks of arms and ammunition. The regiment captured 13 artillery pieces, 6 AT guns and 4 mortars. The 38th captured 6 artillery pieces, 12 AT guns, an SP gun and 9 mortars. U.N. air attacks delivered 260

110-gallon tanks of napalm on the enemy. There was not a single enemy counterattack against the Eighth Army the entire day.

The 23d made plans to cross the Naktong and K and L, 9th Infantry managed to fight their way to within 200 yards of the crest of Hill 201. The regiment sent patrols across the river to reconnoiter. One 22-man patrol was caught by enemy fire trying to cross the Naktong. Three men were killed and another wounded. The rest of the patrol returned to the east side of the river.

Patrols from 2d and 3d Battalions, 38th Infantry crossed the Naktong near Pugong-ni, west of Changnyong on the morning of Sept. 18. They found no enemy on the high ground west of the river. COL Peploe then ordered LTC James H. Skeldon, commanding 2/38th Infantry to send two squads across the river in two-man rubber boats. A platoon was to follow, securing a bridgehead.

Peploe called Division for authority to cross the Naktong in force. At 1:20 p.m., Chief of Staff COL Gerald G. Epley gave permission to cross one battalion. Companies E and F, plus part of G crossed the 100-yard wide and 12-foot deep Naktong before 4 P.M. Thus, the battalion became the first U.N. force to cross the Naktong out of the Perimeter. By 6 p.m., the leading elements of these companies seized Hill 308 a mile west of the Naktong against light resistance. This promontory, dominating the Chogye road, fell so easily because the enemy was taken by surprise by the rapid crossing and advance of U.S. forces. From the crest of Hill 308, men could see an estimated enemy battalion about 1,000 yards to the west. For added support, LTC Skeldon asked for air cover over the bridgehead beginning a half hour after first light the following morning.

On Sept. 19, 3/38th crossed the river, along with some tanks artillery and heavy mortars. Its mission was to protect the bridgehead while the 2d Battalion pushed on against the enemy.

William Temple, I/38th Infantry, recalled his unit crossing the Naktong "in little rubber boats and...form[ed] a bridgehead.... We were not molested that night and the Engineers threw up a pontoon bridge [the next day].... The Second Division is roaring...vehicles, troops, tanks — the works — artillery, and they just bypass us."

However, a bridge was badly needed. By 5 P.M. a bridge site had been selected and every bit of bridging in the 2d Division was on its way to it.

It may have been at this bridge site where LT James F. Malone, D/2d Engineers, recalled, "as we were bridging the Naktong we had trouble getting our rope high-line for the bridge across because we kept snagging Korean bodies in the river and breaking the rope."

LT Thomas K. Voorhis, Assistant Regimental Motor Officer for the 38th, acted as "'beachmaster,' on the Naktong River when we broke out of the Perimeter," he wrote. He came under enemy fire there. "We were ferrying tanks and trucks across and were receiving some mortar fire. My job was to load vehicles according to priority set by the Regt'l CO. It took some scurrying around pounding on tank hatches to get the vehicles in position to load. I was really too busy to be too concerned with the few rounds which came in, although I ducked and took cover like everyone else if they got too close."

2LT Edward B. Quinn recalled that the two or three days before his A/72d Tk Bn crossed the Naktong were " a miserable few days, the rain just came down in buckets." They were supposed to cross immediately, but a bridge had not yet been put in by the engineers. "We finally got enough [barges] out there...and we crossed the Naktong on barges," he wrote. "My platoon went across in the middle of the night...."

Meantime, Eighth Army made no attempt to oust the enemy from Hill 409. Air strikes, artillery fire and patrols from 1/38th Infantry there were used to contain and neutralize elements of the *NK 10th Division* there.

Roy Hill wrote of his experiences when his B/38th Infantry made an attack on Sept. 19, possibly in the vicinity of Hill 409. He was wounded that day. He characterized the action as a combat patrol of "14 men counting Medic Berain." The patrol moved out and reached a "mid-point between hills," he wrote, "in a gully, [where] we left medic Berain." He recalled the hill to be slanted upward at a forty-five degree angle, forcing the men to virtually crawl along on hands and knees. Hill was in the front of the party.

"I approached within about 25 feet of the top of the hill. I lay on my back and took one of the hand grenades from my shoulder web harness and raised it over my head, waving it so the rest of the men could notice and see it. The others got out their grenades and all together, we lobbed them on top of the hill. When they exploded, we rushed the hill. On top I saw a gook running away.... I fired once, without aiming — no time — and hit him in the middle of his back. He threw up both arms, and the shock of the bullet propelled him face forward down the hill."

Hill then ran a few yards to the nearest enemy foxhole, where he saw two enemy soldiers, one on top of the other. He raised his rifle up high over his head so as to shot down in the hole. He fired three shots, all of which hit the top soldier. At that point, he wrote, "'braang,' my empty clip flew out of my rifle. It was empty, so I ran back several feet from the...hole to reload." Instead of taking a clip from his harness, which would have been the easiest and fastest way to reload, Hill began fumbling to extract one from his ammo bandoleer. He finally reloaded his rifle and ran back to the hole to kill the second enemy soldier in it. As he raised his rifle, an enemy bullet struck the front sight and small metal splinters hit his right temple. But for his raised rifle, the enemy bullet would have killed him. Stumbling back, he discovered no blood on his temple. But the enemy had recovered from the initial shock of the GI's attack and were fighting back.

Later, he recalled, it was "guesstimated" [his word] that an enemy company occupied the hill he was on, another on a "hill 50 yards to the north and a gook company on another hilltop a little to the east of the 2d hill." Hill pulled back from the enemy foxhole and found himself standing about five feet to the left of his buddy, Leroy Link. "Bullets were flying around us like flies," he recalled. "One could reach out and grab a hand full anywhere. I was firing back at the other two hill tops when something caused me to look over at Link. A bullet had hit him in the left shoulder and immediately his entire arm and left side of his body was covered with blood." Actually, Link had been hit by four bullets.

Hill called for a litter for Link, not realizing that the unit had none available at the moment. "The call," he wrote, "was an old reflex from [my experience in] World War II. Then he was hit in the left foot. "It felt as if someone had taken a baseball bat and hit the back of my foot trying to knock it out from under me." He discovered blood coming out of a small hole on the left side of his ankle. He thought the shot had come from behind him, but could not locate any enemy there. "Pop" Kiniski came by about this time and Hill yelled "I'm hit!"

Kiniski replied, "What do you want me to do about it?"

Hill responded, "You are supposed to be in charge, so I thought you should know who's hit or not."

Kiniski moved on without answering. An armor piercing machine gun bullet, Hill recalled, had entered his ankle through an eyelet of his combat boot and had gone through four bones in his ankle, "parting each in half," he wrote. "So I now have 8 bones were most people have 4."

Two South Korean civilians loaded Hill on a litter and he gave his rifle and bandoleer to the medic. As the party withdrew, enemy soldiers started over the hill after them. Hill pulled out his 9mm machine pistol and emptied it at them and "Scotty," the platoon machine gunner then opened fire, dispersing the North Koreans. Seven of the 13 men in that patrol were wounded and another was killed.

Meantime, 2/23d Infantry made plans to attack south along the Naktong to help the 9th Infantry to oust the enemy from Hill 201. Men from Companies E, F and H, who participated in this attack later wrote of their experiences.

The attack took place on Sept. 19 along the east bank of the Naktong, in a north-south direction. The attack originated on one ridge line which ran at right angles to the river, followed a connecting ridge along the river to the first objective, then another ridge at a right angle, then on to another ridge further south. 1LT Charles Klipstine's Co. F had the mission of making this main attack, with G on the left, taking a secondary objective. CPT Perry Sager's Co. E was initially in reserve. CPT William Payne's Co. H would support by the fire of its 81mm mortars, machine guns and 75mm recoilless rifles. Two sections from B/82d AAA/AW Battalion, also added their support.

"I was awake at dawn," wrote Donald W. Hoffman, 3d Platoon, Co. F, "had some coffee and we were told to saddle up. We were formed in a long skirmish line. How well I remember LT [James D.] Currie standing on a small knoll in front of us. He...raised [his carbine] over his head and said, 'Let's take those two hills,' and off we went at a slow pace." [Currie had been an enlisted man who had recently been awarded a battlefield commission.] "We took the first hill with little trouble. We paused for a few minutes, then proceeded down the saddle between the two hills when all hell broke loose. I looked to my left and in a flash I saw [squad member] Ricketts get hit in the head and our medic Pete Perletti reel and fall. I knew it was him because he wore white parachute shroud line for shoe strings. Both men were dead. Out of the corner of my eye, I noticed a North Korean running from my right to my left. He was large and heavy and having a

tough time moving." The man was about 50 yards away.

Hoffman fired two "banana" magazines of ammunition at the man and was amazed that he missed. (See Chapter Notes.) Hoffman reloaded his carbine and moved to his right, where he had noted that other GIs had outflanked the enemy. "I joined this group. One of our people by the name of Gomez had the BAR and was firing it on full automatic. All of a sudden the firing stopped." Hoffman was sent to check on Gomez. "I found him slumped over the weapon. I turned him over and a gush of blood came from his throat and went all over the front of me. I was horrified and jumped back. The SGT thought I was hit and he was relieved to see I wasn't. He assigned a new gunner to the BAR who fired short bursts and stayed out of trouble. Gomez was...shot through the jugular vein."

Hoffman was noted in the platoon as a good grenadier, so was often used in that role. "I was told, 'OK, grenade pitcher, pitch 'em in those holes over there,' which I did. When the firefight was over, I found myself at the top of the hill sitting under a small tree, guarding three North Korean prisoners. The Pusan Perimeter was history."

Co. F had two 60mm mortars for this attack. One of them was moved forward and set up, then the other tube was moved up with the first. The company 57mm recoilless rifles also supported. They were credited with knocking out a couple of enemy machine guns.

Co. G seized its objective, a low ridge east of Fox Co.'s hill, by 10 a.m.

Co. E was committed through F to continue the attack. "I was the Co. radio operator," wrote Douglas Graney. "The hill we were to take was steep." As his unit passed through Co. F, Graney "noticed the F Co. radio operator just over the crest of the hill lying dead with a bullet hole in his forehead. I saw he was using his long antenna because of the steep ravine. The SCR 300 [radio] was not good in deep ravines." The long antenna, however, was easier for an enemy to spot and kill the radio operator.

"I took off my long antenna for a short one, thinking the enemy would not see my radio. The 2d Platoon was to be the attacking platoon. CPT Sager and I would be following the 2d Platoon. SGT Rego...was a squad leader in [this]...platoon and would be the first to move out. Artillery [support] was light to none because of other fire missions." There was to be an air strike, he recalled, but the air controller never arrived. "So we jumped off," he continued. "At first enemy fire was light, as were incoming mortar rounds. About half way up [the hill] the soldier carrying the air panel was wounded. Medics carried him and the air panel off the hill. "

About 3/4 of the way up the hill our 1st and 3d Platoons moved closer to us behind the 2d Platoon. Just then four F-51 fighters, with Australian markings, struck us. With no air panel and no [air controller] they thought they'd caught the enemy in the open. It was us they caught. The hill was bald — no cover. Fifty caliber rounds slammed into the hill all around me and CPT Sager. Others were not so lucky. Then they dropped napalm, incinerating many of the 2d Platoon. I kept radioing battalion to tell them to get the air corps off us. They said they were trying to reach the fly boys. One canister of napalm didn't ignite and when the next plane dove at us to strafe, he tried a burst and pulled up. They finally got the word. They circled the hill, dipping their wings in apology.

"We were beginning to move the 1st and 3d Platoons forward when a barrage of mortars from [our] Heavy Weapons Company] all but wiped out what was left of the 2d Platoon. I radioed that Heavy Weapons was hitting friendly troops." He finally got the mortar fire stopped. SGT Rego and a few South Koreans in his squad survived, but most of the 2d Platoon had been killed or wounded by the air strike and mortaring. "Then we heard yelling and thought the enemy was going to attack us. It was K Co....attacking across a ridge that connected to the enemy hill from the east side. (We were attacking from the southwest side.) The enemy began running in all directions, but mostly down the slope toward the river. We caught some of them in a cross fire between us and Co. K. After the hill was taken and secured, E Co. 23d dug in and held while K Co. moved off to rejoin the 3d Bn."

The One That Got Away

After Co. E took the hill, the men saw a lone enemy soldier on the river bank take off his clothing and begin swimming to the far shore. Several men and a machine gunner took him under fire. "We were quite exhausted," Graney wrote, "and didn't really care about one NK making it to safety. But this became a challenge and it became a bit humorous." The enemy soldier kept ducking under water to avoid being hit. Then someone decided to call artillery in on him. In order to get the artillery to fire, they reported an enemy battalion massing at the river's edge. "We blasted the river bank near where it looked like our escaping NK would climb out. Two artillery barrages landed on the bank and in the water near and on our NK soldier. When the dust cleared, our NK soldier climbed out of the river and started to run for cover, but not before he turned toward us and gave us [an obscene gesture] salute. We stood up and gave him a cheer."

LT Phil R. Garn commanded the 75mm Recoilless Rifle Platoon, H/23d Infantry, in this battle. It was the only time in eight months of combat that all four of his 75s were used simultaneously. This was not through choice. "Terrain conditions and shortages of personnel forced the decision," he wrote in "75mm Recoilless Rifle in Korea." (*Infantry School Quarterly*, Jan. 1952) "We found it took about eight men to carry one gun over the Korean terrain. There simply wasn't enough manpower in the platoon to transport all four guns, plus ammunition, over that jumbled mass of real estate.

"In our first attack the 75s were used in a role that later became standard," Garn continued. The guns were placed where they could observe the advancing troops and then fired on targets of opportunity, usually over the heads of the attacking infantry. Most often, this fire was delivered at the request of the rifle company commanders. The fire was continued until masked by the advancing infantrymen. Then the weapons were displaced forward.

For this attack, the two gun sections were initially placed on the ridge to the left of Co. F., in section positions about 250 yards apart. From

these locations, they could observe and fire upon the entire zone over which F Company would advance, as well as the forward slope of the objective itself. The 2d Section was on the far left and in position before the attack started. The 1st Section took up its first position at 8 a.m. and remained there for 30 minutes. It then displaced about 600 yards to the right, from which it directly overlooked the F Co. route of advance. It remained there from 9 a.m. until noon.

On Sept. 19, SGT George E. Vonton led a platoon of tanks from the 23d's Tk Co. to the very top of Hill 201, effectively breaking the enemy's hold on that piece of terrain. That evening, the hill was firmly in 9th Infantry hands. The way was open for the 2d Division to cross the Naktong.

SGT Charles N. Prince was a tank commander in SGT Andrew Reyna's tank platoon. Prince had a series of adventures between Sept. 18 and 20. First, before daylight on Sept. 18, he was walking in front of his tank and a guide when some enemy fire startled him. He stepped off the ridge he was following and rolled downhill some distance before regaining his feet. His tank driver almost drove the tank over the side following Prince.

Later in the day, while his tank was going through a creek, a T-34 took it under fire and 120mm mortar fire began landing nearby. In maneuvering to get a better shot at the enemy tank, Prince's tank flooded out in the water. When it fired, the enemy tank round traveled so close to the lake's surface that one could follow it by the water spray it kicked up in its passage. Prince's tank, and that of SGT Byrd returned the T-34's fire. Byrd's gunner, Robert Lindsey and Prince's gunner, Doyle Smith both fired at the enemy. One or both gunners scored a hit, silencing the enemy tank. Later in the afternoon, the rest of the 3d Tank Platoon moved on, leaving Prince and his stalled tank behind. The water level in his tank was "almost up to the turret deck," Prince wrote, "flooding the driver's compartment and spare 76mm ammo. We were stranded in the creek."

That evening, his platoon leader came up and ordered Prince to have everything salvageable removed from the tank in preparation for the arrival the next day of a retriever. "We were getting the last of the 76mm shells onto the bank about dusk," Prince recalled, "when we were

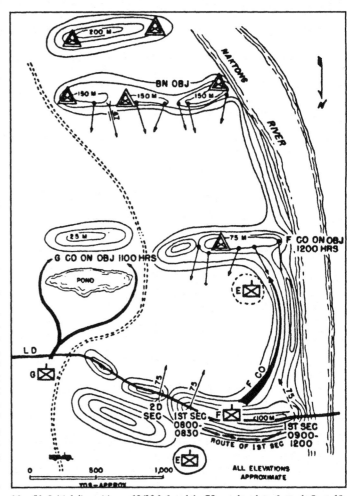

Map 51–Initial dispositions of 2/23 Inf. and the 75mm plt., plan of attack, Sept. 19. OPs are the enemy's. CPT Phil R. Garn, Infantry School Quarterly, Jan. 1952)

treated to some bursts of automatic rifle and burp gun fire, which struck the turret and the water around us. Needless to say, this stopped our unloading program. It also killed our plan to spend the night on the [creek] bank." Periodic enemy sniper fire kept the men, huddled in the tank, awake all night.

The following morning, Prince started to climb out of the turret hatch, but was driven back into the tank by a burst of machine gun fire. Unable to find where the fire originated, he had his machine gun fire into two nearby groves of trees and huts. Enemy fire ceased.

Later in the day, a 1st Cavalry Division unit headquarters and some riflemen set up nearby. Prince and his bow gunner, PFC Barbara, started across the creek to warn the Cavalrymen of the enemy snipers, when shots forced the two men to fall down into the water. One round hit Barbara's helmet, knocking it from his head and into the water. He was furious, because he lost the helmet, but Prince thought the man was lucky to have been wearing one at the time.

Prince and the Cavalrymen then worked out a plan to attack and destroy the enemy snipers. Barbara, still angry, insisted that he accompany the infantrymen. Once they got into position to fire on the enemy, Prince opened up with the tank's .50- and .30- caliber machine guns. "Even our driver fired from the loader's hatch with a rifle on the second group of huts," he wrote, while the tank's machine guns fired into the first group. As the infantrymen closed in the enemy took them under fire with small-arms, burp guns and grenades. The enemy was in the third hut of the first group and a stand of trees nearby. Then a "large volume of fire came from the second group of huts and grove of trees near them," Prince remembered. The tank's machine guns returned this fire, covering the infantrymen as they cleared out the first group of huts. In the end, three enemy soldiers were killed, four were wounded and two were captured. Barbara killed one of the enemy with his rifle.

The next day, Sept. 20, the tank retriever arrived and Prince's tank was brought out of the creek and restored to operation. On Sept. 21, he and his men crossed the Naktong.

Elements of the 3d Transportation Amphibian Truck Co., operating 2 1/2- ton amphibian trucks (DUKWs), supported the 23d Infantry's crossing. The 3d Transportation Amphibian Truck Co. originated from the 74th Transportation Truck Co., which was based in Yokohama in June 1950. The unit was redesignated the 8062d Transportation Amphibian Truck Co. on July 7, 1950, commanded by CPT Robert J. Gilroy. The captain outlined the unit's history and actions in Korea in his article, "Amphibian Truck Company," in Westover's *Combat Support in Korea*. There were originally 3 officers and 94 EM in the unit. Another 100 EM and 2 officers were added to the company after it became the 8062d. Only one person, an enlisted man had been in an amphibian truck company before. Nor were there any men experienced in repairing "Ducks." Further, the unit received 71 vehicles instead of the 38 it was authorized. In Korea, on Aug. 1, the company finally became the 3d Transportation Amphibian Truck Co.

On Sept. 19, the platoons of John F. Williams and LT Claude Payne were ordered to support the 2d Division's crossing of the Naktong. Williams' platoon made a successful crossing. In just forty hours it carried all three battalions of the 23d Infantry and their supplies across the river. During this time, it devised a ferry by lashing a pontoon bridge section between two DUKWs and ferried 138 tanks across the river, probably including those of A/72d Tk Bn. The platoon remained at the crossing site for eight more days to operate a ferry and to help the engineers construct a bridge.

LT Payne's platoon was not so fortunate. It made its crossing and established a ferry, but with the loss of 2 killed and 4 wounded and 10 DUKWs damaged and sunk by enemy fire. All but one of these vehicles was recovered and returned to service. In addition to enemy fire, the mission was hindered by deep mud on both banks of the river. CPT Gilroy commented that mud was the DUKWs "worst enemy."

38th Ordnance Medium Maintenance Co., Night of Sept. 19-20

Small groups of enemy soldiers were still in the 2d Division's rear area on Sept. 19. That night one group attacked the 38th Ordnance Medium Maintenance Co., which was located in the rice paddies along the small Chingdo River, a half mile south of the little village of Songso-do. This company's mission was to provide back-up ordnance maintenance to the 2d

Division. CPT Edward C. Williamson, 4th Historical Detachment, interviewed Lieutenants Edgar E. Dunlap and William E. Peter, Sergeants Claude H. Lusk, George A. Batson, M. J. Thomasson, Thomas E. Griffin and Eugene F. McCracken and CPL Elio Battaglia, all of the 38th. Based on these interviews, he wrote "Ordnance Company Under Attack," (*Combat Support In Korea*). This is their story.

The unit had been scheduled to displace, but was ordered to delay until the following day. In preparation for the move, unit machine guns had been dismounted and unit trash had been dumped into foxholes. No one bothered to remount the machine guns or clean out the foxholes. Korean civilians had been noted in the area; most were dismissed as people from the village. Only SGT Burt Davis had any encounter of note, when he met two Koreans on the four foot high dike which marked the southern boundary of the unit area. He told them to get out and they talked back to him. He reported the incident to several of his comrades.

LT Chris Beaber had been commander of the 38th Maintenance Co. for just one week. The unit numbered 135 officers and EM. Armament consisted of 7 truck-mounted .50- caliber machine guns, three .30-caliber machine guns, 3 rocket launchers, 3 submachineguns, 45 carbines and 76 pistols. In case of emergency, truck sirens were to be sounded. The south and east sides of the perimeter would then be manned by 53 of the unit's men and the north and west sides by another 48 men, the unit automotive section.

That night, unit security consisted of four stationary guards — one at each corner of the unit area, and two roving patrols. The rectangular company perimeter was 800 yards long. The guard was changed at 1 a.m. Some men noted that the nearby MSR was unusually quiet. The ROK National Police were not relaying their usual messages along their chain of posts.

Just before 2 a.m., a party of 35 to 40 guerrillas crawled unnoticed to the southern embankment and attacked with grenades and small-arms fire, centering on the CP, where a 750 gallon gas tanker had been parked. Because of the impending move, however, the tanker and other POL (petroleum, oil and lubricant) supplies had been relocated closer to the MSR. As a result, an enemy grenade tossed into the old site did no damage. It was obvious by the fact that the attack centered on the CP and that they knew the location of POL supplies, that the enemy had carefully reconnoitered beforehand. Enemy grenades exploded and bullets hit trucks and rocks, ricocheting in all directions.

The attack set one truck on fire, brightly illuminating the whole area. The men had little concealment and no foxholes to use. Two more trucks were set afire near the burning one. They were driven away while the fires were put out by Sergeants Ellis and Paul Easlom. A machine-shop truck was then set fiercely ablaze when a grenade was dropped into its gas tank.

Most of the men took shelter and did not fight back. Others were concerned that their fire might hit other men in the unit. The machine guns of an M-24 tank, in the company area for repair, could have been used against the enemy. But the crew climbed into it, buttoned up, and took no part in the battle.

It seems that only SGT Eugene McCracken

initiated any resistance. He was asleep in his underwear when the attack started. First, he assisted LT John J. Moore, an early casualty, then manned the vehicle's .50-caliber machine gun. The attack had been underway about five minutes, and he realized that most of the fire was incoming. At first, he couldn't fire the gun. Then he discovered that the headspace was not properly adjusted. He quickly corrected this. Seeing three of the enemy sitting atop the dike firing small arms, he knocked them off with a few bursts. (See Chapter Notes.)

LT Beaber came by the wrecker and called out, "Can you see any more?" As he did so, the enemy fired a burst of small-arms fire, missing McCracken and the lieutenant, but damaging the vehicle. One round came close to the sergeant, and he swore. Some men under the wrecker, thinking he had been wounded, asked if he had been hit. "No," he responded, "but they're sure trying!"

Two others who engaged the enemy were PFC Daniel LeGaspi, with his .25-caliber pistol and SGT Guy W. Miller, with another .50-caliber machine gun. LeGaspi was wounded and Miller's gun jammed after only a few shots.

Within 15 minutes, the attack ebbed and the unit got a little better organized, although no more machine guns were placed in action. About five minutes later, an enemy whistle blew and the attack was renewed by 12 to 15 enemy soldiers charging down the bank, firing small arms and throwing grenades. One grenade exploded within six feet of McCracken's wrecker. He fired one box of ammunition at the attackers, reloaded the gun and continued to spray the enemy. Within 10 minutes, the second guerrilla attack ended and they covered their withdrawal with a machine gun. McCracken, detecting the muzzle flash of this gun, put it out of action with a few well-aimed bursts. All action ended by 2:30 a.m.

Just before the second attack ended, a messenger had been sent to Chongdo for help from the 622d MP Co. located there. A detail of men from the MPs arrived a few minutes later and another squad of them at about 3 a.m. Meantime, the MP company commander learned that the local police had been attacked just before the ordnance company. A platoon of 25 to 30 policemen arrived shortly before dawn and went after the guerrillas, but they were long gone. A dead North Korean officer was found in the ordnance company area. Papers identified him as the leader of the enemy force. No other enemy bodies were found, but the men believed seven guerrillas had been wounded and taken away.

The company lost one man killed and 5 wounded, three 2 1/2-ton trucks, a jeep, three trailers and 26 cylinders of oxygen and acetylene. Several other vehicles were partially burned or otherwise damaged. At 11 a.m. on Sept. 20, the company finally displaced, having learned a lesson in preparedness.

Visiting the 2d Division on Sept. 19, Walker greatly praised it for its successful crossing of the Naktong. He commented that the 2d had not only inflicted heavy casualties on the enemy but had also forced him to displace his CP.

The 2d Division history records that the 23d Infantry had three companies across the Naktong by 8 a.m. of Sept. 20 and by noon, the 9th in the south was "scouting for a bridge site. The enemy resistance east of the Naktong had all but ceased, the last of it beaten off by the 9th RCT assisted by the Second Battalion of the 23d and the 2d Reconnaissance Company." The history notes that the severe shortage of bridging "throughout the Army area...seriously hampered units of the division in...[transporting] their men and equipment to the western banks of the Naktong from which they could follow up their initial successes."

The 3d Battalion, 23d Infantry slipped across the Naktong before daylight on Sept. 20. It crossed in assault boats at the Sangpo ferry site, south of where the Sinban River enters the Naktong. The surprise was so complete that Co. L captured an enemy lieutenant colonel and his staff asleep. A captured map revealed the locations of the *NK 2d, 4th* and *9th Divisions* in the Sin-ban-ni area. By noon 3/23 had captured Hill 227, which dominated the crossing site on the west side of the river.

Captain Tassey, commanding D/23d Infantry recorded that 3/23d "crossed the Naktong River at 0230 hours [2:30 a.m.] today [Sept. 20] with no enemy resistance. The 1st Battalion is awaiting orders to cross the river some time today." Tassey finally made arrangements with the 38th infantry, on the right, to ferry his mortar platoon across on their rubber bridge floats. That platoon and the 75mm Recoilless Platoon both crossed at 8:40 p.m. The Heavy Machineguns had already crossed at 7 p.m. His CP crossed at 1 a.m. the next day.

That afternoon 1/23d Infantry crossed the river and headed for Hill 207, a mile upstream from the crossing site. This hill dominated the road which crossed the Naktong there. The lead company soon came upon the Sinban River, which no one in the company knew was there. The advance was held up for several hours until DUKWs moved up and carried the unit across that river. That night, they took Hill 207 without a fight; the enemy had left.

The 5th RCT Takes Hill 268, Waegwan and Hill 303 — Sept. 16-21

When the 5th RCT was relieved from the 25th Division sector, it was sent up north into that of the 1st Cavalry Division. The plan called for the 5th RCT, with the 5th Cavalry protecting its right flank, to seize Waegwan and adjacent high ground, then cross the Naktong in assault boats. At the same time, the 24th Division's 19th and 21st Regiments were to cross the Naktong about five miles south of Waegwan, then turn north to link up with the 5th RCT west of the river.

Next, engineers were to construct two bridges at Waegwan; a treadway for infantry and a pontoon bridge for vehicles. Once the 24th Division's heavy equipment had crossed, it was to attack up the main highway to Taejon.

Finally, after assisting the 5th RCT and stopping the enemy in the Bowling Alley area, the 1st Cavalry Division would swing west to follow the 24th Division across the Naktong. It would drop it battalions off along the way to provide area security.

As part of the preparation for this attack, Eighth Army arranged a carpet bombing of the ground on both sides of the river at Waegwan.

The bombing was scheduled for Sept. 16 by over 80 B-29 bombers, but the target area was covered by clouds and the attack was postponed. On Sept. 18, however, visibility had cleared and the strike was carried out at dawn by 42 bombers of the 92d and 98th Bombardment Groups. They struck two target areas 500 X 5000 yards each. Eight hundred 500 lb. bombs were dumped into each target area. GEN Hobart Gay, commanding the 1st Cavalry Division, called the attacks "beautiful." American infantrymen witnessing the attacks stood up and cheered.

Attached to the 1st Cavalry Division on Sept. 14, the 5th RCT moved into an assembly area six miles south of Waegwan. On Sept. 16, it began its operation to seize Waegwan and adjacent high ground. This included Hill 268 to the south of the town and the infamous Hill 303 to the north of it. The initial regimental objective was named "Objective New York." This objective included Hill 268 in the center, a smaller hill to the left, near the Naktong and Hill 160, which lay just south of 268. For the attack, the regiment was short 1,194 men, having a total strength of only 2,599. The three battalions were almost equal in strength, varying from 586 to 595 men.

The 2/5th RCT was the only battalion to be in contact with the enemy Sept. 16. But SGT Charles Shepherd's platoon engaged the enemy that day. Shephard was a tank commander in Tank Co., 5th RCT. LT Lowry, his platoon leader was firing at some enemy AT guns across the Naktong. He called Shepherd on the radio and ordered him to bring his tank up. Shepherd's tank was about 50 yards back, so he drove it up right in rear Lowry's. From this position, he spotted the enemy AT guns from their firing flashes. The guns, apparently fairly small, had hit Lowry's tank several times without knocking it out. Lowry's tank prevented Shepherd from firing on the enemy guns. Lowry backed his tank up to the right and Shepherd moved his up to the left. From there "we peppered the anti-tank gun," he said "I think they were all knocked out."

The 3d Platoon (LT Gaylord) now also came up to join Lowry's. Enemy mortar fire was coming in. Shepherd's loader stuck his head out of the tank. "Get your damned head down before you get it blowed off!" Shepherd ordered. Within five minutes, an enemy mortar round landed on the cupola of the turret. Shepherd had been at the cupola of the turret. The force of the blast from the exploding round knocked him back down in the turret. "I had my hands up on the edge of the cupola," he said. "And I got my hands full of shrapnel and one large piece went across the top of my head and lots of small stuff in my forehead and face."

He was knocked senseless. "I knew everything that was going on, but I couldn't see anything because of blood flowing down my eyes." At first, he thought an enemy AT or tank round had hit and "blew the tank up inside." He expected the crew to get out. "I didn't know what happened," he went on. "I couldn't see...." At first he couldn't move, then slowly, some strength returned and he was able to get himself out of the tank. "I toppled...off the back deck, onto the ground.... I hit the ground, stuck my hand down — had mud on my hands — stuck it up on my head, and I thought, 'My God, I got a

hole in my head! I'll probably be dead in a few minutes.'" Having faced death before, he didn't panic.

Someone got him back some distance and sat him down. LT Jackson offered him a cigarette. But he refused one. His face, he recalled "was like a piece of hamburger...." Of LT Jackson, Shepherd said, "He was a black platoon leader and...the only black in the organization at that time. And that was the bravest man I ever saw. I just wish I could meet this man again to tell him what I think of him as a man, you know."

Rain poured down on Sept. 17. In moving to join the 2d Battalion, 3/5th RCT had to assault and take nearby Hill 160 from the enemy. This hill was on the shore of a lake. COL Daniel R. Beirne, USA, Ret., then a First Lieutenant with K/5th RCT, wrote a detailed account of his experiences during the attacks to take Objective New York and Waegwan.

Hill 160

Co. K attacked up the central finger of the hill while Co. L moved up the one on the left. Almost at once, K Co. saw figures scurrying around the crest of the hill. Once the unit got about half way to the top, it was taken under fire by enemy small-arms and automatic weapons. The men took cover and searched for the sources of this fire. At the same time, K's machine guns and BARs fired toward the crest of the hill. Beirne, commanding the company Weapons Platoon, set up the 60s at the bottom of the hill and began lobbing rounds at the enemy. CPT Lukisch, commanding K, called for artillery support. It soon came in and right on target.

Co. L did not seem to be receiving much fire and was closer to the top of the hill than K, but it wasn't moving forward. About this time Lukisch's radio went out, causing him to lose contact with everyone on the net. He then sent his 3d Platoon to the left to help Co. L and LT Beirne to find out what was happening with that company and to get them moving.

Enroute to Co. L, Beirne dodged a persistent sniper, arriving at their position to find men just sitting around. King's 3d Platoon was moving up the hill to their right. He discovered one group of men around a wounded man, who turned out to be Love's commander, CPT Frank E. Hula, who had been fatally shot in the head. Hula had dashed forward to lead in person when the lead elements of his unit had stalled. An enemy bullet cut him down almost at once. Nearby, a soldier was crying and beating his fist on the ground, shouting, "I'll get 'em! I'll kill 'em all! The dirty so and so's!" His platoon leader knelt by the sobbing man, trying to comfort him. "It was a touching scene," Beirne wrote, "but still nobody was moving forward from L Company."

Beirne found another L Co. officer and had him take charge. Co. L then advanced. But by that time 3/K Co. had already reached the top of the hill and was cleaning out the rest of the enemy. The balance of Co. L also reached the summit and mopped up die-hard enemy soldiers. Sixteen enemy dead were found sprawled outside foxholes, and several more in them. Enemy harassing fire that night inflicted some additional losses on K and L Companies. Sept. 17 was the date that Horace (Andy) Anderson, a squad leader in the 4th platoon, of Co. E, was wounded. He returned to the company a week and a half later.

At 6 p.m. the evening of Sept. 18, the 5th RCT and 6th Medium Tk Battalion were attached to the 24th Infantry Division. But the 5th RCT remained under the operational control of the 1st Cavalry Division for the current operation.

Hill 268

This hill was southeast of Waegwan. It protected the southern approach to the town and was also the left flank of the *NK II Corps*. Loss of the hill would make untenable the enemy advanced position in the 5th Cavalry to the east toward Taegu. There was a gap in the enemy line south of the hill, making its retention even more important; the enemy could oversee and direct fire into this gap from Hill 268. As a result of these factors, some 1,200 men of the *NK 3d Division*, supported by tanks defended 268. (The *3d Division* had its *8th* and *9th Regiments* defending south of Waegwan while *65th Regiment, NK 105th Armored Division* supported in and around Waegwan.) At the southern end of the gap was the British 27th Infantry Brigade holding important terrain just north of the strong *NK 10th Division*.

The 5th RCT began its attack on Hill 268 on Sept. 19. This hill, Beirne wrote resembled "a caterpillar with a long thin body and feelers at both ends. These feelers are fingers. The top of the hill is long and narrow and the sides almost perpendicular except for the fingers. On the top were four knobs, generally in line from south to north. Along the sides [was] a heavy growth of trees, but few trees...on the top."

The plan of attack called for Co. L to attack north up one finger, with Co. B on its left. Co. K attacked up another finger to the right of L. Just south of the knobs was the first objective for Companies L and K. K was also to take the first knob. Once these objectives were seized, Co. I was to assault and take the remaining knobs from the flank, attacking north (right) of King Company.

Co. K attacked at 7 a.m. on Sept. 19. Beirne's mortars and 57mm recoilless rifles supported initially from Hill 160. Enemy small-arms fire, and occasional tank fire fell on Hill 160, but

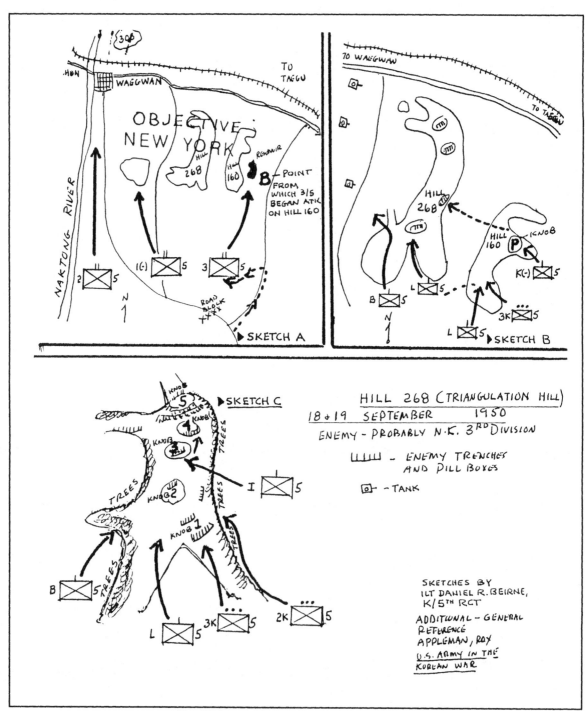

Map 52 (Courtesy of 1st LT Daniel K. Beirne, K/5 RCT)

Waegwan in flames–The town of Waegwan lies along the route of a main highway linking Taegu, Taejon, and Seoul. Its capture was vital to U.N. forces who were striving to link the army in the Seoul sector with the one slugging northwest from the Pusan perimeter. The flames of battle raced through Waegwan's residential district as GIs forced their entrance into the town that required seven days to clear. (Source: P. 204, Pictorial History of the War in Korea, *Veterans of Foreign Wars, 1951)*

As men of the U.S. First Cavalry hacked a path from the beachhead, units of the division's 5th Regimental Combat Team seized the crest of Hill 209. (Source: P. 204, Pictorial History of the War in Korea, *Veterans of Foreign Wars, 1951)*

caused little damage. Item Co. arrived on the hill preparatory to its own attack. Beirne was observing Co. K from behind a rock, when someone called him away. The artillery FO took his place. When Beirne returned, he discovered that the FO had been hit in the leg, fracturing it.

K Co. got about half way up Hill 268 before coming under heavy machine gun fire. Company mortars were ineffective, so artillery was called for. While waiting for the artillery fire, mail for the unit arrived and was distributed to the men near Beirne. "What a contrast!" he commented. "Here in the middle of a battle were men calmly reading their letters."

The rifle platoons began moving again, but under heavy enemy fire. "The 3d Platoon slowly worked its way up a saddle but took ten casualties in doing it," Beirne wrote. An enemy machine gun bunker was the trouble. SGT McCrane, the platoon leader, and CPL Caen, a squad leader, worked their way up on the bunker's left front, tossed in grenades and rushed into the position, killing all the enemy there. This broke the enemy defense. The rest of the platoon rushed up and began mopping up.

The 1st and 2d Platoons, attacking straight up the hill, were also taking heavy casualties. Sergeants James Jackson, Adams, Moran, Finn and Henderson started up the hill after SGT Kermit Jackson (platoon sergeant, 1st Platoon) had formed a skirmish line and got it moving. About this time, BAR-man Gay and a ROK came running downhill and reported that he had spotted three North Koreans in a foxhole, but his rifle jammed when he tried to shoot them. As he said this, three enemy grenades sailed into the midst of the men.

Finn was struck in the jaw by fragments, Adams was hit in the legs and arm and the ROK received a minor face wound. SGT Kermit Jackson quickly threw three grenades back. All three landed in the enemy hole, knocking out the position. The men then surged forward, taking part of the enemy line from the rear. Some of the enemy began running down a path off of Knob #1. (See map) SGT James Jackson waited for them at a bend, killing eight, before the enemy caught on and withdrew off the back slope of the hill. Kermit Jackson, Moran and Henderson had reached the first knob and were killing enemy soldiers with rifles and grenades. Soon Co. K took the first knob. Surviving enemy soldiers made their way to the other knobs and took up position there. Beirne wrote that the unit suffered 40 casualties in the attack.

Co. I then moved to the attack, seizing two of the three remaining knobs. Beirne wrote that the company suffered heavily in this attack. The last knob was even harder. About 10 of the enemy held the top in a trench, from which they threw grenades and fired down on Co. I. Beirne and others could see enemy soldiers pop up, throw a grenade, then disappear. They tried to hit these enemy soldiers with rifle fire, although the range was some 700 yards. Even artillery and mortar fire failed to dislodge these determined North Koreans. Co. I got to within about 25 yards of the crest of the knob, but were stopped there. Beirne recalled that 10 of the company lay dead on the slope.

Robert B. Hardin, of Co. I, wrote, "We got pinned down and our Weapons Platoon was

caught in a saddle and almost all of them were killed."

Meantime, back on the first knob, where Beirne was located, enemy mortar fire caught a group of men who were receiving a distribution of rations. One round hit five of them and another landed in a foxhole, killing both occupants.

All during the day, an enemy tank kept firing at Hill 160. Finally, CPT Lukisch ordered a 57mm recoilless rifle to return the fire. SGT Rushing put his gun into action, firing several rounds, which hit the road. Finally, one hit the tank and bounced off. The tank immediately moved and ceased firing. Rushing and his men claimed the tank as their conquest.

The day was coming to a close, so Co. I was ordered to pull back to the first knob and dig in for the night. Meantime, Beirne was sent with a detail of 20 men to help bring out Item Co.'s wounded. In one instance, he found two men behind a small hummock of ground. He crawled to them pushing a stretcher. One man had been hit in the shoulder and the other through the foot. Both men had been treated and had received morphine. The one with the shoulder wound was in shock, so he was rolled onto the stretcher. Beirne then slid the stretcher down slope where other men took it. He and the other wounded man crawled back to safety. While he was working with these two injured men, SGT MacEnroe, of his rescue detail, ran out onto the third knob, picked up a man and carried him in his arms, while enemy bullets kicked up dirt around his feet. Four other men did the same thing, Beirne wrote, then carried two more wounded out in a shelter half.

Enemy troops, closely following the retreating Co. I, forced Beirne and his rescue party to take a route through woods on the right in order to avoid the bulk of enemy fire.

By nightfall on Sept. 19, the 5th RCT had taken all of Hill 268, except for its northeast slope. The 3d Battalion was on the hill, the 1st was turned northwest of it toward another objective and the 2d Battalion had taken Hill 121. This hill was on the river only a mile south of Waegwan.

The 5th RCT was heavily supported by air strikes which destroyed many enemy weapons and inflicted demoralizing losses on the defenders. The RCT's right flank in this action was protected by the 5th Cavalry and part of the 7th, who fought pitched battles with the enemy on adjacent hills east of Waegwan.

The next morning, following a strike by six planes and a heavy artillery, mortar and 75mm recoilless bombardment, Co. I attacked the last knob again. Over 200 enemy soldiers in logged-in bunkers held the unit off. I Co. asked for help from K. King Co. combined its 1st and 2d Platoons to make a force of 35 men to send to Item's aid. Even so, the combined force could not budge the enemy. SGT Cabral, platoon sergeant of K's 2d Platoon, in the act of rallying his men was severely wounded by a burp gun.

About noon, enemy resistance crumbled, although a few of them still held out. Over 250 enemy dead were left on the hill. "The top of the knoll was completely black from napalm," Beirne wrote. "About 50 burned bodies lay on and around that black spot." Among the dead on Hill 268 was an enemy regimental commander.

Waegwan

The 2/5th RCT entered Waegwan at 2:15 p.m. on Sept. 19. By 2:30 p.m., it joined forces with 1/5th RCT. The 2d Battalion then surprised an enemy party laying mines in front of the town and drove deeper into it. The battalion had passed completely through Waegwan by 3:30 p.m.

Frank Valvo, E/5th RCT was seriously wounded during the battle for Waegwan, so badly that he never returned to Korea.

LT Keith Whitham's most vivid recollection of Waegwan was seeing "a young NK officer in dress uniform, complete with red Russian type shoulder boards sitting up dead on the steps of one of the public buildings in the center of town." At the time, Whitham was platoon leader, 2d Platoon, Tank Co., 5th RCT.

"I remember the town of Waegwan in flames as we passed through...." wrote Gene McClure, H/5th RCT, "and us being shelled by those earth shaking 120mm mortars...on the night before we attacked Hill 268. Also some enemy tank guns on the other side of the river...kept the Naktong River road and my battalion under constant fire as we attacked down the road toward Waegwan." McClure also witnessed one of the infantry assaults up Hill 268, a "by the book" infantry attack using assault fire.

"I recall so well seeing the riflemen walking up Hill 268 in the classic upright infantry assault position, fixed bayonets and all guns held at waist level, including light .30-cal. machine guns [Browning M1919 A6 model], all firing as they went, their bullets all visibly striking the ground...just a few feet in front of them. Some fell after being hit, but not one of the others slowed down or stopped to take cover. Their walk was slow and deliberate all the way to the top. And then walking along the ridgeline of the top, skylined in bold relief against the background of sky and smoke as if to make a statement to the entire world, that here and now, no power on earth could stop them.

"That's what I thought as I watched them.... These infantrymen were indeed 'King of the Mountain.'... A more stirring and inspirational sight I have never seen than these American infantrymen walking upright along that ridgeline of a conquered and savagely contested field of battle. I give all honor to those infantrymen.... It is one of those occasions which must be seen in order to grasp the full impact, and of which I have no words to describe."

Charles Rayoum arrived in Korea "around the first week in September," he wrote. "While on the approach to Waegwan, a sniper shot off the heel of my combat boot, spun me into a fresh-filled rice paddy. When gun fire erupted, everyone went down.... As we were going into the city of Waegwan we had to cross a bridge and were stopped there because of enemy fire." Since it was almost dark, the unit dug in there, "within shooting distance of town," Rayoum recalled. "About 3 a.m., we heard a tank roaring in town. The motor would race and then slow down about every 30 seconds. We found this was because they were pushing a row of tanks...towards us. Our SGT...got the bazookas to fire at the...tank that was doing the pushing. Between the bazookas...57s and 75 recoilless rifles we destroyed all of them — about eight. By daybreak we captured 30 North Koreans and one Russian who came out of the tanks, with hands up, shouting something (Lord only knows)."

Actually, by 9 a.m. on Sept. 19, the *NK 3d Division* in and around Waegwan was in panic-stricken retreat across the river. At that time, aerial observers saw about 1,500 of the enemy cross the Naktong just north of Waegwan. That afternoon, they observed the roads north of town crammed with North Korean groups of varying sizes, from 10 to 300 men, streaming out of town. By midafternoon enemy soldiers were moving through every draw and pass north of Waegwan. That day the 5th RCT captured ten 82mm mortars, twenty-two 45mm AT guns, six heavy machine guns and about 250 rifles and burp guns.

Hill 303

The 2/5th RCT captured Hill 303 in the afternoon of Sept. 20. The 5th RCT War Diary summarized the action this way: "Except for a small pocket of enemy on the northeast slope, the 2d Battalion had secured Hill 303 by 0935 hours [9:35 a.m.]. The enemy pocket on the northeast slope of Hill 303 (known as Objective Philadelphia) was cleaned out by 1630 hours [4:30 p.m.]...."

For Buddy Ford (H/5th RCT) the memory of Hill 303 was sad. "Just before we reached Waegwan I saw a good friend of mine from basic training moving through with his rifle company. They were on their way for the attack on Waegwan and Hill 303. He was carrying a BAR which seemed much too big for him.... [He] smiled a little, but he had that 'blank look' in his eyes. We took Waegwan and Hill 303 that day, but I never saw Archie Leinz again. He was reported killed. In four more days I would be 19 years old."

Under CPT England (CO, E/5th RCT) "our guns were set up properly, in defilade, sighted in and used like mortars are supposed to be used. That ragtag bunch could put one in your hip pocket without scratching your back," wrote Charles Rahn, of E Company's 60mm mortar section. England had come from H Co.'s 81mm mortars.

Rahn recalled one of the gunners, "Pop" Witches, "a 41 year-old professional corporal," he wrote, " a non-conformist of the first rank and an inspiration to us all. Pop wore a soft cap, his pants cuffs were tied with string and he ate a lot of raw garlic to ward off colds and fever.

"We were set up on the edge of Waegwan, throwing an occasional round as the troops worked their way up 303. The night was as black as the inside of your hat. And when a casually dressed soldier, reeking of garlic, walked through our area, the word whispered around, 'Don't shoot. That's Pop.'

"But when that worthy stumbled into a gun pit and fell on top of the crew, it turned out it wasn't Pop at all but one of the E-books [enemy]!

"The guy got out of the hole first and ran for it with the crew hot after him. He hit a board fence and tried to climb over and the fence fell down. Arms, legs, grunts and curses and splintering wood as everyone tried to nail him down. But he got away in the dark and Pop was told to stay in his hole at night or wear a helmet."

Crossing the Naktong

The 1/5th RCT began crossing the Naktong a mile north of Waegwan at 7:45 p.m. on Sept. 20. By midnight it was across and had advanced a mile.

LT Henry E. Emerson's Co. A was the lead company of the battalion across. "The engineers brought up some wooden assault boats and we went across that thing [the Naktong] at night. It was pretty eerie as a matter of fact.... The First Battalion's crossing, however, was unopposed by the enemy.... [W]e got maybe 500 yards inland on the other side before we encountered any resistance. The 2d Battalion followed the 1st across the river and dug in on the west side before midnight.

MG James A. Johnson, USA, Ret., then leader of 1st Platoon, 72d ECC recalled crossing the Naktong. He and other engineers were sent across in boats to clear mines. He was in the first boat with part of a squad. The rest of the men followed in other boats. Johnson recalled that, in all there were about 15 men in this operation. This included two squads and platoon sergeant Emmitt D. Parrish. Johnson's boat hit a shoreline and the men piled out, ran forward on land a short distance, then back into water. In the pitch-dark night they had been inadvertently landed on an island in the dark.

Finally, he and his men got across and began detecting and removing mines. They found the mines, disarmed them and tossed them off the road. LT Kenneth M. Hatch (West Point 1947), leading a detail of men from his the 2d Platoon joined Johnson's party. It was about 10 or 11 p.m.

"The road was almost parallel to the river until it got to [a] cut," Johnson said. "Then it took off north away from the river. The infantry was basically on the left side of the road and fighting for the ridge lines." On the right of the road at this point was what Johnson described as "just a little chocolate drop kind of hill."

Two T-34s, apparently not realizing that the Americans had crossed the river, were on the road on the other side of the pass. A rocket launcher team disabled one of the tanks.

About this time, the infantry on the hills to the left of the road got embroiled in "a hell of a firefight," Johnson recalled. The situation was pretty murky, so he and Hatch, having only one or two squads apiece with them, dug their group in on the reverse slope of the chocolate drop hill for the night. Things finally settled down, he recalled. The next day, they started out toward Kumchon.

"Once we got to the other side of the [Naktong] River," said then-SSG Robert Potter, G/5th RCT, "we were told to take some high ground.... It was dark. We took a position on the high ground; learned...that we were on top of a railroad trestle. And the tracks at the end of the trestle curved around the hill to the north." There were so many wires on the trestle that Potter's unit couldn't dig in. During the night, Potter and his comrades heard an enemy tank approaching from the north on the railroad tracks. They thought that if the tank rounded the curve in front of their position, "that would be the end of our little unit," Potter recalled.

Although that tank, or others, rumbled off and on all night, none came toward Potter's unit.

"The following morning," he wrote, "the Air Force planes took care of the tank."

The 3d Battalion seized Hill 300, four miles north of Waegwan that day.

On the afternoon of Sept. 21, 2/5th Cavalry relieved 3/5th RCT and the latter then crossed the Naktong. The 5th RCT found huge quantities of enemy ammunition and rifles on the west side of the river.

In just five days, the 5th RCT had destroyed the entire right flank and part of the center of the *NK 3d Division.* As a result, the *3d's* advance positions on the Taegu road opposing the 5th Cavalry Regiment were now untenable.

Appleman noted that from Sept. 18 to 21, "Close air support reached its highest peak in the Korean campaign. Fighters and bombers returned several times a day from Japanese bases to napalm, bomb, rocket and strafe enemy strongpoints of resistance and cut down fleeing enemy troops."

24th Infantry Division — Sept. 17-22

The 24th Division was to make the first assault crossings of the Naktong River for the Eighth Army. GEN Church received orders on Sept. 17 to cross in the vicinity of the Hasan-dong ferry west of Taegu. After dark on Sept. 18, the 21st Infantry was to cross in 3d ECB assault boats. Once across the regiment was to attack north to a point opposite Waegwan where it would reach the Kumchon road. At the same time the 24th Recon Co. and 19th Infantry were to cross a little farther south and block the roads leading from Songju, an enemy assembly point, about six miles west of the Naktong. The unanticipated crossing of the river that day by 2/38th infantry farther south did not alter these plans.

I Corps engineers failed to bridge the Kumho River, a tributary of the Naktong, which elements of the 24th Division had to cross in its advance to the Naktong. Divisional engineers were rushed forward and first reinforced the underwater bridge the 5th RCT had already constructed and used, then operated an assault-boat ferry to cross jeeps. The Kumho became a bottleneck which, by nightfall, had backed up vehicles for five miles to the east. GEN Church feared that the regiment would be unable to cross the Naktong before daylight, exposing the troops to heavy casualties. Therefore, he repeatedly urged Stephens to get his troops across before daylight. To support the operation two artillery preparations were fired on known and suspected enemy positions on the west bank of the Naktong.

In spite of almost Herculean efforts to unjam traffic and get troops and equipment beyond the Kumho and to the banks of the Naktong, it was 5:30 a.m. before the first assault troops began crossing the Naktong. On the west side of the river, six miles below Waegwan and just south of the village of Kumnan-dong, Hill 174 and its long southern extension dominated the crossing site.

Fog shrouded the river as the first wave landed and began moving inland. Suddenly, enemy machine gun fire raked the advancing infantrymen from both flanks and North Korean mortar and artillery fire began falling on both sides of the river. The heaviest fire, of course, came from Hill 174 and its southern extension.

The crossing effort was in real trouble. The 1st Battalion completed its crossing under fire, losing about 120 men in the effort. At 7 a.m., an air strike came in on Hill 174. In the meantime, 1/21st reorganized and, supported by more air strikes, captured the hill by noon. The 3/21st infantry crossed that afternoon and captured the next hill to the north of 174. The 2/21st crossed that night (Sept. 19) and the following morning. The next day 1/21 moved north to Hill 170, on the west side of the river from Waegwan. The 3/21 moved onto a higher hill a mile to the northwest.

Lieutenants Charles W. Newcomb (platoon leader, A/21st) and John L. Begley (platoon leader, B/21st) wrote of their experiences crossing the Naktong Sept. 19. Both young officers were 1950 West Point graduates, as were LTs Bruce L. Leiser (E/21st) and Clifton "Bud" Pritchett Jr., of Co. I.

"The river crossing was supposed to take place before dawn and A Company was moved out quite early in the pre-dawn morning," Newcomb wrote. The company was trucked forward to an orchard "a couple hundred yards back from the crossing site," he recalled. Local security was put out and the men got what rest they could. The night was quiet. Newcomb fell asleep. "After what seemed to be just a few minutes, I woke up — to broad daylight! It was deathly quiet and for a moment I panicked. Had everyone gone off and left me?" Looking around, he saw, to his relief, his men sleeping all around him. But he remembered that the crossing was to have been made in the pre-dawn hours. What had gone wrong? "What was supposed to be my first exposure to offensive combat, just didn't seem to be going right."

CPT Babb, the company commander told him to relax; the engineers had not brought the boats forward yet. From that point on, he recalled, all attempt "at security and surprise disappeared. All the officers were taken down to the river bank for reconnaissance and soon people were wandering all over the sandy beach area."

Newcomb went back, briefed his platoon, and they and rest of the company moved forward to the beach, each boatload of soldiers carrying its aluminum boat to the water's edge. As soon as they arrived there, the enemy opened up with machine gun fire and mortars. The machine guns fired into the unit flanks from across the river. Mortar rounds were falling between the tree-line the men had just left and the water's edge. For the moment, Newcomb himself, received none of this fire. But he thought it would be best to get the boats into the water and cross the river as fast as possible.

"This would both accomplish our platoon's assignment," he wrote, "and also get us away from the fire that was landing behind us. It was also rapidly becoming the smartest thing to do because our South Korean soldiers...hadn't had much training and were frantically digging in on the beach [or] firing their rifles in every direction without looking. The boats moved out from the beach but after getting about half way across the river (maybe 50 yards) we grounded on a sandbar.... About that time machine gun rounds began hitting around our boats in a beau-

tiful example of enfilade fire (coming in from both flanks). [It looked] like the movies — little geysers of water erupting in quick straight lines across the surface of the water. The only thing to do was begin wading across. Holding our rifles above our heads, we began slogging toward the beach." The water was about 4 1/2 feet deep.

Reaching the far shore, Newcomb happened to look back and saw some wounded men on the sandbar. Sending the platoon on, he waded back to the sandbar and got the casualties into a boat. With the aid of a few other men, he towed the boat forward to the shore.

Ground masked the enemy machine guns, preventing them from firing on the men once they reached the western shore. Newcomb found CPT Babb and was ordered to attack the objective, "a ridgeline located a couple of hundred yards inland," he wrote. "I got back to my platoon and got everyone coordinated. Then, feeling just a tad silly, gave a typical Fort Benning 'Lets go!' yell and took off for the ridge." Newcomb recalled experiencing what he described as "desultory mortar and machine gun rounds," but when his troops reached the ridgeline, the enemy had pulled out. "Starting next day, Company A, along with the rest of the regiment, began walking towards Seoul...."

Of the five officers in Company B, 21st Infantry, when John Begley joined the unit in mid-August, by Sept. 20, John was one of three who were left. This is what he wrote of the river crossing: "On the A.M. of the 19th [of Sept.] we followed a covered road to the crossing. The entire Co. in single file left the cover and crossed the sandy beach to the river. When the NKPA opened fire the lead element was just getting in boats and the rear element had just left the cover. The entire Co. was spread in a line about 150 yards long. As we advanced people were going down in front, behind and alongside me. When we got to the boats the KATUSAs laid down on their paddles and we had a devil of a time getting across. When we reached the far shore (from soldiers in the water pushing), there was a small ridge which offered protection from enemy fire. Finally, one of our machine guns got into action, which was the sweetest music I'd ever heard. One of our new officers led a platoon on a flanking movement and gradually the NKPA began to withdraw."

LT Earl J. Lochead, FO with 1/21st from the 52d FAB, accompanied by a radioman and a wireman, accompanied the 1st Battalion river crossing. They would be in the second wave of boats. As the first wave landed, the enemy opened a terrible barrage of mortar and artillery fire. Lochead saw one boat literally blown from the water, while thousands of enemy bullets criss-crossed the river's surface, each kicking up its own distinctive water spout. Other enemy bullets slammed into the troop-filled boats, killing and wounding the occupants.

Lochead reached the far shore. When his radioman jumped from the rear of the boat, he fell into the water, ruining the radio. The beach was less than two feet wide, but it was protected from enemy direct fire by a three foot high embankment. While crouched there, Lochead and his party spotted an abandoned 60mm mortar. Retrieving the weapon they fired it on the enemy until the available ammunition was gone.

Soon afterward, a very accurate air strike by four Marine Corsairs broke the enemy resistance and the troops moved inland.

LT Leiser recalled that his E/21st Infantry left a week or so of reserve "in a pup-tent city [in] an apple orchard" to cross the Naktong. "The night before the breakout across the Naktong River, we were lined up with assault boats not far from the river's edge under cover," he wrote. "Needless to say, we did not sleep. Early in the A.M., we moved to the river's edge, some miles south of Waegwan, not far upstream from a dilapidated and shell-torn bridge. Once across the Naktong, Diamond White (2d Bn) of the 21st, passed through some units to take the lead in the attack towards Kumchon along the route of a wide, dry stream-bed."

"The day we crossed the Naktong," said SGT Warren J. Avery (G/21st Inf.), "we had a hill to take and there were probably two North Koreans on [it]. We assaulted.... When we got up the hill there was a North Korean colonel there wounded badly in the chest." A company officer asked if anyone would volunteer to take this colonel down to the aid station. No one would volunteer, and this was the reason Avery gave: "Our men had been found with hands tied behind their backs and shot in the back of the head, so none of us volunteered to carry this colonel down the hill. Bill Jones took his .45 out and put a hole between [the North Korean's] eyes and that was the end of that colonel."

PFC Leonard Korgie, also of G/21st infantry, recalled that the company commander, CPT Syverson, sent out a 50-man patrol north to a point opposite Waegwan. Korgie was a member of that patrol. He thought it would be a tough one, with a lot of casualties. 2LT Williamson, who had been awarded a battlefield commission, led the patrol.

The patrol set off and had no enemy contact until just short of its objective, when it was fired on. The patrol and the enemy were both in a forest thick with underbrush. The patrol was on high ground with the enemy below them. The men in the patrol, he recalled, "were battlewise and mean." They wanted to keep going. After two months of taking it from the enemy, these soldiers wanted to dish it out. They smelled victory and didn't want to be held up by a bunch of the enemy in the valley. One GI raised up to get a look at the enemy, and was cut down at once by a machine gun burst. That brought the patrol back to reality.

LT Williamson decided to charge down the hill. Down they went, swearing, yelling and "firing like hell," Korgie remembered. Some enemy soldiers jumped from their foxholes, to be immediately cut down by the charging Americans. Others held their hands up in surrender, but still held onto potato masher grenades. These men too were shot down. As a result, no prisoners were taken — none of the North Koreans surrendered in an acceptable manner.

The patrol continued and soon spotted two enemy tanks. LT Williamson contacted CPT Syverson on the radio and gave him the map coordinates of the tanks. When the first artillery round came in, Williamson quickly adjusted fire, bringing the artillery down on the tanks, destroying both of them.

When the patrol arrived at its objective, it

discovered that the enemy had abandoned his foxholes. The patrol took possession of them. Shortly thereafter, a party of the enemy came down the road to reoccupy the holes. The patrol waited for them to get within 50 yards, then the men popped up and opened a deadly fire. Men like Korgie, who had survived the terrible early days of the war, took a special delight in cutting down as many enemy soldiers as possible. Remembering the long, hard road from Taejon to the Perimeter, he fired until there was no one else to shoot at. He recalled that he had a ball.

LT "Bud" Pritchett (I/21st Inf.) recalled a reconnaissance of the river similar to that recorded by Newcomb. There was no effort to conceal men or equipment. The officers and EM going on the recon drove to the water's edge. "We got out [of the jeeps], no stealth, no cover or concealment, and went down to the river's edge," he wrote. "People got out their binoculars and stared across the river, waved their hands and pointed their fingers and had a good ol' discussion and then got back into [the] jeeps and drove back to battalion to brief the troops." Pritchett speculated that the North Koreans had observed all this from concealed positions across the Naktong.

Like Co. A, Item Co. assembled the night before the crossing in an apple orchard. Many of the men did not dig in. The next morning an enemy SP gun or tank began firing. Pritchett, new to combat, was frightened. Rounds hitting in the trees produced air bursts. The men who had not bothered to dig a hole, did so now, with whatever came to hand. Finally, an air attack on the enemy silenced this fire. The crossing was unopposed and the company moved onto high ground that he recalled was about a mile west of the Naktong.

Co. I, 21st Infantry crossed the Naktong River by platoons, recalled COL Harry J. Maihafer (then a rifle platoon leader in I/21). His recollection of this and the unit's attack following the crossing are included in his *From the Hudson to the Yalu*. The crossing was made without incident, he wrote. His platoon objective was about two miles inland from the crossing site. As he and his men proceeded, they noted the signs of destruction caused by artillery, bombing and strafing; ground scorched earth, craters, the tail fins of exploded mortar rounds and abandoned enemy positions.

Enroute to the objective the platoon had to cross two intervening hills. The platoon had moved beyond the first platoon, when LT Maihafer received a radio call; since they couldn't see his men, battalion was worried that they were lost.

When his platoon reached the crest of the second hill, an artillery preparation began hitting the objective hill. The route to the objective dipped into a valley, skirted a village, a dry stream bed and a rice paddy. The objective hill was steep, but his platoon struggled to the top, finding it unoccupied. Maihafer reported the objective secured. The company commander, with the 1st Platoon, was now just to the rear, at the objective's base.

The ridge complex constituting the objective was in the form of an H. Two peaks were at the intersections of the legs. His platoon had climbed the right leg to the peak from the south. Now the company commander ordered his platoon to attack across and seize the other peak. The original plan was for the 1st Platoon to pass through Maihafer's and take that objective. With moans of protest, his now exhausted men dragged themselves to their feet and went across and took the second peak. Contrary to expectations, the enemy did not attack them that night.

Two miles south of the 21st, 2/19th Infantry crossed the river at 4 p.m. Sept. 19 and was on the west bank by evening. The battalion lost about 50 men to enemy fire while still east of the Naktong, but once across the river enemy resistance was negligible.

On Sept. 20, the 19th Infantry consolidated its position on the hills west of the Naktong along the Songju road. The 24th Recon Co. crossed the river at night, passed through the 19th Infantry and started to the west on the Songju road. I Corps attached the British 27th Infantry Brigade to the 24th Division that day. The 27th Brigade was relieved in position by 2/7th Cavalry and moved north to the 19th Infantry crossing site.

Elements of the 78th Tk Bn were attached to the 27th Brigade. Among them was the platoon of LT Tomas Carrillo. This is what he recalled of his Naktong crossing: "The bridge for the crossing was under heavy fire and hardly any traffic was going over it. A slow ferry was operating and a lot of artillery and other heavy equipment was using it.... Our side of the river was very congested and chaotic.

"CPT Burke, our company commander, arrived shortly, and after observing the confusion, went into the river and waded across. He found that the river at that point was not deep enough to prevent our tanks from driving across...without problems. In the afternoon we joined the British Brigade and prepared plans to continue the attack within a few days. While waiting in our bivouac area we were subjected to mortar attacks almost daily, without suffering any damage or casualties."

The British 27th Infantry Brigade crossed on what LTC G. I. Malcolm of Poltalloch, in his book *The Argylls in Korea*, described as "a rickety pontoon footbridge which the Yanks had managed to erect." He also wrote of the harassing enemy fire at this crossing site, which "apparently came from the direct fire of a roving...S.P. gun, being especially troublesome to the vehicles which were interminably crossing on an improvised mechanical ferry that not infrequently failed." The Argyll Battalion lost one killed and three wounded in this crossing.

Companies A and C, 3d ECB had the mission of carrying the 19th and 21st Regiments, respectively, across the Naktong. CPT Richard P. Lepke, who commanded Co. C at the time, wrote an account of this venture in "Three River Crossings," *Combat Support in Korea*. The operation, he wrote was to start at 2:45 a.m. on Sept. 19. But there were a number of major problems. First, when the mission was assigned on Sept. 17, none of the engineer officers had seen the sites, nor had an opportunity to examine aerial photos; none of the engineers had received any assault training in Korea; the infantry was without assault river-crossing training; there was little time to coordinate with the infantry commanders; and the engineer battalion had no assault boats. Worst of all, each engineer company had

received a hundred KATUSAs just a few days previously. These ROK soldiers had almost no training, and were completely unfamiliar with assault boats. With the language barrier, there was little time to train them.

On Sept. 18 the engineers did make a recon of the crossing sites. Co. C was reinforced by a platoon from Co. B and another from Co. D. In moving forward by vehicle, the engineers ran into the traffic problem at the Kumho River. In spite of that, CPT Lepke got his unit into its initial assembly area south of Naksan-dong by 7:30 p.m. Lepke took the two platoon leaders who would be making the crossing forward on a recon of the two sites to be used by the 21st. At 9 p.m. his unit closed into its final assembly area, an apple orchard, just 300 yards behind the crossing sites.

The Naktong River, where the 21st Infantry and C/3d ECC were to cross, was about 400 feet wide, and had what Lepke described as "a moderate current." After dark, the 2d Platoon cut down a sheer bank on the approach to one of the sites. A path led down to the beach at the other site. The beach, about 100 yards wide, was flat and sandy. Only some abandoned tactical wire was scattered here and there. The beach, however, was not solid enough to support vehicles.

The 1st Platoon had the first crossing site; the 2d Platoon the other. The 3d Platoon unloaded the boats when they arrived and organized the infantry into boat crews. The B Co. platoon had the job of laying a pierced-plank roadway (airstrip type) over the beach as soon as the first wave had landed. This would provide a road over the beach for litter jeeps and ammo trucks. The attached D Co. platoon was to await orders — a sort of reserve.

The infantry arrived in their forward assembly areas and were oriented on assault boats by the engineers. But the boats did not arrive. COL Stephens got angrier and angrier as the time slipped by. He consulted with LTC Peter C. Hyzer, commanding the 3d ECC. Messengers were sent to locate the boats. They finally arrived at 4 a.m. There were 28 of them. There was further delay to unload many of them which had been placed on 2 1/2-ton trucks. Even worse, the drivers simply left and the engineers had to find drivers of their own to move the trucks away.

Lepke recalled no enemy fire until the boats reached midstream. Then they were taken under what he described as "an extremely high volume of small-arms fire." At the same time, mortar and SP fire hit the near bank and assembly area. Many of the frightened KATUSAs with the infantry refused to leave the boats. One engineer NCO broke his carbine over the hand of one of them to release his hold on the guide rail of one boat. Some of the Koreans even returned to the near shore.

Eight of 28 boats were lost; some to the current and inexperienced paddlers and others to enemy fire. None of the KATUSA engineer troops returned from the first wave. After the battle, the company had only 22 of the original 100 Korean replacements.

As the second wave of infantrymen reached the beach, it too, was taken under enemy fire. The troops dove for the ground. SGT Weird, of the engineers, called on them to load up and cross to help the troops already across. "Hearing this,"

Lepke wrote, "one sergeant jumped up and yelled, 'If the Engineers can stand up and take it so can we!' To a man the infantry hurried to the water's edge and loaded up."

CPT Lepke called battalion for replacement boats; he quickly got 16. A boat-repair detachment was also sent forward, but only its sergeant would go forward to ascertain the damage to the boats.

Enemy fire prevented the B Co. platoon from laying the roadway. In all, C/3d ECC lost 42 men in this operation, eight of whom were GIs.

At noon, Lepke was ordered to take his company and cross the 5th RCT that evening. He found a crossing site just two miles north of Waegwan and radioed his company to meet him on the road. He then started back to Waegwan. The rapid advance of the 21st Infantry on the west shore of the Naktong assured Lepke that the crossing of the 5th RCT would be an administrative one (instead of under fire, or the danger of enemy opposition). As a result, his company was able to cross one battalion in 45 minutes. He was then ordered to cross the other two battalions of the 5th RCT eight miles north of Waegwan opposite Hill 303. The crossing was actually made on the morning of Sept. 20, he recalled. Both battalions of the 5th RCT were crossed before noon and Lepke's company was ready for another mission.

CPT Lepke recalled that the 121st ECB, to which he belonged in WW II, had three months to prepare to cross the Roer River in Germany. This included forming exact crews and making dry run crossings of a similar river with the infantry. But in Korea, his C/3d ECB had, within three days, "received orders for, had planned, and had executed three river crossings, supporting two different regiments," while at the same time giving general engineer support to a third regiment in attack. "How different was Korea," he commented.

Although the infantrymen of the 24th Division were across the Naktong by the close of Sept. 20, no way then existed to get the command's heavy equipment, artillery, tanks and service elements across. A good bridge was necessary, but those which had spanned the river were all destroyed. A major engineer bridging project was necessary and one was undertaken and completed in record time.

The 11th ECB and the 55th Treadway Bridge Co. began work on a 700 foot M2 pontoon float bridge on Sept. 20, completing it by 10 a.m. on Sept. 22. Twenty-fourth Division traffic began crossing at once. Most division vehicles were across the Naktong by midnight. Some carried signs, like "One side, Bud - Seoul Bound," and "We Remember Taejon."

The 1st Cavalry Division Above Taegu — Sept. 16-22

On Sept. 16 the 1st Cavalry and ROK 1st Divisions were almost at a stalemate with the *NK 3d, 1st* and *13th Divisions* on an arc west and north of Taegu. Appleman recorded that fighting in this area was producing the bulk of casualties. Of 373 wounded evacuated to Pusan on Sept. 16, he stated, 200 of them came from the Taegu area. The struggle centered on two avenues of approach to Taegu. The first was the

Treadway Bridge across the Naktong River constructed by U.S. Engineers. Before the bridge was built, the only means of crossing the river was a small ferry operated by South Koreans. (Source: P. 142, Korea, 1950, Chief of Military History, Washington, D.C., 1982)

Artillery moving up over muddy ground into firing position near Taegu. Several tanks and men can be seen in the background. (Source: P. 142, Korea, 1950, Chief of Military History, Washington, D.C., 1982)

highway and railroad route from Waegwan, defended by the 5th Cavalry Regiment against elements of the *NK 3d Division* five miles southeast of Waegwan and eight miles northwest of Taegu. The second was the Tabu-dong route north of Taegu. There, the bulk of the 1st Cavalry and ROK 1st Divisions continued to battle the *NK 13th* and *1st Divisions*. In this area, the enemy was only six miles north of Taegu.

1st Cavalry Division Plan for the Breakout:
5th Cavalry Regt: Attack and hold enemy troops in zone east of the Waegwan-Taegu highway. Protect the right flank of the 5th RCT as it attacks toward Waegwan.

8th Cavalry Regt: Continue to attack in the Chilgok area. Be prepared, on order, to attack north to Tabu-dong. (This was to be a "maximum effort" attack.)

7th Cavalry Regt: On order, shift by successive battalion movements, from the division right flank to the left flank. Make a rapid encircle-

ment of the enemy over a trail and secondary road between Waegwan and Tabu-dong.

The 7th and 8th Cavalry Regiments were to meet at Tabu-dong, encircling enemy troops in the Waegwan-Taegu-Tabu-dong area. The 7th Cavalry began shifting battalions on Sept. 16.

During the first three days of the offensive, the *NK 13th Division* completely stymied the 8th Cavalry. The 2d Battalion clung to Hill 570, beating off repeated enemy attacks. Hill 570 was the dominating terrain east of the Tabu-dong corridor, 10 miles north of Taegu. Meantime, west of the road, 3/8th Cavalry made small gains in the high mountains closer to the city.

The enemy had firmly entrenched both sides of the Tabu-dong road, including mortars and small field pieces dug in on the forward slopes of the hills. For the present, commanders were unable to deploy their men to combine fire and movement. As a result, it was necessary to pro-

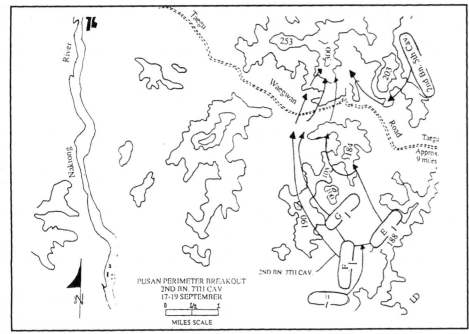

Map 53 (Source: P. 47, Skirmish, Red, White and Blue, Ed Daily, Turner, 1992)

ceed slowly and methodically, or take unacceptable casualties.

Both Generals Walker and Milburn (I Corps) were very unhappy with COL Raymond Palmer's 8th Cavalry; it was moving too slowly. On Sept. 19, Gay attached 3/7th Cavalry to the 8th and COL Holmes, the Chief of Staff, told Palmer that he had to capture Tabu-dong that day. But the *13th Division*, employing artillery and mortars, plus machine gun cross fire, from Kasan on one side and Hill 351 on the other, stopped the regiment with heavy casualties. B/70th Tk Bn (CPT Carlos L. Fraser) lost seven tanks in this area on Sept. 20. CPT Fraser, in an interview for a 1952 Armored School report, *Employment of Armor in Korea - The First Year*, stated that four tanks were lost to mines and two to AT fire. The unit also lost five men wounded.

Meantime, the ROK 1st Division achieved a surprising breakthrough. In the 5th Cavalry zone, Hills 203 and 174 north of the Waegwan-Taegu road and 188 to its south (where 2/7th Cavalry would shortly attack) some 1,000 soldiers of the *8th Regiment, 3d Division* would put up a hard defense. And, as we have seen in Chapter 15, 3/5th Cavalry seized Hill 174 (for the last time) on Sept. 16. The 2/7th Cavalry was attached to the 5th Cavalry and on Sept. 17 began its attack in support of the 5th. It jumped off at 7 a.m. with Co. E moving toward the forward slope of Hill 188 to protect Co. G while it crossed the wide valley on its left. To the left of Co. G, Fox Co. swung southwest of Hill 188 to protect the battalion's left flank. As it did so, it drew heavy fire from Hill 184, which lay northwest of 188. The battalion was ordered to leave enough troops behind to contain the enemy on Hill 184 and continue the attack to seize the ultimate objective, Hill 300, north of the Waegwan road. The attack was slowed somewhat by enemy fire as Companies G and E passed over Hills 105 and 100, respectively. The Co. F artillery FO was wounded.

Companies F and G were ordered to join forces and attack to the northeast toward the road

while Co. E attacked Hill 184 at 2 p.m. Co. E's attack failed until an attack by 2/5th Cavalry helped the unit take the hill. Companies F and G made their attack across the road, forcing the enemy to higher ground. CPT Fred P. DePalina, commanding Co. G was killed in the attack and the two companies became disorganized. This forced their withdrawal south of the road for the night.

The three platoon leaders in G Company were classmates in the West Point Class of 1949 — Lieutenants Harold R. Anderegg, Lawrence J. Ogden and Richard E. Tobin. When the company reached the base of its objective, Hill 253, it began receiving heavy mortar fire, during which the leader of a machinegun squad, nicknamed "Swabbie" was killed. ("Swabbie" had been in the Navy previously.)

As the unit climbed the hill, the shelling intensified. One round landed next to Ogden, killing a man to each side of him, but leaving him untouched. As they neared the crest, enemy small-arms and automatic weapons opened fire. Again, Ogden had a close call when an enemy bullet went through his pant leg without touching him. The company was pinned down by this fierce enemy fire. Suddenly, something motivated the unit, which to a man, jumped up, and yelling, screaming and firing their weapons, charged forward in a quick, sharp assault. The enemy bolted in the face of this crazy attack. The men of George Co., carried on in their rage and enthusiasm, swept down the far slope and into a village where the enemy's mortars were located. Two enemy majors were killed there. The attack went on into a rice paddy in an open valley. On the right a road came down from between two hills, following the contours of the hills, then skirting the paddy's edge.

Suddenly an enemy company appeared, marching in formation down from the hills. A soldier in front carried an unusual green flag. The North Koreans were unaware of Co. G's one man after the other. G Co. was in an untenable position.

CPT DePalina, among the wounded, said he would provide cover while the company withdrew. LT Ogden reached a ditch along the road and crawled along it on hands and knees. He had just crawled over the body of a North Korean when a shot rang out behind him. The North Korean had not been dead, and had raised up to shoot Ogden in the back. As he did so, a man following behind, cut the enemy soldier down with a single shot.

The 2d Battalion continued the attack the next morning (Sept. 18). E and F Companies, with tank support, crossed the road at 5 p.m., but continued to receive heavy enemy fire. The commitment of Co. G to the east of Co. E didn't help; G became pinned down by enemy fire from south of the road. This forced the unit to withdraw to high ground north of the road. Co. F, now only 45 men, remained near the tanks on the road while E and G, with a total of 120 men, attacked to within 200 yards of the summit of Hill 300. There they dug in for the night.

Co. F began the attack to take the final objective at dawn on Sept. 19. Co. E also began its attack, but was forced to withdraw by heavy enemy automatic weapons fire. However, Co. F continued its attack, and after hand-to-hand fighting, attaining the southern tip of Hill 300 by 9 a.m. E and G Companies supported this attack by fire but could not move forward. Within half an hour an enemy counterattack forced Co. F to pull back a hundred yards.

CPT William L. Webb (West Point 1947), F Co.'s C.O., was wounded as he attacked an enemy machine gun. LT Christenson took command. Then a short artillery preparation was fired. Due to the ammunition shortage, only one gun in each battery fired! A coordinated attack by all companies failed. A requested air strike came in at 3:30 p.m. Then the companies tried again. LT Radcliff, commanding Co. E was wounded leading E and G in the assault. At 4:30 p.m., enemy troops observed running from the objective were chased by artillery fire.

At 6:15 p.m. all companies of the battalion attacked again, this time with the help of 1/5th Cavalry. This time Hill 300 was taken and held. This was the dominating terrain in the area. Its capture assured a breakthrough on this axis. The enemy had been deeply dug in. Some positions were dug into solid rock. At least a dozen 120mm and 82mm mortars, tanks and other flat trajectory weapons supported the position. About 200 enemy were killed in the battle, but 2/7th Cavalry also lost 34 killed, 229 wounded and 5 missing. One company commander was among the dead and three company commanders and one company XO were among the wounded. At the end of the battle, the three rifle companies of 2/7th Cavalry had a total of only 165 effectives. Co. F had only 45 men.

Then-Major John W. Callaway commanded 2/7th Cavalry. He recalled this battle. He had sent a platoon out the night before to reconnoiter. Early in the battle, as he scanned enemy terrain looking for their OP he discovered the platoon about a thousand yards west of the key terrain feature. He was amazed. He recalled the mounting casualties throughout the battle. And when the battalion approached the main objective, they encountered "tanks dug in like pillboxes," he wrote. Although the price in killed and wounded was high, the victory "opened the hole for the breakout of Eighth Army...to link up with the X Corps, 180 miles away at Osan, 20 miles south of Seoul," he wrote. "It was a real thrill to look down at the road as hundreds of 2 1/2-ton trucks of the 24th Division moved north. Two days before our tanks could not get to my battalion's line of departure."

1LT Pennel "Joe" Hickey's 3d Platoon of F/7th Cavalry led his unit when it made a coordinated attack with Co. G during the battle. He recalled that the attack began at 8 a.m. on Sept. 19. The company had taken about half of a finger ridge when it began finding enemy foxholes and bunkers. BAR-man CPL James Dady took it upon himself to attack the first three or four of them by dashing forward up the finger, firing a burst from his BAR into each of them. He then turned and dashed back and flopped down next to the other men in his squad. As luck would have it, the foxholes where unoccupied, but that doesn't detract from the courage this young soldier displayed.

Then enemy small-arms and automatic weapons fire came down from higher ground. About 10 or 11 a.m., Dady made another dash up the finger, "blasting everything in sight," Hickey recalled. Returning again to his squad, Dady dropped down about 10 yards to LT Hickey's left. "I moved over to him, and as I got up...to tell him a 'good job'...a shot rang out and took a nip out of the top edge of his right ear. CPL Dady turned white as a ghost, but he wasn't really hurt."

Deciding that Dady was putting the platoon to shame, Hickey jumped up and dashed for the next foxhole, his carbine set for full automatic. "I stood over the foxhole and pulled the trigger," he recalled, "when suddenly the carbine fell into two pieces in my hands. (I hadn't set a retaining clip.) I couldn't help but laugh at myself at the foolishness of the situation, so I hightailed it back to our troops in a hurry."

Shortly thereafter, CPT William L. Webb, commanding F Co., was wounded. He turned the company over to Hickey. The advance continued, but under increasingly heavy opposition. Soon, both companies were pinned down. The ground where Hickey found himself gave cover from the enemy fire. Taking advantage of this, he tried to reorganize the unit. He found only 35 men with him. The others, he recalled, were far behind.

Then he and G Co. were ordered to renew the attack in what he called a "one-inch movement." Both companies advanced about 10 yards before being stopped again. The two units were then both withdrawn to where they had been before.

Edwin Seith was a rifleman in Co. E. He wrote this about one part of the battle: "After a mortar and artillery barrage on the hill, we began to move up. We began to take heavy fire from the very beginning. We were pinned down for quite some time. A mortar round landed nearby with a deafening thud and a few men were hit. We began to move forward again and I heard firing from my left rear. Corporal Elmy had shot two enemy who had come out of their holes just to my left. I did not see them and I would have been a goner if it were not for him.

"Just then, another came out of his hole, run-ning to go over the top [of the hill]. I fired and missed. Then I took a good shoulder aim and hit him in the back. He just leaped in the air and fell dead. After a few more minutes of fighting it was all over. We counted at least a dozen enemy dead in their foxholes and several more bodies strewn across the hill. Several wounded were taken prisoner. We had about a dozen killed and several wounded." Seith removed the identification papers and a cap with a red star on it from one of the enemy dead. His lieutenant made him put them back. He told Seith that if he were ever captured with those items in his possession, he would be tortured by the enemy. "After it was all over, it seemed like a dream," Seith wrote. "Everything happens so quickly, you have no time to think."

Donald Down, a BAR-man with F/7th Cavalry, recalled that when the final objective was reached on Sept. 19, the company had only about 14 or 15 men on the hill. Counting men who had not yet arrived on the hill and possibly mortarmen and company headquarters, the unit actually numbered only 45 men. It is possible that just 15 were in the rifle element that took the hill.

Casualties in 2/7th Cavalry were so heavy that the battalion aid station ran out of supplies. The battalion was attached to the 5th Cavalry, but they were also short of supplies due to their own heavy casualties. CPT John C. Rourke, 2/7th Cavalry Surgeon, remarked that, as a result of the difficulty in obtaining supplies, his medical unit felt like orphans.

PFC James Turner (left) and COL Edwin W. Seith, just before battle near Taegu, Sept. 1950. (Courtesy of Edwin W. Seith, E/7th Cavalry)

7th Cavalry vehicles afer hitting tank mines. (Courtesy of Edwin W. Seith, E/7th Cavalry)

Captured North Korean guerrillas, Pusan Perimeter, 1950. (Courtesy of Edwin W. Seith, E/7th Cavalry)

On the final day of the battle, he personally went back to the supporting 5th Cavalry medical unit for supplies, only to find that it was also short too and could not help. He then traveled several more miles to the rear to Medical Co. 7th Cavalry. He found the unit all loaded up and ready to move out in support of TF 777. As a result, they were also unable to help. (Note: TF 777 is covered in the next chapter.) By this time Rourke was completely frustrated. He located the Catholic Chaplain of the 2d Battalion, CPT McCullough, a close friend, and asked for his help.

"Father, sir," he said, "your old friends in the 2d Battalion are bleeding badly and need help." Rourke outlined the problem and the chaplain immediately set off to see what he could do. "Within 30 minutes after my arrival back at the aid station," Rourke recalled, "he came forward with large amounts of supplies that I had requested. He definitely was a true friend in need."

CPT Rourke recalled CPT Herschel E. "Ug" Fuson (West Point 1947). Fuson got his nickname "Ug" as a star football player at West Point. He was a large, quiet man. Fuson had been struck by a bullet which entered through his right armpit and into the area where the neck and shoulder join. At the aid station, Rourke remembered, Fuson did not seem to be too uncomfortable. But he was hungry. While Rourke was packing his wound, Fuson paid no attention; he was looking for something to eat. "Suddenly he spotted, by accident, a young soldier from one of the mess halls walking around with a large carton of donuts," said Rourke. "These donuts were being distributed to wounded personnel who needed food."

Fuson called the man over, reached into the box with one hand and pulled out seven or eight donuts, and proceeded to eat them with great gusto. Fuson recovered from his wound, only to die of a heart ailment June 14, 1951.

LT Radcliff (Co. E), lived one week after being wounded. He died in a MASH unit.

While 2/7th Cavalry attacked from south of the Waegwan road, the 5th Cavalry was having trouble with Hill 203 north of it. The enemy held on for three bloody days. The men began to say, grimly, "Get Hill 203." On Sept. 17 and 18 A/70th Tk Bn lost nine tanks and a tank dozer. Six were lost to mines, two to enemy tanks and two more to AT guns. On Sept. 18, an American tank knocked out two of three dug-in T-34's.

As Sept. 18 ended, the *NK 3d Division* still held the hill mass centering on Hills 253 and 371, the day the carpet bombing of Waegwan took place.

On Sept. 19, 1/5th Cavalry and 2/7th Cavalry combined their attacks to seize Hills 253 and 300. The enemy defense of these two positions was almost fanatical, resulting in very high casualties in both 2/7 and 1/5. The 2d Battalion's losses have already been mentioned. The 1/5th Cavalry lost almost as many men — American losses were 28 KIA, 147 WIA and 4 MIA. The battalion also lost 28 KATUSA, for a total of 207 men.

During the battle on Sept. 18, Robert R. Byrd, 60mm Mortar Section, C/5th was wounded. "I was Assistant Gunner on a 60mm mortar," he wrote. "The [North] Koreans started dropping mortar [rounds] in the creek bottom [where our mortars were located]. One shell landed about 5 feet behind us and hit a pine tree. Most of the shrapnel hit the gunner in the kidney area and every time his heart would beat, blood would gush out. I helped him get out. He put his arm around my neck and we walked down the creek bed. Another round came in and landed in the water. It splashed water in our faces but didn't explode. We got to the aid station and they put him on a litter. At that time I didn't know I was bleeding too. They sent me to a field hospital for about ten days." Byrd was then given his choice of MP duty or returning to his unit. "I chose to go back to the front with my buddies," he wrote. He also recalled that the man he helped to the Aid Station, called "Gus" by the men, weighed about 250 lbs. Byrd weighed about 150.

The enemy still clung to Hill 371, a mile north

of the Hill 253-300 complex. For the moment, the 5th Cavalry could not budge them.

When the enemy finally did withdraw from this area, the *3d Division* dropped from a strength of about 5,000 men to about 1,800. Panic overtook entire units when the enemy finally began to withdraw. The area occupied by the 5th Cavalry was the old Waegwan pocket. Therein were found 28 enemy tanks — 27 T-34s and an American M-4 refitted by the enemy. These tanks had either been destroyed or captured.

On Sept. 19, GEN Gay began his envisioned encircling movement by moving 1/7th Cavalry from the division's right flank to the left, passing through the badly depleted 2/7th preparatory to its drive on Tabu-dong. The 3d Battalion was placed under the operational control of the 8th Cavalry for the impending operation. He ordered 3/7th Cavalry to move the next morning (Sept. 20) from the right flank to the left. The 3d Battalion moved out on Sept. 20 by truck. Apparently concerned that enemy mortar or artillery fire might interdict the road, COL Nist, 7th Cavalry commander, ordered the men to detruck and walk the rest of the way. They arrived at their destination footsore and late. Gay was furious, because a similar incident had occurred when 2/7th Cavalry had moved to the left flank four days before.

On Sept. 20, 1/7th Cavalry, under LTC Clainos, moved to the attack, took Hill 168, just south of Waegwan by 2:05 p.m., then was well on its way toward Tabu-dong by 8:10 p.m. C/70th Tk Bn, spearheading the battalion attack, lost four tanks to mines in the first 1 1/2 to 2 miles of road. The first mines encountered were carefully buried, but soon they were found randomly scattered. At one point during the advance to Tabu-dong, the troops found an enemy SP gun which had been used to scatter mines as it withdrew. C/70th Tk Bn lost seven men wounded, all to mine explosions. At one point, Appleman stated, the column came to a complete halt when a tank hit a mine. Gay angrily ordered Nist to bypass North Koreans in the hills and "hightail" it to Tabu-dong.

The road of advance to Tabu-dong was a scene of devastation. There were dead oxen, disabled enemy tanks, artillery pieces and stocks of abandoned ammunition and other military supplies and equipment scattered all along the route. By that evening 1/7th Cavalry, with 3/7th following, was only four miles from the town.

The evening of the 20th, Gay, completely unhappy with COL Nist, removed him from command of the 7th Cavalry and appointed LTC William A. "Wild Bill" Harris, commander of the 77th FAB, to take his place.

Harris assumed command of the 7th at 11 p.m. that day and immediately assembled his staff, battalion commanders and commanders of attached units to plan continuation of the attack. The 1st Battalion was to continue its advance. The 3d Battalion, with the I&R Platoon and two tank platoons from C/70th Tk Bn, was to follow. If the 3d Battalion caught up to the 1st, it was to pass on through and continue the attack to Tabu-dong. If the 3d did not catch up to the 1st, it was to go into an assembly area and establish positions to defend the route. Whichever battalion reached Tabu-dong first was to turn south and contact the 8th Cavalry and establish defensive positions to secure the road. All this was to be accomplished by nightfall on Sept. 21.

The 1st Battalion moved out again on Sept. 21, reaching Tabu-dong at 12:55 p.m. Meeting enemy resistance, it made a pincer movement on the village from the southwest and northwest, clearing out the town by 4:35 p.m. An hour later, it moved on down the road to contact the 8th Cavalry. During the advance that day, LTC Clainos was wounded when his jeep hit a mine. Although he refused evacuation, he was evacuated on orders of the regimental commander. LT Frank Maloney received a severe eye injury in the same explosion. LTC Harris led the 3d Battalion as it followed the 1st. MAJ William O. Witherspoon assumed command of the 1st Battalion at 5 p.m.

"Scrappy, this is Skirmish Red. Don't fire." These words, coming over an 8th Cavalry radio, were the prelude to the link up of the 7th and 8th Cavalry Regiments just south of Tabu-dong. GEN Gay, who was accompanying 1/8th Cavalry, was standing with its commander, LTC Robert Kane, when these words came in over a tank radio. A few minutes later, at 6:50 p.m., Sept. 21, SFC Robert P. Goodrow, C/7th Cavalry became the first man to shake hands with a member of the 8th Cavalry. He also received GEN Gay's personal congratulations upon completing the encirclement of the enemy.

The 1st and 3d Battalions, 7th Cavalry had crossed the fronts of the 5th and 8th Cavalry Regiments, cutting off the elements of two enemy divisions.

At Tabu-dong, 3/7th Cavalry turned north and deployed in defensive positions on both sides of the road. The following day, Sept. 22, elements of the ROK 15th Regiment, 1st Division arrived from the north to link up with the 1st Cavalry at Tabu-dong.

ROK 1st Division — Sept. 16-22

The ROK 1st Division orders for the breakthrough were:

1. Attack from Palgong-san to Kasan. Destroy the NKPA 1st Division there.
2. Prepare to cross the Naktong River and attack in concert with the U.S. 1st Cavalry Division toward Sangju.

The ROK 1st Division was to attack at 9 a.m. on Sept. 16. That day dawned with a thick fog and torrential rain. Visibility was zero. Both artillery and air support for the attack were impossible. The division attacked anyway and ran head-on into a similar attack the enemy had launched to take advantage of the bad visibility. Very soon, the troops were so intermixed it was impossible to determine who was attacking and who was defending.

Very quickly, GEN Paik Sun Yup, commanding the ROK 1st Division, lost communications with his 15th Regiment on the division's right for 48 hours. He was greatly concerned because he had no way of knowing what situation was with the 15th. To make matters worse, higher headquarters pressed him for information he couldn't supply.

His 12th Regiment, chosen to spearhead the division attack was stopped by the enemy attack

and the 11th was stymied in the Kasan area. The divisions on his flanks, GEN Paik noted, also had the same problem in making progress. He recalled that GEN Walker "was fit to be tied" because a breakthrough was not accomplished quickly a link-up with the forces from the Inchon landing would be too late.

On the morning of Sept. 17, Walker paid Paik a visit at the ROK 1st Division CP, located in a brewery near the Tongchon airport. Walker asked Paik if he had attended the U.S. Army Command and General Staff College at Ft. Leavenworth, Kansas. Paik had never attended any U.S. Army schools. Walker went on to tell Paik that the Staff College solution to the ROK 1st Division's problem was to bypass the enemy. Turn either right or left and get around the enemy strong resistance. How to accomplish the bypass was up to GEN Paik and his commanders.

Although he still had no communication with the 15th Regiment, Paik learned that it was in a virtual hand-to-hand struggle with the enemy all the way back to its regimental CP, but was intact and fighting well. The 11th Regiment's battle for Kasan, GEN Paik wrote, "remained a melee."

Unknown to the general, his 12th Regiment, under LTC Kim Chum Kon, had achieved a strategically important breakthrough. LTC Kim had discovered a gap in the enemy's lines between the *NK 1st Division* and the *NK 8th Division* to its east. Exploiting this gap, Kim had concentrated his regiment to attack through this gap. By the afternoon of Sept. 18, the ROK 12th Regiment was seven miles behind enemy lines, chewing up his rear areas.

GEN Paik first verified the reports, then reported to Eighth Army. Officials at Eighth Army were incredulous. They couldn't believe it was true. Paik assured them it was and he quickly ordered every available man from the other two regiments to bypass the enemy on the right, leaving only enough men to hold at Kasan. Paik's division drove deep into enemy territory cutting south. At the same time, the 7th Cavalry was driving toward Tabu-dong. The North Korean Army began to crumble, he wrote. He had high praise for the U.S. 10th Antiaircraft Artillery Group, which supported his division "magnificently with its big guns."

As his troops and those of the 1st Cavalry converged, he recalled, the enemy, who had fought so fiercely now disappeared "like fog under a burning sun."

Enemy prisoners revealed that their leaders had kept from them the news that a successful U.S. landing had been achieved at Inchon. His men found enemy machine-gunners chained to their guns, he wrote. So condemned, these gunners resisted to the death. So many enemy troops were killed that his men became disgusted with the killing, he recalled.

On Sept. 19, four days after the counteroffensive started, GEN Paik stood north of Tabudong on the road to Kunwi. Appropriately, Kunwi in Korean, means "military dignity." The scene of carnage and destruction he saw before him was overwhelming. He wrote that it could not be any worse than the look of hell. The air was drenched with the smell of putrefying flesh, both of humans and of animals. "Countless enemy bodies were piled up at the bottom of every

hill," he wrote. The bodies of horses and cows were scattered "everywhere." Enemy tanks, artillery pieces, great numbers of weapons and ammunition were strewn all over the terrain.

The *NK 1st Division*, under MG Hong Rim had defeated Paik and his ROK 1st Division, he wrote, now the *NK 1st Division* "had suffered not just defeat but utter destruction."

Quite large numbers of MG Choi Yong Chin's *NK 13th Division* defected or surrendered, he recalled, resulting in the annihilation of that command. The *NK 3d Division* (MG Lee Yong Ho) "bugged out," he wrote, during the Waegwan fight. A thousand men ran off in panic, he recalled. On Aug. 29, LTC Chung Bong Wuk, who had commanded the *NK 13th Division's* artillery regiment, surrendered. The colonel repudiated Communism, entered the ROK Army, and eventually rose to the rank of major general.

This victory at Tabu-dong, GEN Paik asserted, "served as a primer for the advance of allied forces back up the Korean peninsula and represented one of the war's major turning points." He wrote that the ROK 1st Division's greatest battle started and ended at Tabu-dong. (Note: All quotations are from GEN Paik's book, *From Pusan to Panmunjom*.)

ROK I and II Corps — Sept. 15-22

The ROK II Corps' 6th and 8th Divisions had been battling the *NK 8th* and *15th Divisions* in the mountainous area of central Korea and all four divisions were exhausted. But the *15th Division* was almost destroyed. The ROK 6th Division had fought the attacking *NK 8th Division* to a standstill for two weeks. Then the 6th went on the attack, and in a 4-day battle destroyed the *8th Division* as a combat force. Enemy prisoners said that the division suffered over 4,000 losses at this time. Remnants of the command fled in disorder north to Yechon. By Sept. 21, Appleman wrote, the ROK 6th Division was moving north of Uihung with little opposition.

To the east, the ROK 8th Division got organized and began to move north. It, too, found little opposition, for the enemy's *15th Division* had been all but annihilated.

In the ROK I Corps sector, embracing the much fought-over Kigye-Angang-ni-Kyongju area, elements of the Capital Division battled their way through the streets of Angang-ni on Sept. 16. On its right, the ROK 3d Division had advanced up the north bank of the Hyongsan-gang just short of Pohang-dong. On Sept. 17 a battalion of the ROK 7th Division, coming in from the west, made contact with the Capital Division, closing the two week old gap between the ROK I and II Corps.

The Capital Division had heavy going against stubborn delaying actions by the *NK 12th Division*. As a result, the division did not take Kigye until Sept. 22. Survivors of the *12th*, about 2,000 men, withdrew toward Andong. The *12th* had been one of the enemy divisions composed mostly of Korean veterans of the Chinese Communist Army. As a result, it had been an imposing force.

Appleman likened the enemy and ROK divisions on the eastern flank to exhausted wrestlers, "each too weak to press against the other."

But the ROK divisions were numerically superior, had better supply, daily close air support and, in the Pohang area, naval gunfire support.

ADM Charles C. Hartman's Task Group, including the battleship *USS Missouri*, arrived off Pohang-dong on Sept. 16. Hurling 2,000 lb. shells from its 16 inch guns, the *Missouri* bombarded enemy positions along a dike below the town, north of the Hyonsan-gang. On Sept. 18, COL Emmerich (ROK 3d Division KMAG advisor) directed another bombardment by radio. Following this, ROK troops assaulted across the Hyongsan-gang bridge, but were massacred by enemy machine-gunners. The number of dead is unknown, but 144 of them were wounded in the effort to cross the bridge. Finally, 31 ROK soldiers volunteered to cross the bridge, or die trying. Dummy runs by fighter planes helped keep enemy gunners under cover. Even so, 19 of the volunteers died on that bridge. Other ROK soldiers quickly rushed across to reinforce the few men who had made it to the other side. They found dead enemy machine-gunners tied to their positions.

On the night of Sept. 14-15, naval ships transported the ROK Miryang Guerrilla Battalion, a unit specially trained and armed with Russian-type weapons, to Changso-dong, 10 miles north of Pohang-dong. The battalion landed there after midnight, placing it in rear of the *5th Division*. It was to harass the enemy rear while the ROK 3d Division attacked its front below Pohang-dong. That night, a battalion of the *12th Regiment, 5th Division* was sent back and attacked the ROK battalion in the coastal hills. The ROKs were soon in deep trouble and the U.S. Navy had to rush units to its aid by placing a ring of naval gunfire around the battalion on the beach where the enemy had driven it. On Sept. 18, with great difficulty, "the Navy evacuated 725 of the ROKs, 110 of them wounded, by LST. Thirty-nine dead were left behind, as well as 32 others who refused to try to reach the evacuating ships," Appleman recorded.

Although the Miryang Guerrilla Battalion was of little help to the ROK 3d Division, combat patrols from the division reached the edge of Pohang-dong on the evening of Sept. 19. At 10:15 the next morning, the ROK 3d Division captured the ruined town. One regiment went on to seize the high ground north of it. On Sept. 21 and 22, the hard-driving ROK 3d Division, supported by air strikes and naval gunfire, drove north and captured Hunghae and pushing the now beat-up *NK 5th Division* back to Yongdok in disarray. Yongdok is over 25 miles north of Pohang-dong. The ROK 3d Division was destined to advance to a point on the coast just five miles south of the 38th Parallel by Sept. 30. This feat will be treated in more detail in the next chapter.

The offensive to break out of the Pusan Perimeter, begun on Sept. 16, did not achieve many gains, except where the 23d and 38th Regiments of the 2d Division broke through enemy forces to reach the Naktong. Almost everywhere else, the enemy stubbornly — some places, fanatically — resisted every attack. At times, they mounted short, sharp counterattacks to knock American troops off balance and buy time. Fighting was fierce, and casualties on both sides were very high.

However, on the night of Sept. 18-19, the *NK 6th* and *7th Divisions* began to withdraw. Even so, strong rear guard elements from the *6th Division* executed very effective delaying actions.

The capture of Waegwan by the 5th RCT, plus the pincer movements of the 1st Cavalry and ROK 1st Divisions cracked the resistance of the *NK 1st, 3d* and *13th Divisions*. All three fell back rapidly after this (Sept. 20-21) On Sept. 20, the ROK 3d Division on the east coast, helped by air strikes and naval gunfire, broke loose to drive the *NK 5th Division*, badly depleted, far to the north.

The critical date was Sept. 19, for it was on this day that it became clear that the North Korean High Command gave up trying to penetrate the Perimeter and began to frantically extricate as much of their army from that part of Korea as was possible. By Sept. 23, withdrawal had become headlong flight almost everywhere. There were battles, rear guard actions and ambushes by parties of the enemy in rear areas,

There can be no question that the invasion at Inchon brought this about. In this instance, GEN MacArthur's stubborn adherence to his plan for this invasion paid off as an outstanding strategic victory. Without it, or a similar invasion farther south on the Korean west coast, the alternative would have been a head-on battle by the forces within the Perimeter to break out and defeat the North Korean Army that way. It could have been done, especially if the 1st Marine Division and 7th Infantry Division, plus X Corps artillery, armor, etc., had been added to the Eighth Army instead of being utilized for the Inchon invasion. The avenues for strategic operations and exploitation opened by this invasion far outweigh that course of action.

Considering Another Amphibious Landing

Viewing the Perimeter situation on Sept. 19, GEN MacArthur was disappointed because Walker's Eighth Army seemed to be incapable of breaking out of the Perimeter. It never entered his mind that the Inchon operation had, necessarily, diverted huge quantities of ammunition, including vital artillery ammunition, other supplies and bridging equipment from that Army, severely hampering Walker's attempt to achieve a breakout.

MacArthur was so concerned that, on the evening of Sept. 19, he met with Almond, Struble, Shepherd, Doyle, Wright and other officers to discuss the Perimeter situation. GEN Shepherd made meeting notes. According to them, MacArthur surmised that GEN Collins had been right; the Eighth Army had been bottled up in the Perimeter so long and with so many casualties that it had lost its offensive will. It might be too far between Taegu and Inchon for a link up. MacArthur even said that maybe Walker should be replaced.

MacArthur then suggested that a second amphibious landing should be undertaken. The assembled officers agreed. Struble and Shepherd suggested Posung-myon, fairly close to Inchon. But they then agreed with Doyle, who recommended Kunsan. Ironically, Kunsan is where GEN Walker had wanted the first invasion to take place, not Inchon. The remainder of the meeting

was devoted to discussing technical matters associated with an invasion at that location. At the meeting's conclusion, MacArthur said that if the Eighth Army didn't make progress soon, a second invasion would take place by two American and one ROK division on or about Oct. 15. He directed his G-3, BG Edwin K. "Pinky" Wright to inform planners at GHQ, Tokyo of this decision.

When he learned of the meeting and decision, GEN Walker was both hurt and angry. It demonstrated a complete lack of faith in Eighth Army and its abilities, and indicated that MacArthur was displeased with Walker and had little faith in the latter's ability to successfully lead the Army out of the Perimeter. MacArthur had stated that the 1st Marine Division would remain at Seoul. To Walker, the only other source for the bulk of the troops for a second invasion would have to come from his army. If that happened, Eighth Army would be so weakened that it might not be possible for it to hold onto the Perimeter, let alone break out.

Walker was not shy in letting MacArthur's headquarters know how he felt about a second invasion. In a telephone conversation with Almond's deputy, Doyle Hickey, Walker flatly stated that such a plan would be opposed by Eighth Army; that taking any more troops from his army would almost fatally weaken it. He said that another amphibious landing was ill advised and inappropriate. Clay Blair, in *The Forgotten War*, quoted part of Walker's conversation with Hickey: "We have been bastard children lately, and as far as our engineering equipment is concerned we are in pretty bad shape." Walker was talking about the lack of proper bridging. He went on, "I don't want you to think that I am dragging my heels, but I have a river across my whole front and the two bridges I have don't make much."

The plan for Kunsan did not envision taking troops from Eighth Army, but Walker had no way of knowing that, since he was not privy to the plan. The 7th Division, which had been utilized at Inchon, plus the 3d Division, enroute from the U.S., were to be employed at Kunsan. MacArthur at the time had no authority to employ the 3d in Korea. It had been earmarked by JCS to replace the 7th Division in Japan, but events would overtake this mission.

Within days after the meeting and Walker's response to it, things began to improve in the Perimeter, precluding further consideration of a Kunsan invasion. But the boldness and grandeur of this type operation still appealed to MacArthur, ultimately resulting in his ill-advised creation of a divided command in Korea and the equally bad decision to invade the east coast of North Korea at Wonsan.

The Decision to Liberate Seoul

The primary purposes for invading at Inchon were to make a penetration deep in the enemy's rear, cut off reinforcements and supplies for the enemy troops on the Perimeter and to effect a link-up with Eighth Army breaking out of that Perimeter. Another should have been to exploit the invasion by driving to the east, bypassing Seoul. The decision to liberate Seoul, and making its liberation a primary mission of X Corps was political, not military. Seoul had little military value, except to divert attention, troops, time and supplies. However, the early liberation of the city and highly ceremonial ritual of returning it to President Syngman Rhee, of South Korea, had enormous political import. Its propaganda effect would also be marvelous, giving a large boost to GEN MacArthur. These "spectaculars" had great appeal to the General. (See Chapter Notes.)

Chapter Notes:

P. 346 Allocations of many types of ammunition were severely reduced for the Eighth Army so as to provide for the Inchon invasion. Bridging equipment was given to support X Corps, also at the expense of Eighth Army. MacArthur should have realized that these actions would severely hamper Walker's ability to rapidly displaced the enemy, cross the Nam and Naktong Rivers and move from the Perimeter.

P. 347 CPT Gordon C. Jung, commanding B/ 27th Infantry, recalled that the unit received 75 KATUSAs. Each of them had a number. Those for B/27th were numbered QB 1 to 75. He recalled

that KATUSA "QB-24," a convicted murderer, had been released to the army. In February 1951, QB-24 was granted a short leave to visit his mother. The company officers chipped in and bought him a watch to take along. QB-24 cried when CPT Jung presented it to him. QB-24's mother, in a gesture of thanks for this act of kindness to her son, sent back handmade handkerchiefs for the men who had chipped in to buy the watch.

P. 348 The author knew CPL Collier from Japan and Korea. He was a likable young man and a good soldier.

P. 352 This magazine was called a "banana" because its shape resembled one. It held 30 rounds of ammunition.

P. 354 Headspace is the distance between the face of a machine gun's bolt and the chamber end of the barrel. This space was not fixed on machine guns, since barrels had to be replaced as they wore out from firing. With each new barrel, headspace had to be readjusted. It was also necessary to periodically check headspace on a gun throughout the life of a barrel and make adjustments.

P. 368 There is no unanimity in the belief that

seizing Seoul early on was a mistake. This author believes that it was a mistake, political considerations aside. The Marine Division, and the elements of the 7th Division which were diverted for this action, could have been better employed in achieving an even more spectacular military victory by driving to the east and sealing off more of the enemy's escape routes to the north. ROK marines and other troops could have been employed at the same time opposite Seoul. The city would have fallen, with much less fanfare, if Eighth Army made contact with elements of X Corps to the south and east of it and Eighth had driven north toward the 38th Parallel. If all else failed, Seoul could have been encircled above Uijongbu once the two forces had joined, forcing the enemy from the city. It is futile to lament the decision to make the seizure of Seoul a primary mission once the invasion had been accomplished, but that does not alter the fact that it was a terribly wrong decision if MacArthur hoped to gain the maximum military success possible. A transitory political consideration outweighed taking full advantage of a strategic coup to end or shorten the war.

Tank Co., 23d Infantry getting ready for the "Big Push" out of the perimeter, Sept. 1950. (Courtesy of Charles N. Prince, Tank Co., 23d Infantry, 2d Division)

CHAPTER TWENTY-TWO – Exploitation

Eighth Army Plans and Orders

"We have not had any definite break yet," reported GEN Allen by telephone to GEN Hickey in Tokyo on Sept. 20, "They [the North Koreans] are softening but still no definite indication of any break which we could turn into a pursuit." (Quoted from *South to the Naktong*.) GEN Walker planned to sweep forward along all axes of advance with motorized and armored task forces as soon as he perceived an opportunity.

By Sept. 22, the break had come, and GEN Walker issued the Eighth Army exploitation order. It read:

"Enemy resistance had deteriorated along the Eighth Army front permitting the assumption of a general offensive from present positions. In view of this situation it is mandatory that all efforts be directed toward the destruction of the enemy by effecting deep penetrations, fully exploiting enemy weaknesses, and through the conduct of enveloping or encircling maneuver get astride enemy lines of withdrawal to cut his attempted retreat and destroy him.... Commanders will advance where necessary without regard to lateral security."

I Corps: Continue to make the main attack along the Taegu-Kumchon-Taejon-Suwon axis. Link up with X Corps.

IX Corps (Operational effective 2 p.m., Sept. 23, 1950):

2d Div: Attack along the Hyopchon-Kochang-Anui-Chonju-Kangnyong axis.

25th Div: Attack and seize Chinju. Prepare to attack west or northwest on order.

ROK Army: Attack and destroy enemy in zone by deep penetrations and envelopments.

Eighth Army's Main CP moved back to Taegu, opening there at 2 p.m., Sept. 23.

At the time, total U. N. forces in the Perimeter numbered almost 160,000 men; over 76,000 in Eighth Army and some 75,000 in the ROK Army. And, for the first time in the war, the American and ROK forces had the initiative. Reinforcements arrived in Pusan on Sept. 19, with landing of the Philippine 10th Infantry Battalion Combat Team (BCT). On Sept. 22, the 65th RCT arrived. This command was the first major element of the U.S. 3d Infantry Division to arrive in Korea. Far East Command deactivated the Pusan Logistical Command on Sept. 19, reconstituting it as the 2d Logistical Command, but with no change in mission. The Swedish Red Cross Field Hospital arrived at Pusan on Sept. 20.

The account of the exploitation will begin in the south and move north then east along the Perimeter, but many of these actions were occurring simultaneously.

25th Division — Sept. 22-30

On Sept. 23, GEN Coulter, just placed in command of IX Corps asked GEN Walker for permission to change the 25th division's axis of attack from southwest to west and northwest. He believed that this would allow better coordination of effort with the 2d Division to the north. Walker concurred, so long as Coulter did not change his Corps boundary. Coulter moved the 25th Division's boundary, resulting in the 27th Infantry moving from the division's southern flank to the north (right) flank. There, it crossed the Nam River, as related previously.

TF Torman

GEN Kean formed a special task force whose mission it was to follow the same roads traversed by the Marines in TF Kean and attack Chinju from the south. The task force, named for its leader, CPT Charles J. Torman, CO, 25th Recon Co., consisted of that unit, A/79th Tk Bn, medics, engineers and a TAC party. TF Torman passed through the 27th at 6 p.m., Sept. 23 and headed for Kosang at 20 MPH. Four hours later, it had taken the town without opposition. The captain dashed on to Sachon, taking it by noon the next day, after defeating and scattering about 200 members of the *3/104th Security Regiment* and capturing 15 more. The road between Kosong and Sachon was littered with abandoned, but loaded carts, equipment, and the burned out or otherwise destroyed hulks of tanks, SP guns, vehicles, cannon and small arms, as well as ammunition and stacks of mines. By that evening the task force was at the road junction just three miles south of Chinju, where it was stopped by a stubborn enemy rear guard. CPT Torman called in an air strike then attacked on into the night, driving them away and inflicting some 300 casualties.

On the morning of Sept. 25, TF Torman arrived on the banks of the Nam River opposite Chinju. Enemy gunfire from across the river prevented a crossing. TF Torman dueled with the enemy in Chinju. Enroute to the town, a tank hit a mine, seriously injuring CPT Torman. He was evacuated. CPT Charles M. Matthews replaced Torman.

Meantime, the 35th Infantry was held up at the Chinju Pass until the evening of Sept. 23 by elements of the *NK 6th Division*. But on Sept. 24, the 35th took the Pass area and a patrol reported that the enemy had blown the Nam River bridge at Chinju.

Since the bridge was out, 2/35th crossed the river two and a half miles southeast of Chinju under cover of darkness at 2 a.m. on Sept. 25. Then, supported by tank fire from TF Torman the battalion attacked and seized the town. An enemy force of about 300 men, supported by mortars and artillery had comprised the delaying force in the town.

Both 1/35 and 3/35 crossed the river into Chinju that afternoon. TF Matthews crossed that evening on an underwater bridge constructed by the 65th ECB 200 yards east of the damaged bridge. The 65th, working all night, repaired the highway bridge sufficiently to allow vehicular traffic to begin crossing at noon on Sept. 26.

Meantime, that day, as described in the previous chapter, 1/27th Infantry crossed the Nam River some 16 miles downstream, enroute to Uiryong. The regiment seized the town by noon. On Sept. 28 it moved on to Chinju against little resistance.

Eighth Army altered the IX Corps operations order on Sept. 24, directing it to make unlimited objective attacks to seize Chonju and Kanggyong. To accomplish the 25th Division's part in this mission, GEN Kean organized two principal armor/infantry task forces utilizing troops from the 24th and 35th Regiments. The two forces were known as TF Matthews and TF Dolvin. TF Matthews was the former TF Torman, re-named for the new commander of the 25th Recon Co., CPT Matthews.

Both forces were to begin their drives from Chinju. Two roads left Chinju, one to the west, and one to the north. Both roads skirted the massive Chiri Mountains. This was an almost trackless wasteland of 750 square miles consisting of 6,000 to 7,000-foot high forested mountains forming a rough rectangle some 20 by 25 miles northwest of Chinju. This remote area had long been the hideout for Communist agents and guerrillas. Now, as the enemy forces withdrew, many North Korean stragglers and even some organized units of as many as 200 to 400 men disappeared into the forbidding Chiri Mountains.

It was senseless to fight through this formidable obstacle if it could be bypassed. That is exactly what the two task forces did. Matthews was to head west toward Hadong, then northwest from there to Kurye, Namwon, Sunchang, Kumje, Iri, Kunsan and on to the Kum River estuary. TF Dolvin, starting at the same time, was to head north from Chinju to Hamyang. From there Dolvin was to turn west to Namwon, then northwest from there to Chonju, Iri and Kanggyong on the Kum River.

The troops assigned to TF Matthews were the same ones which were in TF Torman. TF Dolvin included Companies A and B, 89th Tank Bn, Companies B and C, 35th Infantry, 1st Platoon, A/65th Engineers, 2d Platoon, 35th HM Co., the 89th Tk Bn Medical Detachment and the Tk Bn trains.

Two other task forces were also formed. One was TF Blair, named for its leader, LTC Melvin R. Blair, CO, 3/24th Infantry and TF Corley, named for its leader, COL John T. Corley, CO, 24th Infantry.

TF Matthews

The force was delayed in starting on Sept. 27 by three blown bridges. But at 10 a.m., it finally moved out. TF Blair followed Matthews and the rest of the 24th Infantry, known as TF Corley, followed Blair. Matthews reached Hadong at 5:30 p.m. Shortly, the men of TF Matthews began hearing stories of American POWs ahead. Civilians told them; enemy prisoners told them. But the American POWs were always ahead. First, four hours ahead, then two hours, then an hour. Matthews was gaining, but it seemed so slowly. At Hadong they were told that the prisoners were only a half hour away.

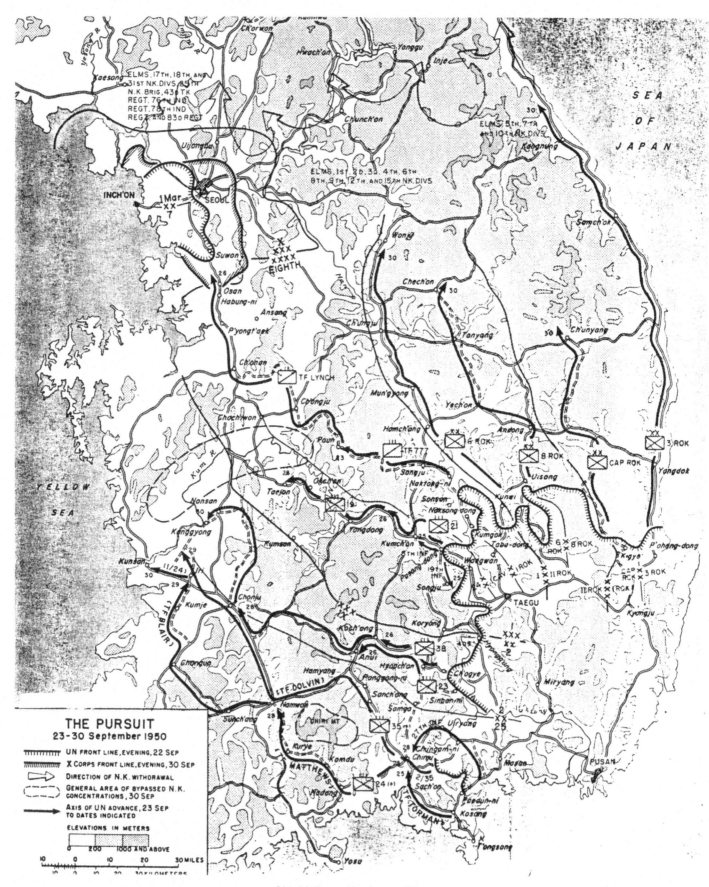

THE PURSUIT
23-30 September 1950

|||||||||| UN FRONT LINE, EVENING, 22 SEP
|||||||||| X CORPS FRONT LINE, EVENING, 30 SEP
▷ DIRECTION OF N.K. WITHDRAWAL
〜〜〜 GENERAL AREA OF BYPASSED N.K. CONCENTRATIONS, 30 SEP
→ AXIS OF UN ADVANCE, 23 SEP TO DATES INDICATED

ELEVATIONS IN METERS

0   200   1000 AND ABOVE

10   0   10   20   30 MILES
10   0   10   20   30 KILOMETERS

Map 54 (Source: South to the Naktong*)*

TF Matthews continued its advance into the night, lit by a bright moon. Some 10 miles northwest of Hadong, in the little village of Komdu, the advance elements of the force freed 11 American POWs — all from 3/29th Infantry. Some still had open wounds and most were unable to walk

About noon the next day (Sept. 28), a number of vehicles at the head of the task force became stuck in the river crossing just below Namwon. SGT Raymond N. Reifers, in the lead tank, however, continued and entered the town. Although Namwon was full of enemy soldiers, their attention had been diverted by two jets which were rocketing and strafing the town. However, as soon as they spotted the American tank, the North Koreans, in a panic, ran madly up and down the streets, jumped over fences or dashed across rooftops to escape. The scene would have been comical to Reifers, he later said, if his own situation had not been so serious. Suddenly, American voices called out, "Don't shoot! American GIs here!" Almost simultaneously a gate leading into a large courtyard burst open and the prisoners, laughing, shouting and crying, poured out into the street.

"Somebody get up here!" commanded Reifers on his tank radio. "I'm all alone in this town! It is full of enemy soldiers and there are American prisoners here. 1LT Robert K. Sawyer, heard the call, and pressed forward in his tank. Other vehicles also got across the river about this time and headed into Namwon. As Sawyer turned his tank into the town's main street, he saw "a large group of bearded, haggard Americans," he said. "Most were barefooted and in tatters, and all were obviously half starved. We had caught up with the American prisoners. There were eighty-six of them." (Quotes from *South to the Naktong*.)

(See Appendix A — Prisoners of War and Missing in Action, for a fuller account of this rescue.)

Task Forces Matthews and Blair combined to clear the enemy from Namwon. TF Dolvin entered the town from the east in midafternoon.

TF Blair

TF Matthews remained in Namwon overnight, while TF Blair pushed on toward Chongup, securing that town by noon of Sept. 29. Iri fell to the force that evening. But the bridge there had been destroyed. TF Blair had to stop and TF Matthews joined it. The port city of Kunsan, on the Kum River estuary, was taken by 1/24th Infantry, without opposition, at 1 p.m., Sept. 30.

"I & R was point for TF Blair during its entire existence," wrote SGT Waymon R. Ransom, a squad leader in the 24th Infantry's I & R Platoon. Ransom recalled that he had no map and didn't know what the final destination was. The orders he remembered were "no EM into Korean houses and don't stop to fight." His squad led the entire force. He was supposed to stop at road junctions and send someone back to the platoon leader to find out which way to go.

"First day out, a lieutenant from somewhere or other was with us. [We] halted overlooking a house surrounded by a hedge. Lieutenant went into the yard and several [enemy] men broke out

of the hedge to the rear of the house. I was standing on the hood of a jeep and snapped a couple of rounds at them as they disappeared into a cornfield. Shot a fanny pack off one of them. Much amusement among the troops. [The] lieutenant was not amused." The officer was not Ransom's platoon leader and did not stay long with the point. Ransom recalled having several encounters with officers, not his platoon leader, while on the point. In one or two instances, his men were checking out buildings for hidden enemy, when questioned by an officer, asking what they were doing. "I sure wasn't moving past buildings as tho they weren't there," Ransom wrote.

"On one evening (2d or 3d day) we came to a road junction just at the edge of a...town just at dusk," he continued. NKs were coming down a street. I put [some of my people] against the wall and grabbed [the enemy soldiers] as they came around the corner, disarmed them and held them. Just as the platoon leader came up I had one and another came around the corner. I was on the ground with two NKs wrestling for my .45. The Lieutenant came up, bent over us and said, 'Don't hit her she's a woman.' I informed him I was well aware of the fact...get her off." The enemy soon became aware of the American presence, and a fire fight broke out. Ransom called for help. A tank came up to his position and took the enemy under fire. The two sides swapped fire all night long, he recalled.

"The NKs faded with the dawn," he wrote, "and the advance continued. Minor fire fights all the way.... Don't recall any major action by TF Blair. The last day before meeting other TFs, a gun truck of the 159th Artillery broke down. Crew, gun and vehicle were left behind. TF Blair met the other force at midday. They crossed in front of us and I & R moved to a RR yard at Iri. In the late afternoon a firefight broke out a short distance away." The I & R Platoon was sent to investigate, but soon returned since the firing didn't amount to much. The guard from the platoon who had been left behind to secure the platoon's equipment reported that he had been assaulted by an officer, who then took an unmarked jeep trailer, which the platoon had found during the advance that day.

That evening, the I & R Platoon was sent to escort an artillery officer and a medical officer back to where the gun crew had been left. The officers insisted on the vehicle headlights being on in order to speed up the rescue effort. As it turned out, the crew had been attacked by a party of North Koreans, but managed to make their way to a ROK unit. Some of the crew were killed. The I & R Platoon recovered them all, dead and alive.

The following morning, Ransom was charged with deserting his post to "loot and pillage." An investigation proved that there was no basis for the charge. Apparently this stemmed from his men having taken possession of the abandoned jeep trailer. There had been personal possessions of at least one officer in the trailer when it was found. Ransom, glancing into the trailer when it was found, saw only a few blankets in it. Unknown to him, under the blankets was an officer's bedroll, including the personal possessions of that officer.

"The next day," he wrote, "I noted a member of I & R rolling up an old WW II type officers'

bedroll. 'Where'd you get that?' [I asked.] 'On the bottom of the trailer,' [he responded]. I told him to take the damn thing down to the sea and bury it in the mud flats at low tide. 'And I do mean all of it!!'" The man was later killed in action. "And if the officer survived," Ransom concluded, "I most humbly beg his forgiveness for the loss of his property."

John S. Komp, the 1/24th Infantry S2 and CPT Richard W. Williams apparently were the first liberators into Kunsan. As the column approached the town, Komp and Williams "took off in [a jeep] by ourselves and ended up being the first ones into Kunsan on the Yellow Sea, which I recall was the 25th Div objective. There was no opposition to us and we were greeted with banners and flags by the locals."

The Great Duck Caper

LT Lyle Rishell's platoon of A/24th Infantry was part of TF Corley. For them, the advance was without any opposition; a ride in the sun. On Sept. 28, the column was stopped by some enemy resistance far up ahead. The column stopped and the men climbed from the trucks to stretch their legs. Some trucks were on the western side of a stream and the remainder were the eastern side. About the same time as the men were dismounting, a flock of ducks came into view on the stream, swimming serenely along.

The troops, seeing this, converged on the river from both sides. Rishell wrote that the two groups of men rushing for the water and jumping in after the ducks, reminded him of "gladiators from another time." There was no escape for the hapless ducks. As the birds darted about in fear, trying to get away, the soldiers splashed after them. Some men actually dove into their midst. It was a race between the men from both sides of the stream to see which truckload of soldiers would win the contest. Not a duck escaped. Men came back to their trucks, proudly clutching "prizes" for all to see. One man brought a duck and handed it to Rishell, who tied it to the running board of his vehicle. After this episode, the men laughingly discussed the affair. As Rishell pointed out, it was a great way to get a bath in clear water, which was a real treat, and the ducks would be a welcome change to the usual diet.

TF Dolvin

TF Dolvin was organized on Sept. 24, with B and C Companies of the 35th Infantry making up the infantry component, as noted. One tank company and one rifle company were paired to form a tank-infantry team. TF Dolvin was thus divided into Team Able and Team Baker. The tank company commander commanded each team. The infantrymen rode on the tank decks. The remainder of 1/35 plus A/64th FAB would follow in motorized support. The task force was to start out on the morning of Monday, Sept. 25, but was held up by a blown bridge at Chinju. Wheeled vehicles had to be towed across. The force actually got started on its epic journey on Sept. 26. The 1/35th Infantry War Diary states that the column moved across the river at Chinju at 3 p.m. About 4,000 yards beyond the crossing the lead tank struck a mine. A three-man engi-

Task Force Dolvin, first day. 3d Plt, A/89th Tk Bn heading for Chinju Pass. The wreckage of an enemy SP gun, knowcked out two days before, sits at the edge of the road. (Courtesy of John W. Akeson, A/89th Tk Bn)

neer team then removed 11 more mines from the road while the column waited. It traversed another 1,000 yards when another tank hit a mine. Another tank caught fire due to faulty wiring. A third minefield was then encountered, but this one was covered by a reinforced enemy platoon, which had to be routed before the mines could be cleared. When the enemy was dispersed and the minefield cleared, the task force discovered 6 AT guns, 9 vehicles and some 7 truckloads of abandoned enemy ammunition.

About 1 p.m., as the task force entered Hajonni, a heavy volume of automatic weapons and mortar fire rained down on the column from a ridge on the right of the road. The infantrymen jumped from the tanks and mounted an attack, supported by tank and heavy mortar fire. An air strike was also called in. After a seven hour battle, the enemy force, estimated at a battalion reinforced with artillery, was dispersed and the column moved off again.

Just before darkness, the North Koreans blew a bridge three miles north of Hajon-ni. The task force was just 30 minutes away at the time. They built a bypass during the night.

On the morning of Sept. 27, Team Able passed through Team Baker. Again, a mine damaged the lead tank. This time, enemy mortar and small arms fire raked the advance elements of the task force from ridges overlooking the road. Tank fire dispersed the enemy on the left side of the road, but an infantry attack on the right was halted by enemy fire. An air strike was called in and sixteen F-51s worked the enemy position over with napalm, bombs, rockets and machine gun fire. GEN Kean, who had come forward in the meantime, ordered Dolvin to break through the enemy and keep going. The force did break through, leaving an estimated 600 enemy soldiers behind near Tangsongmyon and Sandhonmyon. Then another blown bridge halted the column for the night while the engineers built a bypass.

Within the next three miles, four unmanned enemy 45mm AT guns were found, along with a number of hastily abandoned defensive positions.

Team Baker led out at first light on Sept. 28, bypassing another blown bridge near Paekanonni. Dolvin met elements of the 23d Infantry at noon at a road junction just east of Hamyang. The 23d had come from the east. The force was again held up by another blown bridge. Engineers, with the help of 280 Korean laborers, built a bypass in three hours.

As it approached Hamyang, a liaison plane dropped a message to LTC Dolvin advising him that the enemy was preparing another bridge for destruction just to his front. He sent his lead tanks speeding ahead to intercept the enemy at work. The tanks cut down the enemy in the act of planting demolitions and secured the bridge intact. The capture of this bridge upset the *NK 6th Division's* delaying plans. The task force then

sped out at 20 miles per hour the rest of the afternoon, catching up to and killing, capturing or dispersing one group of enemy soldiers after the other. TF Dolvin arrived in Namwon about 3:15 p.m., to meet with TFs Matthews, Blair and Corley.

Dolvin refueled in Namwon and set out just after midnight for Chonju, reaching it in the morning. The town was already occupied by elements of the 38th Infantry. Dolvin continued on through Iri and the Kum River at 3 p.m. The following day, Sept. 30, TF Dolvin was dissolved. Appleman detailed some of its accomplishments:

• Captured or destroyed 16 AT guns, 19 vehicles, 250 mines and 65 tons of ammunition.

• Captured 750 enemy soldiers and killed an estimated 350 more.

TF Dolvin traveled 138 miles, losing 3 tanks to mines and one officer and 45 EM wounded. TF Matthews traveled 220 miles in its operation. On Sept. 29, the 27th Infantry moved north from Chinju to Hamyang and Namwon and established security on the MSR. That same day, ROK marines captured Yosu on the southern coast.

LTC Dolvin summed up the operation by stating teamwork made the operation a success. "The tanks alone could not have done the job. Neither could the infantry do it alone. And the tanks and infantry together would have been able to accomplish nothing without the support of the engineers...constructing bypasses and sweeping minefields.

"The support of the 4.2 mortars was instrumental in overcoming pockets of stubborn enemy resistance. The role of the liaison aircraft cannot be praised highly enough.

"All these elements made up Task Force Dolvin and all of them contributed materially to the success of the operation." (Quoted from "Catching the Enemy Off Guard," Joseph M. Quinn, *Armor*, July-August 1951; copy of article courtesy John W. Akeson, A/89th Tk Bn.

Two members of the 27th Infantry recalled these days of pursuit. Chester E. Main, a medic

Elements of Task Force Dolvin crossing the Kum River, Sept. 1950. (Courtesy of John W. Akeson, A/89th Tk Bn)

American tank on the move with infantry mounted on its rear deck. It became common practice to transport infantrymen this way. (Source: P. 139, Korea, 1950, Chief of Military History, Washington, D.C., 1982)

attached to F/27th, recalled riding tanks until fired upon, then dismounting to drive the enemy away. In one of these episodes, Main had jumped into a rice paddy. His buddy, a man named Bond, called to Main to come to his side of the paddy. "But before I could move," he wrote, "a .51-cal 'Elephant Gun' bullet landed between his legs and exploded on contact. Needless to say, I stayed where I was until we had to move out.... The first three guys I bandaged were all shot in the head, with one having a large hole in the back of his head. His brains were hanging out. I had to poke them in with my fingers before I could put on a bandage. It was my guess that these guys didn't make it, but my job was to get them out of there as long as they were alive."

Milton R. Olazagasti, also of F/27, recalled he and another man moving out of a village in search of a hill position to use to conduct his FO duties. "We came to a cave and we hollered," he said. "I don't know what the heck we hollered, but...some South Korean [civilians] came running to us and they pointed to the cave. I fired a couple of rounds into the air and two North Korean soldiers came out." Using sign language, Olazagasti and his comrade tried to find out if there were more of the enemy in the cave. They had no success and Olazagasti considered tossing a grenade into the cave, but then decided just to take the two captive enemy soldiers back and turn them in. "The next day before we moved out," he continued, I noticed...engineer people...carrying out loads and loads of ammo and shells and stuff from that cave.... "Had I thrown the grenade into that cave, most likely I would not be here telling you this story. I guess I had a guardian angel taking care of me all along in the Korean War."

On Sept. 30, elements of the 27th Infantry made contact with the 2d Division at Anui. For all practical purposes, Sept. 30 marked the end of the exploitation phase for much of the 25th Infantry Division. Front-line units were anything but up to strength. The 27th, for example, numbered only 2,486 personnel. A full regiment had over 3,700. In the first few months of the war, the 25th Division awarded battlefield commissions to 72 NCOs.

2d Division — Sept. 20-30

The 2d Division task organization for the offensive west of the Naktong was prepared at midnight on Sept. 20. The plan of attack was published at noon the following day. This was the organization and plan:

9th RCT (COL Charles C. Sloane) 9th Infantry (- 3d Bn and Tk Co.); B/72d Tk Bn; D/ 82d AAA/AW Bn; 15th FAB; a platoon of the 2d Recon Co.

Mission: Establish bridgehead across the Naktong. Protect Division left flank. Be prepared to attack on order.

23d RCT (COL Paul W. Freeman) 23d Infantry; C/72d Tk Bn; B/82d AAA/AW Bn; 37th FAB.

Mission: Attack from bridgehead with one BCT reinforced with tanks to seize Sinban-ni. Attack south from Sinban-ni toward Hyopchon

in conjunction with an attack from the north by 2/38th Infantry.

38th RCT (COL George Peploe) consisting of the 38th Infantry; A/72d Tk Bn; C/82d AAA/ AW Bn; 38th FAB (-).

Mission: 1/38th Inf, under Division control, patrol south and east of Hill 409 and Hyonpung. 2/38th Inf.: Attack to the west down the Chogye-Hyopchon road. 3/38th: Protect the bridgehead.

503d FAB (155mm): General support.

2/9th Inf and Tk Co., 9th Inf: Eighth Army reserve.

2d Recon Co. (-): Prepare to move through the 9th and 23d RCTs to screen the Division advance south of Hyopchon.

GEN Keiser designated his assistant division commander, BG Sladen Bradley to oversee and control the tactical operations of the 23d and 38th RCTs. Clay Blair, in *The Forgotten War*, relates the upshot of this arrangement. COL Freeman resented the presence of Bradley in tactical command of the two RCTs. Freeman had taken special measures to mount his entire 3d Battalion on trucks and reinforced it with tanks, to form a reinforced mechanized battalion. He expected to employ this force as the regimental spearhead in a drive across the Korean peninsula. Freeman believed that his command was held back by BG Bradley in favor of COL Peploe's 38th.

In one instance early in the breakout effort, Freeman recalled that his command had made "very rapid progress," reaching its objective well ahead of the division's other regiments. From the objective, Freeman said, he could see the enemy fleeing into the 38th Infantry's zone. He asked permission to enter the 38th's area in pursuit, but permission was denied. Freeman took this as an indication that Bradley and Peploe, who were moving the 38th Infantry "very determinedly but slowly,"...resented that we were offering to give them assistance." Other instances of what Freeman regarded as GEN Bradley's favoring Peploe's 38th over Freeman's 23d cropped up during the remainder of the exploitation.

Infantry and tanks in the attack, 23d Infantry, 2d Infantry Division, Korea. (Courtesy of John H. Ramsburg, F/23 Inf & S3, 2/23 Infantry)

Passing through a burned-out village, 23d Infantry, 2d Infantry Division, Korea. (Courtesy of John H. Ramsburg, F/23 Infantry & S3, 2/23d Infantry)

Some elements of the 2d Division had difficulty crossing the Naktong, while others did not. The 23d Infantry's BCT attacking out of the bridgehead made slow progress, as was that of the 38th in its zone. A tank in the 38th attacking force was destroyed by a mine and two others were disabled by AT fire. On Sept. 21, the platoon of L/23d Infantry to which CPL Robert Cooper belonged was holding a position on Hill 409 when it was attacked by a greatly superior enemy force. Cooper remained with his machine gun for four hours under constant enemy mortar and artillery fire. The enemy launched a "banzai" attack, but Cooper, ignoring them, moved his weapon over open terrain to get a more favorable firing position. The machine gun was finally destroyed by enemy grenades and Cooper was wounded. In spite of this, he continued to fight with his pistol until its ammunition was exhausted. He then took his assistant gunner's rifle, ordered his crew to the rear, and fought off the enemy until killed. CPL Robert Cooper was posthumously awarded the DSC.

The 2d Division's attacks were hampered by the shortage of ammunition. Clay Blair, in *The Forgotten War*, records COL Freeman's view of this: "In Korea we were always conserving ammunition. We were always on the brink of running out. Always scared to death that we were going to get caught with no ammunition. I believe it was rationed the whole time I was there. Even small arms ammunition...we never had enough."

On Sept. 21 and 22, E/38th Infantry fought for control of Hill 239. CPL Cecil L. Sherrod wrote of his experiences during the battle: "Planes really pounded Hill 239 Sept. 21. We received light mortar and artillery from [the] enemy [but] didn't have much trouble taking [the] mountain. But did not have the manpower to stay over night.... We moved back off [the] mountain. Assuming it was still clear the next morning we...[started] back up. They [the enemy] had moved back on it during the night. When they opened fire I was one of the first to

get hit. A piece of metal from a mortar, I think, went through my ankle and foot.... A man named Holland bandaged me up. My Plt Sgt [was] shot in the arm at the same time." Later, Sherrod learned that Holland was killed.

Within two days after the 2d Division offensive began, 1/38th and 3/38th were freed to join 2/38th in an attack on Chogye and Hyopchon. The 9th RCT (-) assumed responsibility for security of the bridge and its approaches and also screened south of Hill 409 and in the vicinity of Hyonpung. Five miles south of the town, enemy artillery fired on 1/38th Infantry as it was being relieved by the 9th. Among the casualties was M16 squad leader CPL J. J. Vessel, 2d Platoon, C/82d AAA/AW Bn, who was wounded.

Throughout the afternoon of Sept. 23, the enemy stubbornly fought back with tanks and artillery, trying to cling to Chogye. But, by 6 p.m., K and L/23d Infantry had seized Siban-ni while G/38th Infantry, with some attached tanks of the 38th secured Chogye. The Third Battalion assisted in this attack, having been released from Division control. Two M19s from B/82d AAA/AW Bn supported K/23d Infantry that day.

LT Lou Genuario, a platoon leader with G/23d, was wounded that day. His platoon had assaulted a hill and was thrown back by the enemy. "I called the company commander for tank support," he said. "While talking to him, two rounds hit my right foot. My two machine gunners were hit. We moved down to the bottom of the hill and crawled through a muddy rice paddy. Climbing over one dike, trying to keep low, I was hit through the hip. I fell right on top of one wounded machine gunner. We both started to crawl; we couldn't get far. The six men left tried to get us to cover. Four would stand and fire while a couple of guys would drag the machine gunner and me from bunker to bunker. My platoon sergeant saved my life." Genuario spent the next six months in traction and six more in a cast from the waist down, but finally recovered.

About Sept. 23 or 24, I/38th infantry was trudging up a steep, wooded hill. Young Will-

iam Temple was back in the company, which was strung out in single file. As the men climbed, enemy small-arms and automatic weapons fire began to pop very high over their heads. Since it was so inaccurate, the men paid little attention. Looking down from the crest, Temple and others noticed a band of GIs walking across the valley floor before them. The party crossed the valley, receiving no enemy fire. They climbed a hill to the front and disappeared into a stand of trees. The noise of intense gunfire suddenly erupted in those trees and lasted for seven or eight seconds, Temple recalled.

"As a man, we rose and...went down the forward slope [of our hill], crossed the valley, [and] up the hill into the position [where the firing came from].... There was not a wounded GI there. They were all dead;...at least eight or nine dead, among them LT [Tom] Lombardo," company C.O., and a man named Castro, one of Temple's good friends. Lombardo had been killed by a ROK soldier, who had begun to fire his rifle wildly. The hapless ROK soldier was taken to the bottom of the hill and summarily executed by angry unit members.

Temple recalled that the Lombardo party was making a frontal attack on this hill because LT Lombardo had exhorted his men by calling for volunteers to "banzai (charge) the SOBs." Eight or nine men went with him, and were killed. Temple believed that the hill could have been taken with less loss of life by a flanking maneuver, but he admitted that Lombardo was "a brave guy," but that the unit "lost eight or nine good men and our company commander that day, and that was really the last firefight and the last casualties we took in South Korea."

On Sept. 24, the 9th infantry tried to fight its way into Hyonpung, but was beaten back by the enemy. Meantime, tank-infantry attacks by 2/23d and 3/23d from the south and a similar one by elements of the 38th, formed a pincer movement which closed on Hyopchon. In executing its part in this maneuver, 3/23d made a rapid eight mile drive to enter Hyopchon from the south. The 38th's Second Battalion crossed over the Hwang-gang River just north of the town and cut off an estimated two enemy battalions still in it. As the enemy fled Hyopchon that afternoon, the 2/38th Infantry killed an estimated 300 of the enemy at this roadblock. Two flights of F-51s caught the survivors in the open and continued the slaughter. The whole are near Hyopchon was almost cluttered by groups of fleeing North Koreans that day. The Air Force flew 53 sorties, inflicting terrible casualties on them. That night, elements of 1/38th Infantry entered Hyopchon from the north.

The 38th Infantry started northwest from Hyopchon at daybreak on Sept. 25, headed for Kochang. The road soon became impassable, due to the clutter of destroyed and abandoned enemy vehicles, weapons and equipment. The men had to dismount from their trucks and proceed on foot. Enroute to Kochang, they captured 17 trucks, 10 motorcycles, 14 AT guns, 9 mortars and 4 artillery pieces, over 300 tons of ammunition and 450 enemy soldiers. About 260 North Koreans were killed. The *NK 2d Division*, numbering no more than 2,500 men, along with its commander, MG Choe Hyon, who was ill, dispersed into the mountains.

Late in the afternoon, the Air Force bombed

and strafed Kochang into rubble. The 38th advanced about 30 miles before stopping at 8:30 p.m. a few miles from the town.

Early in the morning of Sept. 26, the 23d Infantry, having covered 40 miles since late the day before, caught up to Peploe's lead battalion, LTC James Skeldon's 2/38, on the road near Kochang. To Freeman, Skeldon's men appeared near exhaustion from marching on foot. Freeman obtained Skeldon's permission to pass through his battalion and seize Kochang with his mechanized force.

But orders from BG Bradley stopped Freeman so that the 38th could pass through the 23d and take Kochang. Freeman was furious. In his mind, Bradley and Peploe wanted to claim some glory for themselves at the expense of the 23d. Freeman said that he had his entire RCT ready to roll, including the artillery, when he got this order. He and Bradley had a bitter exchange of words on the roadside, but the order stuck.

LTC Robert G. Sherrard, commanding Freeman's 3d Battalion, in the lead of the regiment characterized the order as "the most ridiculous order I ever received in my entire career...." He said that his motorized battalion, led by tanks, was progressing at the rate of from five to ten miles per hour, with almost no resistance, when the order came to stop and allow the 38th to move through. Nevertheless, Sherrard stopped his column as quickly as possible to allow the 38th through. While so engaged, GEN Bradley came up to him on foot and proceeded to castigate him for not clearing the road more quickly.

Everyone nearby could here him "ranting and raving," as Sherrard put it. He characterized GEN Bradley's action in shunting the 23d aside, then criticizing Sherrard for not moving to the side fast enough as "cavalier." The men within earshot of Bradley as he upbraided Sherrard, could hear what transpired. Sherrard said the order and his subsequent chastisement by Bradley was "a blow to morale" in his battalion.

Elements of the 38th Infantry entered Kochang at 8:30 a.m. on Sept. 26 and captured an enemy field hospital containing 45 North Korean wounded. From prisoners it was learned that Kochang had been designated as the assembly point for elements of the *NK 2d, 4th, 9th* and *10th Divisions*. The swift American advance foiled this plan.

On Sept. 26, the 65th RCT was attached to the 2d Division. It was immediately assigned the task of taking over responsibility for the entire area formerly held by the Division east of the Naktong. The 65th relieved 2/9th Infantry and began patrolling the north-south MSR between Changnyong to Yongsan and to the river crossing in the former 9th Infantry sector. By midnight, the 9th RCT was advancing to rejoin the rapidly advancing elements of elements of the division, screening the left flank as it progressed.

The 38th remained in Kochang. The 23d rolled on to enter Anui, 14 miles away, at 7:30 p.m. It encountered no opposition. Flooded rice paddies surrounded the village. Sherrard chose a schoolhouse as his CP. Regimental vehicles were dispersed along village streets as much as possible.

It was a trap. At 4 a.m. on Sept. 27,, pre-registered 120mm mortar and artillery fire fell into the 3/23 CP area. The second round struck the CP building, a schoolhouse, killing six senior officers of the battalion outright: the XO, MAJ John C. Brinsmead; the S2; assistant S3; motor officer; the antiaircraft officer, LT William Valachovic and the artillery liaison officer. Twenty-six other officers and enlisted men were wounded, included LTC Sherrard, who barely survived the trip to a mobile hospital. SGT Joseph Orr, of the attached AA unit was among the dead. Three other members of this unit were among the wounded. Sherrard and Freeman blamed GEN Bradley for this disaster, claiming that the 23d would have been far beyond Anui if it had not been stopped by the general.

"Soon after my Tank Platoon [of Tk Co., 23d Infantry] moved into...Anui," wrote SGT Andrew E. Reyna, a tank section leader, "enemy indirect fire began dropping in close by and to the right rear of my position. We immediately moved out toward the north as far as possible and away from the inner town." The next morning Reyna took his section to the top of a ridge and took up defensive positions covering a road running north-northeast. Reyna noticed a farmhouse about 1,000 yards away. He radioed his platoon leader and obtained permission to check out the farm house. Reyna moved out with his two tanks.

"We moved cautiously toward the farmhouse," he wrote.... As we circled to the left and to the rear of the farmhouse, to our surprise, there it was, the NKPA 120 mm mortar...still in firing position. The same gun that hit the 3d Battalion command post, killing the...executive officer [and others].... In addition to the...mortar...there were three Soviet 1/4 ton vehicles...and...other equipment which the enemy abandoned when we approached their position."

Covered by his two tanks and crews, Reyna investigated the area, checking for mines or booby traps. He found none. He had two of the jeeps towed away by his second tank, one by his tank and hauled out the 120mm mortar tube, baseplate and traversing mechanism on the rear deck of his tank. Everything, except one of the Soviet jeeps, was turned in to higher headquarters. The Soviet 1/4-ton truck was repainted and outfitted by company maintenance personnel for use by the company commander.

The 2d Division history relates a humorous incident which occurred at Anui in the early morning hours of Sept. The vehicles of HQ Btry, 37th FAB were in a column on the road in the town. The last vehicle happened to be a captured North Korean truck. Two enemy officers drove up to the rear of this truck in a Russian jeep and promptly fell asleep. Seeing the truck, and not observing anything else, they assumed that they had pulled into the end of a column of their own unit. A GI sentry awakened them, to discover that both officers were very drunk, having been up north in another town having a big time while their unit was being driven from Anui.

The 9th RCT (-) in the south, was still having trouble on Sept. 26, having been repulsed by enemy troops dug in behind minefields about a mile and a half from the town.

On Sept. 27, the last of the enemy on Hill 409 and in Hyonpung, crossed the Naktong before daylight. Patrols from the 9th infantry entered the town that afternoon and two of its companies occupied a portion of Hill 409 without opposition. The next day 2/9th infantry crossed the Naktong after being relieved by elements of the 65th RCT.

South to the Naktong records that the motorized 2/38th Infantry traversed the 73 miles between Kochang and Chonju in nine and one half hours on Sept. 28. At Chonju, the battalion defeated some 300 members of the *NK 102d* and *104th Security Regiments*, killing about 100 of them and capturing 170 more. The entire 38th Regiment closed on Chongju within 12 hours, but was completely out of gas. Luckily, a 2d Division plane flew over the town. The pilot, learning of the situation, reported it to both the 2d Division and IX Corps. Gasoline was rushed forward. After refueling, 3/38 departed Chongju at 3:30 p.m. on Sept. 29, passing through Nonsan and arriving at Kanggyong on the Kum River, without any problem, at 3 a.m. the next day. (See Chapter Notes.)

Officers of K/38th Infantry conferring near Chonju about Sept. 28, 1950. From left, in foreground, 1st LT Rene' Ramos, Co. K; 1st LT Clifford Philipson, Co. K; C.O., Heavy Weapons Co. (a Captain, name not given); 1st LT Robert H. Warden, C.O., Co. K. (Courtesy of Rene' Ramos, K/38th Infantry)

"We pushed [the enemy] for about three days [after the breakout]," wrote SGT Leo Pedroza, of E/38th infantry. "Then we received the order to stop and dig in. My platoon position was on a hill with a long finger in the middle [of it]. We were well dug in when I saw the Bn Ex. Officer checking the line. He saw the M.G. position on the left of the finger. He continued to move and saw an empty M.G. position on the right of the finger. He asked, 'Why is this position here?' I said, 'Because I don't know which way the enemy is coming and we are prepared to face them.' Nothing happened the first night, but the next night they hit us. It was real early in the morning when they came in, in force. The enemy took a bad beating. They had many dead and wounded. My machine gunner, CPL Lopez, fired that gun until it was red hot. [He] never stopped firing until the attack was over. For this action he received the DSC."

Meantime, the 1st and 2d Battalions, 9th infantry were patrolling the roads radiating from the MSR. The 3d Battalion made another attack on Samga, taking it on Sept. 28. Patrols were immediately sent south to meet similar patrols coming north from the 25th Division. The 23d Infantry patrols also made contact with those from the 25th.

"What I remember about the breakout is the speed at which we went forward, but it seemed always a step behind the enemy," wrote CPL Harold W. Brixius, B/37th FAB. "One amusing incident [I recall] is a North Korean jeep with a driver and an officer going south, was halfway down our convoy before anyone noticed him." When he was noticed, however, "everyone" rushed to capture the enemy officer because he was wearing a pistol. An enemy pistol was a prize trophy among the men. "However, when he was disarmed, the pistol he was carrying had no hammer and could not be fired."

Later, in a town Brixius thought might have been Chongju, the battery came upon what appeared to be a prison. "Outside the prison walls were the bodies of 400 to 600 men, women and children," he recalled. These people had been dead less than twenty-four hours. The battery went on to Suwon, he remembered, where it remained for about ten days, "while they were deciding about crossing the 38th Parallel," he concluded.

By Sept. 29, the 2d Division supply line stretched back more than 200 road miles, much of it over mountainous, narrow, twisting, often one-way roads. It took an average of 48 hours to make the trip. Quartermaster drivers supporting the 2d Division, in one 105 hour span averaged just 13 hours' sleep.

On Sept. 30, the 2d Division was spread from the Kum River southward. The 38th was centered on Chonju, the 23d was at Anui and eastward 27 or 28 air miles from there was the 9th Infantry headquartered at Koryong.

The Argyll and Sutherland Battalion Attacks Hill 282 — Sept. 22-23

The British 27th Infantry Brigade, attached to the 24th Division, was to advance along the division's southern (left) flank, just north of the 2d Division. The brigade objective was Songju and its route followed that taken by the retreating NK 10th Division.

At dawn Sept. 22, the 1st Battalion, Middlesex Regiment seized a small hill on the right of the road three miles short of Songju, dubbed Plum Hill by the men. They went on to attack higher ground to the northeast, identified by the British as Point 325, or Middlesex Hill. American tanks and British mortars and machine guns supported this attack and the hill fell to the British before dark. Middlesex Hill is identified on revised maps as Hill 341.

As the Middlesex Battalion was attacking Hill 325, the Argyll and Sutherlanders prepared to attack Hill 282, on the left of the road. The plan was for Co. A to occupy an intermediate position from which to fire in support of Companies B and C later that afternoon. As Co. A moved to its support position, it was supported, in part by tank fire from the 24th Recon Co. LT Tomas Carrillo's platoon, A/78th Tk Bn was attached to the British Brigade and may also have supported Co. A. The unit walked unopposed onto the position and dug in, ready to play their part in the forthcoming attack.

Since it was very late in the day by the time Co. A was in position, LTC Leslie Neilson, commanding the Argylls, obtained permission to launch his battalion's attack the following morning. The attack was scheduled to begin at 5:15 a.m. on Sept. 23.

The leading platoons of Co. B, commanded by LT Mackellar and SGT O'Sullivan, scrambled up the hill. It was not yet light when they started. Within an hour, however, the two platoons reached the crest and surprised the enemy at his breakfast. Shots, shouts and confusion rent the air. Both platoon leaders were wounded, but cheered their men on. "Led by Corporal Sweeney, [the platoons] routed the enemy by a proper Highland charge, and drove them downhill," wrote LTC G. I. Malcolm of Poltalloch in his The Argylls in Korea. The enemy left 15 dead behind and a number of others were shot down as they tried to escape the determined Highlanders.

However, in their eagerness to reach the hilltop, the leading platoons bypassed another party of North Koreans, who opened fire on the Co. CP party and the 5th Platoon as it made their way up the hill. 2LT David Buchanan led his platoon in a charge on this enemy, driving them from their entrenched positions. So, within an hour, the Argylls had seized Hill 282, with but 12 casualties. "The secret," wrote LTC Malcolm, "was the old military principle of surprise, in this case produced by speed and determined leadership."

By this time MAJ Gillies had his Co. C on position. He and MAJ Alistair Gordon-Ingram, CO, Co. B began reorganizing to meet any enemy counterattack. It now appeared to them that they had only part of Hill 282. The part they were on was overlooked by a higher hill on to the left front. 2LT J. R. R. "Jock" Edington's 7th Platoon, Co. C, owing to a slight miscalculation of direction in the darkness, found itself the closest British element to this promontory. The two companies began digging in. Meantime a number of their men from Co. C (since it was farthest from the enemy) were detailed to evacuate the

wounded. This reduced the number of men available to Co. C for defense. About 8 a.m., the enemy started hitting the hill with mortars, creating more casualties. The companies radioed back for stretcher bearers to come forward to evacuate these men.

Then there occurred two things which dramatically influenced the later course of events that day. First, "Jock" Edington reported that the enemy were trying to move closer from the higher hill to the left front. Then the two FOs from the supporting U.S. artillery were withdrawn on 24th Division orders. No amount of protesting by the British unit commanders, nor the brigade commander, himself could get the order rescinded. The FOs, and the artillery they served, had been taken away from the British Brigade at a most critical time. The direct fire of tanks would be useless; the land configuration prevented them from engaging the enemy, who was intent on counterattacking.

Edington's platoon became so badly depleted that it could no longer be termed a platoon. Edington, himself, was one of the casualties. Buchanan and his platoon were sent to bolster the line there, but, by 11 a.m., his platoon was also riddled with casualties. MAJ Gordon-Ingram ordered the survivors to withdraw into the company's main position. "Buchanan skillfully withdrew the remnant of his platoon, still holding the enemy at bay," LTC Malcolm wrote.

About this time, a stretcher bearer party, including some Middlesex volunteers, and the battalion second-in-command, MAJ Kenneth Muir, arrived on the hill. The British had no morphine to ease the pain of their wounded, so swift evacuation was even more important. The stretcher bearers would provide the added speed. SGM Collett organized the treatment and evacuation of casualties.

MAJ Muir found himself the senior officer on the hill. By rights, he should have been back at the main battalion CP. But he had decided to come forward, and now found himself in command on the ground.

Muir reported to the battalion commander that he was on Hill 282 and intended to stay and take charge. LTC Neilson gladly concurred. Muir reorganized the two companies into a single force, relocated some men and weapons to strengthen the position, had ammunition taken from their casualties and redistributed, then called on the radio for the tanks to fire and try to break up enemy troop concentrations. The tanks were unable to deliver the proper fire, since they could not get into position to use their direct fire guns.

LT Tomas Carrillo's tank platoon, A/78th Tk Bn, supported the Argylls at Hill 282. He wrote that his tanks did "knock out at least two enemy automatic weapons."

The enemy build up on the Argylls' left flank continued. With artillery support having been withdrawn by the 24th Division, and the tank support ineffective, Muir had no alternative but to call for an air strike. While awaiting the strike, Muir was literally "everywhere," providing strong, effective leadership to the men. He so energized the defense that it was generally felt that the tide had turned in favor of the Argylls.

About 12:15 p.m., or shortly afterwards, three F-51s came in. The British had out the proper air panels, white in this instance. As the planes circled, the enemy also displayed white panels. CPT Radcliff, of the TAC party, to his dismay, was unable to establish radio contact with the aircraft. Suddenly, the three planes dove in to attack the Argylls, first dropping napalm, then machinegunning the position.

"The whole surprising tragedy was over in two minutes," LTC Malcolm wrote, "leaving the top of the hill a sea of fire which threatened to destroy both fit and wounded alike. The ridge became untenable; the irreplaceable reserve ammunition was exploding everywhere in the flames, and the majority of the defenders were forced to escape the fire by plunging down the sheer slope." This took these men out of further action, because by the time they reached the top again the battle was over.

LT Carrillo, who witnessed the attack, wrote that the aircraft were from the South African Air Force. He also wrote that the strike "by our own air support" created 40 percent casualties among the Argylls on Hill 282. "The Brigade regrouped," Carrillo wrote, "and continued the attack, capturing the objective after some heavy fighting."

On the flame-blackened hill, Muir, Gordon-Ingram, CPT J. A. Penman, M.C., SGM Murray, and others who had not been wounded in the air strike, pulled back to the lower ridge to the C Co. CP. Permission was given to withdraw completely from Hill 282. But MAJ Muir, observing that the enemy had failed to take advantage of the strike and that the wounded PVT W. Watts and a few others still occupied a tiny part of the ridge, was determined to retake the crest. Losses had been appalling, but the officers rounded up about 30 men. Though still shaken by what had happened, the men responded at once to order. MAJ Muir took command of this little band and led them with a cheer back up to the still-smoldering crest in a hail of gunfire. MAJ Gillies' C Co. provided covering fire.

Once the crest was gained, Muir found that he had only 14 men to defend it. A few others joined the group, but the numbers were pitifully small for the task. Ammunition, too, was critical. The hill-top reserve supply had been destroyed by the air attack.

Ammunition on the hill was so short that even a five round burst from a Bren gun was what LTC Malcolm called "a luxury that could rarely be afforded." Taking advantage of the Scotchmen's inability to lay down effective fire, the enemy closed in on three sides. Muir constantly moved around the little perimeter, shouting advice and encouragement to his men. His unyielding ardor encouraged the men to fight even harder.

Muir had been firing a Sten gun at the enemy. When he ran out of ammunition, he grabbed a 2 inch mortar. With Gordon-Ingram as his loader, the Major engaged the North Koreans until mortally wounded by two bursts of automatic fire. Even as he was lifted up by some soldiers, his last words were, "The Gooks will never get the Argylls off this ridge."

But Gordon-Ingram, now in command, found only 10 men fit to fight, and some of them were wounded. The Bren guns were down to only about one magazine each. He had no choice but to pull his men from the crest of Hill 282. But

when he reached Co. C positions, he found that unit almost as bad off as his own. Permission was granted to withdraw completely from Hill 282. Pugnacious to the end, the Argylls came off the hill fighting, one group covering the other by fire. They brought out their weapons and all the wounded. Only six rifles and two Bren guns were needed to rearm the survivors.

The next day, a roll-call revealed losses of 2 officers and 11 EM killed; 4 officers and 70 EM wounded and 2 EM missing. (LTC Malcolm gives 17 personnel killed or missing, but provides no breakdown. The detailed figures are from Page 583, *South to The Naktong*.)

No explanation has ever been given for withdrawing artillery support from the Argylls when they were in the midst of an attack. The tragedy was compounded by the air strike, which produced about 60 of the total casualties suffered by the Argylls this day.

To his everlasting credit, LTG Gordon MacMillan, the Colonel of the Regiment, wrote: "The Regiment's friendship with the United States Air Force personnel can never be impaired by having suffered on one occasion from the risks which are inseparable from operations in modern war."

LT Carrillo recalled that, after this action, "we did not come in contact with the enemy for quite some time and our tank platoon was detached from the British Brigade, who received their own armor support."

24th Division — Sept. 23-30

Just as the 24th Division was ready to jump off on its post-Naktong crossing offensive, enemy artillery fire on the night of Sept. 22 destroyed the only raft at the Naktong River ferry and three times cut the footbridge. This virtually stopped vehicles and supplies.

Because of the tragedy of the Argylls and stiffening enemy resistance, GEN Church had LTC Morris Naudt's 1/19th Infantry attack south toward Songju, then link up with the British. The battalion attacked from Pusang-dong on the

Waegwan-Kumchon road the night of Sept. 23. Songju was captured at 2 a.m. on Sept. 24 and the battalion met the British 27th Brigade below town. Both commands spent the rest of that day and the next mopping up in the area. On the latter date, the British Brigade was detached from the 24th Division and reverted to Eighth Army control.

After daylight on Sept. 24, recalled Willard H. Lee, A/19th Infantry, the first tank moved out, crossed a little bridge and moved on down the road and around the end of a little knoll. "Then all hell broke loose," said Lee. The second tank started over the bridge and hit an enemy mine, which somehow, the first tank had missed. Co. A, 19th Infantry then attacked and took the knoll. In the process, he recalled, they recaptured five U.S. 105mm howitzers, two enemy 122 mm guns and four to six 76 mm guns.

The first tank had advanced so rapidly that it bypassed the enemy 76mm guns before they could fire. The tank crew apparently did not see those guns. That tank went on to engage some enemy 45 mm AT guns. Although hit by those guns, the tank destroyed them, then it started to back up, Lee recalled. When it did, it came under fire of the 76s and was blown into a roadside paddy.

Just before dark, the infantry captured the enemy 76s. U.S. engineers put explosives down their muzzles and blew the tubes apart. On Sept. 26, the battalion rejoined the rest of the regiment near Okchon.

Meantime, the 21st Infantry had led the main 24th Division attack on Sept. 23, heading for Kumchon, site of the North Korean field headquarters on the Perimeter. They were confronted by elements of the *NK 105th Armored Division* with a dozen dug-in tanks, AT guns and vast mine fields.

LT Bruce J. Leiser (West Point, 1950), Weapons Platoon Leader, E/21st, wrote of his experiences during this attack. His unit was advancing along a wide dry river bed. They received sporadic small arms fire until the unit "reached a particular river bed bend, whereupon we came

Tanks of the 24th Division, with infantry aboard, moving to the attack. (Courtesy of Edward N. Arendel, HQ, 34th Infantry & 2/21st Infantry)

Infantrymen passing a U.S. Sherman medium tank of the M4 series near Kumch'on. (Source: P. 174, Korea, 1950, Chief of Military Hisotry, Washington, D.C., 1982)

U.S. soldiers, approaching the outskirts of Kumch'on, take cover at the botom of an embankment. (Source: P. 175, Korea, 1950, Chief of Military Hisotry, Washington, D.C., 1982)

under some damaging small caliber artillery or tank fire which apparently was calculated to burst in the trees along the river banks. My runner beside me was hit in the back of his right thigh. I rendered first aid and had him evacuated. This development very forcefully brought home to me the consequences of ground combat.

"At about the same time, members of the rifle platoons of Easy Company seemed to be rushing to the rear. The company commander was dutifully trying his best to have the men stop and take up firing positions along the river bank. I joined [him] in his efforts. I believe we were about five miles east of Kumchon [at the time]. Eventually we took up static positions along the banks of the river bed for the remainder of the 1st day and the next."

About 2 p.m. on Sept. 24, the platoon leaders were assembled at the Co. CP for a briefing. All at once, they heard the sound of an incoming round, which passed on to detonate in the Weapons Platoon area. No other rounds followed this one. The briefing completed, the platoon leaders returned to their platoons. Leisure found that the round had landed exactly where he had his CP. "My pack and web equipment were all in shreds.... One of my men was killed and several others wounded. I felt very fortunate indeed to have been elsewhere." The 21st, having met stubborn resistance, was halted late on Sept. 23. Just prior to midnight, the 5th RCT, led by its 1st Battalion, passed through the 21st and continued the attack. "That night, I watched in amazement as the 5th RCT ran up the hills with seeming ease around Kumchon in an attack with high success, apparently," Leisure recalled.

LT Keith W. Whitham's 2d Platoon, Tk Co. 5th RCT was the second tank platoon on road in this night attack by 1/5th RCT. 1st Platoon was in the van. Members of B/5th RCT rode his tanks.

"Soon after we began the night attack all hell broke loose, and nothing was moving," he wrote. Two platoons of Tk Co. were on the road, "with companies of the 1st Bn attempting to move on either side of the road. Fierce firing was taking place, and after sitting on the road for some time amid a lot of fire and smoke, I walked forward...to see what was holding us up," Whitham recounted. Behind the third or fourth tank from the front, Whitham found a wounded soldier. If the tank had backed up, the man would have been crushed. He saw to the wounded soldier's treatment and evacuation.

SGT Pearce commanded the lead tank of the column. During the night, a number of enemy soldiers tried to disable Pearce's tank, but he killed or wounded all of the attackers with grenades. If Whitham had not stopped to care for the wounded GI, he might have accidentally mingled with the North Korean attackers and have become a casualty himself.

"After daylight (Sept. 24) the 1st Bn continued the attack with Company A taking a beating on the slope of the hill to the left of the road," Whitham continued. The Battalion Surgeon, Dr. William Headberg (or Hedberg), calmly walked among the wounded, administering to them as enemy mortar rounds dropped all around.

LT Whitham's CO ordered him to take his platoon on down the road "and see what is going on." A short distance down the road, he saw Catholic Chaplain Kapeka administering the last rites to eight or ten dead soldiers from Co. B in the roadside ditch. After proceeding a mile or two, SGT Paeloa stopped his lead tank and radioed that he saw many troops down the road toward Kumchon. "I assured him they were 'our boys' going to Kumchon," Whitham wrote.

"As I stood on the back deck of my tank manning the .50-caliber, MSG John MacMillan in the tank immediately behind mine radioed, asking about two soldiers sitting in the grass to our left, about 100 yards away." Whitham thought they were friendlies, "until they suddenly began to set up and point a machinegun at me.... I turned my .50-caliber on them; when hit they went into what could best be described as a wild dance...." With that, he pulled his tanks back down the road. Whitham wrote that, had he realized that the troops seen on the road were enemy, he would have attacked them and wiped out "what was no doubt at least the remnants of an NK regiment."

1LT Kermit "Pappy" Young led B/5th RCT in this attack. 1SG "Happy" Chandler was his First Sergeant. Young was nicknamed Pappy because he was older than the other first lieutenants of the regiment. The first sergeant got his from the then-baseball commissioner in the U.S. LT Henry E. Emerson, of A/5th RCT, saw essentially the same thing that Whitham did; Co. B was taking heavy casualties in their attack. Co. A, in reserve, watched the stream of wounded from B, passing by enroute to the aid station. Then Emerson was called to report to COL Throckmorton, who informed him that Young and Chandler had both been hit. He ordered Emerson to take Co. A up to Co. B; to take command of both units and continue the attack. And to take the "high ground the road cut through and do it before it got dark," Emerson recalled. Dr. Headberg accompanied Emerson's company up the hill.

"We got up...to the base of the hill and the...killed and wounded were all over the place and the mortar rounds were just raining in," Emerson said. "I had one platoon cut to the right of the road...to attack...and was going to try to take the rest of the force up the left side." He found the B Co. XO, but the man had broken down and was of no help. Calling to some junior NCOs to help Dr. Headberg, Emerson placed some men around the doctor as protection and took the other two platoons of his Co. A and attacked the ridge to the front. Since one platoon was already designated to attack from the right, the other two attacked from the left. Emerson was with the center platoon.

"And it wasn't just an Infantry School standup assault fire," he said. "We crept and crawled, and threw grenades and clawed our way up the thing and I recall very vividly looking back several times.... The mortar rounds still were coming in, especially where the casualties were from B Company, and there's this doctor, just walking around as though he was totally unaware of the danger. One of the bravest feats I ever saw.... He habitually left the aid station and came forward...amongst the [rifle] companies. Its a wonder he wasn't killed or wounded...."

Emerson's unit took the higher ground on the left of the road cut, but the right platoon was being held up. Then they noticed that the enemy was starting to withdraw from that side "and [we] were able to shoot...and kill a bunch of them as they withdrew in front of my right platoon," he said. Suddenly, he saw an enemy machine gun position in front of that platoon and one of his men dashing toward it. It was a man named Silva. "Apparently, the machinegun had been holding him up and he just personally charged it," Emerson recalled.

"We couldn't fire...without risk of hitting [Silva] and he went down real hard.... Right after that the [enemy] machine gunner was killed. I raced over there as fast as I could.... Silva was so close [to the enemy machine gun that] he took five slugs starting from the shoulder right down his side. He was...dying...in my arms." He died before Dr. Headberg could get to him. "[Silva] was a really brave, terrific NCO and a great loss to the company," Emerson concluded.

CPT Claude Baker, then C.O., Co. D, was to become battalion XO, then battalion commander, before being rotated home — a remarkable series of promotions. Emerson considered them well-deserved. "The guy had been a combat company commander and knew what it was like...and [that] made him such a strong battalion commander."

The 2d Battalion launched its attack north of the Kumchon-Waegwan road, relieving 1/5th RCT elements north of the road. At 7 a.m., Throckmorton told the 1st Battalion commander that the 2d Battalion would pass through him.

About three miles east of Kumchon, enemy troops on Hill 140 north of the road, stopped the regiment. The enemy fought a major delaying action to allow a large number of their units to escape. They diverted the *9th Division* southward to Kumchon, along with the remaining tanks of two regiments from the *105th Armored Division* and the *849th Independent Anti-Tank Regiment*, which had recently arrived in Kumchon from the north.

During the battle for Kumchon on Sept. 24, the 24th Division lost six tanks to mines and AT fire. The enemy lost eight tanks — three to ground fire and five to air strikes. The *849th Regiment* was all but wiped out. The 5th RCT lost 12 KIA and 77 WIA.

While the division fought major engagements on its front, bypassed enemy groups attacked at several places in the rear, to include attacks against the 19th Infantry, bringing up the rear of the division.

That night, the 21st Infantry moved to the north of the highway and joined the 5th RCT in a double envelopment of Kumchon. The 3/5th RCT attacked and secured Hill 153 by 7:45 a.m. on Sept. 25, and sent one company toward Kumchon. At the same time, 1/5th RCT was on the southeast slopes of Hill 273 and 2/5th RCT was in contact with the enemy on Hill 140. By 10:25 a.m., the enemy had been driven from Hill 140. Both 1/5th and 2/5th RCT then continued the advance.

K and L Companies, leading 3/5th RCT entered Kumchon at 11:30 a.m., against enemy small-arms and automatic weapons fire. Although the enemy resisted, 3/5th RCT had cleared the town by 2:45 p.m. Advancing beyond the town, it set up a roadblock to the south at 6:30 p.m.

The 1st Battalion, attacking west, was still held up by heavy resistance at 3 p.m. COL Throckmorton then ordered a coordinated attack, with 2/5th RCT attacking to the east, in the enemy's rear, while the 1st Battalion attacked west. The attack began at 5:30 p.m. and succeeded in destroying or driving the enemy from his position. All objectives were secured by 9:40 p.m.

CPL Paul Comi, F/5th RCT, had a memorable experience during the attack out of the Perimeter. His company was going through a little village, mopping up. "I spotted a small opening in the ground near a hut," he wrote. "The hut had a platform with Kimchi rotting in the sun in pots. I had a canvas carrying bag for 60 mm ammo, much like a newspaper boy's bag, with front and back sections. Fearing [it was] a sniper hole, I took a grenade and tried to lob it into the hole. But the back of the ammo bag struck my arm as I was in the process of throwing and the grenade missed the opening and began to roll back toward me. I leaped... behind the rotting kimchi and ended up upsetting one of the crocks. Between that and the explosion, I was drenched with kimchi for almost a week. Until I was able to secure new clean clothing, I was forced to walk long distances from other members of the squad. In the hot daytime sun I was a walking stink bomb."

1LT James A. Johnson's platoon of the 72d ECC supported the 5th RCT during the drive on Kumchon. One day, he recalled, he got into a small town between Waegwan and Kumchon. The main road went through the village and another branched off at a right angle to the right. "I don't know where the damn regiment went," he said. "There was no trace of the 5th. What had happened, the 5th went into town and took the road to the right and let the 21st...attack through." Johnson found himself and one of his squads in the little town by themselves. He didn't know where the 5th RCT was.

Looking back down the road, he saw the leading elements of the 21st Infantry approaching, marching along, with a file of men on each side of the road. There were only a few vehicles with them, since the Naktong ferry was still not operating efficiently.

"I was standing at the road junction...talking to the squad leader and the building we were standing by exploded and a T34 tank came out and turned facing its gun down the road toward the 21st. We were so close to it the North Koreans didn't see us. It let a couple of rounds go at the [approaching] infantry. There was a six foot wall...there at the corner. I went over that and I didn't touch it.... My squad leader ran through the hole that the tank made coming out." The two met on the other side. Their jeep was parked on the side road, but the trailer connected to it was on the main road, in the path and sight of the enemy tank. Johnson and his squad leader tried to pull the trailer onto the side road, and at the same time grope around under its covering tarp in search of a rocket launcher there. Glancing back down the road, Johnson noted that all of the 21st men had disappeared; gone to ground.

Just as he was considering climbing onto the tank to drop something down its turret, "the tank backed up as fast as he would go," he recalled, "to the next little bridge. He had to turn to go down a bypass and was going so fast that he flipped over on his top." The crew climbed out of the bottom of the tank and ran away.

Johnson, still in search of the 5th RCT, started up the branch road. "A short distance up the road there was a little schoolhouse-type building," he said. "The building had a bulge." The bulge had been created by another enemy tank, which had hidden itself in the building. "So we stuck the [rocket launcher] through the window and blew it [the T34]."

Looking up the hill from the village, Johnson spotted two more enemy tanks. He gave up looking for the 5th RCT and went back with his squad and reported to COL Stephens (CO, 21st Infantry). "What the hell is going on up there?" COL Stephens asked.

"I said, 'Sir, I don't know what happened to the 5th. I think they went up there and turned to the right, but I don't know. We had just been playing tic-tac-toe with two tanks. We got ours. On the hill are two more, and they are yours.'"

Johnson recalled that Stephens was unhappy because he felt that the 5th RCT had left him with a "bag of worms" at the point of pass through. This was not Johnson's problem, so he returned to the ferry site and had his platoon bed down for the night. They had been working hard for three days and needed a rest.

The 19th Infantry once more took the lead on Sept. 26. By this time, enemy resistance was rapidly fading away. The 2d Battalion entered Yongdong without meeting any enemy. Three American prisoners were freed from the town jail. The regiment pressed on, reaching Okchon, 10 miles east of Taejon, at 2 a.m. on Sept. 27. It halted in the town long enough to refuel and to give the men a short rest.

The advance continued at 5:30 a.m., but came to a quick halt when the lead tank hit a mine and an enemy AT gun destroyed it. The 1st Battalion then deployed and attacked on both sides of the road. It, too, was soon stopped by enemy occupying the high ground west of Okchon. There, they staged a major delaying action to allow the remnants of a number of enemy divisions to escape from Taejon. Appleman wrote that a GI tanker, moving up to join the fight for Taejon sang, "The last time I saw Taejon, it was not bright and gay. Today I'm going to Taejon and blow the place away."

As expected, Taejon was an assembly point for enemy units retreating from south and west of Waegwan. Some 300 enemy soldiers were captured in the fight for Taejon, representing seven North Korean divisions.

Appleman wrote that the reports of enemy tanks destroyed at Taejon "are confusing, conflicting, and, taken together, certainly exaggerated. The ground forces reported destroying 13 tanks on the approaches to the city, 3 of them by A Company, 19th Infantry, bazooka teams. The Air Force claimed a total of 20 tanks destroyed during the day, 13 of them in the Taejon area, and another 8 damaged."

On the morning of Sept. 28, an air strike was made on the enemy position blocking the route to Taejon, followed by an unopposed advance by 2/19th infantry. Aerial reconnaissance revealed large bodies of the enemy in flight; about 800 moving out of Taejon past the airstrip; more troops assembling at noon at the railroad station, and another large body of them a few miles west of Taejon, heading for Chochiwon. Another force of about 1,000 men was bombed and strafed west of Taejon.

Advance elements of 2/19th Infantry and a party of engineers from C, 3d Engineers entered Taejon at 4:30 p.m. The 19th secured the city by 5:30 p.m., after the engineers had cleared mines ahead of the tanks leading the main force. A 24th DivArty liaison plane landed at the Taejon airstrip at 6 p.m.

The 19th Infantry captured so many enemy soldiers on Sept. 28 that it was unable to maintain an accurate count of them. The capture of large numbers of the enemy continued in the last two days of the month, with 447 of them taken on Sept. 30, alone. Large quantities of enemy equipment was captured by the 24th Division at Taejon. This included four U.S. howitzers, and 50 new North Korean heavy machine guns, still packed in cosmoline. The enemy destroyed equipment at Chochiwon to prevent its capture.

It was sweet revenge, mixed with bitterness, for the 24th Division in retaking Taejon. Nine weeks previously, elements of the division had been driven from it by a relentlessly advancing victorious enemy. The 19th Infantry and 3d Engineers, the last to leave Taejon were, fittingly, the first to re-enter it. Between 5,000 and 7,000 Korean civilians, 17 ROK and 40 U.S. soldiers were executed in Taejon by the enemy between Sept. 23 and the fall of the city to the 24th Division.

Only six people survived — two American soldiers, a ROK soldier and three South Korean civilians. The two Americans had been wounded by their captors, who had tied the prisoners together in batches for execution. The two men, covered by a thin layer of dirt, were able to breathe until they could punch holes to the surface. One of them used a pencil to do so. Of the atrocious acts by the North Koreans during the war, this mass execution was one of the worst.

The 24th Division CP moved to Taejon on Sept. 29. Its mission was to protect the army lines of communications back to the Naktong River. As a result, its units were deployed over nearly 100 miles. The 19th Infantry was responsible for the Taejon area up to the Kum River; the 21st Infantry from Taejon southeast to Yongdong. The 5th RCT was in the Kumchon area while the 24th Recon Co. secured the Waegwan bridges.

1st Cavalry Division — Sept. 21-30

In the original breakout plan, the 1st Cavalry Division was to cross the Naktong at Waegwan and follow the 24th Division. But as the breakout proceeded, I Corps changed the plan and ordered the Cavalry to cross the river above that town then advance to the east of and generally parallel to the route taken by the 24th Division. GEN Gay, his chief of Staff, COL Holmes, and LTC Holley, 8th ECB all agreed on a crossing at Naktong-ni, the site of an enemy underwater bridge. GEN Walker disapproved this site and selected, instead, the ferry site at Sonsan for the division crossing.

The remnants of two enemy divisions, the *3d* and *13th*, the latter near Tabu-dong were retreating in front of the Cavalry. Both were headed for Sangju, the *13th* in complete disorder. The *3d* reportedly numbered a mere 1,800 men when it arrived at the town

Early on the morning of September 21, 30-year-old Senior COL Lee Hak Ku, Chief of Staff, *NK 13th Division*, gently awakened two sleeping soldiers of the 8th Cavalry regiment along the roadside near the village of Samsan-dong, four miles south of Tabu-dong and surrendered to them. Later that morning he revealed that on Sept. 17 the *NK II Corps* had ordered its divisions to go on the defensive and that the *13th Division* knew nothing of the Inchon landing.

Lee was the ranking enemy officer captured during the Korean War. He was very informative. He revealed the location of the division CP, disposition of its troops, remaining artillery, troop morale and supply status. He said the division numbered about 1,500 men. Of this number the *19th Infantry* had about 200 men; the *21st Regiment* some 330 and the *23d* about 300. About 70 to 80 per cent of the troops were South Korean conscripts, but the NCOs and officers were North Korean. The *13th* manned no line, and since communication was out between division and the regiments, each regiment acted on its own and according to necessity.

Many other *13th Division* soldiers captured about this time, confirmed COL Lee's story. He reported that all the tanks attached to the division had been destroyed, and that only two of 16 SP guns remained, but that nine 122mm howitzers and five 120mm mortars were still in operation. The division had only 30 trucks remaining (out of 300). Rations were down one half. He also said that supplies came by rail from Chorwon, through Seoul to Andong.

Task Force 777

GEN Gay spearheaded the 1st Cavalry Division with a task organization named "Task Force 777." The force was built around the 7th Cavalry Regiment. At the time, LTC William A. Harris, commanding the 7th, had but two of his battalions: the 1st and 3d. The 2d Battalion, along with 2d Platoon, Heavy Mortar Company, was in Eighth Army reserve, southwest of Taegu. TF 777 was commanded by LTC Harris. The number 777 was derived from the sevens in each of the number designations of the principal components of the task force. It consisted of HHC, 7th Cav. Regt; 1st and 3d Battalions, 7th Cavalry; 77th FAB; C/70th Tk Bn; two heavy mortar platoons; two medical platoons; the I & R Platoon; TAC party and an SCR 399 Radio Team, 13th Sig Bn.

LTC Harris divided his task force into two subordinate forces, TF Lynch and TF Witherspoon. Each of these forces was named for the commander of the infantry battalion around which it was built: LTC James H. Lynch (3/7th Cav.) and MAJ William O. Witherspoon (1/7th Cav.).

TF Lynch

In addition to 3/7th Cavalry, this force included the 77th FAB (-Btry C); 2d and 3d Platoons, 70th Tk Bn (totaling seven M-4A3E8 tanks); B/8th ECB (-one plat.) but with a dozer; 3d Plat., HM Co.; I & R Plat. and a FAC.

The original mission of TF Lynch was to move out rapidly and secure the river crossing site at Sonsan, about 25 miles from its starting point. The force was to start at 6:30 a.m. on Sept. 22. The planning was completed by 3:30 a.m. and Lynch called a commander's conference for 5:30 a.m. However, about 4 a.m., some 2,000 enemy troops, trapped by the 7th and 8th Cavalry Regiments tried to break through the area of 1/7th Cavalry and to its east. The battalion battled these enemy troops for about two hours, forcing them to move farther west in their escape effort. Harris and Lynch agreed to hold up the commanders' meeting and time of attack until the situation cleared up. As a result the meeting was held at 6 a.m. and the drive kicked off at 8 a.m.

The I & R Platoon led off, followed by the two tank platoons, the engineer company, Lynch's command group, then Companies L, K, Battalion HC, Co. M and Co. I, followed by the 77th FAB (-). Aircraft ranged ahead to attack targets of opportunity. "We went five miles without incident through a devastated country," wrote LTC Lynch in his "Task Force Penetration," in the Jan. 1951 issue of *Combat Forces Journal*. "The Air Force had done a complete job of destroying enemy weapons, tanks and ammunition."

After about five miles, the I & R Platoon in the lead was fired on. It deployed and began to return fire. LTC Lynch came up and told the men to mount up, ignore all enemy fire except determined resistance and keep going. Several more times, the lead elements of the column were delayed by enemy hand grenading from the paddies on the right of the road. The task force had moved so rapidly in those first miles that the enemy did not have time to mine the road. So, after the grenade fight, Lynch moved the tanks into the lead. The I & R Platoon then followed the tanks, and the remainder of the column followed behind them. Once the tanks

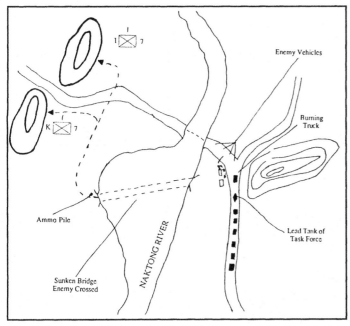

Map 55–Tank Force 777, September 22, 1950. (Source: P. 50, Skirmish, Red, White and Blue, Ed Daily, Turner, 1992)

took the lead, the task force moved along with little resistance. Aircraft attacked fleeing enemy soldiers and vehicles five to ten miles ahead of Lynch.

The lead tank rounded a bend in the road at the crest of a hill at Naksong-dong and was immediately hit and put out of action by fire from two AT guns hidden by the road about 200 yards ahead. GEN Gay, who accompanied TF Lynch, sent four other tanks over the crest of the hill in a rush, firing all their guns. These tanks quickly overran the two AT guns. A short distance later, the lead elements stopped for about ten minutes to wipe out a small enemy party in a culvert in a grenade battle. "One I & R jeep was stalled in the road above the culvert," Lynch wrote. "In trying to place a close one in the culvert, one scout missed and landed his grenade under his own jeep. It caught fire and burned briskly."

As the force turned into the river road at Kumgok, LTC Lynch received an air-dropped message from 1st Cavalry Division headquarters changing his objective from Sonsan to ferry crossing at Naktong-ni. This was 10 miles beyond the original objective. GEN Gay, still with TF Lynch, knew nothing about this change. The message had not been signed or authenticated at division. Gay and Lynch agreed that they would continue on toward Sonsan, while trying to verify the message as they moved.

But the column reached Sonsan at 3:45 p.m., without having received confirmation of the new order. GEN Gay authorized LTC Lynch to stop there for the night and he headed back to the Division CP at Taegu. Lynch had just completed getting his two-hour long column off the road at 6 p.m., when the confirmatory order came in: "Go immediately to Naktong-ni and secure the river crossing site there." During the short halt, Lynch's men found and captured about 50 enemy hiding in the paddies and hills.

As the sun set at 7 p.m., the lead tank set off for Naktong-ni, 10 miles away. This time infantrymen were riding on the tanks. The rest of the column followed. A bright three-quarter moon lit the way. About five miles out, the column began passing burned out villages. Suddenly, in the moonlight, loomed the rear of a retreating North Korean column. The enemy surrendered without a fight. Lynch had no time, nor the manpower, to escort prisoners to the rear. Instead, he wrote, "we merely kicked them in the pants and started them to the rear with their hands on their heads and without guards." Interrogation of enemy prisoners revealed that elements of the *NK 1st, 3d* and *13th Divisions* made up this force.

The head of the column reached a bluff overlooking the Naktong-ni crossing site about 10:30 p.m. Men in the lead tank spotted an enemy AT gun and fired on it. The tank round struck an enemy ammunition truck. Grenades and shells began exploding and a large fire started. By its light, the men spotted about 400 enemy soldiers in the act of crossing the Naktong on an underwater bridge. The tanks took them under fire, but someone passed the word to cease fire.

Lynch and his staff got that straightened out, then a rumor spread in the rear of the column that the explosions being heard were from grenades being thrown down the hill onto forward elements of the column. LTC Lynch took care of that rumor by posting a platoon onto the bluff, thereby securing that flank. Attention was then devoted to shooting up the enemy crossing the river. Lynch recalled that went on for about 10 minutes. It was estimated that about 200 of the enemy were killed.

The explosions from the burning ammunition truck set several other truck afire. Soon, small-arms ammunition, grenades, and all types of shells were, as Lynch put it, "popping and whizzing all over the place." One shell landed in his CP area, wounding one man. Lynch moved the CP back about 100 yards, and kept fighting. By the light of the burning trucks, he could see many abandoned enemy artillery pieces, trucks and several tanks.

Lynch made a quick estimate of the situation: It was 11 p.m. There was a sizable enemy fire block to reduce before the task force could proceed. The task force had to secure the far bank of the Naktong in order to complete the mission. He could only guess at where the road continued on the far shore to select the objective for a river crossing. The road behind was so narrow and jammed with the vehicles of his force that the assault boats in the rear of the column probably could not be brought forward.

The engineers and tanks were set to work clearing the six burning enemy vehicles and guns off the road. This took several hours. The engineers had to work without the dozer, which had broken through a bridge at the rear of the column. The exploding ammunition made the task very dangerous, and Lynch recalled many individual heroic acts during this phase. While the burning vehicles were being removed, undamaged enemy equipment ahead of the them was also pulled aside. In this operation, they found some 50 useable trucks of all sizes, many still bearing their U.S. bumper markings. There were also 20 artillery pieces (Appleman stated 10) and two operable T-34 tanks. Farther to the rear, the task force took possession of two more enemy tanks.

The clearing operation lasted all night, but the colonel used the time to send an engineer reconnaissance party across the river to inspect the crossing site and a squad from the I & R Platoon to reconnoiter the far bank. At 2 a.m., he called his commanders together and issued tentative orders for a crossing to be made in column on the underwater bridge at 4:30 a.m. Order of march: Co. K and Co. I. Co. L to secure the high ground on the near bank. Lynch wrote that this was necessary because POWs had revealed that an enemy battalion had dispersed into the hills on the near bank when his task force got there. He also knew that bypassed North Korean forces might try to attack his rear and cut him off.

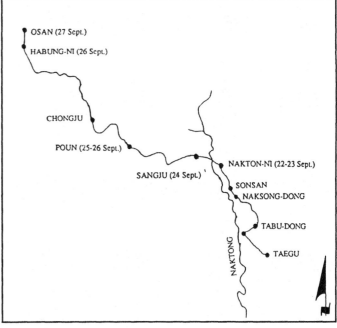

Map 56–Task Force 777, September 22-27, 1950. (Source: P. 50, Skirmish, Red, White and Blue, Ed Daily, Turner, 1992)

Mortars and tanks were positioned to provide covering fire for the crossing. Machine gun sections were attached to Companies K and I and the 75mm recoilless rifle platoon was placed in a blocking position on the near bank on a road leading to the north.

The reconnaissance patrol returned at 3 a.m. and reported that the water was waist deep on the underwater bridge and gave the location of the road on the far shore. However, they were unable to tell how the road ran through the mountain beyond. Lynch, guessing at the lay of the land in the mountain, assigned objectives to I and K Companies. The I & R squad provided guides to the two companies and the attack time of 4:30 a.m. was confirmed.

Promptly at 4:30 a.m., Sept. 23, the men of Item Co. began crossing the icy Naktong River on the underwater bridge. The swift current caused a number of men to lose their footing and had to be pulled up by others. Just as the first men entered the water, a pile of enemy ammunition where the underwater bridge exited the river began to burn and explode. All secrecy was lost. The troops, however, continued to cross in the light of burning and exploding ammunition. On the far side, they ran quickly by this danger and on to their objectives. Within an hour the two companies had crossed, unopposed, except for the self-destructing pile of ammunition, and were moving on to their objectives.

In the early dawn's light, Colonel Lynch, peering through the ground fog, believed that he could see that the road across the river veered to the right of what he had estimated in the night. He called both company commanders on the radio and shifted their objectives. However, about a half hour later, the mist lifted, and he discovered that the road was right where he had first guessed it to be. Lynch called the companies again, and re-routed them. By 7:30 a.m. the crossing site was secured, with K and I Companies occupying the high ground beyond the west bank of the Naktong.

Thus far, there had been few casualties. But one of these was Robert C. "Snuffy" Gray, I & R Platoon Sergeant. He took some shell fragments in the back, but stayed with the platoon. He referred to the rapid advance of Task Force Lynch as "that wild-a——d march."

In 23 hours Task Force Lynch had advanced 36 miles into enemy territory, capturing five tanks, fifty trucks, 20 field pieces, killed or captured over 500 of the enemy; made a night river crossing and secured the division bridgehead.

Later that day, TF Witherspoon passed through TF Lynch and went on to secure Sangju, 10 miles farther north. Frederick A. Duve, Jr., a rifleman in A/7th Cavalry wrote of what he saw the day he crossed the Naktong: "On the south [east] side [of the Naktong] was nothing but dead and burned bodies of the North Korean soldiers. Just about every place you looked you saw the dead enemy.... The Naktong was filled with the enemy corpses. A great many of the bodies were burned and at times it was damn hard to tell that at one time they [had been] human beings.

"Trucks, tanks and every other description of vehicles were scattered and littered the highway and fields.... Nothing for miles and miles but burned out and totally destroyed vehicles and tanks with many of the North Koreans still in them.... Horses and oxen that [had been] used by the enemy littered the highways and rice paddies, along with gaping bomb craters.... It was nothing but total destruction and devastation in all directions and everywhere."

He, like most of the 7th Cavalry troopers, greatly admired and respected the regimental commander, COL William "Wild Bill" Harris. At first, the men were wary of Harris, who was an artilleryman, not infantry. (See Chapter Notes.)

TF Lynch followed Witherspoon to Sangju, closing in there at 6 a.m. on Sept. 24. Meantime, back at Naktong-ni, the engineers put a ferry and raft into operation. Using these, the tanks crossed the river before noon and joined the forces at Sangju. Some 400 Korean laborers were employed to improve the underwater bridge.

At 11 a.m. COL Harris sent CPT John R. Flynn's K Co., with a platoon of tanks on north 30 miles to Poun. King Co. occupied the town without opposition by 5:30 p.m. Harris had authority to concentrate his regiment at Poun, but could go no farther.

That day, too, GEN Gay sent a tank-infantry team south from Sangju toward Kumchon where

Fred A. Duve, Jr., Aug. 31, 1950, Camp Drake, Tokyo, Japan. The next day he was sent to Korea and A/7th Cavalry. (Courtesy of Fred A. Duve, Jr., A/7th Cavalry)

COL William A. Harris, C.O., 7th Cavalry Regt., Korea. Picture taken in 1951. (Courtesy of Walter Raisner, E/7th Calvalry)

Photos above and below are of soldiers crossing the Naktong. G.I.s of the U.S. First Cavalry Division used shallow boats (above), DUKW's, and a pontoon bridge (below) to cross the Naktong River near Taejon. (Source: P. 205, Pictorial History of the War in Korea, *Veterans of Foreign Wars, 1951)*

the 24th Division was engaged in a bitter fight on the main Waegwan-Taejon-Seoul highway. The team made contact with elements of the 24th Division, but, since it had gone beyond the 1st Cavalry Division zone, I Corps ordered it to withdraw.

Meantime, other elements of the 1st Cavalry Division were not idle. The 8th Cavalry Regiment followed the 7th. The 5th Cavalry was still combing the hills for bypassed North Koreans in the old defensive area. However, the entire Cavalry Division, except 2/7th Cavalry, in Eighth Army reserve, was to cross the Naktong by Sept. 25.

On that date, TF Lynch was relieved at Sangju by the 8th Cavalry. All of TF 777 then assembled at Poun that day. Elements of TF Lynch then reconnoitered roads to the north. They found them impassable and returned to Poun that evening.

GEN Gay concentrated the 1st Cavalry Division in the Sangju-Naktong-ni area on Sept. 24-25, while the 7th Cavalry Regiment was at Poun. About dark on Sept. 25, he received radio orders from I Corps forbidding him from advancing his division any farther. Gay was unable to protest the order, since he lost radio contact with Corps. However, he was able to send a message to Eighth Army headquarters by liaison plane requesting clarification of the order and requesting authority to continue the advance and make contact with elements of X Corps near Suwon. Telephone lines were finally laid to Gay's forward CP at the crossing site that night. Just before midnight, he received a phone call from Eighth Army G-1, COL Edgar T. Conley Jr., who told him that Walker authorized the 1st Cavalry to move out and link up with the X Corps if it was possible.

GEN Gay called a commanders' conference early on Sept. 26 in a Sangju schoolhouse. He issued verbal orders that the division would move at noon that day and keep moving night and day until it contacted the X Corps near Suwon. This was the scheme of maneuver: TF Lynch: Lead out from Poun and head for Osan (102 land miles away). The rest of TF 777: Follow TF Lynch. Division Hq and artillery: Follow TF 777. 8th Cav. Regt: Advance on Andong via Koesan. 5th Cav. Regt: Break off its attack toward Hamchang, to be relieved by elements of the ROK 1st Division at noon. Form the division rear guard. Upon reaching Chochiwon and Chonan, halt and block enemy movement from the south and west. Await further orders.

After the conference, COL Harris, at 10 a.m., directed TF Lynch to move out and make contact with the 7th Division, X Corps, near Osan, 102 road miles from Poun. For this mission, the task force artillery contingent was reduced to C/ 77th FAB.

The column moved out at 11:30 a.m., led by an I & R squad and 1LT Robert W. Baker's 3d Platoon, C/70th Tk Bn (three tanks). The task force covered mile after mile without any contact with the enemy, only cheers from Korean civilians they passed. Baker entered Chongju in midafternoon, finding it deserted, except for a few civilians.

The whole column came to a sudden halt at 5:30 p.m. at the village of Ipchang-ni; the tanks had run out of gas and the tanker truck, strangely, had not joined the column. Enough gasoline was

taken from spare gas cans on other vehicles to fill six tanks. At this moment, as if on cue, an enemy maintenance convoy of three trucks suddenly drove up to the head of TF Lynch. The drivers jumped from the trucks and ran. The trucks had enough gasoline to refuel the remaining three tanks and the task force took off again.

As darkness approached, COL Harris, traveling with the task force, authorized Lynch to turn on headlights and keep driving. Lynch gave the order and directed the three leading tanks to "move aggressively to Osan and thence north to Suwon if the 7th Division was not at Suwon." Order of march: Three tanks; an I & R squad; engineer platoon; TF command group; Co. L; Regimental HQ Co.; artillery battery; Co. K; three tanks.

Lynch recalled that the moon was up, but clouds obscured its light. A column of headlights, several miles long moved rapidly through the night. Shortly after dark, Lynch realized that the three lead tanks were moving faster than the column of trucks, but he was unable to contact the tankers by radio to slow them down. Suddenly, Lynch's command group was "point" for the rest of the column. Many miles into the drive, the men began to see parties of 15 to 20 enemy soldiers in each village they passed through. The GIs and enemy soldiers were both surprised. Since the next vehicle was some distance behind him, Lynch held off on firing at these enemy soldiers.

But he found it bizarre that the battalion command group was acting as a point in enemy territory. He stopped the column long enough to put a truck-mounted rifle platoon, with a rocket launcher and .50-cal machine gun in the lead of the convoy. The column moved on, shooting up one truckload of enemy soldiers who refused to surrender.

Well to the front, now, Baker's little force kept moving, meeting small bodies of enemy troops along the way. But Chonan was full of them. Arriving at a street intersection and not knowing which way to go, Baker stopped, pointed and asked an enemy soldier on guard, "Osan?" The North Korean soldier nodded, then realized that these were Americans, and ran away. Baker drove on toward Osan.

The main force was now just 10 miles from Osan and meeting more isolated groups of enemy soldiers, which they killed or dispersed by fire. Suddenly, up ahead, Lynch heard tank or artillery fire and could see what he called "sporadic small-arms tracer fire.... I decided the parade was over and ordered the lights turned off."

Meantime, Baker's three tanks dashed into Osan at full speed and on through the town, stopping just north of it. He was out of radio communication with the task force, but thought he heard the noise of its vehicles approaching. Then he discovered T-34 tank tracks in the road, indicating enemy armor might be nearby. Baker pressed on, encountering enemy fire about three or four miles north of Osan. He ran on through it. Then Baker spotted M-26 tank tracks. At the same time, fire against his tanks increased. AT fire blasted the .50-caliber machine gun mount from the third tank, decapitating one of the crew members.

Unknown to him, his tanks were under the fire of American small arms and 75mm recoil-

less rifle fire from elements of the 31st Infantry, 7th Division. But American tanks with the 31st held their fire because of the great speed of the approaching tanks, the sound of their engines and their headlights created doubt in the minds of the tankers that they were enemy. One of the tank commanders allowed Baker's first tank to pass, intending to fire on the second. Just then, a WP grenade exploded, revealing the white star on the tank's side, identifying it as American. Baker stopped his tanks inside the lines of the 31st Infantry, establishing contact with elements of X Corps. The time was 10:26 p.m., Sept. 26. He had covered 106.4 miles from Poun since 11:30 a.m.

It was miraculous that Baker made it into 31st Infantry lines. His little band had first passed through a strong enemy tank force south of Osan, the North Koreans apparently believing his tanks were theirs, then through an enemy line north of Osan and, finally, into 31st Infantry lines just beyond the enemy. Luckily, too, U.S. AT and anti-personnel mines had been removed from in front of the 31st because it was preparing to make an attack.

Appleman pointed out that Baker's tanks may have escaped destruction by the 31st because MacArthur's headquarters had radioed a message to X Corps, to the Navy and Air Force in the Far East stating that elements of the Eighth Army might appear at any time in the X Corps zone of action. X Corps was directed to take all precautions to prevent bombing, strafing, or firing on these units. At midafternoon, Generals Walker and Partridge flew into the Suwon Airfield from Taegu and conferred with the 31st Infantry staff for about an hour. Walker told them that elements of the 1st Cavalry Division attacking from the south would probably contact the 7th Division in the Osan area within 36 hours.

Lynch, and the rest of his task force, were at least an hour behind Baker. Proceeding blacked out, the force by-passed a bridge just short of the village of Habang-ni then continued on through it. Just beyond the village, Lynch noticed an enemy tank about 20 yards off to the right of the road, its gun tube pointed across the road. He made some joke about it to his S-3, CPT Cecil Curles, thinking it was another enemy tank which had been knocked out by the Air Force. But he ducked under the tube's line of fire, just the same. (Appleman had Lynch telling the joke to the regimental S-3, CPT James Webel.)

As they passed the tank, "the solemn voice of Captain Johnston, commanding the regimental Mortar Company came over the radio," Lynch wrote. "'Don't look now,' said the captain, 'but to your right is a T-34.' Almost at that very moment the tank opened up with machine gun and cannon fire." Lynch and party hit the ditch. So did the rest of the column. Another tank, on the other side of the road, also started firing. Both tanks fired up and down the road, over their heads in every direction.

This continued for several minutes, then LT John Hill (possibly John G. Hill Jr., West Point 1946), the Battalion S-2, went ahead and pulled back the rifle platoon and 3.5 inch rocket launcher which had been on the point. Lynch surmised that the enemy tanks might have infantry with them. LT Nicholas, the artillery liai-

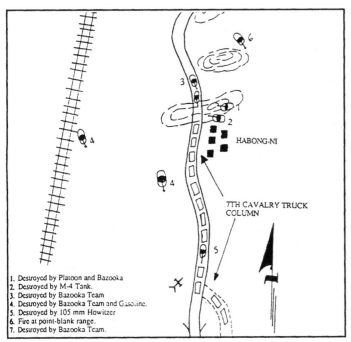

1. Destroyed by Platoon and Bazooka
2. Destroyed by M-4 Tank.
3. Destroyed by Bazooka Team
4. Destroyed by Bazooka Team and Gasoline.
5. Destroyed by 105 mm Howitzer
6. Fire at point-blank range.
7. Destroyed by Bazooka Team.

Map 57–Tank fight at Habang-ni, September 26, 1950. (Source: P. 47, Skirmish, Red, White and Blue, Ed Daily, Turner, 1992)

son officer, took charge of the platoon and bazooka team to attack the enemy tanks.

CPT Curles, meantime, tried to contact LTC Harris by radio, without success. Then Lynch and Curles worked their way across the road as the bazooka team moved toward one of the tanks. As the team got closer, the tanks gunned their engines, but did not move. This proved fatal to one of the tanks, for it was soon knocked out by the rocket launcher. The team set off after the second tank, but it dashed forward into the halted vehicles of the task force and ran over several of them.

The tank then drove several hundred yards out into a paddy and began firing on the column from there. The 3d Battalion XO, MAJ Halden had organized AT defense in the middle of the column. A 75mm recoilless fired at the halted T-34, immobilizing it, but was unable to stop its fire. Finally, another 3.5 inch rocket launcher team with CPT James Webel, regimental S-3 and LT William W. Woodside, L Co. commander, moved in on the tank.

In his account of the action, Lynch wrote that the team destroyed this tank. (Appleman's account, written a few years later, and based on letters and/or manuscript reviews by Lynch, Harris and Webel, stated that the launcher "would not fire.") But CPT Webel grabbed a 5-gallon gas can from one of the vehicles and poured its contents into the engine compartment. The gasoline exploded, blowing Webel about 20 feet to the rear of the tank. He landed on his side, breaking two ribs, but scrambled to his feet and ran to the road, where he realized that he had also suffered minor burns on the face and hands. The tank, afire, lit the entire nearby landscape.

In addition to the tank, the village and several task force vehicles were on fire, casting a dancing, eerie light over the scene. Lynch then heard the sound of approaching tanks, which he hoped were Baker's returning to help. Soon, though, he realized they were probably T-34s, as two of them topped a rise about 800 yards

ahead. He quickly sent his driver, CPL Billie Howard forward to pull the lead 2 1/2-ton truck across the road as a block. The truck brakes failed, but Howard stayed with it until he had it properly placed, then, with the enemy tanks less than 100 yards away, he ran from the vehicle.

The two enemy tanks stopped about 10 yards short of the truck. A voice, in Korean, called out, "What the hell goes on here?" The American reply of a hail of rifle fire made the tanks button up and open up with machine guns and main gun fire which hit the truck and set it on fire. The burning truck delayed the enemy tanks for about 10 minutes, allowing time for the three U.S. tanks still with Lynch to move up and for the infantry to organize more tank-killer teams.

The three M4 tanks moved up and began a battle with the enemy tanks, finally closing to within 10 yards of them. The American tanks soon lost this battle, destroying one enemy tank, while losing two of the three M4s. The enemy tanks then moved down the column and into the paddies on the flank. One of them worked its way down the column, running over several jeeps and firing bursts of machine gun fire into the radiators of each vehicle.

CPT Robert B. McBride, commander of the battalion headquarters company, mistaking the enemy tank for one from the task force, jumped out on the road and gave the enemy tanker hell for running over his jeep. He received a machine gun burst for an answer. One bullet creased the captain and he realized his mistake. Then a 105mm howitzer of C/77th FAB, commanded by CPT Wardlow, which had gone into a hasty firing position, blew the turret off this tank at a range of 30 yards.

When the tank battle erupted, CPT Webel came across several men with a rocket launcher and some ammunition, but none of them were familiar with the weapon. Webel took the weapon and, with it, immobilized two enemy tanks. When the crews ran from their tanks, he took them under fire with a Thompson submachine gun.

SGT Willard H. Hopkins fearlessly mounted one tank and put it out of action by dropping grenades down its hatch. He then organized a launcher team, which some sources credit with knocking out four more enemy tanks. PFC John R. Muhoberac distinguished himself as a member of this team. SGT Hopkins was killed in the cross fire with the tank which was destroyed by the howitzer, while in the act of attacking this tank himself.

When the battle ended, seven enemy tanks had been destroyed and the other three had run away. TF Lynch lost two tanks and 15 vehicles,

along with 2 KIA and 28 WIA. The battle had lasted two hours.

COL Harris decided to reorganize and wait for daylight. By 2 a.m., the task force position was organized and settled. Lynch then sent out a reconnaissance patrol to look for the enemy tanks. They reported back at 5:30: No success. Meantime, at 3 a.m., LTC Harris sent this personal message to GEN Gay, referring to Gay's earlier offer to provide a bottle of champagne for every enemy tank knocked out by ground forces: "Fm TF 777 — Send seven bottles of champagne to CO TF 777. Put three more on ice. I'll get them later. Will continue on mission."

TF Lynch was only four miles from Osan. Lynch organized his force for a foot march to the town. Just as Co. L, the advance guard company, was starting out, a burp gun opened fire from close by. LT Woodside and two enlisted men quickly silenced the gun.

As the column moved out, tank engines were heard just over the hill and tank main gun fire began to fall to the right. A rocket launcher team quickly disposed of the tank. TF Lynch reached Osan, without further incident, at 8 a.m. on Sept. 27.

TF Lynch had covered the 102 miles between Poun and Osan in 21 hours, destroying or overrunning 13 enemy tanks and killing or capturing about 200 North Korean soldiers in the process.

8:26 a.m., Sept. 27. A little bridge north of Osan. At that place and time, Platoon Sergeant Edward C. Mancil, L/7th Cavalry, met elements of H/31st Infantry. TF 777 sent a message to GEN Gay. It read in part: "Contact between H Company, 31st Infantry, 7th Division, and forward elements of Task Force 777 established at 0826 hours just north of Osan, Korea."

The 3/7th Cavalry, with attachments, was awarded the Distinguished Unit Citation for its drive from Taegu to Osan between Sept. 22 and 27, a distance of 196 road miles.

While H/31st Infantry linked up with I/7th Cavalry, the 31st was battling the enemy in the hills north of Osan. TF 777's communications equipment, forward air controllers and medics lent assistance to the 31st. GEN Gay, arriving at Osan about noon, saw the battle in progress and conferred with the commander of the battalion of the 31st which was engaged. He offered to commit the 8th cavalry in support of the battalion by enveloping the enemy, as well as fire from the 77th and 99th FABs and a tank company. The battalion commander responded that he would have to get approval from higher headquarters. How this was handled within the 31st Infantry is unknown, but the regiment had to fight it out on its own, finally taking the enemy position on Sept. 28. GEN Barr, commanding the 7th Division, said that he was never informed of Gay's offer of assistance.

The rapid advance of TF 777 cut off elements of the *NK 105th Armored Division* in the Ansong and Pyongtaek areas plus other units in the Taejon area. On Sept. 28, C/70th Tk Bn and K/7th Cavalry, assisted heavily by air strikes, destroyed at least seven of 10 enemy tanks in the Pyongtaek area. Five of the tanks were knocked out by the air. Part of the 16th Recon Co. had almost been destroyed by these tanks, suffering a number of casualties.

At the end of September, the area occupied by the 1st Cavalry Division was in the general shape of a huge triangle, with the 7th Cavalry at the apex, the 8th Cavalry to the east and the 5th Cavalry to the south.

ROK Army — Sept. 22-30

On Sept. 22, GEN Paik Sun Yup, commanding the ROK 1st Division, ran into TF 777 at a crossroads. The task force was starting out on its memorable drive to Osan. GEN Gay told GEN Paik that they were headed for Osan and then, as TF 777 moved out, he called out "See you in Seoul!" Paik was a very frustrated man at that point. Although the ROK Army lacked the river crossing equipment which the Americans had, he felt that his division had, as he put it, "blasted open the bridgehead that led to this new offensive, and now had to stand helplessly and watch the wind snatch away the glory of victory like the dust dissipating behind Task Force 777."

He immediately called I Corps and protested in the strongest terms, recommending that his division be authorized to head out for Seoul at once. But Corps refused him and restated that the ROK 1st Division's mission was to mop up and advance through Kunwi and Chongju. Paik's men were also bitter about this decision, but, good soldiers that they all were, Paik and his division fulfilled their assigned mission. GEN Paik arrived in Chongju on Oct. 2. There, he awaited further orders.

It must have been even more galling to GEN Paik when he learned that other divisions of the ROK Army were allowed to advance north, unhindered by restraining orders from a corps or army headquarters. ROK troops, although on foot, unlike much of the U.S. Eighth Army, which was motorized, often made remarkable gains in a short time.

The 6th and 8th Divisions of the ROK II Corps advanced close to 16 miles on Sept. 24. The 6th entered Hamchang on the night of Sept. 25. By Sept. 27 it was past Mungyong and across the roughest portion of the Sobaek mountains. On Sept. 30 the 6th came upon enemy delaying action as it neared Wonju.

On the 6th Division's right, the 8th Division also moved rapidly, putting advance elements into Andong before midnight on Sept. 24. There had been a 31-span bridge over the Naktong at Andong, but five spans were down. Parts of the *NK 12th* and *8th Divisions* were withdrawing through Andong at the time. Most of the *12th Division*, except for a rear guard, was already through the town, when the leading elements of the ROK 8th Division arrived. ROK troops arrived there ahead of the *NK 8th Division*, forcing it to move into the mountains to escape.

After a two day battle, during which it came upon extensive enemy minefields, the 8th Division seized Andong on Sept. 26. Advance elements of the division entered Yechon, 20 miles beyond the town, that evening. The next day, elements of the 8th were at Tanyang getting ready to cross the upper Han River. Upon meeting a strong enemy force at Chechon on Sept. 30, the division bypassed the town and moved on north.

The ROK Capital Division, east of the 8th, kept pace in the pursuit, entering Chunyang on

Sept. 27, then continued north through the mountains.

Shortly after midnight on Oct. 1-2, an organized body of the enemy, estimated to be between 1,000 and 2,000 men, which had been bypassed in the mountains, furiously attacked Wonju, site of the ROK II Corps CP. In overrunning the CP, the enemy killed many ROK soldiers plus five American liaison officers. The enemy then ran wild in the town until morning, killing somewhere between 1,000 and 2,000 civilians.

The ROK 3d Division on the east coast, supported by heavy U.S. naval gunfire, captured Yongdok on Sept. 25. The bombardment caused many fires and a large cloud of black smoke hovered over the city. The ROKs' rapid advance caught the *NK 5th Division* by surprise. Some of their trucks were found with their motors running and field pieces were still in position with ammunition stacked nearby. Ponies, still in the traces of North Korean signal carts were found tied to trees. Once Yongdong fell, the remnants of the *5th Division*, estimated at about regimental strength, turned inland into the mountains to escape. One enemy regimental commander distributed his three remaining truckloads of food and ammunition among his men and told them to split up into guerrilla bands.

MAJ Curtis J. Levy, of KMAG, utilized twenty-five 2 1/2-ton trucks, made available to him by COL McPhail, KMAG advisor to the ROK I Corps, to shuttle ROK troops north in pursuit of the enemy. When a roadblock held up the march, Levy was usually the one who led the action to reduce it.

GEN Walker, impressed by the rapid advance of ROK troops, remarked on Sept. 25, "Too little has been said in praise of the South Korean Army which has performed so magnificently in helping turn this war from the defensive to the offensive."

The ROK 3d Division, racing up the east coast, outdistanced all UN units, reaching Samchok on Sept. 29 and a point only five miles south of the 38th Parallel by the following day.

South Korea Freed

By Sept. 24, what was left of the North Korean Peoples Army was in flight, or in hiding. UN aircraft often had to return to base without having seen a single enemy target. In one case, a liaison pilot spotted a body of about 200 enemy soldiers. He dropped a note to them to lay down their weapons and assemble on a nearby hill. They complied and he guided U.N. patrols to them.

On Oct. 1, MacArthur directed the Air Force to cease destroying rail, highway, bridge and other means of communication south of the 38th Parallel, except if they were known to be supporting an enemy force. He also halted attacks on strategic targets in North Korea and attacks on air installations south of the 40th Parallel.

The amount of enemy equipment, weapons and ammunition lost or destroyed during its retreat was, Appleman wrote, "of a scope equal to or greater than that suffered by the ROK Army in the first week of the war. Incomplete records show that more than a dozen operable tanks fell into U.N. hands in the last week of Sept. and

Oct. 1, in addition to a number of SP guns, close to 60 artillery pieces, dozens of AT guns, over 40 mortars and hundreds, if not thousands of tons of ammunition. ROK forces at Uisong captured over 100 tons of rice, other supplies and most of the surviving equipment of an enemy division.

Between Sept. 26 and Oct. 21, seven U.N. survey teams traveled all the principal routes of armor movement between the Perimeter and the 38th Parallel. The survey revealed 239 destroyed or abandoned enemy tanks and seventy-four 76mm SP guns, plus 60 destroyed American tanks.

From Sept. 16 to the end of the month, 9,294 enemy prisoners were placed in the Eighth Army POW stockade. This brought the total of enemy POWs to 12,777. Eighth Army had taken 6,740 of them and the ROK Army 6,037.

Large numbers of the enemy were bypassed in the rapid move out of the Perimeter. One of the largest bodies was an estimated 3,000 soldiers from the *NK 6th* and *7th Divisions*, who, with about 500 civilian officials, initially sought refuge in the Chiri Mountains of southwest Korea.

Just prior to midnight, Oct. 1, about 60 North Koreans, employing rifles, AT and dummy mines set up and held a roadblock for almost 10 hours on the main Seoul highway about 15 miles northwest of Kumchon. A prisoner claimed the roadblock allowed about 2,000 of the enemy and a general officer of the *NK 6th Division* to escape. The enemy divisions which had been fighting along the Perimeter ceased to exist as divisional structures. The number of men from them who actually made their way back to North Korea varied from a few hundred from some divisions to 3,000 to 3,500 in the *12th*. Appleman put the number of enemy troops who escaped to North Korea at from 25,000 to 30,000 men. At this point, the North Korean People's Army had ceased to exist.

Clay Blair, in *The Forgotten War*, states that there was not really a breakout from the Perimeter, but rather pursuit and exploitation actions against an enemy army which had been forced to withdraw because of an invasion deep in its rear. Had the troops committed to the Inchon invasion been assigned to the Eighth Army instead, there would have been a breakout in the style Mr. Blair refers to. The fact is that the rank and file soldier of the North Korean People's Army was not informed about the Inchon landing for a number of days after the event, and fought very stubborn, bloody battles with attacking U.S. and ROK troops. This was before they began to withdraw and execute delaying actions.

The U.S. Eighth Army and ROK Army had been either withdrawing, or defending for so long that, psychologically, many officers and enlisted men had lost "the spirit of the offense." That is, they had devoted so much time and attention to executing withdrawals, or defending, that they had to change to the spirit of aggressive offense, attacking, and attacking to destroy the enemy then pursue him to victory. For some, this was a difficult transition; for others it was a long awaited time.

For the survivors of the early days of the war, when they were forced from one position then another, followed by the defense of the Perimeter, where, time and again, the enemy came close to breaking through the lines, switching to "dishing it out" for a change was exhilarating. It was a time of great joy for them.

Blair also points out that the American and ROK armies failed to "trap" or "pound to pieces" the enemy army in South Korea. He states that Walker's "trap lines" thrown across the peninsula "were too little, too late." He wrote that Walker's decision to send the 1st Cavalry on a dash to link up with elements of the X Corps near Osan contributed significantly to this failure. Blair contends that the Cavalry Division would have been better employed in attacking from the Waegwan area through Taejon.

If the Cavalry had set off in that direction, followed by the 24th Division, then kept moving to the west, perhaps more enemy troops would have been cut off by the rapid advance of these two divisions moving more or less in tandem. The one factor which would inhibit such a maneuver was the lack of adequate river crossing equipment in Eighth Army. It is questionable if the limited facilities installed in the Waegwan area could have adequately supported the crossing of two divisions in a timely fashion. However, in the event the Cavalry crossed the Naktong, it is possible that the two divisions, utilizing both crossing sites, could have executed advances across the peninsula which would have more adequately sealed off the enemy's escape.

Not addressed by either Appleman or Blair is the "might have been" if the 1st Marine Division and part of the 7th Division had been deployed to bar escape routes to the east of the Seoul area, rather than in capturing the city. Although the two divisions were not adequate to stretch across South Korea in a picket line to catch the retreating enemy, they could have blocked most escape routes in the western half of the peninsula and, thereby, have captured more of the fleeing enemy than were taken by the pursuing U.S. and ROK forces from the Perimeter. (See Chapter Notes.)

Blair also surmises that the actual number of enemy troops which made their way back to North Korea was "perhaps as many as 40,000." He also presumes that the majority of enemy troops who managed to reach North Korea were combat-wise veterans, but neither Appleman nor Blair take into consideration the large number of South Korean conscripts in the NKPA at the time. It is conceivable that thousands of these conscripts simply changed into civilian clothing and disappeared. Most of them certainly had no reason to make the long and dangerous trek to the north, when their homes and families were in the south. However, even if only 25,000 of the enemy escaped, this number of officers and enlisted men would have provided cadres for a number of new divisions.

By the first week in October, South Korea had been freed of all organized enemy troops. Bands of so-called guerrillas, some of them fairly large, still existed in the south. Some American and ROK troops were assigned to run down and eliminate these groups.

These were the casualties in Eighth Army to Sept. 30, 1950: 5,145 KIA; 16,461 WIA, of whom 422 died of wounds; 402 POWs; 2,164 MIA. Many of the MIAs were actually POWs or were dead. Total losses: 24,172. The period between July 5 and Sept. 30, 1950 was the bloodiest period of the entire Korean War. Had this casualty rate continued throughout the 37 months of the war, the total losses would have been almost 100,000 more than they actually were. (Korean War losses are discussed in more detail in an appendix to this book.)

Except when the Chinese intervened in the war, these first few months were fraught with the danger of defeat. The defense of the Pusan Perimeter, the first, and most critical campaign of the Korean War was a near run thing. The battle along the Perimeter was, in fact, a series of fights on the brink of disaster. It is to the everlasting credit of Lieutenant General Walton H. Walker, his indomitable spirit, vision and consummate skill as a tactician that this defense was successful. But this does not take any credit from the officers and enlisted men who served under him. Their own spirit, aggressiveness and will to win were the ingredients that Walker needed to implement his desires and orders.

The North Korean Army and its leadership were skillful, daring and very determined to succeed. Their army took huge losses, but continued an uncommon offensive spirit to the end. One must give them credit. It is a tribute to the American and ROK soldier — the men who did the fighting and dying — that they persevered and emerged victorious in this crucial first campaign of the Korean War.

Chapter Notes:

P. 375 The 2d Division history credits the 65th RCT with forcing the enemy from Hill 409 and Hyonpung. It also states that the leading elements of the 38th Infantry departed Kochang at 4 a.m. on Sept. 27, passing through the 23d at Anui and capturing Chonju 10 hours later. The official history, citing 2d Division and 38th Infantry records, interviews and manuscript reviews, states that the 38th departed Kochang on Sept. 28, not Sept. 27.

P. 382 Duve wrote this tribute to COL Harris: "[W]ith him his men came first and whenever our Regiment was in action, you would always see Wild Bill right up there with you giving you encouragement. This made you feel good that the Old Man [commander] was there with you. Wild Bill always rode in his jeep, and you knew that it was him...because mounted on the hood...was a military saddle and the saddle had bullet holes in it. When we were up on line on a perimeter... Wild Bill would see to it that the mess took hot coffee and sometimes doughnuts or hot soup up to us; especially at night or during those cold winter days. How in hell can you not help respecting and admiring with great fondness a man, officer and leader such as that dear trooper, Colonel (then MG) William 'Wild Bill' Harris...."

P. 387 This course of action was tactically, and strategically, more sound than the capture of Seoul, which was politically motivated.

APPENDIX A — Prisoners of War and Missing in Action

Missing in Action

A popular bumper sticker declares that 8,177 men are still missing in action from the Korean War. What is not generally known is that this figure is actually the number of men whose bodies were not recovered and includes men who were killed in action, died of wounds, died while captured and those in a category listed by the Department of Defense as "Died While Missing." There are several things wrong with the figure of 8,177.

Dr. Paul M. Cole, of the RAND Corporation, conducted a study of prisoners of war and missing in action issues. His study and its results were published in *POW/MIA Issues,* Vol. 1, *The Korean War*, RAND, 1994. He states that 37 bodies had been recovered and identified as of 1991, and that the 8,000-plus figure included personnel already accounted for in other categories. The 8,140 figure also includes 859 bodies which were recovered and buried, but not identified.

On Nov. 5, 1954, the Department of Defense issued a press release concerning Korean War era casualties. According to this release, as of Sept. 30, 1954, only 24 men were still officially listed as MIA from the Korean War. Of these, 15 were Air Force fliers and nine were Naval personnel. The press release also stated: "The Army and Marine Corps no longer list any personnel as 'Missing.'"

The Army and Marine Corps declared their missing men as dead, since there was little evidence that any of them were alive (except for a few airmen), even in 1960.

A Department of Defense press release dated March 1, 1960, however, reveals that the United Nations had handed the North Koreans a list of 3,404 members of the UN Command who had not been accounted for and who were believed to have been under "Communist control," in the words of this release. This number included 944 American servicemen. Over half of these men were finally conclusively determined to be dead, according to the press release.

That there were thousands of men not accurately accounted for during the Korean War should be no mystery. Large numbers of men became casualties during several major battles. For example, the 24th Division, in its delaying withdrawal early in the war, lost thousands of men. Many of these were carried as MIA, and later declared dead without their remains to prove this. During other enemy penetrations of the Perimeter, many other men were lost when their positions were overrun. Some North Korean soldiers shot and killed captured, wounded American soldiers; the number of men so murdered is not known.

When the Chinese intervened, the U.S. and UN lost many more troops to the attackers. Two Army battalions, plus attached artillery, etc., were destroyed on the eastern shore of the Chosin Reservoir and the U.S. 2d Division lost 4,037 men in killed, wounded and missing at Kunu-ri on Nov. 30, 1950. Some of the missing were subsequently accounted for as POWs and the remains of some others were discovered and identified. UN forces never regained large areas of North Korea to recover bodies. Many of those missing as a result of battle in those areas were no doubt killed and will never be identified. Others were captured.

The actual number of men truly MIA will never be known. However, this author believes that the number does not approach 8,000. Since the 8,000-plus considered by some as missing includes men already accounted for in one of the other categories, the number is suspect from the start. The number is probably closer to 4,846, the number of men listed as "Died While Missing." No matter how many men are MIA, the heartache of loved ones left behind is all the same.

Prisoners of War

As near as this author can calculate, 7,589 American servicemen became POWs during the Korean War. This figure is derived from several sources: The Nov. 5, 1954, Department of Defense press release states that 5,133 men, "previously reported Captured or Missing" returned to military control. It also notes that 21 American POWs chose to remain in China. The Department of Defense Korean War database, updated to Oct. 1994, lists 33,462 battle deaths in Korea. This figure includes 2,435 men who died while POWs. The 5,133 men returning, plus the 21 who chose to go to China and the 2,435 men who died in captivity total 7,589 men.

The deaths of almost 1/3 of the American POWs during the Korean War amply attests to the horrible treatment accorded them by their North Korean captors. Some men would have died in captivity, but the large number of those who did so in the Korean War can only be attributed to cruel and indifferent treatment by their captors.

The experiences of some of these men, as well as civilian captives of North Korea are further evidence of North Korea's brutal handling of their POWs.

A few men were lucky enough to escape early on and some others were fortunate to be freed at Namwon by advancing U.S. troops. In his *In Enemy Hands: A Prisoner in North Korea*, Larry Zellers, an American missionary, recounts his experiences and those of other missionaries and American soldiers who were prisoners. Zellers wrote of the moral courage of SGT Henry G. Leerkamp (L/34th Inf.) who, on more than one occasion, cared for the dead when no one else did; of the physical strength and courage of MAJ Newton W. Lantron (HQ, 3/34th Inf.), who on the Death March, picked up a man and carried him over his shoulder when the man's weakened and emaciated comrades could no longer help him along; of the great morale booster, CPL Wilbert "Shorty" Estabrook (B/19th Inf.), who even in the worst of times, tried to cheer people up with his jokes; and of the leadership and example of MAJ John J. Dunn (S-3, 34th Inf.), the senior POW; and finally, of the heroic and defiant stance of LT Cordus H. Thornton as he was "tried" then murdered by a North Korean major for allowing POWs under his charge to drop out of the column during the Death March.

Leerkamp had served with MAJ Lantron previously. Leerkamp wrote about the Major: "He carried himself well and was a model officer. He was easy to work with, keeping us informed and organizing transportation. He delegated authority but kept his hand on all units." As a POW, Leerkamp wrote, Lantron "never gave in nor allowed anyone else to do so."

Most of the prisoners captured there were kept in or near Hadong until sometime in September. U.S. aircraft bombed and strafed the town from time to time, beginning about July. During the first raid, all the windows were blown out of the schoolhouse, but the building was not hit.

LT Makarounis and James Yeager (both of the 29th Infantry) were apparently originally in the schoolhouse. Louie M. Hillis (K/29th) did not recall if he was put into the school house or a church. John Napier (L/29) remembered that he was in the church.

In one of the early air strikes the church was hit, reportedly killing 22 of 80 American POWs. Their bodies were left there for two weeks before a detail of POWs was sent to bury them. Louie Hollis, John Napier and Jim Yeager were all in that detail.

The dead men's dogtags were given to LT Max E. Reid (I/29). Hollis said that 15 dead were buried there. Yeager said that a school teacher's house has since been built over the site of this mass grave.

One of the North Korean guards on the burial detail had been in the Japanese Army, Yeager wrote. "After the burial he fired three rounds over the grave and passed a sake bottle to the men and each took a drink in honor of the dead."

That night, Yeager wrote, the walking wounded were separated from those who could not walk. Many of the seriously wounded were killed by the guards.

Makarounis believed that there were about 130 prisoners there — some in caves and some in the orchard. Some of the GIs distributed pears from the orchard to other POWs. Makarounis ate three.

Hollis was never treated for the foot injury he received from a shell fragment. Almost miraculously, it healed by itself. The second day after capture, Makarounis and some other walking wounded were marched to a village four or five miles from Hadong. There, some of the men were treated by a North Korean medic. That was the last time any of them had any medical attention. That night, this group was returned to Hadong and the schoolhouse. There were now about 50 men in the schoolhouse.

Each time Americans bombed and strafed Hadong, the POWs and guards headed for the hill and caves. During this time, Makarounis and CPL Wilson, a WW II Marine combat veteran, developed a scheme to escape. Meantime, POWs began to die — one or more each day — not from bombing, but from wounds.

Makarounis recounted in an article he wrote in the March 1951 issue of *Argosy* magazine, how he, SGT Wilson and PVT Paul Shaffron, escaped for about four days on July 31, being recaptured on Aug. 4.

Makarounis and the others ended up in Seoul on Sept. 11. From there, they began the infamous "Death March" deeper into North Korea. Makarounis wrote that his group started with 376 men. When they reached Pyongyang, he wrote, 296 men remained.

While imprisoned at Pyongyang, LT Makarounis met CPT William Locke, an F-51 pilot who had been shot down, and SGT Takesshi Kumagi (34th Inf.). MAJ William T. McDaniel (former S3, 34th Inf.) was the senior POW of the camp, which was located on the second floor of a schoolhouse.

On Oct. 13, 1950, while he and CPT Locke were, as he put it, "sitting in the school yard, soaking up what sun we could," Locke asked him if he "had a chance to bug off," would he? Makarounis replied he would. On Oct. 14, 1950, the schoolmaster, who was allowed to visit his school from time to time, hid the three men under the school house for several days when he learned that the North Koreans intended to ship the POWs out. Makarounis had a few scraps of bread with him, Locke several loaves of bread, and Kumagi a bottle of water. The hiding place was about three feet high and about 50 feet square, with two tiny windows with bars. Within 15 minutes after they reached this haven, the enemy guards marched the other POWs out and sent them on the way north.

Makarounis wrote that 22 other POWs tried to escape that night, four of them by hiding behind furniture in the schoolhouse. These four, and seven others, were recaptured and summarily executed.

Four other men — a CPL Arikawa and Sergeants Morris, Jones and Eddie Halcomb, all part of the POW burial detail, also escaped. The men marched away from the burial ground and through Pyongyang, with CPL Arikawa, acting as a North Korean guard and shouting *"Habe! Habe!"* at the other three men. Near the city's edge, they found an abandoned house. Taking shelter, they remained there, living on some flour and water until liberated by advancing UN troops.

Makarounis wrote that, of the 376 POWs who had started out from Seoul in 1950, only 45 survived POW camp.

Namwon

CPL William R. Swafford (D, 9th Inf) was captured on Sept. 5, 1950, and marched back and across the Naktong. There, he joined three other POWs. He recalled one of these men was named Scotty. Another he described as "a Mexican." The latter had been shot across the bottom of the foot from the heel to toes. The men carried him in a litter as they were marched further to the rear. The men were marched through one village after the other. One night they were transported by truck. The POWs received a ball of rice or barley every evening.

"In one village," he wrote, "we met a high ranking N.K. soldier. He was wearing a dress uniform. He could speak English fluently. He

asked us questions. When he started to leave he shook our hands, wished us well, and left." This was certainly different treatment by an enemy officer.

"In another village, I heard a dog yelping," Swafford wrote. The guards shot this dog. "That evening we had a bowl of mixed vegetables with some meat in it. I figured it was dog meat [but] I was very hungry and it tasted good."

Swafford and the POWs with him finally arrived in Namwon and were placed in a large building with a number of other POWs. He was near two wounded men. "I could smell the odor coming from the wounds," he wrote, "and could see maggots crawling in their wounds. Some of the men got to complaining about the odor." One day, one of the men with rotting wounds crawled out of the building. Swafford thought the man was going to the toilet. The North Koreans shot him.

In late September the prisoners at Hadong were put on the road north. Barefooted, without shirts, they were force marched. Men fell, exhausted. Others dragged them to their feet. At one point, Hollis and Donald H. Wheldon (also of I/29th Inf.) pulled a SGT Winters to his feet and moved him along between them. LT Reid developed large blisters on his feet, "the size of jumbo olives." Someone found a two-wheel cart along the road. Reid was placed in the cart and pulled along with the column.

In one town they were all put into a prison cell or room. Napier recalled that "at the time there were only about twenty-seven or twenty-eight of [us] still living. No one was to move or talk." Offenders were required to lay their hands on the steel plate of the door where a North Korean beat them with a stick "the size of a broom handle."

"I carried the scars of those beatings for several weeks," Napier wrote. He also lost several fingernails as a result of the beatings.

A North Korean soldier took Yeager's boots early in his captivity, a common practice. "The SOB took my combat boots," Yeager said. "He wore a size five tennis shoe and I wore a size ten. He took these at gunpoint.... I took my C-ration can opener and cut the toes of the tennis shoes."

At Namwon, they were put into a building with about 60 other prisoners and lined up in rows. Hollis was in the second row. The enemy tied the hands of the men in the first two rows. One of the POWs asked for food. It was early in the morning. An enemy officer sent some guards and POWs for rice. "About that time a guy [started] to roll a cigarette out of a page from the New Testament," Hollis wrote. "A Sergeant made him stop and he read what was on the page out loud. It was from John 8:36 — 'If the Son therefore shall make you free; ye shall be free indeed.' In a few moments we heard rifle fire outside and people running." One of the men peeked through a crack in the building and saw an American tank. "The next instant we heard someone yell in English 'Are there any GIs in there?'"

The POWs didn't answer, but broke the door down and swarmed from the building — "one of the happiest times of out lives," Hollis wrote. "There stood a big Swede with a handlebar mustache. His name was Ken Olson, of the 25th Division [TF Blair] I don't know how many hugged him, we were so glad to be free. Thank God...."

In 63 days as a POW, Louis Hollis lost 62 pounds. Others, he wrote, "lost more — their life."

LaVaughn E. Fields' platoon of the 77th ECC was with TF Blair that day. Once into Namwon, the lead tanks, with soldiers riding on them, approached what appeared to be a large school yard. Enemy soldiers were present, but took no action against the Americans. Fields thought they were confused by the big white stars on the tanks and believed them to be Russian. When the tanks stopped, a sergeant dismounted from the lead tank and went up to an enemy guard at the gate to the schoolyard.

"He said something," Fields wrote, "and the guard didn't understand him. So he mumbled and the guard shook his head and opened the gate.... When he opened the gate, we started blasting. As the guards came out of the building; we annihilated them." The POWs, he wrote "didn't believe it.... [We] came in and hollered at them. They just stood there and looked at us. [W]e were black [and] there were no black North Koreans. They broke into a cheer. We fed them.... We...lined up [the guards] and we turned the American prisoners loose on them until [an American officer stopped the POWs' revenge]."

Just before TF Blair arrived, Napier wrote, all the guards left the school building. Someone began untying the men's hands. Napier, Malcolm Steele, and another unidentified man, left the school and made their way to the edge of Namwon. There, they were sheltered by a peasant couple in their home and given what Napier described as "some of the best food we had eaten since being captured." They discovered that it was what the peasant called "meow meat" — cat meat. "Regardless," Napier recalled, "it was good at the time."

Late in the afternoon, the they headed back toward the school. Hearing the rumble of tanks, they quickly hid in a building. But they had been spotted. A tank "roared to a stop in front of the building, [and] we heard someone speak in English," Napier wrote. "He said, 'There is someone in the building to my left, get ready to fire on the building.' (Those were the sweetest words I've ever heard in my life.) Without hesitating we ran out of the building shouting, 'Don't shoot, we are Americans.' They did not shoot. We told them where the other POWs were...."

Among the captured guards was one who Napier wrote "harassed us laughing and asking us if we were hungry." He was under guard along the street. Napier went up to him, "crying and laughing at the same time," he recalled. "As I did he began to cover his face with his hands." Napier asked, "Are you hungry?" Then, "I lost control of myself and before I knew what happened, some of the Americans were pulling me off him."

1LT Thomas T. Jones (D/8th ECB) was captured along with several members of the company near Kasan in mid-September 1950. He wrote an account of his experiences as a POW and of his escape in "Two Hundred Miles to Freedom," in *The Military Engineer*, September-October 1951. Soon after their capture, the men's boots were confiscated. They joined another group of POWs. A few days later, seven more men were added to the group, bringing the number to 21. Some of them had been wounded.

Jones estimated that he walked about 75 miles in the small sneakers. By that time, his right foot was in terrible condition. A North Korean major suggested to him that he discard the sneaker and use a cloth to wrap his foot. He took the major's advice, using some cotton wadding he found, next to his foot. He tied the cloth in place with strips of cloth and used a rice rope as a garter to hold up his socks "and the rope was finally anchored with a double half-hitch above the knee," he wrote.

At one point in the march, an infantry sergeant told Jones that he was worn out - that he would "rather lay down and let them shoot him," Jones recorded. "Dysentery and fatigue had completely wrecked him. However, we took turns in groups of two, supporting him as we walked until he revived enough so that only one man had to help him." A man whose feet were a mass of raw, broken blisters and one of wounded men also required help.

Later in the march, another man, who Jones thought suffered from a ruptured lung, could go no farther. Guards allowed the prisoners to carry him on a litter. Four men carried the stretcher on their shoulders and the others formed up on a column of twos behind them. They relieved the bearers, two at a time, every 75 to 100 yards. They carried the man this way for about six miles. The guards stopped at a North Korean aid station, where the stretcher case, four wounded men and another with raw bloody feet were left. There were then 14 prisoners left of the original 21.

Near dusk on Oct. 1, 1950 shortly after they arrived in Chunchon, "a large tub of steaming rice, a delicacy to us now, was brought to the room," Jones wrote. "Suddenly...there was a lot of shouting and yelling just as we were getting ready to eat." The guards hustled the prisoners outside, ordering them to take what rice they could carry. Braving the burns from the hot rice, the men obeyed. Outside, "the road was clogged with civilians, trucks, carts and soldiers, all rushing toward the north," Jones wrote. "The guards shouted to us to double time down the rough gravel road." Jones and the other lieutenant (Howard C. Smith) in the POW group thought immediately of escape, but that seemed impossible with so many soldiers on the road. "Our group became separated and the lieutenant and I fell behind," he continued. "Then Fate stepped in."

His rag shoe began to fall off. He told the other officer and suggested that they slip into the roadside ditch. They did so and were almost immediately joined by two other prisoners, PFCs Joseph T. Charland and Jack D. Fridley, both members of Jones' platoon. The men all bent over, pretending to fix their shoes, to hide their bearded faces.

They took shelter in a farmhouse that night. The next day, they noticed civilians apparently searching the area. Smith and Jones went to another house. While there, a Korean civilian opened the door to the building, but was stopped when, the two officers said "Chingo, chingo" to him. This was Korean for friend. The four, now ex-POWs were taken by the Korean and four of his friends to a house partly hidden in a wooded gully. They displayed UN and South Korean flags to the Americans and "that they were a democratic people's band."

The men were led down the middle of the road, with Korean civilians waving little Korean flags along the way. About 200 yards beyond was a waiting South Korean Army patrol. Suddenly, the Korean escrots grabbed the mens' hands and began to run. They were only 75 yards from the friendly patrol, but the enemy had arrived and began firing.

The South Korean soldiers returned fire, while the four American soldiers sought refuge in a nearby paddy. The enemy patrol was driven off and a Korean guide came back for them. Only Jones and Fridley were together. They discovered, however, that Charland had already reached safety. A South Korean major in a jeep took Jones and Fridley to the CP of the 2d Regiment, ROK 6th Division, in Chunchon. "Once inside the building, we both burst into tears." They had been POWs for 21 days, during which they had been forced to walk 200 miles. Jones called it "our 200-mile walk to Freedom."

Prisoners in North Korea

The foregoing outlines a few of the experiences of some American POWs who were fortunate enough to be liberated within about two months of their capture. But the bulk of the POWs endured almost three years of brutality and extreme psychological stress in camps and during what became known as a "Death March." This march began Oct. 31, 1950 and lasted over two weeks. The bulk of material for this section comes from Larry Zellers' book, *In Enemy Hands*. He was a teacher at a mission station in Kaesong, just south of the 38th Parallel, when the North attacked, and was soon taken into custody, along with fellow missionaries, male and female. Zellers wrote that he had known 756 military men in POW camps. Of these, only "approximately 250" were returned.

Zellers, the other missionaries, and a number of other civilian prisoners were first sent to Pyongyang. In mid-July 1950, they were placed in a schoolhouse outside the city. On Sept. 5, they were put on a train which made its way to Manpo. As the train was loaded in Pyongyang, some 500 American POWs were put on board. "Long lines of haggard-looking young American soldiers" were marched past his window on the train. He wrote that they were "ragged, dirty [and] hollow-eyed."

He recalled that 726 POWs left Pyongyang. Thirty more joined the group later in the year. But, when he last saw them, Oct. 10, 1951, the number had shrunk to 292. The senior POW was MAJ John J. Dunn (34th Inf.)

Later, during the Death March, the military prisoners were ahead of the civilians in the column. Zellers and his companions passed man after man, lying along the road, awaiting execution. It was pitiful, he wrote, to see these men, many younger than he, lying by the side of the road. One young soldier was singing "God Bless America" as loudly as his weak voice would allow. Tears streamed down his face, and tears also welled up in the eyes of the passing civilian prisoners as they passed him. Zellers wrote that he "was staggered by feelings of hopelessness and grief."

The soldiers were still in summer-weight uniforms, they had had no medical attention and had been fed very little. Many no longer had the strength of body, or of will, to survive.

Howard A. Stevens (HQ/52d FAB) was an 18-year-old PFC when he was wounded and captured near the Kum River on Jul. 18, 1950. Because of his youth, he thought, the enemy didn't bother him too much, but he wrote, a front tooth was broken when he was "unexpectedly hit in the mouth for no reason."

In Taejon he witnessed enemy soldiers throwing concussion grenades into a compound of American POWs. "These guards were laughing and having a ball," Stevens recalled.

Stevens used a little deception early in his captivity. "During my early interrogation," he wrote, "I stuck my finger into my leg wound to get blood to smear on my face and head to make them believe I was in a lot worse shape, physically, than I really was."

The experiences and recollections of these few American POWs are representative of all POWs of the Korean War. Even after almost half a century, it is impossible to forgive and forget. Nor should we!

Postscript

An article appearing in the September 1996 *VFW* magazine states that, as of 1990, 16 sets of the remains of American servicemen were returned by North Korea. Since that time, a total of 208 sets have been returned, but only six have been positively identified. On May 9, 1996, an agreement was made with North Korea permitting a joint U.S.-North Korean search for remains of U.S. missing. However, the search is only a 20-day operation.

A Sept. 18, 1996, article in the Harrisburg, PA, *The Patriot-News* indicates that as many as 900 POWs were unaccounted for in 1953. U.S. Rep. Robert Dornan (R-CA), chairman of a subcommittee examining this issue, is quoted as saying that the latest Pentagon list of unaccounted for numbers 389, although he believed the figure is higher.

The article cites former Czech officer Jan Sejna claiming that hundreds of U.S. POWs were used as guinea pigs in medical experiments in a hospital built in North Korea at Moscow's direction. He said most of the POWs were killed, but that about 100 were sent to the former Eastern Bloc nation of Czechoslovakia at the end of the war for further experiments.

The fate of thousands of men lost in the Korean War will probably never be resolved. Trying to find identifiable remains, or trying to determine if POWs were used in medical experiments and their identities, 50 years after the war will probably prove largely fruitless.

References:

Carroll G. Everist, L/5th Cav. "Bits and Pieces of Korea, Remembered," Military, Aug. 1993. Q&N: 8/24/92.

William R. Swafford, D/9th Inf. Q&N: 7/10/93.

Wilbert R. Estabrook. B/19th Inf. L: Estabrook to Barnett 11/16/90; T: Barnett to Estabrook 4/9/92.

Louie M. Hollis, K/29th Inf. Q&N: 1/19/93.

Alexander Makarounis, I/29th Inf. "I Survived the Korean Death March," Argosy magazine, March 1951. (Copy courtesy Neal Vance, L/29th Inf.)

John L. Napier, I/29th Inf. Undated narrative. (Copy courtesy Frank Myers, 6/28/94.)

James W. Yeager, HQ/3/29th Inf. Q: 1/22/93. Transcript of interview by Lewis Michelony for John Toland. This manuscript was corrected by Yeager for this book in June 1993; there were many errors. Life magazine, May 11, Jun. 8, 1953. "They Buried Me Under the Dead," For Men Only, July 1, 1954.

Henry G. Leerkamp, L/34th Inf. Q: 11/27/92. L: 10/29/92.

Jerene Garges Jones (wife of Thomas T. Jones, D/8th ECC). Copy of Thomas Jones' article, "Two Hundred Miles to Freedom," The Military Engineer, September-October 1951. Thomas T. Jones is deceased.

Harold A. Stevens, HQ/52d FAB. Q&N: 2/2/94.

LaVaugn E. Fields, 77th ECC. T: 9/1/94.

William Locke. 34th Ftr Sqdn, USAF. "The Korean Death March," Military, Dec. 1994.

Larry Zellers, In Enemy Hands, A Prisoner in North Korea (Lexington, KY: The University of Kentucky Press, 1991)

Discussion of MIAs and POWs:
Dr. Paul M. Cole, POW/MIA Issues, Vol. 1, The Korean War, RAND, 1994.

Frank A. Reister, Battle Casualties and Medical Statistics: U.S. Army Experience in the Korean War (Washington, D.C., The Surgeon General, Department of the Army, 1972)

Department of the Army, Office of Public Information. Press releases of Nov. 5, 1954 and March 1, 1960. (Copies courtesy Donald A. Carter, DA Military History.)

Department of Defense Korean Conflict database, as of October 1994. (Does not include 2,452 records for Army non-battle deaths in Korea.)

Letter from Martin J. O'Brien, Augusta, ME, Graybeards magazine, March-April 1995. (Discusses Korean War personnel loss figures.)

"Korea MIA Search Finally Under Way," in "Washington Wire" column, VFW magazine, September 1996

"Files: 900 POWs left in N. Korea," The Associated Press, The Patriot-News, Harrisburg, PA, Sept. 18, 1996.

APPENDIX B — Strength Accounting and Losses

Strength Accounting

When a man was assigned to a company, battery or troop, it became the responsibility of his commander to strictly account for him. This was done by means of a written document called the Morning Report. It was the first sergeant's responsibility to accurately and completely prepare one of these reports daily. It had to show the numbers of officers, warrant officers, NCOs and other ranks assigned to the unit; the number physically present; the number absent and the reasons for the absence of each person from the unit that day. Each report covered the period from one minute after midnight that day to midnight of that day (0001 hours to 2400 hours). No erasures or strikeovers were permitted on this report.

First sergeants often prepared the report late at night (or had the unit clerk prepare it) so that it was ready as early as possible the next morning. Sometimes this efficiency back-fired if someone was killed or wounded just before midnight, if replacements arrived before midnight, or wounded or injured men returned to the unit before midnight.

In the early days of Korea, at least, first sergeants were often stationed with the company "Rear CP," usually co-located with the company's kitchen. Company kitchens (or "messes," as they were known in those days) were usually with the Battalion Rear CP. In addition to the cooks, a company Rear CP could include the supply sergeant, the company armorer-artificer, the company clerk and possibly, the XO. The armorer-artificer made minor repairs to unit weapons and safeguarded any weapons not issued to an individual or crew. Men suffering minor injuries or illness might also be at this rear CP, as well as replacements or returning men, pending their return to the front.

In some commands, company clerks were pooled at battalion or regimental level, and "Feeder Reports" were sent back from the unit front line position daily with strength accounting information on them. The clerks prepared morning reports from these feeders. This did not always prove satisfactory because the tactical situation sometimes prevented preparation of the feeder report, or its dispatch to the rear. This led to inaccuracies on Morning Reports and/or missing reports. Also, the records of some units were lost due to enemy action. As a result of these events, accounting for strengths and losses in the affected units or organizations was incorrect. In such cases, new reports, or corrected reports had to be reconstructed later on when the unit or organization was in reserve and there was time to question the men and investigate the situation leading to the faulty report or no report being rendered.

In some of these instances large numbers of men were carried as MIA because no one knew what had happened to them. Men carried in this status, who were lost in North Korea in places that U.S. troops never returned to, remained MIA until declared dead after the war. This led to a very high number of men initially recorded as MIA (8,177).

Korean War Casualties

U.S. casualties in the Korean War (excluding those in other parts of the world) are listed below. References: DA Korean War database updated Oct. 1994; "Battle Casualties and Medical Statistics: U.S. Army Experience in the Korean War," Frank Reister, DA, 1973; POW/MIA Issues, Vol. 1, *The Korean War*, Dr. Paul M. Cole, RAND, 1994; DOD Press releases, Sept. 30, 1954; March 1, 1960.

KIA:	23,836	
DWM:	4,846	(Died While Missing)
DWC:	2,435	(Died While Captured)
DOW:	2,535	(Died of Wounds)
TOTAL:	33,652	Dead, battle/hostile action
NBD:	3,262	Dead, Non-Battle Deaths (NBD)
TOTAL:	36,914	
MPD:	3,255	(Missing/Presumed Dead)**
TOTAL:	40,169	Dead, all causes in Korea
WIA:	103,284	(Includes only those who survived)
MIA:	39	(24 Air Force and 15 Navy personnel)
DESERTERS:	21	(Chose to go to China from being POWs)
TOTAL LOSSES, ALL CAUSES:	143,513	(Except non-battle injuries/sickness.)

** The figure of 3,255 Missing/Presumed Dead is derived by subtracting the number 4,846 (Died While Missing) and the 39 men still missing from the 8,140 men carried as missing after 1991.

APPENDIX C — Medical Support

Americans associate medical support in the Korean War with the Mobile Army Surgical Hospital (MASH) and helicopter evacuation of the wounded to a MASH.

MASH units came into existence in 1948. The organization was to have fourteen medical officers. two medical service officers, 12 nurses, one warrant officer and 97 EM. One medical officer commanded; one was a radiologist; one an internist; two anesthesiologists; four were general duty medical officers and five were surgeons. The real MASHs in Japan were a bit different. The 8055th in Yokohama, for example, had 10 doctors and 95 EM. But none of its surgeons were considered completely qualified. The Far East Command had no completely trained and experienced surgeons to assign.

The 8055th MASH arrived in Korea on July 6; the 8063d went in with the 1st Cavalry Division in mid-July and the 8076th on July 25. By July 26 all the MASHs were committed to supporting the fight.

Each division had an organic medical battalion, and each infantry regiment had an organic medical company. Each division was authorized a total of 42 doctors. At no time in the early months of the war were there any more than 25 per division. When the 24th deployed to Korea its Medical Battalion had two or three doctors, three Medical Service Corps officers and 124 EM. (TO&E called for 46 officers, two warrant officers and 293 EM.) William H. Wiley (Ambulance Co., 2d Medical Bn, 2d Inf. Div.), wrote that the Ambulance Company of the 2d Med. Bn had three platoons of 10 ambulances each.

There was a driver and an assistant driver in each vehicle. The 1st Platoon supported the 9th Regiment; 2d Platoon the 23d Regiment and the 3d Platoon the 38th Regiment. The 2d Platoon helped the others when the 23d was in reserve. As a result, this platoon was nicknamed "The Rover Boys." Ambulance companies used the 3/4-ton ambulance, configured for four litters. A fifth litter could be placed on the floor of the patient compartment. Because this part of the ambulance resembled a box, they were often called "Box Ambulances."

The regimental medical company was authorized 13 officers and 201 EM, including five doctors among the 13 officers. The unit's ambulance section was equipped with jeeps (called "litter jeeps") which could carry two litters. Riding as a patient in one of these litter jeeps could be a jolting, bone-shaking, agonizing journey for a wounded man.

A battalion medical platoon was attached to each infantry battalion of the regiment. Each platoon was authorized 2 officers and 35 EM. One officer was a doctor. The platoon furnished four-man litter teams and platoon aidmen (medics or corpsmen) to rifle companies.

The chain of evacuation was from the front to the Battalion Aid Station to the Regimental Collecting Station to the Division Clearing Station to a MASH.

Backing the MASHs were evacuation hospitals. One of these, the 8054th Evacuation Hospital (LTC John M. Willis, Jr.) arrived in Pusan on July 6 and set up in a Korean school. It received its first patients the next day. BG (Ret.) Jack Pollock was a maxillo-facial surgeon with the 8054th. He recalled that on three occasions the male officers helped to man a perimeter around the hospital, "because an attack was considered imminent."

The experiences and writings of some of the medical personnel, as recounted in *The Medic's War* by Albert E. Cowdrey (Center for Military History, U.S. Army, 1987) provide some concept of the almost overwhelming problems and primitive conditions which medical personnel overcame to accomplish their mission.

The enemy always targeted the red crosses, which at the time, were painted on some aidmen's helmets, the sides and back of box ambulances and to mark aid stations. Soon, the red crosses were painted out or covered to protect medical personnel and their patients.

CPT Donal L. Duerk's Medical Company, 21st Infantry was "cut to pieces" at Chochiwon. The wounded had to be taken out in a tank. CPT Alexander M. Boysen and his assistant, CPT Clarence L. Anderson, were cut off and captured. A hospital train leaving Taegu at night, heading for Pusan, was hit by small-arms and machine gun fire at one point and rifle fire and grenades at another. Another hospital train leaving Taejon was ambushed and stopped at a railroad tunnel a few miles east of town.

CPT Frank D. Thompson, Jr., Medical Service Corps (MSC), 34th Infantry Medical Co., always placed his collection station on the main road for rapid evacuation, but securely within the perimeter of a combat unit. He spent most of his time at regimental headquarters in order to keep abreast of the combat situation. His battalion aid stations were placed so that they could be reached by litter jeeps. He also insisted on as rapid an evacuation of patients as possible. This kept the aid stations clear of patients and lessened the danger of wounded being lost if the position were overrun by the enemy. At Chochiwon, he located his collecting station close to a railhead. Here, the medics used "Doodlebugs" to shuttle the wounded 30 miles from Chochiwon to Taejon, a gasoline-powered railroad car which could carry 17 litter and 50 ambulatory patients in one haul. The 30-mile trip could be made in about 45 minutes. The Doodlebug released four to five ambulances for use elsewhere. This was important, for ambulances were put to hard use and were in short supply.

The Headquarters and Clearing Co. of the 24th Medical Battalion and the 8055th MASH set up operations in Taejon on July 10 in the Taejon Primary School. The Clearing Co. (MAJ Austin C. Doren) provided basic hospital services to patients, except surgery, before sending them to the rear. The worst cases went directly to the MASH for surgery. The 8055th (MAJ Isaac J. Tender) had its full complement of Army nurses, led by CPT Phyllis M. La Conte. But there were no nurses available for hospital trains nor flight nurses. CPT La Conte volunteered to accompany the train, taking the wounded to Taegu for air evacuation to Japan, then acted as the one and only flight nurse on the trip to Japan.

The shortage of doctors was so acute that MSC officers and, on occasion, even sergeants, had to set up (and operate) battalion aid stations.

On July 20 an enemy tank round exploded over the entrance to the 24th Medical Co. aid station in Taejon, wounding three men. About 4 p.m., the company loaded the last of its casualties onto its three remaining ambulances and got through with a convoy to Yongdong. In the Taejon battle, mortar rounds hit the aid station of the 63d FAB. A battalion aid station of the 21st Regiment at Okchon exhausted all its medical supplies in treating the wounded from Taejon.

The 25th Infantry Division was supported by its medical battalion and the 8063d MASH in the early days. They shared a schoolhouse in Kumchon and were flooded with wounded. CPT Oree Gregory was a nurse with the 8063d. "I'll never forget these casualties," she wrote in her diary. "In all my 17 years of experience I've never seen such patients. Blind, or with legs or buttocks blown off. Many died despite skilled surgery." The July heat was intense and "green, large and heavy" flies swarmed around the school.

A chronic shortage of drivers and ambulances drove the 25th Medical Battalion to improvise. The battalion obtained a self-propelled railroad car, perhaps similar to the Doodlebug the 24th Division had used, and three Korean rail coaches and fitted them with crude litter racks. They coupled the cars to the supply trains headed for Taegu and Pusan. Attendants had to hitch a ride back the same way. The 25th Clearing Co., headed by LTC (Doctor) Paul C. Sheldon, treated 1,086 patients during July 1950.

Before being assigned to support the 25th Division, the 8063d had supported the 24th Division. When this MASH left Kumchon on a flatcar, its commander, MAJ Frank A. Neuman, remained behind with a severely wounded man, who died shortly after. Neuman buried the man in the schoolyard, then he, another doctor and their enlisted driver rejoined the unit in Taegu.

Once the Perimeter was established, medical evacuation routes were shortened, but the fierce heat and savage combat created heavy casualties. Regimental medical companies obtained 25 to 50 Korean civilians to act as litter bearers. It often took four to six men to carry a single litter off the mountains to an aid station — a grueling and, for the patient, very painful journey. Often, one or more litter bearers slipped and fell, throwing the wounded man off the litter onto the ground. Evacuation via litter at night or in rainy weather was very hazardous to the bearers and the patient.

Malaria, heat exhaustion and psychiatric cases added to the number of battle and nonbattle casualties which almost swamped the medical support units in Korea at the time. The number of wounded often overwhelmed a MASH. Further, vermin of every description infested many buildings. The windows of the nurses quarters in one MASH, where 17 nurses shared a single room, had to be kept shut tight in the terrible heat to keep out rats.

"We had patients in every place," wrote CPT Gregory. "Every known type of wound and burn.... One private had lost an arm and was likely to lose a leg.... All the men have blood-stained letters they never had time to read. They're begging for water. But they're mostly due for surgery, so fluids are limited. After that was explained, they just accepted it. Sometimes, when they heard our voices, the boys would think they were back in the States. One private said: 'My God! Not a real American nurse! Rake off my bandages so I can see her!' But he was blind."

MAJ Kryder E. Van Buskirk's 8076th MASH, at Miryang, supported the 24th Division then the 2d Division. It also treated casualties from the 1st Cavalry, further north on the Perimeter. This overburdened MASH was helped by the arrival of the Marine Brigade surgeon, five or six doctors and 30 hospital corpsmen.

MAJ Van Buskirk later recalled, "Everybody worked around the clock without orders." Actually, he had to order people "point blank" to go to bed. "There was no end to the work," he said. The doctors worked 24 hours then napped the next day between cases. A doctor would sleep when he could, be awakened, go back to work, nap again until called again in an endless cycle. The nurses worked "12 to 16 hours a day without rest and some until they collapsed."

Although blood transfusions were never a problem in the 8076th, sponges, bandages, sutures and surgical knives were usually in short supply. Bandages and sponges were washed and re-washed so that they could be re-used several times. Nurses gave "the doctors hell if they so much as wasted a suture," said Van Buskirk.

Nurses of the 8076th were never sent away when danger seemed nearby. They shared the same dangers as the men because Van Buskirk reasoned that the hospital could not work without them.

This MASH seems to have been the inspiration for the movie and TV series, *M*A*S*H*. Between periods of all-out work were those of all-out relaxation — to play and have fun. Van Buskirk strictly observed this rule, too. His people were accomplished scroungers. From the Marines, for example, they got a 220-volt generator and a walk-in refrigerator mounted on a truck.

The 8076th had only 10 doctors, including Van Buskirk. Of these, seven had just completed internships. These seven had all been enlisted men in WW II — most of them combat infantrymen.

American medical personnel and the American field hospital system treated U.S. personnel, ROKs, other allied personnel and even enemy troops.

MASHs were supposed to be 60-bed facilities, but often they were well above capacity. In Aug. 1950, for example, CPT Elizabeth N. Johnson, a nurse with the 8076th, reported that "we are anything but a 60-bed mobile surgical unit. Our holding wards alone held 200 patients." Later in 1950, all MASHs were expanded to support 150-200 bed patients.

Doctors operating in MASHs did not have

the luxury of the refined principles of a private practice. It was, as so aptly expressed in one episode of *M*A*S*H*, "meatball surgery."

They employed triage, the objective of which is to ensure the maximum number of recoveries. The wounded determined to be hopelessly terminal, and those with relatively minor wounds were moved aside. Those with the most severe wounds, but who could probably be saved by immediate surgery, were taken into surgery first. The terminally wounded were made as comfortable as possible, often by the administration of pain-deadening drugs, until they died. The patients with "minor" wounds were treated last.

They had to work quickly and deftly to efficiently treat massive wounds and massive trauma, then move on to the next casualty and do it all over again, and again, and again. Also they eventually learned (or re-learned) that battle fatigue (shell-shock) victims should be treated near the front and returned to the battlefield within a few days. In July through mid-September 1950 these patients were sent back to Japan. As a result, the losses due to this malady further weakened the Army in Korea at a time when manpower losses were critical.

The 2d Division brought in a psychiatrist, CPT Martin J. Schumacher, who set up a one-doctor treatment center in Miryang. His facility treated 612 battle fatigue casualties during Sept. 1950. Of these 71 per cent were returned to duty and only 29 per cent evacuated.

Helicopter Evacuation

The U.S. Air Force first used helicopters for medical evacuation in Korea. In late July a detachment of the 3d Air Rescue Squadron, led by CPT Oscar N. Tibbets, came to Korea. The squadron's mission was to rescue downed pilots. But it had few such missions. Tibbets began to respond to Army requests to rescue casualties which could not be reached by ambulance. By Aug. 1950 these missions became so numerous that the squadron "found itself in the medical evacuation business," said COL Chauncey E. Dovell, (chief medical officer, Eighth Army).

On Aug. 3, as an experiment, COL Dovell had an Air Force helicopter fly two litter cases from Taegu to the 8054th Evacuation Hospital in Pusan. In late October, eight helicopters were purchased and sent to Korea to evacuate casualties by air. But even before this, in early September, the 2d Division surgeon, COL Donald E. Carle, obtained two helicopters through COL Dovell to use in evacuating the most seriously wounded from the division level direct to the supporting MASH. Except for this case and a few others with the Marines, helicopters were not used routinely for medical evacuation to MASHs or elsewhere until late 1950 or early 1951.

Dr. F. T. H'Doubler was assistant regimental surgeon, 5th Marines, in the Perimeter. He recalled the incident which led to the routine use of helicopters by the Marines to evacuate casualties in Korea. During the Pusan Perimeter "the [Marine] medical officers were taken aboard a hospital ship where we met Admiral Boone. He asked us if there was anything we needed that we didn't have. Our immediate reply was helicopters to evacuate the seriously injured. Prior

to that, General Craig...would radio us at our regimental station and ask if we had any serious wounded to be evacuated. He would always come in if requested and take out the wounded on a stretcher. The stretcher would be laid across his lap with the man's head out one window and his feet out the other. Of course, what we needed we got soon, and that was the litters carried on the side (of helicopters).... This was a great help."

Combat Medics and Corpsmen

Combat medics and corpsmen are the unsung heroes of the Korean War. Untold hundreds of them were killed or wounded while treating wounded or dying soldiers or Marines. They crawled or ran from casualty to casualty, doing what they could for each wounded man from the pitiful stock of bandages and morphine syrettes they carried in their aid kits. Often the medic would shelter the patient with his own body; many were killed doing so. They always responded to the call for "Medic!" or "Corpsman!" No group of men, individually or collectively, were ever more brave or less selfish. Almost every combat infantryman knows of at least one medic or corpsman who risked his life, was killed or wounded, in fulfilling his duty.

In the early days of the Korean War, medical support units, although hard-put to evacuate and care for the large number of battle and non-battle casualties, did their best and applied energy and ingenuity to solve problems and care for the wounded and injured at a level higher than in WW II.

Medical Support in the North Korean Army

In organizational charts, North Korean medical support seemed to be on a par with that of the United States. But, in reality, their medical officers were generally of poor caliber; medical equipment and drugs were a mix of American, Russian and Japanese. Communist army political officers distrusted doctors because they were considered intellectuals.

As early as July 1950, the evacuation and treatment of wounded was generally poor, and the delivery of food to the troops was inadequate. The lack of medical attention in the *6th* and *9th Divisions* led to the surrender by many men. The *6th Division* reportedly had no medical doctors and only two medical aidmen per battalion.

Untold hundreds of men were patched up in forward areas and returned to duty. Some POWs had old, ill-treated wounds, often infected. Some had been "bandaged" with leaves and old paper.

So bad was the North Korean medical system that they systematically looted every South Korean medical facility, commandeered almost all hospitals in their part of South Korea and forced almost all of South Korea's 1,800 to 2,000 doctors into the North Korean Army. When the North Korean Army retreated from South Korea in September 1950, it stripped every South Korean hospital of everything portable and carried it north.

Although the ROK Army and U.S. Eighth Army suffered severe losses, the North Koreans had even higher casualties. — sometimes up to 4 to 1. As *The Medic's War*, put it, the "North

Korean medical practice was one of tragic poverty." And later, "The North Koreans lacked [a successful medical system, but] they functioned gallantly without it, and failed in the great gamble because of losses...that no medical service could have restored to duty in sufficient numbers to make is succeed."

References:

Albert E. Cowdrey, *U.S Army in the Korean War, The Medic's War. Center for Military History, U.S. Army, 1987. Ppg. 70-79. (All quotations except those of BG Pollock and Dr. H'Doubler are from this book.)*

BG Jack Pollock (8054th Evac. Hosp): Ltrs to author, July 24 & Aug. 5, 1993.

DR. F. T. H'Doubler (5th Mar.): Tape, 7/23/93.

William H. Wiley, Jr. (Amb. Co., 2d Med Bn, 2d Div.): Material from his response to U.S. Army Military History Korean War Studies questionnaire. Copy in Box, 2d Div, 23d Regiment, O - Z USAMHI, Carlisle Barracks, PA.

TO&E 8-15N, 1948, Medical Battalion.

TO&E 8-7N, 1948, Medical Company, Infantry Regiment.

The author can attest to the jarring, bumpy transportation provided by the front line ambulance.

APPENDIX D — Slang Words and Expressions

This listing is representative of the slang words and expressions prevalent during the Korean War. Some originated in WW II, some were the American version of a Japanese, Korean or Chinese word, and some came directly from the civilian world. The most profane of them have been purposely omitted.

Notations used: C - Chinese; J - Japanese; K - Korean; M - Marine; N - Navy.

Arogato goziamasu (ah-rig-aht-toe go-za-im-mas) (J) — Thank you.

ASAP — As soon as possible.

AWOL (AWHOL) — Absent without leave. To be absent from one's unit without proper authority.

Bed Check Charlie — The name given to an enemy airplane which flew over U.S. troops from time to time to drop a bomb or two. He usually caused no damage. Considered a joke.

Benjo (J) — Toilet

Better believe it! — Phrase meaning, "That's the truth!"

Big Moe — The U.S. battleship, *Missouri.*

Blow it out your barracks bag! — A phrase meaning, "Go to hell!"

Boon Docks (M) — Originally, the jungle; the woods.

Boon Dockers (M) — Drill shoes. These were high-topped shoes.

Boot Camp (M) — Basic training. Initial training for new recruits.

Bought the Farm — Killed or died. To "buy the farm" usually meant killed in action.

Boy-san (Boy-sahn) (J) — Boy

Buddy — Close friend. As in Foxhole Buddy.

Bug Out or Bugout — To leave a place or position rapidly, usually without orders or authority. To retreat rapidly. A song was made up, using the term "Bugging out" and the tune from Hank Snow's country and western song, *Movin' On.*

Burp gun — Enemy hand-held, shoulder-fired machinegun. It had a short barrel and was fed with an ammunition drum. So-named because of its sound when fired.

Chimpo — To have bad luck.

Chinks — Chinese

Choggie (J) — To move. Choggiebearers (chiggie bearers) — Korean men employed to carry supplies to the front and casualties to the rear.

Chop chop — Hurry up.

Chow — Food.

Chow down — to eat.

Chow Hound — One who wanted to eat all the time. A glutton. Men who tried to be among the first in a chow line were called "Chow Hounds."

Chow Line — (1) The line-up of persons waiting to eat, usually cafeteria style. (2) The line-up of foods and servers in the mess area or mess hall.

Church Key — Small can opener used to open C-ration cans or beer cans. Usually carried on the same chain with one's dog tags.

Cow Patties — Anti-personnel mines.

Cut a trail — To leave or depart. "I'm going to cut a trail to the PX": "I am going to the PX."

Dear John letter — A letter from a girlfriend or wife back home announcing that she is breaking off the relationship.

Ding How (C) — Very good.

Dig in — Prepare foxholes and/or a defensive position.

Dog Robber — An enlisted man employed as an aide or servant for an officer.

Dog tags — Small metal identification tags, with one's name, service number, blood type and religious preference imprinted on it. Usually worn on a metal chain around the neck.

Doggies — Infantrymen. Derived from the expression "Dog Face," a front-line soldier who had not shaved and had a full beard.

Doko (Doh-koh) (J) — When.

Dozo (Doh-zoh) (J) — Please

Dud — (1) An unexploded round of ammunition. Usually referred to artillery or mortar rounds. (2) A stupid person. "Joe Zilch is a dud."

First Horse — First Cavalry Division.

First Shirt — First Sergeant.

Fly Boys — Airplane pilots. Anyone in the Air Force.

Frozen Chosen — (1) North Korea. (2) The area in and near the Chosin Reservoir, North Korea.

FUBAR (Foo-bar) — Fouled Up Beyond All Recognition.

GI — (1) A soldier. (2) A soldier who strictly complied with all the regulations. "He was GI."

GI can — Usually, a garbage can, or the large can used with immersion heaters.

Go For Broke — Go all out to win. Overpowering the enemy, disregarding losses and using every means available. From the 442d Infantry in World War II.

Gohang (Go-hawng) (J) — Cooked rice; food.

Gook — An oriental. (Interestingly, an American was known to the Koreans as "Megook.")

Guardhouse Lawyer — a person in a stockade or prison who gave legal advice to other prisoners, but who had no legal training. The advice of these "lawyers" was usually wrong, often leading to more problems for those who took it.

Gung Ho! — (1) An eager or enthusiastic soldier or Marine. (2) One who seemed to enjoy military service or combat.

Hank Snow — Disappear. Run away. Leave quickly, as in "He pulled a 'Hank Snow.'" From the country and western singer Hank Snow's song *Movin' On.*

Hit — Wounded.

Hit the Road — (1) Get out of here. Go away. (2) To start a trip. "I'm going to hit the road to town."

Hiyako (Hai-yawk -ko) (J) — quickly.

Honcho (Hahn-cho) (J) — Boss or leader. The person in charge.

Hot Poop — The latest information about the situation. The latest orders.

Hootch — Where one lived. "Let's go to my hootch for a drink."

How Able — To move out in a hurry. Usually referred to a retreat. "Let's How Able out of here."

Hubba Hubba — (1) An expression usually uttered to express pleasure in seeing a pretty girl. (2) also meant Hurry Up.

Ichi-bahn (Ee-chee-bahn) (J) — Number one; the best.

Incoming or Incoming Mail — Enemy artillery or mortar fire aimed at one's unit or position.

Jaw Bone — On credit; a verbal agreement.

Kilroy was here. — Originated during WW II. The message was scrawled on walls, desks, trees, etc., to let those who followed that U.S. soldiers had been there.

Konbanwa (Kohm-bahn-wha) (J) — Good evening.

Konichiwa (Kohn-ee-chee-wha) (J) — Good day.

LSMFT — Lord Save Me From Truman. Harry S. Truman was President of the United States at the beginning of the Korean War. He issued orders extending the enlistments of men whose time was almost up.

Mac (M) — As in "Hey, Mac!" in calling to another soldier or Marine.

Meat Wagon — Ambulance.

Mess or Mess Hall — a dining facility.

Mezu (Mee-zoo) (J) — Water.

Midnight Requisition or Moonlight Requisition — To take equipment from a warehouse or another unit without permission or authority. Usually, to steal something for use by one's own unit.

Momma-san (Mamma-sahn) (J) — Mother.

Mool (Mool) (K) — Water.

Moving on — Leaving. From the Hank Snow song, *Movin' On*.

Mussamay (Moss-a-may)(J) — Girl or girl friend. Often shortened to "Moose."

Ninety-day Wonder — a 2d Lieutenant graduate of OCS.

OCS — Officer Candidate School. At the time, this course was 90 days long.

On your feet — Stand up and get ready to move out.

Outgoing or Outgoing Mail — Usually, artillery and/or mortar fire aimed at the enemy.

Over the Hill — To go AWOL. "He 'went over the hill.'"

Poggy Bait (M) — Candy.

ROK (ROCK) — Republic of Korea. Used as a word for any South Korean soldier.

Pollye (Poll-yee) (J) — Hurry up!

Poppa-san (Poppa-sahn) (J) — Father.

Rotate — To return to the U.S. from Korea.

Sad Sack — A particularly sloppy and/or stupid soldier. From a cartoon in World War II newspaper for the troops called *Stars and Stripes*.

Saddle Up — Get ready to move out. Get your equipment on and prepare to move out.

Sayonara (J) — Good bye; Sounds like "sigh-o-nada" when pronounced by the Japanese.

Sake (Sah-kee) (J) — Japanese rice wine. Always served hot in very small cups.

Seoul City Sue — Name given to an enemy woman who made radio broadcasts to U. S. troops.

Sexy — Young Korean girl.

Short Round — A soldier who was always in trouble. Similar to Dud, or Sad Sack.

Skoshee (Skoh-shee) (J) — Small or little. (Sometimes shortened to "Skosh."

Scuttlebutt (N) — Rumors or gossip.

SNAFU (Sna-foo) — Situation Normal, All Fouled Up.

S.O.S. — Creamed chipped beef on toast. "S___ on a Shingle."

Swabbies or Swab Jockeys — sailors.

Taksan (Tahk-sahn) (J) — Much or many. "There were taksan enemy there."

Top — First sergeant.

Top Kick — First Sergeant.

Troop and Stomp (M) — Close order drill.

What's up? or What's up, Doc? — "What's going on?" or "What's happening?"

White Money — Cash currency.

Willie Peter — White phosphorous.

Yard Bird — A stupid-acting soldier. See Dud.

You never had it so good. — Phrase meaning that things couldn't be better.

Z.I. — Zone of the Interior. A World War II term for the Continental United States.

Zoomies (M) — Marine pilots.

Sources and Acknowledgements

Viewing historical events from a distance in time is a mixed blessing. On the one hand, the memories of surviving participants in events is dimmed and sometimes distorted by time and the ravages of advanced age. On the other hand, some participants have had the opportunity to put their experiences and recollections into better focus. What they thought was the situation at the time, they now discover was not so in fact. Another plus in waiting to record history is that more data is usually available — more factors bearing in the event(s) have been unearthed. I have carefully considered these negative and positive matters in preparing this history.

A war narrative from the standpoint of the individuals who fought it requires input from hundreds of participants. I have obtained this input, principally from over 500 soldiers and Marines who fought the battles leading to the formation of the Pusan Perimeter, the Perimeter's defense and the breakout.

Many people contributed, one way and another to this project, which has spanned almost seven years.

FIRST: My wife, Ada Joan. When I should have been available to be with her over these years, I was busy working on this book. Over four years of my so-called retirement have been devoted to completing the research, then in writing. Our plans to enjoy retirement together were set aside. Perhaps, now, I will give her the time and attention which she so richly deserves.

SECOND: I am deeply and eternally grateful to the hundreds of soldiers and Marines who contributed their recollections and experiences to me. It was impossible for me to use everything sent to me. I would have had to write several volumes to do so. I intend to donate all the material which they sent to me to the U.S. Army Military History Institute, Carlisle Barracks, PA, where it will be available to historians and other interested persons.

THIRD: No person from one branch of the military service should try to write definitively about the combat operations of another service without employing the best reference sources and having his writing reviewed by members of the other service who took part in the actions described. I did this by using the official Marine history of the Pusan Perimeter as my primary reference for Marine operations in that area and by having what I wrote reviewed and corrected by Marine officers who were there.

These now-retired USMC officers included MG Raymond L. Murray, who commanded the 5th Marine Regiment; COL Ransom M. Wood, then commander of 1-11th Marines; COL Robert D. Taplett, who commanded 3-5th Marines; MG Robert D. Bohn, commander, G-3-5th Marines; COL Francis I. Fenton Jr., commander, B-1-5th Marines; COL Theodore F. Spiker, commander, Wpns-2-5th Marines; LTC John R. Stevens, commander, A-1-5th Marines; COL Christian C. Lee, commander, MATCS-2; COL John H. Cahill, a rifle platoon leader in G-3-5th Marines.

Last, but by far least, was 1LT Francis W. Muetzel, who was so badly wounded as a rifle platoon leader in A-1-5th Marines that he was forced to retire on disability as a young man. These Marine officers ensured that what was written was both accurate and complete. I will say, with some pride, that they had little to change.

MAJ Lacy Barnett, USA, Ret. reviewed the manuscript pertaining to the actions of elements of the 24th Division. David Carlisle, former CO, 77th ECC, reviewed the material on the 24th RCT. Finally, COL Harry J. Maihafer (21st Inf.) and Clay Blair, author of *The Forgotten War*, both reviewed the entire manuscript. I owe each of these men special thanks for taking the time to make these reviews and offer me their very valuable comments and corrections.

FOURTH: I thank the men who sent me the names and addresses of others to contact. This varied from one or two old comrades to the entire roster of divisional and the Marine Brigade veterans' organizations.

FIFTH: Research requires one to consult libraries or other repositories for documents, books, papers and interview transcripts. My research included visits to these facilities:

The FDR Library, Hyde Park, NY. There I was able to obtain tape transcripts and copies of correspondence from the John Toland collection. Archivists Nancy Snedeker, Mark Renovitch and Paul McLaughlin were all extremely helpful. As a result, I was able to obtain a wealth of material in a very short time.

I spent many hours at the USAMHI. The Institute has an outstanding library and thousands of documents, letters, etc., pertaining to all American wars and is open to the public. I was always welcomed by the staff, who were very courteous and helpful. The bulk of my research was done there. I cannot praise enough these staff members: Archivist Historian Dr. Richard J. Sommers; Assistant Archivist Historian David Keough; Archives Technician Pamela A. Cheney; John J. Slonaker, Chief, Historical Reference Branch; Library Technicians Kathleen Gildersleeve, Judy Meck and Judi Provins and Librarian Sandy Bauriedl.

COL William T. Bowers, Dr. Jeffry Clarke, LTC (Ret.) George MacGarrigle and Donald A. Carter, all of the U.S. Army's Center of Military History, Washington, D.C. provided me with material and valuable insights on certain events which took place in the Pusan Perimeter. I was able to visit the Center only once, but that visit was well worth the time. The staff members were outstanding.

My special thanks to Dr. Barry W. Fowle, Historian, Office of History, U.S. Army Corps of Engineers, Alexandria, VA. Dr. Fowle very kindly provided me with an early copy of MG James A. Johnson's oral history. The general was an engineer platoon leader in Korea, but retired as the Deputy Chief of Engineers, U.S. Army.

Although I consulted a number of books in my research, four stand out as most valuable. The principal reference for Army actions and events was *South to the Naktong, North to the Yalu*, by LTC Roy Appleman. Although I have been critical of a few elements of this book, it is the best, most complete and authoritative history of the first year of the Korean War. Appleman devoted over eight years to its preparation. Quite a bit of material was denied to him because it was classified at the time. This material has since been declassified and become available to researchers. This declassified information has sometimes clarified misunderstood or incompletely reported events.

The principal reference for Marine activities was Vol. 1, *The Pusan Perimeter*, by Lynn Montross and CPT Nicholas A. Canzona, USMC. Appleman included a number of individual and small unit actions, along with discussions of battalion, regimental and divisional operations and the "Big Picture." *The Pusan Perimeter*, on the other hand, contains predominantly accounts of individual and small unit actions. As such, it was particularly valuable to me as a reference, since my book includes so many recollections and experiences of individual soldiers and Marines.

Two other books worthy of note are Blair's *The Forgotten War* and *The New Breed* by Andrew Geer. Blair's book contains a wealth of background information on the military leaders and staff officers at all echelons, down to and including the battalion level. His interviews of many of these officers provide new insights on the some of the planning and operations in the Perimeter. *The New Breed* tells the story more from the individual Marine's perspective.

Below, I have listed the names and units of the soldiers, Marines and airmen whose experiences or recollections are recounted. Since the 5th RCT was finally assigned to the 24th Division, it is included in that division's listing. Since the 1st and 3d Battalions, 29th Infantry became battalions of the 27th and 35th Regiments, the men of those two battalions are included in the 25th Division listing. For brevity's sake, a number of abbreviations are used to indicate the source of their contribution. The abbreviation will usually be followed by a date, or dates indicating when the information was received. These abbreviations are: C — card; I — interview; L — letter; LT — letter to N — narrative; NF — narrative for; TA — tape; TF — telephone call from; TI — telephone interview; TT — telephone call to; D — deceased; MC — manuscript comments; Q – Questionnaire; UP – Used by permission.

Chapter references follow this listing.

General:

BG William A. Collier (HQ, Eighth Army) LT Chief, Military History ref. Walker 3/10/58.

COL Norman J. LeMere, USA, Ret. L: 3/21/93.

Robert B. Hardin (I/32 Inf) Q: 3/25/93.

Sal Napolitano (31 FAB) L: 3/18/91.

Francis M. Carpenter (3 Transportation Military Railroad Service) L: 9/14/91; Q: 11/91.

David Livingstone Moffatt (1973 AACS Sqdn, USAF) N: 7/14/92.

William McKinney (Pohang Air Weather Det., USAF) L w/anecdote enclosure 2/14/95.

Dr. Edward Vermillion (Pohang Air Weather Det., USAF) L&N: 2/15/95.

GEN Min Ki Sik, ROKA, Ret. LT Jack Walker, TN Korean Memorial Assn, 7/27/87. (Gen. Min was CO, Task Force Min.)

1st Cavalry Division:

5th Cavalry:
Arthur P. Bartol (Co. G) Q&N: 12/18/93; *New York Times*, 8/14/50.

Adrian B. Brian (Co. B & I) N for Donald Knox; extract L to Mother 8/14/50. WP Brian__L: 11/17/92; 7/7/91; LT Donald Knox 1/19/85; LT COL Tow, father of LT George Tow, who was KIA. L dated 12/14/50. No first name given for COL Tow.

Robert R. Byrd (Co. C) Q: 9/1/94.

Gordon L. Davis (Co. I) L: 7/4/92.

Jerome W. Emer (Co. I) LT Donald Knox 1/7; 1/8; 1/12; 2/3/85; L: 11/23 & 12/14/93; Q: 12/12/93.

Rev. Carroll G. Everist (Co. L) Q: 8/24/92; script for talk: 8/10/92; Memorial to KIA, conducted 10/27/50. Copies of script and memorial courtesy Rev. Everist.

Victor Fox (Co. I) L: 7/19/92 & 7/26/92; comments on video tape about Hill 174 7/26/92; map of Hill 174 area, annotated by Fox 9/84; N: 7/12/92 - Formation of 3/7th Cav to 9/13/50; copies of letters to Donald Knox from: Mark M. Leachman (Co. I) 7/10 & 9/21/86; James Huber (Co. I) 9/5/79 & 2/22/85; Donald Pate (Co. I) 2/14, 2/20 & 3/11/85; Lee Carpenter 1/7 & 2/16/85; Rev. Carroll G. Everist (Co. L) 1/6; 2/13 & 3/28/86. L: 6/12/92, incl. tape transcript, COL Norman F. J. Allen (C.O. Co. I) for Knox 9/83, with Fox's explanation of Allen's terminology used on the tape and Fox's comments on the tape; L: 6/22/92, incl. "Unified Accounts" Fox to Knox 2 & 10/84. These "Accounts" include comments and correspondence from COL Allen, james Cardinal and James Huber, plus copies of the obituaries of COL Allen, GEN Harold K. Johnson (C.O., 3/8th Cav); BG Marcel G. Crombez (C.O., 5th Cav) and CPT James K. Hughes (Co. K); Letter, Allen to Fox 6/18/84; I: Fox of Allen, 5/28/85; Letters Fox to Knox 6/11/84 & 2/4/85; Letters, Knox to Fox, 8/17; 8/19 and 11/19/79; 9/11/82; COL Allen's background written 8/22/83. L: 6/14/92 — name and address list I/5th Cav; Narrative Report 5th Cav, Sep-Oct 1950 and 3/8th

Cav S2-S3 Journal, 1:44 P.M. Sep 13, 1950 - 5:20 P.M. Sep 18, 1950. Fox comments on Journal for Knox 9/84. Copies of all this material furnished to the author courtesy Victor Fox. Mr. Fox deserves high praise for the volume and detail of his contribution to this book.

Dallas Freeburg (Co. D) Q: 2/10/92; T: 2/25/94.

Gerald Gingery (Co. H) Q&N: 3/92; N: 1/15/87, pp. 11-13.

James Keppel (Co. D) L, Q&N: 7/12/94.

Dale M. Larson (Co. I) L: 7/3; 7/16 & 7/17/92; N: 7/16/92; GO 39, HQ, Eighth Army, 1/23/51. Cy courtesy Larson.

Lindsey C. Nelms (HM Co.) Q&N: 7/2/94; GO 102 — Awards; List of men massacred on Hill 303; List of Casualties, 5 Cav., Aug. '50.

Clifford Phillips (Co. G) T: 3/5/94.

Edward Potter (Co. G) Q: 1/94.

Roy F. Richards (Co. I) T: 2/5/93.

Dennis G. Robinson (Co. I) Q&N: 5/10/92; L: 3/11/92.

James M. Rudd (Co. H) Article in *The Sunday Independent*, Ashland, KY 1/18/87.

7th Cavalry:
John W. Callaway (XO & C.O., 2d Bn) Q&N: 8/28/92.

Alfred B. Clair (Co. F) Q&N: 12/21/92; L: 12/3/92; cy of undated ltr, written some time in 1992, enclosed with DD From 149, Application for Correction of Military Record.

Stanley Dahl (Co. D) Q: 1/29/94; N: 1/24/94 & 2/9/94.

James W. Dodgen (Co. B) Q: 6/23/92.

Richard Dowell (Co. B) N: 6/22/94.

Donald D. Down (Co. F) L: 3/18/92; Q: 4/10/92; extract, 7th Cav combat records, 8/14/50.

Frederick A. Duve, Jr. (Co. A) Q: 2/10/92.

Eugene E. Fels (Co. B) Q: 5/27/92; L: 4/1 & 7/2/92; T: 3/5/94; citation & award of the Silver Star.

Lyle Gibbs (Co. E) Q: 1992; N: 4/94; roster Co. E, Christmas 1949.

Robert Gray (I&R Plt) TA: 3/5/94.

Arthur C. Lippincott (Co. E & F) Q: 4/13/92; article by CPL Bobby J. Rushing, "Cav. Squad and ROKs Slip Behind Enemy Lines," *Stars and Stripes*, undated.

BG Richard L. Morton (Co. F) Q & short N: 5/4/92; L: 3/30/92.

John O. Potts (Co. F & H) Q & short N: 4/23/92; L: 3/31/92.

Walter Raisner (Co. E) Q: 5/23/92; L: 8/28/92; T: 3/5/94.

Edwin Seith (Co. E) Q: 2/24/93.

Thomas Stone (Co. F) Q, N&L: 9/3/92

8th Cavalry:
Joe M. Christopher (Co. F) Q&N: 3/4/92; Added information 3/29/92.

Ulmont R. Kendree Jr. (Co. G) N&L: 4/9/93.

Donald Summers (Co. C) Q: 2/92.

8th ECB:
James N. Vandygriff (Co. D) LT: Appleman 5/19/53.

Edward C. West (Co. A) TA: 7/18/94.

2d Infantry Division:

Maurice Holden (G-3) L: 9/28/91; T: 8/13/94.

2d Recon Co:
Wallace A. Kydland Q: 6/28/93; copy GO #67, HQ, 2d Div., 10/17/50.

Roy Mogged L: 9/9/91 & 1/8/92.

9th Infantry:
LTG Julius W. Becton Jr. (Co. I, K & L) L: 9/28/91; T: 8/13/94.

Richard L. Feaser (HM Co.) L: 7/28/93; annotated 1:50,000 scale map, showing positions, etc.

Richard T. Ferrell (Co. G) Q, Korean War Survey, USAMHI.

Willis Fredericks (Co. H) Q: 8/19/93; Item, "Paralyzed by a Dozen Bullets He Kept 500 Reds at bay," Bod Hartford. Bern Price dispatch to Associated Press, 9/2/50 and United Press articles ref. action on 9/2/50. Copies courtesy Willis Fredericks.

Dr. Gene N. Lam, M.D. (Surgeon, 2d Bn) L: 8/28/94.

John L. Mason (Co. G) C: 12/3/93; Q: 4/5/93.

Ronald Peters (Co. B) L: 8/94.

William R. Swafford (Co. D) Q&N: 7/10/93.

Lester M. Thomas (HM Co.) Q&N: 6/17/93; Chap Lewis B. Sheen, Experiences with B/9th Inf., 8/31 - 9/4/50, undated account. Copy courtesy Lester H. Thomas.

23d Infantry:

Richard L. Ballenger (Co. C) Q&N: 9/16/91.

Jesse L. Bishop (Co. F) Daily journal 7/9 - 8/17/50. Copy to author 8/20/91.

Frank C. Butler (Tk Co.) Q: Early 1992.

James Coulos (HM Co.) Q: 9/14/91.

Kenneth C. Dumler Sr. (Co. F) LT: Appleman 1/30/90 (from Korean War Survey USAMHI.)

Morris V. Evans (Co. H) Q&L: 8/21/91.

Robert N. Fogle (Co. K) Outline of action 3/23 Inf, 8/9 - 9/15/50.

Douglas F. Graney (Co. E) Q & short N: Late 1991.

Harlos V. Hatter (Regt. S-4) Q: 8/2/91.

Donald W. Hoffman (Co. F) Q&N: 3/92; L: 7/19/91; annotated map 3/92.

Harold Jennings (Co. I) Q: 8/26/91.

William H. Jones (Co. D) Annotated map.

Roy H. King (Co. B) Q: 8/12/93.

Ralph H. Kroeger (Co. E) L: 6/23/93; T: 5/7/94.

William R. Lamdin (Co. A) Q: 6/26/92.

Charles A. McCave (Co. L) Q: 8/3/91.

John J. McGlue (Co. D) Q&TA: 9/91; Copy of CPT Tassey's daily narrative 9/22 -30/50. (Tassey was CO, Co. D.)

John P. Parsley (Co. H) Q: 8/1091.

Charles N. Prince (Tk Co.) Q&N: 2/2/94.

John H. Ramsburg (Co. F) Q: 8/18/93.

Andrew E. Reyna (Tk Co.) N: Korean War Survey, KOR 337, USAMHI.

Richard H. Shand (Co. E) Q: 8/4/91; roster of CIB awardees, Co. E., courtesy Richard H. Shand 11/22/94.

Leslie C. Sholar (Co. H) L: 7/23/91; Q: 8/22/91.

Harley E. Wilburn (HM Co.) Q: 9/2/93.

Raymond Wisnieski (Medic w/Co. A) Q: 12/2/91.

38th Infantry:

Jerome R. Baker (Co. B) Q: 8/93.

Chap James C Carroll (Regt Chap.) L: 9/4/93.

John E. Fox (Co. F) N: 8/24/93.

John Gamez (Co. K) Q: 9/24/93; copy his citation for Silver Star.

Louis V. Genuario (Co. G) Copy of article by J. Robert Moskin, "The Tragedy of the West Point Class of 1950," *Look* Magazine, Jun. 3, 1952.

George E. Hartley Sr. (Co. K) L: 7/26/93; Q: 9/7/93.

Roy Hill (Co. B) Q: 11/8/93; diary to 9/19/50; LT: Family Sep. 3, 5, 9, 12, 15, 17, 18 & 20, 1950; LT: Mother 9/11 & 9/12/50.

Roger Hallenback (Co. F) "Notes From My Scratchpad: (Jan 1 - May 15, 1991)."

Leonard Lowry (C.O., Co. C) Q: 9/29/93.

Leo Pedroza (Co. C) Q: 11/11/93.

Rene' Ramos (Co. K) Q: 1/19/94.

Bruce Ritter (Co. A) Q: 10/4/93.

Cecil L. Sherrod (Co. E) Q: 10/20/93.

Paul A. Stough (XO, Co. C) Q: 10/28/93; annotated 1:50,000 scale map.

Bradley Sutter (HM Co.) Q&TA: 4/2/93; copy of "The Warrior," a 2d Division newsletter, 8/28; 9/2 & 9/12/50.

William Temple (Co. I) Q: 9/17/93; TA: 6/20/94.

Donald O. Timm (Tk Co.) L: 8/31/93.

Thomas K. Voorhis (Regt. Asst Mtr Off.) Q: 11/19/93.

2d ECB:

John A. Camara (Co. B) Q: 3/29/93; L: 3/15/93 & 4/2/93.

Robert D. Gifford (Co. D) Q: 7/3/93.

Harry L Lohmeyer (HHC) Q: 7/12/93.

James F. Malone (Co. D) Q: 7/21/93; L: 7/31/93.

Glenn O. Roller (Co. B) LT: Camara 2/11/93.

2d Signal Bn:

Fred M. Liddell Q: 8/24/93.

70th Hvy Tank Bn:

Ashley C. Anderson (Co. A) L: 3/23/95; "The Tribute," 70th Heavy Tank Bn, Armor Assn., Dec. 1994.

72d Tank Bn:

Edwin B. Quinn (Co. A) TA: Late 1992.

37th FAB:

Harold W. Brixius (Btry B) Q & short N: 9/20/93.

Earl Dube (HHB) Q&TA: 9/29/93.

82d AAA/AW Bn:

Robert L. Wood (Co. D) L: 8/2/94.

24th Infantry Division:

24th Recon Co:

William F. Coghill LT: Lacy Barnett (Barnett.) This indicates documents from him.

19th Infantry:

Elliot C. Cutler, Jr. (Regt HQ) LT: Clay Blair 12/29/84.

Robert G. Fox (Regt HQ) N: 12/93.

Dr. William W. Garry, PhD (Co. K) L: 8/17/92; Q: 11/12/92.

Buford F. Goff (Co. F.) TA: 9/11/93.

James N. Griffin (P&A Plt, 2d Bn) Q: 8/9/93.

Robert L. Herbert (Co. G) I: Martin Blumenson 8/18 - 24/51. (Barnett)

Forrest Kleinman (G-3 Sec, 24 Div; S-3, 1st Bn) Comments on *South to Naktong* manuscript 6/1/54; L: 10/17/92 & 11/26/93.

Willard H. Lee (Co. A) TI: 8/28/94.

Joseph J. McKeon (HQ, 2d Bn) N: 6/12/91.

Robert E. Nash (2d Bn) I: Martin Blumenson 8/27/51. (Barnett)

Robert A. Spangenberg (Med. Co.) L: 2/28/94; TI: 7/8/94.

Joseph S. Szito (Regt. HQ) I: Martin Blumenson 8/18 - 24/51. (Barnett)

21st Infantry:

Dwight L. Adams (Co. G) Q: 7/10/92.

Warren J. Avery (Co. G) Q: 7/22/93; TA: 9/7/93.

Robert Bayless (Co. G) N: Korean War Survey, USAMHI.

John L. Begley (Co. B) Q: 8/11/93.

Carl Bernard (Co. L) I: Clay Blair 5/18/87 - UP Bernard; Comments on *South To Naktong* manuscript, undated; LT: BG Roy Flint 5/17/90; I: Lewis Micheloy for John Toland, 5/18/87. Transcribed for author at FDR Library 9/18/93.

Russell Bertolf (Adj., 1st Bn) NF: William Wyrick - UP Bertolf & Wyrick 4/1/94.

Earsel Bonds (HQ, 1st Bn) L: 3/22/94; I for TF Smith Survivors 7/7/90 - UP Bonds.

Philip S. Day (Co. C) I: Micheloy for John Toland 6/1/87. Transcript reviewed, corrected and annotated by Day 8/11/93 - UP Day.

Fred Dickerson (Co. G) Korean War Survey, USAMHI; L: 9/2/91; Homer Bigert article, *New York Herald Tribune*, Sep 6, 1950. Copy of article courtesy Fred Dickerson.

John J. Doody (Co. B) Q: 11/30/92.

Dr. Elmer J. Gainok (Co. K) Q: 11/14/92.

William Guinn (C.O., Co. E) L: 8/17/92; Q: 8/28/92.

George Hunnicutt (I & R Plt) TT: 5/23/94; LT: 5/24/84; TF: 6/94.

Joseph Langone (Co. B) TA: 10/92.

Bruce J. Leiser (Co. E) L: 9/92; Q: 9/30/92.

Joe E. Leyba (Co. G) L&N: 8/27/92.

Billy M. McCarthy (HQ, 1st Bn) N: 1/30/94, revised 3/3/94.

Charles W. Newcomb (Co. A) Q&N: 10/15/91.

Dr. Edwin L. Overholt, M.D. (Regt. Surgeon) N: 1990 - UP Overholt.

C. A. "Bud" Pritchett, Jr. (Co. I) Q & TA: 8/18/93.

Robert J. Roy, Jr. (Co. M) L: 1/5/91 & 3/25/94; N: 1/5/91.

BG Charles B. Smith (C.O, 1st Bn) I: Appleman 10/7/51 & COL William J. Davies 1/7 & 8/92.

William Staab (Regt. S-3) TT: 5/12/94; LT: 5/13/94; TF: 5/20/94.

MG Richard W. Stephens (C.O., 21st Inf.) LT: Appleman 4/17/52; comments on *South to the Naktong* manuscript 12/57.

GEN Volney F. Warner (Co. L) Q&N: 9/31/91.

Planter Wilson (XO, HM Co.; C.O., Co. L) L: 10/17/92; Q: 11/13/92.

William E. Wyrick (Co. C) L: 5/31 & 12/20/93; 3/29 & 4/23/94; N: 12/30/92. MC.

34th Infantry:

Albert Alfonso (C.O., Co. A) L: 2/12 & 27/95; 4/25/95. MC.

Edward N. Arendell (HQ, 3d Bn) Q&N: 8/31/93.

Harold B. Ayres (C.O., 1st Bn) LT: Jay Lovless (C.O., 34th Inf.) 8/11/58; LT: Appleman 10/3/52; I: Barnett 3/17/87 w/Ayres' comments; LT: Barnett 5/17/87; 4/7 & 13/89. (All Barnett)

Lacy Barnett (Med. Co.) Review and comments on Chap 5 of this manuscript; TT; Barnett 4/15/94; LT: Charles E. Payne (HQ, 1st Bn) 11/30/89. MC

Robert Bayless (Co. L) N: Korean War Survey, KOR 198, USAMHI.

Charles E. Beauchamp (C.O., 34th Inf.) I: Clay Blair 1984; LT: Barnett 3/27/86. (Both Barnett.)

LTG William B. Caldwell, III (Co. A) Self interview (corrected) 1/24/58 - UP Caldwell; TA for Barnett 2/6/87 (Barnett); TT: 9/25/92.

Spero Calos (Co. A) N: 9/29/92.

Dr. Murray L. Carroll, PhD (Regt. HQ) N: 7/26/93.

Roy E. Collins (Co. A) I: Appleman 8/4/51.

John J. Dunn (Regt. S-3) LT: Appleman 6/17/55. (Barnett)

Robert B. Fahs (S-1, 3d Bn) L: 1/21/95.

Fred M. Hollister (Svc Co.) Q: 9/92.

Robert L. Hysell (Med. Co.) Q: 8/26/92; L: 8/13/92.

James A. Jones (Co. I) TA: 2/17/93.

Leonard Korgie (Co. L) Q: 8/2/92; N: 8/22/92.

Newton W. Lantron (XO & C.O., 3d Bn) T: Barnett to Lantron 4/12/92. (Barnett)

Henry G. Leerkamp (Co. L) Q: 10/30/92.

Joseph E. Leyba (Co. L) N: 9/92.

Donald Luedtke (Regt. HQ) N: 9/92.

William Menninger (Op SGT, 3d Bn) LT: Clay Blair 12/3/84.

Robert W. Moser (Co. B) Q&N: 10/16/92.

Leroy Osburn (C.O, Co. A) LT: Barnett 12/12/85; 3/7 & 10/89; LT: MAJ Leonard C. Friesz, OCMH, 1/21 & 3/5/52. (All Barnett.)

Edgar (Sinnett) Pawelczyk (Co. D) Q&N: 4/19/93.

Charles E. Payne (Regt HQ) LT: Barnett 1/11/90; LT: Donald Knox 3/21/84. (Both Barnett.)

M. Dean Schiller (Co. A) LT: Asst Comdt, the Infantry School, FT Benning, GA 10/28/52; LT: Barnett 7/25/86; LT CPT Kendris 5/14/87 (All Barnett); TI: 2/7 and 2/11/95. MC

Stewart Sizemore (Co. D) Q&TA: 9/4/91.

Maurice Slaney (Svc Co.) N: 8/13/93.

Jack Smith (XO; Acting C.O., 3d Bn) LT: Appleman 6/18 & 21/55. (Barnett)

Matthew R. Thome (Co. K) Q: 12/18/93.

Robert L. Wadlington (XO & C.O., 34th Inf.) LT: MG Dean 7/2/54. (Barnett)

Richard F. Warner (HM Co.) Q: 7/91; TT: 8/21/91.

George L. Wilcox (Co. D) I: Martin Blumenson 8/25/51. (Barnett)

Robert L. Witzig (Co. D) Q&N: 8/2/93.

Miscellaneous:

Russell Gugeler, OCMH LT: Roy E. Collins (Co. A) 12/20/51. (Barnett)

MAJ Leonard C. Friesz, OCMH LT: Leroy Osburn 1/17 & 2/28/52. (Barnett)

The author also wrote to John J. Dunn (Regt. S-3) 9/15/92, Leroy Osburn (C.O., Co. A) and Charles E. Payne (Regt. HQ), both on 9/14/92, but received no responses.

5th RCT:

Horace (Andy) Anderson (Co. E) N: 5th RCT Newsletter, 1991. Copy courtesy Eugene Lakatos (Co. E) - UP Anderson.

Daniel R. Beirne (Co. K) L: 9/4/91; Q: 2/18/92.; L: To family 8/28/50; excerpt of book on Korean War by COL Beirne. L: To family and excerpt UP COL Beirne; Article "Waegwan," 5th RCT Newsletter, 1991. Copy courtesy Eugene Lakatos. T: 4/22/95.

Frank Brooks Jr. (Co. F) Q: 3/19/93; L: 6/3/93; TI: 8/6/94. MC

Francis (Frank) Colbert (Co. D) Q: 1/94.

Paul Comi (Co.F) Q: 7/93.

MG Gordon Duquemin (Co. D) Q: 6/6/94.

James W. "Hap" Easter (Tk Co.) (D) TI: 5/16/95.

David E. Eckert (Co. F) L: 8/15/93; Article in *Taro Leaf*, date unk. Copy courtesy Eckert. *Taro Leaf* is a publication of the 24th Inf. Div. Assn.

LTG Henry E. Emerson (C.O, Co. A) TA: 7/14/92; T: 4/22/95.

Buddy Ford (Co. H) N: 5th RCT Newsletter, Jul. 13, 1990. Copy courtesy Eugene Lakatos.

Kenny Freedman (Co. D) (D) Articles in Feb, Mar & Apr 1995 5th RCT Newsletter.

Robert Hardin (Co. I) Q: 3/25/92.

Eugene R. Lakatos (Co. E) Q: 11/20/92.

Gene McClure (Co. H) Q: 10/14/91; L: 9/4/91; N, undated. Loaned to author 12/91. Hereafter McClure mss.

Robert C. Nelson (Co. B) Q: 6/28/93.

Gerald Pack (Co. F) Q: 6/23/93; copy of his DD 214; copies of Co. F Morning Reports Aug 6 & Sep 1950, courtesy Gerald Pack.

Robert W. Potter (Co. G) TA: 3/18/94.

William G. Price (Co. G) Bio sketch, 5th RCT Newsletter, May 1994.

Charles Rahn (Co. E) L: 5th RCT Newsletter, Jan 1993. Copy courtesy MG Duquemin (Co. D).

Charles Rayoum (Co. A) Q: 11/29/92.

James C. Richardson (Asst S-1/HQ Comdt, 5th RCT) TA: 3/18/94.

Ivan W. Russell (Co. F) (D) Card: 2/23/92; Q: Early 1992.

Charles Shepherd (Tk Co.) Q: 7/3/93; TA: 3/18/94.

Howard W. Stephenson (Regt HHC) Q: 8/12/93.

Toshio Uyeda (Regt HHC) Q: 1/29/94.

Frank Valvo (Co. E) L: 9/1/93; N: 5th RCT Newsletter, Sep 1990; article 5th RCT Newsletter, Aug 1993.

Keith W. Whitham (Tk Co.) N: 12/24/94.

Thomas E. Williams (Co. A) Q: 6/9/93.

555th FAB (part of 5th RCT):

Earl J. Law (Btry B & C) Q: 3/30/93.

Richard Lewis ((HHB) Q&N: 4/21/93.

Wyatt Y. Logan (Btry B) L: 4/12/93.

Eugene Mathews (Btry B) Q: 8/11/93.

William A. Motley, Sr. (Svc Btry) Q: 3/22/93; N: 1/24/94.

Arlen S. Russell (HHB) Q&N: 4/8/93.

Albert F. Semasko (Btry B) Q: 7/8/93.

Kenneth J. Thornton (HQ & B Btries) Q: 8/27/93.

72d ECC (part of 5th RCT):

Raul DeLuna Q: 6/9/93; TA: 7/22/93.

Gerald D. Holler Q: 6/30/93.

MG James A. Johnson I: Dr Charles Hendricks, Office of History, U.S. Corps of Engineers, Feb. 25; Mar 4, 11, 25 and 31; Apr 7, 20 & 21, 1993. Transcript courtesy Dr. Barry W. Fowle, LTC, AUS, Ret., Office of History, Corps of Engineers, 1/6/95. GEN Johnson retired as Deputy Chief of Engineers, U.S. Army.

* * * End 5th RCT * * *

78th Tank Bn:

Tomas Carrillo (Co. A) Q: 2/20/93.

11th FAB:

Ernest Q. Terrell (Btry A) Q&N: 6/12/94; L: 2/12/93.

13th FAB:

Ellsworth "Dutch" Nelsen (Btry B) L: 6/27/94; L: 7/12/94.

52d FAB:

Olin M. Hardy (FO to L/21st Inf.) L: 8/25/92; TF: 7/12/94.

BG Miller O. Perry (C.O., 52d FAB) NF Wyrick 4/94 - UP Wyrick & Perry.

Harold A. Stevens (HHB) Q&N: 2/2/94.

63d FAB:

Art Lombardi N: 4/92.

25th Infantry Division:

Richard G. Jones (HHC) L: 10/27/92.

24th RCT:
John S. Komp (Regt S-2) Q: 2/22/93; N: 7/21/94.

William J. Nelson (Asst. S-3, 2d Bn) TI: 8/27/94.

Isaac S. Smith (Med Co.) Q: 2/12/93.

Trevor Swett (Co. I) Q&N: 10/5/92.

Waymon R. Ransom (I & R Plt) Q: 3/29/93.

Roger S. Walden (C.O., Co. F) Q: 11/12/92; L: 8/10/92 & 7/18/93; TA for David Carlisle. Copy of transcript from the Clay & Joan Blair Collection, USAMHI. Overlay sketch, Co. F disposition and movements Aug 31 - Sep 1, 1950 7/93.

Joel T. Ward (Co. E) Q: 8/1/94.

77th ECC (part of 24th RCT):

Chester Lenon TA for John Toland, Toland Papers, Box 142, FDR Library, Hyde Park, NY. Reviewed and corrected by Chester Lenon - UP Lenon.

Carroll N. LeTellier N: 7/9/94.

David Carlisle MC

27th RCT:

David W. Bradley (HQ & Co. E) Q: Early 1992.

Alfred S. Burnett (C.O., Co. C)(D) Q: 4/19/91; N: 5/91.

Donald Cable (Co. B) L: 2/3/85.

Daniel Cooper (Co. G) L: 6/26/93; Q&N: 8/18/93.

Charles L. Dawson (M/29th & M.27th) I: Clay Blair. Reviewed and corrected by Dawson - UP Dawson.

Glenn V. Ellison (Co. F) Q&N: 6/18/93. Very detailed narrative.

Uzal W. Ent (Co. B) Recollections and experiences as a rifle platoon leader.

Philip File (Co. A) Q: 1991 & 8/14/93; L&N: 10/16/93; map notations for author.

George S. Hearn (Co. B) L: 1/9/91; 11/93; Q: 5/91; N: 10/93.

Cressie Johnson (Co. D) L: 3/19 & 10/22/93; Q&N: 4/2/93; Annotations to the overlay accompanying 27th RCT Historical Report for 9/8/50.

Gordon C. Jung (C.O., Co. B)(D) L&N: 9/5/89; Q: 5/91.

John L. Kirby (L/29th & L/27th) Q&N: 11/20/92.

Harold Lederer (Co. A & C)(D) Q&L: 12/27/90.

Harry Leonard (Co. A) Q&N: 6/11/91.

Chester F. Main (Med & Co. F) Q: 3/22/94.

Richard S. Majcher (Co.C) Q: 7/20/92.

William Molton (M/29 & M/27) Q: Late 1992.

Milton R. Olazagasti (Co. F) Q: 6/30/94; N: 7/18/94; TA: 7/18/94.

Frank U. Roquemore (HHC) Q: 7/16/90; L: 9/2 & 15/93; N: 7/16/90.

Frank W. Sandell (Co. A) Q & TA: 7/22/93.

Ernest N. Smith (Co. B) Q: 4/5/93.

Posey Starkey (Co. D) Q&L: 12/31/90; N: 11/15/93.

Logan Weston (C.O. D/17th Inf & C.O. A/27th) L: 3/24/91; Q: 5/91.

35th RCT:

Edward F. Balbi (A/29th & I/35th) Q: 3/27/93.

LTG Sidney B. Berry (Co. A) L: 9/29/92.

Glenn E. Berry (Co. G) Q: 2/8/92.

Harold Brannon (A/29th & I/35th) Q: 6/2/92.

Donald Cholka (Co. E) L: 5/13/91; Q: Mid 1991.

Anthony Fernandes (Co. G) Q: Mid 1993.

Ray N. Fomby (Co. C) Q: 12/11/92; Card: 10/19/92.

Harold Gamble (Med/29th & K/35th) Q&N: 12/20/93; L: 12/12/94.

Jack J. Gates (Co. F) Q: 5/16/91.

Earl R. Green (Co. G) Q: 2/21/92.

Frank L. Griffin (A&B/29th; I/35th) Article in Columbus, GA *Ledger Enquirer*, Oct 1950; L: 12/10/94.

Robert J. Liberty (Co. A) Q: 8/91.

William J. McCafferty (Co. F) Q: 4/2/94.

Jesus Rodriguez (A/29th & I/35th) TA: 11/22/94.

Grady Vickery (Co. F) Q&L, plus sketch of platoon's defenses at Namji-ri 8/9/93.

James F. Walters (Co. C) TA: 2/25/94; Copy of SO 145, HQ, 35th Inf., 8/7/50.

David Williams (C/29th & L/35th) Q: 6/29/93.

29th Infantry:

Joseph C. Allen (Co. I) Q: 4/29/93.

Edward F. Balbi (Co. A)** Q: 3/27/93; L: 1/1 & 4/30/92.

Robert G. Brown (Surgeon, 1st Bn) L: To Whom It May Concern 12/18/51. Copy courtesy Dennis Nicewanger (Co.D).

Frank E. Byrne (Co. K) N: 12/8/92.

Manuel V. Cabrera (Co. K) Q: 6/93.

Charles Dawson (Co. M)** N&L: 7/20/93.

Clyde Fore (Co. I) LT: A friend 7/20/93.

Harold Gamble (Med Co.)** Q&N: 12/29/92; L: 2/12 & 23/94.

Frank L. Griffin (Co. A & B)** L: 12/10/94.

Louie M. Hillis (Co. K) Q&N: 1/19/93.

Hubert Hotchkiss (Med. Co.) Q: 1/19/93.

John L. Kirby (Co. L)** N: 11/19/92; Q: 11/20/92.

Patrick L. Martin (HQ, 3d Bn) L: 12/16/92; Q: 3/2/93.

Robert W. Mildenberger (Co. M) LT: CSM Frank C. Plass (Co. B), 9/12/92. Copy courtesy CSM Plass.

William M. Molten (Co. M) Q: 1992 - exact date unk.

Baldwin Frank Myers (Co. I) N: undated; I: Lewis Michelony 8/9/87, reviewed & corrected by Myers. Myers' response to John Toland's questions, undated. LT: Secretary of Defense, 2/3/81; Annotated sketch by Myers, showing his route of escape from Hadong, 8/95.

John L. Napier (Co. I) N: Undated; Q: 12/26/92.

Frank C. Plass (Co. B) L: 2/13/93.

Raymond Reis (HQ, 1st Bn) L: 12/8 & 12/19/92.

George F. Sharra (Co. L) Summary of interview for Clay Blair. Clay and Joan Blair Collection, USAMHI.

Neal Vance (Co. L) Q: 5/91; L: 3/20/91; 12/22/92 & 4/25/93.

Charles L. Watson (Co. C) Q: 1993, exact date unk; L: 2/27/93.

David M. Williams (Co. C)** Q: 6/29/93.

Dr James W. Yeager (S-3 Sec., 3d Bn) L: 2/26 & 6/27/93; LT: David G. Strayer, 5/29/92; Q: 1/22/93; I for Clay Blair, reviewed, corrected and annotated by Yeager, 1993 - UP Yeager.
   **Also known to have served later in either the 27th or 35th Inf.

8th FAB:

Robert E. Dingeman (Btry B) Q: 2/8/94; N: Undated,"A Short Tour of the Orient".

Lewis Millett (8th FAB & C.O. E/27th Inf) N: 1988 - UP Millett. Two undated letters to John Toland, commenting on "Above and beyond the Call of Duty," by MG George B. Barth (C.O. 25th DivArty) in *Tropic Lightning Flashes*, June 1953 - UP Millett.

Robert R. Minger (Btry C) Q&L: 9/2/93.

Allen M. Smith (Btry C) Q: 3/12/92.

Joseph W. Terman (C.O., B/31 FAB; HQ, 8 FAB)(D - KIA 8/22/50) LT: Wife 6/15/49, 7/30 & 8/22/50; LT: Parents 9/9, 9/13 & 10/21/49; 1/6/50. All letters UP his son, Dr. James W. Terman, M.D. Series of letters between Dr. Terman and author: 1/5/92 w/chronology of CPT Terman; 1/25; 4/20 & 12/15/92.

Sten Westin (HQ)(D - KIA 8/22/50) L: Janet Westin Bicker (Sten Westin's daughter) to author 10/3/94; Extract CPT Westin's notebook, containing outline of his military service; GO 60, HQ, Eighth Army, 2/8/51, awarding the Silver Star, posthumously, to CPT Westin; L: LTC Augustus T. Terry, Jr. (C.O., 8 FAB) to Mrs. Flora A. Westin (CPT Westin's wife) 9/4/50; L: Chap Walter S. McCloskey (Chap, 25 DivArty) to Mrs. Westin, 9/20/50. All courtesy Janet Westin Bicker.

64th FAB:

Kincheon H. Bailey (Btry B) Q&N: 3/5/95.

Schuyler Berdan (Btry A) Q: late 1991.

Cleo O. Bell (Btry B) Q: 11/29/91.

Donald L. Massey (Btry C) L: 11/5/93.

Benjamin F. Martin (Btry B) Q: 6/5/91.

Fred F. Nelson (Btry B & C) Q: 9/3/91.

89th Tank Bn:

John W. Akeson (Co. A) Q: 1990 (exact date unk.)

28th MP Co:

Milton Melhorn L: 4/19/91; Q: 5/21/91.

Marine Brigade:

1st Battalion:

John R. Baughan (Co. A) Q: 11/15/93.

Delbert R. Bell (Co. B) Q: 12/4/93.

Donald J. Bohlke (Co. A) Q: 12/13/93.

Manuel Brito (Co. B) Q: 11/26/93.

Robert A. Clement (Co. B) Q: 10/17/93.

Joseph Fedin (Co. A) Q: 10/20/93.

Francis I. Fenton, Jr. (C.O., Co. B) Q: 7/7/91 I for John Toland. Reviewed/corrected by COL Fenton - UP COL Fenton. Debriefing of Fenton by USMC History Division upon his return to the U.S. from Korea. Copy courtesy Baker Bandits Archives, 808 Caravan Circle, Austin, TX 78746-3502, 4/19/94. MC

Cornelius E. Finerman (Co. B) Q: 10/2/93.

George C. Fox (Co. A) Q: 10/20/93.

George Hawman (H&S) Q: 10/18/93.

Carl T. Lawendowski (Co. B) Q&N: 4/2/94.

Herbert R. Luster (Co. A) Q&N: 1991.

Edward C. Morris (Co. B) Q: 11/27/93.

Francis W. Muetzel (Co. A) Q&N: 8/2/93; L: 5/14 & 7/29/93; 3/5/95, plus several telephone calls in 1994 and 1995. MC

Billy J. Ogan (Co. A) N: 7/21/94.

Paul Santiago (Co. B) Q: 2/17/94.

Robert C. Sebilian (Co. A) Biographic sketch.

Raymond E. Stephens (Co. A) Q: 8/28/93.

John R. Stevens (C.O., Co. A) Q: 5/19/91. MC

Caspar A. Tartalone (H&S) Q: 12/29/93.

Walter Wolfe, Jr. (Co. B) Q: 1/13/94.

2d Battalion:

Russell A. Albert (Co. D)** L: 10/18/93.

William Albert (Co. D)** L: 10/20/93.

** Russell and William are brothers. Another brother, John (Co. D), was KIA 8/7/50.

Richard C. Blevins (H&S) Q: 11/19/93.

Thomas Burke (Co. E) Q: 10/28/93.

Robert P. Burkhardt (Co. E) Q: 9/29/93.

Esten C. Carper, Jr. (H&S) L: 10/28/93; Q: 11/15/93.

Robert Q. Dickson (Co. E) Q&N: 10/22/93.

Herbert B. Doane (Co. E) Q: 1/6/94.

Edward T. Emmelman (Co. D) Q: 9/2/93.

Dr. John Finn, Ed.D., (C.O., Co. D) TI: 9/6/94.

John Headrick (Co. D) Q&L: 10/15/93.

James I. Higgins (H&S) Diary 7/13 - 9/20/50.

Chick Hitchborn (Wpns) L: 10/26/93; Q: 12/3/93.

Raymond A. Johnson (H&S) Q: 11/30/93.

Alfred R. Jordan (Co. D) L: 5/1/94.

Douglas Koch (Co. D) Recollections in *The Korean War - Oral History*, Donald Knox.

Malachy Lyons (H&S) Q: 11/4/93.

Lloyd W. Pasley (Co. D) L: 10/27/93.

Frank Raponi (Co. D) L: 3/16/94.

Jerry D. Rockey (H&S) TI: 10/26/93.

Richard Tryon, Jr. (Co. E) Q: 2/2/94.

David S. Vandommelen (Co. D) Q: 12/27/93.

Howard Varner (Co. D) L: 11/24/93.

George M. Wiles (Wpns) Q: 12/9/93.

Valente U. Yruegas (Co. D) L: 11/28/93.

3d Battalion:

James W. Abrahamson, Jr. (Co. H) Q: 11/15/93.

MG Robert D. Bohn (Co. G) I for John Toland. Reviewed/corrected by GEN Bohn 4/9/94 - UP GEN Bohn. Annotations to overlay, special map of Obong-ni - Yongsan Area, 1:34,000 scale. MC

John H. Cahill (Co. G) Q: 1991. MC

Paul Stanley Cobane (Co. H) Q: 10/12/93.

Fred F. Davidson (Co. G)(D) Q: 3/16/92, plus numerous letters to author 1991-93.

Edward F. Duncan (Co. G) Q: 11/91.

Dr. Robert J. Harvey, M.D. (Bn Surgeon) Q: 10/18/93.

Wayne K. Knott (Co. H) Q: 11/18/93.

DuWayne A. Philo (Co. G) Q: 1991.

Robert Roberts (Co. G) L: 2/3 & 18/94.

James L. Sanders (Co. G) L: 6/22/93; Q: 7/26/93.

Lloyd P. Summers (Co. G) Q: 1/11/94; TA: 1/13/94.

Robert D. Taplett (C.O, 3d Bn) Q: 7/6/93; L: 7/17/93; I for John Toland. Reviewed and corrected by COL Taplett - UP COL Taplett. TI: 8/24/94. MC

John D. Wagner (Co. H) Q: 12/18/93.

Kermit Wilhelm (Co. G) Q: 9/14/93.

Jack Wright, Jr. (Co. G) Q: 12/26/91; TA: 7/19/93.

Alfred E. Zinn (Co. H) Q: 2/18/94.

1-11th Marines (105mm FAB):

Henry G. Ammer (Btry C) Q: 12/23/93.

Kenneth D. Clothier (Hq Btry) Q: 10/7/93.

Charles C. Marquis (Svc Btry) Q: 12/2/93.

Bill M. Murley (Svc Btry) Q: 11/6/93.

Ernst Rolf (Btry B) Q: 7/9/94.

Donald D. Sisson (Btry B) Q: '1/14/93.

Steve Spanovich (Svc Btry) L: 11/22/93; Q: 1/30/94.

Cleo P. Stapleton (Svc) Btry) Q: 12/13/93.

LeRoy K. Wirth (Btry B) Q: 12/13/93.

Ransom M. Wood (C.O., 1-11th Mar.) Q: 1/19/93. MC

Recon Co:

Richard Orlowski Q, N&L: 6/25/91.

HM Co:

Lester M. Fulcher Q: 2/28/94.

Tom L. Gibson Q: 7/17/93.

Earl J. Graves, Jr. Q: 10/29/93.

Colin S. Jones, Jr. L: 10/30/93; Q: 12/24/93; TA: 5/24/94.

A-1st Tank Bn:

Paul F. DiNoto Q: 10/2/93; copy of statement in support of Post Traumatic Syndrome Condition (PTSD), 9/20/91; Statement by Master Gunnery Sergeant William E. Robinson, USMC, 9/23/90, in support of claim; Marine Corps Tankers Assn Directory; copy A-1st Tk Bn Morning Report, 9/9/50. All courtesy Paul DiNoto.

Harvey G. Frye Q: 6/25/94.

Donald R. Gagnon Q&L: 11/13/93.

Robert C. Solheid L: 1/29/94

Anti-tank Co:

Dr Herbert R. Pierce, M.D. (Corpsman with AT Co.) Q: 11/8/93; LT: Parents 8/13, 15-16/50 - UP Dr. Pierce.

A-1st Engr Bn:

Willard C. Downs Q: 3/94.

Lyle Richard Engle Q&L: 11/29/93.

Elijah G. Gaylor Log & diary 8/24/50 - 5/12/51.

MATCS-2:

Earl H. Falk Q: 10/16/93.

Christian C. Lee (C.O, MATCS-2) L: 11/12/93; 1/12/94. MC

James G. Scott L: 2/3/94 w/copy of the lineage and honors of Marine Air Tactical Control Squadron Two, 1 July 1947 - 15 February 1954.

CHAPTER ONE

William Manchester, *American Caesar, Douglas MacArthur 1880-1964* (New York: Dell Publishing Co. Inc., 1978) pp. 517-18. Hereafter *American Caesar*.

James F. Schnabel, *Policy and Direction: The First year*, in *United States Army in the Korean War* series (Washington, D.C.: Office of the Chief of Military History, 1972) pp.8-11; 16. Hereafter *Policy and Direction*.

MAJ Robert K. Sawyer, Walter G. Hermes, Ed. *Military Advisors in Korea: KMAG in Peace and War* (Washington D.C.: Office of the Chief of Military History, 1962) pp. 7-33; 36-38; 46; 49-52. Hereafter, *Military Advisors*.

Roy E. Appleman, *South to the Naktong, North to the Yalu*, in *United States Army in the Korean War* series (Washington, D.C.: Office of the Chief of Military History, 1961) pp. 1-2; 4-5; 9-11; 13-15. Hereafter, *South to the Naktong*.

Headquarters. U.S. Far east Command, Military Intelligence Section, General Staff, *History of the North Korean Army*, July 31, 1952. pp. 3; 22. Hereafter *History NK Army*.

MAJ Bruce T. Falls, Ed., *The Seventh Division in Korea* (Far East Printing Plant, undated) pp. 40; 47-49; 57; 73; 98. This volume outlines the history of major 7th Infantry Division units, concentrating on their occupation of Korea 1945-49.

Department of the Army Pamphlet 550-30 (DA Pam 550-30), *Area Handbook for Japan*, Sep 1969. Chap 2.

General of the Army Douglas MacArthur, *Reports*, Vol I, Supplement, MacArthur in Japan: The Occupation: Military Phase. pp. 24-25; 27-28; 99; 102; 117; 122; 134; 142-143; 146; 161; 191. Hereafter *MacArthur Reports*.

Robert A. Fearey, *The Occupation of Japan, Second Phase: 1948* reprinted by Greenwood Press, Westport, CT, 1972. Preface.

Edward L. Daily, *Skirmish, Red, White and Blue* Turner Publishing Co., Paducah, KY, 1992) pp. 18-20. Hereafter *Skirmish*. This is a short history of the 7th Cavalry Regiment, 1945-1953.

1LT Charles A. Rogers, *Occupation Diary, First Cavalry Division* (Tokyo: Toppan Publishing Co., May 1950).

Tables of Organization and Equipment (TO&E) 7-7N, Infantry Division; 7-11N, Infantry Regiment; 8-15N, Heavy Tank Battalion; 6-10N, Division Artillery, all dated 1948.

DA Pam 20-196, *A Pocket Guide to Okinawa* (Department of Defense, Washington, D.C., June 8, 1961).

Richard H. Stinson, "Korea Occupation, The Beginning of a Forgotten Era," *Graybeards*, June 1993. Used by permission. *Graybeards* is the publication of the Korean War Veterans Assn, Inc. Stinson was then a member of C/48th FAB.

Albert J. McAdoo (E/5th RCT), *The 5th RCT in Korea. The First Fifty Days. Book One* (Acton, MA, 1990). pp. 1-2. Hereafter *The First Fifty Days*. This is a compilation of the experiences and recollections of veterans of the 5th Regimental Combat Team (RCT) in the Pusan Perimeter.

CHAPTER TWO

South to the Naktong, Chap II.

Military Advisors, pp. 12-45; 67-93.

History NK Army, Sections I, II and III; App I, pp. 19-20; 29-32; 36.

Nigel Thomas and Peter Abbott, *The Korean War 1950-53*, Men-at arms Series 174, Martin Windrow, editor (London: Osprey Publishing, LTD, 1968) pp. 6-7; 9-10; 12.

CHAPTER THREE

John Toland, *In Mortal Combat*, (New York: William Morrow & Co., Inc., 1991) pp 19-20. Hereafter, *Mortal Combat*.

Max Hastings, *The Korean War*, (New York: Simon and Schuster, 1987) pp. 51-52. Hereafter *Korean War*.

Policy and Direction, pp. 30; 38.

Clay Blair, *The Forgotten War* (New York: Times Books, Random House, Inc., 1987) pp. 43-44. Hereafter, *The Forgotten War*.

American Caesar, p. 639.

Bevin Alexander, *Korea, The First War We Lost* (New York: Hippocrene Books, 1968) pp. 18; 21-22. Hereafter, *First War*.

James F. Schnabel and Robert J. Watson, *History of the Joint Chiefs of Staff*, Vol. 3, The Joint Chiefs of Staff and National Policy (Washing-

ton, D.C., The Korean War, Part 1, 1978 and Part 2, 1979) p. 37.

Military Advisors, pp. 110; 112; 114-139.

South to the Naktong, Chapter III.

General Sun Yup Paik, *From Pusan to Panmunjom* (Washington D.C. and New York: Brassey's (US), Inc, 1992) pp. 1-31. Quotations from this book by permission of GEN Paik. Hereafter, *Pusan to Panmunjom*.

Keyes Beech, *Tokyo and Points East*, (Garden City, New York: Doubleday and Co., Inc., 1954) pp. 113-114. Hereafter, *Tokyo/East*.

MG William F. Marquat, "Automatic Artillery in Korea," *Antiaircraft Journal*, Nov - Dec 1950. p. 6. (Hereafter *AA in Korea*.) At the time GEN Marquat was the senior antiaircraft officer in the U.S. Army.

Sergei N. Goncharov, John W. Lewis and Xue Litai, *Uncertain Partners: Stalin, Mao, and the Korean War*, (Stanford University Press, Stanford, CA., 1993) Chap. 5, The Decision for war in Korea.

CHAPTER FOUR

One Year in Korea — A Summary 25 June '50 - 25 June '51, General Headquarters, UN Command, Military Intelligence Section. p. 1. Hereafter, *One Year in Korea*.

South to the Naktong, pp. 46; 59; 61-76.

In Mortal Combat, p. 82.

Forgotten War, p. 89; 95.

Rudy Tomedi, *No Bugles, No Drums* (New York: John Wiley and Sons, Inc., 1993) pp. 10 and 12. Hereafter, *No Bugles*.

Albert E. Cowdrey, *The Medic's War*, in *U.S. Army in the Korean War* series (Washington, D.C.: Office of the Chief of Military History, 1987) pp. 73-74. Hereafter, *Medic's War*.

MG William F. Dean as told to William L. Worden, *General Dean's Story* (New York: The Viking Press, 1954) pp. 16-19. Hereafter, *Dean's Story*.

Donald Knox, *The Korean War. An Oral History. Pusan to Chosin* (New York: Harcourt, Brace Jovanovich, Publishers, 1985) p. 16. Hereafter, *Oral History*.

The First Team. The First Cavalry Division in Korea, 18 July 1950 - 18 january 1952 (No author given) (Atlanta: Albert Love Enterprises, 1952) Pages are unnumbered. Hereafter, *The First Team*.

BG George B. Barth (CG, 25 DivArty) "Tropic Lightning and Taro Leaf in Korea July '50 - May '51," Monograph. Second typewritten version, 1955. pp. 1 and 2. Hereafter, Barth ms.

Paul L. Child, '52, Ed., *Register of Graduates and Former Cadets of the United States Military Academy, 1802 - 1988* (Association of Graduates, West Point, NY, 1988) Hereafter, *Register of Graduates.* This volume was used to obtain the background information of some of the West Point graduates who served in the Pusan Perimeter.

LTC Charles S. Smith (C.O., 1/21st Inf) "Bloody Osan Remembered," *Pacific Stars and Stripes,* July (?) 1951. This is a two-column long first person account of TF Smith at Osan.

Eric C. Ludvigsen, Assoc. Ed. "An Arrogant Display of Strength," *Army* Magazine, Feb 1952.

Carl F. Bernard, as told to SGT A. Mullikan, "The First Brutal Weeks in Korea," in the "World Affairs" section, *The Washington Post,* Sun, June 24, 1951.

BG George B. Barth (25 DivArty), The First Days in Korea," *Combat Forces Journal*, Mar 1952.

William Colon, "Task Force Smith: A study in (Un)Preparedness and (Ir)Responsibility," *Military Review,* Feb, 1988.

MAJ William Pennino, "7 Bloody Hours That Saved Korea," *Real* Magazine, Oct. 1952.

MG John H. Church, Memo for Record, "ADCOM Activities in Korea, 27 June - 15 July 1950," undated, but was prepared in 1950 or 1951. Typewritten and double spaced. pp. 6-8. A copy of this report was obtained at the National Archives by MAJ Lacey Barnett, USA, Ret., and sent to me. Major Barnett was most cooperative to this author by providing a great amount of material — copies of letters, extracts of telephone conversations he had with other Perimeter veterans; command journals and other official reports, etc. He was a member of Medical Co., 34th Infantry during the Korean War. Hereafter, material provided by MAJ Barnett will be identified (Barnett).

DA Memo, Jun 27, 1950, Ridgway Papers, Box 16, U.S. Army Military History Institute, Carlisle Barracks, PA. Hereafter USAMHI.

CHAPTER FIVE

Eighth U.S. Army summary of selected events 30 Jun - 13 Jul 1950. National Archives. (Barnett) It should be noted that MAJ Barnett discovered many of the "new" documents and other material used for the first time in this book.

OPORD 1 062100 July 1950, 24th Inf Div, signed by then-LTC James W. Snee, 24th Division G-3. This document establishes that there was a Task Force Barth. (Barnett)

OPORD 3 082145 July 1950, 24th Inf Div, Taejon, Korea. (Barnett)

GO #51, HQ, 24th Inf Div, 22 Jul 1950, awarding the Silver Star medal to 1LT James C. Little, HC, 3/34 Inf for his actions in Chonan July 8, 1950. (Barnett)

TO&E &-15N, 1948, Infantry Battalion.

34th Infantry Regimental Strength Reports, selected dates between 2 July and 31 Aug 1950. (Barnett)

South to The Naktong, pp. 82-107.

Forgotten War, pp. 89-93; 106-115; 137.

Policy and Direction, p. 89.

General Dean's Story, pp. 8-12; 14; 21-27; 36.

Tokyo/East, pp.148-149.

Skirmish, p. 25.

T.R. Fehrenbach, *This Kind of War* (New York: The Macmillan Co. 1963) Chapter 8. Hereafter *This Kind of War*. This book includes considerable dialog among and between soldiers, but Fehrenbach presents absolutely no reference material or sources for any of it.

Robert F. Futrell, *The United States Air Force in Korea, 1950-1953* (U.S. Air Force, Washington D.C., revised edition 1983) pp. 80;91. Hereafter *USAF in Korea.*

Russell A. Gugeler, *Combat Actions in Korea* (U.S. Army, Washington, D.C., 1970) Chapter 1, "Withdrawal Action." Hereafter *Combat Actions*, citing chapter.

Marguerite Higgins, *War in Korea* (New York: Doubleday & Co., Inc., 1951) p. 6. Hereafter *War in Korea.*

General of the Army Douglas MacArthur, *Reminiscences* (New York: McGraw-Hill Book Co., 1964) p. 335.

Register of Graduates.

Barth ms. pp. 2-6.

Messages from Dean to COL Jay B. Lovless (C.O. 34th Inf). Quoted in *South to the Naktong.* Messages were retained in the Colonel's possession. These two messages are the only orders he received from GEN Dean during the action at Chonan before his relief.

Interview notes by Gugeler of his interviews of 1SG Roy E. Collins and MSG Zack C. Williams (both of A/34th Inf) 8/4/51. and SFC Alfred Beauchamp (A/34th Inf) 8/6/51. (Barnett)

CHAPTER SIX

South to the Naktong, pp. 108-110; 112-120; 195-197; 253; 264; 366;389.

Policy and Direction, pp. 43; 83-84; 124; 299.

Forgotten War, pp. 15-17; 47-48; 144; 156-159; 644-45.

Register of Graduates.

General of the Army Omar N. Bradley and Clay Blair, *A General's Life* (New York: Simon and Schuster, 1983) pp. 111-112.

LTC Charles M. Bussey, USA, Ret., *Firefight at Yechon* (New York: Brassey's (US), 1991) pp. 86-87. Hereafter, *Yechon.*

Louis Galambos, Ed., *The Papers of Dwight David Eisenhower*, Vol. IX, (Baltimore: Johns Hopkins University Press, 1978) p. 2253. "Extraordinary" reference.

Joseph C. Goulden, *Korea The Untold Story of the War* (New York: Time Books, 1982) p. 111. Hereafter *Untold Story.*

Edwin P. Hoyt, *The Pusan Perimeter* (New York: Stein and Day, 1984) Notes to Chapter 8. Hereafter, *Pusan Perimeter.*

William H. Leckie, *The Buffalo Soldiers* (Norman, OK: University of Oklahoma Press, 1967) pp. 8-17; 96-97; 101; 106.

Robert M. Utley, *Frontier Regulars, 1866-1890*, (New York: Macmillan Publishing Co., Inc., 1973) pp. 26-29.

Leckie's work concentrates on the U.S. 9th and 10th Cavalry Regiments; Utley's book deals with the broader scope of all U.S. regular regiments on the American frontier. Pages 26-29 of the latter work provide a capsule of life in a black regiment of the time.

Russell F. Weigley, *Eisenhower's Lieutenants* (Bloomington, Ind., Indiana University Press, 1981) p. 99.

David K. Carlisle and Charles M. Bussey, "In a Higher Tradition." This is a history of the 24th Infantry Regiment and the 77th Engineer Combat Company in Korea. Preface and pp. 20-21; 34. Copy courtesy David K. Carlisle. Bussey commanded the 77th and Carlisle was one of his platoon leaders. Hereafter, Carlisle/Bussey ms.

"Temporary" and "permanent" rank. Author's conversations with his uncle, MG Uzal G. Ent (WP 1924). When promoted to Brigadier General in 1943, he still held the "permanent" rank of Lieutenant Colonel, his pre-war rank.

"The Fair Haired Boy of Eighth Army." Author conversations at the time with other officers. Mt. Fuji anecdote. Author's personal experience as a member of the umpire detail. "Phony Baloney" remark. The officer who made this remark, 1LT Donald F. Darnell, became C.O. of B/27th Infantry.

Lynch Interview 6/25/93; Barnett interview of Lynch 4/22-24/92. (Extract Barnett interview from Barnett).

CHAPTER SEVEN

South to the Naktong, pp. 121-181.

The Forgotten War, pp. 133-144.

U.S. Air Force in Korea, pp. 99-101; 600.

Gen. Dean's Own Story, p. 29

U.S. Army Handbook 1939-1945, pp. 112 and 114 (ref. AA artillery)

Register of Graduates

FM 23-90, *81mm Mortar, M1*, April 1951, p. 59.

History of NK Army, Section V, pp. 41-58.

Periodic Intelligence Report, G2 Section, 24th Division 121800 Jul - 131800 Jul 1950, dtd 132000 Jul 50. (Barnett)

Operations Instructions No. 3, 24th Inf. Div., Jul 14, 1950. (Barnett)

War Diary, 24th Inf. Div., 192400K-202400K Jul 1950. (Barnett)

Journal 1/21 Inf. 20 Jul. Entries for 0131; 0731; 1645 and 1812 hrs. (Barnett)

Extracts, various unit Morning Reports, 24th Div., Jul-Aug 1950. (Barnett)

"The Pineapple Soldiers, The Story of the 24th Infantry Division," Bruce Jacobs, *Saga* magazine, 1955. The account of SGT George D. Libby, 3 ECB. Copy courtesy of Robert G. Fox, 19th Inf.

"Truck Platoon — Withdrawal from Taejon," LT Ralph C. Boyd and CPT John G. Westover, *Combat Forces Journal*, Sept. 1952. Article is based on Westover interview of Boyd.

Newsletter, Tennessee Korean War Memorial Assn, Oct 1990, Lombardi biography. Copy courtesy of Shefield Clark, 63 FAB.

Barnett - Lynch interview 4/22-24/92. Author-Lynch interview 6/25/93.

COL Melicio Montesclaros and COL David N. Smith were unable to help in this project due to severe medical problems. In an effort to obtain additional material and to clarify certain events, the author wrote to these officers on the dates indicated, but had no response: COL Barszcz Osburn and Lantron 9/14/92; MG Beauchamp 9/12/91; MG Marks 12/30/92; COL Dunn 9/5/92; COL Coghill 4/8/93.

CHAPTER EIGHT

South to the Naktong, pp. 184-209; 394.

In Mortal Combat, pp. 109-110; 130-132. Toland bases his Yechon account on interviews of LTC Bussey and Tom Lambert.

The Forgotten War, pp. 152-153; 161-162; 214.

The Pusan Perimeter, p. 109.

Edward L Daily, *The Legacy of Custer's 7th U.S. Cavalry in Korea* (Paducah, KY: The Turner Publishing Co., 1990) pp. 18-25. Hereafter, *Legacy*.

Lyle Rishell, *With a Black Platoon in Combat* (College Station, TX: Texas A&M University Press, 1993) pp. 35-37; 42-43. Hereafter, *With a Black Platoon*. Lyle Rishell led a rifle platoon of A/24th infantry. This book is an account of his experiences and recollections with that platoon.

L. Albert Scipio, II, *Last of the Black Regulars* (Silver Spring, MD: Roman Publications, 1983) pp. 85-87.

Yechon, pp. 34; 37-39; 99-108; 260-261.

Carlisle/Bussey ms. pp. 24-33.

CPT Allan A. David, Ed. and SGT Norwin E. Austin, Assoc. Ed., *Battleground Korea. The Story of the 25th Infantry Division* (Tokyo: Kyoko Co., 1951) Unfortunately, pages are not numbered. Reference here are to the two pages dealing with Yechon. Hereafter, *Battleground Korea*.

Untold Story, pp. 168-169.

LTG James M. Gavin's Forward to *The Triple Nickles* by Bradley Biggs.

From Pusan to Panmunjom, pp. 26-28.

Robert J. Best, *Analysis of Personnel Casualties in the 25th Infantry Division 26-31 July 1950* (Chevy Chase, MD: Operations Research Office, The Johns Hopkins University, Apr 14, 1952) pp. 20-24, casualties of Companies B and C, 27th Infantry on July 28, 1950.

COL Logan E. Weston (C.O., A/27th Inf), *The Fightin' Preacher* (Cheyenne WY: Vision Press, Inc., 1992) pp. 20; 49; 51; 87; 117; 199-200; 203-208.

The Bark of the Wolfhounds, 27th Infantry Regiment Organization Day 2 May 1950, No author given. No pagination. Used to identify names, ranks and units of assignment. Hereafter, *Bark of the Wolfhounds*.

Robert Zoller, *Odyssey of the 27th Infantry Regiment Wolfhounds*, unpublished manuscript, 1991. Chap. 14. Hereafter, *Odyssey of the Wolfhounds*.

Tom Lambert dispatches for July 21,25 and 28, 1950, appearing in the *Los Angeles Examiner*. LT Jung, CPL Grigsby and SSG Bevins quoted in the July 25 dispatch.

Extract, 24th Inf Regt War Diary, 6-31 July 1950.

Historical Report — July 1950, 27th RCT.

Historical Report 10-31 July, 1950, Med Co., 27th Regt, Oct 19, 1950.

Casualty List, 27th RCT, 24-31 July 1950.

History of the NK Army, pp. 55-58. Actions of the *NK 2d, 3d* and *4th Divisions*.

Trial Record, General Court Martial of 1LT Leon A. Gilbert, A/24th Inf. Although found guilty and sentenced, the sentence was commuted by President Harry S. Truman Nov. 27, 1950.

Newsletter of Co A, 27th Infantry, The Wolfhounds, Nov. 1992, profiling Philip File.

CHAPTER NINE

South to the Naktong, pp. 206-208; 210-247.

The Forgotten War, pp. 73-74; 163-172; 179-184; 186-187.

Policy and Direction, p. 91.

MAJ William V. Schmitt, P.I. Officer, Staff Supervision; 1LT Shelby P. Warren, Ed., *24th Division, A Brief History*, (Tokyo, Japan: *Japan News*, 1954) p. 8. Hereafter, *24th Infantry Division*.

War in Korea, pp. 120-130.

Register of Graduates.

Russell Spurr, *Enter the Dragon* (New York: New Market Press, 1988) pp. 24-32.

BG "Mike" Michaelis with Bill Davidson, "This We Learned in Korea," *Colliers*, Aug 18, 1951.

Harold H. Martin, "The Colonel Saved the Day," *The Saturday Evening Post*, Sep 9, 1950. Includes account of the meeting at Chung-ni.

Odyssey of the Wolfhounds, pp. 371-372.

Bark of the Wolfhounds, used to help identify names, ranks and units of assignment.

History of the NK Army, pp. 47-58; 62-63; 79-80. This history states that the *6th (Guards) Division* included the 1st, 13th and 15th Regiments. Other sources, including Appleman for one, state that the division had the *13th, 14th* and *15th Regiments*.

MSG Forrest K. Kleinman, "Haman Notch," *Army* Magazine, Jan 1961. (Forrest Kleinman retired as a Lieutenant Colonel.)

LT Alexander Makarounis, as told to Merle Miller, "I Survived the Korean Death march," *Argosy* Magazine, Mar 1951. (All quotations in the LT Makarounis narrative are from this article.)

Richard J. N. Johnson dispatch to *New York Times*, Aug 5, 1950. (Copy courtesy Robert A.

Spangenberg (Med Co/19th Inf). Quotes of PFC Albin Harp and PVT George Gilbert from this dispatch.

Chicago Daily Tribune, Monday, Oct 23, 1950.

SO #191, HQ, 27th Inf Regt, Aug 25, 1950. These orders, awarding the Combat Infantryman's Badge (CIB) to members of HC and Co. I, 29th Infantry, provided complete names and ranks of some of the survivors of Hadong. Copy courtesy Baldwin Frank Myers (I/29th Inf.)

OPORD 13, HQ, 27th RCT 012300 Aug '50.

Unit Reports #1/2 and 2/3 (1800 hrs 1 Aug - 1800 hrs 2 Aug & 1800 2 hrs 2 Aug - 1800 hrs 3 Aug), 27th RCT, dated 031800 Aug and 041800 Aug 1950.

Operations report 1 Aug - 31 Aug 1950, 1/27th Inf.

Name and address roster , Ex-POWs, 29th RCT, Aug 20, 1990. Copy courtesy Baldwin Frank Myers.

Darold R. Freeman (B/29th Inf) Four page summary history of the 29th Regt., undated. Courtesy the author. Similar historic sketch by Freeman, copy courtesy Charles L. Watson (C/29th Inf.)

Lynch interview 6/25/93.

CHAPTER TEN

South to the Naktong, pp. 248-265; 385-387.

Policy and Direction, p. 128. Cites a GHQ G-1 memo of Aug 5, 1950 giving the total U.S. losses to that date as 7,859.

Lynn Montross and CPT Nicholas A. Canzona, USMC, *The Pusan Perimeter*, Vol. I, U.S. Marine Operations in Korea (Washington D.C., Historical Branch, G-3, HQ, USMC, 1954) pp. 26-27; 51. Hereafter, USMC, *Pusan Perimeter*. Pp. 26-27 discuss the composition of a North Korean division of 1950. Page 51 gives Brigade strength figures.

The USAF in Korea, pp. 59; 79-81; 83; 87; 109; 695.

Dr. William Glenn Robertson, *Counterattack on the Naktong, 1950*. No. 13 in the Leavenworth Papers series, Combat Studies Institute, U.S. Command and General Staff College, Ft. Leavenworth, KS, Dec 1985. pp. 14-18. This is a detailed and accurate study of the 24th Infantry Division's defense of the so-called "Naktong Bulge." Hereafter, *Counterattack on the Naktong*.

TO&E 7N, Infantry Division, 1948.

CHAPTER ELEVEN

South to the Naktong, pp. 263-265; 380-381.

Policy and Direction, pp. 43-46; 89-99; 117-125; 127-131.

USMC *Pusan Perimeter*, pp.48-95; 243; 247-251.

In Mortal Combat, P. 142.

The Forgotten War, pp. 148-149; footnote 15 to Chap 6; 193; 197-198; 202-208; 247-253; 304; 484; 548.

Register of Graduates.

Assembly, USMA, West Point, NY, Jan 1994. Peploe obituary.

The First Fifty Days, pp. 1-3; 7-25. UP the author. Includes narratives by CPT Wyatt Logan, B/555th FAB; LT Frank Brooks, F/5th RCT; SGT Richard Lewis HB/555th FAB; LT Law, B/555th FAB; SGT Eugene Mathews, B/555th FAB; LT William Motley, Svc/555th FAB; SGT Ellis, C/555th FAB.

COL Gerald T. Lochino, USA, Department of the Army Institute of Heraldry. L to SGT Guy E. See, USA, Ret., 4/7/87. SUBJECT: Historical Data on the 5th RCT. (See was a member of G/5th RCT.)

J. Robert Moskin, "The Tragedy of the West Point Class of 1950," *Look* Magazine, Jun 3, 1952. (Copy courtesy LTC Louis V. Genuario (WP '50 & G/38th Inf). Hereafter "Tragedy."

"War in Asia," section, pp. 14-21, *Time* Magazine, aug. 14, 1950. (Copy courtesy Earl T. Graves (4.2" Co/Mar Bde)

Jack Walker, "The 70th Tank Battalion in Korea," *Military* Magazine, May 1993. (Hereafter, *70th Tk Bn in Korea*.

CPT Ike Fenton, "Second Naktong Bulge Battle," *The Guidon*, Sep & Oct 1987. *The Guidon* is a publication of Baker Co., 1-5 Marines, 1950-51, a veteran's organization. The narrative of the battle is not completed in these two issues, but other issues were not available to the author.

CWO Fred W. Merten (HQ, 38th Inf) (D), "Famed for Defense in World War II, the Rock of the Marne Led the Attack in Korea," *The Ranger*, Dec. 19, 1952. Copy courtesy LTC Patrick W. Merten, USA, Ret., Fred's son.

CHAPTER TWELVE

South to the Naktong, pp. 266-288.

The Forgotten War, pp. 183-197; 212; 220; 279; 307; 548; 564-565; 644-645.

USMC *Pusan Perimeter*, pp. 65-66; 68-69; 87-155.
Barth mss. pp. 15-21; 23.

Firefight at Yechon, pp. 140-142; 148-155.

The New Breed, pp. 9-55.

Register of Graduates.

Carlisle/Bussey mss. p. 34.

Battleground Korea, Initial locations of elements of the 5th RCT.

LT Clark C. Munroe, *The Second United States Infantry Division in Korea 1950-1951* (Tokyo, Japan: Toppan Printing Co., LTD., 1951) pp. 4-5; 9. Hereafter *Second Division in Korea*.

Joseph A. Saluzzi, *Red Blood . . . Purple Hearts* (Owings Mills, MD: Watermark Press, 1990) pp. 7-11. This book is a compilation of citations for individual awards made to Marines during the Korean War. Autographed copy courtesy Joseph A. Saluzzi.

The First Fifty Days, pp. 8; 12-21.

Frank Kerr, "The Pusan Perimeter," *Leatherneck* Magazine, Aug. 1990. (Copy courtesy of Edward T. Emmelman (D-2-5th Mar)).

Narrative of Bruce B. Doane (E-2-5th Mar) from *Echoes of Easy*, written and published by Earnest Bagrielson, Cottonwood, AZ., no date given. (Copy of narrative courtesy of Bruce B. Doane.

Historical Division, HQ, U.S. Marine Corps, "The Pusan Perimeter Fight for a Foothold," *Marine Corps Gazette*, June 1951. (One of a series of articles on the actions of the Marines in Korea.) The article contains a few errors of facts pertaining to Army units.

LTC Ransom M. Wood (C.O., 1-11th Marines), "Artillery Support for the Brigade in Korea," *Marine Corps Gazette*, June 1951. Hereafter *Artillery Support*. (Wood retired as a full Colonel.)

1LT Robert D. Bohn (C.O., G-3-5th Mar), "The Approach March in Korea," *Marine Corps Gazette*, Oct 1951. (Bohn retired as a Major General.)

MAJ Francis I. Fenton, Jr., "Changallon Valley," *Marine Corps Gazette*, Nov. 1950. Hereafter, *Changallon*. (Fenton retired as a full Colonel.)

Fred Davidson (G-3-5th Mar) (D), "USMC, Korea - 1950," *Military*, issues in 1991 and 1992. Hereafter "USMC, Korea."

Memorandum for the Record, Aug. 9, 1950, LTC Frank W. Moorman. Box 16, Ridgway Papers, USAMHI.

Casualty List, 25th Division Personnel Interred at Masan. Copy courtesy Gene McClure (H/5th RCT).
Bohn interview.

Taplett interview.

CHAPTER THIRTEEN

South to the Naktong, pp. 163-164; 289-318.

Oral History, Part 3, pp. 127-193.

Pusan Perimeter, Notes to Chap 8.

USMC *Pusan Perimeter*, pp. 173-206.

Forgotten War, pp. 199-201; 204-210.

The Second Division in Korea, pp. 9-12.

This Kind of War, pp. 180-187. Pages 182-187 contain a rather detailed account of action in the 2/9th Infantry. But the frame of reference is muddled. The action described could have been either on August 10th or August 15-16. There is no way to tell.

COL Harry J. Maihafer, USA, Ret. *From the Hudson to the Yalu* (College Station, TX, Texas A&M University Press, 1993) pp. 21-22; 29-30; 34-35. Hereafter, *Hudson to Yalu.*

The National Guard Manual (Basic), prepared under the direction of the Chief, Army Field Forces, U.S. Army, Washington, D.C., Nov. 1948. p. 674 states that company frontages were to be 650 yards [in] "heavily wooded, broken terrain" to 1000 yards, "where the terrain is open and flat, or natural obstacles across a front make it unlikely that the area will be attacked in strength. . . ."

James Bell, *Time-Life* correspondent, "The Brave Men of No-Name Ridge," dispatch account of the Marine fight for Obong-ni Ridge. (Copy courtesy LTC John R. Stevens, USMC, Ret. He was commander of A-1-5th Marines at the time.)

Fight for A Foothold.

Strength Report, 34th Infantry, 2 July - 31 August (1950) and a Partial record of events. These two consist of a 10-page extract of strength and events for selected dates from unit

Morning Reports. Compiled by MAJ Lacy Barnett. Used by his permission. The *Record* shows LTC Perez being assigned to 3/34th Inf. on Aug. 5, 1950.

Unit Reports, 10/11 - 12/13 (111800 - 131800 Aug. 1950), 27th RCT.

Historical Report - August 1950, 27th RCT.

Roster of Casualties of the 27th Infantry Regiment, Consolidated from 1 Aug 50 to 31 Aug 50, dated 1 Nov. 1950.

Summary of Activities, 24 Jul - 31 Aug 1950, HQ, 2d Bn, 27th RCT.
Battalion Narrative, 24 Jul - 31 Aug, HQ, 3d Bn, 27th RCT.

War Diary, 34th Infantry, Aug. 7, 1950. Gives the figure of 20 officers and 417 EM as the 1st Bn strength on Aug. 6, 1950.

Roster, B/34th Inf, Jul-Aug 1950. Copy courtesy Robert W. Moser (B/34th Inf). Includes all unit losses Jul-Aug 1950.

COL Pak Kum Choi, NKPA, Interrogation Report 453. COL Pak gave the strength of the *16th Infantry* on August 6, 1950.

Artillery Support, pp. 18-20.

REFERENCES CONCERNING THE AT-TACK BY CO. A, 34TH INFANTRY, AUG. 15, 1950:

Sometimes referred to as "Attack Along a Ridgeline." This was first related in Chapter 2, *Combat Actions in Korea*. Since then, this account has been found to be inaccurate and incomplete. (This includes the sketch map of the battle, which contains a number of errors.) More survivors of this action, including unit officers, and a study made by CPT Alexander Kendris' student study group, in the Infantry Officer's Advanced Course, FT. Benning, GA in 1987 all combine to discredit the original account and present a more factual and accurate one of the battle. This author will not detail the differences in the Gugeler account and what emerges with the new evidence and input by more survivors. The account in *Fighting on the Brink*, to include the accompanying map, is the most complete, factual and accurate reconstruction of this battle that has been written to date. These are the references used:

Combat Actions in Korea, Chap. 2 — "Attack Along a Ridgeline."

CPT Alexander D. Kendris, Infantry Officer Advance Course 3-87, "Attack Along a Ridgeline, 14 August 1950 — A Leadership Case Study Revisited," June 20, 1987. Kendris interviewed COL Albert Alfonso, USA, Ret., commander of A/34th infantry during the attack, on May 9, 1987. The captain also received letters from CPT George A. Back Leader, 3d Plt) on May 15, 1987 and SFC Regis J. Foley (Plt Sgt, 3d Plt) June 5, 1987. None of these men had been contacted by Gugeler for his narrative, although they were all still in the Army at the time. CPT Kendris attempted to locate LT Shea and 1SG Collins, without success. Columbia, S.C. police visited Collins' last known address in June 1987 and found it abandoned. (All copies courtesy Barnett.)

CPT Russell A. Gugeler, "Attack Along a Ridgeline," *Combat Forces Journal*, May 1954. (Barnett)

"Critique of a Combat Action of Company A, 34th Infantry, Korea, 15 August 1950," Nicholas A. Canzona, 1LT USMC. (Prepared at the request of the Chief of Military History.) The request is undated. Canzona prefaced this critique by stating that his "assumptions must be drawn from speculation as well as material at hand. This situation, of course, gives rise to the possibility of injustices being perpetrated against persons whose actions and decisions might well have been above reproach." Unfortunately, when Canzona's critique was included in Gugeler's *Combat Forces Journal* article (mentioned above), this disclaimer was not included. This was a very negligent oversight on the part of *Journal* editors. Canzona unjustly criticized the leadership and judgement of the company commander, Albert Alfonso and two of his platoon leaders, Lieutenants Edward L. Shea and Melvin D. Schiller. The reputations of all three officers were damaged by this biased and unfounded "critique." Had the disclaimer been included with the Gugeler article, the damage would have been lessened somewhat.

Gugeler notes on his interviews of LT Shea and SFC Roy Collins, both of 2d Plt, A/34th Inf, August 12, 1951. (Barnett)

In addition to studying these references, the author querried Alfonso and Schiller (both retired Colonels). This included three letters to Alfonso, including a copy of the draft manuscript and a map, with overlay, for review, comment and correction. Letters were dated 2/12/95; 3/27/95 and 4/25/95. His responses were dated 2/12/95; 3/27/95 and 4/25/95. He annotated the overlay and reviewed, corrected and commented on the draft. Two letters were sent to COL Schiller (2/7/95 and 5/13/95) including a draft of the manuscript. map and overlay. He responded, annotating the map overlay and reviewing, correcting and commenting on the draft. One phone call was made to him 5/15/95. In addition, through the courtesy of Lacy Barnett, copies of Schiller's letters to the Asst. Comdt, The Infantry School, Ft. Benning, GA, 10/28/52; to the Editor, *Combat Forces Journal*, published 9/54; to Barnett 7/25/86 and to CPT Alexander D. Kendris, 5/4/87 were all made available to the author.

Fenton interview and Fenton debrief.

CHAPTER FOURTEEN

South to the Naktong, pp. 319-333.

Second Division in Korea, pp. 10 & 11.

USAF in Korea, pp. 65; 94-97; 110-112; 123-124; 216; 361; 397.

LTC Walter Killilea, *82d AAA AW Battalion in Korea*, pp. 1 & 2; 5 & 6. Typescript in a loose leaf binder. Undated. Hereafter, *82d AA in Korea.*

Military Advisors, p. 144. The formation of the ROK 26th Regiment.

Register of Graduates.

U.S. Army Handbook, p. 117 (DUKW information).

Weather Service Bulletin #4, 1950, pp.37-44. United Press dispatches, Tokyo, Sat., Aug. 12; Sun, Aug. 13; Wed, Aug. 30, 1950.

W H. Lawrence, *New York Times*, Mon, Aug. 14, 1950.

Trans-Pacifican, Vol. V, No. 13, Fri. Aug. 4, 1950.

POW statements concerning North Korean troops and troop units are all cited in *South to the Naktong*, pp. 320-321; 327; 329; 331-333.

CHAPTER FIFTEEN

South to the Naktong, pp. 254; 263; 334-363; 380-381.

Policy and Direction, p. 94.

The Forgotten War, pp. 211-219; 742 (information on MAJ Claude E. Allen, XO, 2/5th Cav.).

From Pusan to Panmunjom, pp. 31-45; 53; 206; 230; 248.

Hudson to the Yalu, pp. 35-37.

The First Team, Section covering the period Aug 2-17, 1950.

Second Division in Korea, p. 11.

Odyssey of the Wolfhounds, Chap. 14 "Land of the Morning Calm."

Skirmish, pp. 30-38.

History of the NK Army, pp. 69; 97; Charts 4a and 4c, pertaining to the organization of the North Korean anti-tank battalion.

Charles and Eugene Jones, *The Face of War* (New York: Prentice-Hall, Inc., 1951) pp. 45-53.

Edward L. Daily (H/7th Cav), *The Legacy of Custer's 7th U.S. Cavalry in Korea* (Paducah, KY: The Turner Publishing Co., 1990. pp. 26-34. Hereafter, *Legacy*.

"70th Tank Battalion" (Magazine article.)

Robert J. Best, *The Structure of a Battle: Analysis of a UN-NK Action North of Taegu, Korea September 1950* (Chevy Chase, MD: Operations Research Office, John Hopkins University, Jan. 20, 1954.) pp. 102-106. Hereafter *Structure of a Battle*.

The Story of the Wolfhound 27th Infantry Regiment, No author given (Tokyo, Japan: Japan News, 1953) pp. 21-22. Hereafter *Story of the Wolfhounds*.

LTC James W. Edwards, "Action at Tongmyongwon," *The Infantry School Quarterly*, Ft. Benning, GA., Jan. 1951. LTC Edwards commanded 2/23d Infantry at the time.

CPT Charles Multop, "A Heavy Weapons Company in Korea," *The Infantry School Quarterly*, 1951. (Multop commanded a heavy weapons company in Korea.)

CPT Phil Garn, "75mm Recoilless Rifle in Korea," *Combat Forces Journal*, Apr. 1952. (Garn commanded a 75 platoon in Korea.)

Time magazine, 9/4/50, p.21.

Life magazine, 8/22/50, p.22; 9/4/50, account of CPL Roy L. Day, Jr, 5th Cav; 9/11/50, 25th in the Bowling alley; 8/50, pp. 36-38.

Joseph Alsop, *Times,* Roanoke, VA, Aug 3, 1950.

Joseph Alsop, dispatch, Aug 30, 1950.

27th RCT:

Unit Reports, 17-18 through 24-25 Aug. (Aug 18 - 25, 1950.

Historical Report, Aug 1950**

Activity Report, Aug 1950, dated 11/9/50.**

Extract Interrogation Reports (IPW) #12 and #13 from IPW Reports for Aug-Oct 1950.**

Annex 1, OPORD 16, Aug 15, 1950 (Overlay depicting road march from Changwon to Kyongsan.**

Roster of Casualties, Aug 1-31, 1950**

Roster of Officers Present for Duty on Arrival of the Regiment in Korea.** This lists names, ranks and assignments, date joined, date entered combat and casualty status, (if appropriate.)**

Roster of Replacement Officers Since Arrival in Korea. (To Sep 14, 1950). This list contains the same information as that of the officers present for duty when the regiment arrived in Korea.**

1/27th Inf: Operations Report, Aug 1-31, 1950.**

2/27th Inf: Summary of Activities, Aug 1-31, 1950.**

3/27th Inf: Historical Report (Bn Narrative), Jul 24-Aug 31, 1950.**

** Documents so marked courtesy of Cressie Johnson (D-27th Inf).

8th FAB: War Diary, Aug 1950. Copy courtesy Mrs. Janet Bicker, daughter of CPT Sten Westin. (Sten is pronounced Stain.) CPT Westin (HQ, 8th FAB) was KIA Aug. 22, 1950.)

Blair-Lynch interview, 9/9/86. (Walker's flights around Perimeter and GEN Keiser narrative.)

Lynch interview.

CHAPTER SIXTEEN

South to the Naktong, pp. 364-375.
The Medic's War, p. 95.

With a Black Platoon, pp. 51-55; 67-68; 70-72.

Firefight at Yechon, pp. 148-154; 159-163; 165-175; 179-190.

From the Hudson to the Yalu, pp. 29-30; 40-42.

The First 50 Days, pp. 21-23.

Carlisle/Bussey mss — Section relative 77th ECC on the Nam River; note on SFC Collins A. Whitaker.

Barth mss, pp. 23-24.

Battleground Korea — Last four pages of Chap. 2; Chap 3, Fire test.

Michael R. Gordon and GEN Bernard E. Trainor, *General's War* (New York: Little, Brown & Co., 1995) pp. 58-68. These pages tell the sad story of ammunition shortages, air

and sea lift shortfalls and other problems, largely the result of improper preparedness for Desert Storm.

"24th Infantry Command Chart, Aug - Sep 1950," The Clay and Joan Blair Collection, Box 45 - 24th and 25th Divisions, USAMHI.

24th Infantry Casualties on Battle Mountain, from 24th Infantry records, Aug 1950. National Archives, RG 407, unnumbered box.

Johnson interview.

CHAPTER SEVENTEEN

Roy E. Appleman, *East of Chosin* (Texas: Texas A&M University Press, College Station, 1987) Appendix C — 31st RCT, November 27, 1950, Estimated Strength.

LTC Barton O. Baker, "Task Force Baker," *Combat Support in Korea*, John G. Westover (Combat Forces Press, 1955)

Jim Dan Hill, *The Minute Man in Peace and War* (Harrisburg, PA: The Stackpole Press, 1964) pp. 506-507; 543.

The First Century - A History of the 28th Infantry Division, prepared under the direction of COL Uzal W. Ent. Editor, Robert Grant Crist (Harrisburg, PA: Stackpole Books, 1979) pp. 187 & 190.

Military Advisors, pp. 148-151; 153.

Policy and Direction, pp. 118-125; 127-138; 299.

Pusan Perimeter, p. 243.

Frank A. Reister, *Battle Casualties and Medical Statistics. U.S. Army Experience in the Korean War* (Washington, D.C., The Surgeon General, Dept of the Army, 1973) Table 1 - Distribution of U.S. Army division and non-division monthly mean strength, Korea July 1950 - July 1953. Table B-1 - Numbers and annual rates of killed in action, wounded in action and nonbattle causes, admissions and CRO (Carded for Record Only) cases., by year and month, U.S. Army, Korea July 1950 - July 1953.

South to the Naktong, pp. 376-396; 492.

The Forgotten War, p. 222.

USAF in Korea, 1950-1953, pp. 26-27; 33; 46-47; 73-74; 93; 165; 183-187; 325-331; 334-335; 689.

CHAPTER EIGHTEEN

South to the Naktong, pp. 397-435.

From Pusan to Panmunjom, pp. 46-49.

The Forgotten War, pp. 254-262.

From the Hudson to the Yalu, pp. 50-65; 68-79.

Skirmish, pp. 38-44.

Register of Graduates.

The First Team, Narrative for period Aug 29 - Sep 14, 1950.

Oral History, pp. 312-352.

SGM Bryan Shanks, British Army, Ret., Untitled monograph on the British commands which served in Korea Aug 25, 1950 - Dec 1954, dated July 1, 1979. Copy courtesy Victor Fox (I/5th Cav).

Combat Actions in Korea, Chap. 4 - "Attack to the Rear."

COL Thomas T. Jones (D/8th ECB) (D) "Two Hundred Miles to Freedom," *The Military Engineer*, Sep-Oct 1951. Copy courtesy COL Jones' wife, Jerene Garges Jones, 11/2/92.

Robert J. Best, Project FECOM, Technical Memorandum ORO-T-261, Jan 20, 1954, *The Structure of a Battle: Analysis of a UN-NK Action North of Taegu, Korea, September 1950* (Chevy Chase, MD: Operations Research Office, The Johns Hopkins University). pp. 9-42; 48; 54-55; 58; 70; 74-77; 82; 87; 115-117; 122-130; 145-177; 182-188; 195-245; 250; 253; 276-283; 321-336; 339; 241-344; 351-359.

CHAPTER NINETEEN

South to the Naktong, pp. 389-391; 395; 436; 443-470.

USMC *Pusan Perimeter*, pp. 213-237.

The Forgotten War, pp. 246-254.

In Mortal Combat, pp. 163; 165; 167-168.

No Bugles, No Drums, pp. 39-41.

Oral History, pp. 170-193.

The New Breed, pp. 90-100.

The Second Division in Korea, pp. 15-22.

"USMC, Korea 1950"

David Douglas Duncan, *This is War!* (New York: Time, Inc., 1951) Chapter entitled "The Hill."

LTC James W. Edwards, "Naktong Defense," *Infantry School Quarterly*, The Infantry School, Ft. Benning, GA, Apr 1951.

CPT William M. Glasgow, Jr., "Korean Ku Klux Klan," *Combat Forces Journal*, Feb. 1952.

82d AA in Korea, pp. 6-24.

Fight for a Foothold.

CPT Raymond E. Webb, *72d Tank Battalion in Korea 1950 - 1952* (Tokyo, Japan: Toppan Printing Co., 1952), pp. 4-7; 40; 43. Hereafter *72d Tank Bn in Korea.*

"Tragedy."

Artillery Support.

"GIs of 2d Division Slash Way Through Flaming Town in Korea," Associated Press dispatch by Bern Price, Sep 2, 1950. Copy courtesy Courtney Willis Fredericks, H/9th Inf.

Blair-Lynch interview.

Bohn interview

2d Inf. Div, *Operational Directive*, Sep 2, 1950 and Marine Bde *OPORD 19-50*, Sep 2, 1950. These two documents ordered the counterattack for Sep 3, 1950.

CPT Phil R. Garn (H/23d Inf) "75mm Recoilless Rifles in Korea," *Infantry School Quarterly*, Jan 1952.

CPT Charles Multop (H/23d Inf) "A Heavy Weapons Company in Korea," *Infantry School Quarterly*, 1952.

Fenton debriefing.

CHAPTER TWENTY

South to the Naktong, pp. 438-443; 470-487; 546-47.

The Forgotten War pp. 242-246.

Battleground Korea, Chap. 4, The Line Holds.

Combat Actions, Chap. 3, Defense of a Battery Position.

With a Black Platoon, Chap. 6, The Fight Continues.

Yechon, pp. 157-59.

Odyssey of the Wolfhounds, pp. 414-425.

Barth mss, pp. 28-35.

Thrust! The story of the 89th Tank Battalion (No author given) Copyright, 89th Tank Bn, 1953. pp. 21-23. Hereafter *89th Tank Bn.*

The First Fifty Days, pp.22-23.

CPT Robert L. Strouse (65th ECB), "Secondary Mission," *Combat Support in Korea*, Combat Forces Press, 1955.

24th Inf Command Chart.

27th RCT:

Unit Reports, 6 P.M. Aug 31 - 6 P.M. Sep 17, 1950.

OPORD #20, Sep 4, 1950.

OPORD #21, Sep 6, 1950.

OPORD #22, Sep 8, 1950.

OPORD #23, Sep 14, 1950.

Roster of Losses, Sep 14 -18.

Memo, "Organic and Attached Units, 27th RCT September 1950," 11/23/50.

Regimental S1 Narrative report for Sep 1950.

Regimental S2 Summary, Sep 1-26, 1950.

Regimental S2 POW reports for September 1950.

Regimental S3 Activities Report, Sep 1950.

Regimental S3 Historical report, Sep 1950.

Battalion Staff Rosters, Sep 1950.

1/27th Inf Report of Operations, Sep 1-30, 1950.

2/27th Inf Report of Operations, Sep 1-30, 1950.

All of the above listed 27th RCT records were furnished the author courtesy Cressie Johnson (D/27th Inf).

1/35th Inf:

War Diary, 1-15 Sep 1950.

S3 Journal, 1-15 Sep 1950.

Interrogation Reports:

3 Sep - LTC Lee Chun Won (XO, 2/9th Div); PVT Kim Choong Chul (*2d Plt, 9th Co, 3/13th Regt, 6th Div*)

4 Sep - Lyoo Ki Sil (*1st Plt, 1st Co., Engr Combat Bn*, attached to *6th Div*)

6 Sep - Sr LT Kin Gin Kyo (*6th Co, 2d Bn, 3/7th Div*)

7 Sep - PVTs Hong Chong Myn; Ri Dal Shin and Kim Myong Gun (*7th Co. 3d Bn, 3/7th Div*; PVT Lee Sung Ho (*2d Co., 2d Bn, 3/7th Div*).

Roster of *3/13th Regt.*

Morning Report, Aug 31, 1950, for *9th Co, 3/13th Regt.*

Strength of *3d Co., 1/13th Regt, 6th Div* as of Aug 31, 1950.

History of the NK Army, pp. 63; 65; 94-95; 97.

Johnson interview.

CHAPTER TWENTY-ONE

South to the Naktong, pp. 520-522; 538; 542-572.

Policy and Direction, pp. 134-136;155.

The Forgotten War, pp. 278-282; 284-291.

From the Hudson to the Yalu, pp. 101-103.

From Pusan to Panmunjom, pp. 51-53.

Odyssey of the 27th Infantry Regiment, pp. 421-434.

No Bugles, No Drums, Chap 6, Experience of William Glasgow During the Breakout.

KMAG in Korea, pp. 11; 34-35.

With a Black Platoon in Combat, pp. 82-93.

Oral History, pp. 355-363.

The First Team, Narrative for the period Sep 13-21, 1950.

The U.S. 2d Division in Korea, pp. 41-43.

USAF in Korea, pp. 161-162.

Battleground Korea, Chap. 5 — Breakout.

72d Tk Bn in Korea, pp. 6 & 7.

Legacy, pp. 51-66

Skirmish, Chap IV — The Breakout.

The Argylls in Korea, pp. 14-15.

The First Fifty Days, pp. 24-25.

82d AA in Korea, pp. 23-27.

From *Combat Support in Korea*: CPT Robert L. Strouse (65th ECB), "Secondary Mission"

CPT Richard P. Lepke (3d ECB), "Three River Crossings"; CPT Robert J. Gilroy (3d Trans. Amphibian Truck Co.), "Amphibian Truck Company"; CPT Edward C. Williamson, 4th Historical Det., interviewed these officer and enlisted members of the 38th Ordnance Medium Maintenance Co. for "Ordnance Company Under Attack": LTs Edgar E. Dunlap and William E. Peter; SGTs Claude H. Lusk, M. J. Thomasson, Thomas E. Griffin, George A. Batson, Eugene F. McCracken and CPL Elio Battaglia.

Employment of Armor in Korea, VOL II. A research report, The Armored School, Ft. Knox, KY, 1951-52. pp. 78-90.

Barth mss.

CPT William Glasgow, "A Near perfect Attack," *The Infantry School Quarterly*, FT Benning, GA., 1951.

"The 70th Tk Bn in Korea."

27th RCT:

Historical Report, Sep 1950.

Unit Reports, 6 P.M. Sep 9 - 6 P.M. Sep 30, 1950.

OPORD 23, 9/14/50; OPORD 24, 9/19/50; OPORD 25, 9/21/50; OPORD 26, 9/21/50; OPORD 27, 9/22/50; OPORD 28, 9/24/50; OPORD 29, 9/25/50; OPORD 30, 9/28/50.

"Organic and Attached Units, 27th RCT, September 1950," 11/23/50.

S1 Narrative report for Sep 1950, 11/14/50.

S2 Summary for Sep 1950, 11/24/50.

S3 Activities report for Sep 1950, undated.

POW Reports For Sep 1950, 11/24/50.

1/27th Inf: Report of Operations, Sep 10-30, 1950.

2/27th Inf: Report of Operations, Sep 8-30, 1950.

1/35th Inf:

War Diary, 15-30 Sep 1950.

S3 Journal, 15-30 Sep 1950.

5th RCT: (The following 5th RCT records courtesy Gene McClure (H/5th RCT)

Summary, 17-28 Sep 1950.

War Diary, 17-21 Sep 1950.

Unit Reports 38 & 39, 18-21 Sep 1950.

POW Reports, Sep 18 and 21, 1950.

Casualty Statistics, Sep 17-28, 1950.

Special Order #74, 5/26/51, awarding the CIB to certain members.

Roster of G/5th RCT in Hawaii.

5th Cav Regt: Awards and Decorations; Casualties, 1950. (Copy courtesy Lindesy Helms (HM/5th Cav)

TO & E 17N, 1949.

Phil R. Garn (H/23 Inf) *Infantry School Quarterly* article, Jan. 1952.

Johnson interview.

CHAPTER TWENTY-TWO

South to the Naktong, Chap XXVIII (pp. 573-606).

The Forgotten War, pp. 295-319.

The Argylls in Korea, pp. 15-25.

From Pusan to Panmunjom, pp. 55-58.

With a Black Platoon, pp. 87-97.

Battleground Korea — section covering the exploitation phase.

The Second Division in Korea, pp. 43-46.

The First Team — section covering Sep 22-30, 1950.

Odyssey of the 27th Regiment Wolfhounds, pp. 434-440.

82d AA in Korea, pp. 25-27.

THRUST! pp. 24-30

Legacy, pp. 57-58.

Skirmish, pp. 52-57.

Employment of Armor in Korea the First Year, Vol II. Research Report, The Armor School, Ft. Knox, KY, 1951-52. pp. 81-85.

"Tank Company A Holds Frontline Duty Record," *Stars and Stripes*, 2/20/51. An article about A/89th Tank Bn.

Barth mss, pp. 38-39.

Joseph M. Quinn, "Catching the Enemy Off Guard," *Armor* Magazine, Jul-Aug 1951. Copy courtesy John W. Akeson (A.89th Tk Bn).

LTC James H. Lynch (C.O., 3/7th Cav), "Task Force Penetration." *Combat Forces Journal*, Jan 1951.

5th RCT (all courtesy Gene McClure (H/5th RCT):

Summary, Sep 17-28, 1950.

War Diary, Sep 22-28, 1950.

Casualty Statistics, Sep 17-28, 1950.

SO 74, Apr 26, 1951, making the second award of the CIB to certain members of the 5th RCT.

27th RCT (all courtesy Cressie Johnson (D/27th Inf):

Historical Reports, Sep 26-30, 1950.

Unit Reports #28 & 29, Sep 23-30, 1950.

S1 Historical Narrative Report for Sep 1950.

S2 Summary Report, Sep 1-30, 1950.

S3 Activities Report for Sep 1950.

OPORD 30, Sep 28, 1950.

Organic and Attached Units, 27th RCT, Sep 1950.

1/27th Inf Report of Operations, Sep 1-30, 1950.

2/27th Inf Summary of Activities, Sep 1-30, 1950.

35th RCT (courtesy Harold Gamble (Med Co/29th Inf & K/35th Inf):

S3 Journal, Sep 22-30, 1950.

1/35th Inf War Diary, Sep 1-30, 1950.

Johnson (72d ECC) interview.

Basic Military Map Symbols

Symbols within a rectangle indicate a military unit., within a triangle
an observation post, and within a circle a supply point.

Miltary Units – Identification

Antiaircraft Artillery ....

Armored Command ....

Army Air Forces ....

Artillery, except Antiaircraft and Coast Artillery ....

Cavalry, Mechanized (Armored Cavalry) ....

Engineers ....

Infantry ....

Medical Corps ....

Ordnance Corps ....

Quartermaster ....

Signal ....

Mortar ....

Self Propelled Artillery ....

Transportation ....

AA	Anti-aircraft
AAA	Anti-aircraft artillery
AAA/AW	Anti-aircraft artillery, automatic weapons
ABN	Airborne
ACR	Armored Cavalry Regiment
Amd or Armd	Armored
Arty	Artillery
ASP	Ammunition Supply Point
AT	Anti-tank
ATK	Attack
BC	Battery Commander, Border Constabulary (a North Korean military organization)
Bde	Brigade
BG	Brigadier General
BN	Battalion
CID	Criminal Investigation Division C-ration (See-ration) Combat rations. Consisting of canned food, including a main meal, crackers, powdered milk, jam and canned fruit. A box of C-rations provided three meals for one man for a day.
Co.	Company
C.O./CO	Commanding Officer
COL	Colonel
CP	Command Post
CPL	Corporal
CPT	Captain
Def.	Defense
Div.	Division
DOW	Died of wounds
DS	Detached Service. A serviceman detached from his parent unit, serving at another place and/or in another capacity.
ECB	Engineer Combat Battalion. A division had one of these battalions.
ECC	Engineer Combat Company. These companies were organic to the Engineer Combat Battalion. The 5th and 24th Regimental Combat Teams each had its own Engineer Combat Company. The Marine Brigade had its own Engineer Combat Company.
Engr	Engineer
EUSAK	Eight United States Army, Korea
FAB	Field Artillery Battalion
FDC	Fire Direction Center. A central location at an artillery or mortar CP where fire of the guns or mortars is controlled and directed. Personnel in the FDC have a least radio communications with the forward observer and the weapons' site.
FEAF	Far East Air Force
FMF	Fleet Marine Force
FO	Forward Observer
FTAC	Forward Tactical Air Control
1SG	First Sergeant
GEN	General
G.I. or GI	In WWII, this originally stood for "Government Issue." It became a term for a soldier. (1. G.I.s - soldiers; 2. G.I.s - Diarrhea. As in: He had the G.I.s.
GySGT	Gunnery Sergeant
HE	High explosive
HEAT	High explosive, Anti-tank. A type of artillery round for use against tanks.
HHC	Headquarters and Headquarters Company
HM	Heavy mortar
HVAR	High velocity aircraft rockets
I & R	Intelligence and reconnaissance
IU	Independent unit. (This was a North Korean independent infantry formation of about regimental size.)
JCS	Joint Chiefs of Staff
JLC	Japan Logistical Command. A command organized in Japan

to direct logistical operations. Soldiers irreverently referred to it as "Jesus' Little Children." In this case "Jesus" was considered to be GEN MacArthur and the members of this command as his "Little Children."

KATUSA (Ka-too-sa)	Korean augmentation to the U.S. Army. Commonly used as a word referring to any Korean soldier attached to a U.S. unit. ("The unit had 20 KATUSAs." "Three KATUSAs were killed and seven wounded.")
KIA	Killed in action
KMAG (Kay-Mag)	Korean Military Advisory Group. U.S. army organization whose mission was to advise and train the South Korean Constabulary and later, the Republic of Korea Army.
LD	Line of Departure. Usually some easily identifiable terrain feature, such as a road, stream, edge of a field, from which an attack is launched.
LST	Landing ship, tank
LT	Lieutenant. 1LT, First Lieutenant. 2LT, Second Lieutenant
LTC	Lieutenant Colonel
LTG	Lieutenant General
MAJ	Major
MASH	Mobile Army Surgical Hospital. Originally, a small, completely mobile hospital, designed to support an Army division. Although it remained a mobile organization, the MASH bed capacity was dramatically expanded in order to accommodate more patients.
MAW	Marine Air Wing
Med	Medical
MG	Major General
MIA	Mission in action
MLR	Main Line of Resistance. The main battle line or position.
MSG	Master Sergeant
MSR	Main Supply Route. The principal road or highway used to resupply a military organization and to evacuate casualties and damaged equipment
MTACS	Marine Tactical Air Control Squadron
NBC	Non-battle casualty. Anyone injured or who contracts a disease, not due to enemy action.
NCO	Non-commissioned officer. Anyone with the rank of corporal or any of the grades of sergeant.
NK	North Korean
NKPA	North Korean Peoples' Army. In Korean, the Immun Gun.
OP	Observation Post
OPORD	Operations Order. The formal, written order directing a military action. During the Korean War the term was "Field Order."
PFC	Private First Class
PLAT or PLT	Platoon
PM	Provost Marshal. The military equivalent of Chief of Police.
POW	Prisoner of War
PX	Post Exchange. A retail store on an Army post. The Air Force and Navy equivalent was BX - base exchange.
RR	Recoilless rifle
R & R	Rest and Rehabilitation. A short recreational trip to Japan from Korea. This was awarded to men after about four to five months in combat in Korea. Soldiers often crudely referred to this as "Rape and Run."
RCT	Regimental Combat Team. A common sub-structure within a division, or as a separate organization. An RCT consisted of an infantry regiment, a 105mm Field Artillery Battalion, and an engineer combat company. The regiment had its own medical company and tank company, of 22 tanks. At times, a platoon of 4.2" mortars was also attached to the RCT. The RCT was a powerful force.

RECON	Reconnaissance
REGT	Regiment
ROK (Rock)	1. Republic of Korea; 2. Name used by American soldiers for any Korean serviceman.
ROKA	Republic of Korea Army
ROTC	Reserve Officers Training Corps
SCR, as in	
SCR 300	Signal Corps Radio
SD	Special Duty. Assignment to a duty other than what is normal to a person, or for a special project or task.
SGM	Sergeant Major
SGT	Sergeant
SSG	Staff Sergeant
SVC or Svc	Service
TAC	Tactical Air Control or Controller
TACP	Tactical Air Control Party
TDY	Temporary Duty. Temporary assignment to a position, task or mission
TF	Task Force
TO&E	Table of Organization and Equipment. A detailed listing

of the officers, warrant officers and enlisted personnel, by rank and the weapons and equipment by type and numbers of Army units and organizations. Some units are organized under a Table of Distribution (TD) instead of a TO &E. A TD contained the same detailed listing as a TO&E.

TOT	Time On Target. An artillery firing arrangement that placed all of the first rounds of a battery or battalion fire mission on the target at the same time.
TROB	Transportation Railway Operation Battalion
TK	Tank
TSGT	Technical Sergeant
USAFIK	United States Army Forces in Korea
USO	United Services Organization. A non-profit civilian organization dedicated to improving troop morale.
VHF	Very High Frequency
VT	Type of artillery round. Allows air bursts over a target
WIA	Wounded in action
WP	White phosphorous. Also know as "Willie Peter."
XO	Executive Officer

INDEX

A

A-1 Eng. 140
A-25 147
A-6 23
A/1/35th Inf. 90
Abbott, Leroy 236
Able Company 33, 45, 46, 51, 53
Abrahamson, James W. 148, 199
Abt, Freddy 78
Acheson, Dean 26
Adams, Dwight L. 256, 358
Adams, Raymond 33, 38
ADCOM 91
Agok 282, 284, 286, 287, 308
Air National Guard 250
Akeson, John W. 332, 372
Akins, Teddy B. 231
Akridge, Clyde 169
Albert, Russell A. 140
Albert, William 300, 318
Albin, Warren 193
Alcar, David 314
Ales, Benedict 171
Aleutians 26
Alexander, Gerald N. 242
Alfonso 172, 173, 174, 175, 184, 185, 186, 187
Alfonso, Albert F. 170
Alicea, Bob 92
Alkire, Charles R. 51
Allen 275, 276, 277, 279, 280, 369
Allen, Claude E. 225
Allen, Frank 92
Allen, John F. 104
Allen Jr., Frank A. 61, 264
Allen, Levin C. 162
Allen, Norman F. J. 275
Allman 127
Almacy 265, 269
Almond, Eugene 58, 108, 118, 162, 163, 249, 367
Alsop, Joseph 232
Altom 139
American Red Cross 8
Ammer, Henry G. 139
Ancien 164
Anderegg, Harold R. 270, 363
Anderson 139, 147, 258, 331
Anderson, Ashley C. 226
Anderson, Carl 110, 111
Anderson, Clarence L. 393
Anderson, Horace 126, 139, 355
Anderson, Leroy 330
Anderson, William H. 146
Andong 54, 58, 60, 87, 88, 120, 123, 259, 344, 380, 386
Angang-ni 255, 256, 257, 259, 366
Angway 135, 140
Ansong 33, 39, 40, 44, 45, 47, 54, 385
Anui 100, 106, 107, 369, 373, 375, 376, 387
Anzio 100
Applegate, James A. 102, 104, 105
Appleman 43, 47, 53, 55, 60, 62, 63, 67, 69, 71, 78, 79, 81, 84, 86, 87, 90, 98, 100, 106, 109, 111, 113, 118, 119, 122, 123, 124, 142, 156, 161, 163, 175, 189, 194, 218, 219, 225, 236, 237, 240, 243, 244, 247, 251, 252, 264, 266, 267, 268, 282, 284, 289, 290, 316, 319, 320, 323, 324, 326, 337, 340, 345, 359, 362, 366, 372, 380, 381, 385, 386
Aracid, Pop 346
Arawaka, Jack 66
Arendell, Edward 48, 77, 78, 81
Arikawa 389

Arizona 65
Arkadis 193
Arkadis, Nickolas 191
Armed Forces of North Korea 226
Army Chief of Military History 45
Army Special Services 8, 17
Arnold, Charles E. 111
Arnold, Ernest R. 331
Arsenaux, Leroy 216
Arundel 95
Atasugi, Japan 8
Attu 17
Avery, Charles 198
Avery, Warren J. 360
Awashi 15
Awohi, Henry 126, 127
Ayers 63
Aynes, Erman 324
Ayres, Harold B. 43, 45, 46, 47, 51, 53, 55, 64, 68, 69, 71, 72, 74, 75, 77, 79, 85, 168, 169, 170, 172, 175, 186, 187

B

B-26 52, 58
B-29 58
Babb, Earl F. 258, 360
Babbick, John 193
Back, George 185, 186
Badoeng Strait 147
Bai Jun Pal 62
Bailey Jr., Kincheon H. 331
Baker 63, 65, 66, 69, 95, 113, 143, 149, 158, 222, 245, 313
Baker, Barton O. 250
Baker, Claude 155, 379
Baker, Francis 180, 181
Baker, Henry E. 331
Baker, Hubert 113
Baker, Jerome R. 294, 313
Baker, Robert W. 384
Baker, Walter 193
Balaclava 281
Balbi, Edward F. 113, 325, 336
Ballenger, Richard L. 290, 291
Banks 347
Barbara 353
Barker, Harold W. 331
Barner 226
Barnett 108, 137, 193, 347
Barnett, Lacy 43, 46, 55, 69, 75, 85, 124
Barnett, Lonzo 137, 138
Barnwell, Jerome 239
Barr 385
Barrett, Edward F. 141
Barrett Jr., John C. 236
Barstow, CA 132, 133
Barszcz, Michael 65, 67, 68, 76, 79, 105, 109, 110, 188
Barter, Charles T. 62
Barth 237, 243, 319, 325, 331, 334, 346, 350
Barth, Bittman 60, 85, 138, 143, 154, 160, 161, 163, 191
Barth, George B. 31, 33, 34, 42, 43, 45, 47, 55
Bartholdi, Carl S. 291
Bartol, Arthur P. 225, 265
Barton, Charles 217
Bass, Joseph T. 117
Bass, Sam 347
Bastogne 79
Bataan 109, 136, 150
Bater, Lawrence Y. 179
Batson, George A. 354
Battaglia, Elio 354
Battalion Headquarters Hill 309, 310
Battle Mountain 136, 237, 238, 239, 240, 242, 243, 244, 245, 247, 319, 323, 336, 337, 346, 348

Battle of the Bulge 272
Baughman, Bob 198
Baumgartner, William L. 159
Baushmein, Joe 48
Baxter, Earl R. 273
Baxter, Joseph 335
Bayless, Robert 168, 173, 257
Beaber, Chris 354
Beahler, Lee E. 297
Beal, Norman L. 302
Beard 287
Bearden 313
Beauchamp 68, 69, 70, 71, 72, 74, 75, 76, 78, 79, 80, 81, 84, 85, 86, 107, 108, 124, 165, 166, 168, 170, 176, 178, 179, 182, 252
Beauchamp, Alfred 44, 46, 55
Beauchamp, Charles E. 164
Beaullieau 127
Beaver, James 136, 287
Becicka, Leonard 107
Becton Jr., Julius W. 350
Beech, Keyes 30, 42
Beeson, Charles 197, 198
Begley, John L. 360
Behr, Francis J. 159
Beiderlinden, William A. 249
Beijing 11
Beirne, Daniel R. 153, 245, 339, 355, 356
Bell, Cleo O. 90, 91
Bell, Delbert 150
Bell, Douglas 141
Belton, Texas 56
Bemis, Harold 115
Bender, Warren G. 95
Benedict, Richard 263, 264, 266, 267, 272
Bennington, Robert 313
Benziger, Xavier 234
Berain, Manuel 314
Bernard, Carl 32, 33, 36, 38, 40, 52, 53, 86, 258, 327
Bernard, Donald E. 112
Bernotas, Ralph 93
Berry, Glenn E. 97
Berry, Oscar V. 284
Berry, Sidney B. 60
Berryman, Alzondo 93
Bertholf Jr., Russell W. 31, 36, 38, 39
Betencourt 245
Bevins, Ralph 95
Bierne 161
Bigart, Homer 256
Biggs, Bradley 88, 90
Bishop 128, 129, 234, 313
Bishop, Bertram 95, 96, 114, 115
Bishop, Jesse 128, 234, 312
Bissett, David 68, 70
Bivings, Yancy 81
Bixler, Ray 51, 52
Blackmon, Tom 136, 137
Blackwood, Remus M. 102
Blaesing, Donald 159
Blair, Clay 33, 42, 44, 46, 52, 54, 60, 69, 88, 98, 118, 163, 177, 217, 236, 268, 282, 294, 296, 318, 320, 335, 344, 367, 373, 374, 386
Blair, Joan 88, 236
Blair, Melvin R. 335, 337, 369
Blanc, Harold 92, 93
Blevins, Richard C. 138, 302
Bloody Gulch 156, 158, 160, 161, 188
Bloody Knob 238
Bloody Ridge 311, 312, 313
Blumenson, Martin 86
Blunt, Joe 280
Bogard, Eric C. 272
Bogart 127
Bohlke, David J. 302

Bohn, Robert D. 86, 132, 131, 136, 137, 140, 145, 146, 199, 200, 304, 306, 307
Bolkow, George W. 302
Bolo Point, Okinawa 14
Bolté', David E. 263
Bonds, Earsel 36, 40
Bone, Leroy 236
Bonesteel, Charles H. 17
Boone 394
Borgomainerio, Russell J. 193
Borst, Arthur 236
Bosco, Sal 158
Bougainville, Guam 95
Bowhall, Howard 279
Bowling Alley 213, 214, 215, 227, 228, 230, 232, 235, 236, 237, 337, 355
Boxer Rebellion 119
Boyd, Ralph C. 82
Boysen, Alexander M. 393
Bozarth, Grover 289
Bradley 60, 125, 129, 134, 156, 297, 308, 375
Bradley, David W. 347
Bradley, Joseph S. 128, 130, 134, 294
Bradley, Omar 60, 122
Bradley, Sladen 296, 373
Bragg, J.L. 177, 179
Brannon, Harold R. 346
Brennen, Leo M. 186, 187
Brennon 68, 71, 170
Brian, Adrian Beecher 224, 276, 277, 279
Briley, Ray A. 224, 236
Brisco, James F. 290
Bristow, Benjamin 224, 236
Brit. 1st Bn. 250, 281
Brit. 27th Inf. Bde. 250, 253, 260, 281, 295, 296, 313, 345, 356, 361, 376, 377
BRIT Hill 117 34, 39
BRIT Hill 194 53
Brito, Manuel 149, 150, 151, 194, 196, 197
Brixius, Harold W. 227, 376
Bromley, Bruce 287
Brook 127
Brooks 138
Brooks, Frank 135, 137, 140
Brooks, Melvin 137
Brown, Alan G. 268
Brown, Hugh 258
Brown, Jack D. 317
Brown, Melvin L. 266
Brown, Norm E. 257
Brown, Robert 113, 323
Brown, William 93, 113
Bryant, James A. 68, 72, 122
Buchanan, Crawford 221
Buchanan, David 376
Buchanan, Earl W. 111
Buchanan, Neil 281
Buckley 95
Buckley, Harry A. 218, 236
Buckley, John 94, 116, 346
Buettner, Lee 137
Buff, Jack Y. 65
Buffington, Ralph 180
Buford 70, 84
Bullanto, Frank 143
Bunda, Santiago 338
Bunting 52
Burch, Louis 292
Burke, Thomas 193, 302, 361
Burkhardt, Robert P. 193
Burma 68, 126
Burnett, Alfred S. 94, 96, 231, 348
Bussey, Charles M. 60, 89, 90, 142, 239, 243, 247, 320
Buswell 292
Butler, Arthur B. 235

418

McClure, Gene 18, 125, 126, 154, 155, 358
McConnell, Charles B. 165
McCormick 325
McCoy 139, 150
McCracken, Eugene F. 354
McCrane 358
McCullom, Roy E. 273
McCullough 365
McDaniel, Raymond 287
McDaniel, William T. 68, 80, 86, 389
McDermott 316
McDonald, John V. 264
McDoniel, Raymond J. 288, 289
McGee, Charles F. 219
McGhee, Robert B. 157
McGill, Henry T. 65
McGrail, Thomas M. 64, 65, 66, 67, 69, 70, 75, 76, 85, 100, 109, 165, 171, 188
McIntyre, Niles J. 308
McKenna 279
McKenzie, Herbert R. 236
McKeon, Joseph 65, 66, 67, 77, 81
McKinley, Russell 223
McLafferty, William J. 53
McLain, William 272
McMahon 314
McMains 258, 350
McMillan, John 156, 179, 180
McMullen, Orval F. 194, 197, 199, 301
McMurray, Houston M. 320
McNamara, Homer C. 264
McNeely, Morgan J. 139, 146
McPhail 386
McQuitty, Bobbie H. 331
McRoberts 240
McVay 193
McWorter, Vance 143
Meares, Cecil W. 331
Meldrum, Spencer C. 163
Melhorn, Milton 14, 247
Meloy, Guy (Stan) 42, 64, 65, 66, 67, 100
Menninger, Charles W. 51
Menninger, William 165
Menoher, Pearson 42, 47, 66, 67, 80, 84, 111, 176, 177, 180, 187
Mercer 127
Merchant, Martin L. V. 177, 228, 231, 232
Merrill's Marauders 11
Merten, Fred W. 129, 316
Messinger, Edwin J. 130
Metkowski, Ed 168
Mexican Squad 325
Meyer, Henry J. D. 42, 191
Meyer, Walter P. 48
Meyers, Max E. 39
Michaelis, John H. 58, 60, 61, 92, 96, 97, 111, 114, 115, 116, 118, 132, 137, 181, 182, 227, 228, 231, 235, 237, 336, 340
Michelony, Lewis 96, 391
Middlesex Hill 376
Milam, James T. 94, 269
Milburn, Frank W. 344, 363
Mildenberger, Robert W. 105
Millan, William G. 137
Millar, Stanley G. 195
Millard 220
Miller 33, 87, 116, 179, 180
Miller, Earl 87, 347
Miller, Gerald 237, 242, 335
Miller, Guy W. 354
Miller, Kenneth W. 272
Miller, Rolly G. 340
Miller, Stanley G. 144
Milleson, Hugh P. 101
Millett, Lewis 96, 228, 231, 340
Mills 97

Mims 240
Min 112, 113
Min Ki 67
Min Ki Sin 107
Min Sik 107
Min Sik Ki 67
Minger, Robert R. 340
Minietta 48
Miryang 121, 129, 148, 160, 164, 173, 176, 178, 179, 180, 187, 189, 190, 191, 197, 235, 252, 253, 281, 283, 288, 294, 296, 297, 298, 394
Miryang Cemetery 235
Miryang River 190
Mitchell 274
Mitchell, A. 281
Mitchell, Frank G. 122
Mitchell, Harry D. 93
Mitchell, J.H. 273
Mitchell, William 101, 105, 336
Mize, Charles 306, 307
Mlaskac, Milton 236
Mobly 116
Moffatt, David Livingstone 71
Mogged, Roy 297
Mokpo 100
Molotov, V. M. 86
Molton, William 101, 181
Monington, Willis 94
Monohans 97
Monroe 65
Montesclaros, Melicio 62, 64, 65, 67, 76, 85, 86, 105
Montfort, Houston 236
Moody, Jr. Troy E. 177, 178
Moore 101, 105, 106, 107, 109, 110, 111, 112, 113, 115, 170, 171, 172, 174, 176, 178, 180, 183
Moore, John J. 354
Moore, Ned D. 100, 165
Moore, Santford B. 331
Moore, William 110, 179
Moore's Engineer Post 2 180
Moorman, Frank W. 161, 162
Moran 358
Morden, Melvin W. 236
Morgan, Ray 141
Morris, Edward C. 301, 306, 339, 389
Morris, Harold E. 122
Morrison Jr., Harry S. 281, 283
Morrissey, J. 102, 105, 222
Morse, Dale B. 135
Morton, Richard L 262, 264, 265, 268, 269, 270
Moryl 95
Mosan-ni 283, 308, 314, 316
Moser, Robert 67, 68, 71, 82, 169, 170, 174, 175
Moses, Vivian 147
Moskin, J. Robert 315
Motley, William A. 126, 127, 143, 154, 155, 241, 242, 245, 338
Mott, Harold W. 100, 101, 105
Mt. Fuji 8, 10, 11, 15, 60
Mt. Rainier 129
Muan-ni 252, 294
Muccio, John J. 23
Muchon-ni 110, 111, 114, 136, 139, 142, 144, 152, 153, 161
Mudgett, Charles F. 42
Mueller, Robert 263
Muetzel, Francis W. 131, 133, 144, 145, 151, 190, 196, 197, 198, 199, 301, 302, 306, 307, 318
Muhoberac, John R. 385
Muir, Kenneth 376, 377
Muju 61, 91
Mukden 56
Mukhojin-ni 28
Mulligan, Vern 38

Mullins, Junior 338
Multop, Charles 312
Mun Hyong Tae 214
Munger, Clyde O. 309
Mungyong 54, 55, 88, 90, 253, 386
Muñoz, Frank 283, 284
Munsan 17, 26, 27, 29, 248
Munsan-ni 26, 27
Murch, Gordon 60, 111, 132, 177, 178, 179, 181, 326, 329, 332
Murley, Bill M. 138, 139
Murphy, Jack 305
Murphy, John R. 121, 122
Murray, Raymond L. 133, 134, 139, 143, 144, 145, 146, 160, 190, 194, 199, 298, 303, 305, 377
Myang-myon 47
Myers, Frank 103, 104, 105, 110, 391
Myong-ni 298, 299, 300, 304

N

Nagasaki 8
Naha, Okinawa 15, 100
Najin 248
Naksan-dong 361
Naksong-dong 381
Naktong 23, 42, 49, 57, 58, 60, 61, 87, 88, 90, 98, 100, 106, 109, 119, 120, 121, 131, 134, 142, 148, 151, 160, 161, 163, 164, 165, 166, 167, 168, 169, 170, 171, 172, 173, 174, 175, 176, 177, 178, 179, 181, 182, 184, 187, 188, 189, 190, 194, 195, 196, 197, 200, 213, 214, 215, 216, 217, 218, 219, 220, 221, 223, 224, 226, 227, 236, 237, 247, 250, 258, 260, 261, 262, 264, 268, 271, 281, 282, 283, 284, 286, 287, 288, 289, 290, 291, 292, 293, 296, 298, 300, 306, 308, 310, 313, 314, 316, 318, 319, 325, 340, 344, 351, 352, 353, 354, 355, 359, 360, 361, 362, 367, 373, 374, 375, 382, 386, 387
Naktong Bulge 251, 286, 288, 290, 302, 307
Naktong River 58, 83, 108, 109, 119, 120, 121, 134, 161, 164, 166, 167, 200, 213, 214, 215, 217, 219, 223, 237, 269, 288, 303, 319, 344, 351, 355, 358, 359, 366, 368, 377, 382
Naktong-ni 58, 121, 213, 214, 344, 380, 381, 382, 384
Nam 120, 164
Nam River 58, 105, 107, 109, 110, 111, 120, 121, 136, 142, 164, 237, 238, 282, 298, 303, 319, 324, 325, 332, 340, 348, 349, 368, 369
Namji-ri 164, 177, 178, 179, 181, 184, 237, 284, 298, 326
Namji-ri Bridge 319, 332
Namwon 100, 289, 291, 369, 371, 389
Napalm Hill 238
Napier, John L. 105, 388, 389
Napier, John L. 103, 391
Napolitano, Sal 18
Nara 8
Nash, Robert E. 65, 66
National Guard 250
National Press Club 26
Naudt, Morris 377
Nauweiler 222
Nealy 309
Nearhood, John 169
Needham 347
Neisi 143, 153
Nelms, Lindsey C. 224, 236
Nelsen, Ellsworth 70, 71, 166, 168
Nelson 70, 276, 327, 328
Nelson, Bentley 193, 197
Nelson, James H. 80

Nelson, Wally 276
Nelson, William J. 243
Neuman, Cecil, Jr. 236
Neuman, Frank A. 393
Neville, Ward 181
New Georgia 95
New York 30, 44
Newcomb, Charles W. 258, 360
Newman, Cecil 224
Newton, George 139, 143, 144, 145, 148, 149, 150, 191, 194, 195, 197, 199, 298, 301, 302, 305, 309
Ng, Wellington K.S. 127
Nicewander, Dennis 15, 107, 112, 113
Nicholas 384
Nichols 329
Nielson, Leslie 281, 376
Nieman, Robert A. 31
Niemczyk 137
Nisei 125
Nist, Cecil W. 61, 163, 269, 275, 365
NK 1/14th Regt. 273
NK 1/1st Div. 231, 235
NK 102d Sec. Regt. 375
NK 104th Sec. Regt. 375
NK 104th Security Bde 253
NK 105th Armd. Bde. 21, 26, 28, 29, 30
NK 105th Armd. Div. 21, 51, 121, 123, 213, 223, 226, 227, 253, 356, 377, 379, 385
NK 105th Tk. Div. 100
NK 107th Armd. Regt. 28, 37, 40, 42
NK 107th Tk. Regt. 86
NK 109th Armd. Regt. 28, 55
NK 10th Div. 121, 184, 187, 213, 219, 223, 282, 283, 294, 318, 319, 352, 356, 375, 376
NK 11th Regt. 55
NK 12th Div. 54, 55, 87, 120, 121, 123, 253, 254, 255, 259, 366, 386
NK 12th Regt. 367
NK 13th Div. 55, 100, 121, 123, 213, 214, 227, 231, 232, 235, 253, 260, 263, 273, 282, 345, 362, 363, 366, 380, 381
NK 13th Regt. 100, 156, 237
NK 13th Regt./6th Div. 324
NK 14/6th Div. 134
NK 14th Div. 100
NK 14th Regt. 27, 26, 118, 161, 237
NK 15th Div. 54, 55, 98, 100, 121, 123, 213, 214, 227, 230, 240, 253, 258, 259, 260, 345, 366
NK 15th Regt. 109, 118, 121, 161, 237
NK 16th Armd Bde. 253, 296
NK 16th Div. 40, 70
NK 16th Inf. Regt. 40, 63, 167
NK 16th Regt. 37, 62, 86, 182, 191
NK 16th Tk. Bde. 319
NK 17th Armd Bde. 253, 259
NK 17th Motorcycle Regt. 26, 27
NK 17th Regt. 28, 312
NK 18th Inf. 40, 167, 188
NK 18th Regt. 37, 51, 70, 86, 182, 191
NK 19th Inf. 169, 380
NK 19th Regt. 214, 231
NK 1st Border Constabulary Bde. 20
NK 1st Div. 26, 55, 121, 123, 213, 214, 227, 253, 260, 268, 273, 282, 344, 345, 362, 366, 381
NK 1st Peace Preservation Officers' Training Center 19
NK 1st Regt. 232, 235, 237, 296
NK 2/29th Inf. 219
NK 2/2d Regt. 273
NK 203d Armd. Regt. 26
NK 203d Tk. Regt. 86
NK 21st Regt. 380
NK 21st/13 Div. 214
NK 23d Div. 214

424

428

ABOUT THE AUTHOR

General Uzal Ent entered the Army September 1945 and was commissioned in March 1949. He served in Japan and Korea with the 27th Infantry Regiment. He left active service and went with the 28th Division of the Pennsylvania National Guard in March 1954. He served with them until November 1980, retiring as a Brigadier General. During his time in the National Guard, he served as Company Commander, G1, G3, and Chief of Staff.

His awards include the Combat Infantryman's Badge, Legion of Merit, Bronze Star Medal with V device for Valor and two Oak Leaf Clusters (representing a second and third awards of the medal), Meritorious Service Medal, Army Commendation Medal, Pennsylvania Distinguished Service Medal, Presidential Unit Citation with one Oak Leaf Custer, and the Korean Presidential Unit Citation.

General Ent resides in Camp Hill, Pennsylvania with his wife Ada Joan. They have one son and two grandsons.

CPSIA information can be obtained
at www.ICGtesting.com
Printed in the USA
BVOW09*0608030117
472432BV00015B/191/P